INTERNATIONAL LAW IN
HISTORICAL PERSPECTIVE

NOVA ET VETERA IURIS GENTIUM

PUBLICATIONS OF THE INSTITUTE FOR INTERNATIONAL LAW
OF THE UNIVERSITY OF UTRECHT

SERIES A: MODERN INTERNATIONAL LAW
NUMBER 16

MARTINUS NIJHOFF PUBLISHERS
DORDRECHT / BOSTON / LONDON

1992

INTERNATIONAL LAW IN HISTORICAL PERSPECTIVE

BY

J.H.W. VERZIJL†

Late Professor of International Law
Utrecht University

W.P. HEERE J.P.S. OFFERHAUS

PART IX-C

THE LAW OF MARITIME PRIZE

Library of Congress Cataloging-in-Publication Data

(Revised for volume 11, pt. 9C)

Verzijl, J. H. W. (Jan Hendrik Willem), b. 1888.
International law in historical perspective. By J. H. W. Verzijl.

(Nova et vetera iuris gentium. Series A, Modern international law, no. 4, 6-9, 12-14)
Vol. edited by W.P. Heere, J.P.S. Offerhaus.
Vol. published: Dordrecht ; Boston : M. Nijhoff.
Contents: v. 1. General subjects. -- v. 2. International persons. -- [etc.] -- v. 11, pt. 9c. The law of maritime prize.
1. International law--History. I. Heere, Wybo P. II. Offerhaus, J.P.S. III. Title. IV. Series: Nova et vetera iuris gentium. Series A, Modern international law ; no. 4, etc.
JX3695.D8V47 341 68-26728

ISBN: 0-7923-0944-8

Published by Kluwer Academic Publishers,
P.O. Box 17, 3300 AA Dordrecht, The Netherlands.

Kluwer Academic Publishers incorporates the publishing programmes
of D. Reidel, Martinus Nijhoff, Dr W. Junk and MTP Press.

Sold and distributed in the U.S.A. and Canada
by Kluwer Academic Publishers,
101 Philip Drive, Norwell, MA 02061, U.S.A.

In all other countries, sold and distributed
by Kluwer Academic Publishers Group,
P.O. Box 322, 3300 AH Dordrecht, The Netherlands.

Printed on acid-free paper

Printed in the Netherlands

FOREWORD

The publication of the eleventh volume of *International Law in Historical Perspective* occurs more than four years after the death of Professor J.H.W. Verzijl on 21 May 1987.

As mentioned by Verzijl in his own Preface to this volume, the series started in 1968, having been preceded by two volumes on the *Jurisprudence of the World Court* (1965, 1966). Between 1968 and 1979 ten volumes were published with the assistance of Mrs Polona Offerhaus, who joined the staff of the Institute of Public International Law of the University of Utrecht in 1967 for the purpose of assisting Verzijl in the preparation of this work.

After 1979 Verzijl started on the final part of this series, the international law of maritime prize. His previous publications on the subject were already extensive (two books and several long articles), but they covered only the law of prize during the first World War and the inter-war years. What he set out to achieve in two projected volumes, was to analyse the history of the law of prize before 1914, and to give a survey of the developments after 1939, including World War II, the Korean War, the Vietnam War, the War in the Middle East and other armed conflicts.

But he encountered problems when he attempted to collect the necessary printed sources for his great work, which meant that progress was slower than had been foreseen. The author was already 91 when he started the project but he continued to come to the Institute and work at his own desk until 1984, when declining health resulting in periods in hospital forced him to leave his own house and move to a rest-home outside the city of Utrecht. This meant that he could no longer undertake further active work on the manuscript.

When he died in 1987, at the age of 98, about sixty percent of the first volume was ready, with many sections completely unwritten, others only available in a first pencil-written manuscript without accompanying references, and others again in several differing versions. The Preface to this volume is a mixture of several versions, the texts chosen dating from Spring 1980.

In 1988 the Board of Editors decided that Mrs Offerhaus and Mr Heere should finish the first volume concerning the law of prize before 1914. We checked and rechecked the existing text, wrote missing passages, added or corrected source notes, and took various decisions as to what should be the final contents of this volume. We have not indicated what is 'pure Verzijl' and what is ours although references to sources published after 1982 will provide some indication. The Board of Editors also decided not to publish a second volume on the law of prize after 1914 as too little manuscript was available to do so without extensive and time-consuming additional research. We do intend, however, to publish a comprehensive index of the entire series *International Law in Historical Perspective.*

As always, our sincere thanks go to the late Miss Mary Sibthorp, O.B.E., who also corrected this volume and who was instrumental in unifying the text.

Mrs Offerhaus worked with professor Verzijl for twenty years, Mr Heere's collaboration covered some thirty years. It was an intellectual adventure of no mean dimension to have been involved in the research on *International Law in Historical Perspective*. Our memories of the original author, our teacher and fellow-worker, will always be marked by this enormous common project. The publication of this volume may serve as a lasting tribute to the memory of his scholarship and his outstanding contribution to international law.

Utrecht, September 1990

J.P.S. Offerhaus
W.P. Heere

TABLE OF CONTENTS

PREFACE TO PART IX-C

In my foreword to volumes IX, X and XI of the present publication, preceding its volume IX, I have explained the reason why I have split up my systematic Part IX into three separate volumes, each containing a subdivision of that systematic Part IX, namely, Part IX-A, dealing with the Laws of War, Part IX-B with the Law of Neutrality, and Part IX-C with the Law of Maritime Prize. After dealing with the laws of war in Part IX-A and the law of neutrality in Part IX-B, I will now proceed to describe in the present Part IX-C (vol. XI) the law of maritime prize.

PERSONAL PREFACE

"On revient toujours à ses premiers amours". While harbouring certain doubts as to whether this assertion has universal validity as applied to human relationships, it has proved undoubtedly true as regards the present volume and its author.

After receiving my first doctorate in law more than seventy-four years ago (1910) and as I was looking for a subject for my second doctoral thesis, this time in the field of political science, World War I broke out (1914) and my choice fell on the law of maritime prize. This thesis of mine, prepared under the supervision of my teacher and friend Jan de Louter, author of a two-volume Dutch manual *Het stellig volkenrecht* (1910), which was later (1920) republished in Oxford in a French version, *Le droit international public positif*, in a series of the Carnegie Foundation, dates from sixty-seven years ago (1917). It ran to 340 pages and had three basic limitations: it dealt only with prize court decisions pronounced during Word War I; it was of necessity confined to the judgments available to me when finalizing my text, and it was only concerned with the impact of that war on the position of neutrals. Hence its Dutch title *Het prijsrecht tegenover neutralen in den wereldoorlog van 1914 en volgende jaren* (*Prize law in its impact on neutrals during the world war of 1914 and ensuing years*).

It was followed in 1918 by a retrospective survey of how the international law of prize had actually developed during World War I, looked at especially from the point of view of its impact on Dutch interests, which was contributed to the then existing Netherlands *Annuaire Grotius* for the year 1917 (pp. 50-127) in French, entitled "La jurisprudence des prises et le droit des gens".

When, seven years later (1924), at the invitation of the *Institut Intermédiaire International* at The Hague, I produced an enlarged, entirely differently conceived, and amply documented systematic survey in French and various other languages of the case law of 1914-1919 of the prize courts of almost all the belligerent States, the first limitation remained, the second could mainly be remedied by the inclusion of a great deal of additional material, and the third was completely omitted: the survey was no longer confined to the impact of the war on neutrals but also extended to prizes taken from enemies and allies. Hence its title *Le droit des prises de la Grande Guerre* (1924). This new work on prize law burdened me so heavily, and not only by reason of its bulk (about 1500 pages), combined as it was with my new academic duties since 1919 as a young professor of public international law and diplomatic history at the University of Utrecht, that I firmly abjured the subject and vowed never to return to it; this was to be my swan song.

But no one is master of his fate and I felt that I could not refuse the request of the editors of the *Nederlands Juristenblad*, on the outbreak of World War II in 1938, to contribute a series of articles on the state of modern prize law and the resulting prognostication of what was in store for the Netherlands, which were at the time still neutral. This was what I undertook in 1939-1940.

Shortly afterwards fate intervened once more and in a wholly unexpected manner. In May 1940, the Netherlands were invaded by Nazi Germany and in the following month of October I was seized in my bed by servants of the Occupant and transported, together with a group of other opponents of National Socialism, to the German concentration camp of Buchenwald, where we were interned as hostages for the treatment of German nationals in the then Netherlands East Indies. During my stay there I realized that, if I were vouchsafed the mercy of coming out of that place of diabolic horror alive, Seyss-Inquart would dismiss me from my academic post in Holland—a prospect which made me think for the first time of the possibility of filling my prospectively empty days in collecting material for the writing of a broad historical series on the development of international law.

When, after surviving a serious attack of pneumonia, I was suddenly released from Buchenwald in June 1941—by whose intervention I have never been able to discover—things developed as I had foreseen. Just as I was about to resume my lectures in October 1941, at that juncture at the University of Amsterdam, General Rauter's staff stepped in and summarily dismissed me from my University post, obviously on the grounds of my earlier condemnation of the Nuremberg Nazi Race Laws of 1933, my severe censure of the German U-boat practices (though this was parallelled by not less severe criticism of the illegal Allied Reprisals Orders) and my indignation over the surrender by France and England, under the combined blackmail of Hitler and Mussolini, of Czechoslovakia at Munich in 1938, to which I gave vent in my second inaugural speech at Amsterdam on 17 October 1938 (*Na den storm*), which was later inserted in an English version in vol. I of the present publication at pp. 550-556. We all know now from hindsight how that surrender resulted in the ensuing fatal development and acted as a prelude or catalyst to the German holocaust that followed and ended by affecting all mankind.

My dismissal created for me a situation that lasted for three and a half years, during which my Buchenwald plan to write an historical work on the law of nations slowly matured, and I had ample time to engage in the preparatory work of perusing the vast indispensable treaty and other source material and arranging it provisionally into a scientific defensible system.

It was this series of coherent events which led me to undertake the present historical work and it was as a direct consequence of World War II that it has finally seen the light of day.

This short account justifies the paradox that this historical work would probably, and its present Part IX-C would certainly, not have been conceived and published if Germany had not twice in my life-time flouted international law by her major crimes of assaulting her peaceful European neighbours, on the latter occasion including my own country.

After Holland's liberation from the Nazi yoke in May 1945 I had a very busy life, carrying out a variety of functions. At first restored to my academic chair in Amsterdam, thereupon elected to a professorship at the Law Faculty of Leiden, re-appointed to my original chair in Utrecht; engaged in the semi-diplomatic work of the Preparatory Commission for the United Nations and its first session in London in 1945-46 as a representative of the Netherlands; later in charge of the task of a Netherlands State Commission for the extirpation from our national legal system of the scores of Nazi intrusions into that system during five years of Nazi occupation through the channel of spurious German *Verordnungsblätter*, and finally appointed by the Government to serve for several years as Vice-President of the Special Court of Cassation for the Trial of German War Criminals in Holland, I simply lacked the time to start the enormous work involved in writing my planned historical review, especially when I had also to find enough leisure in the meantime to continue and complete a two-volume work on the case law produced by the Permanent Court of International Justice and the International Court of Justice, which I had undertaken from the very beginning of their juridical activity in 1922, and had ever since continued to analyse in an uninterrupted series of articles. I disliked the idea of abandoning this work in its unfinished state after so many years of assiduous study of their case law, even though I realized that its completion would put a heavy additional stress on all my other occupations. But I had the satisfaction of seeing the entire collection after more than forty years work finally printed in book form in 1965 (concerning the old Court) and in 1966 (concerning the new Court).

However, owing to this accumulation of functions following the liberation of our country and the further complications referred to above, it was not until 1967 that I could finally undertake my planned broader historical study, of which ten volumes (I to IX-B) have meanwhile appeared between 1968 and 1979.

My first confrontation with the oldest British judgments in cases of maritime prize dates from a period when I was still unable to lay hands on certain works the existence of which was known to me from literary sources and from the catalogues of the Peace Palace Library at The Hague. So I started the job there. But I soon realized, in particular in respect of the British sources, that that would be wholly insufficient. The result was that I decided to transfer my exploratory work to London, especially in the marvellously rich collection of books and manuscripts kept in the British Museum, complemented by further research in the Record Room of the Guild Hall and the Public Record Office, and later by a visit to the Bodleian Library in Oxford.

But with this decision my real research misery began, in particular due to two different causes.

The first cause, of relatively minor importance, was my discovery at my first visit at the end of 1945 to the vast circular Reading Room of the British Museum of the frequent occurrence of a capital letter D on the sheets of the General Catalogue there. As this letter D seemed to be particularly attached to a number of entries related to the old British books on prize law for which I was seeking, I asked for and got the information that the D meant that the work concerned had been destroyed by a fire caused by an incendiary bomb attack by German aeroplanes during the Blitz of 1939-1940 on a depository where rarely demanded books were being kept. I checked that report as regards my own 1500 page book of 1924 which, of course, I had on account of its weight not carried with me to England for consultation if need be. I learned of its destruction also and was happy to be able to replace it at a subsequent visit with the last duplicate copy which I happened still to have at home.

The second cause of the mounting and far more serious difficulties of my research in loco consisted of the many lacunae in the documentation and the general chaotic state in which the reporting of prize cases in older periods of British legal history proved to have left the subject-matter. I dare to express this criticism because I must acknowledge the same chaos in different variations, with respect to the state of affairs in my own country, in France and in Flemish Malines (Mechelen), once the seat of the appellate *Grand Conseil*, created in 1463 by the then common Sovereign of the Low Countries.

This situation was in part attributable to the same cause as that first mentioned, *viz.*, the destruction of a work that intrigued me in particular, entitled *Law of Contraband of War* (by Frederic Thomas Pratt, London, 1856), one of the richest sources of old customary and judicial law of prize, according to the English tradition. I have sought for it wherever I could expect to track it down, but for years without success. See on this work *infra*, pp. 74-76. The same could also be said of the disappearance of Pratt-Lee-Lloyd's volume of 1854, *Notes on the principles and practice of prize courts*, concerning the War of the Austrian Succession of a century earlier and the references in Sir George Lee's Ms. Notes dating back to again a century earlier, which made it almost impossible for a long time for me to round off my survey of old British case law. Only recently one of my collaborators, Mr Wybo P. Heere, discovered the "Scarlet Pimpernels" in the Peace Palace Library at The Hague, where unfortunately I had missed them by sheer oversight. On the last-mentioned work see *infra*, pp. 74-76.

Before finally quitting the scene, I must once again offer my most sincere and grateful thanks to all those who have supported and helped me and without whose aid this work, with whatever remaining imperfections there may be, could not possibly have been achieved.

There is first Miss Mary M. Sibthorp, O.B.E., who most effectively guided my initially somewhat stumbling steps in English through the legendary maze of facts and illusions which together constitute the history of international law, and who, at the outset of my journey, had to cut away the many linguistic lianas which entangled my feet.

Then there are my two loyal collaborators at the Institute of Public International Law of the University of Utrecht, Mr Wybo P. Heere and Mrs Polona Offerhaus-Stoop, who accompanied me during more than twenty years on my progress, rendering me a great variety of services, drawing my attention to legal sources which I might have overlooked, to repetitions in my text which would have escaped me, to flaws in the system of my exposé, to errors in the dating of treaties and other literary sources quoted, suggesting the filling of certain lacunae which they had discovered and, in the final stage, double-checking the proofs which I have always also controlled myself and indexing all the volumes of this series.

There are further many others, named and unnamed in earlier prefaces, who have given me valuable technical assistance in typing and retyping my drafts.

And there is, last but not least, the publishing house and the printers who performed their part of the job most perfectly.

To all of them I express my heartfelt gratitude for the various ways in which they have enabled me to continue and finish the carrying out of my somewhat rashly undertaken plan.

Spring 1980 *J.H.W. Verzijl*

THE LAW OF MARITIME PRIZE

INTRODUCTION

When facing the arduous task of exposing the origin and growth of the law of maritime prize I had to consider first of all how best to proceed. It was clear to me from the outset that there would be no reasonable possibility of arranging the subject in a systematic manner corresponding to the program of the present series of topics of international law in a historical perspective without considerable preliminary spadework in a *terra* all but *incognita*. So I began my work by exploring the historical data and simply investigating successively the sources most easily accessible or which interested me most at the time without attempting any systematic approach. Not until my research should have resulted in a collection of extracts as complete as possible in the most disparate fields, would I be in a position to form a well-founded judgment on the best possible system of ordering the vast mass of divergent data thus collected, and as to whether the system of arrangement that I had applied sixty years ago in my work of 1924 on *Le droit des prises de la Grande Guerre* was still adequate for the final arrangement of the results of my detailed study on the oldest period.

There was, first, need to open this volume with two essential Chapters: I, a discussion and analysis of its earliest sources, and II, a presentation of a bird's-eye view of the main landmarks of its history from its inception up to the present day. That survey proved to my relief that the order in which I had set out the problems was satisfactory and that therefore the order of arrangement, applied in my previous work, was on the whole still serviceable for this new volume. The lay-out will therefore be broadly parallel with my earlier work, although the latter was confined to the prize law of World War I and, therefore, gave only a summary alphabetical index of older precedents in its Appendix III-B (at pp. 1380-1384). The index which gives guidance through the cases discussed or cited in the present Part IX-C will be considerably larger.

The history of prize law can be divided into two main periods, one extending from its earliest period up to 1907-09, which I will call the pre-codification era, itself divided into two phases, the formative phase until the restoration of Europe after the downfall of Napoleon, and the consolidation phase which followed. This was succeeded by the post-codification period covering Word War I, which was particularly the subject of my work of 1917 and 1924.

There would be ground for adding a chapter earmarked for the 20th century, but for reasons which I will explain later I prefer rather to deal with this post-World War I era in a number of annexes.

Described in a little more detail, the design of this Part is as follows: Chapter I, the sources. While roaming like a knight-errant across the legal wilderness of early times and gradually extending my haphazard spadework there, I found that I could reasonably distinguish eight sources, worth discussion in an equal number of separate sections. These are, however, of very different size and significance *inter se*. Most important among this sequence of sections is section 5, dealing with the decisions of old admiralty courts, and in that section in particular the subsection devoted to the case law of the prize courts of England. This subsection is itself divided into two paragraphs, that *sub* A attempting to describe in a more orderly manner the chaotic sequence of collections of English prize court decrees, and that *sub* B summing up the various legal issues which gradually emerged from the proceedings as topics of judicial examination. This latter review displays a striking picture of the extreme variety of the subjects with which British admiralty courts saw themselves successively confronted in the period between the mid-17th and the end of the 18th century during their country's naval wars.

In Chapter II, I give a very succinct bird's-eye view of the principal landmarks in the history of prize law during its existence, covering approximately sixteen countries, from about 400 A.D. until roughly 1900 A.D.

Chapter III analyses the pre-codification period from the earliest days up to the London Conference on Naval Warfare of 1908-1909. The history of that period is divided on a number of principal issues into a formative and a consolidation phase along what can, in figurative language, be designated as a legal watershed of the first decade of the 19th century. This period will be described and, on the whole in parallel with my studies of 1917 and 1924, will be analysed in three main parts, *viz.*, Part A dealing with the substantive law of prize; Part B dealing with an aggregate of differing issues which I called at the time "droits policiers des belligérants" and for which, because of their variety, I have been unable to invent an appropriate comprehensive name; and Part C dealing with prize procedure.

Part A will be distributed over seven sections, dealing successively with: 1. enemy property at sea; 2. enemy goods on neutral ships and neutral goods on enemy ships; 3. contraband of war; 4. blockade and its breach; 5. unneutral service; 6. the Rule of the War of 1756, and 7. various irregularities committed by non-enemy vessels.

Part B will also be spread over seven sections, devoted successively to: 1. ship's papers; 2. visit and search; 3. possible measures following visit and search; 4. convoy; 5. destruction of the prize; 6. joint capture, and 7. recapture and salvage.

Part C will be divided into eight sections, covering the following subjects: 1. organization of prize jurisdiction; 2. competence of the prize court; 3. law to be applied by it; 4. its procedure; 5. possible dicta and their legal effects; 6. award of damages, freight and general average; 7. award of the proceeds of prizes, and 8. appeal or revision of prize judgments.

An excursus will be intercalated here to commemorate the initial success and ultimate failure of the creation of an International Prize Court in 1907-1909, on which I refer further to Volume VIII of this publication, pp. 345-348.

The main parts A, B and C of this work described above will be preceded by exposés of a general nature which cannot properly be inserted in one or the other of the sections of any of the three main Parts and which I have therefore either entitled preliminary (dealing with the questions: by whom, when, where, and against what objects the right of prize may be exercised), or treated together under the common title "the enemy or neutral (non-enemy) character of prizes", a subsection under I devoted to ships, one under II to goods.

Further divisions of the sections into subsections, paragraphs or subparagraphs will be introduced with regard to subject matter of major importance, such as the carriage of contraband and the breach of blockade.

Seeing that some of the issues examined in the present Part IX-C on prize law also play a role in the law of neutrality (Part IX-B), I have drawn a modest parallel between the two groups of precedents and periods. In order as far as possible to maintain in the following survey of the development a parallel to those chapters and sections, I will arrange the present section 3 on contraband of war, the main ground of belligerent interference with neutral commerce, in such a way that I will divide that era into the same two periods as I distinguished in volume X, *viz.* (*a*) the turbulent formative time extending from the earliest period up to 1815, characterized by a long series of 17th and 18th century wars, and (*b*) the more settled consolidation period between 1815 and 1907 with its own culminating points of the Crimean War (1853-1856), the American Civil War (1861-1865) and the Italo-Abyssinian War (1896).

The division applies, in particular, to § 2 (Destination) and § 3 (Sanctions) of Section 3 (Contraband). It has no special importance for the subject dealt with in § 1 (Categories).

Chapter IV, devoted to the operation of the law of prize during of after World War I, is in its lay-out planned to run parallel to Chapter III. It covers, among others, the same period as analysed in my books of 1917 and 1924, but there is scarcely any question of duplication. Not only do I present the available material in an entirely different manner but I have also had a shot at illustrating the trend of the jurisprudence on certain key questions which characterized naval warfare during World War I in shorter summarizing studies. These will be followed, not by an independent Chapter V that might have set out the developments since the Peace Conference of Versailles (1919), but by three annexes. These are intended to indicate the legal situation at three crucial moments in 20th century history, Annex I giving a critical retrospect on the practice during World War I (which I wrote in 1917), Annex II concerning the prospective state of prize law on the eve of World War II (which I wrote in 1938), and Annex III narrating in brief the actual developments during and after World War II.

I can only hope for a favourable understanding of my choice of a separate treatment of selected recent developments in this last Part IX-C.

"This last Part IX-C". Yes, that remains true from the systematical point of view, which I have never lost sight of. However, both my collaborators and the publishers long ago cautioned me against an over-optimistic view of my standing a chance of incorporating the entire text in one volume. This caution soon proved justified: the text of Part IX-C must be spread over more volumes than one. The contents could, however, from an editorial point of view, fortunately be divided by the abovementioned figurative "watershed" of 1907-1909 into matters belonging to the pre-, and those belonging to the post-codification period.

This is the total scheme of Part IX-C as planned by myself, which is not to say that it will, under present conditions, also be possible to carry it out to its full extent. I have been anxious not to leave the work behind in the state which it has reached up till now, unfinished in the sense that it does not even sketch its planned total design. It is for this reason that I have added a summary of the design for the whole Part IX-C.

CHAPTER I

THE SOURCES OF THE LAW OF PRIZE

GENERAL INTRODUCTION

The rules of prize law have developed in many different ways. Whoever attempts to present a survey of the sources of prize law in past centuries indeed finds himself confronted by an overwhelming mass of sources, both national and international. The development has taken place by means of (1) old regional codifications, (2) bilateral treaties, (3) municipal laws and ordinances, (4) national instructions to the navy, (5) prize court decisions, (6) actual naval practice, (7) arbitral awards and, at a later stage, (8) a few multilateral conventions. I will give some details of this variety of sources below.

Prize cases have already in earlier centuries been the subject of legal analysis in private consultations. Most famous in this field is the consultation which Hugo Grotius wrote about 1605 at the request of the Amsterdam Chamber of the United East India Company concerning the capture, on 25 February 1603 in the Strait of Malacca by the Netherlands Admiral Heemskerck, of a Portuguese carrack, the *Catharina*, which had afterwards been condemned as good and lawful prize by the Admiralty Court of Amsterdam by a judgment of 9 September 1604 (text in annex to W.J.M. van Eysinga's paper "Grotius et la Chine" in *Grotiana*, vol. IX, 1936-1939). This consultation was never published in full at the time. What, however, did appear in 1609, as an anonymous publication, was a treatise under the title *Mare liberum sive de iure quod Batavis competit ad Indiana commercia*, written at the invitation of the Zeeland Chamber of the United East-Indian Company in support of the claim of the Republic of the United Netherlands to freedom of trade with the Indies, disputed by Spain especially during the protracted negotiations for their Twelve Years' Truce of 1609-1621. A manuscript of the original consultation of 1604-1605 was only rediscovered at an auction in 1864 and published by Dr H.G. Hamaker in 1868 under its title *De jure praedae* (edition *Classics*, last vol. (1964); English translation also in the *Bibliotheca Visseriana*, vol. V, pp. 1 *et seq.*). It appeared to consist of twelve chapters, no. XII of which was to all intents and purposes identical with the *Mare liberum*. See for further particulars Part IV of this publication, pp. 31-33.

Many other such consultations have later followed this famous one.

Section 1. REGIONAL CODIFICATIONS

Introduction

A wealth of data concerning such codifications can be found in J.M. Pardessus' *Collection de lois maritimes antérieures au XVIIIe siècle* (Paris, 1828-1845) and in Sir Travers Twiss' *The Black Book of the Admiralty* (London, 1871-1876). The first consists of six volumes with detailed introductory notes regarding each of the inserted documents, grouped under 37 headings. Especially interesting in this context are volumes I and II which contain the texts, introduced by such notes, of the regional codifications, surveyed below. The second collection, printed in a publication entitled *The Chronicles and Memorials of Great Britain and Ireland during the Middle Ages* and published by the authority of H.M. Treasury, under the direction of the Master of the Rolls, also under the title *Monumenta juridica*, consists of four volumes, No. I of which begins with an elaborate Introduction to the said Black Book (pp. vii-xciii), and thereafter reproduces its text (pp. 2-472). Volume IV includes, in addition, twelve other documents relating to maritime law, *viz.*:

— Tabula de Amalfa, Capitula et Ordinationes Curiae Maritimae nobilis Civitatis Amalfae, in 66 articles (pp. 1-51);
— Dat Gotlandsche Water-recht, in 66 articles (pp. 53-129);
— Laws of Wisbuy, in 70 articles (pp. 263-284);
— Codex Livonicus (of the Teutonic Order of Livonia), in 14 articles (pp. 285-299) (Ms. Dreyer in the Library of the University of Göttingen);
— Codex Brugensis or Purple Book of Bruges, or Rolls of Oléron of the Judgments of the Sea, in 24 articles (also numbered 15-39) (pp. 301-333);
— Codex Dantiscensis, in 26 articles (also numbered 40-64) (pp. 335-355);
— Jus maritimum Lubescense in usus Osterlingorum descriptum anno 1299, in 42 articles (pp. 357-383);
— Wisby Stads-Lag van Sciprechte, in 20 chapters (pp. 385-413);
— 't Waterrecht in Vlaanderen, in 24 articles (pp. 415-447);
— L'Ordre Judiciari de la Cort dels Consols de la Mar, in 41 chapters (pp. 449-495);
— Assises Maritimes dou Reaume de Jerusalem, in 7 articles (pp. 497-519) (comp. on this kingdom Part II of this publication, pp. 400 *et seq.*);
— Ordinamenta et consuetudo maris edita per Consules Civitatis Trani, in 32 articles (pp. 521-543) (Introduction to vol. IV, pp. xiv *et seq.*).

One of the oldest surviving manuscripts in this field is the text of the Judgments of the Sea, part of the *Liber Memorandorum*, kept in the Record Room of the Guildhall in London (dating from the early 14th century), see *infra*. The collection in the Guildhall further gives valuable information about a number of other regional codifications, which I will also survey below.

A perusal of all these ancient sources testifies to the very wide extent of old admiralty jurisdiction. This was, however, for by far the greater part exercised in fields which have nothing to do with the law of maritime prize proper. Nevertheless, the regional regulations yield a limited number of rules which, directly or indirectly, do belong to that law. Such rules can be found in Arts. 19 and 20 of Part A of the Black Book of the Admiralty, which bear on the attribution of prize bounties (comp. *infra*, pp. 642 *et seq.*), Arts. 1, 18 and 22 of the Inquisition of Queensborough (1375) in Part D of the Black Book, and Arts. 6-10 of Part B of that Book. According to the latter articles: (6) upon the discovery of an enemy ship, a flag must be hoisted as a warning for the Admiral; (7) upon meeting with a foreign vessel, she must be halted, and her papers examined; in case of suspicion she must be brought before the Admiral; (8) in case of resistance, she must be seized and brought before the Admiral; (9) no prize may be carried out of the fleet without the Admiral's leave, under financial penalty; (10) the captors shall have the goods and armour of a prize above deck. King John specified the rule of Art. 7 in his Ordinance of 1201 (enacted at Hastings) as follows:

> "Item, it was ordained at Hastynges for lawe and custome of the sea in the tyme of King John, in the second yeare of his raigne, by the advice of his temporall lordes, that if the [lieutenant of the Kyng or de admirall of the Kyng or his] lieutenant in any voyage appointed by common counsell of the Kyngdom did at sea meet with any shyps or vessells laden or empty which would not stryke and lower their sailes at the command of the Kyng's lieutenant, or the Kyng's admirall, or his lieutenant, but makeing resistance against those of the ffleet, that if they can be taken that they be reputed as enemies, and their shyps, vessells, and goodes taken and forfeited as goodes of enemies, albeit that the maysters or possessors thereof should afterwards come and alleadge the same shyps, vessells, and goodes to be the goodes of friends of our lorde the Kyng, and that the company therein be chastized by imprisonment of their bodies for their rebellion at discretion."

This is one of the oldest texts which allude to a difference of treatment between ships and cargoes the property of enemies, and those the property of neutrals (designated in those old days by the term "friends").

In the following pages I will survey the main regional codifications.

Lex Rhodia de jactu (Νομὸς Ροδίων ναυτικός)

The, as far as I know, oldest edition of this law, dating from 1596, by Loewencklau, was followed much later by a modern edition by Walter Ashburner, *The Rhodian Sea Law* (Oxford, 1909). See also R. Dareste in

Revue historique du droit 1905, pp. 429 *et seq.*, and Pardessus, *Collection*, I, pp. 209-260.

The chief interest of the Rhodian sea law from the point of view of prize law consists of the fact that it provides a means of determining the pedigree of the various other regional codifications. For, as Travers Twiss remarks in the Introduction to Part IV of his work (comp. also p. cxxx), the surest test of identity of any medieval system of maritime law with the Roman law, or with any contemporaneous body of medieval sea law is to be found in the identity of the rule of contribution of other participants in a maritime adventure to the financial losses suffered by the owners of jettisoned goods, which according to the Law of the Rhodians (expressed in *Digest*, l. xiv, tit. 11, fr. 2, § 2) was to the effect that "jacturae summam pro rerum pretio distribui oportet", but which had different contents in the *Basilica* (l. iii, tit. iii), the *Assises* of Jerusalem

> "— the property which has been cast overboard ought not to be calculated otherwise than at what it cost—'Et por ce comande la lei et lasise que le get ni se qui est remes ne doit estre conte se non tant come il a coste'—with all the 'averages'—in this case meaning: outgivings on account of the cargo—and the property itself which has been rescued ought to be calculated at what it cost, for if one calculated it at the price which one might have for it in the country to which it has been brought, it would work a wrong because by chance there might be certain goods which would sell well and others not [there follows a further explanation]" —;

the Judgments of the Sea (Oléron) and the Consulate of the Sea (Barcelona).

The Assises of Jerusalem

(These I have already mentioned in Part II of this publication, at pp. 400 *et seq.*, when dealing with the Latin Kingdom of Jerusalem).

There have been two such laws, issued by King Amalrik (or Amauri) I (1162-1173), one called the "Livre des Assises de la Court des Barons", the other the "Livre des Assises et des Usages de la Court des Bourgeois du Royaume de Jerusalem", and preceded by the words "Ici orres en quel part establi le roi Amauri qui deust estre la raison des mariniers et des vaiceaus et des naves". They were kept in the treasure-chamber of the Chapel of the Holy Sepulchre until the city was recaptured by Saladin in 1187 and the authentic books disappeared. See on these *Assises* the detailed data in Pardessus, I, pp. 261 *et seq.*, especially pp. 272-282; Travers Twiss, vol. IV, Introduction, pp. xiv-xx and 497-519), and H.L. Zeller in the *Sammlung älterer Seerechtsquellen* (Mainz-Berlin, 1910), Heft 4, pp. 18 *et seq.*

They show a clear affinity with the laws and customs obtaining in France, which is not surprising in view of the fact that many of the Crusaders were French barons. According to these *Assises*, drawn up for the use of the Frankish population, which had emigrated eastward to Syria in the train of the first Crusaders, there were special Courts of the Sea which had a procedure different from that of the ordinary courts of the land and administered justice amongst them in maritime matters, partly *in civilibus*, partly *in criminalibus*. Penal jurisdiction was exercised by the Court of the Burghers and its divisional court, the Court of the Chain, so designated from the chain that was drawn across the entrance of one of the ports of the Latin Kingdom, Acre, for the safeguarding of the vessels within it. It decided the cases pled before it by a jury of six jurors.

The rules according to which the Courts of the Sea were instructed to decide the cases submitted to them were indicated differently in different provisions and manuscripts as "raison", "droit", "assise", "lei", "justice", or "δίκαιον", meaning now *jus civile* or statute law, now judge-made law, now natural law, and sometimes used as identical, sometimes as distinct concepts—"Et por ce comande la lei et lasise"; "εΐς τὸν νομὸν καὶ εΐς τὴν ἄσῆξαν".

More or less reliable MSS. of these *Assises* are still extant in the Vatican, in the Royal Library at Munich (chapters xliii-xlix), in the Imperial Library in Vienna, earlier in the Ducal Library of San Marco in Venice (the MS. Cyprense, chapters xl-xlvi), the Laurian Monastery of Mt. Athos (in Greek)—comp. Dr C.E. Zachariae (von Lingenthal)'s publication of 1839 (Heidelberg), *Historiae juris graeco-romani delineatio*—, and in the *Bibliothèque Nationale* in Paris (MS. Colbert, no. 1390).

The subject-matters dealt with in these Assises in seven long articles were: (5) the carrying of forbidden goods (*merces illicitae, πράγματα κοληµένα*) to the Saracens; (6) the capture of cargo by cruizers (*κουρσάρη*), and (7) the contribution of other cargo-owners to losses caused by jettison (comp. on this subject *supra*, p. 13) and the salvage of flotsam, jetsam and ligan. The prohibition of transport to the land of the Saracens by "mauvais Chrestiens" was in conformity with the formal interdiction of such trade in contraband goods by Christians by Canon 24 of the Third Council of the Lateran (1179):

> "If it happen that a mariner or a merchant .... carries to the country of the Saracens—'Ici orres la raison [in this case: the law] dou mauvais Chrestian qui parte aver devee en terre de Sarasins'—forbidden goods, such as, for instance, armour, coats-of-mail, lances and projectiles, axes or spears of steel or iron, and he is arraigned in the Court of the Chain by the mariners or by the merchants who were there, who knew that he sold or delivered to the Saracens those forbidden goods, and what he carried amounted to more than a mark of silver, all that he possesses ought to be confiscated to the lord of the land, and he ought to be condemned by the other Court of the Burghers to be hanged ..."

Tabula Amalphitana

A MS. of this sea law was discovered in the middle of the 1860's in the Imperial Library of Vienna in the collection MSS. Foscarini no. 184. This collection, which had originally belonged to Marco Foscarini, Doge of

Venice in 1762-1763, was acquired from his heirs by the Emperor of Austria in 1801.

The text of this Tabula, entitled in the MS. "Capitula et Ordinationes Curiae Maritimae nobilis Civitatis Amalphae, quae in vulgari sermone dicuntur La Tabula di Amalfi", containing 66 articles, was published for the first time in 1844 in an appendix to the *Archivio Italiano* (Firenze 1842-1844) and subsequently, after the discovery of the MS. in Vienna, by Dr. L. Goldschmidt in Vol. VII of the *Zeitschrift für das gesamte Handelsrecht* (Erlangen, 1864), pp. 296 *et seq.* with annotations from the pen of Dr. Paul Laband, "Das Seerecht von Amalfi".

This Tabula is of somewhat dubious origin. Some writers considered it to be the oldest subsisting sea law and the source of the *Consolato del Mare*, but Pardessus was in doubt even about its independent existence, still being inclined in 1828 to identify it with the *Ordinamenta et Consuetudo Maris, edita per Consules Civitatis Trani*, a very ancient text in 32 articles (*Black Book*, vol. IV, Introduction, pp. xiv-xvi; pp. 521-543, drafted in Italian, but probably rather of Venetian origin). The sea law, laid down in this *Tabula* of Amalfi, was still applied by the maritime courts of the Kingdom of Naples in the 16th century.

The origin of the town of Amalfi, which still possesses a wonderful ships' museum, is itself a little misty. According to Travers Twiss, in the Introduction to vol. IV of his *Monumenta juridica* of 1874 (pp. vii-xiv), the town was founded by patrician émigrés from Rome, shipwrecked off Ragusa on their way to Constantinople; its dependence on the Byzantine Empire would seem to follow from the fact that its chief magistrate was appointed by the Exarch of Ravenna. The town was in any case an important naval power about the 9th and 10th centuries, together with the Neapolitans fighting the Saracens.

See for the text of the *Tabula Amalphitana* further Travers Twiss' *Monumenta*, vol. IV, pp. 1-51.

The Mediterranean was in any case a centre of maritime legislation. Comp. e.g.:

the Maritime Law of Genoa in Pardessus IV, pp. 419-544; of Pisa (MS. 1342 in the *Libri legali*, kept in the archives of the Chancery of Pisa) (1118), and of Florence in Pardessus IV, pp. 545-609;

the *Statutum navium Bajonensium* (1204-1213), Pardessus IV, pp. 283-289;

the Statutes of Marseille (1253-1255), *ibid.*, IV, pp. 256-283;

the *Siete Partidas* of Castile (initiated by King Alphonso the Wise in 1256, completed in 1266), *ibid.*, VI, pp. 16-57; the fifth *Partida* was framed in accordance with the *Rôles d'Oléron*.

On the *Consulado de Mar* see *infra*, pp. 22 *et seq.*

The same applies to the Adriatic, from which the Venetian Ordinances on sea law of 1255 are handed down to us: Pardessus, V, pp. 20-59; pp. 60 *et seq.*

Rôles d'Oléron

As appears from the collection *Judgments of the Sea*, which, following the indications by Sir Travers Twiss at p. xxi of the Introduction to vol. I of his work on the *Black Book of the Admiralty* and which, thanks to the courtesy of the librarian staff of the Record Room of the Guildhall in London, I could inspect on the spot, those judgments were founded on the *Rôles d'Oléron*, or *Lois de Leyron* (as they were called in a French ordinance of 1364 and in a MS., kept in the Spanish Escorial) as their legal basis, or rather they themselves constituted the said *Rôles*. The legal character of these *Rôles* was in effect not that of ordinances enacted by any State authority, but that of judgments of the Court of the Mayor of the *Commune* of Oléron, vested with jurisdiction by such authority, in casu in virtue of a privilege granted by the Duke of Guyenne to that *Commune*. Hence the heading of the manuscript in the Guildhall: "La Charte d'Oléroun des juggmentz de la miere". They all end with the formula: "Et ceo est le jugement en ceo cas" (Travers Twiss, II, p. 385).

This oldest MS. of the *Judgments of the Sea* is contained in a heavy vellum-bound volume and forms part of a *Liber Memorandorum* of uncertain date, probably from the beginning of the 14th century. Pursuant to data contained in that volume, however, the *Liber Memorandorum* was already preceded by a somewhat older collection, the *Liber Horn*, so named after the Chamberlain of the City during the reign of King Edward II (1307-1327) and also dealing in particular with the laws of Oléron. This famous sea-law is also known as the *Codex Brugensis* or *Purple Book of Bruges*, kept in MS. form in the archives of the library of the City of Bruges (151 folio's), which is a Flemish version of the *Rôles* (*Black Book*, vol. IV, pp. 301-333). The archives of the Bodleian Library in Oxford also contain a MS. Selden of the Rolls under No. B 7 (formerly No. 3341). The manuscripts collection of the British Museum includes a text in MS. Cotton, Nero A VI. Comp. also Add. MS. 10,146, f. 103.

Their origin is controversial. Leibnitz attributed it to the Emperor Otto III who is supposed to have issued them after Richard Cœur-de-Lion's cession to him of Oléron together with Guyenne and Poitou, but this theory is highly improbable. A report of the King's Judges on the Rolls, entitled "Fasciculus de superioritate maris"—a Latin Roll of 12 Edw. III (1339), now kept in the Office of the Rolls—recites that the laws and statutes made by the kings of England in order to maintain peace and justice amongst the peoples of every nation passing through the Sea of England ... were by the Lord Richard [the Lion-hearted] on his return from the Holy Land, corrected, interpreted, and declared, and published in the Island of Oléron, and were named *Gallica lingua* "la ley Olyronn", but in this form the story would seem to be apocryphal because Richard never visited the island. It is beyond doubt that the *Rôles d'Oléron* were officially adopted as law by England at an early date and that the kings of England have naturally had a share in that development. But the rôle of Richard Cœur-de-Lion was more correctly expressed by Sir Leoline Jenkins when he related (at p. 87 of W. Wynne's publication of his *Life*) that "King Richard, being on his return from the Holy War, thought fit to review and reform [the laws of Oléron] and then to give them the stamp of his Royal Authority". The laws were undoubtedly of French origin and existed already as customary rules before his time.

The most plausible theory is that they have been put into writing on the initiative of Eleanor, Duchess of Guyenne (Aquitaine), consort of King Louis VII of France (1137-1180), after her return from the second Crusade in 1147, during which she was informed of the existence of such "customs of the sea" elsewhere. This, at least, is the tradition mentioned in a work of Estienne Cleirac, *Les Us et Coustumes de la Mer* (Bordeaux, 1st ed. 1641), who himself referred as his source to Garcia, *dit* de Ferrande's *Grand Routier de la Mer* of 1541.

The *Rôles d'Oléron* were received as law in the maritime courts of England at the latest about 12 Edw. III (1339), and in the 14th century were also adopted by the Courts of Normandy and Brittanny, and later found their way into the *Coutumier de Normandie*. Their first mention in any French ordinance dates from 1364, when King Charles V of France admitted the Castilians to trade at the ports of Leure and Honfleur (Normandy) and had their causes adjudicated "selon les Coustumes de la mer et les droiz de Leyron dehors".

The *Rôles d'Oléron*, which must already have been known under that name in the 13th century, have developed in two versions, a Gascon and a Norman/Breton text, which differed both in the number of their articles and their substance. A Castilian version of "el fuero de Leyron" can be found in an appendix to Capmany's *Código de las Costumbres Marítimas de Barcelona* (Madrid, 1791), pp. 36 *et seq.* and in Pardessus, VI, pp. 57-63.

There still exist other manuscripts of the *Rôles d'Oléron*, *viz.*, among the Rawlinson collection in the Bodleian Library at Oxford (B 356, f. 43 b, No. 2254; and No. 3341), in the library of the Corpus Christi College at Cambridge and in the British Museum (Cotton collection, Nero A, § 6, No. 30 (1); Vespasian, B xxii, fol. 25).—The text is printed, in different versions, in Pardessus' *Collection*, I, pp. 323-354, in 56 articles, a number considerably larger than those obtaining in the Oxford and London MSS. (24 articles) and in the editions of the abovementioned authors De Ferrande (46) and Cleirac (47). The version which found its way into the *Coutumier de Normandie* of 1539 contained only 25 or 26 articles. The texts published by Travers Twiss (vol. I, pp. 88-131; vol. II, pp. 209-241, with table of contents at pp. 243-251—under the title "Les Costumes d'Oléron et deu Jutgamen de la Mar" in 24 articles, reproducing the text of the MS. in the *Liber Horn*—and vol. VI, pp. 301-333) contain 39 articles. See also the text published by Travers Twiss in vol. II of his work at pp. 253-397 (followed by a table of contents at pp. 399-405), under the heading "Les bons usages et les bonnes costumes et les bons jugemenz de la Commune d'Oléron".

Pardessus explained this continuous growth of the number of provisions by arguing (vol. I, p. 286) that the original *Rôles* of the 24 articles had gradually been extended as a result of accretion with three other groups of rules, two dealing with damage suffered by cargo on its unloading, respectively with fishery associations, eight further provisions, which had never been incorporated in any earlier manuscript until their insertion in Part C of the *Black Book*, and twenty final ones concerned with the breaking of seals, shipwreck, flotsam, etc.

As a result of the reception of the *Rôles* of Oléron in English maritime law, these originally French *Rôles* have become an integral part of the *Black Book of the Admiralty*, intended to serve as a guidance for English admiralty courts. They constitute Part C of that *Black Book* (comp. further *infra*, this section, p. 20). Travers Twiss divided the contents of the *Rôles* in that Part C into three groups, *viz*., 39 original rules, 24 further articles, also identical with an old version of the *Judgments of the Sea*—a statement that cannot be upheld as regards the ensuing ten additional provisions which cannot be found in any other version of those judgments.

The *Rôles* of Oléron include no provisions of prize law proper, but deal with the relations between the ship's captain and the ship-owner (raising of a mortgage on the ship for the sale of provisions; an oath of the master and six mariners as a rebuttal of the presumption of bad tackling), between the captain and the crew (wages; medical care of mariners; consultation before sailing; punishment for offences; conditions for leaving the ship; disputes between them), and between the ship-owner and the charterer (payment of freight for goods saved in a shipwreck; compensation due in case of delay in loading), and further with the responsibility of a pilot, with the jettison of cargo and the felling of masts to save the vessel in case of a storm, and with collisions between ships on roadsteads.

See on these laws Th. Kiesselbach, "Der Ursprung der Rôles d'Oléron und das Seerecht von Damme" in *Hansische Geschichtsblätter* XII (1906), and Karl Fr. Kriger, *Ursprung und Wurzeln der Rôles d'Oléron* (Cologne, 1970). The latter work contains a transcript of the laws, accompanied by a modern German translation at pp. 123-145. Comp. on the contents of the Rôles of Oléron also the scholarly study under the title *Ons oudste zeerecht* [Our—Netherlands—oldest sea-laws] (Zwolle, 1976), by A. Korthals Altes, cited below under the heading "Dutch and Flemish sources", p. 30.

Black Book of the Admiralty

Most complicated is the history of the Black Book of the Admiralty, on the rediscovery of which in 1874 I have already summarily reported in Part IV of this publication, pp. 38-39, but upon which it is now time to enter a little more deeply.

When, in 1871, Sir Travers Twiss published the text of the Black Book of the Admiralty, the original book was missing. Its disappearance from the Admiralty Registry, where it had been seen by Dr. Exton, Judge of the High Court of Admiralty (*The Maritime Dicaeologie*, London, 1664, b. II, ch. xi) and Dr. Christopher Robinson (Introduction to his *Collectanea Maritima* (London, 1801)), was made known for the first time by Mr. Alexander Luders who wished to consult its old French text in 1808, and it had never been found since then. Both Luders and Pardessus made the mistake of holding a certain manuscript, kept in the Bodleian Library in Oxford (Arch. Selden B, 27), which Selden had possessed for a long time and which he has described in his *Vindiciae Maris Clausi* of 1618 (London, 1776) as "Commentarius de Rebus Admiralitatis", to be identical with the missing book. The Bodleian manuscript and the original Black Book were in fact not identical, as was proved by a comparison of certain authentic quotations by Exton and Prynne from the latter with the text of the former. Since the disappearance of the original book from the Admiralty Register two substitute instruments had served, namely, (*a*) a collection of sea laws in the custody of the library of the College of Advocates in Doctors' Commons, received by them as a present from Sir Leoline Jenkins in 1685 and later acquired at an auction of that library by Dr. Th. Spinks, and (*b*) a trustworthy modern transcript, professedly a copy of the original Black Book, which was at one time also found to be missing but which had later been rediscovered in the Admiralty archives in Whitehall. A reconstruction of the text of the genuine Black Book was further made possible by quotations found in a number of other manuscripts in the British Museum: Lansdowne MSS. Nos. 375 and 171 (the Caesar Papers) and Cotton MSS., Vespasian B xxii, Codex Membraneus, "De officio et munere Admirali" dating from the time of the Admirals Sir Thomas Beaufort (1420-1425), John of Lancaster, Duke of Bedford (1425-1436) and John Holland, Earl of Huntingdon, since 1443 Duke of Exeter (1436-1446). In his Introduction to vol. I of his work Travers Twiss explained what sources he had used for the text published. He would have preferred to reproduce that in the MS. Vespasian B xxii, as exhibiting the more ancient and the more accurate text of the documents contained in the first five parts of the Black Book, but as his primary object was to restore the text of the original Black Book, he had decided in favour of adopting the Whitehall MS. and annexing, as notes, the variations to be observed in the text of Cotton's MS. and that of Selden in the Bodleian Library.

As he set out in his Introduction to vol. III of his work (of 1876), however, the original Black Book, which had been lost sight of for more than half a century, had in the meantime come to light, discovered accidentally at the bottom of a chest, which was supposed to contain certain private papers belonging to the late Registrar of the Admiralty Court, and which had been transferred from his private office to the cellars of the existing Registry shortly after its establishment.

In order to bring his publication up to date after the rediscovery of the original Black Book, Travers Twiss gave, at pp. 131-144 of vol. IV of his work a comparative survey of the varying readings of the text of the original *Liber Niger Admiralitatis*, as compared with the texts, previously used by him, of the Whitehall MS. and the Cotton MS. Vespasian B xxii. For a better understanding of the texts of the different codifications of maritime law, moreover, he followed up the abovementioned glossary of Anglo-Norman and Gascon words in the *Rôles* of Oléron at pp. 145-197, with similar glossaries of Catalan words used in the *Consolat de Mar*, at pp. 199-238, and of low-German words, used in certain Baltic sources, at pp. 239-262 of that same volume IV.

The main texts of the Black Book are printed, after Travers Twiss's elaborate Introduction (vol. I, pp. vii-lxxxvi), from p. 2 onwards in four parts.

A, 20 Old Rules for the Lord Admiral (pp. 2-23), concerning the officers of the Admiralty and other related subjects. What this Part A—being an Ordinance issued by the King-in-Council, dating from the early period of Edward III's reign (1327-1377) and contemporaneous with a French Ordinance for the Fleet by Philippe de Valois of 1338—provided in its 20 "Old Rules" related mainly to the Admiral's wages (four shillings per day) and those of his subordinates; the appointment of the ships to the Admiral or his lieutenant, respectively to lower-grade naval officers; the number of lanterns which the different units of the Fleet were bound to carry; and the award of prize money (comp. on the latter subject *infra*, p. 642).

B, 20 Instructions on what the Lord Admiral was to do at sea and land in time of war, including the earliest Articles of War for the King's Navy (pp. 24-39). This Part B—also an Ordinance, issued by the King-in-Council and dating from the same period—added an aggregate of further provisions, dealing with such matters as the Admiral's duty to proclaim against pillaging, robbing the church and ravishing women, upon pain of death; the procedure of the visit of enemy vessels (comp. *infra*, p. 504); the sanction on such vessels offering resistance to their hailing (comp. *infra* p. 505); the dispatch of mariners on shore and their behaviour in enemy country.

C, 39 Rules or Orders about matters belonging to the Admiralty (pp. 40-87). This Part C—a compilation presumably dating from the period 1360-1369—includes, among many other provisions of different purports, an elaborate naval criminal code and various ordinances enacted in the past by Henry I at Ipswich, by Richard I at Grimsby, by King John and Edward I at Hastings. It was also this Part C that, after a remarkable form of oath in old English to be administered to the jurors of the Maritime Inquest, was immediately followed by a series of articles which in the first 24 provisions were undoubtedly identical with the oldest version of the Judgments of the Sea and thus constituted the Laws of Oléron, which at that juncture were already received in England as an integral part of English maritime law (pp. 88-131) (comp. *supra*, p. 18).

D, 81 articles regarding an Inquisition undertaken at Queensborough in 1375 (pp. 132-173), intended to ascertain the customs observed in ancient times "for to keepe and continue them firmly for the future". The latter articles deal with a *mixtum compositum* of old usages relating to *prize bounty*, wages for mariners on different voyages from London, piracy, flotsam, obstruction of rivers by weirs, kiddles, watermills, etc., "royal fishes" (whales, sturgeon and porpoise), felonies, the arrest of vessels for journeys by the King or his Admiral (angary) and their withdrawal from such service; desertion of mariners, unauthorized transport, the catch of oysters and mussels, etc. Only a few articles were concerned with the law of maritime prize (e.g. Articles 1, 18 and 22 relating to the distribution of shares in confiscated prizes). Prize law has, consequently, to use a not inappropriate metaphor, been washed ashore in the early law of nations as a legal flotsam amidst a mass of other "bona weiriata", to become a body of rules of law with a more distinct face of its own only in the course of time.

The main parts A-D of the Black Book surveyed above are followed by six more parts: (5) a treatise on procedure, *Ordo Judiciorum* (pp. 178-220); (6) a Latin text "De officio Admiralitatis", being a translation from the French by Thomas Rowghton (pp. 221-245); (7) various documents connected with the lifelong Admiralty of John Holland, Duke of Exeter (1443-1446) (pp. 246-280), and (8-10) a number of instruments relating to matters which did not properly fall within the province of the High Admiral: (8) Ordinances of war, issued by King Henry V at Nantes upon Seine in 1419, Lansdowne MS. No. 285 (pp. 282-299), (9) the Order of Battle in the Court of Chivalry, Lansdowne, *ibid.*, f. 11 (pp. 300-329), and (10) the *De materia duelli* (Twiss, I, Introduction, xl and pp. 330-344), a sort of commentary on an ordonnance of King Philippe IV of France of 1306 "for the purpose of regulating the waging of battle".

When reading through the main parts of the Black Book, one states again that only a very small portion of their contents has a bearing on the law of prize. This is the case of only Articles 19 and 20 of Part A, dealing with the distribution of the proceeds of prizes and of Articles 6-10 of Part B, regulating the exercise of the right of visit and seizure of enemy vessels. In order to give some idea of their content and of the language in which those ancient texts were drafted, I reproduce below Art. 19 of Part A and Art. 8 of Part B:

A, Art. 19:

Item sil avient que desoubz les gages du Roy sur la mer ou en ports biens des enemys estre gaignez par toute la flotte ou par parcelle dicelles, donques aura et prendra le roy de toutes maneres diceulx biens la quarte partie, et les seigneurs des nefs une autre quarte partie, et lautre moitie diceulx biens auront les gaigneurs diceulx, laquelle moitie doit estre entre eulx également parties...

Item if it happens that under the Kings pay upon the sea or in ports enemies' goods be taken by the whole fleete, or by part thereof, then the King shall have and take the fourth part of all manner of the said goods, and the owners of the shipps another fourth part, and the other halfe of the said goods shall belong to those whoe took them, which halfe ought to be shared equally between them...

B, Art. 8:

Item se aucune de noz nefs ou vesseaulx encontrent sur la mer ou en ports aucunes autres vesseaulx qui facent rebelletees ou defense encontre ceuls de noz nefs ou vesseaulx adoncques bien lise a noz gentz les autres comme ennemys assaillir et par forte mayn les prendre et amener entierement comme ily les ont gaignez devant ladmiral...

Item, if any of our shipps or vessells doe meete upon the sea or in ports any other vessells which doe make any resistance or defence against those of our shipps or vessells, then it is lawfull for our men to assaile the others as enemies, and by force to seize and bring them before the admirall entirely as they have taken them...

The original Black Book, thus fortunately rediscovered, stems from a period anterior to the reign of King Henry VI (1422-1461), but it also includes documents from the period preceding the reign of Edward III (1327-1377).

Pardessus (IV, 199) considered it probable that the laying down of the rules in writing had already begun under the reign of King Edward III and was continued under his successors Richard II (1377-1399) and Henry IV (1399-1413).

The Book was drawn up for the purpose of providing the Court of Admiralty with a body of rules for its guidance in adjudicating upon the causes submitted to their judgment, just as, at a later stage, the Book of the Customs of the Sea (the Consolat of Barcelona) was intended to guide the Courts of the Consuls at Valencia and elsewhere within the dominions of the King of Aragón (see *infra*, p. 25-27).

The Consulate of the Sea

The genesis of the *Libre del Consolat de Mar*—in the original Catalan text—or *Consulado de Mar*—in its Castilian version—has for a long time remained problematical. As Travers Twiss judiciously remarked at p. xxviii of his Introduction to vol. III of his *Black Book of the Admiralty* of 1874, the nationality of the Consulate has formed since the beginning of the 17th century "as interesting a battlefield for disputants as the nationality of the Homeric poems". In his scholarly and penetrating study of the origins of the *Consolat* the author has in a convincing argument, on the negative side, dismissed the claims of both Pisa (defended by the Abbot Gaetano, according to whom the *Consolat* originated in his home town Pisa in 1118) and Marseille, as both being historically equally unfounded, and, on the positive side, proved with a wealth of grounds in support that the origin of the *Consolat* lies in Barcelona and that it is, therefore, of Catalan birth.

The oldest MSS. of the *Consolat* are kept in the *Bibliothèque Nationale* of Paris (Espagnol 124 and 56): these are a century older than the first printed edition and are written in a contemporary Catalan dialect. The demonstrably oldest printed text of the *Consolat* dates from 1494 (although there are certain reliable indications of the existence of an even somewhat older printed edition of about 1484 in semi-Gothic type, mentioned by Capmany in his *Código de las costumbres marítimas*), and was edited by Celelles. The printed *Editio Princeps* of 1494 is still extant in one single copy in the *Bibliothèque Nationale* in Paris, just as is a second edition of 1502, the edition which Capmany knew and mistakenly thought was the oldest. Unable to find any MSS. of the *Consolat* in the British Museum, the Bodleian Library in Oxford or any other depository, I had to content myself with consulting the general catalogue of the Reading Room of the British Museum in order to compare the not less than nineteen editions listed there with those mentioned in Travers Twiss' Introduction. Curiously enough the two lists did not correspond at all. Only one edition appeared to figure in both lists, namely, the Venetian reprint in Italian of 1737, but just that reprint happens to be among the five out of the in total nineteen catalogued editions which are reported as at present missing, namely those of 1567 (*Libro del Consolato dé marinarì*), 1719 (with explanations by Giuseppe M. Casaregi), 1737, 1740 and 1806. The third of these five (1737) was the version referred to by Lord Stowell in his judgment of 1798 concerning the *Aquila* (1 C.Rob., 44) and again in that of 1810 relating to the *Ceylon* (1 Dodson, 110). The last of the five (1806), drafted in Italian, claims to contain "oltre tutto ciò che trovasi nelle edizioni di Firenze, Lucca e Livorno", in addition the laws of Venice on the subject and the so-called *Portolano del Mare*, a document that was also inserted in Alvise da Cà da Mosto's editions of the *Consolato* of 1599 and 1612. Unlike Lord Stowell, Lord Mansfield in 1770 had, in *Luke v. Lyde* (2 Burrows, 289), cited the *Consolat* as a Spanish book. Moreover, I could not find the only Catalan version which, according to Travers Twiss's footnote at p. xxvii of the Introduction to vol. III of his work was kept in the British Museum, *viz.*, that of 1627, at Barcelona.

The oldest version in Italian is that of 1539 by J.B. Pedrezano, but that version deviated considerably from the Catalan *Editio Princeps* of 1494, and had therefore to be corrected in a second edition of 1549 which brought it into line with the text of 1494 and became the standard version in Italy and Northern Europe, until it was superseded by the Lucca edition of 1720, commented upon by Casaregi. Aside from two translations from the Catalan into the Castilian language, one dating from 1539 under the title "Libro llamado Cõsulado de Mar, obra muy vtil y prouechosa, y aun muy necessaria, ansì para todo genere de mercaderes, como de señores de naos, y pilotos y marineros, y todos los que nauegã," and another, dating from 1732, by Cayetano de Pellejá, there were also translations from Spanish and Italian into French by Fr. de Maysson in 1635, and from Catalan into French by P.B. Boucher in 1808; the latter was, however, more a commentary than a translation. An edition of 1549 also included a collection of "Ordinationi supra legni armati" (armed vessels). Further translations were made into Latin, Dutch (by A. Westerveen in 1728) and German. United States Chancellor James Kent complained in his *Commentaries on American Law* (3rd ed., New York, 1836), III, 10, that this "most authentic and most venerable document extant of the commercial usages of the middle ages" had never been translated into English, apart from two chapters (ccxxxi and ccxlv), especially devoted to prize law, published by Chr. Robinson in 1801 (comp. *infra*, pp. 24 and 303). Travers Twiss relates in his Introduction to vol. III of his work on the Black Book of the Admiralty at p. xxvii that he had pondered about the words of Chancellor Kent and had often felt disposed to undertake the task of translating the original Catalan text of 1494, in preference to the texts in the two oldest MSS. Espagnol 124 and 56 in the *Bibliothèque Nationale* in Paris, direct from that language into English, but that he had shrunk from that difficult task, also in view of the fact that Pardessus had meanwhile produced an excellent translation into French in his *Collection* II, pp. 49 *et seq.* Travers Twiss's publication, as a consequence, offers the original Catalan text, juxtaposed by an English text translated from the French (vol. III, pp. 50-57) and accompanied at pp. 199-238 by a glossary of Catalan words. A. de Capmany y de Monpalau inserted the *Consolat* in his two-volume work of 1791 (Madrid), entitled "Código de las Costumbres Marítimas de Barcelona, hasta aquí vulgarmente llamado Libro del Consulado, nuevamente traducido al castellano con el texto lemosín restituido á su original integridad y pureza, é ilustrado con varios apéndices, glosarios y observaciones históricas", in vol. I, pp. 1-134. In his *Memorias históricas sobre la marina, comercio y artes de Barcelona* of 1779, II, 178, Capmany was still rather critical about the authority of the *Libro de Consulado*, but at that moment he had no knowledge of the edition of 1494.

The most recent editions, both dating from 1955, are a facsimile of the manuscript of Valencia edited by the Spanish Ministry of External Affairs, respectively a translation into Castilian by J. Ramón Parallada (Madrid).

Sir Christopher Robinson, in 1801, provided a translation into English of Chapters 273 and 287 relating to prize law. The text of those and a few other Chapters will be quoted in the relevant section 2 of my Chapter III, *sub* A, *infra* pp. 303-304, where they belong systematically.

J.M. Pardessus dealt with the *Consulado de Mar* in vol. II of his *Collection* at pp. 1-363 and gave the text, in 297 Chapters, at pp. 49 *et seq.*; Travers Twiss published it in vol. IV of his work concerning the Black Book of the Admiralty, at pp. 449-495.

Francis Celelles' printed edition of the Book of 1494, upon whose text the Castilian, Italian, French and Dutch translations of the *Consolat de Mar* were all framed, consists of the following elements. After a "dedicatory epistle", a table of contents and an introductory note to the publication of the laws, inclusive of the mode of appointment of the Consuls of the Sea at Valencia and the "Jutge de les appellacions", the Book includes first 42 Chapters, containing the Valencian Regulations on procedure in the Consular Court, ending with the words "Aci acaba lorde judiciari de la Cort dels Consuls". It then continues, after the introductory words "Aci commencen les bones costumes de la mar", with Chapters xxxxvi up to ccxcvii (297), again ending with a passage saying: "Fins aci havem parlat de les leys e ordinacions de actes maritims mercantivols, ara posarem ordinacions e fet de armade maritima".

These "Bonnes costumes de la Mar", in 252 Chapters, are immediately followed by a few Chapters on Cruisers touching, *inter alia*, the distribution of prize among shipowners and officers and crew (comp. on this subject pp. 642-663 *infra*) and finally by 27 more Chapters (cclxxxxviii-cccxxiiii, 298-324), containing "Ordinacions de tot vexell qui armara per anar en cors e de toda armada, que es faca per mar", which in their turn are terminated by a passage stating that "Aci acaba lo libre vulgarment apellat de Consolat en lo qual son los capitols e leys e bones ordinacions que los antichs ordinaran per los fets maritims e mercantivols e encara en fets de cors o armade". Just as the Black Book of the Admiralty was drawn up for the purpose of providing the English Court of Admiralty with a body of rules for the purpose of guiding it in its task of adjudicating upon the causes submitted to its judgment (comp. *supra*, p. 22), so was the *Llibre del Consolat* of Barcelona of 1494 intended to serve as a guidance for the Courts of the Consuls at Valencia and elsewhere within the compass of the Aragonese Kingdom.

Both Pardessus and Travers Twiss have deliberately separated in their collections of mediaeval sources the *Orde judiciari de la Cort dels Consols de la Mar* of Valencia from the *Consolat de Mar* of Barcelona proper, on the consideration that, whereas the former was a strictly Aragonese affair, the latter was a body of rules of a much wider geographical purport (Pardessus, vol. II, pp. 49 *et seq.*, respectively V, pp. 374 *et seq.*; Travers Twiss, vol. III, pp. 35-657, respectively vol. IV, pp. 449-495).

What happened to the *Consolat* after the publication of its text in print in 1494 was its introduction from Barcelona into other areas under Aragonese rule, first Valencia, subsequently Mallorca, Sicily and Roussillon, and its translation into many languages, which made it the common law of the Mediterranean.

The bulk of the contents of the Consolat is concerned with matters foreign to prize law, but there are amongst its Chapters a number which have either a direct or a more remote bearing on the exercise of belligerent rights: questions arising between merchants and captains of ships captured or embargoed in time of war; the repair of damage caused by a failure to fulfil contracts of conveyance as a consequence of a blockade (Chs. 146, 147, 221, 237); ransom of captured ships (Chs. 185-187); contribution to compensation for losses occasioned by exactions by a belligerent (Ch. 203); the legal position in respect of the intermixture of enemy property with the property of friends (Ch. 231, the most famous provisions of the Consolat, discussed *infra*, in Chapter III, *sub* A, section 2, pp. 303-304); participation in gain and loss consequent on resistance to a belligerent cruiser (Ch. 243); and military salvage and recapture (Ch. 245). One would be inclined to cite in this context also Ch. 241 concerning, according to its heading, the case of "convoy", but this term, instead of covering its present legal connotation, rather relates to the practice of an agreed mutual assistance by consort vessels, as regulated in Chs. 48 and 49, called at the time "conservatge"—an institution also treated in Art. 39 of the *Tabula Amalphitana*.

The relevant Chapters and provisions of the Consulate will be set below in Chapter II, *sub* A, B and C in the systematic context in which they belong.

It has always remained a matter of controversy to what extent the *Consolat* of the Sea has in actual fact governed maritime relations between France, England, the Netherlands, the Hanse towns and Spain up to the 15th century. Grotius (*De jure belli ac pacis*, l. III, c. xviii) asserted that it was applied and later authors, such as Capmany (*Código de las costumbres de Barcelona*, p. xxix), H. Wehberg in vol. IV, 1-2 of the *Handbuch des Völkerrechts* (*Das Seekriegsrecht*, Berlin, 1915, p. 22), and A. Veillon in *Die Auswirkungen des Prisenrechts auf die Neutralen* (Winterthur, 1959, p. 11), have later adopted that view. On the contrary, other authors, such as M. Hübner, *De la saisie des bâtiments neutres*, Preface to vol. I (The Hague, 1759); G.F. de Martens, *Essai concernant les armateurs*, etc. (Göttingen, 1795); and the British writers Oppenheim-Lauterpacht (*International Law, II,* § 176) and C.J. Colombos (*International Law of the Sea*), have denied its application. According to G.F. de Martens the auxiliary law in England was the codification known as the *Rôles* of Oléron, not the *Consulado* (comp. Blackstone, *Commentaries*, I, 419 and IV, 423).

But in any case, the rules of the *Consolat* of the Sea have emigrated from their birthplace in the Western Mediterranean to Northern Europe.

The *consulados* after which the *Llibre del Consolat de Mar* was called were institutions which were a combination of a *gremio* (trade union) of sea merchants, ship-owners and mariners and a tribunal for the settlement of disputes arising among them. According to Travers Twiss (vol. IV, Introd., pp. xci-xcii) the office of Consul of the Sea was still unknown in Barcelona in 1258, when the administration of maritime matters seems still to have been in the hands of a corporation, or a group of persons, described as the "probi homines ripariae Barchinonae". The first Consuls of the Sea were established at Valencia in 1283 on the strength of a decree of Pedro III of Aragón: two such functionaries were to be annually selected by the guild or corporation of merchants and navigators from their own body. The Court of the Consuls of the Sea was later complemented by the appointment of a judge of appeal as the representative of the Crown. The *consulados* on Aragonese territory (Valencia, Barcelona, Tortosa, Gerona, etc.) were followed by similar institutions in Castilian cities (Burgos, Bilbao). Outer possessions of the Spanish sovereigns (Mallorca, Rosellón, Nueva España—Lima and Mexico) also harboured such *consulados*.

The genesis of these Consulates of the Sea in Spain, their composition, election, jurisdiction, etc. have been described by Robert Sidney Smith in a study entitled *The Spanish Guild Merchant. A History of the Spanish Consulado 1250-1700* (Duke University Press of Durham, North Carolina, USA, 1940), later translated into Spanish under the title *Historia de los Consulados de Mar (1250-1700)* (Barcelona, 1978). Six appendices give the text of the original *Carta del Consulado de Valencia*, the rules governing the electoral procedure in Barcelona and Bilbao, a few cases decided by the *Tribunal de los Cónsules* in Barcelona and Mallorca, and data concerning the jurisdiction of the Consuls at Valencia.

On the *Consolat de Mar* see also De Pistoye-Duverdy, I, pp. 341 *et seq.*, and L. Perels in *Wörterbuch des Völkerrechts und der Diplomatie* (Strupp), I, 202 *et seq.* The most recent publication of the text of the Consolat de Mar is that of 1975 in a work entitled *Consulate of the Sea and Related Documents*, by Stanley S. Jados (University of Alabama Press).

The maritime laws of the Baltic and the North

Another centre of regional codification was the Baltic. The sea-laws of that area have been collected by Pardessus in vol. III of his *Collection* of 1845 *et seq.*, as regards:

Norway, in Ch. XV (pp. 1-44);
Iceland, in Ch. XVI (pp. 45-88);
Sweden, in Ch. XVII (pp. 89-204);
Denmark, in Ch. XVIII (pp. 205-308);
Bremen, in Ch. XIX (pp. 309-328);
Hamburg, in Ch. XX (pp. 329-390);
Lübeck, in Ch. XXI (pp. 391-448);
the Prussian States of the Teutonic Order in Ch. XXII (p. 449-504), and certain Russian States—Riga, Novgorod, Georgia—in Ch. XXIII (pp. 505-531).

The sea-law of the wider geographical area of the Hanseatic League had already been described by him in vol. II, Ch. XIV (pp. 433-558).

The same North-European areas were covered by Travers Twiss in his vol. IV, where the texts of the following maritime laws can be found:

the Laws of Wisby in 70 articles (pp. 263-284);

the Codex Livonicus of the Teutonic Order of Livonia in 14 articles (pp. 285-299);

the Codex Dantiscensis, or Dantzig Ship-Laws in 26 paragraphs, numbered from 40, § 1 to 64, § 26 (pp. 335-355);

the Jus Maritimum Lubecense, in usum Osterlingorum descriptum anno 1299 in 42 articles (pp. 357-383), the earliest dated code compiled in any of the maritime cities of the Baltic which contains exclusively maritime law;

the Wisby Stads-Lag von Sciprechte in 20 chapters (pp. 385-413).

An extensive study of these Baltic laws has been made by Travers Twiss in the Introduction to vol. IV of his publication on the Black Book of the Admiralty, pp. xvi *et seq.* and xxxviii *et seq.* After a sketch of the gradual laying-down in the course of the 12th century of the unwritten and, as a consequence, barely known and fairly arbitrary customs of feudalism in written formulations, the *Consuetudines Feudorum*, the author argues that a similar development must have taken place in the Baltic region in respect of the customs of the sea. That legal development was determined, politically, by the rise of the town of Wisby, on the island of Gotland, to commercial supremacy in the Baltic and its subsequent supplanting by Lübeck, a course of events that is evidenced, *inter alia*, by the fact that, whereas the oldest of two *Skras*, enacted for a common Gothic-German factory at Novgorod, still emanated from Wisby and all appeals from that factory went to Wisby, the later one, dating from the end of the 13th century, referred them to the Senate of Lübeck. Corresponding events seem to have changed the legal situation as regards Riga (founded about 1200).

The fact that history has handed down to posterity two different codes referred to by the name of Wisby, points to the special position that that town occupied on the island of Gotland, the so-called *Wisby Stads-Lag von Sciprechte* (MS. B 63 in the Royal Library at Stockholm) containing certain rights and franchises secured by King Magnus II Ericson of Sweden about 1320 in the period of the three crowns (Sweden, Denmark and Norway) to the inhabitants of the town, as distinguished from the rest, the countryside, of the island (Travers Twiss, IV, pp. 385 *et seq.*).

The uncertainties prevailing concerning the various Baltic sea-laws are too many and the problem of their interconnection is too complicated to be made the subject of discussion here. There is the less ground for entering further into this subject as all those Northern maritime codes deal, some of them in great detail, with matters other than prize law, such as: vessels aground, the salving of goods, the hiring of ships, loading and unloading, jettison and the cutting of masts or cables, shipwreck, flotsam, ships hypothecated, the sale of ships, and pilots.

None of these regional codes, except that compiled for the "Easterners" (*Osterlingi*) in 1299, carries a sure date, and the determination of the exact year of their enactment is consequently more or less guesswork.

The *Wisby Stads-Lag på Gotland* was contained in two books of exactly the same content, one in Gothic (which has since long disappeared), the other in German (kept in the Town Hall of Wisby and published by Hadorph in the 1680's). The *Maritime laws of Wisby* were printed for the first time in 1505 at Copenhagen, a publication of which only three copies are still extant, but which has been reproduced by Pardessus in vol. I of his *Collection*, pp. 425-502 and by Travers Twiss in vol. IV of his *Black Book*, pp. 263-284. The printed text of 1505 terminated with the words: "Here end the Gotland Sea Laws (het Gotlansche Water-Recht, gemakt te Wisby, MDV.)" The MSS. differ in language, drafted partly in Danish, partly in

Low German (Saxon). As Travers Twiss has set out at p. xxvi of the Introduction to vol. IV of his work on the Black Book of the Admiralty, these elaborate maritime laws of Wisby are not all of Gotlandic origin, but rather a compilation of laws derived from three different sources: Baltic, Flemish or Gascon, and German, *viz.*, the first 14 (except Art. 7) Baltic, the following 25 Flemish or Gascon; 27 further Articles a Saxon version of Netherlands Sea-laws (Ordinance of Amsterdam), the last two again Baltic.

On the *Gotalag* (the Gotland Sea-laws, or *Gotlansche Water-Recht*) in 66 articles see Travers Twiss, vol. IV, pp. 53-129.

On the basis of his penetrating analysis of the Nordic codes Travers Twiss came to the conclusion that the Wisby Laws may rightly be classed as equals of the *Rôles* of Oléron and the Consulate of the Sea, because all three together form a continuous chain of maritime law, extending from the easternmost ports of the Baltic across the North Sea and along the Atlantic coast to Gibraltar, and from there to the eastern coast of the Mediterranean.

Manuscripts of the Gotland Sea-Laws are, according to Travers Twiss, kept in the Royal Library of Copenhagen (MS. 3123), the Library of the University of Copenhagen (Arne-Magnussen Collection, MSS. 22 and 28), the Royal Library in Stockholm (MS. B 74), the archives of the City of Lübeck (MS. Dreyer 65) and the library of the Gymnasium of Lübeck (MS. Petersen).

Dutch and Flemish sources

On the Dutch and Flemish sea-laws, such as the Ordinances of Amsterdam, the Hansa towns of Enkhuizen and Staveren, and Westcapelle, the *Waterrecht* in Vlaanderen—in 24 articles, each beginning with the characteristic words "This is the judgment", and an early 15th century parchment MS. of which was kept in the Danzig archives (Travers Twiss, vol. IV, pp. 415-447)—the Judgments of Damme, possibly a translation of the Rolls of Oléron—and the Purple Book of Bruges, a Flemish version of an early text of the Rolls of Oléron, which does not agree in some respects with either their Gascon or their Breton text, but has a greater affinity to the former, and is free from certain errors which can be found in the Guild Hall MSS. (Travers Twiss, vol. IV, pp. 301-333)—see the Introduction to Part IV of the work of the same author, pp. xxvi and xl *et seq.*

Pardessus has published a long list of legislative sources relating to the same area in vol. IV (Chapter XXIV, pp. 1-188) of his *Collection de lois maritimes*, as to Flanders at pp. 19-29, as to Holland at pp. 29-188. The latter series comprises ordinances of 1537, 1549, 1551, 1563 and 1570 (pp. 37-120) and various regional or municipal ordinances (pp. 120 *et seq.*).

The archives of the cities of Kampen, Dordrecht, Brielle and Danzig contain manuscripts of the sea-law of Flanders.

On the relation between the Baltic and the Dutch and Flemish sea-laws comp. also Travers Twiss's long exposé in the Introduction to vol. IV of his work, at pp. xxi *et seq*.

On the connection between those Netherlands ordinances and the *Rôles d'Oléron* comp. the detailed and profound study by A. Korthals Altes, *Ons oudste zeerecht*, in the publications of the Molengraaff Institute for Private Law of the University of Utrecht, No. 5 (Zwolle, 1976).

Section 2. BILATERAL TREATIES DEALING WITH THE LAW OF PRIZE

An abundant source of old prize law consists of bilateral treaties concluded, in particular, during the 17th century. They have become more rare in the course of time, but many can still be cited from the 18th, and a yet more limited number from the 19th century.

They all have one trait in common, namely, that their content is not restricted to prize law, but also encompasses a number of other subjects, especially neutrality (comp. my remarks in vol. X of this publication, p. 3). In order to give a general idea of how prize law rules were, in earlier times, embedded in treaties of commerce and navigation, alliance of peace, I will quote below a few typical examples of bilateral treaties and texts of this kind. It would be an impossible task to list them all, let alone to cite the provisions of all of them. I can therefore only mention, textually or in summary, the principal types of rules dealing with the subject.

Chr. Robinson's *Collectanea maritima* of 1801 lists a large number of the oldest bilateral treaties, *viz*. between

England and Portugal (1294);

England and Spain (1351, 1357);

England and Flanders (1370, 1417, 1446, 1467, 1495); and

England and Denmark (1490).

See for various of these treaty texts Rymer's *Foedera* V, 717; VI, 659; IX, 434; XI, 144; XII, 383.

From the 17th century I cite the following:

The Netherlands-Sweden, 5 April 1614 (Dumont, V^2, 245), Art. 6: freedom of trade, except to blockaded ports;

The Netherlands-Tunis, 14 November 1622 (*ibid.*, V^2, 411), Arts. 3-6: visit;

The Netherlands-Algier, 15 October 1622 (*ibid.*, V^2, 413), Arts. 5-8: transport of contraband; visit, indebtedness of freight;

England-The Netherlands, Southampton, 17 September 1625 (*ibid.*, V^2, 478), Arts. 12 and 20: joint capture; confiscation of contraband goods;

France-The Netherlands, 18 April 1646 (*ibid.*, VI^1, 342), preamble and Arts. I-III: suspension of the French Ordonnance of 1584 and the doctrine of infection for 4 years; definition of contraband; breach of blockade; modalities of visit;

The Netherlands-Spain, Münster, 30 January 1648 (Dumont, VI[1], 439; Parry, 1, 1), Special Article of 4 February 1648; 17 December 1650 (Dumont, VI[1], 650; Parry, 2, 259), Arts. 5-15: transport of contraband; modalities of visit; neutral goods in enemy ships and *vice versa*;

The Netherlands-Portugal, 6 August 1661 (Dumont, VI[2], 366; Parry, 6, 375), Art. 24: neutral goods in enemy ships;

France-The Netherlands, 27 April 1662 (Dumont, VI[2], 412; Parry, 7, 139), Arts. 27-42: transport of contraband and sanctions; breach of blockade; modalities of visit; neutral goods in enemy ships; adjudication of prizes; revision;

The Netherlands-Sweden, 6/16 July 1667 (Dumont, VII[1], 37; Parry, 10, 187), a detailed "conventio praevia" concerning a variety of subjects: definition of contraband; sanction on its transport and on breach of blockade; requirement of passports; adjudication of prizes, etc.;

the same, 26 November 1675 (Parry, 14, 41), Arts. 2-8;

the same, 2/12 October 1679 (Parry, 15, 331), Arts. 13-23 and 26-36.

The convention of 1667 provided in its main Article 10 for a revision procedure in prize cases and even included a separate Article 3 intended to avoid too high costs of such procedure by prescribing as follows:

> "Praeterea ne impensae Judicii Revisorii, quod beneficio Paragraphi decimi modo dictae Conventionis praeviae institui poterit, eorum, quorum interest singulis nimis graves sint, vel quemquam á persequendo Jure suo deterreant, promittunt itidem D.D. Ordines sese Causas eorum omnes, quibus Diplomata Revisionis indulserunt, iisdem Judicibus extra ordinem deligendis Judicibusque Admiralitatis Ordinariis adjugendis, junctim decidendas commissuros."

Another treaty between the same Powers of 18 July 1667 (Parry, 10, 197) further contained in Article V a compromise solution of a dispute which had arisen over the capture of an individual Swedish vessel, the *C(h)ristina*, by the Netherlands West India Company off the coast of African Guinea (Cabo Corso): Sweden abandoned her action to recover the vessel with its cargo from the Company, in return for an indemnification of 14,000 rixdollars to be paid by the Netherlands to Sweden for the cession of Cabo Corso and the relinquishment of the claim of Sweden and her African Company to the *C(h)ristina* and her cargo;

England-The Netherlands, 17 February 1668 (Parry, 10, 441), Arts. 2-11;

the same, 1/10 December 1674 (Parry, 13, 255), Arts. 2-8 and 11-15. Articles 11-13 of this Treaty of Marine were to the following effect:

> "XI. His Majesty and the said States, being desirous that the subjects of each other may be mutually treated, in all countries under their obedience respectively, with the like kindness as their own subjects, will give all necessary and effectual orders, the judgments upon prizes taken be given according to the rule of justice and equity, by judges beyond all suspicion, and not any way concerned in the case under debate: and his Majesty and the

said States will likewise give strict orders that all sentences already given, and which shall be thereafter given, be (according to the tenor thereof) duly put in execution, and obtain their effect.

XII. And whensoever the ambassadors of the said Lords the States, or any other their public ministers resident at the court of his most Serene Majesty of Great Britain, shall complain of the unjustness of sentences which have been given, his Majesty will cause the same to be reviewed and examined in his council, that it may appear whether the orders and precautions prescribed in this treaty have been observed, and have had their due effect, and will also take care that the same be fully provided for, and that right be done to the party complaining, within the space of three months; and likewise, when the ambassadors or other public ministers of his Majesty, resident with the States General, shall complain on the unjustness of sentences, the said States will cause a review and examination thereof to be made in the assembly of the States General, that it may appear whether the orders and precautions prescribed in this treaty have been observed, and have had their due effect, and they will likewise take care that the same be fully provided for, and that right be done to the party complaining within the space of three months: nevertheless, it shall not any ways be lawful to sell or unlade the goods in controversy, either before the sentence given, or after it, during the review thereof, on either side, unless it be with the consent of the parties interested.

XIII. A suit being commenced between the takers of prizes on the one part, and the claimers thereof on the other, and a sentence or decree being given for the party reclaiming, the said sentence or decree (upon security given) shall be put in execution, notwithstanding the appeal made by him that took the prize, which shall not be observed, in case the sentence shall be given against the claimers."

This treaty of 1674 was said in the *Vlught naa Aegypten* [1747] (Pratt-Lee, p. 128).

> "not to have been made for the sake of the trade and navigation of the Dutch, but for the benefit of the English, who were then at peace with everybody [whereas] the Dutch were then at war with France. Under the circumstances of this case [the Court must consider] the ship not as a Dutch ship under the treaty, but as a neutral ship only; she had no Dutch goods on board."

France-the Netherlands, 10 August 1678 (Dumont, VII[1], 357; Parry, 14, 399), Arts. 3, 13-29; 20 September 1697 (Dumont, VII[2], 386; Parry, 21, 371), Arts. 3, 4, 5, 17-40.

From the 18th century:

France-England, treaty of commerce and navigation, Utrecht, 11 April 1713 (Dumont, VIII[1], 345; Parry, 28, 1), Arts. 17-27;

France-the Netherlands, a corresponding treaty of commerce of 11 April 1713 (Dumont, VIII[1], 377; Parry, 28, 83), entered into for a period of 25 years, Art. 43. This treaty was after its expiry replaced by a new treaty of 21 December 1739 (Wenck, I, 414; Rousset, *Recueil*, XIV, 447; Parry, 35, 459). The latter treaty included the following provisions relating to prize law (Article X):

> "Les Vaisseaux de guerre de Sa Majesté & des dits Seigneurs Etats Généraux, & ceux que leurs Sujets auront armez en guerre, pourront en toute liberté conduire, où bon leur semblera, les prises qu'ils auront faites sur leurs Ennemis, sans être obligez à aucuns

Droits, soit des Sieurs Amiraux, ou de l'Amirauté, ou d'aucuns autres; sans qu'aussi les dits Vaisseaux ou les dites prises entrant dans les Havres ou Ports de Sa Majesté ou des dits Seigneurs Etats Généraux, puissent être arrêtez ou saisis, ni que les Officiers des Lieux puissent prendre connoissance de la validité des dites prises, lesquelles pourront sortir & être conduites franchement & en toute liberté aux lieux portez par les Commissions, dont les Capitaines des dits Vaisseaux seront obligez de faire apparoir, & au contraire ne sera donné azile ni retraite dans leurs Ports ou Havres à ceux qui auront fait des prises sur les Sujets de Sa Majesté ou des dits Etats Généraux; & s'ils sont forcez d'y entrer par tempête ou péril de la Mer, on les fera sortir le plutôt qu'il sera possible."

An example of a bilateral convention of later date which still included, together with articles dealing with neutrality and many other subjects, elaborate provisions on prize law is the Treaty of Commerce and Marine, concluded on 1 April 1769 between France and the Free Imperial City of Hamburg (Martens, R^2, I, 634; Wenck, III, 752; Parry, 44, 255). Matters of prize law were contained in a long series of articles (13-38), in the great majority concerned with the carriage of contraband goods by citizens of Hamburg and with certain mitigations of the French doctrine of infection (comp. *infra*, p. 329).

Another instance which embodied certain mitigations in French prize policy was that of a series of provisions included in the Treaty of Amity and Commerce between France and the United States of 6 February 1778 (Martens, R^2, II, 587; Parry, 46, 447): especially in Articles 14 (12)-19 (17), 22 (20), 23 (21), 25 (23) and 26 (24).

See for a list of treaties on the same subject, entered into by France between 1655 and 1852, De Pistoye and Duverdy's *Traité des prises maritimes*, vol. I, pp. 369-400.

Bilateral formulation of the rules of prize law by treaty was, for that matter, not foreign even to 19th century practice. As an example I cite below the subject matters dealt with in Articles 15 *et seq.* of the treaty of commerce between the United States and New Grenada of 12 December 1846, ratified on 10 June 1848 (B.F.S.P., vol. 36, p. 994; Parry, 100, 363; German translation in Martens, N.R.G.[1], XIII, 653).

Art. 15. Free ship, free good; no arrest of enemy subjects.
16. Neutral goods on enemy ships subject to seizure, unless already loaded before the war.
17. List of contraband goods.
18. Blockade.
19. Only contraband goods subject to confiscation; release of other goods and of the ship. Conduct to a port allowed, if necessary.
20. In case of a master's unawareness of a state of blockade, his ship must be turned away without seizure and confiscation.
21. Limitation of the manners of visit and search.
22. Ship's papers in time of war.
23. Navigation under convoy.
24. Judgment by a prize court.

25. Warlike action only allowed by military forces.
26. No grant of letters of marque by one against the other.
27. Grant of days of grace of six months after the outbreak of hostilities.

See also the Anglo-Portuguese treaty of 19 February 1810 (Hertslet, II, 27, 59; Parry, 61, 41), Art. 28, and the Anglo-Brazilian treaty of 17 August 1827 (Martens, N.R., VII, 479; Parry, 77, 375), Art. 15.

One of the questions which occupied the Admiralty Courts with respect to bilateral treaties was whether they were still subsisting at the date of adjudication. This was controversial, *inter alia*, as regards the Anglo-Swedish treaties of 1661 and 1664. The latter was invoked in 1745-46 to explain the former, but the 1664 treaty was held not to be in force: see the case of the *Hewa* [1745] cited in Pratt-Lee, p. 66: the Court held that it could only judge the case on the basis of subsisting treaties which were its rule. In the *Jonge Tobias* of 1748 the treaty of 1661 was held not to be subsisting as it had been revived in 1720 for only eighteen years: Pratt-Lee, at p. 190. Anglo-Portuguese treaties of 1642 and 1654 were recognized as subsisting: the *Nostra Seignora de Pentha de França* [1746] (Pratt-Lee, p. 92).

A later instance of the dependence of the decision upon the purport or applicability of treaty provisions is that of a cargo of masts, shipped from Riga on a Dutch ship, the *Vrijheid (No. 1)* [1778] (Hay and Marriott, 188; Roscoe, I, 13).

Another case regarded the question of whether an Order in Council, issued in the interval between the signature of a treaty and the exchange of the instruments of its ratification, was valid. The controversy arose in respect of an Order in Council of April 1795 (Instructions to commanders of warships and privateers) in relation to the Anglo-American Jay Treaty of 1794. See the *Recueil des arbitrages internationaux*, I, p. 137.

The retroactivity of a treaty was sometimes also in dispute.

Section 3. NATIONAL LAWS AND ORDINANCES

Introductory

As far as municipal legislative enactments are concerned, their number is no less impressive. Particular attention must, of course, be paid to the Decrees or Instructions issued by the great naval Powers of the time, France, England, the Republic of the United Netherlands, Spain, Portugal and the Scandinavian Kingdoms. As to England and the United States, it has to be borne in mind that the development of national prize rules has traditionally been entrusted, more than in other maritime countries, to the courts. That is why I have inserted so many British and American Admiralty Court decisions in this historical survey. But even where this is not so typically the case, it must be observed that the municipal regulations are often confined to marginal subjects of prize law, such as: the conditions imposed upon privateers, the attribution of prize bounty, the (absolute or relative) competence of Admiralty tribunals, the legal status of prizes recaptured from the enemy captor, etc. I will nevertheless list below a number of municipal regulations on prize law, some of which have in actual fact played a significant rôle in the development of naval practice and of doctrinal opinion.

Municipal laws and ordinances contain provisions of various kinds, relating either to the substantive law of prize, or to the form in which the right of visit and seizure might be exercised, or to the organization of a judicature in prize cases and its proceedings.

But on the whole the vast majority of the provisions included in all those old instruments had no bearing upon the law of maritime prize proper, dealing as they did with such subjects as the chartering of ships (1512, 1538; Pardessus, VI, 115, 121), or maritime insurance (1461, 1484, *ibid.*, V, 521, 523; *ibid.*, VI, 135), or the organization of consular courts vested with jurisdiction in maritime affairs in general.

In the following pages I will deal successively with the legislation on matters of prize law in the main maritime countries.

England

Initially I had the impression that there would probably be only relatively few English laws to be reported on, and the growth of English prize law tradition would have to be described as an almost exclusively judge-made legal system. This original impression seemed to be confirmed by the scarcity of Pardessus' legislative data concerning England in vol. IV of his great legal-historical work up to the 18th century. Although it is true that England's prize law system has developed mainly as a judge-made aggregate of rules, I have only recently been converted to the belief that there have been more legislative enactments in England than I had surmised. My conversion was principally due to the good fortune that I ultimately had, in 1981, after a year-long but vain hunt in libraries and other depositories, in finding a copy of Sir George Lee's MS. Notes of the mid-18th century, which had constantly tricked me by spiriting themselves away like the Scarlet Pimpernel just when I had caught sight of them (comp. on this experience section 5 *infra*, pp. 74-76).

What Pardessus had taught me was that there existed the following series of old English prize law enactments (*Collection de lois maritimes*, vol. IV, pp. 189-220): an ordinance of King William I the Conqueror (p. 203), two enquêtes of 1338 (p. 204) and 1375 (the inquisition of Queensborough, pp. 206-210), a statute of 1601 from the 43rd year of Queen Elisabeth's reign (pp. 210-214), an Act of 1664 (16 Ch. II, pp. 214-219) and the Scottish Laws of the Boroughs (pp. 219-220). The substantive rules of maritime prize in England were indeed mainly judge-made, and legislation was on the whole limited to the regulation of such subjects as the organization of prize jurisdiction and the procedure in prize cases, the award of prize bounty, the distinction between "droits of the Crown" and "droits of Admiralty", etc.

On the special form of legislation in England by the issuance of Royal Instructions to the Navy and to privateers, see *infra*, section 4, pp. 60-61.

The legislative English sources thus collected by Pardessus have, however, later been revealed to be fairly defective, obviously as a result of the fact that that French author had in his day also failed to gain access to certain private English collections of old British legal enactments in the field of maritime prize. Amongst such collections there were, in particular, two which have clarified the legislative situation.

The oldest was a collection of personal papers by Sir Nathaniel Lloyd, D.C.L., a distinguished advocate of Doctors' Commons, who was appointed Advocate-General in 1710 and who held that office for sixteen years.

The later one was the abovementioned collection of personal MS. Notes by Sir George Lee, who still made, in his own handwriting, some corrections in his copy of Sir Nathaniel Lloyd's older collection which he thereupon in 1756 added to his own MS. Notes as three Appendixes A, B and C. These old elusive legislative enactments formed the contents of his Appendix B (see the introduction to that Appendix B in Pratt's edition of Sir George Lee's Notes, p. 249).

The Orders in Council or Instructions thus jumbled together without much chronological order in these two private collections of MS. Notes from different periods are, placed in the order of the successive wars of England, the following (the page numbers refer to Pratt's edition):

4, 22 and 28 February 1664 (pp. 260-261) and 18 May 1665 (pp. 261-264),

22 May/3 June 1672 (pp. 251-253) and 23 May 1672 (pp. 253-256), the first called "Rules and directions", the last "Positions",

2 May 1693 (pp. 205, 264-265),

29 January 1704-5 (p. 267),

11 May 1706 (pp. 205, 268),

18 June 1744 (p. 257),

21 December1780 (pp. 258-260), and

April 1795 (see *R.A.I.*, vol. I, p. 137).

In view of the poor accessibility of the texts of those Orders and Instructions and in order to give an idea of what they contained as national legislative rules of old English prize law, I will insert below extracts from the most important of them, as more or less hidden in Appendix B of Pratt-Lee-Lloyd's collection, parallel to the collection of texts of the main French laws also reproduced below (pp. 45-53).

I choose therefor the "Rules and Directions appointed by his Majesty in Council to be observed by the High Court of Admiralty in the Adjudication of Prizes" of 22 May 1672, published 3 June 1672, with annexed "Positions" dated 23 May 1672. They were issued during England's third naval war with the United Provinces, but these "Rules and Directions" were to all intents and purposes identical with those enacted earlier, during England's second naval war with the United Provinces, on 22 February 1664-1665.

This double dating is connected with the fact that England for a long time (until an Act of Parliament of 1752, 24 Geo. II, c. 23) has continued to adhere to the use of two different kinds of years, one the historical year, commencing on January 1st, the other, the civil or legal year, on March 25th. See Pratt-Lee, footnote at pp. 1 and 2.

I will begin with a summary of those "Rules" and "Positions", as an introduction to their actual text, inserted below at pp. 38-41, to which I will constantly refer. On the other hand, I will not reproduce here the text of any of the other legislative enactments, *viz.*, the Instructions to privateers of 2 May 1693, 29 January 1704-05, 11 May 1706, 18 June 1744 and 21 December 1780. Comp. thereon the introductory section 1, *sub* 1, *infra*, pp. 159 *et seq.*

Several of the articles of the "Rules" and "Positions" of 1672 concern the manner in which proceedings must be instituted (Art. 7 (1) of the Positions), the conditions of the admissibility of claims (Arts. 2 and 3 of the Rules) or of an appeal (Art. 6 of the Rules), or the frequency of sittings of the Court of Admiralty (Art. 7 (2) of the Rules).

Others, of a more substantive nature, concern the following subjects:

— the obligatory observance of treaties (Art. 1 of the Positions);
— the treatment of neutral goods on enemy vessels, *viz.*, in accordance with the principle of "unfree (enemy) ships, unfree goods" (Art. 1 of the Rules), a surprising discovery in the light of the familiar, but obviously mistaken, idea in the current legal doctrine about an England which remained loyal to the system of the Consulate of the Sea (comp. 308).
— the treatment of the inverse position of enemy goods on neutral vessels, *viz.*, their liability to condemnation without, however, "infecting" the carrying vessel (Art. 2 of the Positions);
— the enemy or neutral character of prizes and the proof thereof (Arts. 10-13 and 15 (1) of the Positions);
— the qualification of goods as contraband, their conveyance to an enemy port and the penalty incurred (Art. 4 of the Rules and Art. 7 (1) of the Positions);
— a general exemption from condemnation in favour of vessels whose master was ignorant of the outbreak of war (Art. 14 of the Positions);
— an express prohibition from condemning a neutral ship or her cargo on any of the following specific grounds:
  delivery of a contraband cargo to the enemy on a previous voyage (Art. 7 (2) of the Positions);

the presence of enemy mariners or an enemy master on board (Art. 8 of the Positions);

the fact that the vessel was taken going by the Northern passage (Art. 15 (2) of the Positions);

— the liability of prizes to condemnation on the ground of resistance to visit, the destruction, concealment, or the total absence of ship's papers, or the use of false or double papers (Art. 3 of the Rules and Arts. 4-6 of the Positions).

The actual text of the "Rules and Directions" and "Positions" follows now.

The Court of Whitehall
May 22, 1672
Present
The King's Most Excellent Majesty,
His Highness Prince Rupert,
Lord Archbishop of Canterbury,
etc., etc.

"Rules and Directions appointed by his Majesty in Council to be observed by the High Court of Admiralty in the Adjudication of Prizes.

1. That where the ship or vessell brought in as prize shall belong to the states of the United Provinces, or any or their subjects, or any inhabiting with them, in such case no claim shall be admitted for the goods, but both ship and goods shall receive one and the same judgment, and both be judged and condemned as good and lawful prizes, except sufficient letters of safe-conduct from his Majesty or his Royal Highness be produced, or proved to be granted for the said ship or goods.

2. That where ship and goods seized and brought in as prize shall be claimed to belong wholly to his Majestys friends, allyes, or subjects, or any of them, then the claims shall be allowed to be entered in the Court of Admiralty, yet no claim shall be allowed or suffered to proceed but when sufficient authority from the owners themselves is produced in Court, or made sufficiently to appear but the master shall be allowed to have sufficient power to claim the ship for his owners, and also whatsoever goods pretended to belong to his owners, without any special procuration from them, and also what goods are pretended to belong to himself and mariners, and for so much of the lading as shall belong to the freighters in partnership to claim may be made by any of them, or any other having authority from them, or any of them. But where the lading shall belong to several merchants not in partnership, the claim shall be made by each particular person for his respective part of the lading, or by some that hath authority from the respective persons, and not otherwise.

3. That where any ship met withall by any of the Kings royal navy, or other ships commissioned by his authority, shall fight or make resistance, or the master, or any of the company, shall throw away, burn, tear, or conceal any of the ship's papers or documents, or shall have no papers at all found on board of the said ship, or shall bring or offer to the Court any false or double writings for evidence, thereby to clear her or her goods, or any of them, the said ship and goods shall be judged and condemned as good and lawfull prize.

4. That if any ship or vessell shall be met withall carrying of arms, ammunition, powder, or provision of victuals, or any contraband goods, to any port of the states of the

United Provinces, or into any of their territorys, lands, plantations, or countries, such ship or vessel, together with the said arms, powder, ammunition, provision of victuals, and contraband goods, shall be seized and brought in, and shall be adjudged and condemned as good and lawful prize.

5. That no claim shall be admitted in the Admiralty Court till the claimer first give sufficient security to pay such costs and damages, in case he fails to prove his property, as the Court shall adjudge against him.

6. That if a claim either of a ship or goods, or both, shall be judged against, and the claimant shall make an appeal, such ship and goods shall be forthwith valued and sold, and the money proceeding of the same shall remain deposited till such appeal be determined. But in that case also security shall be given before the Judges in the appeal by such appellant to pay such costs as the Court shall adjudge against him, in case his appeal shall be judged against.

7. That upon notice given to the Court of Admiralty of the seizing and bringing into port of any prize, the Court shall send forth a process to be hanged up upon the Exchange, or other most publick place, whereby all that pretend to have any right to claim may come in and enter their claims in Court in such case where such claim is allowed; and if no person shall come in to claim within 14 days after publication of the said process, then the Court shall forthwith proceed to adjudication, and in case any shall come in to claim, if the goods shall be perishable, the Court shall forthwith order an appraisement and sale; and though they shall not appear to be perishable, yet if the claimers shall have a commission into foreign parts for the proof of their property, then the Court shall also order an appraisement and sale as aforesaid.

The Court of Admiralty shall sit twice a week, or oftner, as occasion shall require, to give dispatch to the affair of prize ships and goods.

It is the day ordered in councel that the aforesaid rules and directions be observed by the High Court of Admiralty in the adjudication of prizes, and that the same be forthwith sent to the Judge of his Majestyes said High Court, to be strictly observed and duly put in execution.

Edwd. Walker
Pub. 3rd June, 1672.

POSITIONS

1. It is not the power of any prince alone to abrogate or disannull that paction or agreement which is made between him and another prince; but is without dispute that the first agreement ought to stand untill a war or falling out happen between them. His Majestyes rules therefore, being of a later date, and his own single act, to which other princes are not parties, cannot countermand or evacuate former treaties, which must necessarily be preferred before them. Neither do the rules themselves gainsay or control any treaties made with foreign princes, however the execution may sometimes seem to the contrary, upon very great suspition that the true intent of the treaty is not duly observed by other princes.

2. The goods of an enemy in a friend's bottom may be lawfully seized; but enemy's goods, neither by the law of nations, nor by his Majestyes present rules, will confiscate a friend's ships. (Vid. Grot. lib. 3. cap. 6. par. 5 et 6)

3. Navis hostilis non afficit res amicorum, quod juris est de toto quoad totum; idem juris est de parte, quoad partem. A part either of ship or goods may be claimed by a friend as well as the whole.

4. The throwing away of paper is such an indication that they were material to the concerns of the ship and lading, that the proof of the contrary will be hardly admitted, for cui bono was the throwing them away, if it were not to save the ship or goods, and missive letters are many times great evidences of the condition both of ships and lading, especially

letters to the master and factors, which frequently discover the whole design, quality, and property both of ships and ladings, from whence come and whither bound. (Vid. the 40th Article of the Placcart of King Philip of Spain, 1624., Cleirac, p. 445)

5. The want of passports and certificates, if there be other writings in her, cannot prejudice the ship; neither are passports and certificates necessary; but some papers are necessary, and these may be dated as well before the war as since, so the war be not of long continuance; and though passports that be after the forms prescribed in treaties be necessary to avoid search and bringing up of ships, and so avoid great trouble and charge, yet the ships and lading may be preserved from confiscation without them, so they be furnished with other writings and proofs that may demonstrate them to belong to friends. But then they are not so free of being seized to undergo a stricter examination, as if they carried such formal pass as by treatys are agreed on.

6. It is not the having aboard false and double writings that is a ground of confiscation, but the offering false or double writings in evidence, to clear the ship, that ought to condemn her. Yet, if they be not reall, or insisted upon, or enforced, for evidence to clear her, they can do nothing to warrant confiscation. Nor do I think that the evidence in the preparatory, whether of master or mariners, or other ship evidence, contradicting the documents, do make them false except there be a positive proof to affect them with falsehood; that is, that they were forged and formed by a false hand, and not so as they pretend to be; for confiscation is never made upon presumptive grounds of falsehood only, but the proof of falsehood must be evident and convincing, to induce a confiscation in this case, except mere presumptions concur to condemn also. Neither do I think the finding of double bills in the ship, the one to make a ship bound to a free port, the other to a port unfree, ought to confiscate the ship, for that artificial colour is lawfull in time of danger, and practised and allowed by all nations. But then, indeed, where double bills are, they that have them must more clearly prove the ship and goods do belong to a friend, and not to an enemy, and were going to a friend's port, and not to an enemy's; and that this is the truth, and the other was but a mere colour, for without an evident proof one enemy will be apt to suspect the worst that may be of another, and will in time of war condemn rather than restore.

7. By the law of nations, a ship carrying contraband goods forfeits itself only and the said goods contraband; but not any other goods besides that are not contraband; and so it is by the King's rule. (Vid. Reg. 4. 1672). Setting aside what are by treaties agreed to be contraband, which must be so esteemed, whatsoever they be, and no other, I also agree that iron, pitch, tar, hemp, clypebard, planks, corn, excepting wainscott, wine, oyle, salt, will be accounted contraband, under which all such things which are of a general use of furnishing the war, and those that are in arms are properly comprehended.

Nothing is forfeited but what is taken going to the enemy; for, after the contraband goods are delivered, neither the ship nor the proceed of the contraband goods, upon the return, will be lyable upon that account singly to confiscation, much less will any other lading in the ship be confiscated.

8. No number of mariners, nor the master, being a Dutchman, will confiscate the ship, neither by the law of nations nor by any rule of the King now in force.

9. If the Dutch property be quite and absolutely bought, and the money paid, the ship is secure both the first voyage before she arrived at the free port, and for ever, so long as it remains out of an enemy's hands; for the ground and cause of confiscation is taken away.

10. Embden was, in the last war with the Dutch (1665-1667), looked upon and adjudged as an enemy, and so accounted still; and if any nation shall consent to entertain a Dutch garrison in any of their territoryes, that part at least where it bears command will be acounted an enemy, but not so if a garrison be brought in and fixed there by constraint and force.

11. The using a Dutch flag is like other colourable things that are made use of to secure and preserve our best friends; and, therefore, if there be nothing else, can be no ground of confiscation. (Vid. Grot. lib. 3. cap. 1. par. 8.)

12. When the enemy runs the risque, the very capture makes it to become and belong to the enemy; and therefore, in that case of insurance, what is insured by the enemy will be confiscate; yet the premium given for insurance ought in equity to be repaid by the taker.

13. If the Dutch let to freight and enter goods for friends and allyes not in any right of their own, they ought not to be judged as goods of the enemy, they being factors merely for other men that are friends; but, indeed, coming from an enemy's country, and let entered by Hollanders, it is lyable to suspition, and will run through a stricter examination; but the truth being made to appear, the law will not confiscate in this case.

14. The ignorance of a war ought to safeguard a ship and goods from confiscation for want of necessary documents or carrying contraband goods or such like, till such time reasonable past; within which time probably a knowledge of the war may incur, and the measure of such time cannot nor is not made certain by the law, because distance of place is so various. It is therefore left to the discretion of the Judge, who must judge one way or other, as the circumstances of the case shall incline him; but doubtless if intelligence thereof can have come by the post, he that shall act contrary will be judged to be in MALA fide.

15. If, by the confession and deposition of the skipper and some of the mariners be intended, the examination in the prepatory, which are taken, when the ship is first brought up, by commissioners specially deputed to take them, in the absence of partyes interested, and whereto they are no partys nor minister any interrogatories, this proof will condemn, if it stand single, and no other comes to the contrary. But contrary proof will be admitted; and if it be well fortifyed, it will and ought to prevail.

It is a suspitious thing in time of war for a ship to be taken going by the northern passage; but it makes no presumption that it is unfree, much less will condemn, especially when any contrary evidence come to assert its freedom; and though it be more suspicious a great deale to take a ship on the enemy's coast with contraband goods, and standing single may condemn her, yet because she may be forced thither by a storm, and that really she might be going to a friend's port, a contrary proof will be admitted; and if it be clear it will free the ship from confiscation.

R.W., Ad.R.

(Sr. Robt. Wiseman, K.'s Advocate)

As to the evaluation of the legal force and binding character of such Orders in Council see Lord Stowell's judgment in the *Courier* [1810] (Edw., 249; Roscoe, II, 50) concerning an Order of 7 January 1807 which prohibited certain voyages:

> "So long as these Orders in Council exist they are to be expounded and applied by this Court; and if they press with any unnecessary severity on the commerce of other nations, that may be a matter very proper for the consideration of His Majesty's Government; but this Court must proceed upon general Rules of interpretation."

Besides Orders in Council and Instructions, certain Statutes were sometimes also enacted to regulate matters of prize law. Examples of such Acts of Parliament were those of 6 Anne, A.D. 1708, issued during the War of the Spanish Succession, and of 17 Victoria, Ch. 18 (1854) issued during the Crimean War, both relating to the grant of prize money to captors, but different in scope. The first was still intended to have a permanent character. The second was an example of the practice which had been introduced since then of enacting a Statute of the traditional type afresh at the beginning of each new war. They were occasionally invoked by the parties to judicial proceedings as the legal ground on which a Court decree could be based, *e.g.*, in the *Providence* [1746] (Lee-Pratt, pp. 82-83), but there in a manner which is very unclear. The case related to the shipowner's responsibility for acts of the master.

Comp. on these old sources also Chr. Robinson's *Collectanea Maritima* (1801), p. 188.

France

When arranging the French sources of the law of prize, of both a legislative and a judicial nature, I found that it was hardly feasible to arrange the available material in two strictly separated sections, one devoted to French legislation, the other to French case law. That is why I had some difficulty in deciding where to deal with one and where with the other. This difficulty was forced upon me specifically by a close study of the famous two-volume collection of A. de Pistoye and Ch. Duverdy, entitled *Traité des prises maritimes* (Paris, 1859). In that scholarly work the authors have arranged the material in such a manner that they set out the French data in a scientific order of their own invention, in each of the successive subdivisions of which they constantly begin by reporting the legislative sources governing the situation in the consecutive phases of the constitutional history of France, and by then distributing among the elements of that systematic framework the pertinent prize court judgments relating to the subject matter under review. That is why I had to cut the knot in some way or another and finally decided to confine this section 3 to a survey of the successive French laws, decrees, etc., as reported in the *Traité*. All other data will be set out in section 5, *infra*, pp. 62-69.

No sharp distinction can be made either between national laws and royal instructions to the fleet. Some of the enactments bore a clear character of the first, some that of the second type, yet others were of a mixed character. The *Ordonnance* of the French King Philippe de Valois of 1338, for instance, was a marked instruction to the French fleet issued in view of his planned, but abortive, expedition against England. The various Statutes and *coutumiers* were examples of local or regional legislation or codification. As I cannot enter into any particulars of the contents of this vast mass of municipal maritime regulations, I will confine myself to adducing below some data concerning the main historical French enactments, *viz.*, those of 1584, 1681, 1778, 1793 and *an* XI (1803) which have played a significant rôle in the development of the customary law of prize.

On naval instructions see section 4, *infra*, pp. 60-61.

The development in France was approximately contemporaneous with that in England. Travers Twiss has informed us also about French legal sources in the Appendices to his study on the *Black Book of the Admiralty*.

Detailed data and full texts of the main French instruments—regional codifications, together with national laws and naval instructions, illustrated by comparative notes—can be found in vol. IV of the great six-volume *Collection de lois maritimes antérieures au 18e siècle* (Paris, 1823-1845) by the French author J.M. Pardessus, Chapter XXVI, pp. 221-418, beginning with the *Statut* of Arles (1150) and the *Coutume* (1223) and *Etablissements* of Montpellier (13th century), continuing with the Statutes of Marseille (1253-1255) and the *Constitutio Societatis Navium Baionensium*, and then giving the complete text of two great national codifications of the 16th and the 17th century. The first is the *Edit sur l'Amirauté* of March 1584, the second the *Ordonnance touchant la Marine* of August 1681. A third codification, which is not included in the Collection of Pardessus because this dates from the 18th century, but which can be found in the *Code des prises* (vol. II, p. 671) and in Martens (R^2, III, 18 *et seq.*) is Louis XV's *Règlement concernant la navigation des bâtiments neutres en tems de guerre* of 26 July 1778 in 15 articles. This *Règlement* was, in its turn, followed during the revolutionary period by a series of legislative enactments and naval instructions, especially a *Décret* of the National Convention "sur le jugement des prises, etc." of 14 February 1793 (Martens, R^2, V, 379) and an *Arrêté* of 2 prairial *an* XI (22 May 1803) "concernant les armements en course et les prises" (*ibid.*, VIII, 9).

The oldest legislative enactments in France on admiralty matters proper date from the beginning of the 14th century. The last part of the Black Book of the Admiralty, under the heading *De materia duelli* (vol. I, Introduction, p. xl; pp. 330-344) is in fact a kind of commentary on an old French ordinance of King Philippe IV of 1306, published for the purpose of regulating "the wager of Battle". In my introductory remarks at p. 42 mention has already been made of the Ordinance of King Philippe de Valois of 23 March 1338, intended to govern his forthcoming expedition against England (*loco cit.*, pp. 420-429), reproducing the texts of the MSS. in the British Museum: Harleian collection No. 3836, and Cotton collection (Claudius E VIII). Further French Ordinances are those of King Charles V of 1364 on the jurisdiction of the Admiral (*Black Book*, vol. I, pp. 430-442) and of 7 December 1373 "sur le fait de l'Amirauté". The latter Ordinance was rediscovered by Fontanon and published in his *Recueil* under a different (wrong) date (7 December 1400). It is kept in manuscript form in the British Museum (MS. Sloane, No. 2423).

One of the later French Ordinances was enacted for Louis Malet, Sire de Greville, who was Admiral from 1486 to 1508 and from 1511 to 1516. It dealt with the jurisdiction of the Admiralty in matters of piracy and for the regulation of maritime prize. Travers Twiss certified that some articles of that Ordinance were still in force in France when he wrote his work on the Black Book in 1871.

The main municipal instruments which have dominated French practice, case law and doctrine in later years are the three Royal Ordonnances of 1584, 1681 and 1778, mentioned above, *viz.*, respectively, the *Edit* of King Henri III "concernant la juridiction de l'Amirauté", of March 1584, the *Ordonnance de la Marine* of King Louis XIV of 15 August 1681 (livre 14, titre 9, see Art. 6) and the *Règlement* of King Louis XVI of 26 July 1778, "concernant la navigation des bâtiments neutres en temps de guerre" (Martens, R^2, III, 18), restored in force after the fall of the monarchy by an *Arrêté* of the Consuls of 29 frimaire *an* VIII (20 December 1799) (*ibid.*, VI, 743), and a fourth legislative instrument, *viz.*, an *Arrêté* signed by the Premier-Consul Bonaparte on 2 prairial *an* XI (22 May 1803) (*Code des Prises*, vol. I, p. 1078; Martens, R^2, VIII, 9-41), which in fact re-enacted in 124 articles all the provisions of earlier legislation declared to be still in force.

The texts of the main instruments follow below.

The Edict of March 1584

The Edict of March 1584, officially entitled "Edit du Roi concernant les ordonnances et réglemens de la juridiction de l'Amirauté" can be found in Pardessus' *Collection*, vol. IV, pp. 295-325. The author relates that the text of this Edict could not be retraced in the collection "Ordonnances du Louvre" and that he had been forced to collate a number of defective texts in circulation with the registers of the *Parlements* of Paris and Rouen. The text as published by Pardessus contains a continuous series of 100 articles, and is divided into titles or paragraphs. It is built on a number of legislative predecessors, in particular the "Ordonnance sur le fait de l'Amirauté" of King Charles V of 7 December 1373, just mentioned.

But many more ordinances on maritime navigation and commerce have preceded the Edict of 1584, such as those enacted by Louis XI on 2 October 1480, by Charles VIII on 12 July 1490, by Louis XII on 15 July 1508 and 10 December 1511, by François I in July 1517 and February 1543, by Henri II in 1555 and 1556. Just as many provisions in other old regional or municipal maritime laws have no bearing on prize law, so the vast majority of the hundred articles of the Edict of 1584 have nothing to do with that subject. Yet a number of them are closely or remotely connected with it. Articles 1 *et seq.* deal with the jurisdiction of the Admiral in maritime cases to the express exclusion of other judges. This in principle exclusive jurisdiction of the Admiral was gradually extended to, or usurped in, other fields outside that of maritime commerce, such as civil and criminal causes involving foreign traders from the Hanse towns, the Baltic, England, Portugal and Spain established in France. It was, however, sometimes exercised concurrently or controversially by other authorities, such as consular courts or the *Chambre des Requêtes* of the *Parlement* of Normandy (comp. *infra*, Chapter III, *sub* C, section 2, pp. 593-594.

Amongst the provisions coming within the description of the law of prize, or traditionally connected with it, I will mention Chapters 20 and 21 (claims to things washed ashore, jetsam, etc.), 25 (grant of safe-conducts by the admiral), 26-31 (equipment of privateers under supervision of the admiral, requirement of a commission, an oath, a deposit and the admiral's consent to put to sea, flying of the banner of the admiral, who should be entitled to a tenth portion of all prizes), 32-38 (capture of vessels and cargoes, guarantees for its regularity, examination by the admiral, punishment of abuses), 39 (distribution of the proceeds of prizes amongst the admiral, ship-owners and mariners) and 69, embodying the eminently French principle of infection of property of friends by the presence of enemy property, which has played an important rôle in the customary development of prize law. Comp. for the text of that provision 69 and its weakening by bilateral treaties my exposé in Chapter III *sub* A, section 2 *infra*, pp. 326-330.

The Ordonnance of 1681

The *Ordonnance touchant la Marine* of August 1681, commented upon by R.J. Valin in his *(Nouveau) Commentaire sur l'Ordonnance* (La Rochelle, 1766) and published by Pardessus in vol. IV, pp. 325-415, with a table of contents at pp. 417-418, is in its turn built on its predecessor of 1584. This *Ordonnance* was arranged in five *livres*, entitled, respectively, "Des officiers de l'Admirauté", "Des gens et des bâtimens de mer", "Des contrats maritimes", "De la police des ports, costes, rades et rivages de la mer" and "De la pesche qui se fait sur mer", each "livre" subdivided in "titres" and "articles". This enumeration of the headings of the "livres" in itself proves that this *Ordonnance*, too, deals with many matters foreign to the law of maritime prize. And one has some difficulties in guessing under which of the five "livres" the prize law is classed. Its rules must be sought and can, somewhat surprisingly, be found in "livre" III under the heading "Des contrats maritimes", under *titre* IX entitled "Des prises", *articles* 1-34 (pp. 384-389).

The five *livres* of the *Ordonnance* were each divided into a different number of *titres* which in their turn each contained a different number of *articles*. *Livre* I (entitled "Des officiers de l'Admirauté et leur jurisdiction") dealt in 14 *titres* with the Admiral, his various officers and Admiralty judges and their competence, France's consuls in foreign countries, and ended with certain principles of procedure, the execution of judgments, the sale of prize vessels and the distribution of their proceeds. *Livre* II (entitled "Des gens et des bâtimens de mer") contained in 10 *titres* provisions on ship's-captains and other persons on board (including chaplains, surgeons, pilots and crew), ship-owners, carpenters and caulkers, and on the various categories of seagoing vessels. *Livre* III (entitled "Des contrats maritimes"), divided into 11 *titres*, gave rules on a variety of subjects: ship-freighting (charter-parties, bills of lading, *prêts à la grosse*, or *emprunts à la grosse aventure*, etc.), conditions of employment for sailors, insurance, contribution to general average in case of jettison, and the inheritance of those who died at sea. But among those *titres* there were two which clearly did not come under the description of maritime contracts, *viz.*, *titre* 10 concerning "lettres de marque et de représailles" (pp. 389-391) and *titre* 9 on "prises" (in 34 *articles*; pp. 384-389).

Livre IV (entitled "De la police des ports, costes, rades et rivages de la mer") again contained, in 10 *titres*, provisions on a variety of subjects: on ports and harbours, roadsteads and beaches; on quay masters, pilots (*lamaneurs* or *locmans*) and coast guards; on the loading and unloading of ballast (*lestage* and *delestage*), on shipwreck and the running-ashore of ships, and on the mysterious subject (*titre* 10) of "La coupe de Varech, Vraicq, Sar ou Goüesmon" (meaning the cutting by the inhabitants of coastal parishes of certain herbs growing in the sea along their coast). *Livre* V (entitled "De la pesche qui se fait en mer"), in 8 *titres*, has again nothing to do with the law of prize.

A subsequent executory *Règlement* of 24 October 1681 (pp. 415-416) finally dealt with subjects that may have a closer connection with prize law, such as: the purchase of foreign vessels in order to enable them to sail under the flag of France, limitations on the grant of "congez" and passports for ships, the building of ships for Frenchmen in a foreign country, etc.

In view of the great historical importance of the *Ordonnance* of 1681, which has for so long dominated the practice of French prize law, I will insert the text of the said *titre* 9 of *livre* III.

"Art. I. Aucun ne pourra Armer Vaisseau en Guerre sans Commission de l'Admiral.

II. Celuy qui aura obtenu Commission pour équiper un Vaisseau en Guerre sera tenu de la faire enregistrer au Greffe de l'Admirauté du lieu où il fera armement, et de donner caution de la somme de quinze mille livres, qui sera receuë par le Lieutenant en presence de nostre Procureur.

III. Défendons à tous nos Sujets de prendre Commission d'aucuns Roys, Princes, ou Estats estrangers, pour armer des Vaisseaux en Guerre et courir la Mer sous leur Banniere, si ce n'est par nostre permission, à peine d'estre traitez comme Pirates.

IV. Seront de bonne prise tous Vaisseaux appartenans à nos ennemis, ou commandez par des Pirates, fourbans et autres gens courans la Mer sans Commission d'aucun Prince, ni Estat souverain.

V. Tout Vaisseau combattant sous autre Pavillon que celuy de l'Estat dont il a Commission, ou ayant Commissions de deux differens Princes ou Estats, sera aussi de bonne prise; et s'il est Armé en Guerre, les Capitaines et Officiers seront punis comme Pirates.

VI. Seront encore de bonne prise les Vaisseaux avec leur chargement, dans lesquels il ne sera trouvé chartes-parties, connoissemens, ni factures: Faisons deffences à tous Capitaines, Officiers et Equipages des Vaisseaux preneurs de les soustraire, à peine de punition corporelle.

VII. Tous Navires qui se trouveront chargez d'effets appartenans à nos ennemys, et les Marchandises de nos Sujets ou Alliez qui se trouveront dans un Navire ennemy, seront pareillement de bonne prise.

VIII. Si aucun Navire de nos Sujets est repris sur nos ennemis, aprés qu'il aura demeuré entre leurs mains pendant vingt-quatre heures, la prise en sera bonne; et si elle est faite avant les vingt-quatre heures, il sera restitué au propriétaire avec tout ce qui estoit dedans, à la reserve du tiers qui sera donné au Navire qui aura fait la recousse.

IX. Si le Navire, sans estre recous est abandonné par les ennemis, ou si par tempeste ou autre cas fortuit il revient en la possession de nos Sujets avant qu'il ait esté conduit dans aucun Port ennemy, il sera rendu au proprietaire qui le reclamera dans l'an et jour, quoy qu'il ait esté plus de vingt-quatre heures entre les mains des ennemis.

X. Les Navires et effets de nos Sujets ou Alliez repris sur les Pirates, et reclamez dans l'an et jour de la declaration qui en aura esté faite en l'Admirauté, seront rendus aux proprietaires en payant le tiers de la valeur du Vaisseau et des Marchandises pour frais de recousse.

XI. Les Armes, Poudres, Boulets, et autres munitions de Guerre, mesme les Chevaux et équipage qui seront transportez pour le service de nos ennemis, seront confisquez en quelque Vaisseau qu'ils soient trouvez, et à quelque personne qu'ils appartiennent, soit de nos Sujets ou Alliez.

XII. Tout Vaisseau qui refusera d'amener ses voiles aprés la semonce qui luy en aura esté faite par nos Vaisseaux, ou ceux de nos Sujets armez en Guerre, pourra y estre contraint par Artillerie ou autrement; et en cas de resistance et de combat, il sera de bonne prise.

XIII. Defendons à tous Capitaines de Vaisseaux armez en guerre d'arrester ceux de nos Sujets, Amis, ou Alliez qui auront amené leurs voiles, et representé leur charte-partie ou police de chargement, et d'y prendre ou souffrir estre pris aucune chose, à peine de la vie.

XIV. Aucuns Vaisseaux pris par Capitaines ayans Commission estrangere ne pourront demeurer plus de vingt-quatre heures dans nos Ports et Havres, s'ils n'y sont retenus par la tempeste, ou si la prise n'a esté faite sur nos ennemis.

XV. Si dans les prises amenées dans nos Ports par les Navires de Guerre armez sous Commission estrangere il se trouve des Marchandises qui soient à nos Sujets ou Alliez, celles de nos Sujets leur seront renduës, et les autres ne pourront estre mises en Magazin, ni acheptées par aucune personne sous quelque pretexte que ce puisse estre.

XVI. Aussi-tost que les Capitaines des Vaisseaux armez en Guerre se seront rendus maistres de quelques Navires, ils se saisiront des Congez, Passe-ports, Lettres de Mer, Chartes-parties, connoissemens, et de tous autres papiers concernant la charge et destination du Vaisseau, ensemble des Coffres, Armoires et Chambres, et feront fermer les Escoutilles et autres lieux où il y aura des Marchandises.

XVII. Enjoignons aux Capitaines qui auront fait quelque prise, de l'amener ou envoyer avec les prisonniers au Port où ils auront armé, à peine de perte de leur droit et d'amende arbitraire; si ce n'est qu'ils fussent forcez par la tempeste ou par les ennemis de relâcher en quelque autre Port, auquel cas ils seront tenus d'en donner incessamment avis aux interessez à l'armement.

XVIII. Faisons defences à peine de la vie à tous Chefs, Soldats et Matelots de couler à fond les Vaisseaux pris, et de descendre les Prisonniers en des Isles ou Costes esloignées pour celer la prise.

XIX. Et où les preneurs, ne pouvans se charger du Vaisseau pris ni de l'équipage, enleveroient seulement les Marchandises ou relâcheroient le tout par composition, ils seront tenus de se saisir des papiers, et d'amener au moins les deux principaux Officiers du Vaisseau pris, à peine d'estre privez de ce qui leur pourroit appartenir en la prise, mesme de punition corporelle s'il y eschet.

XX. Defendons de faire aucune ouverture des Coffres, Balots, Sacs, Pipes, Bariques, Tonneaux et Armoires; de transporter ni vendre aucune Marchandise de la prise; et à toutes personnes d'en achepter ou receler jusques à ce que la prise ait été jugée, ou qu'il ait esté ordonné par Justice, à peine de restitution du quadruple et de punition corporelle.

XXI. Aussi-tost que la prise aura esté amenée en quelques Rades ou Ports de nostre Royaume, le Capitaine qui l'aura faite, s'il y est en personne, sinon celuy qu'il en aura chargé, sera tenu de faire son rapport aux Officiers de l'Admirauté, de leur representer et mettre entre les mains les Papiers et Prisonniers, et de leur déclarer le jour et l'heure que le Vaisseau aura esté pris, en quel lieu, ou à quelle hauteur, si le Capitaine a fait refus d'amener les voiles, ou de faire voir sa Commission ou son Congé, s'il a attaqué, ou s'il s'est défendu, quel Pavillon il portoit, et les autres circonstances de la prise et de son voyage.

XXII. Aprés la Declaration receuë, les Officiers de l'Admirauté se transporteront incessamment sur le Vaisseau pris, soit qu'il soit moüillé en Rade, ou qu'il soit entré dans le Port; dresseront procez verbal de la quantité et qualité des Marchandises, et de l'estat auquel ils trouveront les Chambres, Armoires, Escoutilles, et fond de cale du Vaisseau, qu'ils feront ensuite fermer et sceller du Sceau de l'Admirauté; et ils y establiront des Gardes pour veiller à la conservation du scellé, et pour empécher le divertissement des effets.

XXIII. Le Procés verbal des Officiers de l'Admirauté sera fait en présence du Capitaine ou Maistre du Vaisseau pris, et s'il est absent, en la présence des deux principaux Officiers ou Matelots de son équipage, ensemble du Capitaine ou autre Officier du Vaisseau preneur, et mesme des Reclamateurs s'il s'en présente.

XXIV. Les Officiers de l'Admirauté entendront sur le fait de la prise le Maistre ou Commandant du Vaisseau pris, et les principaux de son équipage, mesme quelques Officiers et Matelots du Vaisseau preneur, s'il est besoin.

XXV. Si le Vaisseau est amené sans prisonnier, chartes-parties, ni connoissement, les Officiers, Soldats et Equipage de celuy qui l'aura pris seront separément examinez sur les circonstances de la prise, et pourquoy le Navire a este amené sans prisonniers, et seront le Vaisseau et les Marchandises visités par Experts, pour connoistre, s'il le peut, sur qui la prise aura esté faite.

XXVI. Si par la déposition de l'Equipage, et la visite du Vaisseau et des Marchandises, on ne peut découvrir sur qui la prise aura esté faite, le tout sera inventorié, apretié, et mis sous bonne et seure garde, pour estre restitué à qui il appartiendra, s'il est reclamé dans l'an et jour, si non partagé comme espave de Mer également entre Nous, l'Admiral et les Armateurs.

XXVII. S'il est nécessaire, avant le Jugement de la prise, de tirer les Marchandises du Vaisseau pour en empescher le déperissement, il en sera fait Inventaire en présence de nostre Procureur et des parties interessées, qui le signeront si elles peuvent signer, pour ensuite estre mises sous la garde d'une personne solvable, ou dans des Magazins fermans à trois clefs differentes, dont l'une sera delivrée aux Armateurs, l'autre au Receveur de l'Admiral, et la troisiéme aux Reclamateurs, si aucun se presente, sinon à nostre Procureur.

XXVIII. Les Marchandises qui ne pourront estre conservées seront venduës sur la requisition des parties interessées, et adjugées au plus offrant en presence de notre Procureur à l'issuë de l'Audience aprés trois remises d'encheres de trois jours en trois jours, les proclamations prealablement faites, et affiches mises en la maniere accoustumée.

XXIX. Le prix de la vente sera mis entre les mains d'un Bourgeois solvable, pour estre délivré, aprés le Jugement de la prise, à qui il appartiendra.

XXX. Enjoignons aux Officiers de l'Admirauté de proceder incessamment à l'exécution des Arrests et Jugemens qui interviendront sur le fait des prises, et de faire faire incontinent et sans delay la délivrance des Vaisseaux, Marchandises et effets, dont la main-levée sera ordonnée, à peine d'interdiction, de cinq cens livres d'amende, et de tous dépens, dommages et interests.

XXXI. Sera prise avant partage la somme à laquelle se trouveront monter les frais du déchargement, et de la garde du Vaisseau et des Marchandises, suivant l'Estat qui en sera arresté par le Lieutenant de l'Admirauté en presence de nostre Procureur et des Interessez.

XXXII. Aprés les distractions cy-dessus, le dixiéme de la prise sera délivré à l'Admiral, et les frais de Justice seront pris sur le restant, qui sera ensuite partagé entre les Interessez conformement aux conditions de leur Société.

XXXIII. S'il n'y a aucun contract de Société, les deux tiers appartiendront à ceux qui auront fourny le Vaisseau avec les Munitions, Armement et Victuailles, et l'autre aux Officiers, Matelots et Soldats.

XXXIV. Faisons defences aux Officiers de l'Admirauté de se rendre adjudicataires directement ou indirectement des Vaisseaux, Marchandises, et autres effets provenans des prises, à peine de confiscation, quinze cens livres d'amende, et d'interdiction de leur Charge."

The Règlement of July 1778

The text of the third instrument in this famous series of legislative enactments, the *Règlement concernant la navigation des bâtimens neutres en tems de guerre* of 26 July 1778 (not to be confounded with an earlier law, of 28 March 1778 (*Code des prises*, II, 623; extract in Martens, R^2, III, 115 *et seq.*), the *Ordonnance concernant les prises faites sur les vaisseaux, frégates et autre bâtimens du Roi* can be found in the *Code des prises*, II, 671, and Martens, R^2, III, 18 *et seq.* It was issued on the eve of the "Armed Neutrality" of 1780, whereupon comp. Chapter II, *infra*, pp. 124-128. Its fifteen provisions regulate a number of issues coming under the traditional rules of the law of maritime prize. Their text runs as follows:

"Le Roi s'étant fait représenter les anciens règlemens concernant la navigation des vaisseaux neutres pendant la guerre, Sa Maj. a jugé à propos d'en renouveller les dispositions et d'y ajouter celles qui lui ont paru les plus capables de conserver les droits de Puissances neutres, et les intérêts de leurs sujets, sans néanmoins autoriser l'abus que l'on pourroit faire de leur pavillon; et en conséquence Sa Maj. a ordonné et ordonne ce qui suit:

Art. I

Fait défense S.M. à tous armateurs, d'arrêter et de conduire dans les ports du Royaume, les navires des Puissances neutres, quand même ils sortiroient des ports ennemis, ou qu'ils y seroient destinés; à l'exception toutefois de ceux qui porteroient des secours à des places bloquées, investies ou assiégées. A l'égard des navires des Etats neutres, qui seroient chargés de marchandises de contrebande destinées à l'ennemi, ils pourront être arrêtés, et lesdites marchandises seront saisies et confisquées; mais les bâtimens et le surplus de leur cargaison seront relachés, à moins que lesdites marchandises de contrebande ne composent les trois quarts de la valeur du chargement; auquel cas les navires et la cargaison seront confisqués en entier. Se réservant au surplus S.M. de révoquer la liberté portée au présent Article, si les Puissances ennemies n'accordent pas le réciproque dans le délai de six mois, à compter du jour de la publication du présent règlement.

Art. II

Les maîtres des bâtimens neutres seront tenus de justifier sur mer de leur propriété neutre, par les passeports, connoissemens, factures et autres pièces de bord; l'une desquelles au moins constatera la propriété neutre, ou en contiendra une énonciation précise. Et quant aux chartes-parties et autres pièces qui ne seroient pas signées, veut S.M. qu'elles soient régardées comme nulles et de nul effet.

Art. III

Tous vaisseaux pris, de quelque nation qu'ils soient, neutres ou alliées, desquels il sera constaté qu'il y a eu des papiers jettés à la mer, ou autrement supprimés ou distraits, seront déclarés de bonne prise avec leurs cargaisons, sur la seule preuve des papiers jettés à la mer, et sans qu'il soit besoin d'examiner quels étoient ces papiers, par qui ils ont été jettés, et s'il en est resté suffisamment à bord pour justifier que le navire et son chargement appartiennent à des amis ou alliés.

Note: Cet Article a été modifié par une lettre du Roi à M. l'Amiral en date du 13 Nov. 1779 v. *Code des Prises* P. II p. 783 dont la teneur fuit: "Mon cousin! je suis informé qu'il se présente fréquemment des difficultés sur l'exécution des mes Ordonnances sur les Prises, au sujet des Papiers qui devroient se trouver à bord des Bâtimens pris ou arrêtés à la mer, et que mon règlement du 26 Juill. 1778, paroissant annoncer implicitement que la preuve du jet des papiers, de quelque nature qu'ils puissent être, emporte avec elle la confiscation du bâtiment, vous ôte, ainsi qu'aux Commissaires du Conseil des Prises, la liberté de peser les circonstances qui auroient pu déterminer à jetter des papiers à la mer, et d'examiner la nature de ces papiers qui pourroient ne pas offrir la preuve d'une propriété ou d'une destination ennemie: cette interprétation exclusive seroit contraire à l'esprit et aux vues dans lesquelles mes Ordonnances ont été dictées, et je vous fais cette lettre pour Vous dire, que je m'en remets entièrement à Vous et aux Commissaires du Conseil des Prises, d'appliquer la rigueur de mes Ordonnnances et de mon règlement du 26 Juillet ou d'en modifier les dispositions, selon que les circonstances particulières vous paroitront l'exiger: et la présente n'ètant à autre fin je prie Dieu etc." Signé Louis et plus bas De Sartine.

Art. IV

Un passeport ou congé ne pourra servir que pour un seul voyage, et sera réputé nul s'il est prouvé que le bâtiment pour lequel il auroit été expédié n'étoit, au moment de l'expédition, dans aucun des ports du Prince qui l'a accordé.

Art. V

On n'aura aucun égard aux passeports des Puissances neutres, lorsque ceux qui les auront obtenus se trouveront y avoir contrevenu, ou lorsque les passeports exprimeront un nom de bâtiment différent de l'énonciation, qui en sera faite dans les autres pièces de bord, à moins que les preuves du changement de nom, avec l'identité du bâtiment, ne faissent partie de ces mêmes pièces, et qu'elles ayent été reçues par des Officiers publics du lieu du départ, et enregistrées par devant le principal Officier public du lieu.

Art. VI
On n'aura pareillement égard aux passeports accordés par les Puissances neutres ou alliées, tant aux propriétaires, qu'aux maîtres des bâtimens, sujets des Etats ennemis de S.M., s'ils n'ont été naturalisés, ou s'ils n'ont transféré leur domicile dans les Etats desdites Puissances, trois mois avant le premier Septembre de la présente année; et ne pourront lesdits propriétaires et maîtres de bâtimens sujets des Etats ennemis, qui auront obtenu lesdites lettres de naturalité jouir de leur effet, si depuis qu'elles ont été obtenues, ils sont retournés dans les Etats ennemis de S.M., pour y continuer leur commerce.

Art. VII
Les bâtimens de fabrique ennemie, ou qui auront eu un propriétaire ennemi, ne pourront être reputés neutres ou alliés, s'il n'est trouvé à bord quelques pièces authentiques passées devant les Officiers publics, qui puissent en assurer la date, et qui justifient que la vente ou cession en a été faite à quelqu'un des sujets des Puissances alliées ou neutres, avant le commencement des hostilités, et si ledit acte translatif de propriété de l'ennemi au sujet neutre ou allié, n'a été duement enregistré par devant le principal Officier du lieu du départ, et signé du propriétaire ou du porteur de ses pouvoirs.

Art. VIII
A l'égard des bâtimens de fabrique ennemie, qui auront été pris par les vaisseaux de S.M., ceux de ses alliés ou de ses sujets, pendant la guerre, et qui auront ensuite été vendues aux sujets des Etats alliés ou neutres, ils ne pourront être reputés de bonne prise s'il ne se trouve à bord des actes en bonne forme passés par devant les Officiers publics à ce préposés, justificatifs, tant de la prise que de la vente, ou adjudication qui en auroit été faite ensuite aux sujets desdits Etats alliés ou neutres, soit en France, soit dans les ports des Etats alliés; faute desquelles pièces justificatives, tant de la prise que de la vente, lesdits bâtimens seront de bonne prise.

Art. IX
Seront de bonne prise tous bâtimens étrangers sur lesquels il y aura un Subrecargue marchand, Commis ou Officier major d'un pays ennemi de S.M., ou dont l'équipage sera composé au delà du tiers de matelots, sujets des Etats ennemis de S.M., ou qui n'auront pas à bord le rôle d'équipage arrêté par les Officiers publics des lieux neutres, d'où les bâtimens seront partis.

Art. X
N'entend S.M. comprendre dans les dispositions du précédent Article, les navires dont les Capitaines ou les maîtres justifieront par actes trouvés à bord, qu'ils ont été obligés de prendre les Officiers-majors ou matelots dans les ports où ils auront rélaché, pour remplacer ceux du pays neutre qui seront morts dans le cours du voyage.

Art. XI
Veut S.M. que dans aucun cas, les pièces qui pourront être rapportées après la prise des bâtimens, puissent faire aucune foi, ni être d'aucune utilité, tant aux propriétaires desdits bâtimens, qu'à ceux des marchandises qui pourroient y avoir chargées: voulant S.M. qu'en toutes occasions l'on n'ait égard qu'aux seules pièces trouvées à bord.

Art. XII
Tous navires des Puissances neutres, sortis des ports du Royaume, qui n'auront à bord d'autres denrées et marchandises, que celles qui y auront été chargées, et qui se trouveront munis de congé de l'Amiral de France, ne pourront être arrêtés par les armateurs françois, ni ramenés par eux dans les ports du Royaume, sous quelques prétexte que ce puisse être.

Art. XIII
En cas de contrevention de la part des armateurs françois, aux dispositions du présent règlement, il sera fait main levée des bâtimens et des marchandises qui composent leur

chargement, autres toutefois que celles sujettes à confiscation, et lesdits armateurs seront condamnés en tels dommages et intérêts qu'il appartiendra.

Art. XIV
Ordonne S.M. que les dispositions du présent règlement auront lieu pour les navires qui auroient échoué sur les côtes dépendantes de ses possessions.

Art. XV
Veut au surplus S.M. que les dispositions du titre des prises de l'Ordonnance de la marine du mois d'Aoùt 1681 soient exécutées selon leur forme et teneur, en tout ce à quoi il n'aura pas été dérogé par le présent règlement; lequel sera lu, publié, et enregistré dans tous les sièges des Amirautés: Mande et ordonne S.M. à M. le Duc de Penthièvre, Amiral de France, de tenir la main à son entière observation.
Fait à Versailles, le vingt six Juillet mil sept cent soixante dix huit."

Signé: Louis
et plus bas De Sartine

The Arrêté of an XI (1803)

The subjects regulated in this *Arrêté* were arranged as follows:

Titre I. Armemens en course (Arts. 1-50)
- Chap. 1. Des sociétés pour la course
- Chap. 2. Équipages
- Chap. 3. Lettres de marque et cautionnemens
- Chap. 4. Encouragemens
- Chap. 5. Police de la course et rançons

Titre 2. Prises (Arts. 51-111)
- Chap. 1. Captures
- Chap. 2. Procédures des prises
- Chap. 3. Déchargement, manutention, vente et liquidation particulière des prises
- Chap. 4. Liquidations générales
- Chap. 5. Repartition

Titre 3. Des armemens en course et des prises dans les colonies et dans les ports étrangers (Arts. 112-121)

Titre 4. Dispositions générales (Arts. 122-124)

The profusion of French *édits*, *ordonnances* and *règlements* dealing with prize law has given rise to their combined publication in a collection of 1784 in two volumes in quarto, reprinted in an augmented edition in four volumes in octavo under the title *Code des prises* (1789-1801). That second edition, to which reference is made above, included also two further enactments, *viz.*, the *Décret* of 14 February 1793, Art. 5 of which maintained in force all earlier laws and regulations (Martens, R^2, V, 379), and the above-mentioned *Arrêté du Gouvernement* of 2 prairial *an* XI (22 May 1803), containing a summary of all the laws issued since 1681, also published in Martens, R^2, VIII, 9-41.

When one collects from De Pistoye and Duverdy's *Traité* all the legislative texts, quoted by the authors, on which the French prize courts were bound to found their judgments, and then places them all in a chronological order, one obtains an impressive series of laws and other enactments. Again a number of them have no bearing on prize law proper, or relate only to marginal subjects—such as slave trading, the composition of the crews of armed vessels, prisoners of war, pirates—but even when eliminating these, one retains a vast number of legislative instruments which lead one through the maze of French prize law, such as it prevailed during the successive wars waged by France in her different constitutional phases. They can be arranged in the order of those wars or according to the subject matters they regulated. In principle I will adopt the latter form of separation.

Spain

As an old sea-faring nation Spain, too, has a long tradition of 13th-15th century maritime law. Apart from a Castilian translation of the *Rôles d'Oléron* in the shorter original version of 25 articles (Pardessus, VI, 57; Capmany, II, 31), Spanish legislation was partly a codification of old local usages—Custom of Valencia, 1250 (Pardessus, V, 333); *Fuero Real*, 1255 (*ibid.*, VI, 15); *Siete Partidas* of King Alfonso X the Wise, 1266 (*ibid.*, VI, 16), *Partida* no. V being framed in accordance with the *Rôles d'Oléron*; *Recopilación de las Ordinanzas de Sevilla* 14th century (*ibid.*, VI, 63)—and partly a sequence of scores of privileges, *ordinanzas*, *pragmáticas*, *cédulas*, etc. on diverse subjects, especially two Ordinances, one on the "policing of navigation" of 1258 (*ibid.*, V, 339), the other a "Maritime Ordinance" of 1340 (*ibid.*, V, 351); a number of ordinances concerning the establishment of consulates and the jurisdiction and procedure of the "judges-consuls" in maritime affairs—1341 (*ibid.*, V, 367), 1343 (*ibid.*, 374), 1381 (*ibid.*, 473), 1405, 1409 and 1432 (*ibid.*, 481, 483 and 485)—and a new Ordinance of the Magistrates of Barcelona on "maritime police" of 1435 (*ibid.*, 487).

The scope of Spanish legislation, initially centered on the Mediterranean, widened, of course, considerably after the discovery of America. From then onward the general picture changed basically and Spanish legislation on maritime affairs developed a pronounced Atlantic aspect. The Mediterranean sources were collected by Pardessus in vol. V of his work, chapter xxxiii, pp. 321-554 (regulations of Cataluña, Aragón, Valencia and Mallorca), the Atlantic sources in vol. VI, pp. 1-300 (southern and western States of Spain). A "pragmática" of 21 July 1494 (Pardessus, VI, 103) set up a consulate at Burgos; an Ordinance of Ferdinand and Isabella of 20 January 1503 (Navarrete, *Colección de los viages*, 1825, II, 245) established a *Casa de Contratación de las Indias* in Sevilla, probably vested with judicial competences, subject to an appeal to the *Consejo de las Indias* (comp. also the subsequent Ordinances of 21 November 1507 (Pardessus, VI, 64) and 1556 (*ibid.*, 76); new *Contrataciones* were established in Burgos (Regulations of

1538, Pardessus, VI, 131), Bilbao (Ordinance of 1560, *ibid.*, 195) and San Sebastián (Ordinance of 1682, *ibid.*, 253). Consular jurisdiction was re-arranged in 1510 and 1599 (*ibid.*, V, 543 and 549). An Ordonnance of King Carlos I (Emperor Charles V) of 1552 (*ibid.*, VI, 66) regulated many subjects of maritime law in more than two hundred articles, but none dealt with prize law.

Portugal

The old prize laws of Portugal are mentioned in Pardessus' *Collection*, vol. VI, pp. 301-318.

At a much later stage the *Código de processo commercial* (Arts. 16, § 2, and 179) conferred jurisdiction over all prize cases "privatívamente" upon the Tribunal of Commerce of Lisbon.

The United Netherlands

In his great historical six-volume work *Collection des lois maritimes* J.M. Pardessus listed a long series of laws and ordinances enacted by the rulers of the countries from which was eventually to emerge the Republic of the United Netherlands, or by the authorities of cities engaged in maritime commercial shipping. The ordinances he cited in vol. IV of his work related in particular to the Counties of Flanders (pp. 19-29) and Holland (pp. 29-188). The latter were issued by the central authorities of the time, the King Emperor of Spain Carlos I (V) in 1532, 1549 and 1551, respectively King Felipe II of Spain in 1563 and 1570, in his capacity of Count of Holland (pp. 62-102, 103-119). Those quotations are followed at pp. 121 *et seq.* by ordinances issued by the municipal authorities of Amsterdam, Enkhuizen, Haarlem and Rotterdam which form together a kind of regional customary law (whereupon comp. *supra*, pp. 29-30).

The first central legislation on prize affairs in the Low Countries prior to the emergence of the independent confederation of the United Netherlands and its Eighty-Years' War with Spain related, according to official Netherlands sources, to the organization of a prize jurisdiction by the then Sovereign of the area, laid down in two Ordinances of 1488 and 1540.

The Ordonnance of 8 January 1487 (*i.e.* 1488), the text of which can be found in the Netherlands *Groot Placaatboek*, vol. IV, pp. 1208 *et seq.*, was enacted at Bruges by the Roman King Maximilian and his son Philip, archduke of Austria, duke of Burgundy, Brabant, Limburg, Luxemburg and Guelder, count of Flanders, Artois and Burgundy, count palatine of Hainault, Holland, Zeeland, Namur and Zutphen, lord of Friesland and Mechelen. This Ordonnance has never been recognized by the county of Holland as binding upon it, so that that county has persisted in maintaining its own judicial organization (the Court of Holland and the Superior Court) as the competent judiciary to deal with legal disputes, including the adjudication of prize cases. Particulars of this controversy can be found in the *Maritieme Geschiedenis der Nederlanden* and in the *Algemeene Geschiedenis der Nederlanden*. Comp. further the data set out *sub* C, section 1, *infra*, pp. 581 *et seq.*

The Ordonnance on maritime navigation of the Netherlands of 27 December 1540, the text of which was inserted in the same *Placaatboek*, vol. IV, pp. 1215 *et seq.*, issued by the Emperor Charles V, King of Spain, at Namur, was to all intents and purposes identical with that of 1488 save for a new Article 18 which expressly permitted an appeal from the Admiral's judgments to the *Grand Conseil* at Mechelen.

The next, third, enactment was the first national document, called "Instruction of the States General of the United Netherlands for the Admiralty Colleges, set up in the respective provinces and quarters", of 13 August 1597 (*Groot Placaatboek*, vol. II, pp. 1530-1558), and was considerably more detailed (99 articles) than the two preceding Ordonnances of the Spanish Kings (24, respectively 23 articles).

After the establishment of the Republic of the United Netherlands the role of legislator in prize law affairs was indeed assumed by the supreme authority of the new confederation who issued a large number of *placaten* (placards) on the subject. Apart from their Instruction of 1597 on the organization of prize jurisdiction (whereupon comp. further section 1 of Chapter III *sub* C, *infra*, pp. 582-584), they enacted *placaten* relating to such subjects as naval blockade, privateering and the award of prize money, recapture and the award of salvage to the recaptors, etc. I will confine myself here to citing a few of the relevant *placaten* and a few selected data.

There is first the well-known series of *placaten* of the States General instituting general prohibitions, also addressed to neutral shipping, from trading with the enemy, an early form of paper blockade, a subject whereupon comp. further III A, section 4, *infra*, pp. 421-423. The States General have indeed in the 16th century exhibited a pronounced tendency, during their Eighty-Years' War of Independence against Spain, to uphold the theory that belligerent Powers were entitled to intercept all trade, also neutral trade, to their enemy. It is only gradually that they have restricted or mitigated that rigid doctrine by either circumscribing it within certain areas of the enemy's territory (the Spanish Southern Low Countries) or confining its scope to two specific harmful activities of neutral subjects, *viz.*, the carriage of contraband to their enemy, or the running of a blockade established by the Republic off an enemy coast or port. A long series of *placaten* (placards) of the States General witnesses to this development.

The *placaten* relative to this principal issue were those of

22 June 1584, confirmed on 17 July, respectively 27 July 1584 by the States of Holland and the States General (*Groot Placaatboek*, vol. I,

pp. 1104, resp. 1076), containing an interdiction, addressed to anyone "of whatever nation, quality or condition he may be", to carry "all goods or merchandise, of whatever kind or quality they may be, none excepted or reserved", to the Spanish Low Countries "from the Netherlands, or from Spain or other kingdoms or countries, either directly or indirectly";

4 April 1586, enacted by Robert Dudley, Earl of Leicester, Queen Elizabeth's Governor in the Netherlands (*ibid.*, I, 1083): differentiating between "residents or natives of the Netherlands provinces" and "ship-captains and merchants of other kingdoms, countries and towns, not living under the jurisdiction nor being natives of the Netherlands provinces", threatening the former with the gallows and confiscation of their ships and goods, but the latter only with forfeiture of their (or their company's) ships and cargo;

18 July 1586 (*ibid.*, I, 1088): extending the operation of the earlier placaten by prohibiting the "entire commerce and traffic with Spain, Portugal and other enemy harbours, countries and towns, both going and coming", and ordering the translation of the text and its sale in the Netherlands, French, English and German languages. This and all previous placaten were, however, in view of strong protests from various foreign quarters, repealed by a new *placaat* of

4 August 1586 (*ibid.*, I, 1092), replacing them by a mitigated interdiction, addressed to non-Netherlands residents and subjects, to carry on trade to the Spanish Low Countries.

This development has been described in detail by J.H. Kernkamp, *De handel op den vijand* (Utrecht, 1931).

The retreat by the States General in August 1586, however, by no means implied that they abandoned their view of the legality of such general trade prohibitions. On the contrary, they maintained that view in subsequent years on various occasions, *inter alia* in diplomatic notes dating from the end of the 16th century and in a new *placaat* of 2 April 1599 (*Groot Placaatboek*, II, 33). The definitive turn in the legal conceptions only occurred at the beginning of the 17th century. The subject matter has been examined, especially with a view to the development of the doctrine of the effectiveness of a blockade, by Professor B.M. Telders in 1939 ("De oorsprong der effectieve blokkade"), in *Rechtsgeleerde Opstellen aangeboden aan Prof. Mr A.S. de Blécourt* (Groningen, 1939) and in *Verzamelde Geschriften van Prof. Mr B.M. Telders* (The Hague, 1948, vol. II, pp. 165-184) and by Dr Johanna Oudendijk in 1974 ("Blockaded seaports in the history of international law", in the Netherlands *Tijdschrift voor Rechtsgeschiedenis* 1974 (42), pp. 1-22).

In the course of the 17th century the States General issued *placaten* on several other subjects, especially during the Nine Years' War of 1688-1697. As example I cite prohibitions of 27 July 1627 and 26 April 1653 to engage in privateering on the strength of commissions granted by foreign Powers, prohibitions repeated much later in a *placaat* of 3 May 1779 (Martens, R^2, III, 62) to the effect that

> "il ne sera permis à aucuns Habitants des Pays-Bas-Unis de mettre en mer ou de faire naviguer leurs Vaisseaux, soit des Ports de cette République, soit d'autres Pays, en vertu de Commissions accordées par des Rois, Républiques, Princes, ou autres Puissances Etrangères, ni d'avoir part à l'armement d'aucuns Vaisseaux, naviguant comme Corsaires en vertu de telles Commissions, d'en partager aucunement les gains ou les pertes, ou étant sortis avec due Commission de M. le Prince d'Orange et de Nassau, en qualité d'Amiral-Général des Pays-Bas-Unis, de prendre en outre une Commission étrangère, de quelque manière que ce soit sans en avoir eu notre permission préalable, à peine etc.";

the system of *convooien en licenten* (the furnishing of protection to merchant ships by warships, and the grant of licenses to trade with the enemy), 9 April 1687 (*Groot Placaatboek*, IV, 1236 *et seq.*);

the regime of recapture in general and the pseudo-recapture of vessels abandoned at sea (*ibid.*, III, 240);

a prohibition to export contraband goods, 9 March 1689 (*Groot Placaatboek*, IV, 220 *et seq.*);

prohibition to ransom vessels captured by the enemy, 2 July 1689 and 12 June 1690 (*ibid.*, IV, 210);

the grant of commissions to private *commissievaarders*, 23 October 1690 (*ibid.*, IV, 211);

the determination of the amount of the rewards to be paid to privateers for their captures, 31 May 1697 (*ibid.*, IV, 217).

Much later, during their fourth Naval War with Great Britain, the States General enacted two new placaten,

one of 12 January 1781, regulating the rewards that their privateers would enjoy (Martens, R^2, III, 153):

(6) in the case of capture, the English ship shall with all goods on board fall to the captor, without any deduction of State portions, with the sole exception of one tenth of the value due to the Admiral (on this particular subject comp. further Chapter III, *sub* C, section 7, *infra*, pp. 649-651, on prize bounty);

(8) in the case of recapture within 48 hours a reward of one fifth, between 48 and 96 hours a reward of one third, and thereafter, a reward of half of the value (on recapture see Chapter III, *sub* B, section 7, *infra*, pp. 549-550).

the other of 13 January 1781, laying down instructions for privateers (Martens, R^2, III, 155), especially Articles

42: prohibition to molest Netherlands, allied or neutral vessels being on their way to England without a contraband cargo, or to offend in any way against those on board;

52: obligation to procure surety to an amount of 30,000 guilders;

53: payment of the rewards pending a possible revision procedure, subject to their restitution in case of an adverse decision, an increase of the surety and a lien on the ship;

The United States of America

The nascent United States of America developed a brisk legislative activity, even during the early years of their existence. Thus, their original Continental Congress in 1778 issued a proclamation ordering their privateers to regard neutral rights as sacred. Initially it was not clearly defined what exactly these rights were. Reference was made to the Treaty of Commerce of Utrecht of 1713 and the famous Report of the Law Officers of the (British) Crown of 1756 during the Seven Years' War, which was itself based on the customary principles laid down in the *Consolat de Mar* (comp. p. 76). On the instructions of Congress the Board of Admiralty in 1776 elaborated a plan for the conclusion of treaties with foreign Powers and a first treaty was entered into on 6 February 1778 with France (Martens, R[2], II, 587; Parry, 46, 417). Following the project for the creation of an Armed Neutrality League, launched by the Russian Tsaritsa Catharina in 1780, the Congress charged the Board of Admiralty with the task of preparing a draft embodying the principles of that Armed Neutrality and on 27 November 1780 adopted the resulting draft, the substantive contents of which were embodied in the Instructions to the captains of American ships of war and privateers. Those Instructions, which were not formally binding upon the early American prize courts which used to apply their own customary rules, in actual fact changed the accepted customary rules as applied by those courts, by introducing the principle "free ship, free goods" instead of the rule of the *Consolat de Mar*. This change gave rise to the usual problem of transitional law: the condemnation by the trial Court of a British-owned cargo on a neutral (Dutch) ship, the *Brunette*, captured before November 1780, was still upheld by the Court of Appeals in 1781 (Bourguignon, *The first federal Court*, p. 281, with footnote 103). The treaty with France on 6 February 1778 (Martens, R[2], II, 587) embodied the principle of "free ship, free goods", but upheld the traditional "infection" doctrine of French prize law in the variant of "unfree ship, unfree goods". See Arts. 23 and 14:

> (Art. 23) "... il est stipulé par le présent Traité qui les bâtimens libres assureront également la liberté des marchandises, et qu'on jugera libres toutes les choses qui se trouveront à bord des navires appartenans aux sujets d'une des deux Parties contractantes, quand même le chargement ou partie d'icelui appartiendroit aux ennemis de l'une des deux ..."

> (Art. 14) "On est convenu au contraire, que tout ce qui se trouvera chargé par les sujets respectifs sur des navires appartenans aux ennemis de l'autre partie, ou à leurs sujets, sera confisqué sans distinction des marchandises prohibées ou non prohibées, ainsi et de même que si elles appartenoient à l'ennemi, à l'exception toutefois des effets et marchandises qui auront été mis à bord des dits navires avant la déclaration de guerre, etc...."

Comp. on this subject further Chapter III, *sub* A, section 2, *infra* pp. 326-331.

Further examples of an earlier or later date are:

the *Tuscan Regolamento* of 1 August 1778 "toccante la navigazione e il commercio in tempo di guerra" (Martens, R[2], III, 24);

the *Danish* Royal Decree of 28 March 1810 "concernant l'armement en course, et la manière de traiter les prises" (Martens, N.R., I, 492), supplemented by a Decree of 27 August 1810 (*ibid.*, 505);

an *Austro-Prussian* agreement of 6 June 1864 concerning maritime prizes made during the war with Denmark, followed by common instructions to the commanders of their warships (Martens, N.R.G.[1], XX, 254, 258);

Governmental Decrees of *Austria, Prussia* and *Italy* of 13 May, 19 May and 20 June 1866 concerning the capture of enemy merchant ships during the hostilities of 1866 (Martens, N.R.G.[1], XVIII, 308-309);

similar ordinances of the *North-German Federation* of 8 July 1870 (cancelled by Decree of the German Emperor of 19 January 1871) and of *France* of 13 August 1870 (*ibid.*, XIX, 588-590);

the *Russian* Imperial Ukaz of 24 May 1877 "concerning the rules to be observed, during the war with Turkey, vis-à-vis the enemy Power and its subjects and the neutral States and their subjects" (Martens, N.R.G.[2], III, 216);

the *Turkish Règlement* of 7 June 1877 (*ibid.*, III, 218), limited to the organization of a prize jurisdiction;

the *Japanese* Regulations of 20 August 1894 enacted during Japan's war with China (text in Hurst & Bray, II, 416);

the *Russian* Regulations as to Naval Prize etc. of 14 July 1895 (text in 93 articles in Hurst & Bray, I, Appendix A, at pp. 311-331).

When the Russo-Japanese War broke out in February 1904, both the Japanese Regulations of 1894 and the Russian Regulations of 1895 were still in force. The same applies to the Instructions of 20 September 1900 which the Admiralty Council of Japan had in the meantime approved in virtue of Art. 26 of the Regulations of 1895 (text, *ibid.*, I, Appendix B at pp. 331-346). See on the general contents of those Instructions section 4, *infra*, p. 61.

What further occurred after the opening of hostilities was

as to Russia the issuance of an Imperial Ordinance of 14 February 1904 under the heading "Rules which the Imperial Government will enforce during the War with Japan" (text, *ibid.*, I, Appendix C, at pp. 346-349, with five additional Appendixes D-G on contraband, at pp. 349-351), and

as to Japan, the issuance of new Regulations relating to Capture at Sea on 7 March 1904 in 98 articles (text, *ibid.*, II, Appendix B at pp. 422-444).

It is worth-while consulting the Rules enacted in 1904 as authentic evidence of the views held by a great Continental and a great maritime Power respectively on the law of prize at the very end of the pre-codification period.

A collection of national prize regulations, complete in so far as is possible, which either were issued by the belligerent Powers during World War I, or were of earlier date but still in force at the time, can be found in my *Le droit des prises de la Grande Guerre* of 1924, Annexe II, at pp. 1355-1370. They are partly of a legislative nature, partly in the form of instructions to the Navy.

Section 4. INSTRUCTIONS FOR THE ADMIRAL OR FOR PRIVATEERS

When reporting in section 1 above, pp. 16 *et seq.*, on the part which the Rolls of Oléron have played in English maritime jurisdiction, I have already alluded to old instructions, dating from the 15th century, which were given by the King of England to his Admiral, on how to behave in time of war.

The same applies to France. Thus, an appendix to vol. I of Travers Twiss's work on the *Black Book of the Admiralty* reproduces

at pp. 420-429 from two MSS. in the British Museum (Harleian Collection No. 3836 and Cotton Collection Claudius E viii) the text of the abovementioned (p. 43) Ordinance of King Philippe de Valois of France of 23 March 1338 for the French fleet, intended to govern its expedition to be dispatched under the Duke of Normandy for the conquest of England, and captured on board the French Admiral's ship in the disastrous battle of 1340 on the Swyn near Sluys;

at pp. 430-442 from the British Museum Sloane MS. No. 2423, fol. 1^{b}-10, the text of a "Règlement sur le faict de l'Admiraulté", being laid down in an Ordinance of King Charles V (1364-1380) on the jurisdiction of the Admiralty against piracy and for the regulation of war prize of 7 December 1373, in subsequent publications (Fontanon's *Recueil des Edits et Ordonnances des Rois de France*, III, 864; Secousse's *Ordonnances du Louvre*, VIII, 640) erroneously dated 7 December 1400;

at pp. 443-448 from the same Sloane MS., fol. 10^{b}-14, the text of an *Ordonnance* of uncertain date concerning *Droitz et preeminences de Monsieur l'Admiral*;

at pp. 448-452, again from the same Sloane MS., fol. 14^{b}-15^{b}, the text of an *Ordonnance touchant la dixième*, also without date.

In earlier periods government instructions were often specifically addressed to privateers. Those instructions used to be very elaborate. Their contents will be analysed in a separate exposé on privateering in Chapter III (General issues, section 1), *infra*, pp. 159-164.

For the rest, as already remarked above (p. 42), it is difficult to draw a sharp distinction between legislative enactments and royal instructions to the Navy.

In Sir George Lee's MS. Notes concerning the *Med Guds Hielpe* [1750], as edited by Fr.Th. Pratt in 1856, one comes across the following sentence regarding the legal force of such instructions (at p. 196);

> "Instructions in casu those of 1706 are very different from rules to this Court by the Crown or public notification to all Crowns".

In the same Notes, this time relating to the *De Vlught naa Aegypten* [1747] (at p. 128), another sentence says that

"Instructions can not alter the Law of Nations".

These remarks relate to a legal problem that has later proved to be a keystone of the English doctrine concerning the controversial question of the interrelation between national and international law in matters of prize, whereupon comp. further section 3 of Part C of Chapter III, *infra*, pp. 595-610.

A footnote 2 at the same page 128 of Pratt-Lee contains certain references in support of his succinct thesis concerning the force of the King's instructions, *viz.*, 2 C.Rob., 202 and Edwards, p. 604, and the *Snipe* case of 1812, reported *in extenso* in Edwards, pp. 381-417. But I have been unable to find anything about this basic issue at the places he cites. There must be mistakes in that footnote; C. Robinson does not mention the subject at the place indicated; Edwards, p. 604, must be wrong, if only because this collection of reports ends at p. 417; and neither could I find the *Snipe* case of 1812 at the places referred to in that footnote 2 (said to be at pp. 119 and 122, of what collection, probably again of Pratt-Lee). In any case, such footnotes are more misleading than helpful.

Instructions concerning the treatment of contraband goods were issued, *inter alia*, by King William and Queen Mary on 2 May 1693 and by Queen Anne on 11 May 1706 (Pratt-Lee, p. 205.)

Government instructions have throughout the centuries continued to be issued. In section 3 above (p. 59) I have already mentioned the Instructions approved by the Russian Admiralty Council on 20 September 1900 (text in Hurst & Bray, I, Appendix B, at pp. 331-346). As these Instructions are the latest of their kind in the pre-codification period, I will summarily indicate here their contents. They deal successively with Stopping (2-3), Examination—including search (4-31), Detention (32-38), Bringing-in—including destruction and entry of neutral ports (39-42), and Handing-over of prizes (43-45).

Section 5. ADMIRALTY AND PRIZE COURT DECISIONS

The law regarding the exercise of the right of prize is laid down in a large number of collections of national prize court decisions.

As I have reported in section 1 (*supra*, p. 16), the oldest surviving judgments, the so-called "Judgments of the Sea", date from the early 14th century and are based on, or themselves constituted, the Rolls of Oléron, which are of French origin. Those judgments appeared to have been indeed rendered in maritime disputes, but on inspecting them in the Record Room of the Guildhall in London (facilitated by a transcript of later date) I found them disappointing inasmuch as that they have no bearing on prize law proper, but only on legal relations between five particular groups of people, *viz.*, ship-owners, ship's captains, crews, charterers and pilots. There was, therefore, no ground for having them reproduced in this volume, the less so because their text is known since they have been printed in other collections. They were mainly localized in the region of Bordeaux, La Rochelle and the island of Oléron, and in the wine-cultivating area of southwestern France, but their operation extended northward up to the Zwin near Damme (Flanders). The crews mainly came from Normandy and Brittany. See on these Judgments of the Sea further section 1, *supra*, pp. 16 *et seq*.

In the following pages I will deal successively with the collections of judgments of French prize tribunals, of English Admiralty courts and of prize courts of other maritime Powers.

The French collections

While, as will be set out below, the quick succession of British prize court decrees reached its peak on the threshold and at the outset of the 19th century, the various adjudicative instances which succeeded one another in France under the consecutive constitutional régimes also made their contribution to the creation of a coherent body of prize law.

The adjudication of prize cases in the earlier period of French legal history was described by Auguste Dumas in an academic thesis (Paris, 1908) *Étude sur le jugement des prises maritimes en France jusqu'à la suppression de l'office d'Amiral (1627)* (comp. on this latter development the details given in Chapter III, *sub* C, introductory section, *infra*, p. 575).

French case law on maritime prize, based on old French legislation, was surveyed for the first time by René-Josué Valin, *Avocat et Procureur du Roi au Siège de l'Amirauté de la Rochelle*, in a work entitled *Nouveau Commentaire sur l'Ordonnance de la Marine du mois d'août 1681.* This work was presented as a "traité des prises ou principes de la jurisprudence françoise concernant les prises qui se font en mer, etc.". This work, first published in La Rochelle in 1763 and again in new editions of 1766 and 1776, also gave information on that legislation and on the procedure which was to be observed. Valin's work was very recently (1981) reproduced in a beautiful new two-volume edition by the *Association française du droit maritime* to commemorate the three-hundredth anniversary of Colbert's *Ordonnance de la Marine* of August 1681.

Almost a century after its first appearance Valin's work was resumed by two successors, A. de Pistoye and Ch. Duverdy, who published another two-volume study under the title *Traité des prises maritimes dans lequel on a refondu en partie le traité de Valin* (Paris, 1855, 2nd edition 1859). In this work the authors have arranged their subject-matter systematically by dealing with it in ten *titres* (see *infra*).

The work contains elaborate historical introductions to the main substance of the study which consists of the texts of the relevant French laws and decrees on prize law, and the texts of French prize tribunal decisions implementing those laws and decrees.

Legislation and prize court decrees of the 1790's were dated in France in accordance with her artificial 30 days-a-month calendar of vendémiaire/brumaire/frimaire, pluviôse/ventôse/nivôse, germinal/floréal/prairial and thermidor/messidor/fructidor from *an* I up to *an* XI, starting with the 1st vendémiaire *an* I (3 October 1793).

A student of prize law who has completed a detailed research into old British sources and then passes on to a corresponding research into old French precedents gets the strange impression of landing in a completely different world of thought.

When examining the British cases one fancies oneself roving through a nature reserve, full of wild growth and entangling lianas—a landscape in which the judges, tempted by differing, sometimes exotic flowers, are seen following separate paths towards their common goal. When one then crosses the fence into the French cases the scenery changes completely: the observer enters a Le Nôtre garden where he perceives the judges walking under an official guide along paths strictly laid out by the owner of the estate.

This striking difference between the landscapes is bound to cause difficulties to a writer who endeavours to spread the available case material over a logical system of juristic exposition. Whereas the English courts were far more independent in their judgment, less bound by legislative fetters, the French courts had to keep strictly within the bounds set by their legislator. One who surveys British prize cases is therefore justified in describing them as free decisions of the adjudicating court, but one who examines French prize law must realize that the judgments can only be evaluated as interpretations or applications of rules enacted by a superior authority. This would, strictly speaking, necessitate the previous drafting of a summary of the contents of these legislative enactments but, as I have set out in section 3, these are so numerous, from the 14th century onward, and so elaborate that it is hardly feasible to apply this logical method of arrangement. I have consequently been compelled to seek a middle course with regard to old French prize law. In order to form a personal idea of what this impressive series of laws, decrees, ordonnances, etc., includes, I have for my personal guidance made a brief inventory of them from De Pistoye and Duverdy's scholarly work. One has to state, then, just as one finds when one goes through the British judicial precedents, that the French collection contains a fair number of data which are not usually considered to be the subject matter of a body of maritime prize law, such as the capture of pirate ships and of slavers—dealt with by the authors under the common heading "Du droit de prise en temps de paix" in section 1 (pp. 33-66), respectively section 2 (pp. 67-85) of Chapter III of title I of their work.

As it is fairly difficult to follow the authors of the *Traité* in the logic of their system of arrangement and as, moreover, they have applied in their two-volume work a most awkward caesura precisely between two §§ (2 and 3) of section IV of Chapter II of title VI and right through the period of the Crimean War, I will begin with a summary enumeration of the headings of the ten *titres* of their work and follow that up with a more detailed survey of their contents, with references between brackets to the places where specific legal issues are examined in one or the other of the two volumes. The authors themselves have offered at pp. 507-509 of vol. II a chronological list of French laws, ordinances, decrees and *arrêtés* dating from 1638-1854.

I begin by recalling my above remark that *titre* I of the work deals with subjects that do not properly belong to the law of prize in the usual meaning of the term, *viz.*, "prize law in time of peace".

The examination of French practice of maritime prizes in time of war proper commences with *titre* II under the heading "Les lieux où peut s'exercer le droit de prise" (vol. I, pp. 92-118). The further *titres* are successively presented under the headings:

titre III (vol. I, pp. 119-156) "Des temps dans lesquels s'exerce le droit de prise";

titre IV (vol. I, pp. 157-229) "Les personnes qui peuvent exercer le droit de prise";

titre V (vol. I, pp. 230-312) "Devoirs des croiseurs";

titre VI (vol. I, pp. 313-463 and vol. II, pp. 1-103) "Des choses de bonne prise", the main body of substantive prize law;

titre VII (vol. II, pp. 104-139) "Des navires recous sur l'ennemi ou abandonnés par lui";

titre VIII (vol. II, pp. 140-364) "Du jugement des prises";

titre IX (vol. II, pp. 365-448) "Vente, liquidation et partage des prises";

titre X (vol. II, pp. 449-465) "Des prises étrangères amenées dans les ports de l'Empire lorsque la France est neutre".

This arrangement is not very conducive to an adequate understanding of where exactly in particular the rules of the different chapters of substantive prize law can be found. For that one has to consult the subdivisions of the *titres* in *chapitres*, *sections* and *paragraphes*, and even then there is some considerable difficulty.

Under each of these ten headings the authors first set out the relevant legal provisions in force at the time—successively under the long reign of the Kings of France up to 1793, the revolutionary period 1793-*an* VIII under the *Convention* and the *Directoire exécutif*, the era of the *Consulat* and Napoleon's Empire, and the ensuing period of the Restoration from 1814 up to and including the Crimean War—and then report, as an illustration or construction of such legal provisions, the relevant decisions of French prize courts, re-incorporating those already recorded by Valin.

The details of French prize case law are thus scattered over De Pistoye and Duverdy's *Traité* in the arrangement sketched above. They had a bearing, in particular, upon the following subject matters: the criteria of the enemy or non-enemy character of ships and the transfer of enemy ships to a neutral flag; the requirement of ship's papers and the composition of the crews; the regime of privateering; the various grounds of confiscation of prizes; naval blockade; the transportation of contraband goods and the sanctions thereon; the distribution of the proceeds of prizes, inclusive of the award of prize money to the captors, and the regime of recaptures and the award of salvage. All these subject matters, as reflected in French prize jurisprudence, will be examined at their appropriate places in my systematic arrangement in Chapter III below.

I will enter into some greater detail concerning the contents of the authors' further exposé of French legislation and jurisprudence with constant references to volumes and pages where the issues are discussed.

The admissible theatre of the exercise of the right of prize is determined in *titre* II, 26 pages (vol. I, pp. 92-118), the admissible period during which it could be exercised in *titre* III (vol. I, pp. 119-156), and the group of persons who were entitled to exercise it in *titre* IV, 72 pages (vol. I, pp. 157-229), a long titre necessary to relate all interesting facts about the practice of privateering, from King Charles VI's regulation of 13 November 1372 onward.

The formalities in earlier times prescribed for the exercise of the right of prize are set out in *titre* V of 82 pages (vol. I, pp. 230-312), dealing successively with the introductory warning shot (*coup de semonce*), the procedure of visit, putting the cargo under seal, seizure of the ship's papers, the bringing of the prize into port (*amarinage*), the treatment of those on board as prisoners, the practice of ransoming the prize, and the captor's duty to report to the naval authorities (*déclaration de prise*). The formalities of visit and seizure were laid down, *inter alia*, in an Ordonnance of 1696, the *Arrêté* of 2 prairial *an* XI and a Law of 10 April 1825 (vol. I, pp. 230-238, 243-245 and 248-258).

The substantive law of prize is then exposed in a very long *titre* VI, the capture of enemy property being dealt with in chapter I (vol. I, pp. 313-337), that of neutral property in chapter II (vol. I, pp. 337-509, continued in vol. II, pp. 1-103). These latter 275 pages on the right of prize against neutrals range over a wide field, dealing not only with the two main grounds of capture and condemnation—violation of a blockade (section II, vol. I, pp. 365-392) and the carriage of contraband (section III, vol. I, pp. 392-415)—but also

in section IV, with the various aspects of ship's papers, in a very detailed survey amounting to not less than 163 pages (vol. I, pp. 416-509 and vol. II, pp. 1-70), spread over four paragraphs: § 1 devoted to the "justification of neutrality" (vol. I, pp. 416-462), the conclusive force of ship's papers and the moment when they must be produced, unsigned documents and bills of lading (*connaissements*); § 2 to the validity of passports (vol. I, pp. 463-509);

§ 3 to deeds stating changes in the ownership of ships (vol. II, pp. 1-30) and § 4 to the composition of their crew (vol. II, pp. 31-70);

in section V, with the jettison of ship's papers (vol. II, pp. 70-85);

in section VI, with ships provided with authorizations (*sauf-conduits*) of the French government, the counterpart of the British licenses (vol. II, pp. 85-89);

in section VII, with vessels run ashore on the coasts of France or her possessions (vol. II, pp. 89-94); and

in section VIII, with the refusal to obey a *semonce* (vol. II, pp. 95-103).

The work then continues with an elaborate exposé in *titre* VII of the rules on the recapture (*recousse*) of ships from, or their abandonment by, the enemy, chapter I (vol. II, pp. 104-119) dealing with French or allied ships, chapter II (vol. II, pp. 120-139) with neutral vessels.

Titre VIII, divided into four chapters, sets out the rules on the adjudication of prizes,

in chapter I (vol. II, pp. 140-193) devoted to an historical survey of their judgments in the four successive periods: the old monarchy (from 1400 onward, via subsequent ordinances of 1527, 1584, 1643, 1681 and 1778; section I, vol. II, pp. 140-149), the revolutionary period of 1793 up to *an* VIII, under the *Convention* and the *Directoire exécutif* (section II, vol. II, pp. 149-158), the ensuing period under the *Consulat* and Napoleon (section III, vol. II, pp. 158-177), and the years between 1814 and the Crimean War, 1854 (section IV, vol. II, pp. 177-193);

in chapter II (vol. II, pp. 193-228) dealing with prize proceedings in the port where the prize was brought in (*port d'amarinage*)—instruction (i) of prizes brought into ports of France or her colonies, (ii) of cases of stranding or shipwreck, and (iii) of prizes conducted into a foreign port—;

in chapter III (vol. II, pp. 228-345), a long chapter concerning the new *Conseil des prises*, set up by a Decree of 18 July 1854;

and in chapter IV (vol. II, pp. 345-364) setting out the special subject of the admissibility of transactions in prize cases.

An exposé of the rules on the sale, liquidation and partition of prizes follows in *titre* IX (vol. II, pp. 365-448). It describes in great detail the formalities of the sale; the partition of prizes made by privateers according to the *Arrêté* of 2 prairial *an* XI—determining the parts owing to the crew (1/3), the ship-owners (2/3), the master (*préciput du capitaine*), the *Caisse des Invalides de la Marine* and the "tenth of the Admiral", both in normal cases of capture by a single privateer and of joint capture by more than one—and the partition of prizes made by the Imperial Navy; and regulates (*Arrêté* of 6 germinal *an* VIII) the settlement of disputes arising between those entitled to a part of the prize.

Titre X (vol. II, pp. 449-465) finally deals with a neutrality, rather than a prize law, problem; namely, the régime of foreign prizes brought into French ports when France was neutral.

I insert this brief survey of the contents and arrangement of De Pistoye and Duverdy's study in order that it may be of some help as a guide through the vast material in which, as my experience taught me, I found myself more than once at a loss as to the exact place in their system where the subject matter I was looking for was to be found.

I therefore add a few more references.

— The subject of the enemy or neutral character of prizes is hidden under two separate headings where one would not expect to find it, namely, under "Des pièces de bord" in vol. I, pp. 416-462 (where the title of § 1 "justification de la neutralité" is missing) and pp. 463-509 (title of § 2 "De la validité des passeports"), and further under the surprising heading "De la composition des équipages. Du rôle d'équipage" in vol. II, pp. 30-70. These two separate groups of data are connected by cross-references from vol. I to vol. II but, as said before, that has been done in a manner which makes it very awkward to find in vol. II the cases to which reference is made in vol. I as a result of the fact that this reference is not made to pages in that vol. II, but to the very complicated system of arrangement of the source material in titres (VI), chapters, sections and paragraphs.
— A long exposé of the problem "free ship, free goods" can be found in vol. I, pp. 340 *et seq*.
— The *crû ennemi* is dealt with in vol. I, pp. 360-361: *Règlement* of 21 October 1744.
— On *sauf-conduits* and *licenses* see vol. II, p. 85: *Règlement* of 26 July 1778.
— Exemption from condemnation of enemy property was decreed already by an early stage in favour of small coastal fishing vessels by a Decree of 1 October 1692 (vol. I, p. 314).
— The obligation of the captor to pay freight to the ship-owner in the case of his recapturing a prize was laid down in a Law of 18 vendémiaire *an* II (1794) (vol. I, p. 171).
— On recaptures (*recousses*) themselves see vol. II, p. 104 (of French or allied vessels) and p. 120 (of neutral vessels).
— A number of Ordinances contained rules on the sale and repartition of the proceeds of prizes and the grant of prize money (*parts de prises*) to the Admiral, the captain and the crew of the capturing vessel and the *Caisse des Invalides de la Marine*. In earlier times the *Admiral de France* had the right to receive one-tenth of the proceeds of every prize, but his privilege was abrogated by an Edict of 1758 (vol. II, p. 397). See further *ibid.*, *titre* IX, *chapitres* II (section II, §§ 1-5), III and IV in vol. II, pp. 380-443; 443-447. The exposé follows the order of Arts. 99-111 of the *Arrêté* of 2 prairial *an* XI. How uncertain the legal position was, also in France, appears from a judgment of the Court of Cassation of 12 floréal *an* IX in the case of *Bellas contre l'Epervier* (vol. II, p. 403) on appeal from a decision of the *Tribunal des Basses-Pyrenées* which had denied Bellas the right to invoke, in support of his claim to a share, a *Règlement* of 1 August 1743 and a Law of 1 October 1793. The Court of Cassation could not but state that it had been

unable to ascertain the contents of the *Règlement* of 1743 invoked by the lower tribunal (vol. II, p. 404):

> "Le Tribunal des Basses-Pyrenées n'en a parlé que d'une manière très vague: il n'en a pas cité une seule disposition, et nous ne l'avons trouvé ni dans le Code des prises de Chardon, imprimé en 1783, ni dans celui de Lebeau, publié en l'an VIII, ni dans les différents recueils que nous avons parcourus."

And as to the Law of 1793, which did exist, the Court of Cassation rejected its construction by the lower tribunal.

— On the *préciput* of the ship's captain, see vol. II, p. 387; on the rights of the *Caisse des Invalides de la Marine* vol II, p. 389; on the repartition of the proceeds of prizes among the crew of privateers, vol. II, pp. 397 and 415 (the special case of joint capture), and on the liquidation and distribution of prizes made by the Imperial Marine, vol. II, p. 425.

The Law of brumaire *an* IV on the administration of prizes made no distinction of any kind between prizes made by warships of the State and prizes made by privateers.

Comp. for further details of this subject Chapter III, *sub* C, section 7, *infra*, pp. 647-649.

— On the *jet de papiers* see vol. II, p. 70; on a refusal by the arrested vessel to heave to vol. II, p. 95.

— An Ordonnance of Louis XIV of 23 February 1674 cautioned against sailing under a false flag and carrying different flags on board.

— The obligation of captors to bring their prizes into a French port was laid down, *inter alia*, in Ordinances of 6 June 1674 and 15 April 1689 (vol. I, p. 264), which expressly forbade the captors to conduct them to foreign ports or to abandon them at sea, and of 5 April 1710 (*ibid.*).

The ransoming of prizes was regulated by *Règlements* of 27 January 1706 (vol. I, p. 301) and June 1759 (vol. I, p. 284).

— Prizes made in neutral waters were, according to the elements of the cases, either released or condemned on the basis of legal rules enacted in 1667, 1681, 1778 and *an* XI, referred to, *inter alia*, in the *Saint-Michel* (vol. I, pp. 99-100).

— Rules on the escort of merchant vessels (convoy) were laid down in a Decree of 14 May 1745.

— The fate of shipwrecks (*navires échoués* or *abandonnés*) was determined by rules set out in vol. II, pp. 89 and 220.

— On the transfer of enemy vessels to a neutral flag see *titre* VI, *chapitre* II, *section* IV ("Des pièces de bord"), § 3 ("Des actes constatant les changements de propriété des navires") in vol. II, pp. 1-30 and 499-505.

— On the history of the organization of prize jurisdiction in France during her successive constitutional phases—the old monarchy, the *Convention* and the *Directoire*, the *Consulat* and Napoleon I, and the restoration of the monarchy—comp. vol. II, pp. 140-186 and 228-238, in particular the *Arrêté* of the Consuls of 6 germinal *an* VIII (1800), establishing a *Conseil des prises* (vol. II, p. 161), the *Décret* of 11 June 1806 (vol. II, p. 176), the *Décret* of 18 July 1854 during the Crimean War (vol. II, p. 228) and the *Décret* of 9 May 1859 during the war over Savoy.

— Proceedings in prize cases were regulated in an early period by an *Arrêt du Conseil* of 31 July 1661 and a *Règlement* of 6 June 1672 (vol. I, p. 307), at a much later stage by the *Arrêté* of 2 prairial *an* XI, differently as regards prizes in the ports of France and her colonies (vol. II, p. 197), shipwrecks (vol. II, p. 220) and prizes in foreign ports (vol. II, p. 225).

The case law during the Franco-German War was later described by H.M. Barboux in his *Jurisprudence du Conseil des prises pendant la guerre 1870-1871* (Paris, 1872).

The British collections

Every student of old British prize law must be struck by the diversity of the sources he has to consult for information about its origins and gradual development, in particular through the action of Admiralty tribunals, which has produced an unwieldy mass of prize law judgments, which will need some form of systematic exposition in my Chapter III. In the context of the present Chapter I concerning the historical sources of the law of maritime prize it seemed to me apposite to attempt to create some provisional order in this documentary chaos by first setting out what collections of early British prize cases exist and to what historical periods they relate, and by then arranging the older available source material in a manner which I have not found applied anywhere else but which seems to me to have some practical advantage in order to make it clearer through what sequence of political events the law has developed during the 17th and 18th centuries and what States were belligerent, respectively neutral or allied, during the successive periods of hostilities. This could be done by listing the most important early court decisions and further documents and publications in the chronological order of the naval wars to which they successively relate (see *infra*, pp. 85-102). I will therefore begin by reviewing under A the existing British collections themselves, and then, under B, deal with the main types of cases which gradually emerged during the successive wars in which England became involved, in order to illustrate how a customary law of prize has gradually emerged from the pronouncements of British courts of Admiralty.

A. The English collections themselves

As I have already explained, my research in this field was seriously hampered by the fact that some of the oldest collections of English prize cases were difficult to unearth from the various depositories of manuscripts and printed books, and further by the unfortunate fact that entire sections thereof in depositories of the Reading Room of the British Museum proved to have been destroyed as a result of the air bombardment of London during World War II. I therefore have only been able to retrace certain of the missing texts in other libraries or record rooms, or in references to them in publications of later dates.

As I have also pointed out, English prize case law presents every student of the subject with the difficulty that the reports of the judgments exhibit a rather chaotic picture, at least up to about 1800. Most of the 17th and 18th century English judgments in prize cases are indeed handed down to us in summary, often defectively worded texts and personal notes of the judges who delivered them or were in office at the time, which were subsequently found and edited by other lawyers. The scene only changed to a more orderly form of recording when Sir Christopher Robinson, who never acted in prize cases himself, began his chronological publication of "cases heard and determined by the High Court of Admiralty" in 1798, a publication which was subsequently continued, from 1808 onward, by four other lawyers (Th. Edwards, J. Dodson, J. Haggard and W. Robinson) up to 1850, thus constituting together a series of 16 volumes (see *infra*, p. 82).

The oldest history of English Admiralty law has been described in a work published in London in 1724 by William Wynne of the Middle Temple in two folio volumes under the title *The life of Sir Leoline Jenkins, Judge of the High Court of Admiralty, and Prerogative Court of Canterbury & c., Ambassador and Plenipotentiary for the general peace of Cologn and Nimeguen, and Secretary of State to King Charles II, etc.* According to data which I came across in the Public Records Office in London, 1500 cases were determined in his time, 1000 resulting in condemnation, 500 in release of the prize. One of the oldest reported cases was that of the *Arms of Plymouth* of 1692 during the Nine Years' War (1688-1697), said in a note at p. 2 in vol. I of E.C. Roscoe's *Collection of Reports of Prize Cases* of 1905 to have been the first precedent of the condemnation of a ship on the ground of the transport of contraband of war. Comp., however, Chapter III, *infra*, pp. 333-336.

Another author to whom we are particularly indebted in this field is Sir Reginald G. Marsden, who assumed the task of reporting quite a number of old Admiralty decisions, either in an independent personal capacity, or on behalf of two scientific institutions, the Selden Society and the Naval Records Society.

The publication for the Selden Society (vol. VI of the year 1892) under the title *Select Pleas in the Court of Admiralty, vol. I. The Court of the Admiralty of the West (A.D. 1390-1404) and the High Court of Admiralty (A.D. 1527-1545), edited for the Selden Society by Reginald G. Marsden* (London, 1894), contains the oldest judgments, *viz.*, in Part I (pp. 1-26), two records of the Court of John Earl of Huntingdon, Admiral of the West (under Richard II), and

in Part II (pp. 27-148, at pp. 88 *et seq.*), extracts from the records of the High Court of Admiralty (under Henry VIII), only a very limited number of which, however, have a closer or wider bearing on prize law proper. The volume is preceded by an Introduction (pp. xi-lxxxviii), followed by translations (pp. 149-242) and complemented by an Index. The main part of the volume includes, amongst a mass of judgments on other subjects (jettison, piracy (treaty of Bruges of 1297), collision, fish, flotsam, obstruction in waterways, etc.), several decisions dealing directly or indirectly with prize law proper, such as: letters of marque and reprisals, capture and recapture, property in goods recaptured and rights to salvage, freight claims (*pro rata itineris*), contributions to general average, jurisdiction (in general; with or without jury; delimitation as against other rival marine or seaport courts), appeal to Delegate judges, enemy ownership of goods and ships, hypothecation of ships, bottomry bonds and other liens on ships, transfer of property in transit, proceeds and distribution of prizes, droits of Admiralty, procedure, etc.

In his introduction, the author relates in detail the various judicial instances to which maritime cases were submitted in the course of time, such as: courts of common law, the King's Council, the Chancellor, the Admiral and his council, or arbitrators. The Admiralty Court was a Court of Record, but its early records have disappeared (Introduction, pp. xlv, xlvi, lvi, lx, lxi).

Reginald Marsden's publication for the Naval Records Society (vol. 49 of 1915), entitled *Documents relating to Law and Custom of the Sea*, contains documents from the period 1205-1648. I will confine myself to quoting here a few of the oldest decisions reported in that volume on issues which arose in the field of prize law in the course of the 13th and 14th centuries.

A case of the arrest of ships on account of the transportation of contraband goods occurred in 1293 (p. 21), when nearly a hundred German and French vessels which had been driven by bad weather into Newcastle upon Tyne and Scarborough were detained because they were suspected of having on board provisions and war material for the King's enemies in Flanders and France.

At p. 42 Marsden relates that it is not clear whether friends' goods in an enemy's ship shared the fate of the ship. According to him in most cases they probably did, but sometimes restitution of the goods to their owners was ordered by the King, as happened in 1296.

On the other hand, in 1337 a Flemish (neutral) ship with enemy (Spanish) goods on board was given by the King as good and lawful prize to the master of the galley that captured her (p. 66); the source from which Marsden borrowed his knowledge of this case was an entry in the *Close Rolls*, 11 Edw. III, part 2, m. 32.

Data on the manner of adjudication of prize cases in those early days can also be found in this volume. Since there existed no admiralty court in the 13th century, questions of the legality or illegality of capture at sea or of the distribution of the proceeds of condemned prizes were still tried before the King in Council or before courts of common law. Thus, the *Documents* mention (at p. 12) the process of a suit, heard in 1293 at Canterbury before the King and Council between merchants from Spain, Portugal and Piacenza and captors of their property. A certain Herbert de Newerk, formerly Dean of York, and others were assigned by the King to try the facts. Judgment was given for the defendants, the captors, who should keep the goods as prize legally captured from open enemies of the King.

The King himself sued for the proceeds of prizes before his own courts of common law:

in 1276, by an action relating to the King's half of goods captured from the enemy, he having granted the other half to the captor—see the text at p. 8, taken from the *Coram Rege Rolls*, No. 22;

in 1341, by an action in the Exchequer Court touching enemy goods detained by the captors and claimed by the King, the ship having been given to the captors—see the text at p. 69, taken from the *Exchequer Plea Rolls* (14 & 15 Edw. III, m. 13 d).

The King also used other means in order to stop supplies, *e.g.*, ships reaching his Scotch enemies, *viz.*, by friendly requests to neutral Sovereigns. See King Edward III's requests to that effect, addressed in 1336 to the Count of Holland (at p. 64, taken from the *Close Rolls*, 10 Edw. III, m. 9 d), the King of Norway and the Count of Guelder (Rymer, IV, 715).

In its appellate judgment of 20 March 1953, and therefore dating from after the Second World War, concerning the *Hermes and other hulls* (*Ll.P.C.* (2nd.), pp. 347 *et seq.*, at pp. 360-361) the Judicial Committee of the Privy Council still quoted with approval the narrative by E.S. Roscoe in his *History of the English Prize Court* (London, 1924) of how the Lord High Admiral was authorized in early days by the Crown to investigate "with a delegated authority in the nature of prize jurisdiction" complaints by neutrals or allies that their ships had been seized; how in the course of time a personage—called the Admiral's deputy—came into existence, who exercised a Prize Jurisdiction (Marsden's *Select Pleas*, at p. xiii), and how by the sixteenth century a rudimentary Prize Court undoubtedly existed (Roscoe, *loco cit.*, p. 11). This jurisdiction was to decide about "Prizes", *i.e.*, captures of ships. At the time of the Armada in 1589, for example, Dr Julius Caesar, "doctor of laws, the duly appointed Judge-Lieutenant of the High Court of Admiralty of England", was pronouncing a sentence of condemnation of a Spanish ship as lawful prize (Marsden's *Law and Custom of the Sea*, p. 254).

Valuable information on several subjects of old prize law is further contained in Chr. Robinson's *Collectanea Maritima* of 1801, a richly documented collection of public instruments, etc., often consisting more of footnotes than of text, designed, as the author explains in his Advertisement, "to illustrate the history and practice of Prize Courts" and to "connect ancient precedents of the practice of prize law, showing the antiquity of the main principles, as part of the immemorial usage and customs of the sea". This collection begins at p. 1 with the Instructions of 1512 to the Admiral of the Sea Sir Edward Haward during the voyage and enterprise to be made against the French King in Guyenne (Rymer, *Foedera*, XIII, 229), including among their 28 provisions articles on visitation and search (Art. 18) and on resistance of neutral vessels (Art. 20). They are followed at p. 21 by a Proclamation of 1602 "ad reprimendas depredationes super mare" (44 Eliz.), providing, *inter alia*, against the use of neutral ports by captors and for the bringing of prizes into one of the captor's own ports. Arts. 2 and 3 are to the following effect:

> "Item, that if any person whatsoever shall upon the sea take any ship that doth belong to any of her Majestie's freynds and allies, or to any of their subjects, and after knowledge had that the said shippe doth belonge to her freyndes, doth not forbeare to stay the same, unlesse it shall be laden with goods of her Majestie's enemyes, or with merchandizes of such nature or quallety as may serve to furnish the Kynge of Spayne, his armyes or navyes, and going into the kingdome of Spayne and Portugall, or shall take out of it anie goodes belonging to her sayde freyndes, except foods of the aforesaid nature or quallity bound for Spayne or Portugall, hee or they soe offending, shall suffer death ...
> Item, that all admyrall causes ... shall be summarily heard by the Judge of the High Court of the Admyralty, without admitting any unnecessary delay".

But in a series of footnotes at pp. 36 *et seq.* the author falls back on much older sources, mainly treaties, from 1294 onwards, several of which throw light on the oldest practices of prize law, for example, on the question of whether a non-enemy ship carrying an enemy's property was liable to confiscation. Comp. on this confused subject Chapter III, *sub* A, section 2, *infra*, pp. 300-301.

Among those treaties I cite those of 1294 between England and Portugal, of 1351 and 1357 between England and Spain, of 1370, 1417, 1430, 1446, 1467 and 1495 between England and Flanders, and of 1490 between England and Denmark (see for their texts the *Foedera* of Rymer, V, 717; VI, 659; IX, 434; XI, 144; XII, 383).

Besides such treaties, the footnotes also list documents of another type, such as:

royal ordinances (Edw., A.D., 1294; Rymer, II, 632);

royal mandates, *e.g.*, of 1327 for the restitution of a Flemish ship taken during the then Anglo-Scottish war (Rymer, IV, 328) and of 1373 for the restitution of a Portuguese vessel (Rymer, VII, 3).

Following all those footnotes, the collection continues by giving the texts of a variety of further documents, both British and foreign, especially French, such as two Royal Proclamations of 1625 and 1626 against Spain (pp. 54 and 63 *et seq.*) and a Commission to Lord Carleton of 1626 (p. 69), data concerning a number of French Ordinances of 1400, 1543, 1584, 1681, 1704, 1744 and 1778 (pp. 75 *et seq.*, 119 *et seq.*), etc.

The period of the War of the Austrian Succession in the 1740's is represented by a book, only published in 1856, entitled *Law of Contraband of War, with a selection of cases from the papers of the Rt. Hon. Sir George Lee ... and an appendix containing extracts from treaties, miscellaneous papers, and forms of proceedings, with the cases to the present time*, by Frederic Thomas Pratt. The same author also edited Judge Story's *Notes on the Principles and Practice of Prize Courts* (1854)—a work that, according to Roscoe, II, at p. 631, had seen selected by the British Government for the use of its naval officers as the best code of instruction in prize law. The publication of 1856 contains the collection of "MS. Notes of Sir George Lee", referred to by E.S. Roscoe in footnote *a* at p. 38 of vol. I of his *Reports*, published in 1905. The author of these MS. Notes (1700-1758), who from 1751 to 1758 was Dean of The Arches, must not be confounded with Richard Lee, another writer on prize law (*A Treatise on Captures in War*, London, 1803), on whom some less flattering notes can be found in Alice Clare Carter's *The Dutch Republic in Europe in the Seven Years' War* (Edinburgh, 1971, p. 85 and footnote), but who is obviously more highly appreciated by Bourguignon in his recent study of 1977 on *The First Federal Court* in the United States.

The discovery of the manuscripts. In the early 1850's a distinguished lawyer, Mr Frederic Thomas Pratt happened to pay a chance visit to a Dr Lee at his home in Hartwell, who drew his attention to a manuscript in his possession which had belonged to an older relative of his, Sir George Lee, and which he thought might interest his visitor. Upon inspection of that manuscript, which I will further call Sir George Lee's "Notes", Mr Pratt found it so valuable that he asked and was given permission to undertake its publication.

The entire collection, as it stood, was printed during the Crimean War in book form in accordance with Mr Pratt's instructions (1856). He has deserved well of the legal profession by this publication of a manuscript that had almost been completely forgotten, and also, in addition, by providing the "Notes" with a personal contribution of his own, laid down in an analytical survey of old British practice and rules of contraband of war, based on the "Notes". This survey inserted in the first section of the book is paged by the Roman ciphers xxvii-lxx. I will further refer to it as Mr Pratt's "Preface".

The main substance of the book consists of a reproduction in print of the "Notes" covering pp. 1-205. In contradistinction to the (handwritten) "Notes" I will further entitle their printed reproduction as did Pratt: "Reports of cases decided by the Court of Admiralty", or simply: "Reports". The rest of the book is chiefly filled with "Appendixes" of different kinds or by footnotes, which are not always correct, or some cases of uncertain authorship. The "Notes" and "Reports" contain the texts of thirty-seven judgments pronounced by Sir Henry Penrice, President of the High Admiralty Court of the time (the War of the Austrian Succession of the 1740's). The "Appendixes" form a wide mixture of data (pp. 207-310): Appendix A (pp. 207 *et seq.*) including the texts of British treaty provisions on contraband, Appendix B (pp. 249 *et seq.*) containing the texts of British Orders in Council and Instructions to the Navy and to privateers, and Appendix C (pp. 269 *et seq.*) continuing with a *mixtum compositum* of data relating to prize proceedings, interrogations, monitions, etc., etc. These Appendixes A-C, originally again in the form of manuscript notes, are not, however, from the hand of either Sir George Lee himself nor of his editor Mr Pratt, but from that of another, earlier private collector who thus passively contributed to the general systematic chaos by providing Sir George Lee with another older set of manuscript notes to add, with a few corrections, as additional appendixes to his own "Notes". The author of this collection was Sir Nathaniel Lloyd, D.C.L., another distinguished advocate of Doctors' Commons, who was appointed Advocate-General in 1710 and held that office for sixteen years. This is why for the sake of brevity I sometimes indicate this peculiar hotchpotch work as "Pratt-Lee" or "Pratt-Lee-Lloyd".

Mr Pratt's survey in his "Preface" deals successively with the following main topics: the concept of contraband itself; the determination of its enemy destination *in concreto* (ports in the same bay, change of destination in transit, discretionary destination, the effect of territorial change *in transitu*, several destinations); the main categories of contraband goods, either warlike or of promiscuous use; indulgence in favour of the native growth and produce of the exporting neutral country (pre-emption); destination as a test of contraband character; a long and very detailed list of all possible sorts of contraband goods (such as "provisions" (*commeatus*), naval stores, metals and timber, saltpetre, coals, etc.), which have occupied the courts in the course of history ("Preface", pp. lxi-lxv), and on "contraband by notification" (*ibid.*, pp. lxvi-lxxx). This analytical survey, again followed by various further data in appendixes, hardly excels for its strict logical arrangement.

Sir George Lee's "Notes" make difficult reading. They all relate to cases which came before the High Court of Admiralty (and the Lords Commissioners of Appeal) during the period of England's participation in the War of the Austrian Succession (1744-1748). They begin with an exposé of the facts, which is followed by a summary in telegraphese of the, often contradictory, statements of the law by all the procedural actors: the captors, the claimants and their respective Counsel, the famous lawyers of their days, such as Dr Paul, and the Attorney-General, etc. Each "Note" ends with the text of the decision of the case pronounced by the President of the High Court of Admiralty at the time, Sir Henry Penrice, introduced by the formula *Per Curiam*. As compared with the boringly long lists of documents produced by the contesting parties and the interrogatories of witnesses, the *Per Curiam*'s are extremely summary and of little interest.

The references by Sir George Lee to older judgments with which the "Notes" are interspersed date from Britain's Second and Third Naval Wars against the Republic of the United Netherlands of 1665-1667 and 1672-1674, the Nine Years' War of 1688-1697, and the War of the Spanish Succession of 1702-1713. The "Notes", as printed, are, moreover, provided with footnotes, again not always correct and sometimes of uncertain authorship.

This confusing and unusual arrangement of the source material makes wading through the "Notes" a fairly hard job and anyhow thwarts a clear understanding of the legal situation in the middle of the 18th century. One gets the impression that it was very confused, not only in the days of the War of the Austrian Succession, but also in earlier and subsequent periods. As remarked above, the statements made by the different parties and their Counsel often contradicted one another, so that it proved hardly feasible to obtain an adequate picture of what the prevailing situation actually was. And to a certain extent Mr Pratt's analysis of the case law strengthens this impression.

One of the doubtful points was the liability of the contraband-carrier and of the innocent goods on board to confiscation together with the contraband. Another is the extent of the applicability of the rule concerning the exemption of the native produce or manufacture of the exporting country from condemnation. Furthermore there was the greatest divergence further as to the character of specific goods *ancipitis usus* as contraband of war.

Details of the many varying subjects jotted down by Sir George Lee in his "Notes" and their scientific analysis by Mr Pratt in his "Preface" will be distributed over the relevant parts, sections and paragraphs of Chapter III A *infra*, according to their logical place in my general system of exposition. See on the abovementioned more specific points §§ 1, 2 and 3 of section 3 *infra*, pp. 331-414.

It was during the War of the Austrian Succession that the famous controversy between the Courts of St James and Berlin over the Silesian loan arose. Although this dispute, from a systematic point of view, belongs rather to B, *infra*, I will mention it here because of Sir George Lee's personal deep involvement in it.

It had a bearing on Prussia's suspension of the payments due on Emperor Charles VI's loan of 1735 of 1,000,000 crowns borrowed from British bankers on the security of the revenues of Silesian mines, a loan which had been taken over by King Frederick II of Prussia in the peace treaty of Breslau of 1742 by which the Empress Maria Theresia was forced to cede her land of Silesia to Prussia. This suspension of payments was defended by the Court of Berlin as a measure of reprisal against certain captures of Prussian ships, made by Great Britain during her war with France and Spain, which broke out in 1744. The task of replying to the elaborate statement of reasons by the Court of Berlin, prepared by a commission countersigned by the celebrated lawyer Cocceji and three further members, Podewils, Bismarck and Finkenstein, was as a matter of fact entrusted to a British committee consisting of Sir George Lee, Judge of the Admiralty Court; Dr Paul, Advocate General; Sir J. Ryder, Attorney General and Mr W. Murray, Solicitor General. The British reply of 18 January 1753 (reproduced by T. Baty at pp. 116 *et seq.* of his study of 1915 on *Prize Law and Continuous Voyage*) contained a number of principles which the prize courts of their days used, and indeed were bound to decide the cases submitted to their judgment and which subsequent British prize courts would have been well advised to remember, but which they have in an increasing degree in fact ignored. I only quote a few of them:

> "The evidence to acquit or condemn ... must, in the first instance, come merely from the ship taken" (in another version: a ship could only be condemned "out of her own mouth").
> "No order or intimation is ever given to any judge."
> "All captures at sea, as prize, in time of war, must be judged of in a court of admiralty, according to the law of nations ... There never existed a case where a court, judging according to the laws of England only, took cognizance of prize ... It never was imagined that the property of a foreign subject, taken as prize on the high seas, could be affected by laws peculiar to England."

This dispute between the two countries lasted for a long time and was not finally resolved until 1756, when on 16 January the following declaration on the part of Great Britain in Council was made with reference to it:

> "In order to put an end to the disputes which have arisen between their Britannic and Prussian Majesties, it is declared that upon his Prussian Majesty taking off the attachment put upon the Silesian debt, and causing to be paid to his Britannic Majesty's subjects what remains due to them thereon according to the original contract, as well interest as principal, his Britannic Majesty does promise and engage on his part to cause to be paid to his Prussian Majesty the sum of 20.000 l. sterling, for extinguishing all and every claim from his said Majesty, or his subjects, upon his Britannic Majesty under any pretence whatever" (Pratt-Lee's Preface, footnote 1 at pp. v and vi).

A further publication is the one we owe originally to Sir William Burrell. The title of that work was *Reports of Cases determined by the High Court of Admiralty and upon appeal therefrom temp. Sir Thomas Salusbury and Sir George Hay, Judges, 1758-1774, by Sir William Burrell, Bart. (1732-1796)*, together with two appendices. This work was re-edited, again by the same Sir Reginald Marsden, in an independent personal publication (London, 1885), and presents difficulties of another kind. The original author, at p. iv of his Introduction, echoed the general compliant about "the absence of any published Admiralty reports of earlier dates than the end of the 18th century" and "therefore offered his compilation in the hope that it might be not without interest to Admiralty lawyers". It is indeed a somewhat strange compilation despite the interest which it inspires, as it contains a most curious hotchpotch of documents. Although Burrell's work deals in the main with a later period, *viz.*, the Seven Years' War of 1756-1763 (in Marsden's edition at pp. 1-299, the first 153 pp., however, dealing with admiralty cases other than prize cases), it also includes, at pp. 231-339, as appendices,

Extracts from the Books and Records of the High Court of Admiralty and the Court of Judges Delegates, dating from different periods from the 16th century onward. As far as they date from the time before the institution of the Judicial Committee of the Privy Council (1834), they are now in the keeping of the Public Record Office in London.

The work continues at pp. 351-392 with a collection of Cases and Opinions on Admiralty Matters 1701-1781. No wonder that, when the editors of *The English Reports* (see *infra*, pp. 80-81) resolved to re-publish several old collections of Admiralty cases (prize cases and others) in an orderly series, they were at a loss what to do with the "Opinions", inserted in Burrell's second appendix "Cases and Opinions". These opinions did not, in fact, fit into the plan of the great new publication and they were therefore simply omitted as falling outside the scope of the project (*The English Reports*, vol. 167, *sub* iii, pp. 443-615).

On a closer perusal of this compilation by Burrell one sees that it is a mixed composition, consisting of varying elements and subjects, each from a different period. As a guide through this curious collection of documents I will give a brief table of contents. After a section of 153 pages of mixed Admiralty cases, the volume continues with a section on prize cases proper, dating from the Seven Years' War of 1756-1763 and encompassing pp. 155-229. The ensuing pp. 231-350 follow with the abovementioned Books and Records of the High Court of Admiralty and the Court of the Judges Delegates (the ancient Court of Appeal from the Admiralty before the institution of the Judicial Committee of the Privy Council in 1834 (1584-1859), then deposited in the Public Record Office. The compilation is composed of seven series, every one covering a different period: 1677-1767 (Registrar's notes of all proceedings in the Admiralty Court); 1524-1744 (Act Books of the Admiralty Court, formal entries of Acts); 1538-1834 (Assignation Books of the Court of the Judges Delegates); 1538-1684 (Delegates' Act Books); 1619-1834 (Delegates' Process Books, complete statements of all proceedings, the only record of the formal sentence of the Admiralty Court "which the present writer [Burrell] has hitherto been able to discover"); 1585 *et seq*., an incomplete collection "in a bad state of preservation" and "in a state of great confusion"; and a collection of miscellaneous papers "in a state of confusion". The compilation concludes at pp. 351-401 with a selection of ecclesiastical cases from documents in Burrell's own handwriting, reproduced *verbatim* in old spelling and "erratic in proper names".

Small wonder that I found it rather difficult to make my way through this maze of sources, in order to form a somewhat adequate idea of how British prize case law has actually developed. That difficulty was not alleviated by the proceedings and records being drafted up to Cromwell's time in Latin, then for a short period during his rule mostly in English, from 1666 onwards, when jurisdiction returned to Doctors' Commons, again in Latin, until they finally turned to English in 1733.

Sir William Burrell's collection of judgments from the time of Judges

Thomas Salusbury and George Hay (1758-1774) covers, as the dates indicate, the period of the Seven Years' Naval War between England and France. Some of them have a bearing on reserved colonial trade engaged in by neutrals, the practice which was responsible for the emergence of what has become known as "the rule of the War of 1756". This trade was mainly with the French or French-occupied West Indian islands, such as Guadeloupe and Hispaniola. Comp. on this type of trade Chapter III, *sub* A, section 6, *infra*, pp. 471-477. But apart from those cases the collection contains decisions on the ordinary subjects of prize law: the transportation of contraband, violation of a blockade, hostile assistance, uncertainty concerning the enemy or neutral character of prizes, or their transfer *in transitu*, the treatment of neutral property on board an enemy vessel or on its way to enemy territory, the exemption from capture of ships sailing under a licence, joint capture and the captor's right to prize money, instances of fraudulent behaviour, and the legal effects of a preliminary peace treaty, or of the capitulation of enemy (respectively neutral) territory to a neutral (respectively enemy) State upon the confiscability of sea-borne cargoes.

As appears from the survey above, the state of the written sources of early prize law available in England is fairly chaotic. I have already had occasion earlier, in section 1 (pp. 22-23), to mention the unfortunate fact that the collection of editions of the *Consolat de Mar* of Barcelona, listed in the general catalogue in the Reading Room of the British Museum, does not correspond at all with another series of editions I found mentioned in Travers Twiss's *Black Book of the Admiralty*, and that it shows a serious lacuna in that five of their total number of nineteen are designated as "presently missing". In another context (p. 18) I recalled Travers Twiss's misfortune in publishing the first volume of his famous work on the *Black Book of the Admiralty* from a copy of it, in default at the moment of the original Black Book which, to all appearances, had vanished for good, whereas that original was rediscovered only a short time after the publication in an entirely unexpected place, which forced the author to slightly correct the text given in his first volume in a subsequent one. During my research into the more recent written sources of British prize law from the 16th to the 18th century inclusive I came across many complaints by English writers themselves about the defective state in which prize court decisions have been handed down to past generations, either in that they were simply laid down in personal notes of judges or other contemporary lawyers, only subsequently discovered, or were incomplete, confused or badly drafted, with constant misspelling of ships' names, or mixed up with judgments of an entirely different nature, such as ecclesiastical affairs.

A further illustration of my difficulties was my hunt for the collection of judgments from the War of the Austrian Succession, published in 1856 in London by F.Th. Pratt in a curious work under the comprehensive title *Law of Contraband of War*.

The collections surveyed above and the decisions dating from the first decade of the second half of the 19th century, collected by Thomas Spinks in his publication of *Reports of cases decided during the present* [Crimean] *war in the Admiralty Prize Court and the Court of Appeal (1854-1856)*, were finally reprinted in 1923-1924 in a new series under the title *The English Reports*, partly—as concerns the publications by Th.H. Acton, J.W. Knapp and E.F. Moore—in a *Privy Council Series*, vols. 12 *et seq.*, partly—as concerns the publications by Burrell, Hay and Marriott, Chr. Robinson and his successors—in an *Ecclesiastical, Admiralty, and Probate and Divorce Series* (a curious, typically English combination of subjects, only attributable to an age-old apportionment of jurisdictional powers amongst particular branches of the Judiciary), vols. 165-167 (Edinburgh-London), and in the latter series again subdivided into three vols. V, VI and VII (see *infra*).

The general titles of these volumes 12 *et seq.* and 165-167 highlight another difficulty for a student of old British prize law, *viz.* that they include a great number of cases which—even in the field of Admiralty alone—have nothing to do with the law of prize (such as disputes on collision, salvage, compulsory pilotage, seamen's wages, forfeiture on account of unauthorized import, etc.) and he therefore finds himself faced with the tedious task of collecting the prize cases proper from this vast *mixtum compositum* of judicial pronouncements. These volumes of *The English Reports* contain, respectively, in the two series mentioned:

A. in the *Privy Council Reports*:

— in vol. 12

the judgments, reported earlier by Th.H. Acton in two volumes:

I (pp. 1-155) from the period June 1809 to July 1810;

II (pp. 156-221) from the period 1810-1811;

the judgments, reported earlier by Jerome Th. Knapp in three volumes:

I (pp. 222-377) from the period 1829-1831;

II (pp. 378-545) from the period August 1831 to June 1834;

III (pp.546-709) from the period 1834-1836;

the judgments reported earlier by Edmund F. Moore in two volumes:

I (pp. 710-901) from the period 1836-1837;

II (pp. 902-1096) from the period 1837-1838;

with a table of cases at p. 1097;

— in vol. 13

the judgments reported earlier also by E.F. Moore in a series of five more volumes:

III (pp. 1-199) from the period 1839-1841;

IV (pp. 200-388) from the period 1841-1845;

V (pp. 389-581) from the period 1845-1847;

VI (pp. 582-778) from the period 1846-1849;

VII (pp. 779-975) from the period 1849-1851;

with a table of cases at p. 997;

— in vol. 14, leading into the period of the Crimean War, the judgments reported earlier, again by E.F. Moore, in a series of further volumes:

VIII (pp. 1-196) from the period 1852-1854;
IX (pp. 197-388) from the period 1854-1855;
X (pp. 389-594) from the period 1855-1857;
XI (pp. 595-811) from the period 1856-1858;
XII and so on;

B. in the *Ecclesiastical, Admiralty, and Probate and Divorce Reports*:

— vol. 165, the judgments reported earlier by
(i) Hay and Marriott (pp. 1-71), with, in an appendix, the French *Règlement* of 21 October 1744 (pp. 71-73);
(ii) Chr. Robinson, 6 vols., ending with the *Caroline* case [1808] (pp. 74-1002);
(iii) Th. Edwards (pp. 1011-1159);
(iv) J. Dodson, 2 vols. (pp. 1211-1568);
with a table of cases at pp. 1575-1578;

— vol. 166, the judgments reported earlier by
(i) J. Haggard, 3 vols., during the time of Lord Stowell, I, 1822-1825 (pp. 1-144); II, 1825-1832 (pp. 145-307); and III, 1833-1838 (pp. 308-473);
(ii) W. Robinson, 3 vols., commencing with the judgments of Dr. Stephen Lushington, I, 1838-1842 (pp. 474-655); II, 1843-1847 (pp. 656-862); III, 1847-1850 (pp. 863-985);
(iii) Maurice C. Merttins Swabey (London, 1858-1860), covering the period 1855-1859 (pp. 986-1254);
with a table of cases at pp. 1255-1264;

— vol. 167, the cases decided in the High Court of Admiralty of England and on appeal to the Privy Council, 1859-1862, reprinted from the collections by
(i) Vernon Lushington, vol. I (London, 1864), (pp. 1-267);
(ii) Ernst Browning and Vernon Lushington (London, 1868), for the period 1863-1865 (pp. 268-441);
(iii) Th. Salusbury and G. Hay/Burrell/Reginald Marsden, 1758-1774 (London, 1885), with a Preface (pp. 442-605), but missing Burrell's "Opinions upon Admiralty matters (1701-1781)" (comp. *supra*, p. 78), which did not fit into the general scheme of *The English Reports*.

The latter series has meanwhile been re-edited again recently, but only in microfilm form, which does not make its consultation any easier.

A collection that covers the case law of the first period (1776-1779) of the American War of Independence and connected wars on the British side contains a series of sixty-five judgments presented under the title *Decisions of the High Court of Admiralty during the time of Sir George Hay and Sir James*

Marriott, late judges of that Court, some of which were later reproduced in Roscoe's *Reports* of 1905, I, pp. 12-28. This collection was originally published in 1801 and later re-edited by G. Minot (Boston, 1853). This re-edition includes cases selected from vols. II and III of Jerome W. Knapp's *Privy Council Reports* (1831-1836) and vols. I, IV, VI and VII of Edmund F. Moore's *Privy Council Reports* (1836 *et seq.*), on which comp. further *infra*, pp. 82-84. Both collections, of 1801 and 1853, again proved to have been destroyed in the depositories of the library of the British Museum during the Blitz, together with Sir James Marriott's *Mémoire justificatif de la conduite de la Grande Bretagne en arrêtant les navires étrangers et les munitions de guerre destinées aux insurgens de l'Amérique* (1779). The collection has later been inserted in *The English Reports*, vol. 165, pp. 1-71 (see *supra*, p. 81).

Two other publications, intended especially to defend England's action during these wars, were those of Sir James Marriott, the first of 1778, the second (the above-mentioned *Mémoire justificatif*) of 1779. The first was originally written in the days of the Seven Years' War under the title *The case of the Dutch ships considered by Sir James Marriott* (2nd and 3rd editions of 1759, *infra*, p. 471), but was reprinted in 1778 in a 4th edition.

A better arranged publication of decisions was undertaken in 1798 by Sir Christopher Robinson in a six-volume series under the title *Reports of Cases argued and determined in the High Court of Admiralty, commencing with the judgments of Sir William Scott, Michaelmas Term 1798*. This series (1st edition of vol. I in 1799; 2nd ed. in 1801, London) covered the period 1799-1808. It was continued later by a number of other lawyers who extended it up to the middle of the 19th century, *viz.*:

Thomas Edwards, *Reports of Cases argued and determined in the High Court of Admiralty commencing with the judgments of Sir William Scott etc., Easter Term 1808 to 3rd July 1812* (London, 1812);

Sir John Dodson, *Reports of Cases argued and determined in the High Court of Admiralty commencing with the judgments of Sir William Scott, etc. Trinity Term 1811, and continued to March 1822*, vols. I (1811-1815) and II (1815-1822);

John Haggard, *Reports of Cases argued and determined in the High Court of Admiralty commencing with the judgments of Sir William Scott, etc.* (1822-1838);

and William Robinson, *Reports of Cases argued and determined in the High Court of Admiralty, commencing with the judgments of ... Dr. Stephen Lushington (1838-1850)*, 3 vols. (1st ed. 1844 *et seq.*).

The case law reported in this series has been made more easily accessible by J. Greene in his *A digested index of the cases determined in the High Court of Admiralty, contained in the Reports of Robinson, etc.*

A new edition of this series of Chr. Robinson and his successors was undertaken by G. Minot in 1853 (printed in the United States, Boston-

Cambridge), which I found again registered in the general catalogue of the Reading Room in the British Museum as having been destroyed in its depositories in 1939-1940.

Falling more or less outside the series of Chr. Robinson and his successors, but forming an integral part of it, is Thomas Harman Acton's collection of *Reports of cases argued and determined*

(volume I (1)) *before the Most Noble and Right Honourable the Lords Commissioners of Appeals in Prize Cases, also on Appeal to the King's Most Excellent Majesty in Council* (containing the judgments from the period June 1809 to July 1810),

and (volume I (2)) *before the Lords Commissioners of Appeals in Prize Cases* (containing the judgments from the period Michaelmas Term 1810 to Trinity Term 1811, both inclusive (London, 1811)).

As Acton relates in his Advertisement, decisions of the High Court of Appeals had never until then been published. The Lord Commissioners of Appeal of his time were the Earl of Camden (Lord President of the Council), Sir William Grant (Master of the Rolls), Sir William Scott (Judge of the High Court of Admiralty), Sir William Wynne (Sir Leoline Jenkins' biographer), Sir John Nicholl (Judge of the Arches Court) and Sir Christopher Robinson (King's Advocate General).

The appellate judgments of the period June 1809 to July 1810, contained in Acton's first volume, make an uninteresting, indeed tedious impression, which I found confirmed by the author himself in his Advertisement to a second volume reporting the judgments covering the ensuing period of Michaelmas Term 1810 to Trinity Term 1811. In that advertisement the author apologized for the imperfections of his first volume and the slight importance of many of the decisions reported therein, and explained that he had therefore adopted a new, different method of recording them. Yet, Acton's volumes I (1) and II (2) include a variety of cases, quite a number dealing with violations of the blockade of French or French-occupied ports or river mouths (in the West Indies—Martinique, St. Pierre, Trinidad—, Spain—Cádiz—, North West Germany—Elbe, Weser, Ems), or with the transportation of contraband, reserved colonial or coastal trade (*e.g.*, to the Isle de France, between two ports of the French-occupied Netherlands island of Java, or from Batavia to Decima), illicit, in particular slave trade, trade with the enemy under a misused licence, the enemy or neutral character of ships and cargoes, transfers of property in transit, the use of false papers or navigation to a false destination, or other fraud, joint capture or recapture, resistance to visitation, and claims to prize money or freight. A number of these cases will be digested *infra* in Chapter III at their appropriate place.

Acton's work has subsequently been continued by H. Wheaton and Edm.F. Moore: *Privy Council 1854-1859; Reports of Cases heard and determined by the Judicial Committee and the Lords of H.M.'s Privy Council*

1836-1873 (London, 1840 *et seq.*), followed by a new series in 9 vols. (London, 1862-1873).

As Roscoe remarked in his *Reports* of 1905 in footnote *b* appended to the *Pennsylvania* case of 1809 (vol. II, 103), Acton's work also caused him difficulties: although in his own collection he applied a chronological order of reproduction, he had been compelled to make a slight alteration in that order in the case of Acton's *Reports* in order to keep the cases grouped under the titles of the original reports.

There is no separate collection of judgments pronounced on British captures operated during the Anglo-American War of 1812-1814. However, these can be found in J. Dodson's collection of reports, from where they have been reproduced in vol. II of Roscoe's collection of 1905. The American judgments dating from that war are inserted in the collection of William Cranch, covering the period 1801-1815 (see *infra*, p. 114).

The entire period of prize court activity between the last decade of the 18th century and the end of World War I is covered by a publication by John Brown Scott under the title *Prize cases decided in the United States Supreme Court 1789-1918, including also cases on the instance side in which questions of Prize Law were involved* (Oxford, 1923, 3 vols.).

B. The types of issues determined in decisions during England's successive wars

In order to give some impression of the types of cases with which the British prize courts had to deal during the successive wars in which their country became involved, in particular in the period from the middle of the 17th century up to about 1800, and to enliven a little the arid picture of a series of prize law decrees by placing them in the historical context to which they belong, I will for that purpose give below a summary account of the subject matters which successively occupied the English courts and which reflect the slow growth of an English law of prize, arranged in the context of those wars. I intend to continue that summary survey up to the last decade of the 18th century when the torrent of prize court judgments became so overwhelming during the Coalition Wars against Revolutionary France that they practically covered the whole field of prize law.

In the following pages I will apply, as far as is practicable, the same arrangement of the source material as I have applied in my exposé of the Neutrality régime in vol. X of this publication, namely, the formative period from the earliest time up to 1815 (Chapter III of that volume, pp. 46-100) and the consolidation period of 1815-1907 (Chapter IV of that volume, pp. 101-149). This arrangement applies, in particular to the formative period up to 1815. The consolidation period, in its turn, shows a characteristic new development and, consequently, a new temporal demarcation line in the American Civil War of 1861 and its effects on the law of prize.

In accordance with this arrangement I will first deal with the period up to the restoration of Europe after the Napoleonic era, still including the War of the American Independence of 1776 *et seq.* and the connected wars of the 1780's, the wars against Revolutionary France of 1793 *et seq.* and the Anglo-American War of 1812-1814.

The formative period

The earliest wars. I will begin my survey with England's war with Spain at the beginning of the 17th century. This caused King James I to issue his proclamation of 2 March 1604, recorded at fol. 727 of vol. II of W. Wynne's *The life of Sir Leoline Jenkins*, to the effect that in case foreign vessels had been, or should be, captured within his waters after having lawfully entered them, they would be restored to their owners. On 23 September 1609 an order was issued for the release of certain Portuguese ships (Roscoe, I, footnote *a* at p. 452).

Two of the oldest prize cases which I found mentioned relate to the final period of the eighty Years' War between the Netherlands and Spain and date back to 1643. They were discussed during the Anglo-Netherlands negotiations which led up to the conclusion of the Treaty of Alliance of Whitehall of 4/14 September 1662 (Dumont, VI^2, 422; Parry, 7, 193). Article 15 of that Treaty prescribed that a group of reciprocal private claims should be submitted to arbitration if previous attempts to settle them by a conciliation procedure should fail. That article did not specify the cases which the parties had in view, but from what is known from the preceding negotiations this group of claims was to include a number of unresolved prize cases, to the express exclusion, however, of two of them, dating back to 1643, in which two Spanish vessels, the *Bonaventura* and the *Bona Esperanza*, were involved. The others were retraced by E.O. van Boetzelaer in his Leiden dissertation of 1929, partly written in Dutch, partly in French, on *Netherlands international arbitrations between 1581 and 1794*, pp. 88 *et seq.* (comp. Part VIII of this publication, pp. 217 and 319).

On certain details of the prize law history during

— the first Anglo-Netherlands naval war of 1652-1654 see Reginald Marsden's *Narrative* of the proceedings in the cases of the *Simpson*, *St. George* and *St. Salvador*. Although I found this *Narrative* registered in the general index of the Reading Room of the British Museum under the number E 1952 (12), the staff of the library proved unable to produce it for my inspection. But it must have been these cases to which the Peace Treaty of Westminster of 5 April 1654 between the Netherlands and England (Dumont, VI^2, 74; Parry, 3, 225) referred when in Art. 28 it arranged for arbitration to settle a claim by England on account of the detention and seizure by Denmark in May 1652, at the express request of the United

Netherlands, of British ships and goods which were at that time within her territory. The award was made on 31 July 1654 (Dumont, VI², 85; Parry, 3, 303). Comp. Part VIII of this publication, pp. 216-217.
— the second Anglo-Netherlands naval war of 1665-1667, in which, on opposite sides, France, Denmark and Sweden also joined.
— the third Anglo-Netherlands naval war of 1672, ended between these two States in 1674, but continued between some of the other participants, Louis XIV of France, two ecclesiastical German Rulers, the bishops of Münster and Cologne, the Margrave of Brandenburg and the King of Sweden, until the final Peace Treaties of 1678 and 1679. It was during this war, on 11 October 1675, that Sir Leoline Jenkins, then Judge of the Court of the Admiralty, requested the Council of King Charles II to release a vessel from neutral Hamburg that had been captured within the dominions of the French King on her way to an English harbour.

The Peace Treaty of Nijmegen of 2/12 October 1679 between the Netherlands and Sweden (Dumont, VII¹, 432; Parry, 15, 328) in a separate Article 2 contained a settlement concerning seven Netherlands merchant ships which had been captured during the war by privateers, three of them—the *Mouthaan*, the *Buys* and the *Hoop*—by Swedish raiders, the other four—the *St. Jacob*, the *Witte Roos*, the *Maria Boodschap* and the *Nieuwe Heeren Logement*—irregularly by raiders provided with French commissions. See for further details of this settlement Part VIII of this publication, p. 219.
— the Nine Years' War of 1688-1697 (ended by the Peace Treaties of Rijswijk), in which the parties were England, the Netherlands and Spain versus France.

This war is renowned in the history of the law of maritime prize for having produced the first case of the condemnation of a neutral vessel that had carried contraband goods to the captor's enemy together with those contraband goods. That was the case of the *Arms of Plymouth* [1692], whereupon comp. further Chapter III, *sub* A, section 3 (Contraband), § 3 (Sanctions) under A (Extension of the sanctions), *infra*, p. 380. A long series of judgments cited there, dating from between 1691 and 1696, dealt with the same issue.

Another case that occurred during that war was that of the *Constant Mary* [1696-1697], commemorated by Sir William Scott as "a case of great antiquity in the Court". This *Constant Mary* was a prize vessel that was condemned when lying in a neutral port, was purchased there by a neutral person and was later recaptured. She was restored by the Prize Court to her original owner. When on her restoration the neutral buyer demanded from the original owner compensation for the costs which he had meanwhile made for the amelioration of the ship, this demand was refused by the Prize Court. See the quotation of this judgment in the *Kierlighett* [1800] (3 C.Rob., 96; Roscoe, I, at p. 260).

As appears from Pratt-Lee's collection, it was during this war that the issue of the exemption of contraband goods from confiscation when they were the produce of the neutral shipper's own country reached the *forum* of the British prize court, where they began to be privileged on condition that the Crown was entitled to appropriate them by pre-emption.

During this war an Order in Council of 15 August 1689 was issued for the release of certain Danish ships (Roscoe, I, footnote *a* at p. 452).

— the War of the Spanish Succession of 1702-1715 (ended by the Peace Treaties of Utrecht and Baden), in which the parties were England, the United Netherlands, the Empire, Prussia, Savoy and Portugal *versus* France and Spain.

The judgments rendered during this war have been collected and edited by Sir Reginald G. Marsden in his publication entitled *Cases and Opinions upon Admiralty Matters, 1701-1781*, appendixed at pp. 351-392 to another publication by Sir William Burrell, under the heading *Reports of Cases determined by the High Court of Admiralty and upon appeal therefrom, temp. Sir Thomas Salusbury and Sir George Hay, Judges, 1758-1774* (London, 1885) (pp. 78-79 *supra*).

Information regarding the state of affairs in this war can also be found in Pratt-Lee, this time in a separate collection of "Notes for argument in the case of the *Med Guds Hielpe*" (pp. 201-203).

These additional notes are preceded by references to three writers on the subject (van Bynkershoek, *Quaestiones juris publici*, I, ch. 10, pp. 77, 79; Grotius, *De jure belli ac pacis*, l. III, c. I, s. 5, nos. 1 and 2; and J.F. Gronovius, *Notae*, *in voce* "belli rigorem"), and to certain legislative instruments (a Royal Declaration of 22 February 1664, an Order by H.M. Principal Commissioners of Prize of 18 May 1665 and "Rules for condemning prizes" of 22 May 1672). The judgments of 1702 *et seq.*, mentioned in the notes, all related to Swedish ships laden with cargoes of pitch and tar, the native produce of Sweden. They were all restored to their owners, paying expenses, and so also were almost all the cargoes. As to the latter, the Court of first instance restored them subject to the condition of their sale in England. But these instances of 1706 were the last in which the courts imposed the condition of such a compulsory sale, for the judgments concerned were on this point reversed in appeal by the Lords who ordered the ships and goods to be restored absolutely. See the cases of 1706 concerning the *Concordia* and the *Town of Rotterdam*, reported by Pratt-Lee at p. 196.

I have been unable to infer with certainty from the sources whether in this period a ship that was carrying contraband to the enemy was or was not liable to punishment for such action, and on what grounds either the release or the condemnation was decreed. The sources are on these points confusing. One of the ships, the *Christiana Margaretta* [1702], cited by Sir George Lee at pp. 192 and 202 of Pratt's edition as restored to her owners (see also Wynne's *Life of Sir Leoline Jenkins*, fol. 751), was a Danish ship bound from Denmark to the French port of Le Havre de Grâce, laden with various goods, including fourteen barrels of tar. The latter were condemned as contraband, although they were the native produce of Sweden, which seems to testify to the non-recognition of the rule relative thereto at that juncture. The other parts of the lading were likewise restored to the subjects of Denmark, which might justify the conclusion that the contraband did not (yet) "infect" other objects, although the owners-claimants had to pay the captor's expenses.

During this war prizes were sometimes released in virtue of an Order in Council, see the cases of the *Salvador* [31 January 1704], one of a number of Swedish ships, captured while sailing under a Swedish convoy, and of certain Dutch ships seized and brought in for trading with the common enemy [1705] (Roscoe, I, footnote *a* at p. 452).

Insofar as in cases of this kind the Crown *a posteriori* released a prize (either the contraband goods themselves, or the carrying ship or the innocent parts of the cargo) despite their condemnation by the judiciary (subject or not to the Crown's right of pre-emption), this may have had something to do with a difference of opinion between the Crown and the courts about the interpretation of, *e.g.*, the Swedish treaty, or with Sir Leoline Jenkins's protests against the confiscation of the native produce of the exporting country. But I really cannot tell which it may have been.

It was during this War of the Spanish Succession too that a change was made in the allocation of condemned prizes. Ships and goods seized in port were until 1706 condemned to the Lord High Admiral as "droits of Admiralty", even if the seizure had been made by warships—cases of the *St Nicholas du Tot* and the *John* of 1702. However, pursuant to Queen Anne's *Cruizers Act* of 1708, sole property of such prizes would be given to the captors, although they were by an Order in Council stated to be officially condemned to the Queen in her name; the proceedings would remain as usual. Thenceforth the Lord High Admiral had no "droits" of vessels seized in port by the Queen's men-of-war—cases of the *Voorsigtigheit*, taken in the port of Falmouth by a Queen's ship in 1709, and of the *Adventure* [1709], the *Hope* [1710], the *Anne Galley* and the *St Nicholas* [1712]. Only in exceptional circumstances did the Courts still maintain the Lord High Admiral in his old position. Thus the *Nostra Signora del Carmen*, seized in 1708 in the harbour of Gibraltar by its garrison, was on 25 June 1708 condemned to the Lord High Admiral as "perquisite of Admiralty" (Roscoe, I, footnote at p. 119). Comp. on this particular subject of two kinds of "droits" the exposé in Chapter III, *sub* C, section 7, *infra*, pp. 653-658.

As to France, the War of the Spanish Succession caused the issuance of new prize regulations there.

— the Nordic War of 1700-1721 between Sweden, on the one hand, and Denmark, Saxony-Poland and Russia, on the other.

The Prize Ordinance, with executive regulations, which Sweden enacted in 1715 during the Nordic War (*Collectanea Maritima*, pp. 167 *et seq.*, 172 *et seq.*) included provisions concerning resistance to visitation opposed by neutral vessels (ground of confiscation, p. 168), the confiscation of enemy goods on board neutral ships (p. 171, Article 12), the condemnation of vessels any part of which was enemy property (p. 175, Article 22) and the award of prizes to the captor, but nothing about the fate of the transporting vessel or of innocent goods on board.

— the War of the Austrian Succession, ended by the Peace Treaties of Breslau of 1742 and of Aachen (Aix-la-Chapelle) of 1748, in which England (since 1744) and at a very late stage France and (after France's intervention) the United Netherlands also joined (on the curious Anglo-French attitude at the first stage of this war comp. vol. IX of this publication, p. 52).

Despite the continental origin of this war the number of prize cases was considerable. One is analysed by J. Andrew in an "Opinion" of 31 March 1741, which can be found inserted in Reginald Marsden's *Admiralty Cases*, pp. 337 *et seq.* The elements discussed were, *inter alia*, the contraband character of ropes, sails and other ship's material under the treaties then in force; the legal position of British property seized on board a neutral vessel by belligerent Spain; the award of head money (*in lieu* of gun money) in a case of unopposed seizure, and the indebtedness for damages in the case of the release of a captured ship.

Thirty-seven prize cases decided during this war are known from the abovementioned publication of 1856 by Fr.Th. Pratt entitled *Law of Contraband of War*. In that publication, on which comp. further pp. 74 *et seq.*, the writer edited the personal MS. Notes of Sir George Lee (1700-1758), once Chief Justice, concerning those thirty-seven cases, which were decided in the first instance by the then President of the High Court of Admiralty, Sir Henry Penrice. They were referred to much later by Lord Merriman, the President of the Admiralty Court during World War II in the case of the *Hermes and other hulls* (*Ll.P.C.* (2nd), at p. 303).

As appears from this and other sources (such as Reginald Marsden's collection, pp. 377-397, and that of Hay and Marriott), the judgments pronounced during or immediately after the War of the Austrian Succession dealt with the following subjects:

1741: the *Charles Havernerswerth* (cited in the *Sally* of 1795, Roscoe, I, at p. 30), relating to the requirement of proof of the neutral property of goods carried overseas;

1743: the *Pretty Betsy*, discussed in Burrell-Reginald Marsden's *Reports of Cases* (London, 1885), at pp. 388 *et seq.* This was the case of an English plantation-built brigantine, the property of British subjects, which was first seized by a Spanish-registered ship while bound with a cargo from Portuguese Madeira for Virginia, but was recaptured a few weeks later by the English brig *St George*, a merchant ship engaged in trade only, not a privateer or letter of marque ship, whose master was subsequently ordered by a British man-of-war to sail back to Madeira. There the brigantine was sold by public auction and bought by the master of the *St George* without having been first condemned by a prize court. When the brigantine later entered the port of Liverpool, she was claimed there on behalf of the original owner. The experts, consulted on the issues of ownership and salvage, were of the opinion that the property of the ship and cargo was not altered by the events and that salvage was due to the *St George* who retook the *Pretty Betsy*, although she did not have a letter of marque, in the same manner and proportion as if she had been retaken by a privateer, *i.e.*, one-third should she have been in possession of the enemy above forty-eight hours and under ninety-six, if above ninety-six hours a moiety;

1745: the *Med Guds Hielpe* (Pratt-Lee, 191; Roscoe, I, 1), confiscatability of a neutral vessel that carried pitch and tar, considered as contraband (*infra*, p. 311);

— the *Nostra Signora de Cabadonga* (Roscoe, I, footnote *a* at p. 568) concerning the right to share in the distribution of prize money;

1747: the *Young Andreas* and the *Jonge Tobias* (Pratt-Lee, 99, respectively 187; Roscoe, I, 3), contraband character of tallow and butter, respectively salt;

— the *Santa Bo(n)a Ventura* (Roscoe, I, footnote at p. 433), Nantes recognized as a mercantile port;

— the *Ringende Jacob* and the *Deergarden* (Roscoe, I, at p. 108): condemnation because of false destinations;

1748: the *Adolphus Frederick* (Roscoe, I, footnote at p. 453): capture after the cessation of hostilities;

1749: the *Elizabeth* and the *Lady Jane* (Roscoe, I, at p. 108): cases of trading with the enemy.

During this war France issued her new *Règlement* of 21 October 1744 on the "crû ennemi" (see *infra*, 272).

— the Seven Years' War of 1756-1763 (ended, as to its naval section, by the Peace Treaty of Paris), in which the parties were Prussia and England *versus* Austria, France, Russia and Saxony/Poland (on the famous "renversement des alliances" during this war, in which France, contrary to her tradition, took sides with Austria against Prussia, comp. vol. IX of this publication, p. 50).

The prize cases adjudicated upon during this war by British prize courts had first been collected by Sir William Burrell (1732-1796) from the papers of Judges Sir Thomas Salusbury and Sir George Hay in his publication covering the period 1758-1774, a collection re-edited in 1885 by Sir Reginald Marsden, in whose work the prize cases adjudged during the Seven Years' War are reported at pp. 154-229 (comp. on the character and contents of this work the details given above under *A*, pp. 77 *et seq.*).

Detailed data concerning the operation of the law of maritime prize during this war have been gathered further, especially as regards the application of the doctrine of continuous voyage and the new English action against the involvement of neutrals in wartime trade with the colonies of a belligerent, usually closed to them in peace-time, by H.W. Briggs in his study of 1925 on *The doctrine of continuous voyage* in series XLIV, No. 2, of Johns Hopkins University Studies in Historical and Political Science (Baltimore, 1926).

But the most elaborate analysis of British prize law practice during that war we owe recently to Henry J. Bourguignon, Associate Professor, University of Toledo College of Law, in the introductory retrospective historical sections I-III of Part One (Historical development) of his thorough study on *The First Federal Court. The Federal Appellate Prize Court of the American Revolution 1775-1787* (Philadelphia, 1977), a remarkable work of 362 pages. In that study the author included under the heading " Roots in the past " the results of his meticulous research into the law and practice of maritime prize in the British Empire during the Seven Years' War, collected from all possible sources available in manuscript or in printed form. Occasionally he cites still older precedents from the War of the Austrian Succession (1744-1750), *inter alia*, the *Grande Juste* and the *Amsterdam Post* of the Massachusetts Vice-Admiralty Court (p. 158, footnotes 46 and 49), and a case from Rhode Island that dragged on from the latter war into the Seven Years' War from 1745 to 1763, the *William Galley* (footnote 103 at pp. 176-177). The sources tracked down and analysed by the author are manifold: manuscripts—public (court and government) records and twenty-six collections of personal papers and published sources—public (court and government) records, legal and political treatises, collected personal papers and writings, and newspapers. They come from a wide range of depositories: from the Public Record Office in London to the British Museum, from the Library of Congress to the Rare Book Room of New York Public Library, from the Public Records, Statute Books or Archives of one British colony to those of another, and from one Vice-Admiralty Court Minute Book to another. Bourguignon's work contains precise statistical data on the cases adjudicated during the period 1758-1766 (p. 163, footnote), on the frequency with which the several colonial prize courts were called upon to decide, and on the composition and actual presence at the hearings of the Lords Commissioners of Appeal. The 253 prize court judgments of the first instance emanated from the High Court of Admiralty in London, the Irish Vice-Admiralty Court and the Vice-Admiralty Courts of Jamaica (88) and of 8 of the 13 North-American colonies. The appeals lay either to the Lords Commissioners of Appeal, amongst whom only six took an active part in the hearings and only one, the Earl of Mansfield, had legal experience (p. 162), or to the so-called Surrogate's Court, staffed by one of the members of Doctors' Commons (p. 166). The author pays special attention to the procedural practice of the period. In his footnotes he quotes the names of some 70 ships involved in the prize proceedings. In order to get a comprehensive view of the British case law during the Seven Years' War I compared the list of cases reported in the collections of Burrell-Marsden (pp. 154-229) and Roscoe (I, 3-11) with a list compiled from Bourguignon's footnotes (pp. 139-178). If I have made no mistakes in my arithmetical and comparative operation, the two lists do not correspond completely: on the one hand, Bourguignon cites a small number of judgments which I could not retrace in the other list, whereas, on the other, Burrell-Marsden reports a (larger) number not mentioned in these footnotes. Bourguignon also cites many works or monographs on the subject and enlightens us on the sources which the American admiralty court judges of the first hour could consult in their days.

In the following survey I will summarily illustrate the variety of issues which arose during the Seven Years' War. Where no other source is mentioned, the references are to pages in Burrell-Marsden's collection.

The Seven Years' War was preceded by irregular peace-time captures in 1755: the cases of the *Lis* and the *Alcide* (comp. vol. IX of this publication, p. 61) and produced a notorious case of a capture by forcible action in neutral (Spanish) waters: the Dutch vessel *De Fortuyn* [1760] was condemned, despite the place of capture, by the lower court, but restored by the Lords of Appeal (Burrell, 175; Roscoe, I, 7).

It gave, moreover, rise to the emergence of the new rule threatening the sanction of condemnation in prize against the involvement of neutral vessels in (especially colonial) trade which was reserved in peace-time to the enemy's own subjects (see *infra*, pp. 471-477).

Already in the middle of the 18th century the prize court sometimes based its decision on old treaty provisions, such as those of the Anglo-Iberian treaties of 1654 in the case of the Portuguese vessel *San Antonio y Almas* (Burrell-Marsden, 176) and of 1667 in the cases of the Spanish vessels *San Vincent* and *San Sebastián* (155, 156). These treaties were invoked with regard to their provisions concerning the validity and effects of passes mutually delivered to each other's merchant ships.

The impact of the preliminary Peace Treaty between England, France and Spain of 1762 on the legal status of a prize was considered in the case of the Dutch vessel *King William the Third* (183).

The qualification of specific cargoes as contraband was at issue in the cases of a number of neutral (Spanish, Dutch or Danish) vessels: the *Vriendschap* (timber, 155), the *San Vincent* (wine, 155), the *St. Jacob* (oil and lemons, 160), the *Nostra Signora del Carmen* (China tea, 164), the *San Juan Baptista* (tea, coffee, longwood, 164), the *Jesús* (or *Jesús, Maria y Joseph*) (saltpetre, 164), the *Juffrouw Titia* (planks, 176), the *Young Weybe* (salt, 177), the *Dolphin* (wine, brandy, 181). In some of these cases and in others the hostile destination of the goods was doubtful: the *Vriendschap* (a Dutch ship, captured on her return voyage, 155), the *Young Peter* (real destination Dutch Surinam or French Guyenne?, 184), the *Dolphin* (destination of a Danish vessel, Lübeck or a French port, 181). In some of these or in some others the question was whether the ship or the innocent part of her cargo was liable to condemnation together with her contraband cargo: *Il*

Santo Crucifixo (160), *Jesús* (164), *San Juan Baptista* (164), *Dolphin* (181) and *Ravens* (182).

I have found no instance during this war of an exemption from confiscation of contraband goods, the produce of the neutral shipper's native soil.

In a number of cases ships or their cargoes were exempted from condemnation on the ground that they were sailing under the protection of a pass or licence: the *Vigilante*, an enemy (French) vessel, sailing with a British pass (183), or they claimed such protection by a flag of truce or cartel: the *Beaver* (165) and certain others (166, 167).

The controversy often had a bearing on the enemy or non-enemy character of a prize: the *Yong Vrow* (read: Jonge Vrouw) *Adriana* (178; Roscoe, I, 8), the *Ravens* (182), the *San Antonio de Padua* alias the *Dragon* (189).

Co-ownership was one of the elements of the case of the *Il Santo Crucifixo* (160), in which the judgment also bore on the alleged privileged position of a consul of Genoa. The hypothecation of a ship played a certain rôle in the *Grand Duke of Tuscany* (188).

A case of the capture of neutral property on board enemy vessels, which was sold during the war to a Spaniard, was that of the *Félicité* and the *Nuestra Señora del Rosario y San Antonio* (175).

Grounds of condemnation other than enemy ownership and the carriage of contraband were

the violation of a blockade: the *Vier Gebroeders* [1759-1760] (159; Roscoe, I, 5), relating to the (uncertain) blockade of Dunkirk (ship released, but cargo condemned);

engagement of neutral vessels in a reserved colonial trade with the enemy, the famous new ground of lawful capture developed during the Seven Years' War. See the cases of the Dutch ships, sailing to French West-Indian colonies under a French licence (to be examined in Chapter III, *sub* A, section 6, *infra*, pp. 471-473), discussed in a publication of 1756 entitled *The case of the Dutch ships considered by Sir James Marriott* (2nd and 3rd editions of 1759); and the *Fortuyn* (175), a Dutch vessel sailing under a French licence to trade with French-occupied Spanish Monte Christi on Hispaniola. Other destinations were the French possessions Guadeloupe (137) and in East India (164, 165).

Application of this "rule of the war of 1756" was, however, refused by the Lords in the case of the Danish vessel *Good Christian* [1760] (216, 217; Roscoe, I, 11): release on appeal, with her cargo, of a ship seized when sailing from Danish Ste Croix to Cape François in the French colonial territory of Santo Domingo with a Dutch pass for trade amongst all the West Indian islands. In a footnote at p. 11 of vol. I of his *Reports of Prize Cases*, Roscoe says that this case illustrates an attempt to extend the rule of the war of 1756.

Capture was held to be justified by fraudulent behaviour of the shipper or master. A vessel sailing under the Tuscan flag, the *Grand Duke of Tuscany*

(188), was condemned by the Vice-Admiralty Court of Gibraltar on the ground of her sailing with false and colourable papers, but this judgment of confiscation was reversed on appeal.

The records of the decisions made during the Seven Years' War frequently relate to joint captures, operated under the most varying circumstances:

Augusta et al., *Marlborough*, *Princess Mary* (167), *Touraine* (169), *Le Hazard* (170), *Arc-en-Ciel* (171), *Nostra Señora de la Concepción*, *San Francisco de Assisi* (172), *Industrie* (173), *San Juan*, *San Antonio de Padua* (174).

Cases concerning claims to the award of prize money were: the *La Pacifique* [1761-1764] (158; Roscoe, I, 3) (Admiral's claim of one-eighth); the *Helena* (190) (forfeiture of the prize in the first instance to the captor (a privateer), the Admiral and the King, each for one-third; in appeal entirely to the captor); the *Catharine* (196), a case of "collusive capture" (award in the first instance of one-half to the capturing privateer, the other half to His Majesty; on appeal to the captors only).

One of the more complicated cases decided in this period was that of the *Charming Elizabeth* [1757-1760] (197), a British-owned ship that was captured by a French privateer on her way from London to Jamaica and condemned as prize at Port-au-Prince (Cuba). Some time later she was bought there by the master of an English cartel-ship and sent to Jamaica. On her arrival there she was seized by the English man-of-war *Marlborough* and proceeded against as prize. Both the former owners and the purchaser claimed the ship as their property, but the Vice-Admiralty judge in Jamaica dismissed both claims and condemned the ship as lawful prize on 24 October 1757. This condemnation was, however, reversed on appeal in 1760: the original British owners got their ship back, subject to payment to the recaptor of one-eighth of her value due for salvage and his usual expenses. A similar case was that of the *Florence* [1760] (198).

Another such dispute was that reported by another collector, Roscoe, in a note in vol. I of his work at pp. 347-348, concerning a British ship captured by the French in 1761 and carried by them to neutral Christiansand; she was condemned in the courts of France and sold to a Danish merchant, who sent her in the course of her trade to a port in Scotland. There the original proprietors arrested the vessel by precept from the Court of Admiralty on the ground of the invalidity of such a sentence to change the property. The Judge of Admiralty sustained the objections and decreed the vessel to belong to the original owners. An appeal was prosecuted to the Court of Sessions: *Benton v. Brink* (6 C.Rob., at 138; Roscoe, I, at 347), which directed an inquiry to be made into the practice of the High Court of Admiralty of England on this subject. Comp. on this complicated case further Chapter III, General Issues, section 3, under B, § 3, *infra*, p. 194.

The effect of a territorial capitulation was at issue in two cases of delivery of Spanish goods to the British forces after the surrender to them of Havana: the *Constanza* (161), respectively Manila: the *Santísima Trinidad, alias el*

Poderoso (162). Other cases concerned trading with the enemy (104, 127), the transfer of an enemy ship to a neutral flag (127) and fraudulent behaviour (126, 127 note).

See for the rest of the case law produced by English Admiralty Courts during the War of 1756-1763 the relevant subsections in Chapter III, *sub* A, sections 3 (Contraband), 4 (Blockade), 5 (Unneutral service) and 6 (Reserved colonial and coasting trade), *infra*.

Data on the events during the Seven Years' War can be found, *inter alia*, in R. Pares, *Colonial blockade and neutral rights 1739-1763* (Oxford, 1938), and in Alice Clare Carter, *The Dutch as neutrals in the Seven Years' War* (London and Basingstoke, 1971). The Treaty of Marine of 1674 between the Netherlands and England, which has dominated their relations for such a long period of time, was still invoked during the Seven Years' War also on the British side and remained in force until their fourth naval war of 1780.

— the American War of Independence and connected wars of 1775-1784.

This group of wars originated in the revolt of Great Britain's North-American colonies against the mother-country in 1775. The colonies were ideologically, diplomatically and in fact supported by France. France thus became implicated in a war with Great Britain, which at a later stage also got involved in tension with Spain and, in 1780, in hostilities against the United Netherlands (the fourth and last of the Anglo-Dutch naval wars).

From the systematic point of view I must differentiate here between these various wars and the various bodies of case law during the period 1775-1784.

The prize court decrees to be surveyed in the present subsection can only be those pronounced by British judges; all others belong elsewhere, those rendered by the courts of the North-American colonies-in-rebellion *infra*, pp. 111 *et seq.*, in the sub-division concerning the case law of the United States tribunals, those made by the French tribunals *supra*, pp. 62 *et seq.*, those emanating from Spanish and Netherlands tribunals, in so far as there is any possibility of retracing their texts, *infra*, pp. 106-111. The political constellation in the period concerned entailed indeed, as the central conflagration, England's efforts to quell the rebellion of her colonies (1775/6-1783), which proved abortive, and as contributory elements the hostilities between England, on the one hand, and the three States which supported the rebellious colonies—or otherwise became involved in the colonial wars—on the other.

The prolonged struggle between England and her colonies, the central conflagration, was terminated by preliminary articles of peace signed at Paris on 30 November 1782 (Martens, R², III, 497; Parry, 48, 223) in virtue of an Act of Parliament of January 1782 which authorized the King to conclude a peace or armistice treaty with the American colonies (Martens, R², III, 495), followed by their final peace treaty of Paris of 3 September 1783 (Martens,

R^2, III, 553; Parry, 48, 487), which included a vague determination of the future State boundary between the independent United States and the remaining British colony of Canada (Art. II), and later gave rise to a series of arbitral proceedings under the Anglo-American Jay Treaty of 19 November 1794 (Martens, R^2, V, 642; Parry, 52, 243).

The conclusion of peace between England and each of her three European adversaries took place in two successive stages, first by a preliminary convention and after that by a definitive treaty.

As to France, see their preliminary articles of peace signed at Versailles already prior to the final termination of the Anglo-American War, namely on 20 January 1783 (Martens, R^2, III, 503; Parry, 48, 231), followed by their final peace treaty concluded at the comprehensive Peace Conference of Versailles on 3 September 1783 (*ibid.*, III, 519; Parry, 48, 437) accompanied by certain diplomatic instruments, *inter alia*, on the mediation by the Emperor and the Tsaritsa (ibid., III, 533, 536-540) and a reservation regarding the use of French as the treaty language (*ibid.*, III, 528).

As to Spain, see their preliminary articles of peace signed at Versailles on 20 January 1783 (*ibid.*, III, 510), followed by their final peace treaty of Versailles of 3 September 1783 (*ibid.*, III, 541; Parry, 48, 481), attended with yet another (mutual) reservation by the two Sovereigns concerning their use of obsolete royal titles (*ibid.*, III, 549, 550).

As to the Republic of the United Netherlands, see their preliminary articles of peace of 2 September 1783 (*ibid.*, III, 514), followed by their final peace treaty of Paris of 20 May 1784 (*ibid.*, III, 560; Parry, 49, 65).

The scientific operation of splitting-up my systematic exposé of the legal development during the formative period since the War of the American Independence, which was thus forced upon me by the course of political history towards the last quarter of the 18th century (*supra*, p. 84), has of course exerted its inescapable impact also on my handling of the two remaining groups of hostilities between 1793 and 1815, *viz.*, the Revolutionary Wars of France and the Anglo-American War of 1812. In order nevertheless to round-off and complete my sketch of the formative period, I make bold to continue my exposé as if nothing fundamental had happened and to describe the last two decades of the 18th century in the same manner as I have done up to now.

As far as England was concerned, the prize court decrees emanated, in the first instance, from British Vice-Admiralty Courts overseas or the Court of Admiralty in London and, in appeal, from the Lords Commissioners of Appeal in London.

The events and judgments of this period show the following picture.

The Anglo-French and Anglo-Dutch hostilities were, just as in the Seven Years' War, preceded by peace-time (1778) captures of prospective enemy

(French) ships, the *Belle Poule*, the *Pallas*, the *Licorne* and the *Coureur*. I have reported on these captures in Part IX of this publication, at p. 61.

The prize cases decided during these wars, as reported by Hay and Marriott in their collection, on the whole make a monotonous impression, although they deal with a multiplicity of subjects, beginning with a very elaborate judgment (pp. 1 *et seq.*) concerning the question of whether the *Dickenson*, a ship of the American rebels of Philadelphia, captured in 1776, was to be condemned to the Lord High Admiral or to the Queen. See also the case of *Le Grand Terrain*, and comp. further on this controversy *supra*, p. 88 (War of the Spanish Succession) and *infra*, (Chapter III, *sub* C, section 7), pp. 652-658.

Many of the judgments reported in Hay and Marriott's collection concern the capture of ships and goods, whether American or others, going to or coming from the rebellious colonies, which were decreed by "an Act of the Legislature for Stopping all Trade and Intercourse with British American Colonies in Rebellion" to be subject to forfeiture after a limited period of time: the *William and Grace* [1777] (p. 76).

An exemption from forfeiture was granted on different occasions to property of residents of the colonies, either because, in one case, the owner, ex-Governor of South Carolina, had been deprived of authority by the American Congress: the *Commerce* [1777] (p. 80), or because, in other cases, the owner had been forced to emigrate after his refusal to abjure King George III and the British Parliament, as "the pretended new Governor of the province" demanded: the *Sally* [1777] (p. 83) and the *Rebecca* [1778] (p. 197).

Several judgments dealt with the proof of ownership, American or British (respectively neutral): the *Louisa* [1778] (p. 143); the *Vro(u)w Antoinette* [1778] (p. 142); the *Jeanne Isabelle* [1778] (p. 185). Other instances of the necessity to determine the enemy or non-enemy character of prizes concerned either property belonging to subjects or residents of the rebellious colonies, or property claimed by subjects of third Powers: the Swedish *Maria Magdalena* [1779] (p. 247; Roscoe, I, 20): English or French ownership?

The validity of the transfer of an enemy ship to a neutral flag was discussed in the *Hendric and Alida* [1777] (p. 96), a case relating to an originally British ship, captured off Antigua by American privateers, carried by them to Dutch St Eustatius and sold there to a Dutchman.

In a number of cases it was a matter of controversy whether a seizure made prior to the declaration of war should be held valid. The answer was in the affirmative "because a commission of general reprisals is stronger than even a declaration of war" and could be effected without the observance of the six months' term of exemption stipulated by treaty: the *Père Adam* [1778] (p. 141).

Many decisions admitted the lawfulness of the pre-emption of cargoes (in particular masts and other ship's materials) for His Majesty's use at a fair evaluation, or themselves ordered their sale: the *Vro(u)w Antoinette* [1778] (p. 142); the *Vrijheid* [1778] (p. 188).

The freedom for neutrals to carry free the goods of an enemy was at issue in *Les Quatre Frères* [1778] (p. 170) and the *Veranderen* (or *Le Changement*) [1778] (p. 180). In the first case the claimant, a Danish shipowner, invoked a most-favoured-nation clause obtaining in the treaty of Copenhagen of 11 July 1670 which established such freedom; in the latter case the Court held that the ship, a Prussian vessel, could lay no claim, either by treaty or by the custom of nations, to the privilege to carry free the goods of enemies.

Interesting judgments were concerned with the fate of vessels, recaptured from the enemy: the *Renard* [1778] (p. 222), and with the amount of salvage due for such recapture: the *Betsey* (p. 80); the *John* (p. 152), and the *Lucretia* (p. 227), analysed in more detail in Chapter III, *sub* B, section 7, *infra*, p. 552.

Questions of the captor's indebtedness of freight to the neutral carrier arose in the case of the Swedish *Anna Christiana* [1778] (p. 161):

> "The Court will allow all neutral carriers the full freightage, even as to the farther port of destination. That is their right, and a charge hypothecated on the goods of enemies, of which they should have the full benefit, provided masters of neutral ships are guilty of no falsity or prevarications in their evidence or conduct."

Sometimes the captors did not have letters of marque: the *La Mignonne* [1778] (p. 51).

The Netherlands vessel *Zelden Rust* [1778] (p. 51) was restored to her owners on the ground of the special circumstances under which she had been captured by an English privateer: she had indeed been forced by a Spanish man-of-war during a voyage to take on board a quantity of gold and silver and a Spanish supercargo for the purpose of their transportation to the enemy port of Le Havre.

Other issues which came up for adjudication in this period related to the following subjects:

— the beginning of a *de facto* war by an Order of Reprisals, of 29 July 1778 against France, respectively of December 1780 against Holland: the *Maria Magdalena* [1779] (Hay and Marriott, 247; Roscoe, I, 20); the *Snelle Zeylder* (Roscoe, I, footnote *b* at p. 254). This ship was captured when sailing from London to Nantes. Should the cargo have reached that place, then it would have become the property of French citizens, but having been seized at sea it had remained the property of the British consignors. There was no British declaration of war yet against France, but only a declaration of general reprisals. This was, however, held by the Court to be equivalent, as to its legal effects, to a declaration of war. The cargo was condemned in accordance with the British Declaration of Reprisals of 29 July 1778.

— the enemy or neutral character of cargoes: the *Postilion* [1779] (Hay and Marriott, 245; Roscoe, I, 20), concerning the cargo, property of a French-

man domiciled in Hamburg, seized on a Lübeck ship; the *Concordia Affinitatis* [1779] (Hay and Marriott, 289; Roscoe, I, 25): affidavits in proof of neutral property in a cargo must be unequivocal as to when it was first laden, when taken and finally landed; the *Juffrouw Louisa Margaretha* [1781] (Roscoe, I, at p. 108), wines shipped in a Dutch vessel by a house of trade in London with an established house of trade in Spanish Málaga; the *St. Louis/El Alessandro* (Roscoe, I, 109);
— the character of masts as contraband under the Anglo-Dutch treaty of 1 December 1674, their enemy destination and their pre-emption for the use of His Britannic Majesty: the *Vrijheid (No. 1)* [1778](Hay and Marriott, 188; Roscoe, I, 13);
— relaxation of the law of contraband in favour of the produce or the manufacture of the neutral shipper's own country: the *Jonge Pieter* [1781-1783] (Roscoe, I, at p. 369): hemp, being Prussian property but of uncertain produce, sent to France on a Dutch ship; the *Goede Vreede* [1780], the *Sanctissimo Sacramento* [1781] and the *Juffrouw Wobetha* [1781-1782] (the latter three cited in Roscoe, I, at p. 369); comp. on this subject Chapter III, *sub* A, section 3 (Contraband), § 3 (Sanctions), *sub* B (Relaxations), *infra*, pp. 401-413;
— trading with the enemy: the *Comte de Wohronzoff* [1781] (Roscoe, I, at p. 110), wine trade from Bordeaux to Ireland; the *Expeditie van Rotterdam* [1782] (Roscoe, I, at p. 111);
— destruction of a prize by fire on the Thames: the *Creighton* [1782] (Roscoe, I, 390, footnote);
— the impact of the surrender, respectively the military occupation of territory on the exercise of the right of prize: the *Negotie en Zeevaart* [1782] (Roscoe, I, at p. 74), adjudicated after the surrender of Dutch Demerara to the British forces, and the *Bella Giudita* [1785] (Roscoe, I, at p. 112), after the capitulation of the West-Indian island of Grenada to the French;
— joint capture and prize money: *Twee Gesusters* [1780-1785] (Roscoe, I, footnote *a* at p. 230); the *Buen Consejo* [1780] (Roscoe, I, footnote *a* at p. 256) and the *Signior San Joseph* [1784] (Roscoe, I, at p. 182);
— the admissibility of belligerent reprisals against the enemy which in their effects were harmful to neutrals: the Swedish *Concordia Affinitatis* [1779] (supra);
— recapture: the *John* [1778] (Hay and Marriott, 152; Roscoe; I, 12), a British ship captured by the French, detained by them for ninety-six hours, but recaptured by a British privateer; the recaptors were awarded as salvage one-eighth of the ship's value on her restoration to the owners (on this particular aspect of the case comp. *infra*, p. 552); the *Renard* [1778] (Hay and Marriott, 222; Roscoe, I, 17);
— denial of jurisdiction: the *Ooster Eems* [1784] (Roscoe, I, footnote *a* at p. 136), relating to the claim by the warden of the Cinque Ports to the cargo of a Prussian vessel, stranded on the Goodwin Sands.

— the four successive Wars of Coalition against Revolutionary France:

the *first*, of 1793-1797 (ended between the continental belligerents, Austria and France, by their Peace Treaties of Leoben and Campo Formio);

the *second*, of 1799-1802 (terminated between the continental belligerents by their Peace Treaty of Lunéville, 1801, and between Great Britain, France, Spain and the United Netherlands by their Peace Treaty of Amiens, 1802);

> "It was during these two wars that the famous prize court judge Sir William Scott (later: Lord Stowell), began his career as the unchallenged progenitor of British prize law and that sir Christopher Robinson undertook his six-volume publication (1798-1808)."

the *third*, of 1805-1807, in the course of which the European allies Austria, Prussia and Russia were successively forced to make peace with France (Schönbrunn, 1806 and Tilsit, 1807);

the *fourth*, of 1813-1815, the period of Napoleon's ultimate downfall, described in vol. IX of this publication, pp. 471 *et seq.*, by an enumeration of the treaties which sealed his fate.

Many prize court decrees which accompanied this prolonged European struggle can be found in the abovementioned six-volume publication. See for instance the judgments, reproduced by Roscoe (II, 200 *et seq.*) from Dodson's collection, concerning the *La Clorinde*, *Genoa and Savona* cases, the *La Henriette*, the *La Mélanie*, the *Ville de Varsovie* and the *La Bellone*.

It was during this long sequence of wars, which was—as far as the relation of England with France and her reluctant allies was concerned—only interrupted for a short period after the Peace of Amiens, 1802, that the massive bulk of authoritative British precedents in the field of maritime prize was produced.

As Roscoe rightly remarked, when in 1798 Sir William Scott was appointed judge of the High Court of Admiralty, there were still only very few definite rules of British prize law to guide either Bench or Bar. There was no code of British prize law, there were but few judicial decisions recorded and those few were often imperfectly drafted.

In his judgment of 19 November 1798 concerning the *Staadt Embden* (1 C.Rob., 26; Roscoe, I, 37), for instance, Sir William Scott mentioned that he only possessed a manuscript note of Sir George Lee (1700-1758), recording the confirmation "by a solemn judgment of the Lords" (of 29 June 1750) of a decision by Sir Henry Penrice (*per Curiam*) on 9 August 1745 relative to the Swedish vessel *Med Guds Hielpe* (Pratt-Lee, 191; Roscoe, I, 1).

Sir William Scott has in fact created much of British prize law. Not all publicists, however, were equally impressed by this British—nor, for that matter, the French—prize jurisprudence of the period; witness a German publication of 1802 entitled *Merkwürdige Entscheidungen der Londoner und Pariser Schiedsgerichte*. Recently (1987) Henry J. Bourguignon has dedicated a study to *Sir William Scott, Lord Stowell. Judge of the High Court of Admiralty, (1798-1828)* (Cambridge University Press); Bourguignon gives us a biographical sketch of Sir William's life, an analysis of the prize law of the period and Sir William's "judicial philosophy" and "influence".

— the Anglo-American War of 1812-1814.

There exists no separate collection of the texts of judgments pronounced on the legality or otherwise of captures made during this war. They were, on the English side, inserted in the collection of Dodson, later republished in vol. II of Roscoe's *Reports* (see, for example, the cases of the *Georgiana* (p. 193), the *Fanny* (p. 202), the *Actaeon* (p. 209), the *London* (p. 213), the *John (No. 2)* (p. 232) and the *Felicity* (p. 233)), and on the American side in the collection of Cranch (see *infra*, p. 114).

Besides decisions concerning captures made during the Anglo-American War, the same period has also continued to produce judgments relating to captures made during the contemporaneous fourth Coalition War against France.

— the Crimean War.

This war (1853-1856) gave rise to the publication of an new collection of cases by Thomas Spinks: *Reports of cases decided during the present* [Crimean] *War in the Admiralty Prize Court and the Court of Appeal* (London, 1854-1856), followed in its turn by collections of reports by Maurice C.M. Swabey and Vernon Lushington (1855 *et seq.*).

Apart from the reprint of earlier prize court decisions in vols. 12-14 and 165-167 of *The English Reports* in 1923-1924 (*supra*) which carried the systematic reporting of older British prize case law into the first decade of the second half of the 19th century, an early 20th century publication, undertaken by E.S. Roscoe, offered a broad retrospective review of over a century of legal development from the middle of the 18th century to the middle of the 19th century, under the title *Reports of Prize Cases determined in the High Court of Admiralty, before the Lords Commissioners of Appeals in prize cases, and before the Judicial Committee of the Privy Council from 1745-1859*, in two vols. (London, 1905). This publication was intended to include old judgments which had still retained their legal importance at the time of the publication. The oldest case briefly reported in this collection was that of the Swedish vessel *Med Guds Hielpe* of 1745, confirmed in appeal in 1750—a case of condemnation of a ship for the carriage of a contraband load of pitch and tar. This judgment, for the first time reported *in extenso* in Pratt-Lee's collection of 1856 (at p. 191) and praised by Sir William Scott as "famous" (in the *Staadt Embden* [1798] (1 C.Rob. 26; Roscoe, I, 37) and as "memorable" (in the *Maria (No. 1)* [1799] (1 C.Rob. 340; Roscoe, I, 152)), had already been preceded by two judgments pronounced in the first years of the War of the Spanish Succession concerning the Danish *Christiana Margaretta*

[1702] (Pratt-Lee, pp. 146, 192, 202) and the *Concordia* [1706] (Pratt-Lee, p. 196), in both of which, however, the ship was restored, and it was followed by two other cases which arose during the War of the Austrian Succession in 1747: the Prussian vessel *Young Andreas* (Pratt-Lee, pp. 99) and the Swedish vessel *Jonge Tobias* (*ibid.*, p. 187), in both of which cases the ship was also restored.

Retrospect

Looking back at my lengthy account of the gradual emergence of a comprehensive body of detailed rules on the most divergent subjects of maritime prize from the judgments of the British Admiralty Courts, I will conclude this section with a brief commentary on the functioning and practical effect as a subsidiary source of prize law of a principle that is peculiar to the English legal system in general. One of the peculiarities of that system was indeed and still is that the courts considered themselves bound, also in this domain, though not too strictly by judicial precedents. Whereas there were only scarce legislative enactments in the field of substantive prize law available to guide them in their judgments, this lacuna was amply filled by rulings given in the past according to what was indicated as the doctrine of *stare decisis*.

It is hardly necessary to state that this doctrine applied only to the relation between earlier and later English judgments and had nothing to do with earlier decisions of foreign courts, which, moreover, were only quoted in exceptional cases. One of the rare occasions on which an English prize court invoked foreign decisions and authorities was in the appeal decision in the *Ostsee* [1855] (Spinks, 174; 9 Moore P.C., 150; Roscoe, II, 432), where the issue was whether a captor was liable to damages even if he had acted under an honest mistake. Reference was made there by the Judicial Committee of the Privy Council, *inter alia*, to the opinion of the Commissary of the French Government at the *Conseil des prises* M. Portalis in the case of the *Pégou* [1799] (Roscoe, II, at pp. 437-438).

Stare decisis

Cases in which preceding judgments were invoked and recognized as binding precedents and consequently served as direct and genuine sources of British prize law were legion. I will cite below a few examples and add some remarks about the operation of the principle in this field.

One of its simplest formulations was that given by Sir William Scott in the *Apollo (No. 1)* case [1802] (4 C.Rob., 158; Roscoe, I, 368), which concerned the exemption from condemnation in prize of contraband goods being the produce of the neutral shipper's native soil. In that instance the President, referring to the earlier case of the *Jonge Pieter* of 1781-1783 decided in both instances in favour of the owner, stating the legal position as follows:

> "It is, therefore, a direct precedent binding on this Court, and in conformity to that authority I shall direct this cargo to be restored".

The principle was formulated more elaborately by the same judge in the case of the *Lisette* [1806] (6 C.Rob., 387; Roscoe, I, 587), in which he referred to his earlier judgment in the *Charlotte Sophia* case of the same year (Roscoe, I, 547, footnote *b*), dealing with a transport of goods organized under a charter-party formed at Hamburg to take on board a cargo for Málaga, which was to be sent from the blockaded river Elbe in lighters (comp. on this operation Chapter III, *sub* A, section 4 (Blockade), *infra*, p. 441). In that *Lisette* judgment Lord Stowell said:

> "In the former case of the *Charlotte Sophia*, both the ship and the cargo were condemned; and this ship (the *Lisette*) had been engaged in precisely the same course of trade. There is no doubt, then, that this vessel must have been condemned upon the authority of that (*Charlotte Sophia*) case, unless one other material distinction of fact had existed, leading to a rule of law to which the Court is strongly disposed to adhere. It is this, that this vessel (the *Lisette*) was not captured till the blockade had ceased. It is said that the offence was consummated by the act of sailing; so it is in a certain sense [comp. on this asserted 'droit de prévention' Chapter III, *sub* A, section 4, *infra*, pp. 432-434]. But the ship was not taken *in delicto*, and I have not had any case pointed out to me in which the Court has pronounced an unfavourable judgment on a ship seized for the breach of a by-gone blockade. I know of no such case, and certainly the same reason for rigour does not exist, because the blockade being gone, the necessity of applying the penalty to prevent future transgression cannot continue. That was the ground on which my opinion was formed in restoring the ship ...".

From a judgment of Sir Henry Penrice in the case of the *T'Slots Copenhagen* [1745-1746], reported by Sir George Lee in his MS. Notes, it is apparent that the binding force of a precedent was denied when it was still *sub judice* in appeal: case of the *Vierge Marie* (Pratt-Lee, p. 48).

There is, moreover, a trend in British case law to consider the doctrine of *stare decisis* in the field of prize law as less stringent than in other fields and to apply it *cum grano salis*. There was also an easy way of escape available from the oppressive fetters of sometimes obsolete precedents in the practice of "distinguishing" between the new case and the old. The acceptance of the presence of such a distinguishing element was often arbitrary, depending upon the degree of the Court's dissatisfaction with the earlier decision and the resulting desirability of changing the traditional trend of the judgments, frequently few and far between, or hardly known to the adjudicating Court. But there were, of course, also cases in which it was seriously debatable whether an earlier judgment showed exactly the same elements as the later one. One of the cases in which the Court found itself faced with this doubt was that of the *Danckebaar Africaan* [1798] (1 C.Rob., 107; Roscoe, I, 74) in its relation to that of the *Negotie en Zeevaart* [1782]. It was in the 1798 case that Sir William Scott analysed the proceedings in the former case in order to form an opinion on his freedom to decide differently from the older precedent. He argued as follows:

"I am of opinion that this is a decided case on the authority of the Supreme Court in the *Negotie en Zeevaart* [Lords, 18 July 1782]. I remember that case well, having been junior counsel in it, and having attended much to it, as there was much difference of opinion respecting it in the Court below.

It was the case of a ship sailing from Demerara to Middlebourg in Holland, on the 30th of January, 1781, about six weeks after the declaration of hostilities against Holland. Demerara surrendered to the British forces on the 14th of March, and the capture was made on the 25th.

The terms of capitulation were very favourable: "The inhabitants were to take the oath of allegiance; to be permitted to export their own property, and to be treated in all respects like British subjects, till his Majesty's pleasure could be known;" and although this was in the first instance only under the proclamation of the captor, still, that being accepted, it took complete effect. These terms were afterwards confirmed by the King. There was, therefore, in that case as strong a promise of protection as could be, and recognised and confirmed by the supreme authority of the State. Under these circumstances, the Judge of the Admiralty thought the claim so strong that he actually restored: and it was not his opinion alone.

On appeal, however, the Lords were of opinion that property sailing after declaration of hostilities, but before a capitulation, and taken on the voyage, was not protected by the intermediate capitulation. It was not determined on any ground of illegal trade, nor on any surmise, that when the owners became British subjects the trade in which the property was embarked became, *ex post facto*, illegal; nor was it at all taken into consideration that Demerara had again become a Dutch colony at the time of adjudication. It was declared to be adjudged on the same principles as if the cause had come on at the time of capture. It was not on any of these grounds, but simply on the ground of Dutch property, that condemnation passed in that case. I remember a *dictum* of a great Law Lord then present, Lord Camden, "that the ship, as Dutch, could not change her character *in transitu.*"

This decision of the Supreme Court must be binding on me, unless there are in the present case any distinctions that take it out of the law of that decision. The distinctions made are: 1st, that the colony in this case was not hostile; and, 2ndly, that the ship was not going into the hands of the enemy, but that she was coming first to the Cape into the hands of the owners, now become British subjects, and that they would have altered the ulterior destination to Holland.

On the first point, that Holland was not hostile, it is enough that hostilities have since followed, and with a retrospective operation. The state of affairs was at that time at best but very doubtful; and all property taken during that doubtful state of things has been since condemned; but it is said that, although Holland has become hostile, the Cape has not. If it could be proved that the colony adhered to the old government, it might entitle them to be exempted from this hostile character; but that is not shown, and there is no reason to presume it. They surrendered as Dutch subjects, and, therefore, there is no pretence now to contend for a different character.

The other distinction is, that this property was coming to the hands of the owners, whilst in the Demerara case it was gone from them, and must have fallen into the possession of the mother country; but there is no decided proof that this ship was coming to the Cape, and, if so, she is still to be considered as taken merely *in transitu* towards Holland, where the voyage was clearly to have ended; and in what character?—As a Dutch ship, in a Dutch port. If the vessel had arrived at the Cape, I will not say, that coming actually into the hands of the capitulants, she might not have been protected as property in possession; but being taken before she arrived there, as Dutch property, I am bound down by the decision of the Lords, and I think myself obliged to say that her character could not be changed *in transitu*, and that she must be condemned as Dutch property."

In his subsequent decree of 1799 in the case of the *Herstelder* (1 C.Rob., 113), however, Sir William Scott frankly gave vent to his misgivings about the legal situation:

> "If I am right in considering the property in this case in the same light as other Dutch property taken at that time, it must follow the same course. I am aware, this is to act on a principle sufficiently strong; but it is one that has been laid down by the Superior Court; and therefore, it is one that I am undoubtedly bound to obey; although I have no scruple to declare, that it is a principle which I am not disposed to carry a step further than authority leads me."

The case ended, moreover, with an annulment of the decree on the ground that the vessel had been described in the documents of the case as lying at Plymouth, whereas on capture she had in fact been taken to a port in Norway and lay there at the time of adjudication: the Court was not prepared to condemn a vessel lying in a neutral port.

Another instance of doubt about the binding force of a precedent was the case of the *Charlotte (No. 2)* of 1804 (5 C.Rob., 305; Roscoe, I, 490) in its relation to an earlier one, the *Graeffen van Gottland* of 1803. In both cases the claim, brought by merchants in Russia, related to the interception of a cargo of contraband (masts), the produce of Russia, carried from that country westward in a non-Russian vessel (in 1803 Swedish, in 1804 from Lübeck) to an enemy port of naval equipment (in 1803 Cádiz, in 1804 Nantes). In the *Charlotte* case Lord Stowell was asked to ignore the precedent of 1803 on the ground of a triple distinction to be made between the two cases. But, while recognizing his duty under the principle of *stare decisis*, he dismissed the request, arguing that none of the three distinctions advanced applied. His elaborate argument in the *Charlotte* case of 1804 indeed proceeded along the following lines:

> "If there is a decision by the Supreme Court on a similar point, especially such a recent one as 1803, it will be conclusive upon my judgment, and I shall have only to follow the rule of law there laid down and to act under the authority of that decision. Let us see, then, whether the cases are so far parallel cases as to be subject to application of the same principle."

Stating that the two cases ran parallel insofar as both were brought by merchants domiciled in Russia, exporting the produce of that country in non-Russian vessels, Lord Stowell examined the three alleged distinctions and concluded that neither was there any solid ground for deviating from the earlier decision:

a. the principle was not varied by the fact that the claimant was a Swedish consul trading in Riga;

b. although the Spanish port of Cádiz was a place of great mercantile equipment also, this did not alter the fact that it was a public arsenal of the enemy and, consequently, should be considered, just as the French port of Nantes, to be a place of great military equipment;

c. although the political relations between England and Russia under their treaty of 1797 were different from those existing in 1804, that circumstance was no ground for distinction, either.

In other instances it was not so much the direct applicability of a precedent to the later case that was at issue as the asserted similarity of the elements of the two cases which justified the decision of the later case on the same broad principles as had governed earlier cases. An example of this situation was that of the *Gerasimo* [1857] (11 Moore P.C., 88; Roscoe, II, 577) in which the Judicial Committee of the Privy Council was confronted with the problem of whether the neutral claimants' residence in belligerent-occupied neutral territory resulted in their acquiring enemy character on the same footing as inhabitants of territory under the sovereignty of the enemy. This was *in casu* denied on the analogy of the events concerned (military occupation of Moldavia and Wallachia by Russia in 1853) with those of the ineffective cession of Louisiana by France to the USA in 1803 (comp. on this subject my exposé of the question of enemy character of prizes, *infra*, pp. 258-259).

My general impression is that the legal dogma of the binding force of older judgments either of a superior court or of a court on the adjudicating body's own hierarchical level was not yet so strongly grounded at an earlier period of prize law history as it may have become later.

At a later stage British prize courts have cudgelled their brains over another problem. *viz.* whether, in their capacity of municipal courts, they were bound to observe the English theorem of *stare decisis*, even if this should result in judgments contrary to a developing international law of maritime prize. Their doubts were partly alleviated by the transparent fiction that British prize law was identical with the true law of nations.

Municipal regulations, either couched in laws, ordinances or other legislative instruments, or laid down in instructions to the Navy, were as a rule considered by the courts as also binding upon them. The testing of such legislative enactments or naval instructions by higher-ranking municipal legal rules was extremely rare in earlier periods, but it sometimes occurred later, when an Order in Council was tested by the contents of an Act of Parliament. This happened in the famous *Fox* and *Zamora* cases of 1811 and 1916, analysed *infra sub* C, section 3, pp. 598 and 606.

Issues concerning other States

The Netherlands

As a seafaring nation the Netherlands must also have produced a considerable number of prize court decisions during its successive naval wars. An inquiry into the survival of the texts of such decisions in the various depositories of historical documents, such as the General State Archives in The Hague (including the autonomous section of the archives of the former (united) province of Holland, deposited there), the sections of the State archives in the provinces of Friesland and Zeeland and the historical archives of the city of Amsterdam, has confirmed my earlier finding that the texts of the judgments of the former Admiralty Colleges have for by far the greater part been destroyed as the result of two fires. See for further details concerning these Admiralty Colleges my exposé in Chapter III under C, section 1, *infra*, pp. 581 *et seq*.

The study of the development of Netherlands prize case law in earlier centuries has remained neglected for a long time and its history, as a result, unexplored. This was partly due to the calamities which befell the prize tribunals and their archives, and the political upheavals and resulting removals of their seats, and partly to the deplorable state in which the archives of the *Grand Conseil de Malines*, an old court of appeal for the Low Countries (on which comp. further Chapter III under C, section 8, *infra*, pp. 663 *et seq*.) were found to be after their wandering through different countries of Europe prior to their ultimate return to Brussels. The state of these archives has been set out in a report following an inspection *in loco* which the present writer and an historian, senior lecturer at the Institute of Public International Law of the University of Utrecht, Dr Johanna Oudendijk, made in 1956 of their contents in the Belgian State Archives in Brussels, a report published in the *Handelingen van de Koninklijke Commissie voor de Uitgave der Oude Wetten en Verordeningen van België*, vol. XIX, issue II, 1957, pp. 315-323 (see vol. I of this publication, p. 430 and vol. VII, pp. 32-34).

The situation has meanwhile been considerably improved as the result of a systematic inquiry by a mixed Belgo-Netherlands commission for the publication of the jurisprudence of the *Grand Conseil*, composed of lawyers and historians, which has since been initiated. It may be, and I sincerely hope so, that this inquiry will yield valuable results. Although I am personally rather pessimistic about the real value of their future legal harvest, I wish them all possible success. Be this as it may, it is still too early to draw more definite conclusions from the finds in the still extant remains of the judicial archives, and the start of this systematic investigation has in any case come too late for me to take advantage of the results in the present volume. The scarce data which are already available are anyway too detailed and scrappy to fit into the general much wider context of this publication.

I must confine myself here to a few details relating, in particular, to the situation in the 15th and 16th centuries.

One of the oldest court decisions in the Low Countries that I know of, dates back to 1477-1482, a period when the counties of Holland and Zeeland formed part of the possessions of the Dukes of Burgundy and their successors. The case I have in view occurred shortly after the death of Duke Charles the Bold and related to the capture of a neutral (English) vessel, the

Mary Hampton of London, by a group of captors, the *Trygo* and other vessels, equipped by four towns of the county of Holland, which were engaging in a joint venture at sea. On this particular feature of these naval operations comp. my remarks in Chapter III, the preliminary chapter on general issues at the end of section 1, *sub* A, *infra*, p. 152. The events in that case developed as follows.

After having already been hailed by the *Trygo* in the English Channel on her outward voyage to France, the *Mary Hampton* was met again on her return voyage from Rouen. When she attempted to offer resistance to a visit of inspection she was brought into the Holland port of Brouwershaven, where she was appropriated as a prize by the crew and the owners of the capturing vessel jointly. However, when the London owners of the *Mary Hampton* instituted proceedings before the Court of Holland against the towns which had equipped the *Trygo*, that body decreed by a judgment of 23 June 1478 that the prize should be restored to them, as having been unlawfully captured because the suspicions against her (carrying French (enemy) goods, possibly of a contraband nature, to an enemy port and resistance to visitation), were not sufficiently well-founded. The case was subsequently brought in appeal before the *Grand Conseil de Malines*. This body confirmed the sentence of restitution of the prize to the British owners in 1482.

It was this case to which my attention was drawn by C.G. Roelofsen, another historian, a member of the staff and senior lecturer of the Institute of Public International Law at the University of Utrecht, who is actually engaged in an investigation into old Netherlands prize cases, including a number brought in appeal before the said *Conseil*. Comp. for a thorough analysis of this early instance of a 15th century Netherlands prize case Mr Roelofsen's contribution to the *Netherlands International Law Review*, vol. 27 (1980), pp. 218 *et seq*., under the title "Early Dutch prize law. Some thoughts on a case before the Court of Holland and the Grand Conseil of Mechelen (1477-1482)".

This *Mary Hampton* case was only one of the instances in which the *Grand Conseil* has exercised appellate jurisdiction in prize cases within the compass of the Burgundian Circle of the Low Countries.

Another case that was brought in appeal before the *Grand Conseil de Malines* occurred in 1508, when a shipment of fourteen oxen, the property of a merchant and cattle fattener, a citizen and resident of the Overijssel town of Zwolle, was intercepted near the Guelder town of Elburg on the Zuiderzee on a voyage from another small Overijssel town Genemuiden to Amsterdam. Those intercepting the ship and her cargo were ship's captains from the province of Holland which was involved at the time in naval hostilities against the then Sovereign of Guelder, Duke Charles, who was himself at war with the Burgundians. Parties to the proceedings were consequently, on the one hand, the Zwolle merchant and, on the other, the ship's captains from Amsterdam. The bishop of Utrecht, sovereign of the province of

Overijssel, had remained neutral in the conflict between Holland and Guelder until October 1508 when he was forced, in his turn, to join in the fighting to defend himself against Gueldrish attacks.

The incident, near Elburg, consequently related to a hostile act, bordering on piracy, committed by a belligerent naval force against neutral property carried on a neutral vessel. The capturing vessels belonged to the flotilla of Amsterdam, whose crews, though in the service of the Count of Holland, received their wages from the town of Amsterdam. It is not clear whether, but improbable that, the Amsterdam flotilla had the task of preventing all contact between neutrals and Gueldrish towns. On their side, the commanders of the Amsterdam flotilla asserted that the Gueldrians had first seized the Genemuiden vessel near Elburg and conducted her *intra praesidia* and that they (the Amsterdam captains) themselves had later recaptured her.

The owner of the oxen instituted proceedings against the captors, not in the Admiralty Court, set up in 1488 by an Ordonnance of Maximilian (which was not recognized in the County of Holland) but before the Provincial Court of Holland, which pronounced in his favour by a sentence of September 1511. In appeal, the *Grand Conseil de Malines* confirmed the lower sentence on 4 March 1513, but its execution proved impracticable because the captors were insolvent. The cattle owner thereupon instituted new proceedings, this time against the town of Amsterdam, which argued in vain that it was not responsible because the flotilla had acted in the service of the Count of Holland. When the new sentence of the Court of Holland of 1517 was again favourable to the owner of the oxen, the town appealed from it to the *Grand Conseil*, but again in vain: the town was, on 20 May 1519, sentenced to pay damages to the cattle owner; the only concession the *Grand Conseil* granted to the town of Amsterdam was that it authorized the latter to recuperate the damages from its responsible magistrates.

It was again Mr Roelofsen who analysed the events and their legal aftermath at a congress at Namur in May 1982 of the *Société d'histoire du droit et des institutions des pays flamands, picards et wallons.*

The same sea area of the Zuiderzee (at present: the IJsselmeer) was later the scene of another dispute, adjudicated by the *Grand Conseil* on 29 April 1559, on the basis of an Edict of the King-Emperor Charles V of 12 November 1547 on sea fisheries, in a controversy between the fishermen of the at the time independent States of Holland and Overijssel who had accidentally crossed into each other's fishing waters. See on that controversy the data inserted in a judgment of the District Court of Utrecht of 1941, summarized in the *Annual Digest and Reports of Public International Law Cases*, years 1919-1942 (supplem. vol.), Case No. 91 (pp. 175-176).

When the provinces were still members of the Burgundian Empire, the decrees of their provincial courts in prize cases and those of the Admiralty

Colleges were, as set out above, subject to appeal to a common superior tribunal, the *Grote Raad van Mechelen* (*Grand Conseil de Malines*).

The history of Netherlands prize jurisdiction following the Burgundo-Habsburg era must be divided into four successive periods, *viz.*, from early days up to 1795, under French rule up to 1813, from 1813 to 1940, and from 1940 onward.

The first, longest and in fact, the only important period extends from the days when the United Provinces began their insurrection against Spain and engaged in maritime warfare, up to the end of the 18th century when the Republic fell a victim to French expansionism. During that period jurisdiction was exercised by the so-called Admiralty Colleges. See on their history *infra*, pp. 581-586. The texts of prize court judgments rendered by the Admiralty Colleges of the Republic of the United Netherlands have never been published systematically, so that they can only be unearthed from records or archives.

A few special cases have received more attention or can still be consulted in the provincial sections of the State Archives in Zeeland or The Hague (autonomous section of Holland province, transferred there). The most famous of those cases is that of the Portuguese carrack *Catharina*, which in 1606 inspired the young Huigh de Groot (Grotius) to write his first dissertation *De jure praedae*. The case was adjudicated upon by the Admiralty College of Amsterdam in 1604 and dealt with the capture of a Portuguese carrack which returned from the East Indies with a valuable cargo (text of the judgment in W.J.M. van Eysinga's contribution to the *Grotiana*, vol. VII (1936-1939) pp. 28-33, reproduced in *Sparsa Collecta van Eysinga*, Leyden 1958, pp. 255 and 261).

Another prize case dating from the same period (1607) was that of the *San Jago*, also a Portuguese vessel, this one decided by the Admiralty Court of Zeeland. The case was analysed in detail by the same historian Mr Roelofsen in a contribution to the publications of the Netherlands Society for Maritime History (March 1970) under the title "Het trieste slot van een reis om de wereld in het begin van de zeventiende eeuw, de affaire Carletti" ("The sad end of a journey around the world at the beginning of the 17th century, the Carletti affair").

Another case that has attracted the attention of writers dates from the beginning of the 18th century and concerned the *Oude Roos*, a Netherlands merchant-man, which was captured by two Dunkirk privateers on 2 December 1710, was recaptured by a Netherlands privateer on 19 December and lost again, on 25 December, to another French privateer who later abandoned her. The ship ultimately succeeded in reaching a place of safety. G.F. de Martens, in his *Essai concernant les armateurs etc.*, related that he had been unable to find the judgment, but the complicated case had in fact been decided in the first instance and in appeal by successive judgments of 19 May 1711, 1 March and 4 July 1713. It was discussed in a publication under the title *Memorien, Advertissementen van regten en Advysen van*

Regtsgeleerden, etc. (Amsterdam, 1713), kept in the library of the Peace Palace at The Hague.

More information on prize law and prize cases in the first quarter of the eighteenth century can be found in Bynkershoek's *Observationes tumultuariae* where he surveys the jurisprudence of the High Court of Holland and Zeeland; this Court was competent for revision cases when there was an "appeal" from judgments of the provincial Admiralty Colleges, which often differed considerably in the interpretation of the placards of the States General concerning prize cases.

The provincial Zeeland section of the State Archives still contains documents relating to the capture of an English vessel, *The Endeavour*, in the last part of the 18th century (1782).

The rare old judgments the text of which I could thus retrace as still extant were so unimportant in the whole context of Netherlands prize jurisprudence that I cannot enter upon them in a general work such as the present one. I am afraid that even continued research in archival sources which might still become available in the future, will only yield a poor harvest and that one must, as a consequence, accept the fact that many texts have vanished for good. Moreover, many judgments have regrettably perished as a result of fires, mainly in a depository of the Ministry of Marine in 1844. Still, studies made by British historians, such as J.S. Bromley (*The North Sea in wartime* (1688-1713), 1977), may perhaps justify some optimism.

The preceding data relate to the situation from the 15th to the 19th century. During the 19th century only three prize court decisions have been rendered, and those were pronounced by a Netherlands-Indies civil court, the *Raad van Justitie* at Batavia, during a colonial war between the Kingdom of the Netherlands and the self-governing indigenous State of Atjeh (Acheen) in northern Sumatra. Since all three of these judgments related to a regional blockade, I will deal with their content in Chapter III, *Sub* A, section 4, *infra*, p. 451.

American collections

The political scene in North America changed in 1775 as a result of the rebellion of Great Britain's colonies there against the mother-country, followed by the creation of an autonomous American prize law judiciary. From that moment onward the adjudication of prize cases in North America altered.

The most elaborate study of early autonomous American case law in the field of maritime prize we owe to Henry J. Bourguignon in his thorough study *The First Federal Court. The Federal Appellate Prize Court of the American Revolution, 1775-1787* (Philadelphia, 1977) (comp. on this work the review in *A.J.I.L.*, vol. 73 (1979), pp. 728-729). This is not a collection of texts of prize court decrees pronounced during the War of Independence, but a very thorough analysis of their contents, as I have already had occasion to describe under "The Seven Years' War" (1756-1763), when the British colonial vice-admiralty courts still functioned there.

As the author says, the records of this first prize court of the United States, the "Court of Appeals in Cases of Capture", established in January 1780, are kept in 114 case files in the U.S. National Archives. According to Bourguignon this first Federal Appellate Prize Court in its case law still followed the judicial practice of the British colonial vice-admiralty courts rather than that of the Lords Commissioners for Prize Appeals in London.

In order to give some impression of the types of cases which arose during the revolutionary struggle for independence of Great Britain's American colonies and which were examined and decided by the first Federal American Prize Court, I will make a summary selection from those cases as analysed by Henry J. Bourguignon.

The complicated *Lusanna* case, which was very elaborately discussed before the Court (pp. 242 *et seq.*), mainly on the theoretical basis of Éméric de Vattel's writings, concerned two successive captures of a brig of an American owner Doane who originally, in the troubled summer of 1775, sent her off from Massachusetts with the aim of having her cargo of whale-oil, staves and wood sold in Europe by his son-in-law Bourne as supercargo, whom he instructed to return with another cargo to America. The first capture took place in the harbour of British Halifax where the brig had been forced to take shelter by a severe gale. After a long detention there, her owner saw no better chance of saving his property than by taking out a new register, listing the ship as belonging to the British port of Halifax. In that capacity she then sailed to Europe (London, Gibraltar) where Bourne planned a return voyage, again under a British register, ostensibly to Halifax, but in the hope of getting a chance to slip through the British fleet into some Massachusetts port. In carrying out this scheme Bourne posed as an American loyalist who had fled from the wrath of the rebels at home. This plan, however, unfortunately miscarried: on his return voyage to Halifax with a partly military cargo the brig was captured again, this time not by the British, but by an American privateer (October 1777). On the basis of Bourne's own earlier assertions (loyalist ownership; supply to British military forces) the brig was condemned by the American maritime court of New Hampshire and, on appeal, by that State's Superior Court. However, the Federal Court ultimately reversed those judgments of condemnation and restored the property to Doane c.s.

In other comparable *prima facie* suspicious cases, the Federal Court also showed a remarkable fairness of judgment: cases of the American vessels *Frank*, *Hope*, *Hawke*, *Minerva*, *Fancy* and *Hannah* (pp. 253-254, with footnotes 31 and 32, and p. 257). In the only case of this kind which resulted in final condemnation by the Federal Court, that of the *Fame* (1780), the suspicions against the prize were held to be too strong (pp. 254-256, with footnote 33).

A series of cases of a different type concerned the question of how to determine the enemy character of property when the enemy State (Great Britain) was in possession of large parts of a nearby American State. This variant occurred repeatedly in maritime intercourse between the American State of Connecticut and British-controlled Long Island (pp. 257-263) and resulted in the final restoration of the prizes to their owners in 1783.

Cases of fraud or collusion in the original capture were those of the schooner *Dolphin* and the sloop *Diamond* (pp. 263-264 with footnote 59), of the *Four Sisters* and the *Good Intent* (p. 264 with footnote 60) and of the *Sally* (pp. 264-265, with footnote 61).

The old question of the fate of neutral property carried by an enemy ship only came before the Commissioners of Appeals in November 1779, see the cases of the *Nuestra Señora de Merced* (pp. 278-279, with footnote 96), the *Valenciano* (pp. 279-280, with footnote 98), the *Santander y los Santos Mártires* and the *Good Intent* (p. 280, with footnotes 101 and 102). In the case of an enemy (British) cargo carried by the neutral (Dutch) ship *Brunette* the well-known problem of transitional law arose in the Court of Appeals: seizure prior, final adjudication subsequent to the new Instructions of November 1780 (comp. *infra*, p. 330).

Further cases related to the effects of a recapture and the award of prize salvage. This issue was discussed for the first time in respect of the recapture of French vessels by American privateers from the British under the Treaty of Amity and Commerce with France of 6 February 1778 (Martens, R^2, II, 587; Parry, 46, 417): cases of *Le Vern* and *Maria Theresa* (pp. 276-277, with footnote 91). The majority of cases, however, during the first period of the War of Independence had a bearing on the recapture by American privateers of American vessels, previously captured by the British. Cases of the recapture of neutral vessels by American privateers only came up later under the new regime of the Congressional Instructions of November 1780: cases of 1783 and 1784 concerning the *Minerva*, the *Nostra Seigniora da Solidade e St. Miguel e Almas* and the *Hope* (pp. 282-283, with footnotes 108 and 109). For details on this subject comp. further Chapter III *sub* B, section 7, *infra* p. 563.

Joint capture was asserted in the cases of the *Anna Maria*, the *Mermaid*, the *Barbary*, the *Countess of Eglinton* and the *Squirrel* (pp. 268-273, with footnotes 78, 79, 80 and 82). Comp. on this subject further Chapter III *sub* B, section 6, *infra* pp. 533-536.

On the capture of further neutral vessels, such as the *Resolution* [1781], the *Eersten* [1782], the *Chester* [1787] (captured in 1777) and the *Good Fortune* [1787], see the detailed data, published by Bourguignon, respectively at pp. 284-289, with footnote 112; pp. 289-293, with footnote 116; pp. 293-295, with footnote 114; and p. 294, with footnote 125.

Regular printed collections of American prize cases were started in the first years of the 19th century:

William Cranch (an Assistant Judge of the Circuit Court of the District Court of Columbia), *Reports of Cases adjudged by the Supreme Court of the United States, 1801-1815*, in nine volumes, the first of which (published in Washington City, 1804) comprises the judgments pronounced in the August and December terms, 1801, and the February term, 1803, and is introduced by a Preface which explains the reasons for the publication: the frequent complaint in the United States about the uncertainty of the law, attributable mainly to the lack of American reports, and to the resulting absence of uniformity in the case law owing to the judicial authority being shared among a vast number of independent tribunals which, even in the same court, were scarcely aware of each other's decisions. The last volume (IX) of this series contains the decisions made during the February term, 1815. It was followed by a volume of corresponding reports by Henry Wheaton, covering the February term, 1816.

Samuel Blatchford, *Reports of Cases in Prize, argued and decided in the Circuit and District Courts of the United States for the Southern District of New York (1861-1865)* (New York, 1866), published at the request of the Department of State and comprising the prize cases decided during the rebellion; this collection, therefore, includes no decisions of the Supreme Court. The jurisprudence of the New York court has been analysed by Madeline Russell Robinton in her study *An introduction to the papers of the New York Prize Court, 1861-1865* (New York, 1945); an excellent bibliography on pp. 189-195 surveys the printed collections and documents relating to the law of prize in the Civil War period.

Wallace, *United States Supreme Court Reports*. A reference table, inserted in each of the volumes 66-93 of these Reports, refers to the numbers of the corresponding volumes and pages of this special collection of prize cases (vols. 1-23).

The most famous Chief Justices of the period were John Jay (1789-1795) and John Marshall (1801-1835). Other (Associate) Judges were W. Cushing, W. Paterson, S. Chase, B. Washington, A. Moore and J. Story.

In 1923 J. Brown Scott reprinted the American prize court decisions since 1789 in his three-volume collection *Prize cases decided by the United States Supreme Court* (Oxford, 1923).

Italian cases

A limited number of Italian judgments which related to the law of prize, were quoted in the Italian contribution to the preparatory documents for the London Conference of 1908 on Naval Warfare. They relate to the following subject matters:

1857/58, the *Cagliari*: restitution because innocence was established;

1859, the *Fama Argentina*: destruction of a neutral vessel;

1866, the *Venezia*: transfer of an enemy ship to a neutral flag;

1878, the *Britannia* and the *Matilde Bellagamba*: effectiveness of a blockade of sea areas which gave access to neutral coasts;

1896: the *Doelwijk*: application of the doctrine of continuous voyage to conditional contraband.

As those references give scarcely any information on the actual content of the decisions quoted, I have tried to find their text in the collection where one would expect them to be reported, namely, the publication *La prassi italiana di diritto internazionale, Prima serie (1861-1887)*, vol. 2 (Dobbs Ferry, 1970), but in vain.

The second half of the nineteenth century

During the half century between the Crimean War and the codification of 1907-1909 the flood of prize court judgments gradually decreased, and as a result there was little reason to start the publication of new collections. A brief survey of the events during this period may suffice.

The American Civil War of 1861-1865 still produced a large number of famous prize court decisions, especially concerned with the carriage of contraband and violation of blockade. Their texts can be found in the above-mentioned American collection by S. Blatchford, entitled *Reports of Cases in Prize argued .... in the Circuit and District Courts of the U.S. for the Southern District of New York* (1866). In 1945 Madeline Russell Robinton published *An introduction to the papers of the New York prize court, 1861-1865* (New York), a study of the cases found in Blatchford's *Reports* and several other printed collections (p. 190). This Civil War also produced the *Trent* incident, described in vol. X of this publication, pp. 97 *in fine* and 116, from its neutrality aspect, and further *infra* in Chapter III *sub* A, section 5 (pp. 460-461) from the point of view of prize law.

The war between the German Bund and Denmark of 1864 was characterized by reciprocal exemptions of enemy vessels from condemnation as maritime prize (comp. Chapter III, *sub* A, section 2, *infra*, pp. 275-278 *et seq.*), by a Danish blockade of the North German coast, and by a national Danish Ordinance on the exercise of the law of prize (see Deák and Jessup, *Neutrality Law*, I, pp. 473 *et seq.*), but I have not come across actual prize cases.

Neither would the ensuing war of 1866 between Prussia and Austria for the supremacy within the area of the former Holy Roman Empire of the Germanic Nation (comp. Part II of this publication, p. 182) seem to have given rise to prize proceedings, for instance in implementation of corresponding mutual exemptions of each other's merchantmen from confiscation. What I did find, however, was a case brought not before a prize court, but before the Italian *Contenziosa Diplomatica*, during the contemporaneous war between Austria and Italy relating to the affair of the *Venezia*, to which reference is made in a note in the Italian Memorandum for the Naval Conference of London (1908-1909), p. 45.

A number of prize cases arising from the Franco-German War of

1870-1871, decided by the French *Conseil des prises*, were collected in a special publication by H.M. Barboux (Paris, 1872) *Jurisprudence du Conseil des prises*.

A few years later (1873) a colonial war between the Netherlands and the indigenous State of Atjeh (Acheen), including a Dutch naval blockade of that State, treated as an international war, led to a few prize court decisions which I will briefly digest in Chapter III, *sub* A, section 4, *infra*, pp. 451 *et seq*., because they are hardly known to foreign writers.

During the Balkan War between Russia and Turkey of 1877-1878 the blockade of the Adriatic Sea by Russia caused controversy over its lawfulness on the ground that it also barred the access to neutral (Italian) territory. This controversy obviously came up before the Italian *Contenziosa Diplomatica* as is mentioned in another note, at p. 43, of the Italian Memorandum, referred to above.

Prize cases from the Japanese wars can be found in:

S. Takahashi, *Cases on international law during the Chino-Japanese* War (edition by T.E. Holland and J. Westlake, 1899);

S. Takahashi, *International law applied to the Russo-Japanese War, with the decisions of the Japanese Prize Courts* (English edition, London, 1908);

C.J.B. Hurst-F.E. Bray, *Prize cases, being a collection of translations and summaries of the principal cases decided by the Russian and Japanese Prize Courts arising out of the Russo-Japanese War, 1904-1905*, 2 vols. (London, 1912-1913).

Section 6. CUSTOMARY PRACTICE

When treaties are lacking, when municipal rules of prize law were silent or needed interpretation, or when the validity of the latter had to be tested by the law of nations, the prize courts were forced to seek the solution of controversial questions in customary international law. In doing so, they engaged in historical investigation and employed widely divergent reasoning based upon a great diversity of methodological conception, either deduction from general principles of international law, or comparison of the laws and regulations of the various maritime powers, or a study of judicial precedents, both national and foreign, or of the opinions of legal writers, a postulation of maxims of equity, or even invocation of Roman law.

When compared, a detailed analysis of all such methods clearly demonstrates a lack of consistency and a choice of arguments according to the need in each particular case to reach a decision subservient so far as possible to the national interest, illustrating the need for the creation of an impartial prize jurisdiction.

Section 7. ARBITRAL AWARDS

Arbitral awards have also been a source of prize law, but only to a limited extent, *viz.*, insofar as their findings enunciated or confirmed rules or principles which were thenceforth accepted as the law of the international community and thus had a lasting influence on its consolidation or development. This applies to the role of arbitration in the field of maritime prize just as in other domains of the law of nations. Viewed from this angle, the effect of arbitral awards dealing with the law of maritime prize has been limited either because the awards were merely of a factual nature, or because they bore the character of a compromise settlement instead of a statement of the law, or because they were rejected by interstate society, or because they have only subsisted as almost forgotten *petrifacts*, not to mention in this context the many cases in which for one reason or another the proceedings broke down, or the awards were given without any statement of reasons.

In particular, there have been two historical periods in which arbitral settlements played a somewhat more significant part in the solution of disputes over captures of ships or cargoes in prize, namely, the middle of the 17th and the end of the 18th century. I will not however go into this more thoroughly here, but refer instead to my exposition in Chapter III *sub* C, section 8, *infra*, p. 663.

One of the most famous instances of the settlement of international controversies, including prize law disputes, by arbitration (in the form of mixed claims commissions) is the agreement reached by Great Britain and the United States in their Jay Treaty of 19 November 1794 (Martens, R^2, V, 642; Parry, 52, 243) to submit certain controversies over seizures made by Great Britain during the first period of her Coalition Wars against France to third-party judgment. But again, although these proceedings have had considerable impact, I will not expatiate upon them here, but refer to analyses of the points of law involved, which I will insert in Chapter III below, especially *sub* A (Enemy or non-enemy character of prizes), pp. 245-246 and *sub* C, section 8 (Review of arbitral awards) at p. 669.

The *Betsey* case (1797-1798). This arbitration has become notorious as a result of the manner in which the British Agent attempted to block the orderly course of adjudication by the advancement of two preliminary objections which I cannot but consider as procedural chicaneries. The first was his pretension in the *Betsey* case that the Mixed Claims Commission could not take cognizance of the American claims for the review of a series of condemnatory British prize court decrees on the ground that they had the force of *res judicata* also on the interstate level. As has been set out from American sources by the editors of the *Recueil des arbitrages internationaux* (R.A.I.), the British Government has quietly abandoned this extraordinary procedural defence advanced by their Agent by prohibiting their Commissioners, first from discussing it in writing with their fellow Commissioners and later (express orders of Lord Grenville on the advice of the Lord

Chancellor) from moving it again at all (*R.A.I.*, vol. I, pp. 52-53). This course of events has hindered a full-scale discussion of this vital issue by the Mixed Commission. The only Commissioner who still paid attention to it was the American Commissioner Gore (*ibid.*, I, pp. 56 *et seq.*); his colleague Pinkney was interested in other elements of the case (*ibid.*, I, pp. 73 *et seq.*), and the presiding Commissioner Trumbull did not even mention it in his verdict (*ibid.*, I, pp. 82 *et seq.*). Anyway, the judicial debate resulted in a silent, but not therefore less impressive victory for the adoption of sound conceptions on international arbitration. Another very valuable contribution to the future of arbitral settlement of disputes was made by the Commission with respect to a valid procedural defence advanced by the British Agent, *viz.*, that, although an arbitral tribunal was in principle competent to determine its award by a majority of votes, this should not apply to controversies over its own competence, which should therefore be decided unanimously, or else be referred back to the contesting parties for their decision. This defence was also abandoned or rejected (*ibid.*, I, pp. 63 *et seq.*).

There is another reason why I confine myself in this section to these few summary remarks, *viz.*, that I have already had occasion in several places in Parts VI and VIII of this publication to cite a number of cases of the solution of specific disputes over captures in prize by arbitration, in particular vol. VI, pp. 647 *et seq.* and vol. VIII, pp. 276-277 and 319-320.

As I will also set out below *sub* C in section 8, at p. 663, the arbitral proceedings could take two different forms, either as a conferment of arbitral jurisdiction "by prorogation", *i.e.* directly upon the international tribunal, or as a continuation of previous proceedings conducted in the municipal sphere.

A non-European example of the arbitral solution of a dispute relative to a prize case is that recorded from the Russo-Japanese War of 1904-1905 concerning a controversy between the owners of the steamship *Prometheus* and the Osaka Shosen Kaisha about the lasting validity or obsolete character of the old Rule of the War of 1756: *Hong Kong Law Reports*, vol. II, Part VI, December 1907, p. 207. See on that arbitration Chapter III *sub* A, section 6, of this volume, *infra*, p. 476, and the exposé in Hurst and Bray, vol. II, p. 451.

Section 8. COLLECTIVE TREATIES

The few multilateral treaties which have created, or been intended to create, new positive rules of law to cover the field of maritime prize will be surveyed in my historical exposé in Chapter II *sub* A, B, C and D at pp. 124-133. They are the Declaration of Paris (1856), the treaties which constitute together the

"Armed Neutrality" (1780 and 1800), certain Conventions or Articles of Conventions concluded at the Second Hague Peace Conference of 1907, and the London Declaration on Naval Warfare of 1909. The contents of the latter two will be set out in more detail below in the various sections of my systematic survey in Chapter III.

CHAPTER II

A BRIEF HISTORY OF THE LAW OF PRIZE

GENERAL INTRODUCTION

As I set out in my Introduction to Chapter I at pp. 6-7, I will, before starting with a systematic exposé of the various issues of prize law in the period preceding the codification of 1907-1909 in Chapter III, begin by giving in this Chapter II a broad outline of the historical development of the law of prize from its earliest appearance up to the present time.

Before engaging, in Chapter III, in a systematic historical exposé of the different subject-matters that call for survey, I will briefly describe the three principal earlier attempts which have been made in the course of history to codify the laws to be observed in naval warfare against enemy and neutral shipping, *viz.*, *sub* A, the Armed Neutrality Alliances of 1780 and 1800, followed by the abuses of the Continental System; *sub* B, the Declaration of Paris of 1856 and *sub* C, the Conventions of the Second Hague Peace Conference of 1907, which were followed by the London Declaration on Naval Warfare of 1909, with which Chapter III ends. A sketch of the development that took place after the London Conference will follow *sub* D.

The law of prize dates back to a very old historical period, in fact to the origins of naval warfare, and so does prize jurisdiction, initially exercised by the Admiral and his courts. In those early days a rough distinction was made between enemy property at sea, which was subject to seizure and confiscation, and property belonging to owners of non-enemy nationality ("friends" and allies), which was not. The intertwinement of enemy and non-enemy property as a result of the presence of enemy goods on board non-enemy vessels or of non-enemy goods on board enemy vessels already gave rise in past centuries to differing systems of treatment: the fate of the cargo could be determined either (*a*) by the enemy or non-enemy character of the transporting ship, or (*b*) by its own character. In the first case (*a*) non-enemy cargo was subject to confiscation together with the enemy ship, whereas enemy cargo was protected by the ship's non-enemy character. In the second case (*b*) the distinction between the enemy and non-enemy character of the cargo was strictly applied as a matter of principle: *separatorum separata fit ratio*. This simple legal solution was, however, complicated to the detriment of non-enemy owners by the theory of infection of innocent by non-innocent property on the ground of their intertwinement, resulting for example in the confiscation of non-enemy cargo found on board an enemy ship, or of a non-enemy vessel because of her conveying enemy goods. That theory of infection was also applied to other sea transports. For, apart from the basic confiscatability of enemy property at sea, there were also other grounds of condemnation, which directly affected non-enemy property, in particular (i) the carriage of contraband goods to the enemy by non-enemy ships, entailing the confiscation not only of those contraband goods, but in different variants also of innocent goods of the same owner on board and of the transporting non-enemy vessel herself, and (ii) the carriage even of innocent goods by a non-enemy ship to a blockaded enemy port or coast. And gradually still other grounds of seizure were introduced, such as (iii) the transport of soldiers or sailors to an enemy country or navy in non-enemy ships (quasi-contraband). It goes without saying that all these variants of treatment and grounds of seizure caused a complicated and incoherent system of legal rules to emerge.

That aggregate of rules was already in early times subjected to a system of judicial control by admiralty courts, which was the more necessary as naval warfare was for some centuries mainly delegated by belligerent States to privateers commissioned by them for that purpose, a practice of warfare which in fact lasted until the middle of the 19th century.

Admiralty court decisions have been handed down to us from early days. In the preceding Chapter I, I have already listed a number of collections of national prize court decisions since the middle of the 17th century. Netherlands Admiralty Tribunals must also have left behind a trail of prize court judgments, but extensive fires, especially in the Ministry of Marine in 1844, have proved fatal as regards their legal inheritance, as is witnessed by a sad remainder of charred documents in the General State Archives.

When we look back at the legal position as it existed in the last decades of the 16th century, we are justified in stating that the old practice by belligerent States of intercepting all, including "neutral", commerce with their enemies was at that juncture still in frequent use and fairly generally recognized as accepted law, but that nations not involved in the war showed growing opposition to that practice, as testified by many historical protests against it.

Certain *placaten* of the States General of the United Netherlands in the last decades of the 16th century are notorious for the boldness with which that body deemed itself entitled to encroach upon the rights and interests of neutrals. Whereas they still limited the interception of shipping to Spain and her possessions in the Southern Low Countries to transport carried out by their own subjects (21 December 1580, 22 May 1582, 23 March 1583 in *Groot*

Placaatboek, I, 1099, 1100, 1103), their policy changed in July 1584 (*ibid.*, I, 1976, 1104), when they expressly put a ban also on such shipments by neutrals and from neutral ports, still restricting, however, the interdiction to trade to the Spanish Netherlands and not extending it to trade to Spain herself. Robert Dudley, Earl of Leicester, Queen Elisabeth's representative in the United Netherlands, tightened the measures still further by his proclamations of 4 April 1586 (*ibid.*, I, 1083) and 18 July 1586 (*ibid.*, I, 1088) which extended the prohibition to neutral shipping, directed not only towards the Southern Low Countries but also towards Spain and Portugal, although still differentiating between the penalties threatened against Netherlanders (the gallows) and foreigners (confiscation of ships and cargoes). Queen Elisabeth, however, out of fear of reprisals by King Henry III of France, caused the prohibitions to be mitigated again by a new proclamation of 4 August 1586 (*ibid.*, I, 1092) that no longer threatened the penalty of confiscation in respect of trade by neutrals to Spain and Portugal themselves. This complicated history of the Netherlands trade prohibitions in the 1580's is described in detail by J.H. Kernkamp, *De handel op den vijand* (Utrecht, 1931), vol. I. Comp. the Summary in B.M. Telders' excellent paper of 1939 on *De oorsprong der effectieve blokkade* (at pp. 165 *et seq.* of volume II of his *Verzamelde geschriften*, edited in 1948 after his death in 1945 in the concentration camp of Bergen Belsen as a victim of German brutality). A new prohibition by the States General of 2 April 1599 (*Groot Placaatboek*, II, B, 33) was still resolutely defended by that body against protests by the Kings of France and of Scotland as a measure (in translation) "which was not new, but always employed, in conformity with the law of nations and the customs of all kings, princes and republics being at war, *viz.*, that they forbid and prevent all supply to their enemies", it being "tout notoire et évident que selon la disposition et l'usage irréfragable de tous roys, princes et républiques d'Europe l'on peulx empescher aux ennemis de tout ce quy peult aulcunement servir à leur commodité et service".

A basic reversal of this trend only took place in the first half of the 17th century, when the clash between the interests of belligerent and neutral countries, which was in any case due to result in the event in some sort of compromise, in actual fact led to a double mitigation of the customary practice, consisting of a limitation of the traditional interception of neutral trade to (*a*) those goods which could be of vital interest to the enemy (contraband of war) and (*b*) those ships that attempted to establish communication between the high seas and besieged ports (blockade). This twofold mitigation of the pre-existing severe customary rules took place about 1600. It leads quite naturally to a bifurcation of the historical exposé into a chapter concerning the carriage of contraband of war and a chapter relating to blockade and its violation.

On the basis of these two branches of the law of prize affecting neutrals, the law of contraband and the law of blockade, the system of prize law has further developed in the course of the 17th and 18th centuries, partly by means of treaties, partly through municipal legislation or navy instructions, partly as a result of decisions of admiralty courts, as described in Chapter I. Each of the successive major wars of that period has in its own way contributed to that development, especially in the Nine Years' War of 1688-1697, the War of the Spanish Succession of 1702-1713, the War of the Austrian Succession of 1740-1748, the Seven Years' War of 1756-1763, the American War of Independence of 1776-1783 and the Wars of Revolutionary France from 1793 onwards.

Provisions against the transportation of contraband were inserted, for example, in the treaties of

11 July 1670 between Denmark and England (Parry, 11, 347);

25 April 1741 between Sweden and France (Wenck, II, 5; Parry, 36, 183), 15 March 1742 (Parry, 36, 267) and 23 August 1742 between Denmark and France (Wenck, I, 591; Parry, 36, 425), and

20 June 1766 between Russia and England (Martens, R^2, I, 390; Parry, 43, 365), Arts. X and XI.

The case law of English and French prize courts illustrates the practice of maritime blockades, the gradual extension and sharpening of belligerent action against the transportation of contraband of war and the emergence of new rules concerning unneutral assistance, reserved colonial or coastal trade and the interception of produce of the enemy soil.

The last two decades of the 18th and the first decade of the 19th century were a period during which the law of maritime prize came most spectacularly to the forefront of events as a result of the actions of both neutral and belligerent States.

Neutral States initiated the change by uniting in an alliance against belligerent abuses, first in 1780, again in 1800, under the leadership of the Russian Tsaritsa Catharina II—an alliance which was historically designated as "Armed Neutrality". After the final breakdown of that alliance in 1801, the main belligerents of that time, France and England, engaged, to the detriment of neutrals, in a fierce struggle for supremacy in Europe. This struggle gave rise, in 1800, to a system of mutual reprisals which became known as the "Continental System".

Under that Continental System the development of the practice of prize law went from bad to worse during the Napoleonic Wars. The series of belligerent measures began with a declaration by the First Secretary of State of the Department of Foreign Relations of his Britannic Majesty, addressed to the diplomatic representatives of the neutral Powers in London, dated 16 May 1806 (French text in Martens, N.R., I, 436; English text in B.F.S.P. 1812-1814, 1512), by which he announced that the King

> "taking into consideration the new and extraordinary means resorted to by the Enemy for the purpose of distressing the commerce of his Subjects, has thought fit to direct that the necessary measures should be taken for the Blockade of the Coast, Rivers, and Ports, from the River Elbe to the Port of Brest, both inclusive; and that the said Coast, Rivers, and Ports, are and must be considered as blockaded; ...".

This declaration was reciprocated by the French Emperor Napoleon in a Decree issued in Berlin—and therefore historically known as the Decree of Berlin—on 21 November 1806 (text in Martens, N.R., I, 439), in which, after enumerating the various infractions of the law of nations, assertedly committed by England, he decreed:

> "Art. I. Les Isles Britanniques sont déclarées en état de blocus.
> Art. II. Tout commerce, et toutes correspondances avec les Isles Britanniques sont interdits.—En conséquence, les lettres ou paquets adressés ou en Angleterre, ou à un Anglais, ou écrites en langue Anglaise, n'auront pas cours aux postes, et seront saisies.
> Art. III. Tout individu sujet de l'Angleterre, de quelque état et condition qu'il soit, qui sera trouvé dans les pays occupés par nos troupes ou par celles de nos alliés, sera fait prisonnier de guerre.
> Art. IV. Tout magazin, toute marchandise, toute propriété de quelque nature qu'elle puisse être, appartenant à un sujet de l'Angleterre, sera déclarée de bonne prise.
> Art. V. Le commerce des marchandises Angloises est défendu, et toute marchandise appartenant à l'Angleterre ou provenant de ses fabriques, et de ses colonies, est déclarée de bonne prise.
> etc.".

These introductory measures of the two main belligerents were followed by a further series of decrees or ordinances, which successively and progressively violated the law of nations by the enactment of illegal trade prohibitions. The entire series of these decrees and orders during the period 1806-1810, which together constitute the Continental System, can be found in Martens, N.R., I, 433-549 under the letters *a-z* and *aa-ww*. It included, apart from an English order of 21 May 1806 (*ibid.*, 438), that English warships and other commissioned vessels would not arrest and seize any ship navigating on the Baltic Sea, an English counter-declaration against blockades to the detriment of neutrals of 7 January 1807 (*ibid.*, 444) and certain further English countermeasures of 11 and 25 November 1807 (*ibid.*, 446, 449), and Napoleon's second Decree of 17 December 1807, known as the Decree of Milan (*ibid.*, 452). Prussia joined in the struggle between belligerents and neutrals by her rupture with England on 1 December 1807 after the Franco-Prussian Peace Treaty of Tilsit (*ibid.*, 454) and the United States by putting an embargo on all merchant vessels in its harbours (Embargo Act of 22 December 1807, complemented on 9 March 1808, *ibid.*, 455, 459). Further details of this Continental System and of the contents of the Reprisals Orders which established it will be given in Chapter III, *sub* C, section, 3, *infra*, pp. 601-606.

A. THE ARMED NEUTRALITY ALLIANCE, FOLLOWED BY THE CONTINENTAL SYSTEM

As I remarked in Part IX-B (vol. X) of this publication, pp. 50-56, the programme of the famous "Armed Neutrality", propagated on 28 February 1780 by the Russian Tsaritsa Catharina II, was in actual fact concerned, in particular, with certain principles of the law of prize. Her Declaration, made to the Courts of Paris, London and Madrid and communicated to the neutral Powers of the time, was to the following effect (text in Martens, R², III, 158; Parry, Suppl. 1, 44).

Referring to the moderation that she had shown in respect of neutral Powers and their subjects during the preceding war between Russia and the Ottoman Porte of 1768-1774 and expressing her disappointment over the many impediments placed in the way of neutral commerce by other belligerent Powers since then, the Empress proposed to the Courts of France, Great Britain and Spain that they should adopt as their future policy the following principles, said to be "consignés dans le droit primitif des peuples, que toute nation est fondée à réclamer, et que les Puissances belligérantes ne sauraient invalider sans violer les loix de la neutralité" (called elsewhere also "principles of natural law"):

"1. Que les vaisseaux neutres puissent naviguer librement de port en port et sur les côtes des nations en guerre.

2. Que les effets appartenans aux sujets des dites Puissances en guerre, soyent libres sur les vaisseaux neutres, à l'exception des marchandises de contrebande.

3. Que l'impératrice se tient quant à la fixation de celles-ci à ce qui est énoncé dans l'Art. X et XI de son traité de commerce avec la Grande-Bretagne [of 20 June 1766, Martens, R², I, 390; Parry, 43, 365], en étendant ces obligations à toutes les Puissances en guerre.

4. Que pour déterminer ce qui caractérise un port bloqué, on n'accorde cette dénomination qu'à celui, où il y a, par la disposition de la Puissance qui l'attaque avec des vaisseaux arrêtés et suffisamment proches, un danger évident d'entrer.

5. Que ces principes servent de règle dans les procédures et les jugemens sur la légalité des prises."

The reactions of the Powers, thus approached by Russia, to these suggestions were on the whole not unfavourable, although the British Government, on a later occasion (1800), expressly declared that the principles of 1780 were in clear deviation from those always adopted by Great Britain in the past (Martens, R², VII, 203). See on the answers of the three belligerent Powers of the time (April 1780): Martens, R², III, 160, 162 and 164. As to the neutral Powers, invited to accept the policy, several of them did so, first by notifying their acceptance, later by entering into detailed treaties with Russia. See as regards:

the Netherlands: Resolution of the States-General of 13/24 April 1780 (Martens, R², III, 166, 168) and Treaty of 3 January 1781 (*ibid.*, 215, 219);

Denmark: Declaration of 8 July 1780 (*ibid.*, 178)—following another Declaration of 2 May 1780 concerning the proclamation of the status of the Baltic as a "closed sea" (*ibid.*, 175; comp. Part IV of this publication, p. 112)—and Treaty of 9 July 1780 (*ibid.*, 189, 195; Parry, 47, 345);

Sweden: Declaration of 21 July 1780 (Martens, R², III, 185) and Treaty of 1 August 1780 (Martens, R², III, 198, 205; Parry, 47, 357);

Austria: Act of Adhesion of 9 October 1780 (Martens, R^2, III, 257) and Treaty of 10 July 1781 (Martens, R^2, III, 252, 260: Parry, 47, 495);

Prussia: two Ordinances of 3 November and 8 December 1781 (Martens, R^2, III, 290, 293) and Treaty of 8 May 1781 (Martens, R^2, III, 245; Parry, 47, 463);

Portugal: Treaty of 13 July 1782 (Martens, R^2, III, 263; Parry, 48, 105);

the Two Sicilies: Treaty of 10 February 1783 (Martens, R^2, III, 267; Parry, 48, 253).

In order to enforce the observance of these principles by belligerent States, the Empress announced her intention to cause a considerable part of her naval forces to be equipped against possible violators of the same. It was especially on this element of Russia's proposals that Sweden asked more detailed information, comp. the Note of the Swedish Government in Martens, R^2, III, 170 and the Russian answer (*ibid.*, 171).

At a later period, however, Russia became disloyal to her own principles of the "natural law" of neutrality when, in 1793, she concluded her treaty of 25 March with Great Britain (Martens, R^2, V, 438; Parry, 52, 1), by Article IV of which

> "Their Majesties engage to unite all their efforts to prevent other Powers, not implicated in this war, from giving... any protection whatever, directly, or indirectly in consequence of their neutrality, to the commerce or property of the French, on the sea, or in the ports of France",

but this engagement was said to be made "on this occasion of common concern to every civilized State". It was therefore presented as an exceptional measure.

The system of Armed Neutrality was revived in 1800 when Tsar Paul I invited the other Baltic States, Sweden, Denmark and Prussia, by a Declaration of 29 August (Martens, R^2, VII, 150) to re-establish the rights of neutrality. The occasion for this invitation was a series of incidents caused by Great Britain, which prompted the Tsar to reunite the neutral Powers in a common front, directed especially against England. The long diplomatic exchanges of 1800-1801 between the Powers concerned, reproduced (with connecting notes) in Martens, R^2, VII, 127-286, reveal the following causes of the new discord between belligerent England and the four neutral countries encircling the Baltic.

A conflict which developed in December 1799 off Gibraltar between the Danish frigate *Havfruen*, convoying a number of Danish merchant vessels, and two British frigates, *Emerald* and *Flora*, whose commanders claimed the right to visit the Danish merchantmen despite their sailing under Danish convoy (Martens, R^2, VII, 127-133; Ortolan, *Règles internationales et diplomatie de la mer*, II, 268, footnote; 412-415).

A similar incident occurred on 25 July 1800 in the entry to the British Channel between the Danish frigate *Freya* and a British squadron, when the

Danish commander likewise refused to permit the visiting by the British navy of the merchant vessels under his convoy (Martens, *loco cit.*, 133-153; Ortolan, II, 268, 415-424).

Tsar Paul I's resentment over England's refusal to fulfil her promise of 1798 to restore the island of Malta, after its reconquest from France, to the Knightly Order of Saint John of Jerusalem, whose Grand Master the Tsar had become in 1798 (comp. Part II of this publication, p. 30), induced him to lay an embargo upon all British vessels in Russian ports on 29 August 1800 (Martens, *loco cit.*, 153-154), a measure which was followed by an incident caused by two British ships in the port of Narva (*ibid.*, 155).

A serious incident was provoked by an English frigate near Barcelona on 4 September 1800: after having occupied the Swedish galliot *Hoffnung* with a prize crew, the commander of the frigate reached the roadstead of Barcelona under the cover of the Swedish flag and thereupon captured two Spanish frigates, a treacherous British action which resulted in a diplomatic conflict between Spain and Sweden, whose Government did not, in Spain's opinion, protest strongly enough to the British Government, whereas Sweden denied all legal responsibility for a delinquency committed by a third Power (Martens, *loco cit.*, 156-164; Ortolan, II, 31, 375-379).

Another incident, the seizure by a British warship off the Netherlands island of Texel of the *Triton*, a Prussian merchant vessel sailing with a cargo of wood from Emden to Amsterdam, and her subsequent bringing-in to the port of Cuxhaven belonging to the neutral Free City of Hamburg. When Prussia sent troops to this port to claim the release of the vessel with a view to upholding the regime of Armed Neutrality of Northern Germany (Martens, *loco cit.*, 165), the King of Great Britain protested in order to protect his own interests as Elector of Hanover (*ibid.*, 164-170).

All these incidents combined prompted the Emperor Paul I of Russia to suggest by his Declaration of 29 August 1800 mentioned above to the other countries surrounding the Baltic the re-establishment of the system of Armed Neutrality created in 1780. This suggestion was accepted and resulted in three separate Conventions, dated 16/18 December 1800, between Russia, on the one hand, and Sweden (Martens, R^2, VII, 172; Parry, 55, 411), Denmark (Martens, R^2, VII, 181; Parry, 55, 425), and Prussia (Martens, R^2, VII, 188; Parry, 55, 427), on the other. These Conventions reconfirmed the principles of 1780 and complemented them by a few others, which prescribed a special warning to neutral vessels by the blockading force and respect for a neutral convoy;

Art. III (3) "... et que tout bâtiment naviguant vers un port bloqué ne pourra être regardé d'avoir contrevenu à la présente convention que, lorsqu'après avoir été averti par le commandant du blocus de l'état du port, il tâchera d'y pénétrer en employant la force ou la ruse".

Art. III (5): "que la déclaration de l'officier commandant le vaisseau ou les vaisseaux de la marine royale ou impériale, qui accompagneront le convoi d'un ou de plusieurs bâtiments marchands, que son convoi n'a à bord aucune marchandise de contrebande, doit

> suffire pour qu'il n'y ait lieu à aucune visite sur son bord ni à celui des bâtimens de son convoi".

However, after Tsar Paul I's death on 23 March 1801, his successor Alexander I, less antagonistic to Great Britain, again disowned Russia's principles of neutrality law by concluding a maritime convention with England on 17 June 1801 (Martens, R², VII, 260; Parry, 56, 105), with an explanatory declaration of 20 October 1801 (Martens, R², VII, 271; Parry, 56, 123), which shifted the balance between neutrals and belligerents in the latter's favour. The changes made signalled the final failure of the policy of Armed Neutrality, because Denmark and Sweden also accepted them (Martens, R², VII, 273 and 276). The changes of 1801 were mainly twofold: (*a*) the neutral flag would no longer protect enemy goods, nor produce of the enemy soil, nor reserved colonial trade; (*b*) the belligerent's right to visit neutral merchant ships notwithstanding their sailing under neutral convoy was recognized, albeit under strictly defined conditions:

Art. III (2) of the Convention laid down

> "Que les effets embarqués sur les vaisseaux neutres seront libres, à l'exception de la contrebande *et des propriétés ennemies*; et il est convenu de ne pas comprendre au nombre des dernières *les marchandises du produit, du crû, ou de la manufacture des pays en guerre* qui auroient été acquises par des sujets de la puissance neutre, et seroient transportées pour leur compte; lesquelles marchandises ne peuvent être exceptées en aucun cas de la franchise accordée au pavillon de la dite puissance."

The explanatory Declaration was to the effect that

> "la liberté du commerce et de la navigation accordée par [l'article III (2)] aux sujets de la puissance neutre, ne les autorise point à transporter directement, en temps de guerre, *les marchandises et les denrées des colonies de la Puissance belligérante* dans les possessions continentales, ni vice versa de la Métropole dans les colonies enemies [except in virtue of a most-favoured-nation clause]".

Articles IV and V of the Convention detailed the conditions under which the belligerent Party would be entitled to visit merchant vessels sailing under convoy. The right of visitation, now recognized, would, however, be limited "aux seuls cas où la puissance belligérante pourroit essuyer un préjudice réel par l'abus du pavillon neutre" and would be conditional upon the observance of six strict obligations.

B. THE DECLARATION OF PARIS

The Declaration of Paris of 16 April 1856 "pour régler divers points de droit maritime" (Martens, N.R.G.¹, XV, 791 = XVI², 641; Parry, 115, 1) was a direct consequence of the necessity during the Crimean War for the Allied Powers to agree upon a parallel course of action vis-à-vis neutral property at sea. Corresponding instructions were for that purpose issued by France and England on 28 and 31 March 1854 in order to inaugurate a common policy of prize law to cover the War. The Declaration of the Emperor of France, while maintaining the right to seize contraband goods and to prevent neutrals from carrying dispatches to the enemy, as well as the right to prevent them from violating an effective blockade, renounced the right to seize enemy property on neutral vessels and the right to confiscate neutral property on enemy vessels. The Emperor furthermore declared his intention not to deliver for the time being *lettres de marque* authorizing privateering. The corresponding British declaration was a much longer document in 21 articles that was far more specific and also regulated a number of other matters (nationality of trading houses, recapture, action against Russian privateers, the forms of visit, convoy, prize jurisdiction, etc.). See for the texts of the two declarations: Ortolan, *Diplomatie de la mer*, II, 446-455. An Ordinance of neutral Sweden can be found *ibid.*, at pp. 460-463.

The main purport of the agreement was to sanction definitively the principle of "free ship, free good" and to finally abolish the doctrine of hostile infection of neutral property by its transportation on enemy ships. The same rules were laid down in small numbers of bilateral treaties which adopted as "permanent and immutable principles" the twin rules "free ships make free goods" and exemption of neutral property on board enemy ships from confiscation. See the treaties of the United States with Russia of 22 July 1854 (Martens, N.R.G.[1], XVI[1], 571; Parry, 112, 87) and with the Two Sicilies of 13 January 1855 (Martens, N.R.G.[1], XVI[1], 569; Parry, 112, 399).

The reasons which compelled the main maritime Powers to agree on the four principles set forth in the Declaration of Paris are explained in its preamble in the following paragraphs:

> "Considérant
> Que le droit maritime, en temps de guerre, a été pendant longtemps l'objet de contestations regrettables;
> Que l'incertitude du droit et des devoirs en pareille matière donne lieu, entre les neutres et les belligérants, à des divergences d'opinion qui peuvent faire naître des difficultés sérieuses et même des conflits;
> Qu'il y a avantage, par conséquence, à établir une doctrine uniforme sur un point ainsi important;
> Que les Plénipotentiaires, assemblés au Congrès de Paris, ne sauraient mieux répondre aux intentions dont leurs Gouvernements sont animés, qu'en cherchant à introduire dans les rapports internationaux des principes fixes à cet égard."

The four principles mentioned in the Rules of the Declaration of Paris were themselves worded as follows:

> "1. La course est et demeure abolie;
> 2. La pavillon neutre couvre la marchandise ennemie, à l'exception de la contrabande de guerre;
> 3. La marchandise neutre, à l'exception de la contrebande de guerre, n'est pas saisissable sous pavillon ennemi;
> 4. Les blocus, pour être obligatoires, doivent être effectifs, c'est à dire, maintenus par une force suffisante pour interdire réellement l'accés du littoral de l'ennemi."

The Declaration concluded by an invitation addressed to other Powers to accede to it and by an expression of confidence that they would in fact do so, but it was complemented by a special clause which threatened to become fatal for the operation of the new rules in the future:

> "La présente Déclaration n'est et ne sera obligatoire qu'entre les Puissances qui y ont ou qui y auront accédé."

The principles, enunciated in Rules 2 and 3, were already inserted a few months later, in a different wording, in Article 1 (1 and 2), of the treaty of Lima of 22 July 1856 between the United States and Perú (Martens, N.R.G.[1], XVII[1], 191; Parry, 115, 301), and intended, together with the repeal of certain contrary provisions of an earlier treaty of 26 July 1851, "to establish a uniform system of maritime legislation in time of war, in accordance with the present state of civilization". The two principles of Paris were recognized on a bilateral footing as "the bases of the rights of neutrals at sea" and declared "as permanent and immutable, as the true and indispensable conditions of all freedom of navigation and maritime commerce and trade". Art. 1 (1) extended the freedom from capture of enemy goods, carried on neutral vessels, to property belonging to the enemy State, and expressly laid down that even warlike articles would not be considered to be contraband of war if they were destined for the use of either of the parties. Art. IV provided for steps to be taken by them in order to induce other States to join the principles by formal declarations of adhesion.

C. THE SECOND HAGUE PEACE CONFERENCE AND THE LONDON CONFERENCE ON NAVAL WARFARE

The Second Peace Conference of 1907 produced, besides other Conventions concerning the laws of war (Nos. III, IV, VII, VIII and IX) and neutrality (Nos. V and XIII), three Conventions which belong systematically to the law of prize, *viz.*, Conventions VI (relative to the régime of enemy merchant ships at the commencement of hostilities), XI (concerning certain restrictions of the exercise of the right of capture in maritime war) and XII (relating to the establishment of an International Prize Court), whereas Convention X (for the adaptation of the principles of the Convention of Geneva to maritime war) has its roots in all three fields surveyed in Parts IX-A/B/C of this publication.

Since Convention XII of 1907 soon proved to be doomed in any case to remain a dead letter if no complementary Convention were adopted defining the substantive law of prize to be applied by the projected Court, a further Conference was convened in London in 1908 in order to achieve that aim. Although that Conference was successful and resulted in the adoption of a Declaration on Maritime Warfare, dated 26 February 1909, as carefully balanced as was thought possible at the time, this Declaration also failed to gain ratification and was finally destroyed as a codification of international prize law by the developments during World War I.

D. DEVELOPMENTS AFTER THE NAVAL CONFERENCE OF LONDON OF 1908/1909

A number of States began by incorporating without delay the rules of the London Declaration on Naval Warfare of 26 February 1909 (Martens, N.R.G.[3], VII, 39; *R.G.D.I.P.*, XVI, Doc., p. 1; B.F.S.P., 104, 242; Strupp, *Urkunden* II, 493) into their national legislation or into instructions for their Navy pending the ultimate acceptance of the new Code by the principal maritime Powers, thus intimating their intention to adopt them as the law of maritime prize of the future. So for instance, did Germany by inserting the rules in her *Prisenordnung* of 30 September 1909, published in Berlin 3 August 1914 (*R.G.Bl.* 1914, p. 275; Martens, N.R.G.[3], X, 505; *R.G.D.I.P.* 1918 (XXV), Doc., p. 1; Niemeyer's *Z.f.i.R.* 1915 (XXV), 569), and Austria-Hungary by incorporating them into the annex to the *Dienstreglement für die k.u.k. Kriegsmarine*, sanctioned by Imperial Decree of 2 May 1913 (*Dienstbuch* XXI-1 a) (*Normalverordnungsblatt für die k.u.k. Kriegsmarine*, 1913, No. 15). As a result the new rules were in actual fact in force during the wars of 1911-1913.

These wars proved to what extent the compromise solutions, reached by the London Conference of 1908-1909, had really gained a foothold and were "received" by the belligerents as part of the modern international law of prize.

As to the Italo-Turkish war of 1911-1912, the blockade by Italy of the coast of Tripolitania and Cyrenaica was conformable to Chapter I of the Declaration, and the Ottoman Empire adopted Chapter II on contraband as its guideline. Comp. Strupp's *Urkunden*, *Ergänzungsheft*, pp. 85 and 87 *et seq.* and the arbitration cases before the Permanent Court of Arbitration of 1913 relating to the seizure of the French vessels *Manouba* and *Carthage* in 1911 (Part VIII of this publication, p. 238).

As to the (first) Balkan war of 1912 the same can be said in respect of the blockade by Greece of the bight of Preveza and the temporary blockade of the island of Lemnos, and her initial adoption of the contraband provisions of 1909 (contraband lists; definition of enemy destination); later, however, she changed her attitude by first transferring fuel from the list of relative to that of absolute contraband and by subsequently abandoning the whole category of relative contraband. Comp. on the law of prize during the (first) Balkan war *Z.f.VR.* 1913 (VI), pp. 593 *et seq.* Turkey, in her turn, took the Declaration as embodying her view on modern contraband law, even in a yet more liberal manner than during the Tripoli war (C. Dupuis, *Le droit de la guerre maritime d'après les Conférences de la Haye et Londres* (Paris, 1911), p. 601), and her blockade of the Bulgarian coast was in conformity with Chapter I of the Declaration.

See for Turkey the Rules on maritime prizes of 31 January 1912 (French translation in *Bulletin I.I.I.*, V, 137) and for Greece the laws of 8/21 October 1912 on the transfer of the flag of merchant vessels and of 16/29 March 1913 on the institution of the prize court (French translation in *R.G.D.I.P.* 1914 (XXI), Doc., p. 34; *Jb.VR.*, II-2, p. 323).

Even after the outbreak of the First World War a certain optimism seemed to be justified about the final "reception" of the rules of the London Declaration by all the great Naval Powers despite the lack of ratifications. England, France and Russia indeed began, in August-September 1914, by declaring the provisions of the Declaration applicable, save for certain additions and modifications:

England: by Order in Council of 20 August 1914 (Martens, N.R.G.[3], X, 435);

France: by Decree of 25 August 1914 (*R.G.D.I.P.* 1915 (XXII), Doc., p. 23; Martens, N.R.G.[3], X, 437);

Russia: by Imperial Ukaz of September 1914, with official commentary of 9 September 1914 in Russian, explaining in what way the Rules of 27 March 1895 (French translation in *R.G.D.I.P.* 1897 (IV), Doc., p. 6; German translation in *Z.f.VR.* 1908 (II), p. 144) had to be modified in order to harmonize them with the Declaration of London;

Japan by Imperial Decree of 11 September and 6 October 1914, abolishing the Decree of 7 March 1904 (Japanese texts in a collection of "Laws and Regulations of Naval War", Tokyo);

Italy followed suit by a *Decreto Luogotenenziale* of 3 June 1915 (Martens, N.R.G.[3], X, 443; French translation in *R.G.D.I.P.* 1917 (XXIV), Doc., p. 117).

Further detailed data concerning all the national Ordinances and Instructions in force during World War I (Germany, Austria-Hungary, Belgium, Brazil, China, United States, France, Great Britain, Greece, Italy, Japan, Portugal, Romania, Russia, Siam and Turkey) can be found in my *Le droit des prises de la Grande Guerre* of 1924, Annex II at pp. 1355-1370.

The situation had in the meantime deteriorated still further, and considerably, by the issuance of a number of Reprisals Orders, beginning with a British Order in Council of 11 March 1915, followed by Orders of 10 January and 16 February 1917, paralleled by a French Decree of 1/13 March 1915, the full texts of all of which are also reproduced at pp. 55-59, respectively pp. 65-66 of my abovementioned thesis of 1917.

The Naval Declaration of London has since almost completely disappeared from sight as a formulation of the positive law of prize, although in its preliminary provision "les Puissances Signataires (étaient) d'accord pour constater que les règles contenues dans les chapitres suivants, répondent, en substance, aux principes généralement reconnus du droit international".

As a result, the international community has fallen back into the chaotic state which had characterized the legal situation prior to the Naval Conference of London.

PRIVATE CODIFICATIONS OF THE LAW OF MARITIME PRIZE

1. Institut de droit international

The rules of the law of maritime prize have repeatedly formed the subject of discussion in the *Institut de droit international.* It has indeed dealt with the rules of the law of prize more especially in the first decades of its existence.

Already at its session of The Hague, more than a century ago (1875), it championed in the form of a *vœu* (*sub* II) the principle of the inviolability of private enemy property sailing under enemy flag ("conclusion", *sub* II), subject to two self-evident exceptions (for the text see *infra*, Chapter III, *sub* A, section 1 under (a), p. 278).

This *vœu* was confirmed at its second session at Zürich (1877) in a far more positive and imperative wording ("conclusion" *sub* I):

> "La propriété privée neutre ou ennemie naviguant sous pavillon ennemi ou sous pavillon neutre est inviolable",

a declaration of principle which in the light of later experience has now the sound of a *vox clamantis in deserto*.

The same resolution of 1877 formulated in the "conclusions" II-VI clearly and concisely certain basic principles of prize law (contraband, blockade, abolition of privateering, visit and search).

The adoption of these first "conclusions" was later followed by a comprehensive series of resolutions which together were to constitute an exhaustive codification of the law of maritime prize. This great work of scientific codification was started in the 1880's. In five consecutive sessions between 1882 and 1897 the entire prize law was thus laid down in a *Règlement international des prises maritimes.* It was successively adopted at the sessions of Turin (1882), Munich (1883), Heidelberg (1887) and Copenhagen (1897). An intermediate session at Venice (1896), convened after introductory discussions in Paris (1894) and Cambridge (1895), had in the meantime dealt especially with the law of contraband.

The general *Règlement*, thus finally adopted in 1897, regulated the relations between belligerents and neutrals as well as those between belligerents *inter se*.

The *Institut* has only resumed its activity in this field in the post-codification period, *viz.*, at its session of Oxford in 1913, where it adopted a *Manuel des lois de la guerre maritime*, which, however, unlike the *Règlement* of 1882-1897, was on the one hand confined to relations between belligerents, but on the other, extended beyond the field of prize law.

The basic *Règlement* of 1882-1897 was in fact a scientific codification of the entire law of prize in 122 articles (see *Annuaire*, II, 121; III, 109; V, 131; VI, 12, 105, 129, 139, 164, 174, 213-223; VII, 185-190; VIII, 167; IX, 202-217; XIII, 102; XIV, 65; XV, 230).

A guide through the various stages in which the vast enterprise was carried out can be found in Ernest Lehr's *Tableau général de l'organisation, des travaux et du personnel de l'Institut de droit international pendant les deux premières périodes décennales de son existence (1873-1892)* (Paris, 1893), and in Albéric Rolin's *Tableau général de l'organisation, des travaux et du personnel de l'Institut pendant la période décennale 1904-1914* (The Hague-Paris, 1919), the latter of which also gives a retrospective survey over the whole period 1875-1914 at pp. 166 *et seq.* under the Nos. IX, X, XII, XIII and XVI. See also Hans Wehberg's *Tableau général des résolutions (1873-1956)*, footnote at p. 209.

Further particulars concerning this basic scientific codification will be given in Chapter III of this volume at their appropriate place. I limit myself here to reproducing the headings of the sub-divisions of the *Règlement* in order to illustrate its compass and the method of its exposition of the matter.

I. Dispositons générales (§§ 1-9)
II. Dispositions spéciales
   1. De l'arrêt (§§ 10-13)
   2. De la visite (§§ 14-18)
   3. De la recherche (§§ 19-22)
   4. De la saisie (§ 23)
   5. De la nationalité du navire, de la cargaison et de l'équipage (§§ 24-29)
   6. Des transports interdits durant la guerre (§§ 30-34)
   7. Du blocus (§§ 35-44)
   8. Des formalités qui suivent la saisie (§§ 45-57)
   9. Du transport du navire saisi en un port de mer (§§ 58-62)
   10. De l'organisation et de la procédure du tribunal d'instruction des prises dans le port d'arrivée (§§ 63-84)
   11. De l'organisation et de la procédure du tribunal des prises maritimes (§§ 85-99)
   12. De l'organisation et de la procédure du tribunal international des prises maritimes (§§ 100-109)
   13. Du droit matériel concernant le jugement de prise et de reprise
       A. Procès de prise (§§ 110-118)
       B. Procès de reprise (§§ 119-122)

2. *The Harvard Research Draft (1939)*

Another scientific effort to formulate the rules of modern prize law is of much later date. It was made in the United States at the end of the inter-war period (1939). Just before the Second World War broke out, a private Research Group in International Law of the Harvard Law School prepared and produced a detailed Draft Convention on the Rights and Duties of Neutral States in Naval and Aerial War. It was published (with a commentary) in a Special Supplement (Codification) of the *A.J.I.L.*, July 1939 (vol. 33), pp. 167-817.

The draft was not confined to neutrality law proper, as it contains a great number of rules which in my systematic lay-out belong to the law of prize. There were therefore reasons to spread the contents of the Draft, which again from a systematic point of view, I must confess, makes a somewhat disorderly impression, over Parts IX-B (vol. X) and the present Part IX-C of my publication. I did that therefore in this manner, in that I quoted the provisions concerning the law of neutrality proper—forming Articles 4-48 and 87 of the Draft—in § 4 of section 3 of Chapter VI (pp. 267-274) of my preceding Part IX-B (vol. X) on Neutrality Law. What remains to be surveyed in the present Part IX-C is consequently the aggregate of rules of prize law in naval war, contained in Articles 49-82, and of rules of prize law in aerial war, contained in a number of dispersed provisions. All these provisions together would have constituted a new international code of prize law, and might have governed the events during World War II if they had been drafted earlier and if this private codification had been adopted at an international conference and had then been laid down in a law-making treaty, subsequently ratified by the contracting States.

The systematic arrangement of the rules on naval prize law in the Draft Convention deviates considerably from that applied in the Declaration of London of 1909. The subject matters are indeed grouped in Part II as follows:

section 6 (Arts. 49-63), Visit, search and capture, spread over five sub-sections: A. General (Arts. 49-55), B. Neutral convoys (Arts. 56-58), C. Unconvoyed certified vessels (Arts. 59-60), D. Uncertified vessels (Arts. 61-62) and E. Rules of prize law (Art. 63);

section 7 (Arts. 64-66), Unneutral service;

section 8 (Art. 67), Transfer of flag;

section 9 (Arts. 68-82), Maritime blockade.

These Articles are complemented by a provision on "Quotas" (Art. 47 in Part II of the Draft, section 5, *sub* C), which is balanced on the ridge between the laws of neutrality and prize, but which to my mind belongs more typically to the latter field.

Art. 63 of the Draft makes, so to speak, an inventory of the rules of substantive prize law. It lists the provisions in yet another different order, as it deals under (*a*)-(*d*) with the breach of a blockade, under (*e*)-(*f*) with the transport of contraband and under (*g*)-(*n*) with a medley of subjects: denial of the principle of infection of neutral goods by enemy property; preemption of non-contraband goods; the rule "free ship, free good"; damages due in the absence of a "probable cause" for interference; illegal diversion of merchant ships to an enemy port, and postal matters.

I will reproduce the prize law provisions of the Draft below, not in the order in which they are arranged there, but in the same order as I have applied in my systematic exposition of the law of prize in Chapter III of this Part IX-C. From that survey it will also emerge which of the subjects are not covered by the Draft.

The Draft reflects on the whole the familiar picture of traditional provisions of prize law, but makes a somewhat complicated impression as a result of a constant distinction in Arts. 41 *et seq.* and 59 *et seq.* between certified and uncertified (neutral) vessels. Art. 41 indeed suggests the introduction with regard to sea-going vessels in wartime of a new and fairly complicated system of "certificates of neutrality", in accordance with a set of ten Rules, laid down in an Annex II, and subsequent Articles draw certain consequences from the introduction of that system, prescribing, for instance, a public notice of departure before clearance, with details concerning the time of sailing, the vessel's destination, her cargo, etc. Those provisions entail a difference in treatment of certified and uncertified neutral ships in respect of the belligerent rights of visit and search.

Arts. 41, 42, 44 and 48 run as follows:

"(41) A neutral State may issue certificates of neutrality in accordance with the rules laid down in Annex II to this Convention.

(42) (1) Prior to the clearance of a vessel with a certificate of neutrality from its territory, a neutral State shall give a public notice of departure containing: (*a*) The name of the vessel, its tonnage, time of departure, approximate route, destination, probable time of arrival thereat and general description of the ship and its cargo; (*b*) If the vessel is convoyed, an adequate identification of the convoying warship or warships.

(2) If the announced departure of the vessel is delayed, or if other announced details are altered, a corrected notice shall be issued.

(3) A certified copy of the notice shall be given to the master of each vessel named therein.

(4) A neutral State may also give publicity by radio to notices of departure. Upon the request of a belligerent, a neutral State shall use the radio facilities at its disposal to bring to the knowledge of belligerent warships or aircraft at sea notices of departure, but such messages may not be sent in code.

(44) A neutral State shall require vessels to which it issues certificates of neutrality, and its warships while engaged in convoying certified vessels, to observe the following rules: (*a*) All such vessels and warships shall be painted white, and shall have painted prominently on both sides of the ship's hull and superstructure amidships, their national colors in vertical stripes not less than one meter wide. Similar stripes shall be painted horizontally on the decks or superstructure in a manner readily distinguishable by aircraft. (*b*) All such vessels and warships while at sea shall continuously display their flags and the usual running lights, and shall be equipped with searchlights or floodlights casting special illumination upon the flag and upon the vertically and horizontally painted stripes.

(48) (1) A neutral State may also issue a certificate of neutrality to a vessel covered by an agreement made by the neutral State with both belligerents.

(2) Such an agreement may specify the commodities and define the quantities thereof which may be shipped from the neutral State by private persons to a belligerent or from a belligerent to a neutral State under guarantee of safe passage.

(3) Such an agreement may be made for specific voyages or for specified periods of time. It may provide for cancellation upon notice in case of fraud or violation of its terms.

(4) Such an agreement may specify that certificates of neutrality may be issued even though the shipment be made in a vessel flying a belligerent flag.

(5) Beyond supervision of loading and certification, the neutral State is not responsible for the execution of such an agreement."

Arts. 45 and 46 caution against the departure of uncertified merchant ships and against fraud:

"(45) A neutral State shall use the means at its disposal to prevent uncertified vessels from departing from its territory with any simulation of the distinctive markings required of certified merchant vessels.

(46) (1) If an uncertified neutral vessel adopts the distinctive markings of a certified vessel, or if a certified neutral vessel violates the privileges of a certificate by taking on board, subsequent to certification, any goods or persons except in the case of salvage at sea, or by going voluntarily to a destination other than that specified in the certificate, the neutral State whose flag the vessel is entitled to fly shall: (*a*) If the vessel is within its territory, provide that the vessel be sequestered for the duration of the war or forfeited to the State; (*b*) If the vessel is not within its territory cancel the registration thereof and immediately give notice of the fact to the belligerents and to other neutral States. If the vessel subsequently comes within its territory, the neutral State shall proceed under paragraph (*a*) of this article. If such vessel is not forfeited under paragraph (*a*), it may not subsequently, during the war, be granted registration or a certificate of neutrality by the same or by any other neutral State.

(2) If the flag State does not take the action required by paragraph (*a*) or (*b*) of this article, any other neutral State may decline to admit that vessel to its territory during the war, or, if it enters, may sequester it for the duration of the war.

Articles 43 and 44, which are embedded between those two groups of provisions, deal, *inter alia*, with ships sailing under neutral convoy, see *infra*, p. 144.

A, to my mind displaced, Art. 47, slipped in between the others, belongs to the law of contraband: it suggests the introduction of a new semi-obligatory quota system with a view to avoiding disputes arising from the application of the doctrine of continuous voyage to the transportation of contraband goods to neutral ports. I have already quoted it in my exposé in Chapter VI, section 4, § 2 of Part IX-B of this publication on the law of neutrality, p. 283.

Further Arts. 59-61 define the above-mentioned differentiation in treatment between certified and uncertified neutral vessels with regard to belligerent visit and search, whereupon comp. *infra*, p. 143.

Arranging my survey of the contents of the prize law provisions in the Draft as indicated above, I will begin with a few general issues.

1. Who is qualified to exercise the right of visit and seizure?

"Art. 49 (2). A belligerent may exercise the right of visit and search only by a commissioned warship or commissioned military aircraft. Belligerent armed merchant vessels or armed non-military aircraft may not exercise the right of visit and search.

Art. 50. Privateering is and remains abolished."

Arts. 54 and 55 recognize the right of submarines and aircraft to exercise the right of prize.

2. When may it be exercised? No provision.
3. Where may it be exercised?

"Art. 49 (1). A belligerent has the right of visit and search on and over the high seas and on or over territorial waters that are not neutral.

4. What objects are liable to its exercise?

The Draft is not specific about this. It only contains a sidelong reference to armed merchant vessels in Art. 2 *jis.* Arts. 19 and 32-39, which systematically belong rather to the law of neutrality: belligerent merchant vessels, whether surface or submarine, shall, if armed for defense or offense, be assimilated to warships, but only for the purposes of the Articles 19 and 32-39 (relating to their admission to, and stay in, neutral waters).

Art. 55 lays down that

"In their action with regard to enemy armed merchant vessels, belligerent warships, whether surface or submarine, and belligerent military aircraft are governed by the rules applicable to their action with regard to enemy warships."

On the enemy or neutral character of prizes the Draft is very summary.

As regards ships, it does not define the criterion or criteria of their character and only deals with the case of the transfer of enemy vessels to a neutral flag. See Art. 67:

"A prize court may treat as an enemy vessel:

(a) A vessel transferred after the outbreak of war from the flag of a belligerent to the flag of a neutral State unless it is proved that such transfer was not made in order to evade capture by the enemy. But the court may decline to receive such proof:

(1) If the transfer has been made while the vessel was on a voyage or was in blockaded territory;

(2) If a right to repurchase or recover the vessel is reserved to the vendor;

(3) If the requirements of the municipal law governing the right to fly the flag under which the vessel is sailing, have not been fulfilled.

(b) A vessel transferred within thirty days before the outbreak of war, if it is proved that such transfer was made in anticipation of the outbreak of war and for the purpose of evading capture by an enemy of the State from whose flag the vessel was transferred."

Neither does the Draft define the exact criterion of the enemy or neutral character of cargoes, although Art. 63 *sub* j mentions "enemy ownership or origin", nor does it mention the old doctrine concerning produce of the enemy soil.

A. *Substantive prize law.* Art. 21 regulates the belligerents' asserted right to requisition neutral vessels, privately-owned or operated (angary), but that right lies outside the domain of prize law.

Resort by a belligerent to acts of reprisal to the prejudice of neutrals is prohibited in express terms by Arts. 23 and 24, running as follows:

(23) "A belligerent is not relieved of its duty to respect the rights of a neutral State as provided in this Convention, even when engaged in acts of reprisal or retaliation for illegal acts of its enemy".

(24) "A belligerent may not resort to acts of reprisal or retaliation against a neutral State except for illegal acts of the latter, and a State is not to be charged with failure to perform its duties as a neutral state because it has not succeeded in inducing a belligerent to respect its rights as a neutral State".

These two provisions are a basic refutation of entirely unjustified belligerent pretensions to the contrary.

1. *Enemy property. Exemptions from condemnation*
   Art. 63 exempts *sub* (*m*) and (*n*) postal correspondence from confiscation.
2. *Enemy goods on neutral ships and neutral goods on enemy ships*
   Art. 63 excludes *sub* (*g*) the infection of neutral cargo by the enemy character of the transporting vessel, and proclaims *sub* (*j*) the principle "free ship, free goods".
3. *Carriage of contraband*
   The Draft introduces in a long Art. 47 a novel system of quota which is intended to preclude the many disputes which have arisen in the past as a consequence of the capture of contraband goods on their way to neutral ports by the application of the rule of continuous voyage. The text of that Art. 47 is worth reproduction:

"(1) A quota limitation is required for imports into a neutral State if demanded by a belligerent in accordance with the provisions of this article.

(2) A belligerent may demand that a neutral State publish monthly data as to its imports, their amount, value, disposition or ultimate utilization, and data as to its exports, their amount, value and destination, if there are being imported into the neutral State goods which

(a) are publicly listed by any of the belligerents as of use in war; and
(b) are of a kind which the enemy of the demanding belligerent imports directly or indirectly; and
(c) are either imported into the neutral State for export in their original or in a processed state, or imported in amounts exceeding normal peace time imports, taking into account normal expansion not due to supplying war demands in belligerent markets.

(3) A neutral State shall at once proceed with the publication as demanded.

(4) However, if the neutral State does not agree that factual conditions exist justifying the demand, it shall so notify the demanding belligerent. At the same time it shall designate one of its nationals who, with a person designated by the belligerent, shall choose a national of a third State; and these three persons shall constitute an arbitral board to determine whether the factual conditions exist justifying the demand. If a majority of the board decides that the belligerent has made out a *prima facie* case under paragraphs (a), (b) and (c) of section (2) of this article, the neutral State shall continue the publication as demanded; if a majority of the board decides that the belligerent has not made out such a *prima facie* case, the neutral State may cease publication.

(5) If the belligerent is not satisfied by the neutral State's published statements that goods imported by the neutral State are not reaching its enemy in their original or in a processed state, it may notify all neutral States that it demands the fixing of a quota in accordance with Annex III to this Convention.

(6) The publication of data as required under section (2) of this article may be dispensed with if the neutral State consents to the fixing of a quota under section (5)."

The Draft includes further the following rules on the sanction of condemnation:

Art. 63:
"(*e*) Cargo destined for belligerent territory either directly or through a neutral port, may be condemned in so far as it is composed of arms, ammunition or implements of war, or of other goods shipped in violation of a neutral State's prohibition under Article 11. If more than half of the cargo by value, weight, volume or freight is composed of goods which may be condemned, the rest of the cargo and the vessel are similarly subject to condemnation.

(*f*) Any commodity in a cargo destined for a neutral State upon whose imports of that commodity a quota has been fixed under Article 47, but not included within a portion of the quota allocation to the State from which the commodity was shipped, may be condemned."

4. *Blockade.*

The rules on blockade, on the other hand, are very detailed:

Art. 60:
"Notwithstanding the provisions of Article 59, if an unconvoyed certified vessel is found within a blockade zone, the belligerent may seize it and conduct or send it to one of its ports. Under no circumstances, except as provided in Article 53, may a certified vessel be fired upon or destroyed."

Art. 63, *sub* (*a-d*):
"A prize court shall be bound by the following rules:

(*a*) A vessel which intended to run a blockade, may be condemned together with its cargo.

(*b*) Cargo destined for a blockaded port by sea, may be condemned; the vessel may also be condemned if the destination of the cargo was known to the owner, charterer or master of the vessel.

(*c*) The presence of an uncertified vessel within a blockade zone is presumptive evidence of an intention to break the blockade; the presumption may be rebutted by proof that neither the vessel nor the cargo was in fact destined for a blockaded port or place by sea.

(*d*) A certified vessel seized in a blockade zone may be condemned together with the cargo on board, unless it is proved that the vessel entered the blockade zone by mistake or in distress."

Art. 68:
"A belligerent may blockade the ports and coasts belonging to or occupied by its enemy, but may not bar access to the ports or to the coasts of neutral States."

Art. 69:
"A belligerent may support the enforcement of a blockade by proclaiming a blockade zone. Where the coast of a neutral State adjoins a belligerent coast, the limit of the blockade zone shall follow a projection of the frontier between the neutral State and the belligerent but shall not be such as to hinder access to neutral ports. In no case may a blockade zone close international straits."

Art. 70:
"A belligerent may not establish on the high seas outside of a blockade zone a barred zone or other area however described in which it seeks to impose special prohibition, restriction or regulation upon the passage of neutral vessels. However, a belligerent may require neutral vessels in the immediate vicinity of its armed forces not to make use of their radio transmitting apparatus except for S O S calls while in the immediate vicinity of such forces."

Art. 71:

"Blockading forces, subject to the provisions of Article 54, may control the movement of all vessels and persons within a blockade zone."

Art. 72:

"A blockade in order to be binding must be effective, that is to say, it must be maintained by a naval or aërial force sufficient really to prevent access to and egress from the blockaded territory by sea. The question whether a blockade is effective is a question of fact, but no blockade shall be considered effective unless surface or submarine vessels or aircraft of the blockading belligerent are actually patrolling or cruising off the blockaded territory."

Art. 73:

"For the purpose of establishment and maintenance of a blockade, a belligerent must use surface or submarine vessels or aircraft, and may also use fixed obstacles and anchored automatic contact mines which become harmless on becoming unanchored."

Art. 74:

"(1) A blockade must be applied impartially to all vessels, including those of the blockading belligerent.

(2) Subject to Article 76, if a belligerent licenses or knowingly permits its own or any other vessels to pass through the blockade, the blockade is regarded as raised."

Art. 75:

"A blockade is not regarded as raised if the blockading forces are temporarily driven off by bad weather."

Art. 76:

"In circumstances of distress, acknowledged by an authority of the blockading forces, a neutral vessel may enter a blockaded place and subsequently leave it, provided that it has neither discharged nor shipped any cargo there."

Art. 77:

"A blockade, in order to be binding, must be declared in accordance with Article 78 (1) and notified in accordance with Article 79."

Art. 78:

"(1) A declaration of blockade is made either by the belligerent or by the naval authorities acting in its name. It specifies:
(a) The time when the blockade begins;
(b) The geographical limits of the coast blockaded and of the blockade zone;
(c) The time to be allowed for the departure of neutral vessels.

(2) If the blockading belligerent or the naval authorities acting in its name, fail to establish the blockade in accordance with the declaration, the declaration is void and a new declaration is necessary in order to make the blockade operative."

Art. 79:

"A declaration of blockade is notified:

(a) to neutral States, by the blockading belligerent;

(b) to the local authorities of the territory covered by the declaration of blockade, by the officer commanding the blockading force."

Art. 80:

"The voluntary raising of a blockade, as also any restrictions in the limits of the blockade which may be introduced, must be notified in the manner prescribed by Article 79."

Art. 81:

"A belligerent may capture an uncertified neutral vessel for breach of blockade at any time during the vessel's voyage to or from a port or place against which an effective blockade existed at the time when the vessel commenced its voyage, provided that:
(*a*) The liability of a neutral vessel to capture for breach of blockade is contingent on its knowledge, actual or presumptive, of the blockade;
(*b*) Failing proof to the contrary, knowledge of the blockade is presumed if the vessel left a

neutral port subsequently to the notification of the blockade to the State to which such port belongs, if such notification was made in sufficient time."

Art. 82:

"(1) If a vessel otherwise liable to seizure for breach of blockade does not know or cannot be presumed to know of the blockade, notification must be made to the vessel itself by an officer of the visiting warship. This notification must be entered in the vessel's log book, with indication of the day and the hour, and of the geographical position of the vessel at the time.

(2) A neutral vessel which leaves a blockaded port must be allowed to pass free if, through the negligence of the officer commanding the blockading force, no declaration of blockade has been notified to the local authorities or if in the declaration as notified no time for departure has been indicated."

5. *Unneutral service.*

The provisions on "hostile assistance" are preceded by an Art. 62 to the following effect:

"(1) A belligerent may arrest on board an uncertified neutral vessel and hold as a prisoner of war:
(*a*) A person incorporated in the armed forces of the enemy;
(*b*) A person travelling to the territory of the enemy or to territory under enemy occupation, in order to join the armed forces of the enemy;
(*c*) A person of enemy nationality travelling as an agent of the enemy for the purpose of assisting its military or naval operations, provided he is not a member of a diplomatic mission or a person charged with a diplomatic function.
(2) A person arrested under this article may be removed from the vessel on which he is found, or if the vessel is brought in for adjudication, may be brought into port on the vessel. If the neutral State whose flag the vessel flies, disputes the liability to arrest of the person concerned, the belligerent shall afford to the neutral State an opportunity to have the question promptly determined in a court of the belligerent."

Art. 64:

"A belligerent may treat as an enemy merchant vessel:
(*a*) A neutral vessel under the orders or immediate control of an agent of the enemy, or sailing under the convoy of enemy warships;
(*b*) A neutral vessel in the exclusive employment of the enemy;
(*c*) A neutral vessel on a voyage specially undertaken with a view to the transportation of individual passengers who are incorporated in the armed forces of the enemy, or with a view to the transmission of intelligence in the interest of the enemy;
(*d*) A neutral vessel transporting, with the knowledge of either the owner, the charterer, or the master, a military detachment of the enemy, or one or more persons who, in the course of the voyage, with the consent of either the owner, the charterer or the master, directly assist the operations of the enemy."

Art. 65:

"A belligerent may treat as an enemy warship:
(*a*) A neutral vessel taking a direct part in hostilities on the side of the enemy;
(*b*) A neutral vessel exclusively engaged at the time in the transportation of enemy troops."

Art. 66:

"Articles 64 and 65 (*b*) do not apply if the vessel began its voyage before the outbreak of war, but in such case the vessel may be required to return to a neutral port."

6. *Reserved navigation.* No mention is made of this old ground of confiscation.

7. *Encroachments on the policing rights of the belligerents.* See Art. 53 (2):

"If the vessel when summoned does not stop, attempts to escape, or resists visit and search, it may be compelled to stop by force and the belligerent shall not be responsible for resulting injury to life or property,"

and further *sub* B, 2.

B. Formalities to be observed in the exercise of the rights of visit and capture

1. *Ship's papers.* Comp. my above remarks on certified and uncertified neutral vessels (Arts. 41 *et seq.*; 59 *et seq.*).

2. *Visit and search.*

Art. 51:

"A certified merchant vessel at sea shall respond to radio or other inquiries from any public vessel, giving full details of its name, flag, certificate, route and destination."

Art. 53:

"(1) In order to exercise the right of visit and search, a warship signals the vessel as by radio or by firing a blank charge. If such notice does not suffice, the warship may fire a projectile across the bow of the vessel. Before this or simultaneously, the warship shall hoist its flag, above which at night a light shall be placed. The vessel shall reply to the signal by hoisting its flag and by stopping at once. Thereupon the warship sends to the vessel a boat manned by an officer and by unarmed men of whom not more than two shall accompany the officer on board the vessel. The boarding party may examine the ship's papers and may interrogate persons on board. It may inspect the cargo but the cargo may not be broken open or removed. Postal correspondence may not be opened or removed".

"(2) If the vessel when summoned does not stop, attempts to escape, or resists visit and search, it may be compelled to stop by force and the belligerent shall not be responsible for resulting injury to life or property".

"(3) If the visit and search gives rise to a reasonable suspicion that the vessel or its cargo is subject to condemnation or preemption, the vessel may be captured and brought or sent into port for prize proceedings".

Art. 59 (2):

"If the vessel is visited and is found to carry a certificate of neutrality, it shall be allowed to proceed immediately without further hindrance, but the officer of the warship shall endorse a memorandum of the visit upon the certificate."

Art. 61 (1), 1st sentence:

"If a vessel does not display the distinctive colors and markings required of a certified vessel under Article 44, or fails to produce a certificate of neutrality, and if the belligerent as a result of visit and search has reasonable grounds for belief that the vessel or its cargo is subject to condemnation or preemption, the belligerent may capture the vessel and conduct or send it to one of its ports for prize proceedings."

Art. 61 (2):

"If sea conditions make it impossible to launch a small boat for the purpose of examining the vessel's papers, the warship may by radio require the vessel to proceed under its escort and under instructions as to speed upon an indicated route until the sea moderates. The vessel shall display at night the usual lights and failure to do so or any attempt at resistance or escape justifies the warship in firing upon the vessel and destroying it."

Art. 61 (3):

"In no case may a warship divert a vessel to port to facilitate search unless the vessel has been captured in accordance with the provisions of this article".

3. *Possible measures following visit and search.* Art. 49 (3):

"After a captured vessel is in port, or if a neutral vessel is voluntarily in port, the vessel may be searched by the public authorities of the belligerent; but a neutral vessel may not be diverted to port to facilitate search except as provided in Art. 61 (3)".

4. *Sailing under neutral convoy.* Arts. 43, 56-58.

Art. 43:

"A neutral State may convoy by its warships its own merchant vessels or those of any other neutral State; provided that all the vessels so convoyed have certificates of neutrality issued or countersigned by the convoying State; and provided further that no vessel shall be permitted to join the convoyed vessels after they leave port."

Art. 56:

"A belligerent warship may not visit and search vessels under neutral convoy. The commander of a convoy shall, upon request of the commander of a belligerent warship, give, by radio or otherwise, all information as to the character of the vessels and their cargoes which could be obtained by visit and search."

Art. 57:

"If the commander of the belligerent warship has reason to suspect that the convoy includes an uncertified vessel, he may communicate his suspicion to the commander of the convoy. In such a case it is for the commander of the convoy alone to conduct an investigation; he must state the result of such investigation in a memorandum, of which a copy is furnished to the officer of the warship. If, in the opinion of the commander of the convoy, the facts thus stated prove the correctness of the belligerent's charges, the protection of the convoy must be withdrawn from the vessel concerned."

Art. 58:

"If the commander of the convoy and the commander of the belligerent warship are not agreed as to the character of the convoyed vessels, the former shall, upon arrival at the neutral port of destination, give a copy of his memorandum with the objections of the commander of the warship to an official of the neutral State of discharge. The neutral State of discharge shall forthwith provide for the procedure prescribed in Rule 10 of Annex II."

5. *Destruction of prizes.*

Art. 54 (3):

"In particular, except in the case of persistent refusal to stop on being duly summoned, or of active resistance to visit or search, a warship, whether surface or submarine, or a military aircraft, may not sink or render incapable of navigation an unarmed merchant vessel without having first placed passengers, crew and ship's papers in a place of safety. For this purpose the ship's boats are not regarded as a place of safety unless the safety of the passengers and crew is assured, in the existing sea and weather conditions, by the proximity of land, or by the presence of another vessel which is in a position to take them on board."

Art. 61 (1), 2nd sentence:

"If to conduct or send the captured vessel to port would involve danger to the safety of the captor or to the success of the operations in which he is engaged at the time, the captured vessel may be destroyed subject to compliance with the rules laid down in

Article 54. In such cases prize proceedings shall be held on the basis of the ship's papers and other lawful evidence."

6. *Joint capture*. No rules

7. *Recapture, Prize salvage*. No rules.

C. Prize jurisdiction

The only provisions in the Draft which concern the adjudication of prizes relate to the award of damages in cases of unjust treatment.

Art. 63:
(k) When a vessel has been captured and brought into port for prize proceedings and the prize court finds that there was no probable cause for the capture, damages must be paid for losses suffered by the vessel and by the owners of the cargo.
(l) A vessel which has been diverted to port in violation of the provisions of Article 61 (3), regardless of the nature of its voyage or of its cargo, shall be released and the capturing belligerent must pay damages for the delay."

CHAPTER III

THE PRE-CODIFICATION PERIOD UP TO 1907-1909

PREFACE

As I have set out in my General Introduction, p. 7 above, the systematic exposé in this Chapter will be arranged in three main Parts, that under A exposing the substantive law of prize, that under B describing the modalities of the exercise of the belligerents' rights, and that under C regarding prize jurisdiction. These three main Parts will be preceded by two preliminary sections devoted to the discussion of themes of a general character which are of equal interest for all three without belonging systematically to any one of them in particular. The first of these two preliminary sections relates to the quadruple question by whom, when, where and against what objects the right of capture may be exercised, and is therefore presented under the comprehensive heading General issues; the second is that of the problem of the enemy or non-enemy character of prizes. Each of the three main Parts will also be further divided into a number of sections relative to the great many issues which together constitute the law of prize in naval warfare.

Applying this system of arrangement and before entering upon the subject-matter of Part A, setting out the various specific grounds on which a belligerent State is, or deems itself to be, entitled to seize foreign property under the law of prize, I will accordingly discuss in my preliminary section I the quadruple group of general issues and in my preliminary section II the problem of the (non-)enemy character of prizes. When I use the term "foreign" property here, I have in view principally enemy and neutral property, but also the property of allied subjects. Moreover, some countries (mainly Great Britain, but also Japan, Arts. 36 and 41 of her Regulations relating to Captures at Sea of 7 March 1904) apply the international law of prize even to the property of nationals, a practice which in other legal systems falls within the realm of municipal, in particular penal law.

Preliminary Section I. GENERAL ISSUES

What I intend to do in the present first preliminary section is to set out:

Section 1. Who are qualified to exercise the right of prize;
Section 2. When such exercise is permitted;
Section 3. Where the right of prize may be exercised;
Section 4. What objects are liable to such exercise.

These are the four headings under which these general issues will be discussed.

The same quadruple set of questions formed the object of discussion and regulation by the *Institut de droit international* in the first years of its existence. The following survey illustrates the ideas then adopted.

By whom?

Zürich (1877), "conclusion" IV: "La course est interdite".

Turin (1882), *Règlement international*, §§ 1-3: "Les navires de guerre et les forces militaires d'Etats belligérants sont seuls autorisés à exercer le droit de prise ... La course est interdite", but "L'armement en course demeure permis à titre de rétorsion contre les belligérants qui ne respectent pas ce principe. En ce cas il est interdit de délivrer des commissions à des étrangers."

When?

Zürich (1877), "conclusion" V: "Le droit de visite peut être exercé depuis le moment où la déclaration de guerre a été notifiée jusqu'à la conclusion de la paix. Il est suspendu pendant une trève ou un armistice."

Turin (1882), *Règlement international*, § 5: "Le droit de prise entre belligérants ne s'ouvre qu'après le commencement des hostilités. Il cesse durant l'armistice et avec les préliminaires de la paix. A l'égard des neutres le droit de prise ne peut être exercé qu'après que les belligérants leur ont notifié l'existence de la guerre."

Where?

Zürich (1877), "conclusion" V: "(Le droit de visite) peut s'exercer dans les eaux des belligérants comme dans la haute mer ..."

Turin (1882), *Règlement international*, §§ 8-9: "Le droit de prise ne peut être exercé que dans les eaux des belligérants et en haute mer; il ne peut pas être exercé dans les eaux neutres ni dans les eaux qui sont expressément, par traité, mises à l'abri des faits de guerre. Le belligérant ne peut pas non plus poursuivre dans les eaux des deux dernières espèces une attaque commencée.—Les prises faites dans les eaux neutres, ou dans les eaux qui sont mises, par traité, à l'abri des faits de guerre, sont nulles. Les navires ou objets capturés doivent être livrés à l'Etat neutre ou riverain pour être restitués par cet Etat à leur propriétaire primitif. En outre, l'Etat du capteur est responsable de tous les dommages et pertes."

Against what objects?

Zürich (1877), "conclusion" V: "(Le droit de visite ne peut s'exercer) sur les vaisseaux de guerre neutres ni sur ceux qui appartiennent ostensiblement à un Etat neutre."

Turin (1882), *Règlement international*, § 14: rule to the same effect.

Enemy warships and State ships are not subject to the exercise of the right of prize proper, because they fall automatically to the capturing belligerent as spoils of war.

Section 1. WHO ARE QUALIFIED TO EXERCISE THE RIGHT OF PRIZE?

Introductory

The first general issue to be discussed under this heading is to define who were the persons qualified to act as captors. Since captures of ships and sea-borne goods by a belligerent are essentially acts of State, it is self-evident that attention must in the first place be paid to State organs. Amongst those State organs warships—in the old English terminology "King's ships"—were naturally foremost, but other State organs, such as port authorities, customs officers and such-like, were from early days also competent to carry out seizures in prize.

Equally important was, however, the rôle which the practice of privateering, now obsolete, has played in the course of the centuries.

Unlike the present day legal situation when the exercise of the right of visit and capture by a belligerent is reserved to State organs, in particular warships, this issue was dominated in earlier centuries, in this case even up to the Crimean War, by the legitimate practice of privateering. Since this practice is, at least in principle, now entirely a matter of the past, I will in this section give a separate exposé of this historical subject. However, before entering upon it, I must make a few introductory remarks on the conceptual delimitation of privateering towards four other practices that have played an historic rôle, *viz.*, (*a*) piracy; (*b*) the grant of letters of reprisal or letters of marque; (*c*) the *ad hoc* conversion of merchant ships into State warships; (*d*) the arming of merchant vessels.

What then remains to be examined is the possibility that other actors than State organs and privateers were exceptionally allowed to act as captors.

These preliminary remarks explain the order in which the question of who may exercise the right of prize will be discussed.

A. State organs

1. *Warships and other State ships*

The task of exercising the right of visit and seizure of ships and sea-borne goods was in the first place entrusted to "King's ships", warships or other naval units of the State. Occasionally other State vessels also acted as captors, in particular in the role of recaptors. Thus, the British *Helen* [1801] (3 C.Rob., 224; Roscoe, I, 299) was recaptured by a British revenue cutter, the *Robert*, but this vessel carried a letter of marque and consequently acted on the footing of a private ship of war. This case was one in which doubts arose about the legal status of a capturing vessel as either a King's ship or a privateer.

In other cases it was dubious whether the capturing vessel was a warship or a merchant vessel. A type of vessel which has given rise to this doubt about her legal status under the law of prize in England was a transport. This status was questionable from two different point of view: (*a*) Could, from the active aspect, a transport participate in capture operations and then lay claim to a share in the proceeds of the prize? (*b*) Was she, from the passive aspect, to be considered as an object of the law of prize proper or rather as susceptible of direct appropriation by the captor as booty of war on the same footing with warships?

On the first question, which alone belongs to the subject discussed in the present preliminary section 1, see further *sub* C, section 7, *infra*, pp. 656-659.

The second question is not relevant here and will be set out in section 4 *infra*, pp. 197-203.

In France, the distinction between a warship and a merchant vessel arose in respect of the American armed vessel the *Pégou* [*an* VIII] (de Pistoye and Duverdy, II, 51), but in that case again not from its active, but from its passive aspect of her treatment in case of capture. Comp. therefore section 4, *infra*, pp. 198-199.

According to a footnote in Roscoe, I, 233, the Advocate of the Admiralty declared that in the case of the capture of *Negapatnam* he had received the authority of the Admiral of the fleet Lord Hood to state, as his opinion, "that the permission of the Admiral of the fleet to merchant vessels to wear pennants was considered as an act adopting them into the King's service for that occasion". However, in the case of *The Cape of Good Hope and its dependencies* [1799-1802] (2 C.Rob., 274; Roscoe, I, 227 *et seq.*, at p. 233), Sir William Scott denied that the permission to wear the pennant gave the vessel concerned the character of a King's ship: such a vessel was not to be considered in a military character, but as a transport; the mere circumstance that she had before carried pennants, having taken them down only out of respect to the King's ships and that she desired to hoist them again could not be held "to be a sufficient proof that she was by that act taken and adopted into the military character." Sir W. Scott could attribute no such effect to a mere act of civility and condescension. Neither could he admit that the employment of vessels in carrying provisions and military stores on shore amounted to their employment in military service beyond the common extent of transport duty, nor that this conclusion could be drawn from their receiving military orders.

Reference may, in this context, also be made to the *Rebeckah* case [1799] (1 C.Rob., 227; Roscoe, I, 118), one of the instances of a capture made by the crews of boats sent from a naval station. The issue in that case was whether the vessel so captured was to be treated as prize or as "droit of the Admiralty". For the discussion of that question I must refer again to the exposé *sub* C, section 7, *infra*, pp. 653-658. In this judgment the Court examined two earlier cases, invoked by the parties, but dismissed them both as binding precedents. The first case bore a slight resemblance to that of the *Rebeckah*, *viz.*, the *Trautmansdorff*, decided by the Lords of Appeal on 1 August 1795 (cited in Roscoe, I, 119) against the Admiralty's claim to the prize: it concerned a capture made in the open sea off the bold shore of St. Helena, with regard to which it remained doubtful in what manner possession of the vessel was first taken, either by boats sent from the warship *Powerful*, or by the act of firing a shot from the fort on the island. The second case was the much older one of the *Nostra Signora del Carmen* (cited in footnote *a* at p. 119), captured in the port of Gibraltar by its garrison in 1708 by order of the Lieutenant-General of the colony: she was condemned to the Lord High Admiral on 25 June 1708 as a "perquisite of Admiralty" (on this qualification comp. again *sub* C, section 7, *infra*, p. 656).

Another unusual instance was the occupation of a neutral merchant vessel, at anchor in the vicinity of a stranded British frigate, the *Apollo*, by the latter's officer and men, see the case of the *Jonge Jacobus Bauman* [1799] (1 C.Rob. 243), described *sub* B, section, 3, under (*b*) *infra*, p. 513.

2. *Port authorities*

Another category of State organs whose natural task it was to exercise the right of capture consisted of the authorities of seaports where foreign vessels or cargoes liable to seizure were found at the outbreak of hostilities, or where foreign ships ventured to enter during the war. British cases offer many instances of this action.

3. *Customs officers*

In France seizures by customs officers have given rise to doubts about the effects of their action, not so much as regards the validity of such seizures under the law of prize, but rather as regards their right to receive a "part de prise", a share in the proceeds of the prize, and in particular as far as recaptures were concerned. Comp. therefore on this subject also the sections on recapture (*infra*, *sub* B, section 7, pp. 558-563) and on the partition of the proceeds of prizes and the award of prize money (*infra*, *sub* III C, section 7, pp. 647-661.

In later years the growing practice of applying the law of prize also in ports and other internal waters, and even on land on harbour quays, in warehouses, etc., has entailed a corresponding extension of the group of State organs qualified to exercise the right of prize. This aspect links the subject under review in this section 1 with section 3, dealing with the place where the right of prize may be exercised (*infra*, pp. 180-182). All these questions are interconnected to such an extent that it is difficult to divide the legislative and jurisprudential data strictly logically between the various sections.

A typical example of the practice and of the uncertainty in France is that of *Le Merle contre la Fortunée* [*an* IX] (de Pistoye and Duverdy, I, 166-167). The *Fortunée* was a French *tartane*, captured by an English privateer, abandoned by her crew, manned by an English prize crew and recaptured after thirty hours by the crew of an armed vessel of the French *Régie des douanes*, the *Merle*, who took the enemy prize crew prisoner. The regularity of that recapture was not doubted, nor was it doubtful that the *Fortunée* was good and lawful prize after having remained in the possession of the first captors during more than twenty-four hours, but a dispute arose over the question whether the crew of the *Merle* was entitled to any part of the prize. What the Commissary of the Government advised the *Conseil des prises* on this issue was to the following effect:

> "Il s'agit de savoir à qui cette capture doit être adjugée. Il est constant, dans le fait, que le bâtiment la *Fortunée* a été recous; que trente heures se sont écoulées entre la prise et la recousse. Il est de principe qu'après les vingt-quatre heures la prise appartient à ceux qui l'ont faite; cela est convenu par les propriétaires primitifs du navire recous.
>
> En faveur de qui doit être adjugée la prise? Ce serait incontestablement au dernier capteur, si le gouvernement lui avait conféré des lettres de marque. Mais les employés de la régie n'étaient point autorisés à armer en course, et si, dans la circonstance actuelle, ils ont fait une action utile et courageuse, il n'en est pas moins vrai que, dans la rigueur des principes, le produit de cette reprise ne peut appartenir qu'au gouvernement et que mon ministère m'impose le devoir de la réclamer à son profit."

However, the Commissary added, both the importance of the encouragement of such actions and a certain practice of the old monarchical government in respect of the recapture of French prizes not to exercise its rights too rigorously, but rather to grant two-thirds of the proceeds to the former owners of the prize and one-third to the recaptors, induced the Commissary to suggest that the new republican government should not be less generous.

This whole extra-legal and artificial argument was very soon afterwards overthrown by an *Avis du Conseil d'Etat* of 4 April 1809, approved by the Emperor, to assimilate customs officials to State vessels and land troops, the latter evidently also to be henceforth considered as authorized to make maritime prizes (*loco cit*., II, 431-432).

4. *Land troops*

In the English case of *La Rosine* [1800] (2 C.Rob., 372), cited in the *Johanna Emilie, otherwise Emilia* of 1854 (Roscoe, II, footnote *q* at p. 254), the seizure of several boxes of tin plate was made on a cartel ship by orders of the officers of the Fife Dragoons. This prize was condemned as "Droits of Admiralty":

> "It is common for captures to be made by non-commissioned persons. The capture is equally good, but it belongs to the Queen in her office of Admiralty".

5. *Exceptional old instances: towns as captors*

A peculiar belligerent naval operation against enemy shipping took place in the middle of the 15th century under the Burgundian Empire. It was an expedition which, in a sense, fell between an action by naval forces of the Sovereign of the country concerned and an act of authorized privateering. On the one hand, those who organized it carried it out at their own cost and risk—the characteristic feature of privateering. On the other hand, the actors were not simple private individuals but a group of cities, and as such part of the constitutional structure of the Sovereign Power concerned, the Duke of Burgundy in his capacity of Count of Holland. On the prize court proceedings that followed these naval operations in appeal before the Grand Council of Malines comp. Chapter I, section 5, *supra*, pp. 107 *et seq.*

B. *Privateering*

Introductory remarks on the delimitation of privateering towards other somewhat similar practices.

Before entering into this subject of privateering I will deal with four other practices which exhibit some superficial resemblance to privateering, but are notionally distinct from it.

(a) *Piracy*

Differing from the situation in antiquity, there has existed for centuries a clear notional distinction between privateering and piracy in that pirates are acting for their own profit against private shipping without any official authorization by their government (on piracy comp. the exposé in Part IV of this publication, pp. 248 *et seq.*). Hence the frequent provisions in treaties and municipal regulations of the past by which those on board of vessels engaged in acts of violence against harmless foreign merchantmen without an official commission of their government were equated with pirates (see *infra*).

(b) *The grant of letters of marque*

Privateering as a means of warfare has a strong conceptual affinity with another historical institution, with which it is consequently often mentioned in the same breath, namely, the taking of (private) reprisals. This latter type of action was equally taken by private persons with the authorization of their government. In both cases the authorization was embodied in an official document of corresponding tenor. This older type was called *lettre de représaille* or *lettre de marque* (*literae repressaliae*, *marcae vel contramarcae*), once theoretically distinguished *inter se* by the place where the authorization could be carried out: either only within the Sovereign's own jurisdiction or also outside the boundary (*marca*) of his territory. They were also known under the name *kaperbrief* or *commission.*

The institution of private reprisals served the purpose of providing private persons with a means of recovering from wrongdoers, especially foreigners, the damage which these had caused them and for which no official instance had awarded them due reparation. The oldest text of such a commission which I found reported is taken from an instrument issued to the Lord of Rye, one of the Cinque Ports.

It was granted by King John of England to John, the baron of Rye, on 28 June 1216, authorizing him to arrest so many goods of "those of Damme" as represent the value of one of his ships which they had robbed. See *Hansisches Urkundenbuch*, I, no. 139. Rye was at that juncture still one of the seven head-ports of South-Eastern England until it lost its eastern quester territory as a result of inundation by the sea and so declined, to live on only as an "old town". The fate which its sister-town of Winchelsea suffered was still worse: it was completely overwhelmed by the sea at the end of the 13th century and even the exact site where it once stood can no longer be identified. As a result only five of the original seven head-ports survived as the Cinque Ports proper: Dover, Sandwich, Hythe, Romney and Hastings, already mentioned in a letter of King John of 29 July 1204 (*loco cit.*, I, no. 65). The old dignity of Lord Warden of the Cinque Ports is at present vested in Queen Elizabeth, the Queen Mother.

De Pistoye and Duverdy, in their *Traité des prises maritimes* (I, p. 90), relate a famous case from the 16th century, when a citizen of Dieppe, Ango, in 1530 launched an expedition against the King of Portugal whose men had sunk one of Ango's ships. After the King's refusal to give him due compensation, Ango obtained authorization from King François I to exercise reprisals, which were carried out by sending a squadron of seventeen ships to the river Tagus.

See on this institution of private reprisals, for example, Art. 17 of the Franco-Netherlands treaty of 27 April 1662 (Dumont, VI², 412; Parry, 7, 139):

"Toutes Lettres de Marque ou de Represailles, qui pourroient avoir esté cy-devant accordées pour quelque cause que ce soit, sont declarées nulles, & n'en pourra être cy-après donné par l'un desdits Alliez au prejudice des Sujets de l'autre, si ce n'est seulement en cas de manifeste dény de Justice, lequel ne pourra être tenu pour verifié, si la Requeste de celuy qui demande lesdites Repressailles, n'est communiqueé au Ministre qui se trouvera sur les lieux de la part de l'Estat, contre les Sujets duquel elles devroient estre données, afin que dans le terme de quatre mois, ou plutost s'il se peut, il puisse informer du contraire, ou procurer l'accomplissement de Justice qui sera dû."

Another, older example of regulation of the practice by international Convention was Art. 39 of the Anglo-Netherlands Treaty of Alliance of 17 September 1625 (Dumont, V^2, 478):

"Toutes lettres de Represailles, Marque, Arrest, & autres semblables, qui ont esté cy-devant octroyées & decernées contre les Subjects de l'un ou l'autre des confoederez pour quelque cause que ce soit, n'auront lieu de part & d'autre, ains sont dès maintenant & demeureront nulles & de nul effect, & pour l'advenir n'en seront aucunes octroyées, mais justice sera rendue & administrée, ainsi que de droit appartiendra".

The last letters of reprisals which were delivered in France were those granted in 1778 by Louis XVI to merchants of Bordeaux against the English and the last treaty that dealt with this matter between France and England was their Treaty of Commerce signed at Versailles on 26 September 1786 (Parry, 50, 71), Art. 3 of which disposed as follows:

"... et ne seront données à l'avenir, par l'une des deux Hautes-Parties Contractantes, au préjudice et au dommage des sujets de l'autre, aucunes lettres de représailles, si ce n'est seulement au cas de refus ou de délai de justice; lequel refus ou délai de justice ne sera pas tenu pour vérifié, si la requête de celui qui demande lesdites lettres de représailles, n'est communiquée au Ministre qui se trouvera sur les lieux de la part du Prince contre les sujets duquel elles doivent être données, afin que, dans le terme de quatre mois, ou plutôt s'il se peut, il puisse faire connoître le contraire, ou procurer la juste satisfaction qui sera dûe."

(c) *Conversion of merchant ships to warships*

Neither must the practice of privateering be confounded with the employment of private merchant vessels in naval State service as auxiliary cruisers. It already occurred indeed in earlier centuries that a belligerent adopted the policy of reinforcing its navy, as a temporary measure, by placing ordinary merchant ships fit for the purpose of combating the enemy at sea under direct naval command. The British Government alluded to that practice in its memorandum for the Naval Conference of London of 1908-1909, in connection with the controversy over the question of whether the transformation of merchant vessels into State warships could be lawfully effected on the high seas. The British Government, though itself disputing the permissibility of such transformation on the open sea, conceded that no generally recognized international practice in this field existed so that no rule of positive international law concerning the controversy could be derived from such practice, and that neither would there seem to be any judicial precedents governing the question. The only cases which had in the past occupied

British prize courts and showed some distant affinity with the theme of privateering related to the right of British owners of ships, captured by the enemy, to the restoration of their property after its recapture by British, allied or even neutral forces, whether warships or privateers: the *Ceylon* [1811] (Dodson, I, 105; Roscoe, II, 133); the *Georgiana* (Dodson, I, 397); Roscoe, II, 193). Comp. the *Proceedings of the International Naval Conference (Miscellaneous No. 5)* (1909, Cd. 4555), p. 40; and, for the rest, on the failure of the Second Hague Peace Conference of 1907 to solve the particular problem of the admissibility of transformation on the high seas, Chapter III, *infra*, p. 244.

(d) *The arming of (non-commissioned) merchant ships*

I have already had an opportunity of mentioning armed merchantmen in previous volumes of this publication, *viz.*:

in Part IV, pp. 74-75, where, after alluding to the controversy which arose during World War I over the permissibility of the arming of merchant ships, I have cited an Edict of King Felipe II of Spain of 1563 (*Groot Placaatboek*, I, 796) (Art. 26) and three 17th century treaties, of Westminster 1654 (Art. 20), Helsingör 1659 (Art. 3) and Nijmegen 1679 (Art. 7, *in fine*), in support of the statement that the arming of merchant ships was generally held to be perfectly lawful;

in Part IX-A (vol. IX), pp. 292-293, where I adduced a few additional data on their traditional right to carry arms for their defence, including a provision in an American Act of Congress of March 1805;

and in Part IX-B (vol. X), pp. 229 *et seq.*, where the neutrality aspect of armed merchantmen was set out.

From the point of view of prize law three aspects of armed merchant vessels must be considered, *viz.*:

(i) in this section 1, *sub* C (pp. 171-173) the possible exercise by merchant vessels, in an active rôle, of the right of visit and seizure—a question which, for the rest, is not strictly limited to *armed* merchantmen;

(ii) in section 4 (pp. 179-203 *et seq.*) their liability, in a passive rôle, to belligerent action in virtue of the law of prize proper; and

(iii) in the present Chapter III, Part B, section 2 (pp. 504-511 *et seq.*) the impact on the modalities of the exercise of the right of visit which their particular character may produce.

At the end of the pre-codification period the Japanese Regulations of 7 March 1904 relating to Capture at Sea in Art. 40 made express mention of enemy ships "equipped for fighting"; the whole of their cargo was to be included in their condemnation.

In former centuries it was beyond all doubt that merchant ships could lawfully be armed as a protection against piracy and belligerent action: not only did they have the right to take this precautionary measure, but they were often instructed by their national authority to arm themselves before putting to sea. This obligation was laid down, for instance, in Articles 59 and

60 of the Edict of King Henri III of France of March 1584 to the following effect (extracts):

> "59. Nous avons declaré, voulu et ordonné, declarons, voulons et ordonnons, et nous plaist, que chacun bourgeois de navire sera tenu fournir et agreer son-dict vaisseau bien et deuëment d'artillerie, bouletz, picques, maches, toises, coings de toutes sortes, et aultres menus ustencilles servans à ladicte artillerie, plomb et latine, cuirs vers, soultes, avirons, picques, arbalestres et aultres armes, planches, brey, goutren, clouz, fiches, compas, orloges, plombz et lignes à sonder, et autres choses requises à porter en mer pour la seureté desdicts navires ...
> 60. Pour ce qu'il s'est perdu, pris et depredé grand nombre de navires et vaisseaulx appartenans à nos subiects, faulte d'estre accompaignez et armez ainsi qu'il appartient, pour la seureté et deffence de leursdicts navires et vaisseaulx, en quoy non-seulement nosdicts subiectz demeurent endommagez et interessez, mais aussi nous et la chose publique de nostre Royaume, Nous avons ordonné que doresnavant quant nosdicts subiects voudront sortir leurs navires en mer quelque part en route qu'ils veulent tirer, et pour quelque effect que ce soit, seront tenus armer leursdicts navires, et les mettre en l'équipage qui s'ensuit, à scavoir ...".

The provisions further entered into great detail on the obligatory armament and the required number of mariners.

In the case of the American vessel the *Pégou* (Pistoye-Duverdy, II, 51) the *Conseil des prises* decided that a vessel which only carried a normal armament did not by that fact become a warship. Since this case concerned the controversy as to whether the ship was subject to condemnation in prize, I refer for it to section 4, *infra*, p. 198.

General introduction

(a) *Historical*

Up to 1856 the exercise of the right of prize was to a large extent assigned to privateers acting under a commission obtained from their government. In view of the important rôle which privateers have played in past centuries concurrently with State warships, I will begin by sketching their activity and the conditions on which the legality of that activity depended.

In an Anglo-Netherlands treaty of 1674 privateers were designated by the following description (Parry, 13, 255):

> "Nav(es) Ordinum aut ejus (*sic*) subditorum, qui privatis sumptibus & cum Diplomate tamen publico eas Naves instruxerunt".

The institution of privateering was very useful in assisting the belligerent government to do as much harm to its adversary as possible and in intercepting the ships which maintained its overseas communications. The privateer masters concerned were rewarded for their expenses and for their success, and were consequently financially interested in their enterprise. This method, particularly valuable in a period of history in which powerful navies had not yet developed, had, however, its obvious drawbacks since it encouraged abuse, and it was therefore necessary to constrain the freedom of action of privateers by severe prescriptions and prohibitions. Treaties and municipal regulations are full of such instructions and restrictions.

The main seafaring nations have introduced three different names to indicate the activity of private ships authorized by their government to seize foreign, in particular enemy but also allied and neutral ships at sea in time of war:

Kaperei in German (*Kaperi* in Swedish and Danish, *kaapvaart* in Dutch, even каперство in Russian);

Course or *armement en course* in French (*corso* in Italian, Spanish and Portuguese);

privateering in English,

with the corresponding terms *Kaper*, *corsaire* (*armateur*) and privateer to designate those practising it.

Dutch circles also called it *commissievaart* (comp. Art. 14 of the Netherlands-Swedish Treaty of Commerce of 26 November 1675 (Dumont, VII[1], 316; Parry, 14, 41)), quoted below at p. 165.

Privateers in earlier times needed a commission from their national authorities entitling them to take action against enemy vessels. Such commissions could, in principle, only be issued by a belligerent Sovereign to his own subjects, specified by name. Acceptance of a commission from both belligerents was strictly forbidden. Operation without any commission was equated with piracy. Privateers also fell under the category of pirates when they sailed under a false flag, or continued their action after the conclusion of peace, or after the expiry or withdrawal of their commission. They were bound to observe the rules and customs of war and the instructions laid down in their commission, and to submit their seizures to adjudication by an admiralty court. They were often specifically prohibited from carrying their activity in rivers or other inland waters of the enemy country. They were usually obliged to pay a deposit or to give surety as a guarantee for their lawful behaviour.

The first Sovereign who introduced the requirement of such a commission would seem to have been the French King Charles V the Wise of Valois who, by his Ordonnance of 1373, often erroneously dated 1400 (comp. Chapter I, *supra*, p. 43), empowered his Admiral to grant commissions and to adjudicate upon possible infractions committed by their holders. This requirement was never cancelled. See for the text of such a commission, which I select from a later period, the "formule à employer pour les lettres de marque", annexed to the Decree of the French National Convention of 31 January 1793, in Martens, R[2], V, 378:

"Liberté, Egalité.
Au nom de la République Française.
Le conseil exécutif de la République française permet, par ces présentes, à ... de faire armer et équiper en guerre un ... nommé le ... du port de ... tonneaux ou environ, actuellement au

port de ... avec tel nombre de canons, boulets, et telle quantité de poudre, plomb et autres munitions de guerre et vivres qu'il jugera nécessaires pour le mettre en état de courir sur les pirates, forbans, gens sans aveu, et généralement sur tous les ennemis de la République française, en quelque lieu qu'il pourra les rencontrer; de les prendre et amener prisonniers avec leurs navires, armes et autres objets dont ils seront saisis, à la charge par le dit ... de se conformer aux ordonnances de la marine, aux lois décrètées par les representans du peuple Français, et notamment à l'article IV de la loi du 31 Janvier, concernant le nombre d'hommes devant former son équipage; de faire enregistrer les présentes lettres au bureau des classes du lieu de son départ, d'y déposer un rôle signé et certifié de lui, contenant les noms et surnoms, âge, lieu de naissance et demeure des gens de son équipage; et à son retour, de faire son rapport pardevant l'officier chargé de l'administration des classes, de ce qui se sera passé pendant son voyage.

Le conseil-exécutif-provisoire requiert tous les peuples amis et alliés de la République française et leurs agens, de donner au dit ... toute assistance, passage et rétraite en leurs ports avec son dit vaisseau et les prises qui'il aura pu faire, offrant d'en user de même en pareille circonstance. Mande et ordonne aux commandans des bâtiments de l'état, de laisser passer le dit ... avec son vaisseau, et ceux qu'il aura pu prendre sur l'ennemi, et de lui donner secours et assistance. Ne pourront les présentes servir que pour ... mois seulement, à compter de la date de leur enregistrement.

En foi de quoi le conseil exécutif provisoire de la République a fait signer les présentes lettres par le ministre de la marine et y a fait apposer le sceau de la République.

Donné à Paris, le ..."

Data concerning older municipal rules on privateering can be found in *French* instructions of 1584 (extract in *Code des prises*, I, 17);

Netherlands instructions of 1597 (*Recueil van Placaaten, etc*., I, 1-16);

Spanish Ordenanzas para navegar en corso of 1621 (Abreu y Bertodano, *Colección de los tratados*, under King Felipe IV, vol. I), 1718 and 1779; *infra*, pp. 163-164;

British Act of Parliament of 1707 (6 Anne, ch. 13), see Roscoe, *History of the English prize court* (1924), p. 38;

Privateering was also regulated in a long series of treaties, dating from the 15th up to the end of the 18th century, *infra*, pp. 164-168.

Repeated attempts have been made in the course of the centuries to achieve the abolition of privateering but up to 1856 they have all failed, comp. *infra*, p. 168.

(b) *Bibliographical*

One of the most elaborate dissertations on privateering is that of G.F. de Martens in his work of 1795 (Göttingen) *Essai concernant les armateurs, les prises et surtout les reprises* (translated in 1801 in London by Th.H. Horne). In Chapter I (§§ 1-9) of his work he dealt with the history of privateering in the wars of the Middle Ages; with the origin of, and the difference between letters of marque and of reprisals in time of peace, on the one hand and letters of marque in case of war, on the other; with privateers in the 15th century; with the actions of privateers in the Eighty Years' War of the Low Countries with Spain (the so-called *Watergeuzen*, "beggars of the sea") and other types of private expeditions on the sea (those of the early "Victualienbrüder" or Vitalians in the Baltic, and later the freebooters, "flibustiers" (filibusters) or buccaneers, especially on Hispaniola (Santo Domingo)); and with the general use of privateers since the end of the 17th century. In Chapter II (§§ 10-39) he set out the (then) modern rights of privateers, comprising such questions as: to whom the right of granting letters of marque belonged; whether they might be granted to foreigners; whether it was allowed to take commissions from two princes; the guarantees a privateer should give previous to his setting sail; the conditions and the limits of the rights of privateers to visit and seize ships sailing either under an enemy or under a neutral flag, either convoyed or sailing alone; the right to ransom the goods of an enemy; the conduct of a prize to a national or a foreign port; the institution of prize proceedings; the sanction of condemnation of the privateer in costs and damages in case of his breach of the rules; distribution of the prize and the grant of rewards, and the revocation of the letters of marque. All these issues would, however, need such circumstantial exposition that I will refrain from entering upon them in detail here.

See for a thorough French monograph on the subject, of much later date, C. la Mache, *La guerre de course dans le passé, dans le présent, et dans l'avenir* (Paris, 1901).

A detailed exposé of the importance of privateering for the Republic of the United Netherlands was given by Prof. Dr J.A. van Hamel in his article in *Varia juris gentium (Liber amicorum J.P.A. François)* (Leiden, 1959), pp. 140-159: "De betekenis van kaapvaart- en blokkaderecht in de Republiek der Verenigde Nederlanden."

I. *Legislation*

The conditions on which private persons could be authorized to engage in privateering were more or less strictly defined in earlier centuries in numerous municipal regulations.

England

As regards Great Britain, see the Statutes of 16 Geo. III, ch. 5 (Martens, R^2, III, 105); 17 Geo. III, ch. 7 (*ibid.*, 110) and 22 Geo. III, ch. 25 (*ibid.*, 113), and the Instructions to British privateers of 1664 and 1665 (not found by Sir George Lee in the registry of the Admiralty Court or in the Council Office), 1693, 1704/5, 1706, 1744 and 1780 in Appendix B to Pratt-Lee's work of 1856 on the *Law of Contraband of War*, pp. 257 *et seq.*, and those of 1793 and 1794 in Martens, R^2, V, pp. 596 *et seq.* As appears from a footnote at p. 596, the Instructions of 8 June 1793 seem to have been countermanded or suspended half an hour later, but obviously without any real effect since the subsequent Instructions of 8 January (p. 600) and 18 August 1794 (p. 604) witness to their continued operation.

The formalities regarding the issuance of letters of marque in England at the end of the 18th century appear from data collected by Judge Story in his *Notes on the principles and practice of Prize Courts* (ed. Pratt, 1854). See the forms for a petition for letters of marque and for a commission to grant them (1793), and those of a warrant from the Lords of the Admiralty to issue letters of marque (1798) and of a bail and affidavit by sureties on obtaining them (pp. 141, 161, 165, 167).

By a declaration of 28 March 1854 (*loco cit*., pp. 148-149), made at the beginning of the Crimean War, the British Government announced, in agreement with the French Government, that they had no intention of issuing letters of marque for the commissioning of privateers.

As an example of the text of such Instructions I insert below Arts. IV, V, IX and XVII of those of 18 June 1744:

> "Article IV.—That all captains and commanders of ships who have or shall have letters of marque or commissions for private men-of-war, are hereby required and enjoined to observe carefully and religiously the terms of the treaty-marine between his late Majesty King Charles II, and their High Mightinesses the States General of the *United Netherlands*, concluded at London the 1st day of December, 1674, old style, and confirmed by subsequent treaties; and they are hereby required to give security pursuant to the tenth article of the aforesaid treaty-marine for the due performance thereof.
>
> Article V.—That all sorts of fire-works and things thereto belonging, as cannon, muskets, mortars, petards, bombs, grenadoes, saucisses, peckransen, carriages, rests, bandoleers, powder, match, saltpetre, bullets, pikes, swords, head-pieces, cuirasses, halberts, horses, saddles, holsters, belts, sailwork, rigging, cables, cordage, masts, lead, pitch, tar, hemp, together with all other equipage that serves for sea and land, laden in *Danish or Swedish* ships, or ships belonging to neutral countries, and bound to the enemies' country, are accounted contraband goods.
>
> Article IX.—That the said commanders of such merchant ships or vessels who shall obtain the said letters of marque or commission as aforesaid for private men-of-war, shall not do or attempt any thing against the true meaning of any article or articles, treaty or treaties, depending between us and *any of our allies*, touching the freedom of commerce in the time of war, and the authority of the passports or certificates under a certain form in some one of the articles or treaties so depending between us and our allies as aforesaid, when produced and shewed by any of the subjects of our said allies, and shall not do or attempt anything against our loving subjects, or the subject of any prince or state in amity with us, nor against their ships, vessels, or goods; but only against *France and Spain*, their vassals and subjects, and others inhabiting within their countries, territories, or dominions, their ships, vessels, and goods, except as before excepted; and against such other ships, vessels, and goods as are or shall be liable to confiscation.
>
> Article XVII.—That all persons who shall violate these instructions shall be severely punished, and also required to make full reparation to persons injured contrary to these instructions, for all damages they shall sustain by any capture, embezzlement, demurrage, or otherwise."

Those of 21 December 1780 were intended to protect also the subjects of Portugal, Denmark and Russia.

France

The oldest French Edict dates back to the second half of the 14th century, namely, to 1373. The rules laid down therein were virtually reproduced in a long series of subsequent *Ordonnances*, of François I (1517 and 1543),

Henri III (1584) and Louis XIV (1650 and 1681), and finally redrafted in an *Arrêté* of 2 prairial *an* XI (22 May 1803).

The activity of privateers belongs indeed to the oldest matters of regulation, to begin with the *Ordonnance* of King Charles VI of 13 November 1400 (or 7 December 1373, see p. 43) just mentioned (de Pistoye and Duverdy, I, 158), which required privateers to apply for a commission, to be laid down in a "lettre de marque", and to deposit a security. This regulation was repeatedly renewed.

Arts. 33 and 34 of the *Arrêté* (*ibid.*, I, 230) contained the following rules:

(33) "Les capitaines de bâtiments armés en course seront tenus d'arborer pavillon français avant de tirer à boulet sur le bâtiment chassé, sous peine d'être privés, eux et les armateurs, de tout le produit de la prise, qui sera confisquée au profit de la République, si le bâtiment capturé est ennemi, ...
(34) Tout capitaine convaincu d'avoir fait la course sous plusieurs pavillons sera, ainsi que ses fauteurs et complices, poursuivi et jugé comme pirate".

A law of 10 April 1825 (*ibid.*, I, 230) threatened privateers acting against certain rules with treatment as pirates:

(Art. 3) "Seront poursuivis et jugés comme pirates: 3°. Le capitaine et les officiers de tout navire ou bâtiment de mer quelqonque qui aurait commis des actes d'hostilités sous un pavillon autre que celui de l'Etat dont il aurait commission".

Art. 30 of the Edict of March 1584 (Pardessus, IV, at p. 302), stipulated as follows:

"Ne pourra aucun de quelque estat qu'il soit mettre aucun Navire à ses despens, pour faire la guerre à noz ennemis, sinon par le congé dudit Admiral ou de sondict Visadmiral et Lieutenant ..."

Arts. 31-33 continued by lying down directions concerning equipment, a "caution juratoire"—of unspecified amount—, the requirement of previous leave to sail out, and on how to act after a capture pending the judgment on the legality of the seizure.

Articles 1 *et seq.* of *titre* IX of *livre* III of the *Ordonnance de la Marine* of August 1681 (Pardessus, IV, 325) contained an injunction to have the Admiral's commission registered against the deposit of a security of 15,000 *livres*; a prohibition to accept without Royal permission a commission of any foreign sovereign and to sail under his banner on penalty of being treated as pirates; an interdiction to fly a flag other than that of the State which granted the commission, or to have commissions of two different States.

New rules on the subject were enacted in 1778:

a Royal Declaration of 24 June (*Code des prises*, vol. II, p. 654; extract in Martens, R^2, III, 117), dealing, *inter alia*, with the premiums which privateers could claim from the proceeds of the prizes made by them;

a Royal *Règlement* of 26 July "concernant la navigation des bâtiments neutres en tems de guerre" (*Code des prises*, vol. II, p. 671; Martens, R^2, III,

18), including a few articles equally binding upon King's ships and privateers;

a Royal *Règlement* of 27 September (*Code des prises*, vol. II, p. 692; Martens, R^2, III, 123), relating in particular to prizes which French privateers might bring into ports of the United States, and *vice versa* (comp. also the footnote by Martens at p. 127 relative to further developments in 1781);

a special *Règlement* of 8 November 1779 (*Code des prises*, vol. II, p. 761; Martens R^2, III 129; Th. Ortolan, *Diplomatie de la mer*, pp. 403-409) regulating the procedure to be followed, in case of the conduct of prizes into foreign (neutral) ports, by the French Consuls established there. Comp. on this particular subject my historical survey in Part IX-B (vol. X) of this publication on neutrality law, p. 83.

One of the most elaborate regulations of privateering is that laid down in the French *Arrêté* of 2 prairial *an* XI (22 May 1803) "contenant règlement sur les armements en course" (Th. Ortolan, *loco cit.*, II, pp. 380-403; Martens, R^2, VIII, 9), an instrument of 123 Articles, in which the subject was set out in four "titres", the first (Arts. 1-50) on "Armements en course", dealing in 5 chapters respectively with "sociétés pour la course", "équipages", "lettres de marque et cautionnements", "encouragements" and "police de la course et rançons", the second (Arts. 51-111) on "Prises", dealing in 5 more chapters respectively with "captures", "procédure des prises", "déchargement, manutention, vente et liquidation particulière des prises", "liquidations générales" and "répartition", the third (Arts. 112-121) with "Armements en course et prises dans les colonies et ports étrangers", and the fourth (Arts. 122-123) containing a few general provisions.

This *Arrêté* organized the practice of privateering by setting up "sociétés en commandite pour la course", in which individual ship-owners took part, for the construction and equipment of the vessels as well as for the subsequent repartition of the proceeds of their prizes. The crews could consist for no more than 1/8 of conscripts for the State Navy. Only French citizens could obtain *lettres de marque*. They were obliged to give security in writing of 37,000 to 74,000 francs, depending on whether the crew numbered up to 150 men or more. A system of bonuses was introduced to encourage the taking of prizes. The privateers were subject to disciplinary control and penal prosecution in case of offences. Release of their prizes on the high seas against ransom was only allowed in virtue of a special authorization. Elaborate rules further dealt with captures, recaptures, the bringing of prizes into port, prize proceedings and the distribution of the proceeds of the prizes among the ship-owners and the crews.

Art. 15 of the *Arrêté* distinguished between two kinds of commission, *viz.*, (*a*) the *lettre de marque pure et simple* or *pour les armements en course*, and (*b*) the *lettre de marque pour des armements en guerre et marchandises*. Comp. De Pistoye and Duverdy, *Traité des prises maritimes*, I, 159 *et seq.*:

"Les lettres de marque peuvent être délivrées à deux sortes de navires: 1°. à ceux dont le but unique est de courir sus à l'ennemi; 2°. à ceux dont le but principal est le commerce, mais qui veulent se ménager la possibilité de profiter d'une bonne occasion qui pourrait se présenter de capturer un navire ennemi ... Les Commissions en guerre et marchandises sont donc des lettres que prennent les navires marchands pour s'assurer le propriété des prises qu'ils pourraient faire, et pour éviter d'être considérés comme pirates".

The Netherlands

Already at an early date the States General of the United Netherlands issued placards against the application by the inhabitants of their country for, and their acceptance of, commissions from foreign Powers. Those placards dated from 27 July 1627 and 26 April 1653 and were renewed by a placard of 3 May 1779 (a French translation of which can be found in Martens, R[2], III, 62).

Subsequent ordinances followed this up by

a placard of 12 January 1781 concerning the recompenses which privateers would enjoy (extract in French in Martens, R[2], III, 153);

and an instruction for privateers of 13 January 1781 (extract in French *ibid.*, III, 155).

After the restoration of the country's independence in 1813 an elaborate Royal Decree of 13 December 1818 (*Staatsblad* N° 44) enacted rules concerning the capture of prize vessels and the distribution of *prijs- en buitgelden* (prize and booty money). This Decree, that regulated the award of prize bounty in a very complicated manner (*e.g.*, 2/8 of the value of the prize destined for the crew and 1/3 thereof for the commanding officer), was still in force on the outbreak of World War II. See *infra*, pp. 586-587.

Spain

A Spanish version of the rules enacted for the regulation of the practice of privateering—of special historical interest because Spain was one of the few Powers which failed for a long time to ratify the Declaration of Paris of 16 April 1856 against that practice—can be found in Pardessus' *Collection*, vol. V, pp. 396-432, on the subject "Privileges granted to privateers" as "Chapitres sur les armemens en course" from the beginning of the 14th century (dated 1330) and at the time annexed as a sequel or complement to the *Consolat de Mar* in its edition of 1494. These "Chapters on privateering" consisted of two groups of provisions, Chapters I-VIII (§§ 298-305) and Chapters IX-XXXVII (§§ 306-334),—upon which comp. Pardessus' footnotes (1)-(3) at p. 397 and (1) at p. 404.

See also the Spanish *Ordonnance* on privateering, dated 1356 (*ibid.*, p. 465) and from a later period the *Ordonnance* of (belligerent) Spain of 1 July 1779 (in a Dutch translation in Martens, R[2], III, 139) concerning privateers acting under the Spanish flag, and the letter of Count Florida-Blanca, Spanish

Secretary of State to the Spanish Minister of Marine, of 13 March 1780 (*ibid.* p. 92).

The United States

The United States already enacted rules on privateering in the first stage of their fight for independence. See the Instruction for privateers of 10 April 1776 (Martens, R^2, III, 100); the letter of the Commissioners of the Congress to the Commanders of warships, armed vessels, or privateers of 21 November 1777 (Martens, R^2, III, 16), and the Proclamation of Congress of 9 May 1778 (*ibid.*, 17). See also Bourguignon, *The first federal Court* at pp. 52 *et seq.* and 125 *et seq.*

Other States

During the same period decrees on the subject of their attitude toward foreign privateers were enacted by a number of neutral States:

by Tuscany on 1 August 1778 (*ibid.*, 24);

by the Two Sicilies on 19 September 1778 (Martens, R^2, III, 46);

by the Pope as Head of the Ecclesiastical States on 4 March 1779 (*ibid.*, 52);

by Sweden in March 1779 (*ibid.*, 60);

by Genova on 1 July 1779 (*ibid.*, 64);

by Venice on 9 September 1779 (*ibid.*, 74);

by the Ottoman Porte on 12 February 1780 (*ibid.*, 88); and

by Portugal on 30 August 1780 (*bid.*, 157).

As an example of those decrees I quote the main passages of Art. 7 of the Tuscan *Regolamento* of 1 August 1778;

> "Vietiamo espressamente tanto ai Nostri sudditi quanto ad ogni altro domiciliato, o commorante ancorchè di passagio nel Gran Ducato, l'armare in Corso o in Guerra in veruno dei Porti, o Luoghi dei Nostri Stati, Navi, Vascelli e qualunque altra sorta di Bastimenti tanto Quadri, che Latini, da Vela, o da Remo, niuno eccettuato, non volendo che ciò possa farsi nè par se nè per altri, nè direttamente nè indirettamente. Siccome non vogliamo che si possa prendere da' detti nostri Sudditi, abitanti o commoranti come sopra alcuno interesse, partito, o partecipazione in detti armamenti di Guerra o di corso sebbene fossero fatti anco fuori di stato, alla pena etc. ..."

II. *Treaty provisions or international complications*

After my preceding summary of municipal legislation concerning privateering I will now pass on to a short survey of the numerous relevant treaty provisions and to some ensuing international complications. In this selection from the available source material, intended to exemplify the legal situation, I will follow, as far as is practicable, a certain systematic order according to the various elements of the subject matter under review, and take my examples mainly from Netherlands treaties of the 17th century, which do not differ in this respect from conventions concluded by other States.

(a) *Requirement of a commission*

Treaties sometimes laid down in express terms that private warships acting without a commission would be treated as pirates. Commissions were as a rule issued to privateers by their own national authorities. There were even express prohibitions in force forbidding the acceptance of "foreign commissions" in general.

Occasionally, however, irregular practices were resorted to. Thus, it occurred that a belligerent State took into its service as privateers ships equipped in a foreign, even neutral, State, or allowed such an action. An example is the fitting-out of privateers by nobles of Genoa in 1617 for the purpose, in the service of Spain, to capture Netherlands vessels. The neutral Government of Genoa did not dare to stop this activity, which was carried out under the command of the Genoese Admiral Doria, by the use of force for fear of provoking a war with Spain (*Levantsche Handel*, *R.G.P.*, no. 9, pp. 119-120). It was these privateers which, in 1617, captured the Netherlands merchantman *St. Jacob* within sight of the French coast (Yperen?).

Another uncommon instance was that of the action by privateers in the service of Sweden, operating against Netherlands shipping under a French commission during the peculiar Swedish-Netherlands war which ended with the Peace Treaty of Nijmegen of 2/12 October 1679 (Dumont, VII[1], 432; Parry, 15, 328). The captures made under those irregular conditions gave rise to the organization of an arbitral settlement through the Peace Treaty, achieved especially with a view to the peculiar character of the events. Comp. on this arbitration Part VIII of this publication, p. 319 and Chapter I of this volume, section 5, p. 86.

(b) *Prohibition against accepting a commission from an enemy government (or engaging in privateering together with enemy privateers)*

Art. 16 of the Franco-Netherlands treaty of 27 April 1662 (Dumont, VI[2], 412; Parry, 7, 139);

The Netherlands-France, 10 August 1678 (Dumont, VII[1], 357; Parry, 14, 399) Art. 25;

The Netherlands-England, Peace Treaty of Breda of 21/31 July 1667 (Dumont, VII[1], 44; Parry, 10, 231), Art. 21, repeated in Art. 15 of their Marine Treaty of 1 December 1674 (Dumont, VII[1], 283; Parry, 13, 255) which included a provision by which the Parties undertook to punish those of their subjects, found in possession of an enemy commission contrary to Art. 21 of the Treaty of 1667;

The Netherlands-Sweden, 26 November 1675 (Dumont, VII[1], 316; Parry, 14, 41), Art. 10; 2/12 October 1679 (Dumont, VII[1], 437; Parry, 15, 331), Art. 3:

"Quòd praedictae Suae Majestatis praedictorumque Ordinum Generalium Subditi & Incolae nullos imposterùm inter se exerceant hostilitatum actus aut violentias, nec Mari nec Terrâ, nec in Fluviis, Fluminibus aut Stationibus, sub quocunque nomine aut praetextu, ita ut Subditi Suae Regiae Majestatis nullum Diploma, Commissionem vel

Instructionem pro privatis Armaturis Navalibus exercendis, neque Literas Repressaliarum (ut vulgò vocant) aliquorum Principum vel Statuum, qui praefatorum Dominorum Ordinum Generalium Hostes sunt recipiant, neque vi aut praetextu eorundem Diplomatum, Commissionumque vel Repressaliarum praedictos Dominorum Ordinum Generalium Subditos & Incolas turbent, infestent vel incommodo damnove aliquo afficiant, neque ejusmodi vel Armaturam exerceant, vel eâ in altum procedant: qui secus fecerint, ut Piratae prosequendi sunto & plectendi. Id quod reciprocè respectu & ratione Suae Majestatis Subditorum & Incolarum ab Unitarum Belgii Provinciarum Subditis & Incolis observandum fit".

The Netherlands-Spain, 26 June 1714 (Dumont, VIII[1], 427; Parry, 29, 97), Art. 5:

"Les Sujets dudit Seigneur Roy ne pourront prendre aucunes Commissions pour des Armemens particuliers, ou Lettres de représailles des Princes ou Etats, Ennemis desdits Seigneurs Etats Généraux, moins les troubler, ni endommager en aucune manière, en vertu de telles Commissions ou Lettres de représailles, ni aller en course avec elles, sous peine d'être poursuivis & chatiés comme des Pirates, ce qui sera pareillement observé par les Sujets des Provinces-Unies à l'égard des Sujets dudit Seigneur Roy, & seront à cette fin toutes & quantes fois, que cela sera requis, de part & d'autre, dans les Terres de l'obéissance desdits Seigneurs Roy & Etats Généraux publiées, & renouvellées, défenses très-expresses, & très précises de se servir en aucune manière de telles Commissions ou Lettres de représailles, sous la peine susmentionnée, qui sera exécutée sévèrement contre les contrevenants outre la restitution entière, à laquelle ils seront tenus envers ceux auxquels ils auront causé dommage".

(c) *Instruction to hand in the commission after return to the home port and prohibition of its further use*

The Netherlands-Sweden, 26 November 1675 (Dumont, VII[1], 316; Parry, 14, 41), Arts. 12 and 13:

"XII. Avocabunt praeterea tam Sacra Regia Majestas Sueciae, quam Celsitudo Dominorum Ordinum Generalium, omnes & singulos Subditos, qui a infestandas praedictas Naves Mercatorias, Merces & Bona aut quicquam eorum operam suam alteri cuicunque Principi aut Statui jam nunc addixerunt, quatenus illi nondum ancoras & vela solverint, sub poena corporis & bonorum.

XIII. Respectu vero eorum qui jam ante vela solverunt curabunt Sacra Regia Majestas Sueciae & Celsitudo Dominorum Ordinum Generalium, ut hi intra spatium trium mensium ab incoepto desistant, eamque quam aliis Principibus aut Statibus addixerunt operam, renuntient, sub praefata poena corporis & bonorum."

(d) *Obligation imposed upon masters and owners of privateers to give surety against misbehaviour*

The Netherlands-Algiers, 15 October 1622 (Dumont, V[2], 413), Art. 11;

The Netherlands-France, 18 April 1646 (Dumont, VI[1], 342), Art. IV: a surety of 12,000 *livres tournois* for what might happen during the course and a couple of days afterwards;

The Netherlands-England, 5 April 1654 (Dumont, VI[2], 74; Parry, 3, 225), Art. 25;

The Netherlands-France, 27 April 1662 (Dumont, VI[2], 412; Parry, 7, 139), Art. 38: 15,000 *livres tournois* under penalty of the lapse or the nullity of the commission. The text ran as follows:

"Et pour cette cause seront doresnavant les Capitaines & Armateurs obligez chacun d'eux avant leur partement, de bailler caution bonne & solvable pardevant les Juges compétens, de la somme de quinze mille Livres tournois, pour répondre chacun d'eux solidairement des malversations qu'ils pourroient commettre en leurs courses, & pour les contraventions de leurs Capitaines & Officiers au présent Traité, & aux Ordonnances & Edits de sa Majesté, qui seront publiez en vertu & conformément à la disposition d'iceluy, à peine de déchéance & nullité desdites Commissions & Congez, ce qui sera pareillement pratiqué par les Sujets desdits Seigneurs Estats Généraux";

The Netherlands-England, 4/14 September 1662 (Dumont, VI^2, 422; Parry, 7, 193), Art. 24; 1/10 December 1674 (Dumont, VII^1, 283; Parry, 13, 255), Art. 10;

The Netherlands-France, 10 August 1678 (Dumont, VII^1, 357; Parry, 14, 399), Art. 25: surety by captain and shipowner;

The Netherlands-Sweden, 2/12 October 1679 (Dumont, VII^1, 437; Parry, 15, 331), Art. 25, and from a later period

France-United States, 6 February 1778 (Martens, R^2, II, 587; Parry, 46, 417), Art. 21.

(e) *Obligatory modalities of visit and seizure*

Prescriptions relating to the formalities to be observed by privateers when exercising the right of prize can be found, *e.g.*, in Art. 11 of the Netherlands-Spanish Treaty of Marine of 17 December 1650 (Dumont, VI^1, 570; Parry, 2, 259), which equally applied to State warships:

"Que s'ils sont entrés en Rades, ou rencontrés en pleine Mer, par quelques Navires dudit Seigneur Roy, ou des Armeurs particuliers, ses Subjects, lesdits Navires, pour eviter toutes desordres, demeurants esloignés de la portée du Canon, pouront envoyer leur Bateau, ou Chalouppe à bord du Navire des Subjects et Habitants des Provinces Unies, et faire entrer en iceluy deux, ou trois hommes seulement, auxquels seront monstrés les Passeports par le Maistre, ou Patron dudit Navire des Provinces Unies en la forme specifiée aux Articles anterieurs, et aussi les Lettres de Mer, couchées selon le formulaire, qui sera inseré à la fin du present Traité, par ou devra conster non seulement de la charge, mais aussi du lieu de sa demeure, et residence aux Provinces Unies, et du nom tant du Maître, ou Patron, que du Navire, afin que par ces deux moiens on puisse cognoistre s'il y a Marchandise de Contrebande, et qu'il apparoisse suffisament de la qualité du Navire, comme aussi du Maistre, ou Patron d'iceluy, auxquels Passeports, et Lettres de Mer sera donnée entiere foy, et creance, d'autant plus, que tant de la part dudit Seigneur Roy que de celle desdits Seigneurs Estats seront données des contremarques, pour en mieux recognoistre la validité, et afin qu'elles ne puissent estre aucunement falsifiées".

(f) *Sanctions on irregularities and abuses*

Treatment of privateers as pirates in case of the contravention of their instructions was often threatened by treaty. See, *e.g.*, Art. 2 of the Franco-Netherlands treaty of commerce of 10 August 1678 (Dumont, VII^1, 357; Parry, 14, 399):

"Et ainsi n'exerceront plus à l'avenir aucunes sortes d'hostilitez ni de violences les uns contre les autres tant sur la Mer, que sur la Terre, ou dans les Rivières, Rades, & Eaux douces, sous quelque nom & prétexte que ce soit; & aussi ne pourront les Sujets de Sa Majesté prendre aucunes Commissions pour des Armemens particuliers, ou Lettres de

> Représailles des Princes & Etats Ennemis desdits Seigneurs Etats Généraux, & moins les troubler ni endommager d'aucune sorte, en vertu de telles Commissions ou Lettres de Représailles, ni mesme aller en course avec elles, ... sous peine d'estre poursuivis & châtiez comme Pirates."

Many national regulations on privateering ran parallel with and referred to the abovementioned treaty provisions. They were frequently issued during the Anglo-American War of Independence and the period of the Armed Neutrality.

Returning to my preceding more detailed survey of the international régime of privateering, which has dominated so many centuries of prize law practice, I conclude by stating that the main instances of irregularities (which exposed the private belligerent vessel herself to the penalty of confiscation and her owner or master to heavy, in graver cases even capital, punishment as pirates) consisted of the following activities:
— operating without a commission (Art. 30 of the French Edict of 1584);
— accepting without Royal permission a commission from a foreign Sovereign (Art. 3 of *titre* IX of *livre* III of the *Ordonnance de la Marine* of 1681);
— flying the flag of a State other than that which granted the commission (Art. 5 of the same *titre*);
— sailing under commissions of two different States (the same Art. 5):

> "Tout Vaisseau combattant sous autre Pavillon que celuy de l'Estat dont il a Commission, ou ayant Commissions de deux différens Princes ou Estats, sera aussi de bonne prise; et s'il est Armé en Guerre, les Capitaines et Officiers seront punis comme Pirates."

III. *Attempts to abolish privateering*

The practice of privateering, which is thus reflected in hundreds of treaty provisions and municipal regulations especially of the 17th and the 18th century came under attack following the end of the 18th century, when in particular the United States took the initiative in an attempt to abolish it.

This was, for the rest, not the first time that such a proposal had been made to put an end to its legal existence. A suggestion to that effect was indeed already included in Article 14 of the Netherlands-Swedish treaty of commerce of 26 November 1675 (Dumont, VII[1], 316; Parry, 14, 41) to the following effect:

> "Quemadmodum vero exiguum paene pro securitate Commerciorum & Navigationis, quae Pactis hisce intenditur actum videbitur, nisi a reliquarum etiam Partium Armatoriis infestationibus, *Commissievaerders* dictis, Mare omnimodo liberum evadat, ita proinde desuper in majorem horum Pactorum observantiam, utrinque conventum est, ut tam à parte Sacrae Regiae Majestatis, quam Celsitudinum Dominorum Ordinum Generalium omnis cura studiumque impendatur, quo suos uterque Confoederatos ad consimilem dictarum infestationum prohibitionem, quam fieri poterit ocius persuadeant, quemadmodum certa satis spes etiam affulget, eos ad Negotium tam salutare induci posse."

A hint of this disposition of the Parties can be found in Article 3 of their subsequent treaty of commerce of 2/12 October 1679 (Dumont, VII[1], 437; Parry, 15, 331) in which a rule on privateering was followed by the optional clause that privateering could mutually be prohibited by *placaat*.

As appears from a footnote in Martens, R^2, V, 376, the collector has been unable to find any confirmation of the assertion by Büsch in his work *Über das Bestreben der Völker einander in ihrem Seehandel wehe zu thun* (Hamburg, 1800), p. 290, that the French Constituent Assembly has at one moment decided in favour of the abolition of all *armements en course*. The only thing which seems to be uncontroversial is that the French *Constituante* has deliberated upon it and that certain diplomatic soundings have been made in foreign capitals (to which only the Hanse Towns have responded favourably). Be this as it may, France has soon abandoned the idea, witness the series of successive decrees concerning the conduct of, and containing encouragements to, privateers, starting with a Decree of the National Convention of 31 January 1793 (provoked, according to its preamble, by threats from England) which authorized *armement en course* and enacted administrative provisions (Martens, R^2, V, 376), explained as to Art. IV by a Decree of 17 February 1793 (*ibid.*, 377, footnote). This Decree of 31 January 1793 was followed by further Decrees of 10 August 1795 (*ibid.*, 378, footnote) and 22 May 1803 (*ibid.*, VIII, 9). The Decree of 1795 prescribed the deposit of a cautionary sum of 50,000 *livres* (Art. 6), maintained earlier proclamations on privateering, and dealt with the distribution of the proceeds of the prizes and with the allowance of damages.

As far as the United States was concerned, Art. XXIII, *in fine*, of the Prussian-American treaty of commerce of 10 September 1785 (Martens, R^2, IV, 37; Parry, 49, 331) disposed as follows:

> "... Et les deux Puissances Contractantes s'engagent à n'accorder aucune commission à des vaisseaux armés en course, qui les autorisât à prendre ou à détruire ces sortes de vaisseaux marchands, ou à interrompre le commerce".

A *Manifesto* of the Commander in chief of the Russian forces in the Levant, Count Orlov, of 1 May 1772 (Martens, R^2, II, 33 at p. 34) recalled that he had, by an earlier *Manifesto* of 12 July 1770, made the "essential sacrifice" of not admitting any privateer under the Russian flag and that he had even resolved to

> "détacher, au milieu de [ses] opérations militaires [in the Mediterranean] les plus importantes, une escadre suffisante pour nettoyer les différentes parages de ces mers des corsaires, qui profitant des troubles de la guerre et croyant déguiser plus sûrement leurs forfaits, poussoient l'audace jusqu'à se servir du pavillon supposé de la Russie".

The movement in favour of the abolition of privateering, however, only bore fruit in the middle of the 19th century during and after the Crimean War, when on a British proposal, already preceded by unilateral declarations of both England and France, Article 1 of the famous Declaration of Paris of

16 April 1856 (Martens, N.R.G.[1], XV, 791 = XVI[2], 641; Parry, 115, 1) decreed in apodictic terms:

> "La course est et demeure abolie".

But even then the abolition was not yet universally adopted.

Perú, on the occasion of her war with Spain of 1856-1867 (declaration of war in *B.F.S.P.*, vol. 56, p. 709), still issued instructions to the commanders of her warships and to privateers (*ibid.*, p. 913).

Italy, in Art. 208 of her *Codice per la marina mercantile* of 24 October 1877, adhered to the abolition conditionally:

> "L'armamento in corso è abolito. Tuttavia, salvi gli impegni assunti dallo Stato nella convenzione di Parigi del 16 aprile 1856, l'armamento in corso contro le Potenze che non avessero aderito alla convenzione medesima o che ne recedessero, potrà essere autorizzato come rappresaglia delle prede che fossero commesse a danno della marina mercantile nazionale.
>
> In questo caso le condizioni per le concessioni delle lettere di marca e per l'esercizio della corsa saranno determinate con regio decreto. A questo effetto, se la Potenza nemica non avesse previamente rinunciato a commettere prede, potranno gli armatori delle navi nazionali, facendone richiesta all' autorità marittima, ottenere l'autorizzazione per un aumento d'armi, di munizioni e di equipaggio oltre il consueto".

In particular three States—the United States, Spain and Mexico—refused to be bound by the abolition, partly (Spain and Mexico) because they possessed only a disproportionally weak navy, partly (the United States) because the abolition of privateering was not paralelled by another abolition, *viz.*, that of the right of capture of private enemy ships, already proposed by the United States government at the end of the 18th century. These three States have, however, subsequently also adopted the principle of 1856.

The fact that the Declaration of Paris was not ratified by all maritime Powers was one of the causes of the continued mention of privateers in a number of municipal enactments dating from after 1856. See, *e.g.*, those of

Bremen. The Senate of the Free City of Bremen, which had prohibited the admittance of privateers to its waters and their equipment and supply there during the Crimean War on 29 April 1854 (Deák-Jessup, I, 632), still renewed that prohibition during the American Civil War on 4 July 1861 (Deák-Jessup, I, 633).

Japan. The admission of privateers to national waters was still regulated, *i.e.* in principle prohibited, by Japan during the Spanish-American War (Ordinance No. 87 of 30 April 1898; Deák-Jessup, I, 740, Art. 1).

Denmark. Even a Royal Danish Order of 20 December 1912 (*ibid.*, I, 476) still contained a corresponding prohibition in paragraph 2.

Privateers have continued to play a modest rôle, even in neutrality legislation in force during World War I, owing to the fact that the Declaration of Paris of 1856 had not yet, even then, been ratified by certain Powers, so that account had to be taken of the possibility that in the second decade of the

20th century privateering would still re-appear, even though as a superannuated method of warfare.

C. *Captors other than State organs and privateers*

This relates, in particular, to merchant ships, but also to individuals who found themselves in the position of being able to capture or recapture a prize. In this respect, also, the question has indeed often arisen on the occasion of a recapture, combined with a claim to the award of prize salvage.

In the abovementioned case of the *Helen* [1801] Sir William Scott developed a general theory on the right of individuals to proceed to, or participate in, a recapture, arguing with regard to a claim of recaptors to salvage that

> "In a recapture no commission is necessary to vest a salvage interest in the recaptors. It is the duty of every subject of the King to assist his fellow subjects in war, and to retake their property in the possession of the enemy. No commission is necessary to give a person so employed a title to the award which the policy of the law allots to that meritorious act of duty ...".

The recaptor was *in casu* rewarded with one-sixth of the ship's value on the footing of a privateer and not with one-eighth on the footing of a King's ship.

Merchantmen were often held to be entitled to take prizes and to recapture them, albeit only in exceptional circumstances, for they had, at least in later periods, no authority to play an active rôle as captors.

In a more remote past the practice of ordinary, non-commissioned merchant ships attempting to capture enemy merchant ships was not unknown and even regulated in detail. See Chapter 288 of the *Consulat de Mar* (Pardessus, II, 334):

> "Lorsque un navire marchand en rencontre un d'ennemis, s'il porte un ou quelques marchands, le patron doit leur demander s'ils veulent aller à l'abordage et combattre afin de prendre ce navire ennemi. Si le marchand ou les marchands, en totalité ou en majorité, y consentent, le patron peut le faire, et, quels que soient le dommage et le préjudice que les marchands en souffrent, il ne leur doit aucune indemnité, puisqu'ils ont donné leur consentement et que tout a été fait par leur volonté.
>
> Mais, si le patron fait ce qui vient d'être dit à l'insu et sans la volonté des marchands, de tous ou de la majeure partie, ce qu'ils en souffriront de dommage ou préjudice, le patron doit le supporter et le payer sans aucune dispute, quand même le navire devroit être vendu, ou même le bien du patron, si l'on en trouve quelque part, parce qu'il aura fait l'attaque à l'insu et sans la volonté des marchands, de tous ou de la majeure partie."

Curious echoes of that practice could still be heard much later in Article 209 of the *Codice per la marina mercantile* of Italy of 24 October 1877, worded as follows:

> "Le navi mercantili essendo aggredite da navi, anche da guerra, potranno difendersi e predarle, come pure accorrere alla difesa di altre navi nazionali od alleate aggredite, e concorrere colle medesime alla preda."

Art. 210 added another form of action by private captors:

"Se una nave nemica tentasse di far preda in vista delle coste dello Stato, oltre i provvedimenti che fossero presi dalla forza militare per respingere il tentativo, sarà lecito a qualunque cittadino di formare armamenti per correre in soccorso della nave aggredita. Se la nave aggredita è salvata, le persone avranno un premio a carico della proprietà salvata, da determinarsi, in caso di disaccordo, dall'autorità marittima competente".

The same echo can be heard in Article 15 of the Russian Prize Regulations of 14 July 1895, pursuant to which merchantmen were exceptionally entitled to exercise the right of prize against enemy or suspected vessels. The text of that Art. 15 has puzzled me because it set me the task of solving a linguistic riddle. The French translation of that Article read as follows:

"[Le] droit [d'arrêter, de visiter et de capturer les navires et chargements ennemis ou suspects] n'est accordé aux navires de commerce que dans les cas suivants:
1. en cas d'attaque de la part des navires ennemis ou suspects, et
2. s'il y a lieu de venir en aide aux navires russes ou *neutres* attaqués par l'ennemi."

However, in the German translation of the Regulations in the *Z.f.VR.* II (1908), pp. 144 *et seq.*, this word "neutres" has the word "Verbündete" as its counterpart. Only the original Russian text could have solved the problem convincingly, but I have failed to lay hands on it, in order to verify which of the two words represents the correct translation. Finally, a fourth language to which I must give credit, came to my aid: the English version of Art. 15, *sub* 2, proves that the French translation was wrong and the German translation right. The text in Hurst & Bray's volume I, Appendix A, at p. 315, indeed runs as follows:

"when they come to the assistance of Russian or *allied* ships exposed to attack".

The German translation already seemed to be more likely from the logical point of view, but had the drawback of contrasting the Russian provision with the Turkish Prize Law of 31 January 1912, which on the whole presents a strong resemblance to the Russian Regulations and reproduces in effect (again in a French version) the text "... ou si c'est pour prêter main forte à des navires ottomans ou à des navires battant pavillon neutre, attaqués par l'ennemi".

The right of Russian merchantmen to capture prizes was obviously so far above all doubt that the Prize Regulations of 1895 included two other Articles (48 and 49) which fixed in advance the amount of prize money to which their owners could lay claim: from one-fourth to one-half of its total according to the damage suffered by their vessels in capturing the prize.

Examples from the French past in which the right of merchantmen to act as captors was acknowledged were those of the *Marie-Louise* and the *Vierge du Rosaire*.

The *Marie-Louise* [*an* X] (de Pistoye and Duverdy, I, 167) was a French merchant vessel that was recaptured from the British within twenty-four hours by certain other French merchantmen, not provided with letters of marque; her recapture was held valid; while one-third of the value of ship and cargo was adjudged to the Republic, the crews of the recapturing merchantmen were referred to the Government with a recommendation by the *Conseil des prises* that they should be recompensed.

The *La Vierge du Rosaire* [1807] (*ibid.*, I, 168) was a French merchant ship that, together with two Spanish ships, had succeeded in recapturing three other merchant ships, and was granted a share of one-third of the value of the three recaptured vessels in virtue of Art. 54 of the *Arrêté* of 2 prairial *an* XI, which in this respect assimilated ordinary merchant ships in case of legitimate defence to vessels "armés en course":

> "Les bâtiments de commerce qui sont attaqués et qui, dans un combat pour leur légitime défense, reprennent des bâtiments capturés par l'ennemi, jouissent des mêmes droits de recousse que les bâtiments armés en course."

See also the case of the *Anonyme* [*an* IX] (*ibid.*, I, 165), a French vessel, captured by the enemy and recaptured by three fishing-boats, not provided with letters of marque, after she had remained in the possession of the enemy during more than twenty-four hours; she was adjudged to the French Republic.

Old French prize court judgements have sometimes dealt with cases in which a capture had been made by or on the authority of someone who was not regularly empowered to act. If in such a case the validity of the action was upheld, the prize fell to the State. Otherwise the prize was released. See the cases of

the inhabitants of the *Commune of Sanary* [*an* IX] who organized an expedition to secure a ship that had cast anchor in a creek of their coast and which later proved to be a prize taken by an English privateer from the Spaniards (*ibid.*, I, 165);

the *Ulrick Cock* [*an* VIII] (*ibid.*, I, 30), a Danish vessel, anchored in the port of Cayenne, seized on the strength of an illegal *Arrêté* of the colonial Governor of French Guyana, an agent of the *Directoire*;

the *Cornwalis* [*an* XIII], reported I, 172 under the heading *Le capitaine Gaultier contre le Contrôleur de la marine*. This was a ship of the British East India Company which was sailing under the escort of the British frigate the *Brave* from Bombay to England with ninety-five French prisoners of war on board. During the voyage those prisoners of war succeeded in overpowering the crew and capturing the *Cornwalis*.

Section 2. WHEN MAY THE RIGHT OF PRIZE BE EXERCISED?

The answer to this question is obvious: only during the war, *i.e.*, neither (A) prior to its outbreak, nor (B) after its termination.

This period problem, including related questions of transitional law, has been examined in great detail by De Pistoye and Duverdy in their *Traité des prises maritimes*, vol. I, 119-156:

Titre III. Des temps dans lesquels s'exerce le droit de prise.

- Chap. I. Prooemium. Du temps à partir duquel l'exercice du droit de prise peut commencer (pp. 119-133).
- Chap. II. L'exercice du droit de prise pendant la guerre (pp. 133-140).
- Chap. III. Des temps à partir desquels cesse l'exercice du droit de prise (pp. 141-156).

A. Captures made prior to the outbreak of war

Visits or captures effected before the war, even in expectation of its outbreak, were illegal. The fact that the commander of the warship or the privateer concerned was under the conviction, wrongly, that war had already begun, was no ground of exculpation: the action remained an international delinquency. A case of this type is recorded from 1812, when the American brig *Oneida* seized the British merchant vessel *Lord Nelson* thirteen days before the official declaration of war. This case was much later, in 1854, still submitted to arbitration by the Mixed Commission of London (1853). Its umpire could not, however, award damages to the ship's proprietors because the Commission lacked competence to adjudicate upon the case *ratione temporis* (see *R.A.I.*, I, pp. 685-686).

It might of course be doubtful in a given case whether a state of war had already existed at the moment of visit or capture, but that doubt did not affect the principle.

Old cases are recorded in which a capture took place after the issuance of an order of general reprisals but before war was officially declared. See the case of British cargo on board the Swedish *Maria Magdalena* [1779] (Hay and Marriott, 247; Roscoe, I, 20), captured under the Order of Reprisals of 29 July 1778 against France, and the Dutch *Snelle Zeylder* [1781] (Roscoe, I, footnote *b* at p. 254), captured under the Order of December 1780 against Holland. Despite the argument of the claimants in the first case that "the present state of hostilities was not such a state of war as to make British subjects liable to confiscation, or any other legal inconvenience", and that "nothing but a declaration of war could restrain the subject", Judge Sir J. Marriott showed himself very generous towards the captor by arguing that he saw no difference between the case of the engagement of the King of France in actual hostilities with England and other cases in which "a war is proclaimed by a herald at the Royal Exchange, with his trumpets, and on the Pont Neuf at Paris, and by reading and affixing a printed paper on public buildings".

An historical case of much later date in which the exact dating of the outbreak of war was of primary importance for the assessment of the legality of the exercise of the right of prize was that of the seizure and sinking on

25 July 1894 by a Japanese warship of the British (neutral) vessel *Kow Shing*, temporarily employed as a Chinese troop transport on a voyage from Shanghai to Taku. Apart from other different questions—(*a*) whether a state of war could be held to exist without a formal declaration (whereupon comp. Part IX-A (vol. IX) of this publication at pp. 58 *et seq.*); (*b*) whether Japan's naval action was lawful in view of the fact that it took place in neutral Korean waters (whereupon comp. vol. X of this publication, p. 135); (*c*) how the transport of enemy troops should be qualified juridically (whereupon comp. *infra sub* A, section 5, pp. 458-461), and (*d*) whether the sinking of a neutral ship was lawful at all (whereupon comp. *infra sub* B, section 5, pp. 528-533), the exact moment of Japan's naval action also gave rise to controversy. The Sino-Japanese war having been started without a formal declaration (which was only made at 1 August 1894), the question was by what precise events had it broken out *de facto*? The different points of time which came under consideration—the first actual exchange of fire between the respective navies, or the initial warning shot intended to summon the *Kow-shing* to submit to visit, or even already perhaps the sailing of the Japanese fleet with aggressive intent—were discussed in great detail by S. Takahashi in his *Cases on international law during the Chino-Japanese War*, pp. 24 *et seq.*, pp. 42 *et seq.*

It might also be doubtful whether a state of war between the captor State and another State had existed at all. This was questionable in an old case of 1807 relating to the Ragusan merchant vessel *Assomption* (de Pistoye and Duverdy, I, p. 29) that had been captured by a French privateer. As the validity of that capture depended on the existence of a state of war between France and Sardinia, French prize courts examined the question. Both the *Conseil impérial des prises* and, in appeal, Napoleon decided that during the years IX and X the French Government had taken no steps against Sardinia which authorized France to exercise belligerent rights against foreign shipping.

The principle applied in France was in the cases of *Le Hoop contre le Renard, le Pas-de-Calais et le Ricochet* and *Le Cérès contre la Sophie* [November 1815] (*ibid.*, I, 145) formulated by the *Conseil d'Etat* as follows:

in the first case:

> "C'est à l'époque de la prise qu'on doit s'arrêter, sans égard au temps postérieur, pour savoir s'il y avait hostilité entre la France et le pays auquel appartient le navire capturé ...";

and in the second case:

> "On doit décider les contestations en matière de prises d'après les règles et circonstances existantes à l'époque de la saisie sans tenir compte de ce qui existe lors du jugement."

Historical cases in which captures of French ships—both warships and private merchant vessels—were made by British warships or privateers prior to the official outbreak of hostilities are those of the *Lis* and the *Alcide* [June

1755] and the *Belle-Poule*, *Pallas*, *Licorne* and *Coureur* [June 1778], recorded in Part IX-A (vol. IX) of this publication, p. 61.

When, in 1809, the Spanish ship *Nuestra Señora de los Dolores* (Edw., 60; Roscoe, II, 20) was captured prior to be outbreak of hostilities, her restitution to the owners with costs and damages was decreed, but war actually broke out before this decree was executed. No further step was taken during the war to obtain her condemnation. When peace was made, the claimant owner was held to be replaced in the same position as before the war: he was entitled to restoration of his ship and to costs and damages.

Since I have not dealt with Japan's aggression against Russia in 1904 at p. 62 of Chapter II (on the opening of hostilities) of Part IX-A (vol. IX) of this publication, in order to reserve it for discussion in the present Part IX-C, I must now briefly consider it here to illustrate the arguments with which the Imperial Government has glossed over their action and the Japanese prize courts have sanctioned them on the eve of the codification.

In the *Mukden* case appeal proceedings (Hurst & Bray, II, 12 *et seq.*) the Government's justification was set out by the Procurator and the Higher Prize Court adopted the latter's view in the following wording (at pp. 15-16):

> "a state of war does not necessarily commence at the moment when opposing armed forces open fire upon each other, nor when a declaration of war or any such notice is given, but rather when the intention of going to war is carried into effect or when such intention is made manifest. When, by reason of Russia's unreasonable behaviour, the prospect of an amicable settlement of the diplomatic negotiations between Japan and Russia became utterly hopeless, and it became certain that Russia's intention was to make preparations for war, and to compel Japan to submission by force of arms, our Government, on the 5th of February, 1904, despatched instructions to the Japanese Minister accredited to Russia to give notice to that State that diplomatic relations with her were at an end. At the same time, the Imperial fleet made preparation for war and left Sasebo on the following day, the 6th, at 7 a.m., with the intention of opening hostilities. On the way the Japanese fleet captured the steamship "Ekaterinoslav," of the Russian Volunteer Fleet Company, which was a vessel liable to naval service in time of war. This was nothing less than the carrying out of the intention of making war, and any capture made after that time is lawful. Moreover, the ship was captured after the Imperial Government had, on the 6th of February, at 2 p.m., notified the Russian Minister at Tokio of the rupture of diplomatic relations. Thus the first and second points of the appeal fail."

B. Captures made after the cessation of hostilities

The answer to the question when the right of visit and capture lapsed, although equally obvious in principle, *i.e.* with the termination of hostilities, was not in the past so easy to determine in actual practice.

An old instance of the capture of an English ship by a Spanish privateer within the term fixed in Article 2 of the Anglo-Spanish peace treaty of 15 November 1630 (Dumont, V^2, 619) gave rise to a legal "consultation" in support of the claim of her owners for restitution. This "consultation" was dated 1 March 1632 and is inserted in the Dutch collection of Pamphlets by Knuttel, no. 4184. It was based on the law of nations generally and cited, in particular, Hugo Grotius, *De jure belli ac pacis*, l. III, c. II, § 5 and c. XX, §§ 2 and 24.

Another old case, in which a neutral ship was restored on the ground of her capture after the conclusion of peace, was that of the *Adolphus Frederick*. This ship was captured at the end of the War of the Austrian Succession on 2 May 1748; a proclamation of 5 May 1748 announced the cessation of hostilities in the Channel from twelve days after 19 April 1748, the date of signature of the preliminary Articles of peace of Aachen, which terminated that War. The Court decreed her restitution on 17 May 1748 (Roscoe, I, footnote *a* at p. 453).

A well-known difficulty experienced in earlier centuries was the uncertainty about the conclusion of peace as a result of lack of speedy communications between the government and its operating navy units. This led to the insertion in peace treaties of special stipulations dealing with the prevailing situation.

Legal doubts could also be more easily provoked because customary law gave no clear answer to the question at what precise moment a war ended: with the signature of the peace treaty, with its ratification, or with its entry into force?

The case of the *John (No. 2)* [1818] (2 Dodson, 336; Roscoe, II, 232) presented the picture of the capture on 5 March 1815 of an American merchantman by an English privateer, acting in ignorance of the conclusion of the Anglo-American peace treaty of Ghent of 24 December 1814. The prize was afterwards lost without negligence on the part of the captor. He was exonerated and held not liable to damages because he could not have been aware of the conclusion of peace.

It might further be uncertain as to what was the effect of the conclusion of an armistice upon the continuance of the right of capture: did it terminate that right when the armistice was silent on the issue? The answer was generally negative: the belligerents could and did continue to exercise the right of visit and seizure, at least against enemy vessels. The legality of its exercise against neutral shipping was more controversial. During the Sino-Japanese War of 1894-1895 the Japanese searched and captured the British SS *Yik-sang* after the conclusion of the armistice, but in that case Article 4 of the armistice convention permitted in so many words the continuation of the measures of visit, search and capture (S. Takahashi, *loco cit.*, pp. 73 *et seq.*). The question was examined by E. Kappelhoff-Wulff in an academic dissertation at the University of Hamburg (1973) under the title *Die Zulässigkeit der Ausübung des Prisenrechts während eines Waffenstillstands*.

The fact that the right of visit and capture ended with the conclusion of peace did not, of course, imply that prizes once made were to be released. This might be, and was occasionally, stipulated by an express treaty provision, but that was an exception: prize jurisdiction normally prevailed after the end of hostilities with regard to seizures made prior to that end.

This was decided in express terms by the *Conseil des prises* in the abovementioned case of *Le Cérès contre la Sophie* of November 1815 (de Pistoye and Duverdy, I, 145) concerning the capture of a Netherlands vessel with an English cargo on board, made prior to the conclusion of peace on 16 May 1814: the *Conseil* saw no objection to a validation of the prize after the conclusion of peace. The same ruling was constantly decided by the Japanese Prize Courts in 1905-1906.

Historical instances of treaty stipulations that provided for the release of prizes captured during the war, but not yet adjudged by a prize court at the moment of the conclusion of peace were, for example, the treaties of commerce of 6/16 July 1667 between Sweden and the Netherlands (Dumont, VII[1], 37; Parry, 10, 187), Article 9:

> "Denique D.D. Ordines statim post subscriptionem harum Tabularum mandabunt, ut Naves Merxque omnis ad Subditos Suecanae Ditionis pertinentes, atque ex auctoritate Paragraphorum superiorum pro licitis habendae, quas in potestate occupantium, aut in Custodia Admiralitatis Belgicae liquebit etiamnum detineri, nec Fisco hactenus addictas esse, quasve occupari, postquam Pactis hisce jam subscriptum erit, continget, quantocius Proprietariis restituantur."

and of 26 November 1675 between the same countries (Dumont, VII[1], 316; Parry, 14, 41), Art. 16:

> "Denique Sacra Regia Majestas Sueciae & Celsitudines Dominorum Ordinum Generalium statim post Ratificationem harum Tabularum mandabunt, ut Subditi alterutrius quantocius libertati reddantur, & Naves, Merces, Pecuniae, caeteraque denique omnia bona ad Subditos alterutrius pertinentia, & occasione hujus Belli capta, vel arresto detenta, Proprietariis restituantur".

Restitution of prizes which had still been made after the cessation of hostilities was more normal because they were in any case irregular. Since, however, as remarked *supra*, such captures were often effected at a moment when the termination of hostilities was not yet known to the captors owing to the lack of means of communications, many treaties included time limits: prizes made after the termination of the war were only to be restored if the capture had been effected after the expiry of those time limits. See, *inter alia*, the treaties entered into by the United Netherlands with:

Portugal on 6 August 1661 (Dumont, VI[2], 366; Parry, 6, 375):

> "Cui consequenter cessent inter Regem & Regnum Lusitaniae ab una & Foederatum Belgium ab altera parte, ac utriusque Subditos & Incolas omnis actus hostilitatis & injuriarum, idque in Europa post elapsum bimestre spatium ab eo die quo huic Foederi utrimque subscriptum erit, in caeteris vero Mundi partibus à publicatione harum Tabularum omnesque captivi hinc inde ilico post Ratihabitionem hujus Tractatus pristinae libertati restituantur; omnes itaque Ditiones, omnia Loca, Naves, Bonaque, quae temporis inter ea ab alterutro occupabuntur, ut & quae antea occupata fuerunt in India Orientali, Occidentali, vel alicubi locorum, in Dominio permanebunt eorum, qui praefatis tempori-

bus eorum possessores fuisse comperientur; ea vero, quae elapsis duobus post factam eandem subscriptionem mensibus in Europa & post publicationem in caeteris Mundi partibus occupabuntur aut capientur, prioribus eorundem Dominis absque ulla mora aut exceptione restituentur";

England on 21/31 July 1667 (Dumont, VII[1], 44; Parry, 10, 231), Art. 7, [identical with Art. 3 of the preceding treaty of Westminster of 5 April 1654 (Dumont, VI[2], 74; Parry, 3, 225)]:

"Sed ad evitandam porrò omnem litis & contentionum materiam, quae oriri interdum solet ex causa restitutionis aut liquidationis ejusmodi Navium, Mercium aliarumque rerum mobilium, quas in locis & oris longè dissitis, post conclusam Pacem & priusquam ea ipsa Pax ibidem innotuerit, captas aut occupatas fuisse, utraque Pars aut alterutra causari possit. Conventum est, uti omnes ejusmodi Naves, Merces aliaque bona mobilia, quae fortè post conclusionem & publicationem praesentis Instrumenti occupari possent, intra spatium duodecim dierum in Freto Britannico, atque in Mari Boreali; intra spatium sex septimanarum ab Ostio dicti Freti Britannici usque ad Promontorium Sancti Vincentii, ut & intra spatium decem hebdomadarum ultra praedictum Promontorium & cis Lineam Æquinoctialem vel Æquatorem, tam in Oceano & Mari Mediterraneo, quam alibi; tum inde intra spatium octimestre trans terminos praedictae Lineae per universum Orbem, sine aliqua exceptione vel ulteriore temporis locive distinctione, ullave restitutionis aut compensationis ratione habitâ, occupantium sint & maneant";

France on 10 August 1678 (Dumont, VII[1], 350 (Peace Treaty) and 357 (Treaty of Commerce); Parry, 14, 365 resp. 399), resp. Arts. 2 and 3, and on 20 September 1697 (Dumont, VII[2], 386; Parry, 21, 371), Art. 3;

Sweden on 2/12 October 1679 (Dumont, VII[1], 437; Parry, 15, 331), Art. 22;

Spain on 26 June 1714 (Dumont, VIII[1], 427; Parry, 29, 97), Art. 6.

Judgments quoted in the context of this timing problem sometimes come within the domain of transitional law. This is in particular the case of a number of French prize courts judgments which I will quote below although, strictly speaking, they do not come within the scope of the subject matter surveyed in the present section.

Such questions of transitional law were decided by the *Conseil des Prises*, *e.g.*:

in the case of *L'Ariadne contre la Laure* [*an* IX] (Pistoye-Duverdy, I, 146):

"Les traités internationaux, même non promulgués lois de l'Etat, peuvent avoir un effet rétroactif, lorsque tel est leur dispositif.—Une prise faite avant un traité, et qui eût été déclarée valable si elle avait été vérifiée avant sa conclusion, peut être annulée en vertu du traité, quand elle est jugée après sa promulgation, mais, dans ce cas, aucune condamnation en dommages et intérêts ne peut être prononcée contre le capteur";

in the case of *La Thétis contre le Serpent* [*an* X] (*ibid.*, I, 147):

"N'est pas valable une prise faite après la signature d'un traité de paix même avant sa ratification, alors qu'aucune stipulation spéciale n'est faite à cet égard. Il en est ainsi même quand la paix est connue ni du capteur, ni du capturé";

in the case of *La Bellone contre Le Porcher; La Petite-Renommée contre La Nymphe* [*an* XI] (*ibid.*, I, 149, 154):

> "Lorsqu'un traité de paix détermine des délais à l'expiration desquels les prises ne seront plus faites valablement, l'ignorance absolue de la paix n'est pas indispensable pour la validité d'une saisie faite dans les délais réservés.—Dans les délais où les prises peuvent être encore légitimement faites, la présomption d'ignorance de la paix est de droit, et elle ne doit céder que devant la preuve complète que le capteur a eu une connaissance positive de la paix.
>
> Connaissance doit être certaine, assurée, indubitable. Elle ne peut résulter de renseignements verbaux, ni même de documents non-authentiques fournis par l'ennemi. Elle doit émaner immédiatement ou médiatement de la puissance à laquelle appartient le capteur. Elle peut, néanmoins, résulter de communications faites par la voie de l'ennemi en vertu d'instructions spéciales et officielles dont il serait porteur";

or by the *Conseil d'Etat* in the case of *Le Dolly et Le Télégraphe contre La Méduse* [1819] (*ibid.*, I, 155):

> "Sont valables les prises faites en vertu d'une loi en vigueur au moment de la capture et qui n'a été révoquée que depuis ce moment; si la révocation a eu lieu avant le jugement de ces prises, elles doivent néanmoins être validées".

Section 3. WHERE MAY THE RIGHT OF PRIZE BE EXERCISED?

A. *Places where the exercise is normal*

Open sea

The law of prize was a body of rules destined to govern naval warfare so that the right of visit and capture was in principle to be exercised at sea. Already in earlier periods, however, it was not uncommon that captures were in actual fact effected, for example, on a river. The accounts of the municipality of Cologne of 1645, *e.g.*, reveal that captures were made on the river Rhine. The Netherlands *Groot Placaatboek* publishes on p. 978 of volume I Decrees for capturing enemy vessels on inland rivers, especially on the Upper-Rhine (8 August 1625 and 11 June 1639).

Territorial waters of the belligerents

It is clear that territorial waters near the sea were also often considered by naval units and privateers as appropriate places where the right of prize could be exercised. However, the sources witness to the occasional insertion in treaty provisions or municipal regulations of an express prohibition of privateers taking any action in territorial waters. Comp. section 1 *supra*.

Internal waters or inland lakes

Subsequently, the practice of effecting seizures on internal waters slowly insinuated itself into the customary law of prize. That extension was not surprising in so far as inland waters in open communication with the high seas were concerned. Thus, there was nothing unusual in the seizure of a Russian ship, the *Johanna Emilie,* as prize in the port of London during the Crimean War by non-commissioned captors (customs officers) [1854] (Spinks, 12; Roscoe, II, 252).

When, however, the practice gradually extended to other inland waters, prize courts began to discuss whether and to what extent that was permissible. The first prize tribunals to busy themselves with this problem would seem to have been the prize courts of the United States, when captures in prize had been made on the Great Lakes between their country and Canada during the 1812 war. Those captures were validated, although even an indirect communication between the Lakes and the Atlantic Ocean, as there is at present, did not at the time yet exist; there was indeed no navigable connection between the two prior to 1817. See on these facts the historical survey in the judgment concerning *Craft captured on Victoria Nyanza* (*B.C.P.C.*, III, 295), adjudicated upon at the end of World War I (25 November 1918). Not many comparable cases of captures on inland lakes or rivers seem to have occurred since then. One further case was the seizure of the *Cotton Plant* by the United States authorities on the river Roanoke during the Civil War in 1864 [1870] (10 Wallace (Amer.), 577).

Seizures on land

The Canadian cases had, for that matter, already been preceded by quite a different form of the exercise of the right of prize elsewhere than on the sea, namely on land. The surrender of the Netherlands island of Saint Eustatius in the Caribbean to the British naval and military forces during the Anglo-Netherlands war of 1780 was followed by the seizure of Netherlands property on that island and that gave rise to a case of 1782, decided by Lord Mansfield and known as *Lindo v. Rodney* (2 Douglas, footnote at p. 613), which resulted in the condemnation of that property as good and lawful prize. That decision was still invoked much later by Lord Merriman, the Prize Court judge in England during World War II, in the case of the *Hermes and other Hulls* of 1951 (*Ll.Rep.P.C.* (2nd), at p. 303).

Many more such seizures on land, on harbour quays, in custom houses, harbour tanks, etc. have since been made by belligerent forces, and not exclusively by American and British captors.

Such captures have, however, given rise in England to constant contests and quarrels between the Common Law Courts and the Courts of Admiralty concerning the jurisdiction claimed by the latter to deal with causes, civil and marine, in ports and harbours, and also in rivers or creeks, within the interior of a country, which the Common Law Courts asserted could only be tried at law. Lord Mansfield, however, decided in the abovementioned case of *Lindo v. Rodney*, with the subsequent approval of the House of Lords, that "the nature of the ground of the action—prize or not prize—not only authorizes the prize court, but excludes the common law".

When Sir William Scott in the case of *The Two Friends* [1799] (1 C.Rob.,

271; Roscoe, I, 130), observed that he knew "no other definition of prize goods than that they are goods taken on the high seas *jure belli* out of the hands of the enemy", he obviously employed the word in a more limited meaning. Comp. also *infra*, section 4, p. 197.

On the admissibility of the exercise of the right of capture on land at the end of the pre-codification period see the elaborate reasoning of the Higher Prize Court of Japan in the *Thalia* [1905] (Hurst & Bray, II, at pp. 118-129) resulting in the following succinct *dictum*:

> "Putting a vessel in dock or on the building yard of the dock for repairs is no more than a temporary removal from the water during the work with the object of restoring her to her proper efficiency. In such a case it must be held that the right of capture may be enforced upon the vessel, even if the place where she lies is not covered with water."

After my above survey under A of the places where the right of prize may normally be exercised, I now turn to

B. *Places where the exercise is disputable*

Neutral or neutralized waters

The famous issue of the illegality and invalidity of captures made in neutral waters has both a neutrality and a prize law aspect. As far as the former is concerned, I refer to my detailed surveys in Part IX-B (vol. X) of this publication, Chapter III, section 2, pp. 61 *et seq.* and Chapter IV, section 2, pp. 106 *et seq.* I will confine myself here mainly to setting out, in addition to those surveys, its prize law aspect, although the two are closely interwoven.

In Part I (p. 202) of their *Recueil des arbitrages internationaux* the editors remarked on this subject that

> "peu d'histoires sont plus obscures que celle de l'abus du territoire neutre dans la guerre maritime".

The history of this chapter of the law of nations has also been described, *e.g.*, in Holtzendorff's *Handbuch des Völkerrechts*, IV, § 128, pp. 605 *et seq.* and in Walker's *History of the law of nations*, I, pp. 148 *et seq.*

Cases of the seizure of an enemy or neutral ship or cargo in neutral waters are reported from early dates. Reginald Marsden, in his work for the Selden Society, pp. 355-356, mentions an old case of this kind, dating from the War of the Austrian Succession (1740-1748): *The Two Sisters*, sailing under English colours from Norway to the then neutral French port of Havre de Grâce, from where she was due to continue her voyage to England, and captured on 22 August 1740 by a Spanish privateer whilst she was weighing anchor off that port at a distance of a mile from the French coast.

Under this heading "neutral or neutralized waters" I will deal successively, under I with the illegality of such captures in general, under II with the judicial treatment of the same, and under III with the connected problem of the admissibility of the adjudication of prizes brought into and lying in neutral harbours.

I. *Illegality of captures in neutral or neutralized waters in general*

It was not seriously disputed even in early days that such captures were illegal. See already Art. 19 on the Anglo-Burgundian treaty of 24 February 1496 (Dumont, III^2, 336):

> "Item, Conventum est ut suprà: Quod si aliqua Navis per aliquem non Subditum Principibus praedictis, capta fuerit in portu aliquo, aut Franchisiis alicujus Principum praedictorum, tenebitur ille Princeps, in cujus portu aut Franchisiis Navis illa capta fuerit, una cum altero Principe pro restitutione dictae Navis prosequi, sumptibus tamen & expensis Partis damnificatae."

Several treaties prohibited them during the 17th and the 18th century. In addition to the data given in vol. X of this publication, at pp. 69-71, I cite those of

Spain-England, 18 August 1604 (Dumont, V^2, 35), Art. 32, repeated in 1630, 1667 and 1670;

Spain-Denmark, 19 March 1641 (Dumont, VI^1, 209), Art. 12;

France-Denmark/Norway, 23 August 1742 (Wenck, I, 591; Parry, 36, 425), Art. 33;

France-United States, 6 February 1778 (Martens, R^2, II, 587; Parry, 46, 417), Art. 6:

> "Le Roi Très-Chrétien fera usage de tous les moyens qui sont en son pouvoir, pour protéger et défendre tous les Vaisseaux et Effets, appartenants aux Sujets, Peuples et Habitans des dits Etats-Unis et de chacun d'iceux, qui seront dans ses Ports, Havres ou Rades, ou dans les Mers près de ses Pays, Contrées, Isles, Villes et Places, et fera tous ses efforts pour recouvrir et faire restituer aux Propriétaires légitimes, leurs Agens ou Mandataires, tous les Vaisseaux et Effets qui leur seront pris dans l'étendue de sa Juridiction",

and *vice-versa* (Art. 7);

United States-Sweden, 3 April 1783 (Martens, R^2, III, 565; Parry, 48, 269), Art. 18;

England-France, 26 September 1786 (Martens, R^2, IV, 155; Parry, 50, 71), Art. 41;

France-Russia, 11/22 January 1787 (Martens, R^2, IV, 196; Parry, 50, 103), Art. 28;

Spain-United States, 27 October 1795 (Martens, R^2, VI, 142; Parry, 53, 9), Art. 6;

and, still from the 19th century:

peace treaty between Portugal and Algiers of 14 July 1813 (Martens, N.R., III, 268; Parry, 62, 281), Art. 4:

> "No Algerian corsaire shall cruise within the distance of six miles from the coast of Portugal and its isles, or remain in those waters for the purpose of giving chase to or visiting Portuguese ships or those of any other Nation ...".

There are also examples of old treaty stipulations that prohibited the exercise of the right of prize in certain sea areas other than those forming part of the territorial sea in its normal sense. See the express interdiction of the visiting by a belligerent State of ships passing the Sound, embodied in Art. 3 of the Netherlands-Danish convention of 13 August 1645 (Dumont, VI[1], 312), Art. 24 of that of 12 February 1647 (*ibid.*, VI[1], 367) and Art. 3 of that of 6 July 1688 (*ibid.*, VII[2], 157; Parry, 18, 245).

The same prohibitions were included in various national regulations which can be found in Martens, R[2]:

United States, 9 May 1778 (III, 17);
Tuscany, 1 August 1778 (III, 24), Arts. 1 and 2;
Genoa, 1 July 1779 (III, 64), Art. 1;
Venice, 9 September 1779 (III, 74), Art. 9;
Russia, 31 December 1787 (IV, 336), Art. 2;
Austria, 7 August 1803 (VIII, 105), Art. 11.

See also Art. 14 of the British Act of 9 August 1870 in Deák-Jessup's *Neutrality Law*, vol. I, p. 138, under the heading "Illegal prize".

As to the practical application of the generally recognized principle, the question of the validity, or otherwise, of captures made in neutral territorial waters has also been a subject of discussion for a very long time in prize courts. As stated in vol. II of W. Wynne's *The life of Sir Leoline Jenkins*, p. 727, King James, in a proclamation of 2 March 1604, already ordained that all foreign vessels, once they had lawfully entered his waters, would be safe and that in case of their capture they would be restored. It was on the strength of this precedent that Sir Leoline Jenkins, Judge of the Court of Admiralty, on 14 October 1675 requested the Council of King Charles II to release a Hamburgian vessel that had been captured within the dominions of that King whilst on her way to an English harbour.

Prize courts of belligerent States have more than once been seised of cases in which it was alleged that the capture had taken place in neutral waters.

One of the oldest reported cases is that of the *De Fortuyn* [1760] (Burrell, 175; Roscoe, I, 7), a Dutch ship seized by three English privateers whilst at anchor in the Spanish port of Monte Christi (Hispaniola). The Lords of Appeal decided that although the ship and her cargo were liable to condemnation (on the ground of her trading with a French colony under the licence of the King of France), the condemnatory sentence of the lower court must be reversed, and the ship restored to her owners "by reason that she was attacked and taken whilst she lay at anchor in one of the ports of the King of Spain within reach of his cannon and under his protection contrary to the remonstrances of his Governor".

In adjudicating upon such captures the courts were sometimes faced with doubts about the exact boundaries of the territorial sea of the neutral country concerned or with other comparable uncertainties. Such were the circumstances in two of the oldest recorded instances of doubts of this nature, *viz.*, the famous cases of two Dutch vessels with the same name *Twee Gebroeders* but with different masters, dating from 1800 and 1801, both occurring in the same maritime area, the Shallows (*Wadden*) north of the Netherlands province of Groningen, and in both of which it was the neutral Government of Prussia that intervened in the prize court proceedings. I call them famous because at the present time they still provide legal material for the solution of the never definitively solved dispute between the Netherlands and (West-)Germany over their State frontier in the mouth of the German river the Ems, whereupon comp. vol. II of this publication, pp. 4 and 599, and vol. X, p. 71. They are also interesting because they cast light upon old views on the admissibility of maritime blockades which affected neutral countries. On this latter aspect of England's naval operations of about 1800 comp. my remarks *infra*, III A, section 4, p. 427.

In the present context I will confine my exposé to the question of the alleged violation of neutral water territory.

The *Twee Gebroeders (No. 1)* (Alberts, Master) [1800] (3 C.Rob., 162; Roscoe, I, 286) resulted in the restoration of the four Dutch vessels concerned on the ground that when a warship lying in neutral water territory sends out boats which capture an enemy ship outside the neutral territory, she commits an act of hostility that cannot be tolerated: no such action may commence within the territory of a neutral State.

The *Twee Gebroeders (No. 2)* (Northolt, Master) [1801] (3 C.Rob., 336; Roscoe, I, 323) resulted in the condemnation of the vessel concerned on the ground that the Court was not convinced of the validity of Prussia's claim to territorial sovereignty over he place of the actual capture.

The two cases were very similar: in both the capture had been made by the crews of English boats operating from a British warship, the *Espiègle*, anchored in the Prussian waters of the Easter-Ems, and in both the captures had actually been made in or on the Uithuizer Wad, the shallow north of the Netherlands province of Groningen, albeit at different spots (see the maps in Robinson's *Reports* of the cases). In both, too, the Dutch (enemy) merchant vessels were on their way from East Frisian waters across the shallows and the then still existing Dutch inland sea, the Zuiderzee, to blockaded Amsterdam.

The Court upheld the basic principle of the unlawfulness and resulting invalidity of captures made in neutral waters, but reached contrary conclusions as to some other points which were decisive of the ultimate fate of the captured vessels.

During the discussion it was contended on the Prussian side that the captures had been made within Prussian territory, but that even if the act of actual capture might not have taken place within neutral territory, yet the capture was unlawful because the warship to which the boats belonged was lying within the neutral limits, and that therefore, wherever the place of actual capture might have been, the station of the warship was in itself sufficient to affect the legality of the capture.

In view of the historical and doctrinal interest of these two judgments I will insert below the main relevant passages from the statements of reasons obtaining in the two decrees. The first question—partly factual, partly juridical—dealt with was whether the captures were actually made in a sea passage to the Zuiderzee that belonged to the neutral State of Prussia. The second question was whether the captures, even if made within Dutch (enemy) waters, was perhaps invalidated by the fact that the captors had passed through neutral territorial waters before reaching the actual places of capture.

From the *Twee Gebroeders (No. 1)* [1800] I quote:

"Upon the question so proposed, the first fact to be determined is the character of the place where the capturing ship lay, whether she was actually stationed within those portions of land and water, or of something between water and land, which are considered to be within the limits of the Prussian territory. On this point I am inclined to think, on an inspection of the charts, and on hearing what has been urged, that she was lying within the limits to which neutral immunity is usually conceded. She was lying in the eastern branch of the Ems, within what may, I think, be considered as a distance of three miles at most from East Friesland. An exact measurement cannot easily be obtained; but in a case of this nature, in which the Court would not willingly act with an unfavourable minuteness towards a neutral state, it will be disposed to calculate the distance very liberally, and more especially as the spot in question is a sand covered with water only on the flow of the tide, but immediately connected with the land of East Friesland, and when dry may be considered as making part of it. I am of opinion that the ship was lying within those limits, in which all direct hostile operations are by the law of nations forbidden to be exercised. That fact being assumed, I have only to inquire whether, the ship being so stationed, the capture which took place was made under such circumstances as oblige us to consider it as an act of violence, committed within the protection of a neutral territory.

It is said that the ship was in all respects observant of the peace of the neutral territory, that nothing was done by her which could affect the right of territory, or from which any inconvenience could arise to the country within whose limits she was lying, inasmuch as the hostile force which she employed was applied to the captured vessel lying out of the territory. But that is a doctrine that goes a great deal too far. I am of opinion that no use of a neutral territory for the purposes of war is to be permitted. I do not say remote uses, such as procuring provisions and refreshments, and acts of that nature, which the law of nations universally tolerates; but that no proximate acts of war are in any manner to be allowed to originate on neutral grounds; and I cannot but think that such an act as this, that a ship should station herself on neutral territory, and send out her boats on hostile enterprises, is an act of hostility much too immediate to be permitted; for, suppose that even a direct hostile use should be required to bring it within the prohibition of the law of nations, nobody will say that the very act of sending out boats to effect a capture is not itself an act directly hostile—not complete, indeed, but inchoate, and clothed with all the characters of hostility. If this could be defended, it might as well be said that a ship lying in a neutral station might fire shot on a vessel lying out of the neutral territory. The injury in that case would not be consummated, nor received on neutral ground; but no one would say that such an act would not be an hostile act, immediately commenced within the neutral territory: and what does it signify to the nature of the act, considered for the present purpose, whether I send out a cannon-shot which shall compel the submission of a vessel lying at two miles distance, or whether I send out a boat armed and manned to effect the very same thing at the same distance? It is in both cases the direct act of the vessel lying in neutral ground; the act of hostility actually begins, in the latter case, with the launching and manning and arming the boat that is sent out on such an errand of force.

If it were necessary, therefore, to prove that a direct and immediate act of hostility had been committed, I should be disposed to hold that it was sufficiently made out by the facts of this case. But direct hostility appears not to be necessary, for whatever has an immediate connection with it is forbidden."

The Court concluded by decreeing that the captures could not be maintained and directing the vessels to be restored, but the President added, with respect to the prayer for costs and damages:

"With respect to that, I think the situation in which the vessels were stationed was too dubious to affect the parties with any intentional violation of neutral rights. The capture may have arisen from misapprehension and mistake. It is very different from a case of actual attack on clear neutral territory. There is no sufficient reason to induce me to give costs and damages against the captors."

In the *Twee Gebroeders (No. 2)* [1801] the Court concluded that, on the evidence produced, it was impossible for it to pronounce that the captures were invalidated by being actually made on Prussian territory, and continued as follows:

"There remains the other question, whether the captures are not vitiated by the capturing ship having passed over neutral territory to accomplish the capture—as it is alleged they passed up the Western Eems, and that the whole of that is Prussian territory. I have already intimated some doubts that might possibly be entertained upon the present evidence, whether the Western Eems is to be deemed at all times and in all parts of it clearly Prussian territory; but supposing it to be so, is it a violation of territory to have committed an act of capture after having passed over this territory to effect it? On this point there are some observations of law and some of fact that appear not unworthy of notice. In the first place, the place of capture is accessible by other passages not asserted to be neutral; it is not alleged that a hostile force might not have reached these ships by another route through the Lower Zee or other communications; it is not to be said that they were so inclosed and protected on all sides by neutral territory that you could not approach them without passing over it. In the next place, it is not the case of an internal passage into the heart of the country, into the Homegat, if I may adopt their own term; it is a passage over an external portion of water which you may prescribe for as territory, but not as inland river or as part of the internal territory; it is not an entrance of an armed force up an inward passage to reach an enemy lying in the interior of the land. Thirdly, it is an observation of law that the passage of ships over territorial portions of the sea or external water is a thing less guarded than the passage of armies over-land, and for obvious reasons: an army in the strictest state of discipline can hardly pass into a country without great inconvenience to the inhabitants; roads are broken up, the price of provisions is raised, the sick are quartered on individuals, and a general uneasiness and terror is excited; but the passage of two or three vessels, or of a fleet, over external waters, may be neither felt nor perceived. For this reason, the act of inoffensively passing over such portions of water, without any violence committed there, is not considered as any violation of territory belonging to a neutral State; permission is not usually required. Such waters are considered as the common thorough-fare of nations, though they may be so far territory, as that any actual exercise of hostility is prohibited therein. Fourthly, it is to be observed that the right of refusal of passage, even upon land, is supposed to depend more on the inconvenience falling on the neutral State than on any injustice committed to the third party who is to be affected by the permission. Grotius and Vattel both agree that it is no ground of complaint nor cause of war against the intermediate neutral State if it grants passage to the troops of a belligerent, though inconvenience may ensue to the State beyond; the ground of the right of refusal being the inconvenience that such passages bring with them to the neutral State itself. This being the general state of the fact and of the law, it would be a proposition which could not be maintained in a full universal extent that the passing over water, claimed as neutral territory, would vitiate any ulterior capture made on a third party. Suppose the case of a war between England and Russia, and that the Sound was the pass in question, over which Denmark claims and exercises imperial rights on stronger grounds than can be maintained in support of this claim; or suppose a war between France and Russia, and the Dardanelles to be the pass in question; or suppose any two powers exercising hostilities in the Mediterranean, after having passed through the Straits of Gibraltar, occupied by an English fortress on one side and by Tangier on the other, formerly in possession of this country—could it be said in any of these cases that captures made beyond this point of passage over neutral water territory would be invalidated on any principle of the law of nations? Where a free passage is generally enjoyed, notwithstanding a claim of territory may exist for certain purposes, no violation of territory is committed if the party, after an inoffensive passage, conducted in the usual manner, begins an act of hostility in open ground. In order to have an invalidating effect it must at least be either an unpermitted passage over territory where permission is regularly requested, or a passage under a permission obtained on false representation and suggestions of the purpose designed. In either of these cases there might be an original misfeasance, and trespass, that travelled throughout and contaminated the whole; but if nothing of this sort can be objected I am of opinion that a capture, otherwise legal is in no degree affected by a passage over territory in itself otherwise legal and permitted."

Subsequent cases relating to captures allegedly effected in neutral waters were the following:

In the *Vro(u)w Anna Catherina (No. 1)* [1803] (5 C.Rob., 15; Roscoe, I, 412), a Dutch (enemy) vessel, captured near the Portuguese island of São Miguel (Açores), Sir William Scott decided as follows:

"The sanctity of a claim of territory is undoubtedly very high. The Court is at all times very much disposed to pay attention to claims of this special kind. When the fact is established it overrules every other consideration. The capture is done away, the property must be restored notwithstanding that it may actually belong to the enemy, and if the captor should appear to have acted wilfully, and not merely through ignorance, he would be subject to further punishment. It is to be remembered, however, at the same time, that it is a point on which foreign States are extremely liable to be misinformed and abused by the interested representations of those who are anxious to catch at their protection. The claim of territory is therefore to be taken as a matter *stricti juris* and to be made out by clear and unempeached evidence ..."

On the evidence produced the claim of territory was rejected.

The *Anna* [1805] (5 C.Rob., 373; Roscoe, I, 499) related to the capture of a Spanish merchantman by an English privateer in the maritime belt of the neutral United States within three miles from some uninhabited island at the mouth of the Mississippi. See on this case Part IX-B (vol. X) of this publication, p. 61, and Oppenheim's *International Law*, vol. I, § 234 and II, § 362, footnote 1, at p. 756.

In this case the Court held as follows:

"If the chase of the captured vessel had begun at a greater distance than three miles from these islands the capture might, having regard to the fact that they were uninhabited, have been valid, but in the present case it was invalid because the captors have behaved illegally in stationing their ships within the mouth of a neutral river."

An unusual case of a capture in waters the international status of which was doubtful was that of the *Foltina* [1814] (1 Dodson, 450; Roscoe, II, 206). She was captured in the roadstead of Heligoland in 1811.This island had been conquered by the British navy in 1807 but had not been officially ceded by Denmark to Great Britain by treaty. The prize court stated that the case was without precedent, but held the capture to have been validly made. The prize was condemned as "droits of Admiralty" (whereupon comp. *sub* C, section 7, *infra*, pp. 642 *et seq.*

In the case of the *Eliza Ann and others* [1812-1813] (1 Dodson, 244; Roscoe, II, 162), American ships, captured in waters claimed to be neutral Swedish territory (Hanoe Bay) within a mile of the mainland of Sweden, the Court rejected the claim on the special ground that the government whose territory was alleged to have been violated on 11 August 1812 was not in fact neutral.

Captures made in neutral or neutralized waters sometimes gave rise to the award of claims for reparation of the damage inflicted by such illegal actions. An example thereof is the *Anna* case of 1805, just mentioned.

Apart from the difference between the legal fate of a captured enemy warship and a captured enemy merchant vessel (comp. on this difference under General Issues, section 4, *infra*, p. 198), no further distinction was made in France between the two as regards the obligation of a neutral Power to protect them against attacks by belligerent warships or privateers within its territorial waters. On the French views in this respect comp. De Pistoye-Duverdy's *Traité*, vol. I, p. 107 (attack by an English fleet of sixteen warships against a French squadron of four warships which had taken refuge in Portuguese waters).

On an actual capture of a neutral Danish vessel, the *Christiania Colbiornsen*, by a French privateer, the *Patriote*, in the neutral port of Livorno [*an* VII] see the judgment of the French Cassation Tribunal (*ibid.*, I, 123).

Captures in neutral waters have played a prominent rôle in the Anglo-American arbitration under Art. VII of the Jay Treaty of 19 November 1794, but the cases concerned, the *Jamaica*, the *Fanny* and the *Elizabeth* (distinguished by the editors of the *Recueil des arbitrages internationaux* as a separate fourth group of issues in vol. I of their work at pp. 178, 185 and 188) did not centre on the prize law aspects of the cases, but rather on their neutrality aspect, *viz.*, the problem of the responsibility of a neutral State for inadequate protection of foreign property against belligerent violation of its territorial waters; comp. on that aspect Part IX-B (vol. X) of this publication, pp. 56-58, 66.

British lawyers and prize courts during World War I fell back on decisions of Sir William Scott concerning such claims for reparation as rendered in the two abovementioned cases of the *Twee Gebroeders* [1800] and the subsequent case of the *Anna* [1805], with regard to which it must, however, be remarked that the former two and the latter were not in complete harmony.

In the case of the *Anna* the court awarded damages for a seizure effected in neutral American waters, in that of the *Twee Gebroeders* [1800] the claim for damages was dismissed on the ground that there had not been "an intentional violation of neutral rights". Comp. on these precedents the later case of the *Düsseldorf*, adjudicated after World War I (*B.C.P.C.*, III, 466; appeal, III, 664), and further the case of the *Pellworm and other vessels* (*B.C.P.C.*, III, 705; appeal, III, 1053).

Another case of a capture in neutral waters, dating from the American Civil War, was that of the *Florida*, a Confederate cruiser captured in October 1864 by the Federal cruiser *Wachusett* in the neutral Brazilian port of Bahia. Brazil claimed the prize which had in the meantime sunk while at anchor in Hampton Roads. As the Confederate cruiser could not be delivered to Brazil, the United States Government expiated the violation of Brazilian waters by court martialling the commander of the *Wachusett*, by dismissing their consul at Bahia for having advised the capture and finally, by sending a man of war to the spot where the violation of neutrality had taken place for the special purpose of giving a solemn salute to the Brazilian flag. The dispute over that capture was ultimately settled by the United States Supreme Court in 1879 (101 U.S. 37). See Moore's *Digest*, vol. VII, 1334.

The succinct argument of the Higher Prize Court of Japan during the War with Russia of 1904-1905 when rejecting the claimant's reference to the neutrality of Korea in the *Michael* (Hurst & Bray, II, 80 *et seq.*, at p. 85) ran as follows:

> "the third ground of appeal was that the capture was illegal, because effected within the territorial waters of Korea, a neutral State. As regards the hostilities between Japan and Russia, not only did Korea from the first consent to the landing and transit of Japanese troops, but also the fighting at the commencement of hostilities took place within the territory of that country. For this reason Korea cannot be regarded as a neutral State in the ordinary sense ...".

II. *The judicial treatment of cases of capture in neutral waters: illegality or also invalidity?*

A special problem arose, however, in respect of the judicial treatment of captures in neutral waters, namely, whether a prize court had to take into account the irregularity of the capture *ex officio* to the effect of denying its validity vis-à-vis the owners of the property seized, or whether such property could not be condemned as good and lawful prize in accordance with the general rules of substantive prize law unless the neutral Power whose territory was violated intervened in the prize proceedings with the object of demanding the release of the prize, as happened in the above-mentioned *Twee Gebroeders* cases—a problem which has never been unanimously and finally resolved and over which the opinions of lawyers, including prize courts, are divided up to the present time.

There was general agreement that the government of a captor State was perfectly competent to release on its own authority, and to restore to a neutral government without an intervening prize court decision, a prize made inside its territorial waters, as happened in the case of the British brig *Grange*, captured by the French frigate *Embuscade* in American territorial waters within the capes of Delaware in 1793, cited in vol. X of this publication, at p. 66. But the belligerent prize courts which were faced with such seizures differed as to the question how to deal with them if they were submitted to their judgment by the private persons interested in the prize. Whereas some belligerents—France, and at a later stage Germany—considered a capture in neutral waters as absolutely null and void, others—Great Britain, the United States and Russia—deemed it only invalid in regard to the neutral State whose territorial waters were violated and only if that State protested or opposed the capture in the prize court, otherwise the capture could be held valid with regard to the victim of the seizure.

The English, and in its footsteps the American, doctrine consequently was to the effect that the capture of an enemy ship, although made within neutral jurisdiction, was valid between the belligerents, as enemy property may be taken wherever found, and that it was the business of the neutral State, not of the enemy victim of the capture, to protest.

This was already decided in England by the Lords of Appeal as early as 1798 in the case of the *Etrusco* (Roscoe, I, 286, footnote *a*): intervention by the neutral State was required to gain the release of the prize thus made, or, as it was expressed according to 3 C.Rob., 162, note:

> "A suggestion of neutral territory cannot be set up by an individual claimant but must proceed from the government whose territory is asserted to have been violated".

British and American prize courts consequently did not acknowledge the absolute nullity also vis-à-vis the owners of the ship or cargo seized, of captures made within neutral waters.

The Anglo-American doctrine was, however, repudiated by the Anglo-American Mixed Claims Commission, set up by Art. 12 of the Treaty of Washington of 8 May 1871 (Martens, N.R.G.[1], XX, 698; Parry, 143, 145), charged with the task of settling all private American claims upon the British Government "arising out of acts committed against the persons and property of United States citizens during the period between 13 April 1861 and 9 April 1865 inclusive", other than those belonging to the "Alabama claims" for the settlement of which an international arbitral tribunal was created. Among the cases falling within that description was also the *Sir William Peel* case, decided in 1862 by the Supreme Court of the United States adversely to that vessel (Lawrence's edition of Wheaton, 3rd ed., 716; 5 Wall. (Amer.), 517), but which was later brought before the Mixed Commission to be decided on the interstate level. The case concerned a British ship captured by the United States Navy in the waters of neutral Mexico. In its decision of 1871 (Moore, *Arbitrations*, p. 3948) the Commission held that the owners of a neutral vessel could institute a claim for capture in neutral waters, regardless of any protest by the territorial neutral State.

Despite this repudiation of the doctrine by an international arbitral tribunal, Sir Samuel Evans revived it in his *Bangor* judgment during World War I relating to a capture in the neutral Strait of Magellan [1916] (*B.C.P.C.*, II, 207) in the following wording:

> "Neither an enemy, nor a neutral, acting the part of an enemy, can demand restitution of captured property on the sole ground of capture in neutral waters."

The issue was, however, confused by the old traditional rule of English law which denied to enemy subjects the *jus standi in judicio* (comp. on this subject Part IX-A (vol. IX) of this publication, pp. 26 *et seq.*). It could, therefore, arise in a pure form only with regard to neutral or other non-enemy prizes.

This revival of the old doctrine has not met with any disapproval from the editors of the *A.J.I.L.* 1915, pp. 142 and 181 *et seq.* However, to my mind the theory is unacceptable at the present time because of its inconsistency with the spirit of Convention XIII of The Hague of 1907.

As regards French case law, based on the *Règlement* of 1778, the following judgments can be cited from vol. I of De Pistoye and Duverdy's *Traité des prises maritimes*:

the *Saint-Michel* [*an* VII], (p. 99), captured under the cannons of Spanish Bilbao and released despite certain irregularities in her passport and crew list;

the *Christiania Colbiornsen* [*an* VII] (p. 123), a Danish vessel, captured by the French privateer the *Patriote*, operating from the neutral Tuscan port of Livorno, and brought into the Corsican port of Ajaccio, released in appeal;

La Nostra Segnora del Carmel contre la Vénus-de-Medicis [*an* VIII] (p. 106), a Portuguese ship, captured in the territorial waters of Morocco; the capture was declared illegal and void, even though no fortress or battery defended the coast;

La Perle [*an* VIII] (p. 100), an American vessel, captured at a distance of half a mile from the Spanish port of San Sebastián and released;

the *Daniel Frederick* [1808] (p. 102), another American vessel, captured at the Prussian roadstead of Pillau, at a distance of 3 or 4 miles from land; she was condemned because roadsteads were generally considered at the time not to be covered by the immunity of territorial waters beyond the reach of a cannon shot;

the *Two Generals* [1819] (p. 104), a third American vessel, captured in the territorial sea of Denmark; although the capture was held illegal, the claim by her owner-master for damages was rejected because he alleged no circumstances establishing the captor's bad faith.

Amongst the instances of the application of the theory by United States prize courts in earlier years see further the case of the *Anne* [1818] (3 Wheaton, 435, 447; Scott's *Cases*, p. 1012), and the *Lilla* [1862] (2 Sprague, 177; Scott's Cases, p. 1851) and other vessels such as the *Adela* [1867] (6 Wall., 266), during the Civil War.

The Russian rule was still at the end of the pre-codification period formulated in Arts. 31 and 74 of the Prize Regulations of 1895 which laid down that the original owner of a cargo seized inside the territorial waters of a neutral State (or in waters neutralized by a special Agreement) could not obtain restitution of that cargo nor receive damages for its loss unless at the demand of that neutral State (or a signatory of such Agreement), and on condition that the demand be made within a year's time from the date of the seizure. If not, the prize was not to be condemned for the benefit of the State and no prize-money was to be paid to the captor. The full text of the two articles can be found in Hurst & Bray, vol. I, Appendix A at pp. 317-318 and 327.

Japanese prize courts did not adhere to the Anglo-American doctrine. I conclude this from the following consideration. Among a number of cases adjudicated at the end of the pre-codification period, in which captures in neutral waters were held not to be invalid vis-à-vis their victims were a number that were brought before the Japanese prize courts during the Russo-Japanese War of 1904-05. In those cases the territorial waters concerned, although belonging to a formally neutral State (Korea), were not considered to have remained neutral waters after the Japanese military operations in Korea. That is to say that if Korea's status had remained that of a genuinely neutral State, the captures would have been decreed to be illegal and invalid. See the judgments concerning the *Ekaterinoslav*, the *Mukden* and the *Argun*, mentioned in Hurst & Bray's *Russian and Japanese Prize Cases*, vol. II, pp. 1, 12 and 46. The Japanese prize court decrees were later, again during World War I, cited as precedents by the French *Conseil des prises* in the case of the *Tinos, Bogados, Kythnos and others* [1917] (Fauch. Fra., I, 390; appeal, *sub nomine Korana, Marienbad, Sabbadino et Salona* [1919] (*R.G.D.I.P.* 1920, p. 10 jur.), captured in the waters of neutral Greece.

III. *Adjudication of prizes lying in neutral waters*

Quite a different problem from that of the validity of captures made in neutral waters, discussed above, is the problem of the validity of condemnatory judgments concerning prizes brought by the captor into a neutral port. This type of case can again present two different aspects: the prize proceedings may have taken place either before a (consular) court established by the captor in the neutral country concerned, or normally before a prize court in the captor's own country.

The neutrality aspect of these two forms of irregular proceeding has been analysed in vol. X of this publication at pp. 83-85, where I have provisionally sketched the complications which arose in four old cases, respectively those of the *Constant Mary* [1696-1697], the *Flad Oyen* [1799], the *Kierlighett* [1800] and the *Cosmopolite* [1801].

(*a*) Adjudication of prizes, brought by the captors to a neutral port, by a prize court established in the captor's own country.

This least objectionable of the two variants has already been the object of prize court decrees in early days.

One dated from the Nine Years' War—"a case of great antiquity"—finally decided in 1697: the *Constant Mary*, a British ship captured by the French in 1691, brought to a neutral (Norwegian) port, confiscated by a French prize court in Dunkirk, sold in Norway, subsequently arrested in the port of London by her former owner and restored to him by a British prize court (comp. vol. X of this publication, p. 84).

Another case dating from the Seven Years' War was adjudicated upon by prize courts in Scotland in 1761: the case of *Benton v. Brink*, decided by the lower court against the validity of the condemnation on 23 July 1761, but reversed in appeal by the Scottish Court of Sessions (*Decisions reported, from 1760 to 1764*, I, 104; Roscoe, I, 347-348). This case concerned a British ship, captured by the French, carried to Christiansand (Denmark), condemned in the courts of France and sold to a Danish merchant. In the course of her trade to Scotland the original proprietor had the vessel arrested in a Scottish port by precept from the Court of Admiralty on the ground that such a sentence of condemnation could not have the legal effect of changing the property of the prize. The Court of Admiralty sustained the objection to the validity of the condemnation and decreed that the vessel belonged to the original British owner: a condemnation of a prize by the consul of a belligerent nation on neutral territory could not be recognized as a legal title. On appeal to the Court of Sessions, however, an inquiry was directed to be made into the practice of the High Court of Admiralty of England on the subject. That practice was certified to be to condemn prizes lying in neutral ports. This finding resulted in the reversal of the judgment of the lower Scottish court and the restitution of the ship to the Danish buyer, a sentence in which the original British owner seems to have acquiesced.

The same issue came up for adjudication by British prize courts some forty years later in the cases of 1799-1807 concerning the *Henrick and Maria*, and concerning the *Glückliche Peter* and the *Jonge Jan*.

The *Henrick and Maria (No. 2)* (4 C.Rob., 43; Roscoe, I, 339) was a British vessel, captured by a Dutch privateer in October 1795 and carried into a Norwegian port. A sentence was passed in March 1796 at The Hague before a court styled "the Committee of the Affairs of the Marine of the Batavian Republic". The ship was thereupon sold in 1796 in Christiansand to a Danish merchant and captured a few days later by the British while on her way to the assertedly blockaded port of Amsterdam with a cargo of timber:

> "On principle, the condemnation of a vessel of a belligerent lying in a neutral port is invalid, and a sale arising out of such condemnation is also invalid. But [said the Lords Commissioners of Appeal] as the British Prize Court had condemned vessels in neutral ports, a title arising from a sale on a decree of a foreign Court as above must be recognized as valid" (decree of 26 November 1799, affirmed 7 August 1807).

The judgment gave an elaborate statement of reasons in support.

In the *Glückliche Peter* and the *Jonge Jan* (6 C.Rob., 138, note; Roscoe, I, 347) the Court of Appeal (*per* Sir William Grant) said about condemnations pronounced in a belligerent country on prizes carried into neutral ports that

> "The acknowledged practice of this country must have the effect of making those sentences valid whilst the practice continued. For there should be no equity on which we could deny the validity of that title to neutrals purchasing of the enemy at the same time that they were invited to take them from ourselves.
>
> After the declaration of the practice of our own Courts [in the Scottish case] it would be a very great hardship on Danish merchants to expect that they should know the law better than the Courts of Scotland or that they should abstain from purchases of this kind on a mere surmise that a different doctrine might be held forty years later. The equitable mode of correcting the principle of law, if it is wrong, would be to correct in the first instances the practice of our own courts. If that is altered so as to be brought to the knowledge of neutral merchants, the question as to them will be materially changed. They will no longer be at liberty to stand on our practice and the title is allowed to be good amongst ourselves ... The Court is of opinion that neutrals are sufficiently confirmed in their title by the practice which has prevailed amongst ourselves."

As a result, the reasoning in the *Henrick and Maria* case was affirmed and the sentences of the Vice-Admiralty Courts restoring the *Glückliche Peter* and the *Jonge Jan* to their former owners were reversed.

There is, as far as I know, only one reported exception to the general rule, *viz.*, the *Polka* case of 1854 (Spinks, 54; Roscoe, II, 301), in which the British Prize Court condemned a number of Russian prize vessels despite the fact that they had been brought from the enemy harbour of Libau into the neutral port of Memel. The special circumstances under which this irregular action had taken place, are described under B, section 3, *infra*, p. 517.

The British vessel *Christopher* [1799] (2. C.Rob., 210; Roscoe, I, 225), captured by a French privateer, although brought into the (allied) port of Spanish San Sebastián, was not condemned there, but by a prize court at Bayonne.

(*b*) Adjudication of prizes, brought by the captor into a neutral port, by a prize court established there by the captor State.

This more objectionable of the two variants distinguished above has led to sometimes complicated judicial proceedings.

There is first the case of the *Flad Oyen* [1799] (1 C.Rob., 135; Roscoe, I, 78), a Danish vessel, captured by a French privateer and condemned by a

French consular court, set up in Bergen (Norway), later captured by the British on the high seas, and claimed by the original Danish owner. The British prize court held that a prize court could not legally be established by a belligerent in neutral territory.

Then the case of the *Kierlighett* [1800] (3 C.Rob. 96; Roscoe, I, 258), a British ship, captured by a French warship, brought to a neutral Norwegian port, condemned there by a French consular court and sold to a Danish shipowner; later captured again by the French and on that occasion brought to a port of allied Spain, where she was again confiscated by a French consul, despite the property claim of her Danish buyer, who, however, succeeded in achieving the reversal of this second consular decree by the Court of Appeal in Paris. When subsequently calling at the port of Liverpool flying the Danish flag, she was arrested by her original British owner, who won his suit and so finally regained his property. Comp. on this complicated case and Sir William Scott's disapproval of the novel French practice of setting up consular courts in neutral towns vol. X of this publication, pp. 83-84.

The *Cosmopolite (No. 1)* [1801] (3 C.Rob., 333; Roscoe, I, 321) was again a case of the bringing into a Spanish (allied) port (Tenerife) of an (American) merchant ship by the French. The vessel was condemned by a consular court set up on the island, sold to a neutral (Danish) merchant and later captured again by an English cruiser. In that case the British Admiralty Court refused to restore the vessel to her original American owner, but on the special grounds that it could not do so because this would mean (*a*) a legal assessment of the at the time ambiguous relations between the United States and France, which it was neither entitled nor obliged to make, and (*b*) a judgment on the conditions under which Spain was entitled to open her port to French captors of American ships. The vessel was, consequently, adjudged not, as in the *Flad Oyen* case, to the original American owner, but to the Danish buyer. Comp. on this case vol. X of this publication, pp. 84-85.

In the *Perseverance* [1799-1803] (2 C.Rob., 239; Roscoe, I, 226), another case of illegal condemnation (of a British prize in Norway), followed by its sale to a Swedish merchant, a special problem of transitional law emerged. Though upholding the general rule that whoever purchases under an illegal title does it at his own peril, Sir William Scott admitted certain exceptions or relaxations of the principle under special circumstances:

> "If, henceforth, neutrals shall continue to purchase under such flimsy titles, they must take the consequences of their own imprudence. But it may be too much to apply this maxim without any alleviation to a person who has heretofore bought under a practice, which, although illegal, was too prevalent in some parts of the north of Europe."

See further on this case *infra*, p. 234 (restitution to the Swedish buyer of certain of his expenses for repairs between the sale of the vessel and the decree for its restoration to the British owner).

An old case, of 1793, was that of two British vessels, the *William* (from

Glasgow) and the *Fanny* (Piles, Master), which were captured during the American War of Independence, outside the American three-mile territorial sea by French privateers which had been equipped in an American port and now conducted their prizes into the American port of Philadelphia. There they were adjudicated upon by a French consular Court set up in Philadelphia and condemned. The United States District Court, seised of the case by the United States Government, considered itself without jurisdiction to restore the vessels to their owners. George Washington, thus let down by the Judiciary, had to invoke the help of the Executive to achieve their restoration.

Finally the case came before the commission ex Article VII of the Jay Treaty and dismissed on 24 October 1798 as lying outside the provisions of the Treaty.

See for a survey of the case R.A.I., I, pp. 36 and 185, and Moore, *International adjudications*, Modern series, vol. 4, pp. 518 *et seq.* and 551.

The illegality of the adjudication of prizes, conducted by a belligerent into a neutral port was not always recognized. On the contrary, there are well-known examples of provisions obtaining in bilateral treaties which permitted such adjudication in express terms. See the treaties of 1782 and 1783 between the United States on the one hand, and the Netherlands, respectively Sweden, on the other.

Art. 5 of the American-Netherlands Convention of 8 October 1782 (Martens, R^2, III, 462/463 *et seq.*) was to the following effect:

> "The vessels of war and privateers, of one and of the other of the two Nations, shall be reciprocally, both in Europe and in the other ports of the world, admitted in the respective ports of each, with their prizes, which may be unloaded and sold, according to the formalities used in the State, where the prize shall have been conducted, as far as may be consistent with the 22nd Art. of the Treaty of Commerce, provided always, that the legality of prizes, by the vessels of the Low Countries, shall be decided conformably to the laws and regulations established in the United Netherlands; and likewise, that of prizes, made by American vessels, shall be judged according to the laws and regulations, determined by the United States of America".

Art. 18 of the American-Swedish Treaty of Commerce of 3 April 1783 (*ibid.*, III, 565) included a corresponding rule *sub* (4).

Section 4. WHAT OBJECTS ARE LIABLE TO SEIZURE IN PRIZE?

The exercise of the right of prize being in origin an action of naval warfare, its objects were in principle seagoing vessels and sea-borne goods.

Prize practice has, however, shown, a tendency, together with its penetration into land (section 3 above), to include other objects in its operation, in particular, goods stored in ports, on quays, in warehouses, in tanks, etc.

Apart from this close connection with the place of the seizure—oil in a tank in a port, locomotives unloaded from a ship on a quay, launches on a lake or river—the question arose with regard to the extent of the jurisdiction of a prize court.

In the *Two Friends* [1799] (1 C.Rob., 271; Roscoe, I, 130) Sir William Scott still said that he knew no other definition of prize goods than that they were goods taken on the high seas *jure belli* out of the hand of the enemy, but at a later stage another judge remarked that a source of danger lies in the two meanings contained in the word "prize"; sometimes it is applied generally and indiscriminately to all property condemnable by the Court, sometimes it is confined to goods captured at sea in contrast to such as are taken in ports as droits of Admiralty: *Ten bales of silk at Port Said* (*B.C.P.C.*, II, 247).

A further question is whether the law of prize applies to enemy warships and other public vessels, or whether these ships fall to the captor State *ipso jure* as booty of war without the necessity of intervention of any prize court decision. The general practice was in the latter sense. An American case was that of the *Schooner Charity* [1861], cited by M.R. Robinton, *Introduction to the papers of the New York Prize Court 1861-1865* (1945), p. 139.

Art. 10 of the Russian Prize Regulations of 14 July 1895 gave the impression of putting enemy warships on a par with enemy merchant ships by decreeing that

> "Ships of war and merchant vessels of the enemy are subject to condemnation as prizes,"

but from Art. 20 it followed that this did not imply that enemy warships had to be adjudicated by a prize court in the same way as enemy merchantmen, since it enjoined the Commander of the ship making the capture to proceed in accordance with another instruction, laid down in Art. 351 of the Naval Regulations, a conclusion which was still more clearly corroborated by Art. 27:

> "The condemnation of captured ships of war and their cargoes is to be carried out in accordance with the orders of the competent naval authority. The condemnation of other vessels and cargoes which have been seized can only be carried out in accordance with the decisions of the Prize Court."

The Japanese practice under the regulations of 7 March 1904 was not different.

When public vessels of the enemy State(s) fall to the capturing State *ipso jure*, the question of the status of State merchant ships and their cargoes arises.

Sometimes there were doubts about whether a particular ship was a (private) warship or a merchant vessel. An old case in which this occurred was that of the *Pégou* [*an* VIII], officially called *Le navire américain Le Pégou contre les frégates françaises La Bravoure et La Cocarde* (Pistoye-Duverdy, II, 51), in which the *Conseil des prises* was faced with the question. In accordance with the conclusions of the Commissary of the Government M. Portalis the

Conseil decided that there was no ground for regarding as a " navire armé en guerre " a vessel that carried no further armament than " les navires n'en portent ordinairement pour leur propre défense, et qui, au moment de son arrestation, n'en a pas fait usage ". Comp. on this subject further my remarks introductory to subsection B of the preliminary section 1 above on the delimitation of privateering towards four other somewhat similar practices, *sub* (*d*) at p. 156.

It was occasionally also doubtful whether a company, the owner of a ship, was a private undertaking or a State institution. This was the case of certain companies whose vessels were captured by the Japanese after the outbreak of hostilities with Russia in 1904. Ships of the semi-governmental Russian Volunteer Fleet Company, such as the *Ekaterinoslav* (Hurst & Bray, II, 1), and the Chinese Eastern Railway Company, such as the *Mukden* (*ibid.*, II, 12) and the *Argun* (*ibid.*, II, 46), were early specimens of a middle category of vessels between State and private ships:

> " The Chinese Eastern Railway Company is ostensibly a private corporation, but—according to the statistics of the vessels in Russian dominions in Asia, published by the Russian Department of Communications—all the vessels of the Company are included in the list of Government vessels. Again, after the North China riots of 1900 the Russian Government demanded an indemnity from China for the loss sustained by that Company as damages sustained by the State. Thus the Russian Government itself admits that the Chinese Eastern Railway is a State institution ... "

The status of ships requisitioned or usurped by the enemy government has sometimes been construed as, or placed on the same footing with, that of enemy State ships.

The legal status of mails as objects of the law of prize has been discussed by prize courts mostly in combination with that of mailships. The latter have drawn the special attention of the prize courts in the Far East in 1904-05, both as regards their capacity as potential objects of the exercise of the right of capture as meant in the context of the present section in general, and as regards their possible employment by the enemy as carriers of " contraband persons " or of harmful correspondence, on which comp. section 5 (Unneutral service) *infra*, p. 456.

Doubts have arisen in the past about the status of vessels under construction: did they fall within the description of ships or rather within that of property on land?

On harbour launches see the Japanese case of the *Juliette* [1905] (Hurst & Bray, II, 103).

On vessels found by a belligerent in a disabled state in one of its harbours at the outbreak of hostilities see the Japanese case of the *Manchuria (No. 2)* [1905] (*ibid.*, II, 100).

On the qualification of a ship, transported on another Japanese steamer, the *Progress*, to Hakadate dockyard to be repaired there, as an object of the exercise of the right of capture see the case of 1905 concerning the *Thalia* (*ibid.*, II, 129-130).

Special attention has further been paid, in particular by French prize courts, to the status of wrecks and abandoned vessels.

Wrecks and other ships found in a comparable situation, such as vessels sunk by enemy action or, for that matter, as a result of voluntary action by their own crew, have already in the old law of prize occupied a special position, I do not understand exactly why, in so far, at least, as that special consideration was not connected with the text of provisions conferring jurisdiction upon the prize tribunal. See on "navires échoués ou naufragés" the French *Ordonnance* of 12 May 1696, Art. 14 of the *Règlement* of 1778, Arts. 2, 6, 8 and 19 of the *Arrêté* of 6 germinal *an* VIII and Art. 2 of the *Décret* of 18 July 1854 (De Pistoye and Duverdy, *Traité*, I, 113-114).

Instances of French judgments on this subject were, *inter alia*, those of the *Conseil des prises* of

29 fructidor *an* VIII concerning the *Maria-Arendz*, owned by merchants from Emden (*ibid.*, I, 116), which specified the position as follows: an enemy merchant ship was liable to condemnation even if run ashore, wrecked or abandoned on the coasts of France; any other vessel could in such circumstances only be released if her neutral character was duly established; her state of disablement in itself was insufficient;

3 messidor *an* IX, concerning the Oldenburg vessel *Juffrouw Anna-Catharina* (*ibid.*, II, 91), which had stranded during a storm on the sandbanks in the mouth of the river Somme:

> "Les navires échoués sur les côtes de France sont obligés de prouver leur neutralité comme ceux qui sont arrêtés en pleine mer. Si la cargaison est ennemie, et que par droit de représailles on cesse d'appliquer la maxime que le pavillon couvre la marchandise, la cargaison doit être confisquée, mais le bâtiment doit être relaxé";

13 ventôse *an* IX, concerning the Prussian vessel *Diana* (*ibid.*, II, 91), which had been forced by the storm to seek refuge on the roadstead of Dunkirk; the seizure of this vessel and her cargo by the commander of a floating battery there was declared invalid.

In its decision of 23 November 1811 concerning the wreck of the *Jeune-Annette* (*ibid.*, II, 93), based on the *Ordonnance* of 1696, the *Conseil d'Etat* made a distinction between vessels which had run ashore by accident and those stranded deliberately. This distinction related to the allocation of the proceeds of the sale of the wreck either, in the first case, to the *Caisse des invalides de la Marine*, or, in the second case, to the State:

> "Napoleon, etc.—Considérant que dans l'espèce présente, l'échouement du navire Jeune-Annette ne peut être considéré comme un malheur indépendant de la volonté de l'équipage, puisqu'il résulte des pièces produites par l'administration des douanes depuis la décision du Conseil des prises que c'est à dessein que le navire a échoué et que c'est par une manoeuvre généralement pratiquée dans ces parages, pour introduire plus facilement sur le continent les marchandises prohibées; Que, par conséquent, le produit de la saisie ne peut entrer dans la Caisse des invalides, à laquelle la loi n'accorde que le produit des échouements fortuits".

Comp. on this subject further De Pistoye and Duverdy's exposé at pp. 117

et seq. of their vol. II, which in addition refers to two old ordinances of the King of Spain of 1702 and 1718.

As remarked above, ships abandoned at sea have in French legislation always been considered as closely connected with wrecks. Although this traditional coupling of vessels in two different conditions is not so conspicuous in English case law, it goes without saying that British prize courts have also had to deal with cases of abandoned ships. I will quote two of them. The first was simple; the second was far more complicated because it resulted in a legal battle between two English admirals, and their crews, both theoretically eligible for prize money, depending upon what was the legal effect of a decision by Admiral A no longer to consider certain captured ships as prizes and its impact upon rival claims of his successor B who took a different view and captured them in his turn. The two cases were:

the *Gage* [1806-1807] (6 C.Rob., 273; Roscoe, I, 554), a British ship which had been captured by a French privateer, but was found abandoned at sea, with a fire burning in her cabin:

> "If a British vessel in a derelict state is recaptured, the Court will award a larger amount of salvage than is presented by the Prize Act";

the *Diligentia* [1814] (1 Dods., 404; Roscoe, II, 197), one of a group of Danish vessels lying in the river Tagus in August 1808 and there blockaded by a fleet of British warships under the command of Vice-Admiral Sir C. Cotton; upon the evacuation of Portugal by the French forces in virtue of the Convention of Cintra (22 August 1808), the Danish ships in the Portuguese ports were taken possession of by the squadron under the command of Vice-Admiral Cotton, but they were released by orders from him before his return to England. Upon the arrival of his successor Admiral Berkeley in January 1809 the vessels were again seized and sent to England in consequence of an order of the Lords Commissioners of the Admiralty to send home for legal adjudication all Danish and other foreign vessels in the Tagus which were in that river prior to the evacuation of Portugal by the French. A legal discussion followed on the question which of the two fleets was as captor entitled to the benefit of the prize. The decision of Sir William Scott was in favour of Admiral Berkeley's claim, arguing that Vice-Admiral Cotton, from motives of delicacy and a nice interpretation of the Convention of Cintra, thought these vessels were not liable to be considered as prize, and either by mistake of fact or law relinquished possession; that, by so doing, he abandoned the right of himself and of those under him; and that the ships thus became the lawful prize of a subsequent captor.

One would expect the *Institut de droit international* to have determined already in its *Règlement international des prises maritimes* of 1882 the criterion or criteria of the enemy or neutral (non-enemy) character of prizes, but the result of its deliberations on this subject was completely disappointing since neither in its resolution of Turin (1882) nor in the final text of

Copenhagen (1897) it contained anything substantial either on the enemy or non-enemy character of a ship or on that of sea-borne cargoes. The only rules included in section 5 of the *Règlement* concerning ships decided nothing:

> "§ 24. La nationalité du navire, de sa cargaison, de son équipage doit être constatée par les papiers de bord trouvés sur le navire saisi, sans exclusion, toutefois, d'une production ultérieure devant les tribunaux de prises.
>
> § 25. La question de savoir si les conditions de nationalité sont remplies est décidée selon la législation de l'Etat auquel le navire est ressortissant",

whereas §§ 27-29 relating to ship's papers kept the reader equally in the dark in respect of the enemy or non-enemy character of goods.

The last occasion on which it might have become clearer from judicial decisions how far the ideas about this vital problem had progressed up to the end of the pre-codification period would have been the last great war of that period, between Russia and Japan of 1904-1905. However, a close study of the copious pronouncements made by the prize courts of the two belligerents, containing together about 850 pages in Hurst & Bray's two-volume work on *Russian and Japanese prize cases* (printed in 1912-1913, and reprinted as vols. VI and VII of the International Military Law History Reprint Series) only admits of the conclusion that the issue had remained as unsettled as before up to the eve of the Codification Conference of London on Naval Warfare. And as far as the scientific activity of the *Institut* is concerned, it is not different. The existing uncertainty in these domains has indeed, in the *Institut* also, lasted until after the London Conference when in 1913, in its session at Oxford, it resumed its deliberations in this field by adopting a "Manuel des lois de la guerre maritime dans les rapports entre belligérants" and in Art. 51 thereof filling certain gaps which even that Conference had been unable to fill in its Declaration of 1909. The solution reached by the *Institut* in 1913 was to the following effect:

> "Le caractère ennemi ou neutre d'un navire est déterminé par le pavillon qu'il a le droit de porter.
>
> Le caractère ennemi ou neutre des marchandises trouvées à bord d'un navire ennemi est déterminé par le caractère ennemi ou neutre de leur propriétaire. Chaque Etat doit déclarer, au plus tard dès le début des hostilités, si le caractère ennemi ou neutre du propriétaire des marchandises est déterminé par le domicile ou par la nationalité de ce propriétaire."

A rare type of legal battle, caused inversely by those on board a British (State) vessel in distress, developed in 1799 between her crew and a perfectly seaworthy neutral merchantman, the *Jonge Jacobus Baumann* (1 C.Rob., 243), described in detail *sub* III B, section 3 under (*b*), *infra*, p. 513.

The bottom of the North Sea beyond the outer boundary of the maritime belt of the Kingdom of the Netherlands still preserves the wreck of a Batavian vessel that had been captured by the British Navy during Holland's brief metamorphosis as the Batavian Republic (1798-1806), but was abandoned by the captors on account of its unseaworthiness and afterwards sunk.

This wreck might give rise to an interesting discussion on its present legal status and ownership: English, Dutch or nobody's? Great Britain never submitted the prize to an Admiralty Court for adjudication and never had more than a temporary grip on the vessel; the Netherlands as successor to the Batavian Republic can hardly claim the automatic return of the vessel to her owner as a consequence of the British abandonment of the wreck, so that the third solution: the status of a *res nullius*, capable of appropriation by whoever might attempt to recover it from its resting place, seems to be the correct one.

The legal status of wrecks has formed the subject of a thorough study in the Hamburg series *Das geltende Seevölkerrecht in Einzeldarstellungen* by Heidi Engert-Schülert under the title *Völkerrechtliche Fragen des Eigentums an Wracks auf dem Hohen Meer* (1979). I can only say that its contents have failed to convince me of the incorrectness of the third conclusion, just expressed, but the thoroughness of the reasoning of the writer on the problem as a whole would deserve a counter-argument in another monograph of equal size.

Another recent and interesting article in the *Netherlands Yearbook of International Law* (1982) by Lucius Caflisch (pp. 3-32) deals with a related problem, this one restricted to "Submarine antiquities and the international law of the sea" in the light of the new Draft Convention on that wide subject (UNCLOS).

Preliminary Section II. THE PROBLEM OF THE ENEMY OR NON-ENEMY CHARACTER OF PRIZES

After my discussion of the four General Issues in the preceding preliminary sections 1-4, I now come first to another general subject that likewise deserves such preliminary treatment because it is of equal importance for the whole contents of the following exposé of the law of maritime prize without being peculiar to any of the three Parts A, B and C over which that exposé will be spread, namely the problem of the enemy or non-enemy character of prizes.

Prefatory

One of the principal questions which required an answer in the operation of the law of prize has of course always been that of the criterion applied to make the distinction between enemy and non-enemy (neutral, allied or national) property at sea. The national character of ships and cargoes, either enemy or non-enemy (at a later stage: enemy or neutral) naturally depended in the early days on their ownership. In the course of time this criterion did not, however, remain the only one.

As far as *ships* were concerned, the flag that a vessel was flying acquired increasing importance as a rival criterion. This criterion appeared for the first time, it would seem, implied in the Capitulation granted by the Ottoman Sultan to King Henry IV of France in 1604. The text of that Capitulation (Noradounghian I, 93) repeatedly refers to French vessels in the formula "sous l'aveu et sûreté de la bannière de France". Occasionally legal importance was attached to yet other factors, such as the place where the ship was built, or from where the shipping business was run, or where the ship was registered or had her home port. As ships were often run by companies or partnerships, the problem of the national character of the latter also played a part. Moreover, the question often arose of what was the impact of the fact that persons other than the owner had a claim on the ship from a mortgage or a bottomry bond.

As regards *cargoes*, considerations other than ownership began to be taken into account. In their respect, also, an analogous question gave rise to doubt whether ownership was the exclusive key to the solution of the problem: did security rights or the financial risks run by money lenders, insurers or buyers indeed carry no weight? And as far as ownership was decisive, what element determined the owner's enemy or non-enemy character: his nationality or his domicile, and what was to be understood by a merchant's domicile? This, in its turn, raised the question of the status of trading houses in foreign countries. A special ground of enemy property turned up in the form of the qualification as such of products of, or manufacture on, enemy soil. Requirements for the proof of non-enemy ownership became stricter in the face of many devious attempts to conceal an enemy character.

And as regards both ships and cargoes, more and more attention was given to the suspect character of their transfer by enemy owners to non-enemy buyers during the war or in contemplation of the outbreak of war, or while in transit. Such transfers, either of a ship or of a cargo, by an enemy owner to a neutral buyer during the war or shortly before the outbreak of hostilities were always considered as highly suspect. Although it is somewhat difficult to group the numerous prize cases on this subject under different headings because the pronouncements often related in general terms to both ships and cargoes, or were in actual fact concerned with both in the same case, I will nevertheless attempt to survey the case law below, first as to the transfer of enemy ships to non-enemy buyers and then as to the transfer of enemy cargoes *in transitu.*

A more exceptional complication emerged as a result of the fact that not a prize, but a territory towards which a ship or cargo was sailing was, during the voyage, transferred from one sovereignty to another.

As experiments with a number of possible modes of arrangement of the details of this complicated subject matter have shown, the differing features of ships and cargoes do not allow of a strict parallelism in the exposé. And other circumstances also render this impracticable, such as the differences between the English and French systems, the presence in one system of legal elements which are almost absent in another, and the identity or similarity of solutions reached in one and the same system in respect of both ships and cargoes, *e.g.*, in the field of transfers in transit, the legal impact of non-proprietary rights to prizes on their ultimate fate, and the legal effect of territorial changes.

That is why I have felt compelled to abandon the idea of a strict congruity in the arrangement and to adopt the following order of exposition.

Although this order of arrangement in two Sub-Divisions is perfectly justified, there was a slight obstacle of a simple systematic nature. When arranging the available case law, I found it somewhat difficult to make a sharp distinction between judgments concerning ships and those concerning cargoes owing to the fact that the arguments and precedents adduced by the courts in support of their findings were often the same for both categories of prizes so that the judgments contained many cross-references from one to the other, and even the clear boundaries between Sub-Divisions I and II became confused. Where that happened, especially where arguments and precedents dealing with cargoes were invoked in proceedings which related essentially to vessels, I decided in favour of classing them under Sub-Division I, the most interesting of the two.

Sub-Division I. ENEMY OR NON-ENEMY CHARACTER OF SHIPS

Introductory section

The search for a clear criterion for the determination of the enemy or neutral (non-enemy) character of a vessel has never throughout history led to a final, generally agreed result. The rules which governed this vital issue were indeed always rather chaotic. This applies to England as well as to France, the two main belligerents who put their stamp upon the early development, in both of which countries judicial pronouncements or legislative texts constantly alluded to a variety of possible criteria without making a definitive choice.

A bird's-eye view shows that the normal criterion of the character of a ship was either her ownership or her flag, but various other criteria, such as the place where the ship was built, the passport she carried, or the nationality or residence of her master or crew, were also applied or at least invoked, as will appear from the summary below.

And when we take a look at the wider international field, we see that there also such additional criteria were sometimes alluded to. Thus, the Swedish-Netherlands treaty of Elsenör of 9 December 1659 (Dumont, VI², 293; Parry, 5, 445) stipulated in express terms that for the determination of the national character of a ship it made no difference whether she had been built in Sweden, respectively the Netherlands, or elsewhere. A later treaty, of 28 September 1716 between France and the three main Hanse Towns (Dumont, VIII¹, 478; Parry, 13, 19), however, prescribed in Article 30 that in principle a ship sould be "de leur [*i.e.*, of the Hanse Towns'] fabrique ou de celle d'une nation neutre."

In the following pages I will first illustrate by quotations from the judgments pronounced by English, respectively French courts in the formative phase of the pre-codification period how the views of those courts on the criteria for the determination of the enemy or non-enemy character of ships—the subject of my Section 1—developed in that early period, and after that I will continue the story under Section 1 up to the end of that period, concluding with the Russo-Japanese War of 1904-05, the last occasion on which the belligerents could demonstrate how far their views had progressed on the eve of the codification.

Section. 1. CRITERIA FOR THE DETERMINATION OF THE ENEMY OR NON-ENEMY CHARACTER OF SHIPS: OWNERSHIP, FLAG OR POSSIBLY ADDITIONAL OTHERS?

Old English case law

Elaborating now on the summary data given in my introductory paragraph above, I will first pass on to a brief survey of the English case law on the criteria for the determination of the (non-)enemy character of ships during the formative phase of the pre-codification period.

When, in order to form an idea of the criteria applied in England for that determination in former times, one peruses the data collected by Sir George Lee in his Ms. Notes, specially devoted to the jurisprudence during the War of the Austrian Succession in the period 1744-1748, the following conclusions can be drawn.

In accordance with the precedents of earlier wars, *viz.*, the three naval wars of 1652, 1655 and 1672 with the Netherlands, the Nine Years' War of 1688 and the War of the Spanish Succession of 1702, quoted by Sir George Lee in the texture of his Notes, the Court of Admiralty (Sir Henry Penrice) and the Lords of Appeal of the period kept to the simple and traditional criterion of the ownership of a merchant vessel. This is especially apparent from the first judgments delivered by the Admiralty Court, *viz.* the series relating to the *Anna Galley* (Pratt-Lee, pp. 1, 11 and 18), the *Marlborough* (p. 24), the *Fortune de la Mer* (p. 33), the *T'Slots Copenhagen* (p. 40) and the *Louissa* (p. 49). The national character of the vessel was constantly determined by her ownership as the self-evident criterion of nationality. True, reference was repeatedly made to other elements, but there is no indication that they were in any way conclusive; their mention was only meant to serve as an argument *ex abundantia.* Thus, the *Marlborough* was "sailing under French colours" and had been "built at Bristol" (p. 25), but "the property of the ship was clear" (p. 32), as "belonging to natives and inhabitants of France and Holland" (p. 29). The *Fortune de la Mer* had been built in Danzig, her master was a Prussian living in that town, her crew consisted of Danzigers, but her national character was determined by the fact that her two owners were born and resident in Danzig. The *T'Slots Copenhagen* had a Danish crew, but her Danish character was determined by the fact that her owner was a Dane residing at Elsenör. The *Louissa*, which had a Swedish crew, belonged to a group of co-owners established in Sweden, among them her master for one-eighth. It was obviously on this basis that the national character of a ship was determined by the Courts in England during the 17th and 18th centuries.

Pratt, in his own analysis of the precedents, hardly pays any attention to this question of the criterion for the determination of the neutral or enemy character of a ship.

Sir William Scott, in his decree on the *Vigilantia* [1798] (1 C.Rob., pp. 1 *et seq.*, at p. 13; Roscoe, I, 31) expressed himself as follows:

> "I conceive the rule to be, that where there is nothing particular or special in the conduct of the vessel itself, the national character is determined by the residence of the owner; but there may be circumstances arising from that conduct, which will lead to a contrary conclusion. It is a known and established rule with respect to a vessel, that if she is navigating under the pass of a foreign country, she is considered as bearing the national character of that nation under whose pass she sails: she makes a part of its navigation, and is in every respect liable to be considered as a vessel of that country. In like manner, and upon similar principles, if a vessel purchased in the enemy's country is, by constant and habitual occupation, continually employed in the trade of that country, commencing with the war, continuing during the war, and evidently on account of the war, on what ground is it to be asserted, that vessel is not to be deemed a ship of the country from which she is so navigating, in the same manner as if she evidently belonged to the inhabitants of it?"

Sir William Scott's statement in a single sentence in which he specified the criterion of ownership of a vessel as referring to the owner's *residence*, seems to me to be hardly substantiated by the case law produced by Sir Henry Penrice in the 1740's.

What follows in Sir William Scott's judgment of 1798 has again only a marginal interest for the central problem, as it refers to the *conduct* of a vessel rather than to its national character. See, however, the extensive study of Sir William Scott's ideas about the nationality aspect in prize proceedings in Bourguignon's *Sir William Scott, Lord Stowell* (Cambridge, 1987), chapter 4 (Prize law: nationality—A study in detail, at pp. 115-171).

Be this as it may, the above quotation seems to prove that in England there was no generally recognized single criterion for the determination of a ship's national character in wartime. And that has remained so up to the present day despite the efforts of the London Conference on Naval Warfare of 1908-1909 to agree upon a single criterion, *viz.*, the flag which a ship is entitled to fly.

In the case of the *Vreede Scholtys* [1804] (5 C.Rob., p. 5, footnote *a*; Roscoe, I, footnote *a* at p. 410) the ship was held "bound by the character imposed upon it by the authority of the government from which all the documents issued".

Insofar as the enemy or non-enemy (neutral or allied) character of the ship was determined by her flag, that was in principle the flag which she had the right to fly, but it would also be the flag she actually flew, if this was the enemy flag. On the other hand, prize courts used to look behind the neutral flag actually flown if there were grounds for doing so. This was the case, for example, when the neutral flag was suspected of covering enemy interests, or when the ship appeared to have been transferred to neutral ownership during or even in view of the outbreak of war. But there are also British precedents which attached primary importance to the (enemy) place of residence of her owner, or drew unfavourable conclusions from the fact that the ship had previously formed part of the armed forces of the enemy. The English case law was thus weighted heavily against the neutral character of a vessel.

As far a I have been able to infer from the available case law, especially that collected by Sir George Lee in his Ms. Notes, the criterion of the flag as a decisive element had only a limited importance for the central problem of the determination of the national character of a vessel in the law of prize since judgments on ships flying an enemy flag argued more on the basis of their *conduct* than on that of their *nationality*, whereas the fact of a ship's flying a neutral (non-enemy) flag had to give way to arguments based on her enemy property relations.

Other judgments, dating from the Napoleonic period, related to the following cases.

The fact that a ship had previously been in the service of the enemy was held to be a valid ground for considering her as vested with enemy character. It was not necessary, for a ship to be subject to treatment as such, that she was formally incorporated into the enemy navy; her actual employment by that navy was sufficient. See the *Ceylon* [1811] (1 Dods., 105; Roscoe, II, 133), *infra*, p. 568. Even her having been forced by the enemy to render military service was no ground for exemption, see the cases of the *Minerva* [1807] (Knuttell, Master) (6 C.Rob., 396; Roscoe, I, 591) and the *Cousine Marianne* [1810] (Deboer, Master) (Edw., 346; Roscoe, II, 85), *infra*.

The enemy character of a ship was sometimes inferred from the finding that she was hired upon charter-party by the enemy, a fact that was construed as a lending of the ship to them. See the earlier cases of the *Elizabeth Catherina* and the *Vro(u)w Anna Maria* [1747], reported by Pratt-Lee, pp. 115 *et seq.* and pp. 119 *et seq.* (at pp. 118-119). But I will not expatiate here upon cases of this kind because they are too closely related to the subject of unneutral service which will be discussed *infra*, *sub* A in section 5, pp. 467 *et seq.* I will only still mention that enemy character also attached to neutral ships sailing under the protection of a safe-conduct of the enemy State.

Returning to the great variety of criteria for the determination of the enemy character of vessels applied by the British prize courts, I state that there is one among them which I purposely left out of my summing-up, *viz.*, that of risk, *i.e.*, the question as to who would suffer the loss if the vessel were condemned. It is again a judgment of Sir William Scott in which this criterion was invoked, but this in a manner that has caused more confusion than clarity by its formulation. What the President said in this early judgment concerning certain cargo in the *Packet de Bilboa* [1799] (2 C.Rob., 133; Roscoe, I, 209) in effect gave the strong impression of representing ownership of the prize and risk of its loss as to all intents and purposes identical or interchangeable. The passages which caused the confusion were worded as follows:

> "The goods are sent at the risk of the shipper. If they had been lost, on whom would the loss have fallen but on him? What surer test of property can there be than this? It is the true criterion of property that, if you are the person on whom the loss will fall, you are to be considered as the proprietor."

This view has later been expressed again, in differing and more elaborate versions, in comparable cases or situations, such as that of the *Belvidere* [1813] (1 Dodson, 353; Roscoe, II, 183), to which I will have to return in due course.

There were rare cases in which the strange question was asked, what was "the effect of the cargo on the character of the ship": the *Vro(u)w Elizabeth* (Probst, Master) [1803] (5 C.Rob, 2; Roscoe, I, 409) and the *Friendship* (Collard, Master) [1807] (6 C.Rob., 420; Roscoe, I, 599). I cannot but consider such formulations as logically wrong.

The *Vro(u)w Elizabeth*, sailing under the Dutch (enemy) flag and with a Dutch pass from Surinam to Amsterdam, was after capture claimed by a merchant in (neutral) Bremen as her *bona fide* owner on the ground that her nominal transfer to a Dutch merchant and her placing under a Dutch flag and pass was explained by the owner's purpose of enabling her to trade between the Dutch colonies and Holland. However, the judgment of 6 September 1803 held against the claimant:

> "A ship under the colours and pass of a nation is to be considered as a ship of such nation, to whatever nationality her actual owner may belong."

When by exception a shipowner was granted a British licence to sail under any flag, except the French, he should have been protected by such licence when his ship sailed under the Prussian flag. The British prize court, nevertheless, held this ship liable to capture and confiscation in prize on the ground that she was owned by a Frenchman: the *Cousine Marianne* [1810] (Edw., 346; Roscoe, II, 85).

The decisive criterion of the flag actually flown was also applied in the case of the *Oelbaum*, mentioned in a study of 1851 by Jacobson (pp. 450-451), a vessel claimed to be in actual fact a ship based at (neutral) Altona.

The preceding selection from judgments pronounced during the formative phase of the pre-codification period testifies to the great variety of possible criteria for the determination of the (non-)enemy character of captured ships. But it was not that variety alone that made their ultimate fate more or less of a gamble.

The issue was indeed complicated by the fact that various external factors began to throw their weight into the scales in the process of determining the final solution of the central problem of condemnation or release of the prize. Such external factors were, for instance, the existence of neutral non-proprietary rights on a vessel whose enemy character was duly established by the Court or, inversely, the occurrence of certain territorial changes which might adversely affect the national character of a vessel whose neutral character had been duly established. The impact of such factors will be discussed below in a separate Section 2 at pp. 219 *et seq*. They did not in reality interfere with the conclusiveness of the criteria for the allocation to a vessel of enemy or neutral character and, consequently, do not fit into Section 1.

A new upsurge of judgments again dealt with the subject during the Crimean War, when Dr Stephen Lushington and the Judicial Committee of the Privy Council in appeal critically reviewed the precedents from the time of Sir William Scott, and neutral claimants made new attempts, but unsuccessfully, to reverse the trend of those precedents in their favour.

I will not enter into this case law here because it belongs to the consolidation period, and I therefore refer to pp. 222-224.

A very special case was that of the *Ocean Bride* [1854] (Spinks, 66; Roscoe, II, 309), a British ship that, after sailing from England to Archangel in September 1853, was frozen-in there and held by the ice until some time after the outbreak of the Crimean War. She was for practical reasons transferred to Russian merchants. She sailed in the beginning of June 1854 and arrived about 10 July at Leith where she was seized with her cargo by Customs House Officers as a Russian prize. The Court stated that it was settled by various cases that property claimed by British merchants could not be restored if, at the time of capture, their trade was contrary to British statute law: condemnation of the *Walsingham Packet* [1799] (2 C.Rob., 77; Roscoe, I, 149) and the *Etrusco* [1803] (Roscoe, I, 388, footnote). However, in the case of the *Ocean Bride* the circumstances were found to be such that the ship should be restored:

> " If a British shipowner is entitled to restoration, the Prize Court will generally not inquire into questions of municipal law—such as the registration of ownership—unless it is shown without doubt that the owner has committed a clear breach of his municipal law. A British-owned ship fictitiously transferred to Russian merchants to prevent her seizure by the Russian authorities as enemy property, while lying ice-bound in a Russian port at the outbreak of the war, but seized as Russian property by the officers of the Customs on her arrival at Leith, was to be restored to the British owners on payment of the seizor's expenses."

Old French legislation and jurisprudence

After the preceding survey of old English case law concerning the enemy or non-enemy character of ships I now pass to a corresponding survey of old French legislation and jurisprudence.

The precedents reported by De Pistoye and Duverdy in vol. II of their *Traité des prises maritimes* and dating from the beginning of the nineteenth century, relate in part directly to the practice of transfer of enemy vessels to a neutral flag during, or in expectation of, a war, which will form the subject of the following section 3. In so far the French courts were bound by the specific rules of their national legislation. These will be set out in that section 3. See, for instance, the following judgments:

A vessel of enemy construction must be able to prove with reliable documents, preferably by a deed drawn up by public officers, that she has become neutral property before the war: the *Haabet* (p. 4); *Four merchantmen of Tungeln* (Varel) (p. 9); the *Carl Ludwig* (*ibid.*).

An enemy vessel sold to neutrals (Danes) after the outbreak of war was to be condemned as good and lawful prize: the *Caninholm* (p. 34).

But that close relation to *transfert de pavillon* was not always present in the cases to be adjudicated and then the courts could take up a more independent position.

The sanction of condemnation also applied, for example, to vessels of neutral origin and ownership if they sailed without a regular deed, or if doubts arose about their identity (bearing the same name, but being of different tonnage): the *Hoffnung, alias Corn Planter* (p. 12); see also the *Elisabeth* (p. 11).

The owner of a vessel of enemy construction sailing under neutral colours after her asserted capture by a French privateer and her subsequent sale to a neutral person must prove these facts by an uninterrupted series of deeds:

the *Anna Maria* (p. 20); the *Bucking* (p. 23); the *Anna O'Neil, alias Altée* (p. 26). The same applied to an ex-enemy merchantman, claimed to have been sold to neutrals (Norwegians) after her capture by the naval forces of Holland, then the ally of France: the *Normanden, alias Jeune-Jean* (p. 21).

The doctrinal discussion of the subject of the enemy or neutral character of ships is in the *Traité des prises maritimes* concealed under two separate headings where one would not expect to find it, namely under "Des pièces de bord" in vol. I, pp. 416-462 (where the title of § 1 "justification de la neutralité" has dropped out by negligence) and pp. 463-509 (title of § 2 "De la validité des passeports"), and further under the surprising heading "De la composition des équipages. Rôle d'équipage" in vol. II, pp. 30-70.

These two separate groups of data are connected by cross-references from vol. I to vol. II, but that has been done in a manner which makes it very awkward to find in vol. II the cases to which reference is made in vol. I, as a result of the fact that this reference is made not to pages in vol. II, but to the very complicated system of arrangement of the source material in titles (VI), chapters, sections and paragraphs.

The legal situation in France was just as uncertain as in England.

The criterion of the flag as determinant of the national character of a ship seems to have emerged for the first time in France in her Capitulation of 1604 with the Ottoman Sultan (text in Noradounghian I, p. 93). Although this Capitulation mostly used the general term "vaisseaux français" (Arts. 2, 14, 15, 44) and in Art. 10 promised protection to French subjects "qui naviguent sur des vaisseaux appartenant à nos [*i.e.* the Sultan's] ennemis", it also included provisions in which mention was made of vessels sailing "sous la bannière de France" (Arts. 4, 6, 8 and 23).

French prize law was on the whole very severe.

The enemy or non-enemy (neutral or allied) character of a ship was also determined in old French prize law by uncertain factors. The general rule was that it depended on who was her owner.

Art. 1 of the Law of 29 nivôse *an* VI (Pistoye et Duverdy, I, 123) provided that

> "L'état des navires, en ce qui concerne leur qualité de neutre et d'ennemi, sera déterminé par leur cargaison...",

but that was obviously a strange formulation of the French doctrine of infection (comp. *infra sub* A, section 2, pp. 350-352) and was not meant as a criterion of the enemy character of the ship.

Pursuant to the *Arrêté* of 2 prairial *an* XI (Pistoye et Duverdy, I, 313)

> "seront de bonne prise tous bâtiments appartenant aux ennemis de l'Etat".

A vessel owned by an enemy national had enemy character, one owned by a neutral or allied subject had non-enemy character. The first of these two rules naturally applied to ships sailing under an enemy flag. But even if a ship sailed under a neutral pass and belonged to neutrals, she could nevertheless be held to have enemy character on the ground of circumstances which made her character suspect, in particular if she sailed under the command of a master, born in an enemy country.

Pursuant to Article 6 of the French *Règlement* of 1778:

> "On n'aura pareillement pas égard aux passe-ports accordés, par les puissances neutres ou alliées, tant aux propriétaires qu'aux maîtres des bâtiments sujets des Etats ennemis de Sa Majesté, s'ils n'ont été naturalisés, ou s'ils n'ont transféré leur domicile dans les Etats desdites puissances, trois mois avant le 1er septembre de la présente année; et ne pourront lesdits propriétaires et maîtres de bâtiments, sujets des Etats ennemis, qui auront obtenu lesdites lettres de naturalité, jouir de leur effet, si, depuis qu'elles ont été obtenues, ils sont retournés dans les Etats ennemis de Sa Majesté, pour y continuer leur commerce".

This text proves, moreover, that the owner's domicile also played a certain rôle and that it was not only the nationality or domicile of the owner but also that of the ship's captain which had to be taken into account. This extension of the criterion of the enemy character of a vessel was applied by the *Tribunal de Cassation* in a judgment of 18 thermidor *an* VII in the case of the *Friendship*, captured on a voyage to London by the French privateer *Actéon* (Pistoye et Duverdy, I, 505). The master of the *Friendship* was an Englishman by origin, but an American citizen by naturalization, which he had obtained less than five months prior to the Franco-English war; he had never had his domicile in a neutral country before that war:

> "Il résulte évidemment de l'esprit du règlement de 1778, qu'une seule [des deux conditions requises, *i.e.*: antériorité du domicile et antériorité de la naturalisation à la déclaration de guerre] ne peut suffire; que toutes les deux sont nécessaires, les lettres de naturalisation n'étant que le résultat de la translation de domicile".

To the same effect the decision of the *Conseil des prises* of 7 vendémiaire *an* X concerning the *Ams* (*ibid.*, I, 506), whose master was a native of Guernsey, but was naturalized in November 1798 by the Senate of the city of Emden. The master's defence that he had for a very long time been an "habitant domicilié en Prusse" was rejected on the ground that he had failed to prove "son habitation en Prusse, trois mois seulement avant la déclaration de guerre entre la France et l'Angleterre, pour que sa qualité d'originaire de Guernsey ne lui fît pas perdre celle de neutre".

The Commissary of the French Government, M. Portalis, advocated a mitigation of these rules in the special case of the *Ruby*, whose captain was of British origin, but had been a resident of Boston (U.S.A.) for fourteen years and was considered by the local authorities as an American citizen. However, contrary to the Commissary's advice the *Conseil des prises* condemned his vessel (comp. I, 508-509).

In the case of the *Libérateur* (II, p. 42) it was decided that a ship did not acquire enemy character on the ground that her pilot and ex-master, at the same time her part-owner, was born in, and resident of, a neutral area (the

Adriatic district of the Bocche di Cattaro, belonging to Austria) which was then (1807) militarily occupied by Russia, at the time the enemy of France, the less so because he had since ceased to live in that area.

The French *Conseil des prises* attached great importance to the place where a vessel was built. Thus, in the case of *Le Haabet contre l'Heureux* [*an* XIII] (*ibid.*, I, 239) the *Conseil* held that a vessel sailing under a neutral (Danish) flag, but of enemy construction, had to prove by documents in due form that she had been acquired by the neutral buyer prior to the war and that the grant of a passport by the neutral Sovereign had taken place outside his port area.

De Pistoye and Duverdy further report two cases of "constructive" enemy character on account of the actions of the ships concerned:

the *Amphitrite* and the *Notre-Dame-des-Carmes*, two Spanish vessels captured by five French State vessels and condemned as good and lawful prize by the *Conseil des prises* in December 1809 on the ground that they flew the flag of the deposed Spanish Government and carried a cargo of tobacco abroad for sale for the benefit of the Spanish insurgents who fought against Napoleon's brother, the new King of Spain, Joseph Napoleon (I, 327);

the *Carlo Alberto*, a Sardinian steamship, chartered by the French Duchess De Berry for the purpose of landing a group of passengers in Marseille who intended as insurgents to fight the Government of France in office at the time (1832). When the ship was damaged and forced to take shelter in the roadstead of Ciotat, a number of the passengers were arrested. A claim for reparation was rejected by the *Cour de Cassation* on 8 September 1832 (I, 328):

> "Attendu que le privilège établi par le droit des gens, en faveur des navires alliés ou neutres, cesse dès que ces navires au moyen de l'alliance ou de la neutralité du pavillon qu'ils portent commettent des actes d'hostilités; que, dans ce cas, ils deviennent ennemis".

A case like this can be classed equally well under the heading "Unneutral service".

The same authors, stating in vol. I, 314 that it was often very difficult to decide whether a ship had enemy character, asserted that it was impossible to formulate fixed rules for the determination of such a character. They felt it was a *quaestio facti* and seemed to approve the practice of prize courts to base their findings concerning the enemy or non-enemy character of a vessel on her actions rather than or her "nationalité apparente"—a dilemma which I fail to understand and which seems to me to be at any rate logically inadmissible as a criterion of the national character of a ship.

What *is* admissible is, however, the assimilation of a neutral vessel to an enemy ship on account of her behaviour, but that again is rather a case of unneutral service by a neutral ship.

A normal instance of the attribution of enemy character to a captured vessel was the case of the brig *Oack* (I, 318), captured by the French privateer *Le Voltigeur* on 21 ventôse *an* IX: she was built at Scarborough near Newcastle, was the property of two British merchants in Brighton, was sailing under English command and under the English flag, and carried an English passport.

The neutral nationality of the owner was indeed not always decisive for the above-quoted Art. 6 of the *Règlement* of 1778, re-enacting earlier regulations of 1704 and 1744 (kept in force by a subsequent law of 4 February 1795), laid down the additional rule that that nationality could not be attributed to an owner who had only recently changed his previous enemy nationality into allied or neutral citizenship in virtue of naturalization.

This same *Règlement*, moreover, introduced other persons whose presence on board a neutral vessel could impose enemy character on the vessel. Art. 9 decreed on this point as follows:

> "Seront de bonne prise tous bâtiments étrangers sur lesquels il y aura un subrécargue marchand, commis ou officier-major d'un ennemi de Sa Majesté, ou dont l'équipage sera composé au delà du tiers de matelots, sujets des Etats ennemis de Sa Majesté, ou qui n'auront pas à bord le rôle d'équipage arrêté par les officiers publics des lieux neutres d'où les bâtiments seront partis."

The rule concerning an "officier major ennemi" was extended to a ship's captain of enemy origin who had only recently been naturalized in a neutral country. The latter rule was applied in the *Caninholm* (De Pistoye-Duverdy, II, 34): the chief officers of this neutral (Danish) vessel were enemy subjects; on that and on other grounds she was condemned as enemy property.

French legislation contained no provision as how to decide if a ship belonged partly to enemies, partly to neutrals (see *infra*, p. 221).

In exceptional circumstances the fact of flying an enemy flag could be disregarded as a ground for condemnation. This appears from two French cases of later dates (in the 1870's).

The *Palme* (Wheaton's *International Law*, II, 7th ed., pp. 152-153; Dalloz, *Jurisprudence générale* (1872), Pt. III, p. 94), captured by the French during the Franco-German War, was a German vessel purchased by the Swiss Red Cross from German owners. The Swiss Government would not allow their flag to be flown and the French Government forbade the use of their flag. In default of any other the German flag was retained and a German agent appointed. Because of the peculiarity of the circumstances and their exceptional character the French *Conseil des prises* decreed her release.

The *Taxiarchis*, also referred to by Wheaton, was a British-owned ship, registered in Cyprus, an island which at the time was nominally under Turkish rule but was actually administered by Great Britain. Cyprus did not have a national flag and therefore the *Taxiarchis* flew the Turkish flag. (See also *R.G.D.I.P.* XX (1913), p. 510)

In both these cases the absence of a national flag, coupled with the neutral or friendly nationality of the owners, was the deciding factor.

As appears from judgments inserted in vol. I of the *Traité*, special rules were applied when the consul of a neutral State in an enemy country was involved in the transaction. In this respect French and English case law diverged: contrary to the English view (*infra*, p. 260), it was indeed decided in the *La Paix* [*an* IX] (I, p. 321), *the Hardy* [*an* VII] (*ibid.*) and the *Marthe-Magdeleine* [*an* IX] (I, p. 378) that a neutral trader did not lose his neutral character by acting as the consul of his country in an enemy country. Comp. also the case of the Austrian (neutral) vessel *Gentil-Faucon* [*an* IX] (I, p. 355) to which an English (enemy) consul had delivered a certificate of neutrality for the purpose of deceiving possible French privateers.

International practice has continued to show up to the end of the pre-codification period the traditional reluctance of the prize courts to take notice of certain non-proprietary interests in ships liable to condemnation in their established capacity of enemy vessels which were invoked for their protection by third parties, such as bankers, insurers, holders of liens, bottomry bonds, etc.

See for Japan, *e.g.*, the cases of 1904 concerning

the *Rossia* (W.H. Gill's claim) (Hurst & Bray, II, at p. 45):

> "not only do the Japanese Prize Court Regulations make no mention of preferential rights in respect of a prize, but according to International Law the rights of a captor over a prize which is condemned as enemy property are absolute, and a third party has no right to make a claim in respect of such property ... It follows ... that the claimants [who had defrayed expenses for the continuation of the ship's voyage] can have no right to claim compensation from the Treasury, but the question of compensation by the Treasury is beyond the jurisdiction of this Court",

and a petition to the Sasebo Prize Court by the Chinese charterers of the British s.s. *Nigretia* (*ibid.*, II, 208), claiming a preferential right against the ship for the amount they had spent for her salvage after her stranding down a river and requesting the establishment of a lien upon the ship. The Prize Courts denied their jurisdiction to examine such petitions for the recognition of preferential rights.

The same applies to the tradition of prize courts to deny any protective force to rights of joint-ownership, in one form or another, invoked by neutrals in ships liable to condemnation in their capacity of enemy vessels. See as a late instance the case of

the *Manchuria (No. 1)* [1905] (*ibid.*, II, at pp. 55-56):

> "The *Manchuria* was registered as a Russian ship, and, at the time of capture, was flying the flag of the enemy merchant marine, sailed under an enemy licence, and was owned by the East Asiatic Company of St. Petersburg. There is thus no room for doubt that she was in International Law an enemy ship. The appellants argued that as the greater part of the shares in the East Asiatic Steamship Company are held by Danish subjects, her condemnation would injure the rights of Danish, that is neutral, subjects, and therefore she should be released. But the fact that most of the shares in the company which owns the vessel, belong to neutral subjects does not affect the character of the vessel ...".

The condemnation of a ship on the ground of her enemy character indeed brought of old in its train the condemnation of neutral shares in the ship, by whose enemy character the neutral person concerned was held to be bound: case of the Russian *Primus*, in which a Danish merchant had a share [1854] (Roscoe, II, 290). To the same effect the case of another Russian vessel *Industrie* in which the neutral (Danish) master had a one-fourth share [1854] (Roscoe, II, 297).

Sweden specified already in her Prize Regulations of 19 February 1715 during the Nordic War of 1700-1721 that any enemy part in a vessel rendered the whole ship liable to condemnation, see Article 22 (*Collectanea Maritima*, p. 175):

> "En cas qu'une partie du vaisseau ne soit pas libre & que l'autre le soit, toutes les parties dudit vaisseau seront confiscables."

The issue of the true criterion of the enemy or non-enemy character of ships has remained unsettled up to the eve of the codification in 1908-09.

Russia's Regulations as to Naval Prizes of 14 July 1895 (Hurst & Bray, I, Appendix A, pp. 311-331) persisted in delegating the issue to the national legislation of the vessel concerned. Art. 7 said in effect:

> "The nationality of a vessel is to be decided in accordance with the laws of the country under the flag of which she is sailing, or to the fleet of which she claims to belong",

subject to the traditional deviation from that rule in the case of the transfer of the vessel by her enemy owner to the neutral claimant during the war. And the prize courts applied that principle of Art. 7 by holding (Hurst & Bray, I, pp. 96 *et seq.*, 107 *et seq.* at p. 108) in the case of a captured German ship:

> "as the *Thea* was flying the German flag and was registered at the German port of Kiel, the nationality must be determined by the laws of the German Empire, *in casu* its Merchant Shipping Law of 25 October 1867, supplemented by the Law of 23 December 1888, relating to the nationality of merchant vessels and their rights to hoist the Federal flag ..., governed only by two conditions: that she should belong to a native of one of the Federal States, and should be registered in the ships' register at a German port. No other restrictions on the flying of the German flag exist in German law, which, differing from the laws of some of the other countries, does not require the whole or part of the crew to be German subjects."

Japan's Regulations relating to Capture at Sea of 7 March 1904 (Hurst & Bray, II, Appendix B, pp. 422-439) included two definitions, one of enemy ships in Article 6, the other of national ships of Japan in Article 7. By enemy ships were meant according to Art. 6:

> "1. Ships used by the enemy. This rule applies even when the use is the result of intimidation.
> 2. Ships which sail under the enemy's flag or with a special licence from the enemy.
> 3. Ships the whole or part of which is owned by the hostile State or by individuals of that nation. Ships, however, which hold certificates of registry (nationality) as Japanese vessels, or which ply under special licence from Japan, are not included in this category."

[Item 4 dealt with ex-enemy ships irregularly transferred to a person domiciled in Japan or in a neutral country.]

By Japanese ships were meant according to Art. 7:

"1. Ships which ply with a Japanese certificate of registry (nationality) or with a special licence from the Imperial Government.
2. Ships owned by persons domiciled in Japan."

Vessels of a "neutral nationality" (which I found mentioned in the Russian Regulations of 1895, namely in Art. 11) were not defined but their confrontation with "enemy ships" in Art. 6 (3) admits of no other conclusion than that they were not protected by their neutral flag when they were, even in part, the property of an enemy subject. Officers carrying out a visit or search were, moreover, instructed in different articles of the Regulations to inquire into such details as the ownership of the vessel, the place where she was built, the nationality of their crew, etc.

Many of the prize ships seem to have presented no difficulties because their enemy character could not be contested and the Court could confine itself to adducing their being the property of the Russian Government or of a Russian subject or company, and/or their registry in a Russian home port. Occasionally, however, when there was reason for doubt, especially in the case of companies or partnerships, other elements came to the fore, such as their status under Russian public law—the cases of ships belonging to the semi-governmental institutions of the Russian Voluntary Fleet Company and the Chinese Eastern Railway Company: the *Mukden* (Hurst & Bray, II, 12), the *Argun* (*ibid.*, 46) (comp. *supra*, p. 199), or the neutral nationality of the majority of their shareholders: the *Manchuria (No. 1)* (*ibid.*, 52):

"the fact that most of the shares in the company which owns the vessel belong to neutral subjects does not affect the enemy character of the vessel".

According to the *Rossia* (*ibid.*, 39):

"In the absence of clear proof to the contrary, the ownership of a captured vessel must be concluded from the ship's papers."

On the question whether the character of a ship as enemy or non-enemy was affected by a lien see *infra*, p. 221.

I may be allowed further to refer to the corresponding Sub-Division II on the (non-)enemy character of cargoes, which is far more profuse in presenting legal puzzles.

A remarkable safety-measure against the risk that enemy subjects should attempt to elude the consequences of their enemy character, not by the usual way of a *transfert de pavillon*, but by a change of their own enemy nationality to that of neutral Denmark in order in that manner to assist the common enemy by means of her commercial fleet, England and the United Netherlands, with the object of preventing this during their Nine Year's War against France, in their treaty of 20(30) June 1691 (Dumont, VII[2], 292; Parry, 19, 297) in Article V even forced on Denmark the undertaking that no naturalization would be granted to foreigners without their having previously taken an oath that they would remain domiciled with their family in Denmark for at least ten years.

The jurisprudence, thus formed in the pre-codification period, was continued afterwards in the *Miramichi* [1915] (*B.C.P.C.*, I, 137). In that case (which concerned a captured British ship, but left undecided whether an English company, consisting entirely of aliens, could own a British ship) invoked as precedents two judgments dating from the pre-codification period, *viz.*, those of the above-cited *Cousine Marianne* [1810] and the *Ida* [1854] (Spinks, 26; Roscoe, II, 268), but those judgments would seem to have related especially to seized cargoes.

The enemy or non-enemy character of cargoes has always been determined by the enemy or non-enemy character of their owner, which was itself determined by either his citizenship or his residence. I have been unable to infer with certainty, for example from Sir George Lee's Ms. Notes on the case law of the War of the Austrian Succession, which of these two criteria was held by the prize courts to be paramount.

The prize courts of World War I have again reviewed the old cases and quoted them, sometimes in great detail. See, among many others, the *Southfield* [1915] (*B.C.P.C.*, I, 332) and the "*Trinks cases*" of 1917 (*Posteiro and eighteen other vessels*) (*B.C.P.C.*, III, 275). This *Southfield* case was in its turn quoted as a precedent in the subsequent prolix judgment concerning the *Kronprinsessan Margareta, Rena, Paraná and Hilding* [1920] (*B.C.P.C.*, III, 803; *A.J.I.L.* 1921, p. 593), in which the Judicial Committee of the Privy Council examined afresh and retrospectively the origin and *ratio* of the rule against the validity, as regards the captor, of the transfer of seaborne goods in war-time.

The principles thus adopted by British prize courts for normal cases were also applied in the abnormal case of the application of Reprisals Orders, decreeing the interception of "goods of enemy origin": see the judgment in the World War I case of the *United States (No. 1)* [1916] (*B.C.P.C.*, II, 390).

Section 2. EXTERNAL FACTORS WHICH MAY THWART THE NORMAL EFFECTS OF THE ALLOCATION OF ENEMY OR NON-ENEMY CHARACTER TO SHIPS

What I have described in section 1 is the great variety of positive grounds on which British prize courts deemed themselves justified in basing their conclusion that a captured ship was vested with enemy character. What I must describe in the present section 2 is the impact which various external factors may make on the ultimate fate of a ship whose enemy, respectively non-enemy character had been established by the court, to the effect that in despite of the establishment of the vessel's enemy character no condemnation could follow or, inversely, that in despite of her established neutral character no release was justified, two possibilities at which I have already hinted earlier. These counteractive elements may result in the release of an enemy ship as well as in the condemnation of a non-enemy ship.

There are, in particular, three groups of such counteractive factors which I will discuss separately below, *viz.*:

1. some form of intertwinement of neutral and enemy interests in the same vessel, either (*a*) co-ownership or (*b*) neutral non-proprietary rights in an enemy ship;
2. change of the territorial situation during the vessel's voyage as a result of (*a*) cession or (*b*) military occupation;
3. an intervening termination of hostilities.

1. *Impact of some form of intertwinement of neutral and enemy interests in the same vessel*

Just as in the case of sea-borne goods (*infra*), neutral or other non-enemy holders of rights in respect of enemy vessels have often attempted to save their interests by claiming that such rights should be respected when the vessels were condemned in their capacity of enemy ships. Lengthy judicial battles have been fought over this issue, but have finally resulted in the dismissal of such claims.

The status of captured vessels under the law of prize could indeed be affected by the fact that enemy and neutral (non-enemy) interests in the same ship were interlaced, either (*a*) because neutrals had a share in the property of an enemy vessel, or (*b*) because they had a lien on, or any other non-proprietary interest in, it. The solution of such situations was already in early periods often to the effect that the neutral interests were lost together with the ship.

(*a*) *Mixed enemy and non-enemy co-ownership*

Instances of this first variant which came up before the British prize courts during the Crimean War were those of two Russian ships, the *Primus* (Spinks, 48; Roscoe, II, 290) and the *Industrie* (Spinks, 54; Roscoe, II, 297), the latter for one-quarter the property of her neutral (Danish) master. In those cases Dr Lushington decided that the claims could not be sustained because the enemy's flag and pass imprinted a hostile character on the whole ship, and her owner was bound by that character.

A special case was that of 1812 respecting the *Success* (1 Dods., 131; Roscoe, II, 140) which concerned a vessel sailing under the flag of Sweden but belonging by half to Swedish subjects, and by half to a British owner: the ship sailed under the protection of Royal British Instructions of 20 June 1810, allowing neutrals to trade with an enemy country, in deviation from an Order in Council of 7 January 1807. The Court in that case held that, in order to be entitled to avail itself of the Instructions of 1810, a ship so trading must be wholly the property of neutrals. As this was not the case, the *Success* was condemned in its entirety.

This same question of what was the fate of neutral shares in the property of a vessel found to have enemy character, was answered also by French prize courts to the effect that such shares were condemned together with the ship. See De Pistoye and Duverdy in their *Traité des prises maritimes*, vol. I, pp. 313-314, who referred to the corresponding precedents of the British Prize Court in the *Industrie* (*supra*) and the *John* [1854] (*ibid*., I, 336-337), a third case of the same type, which, however, related not to co-ownership, but to a lien on a ship or her freight (*infra sub b*).

(*b*) *Other than proprietary rights of neutrals*

However, the question arose in particular in the latter of the two variants in which the test of ownership was generally held to be decisive, so that neutral liens, bottomry bonds and similar rights of neutrals on enemy vessels could not save the ship from condemnation as enemy property. Just as in the case of seized enemy cargoes (*infra*, pp. 251-253), British prize courts disregarded also in respect of enemy ships any liens or other non-proprietary rights of neutrals (non-enemies) on such ships. See, *e.g.*, Sir William Scott's judgment in the cases of the *Tobago* [1804] (5 C.Rob., 218; Roscoe, I, 456), the *Marianna* [1805] (6 C.Rob., 24; Roscoe, I, 518), the *Constantia Harlessen* [1810] (Edw., 332; Roscoe, II, 27-28, footnote *a*) and the *Belvidere* [1813] (1 Dods., 353; Roscoe, II, 183).

In the case of the French ship the *Tobago*, whose master had contracted a loan from a British merchant on a bottomry bond previous to hostilities, Lord Stowell refused to allow the claim of the British money-lender as against the captors, saying that there was no instance in which the courts had recognized bonds of this kind as titles to property and that such bonds were not entitled to be recognized as such in prize courts. It was this precedent that Dr Lushington later invoked in his judgment during the Crimean War concerning certain cargoes on board the *Ida* [1854] (Spinks, 26; Roscoe, II, 268):

> "It is an established principle of this Court that no lien, however honest, affords sufficient ground for restitution. This was asserted to its fullest extent in the *Tobago* than which a harder case can scarcely be conceived."

Dr Lushington continued his reference to the older precedents by saying:

> "The total silence of those who have argued for the claimant as to any precedents for this demand, strongly shows that it has not been the practice of this Court to consider such

bonds as property entitled to protection and I think, I may venture to say, that there has been no such instance. ... This Court, therefore, excludes all considerations of liens or circumstances of this species. On the whole, I am of opinion that there is no instance in which the Court has recognized bonds of this kind as titles of property, and that they are not entitled to be recognized as such in the Prize Court, however much the Court of Admiralty may be disposed to uphold them in the other branch of its jurisdiction when they are brought directly before it."

In the *Marianna* Sir William Scott disregarded liens arising out of the purchase of a ship, originally an American vessel, which was sold to a Spanish merchant at Buenos Aires, was seized on a voyage to England while sailing under the flag and pass of Spain. A claim was given on behalf of the former American proprietor in virtue of a lien which he had retained on the property for the payment of purchase money. Sir William Scott held, however, that such an interest could not be deemed sufficient to support a claim of property in a court of prize:

"It will be sufficient that a legal transfer has been made, and that the mode of payment, whatever it is, has been accepted" (at p. 26).

The case of the *Constantia Harlessen* concerned an advance of money made by a cargo-owner to the Danish master in order to prevent his borrowing money on a bottomry bond; the money was to be applied at the end of the voyage to average or to be regarded as a payment in respect of freight. In this case, however, Lord Stowell held as follows:

"Where the Crown takes to itself the rights of one of the parties against the other, so far as they arise out of the individual transaction, I am of opinion that it is to the same extent bound by the obligations of that party towards the other and, therefore, without breaking in upon the principle that the Crown is not to regard latent remote claims of third parties arising on foreign transactions, I shall allow the money which had been advanced to be deducted from the freight."

In the case of the American *Belvidere* the money was advanced not for the immediate outfit of the vessel, but for the general mercantile transactions of her owners. In this case Lord Stowell rejected claims based on general liens, but seemed to admit them in principle if the claimant was in possession of specific security:

"Cases have been stated in which the Court has attended to claims somewhat similar: but in all those cases the parties had some certain evidence of their right; they had either a positive lien upon the ship, or were in possession of a bottomry bond, or some specific security. In this case nothing of the kind is made out by the claimants; and this does, I think, materially distinguish it from the cases which have been mentioned. Here is nothing but an affidavit of the claimants themselves, stating that they have at various times advanced money for the uses of this ship, and that the American owner had put them in possession of it as a security for the debt contracted. No bottomry bond, or any instrument of any kind, is produced in support of the claim, which is left to rest upon the mere averment of the parties interested."

During the proceedings regarding captures made in the course of the Crimean War new attempts were made by neutral claimants, but unsuccessfully, to reverse the trend of the precedents by invoking, in support of their non-proprietary rights, the above-quoted passages obtaining in Sir William Scott's judgment concerning the *Belvidere*, in which he rejected claims based on secret liens but seemed to admit them when the claimant had some specific security. But those attempts failed to convince Dr. Lushington.

The traditional rule was, for example, confirmed in the case of the *Aina (No. 1)* [1854] (Spinks, 8; Roscoe, II, 247), a Russian ship captured by the British warship *Alban* in the Kattegat while sailing under Danish colours on a voyage from Lisbon to Elsenör. Counsel for the claimant, a citizen of Lübeck, resident in Helsingfors (Finland) as Consul of the Netherlands, invoked certain precedents in support of his demand for one-third of the proceeds of the ship, based on a mortgage deed, but his plea was in vain. Dr. Lushington asked whether there was any case where such a claim had been allowed to any but British merchants, but Counsel was unable to furnish him with any. Eliminating the *Belvidere* case (in which Lord Stowell had rejected secret liens, but had admitted such claims in principle when the claimant had some specific security) as being a case of quite a different character, the President condemned the *Aina*:

> "Foreigners cannot set up a mortgage deed on a ship against the captors, though under certain circumstances the claim of British merchants may be allowed".

In the appeal case concerning the *Ariel* [1857] (11 Moore P.C. 119; Roscoe, II, 600) both the parties and the Court (*per* Sir John Patteson) reviewed a large number of precedents.

In his judgment the President, Patteson, asked:

> "Supposing, however, that a lien on the freight or even on the ship in favour of the vendor, who is to be considered as an enemy, did exist, would that lien render the ship in the possession of the neutral owner liable to be captured? That such a lien on an enemy's ship would not be sufficient to found a claim by a neutral in a Court of Prize is clear".

After quoting in support of this view the English precedents of the *Tobago*, the *Marianna* and the *Christine* [1854] (Spinks, 82; Roscoe, II, 320), and the American precedents of the *Frances* (Irvin's claim) (8 Cranch, 418) and the *San José Indiano* (2 Gallison's Rep., 283), his Lordship turned to the inverse case of a neutral prize burdened by an enemy lien:

> "The converse of the proposition was contended not to be true, and that, although the lien of a neutral on an enemy's ship or its freight is not sufficient to found a claim, yet the lien of an enemy on a neutral ship or its freight is sufficient to show an interest in the enemy, of which the belligerent captor is entitled to avail himself, and to defeat the neutral's claim; that a lien on an enemy's ship which would not be recognized in favour of a neutral, would be recognized against a neutral for the purpose of condemnation if the lien be in favour of an enemy. Their Lordships asked, and asked in vain, for some authority which went to establish that distinction. No such authority was produced, but their Lordships were referred again to the language of Lord Stowell in the case of the *Sechs Geschwistern*, which ... was a question as to the right of property, not of lien. Their Lordships have been unable to find any authority for the alleged distinction, and, on the contrary, they are of opinion that the cases of the *Tobago* and of the *Frances* (Irvin's claim) are plainly against

> the distinction... Their Lordships have come to the conclusion that the supposed distinction does not exist, and that liens, whether in favour of a neutral on an enemy's ship, or in favour of an enemy on a neutral ship, are equally to be disregarded in a Court of Prize".

In these appeal proceedings the parties also invoked a number of other pronouncements dealing with the doctrine against the recognition of neutral liens on enemy ships, and placing the controversy in a much wider context, such as Lord Eldon's remarks in the *Warre* case (note to 8 Price's Reports, 269) and the cases of *Stephenson v. Dowson* (3 Beav., 342), *Langton v. Horton* (1 Hare, 549) and *Leslie v. Guthrie* (1 Bing. N.C. 697):

> "There are no means by which according to contract the ship could in any manner be affected either in the Admiralty, the Courts of Common Law or the Court of Chancery. It may be doubtful, considering the loose terms of the contract, and as it was made between foreigners, whether the Court of Chancery would interfere by appointing a receiver of the freight if the ship arrived in England and the owner had not applied the earnings toward payment of the purchase-money... It was said in argument that, by the law, either of Russia or Denmark, some lien might be created on the ship; but that is a matter of foreign law, and therefore a fact to be proved by those who rely upon it, and no proof was offered".

Reference was also made during these appeals proceedings to certain passages in Sir William Scott's judgment of 1799 in a case not relating to a ship but to a cargo: the *Packet de Bilboa* (2 C.Rob., 133; Roscoe, I, 209), which seemed to recognize the validity of claims of neutral mortgagees, holders of maritime liens or bottomry bonds for the recovery from the proceeds of the prize in case of its condemnation the sums of money which they had advanced on security to its owners.

All of Sir William Scott's earlier hesitant allusions to a possible recognition of non-proprietary interests in captured enemy vessels were in fact "construed away".

The net result of all these somewhat inconsistent considerations was that the case law of the Crimean War reaffirmed the older decisions that the only cases in which British prize law respected liens and other similar non-proprietary interests in enemy vessels concerned claims of this nature brought by British claimants. It is not clear what justification there was in this discrimination against neutral holders of liens, bottomry bonds, etc., on enemy vessels. See for a case in which the Court recognized this privileged position of British claimants the *Onderneeming* [1803] (5 C.Rob., 7 footnote *a*; Roscoe, I, 411, footnote *a* and II, 299): award of a seven-eighths' share in the confiscated Dutch (enemy) vessel. For the rest, neutral shares or interests in a vessel captured under an enemy flag were swept away by her condemnation, in accordance with the old precedent of the *Vreede Scholtys* [1804] (5 C.Rob., 5-6, footnote *a*; Roscoe, I, 410, footnote *a*).

See also the case of the *Broders Lust* (5 C.Rob., 6, footnote): the part owner of the ship, and supercargo on board the vessel, obtained restitution of his claim for parts of the cargo, though his claim to the ship was rejected.

The prize courts of World War I have again reviewed the old cases and quoted them, sometimes in great detail. See, among many others, the *Southfield* [1915] (*B.C.P.C.*, I, 332) and the "*Trinks*" cases of 1917 (*Posteiro* and eighteen other vessels) (*B.C.P.C.*, III, 275). The *Southfield* case was in its turn quoted as a precedent in the subsequent judgment concerning the *Kronprinsessan Margareta*, *Rena*, *Paraná* and *Hilding* [1920] (*B.C.P.C.*, III, 803; *A.J.I.L.* 1921, p. 593), in which the Judicial Committee of the Privy Council examined afresh and retrospectively the origin and ration of the rule as against the validity, as regards the captor, of the transfer of seaborne goods in wartime.

The principles thus adopted by British prize courts for normal cases were also applied in the abnormal case of the application of Reprisals Orders, decreeing the interception of "goods of enemy origin": see the judgment in the World War I case of the *United States (No. 1)* [1916] (*B.C.P.C.*, II, 390).

2. *Impact of a change of the territorial situation during the vessel's voyage*

The change envisaged here can consist either in (*a*) cession, or (*b*) a military occupation.

(*a*) *Territorial cession*

I will deal with this particular event in the present sub-paragraph because it has acquired some renown in English prize law owing to its frequent quotation, in season and out of season, by English prize courts, not paralleled by cases of a corresponding fame in French jurisprudence. Two historical cases are in particular prominent: one relating to the conquest of Dutch Demerara (Guyana) by the British in 1782, the other to the capitulation of the Dutch Cape Colony in 1798. Although, from a systematic point of view, these two cases must be distinguished because the former concerned the character of a ship, the latter that of a cargo, the Courts made no difference between them.

I shall for the moment mainly confine myself to the first of the two cases, the *Negotie en Zeevaart* [1782] (Lords of Appeal, 18 July 1782), while referring for the second case, the *Danckebaar Africaan* [1798] (1 C.Rob., 107; Roscoe, I, 74), to section 3 of Sub-Division II on the character of goods, *infra*, pp. 268-271.

These cases of a territorial change *in transitu* of the vessels presented some superficial resemblance to that of a *transfert de pavillon* (where-upon comp. section 3 *infra*, pp. 229-244): in both cases the issue was whether the change in the situation had any impact on the legal status of the ship, but in the first case the new situation was caused by a shift in territorial sovereignty, in the second by a change in ownership, consequently two entirely different causes. Be this as it may, the comparable situation in the two famous cases of 1782 and 1798 was as follows.

The first of the two ships, the *Negotie en Zeevaart*, was sailing under Dutch colours from the Dutch colony of Demerara to Middelburg in Zeeland when she was captured by British forces on 25 March 1781. England had declared war against the Netherlands on 30 January 1781 and six weeks later, on 14 March 1781, Demerara had surrendered to the British. When the ship left Demerara, Holland had not yet ceased to be an ally of England. In appeal the Lords were of opinion that property captured after a declaration of hostilities but before a capitulation, and taken on a voyage, was not protected by the intermediate capitulation. The case was not determined on any ground of illegal trade, nor on any surmise that when the colony became British the trade in which the property was embarked, became *ex post facto* illegal, nor was any consideration given to the fact that Demerara had again become a Dutch colony at the time of adjudication. It was declared to be adjudged on the same principles as if the cause had come on at time of capture. It was not on these grounds, but simply on the ground of Dutch property, that condemnation was passed in that case: "the ship as Dutch could not change her character *in transitu*".

It was this precedent that the claimants in the subsequent *Danckebaar Africaan* case of 1798 invoked in support of their claim for restoration of certain cargoes on board. That Dutch ship was bound from Batavia to Holland. On coming to the Cape of Good Hope, a claim was made on the part of Goetz and Brothers, inhabitants of the Dutch Cape colony. The ship sailed from the Cape on 21 May 1795 with her cargo, which had been reshipped and delivered to her on bail to answer adjudication. On that further voyage she was captured by the British on 16 November 1795 after the capitulation of the colony to the British on 15 September, which caused the claimants to become British subjects. There was elaborate discussion in this case on whether it was distinguishable from the *Negotie en Zeevaart* case of 1782, but the prize court of 1798 (*per* Sir William Scott) denied that: the ship failed to dispel her hostile character and the Court clung to the principle that the ship could not change her character *in transitu*. The Court further argued that on 21 May it must have been known at the Cape what was the state of Holland; the Stadholder had left it, and the country was in possession of the French. The ship was despatched as a Dutch ship, with directions to make a vigorous resistance against cruisers; that is, as it must have meant, against English cruisers. With respect to the intermediate capitulation on 15 September, nothing is more clear than that the general articles, protecting the property of inhabitants, apply only to such property as is then within the colony, and not to any other which they may possess elsewhere on the surrender of a colony, and which devolves to the conquering power. The protection arises as exceptions under capitulation, and it is not to be extended beyond the terms of the Article.

Commenting upon the case of the *Danckebaar Africaan*, Hall (*International Law*, 6th ed., p. 502) considered it reasonable that neutral property which had become hostile through the conquest by an enemy State of the port at which its owners were domiciled should be condemned, but felt that, if this were done, no good cause could be shown for deciding that hostile property should not, inversely, become friendly to a belligerent State from the moment at which the latter obtained possession of the port to which the property belonged. However, in the case of the *Danckebaar Africaan* the Court ruled otherwise: property sent from a hostile colony could not change its character *in transitu*, even if the owners became British subjects by a capitulation preceding the capture.

The same principle was applied again in the case of the *Boedes Lust* [1804] (5 C.Rob., 233; Roscoe, I, 459) carrying a cargo shipped from Demerara in January-February 1804 and seized 10 May 1804, a month before Great Britain's declaration of war against Holland. At the time of adjudication the owners, as inhabitants of Demerara, had become British subjects. They had not settled there during the time of British possession nor had they averred an intention of retiring when that possession ceased. This complication gave rise to the following argument:

> "[The claimants] are therefore to be treated under this general view as Dutch [enemy] subjects, unless it can be shown that there any other circumstances by which they are protected. It is contended (but without success) that the property was taken in a state of peace, and that the proprietors are now become British subjects, and consequently that this property could not be considered as the property of an enemy, either at the time of capture or of adjudication".

(*b*) *Belligerent occupation*

Parallel with the cases in which the enemy or neutral character of the owner of a prize depended on the relevancy or otherwise of a change of territorial sovereignty over the country of the owner's domicile *in transitu* were other cases in which the country concerned fell temporarily under foreign military occupation or found itself in a comparable transitional situation. An analysis of the effects of such an event would fit here in this sub-paragraph if I had come across a case affecting the status of a ship, but all the cases I found related to the enemy or non-enemy status of cargoes. I must therefore refer to the corresponding sub-paragraph in Sub-Division II, *infra*, pp. 260-261, concerning especially the *Gerasimo* case.

Did such a temporary change also have adverse consequences for the owner of the prize? This question was most elaborately discussed by the Judicial Committee of the Privy Council (*per* Sir Pemberton Leigh) in the *Gerasimo* case of 1857 after the Crimean War (11 Moore P.C., 88; Roscoe, II, 577). This case related to the impact that the temporary Russian occupation of the Danubian principalities of Moldavia and Wallachia in 1853 had on the enemy or non-enemy character of their inhabitants. When adjudicating the appeal of the owners of the *Gerasimo* from a judgment of the High Court of Admiralty (*per* Dr. Lushington) which had admitted such impact (Roscoe, II, at p. 579), the Judicial Committee began by quoting an old precedent, the

Fama [1803] (5 C.Rob., 115; Roscoe, II, at p. 583), decided by the then Court of Admiralty (*per* Sir William Scott) which related to another part of the world, North-American Louisiana, and had no bearing on a military occupation of that territory, but on its cession by Spain to France by their treaty of San Ildefonso of 19 August 1796 (Parry, 53, 257) which had remained without effect. It was this early decision by Sir William Scott that the Judicial Committee took as its point of departure in 1857, joining their predecessor of 1803 in his general theoretical outlook, expressed as follows:

> "In order to complete the right of property there must be both right to the thing and possession of it, both *jus ad rem* and *jus in re*. All writers concur in holding it to be a necessary principle of jurisprudence that to complete the right of property the right to the thing and the possession of the thing should be united. This is the general law of property and applies, I conceive, no less to the right of territory than to other rights. Even in newly-discovered countries, when a title is meant to be established for the first time, some act of possession is usually done and proclaimed as a notification of the fact [an allusion to old principles covering the famous event of acquisition of territorial sovereignty by occupation]".

That was why Sir William Scott was of the opinion that the act of cession of Louisiana by Spain to France by the treaty of San Ildefonso could not be recognized as having actually taken place, and why Louisiana had still to be considered a Spanish colony in May 1803.

Continuing then to deal with the special case of the *Gerasimo*, relating to the in their view comparable case of temporary military occupation, the Judicial Committee surveyed a number of kindred earlier historical cases in which the situation had been inquired into:

the Santo Domingo cases, decided in appeal by the Lords in 1808, relating to the fact that specified places in this insular colonial possession of France were at the time in the actual possession of insurgent negroes who had detached them, as far as actual occupancy could do so, from the mother country (Edw., 1; Roscoe, II, 584):

the *Manilla* [1807] (Edw., 1; Roscoe, II, 584, footnote *m*);

the *Dart* and the *Happy Couple* in appeal: 1808;

the *Santa Anna* [1808] (Edw., 180; Roscoe, II, 585, footnote *n*), concerning parts of Spain (Cádiz), occupied by France during her war with England;

Donaldson v. Thompson, decided by a court of common law in respect of the occupation of Corfú and other Ionian islands by Russian troops [1800] (1 Campb., 429; Roscoe, II, 585, footnote *p*);

the *Bolletta* [1809] (Edw., 171; Roscoe, II, at p. 586), where the issue was whether the Ionian island of Zante was Russian or French territory;

Hagedorn v. Bell (Roscoe, II, at p. 586, footnote *q*), again a case of common law, regarding the occupation of Hamburg by French troops.

On the basis of this wealth of precedents the Lords of Appeal reached the conclusion that the national character of the cargo of the *Gerasimo* was not influenced to its disfavour by the fact that its owner was the inhabitant of a neutral territory which had temporarily fallen under the military occupation of a belligerent State. This conclusion was amply motivated by interesting legal observations.

3. *Impact of a peace treaty on the character of a prize*

There is a third possibility which may produce a similar impact, namely, the conclusion of a peace treaty *in transitu*. A change of character of the prize may indeed exceptionally be the consequence of a change of nationality of the owner in virtue of a peace treaty. I have not come across older instances which provide a clear answer to this supposed contingency, apart from a certain resemblance to it of French prize decrees which refused to accept the neutral character of captured objects claimed by persons who appeared to have been naturalized from enemy to neutral nationality (comp. *supra*, p. 215).

The effect of a peace treaty on the fate of captured property was, however, discussed much later, as an aftermath to World War I, in the case of the *Blonde, Prosper and Hercules* (*B.C.P.C.*, III, 875). See also the case of the *Pellworm and other vessels* [1919] (*B.C.P.C.*, III, 702), in which the lower court referred to an old judgment of the American Supreme Court (*per* Marshall, C.J.) in the case of the *United States v. Schooner Peggy* [1801] (1 Cranch (Amer.), 103), in which the Court said that:

> "where a treaty is the law of the land, and as such affects the rights of parties litigating in Court, that treaty as much binds those rights, and is as much to be regarded by the Courts as an Act of Congress."

The treaty in question was by certain of its general provisions held to operate to divest the rights of a captor which had been established by a court of first instance before the date at which the treaty took effect.

Section 3. TRANSFER OF ENEMY SHIPS TO A NON-ENEMY FLAG DURING OR IN CONTEMPLATION OF WAR

Introductory remarks

As has been said before (p. 204), belligerents have already in early days opposed, as being a device to frustrate their rights, the transfer of enemy vessels to a non-enemy (allied or neutral) flag in wartime or in contemplation of an expected war. Both municipal laws and prize court decrees testify to the general recognition of this principle, and there were also treaty provisions which incorporated it, or hinted at it. Thus, a possible *transfert de pavillon* was considered in Art. 30 of the treaty between France and the three main

Hanse towns of 28 September 1716 (Dumont, VIII[1], 478; Parry 13, 19). After stating the principle that a ship should be "de leur [*i.e.* of the Hanse towns] fabrique ou de celle d'une nation neutre", the article continued by providing that

> "si néanmoins étant de fabrique ennemie ou ayant apartenu aux ennemis, il a été acheté avant la déclaration de la guerre, soit par des sujets des Villes Anséatiques, soit par ceux d'une nation neutre, il ne sera point sujet à confiscation".

This allusion to a sale prior to the declaration of war implies, *a contrario*, that such a transfer effected after the outbreak of hostilities would not be considered as causing a valid change of enemy character of a vessel.

As to the invalidity vis-à-vis the belligerents of the transfer of enemy ships to neutral purchasers a distinction was developed between *post bellum* and *ante bellum* contracts of sale. The latter were only suspect in exceptional circumstances whereas the former were suspect in any case unless their *bona fides* were duly proven.

One of the principal issues dealt with by prize courts was to define the conditions under which an *ante bellum* contract of sale was nevertheless invalid or a *post bellum* sale was nevertheless valid vis-à-vis the captor State.

There were, in particular, two classes of transfers which were looked at with extreme suspicion, *viz.*, the sale of enemy vessels lying in a blockaded port and the sale of enemy public vessels. This will become apparent from a survey of English and American precedents dating back respectively to the Napoleonic period, the years of the Crimean War and the American Civil War.

These various topics will be set out in the following pages, devoted first to old French legislation and jurisprudence (pp. 230-231) and then to old Anglo-American case law (pp. 232-242).

1. *Old French legislation and jurisprudence*

Old French legislation had dealt with the issue of *transfert de pavillon* in detail.

It was originally regulated by Art. 4 of the *Règlement* of 17 February 1694, confirmed by those of 12 May 1696, 23 July 1704 (Art. 7) and 21 October 1744 (Art. 10). Art. 7 of the *Règlement* of 26 July 1778 finally defined the régime of enemy vessels sold to neutrals prior to, or during the hostilities as follows:

> "Les bâtiments de fabrique ennemie, ou qui auront eu un propriétaire ennemi, ne pourront être réputés neutres ou alliés, s'il n'est trouvé à bord quelques pièces authentiques passées devant des officiers publics qui puissent en assurer la date, et qui justifient que la vente ou cession en a été faite à quelqu'un des sujets des puissances alliées ou neutres, avant le commencement des hostilités, et si ledit acte translatif de propriété de l'ennemi, au

sujet neutre ou allié, n'a été dûment enregistré par-devant le principal officier du lieu du départ, et signé du propriétaire ou du porteur de ses pouvoirs."

Art. 8 of the same *Règlement* added in respect of enemy vessels captured and sold by the captors to neutrals:

"A l'égard des bâtiments de fabrique ennemie qui auront été pris par les vaisseaux de Sa Majesté, ceux de ses alliés ou de ses sujets, pendant la guerre, et qui auront ensuite été vendus aux sujets des Etats alliés ou neutres, ils ne pourront être réputés de bonne prise s'il se trouve à bord des actes en bonne forme, passés par-devant les officiers publics à ce préposés, justificatifs tant de la prise que de la vente ou adjudication qui en aurait été faite ensuite aux sujets desdits Etats alliés ou neutres, soit en France, soit dans les ports des Etats alliés; faute desquelles pièces justificatives, tant de la prise que de la vente, lesdits bâtiments seront de bonne prise."

Later French cases that had a bearing on the validity or invalidity of the transfer of enemy ships to neutral owners date from the Crimean War.

In 1854 the new *Conseil des prises* of France condemned the Russian ship *Orione* of Odessa as an enemy vessel despite her asserted transfer to a Tuscan buyer at Livorno (*Traité*, II, 499, under the heading *L'Orione contre l'Averne*). The grounds of her condemnation, set out in detail in the judgment, were convincing. The ship, captured by a French warship when leaving the port of Livorno on a voyage from Odessa to the English Channel, had assertedly been sold to a Tuscan banker by an "acte sous seing privé" subsequent to the outbreak of hostilities between the Porte and Russia, but only a copy of that act was produced; therein the banker, who was in habitual relations with Russia, was not mentioned in any way; the ship sailed under the apparent command of a Tuscan citizen, usually engaged in local cabotage, who could neither read nor write; the former master of the ship, who represented the interests of the Russian owners, had, with all the original crew, remained on board and actually continued to direct the navigation and operations; he had even signed the bill of lading:

"Considérant que le navire portait illégalement le pavillon toscan, en vertu d'un passavant délivré par le consul général de Toscane à Odessa, contrairement à l'art. 8 du règlement du 14 avril 1826 qui interdit aux consuls de délivrer aucun passeport pour arborer le pavillon toscan; Considérant qu'en rélachant à Livourne, le capitaine ne s'est pas même consigné au sieur Adami, son prétendu armateur, mais qu'il s'est consigné à ordre;
Considérant que cette relâche à Livourne n'a eu pour but que de changer d'équipage et de se munir de nouveaux papiers de bord, contrairement au principe généralement établi qui ne permet à aucun navire, en temps de guerre, de changer de propriété, de nationalité et de papiers de bord, au cours de voyage".

The *Christiane* [1854] (*Traité*, II, 502), was a vessel built in Russia, which had belonged to a Russian subject and which had still flown the Russian flag in the Danish port of Copenhagen under the name *Weljet* five days before leaving that port flying the Danish flag, under which she was captured off the coast of France. The defence that the ship had been transferred to a Danish buyer in a Danish port prior to the war, was dismissed: there was no proof by authentic documents in support.

2. *Old Anglo-American case law*

After this summary survey of French case law I will now pass to the practice of English and American prize courts, arranged in the order of the successive naval wars in which the two countries became involved.

A vast number of English prize cases have sanctioned the rule concerning the invalidity vis-à-vis the captor of the transfer of enemy vessels to a neutral flag. The transfer operation was particularly suspect when it either took place with regard to a ship lying in a blockaded port, or related to a public vessel of the enemy.

(*a*) *Seven Years' War*

One of the oldest reported instances of an enemy ship sold to a neutral subject in a blockaded port is that of the *Felicity* [1756], referred to by Sir William Scott in his judgment concerning the *Minerva* [1807] (6 C.Rob., 396; Roscoe, I, 591) (see *infra*). That *Felicity* case related to a French merchant vessel that had sailed during the Seven Years' War from Martinique and put into the Spanish port of Cádiz where she was condemned and sold; her condemnation was, however, reversed by the Court of Appeal (comp. Roscoe's footnote *a* at p. 592 of vol. I of his *Reports*).

(*b*) *The fourth Anglo-Dutch naval war*

The first cases of this type, with which Sir William Scott himself was confronted, came before him during his early years of office in the Prize Court and the Court of Appeal; they related to the Dutch vessel *Nieuwe Vriendschap* and other Dutch ships that had lain in the harbour of Dutch Curaçao for nearly two years with their cargoes on board during the fourth Anglo-Dutch naval war of the 1780's, in expectation of convoy, and had assertedly been sold in that situation to subjects of the German Empire and other neutral claimants. The Court of Appeal [1786] (Roscoe, I, footnote at p. 592) seems in that case to have inclined to the argument of the purchasers, but did not give any decision upon the question of law when it affirmed the sentence of condemnation by the Vice-Admiralty Court expressly on the ground of the lack of an actual *bona fide* transfer.

During this war the Prize Court also laid down the rule that "a ship cannot change its character in transit". This was decreed by Lord Camden in a case of territorial cession, which has been discussed *supra*, at p. 226, relating to the Dutch vessel *Negotie en Zeevaart* [1782] (1 C.Rob., 112; Roscoe, I, 75 n).

(*c*) *Revolutionary Wars of France*

The *Vigilantia* [1798] (1 C.Rob., 1; Roscoe, I, 31) was originally a Dutch (enemy) vessel, assertedly sold to a (neutral) merchant at Emden. When afterwards sailing under Prussian colours, she was taken on a voyage from Amsterdam to Greenland, whilst fitted out with stores necessary for the Greenland fisheries. She was held by the Prize Court still to continue *de facto* to be the property of the former Dutch (enemy) owner: the ship was Dutch-built and had sailed regularly and habitually to Greenland whither she continued to sail after having been bought by the Emden merchant. In that case the Court adopted the principle that the national character of a ship was generally determined by the place of residence of her owner, but held that special circumstances might negate that general rule, for instance, the fact that she was navigating under the pass of a foreign country or was, by constant and habitual occupation, continually employed in the trade of that country, commencing with the war, continuing during the war, and evidently on account of the war. Sir William Scott expressed his opinion on the "abstract question of law" and "subject to the correction of a superior Court" as follows:

> "Supposing [the claimant, a merchant resident at Emden] to be the actual proprietor of this vessel, yet this vessel and her concerns ... are liable to be treated and considered as Dutch [enemy] property. In the first place, she is a Dutch-built vessel, a Dutch fishing vessel, that went from Amsterdam regularly, and habitually, to Greenland, and to return to Amsterdam, there to deliver her cargo; she is purchased [by the Emden merchant] in Holland; she is purchased avowedly for the purpose of pursuing the same course of commerce, the fishing trade of Holland; she is purchased at a time when, it is said, there was a defect of conveniences for carrying on this trade at Emden; but I am satisfied it was the intention of the parties to carry on this trade to and from Amsterdam. Now, I ask upon what grounds is it that this vessel, so purchased and so employed, is to be considered merely as a Prussian vessel? Here is a ship as thoroughly engaged and incorporated in Dutch commerce as a ship can possibly be; she is fitted out uniformly from Amsterdam; she is fitted out with Dutch manufacture, she is fitted out for Dutch importation in all these respects employing and feeding the industry of that country; she is managed by a Dutch ship's husband, and finding occupation for the commercial knowledge and industry of the subjects of that country; she is commanded by a Dutch captain; she is manned by a Dutch crew, and brings back the produce of her voyage for the purpose of Dutch consumption and Dutch revenue. If to this you add that the vessel is transferred by the Dutch because they themselves are unable to carry on the trade avowedly in their own persons it is truly a Dutch commerce in a very eminent degree, not only in its essence, but for the very hostile purpose of rescuing and protecting the Dutch from the naval superiority of their British enemy. In my apprehension, unless it could be maintained as a rule, without any exception whatever, that the domicile of the proprietor constitutes the national character of the vessel, this ship must be condemned, even if she had been really transferred."

In a parallel case, of the *Embden* (Meyer, Master) [1781] (1 C.Rob., 16; Roscoe, I, 35) the President held that the same conclusion applied, although that case was distinguishable from the *Vigilantia* in the point that the ship's master was a Prussian by birth.

The *Staadt Embden* (Jacobs, Master) [1798] (1 C.Rob., 26; Roscoe, I, 37) was a British vessel taken by the enemy (France) and carried by him as prize to Christiansand (Norway), where she was condemned and sold to a Emden merchant. During a subsequent voyage from Riga to Amsterdam she was captured by the British. The Prize Court held that the sale had not been a *bona fide* sale. She was condemned together with her cargo of masts and deals, qualified as contraband.

The *Bernon* [1798] (1 C.Rob., 101; Roscoe, I, 70) was a case of the sale of a ship by a Frenchman in France to an American during the war: the purchase of an enemy vessel by a neutral in time of war was liable to arouse great suspicion, still more increased when the asserted neutral purchaser appeared to be personally residing in the enemy country at the time of sale of this ship (condemnation on want of proof of *bona fides*).

Other variants of this aggregate of problems turning on the transfer of ships to a neutral flag in wartime or in contemplation of war were those which arose after the capture of

the *Perseverance* [1799] (2 C.Rob., 239; Roscoe, I, 226), purchased by a neutral (Swedish) subject under an illegal condemnation pronounced by a French court while the ship lay in neutral (Norwegian) waters. She was seized on the part of her former owner on coming to the Isle of Guernsey. In this case the British Court argued:

> "It is a general rule, undoubtedly, that whoever purchases under an illegal title does it at his own peril, and must take the consequences (both in his purchase and in his own subsequent expenditure upon it) of his inattention to his own security; but I think this was not a title so notoriously bad, at the time when this purchase was made, as to bring it fairly under the application of the general rule to its utmost extent.
>
> The Court has had occasion to inquire into the validity of such purchases and has, upon a regular discussion, pronounced them invalid; and if, henceforth, neutrals shall continue to purchase under such flimsy titles, they must take the consequences of their own imprudence. But it may be too much to apply this maxim without any alleviation to a person who has heretofore bought under a practice which, though illegal, was too prevalent in some ports of the North of Europe: it appears that a sum of money has been expended on the repairs of this vessel, by which the claimant (the original owner) will be benefited, though not to the whole amount of the sum laid out; something must be allowed for wear and tear; and besides, the party who has expended this sum, has had the use of the vessel in the meantime; I shall therefore not allow the whole sum, but I shall take a moiety, and I shall allow that, in consideration of the benefit which the original owners are likely to receive from the amelioration".

[The ship was restored to her original owner on salvage, subject to an allowance of the moiety of that sum, owed by him to the purchaser for his expenses];

Vrouw Hermina (Jonker, Master) [1799] (1 C.Rob., 163), a Dutch (enemy) vessel, asserted to have been sold to a buyer resident in neutral Eastern Friesland; the latter's petition for a rehearing for the production of newly collected evidence was refused by Sir William Scott because he considered the case to be incapable of fair explanation;

the *Juffrouw Anna* (Greeson, Master) [1799] (1 C.Rob., 124 a; Roscoe, I, 76), an English ship, captured by the French, condemned and assertedly purchased again by an Emden merchant, who claimed her as his property. The claimant was, however, convicted of fraudulent conduct and of departing from a fair neutral character, and the ship was condemned;

the *Copenhagen* (Mening, Master) [1799] (1 C.Rob., 289; Roscoe, I, 138), a ship duly certified as Danish, but bought in an enemy country during the war, driven into an English port by bad weather. The cargo was restored and after further proof the ship was also released; no damages on account of her detention, but award of *pro rata* freight (comp. on this latter feature of the case *sub* C, section 6, *sub a*, *infra*, p. 632).

The transfer of a ship to a neutral flag was sometimes made not by an enemy, but by a national (British) shipowner and in that case for the purpose of concealing his trading with the enemy. This was, *e.g.*, the case of the *Odin (No. 1)* [1799] (1 C.Rob., 248; Roscoe, I, 127), a British vessel, ostensibly transferred to a Dane and later captured by a British man-of-war while she was sailing on a voyage from Dutch (enemy) Batavia to neutral Copenhagen, after having first made a voyage to that (at the time French-occupied and consequently enemy) town from the Danish settlement of Fredericksnagore near Calcutta, where the claimant, described as a Norwegian by birth, carried on his business:

> "If this had been the whole of the case the consequence must have been an immediate restitution, because this Court has not taken upon itself to lay down that a Danish merchant at Fredericksnagore may not send a cargo of his own in his own ship to Batavia, there dispose of that cargo and purchase another, and bring that to his own country in Europe. But ... a fundamental fact appears in the use ..., namely, that this had been a very short time before the voyage, the property of ... British subjects, residing at Calcutta; this fact leads to the question whether this ship had been actually and *bona fide* transferred from them to this Danish merchant? For if not, if she continued the property of these British merchants, going on their commercial errands to Batavia, then a port of the public ennemies of his Majesty, she is going illegally ... so as to subject her to confiscation, there being no maxim better or more firmly established in the maritime law of this country than this, that no subject of the King can trade directly with the public enemy but under a licence authorising him to do so ..." (comp. on this subject *infra*, *sub A*, section 1, p. 281).

Further cases, adjudged in the beginning of the 19th century, were the following.

In the case of the *Jemmy* [1801] (4 C.Rob., 31; Roscoe, I, 331), a French ship, pretendedly bought at Dunkirk by a merchant of neutral Altona, the Prize Court decreed her condemnation. The possibility of further proof by the claimant was refused, because the case against him was too clear: the ship had been left under the same management and in the same trade as before the asserted transfer; the conclusive presumption was that the transfer was not genuine.

In the case of the *Sechs Geschwistern* [1801] (4 C.Rob., 100; Roscoe, I, 363), a ship assertedly purchased from the enemy in France by a neutral merchant, but not wholly transferred,—a liberty which England had not denied to neutral merchants, unlike the regulation of France by which it was entirely forbidden—, the Court said:

> "The rule which this country has been content to apply is that property so transferred must be *bona fide* and absolutely transferred, that there must be a sale divesting the enemy of all further interest in it; and that anything tending to continue his interest vitiates a contract of this discription altogether. This is the rule which this country has always

> considered itself justified in enforcing; not forbidding the transfer as illegal, but prescribing such rules as reason and common sense suggest to guard against collusion and cover, and to enable it to ascertain, as much as possible, that the enemy's title is absolutely and completely divested.—In the present case there are covenants which preserve and retain the interest of the enemy seller ... Looking to the control which the French Government and the vendor still retain over this property, it is impossible for me to hold that all the interest of the enemy is completely divested."

The ship was accordingly condemned.

The validity of the always suspect transfer of a vessel in a blockaded port depended on the question between whom and whom the transfer took place:

the transfer of a ship effected in a blockaded port by a neutral citizen to another neutral citizen was valid: the *Potsdam* [1801] (4 C.Rob., 89; Roscoe, I, 355); the vessel was permitted to come out in ballast;

a transfer operated by an enemy owner to a neutral buyer was held invalid in the case of the *General Hamilton* [1805] (6 C.Rob., 61; Roscoe, I, 528), relating to the purchase of an enemy ship by an American merchant in a blockaded French port and seized on a voyage from the Seine to New Orleans when she had been driven by stress of weather into a British port. Sir William Scott rejected both defences, put forward by the neutral claimant, *viz.*, (*a*) that the vessel had been bought out of the proceeds of the cargo of another vessel:

> "That circumstances cannot avail on a question of blockade. If the ship has been purchased in a blockaded port, that alone is the illegal act, and it is perfectly immaterial out of what funds the purchase was effected";

and (*b*) that the vessel had terminated her voyage and, therefore, the penalty would no longer attach:

> "It is true that she had been driven into a port of this country by stress of weather, but that is not described by the master as forming any part of the original destination, which is represented to have been New Orleans. It is impossible to consider this action as any discontinuance of the voyage or as a defeasance of the penalty which has been incurred."

On these grounds the *General Hamilton* was condemned.

When, however, two years later the Court was faced by a slightly different case concerning the asserted sale of a former enemy warship in a neutral port to a neutral purchaser—the case of the *Minerva* (Knuttell, Master) [1807] (6 C.Rob., 396; Roscoe, I, 591)— the Court hesitated what to decide because there were no precedents concerning enemy warships having been sold in the same circumstances. The *Minerva*, a ship of war that belonged to the Dutch East India Company, carrying eighteen guns and armament, had been chased by a British frigate into the port of (Norwegian) Bergen at the beginning of the war and had been lying in that port ever since. She was claimed by Count Bentinck, Lord or Prince of the small State of Kniphausen, whose legal representative alleged that he had purchased her in

April 1807 in the port of Bergen in order to allow her to sail to his port on the river Jade under Kniphausen colours. Sir William Scott was not aware of any case in the Prize Court or in the Court of Appeal in which the legality of such a purchase had been recognized. The President, therefore, started on a fresh evaluation of the legal situation created by this claim of the "highly distinguished person, described to be the Prince of Kniphausen". His first question was whether such a purchase could be legally made. Even as regards private merchant vessels in that situation the President preferred to wait for the authority of the Superior Court before he admitted the validity of such a transfer:

> "That a private merchant could lawfully do this I shall not hold till I am so instructed by the Superior Court. That a sovereign prince should embark in such a transaction, unless under such guards as would effectually remove all possibility of abuse is what, but for the instance before us, could scarcely have been expected. Some communication, at least, we might suppose would be made to the belligerent government, accompanied with a disclosure of any circumstance of caution that should exclude the suspicion of what is always to be apprehended, the danger of such a vessel finding her way back again into the navy of her own country."

After circumstantial argument to the effect, *inter alia*, that it had not appeared that Count Bentinck was the owner of merchant vessels, or that he was engaged in mercantile adventures, and that, therefore, some imposition must have been practised on "the august person" by those who had asked for the restitution of the ship on his behalf, the claim was rejected.

On the re-appearance of this issue during the American Civil War see *infra*, *sub* (*e*).

The *Falcon* [1805] (6 C.Rob., 104) was the complicated case of the transfer of an originally British vessel that was captured by the French on 2 June 1803, condemned by a French Consular Court in Livorno and there sold to an American consul in France. The condemnation was subsequently (on 26 March 1805) on rehearing (in appeal) confirmed by the *Conseil des prises* in Paris. The first buyer under the consular judgment had in the meantime taken the ship to New Orleans (U.S.A.) and in December 1804 back again to Bordeaux, where she became the subject of further transfers, finally to another American buyer, a resident of Bordeaux who was an American consul. The main issues in this case were the questions of whether (*a*) an American consul in France was disqualified by his place of residence from producing evidence before a British court (a question *in casu* answered in the negative because "the mere intention to settle in France as a French merchant could not be held to clothe him immediately with the French character and to deprive him of the right of being considered at the present time as an American merchant"), and (*b*) the title of condemnation under which the property had been acquired was valid. On the latter point the Court decided that the condemnation of the vessel by the French consul in Livorno would not have vested the buyer with a sufficient title if the matter had rested there, but that the question appeared in a different light as a result of the fact that the consular judgment had since been confirmed in appeal by the *Conseil des prises* in Paris, although "the state of that tribunal as a court of original jurisdiction and also as a court of appeal with the power of evocation was extremely vacillating during the [then] turbulent times."

The *Clio* [1805] (6 C.Rob., 67; Roscoe, I, 529) was a ship purchased by a London house from an (enemy) French merchant on the strength of a licence granted to them with a view to recovering a bad debt; the fact that the transaction was attended with a bond to the French Government for the restitution of the ship at the conclusion of the war and that the claimant ought to have fairly represented that to the British Government at the time of obtaining the licence, nevertheless did not in the circumstances of the case vitiate the licence, because the transaction was *bona fide* and in accordance with its intention.

The *Marianna* (Pasadillo, Master) [1805] (6 C.Rob., 24; Roscoe, I, 518) was originally an American (neutral) ship, later sold to a Spanish (enemy) merchant at Buenos Aires. A claim to her property was given in virtue of a lien retained on the ship by the seller for the payment of the purchase money. In accordance with a constant judicial practice such an interest was deemed insufficient to support a claim of property in a Court of Prize:

> "a legal transfer in casu by a neutral to an enemy subject has been made and the mode of payment, whatever it is, has been accepted. Upon this view of the principle upon which the Prize Court has always acted, the ship must be considered to have been legally transferred, and must be pronounced subject to condemnation as Spanish property."

A more complicated case was that of the *Baltic* [1809] (1 Acton, 25), formerly called *Hazen* when she was still the property of traders in Bordeaux. This was a case of continuous voyage from an (enemy) French harbour to an (enemy) French colony. The ship and the cargo were sold in the port of Philadelphia to a nominal American buyer; the ship obtained the new name of *Baltic* in the shipping register; a new master was appointed, but the same American supercargo remained in charge. This man was proved to be an agent for the enemy and subject of France. The vessel, that was sailing under false papers, was condemned despite her (fraudulent) sale to a neutral citizen.

The *Fortuna* [1811] (1 Dodson, 81; Roscoe, I, 193, footnote) was an American vessel that was sold under suspect circumstances to a Portuguese on the island of Madeira. She was proved to have been sold for the purpose of engaging in the slave trade from West Africa and was condemned also for that reason (comp. *infra* Ch. III A, section 6 A, p. 478).

(*d*) *The Crimean War*

The following British cases, dating from the Crimean War, relate to Russian ships assertedly transferred *bona fide* to neutral buyers and claimed by subjects of

Hanover: the *Johanna Emilie* or *Emilia* [1854] (Spinks, 12; Roscoe, II, 252), a ship built in Hanover in 1853, which after having first sailed under

Russian colours, with a crew of Hanoverians, via Riga and Lisbon to London, was seized there by the Customs Officers. A Hanoverian claimed the ship as his property, asserting that, while she passed Newcastle, she had been sold to him on 23 January 1854, *i.e.*, prior to the outbreak of war, under a power of attorney given by her Russian owner to her master. The case was suspect: no money had passed at the time of the alleged sale, the ship had carried on the same trade as before, there was no Hanoverian flag on board and even after the transfer she had still sailed under Russian colours, so that further proof of *bona fides* was required;

Denmark: the *Johann Christoph* [1854] (Spinks, 60; Roscoe, II, 302), relating to the asserted sale of a vessel by her Russian owner to her neutral (Danish) master, which was qualified by the Court as merely colourable and fictitious; the *Soglasie* [1854] (Spinks, 104) and the *Rapid (No. 2)* [1854] (Spinks, 80; Roscoe, II, 317), relating to the assertedly *bona fide* sale by her Russian owner to a Dane immediately antecedent to the war, a sale that could not be upheld against the captors;

the *Ariel* [1857] (11 Moore P.C., 119; Roscoe, II, 600), a very elaborate judgment concerning a sale made immediately before the war; the lower court condemned the vessel as enemy property because it was not convinced that the alleged transfer was absolute and *bona fide*; only part of the purchase price had been paid, the rest to be paid out of the ship's earnings. This judgment was, however, reversed in appeal [1857] on the ground that the non-payment of part of the purchase price did not create a lien on the freight and ship in favour of the Russian seller so as to render the ship of a neutral owner liable to seizure by a belligerent (Roscoe, II, 614, note);

the *Benedict* [1857] (Spinks, 314; Roscoe, II, 527), a ship sold by a Russian father to his Danish son as an advance on his inheritance for his education; the ship was restored to the son as having been validly and *bona fide* transferred to him;

the *Baltica* (Pygelstrom, Master) [1857] (11 Moore P.C., 141; Spinks, 264, not republished by Roscoe, see his note *c* at p. 629 of vol. II), the case of a sale made by a neutral father, residing in enemy territory as a consul of the neutral Netherlands, to his Danish son, whilst the ship was sailing from Russian Libau to neutral Copenhagen where the buyer took possession of the ship. The vessel was sold *bona fide* and absolutely to a neutral subject at a moment when war between England and Russia was imminent;

Lübeck: the *Christine* (Schwartz, Master) [1854] (Spinks, 82; Roscoe, II, 320), a case in which the Lübeck purchaser had made no payment nor given security to the Russian seller; there was no certificate of sale on board; further proof was refused;

Mecklenburg-Schwerin: the *Ernst Merck* [1854] (Spinks, 98; Roscoe, II, 338) regarding a transfer made immediately before the outbreak of war; the *onus* of proof of its *bona fide* character was held to rest on the neutral buyer, who must have a good legal title in order to obtain restoration;

Belgium: the *Maria (No. 2)* [1857] (11 Moore P.C., 271; Roscoe, II, 616):

restoration of the vessel, which had been transferred before the declaration of war; application of the same rule on the *onus* of proof: every circumstance of fraud, contrivance or attempt at imposition on the Court in making out his title was held to be fatal to the claimant; in the *Maria (No. 1)* (Petit, Master) [1855] (Spinks, 321; Roscoe, II, 536) the Court had held that further proof was required seeing that there was no bill of sale on board and that the master was ignorant of the real ownership of the vessel; should the claimant proceed by plea and proof, then the cause would be open to further proof on the part of the captors;

Austria: the *Nina* [1855] (Spinks, 276, appeal: 347; Roscoe, II, 514), sold by her Russian owner in 1853;

England: the *Neptune* (Keetley, Master) [1855] (Spinks, 281; Roscoe, II, 520), a vessel sailing under the Russian flag, but protected by an Order in Council that authorized her to sail from a British port. She had, however, remained in the port and had here been sold to a British subject. Although this fact gave rise to doubt about the legality of this form of trading with the enemy, the ship was with the consent of the captors released to the British buyer.

The abovementioned *Baltica* case was a sequel to that of the *Ariel.* Both these ships formed part of a larger group which, prior to the outbreak of the Crimean War, had been sold by a neutral (Danish) owner, Sörensen, to his Danish son. As Sörensen Sr. was established on Russian territory, where he carried on his trade, the English authorities, after the commencement of the war, considered him as an enemy on account of that domicile and his trade, despite his acting in his town of residence as a consul of the neutral Netherlands.

The sale of the vessels had taken place whilst they were lying in Russian or neutral harbours, except one which was sailing at that moment, but had safely reached Copenhagen, where Sörensen Jr. had taken possession of her. All these ships had subsequently left their ports and sailed under Danish colours to England where they were seized by the customs officers of Leith on the ground of illegal transfer to a neutral flag. Proceedings were instituted against all the vessels. One ship, the *Ariel*, was selected as a test case. Dr. Lushington condemned her, but his decree was reversed on appeal by the Lords of the Privy Council and the ship was restored to her owner, Sörensen Jr. The British authorities thereupon also released all the others, except the *Baltica*, the only vessel that had been sold *in transitu.* Dr. Lushington again pronounced a decree of condemnation, distinguishing the *Baltica* case from the others, but his decision was once more reversed. The Lords took some time in reaching their final decision on the validity of the plea of the Crown that the case was distinguishable from the *Ariel.* The case was re-argued in the appeal proceedings but ended in a decree that denied the validity of the distinction. The *Baltica* was accordingly restored to her owner, just as the *Ariel*:

"the sale, though *in transitu*, was valid, and the *transitus* had ceased, when the vessel had come into possession of the purchaser, which took place before the seizure [in the port of Leith]".

This succession of hearings and contradictory decrees is very interesting. The appellate decision in the *Ariel* case of 1857 can be found in 11 Moore P.C., 119; Roscoe, II, 600 *et seq.* at pp. 604-615, that in the *Baltica* in 11 Moore P.C. 141; Roscoe, II, 628 *et seq.*, at pp. 630-635.

From the *Baltica* judgment in appeal I quote the following passages (*per* Sir P. Leigh):

"The only question of law which can be raised in this case, is not whether a transfer of a ship or goods *in transitu* is ineffectual to change the property, as long as the state of *transitus* lasts; but how long that state continues, and when, and by what means, it is terminated.

In order to determine the question, it is necessary to consider upon what principle the rule rests, and why it is that a sale which would be perfectly good if made while the property was in a neutral port, or while it was in an enemy's port, is ineffectual if made while the ship is on her voyage from one port to the other. There seem to be but two possible grounds of distinction. The one is, that while the ship is on the seas, the title of the vendee cannot be completed by actual delivery of the vessel or goods; the other is, that the ship and goods having incurred the risk of capture by putting to sea, shall not be permitted to defeat the inchoate right of capture by the belligerent Powers, until the voyage is at an end.

The former, however, appears to be the true ground on which the rule rests. Such transactions during war, or in contemplation of war, are so likely to be merely colourable, to be set up for the purpose of misleading, or defrauding captors, the difficulty of detecting such frauds, if mere paper transfers are held sufficient, is so great, that the Courts have laid down as a general rule, that such transfers, without actual delivery, shall be insufficient; that in order to defeat the captors, the possession, as well as the property, must be changed before the seizure. It is true that, in one sense, the ship and goods may be said to be *in transitu* till they have reached their original port of destination; but their Lordships have found no case where the transfer was held to be inoperative after the actual delivery of the property to the owner. That the *transitus* ceases when the property has come into the actual possession of the transferee is a doctrine perfectly consistent with the decisions in the *Danckebaar Africaan* and in the *Negotie en Zeevaart* on the authority of which the former case was decided."

A curious case of two successive transfers of the same vessel, or rather a transfer, later followed by a retransfer, occurred in the 1850's. During the hostilities between Denmark and Prussia of 1849-1850 the Prussian vessel *Caroline* (Kraft, Master) was fictitiously sold by her owner to a Russian subject and assumed (neutral) Russian colours, which she continued to carry long after Prussia's peace with Denmark and even up to 1855, after the Crimean War had broken out between England and Russia. The vessel was captured by the British as an enemy Russian ship, but she was released by the British Prize Court in her real capacity of a Prussian-built neutral Prussian vessel, but without the captor being condemned in costs and damages (Spinks, 252; Roscoe, II, 501).

(*e*) *The American Civil War*

Instances of transfers to a neutral flag which occurred during the American

Civil War were those of the *Georgia* [1868] (7 Wall., 32) and *in re United States v. Etta* [1868] (7 Wall., 42; 4 Amer. Law Reports (N.S.), 387), both concerning the special case of the sale of an enemy warship to a neutral purchaser, and much later, after World War I, invoked as precedents in the *Edna-Mazatlán* [1921] (*B.C.P.C.*, III, 926):

> "That a vessel, which is, or has been, a portion of the armed forces of a belligerent, cannot by a mere private transaction be placed beyond the reach of capture on the high seas is well settled, and there is authority for the proposition that while a vessel formally incorporated in the enemy forces is, and continues to be, for this and cognate purposes a public ship of war, her mere actual employment in that capacity without formal incorporation or commission will also bring upon her the like disability."

The Prize Court in office in the first phase of World War I has discussed precedents concerning the transfer of enemy vessels to a neutral flag in the *Tommi and the Rothersand* [1914] (*B.C.P.C.*, I, 16), two German sailing-vessels, but that case was in actual fact decided on the ground of their enemy character, and Sir Samuel Evans' reference to the precedents of the *Jan Frederick* (Bloedorne, Master) [1804] (5 C.Rob., 128; Roscoe, I, 434) and the *Baltica* (Pygelstrom, Master) [1857] was merely hypothetical in case the claimants should rightly plead the transfer of their vessels to a neutral buyer.

The manner in which the *Institut de droit international* has handled the subject of the transfer of an enemy vessel to a neutral flag in its *Règlement international des prises maritimes* of 1882 appears from its § 26, running as follows:

> "L'acte juridique constatant la vente d'un navire ennemi faite pendant la guerre doit être parfait, et le navire doit être enregistré conformément à la législation du pays dont il acquiert la nationalité, avant qu'il quitte le port de sortie. La nouvelle nationalité ne peut être acquise au navire par une vente faite en cours de voyage."

This summary rule was in the post-codification period replaced in the *Institut's* Manual of Oxford (1913) with a far more elaborate Article 52:

> "*Du transfert de pavillon.*—Le transfert sous pavillon neutre d'un navire ennemi, effectué avant l'ouverture des hostilités, est valable, à moins qu'il soit établi que ce transfert a été effectué en vue d'éluder les conséquences qu'entraîne le caractère de navire ennemi. Il y a néanmoins présomption de nullité si l'acte de transfert ne se trouve pas à bord, alors que le navire a perdu la nationalité belligérante moins de soixante jours avant l'ouverture des hostilités; la preuve contraire est admise.
>
> Il y a présomption absolue de validité d'un transfert effectué plus de trente jours avant l'ouverture des hostilités, s'il est absolu, complet, conforme à la législation des pays intéressés, et s'il a cet effet que le contrôle du navire et le bénéfice de son emploi ne restent pas entre les mêmes mains qu'avant le transfert. Toutefois, si le navire a perdu la nationalité belligérante moins de soixante jours avant l'ouverture des hostilités, et si l'acte de transfert ne se trouve pas à bord, la saisie du navire ne pourra donner lieu à des dommages et intérêts.
>
> Le transfert sous pavillon neutre d'un navire ennemi, effectué après l'ouverture des hostilités, est nul, à moins qu'il soit établi que ce transfert n'a pas été effectué en vue d'éluder les conséquences qu'entraîne le caractère de navire ennemi.

> Toutefois, il y a présomption absolue de nullité: 1°. si le transfert a été effectué pendant que le navire est en voyage ou dans un port bloqué; 2°. s'il y a faculté de réméré ou de retour; 3°. si les conditions, auxquelles est soumis le droit de pavillon, d'après la législation du pavillon arboré, n'ont pas été observées."

Conclusions

Summarizing the various older cases of transfer digested above and a few others which are reported later, I draw the following conclusions.

The assignment, either by sale or gift, to a neutral citizen of an enemy ship, other than a ship of war, was not rendered invalid merely by the fact that it was made during or in contemplation of hostilities: *Minerva* (Knuttell, Master) [1807] (6 C.Rob., 396; Roscoe, I, 591).

In special circumstances, however, such an assignment was held to be null and void vis-à-vis the captor. This was in particular the case if

(i) the transfer was made in a blockaded port: *General Hamilton* [1805] (6 C.Rob., 61; Roscoe, I, 528);

(ii) the transfer was made in the course of a voyage. For this purpose a voyage was at an end as soon as the ship reached a port where she could actually be delivered into the possession of the transferee: *Danckebaar Africaan* [1798] (1 C.Rob., 112; Roscoe, I, 74); *Vro(u)w Margaretha* (Crigsman, Master) [1799] (1 C.Rob., 336; Roscoe, I, 149); *Baltica* [1857] (11 Moore P.C., 141; Spinks, 264);

(iii) the vendor retained any share in the ship, or if there was an agreement to recover her at the end of the war: *Sechs Geschwistern* [1801] (4 C.Rob., 100); *Noydt Gedacht* [1799] (2 C.Rob., 137, footnote).

The claimant was burdened by the onus of proving that the transfer was genuine, and that the assignment was complete, *bona fide*, and for a good consideration. A vessel transferred to a neutral flag was, therefore, still liable to be condemned by the prize court if the circumstances of the transfer were attended with suspicion, not removed by the claimant: *Vigilantia* (Gerritz, Master) [1798] (1 C.Rob., 1; Roscoe, I, 31); *Endraught* (*Eendracht?*) (Bonkins, Master) [1798] (1 C.Rob., 22); *Welvaart* (Cornelis, Master) [1799] (1 C.Rob., 122); *Juffrouw Anna* (Greeson, Master) [1799] (1 C.Rob., 124; Roscoe, I, 76); *Noydt Gedacht* [1799] (see *supra*); *Jemmy* [1801] (4 C.Rob., 31; Roscoe, I, 331), for example if:

(*a*) no documentary evidence of the assignment was found on board at the time of the seizure;

(*b*) the transferor retained any control over the ship, reservation of profits, or power to revoke the assignment;

(*c*) possession had not been taken by the alleged transferee, or by some agent of his who was not an enemy;

(*d*) the ship was under the control of the enemy;

(*e*) the master or other person in command was in the service of the enemy.

The principles adopted by the British prize courts from early days with regard to the transfer of enemy ships to a neutral or other non-enemy flag and their subsequent sailing under such non-enemy colours, have been upheld ever since.

Originally there was no question of the fixing of any specified period of time preceding the outbreak of war which would make the sale or other form of transfer suspect as having been made "in contemplation of the war", as was attempted at the beginning of the 20th century at the London Conference on Naval Warfare of 1908-1909. But the principle of the invalidity *vis-à-vis* the capturing State of transfers effected during the war, or with that prospect in view, was unshakable and not only in the opinion of British courts. It was in fact universally recognized. The attempts of 1909 to fix the conditions under which the rule would apply and certain legal presumptions for or against the sincerity of the transaction more precisely, and to gain general support for such specification, have come to nothing.

Sub-Division II. THE ENEMY OR NON-ENEMY CHARACTER OF CARGOES

Introductory paragraph

As I have set out in sections 1, 3 and 5 of Chapter I, the distinction between enemy and non-enemy property at sea has already formed the subject of regulation very early on, but no very clear criteria have developed until much later. Sea-borne goods were considered, as a matter of course, to have enemy or non-enemy character according to whether their owner was enemy or non-enemy, but the enemy or non-enemy character of the owner of a captured cargo was still for a long time indicated in terms of nationality and/or residence without a conscious and very clear distinction between these two criteria. This becomes apparent especially from a perusal of Sir George Lee's detailed Ms. Notes on the particulars of each of the 37 reports concerning captures made during the War of the Austrian Succession (1744-1750) and of the numerous references to other judicial precedents of earlier or later dates, dispersed by the author all over those Notes. The objects seized were indicated indeterminately by such expressions as "the property of a Frenchman in Hamburg", or "belonging to nationals or/and inhabitants of Holland". It does not become clear whether such indications were meant to be cumulative or optional requirements, but they generally make the impression of testifying to legal uncertainty about the true criterion of the enemy or non-enemy character of seaborne goods, or of reflecting a more general lack of clarity in the doctrine of public law about the conceptual difference between the two criteria.

What, for example, to think of such strange passages as can be found in the case of a cargo of salt in the *Jonge Tobias* [1748] (Pratt-Lee, p. 190) where the *Per Curiam* ran as follows:

> "Though the cargo is Dutch property, yet being on board a Swedish ship must be considered as Swedish property, and has not Dutch privilege" (under Article 2 of the Anglo-Netherlands treaty of 10 December 1674 (Dumont, VIII[1], 282; Parry, 13, 255)).

When wading through the dull notes, which cover periods up to the middle of the 19th century, for the purpose of getting a clear answer to one's query about the basic ideas of the past concerning the criterion or criteria of the (non-)enemy character of seaborne goods, current in England, one meets with so many reported cases in which it is hardly possible to identify the real or principal grounds on which a cargo was either condemned or restored, that one is inclined to close the book in despair. Anyway, I refrain from citing from the Nine Years' War, the Wars of the Spanish or the Austrian Succession, the Seven Years' War or the American War of Independence examples to explain my feeling of uncertainty. Others may perhaps be more fortunate in their research.

It is, moreover, often unclear on what legal ground(s) a seized cargo was confiscated, respectively restored to the claimers: it may have been defective evidence of ownership or of the owner's nationality or residence, but it may as well have been the applicability or otherwise of specific treaty provisions, or of the judicial practice of exempting seaborne goods from confiscation because of their being the native produce of the neutral shipper's soil (on this particular subject comp. Chapter III *sub* A, section 3 (Contraband), § 3 (Sanctions) under B (Relaxations), pp. 401 *et seq.*).

My impression is that it has taken in particular British Admiralty Courts a very long time to make a final choice between the two most obvious criteria for the determination of the enemy or non-enemy character of seaborne goods, namely, the domicile of their owner, this in contrast to French legislation which preferred the criterion of his nationality.

Referring to my remark above in Sub-Division I, p. 207, concerning Sir William Scott's fleeting statement in the *Vigilantia* [1798] (1 C.Rob., 1; Roscoe, I, 31) with respect to the enemy or non-enemy character of ships, as though the criterion of the owner's residence was decisive, I must repeat that neither in respect of the character of cargoes does that statement seem to be sufficiently substantiated by Sir George Lee's Ms. Notes concerning older British case law.

After the gradual emergence in British prize jurisprudence of the criterion of domicile as the paramount or exclusive criterion of the enemy or non-enemy character of seaborne goods the controversy has reached the international scene as a consequence of the Anglo-American agreement by Art. 7 of the Jay Treaty of 19 November 1794 (Martens, R[2], V, 641; Parry, 52, 243) to submit certain groups of prize cases to third-party decision in the form of a mixed claims commission. The controversies concerned related to events which had occurred during the first years of England's wars against Revolutionary France (1793-1794). In the interval between those events and the adjudication by the Mixed Claims Commission, British prize courts had pronounced against the claims of the American owners, victims of the British seizures. Hence the appearance of those arbitral proceedings as the prolongation, in a second, international instance, of decisions made in the first by national courts.

Amongst the disputes brought before the Mixed Claims Commission under Article 7 of the Jay Treaty there were two which had a remote bearing on the question of the enemy or non-enemy character of cargoes, namely, that relating to the *Betsey* (*R.A.I.*, I, 51-119) and that concerning a group of more or less identical cases, presented by the editors under the heading (*sub* A) *Présomptions de condamnation* (*R.A.I.*, I, 120-123), consisting of the *Fame*, the *Farmer*, the *Molly*, the *Sally* (Griffiths, Master) and the *Active* (comp. my exposé on the review of prize court decrees by arbitration below III *sub* C, section 8, at pp. 663-667). But none of those cases has contributed anything of importance to the final solution of the central issue. I will only enter into some detail on the *Betsey* case in section 2 *ad* (*c*) at p. 263 *infra*, because this case fits in with the subject of domicile as a determining factor of enemy character, discussed there.

Since there has always been a great difference in treatment between enemy and neutral or otherwise non-enemy seaborne goods, it goes without saying that prize courts must have been alive to the necessity of distinguishing between the two groups of cargoes, but I have been unable to discover in the mass of defective reports of older British Admiralty decrees any dependable foothold for drawing convincing conclusions about how their authors looked at the problem of the enemy or non-enemy character of cargoes, and how exactly they gradually developed a coherent system of jurisprudence. For the problems which successively arose were multiple.

When we try to summarize the whole aggregate of questions with which the adjudicating bodies became confronted in the course of time, the following general picture emerges.

Was legal ownership the true criterion, or could other interests in the goods be considered as well? Could in the latter case account also be taken of persons who were running the actual risk of their loss, such as: buyers or consignees to whom the legal ownership had not yet been transferred, bankers who had lent money to the owner on security of the goods, or houses that had insured them against loss? And if legal ownership was the criterion, at what moment should it have passed from the seller or consignor to the buyer or consignee? Was there reason to distinguish in this respect between *ante bellum* and *post bellum* shipments? Furthermore, how should the enemy or neutral character of the owner be determined? This might be done by holding his nationality decisive, but attention or preference could also be given to his domicile in an enemy or neutral country. And what kind of domicile was then to be considered: his personal residence or a possible commercial or trade domicile? And what was the legal situation with regard to goods handled by a branch establishment of a neutral trading concern in the enemy country? How should the transfer of cargoes in transit be assessed? Was it, in addition, lawful to take yet other factual elements into account, such as the fact that the goods were a procedure of the enemy soil or were on their way to an enemy country?

All these questions were due to play an increasingly important part in prize court proceedings. English and American case law, in particular, have gradually built up a coherent and comprehensive legal system concerning these various problems. The general trend of that Anglo-American case law amounts to the following.

Legal ownership of the goods is as a rule decisive. Prize law has its own rules concerning the exact moment when that ownership must be held to have passed, differing from those obtaining in civil law. The enemy or neutral character of the owner depends on his domicile, in particular his trade domicile. The goods being a produce of the enemy soil is an additional criterion of enemy character. Transfer of the goods *in transitu* cannot be recognized as a valid transfer in wartime.

On a number of the questions listed above concerning the determination of the enemy or non-enemy character of seaborne goods, a marked difference has gradually developed between the principles adopted by the British and by the continental courts.

In the English system a sharp distinction was made between *ante* and *post bellum* shipments. Whereas *ante bellum* shipments were, in principle, governed by the ordinary rules of civil or commercial law, the solution was totally different as regards *post bellum* shipments or shipments effected *imminente bello*: questions relating to such property were on an entirely different footing from those relating to transactions initiated during a time of peace, determined as they largely or mainly were upon considerations concerning the rights of the belligerent States and attempts by neutral shippers to defeat such rights. This distinction implied two important legal consequences. The first was that the consignors of goods forwarded in wartime towards an enemy country could not legally retain the *jus disponendi*. The second was that transfers of goods effected *in transitu* during a war were considered by the belligerents as null and void in their respect.

As regards the first of these principles, Sir William Scott set out the law in the *Vro(u)w Margaretha* case of 1799 (1 C.Rob., 336; Roscoe, I, 149). This case related to a cargo of brandy, shipped by Spanish merchants in Spain in May 1794, before Spanish hostilities commenced and transferred to a citizen of neutral Hamburg during its voyage to Holland on a Dutch vessel. The application of the English rule according to which property of seaborne goods was considered in wartime to remain in the shipper until delivery and that its transfer *in transitu* by an enemy owner to a neutral purchaser was invalid if war was existing or imminent at the time of such transfer, was in that case motivated by Sir William Scott as follows:

> "In the ordinary course of things in time of peace—for it is not denied that such a contract may be made, and effectually made (according to the usage of merchants)—such a transfer *in transitu* might certainly be made. It has even been contended that a mere delivering of the bill of lading is a transfer of the property. But it might be more correctly expressed, perhaps, if said that it transfers only the right of delivery ... When war intervenes, another rule is set up by Courts of Admiralty which interferes with the ordinary practice. In a state of war, existing or imminent, it is held that the property shall be deemed to continue as it was at the time of shipment till the actual delivery; this arises out of the state of war which gives a belligerent a right to stop the goods of his enemy. If such a rule did not exist, all goods shipped in the enemy's country would be protected by transfers which it would be impossible to detect. It is on that principle held, I believe, as a general rule that property cannot be converted *in transitu*, and in that sense I recognize it as the rule of this Court. But this arises ... out of a state of war, which creates new rights in other parties, and cannot be applied to transactions originating, like this, in a time of peace. The transfer, therefore, must be considered as not invalid in point of law at the time of the contract, and being made before the war it must be judged according to the ordinary rules of commerce.
>
> It has been further objected to the validity of the contract that a part of the wines did actually reach Holland, where they were sold... It comes then to a question of fact, whether it was a *bona fide* transfer or not. I think the time is a strong circumstance to prove the fairness of the transaction. Had it happened three months later there might have been reason to alarm the prudence of Spanish merchants and induce them to resort to the expedient of covering their property. But at the time of the contract there seems to have been no reason for apprehension..."

On these grounds the claims of the Hamburg citizen were allowed without opposition.

Examples of how the British principles operated in actual practice were the cases of the *Sally* (Griffiths, Master) [1795] (3 C.Rob., 300, footnote *a*; Roscoe, I, 28) and the *Atlas* [1801] (3 C.Rob., 299; Roscoe, I, 31, footnote *a*).

In the first case the Lords of Appeal decided that property shipped by a neutral, ostensibly for the account and at the risk of a firm in Philadelphia and consigned to them or their assignees, was liable to condemnation because by an endorsement on the bill of lading, it was agreed that the ship should proceed to the enemy port of Le Havre de Grâce and there wait for orders for such time as might be necessary. In the second comparable case, which he refused to distinguish from the *Sally* case, Lord Stowell condemned a cargo carried on an American vessel and seized on a voyage from the United States via Spanish Vigo, where it was sold to the Spanish Government, to Sevilla; in this case also, the cargo was held to be liable to condemnation on the ground that it was taken whilst going in fact to an enemy port to be delivered there to an enemy, and to be paid for by him.

These general basic principles of English law (whereupon comp., *inter alia* Benjamin's *Sale of goods*) were applied by Sir William Scott in the special domain of the law of prize in various other judgments, such as the *Packet de Bilboa* [1799] (2 C.Rob., 133; Roscoe, I, 209) and the *Anna Catharina* [1802] (4 C.Rob., 107).

These and other similar precedents from Sir William Scott's time were, for that matter, not the oldest cases recorded, for in the *Sally* case [1795] (*supra*) reference was made to a much older precedent of 1741 during the War of the Austrian Succession, the *Charles Havernerswerth* case, in which the Lords Commissioners of Appeals stated the principle as follows:

> "It has always been the rule of the Prize Courts that property going to be delivered in the enemy's country, and under a contract to become the property of the enemy immediately on arrival, if taken in *transitu*, is to be considered as ennemies' property. When the contract is made in time of peace or without any contemplation of a war, no such rule exists. But in a case like the present, where the form of the contract was framed directly for the purpose of obviating the danger apprehended from approaching hostilities, it is a rule which unavoidably must take place."

The cargo was accordingly condemned as enemy's property.

This precedent was followed by Sir William Scott in 1801 in the case of the *Atlas*.

In the case of the *Cousine Marianne* [1810] (Edw., 346; Roscoe, II, 85), a Prussian vessel sailing from Bordeaux to London with a licence granted to British merchants which did not contain the obligatory words "to whomsoever the property may appear to belong" and therefore did not protect enemy property on board, the Prize Court said:

> "It is a settled principle in this Court that in order to constitute an effectual transfer of the property there must be either an order for the goods, or an acceptance of them by the consignee prior to the capture. If the capture takes place, where no order has been given, and before the goods have been accepted, they must be considered as the property of the persons who have so consigned them."

The Court then continued by arguing that, although there might exist an expectation on the part of the British merchants that the goods would be accepted and paid for, there was no legal obligation on them, and concluded that the legal property still remained with the enemy.

These old principles were later, during the Crimean War, reaffirmed by Dr. Lushington and the Judicial Committee of the Privy Council in the *Baltica* case, relating to a cargo of linseed on board a Russian ship. The ownership of that cargo was disputed (11 Moore P.C., 141; Roscoe, II, 628). In that case the Privy Council (*per* Lord Kingsdown) set out the origin of the traditional English doctrine as follows:

> "The general rule is open to no doubt. A neutral, while a war is imminent, or after it has commenced, is at liberty to purchase either goods or ships (not being ships of war) from either belligerent, and the purchase is valid, whether the subject of it be lying in a neutral port or in an enemy's port. During a time of peace, without prospect of war, any transfer which is sufficient to transfer the property between the vendor and vendee is good also against a captor, if war afterwards unexpectedly break out. But in case of war, either actual or imminent, this rule is subject to qualification, and it is settled in such case that a mere transfer by documents which would be sufficient to bind the parties, is not sufficient to change the property as against captors, as long as the ship or goods remain *in transitu*".

Of the two possible grounds of justification of the rule the Court gave preference to the ground that, while the ship is on the seas, the title of the vendee cannot be completed by actual delivery, over the other ground that the ship and goods, having incurred the risk of capture by putting to sea, shall not be permitted to defeat the inchoate right of capture by belligerents until the voyage ends.

Continental prize courts were guided by quite different principles. They made no distinction as regards the determination of the moment of the transfer of property between ordinary commercial transaction in peacetime and such transaction in time of war. The only deviation from the ordinary rules on the transfer was that continental prize courts, also, denied the validity vis-à-vis the belligerents of transfers of property of goods in overseas transit during or in contemplation of a war.

Apart from this basic difference of views, there existed another equally basic contrast between the two systems: was the ownership of seaborne goods in wartime to be determined by the nationality or by the domicile of the owner? The English system clung to his domicile, the continental system to his nationality.

No serious conflicting views were held as regards a further controversy, *viz.*, whether on the determination of the enemy or non-enemy character of seaborne cargoes other rights and interests than legal ownership, such as mortgages and liens, could also be taken into account. The general answer was negative.

All these, and a number of connected controversial issues will be set out in the following sections of the present Sub-Division II. At an early stage of this publication, I had already occasion to mention briefly this aggregate of problems, see vol. I, pp. 70-71.

Comment must finally be made on a special rule, imprinting enemy character upon produce of the enemy soil.

My exposé will, therefore, be arranged as follows.

A first section, common to both systems, will deal with the question of how far rights and interests other than legal ownership of cargoes were recognized as a determining factor of their enemy or non-enemy character (pp. 251-254).

A second section will set out the rules concerning the determination of enemy or neutral ownership: (*a*) the decisive moment of such determination, (*b*) the proof of ownership, and (*c*) the criteria for the owner's enemy or neutral character according, respectively, to the simple continental idea (the owner's nationality) or to the artfully ramified English doctrine (the owner's residence or domicile) (pp. 254-268). A certain overlapping of the various subjects of discussion proved, however, to be unavoidable.

A third section will deal with a number of special, in particular English, cases of transfer, in addition to what I have already set out in my introductory paragraph about the essentials of the English system of rules concerning the transfer of the property of goods in wartime, including their transfer *in transitu*.

A fourth section will finally explain the special rule relative to the enemy character of the produce of the enemy soil, again common to both systems.

After this lengthy introductory orientation in the wide field of issues connected with the allocation of enemy or non-enemy character to cargoes, I will now turn to the various elements of the problem separately.

Section 1. LEGAL OWNERSHIP OR (ALSO) OTHER, NON-PROPRIETARY INTERESTS? MIXED CO-OWNERSHIP

(*a*) *Other than proprietary interests of neutrals*

Pursuant to an old practice it was the criterion of ownership of the prize that decided the enemy or non-enemy character of prizes under the law of prize. Yet, there are precedents in which allusion was made to another criterion, namely: who was to bear the loss of the prize in case of its condemnation?

This happened in proceedings before Sir William Scott concerning certain cargo in the *Packet de Bilboa* [1799] (2 C.Rob., 133; Roscoe, I, 209), a case in which an English business house claimed for goods shipped on board a Spanish vessel by the order of Spanish merchants before the outbreak of hostilities between England and Spain at a moment when the exact relation between the two countries was unknown even to the British Government. The goods, captured in December 1796 on a voyage from London to La Coruña, had consequently been shipped at the risk of a neutral consignor to a neutral consignee who only became an enemy after the outbreak of war. In view of this position Sir William Scott, restoring the goods to the shippers, argued as follows:

> "There appears to be no ground to say that this contract was influenced by speculations on the prospect of a war or that anything has been specially done to avoid the risks of war... The question is, in whom is the legal title? Because if I should find that the interest was in the Spanish consignee I must then condemn, and leave the British party to apply to the Crown for that grace and favour which it is always ready to show, the property being condemnable to the Crown as taken before hostilities... The ordinary state of commerce is that goods ordered and delivered to the master are considered as delivered to the consignee, whose agent the master is in this respect, but that general contract of the law may be varied by special agreement, or by a particular prevailing practice that presupposes an agreement amongst such a description of merchants. In time of profound peace, when there is no prospect of approaching war, there would unquestionably be nothing illegal in contracting that the whole risk should fall on the consignor till the goods came into possession of the consignee. In time of peace they may divide their risk as they please... In time of war this cannot be permitted, for it would at once put an end to all captures at sea... The present contract is not of this sort."

The passages in which Sir William Scott made his allusion to the criterion of risk ran as follows:

> "The present contract ... stands as a lawful agreement being made whilst there was neither war nor prospect of war. The goods are sent at the risk of the shipper. If they had been lost, on whom would the loss have fallen but on him? What surer test of property can there be than this? It is the true criterion of property that, if you are the person on whom the loss will fall, you are to be considered as the proprietor".

These passages prove clearly that they were written by Sir W. Scott in the context of his thesis that the risk of losing one's property is the truest criterion of ownership, but they have understandably given rise to speculation about their implications.

In actual fact, the criterion of legal ownership has remained the true criterion of the enemy or neutral (non-enemy) character of seaborne goods. See for an example of such a case in which non-enemy liens on an enemy vessel were in so many words ignored, the *Marianna* [1805] (6 C.Rob., 24; Roscoe, I, 518), in which the Court disregarded liens arising out of the purchase and condemnation of a ship and her cargo, even though the latter was bound by a lien as between the shipowner and the vendor of the ship.

In the following pages I will give a brief survey of the legal situation in the field of non-enemy non-proprietary rights in condemned enemy prizes.

I use the general word "prizes" here because the prize courts often formulated their arguments on the subject in the same way, no matter whether they related to non-proprietary interests on enemy ships or to such interests in enemy cargoes. Referring back here to what I have already said in the preceding Sub-Division I (*supra*, pp. 221-225) about non-enemy liens, bottomry bonds, etc., on enemy vessels, I will confine myself here to a few cases regarding in particular the fate of cargoes.

In the case of certain goods on board the *Abo* [1854] (Spinks, 42; Roscoe, II, 285) the same vacillation as shown by Sir William Scott in the *Packet de Bilboa* case re-appeared: when being reminded by Counsel for the neutral shipowner-claimant of Sir William Scott's argument, Dr Lushington in fact "construed it away" by virtually eliminating the suggested idea of the owner's risk of the loss of his property as the legal criterion of enemy or non-enemy character, and upholding the criterion of ownership as decisive of the national character under the law of prize, but he nevertheless added in his turn that "account could also be taken of the question of who would bear the loss". The uncertain case law of the earlier period was thus continued along the same lines during the Crimean War. But in the case of the *Ida* [1854] (Spinks, 26; Roscoe, II, 268) relating to a cargo of coffee seized on this Russian ship and claimed by the neutral Danish holder of a lien, the Court held that the existence of that lien could be no ground for restitution of the goods to a third party, however honest. The rule concerning disregard of liens and other similar interests was re-affirmed in appeal by the Privy Council (*per* Lord Kingsdown) in the *Baltica* [1857] (11 Moore, P.C., 141; Roscoe, II, 628).

This older case law was recapitulated in an historical survey of the development in an early case of 1914, the *Marie Glaeser* (*B.C.P.C.*, I, 38) in which the consignee of the seized goods claimed them on the ground of a lien on the cargo, invoked on the credit of advances made by him to the enemy owner.

As the Prize Court of World War I remarked in its decision concerning the *Miramichi* [1915] (*B.C.P.C.*, I, 137), in which it summarized the respective lines of argument followed by the Attorney General for the Crown and by Counsel for the claimants:

> "Very difficult questions arise at law as to when the property in goods carried by sea is transferred, or vests; and at whose risk goods are at a particular time, or who suffers by their loss ... Where goods are contracted to be sold and are shipped during peace without any anticipation of imminent war, and are seized or captured afloat after war has supervened, the cardinal principle is, in my opinion, that they are not subject to seizure or capture unless under the contract the property in the goods has by that time passed to the enemy. It may be that the element of risk may legitimately enter into the consideration of the question whether the property has passed or has become transferred. But the incidence of risk or loss is not by any means the determining factor of property or ownership. The main determining factor is whether, according to the intention of seller and buyer, the property had passed. The question which governs this case, therefore, is, whose property were the goods at the time of seizure? This principle is consonant with good sense and with the notion of what is right in commercial dealings [further reference is made to the opinion of eminent jurists and to judicial precedents]".

It seems to have been only in special circumstances that certain liens were recognized. See for such an exceptional case the *Two Friends* [1799] (1 C.Rob., 271; Roscoe, I, 130) where the Prize Court had to decide on a particular sort of claim, *viz*., that of the partly British crew of an American merchant vessel who, after her capture by the French, succeeded in recapturing her from the enemy prize crew. The Court recognized the lien claimed by the crew on that part of the salvaged cargo which had meanwhile been landed. Every person assisting in a rescue was held to have a lien on the thing seized.

(*b*) *Mixed enemy and non-enemy property*

Apart from the existence of liens on a captured cargo, complications could also arise from the fact that the cargo of an enemy vessel was of mixed ownership, as happened in France, where the national laws contained no rule for the solution of this contingency. Filling the legislative gap, the French Court of Cassation in the case of a cargo on board the *Nordel-Falk* [*an* VII] (Pistoye-Duverdy, I, 336) decreed that:

> "Lorsque la cargaison d'un navire ennemi est composée mi-partie de marchandises ennemies, mi-partie de marchandises neutres, les premières doivent être confisquées et les secondes relâchées".

This seems to have been the rule also observed in England. In the

Vro(u)w Elizabeth (Probst, Master) [1803] (5 C.Rob., 2; Roscoe, I, 409), concerning the claim of a merchant of neutral Bremen for a share in an enemy vessel, taken under the Dutch (enemy) flag and pass, in which it was decided that a vessel sailing under the colours and pass of a nation was to be considered as clothed with the national character of that country, the Court remarked "that with goods it might be otherwise". In the same case indeed, the captor contested the ship-owner's additional claim for an undivided part of the cargo, documented as Dutch (enemy) property, a claim which, according to the captor, should likewise be precluded by the documentary character of the goods and their incorporation into Dutch commerce, but this argument was overruled by the Court. In this context Roscoe, in a long note at p. 410 of vol. I, annexed to the *Vro(u)w Elizabeth* case, quoted the decision in the somewhat older *Vreede Scholtys* case concerning the equally unsuccessful claim of another merchant of Bremen for a share in another vessel taken under the Dutch flag and pass. In those proceedings also, the captor's further objection to the claimant's additional claim for his undivided part of the cargo, likewise documented as Dutch property, was overruled by the Court and that claim was allowed:

> "A great distinction has been always made by the nations of Europe between ships and goods. Some countries have gone so far as to make the flag and pass of the ship conclusive on the cargo also, but this country has never carried the principle to that extent. It holds the ship bound by the character imposed upon it by the authority of the government from which all the documents issue. But goods which have no such dependence upon the authority of the State may be differently considered. Then comes the question whether the Court will make the separation. Generally, it cannot be doubted that such separation may be made. It is in every day's practice to make such distinctions. Are there, then, any particular circumstances to prevent the Court from doing it in the present instance? Has the claimant assumed the character of a Dutchman so as to render the property liable to be considered as Dutch property? I know of no case that has fixed such a consequence upon a transaction of this kind in time of peace. On the contrary, we all remember the cases of the Swiss who had shipped property from Curaçao under Dutch names to avoid the Alien Duties, and yet obtained restitution of their claims. Had the trade in the present instance been even an exclusive trade, it might have been questionable how far the party could have been held to the Dutch character merely on account of a false representation practised against the Dutch revenue laws—unless, indeed, it had appeared that there had been some pass or licence conferring on him the special privileges of a Dutch merchant, or unless it was a trade arising out of the circumstances of war, or the expectation of such an event. Here the party appears only to be availing himself of Dutch names in time of peace for the benefit of avoiding particular duties; in such a case it would be going further than the Court has hitherto gone to declare that the person is to be held to all the revolutions which may attend the Dutch character. In time of war a more strict principle may be necessary. But it is needless to decide what considerations might be fit to be applied to such a transaction in time of war, as this case arose altogether in time of peace, and without any expectation of war. I see nothing to prevent the Court from performing the office of separating this undivided share, and as the property is fully proved, I shall decree it to be restored."

Section 2. DETERMINATION OF ENEMY OR NON-ENEMY OWNERSHIP

If we further assume that legal ownership is the determining factor, new questions arise, *viz.*:

(*a*) what moment is decisive for that determination?

(*b*) how must the ownership of seaborne goods at that moment be proven?

(*c*) what criterion decides the enemy or non-enemy character of the owner: his nationality or his residence or domicile? And what is the meaning of domicile in this context?

(*a*) *Decisive moment*

There are three moments which may in theory be held decisive: that of the shipment of the cargo, that of its seizure, and that of the adjudication of the prize. The answers to these questions varied.

(i) The *date of the shipment* was taken into account when a cargo was shipped either from, or to an enemy's port. In such cases the English prize courts acted on the principle that such cargoes were presumably enemy property. On the first supposition see the decision in the *Juno (No. 2)* [1799] (Roscoe, I, 202): goods shipped in the enemy country were to be considered *prima facie* as the property of the enemy, and could only escape that presumption by fair and unbiassed evidence, especially the master's papers. On the second supposition see the decision in the *Sally* (Griffiths, Master) [1795] (3 C.Rob., 300, footnote *a*; Roscoe, I, 28): property shipped by a neutral and consigned to a hostile port to become the property of an enemy on arrival, if captured *in transitu*, was liable to condemnation as enemy property. However, this rule applied only to wartime shipments, as was held in the abovementioned case of the *Packet de Bilboa* [1799] (2 C.Rob., 133; Roscoe, I, 209).

In a later case, of 1920, the *Kronprinsessan Margareta, Rena, Paraná and Hilding* (*B.C.P.C.*, III, 803; *A.J.I.L.* 1921, p. 593) the then Prize Court stated that it was already in Lord Stowell's time the invariable practice of the High Court to look to the time of shipment. Comp. further section 3 *infra*.

(ii) Other courts attached more importance to the *date of the seizure* as the decisive moment for the determination of the enemy or non-enemy character of a cargo. In their view the general rule was to the effect that the moment of seizure was in principle decisive for the determination of the enemy or non-enemy character of prizes. However, this rule did not apply to cases in which the neutral property concerned was sold to an enemy after the seizure. See *sub* (iii). Then, of course, the further question was whether the ownership had already passed at that moment from the consignor to the consignee. As set out above, p. 247, with regard to this question the English courts have developed a clear distinction between the rules governing the transfer of seaborne goods under ordinary civil law and those adopted for cases coming under the law of prize, at least in so far as *post bellum* or *imminente bello* shipments were concerned. The problem was, as to *ante bellum* shipments, generally solved in conformity with the ordinary provisions of English civil or commercial law, according to which the intention of the parties plays a major rôle, and the solution depends on specific contract clauses, such as: "no arrival, no sale", "documents against acceptance of the seller's draft", "f.o.b." or "c.i.f.". On the effects of f.o.b. or c.i.f. contracts comp. the case of *Biddell Brothers v. E. Clemens Horst Co.* [1911-12] (first instance; 80 *L.J.K.B.*, 584; 1 *K.B.*, 934; appeal: 81 *L.J.K.B.*, 42; *A.C.*, 18).

(iii) The *date of adjudication* was only decisive when the prize which was still neutral (non-enemy) at the moment of seizure had in the meantime been sold to an enemy. Then it was subject to condemnation despite its original character of neutral property. See, *inter alia*, the case of the *Schooner Adeline* [1815] (9 Cranch (Amer.), 244).

(*b*) *Requirement of proof*

It was frequently doubtful to whom the property of seaborne goods belonged; the issue was in such cases often fined down to a question of proof.

In the *Concordia Affinitatis* [1779] (Hay and Marriott, 289; Roscoe, I, 25), Judge Sir J. Marriott specified the requirements of proof of the national character by stressing that the affidavits presented to the Court must be unequivocal and must cover the property of the goods at the periods when first laden, when taken and when finally landed, and that they ought to be negative as well as affirmative that no enemies of the Crown of Great Britain, or its subjects trading with its enemies, had had, had, or would have, at any of these times, any right, share, title, or interest therein, directly or indirectly without fraud, collusion, equivocation, or mental reservation.

It goes without saying that British Prize Courts looked with special disfavour at the suppression of an enemy's interest in a prize by a neutral cargo-owner with a fraudulent intent, see the case of the Danish vessel *Graaff Bernstorff* [1800] (3 C.Rob., 109; Roscoe, I, 265).

In the case of the *Adelaide* [1801] (3 C.Rob., 281; Roscoe, I, 306) it was uncertain to whom the property of a cargo, ordered from a Dutch (enemy) merchant by the claimants, American (neutral) merchants figuring in the bill of lading as its owners, really belonged, and equally uncertain whether the claimants had been aware of the existing blockade of Amsterdam. This was one of the many cases in which the question arose of whether a merchant, in his legal capacity of a principal, was liable for the acts of his agent. The answer was in the affirmative in principle, but the rule could not be applied too rigorously. Thus, in the case of the *Adelaide*, the second uncertainty gave rise to the following reservation by the Court:

"The rule which the Court has already laid down on this point is, that in cases of agency of persons in an enemy's country during a blockade, something more than the mere strict principle of law is necessary in order to bind employers by their acts. There must be time to give the principal an opportunity of countermanding".

In casu it was held that there had not been sufficient time, and that the claimants accordingly were not, either in respect to proof of property or on the ground of the blockade, incapacitated from receiving restitution. I will return to this subject below under III A, section 4 (Blockade), pp. 424-425.

For the rest, the question of the sufficiency of the evidence produced is too much a *quaestio facti* to be discussed in detail. Comp. my observations *sub* III C (Procedure), section 4, *infra*, p. 614.

In the later case of the *Nina (No. 1)* [1855] (Spinks, 276; Roscoe, II, 514), the claimant alleged his sole ownership of a cargo, but other persons also claimed an interest in it. Under those conditions the Court did not allow the production of further proof of ownership because it was satisfied that no trustworthy proof could alter the complexion of the case.

(*c*) *Nationality of the owner versus his domicile as the criterion for his enemy or neutral character*

Whereas continental prize law generally upheld the criterion of the nationality of the owner of seaborne goods, Anglo-American prize law has, at least by degrees, adopted the owner's residence or domicile as the true criterion for the determination of his enemy or neutral character in prize cases.

The criterion of nationality may in more exceptional cases give rise to doubts (possibility of dual citizenship, in which case the enemy nationality of the owner will prevail, or of naturalization of an enemy subject in a neutral country in wartime, as foreseen by the French prize law regulations), but I have not come across any such clear case in earlier times. These possibilities are at any rate more rare than complications that may arise from doubts about a merchant's residence or domicile.

In the case of the *Libérateur contre Le Napoléon* [1807] (Pistoye-Duverdy, *Traité*, II, 42), the *Conseil d'Etat* decided that the subject of a neutral State whose territory was under the military occupation of an enemy State did not thereby lose his neutral character.

Occasionally in France enemy subjects were not treated as enemies because they had long since been established in neutral territory, or because they had acquired there a *droit de cité* and had never returned to their country of origin. See, for instance, the case of the Algerian *Gioseppino* [1816], decided in this sense by the *Conseil d'Etat* in appeal (Pistoye-Duverdy, I, 134).

In the *La Paix* case of *an* IX (*ibid.*, I, 321), which related to a neutral consul in an enemy country—a subject of Ragusa, acting as the consul of that republic in Messina in the Kingdom of the Two Sicilies with which France was at war at the time—, who carried on trade there, it was decided that neither did such a consul thereby lose his neutral character.

Probably from early on English prize courts have preferred the residence or domicile of the owner of the goods to his nationality as the criterion for the determination of his enemy or neutral character. Already in the case of the *Postilion* of 1779 (Hay and Marriott, 245; Roscoe, I, 20) that determination was made dependent on his residence. The case concerned property of a native of Hamburg resident in France, who had to be considered as an adopted Frenchman *pro hac vice*. This criterion applied *in ambas partes*, to enemy subjects domiciled in a neutral country as well as to neutral subjects domiciled in an enemy country, and to private residents as well as to merchants. An exception was made, however, for enemy nationals resident in a neutral Capitulatory country, such as China (see *infra*, p. 259).

The case law has in particular developed the doctrine with regard to traders. In respect of them the Prize Courts have elaborated the theory of a trade or commercial domicile. The origin of this term seems not to be quite certain: Sir Samuel Evans at least stated, in the *Annaberg* case of World War I [1916] (*B.C.P.C.* II, 241), that, as far as he was aware, the term was never made use of by Lord Stowell. He believed it to be a phrase coined at a later date, which expresses in convenient form the idea of a man who trades in a country and to all appearance lives there permanently, and he felt no doubt that Lord Stowell had such an idea in his mind on many occasions when he spoke of a man having made himself a trader of a country.

In any case the idea was applied in a large number of prize cases. See for instance the judgments relating to the *Vigilantia* [1798] (1 C.Rob., 1; Roscoe, I, 31), a case concerning the national character of a ship, and the *San José Indiano* [1814] (2 Gallison, 268; Scott's Cases at p. 1546), and those of 1800 concerning the *Harmony* (2 C.Rob., 322; Roscoe, I, 241) and the *Indian Chief* (3 C.Rob., 12; Roscoe, I, 251). See also the American case of the *Freundschaft* [1819] (4 Wheaton, 105).

A neutral trader could only divest himself of an enemy trade domicile and thus escape treatment as an enemy by abandoning his commercial domicile as soon as possible after the outbreak of war between his country of residence and a third State.

In the *Packet de Bilboa* case [1799] (2 C.Rob., 133; Roscoe, I, 209) the Court inserted a passage concerning the length of time of a person's stay in a foreign country as a criterion of his enemy or non-enemy character.

The trader concerned was, moreover, to be granted a reasonable period of time to withdraw from an enemy country. This was expressed by Dr. Lushington during the Crimean War in the case of a cargo of corn, the property of merchants of Galatz in Moldavia, subjects of the Ionian Islands, carried on a ship sailing under Wallachian colours and captured in the Sulina mouth of the Danube after Russia's military occupation of the Danubian principalities (on this special feature of the case see *infra* p. 260). In that case, the *Gerasimo* [1857] (11 Moore P.C. 88; Roscoe, II, 577), Dr. Lushington said:

> "The national character of a trader is to be decided, for the purposes of the trade, by the national character of the place in which it is carried on. If a war breaks out, a foreign merchant carrying on trade in a belligerent country has a reasonable time allowed him for transferring himself and his property to another country. If he does not avail himself of the opportunity, he is to be treated, for the purpose of trade, as a subject of the Power under whose dominion he carries it on, and as an enemy of those with whom that Power is at war".

Lord Stowell seems to have been of the opinion that a trader could acquire a trade domicile in two or more foreign countries. Certain passage to that effect can, in effect, be read in the *Jonge Klassina* [1804] (5 C.Rob., 297; Roscoe, I, 485), a case in which a licence granted to a trader in Birmingham for the importation of certain goods from (enemy) Holland into England was held to be invalid because the licensee was likewise the exporter from Holland. Subsequent British Prize Courts, however, have not been sure of that, as appears from certain hesitant passages appearing in the judgments of World War I, such as those concerning the *Derfflinger (No. 1)* (*B.C.P.C.*, I, 386) and the *Lützow (No. 4)* (*B.C.P.C.*, II, 122). Commenting upon the precedent of the *Jonge Klassina*, the President of the British Prize Court in the *Derfflinger* case [1915] made the following remarks:

> "It is sometimes said that Lord Stowell in the *Jonge Klassina* expressed the opinion that a man may acquire a commercial domicile in more countries than one. The passage referred to is as follows: "A man may have mercantile concerns in two countries and if he acts as a merchant of both, he must be liable to be considered as a subject of both with regard to the transactions originating respectively in those countries..." It must not be taken that I am expressing any opinion as to whether a man can have a commercial domicil in two neutral countries which would entitle him to be regarded as a neutral trader in both, I can conceive that it is possible that he might establish a sufficient residence in both for the purpose".

The same indecision was apparent in the case of the *Lützow (No. 4)*.

The principle that enemy merchants resident in a neutral country were as a rule exempt from treatment as enemies did not apply to the case of their having a trade domicile in an Oriental country where foreigners enjoyed the privilege of extra-territorial jurisdiction in virtue of a Capitulation, such as China. In this respect Sir William Scott observed in the case of the *Indian Chief* of 1800 (3 C.Rob., 29; Roscoe, I, 251):

> "In the East, from the oldest times, an immiscible character has been kept up; foreigners are not admitted into the general body and mass of the society of the nation; they continue strangers and sojourners as all their fathers were—*Doris amara suam non intermiscuit undam*; not acquiring any national character under the general sovereignity of the country, and not trading under any recognised authority of their own original country, they have been held to derive their present character from that of the association or factory under whose protection they live and carry on their trade".

This passage was later quoted in the case of the *Derfflinger (No. 1)* by the British Prize Court for Egypt (*supra*).

American jurisprudence, on the other hand, admits the possibility of the establishment of a "civil domicile" in China. See the judgment in *Mather v. Cunningham* [1909] (*A.J.I.L.*, 1910, p. 446) and my *Le droit des prises de la Grande Guerre* (1924), pp. 537 *et seq*.

Doubts have arisen with respect to

(*a*) traders of enemy nationality, expelled from a neutral country: the *Venus* case of 1814 (*England v. U.S.*) reported in 8 Cranch, 253, and Scott's *Cases*, p. 530, but later repudiated by *Nigel Gold Mining Co. v. Hoade* [1901], and

(*b*) consular agents of a neutral State carrying on trade in an enemy country.

In the *Baltica* [1857] (11 Moore P.C., 141; Roscoe, II, 628), during the Crimean War, the solution depended on whether a neutral subject, established on enemy territory, was by that fact divested of his neutral character even if his residence there was the consequence of his function as the consul of his home country. The claimant in that case was a Dane by birth, who had long resided as Danish consul in Libau, where he traded as a merchant. Dr. Lushington decided that, from the fact of the seller of the goods being consul of a neutral State and also a merchant trading in the enemy's country, he was to be regarded as an enemy, but his judgment was reversed in appeal on other grounds.

The same question had already arisen in the *Aina (No. 1)* [1854] in respect of a merchant citizen of Lübeck, who acted as a Netherlands consul in Finland. The Court decided that he lost his neutral character by his residence in an enemy country in that capacity (Spinks, 8; Roscoe, II, 247):

> "I take it to be a point beyond controversy that where a neutral, after the commencement of war, continues to reside in the enemy's country for the purpose of trade, he is considered as adhering to the enemy, and as disqualified for claiming as a neutral altogether".

On the other hand French jurisprudence was to the opposite effect, see the case of the *La Paix* [*an* IX] (De Pistoye-Duverdy, I, 321), cited *supra*, p. 257.

What applied to a trade domicile in enemy territory equally applied to such a domicile in militarily occupied neutral territory. See in particular the above mentioned case of the *Gerasimo* [1857] (11 Moore P.C., 88; Roscoe, II, 577), in which Dr. Lushington also held that circumstances which convert a friendly or neutral territory into an enemy's country did not by themselves necessarily convert its inhabitants into enemies:

> "the mere fact of a State being in occupation of a country does not turn the traders in that country into enemy traders or make their goods enemy goods".

This was the case of certain merchandise originating from Moldavia, then Turkish (allied) territory, which was however under the military occupation of (enemy) Russian forces.

The case law developed during the period covered by vol. I of Roscoe's collection of reports of prize cases (1745-1808) was confirmed by judgments, pronounced during the period 1808-1859, including the Crimean War reproduced in his vol. II. In addition to the judgments reported by Roscoe, British Prize Courts have rendered a series of other decisions, which I could not find in Roscoe's collection, but which were also made on the principle of the residence of the owner of both ships and cargoes as the true criterion for the determination of their enemy or non-enemy character.

Comp. the following cases:

the *Bella Giudita* [1785] (1 C.Rob., 207); the *William* [1795-1801] (1 C.Rob., note at p. 214); the *Hoop* [1799] (1 C.Rob., 196); the *Fama* [1804] (5 C.Rob., 106); the *Dart*, the *Happy Couple* and the *Manilla* [1808 and 1809] (Edw. 1); the *Bolletta* [1809] (Edw., 171); the *Santa Anna* [1809] (Edw., 180). A number of these cases also present the special feature of relating to prizes belonging to owners resident in territories under belligerent occupation (British Grenada, British Guadaloupe, Spanish Louisiana, Danish Heligoland and St. Croix, American Castine (Maine), French Zante and Korfú, Spanish Santo Domingo, Cádiz, Hamburg, Transvaal and Holland).

Further judgments which demonstrate the import of the basic rule on the enemy or non-enemy character of persons on the ground of their residence on enemy territory are the following.

According to the *Harmony* [1800] (2 C.Rob., 322; Roscoe, I, 241) the chief test of the owner's domicile was the length of time which he remained in the country; if he visited a foreign country for a special purpose the length of time during which he remained in it might negative the inference to be drawn from the temporary character of the stay in the first instance.

In the *President* [1804] (5 C.Rob., 277; Roscoe, I, 475) evidence of the intention of a merchant settled for a long time in a foreign country to leave it, was held insufficient to divest him of the national character which he had obtained, without some overt act in addition.

In the *Indian Chief* [1809] (3 C.Rob., 12; Roscoe, I, 251) the national character gained by residence was held to cease with residence the moment the person concerned set himself *bona fide* to change his place of residence.

Other judgments dealt with the not uncommon case that a trader had a house or transacted business in different countries:

the *Herman* [1802] (4 C.Rob., 228; Roscoe, I, footnote (*a*) at p. 270):

> "Where a person has a house of trade in a neutral country, and one in Great Britain secondary to his house in the neutral country, his right to carry on trade with the enemy from his house in the neutral country cannot be denied, provided it does not originate from his house in London, nor vest an interest in that house";

or with the case of a partnership between a resident in neutral and one in enemy territory:

the *Jacobus Johannes* [1785] (Roscoe, I, at p. 34): two partners in a house of trade at (Dutch) Sint Eustatius, one resident there, the other resident in Denmark, the first forwarding the goods to Europe, the second receiving them and disposing of them there. The share of the person resident in Sint Eustatius was liable to condemnation as the property of a domiciled Dutchman, the share of the other should be restored. A similar situation occurred in the case of the *Osprey* [1795] (*loc.cit.*) where one partner was domiciled in France, the other in America.

In a subsequent judgment in appeal the Lords, in the case of *Zacharia Coopman & Co.*, *sub nomine* the *Nancy* [1798] (*eod.loco*), argued on a different line: eliminating the former cases which occurred merely at the commencement of a war, the Lords held that

> "in the case of a person carrying on trade habitually in the country of the enemy, though not resident there, he should have time to withdraw himself from that commerce, because it would press too heavily on neutrals to say that immediately on the first breaking out of a war, their goods should become subject to confiscation as enemy property".

The judgment continued, however, by expressly laying down that

> "if a person entered into a house of trade in the enemy's country in time of war, or continued that connection during the war, he could not protect himself by mere residence in a neutral country ... There is a traffic which stamps a national character on the individual independent of that character, which mere personal residence may give him".

The British memorandum for the Naval Conference of London of 1908-1909 defined the legal situation in this field as follows:

> "The principle adopted by the British tribunals has been to treat the domicile of the owner as the dominant element to decide whether the captured property is enemy property. But this principle was not, in this respect, from every point of view limited to a domicile of origin or to residence: *Postilion* [1799] (Hay and Marriott, 245; Roscoe, I, 20); *Harmony* [1800] (2 C.Rob., 322; Roscoe, I, 241); *Aina (No. 1)* [1854] (Spinks, 8; Roscoe, II, 247); *Gerasimo* [1857] (Roscoe, II, 577, at p. 582; 11 Moore P.C., 88)."

The principle was in fact applied as follows:

A person domiciled in a neutral country, but having a trading house in an enemy country, was deemed to acquire thereby a commercial domicile in the enemy country in respect of trade operations which originated there: *Jonge Klassina* [1804] (5 C.Rob., 297, at p. 302; Roscoe, I, 485-488); cases cited in the *Vigilantia* [1798] (1 C.Rob., 1; Roscoe, I, 31). Other properties of such an owner were not affected thereby: *Portland* (3 C.Rob., 43).

A commercial domicile which was not the domicile of nationality was lost when effective measure were taken *bona fide* to abandon it in favour of another domicile, without intention to return: *Indian Chief* [1800] (3 C.Rob., 12; Roscoe, I, 251).

The principle of a commercial domicile applied equally in the case of an individual, a society or a corporation, residence in the latter two cases meaning the place from where the business was conducted: cases cited in the

Vigilantia (*supra*) and in the judgment of Lord Lindley in the affair of *Jansen v. Driefontein Consolidated Mines, Ltd.* (Law Reports 1902, Court of Appeal, 505; A.C., 484).

In case a society or one or several associates were domiciled in enemy territory, ownership was apportioned proportionately among the associates, and the portion attributed to an associate domiciled on enemy territory was presumed to be enemy property: *Citto* [1800] (3 C.Rob., 38); *Harmony* [1800] (2 C.Rob., 322; Roscoe, I, 241).

See for another case of partnership the *Franklin (No. 3)* [1805] (6 C.Rob., 127; Roscoe, I, 539), a case of trading with the enemy by a firm in London in which an American citizen was a partner together with an Englishman. The issue was whether the American share was liable to forfeiture. The Court denied this.

In support of the doctrine that neutral subjects established in an enemy country could only divest themselves of their enemy character by severing all links with such country as soon as possible, English courts sometimes invoked parallel precedents which had arisen in the field of trading with the enemy. See the case of the *Hoop* [1799] (1 C.Rob., 196; Roscoe, I, 104), in which Lord Stowell referred to the rigid rule against trading with the enemy "where cargoes had been laden before the war but where the parties had not used all possible means to countermand the voyage after the first notice of hostilities"; see also Chief Justice Marshall's "celebrated dissenting judgment" in the *Venus* [1814] (comp. my *Le droit des prises de la Grande Guerre*, p. 532).

In the above survey I have only dealt with the contrast between domicile and nationality as criteria of enemy character. But there was also a contrast between domicile and temporary residence. This contrast was examined by the Mixed Claims Commission set up by Article VII (2) of the Anglo-American Jay Treaty of 19 November 1794 (Martens, R^1, VI, 336; Parry, 52, 243). The case in question concerned the temporary stay of an American ship-owner on the enemy island of Guadeloupe was held insufficient to establish his enemy character: the *Betsey* case of 1797.

The *Betsey* was an American vessel that was captured by an English privateer on 20 March 1794 on a (second) voyage from Baltimore to French Guadeloupe, and was declared good and lawful prize by a British Admiralty Court at Bermuda by a Decree of 20 May 1794, confirmed on 25 July 1794 by the Lords Commissioners of Appeal. The claimants were two Patterson brothers, one, George, owner of the ship, the other, William, co-owner by half of the lading jointly with George. They were both American citizens and domiciled in Baltimore, but George had temporarily remained on Guadeloupe, after a first voyage of the ship, for the purpose of winding-up a business affair with the French authorities on the island. This was the factual situation with which the Mixed Claims Commission was faced when the American Government claimed on behalf of the Patterson brothers compensation for the loss of their property, for costs and damages, and for the loss of benefits as a result of the interruption of the ship's (second) voyage, and the British Agent in the case opposed the claim on the ground of an asserted enemy domicile of brother George on Guadeloupe at the moment of capture. His argument was that George's stay on Guadeloupe sufficed to constitute the enemy character of the claimants, if not as a conclusive evidence of that character, at least as a presumption *juris tantum* which reversed the *onus probandi* from the captor upon the claimants. The controversy related, therefore, not to a collision between the basic criteria of citizenship and domicile, but to that between domicile and temporary stay. Although this case has thus only a very reduced legal importance for the problem of the criterion or the criteria of the enemy or non-enemy character of sea-borne goods, it is not without interest because of the attention which was paid to the plea advanced by the British Agent which was, of course, dismissed by the majority of the five Commissioners. See for the opinion of the American Commissioner Mr Gore *R.A.I.*, I, pp. 69-73, for that of his colleague Mr Pinkney *ibid.*, pp. 73-79, and for that of the presiding Commissioner Mr Trumbull *ibid.*, pp. 82-86. In the course of their arguments the Commissioners, apart from invoking the authority of Grotius, Vattel, Barbeyrac and Burlamaqui, cited certain judicial precedents, *viz.*, those of the *Harmonie* and the *Jacobus Johannes* [1785] concerning claims advanced by residents of the (enemy) Caribbean island of Saint Eustatius and rejected on the ground of their permanent residence there, with the exception of one claim which was allowed because the claimant had only an accidental residence in enemy territory.

See on the legal value of the arguments adduced by the parties in the *Betsey* case the elaborate doctrinal opinion of the editors of the *R.A.I. sub* IV at pp. 86 *et seq.* of vol. I.

The second category of cases submitted to the Mixed Claims Commission, consisting of the *Fame*, the *Farmer*, the *Molly* and the *Sally* (captain Griffiths), and the *Active*, is still less important for the general problem of enemy character. They relate to the justification of certain presumptions, even *juris* and *de jure*, of enemy property, such as, in particular, suspect manoeuvres and fraudulent behaviour. See *R.A.I.*, I, pp. 119-123, *sub* A.

The judicial practice of ignoring non-proprietary interests in cargoes has remained unchanged up to the very end of the pre-codification period. See as to Japan:

the *Manchuria (No. 1)* [1905] (Hurst & Bray, II, 52 *et seq.*, at p. 56):

> "With regard to the goods shipped in an enemy vessel, and despatched to enemy territory, they are liable to capture, and even if, as the appellants assert, they were insured by neutrals, the existence of an insurance contract cannot be made a reason for the release of goods having an enemy character."

the *Frederick Huth & Co's* claim to a cargo of tea in the same vessel (*ibid.*, II, 69 *et seq.*, at p. 74) was introduced by a neutral (British) bankers' firm in

London which had accepted a bill of exchange drawn by the (neutral) consignors. The decision was the same:

> "capture cannot be avoided on the ground of the acceptance by a neutral of a bill of exchange drawn against the goods."

A third case, in which a neutral insurance company of Canton claimed directly the release of innocent goods found on board the British contraband carrier *Hsiping* [1905] (*ibid.*, II, 135 *et seq.*), petered out in an appeal decision of dismissal on the ground that the claimants had procured no evidence to show that they had any interest in the goods.

A fourth claim by a German Boeddinghaus (cargo *ex Mukden*) (*ibid.*, II, 19) was wrecked on a general *dictum* that a claim for freight, insurance and expenses was not within the jurisdiction of the Prize Court.

The Russian view was equally adverse to such non-proprietary claims.

The series of Russian judgments concerned in particular cases of the conveyance of contraband of war to the enemy by neutral vessels and the admissibility of their destruction. As they present hardly any interest for the subject of the enemy or non-enemy character of cargoes and the Russian Prize Regulations are also silent on it, I will pass on at once to the series of Japanese Court decrees.

The Japanese rule on the character of cargoes was laid down in Art. 8 of the Regulations relating to Capture at Sea of 7 March 1904:

> "the nationality of cargo is determined by the nationality of the owner",

but Art. 9 added *sub* 1 concerning the transfer of property in wartime that

> "Cargo which has been despatched, either before the war began in anticipation of hostilities breaking out, or while the war was in actual progress, by a person domiciled in Japan or in a neutral country, or by someone deputed by him to do so, to the hostile State, to individuals of that nation, or to a person deputed by the enemy to receive it, shall be held in all cases to be enemy cargo."

The Japanese courts on the whole adhered to the British system and, consequently, replaced the criterion of the owner's nationality by that of his domicile.

The essential elements of that system were already succinctly defined by the Higher Prize Court in its very first judgments concerning *Cargo ex-Ekaterinoslav* (*Kunst and Albers' claim*) and *Mukden* (Hurst & Bray, II, at pp. 10-11 and 16, respectively):

> "The question whether goods are enemy goods or not depends, not on the nationality of their owner, but on his domicile, or, in the case of a merchant, the place of his business";
> "goods shipped by a person living outside the enemy territory, in an enemy vessel and consigned to a person residing in the enemy territory, are enemy property and liable to confiscation. This is a rule recognised by international usage, and this Court considers it fair and reasonable."

This principle was held to apply even when the goods were despatched prior to the outbreak of war and were seized *in transitu*: see the decisions of the

Sasebo Prize Court on the Boeddinghaus' and Yak Yuk Chang's claims to goods in the same *Mukden* (*ibid.*, II, pp. 19-20, respectively 25-26):

> "It is recognised by International Law that when goods are placed on board a vessel and despatched to the address of a person residing in the enemy country, unless there is evidence to the contrary, the ownership of such goods passes to the consignee from the moment they are shipped."

The rule concerning a merchant's place of business gave rise to the theory of a "trade domicile". Just as in the case law of the English courts it was this trade domicile that in its application caused, in Japan also, difficulties in the various divergent situations in which it was invoked (*infra*).

Other principles, bearing the English stamp, which were adhered to by the Japanese prize courts from the very beginning, were embodied in the series of early judgments concerning the fifteen Russian ships condemned with their enemy cargoes as enemy property—the *Ekaterinoslav*, the *Mukden*, the *Rossia*, the *Argun*, the *Manchuria et al.* As far as they had a bearing, in particular, on the transporting ships themselves, I refer back to Sub-Division I *supra*, pp. 216-218, restricting myself here to the problems arising from doubts about the enemy or non-enemy character of cargoes.

I can only make a succinct selection from the abundant mass of case material available, telescoping it for the sake of brevity in a necessarily shallow summary that neglects the tentative systematic differentiations which I have introduced above (sections 2-4 of this Sub-Division II) in an effort to unravel in a sequence of separate sections and paragraphs the various aspects of the English system.

The Japanese prize courts have displayed great virtuosity in disentangling, in accordance with the British-inspired decisive criterion of a trade domicile, many intricate problems concerning the enemy or non-enemy character of natural and, in particular, legal persons operating in the Far Eastern labyrinth of those days. Such complications could arise from trade relations between neutral (respectively enemy-based) branch offices and enemy-based (respectively neutral) counterparts elsewhere, from mixed partnerships, from limited liability companies of international composition of either their board of directors or their shareholders, from the transfers of business seats from neutral to enemy territory, or conversely, from belligerent occupation of neutral territory, from temporary residence in enemy territory, etc.

One of the most striking examples was that of a consignment by the neutral Chinese branch office of a neutral German-based bank to its branch office in neutral Korea that was at the time under the military occupation partly of Russian, partly of Japanese troops.

The legal battle hinged mainly on two groups of factors:

(*a*) the conditions of the commercial transaction involved, under the traditional doctrine on the moment at which the property passed from the consignor to the consignee, in the light of their respective domiciles;

(*b*) the conditions of the capture, in particular from its temporal or local aspect: prior or subsequent to the commencement of the war; at a permissible place or not; against admissible objects or not; contrary or conformably to the Imperial Japanese Days of Grace Ordinance of 9 February 1904.

More often than not the elements *sub a* and *b* presented themselves in combination, so that the cases were of a complex nature. This already happened from the outset, when the prize courts still had to find their way through the maze of controversial issues raised by the parties. When dealing with them, the Higher Prize Court, in particular, exhibited a remarkable systematic logic in first setting out in detail the arguments of the appellants, then the counter-arguments of the Procurator of the Sasebo Prize Court, and concluding with its elaborate own decision on each of the arguments, point by point.

A few instances may illustrate the way in which the Japanese prize courts have solved from the very beginning the many problems arising from the variety of situations in which their decision was invoked (the references are to the pages of Hurst & Bray, vol. II).

Among the goods found on board a captured enemy ship were condemned as enemy property, *inter alia*,

cargoes sent, no matter under what circumstances, even if despatched before the outbreak of war, to a consignee in territory which later became hostile: in the absence of proof to the contrary the consignee was to be presumed to be the owner if he was permanently residing and carrying on business in such territory (p. 31);

specie sent by the Japanese branch of the Russo-Chinese Banking Corporation to its head office notwithstanding the registry of that branch in Japan according to Japanese law (p. 36);

goods shipped by a neutral consignor on the order of an enemy consignee (p. 59);

goods claimed by the neutral acceptor of a bill of exchange (p. 69);

cargoes consigned by one enemy branch of a neutral company to another enemy branch of the same neutral company (p. 10).

Enemy goods were not protected by the fact that they were insured by neutral undertakers (p. 52).

A petition by a neutral subject, defendant in a pending action, to attach, in virtue of a general order of a civil court, the movable property of his adversary captured as prize, was refused for lack of the prize court's competence (p. 21).

A claim to certain goods in an enemy ship, filed by a neutral (Danish) consul, was stranded on his non-recognition as a "party interested" in the goods (p. 57).

On the other hand, among the goods found on board an enemy ship which were released were cargoes

consigned by neutral subjects or by subjects of the captor State to neutral or Japanese subjects resident in (partly enemy-occupied) Korea (p. 18);

sent by a neutral government to its commercial agent or trade commissioner in enemy territory (pp. 12, 52);

consigned to a person only temporarily resident in enemy territory (pp. 52, 65).

Section 3. SPECIAL CASES OF TRANSFER

Unlike the situation in respect of ships where a separate analysis of the legal effects of their transfer from enemy to neutral (non-enemy) ownership (*transfert de pavillon*) is apposite, such a separate analysis has hardly any sense, insofar as England is concerned, because the transfer of cargoes *in transitu* is so closely connected with the general English doctrine on *post bellum* shipments and their effect, described in my introductory paragraph *supra*, pp. 247 *et seq.*, that a separate treatment would only in fact mean a repetition of principles already set out. What I stated in that introductory paragraph was that enemy goods could not change their character to neutral when sailing in war-time, a rule formulated in the *Vro(u)w Margaretha* [1799] (1 C.Rob., 336; Roscoe, I, 149) in the wording that goods were considered to be vested in the shipper until delivery. This rule that a transfer *in transitu* was invalid only applied when at the date of such transfer a state of war was existing or imminent.

In this respect the transfer of goods *in transitu* was governed by the same principles as applied to the transfer of ships so that there is no need to return to the subject after what I have already set out earlier. Nor does it seem worth while to classify the older cases of transfer of cargoes *in transitu* according to whether they concerned *ante* or *post bellum* shipments.

One of the most important examples of the application of the rule was that of a large-scale business transaction of this type by sellers in Batavia, the V.O.I.C. (United East India Company), of vast quantities of coffee, the produce of the Dutch East Indies, shipped in several vessels from there to a trading house in Denmark. The case was submitted to the British Prize Court in 1802 after the capture of one of those vessels, the *Rendsborg* (4 C.Rob., 121; Roscoe, II, 614, Note). As the Dutch colonies were at that time under the military occupation of France, the validity of the sale in regard of the captor was disputed and finally denied in a judgment elaborately motivated owing to the magnitude of the transaction. The entire shipment was confiscated.

Another instance of major importance to the disputed validity of transfers of seaborne goods *in transitu* was that of the *Jan Frederick* and a number of other Dutch vessels [1804] (5 C.Rob., 128; Roscoe, I, 434). This case related to a very considerable quantity of colonial produce shipped in January-February 1803 from Dutch Surinam for the account and at the risk of certain estates there, documented as Dutch property, on board of Dutch vessels bound to Holland. While *in itinere* these colonial products were bought by a resident of neutral Emden under a contract of 10 May 1803 at a moment when England had already put a general embargo on Dutch property previous to the outbreak of hostilities. The purchase was still made in time of peace, but probably in contemplation of an imminent Anglo-Dutch war, and the issue was, obviously for the first time, whether the rule against transfers of cargoes *in transitu* in time of war also applied to cases of transfers made on the prospect of war. The Court began by defending the general rule against transfers *in transitu* effected by the transfer of the bills of lading, in a wording which suggests that the validity or effectiveness of such a type of commercial transaction was not yet firmly established even about 1800:

> "The Court has opened a door to claims in opposition to the averment of the ship's papers, and it has done this on a consideration of the fair course of mercantile speculation in time of peace. It has even allowed a change of property *in transitu* by the transfer of the bills of lading, where it had been done without any view of accommodation to relieve the seller from the pressure or prospect of war. ... That a transfer may take place *in transitu* has ... been decided in two or three cases where there had been no actual war, nor any prospect of war, mixing itself with the transaction of the parties. But", the Court continued, "in time of war this is prohibited as a vicious contract, being a fraud on belligerent rights, not only in the particular transaction, but in the great facility which it would necessarily introduce of evading those rights beyond the possibility of detection. It is a road that in time of war must be shut up; for although honest men might be induced to travel it with very innocent intentions, the far greater proportion of those who passed would use it only for sinister purposes, and with views of fraud on the rights of the belligerent".

After that argument the Court passed on to "the important question raised whether the contemplation of war would have the same effect in vitiating the contracts as actual war?" Sir William Scott answers the question in the affirmative.

An entirely different subject is that of the impact, not of a transfer of the property of goods, but of a change in the sovereignty over territory "in transit" of the vessel upon the fate of prizes. The precedents, rather illogically, deal indiscriminately with these two wholly dissimilar contingencies on the same footing, illustrating the rule by frequent cross-references from one category of cases to the other. This was still done especially by the Judicial Committee of the Privy Council after World War I in a case of December 1920 in which this court of appeal investigated the uncertain origin and foundation of the rule against the validity of transfers of seaborne goods *in transitu* vis-à-vis the captor. That case concerned the seizure by British forces of certain cargoes unloaded from the neutral (Swedish and Brazilian) vessels *Kronprinsessan Margareta, Rena, Paraná* and *Hilding* (*B.C.P.C.*, III, 803). In that judgment the court of appeal connected the rule, somewhat inconsistently, with two old precedents of the end of the 18th century relating to the impact of a territorial change from enemy to non-enemy, or inversely, on the enemy or non-enemy character of prizes, while in transit towards or from the territory concerned. Those precedents were the cases of the *Danckebaar Africaan* [1798] (1 C.Rob., 107; Roscoe, I, 74) relating to cargoes, in connection with an earlier judgment of 1782 relating to a vessel, the *Negotie en Zeevaart* (already referred to in section 3 of Sub-Division I, *supra*, pp. 225-227). It was these two precedents which were recapitulated together in the appellate judgment of December 1920, cited above:

> "The rule against recognising transfers of enemy goods while at sea, if unaccompanied by actual delivery and transfer of possession, is so well established and is now so ancient that its authority cannot be questioned or its utility impugned for the purposes of a judicial determination...
>
> The history and the theory of the rule, neither of which is now very clear, are too inconclusive to add weight to the rule itself or throw light on its true application. It appears to have been regarded as a particular example of a wider principle—that the national character of moveables cannot be changed while they are at sea by any independent dealings or occurrences. Thus, in The *Negotie en Zeevaart*, decided on appeal in 1782, the question was whether a ship, which went to sea a Dutch ship, has ceased to bear that national character when she was taken because the Dutch colony of Demerara, from which she sailed, had before her capture become British by capitulation to the British Crown. It was held that she had not. This was followed in the *Danckebaar Africaan*, where the question was whether the capitulation of the Cape of Good Hope, which had taken place after the ship sailed, but before her capture, and had made British subjects of the Dutch owners, had not also entitled them to claim their ship on arrival at the Cape as prize on the ground that there had been in fact a capture of British property. So strict was the rule even then that the claimants, although British subjects themselves at the time of capture, could not be heard to assert that title against the presumptions, arising when the ship sailed. Shortly afterwards it was accepted in The *Vrow Margaretha* [1799] (1 C.Rob., 336; Roscoe, I, 149) that there was no recorded instance of a claim being sustained for goods purchased of an enemy in transit in time of war, for the practice of the High Court to look only to the time of shipment was already invariable".

To conclude these references to a few special cases in which the rule against the validity of transfers *in transitu* was applied, I will make two additional remarks.

The first is that the rule against the validity of the transfer to a neutral flag of a ship lying in a blockaded port was equally applied to the sale of goods being in the same position: invalidity vis-à-vis the captor of the sale to a neutral buyer of a cargo lying in a blockaded port, effected prior to, but in contemplation of, the war.

The second additional remark concerns the confusion which, at a much later stage, during World War I, led the British Prize Court to ignore or neglect the obvious distinction between two operations of a totally different nature, *viz.*, the *transhipment* of goods from an enemy to a neutral ship in transit, and the *transfer of their ownership* to neutral persons in transit. I did not come across any old cases in which the two operations were legally mixed up in the same manner. The case I have in view is that of certain cargoes on board the enemy (German) ship *Neuenfels*, transhipped in April 1915 in the Spanish port of Vigo to the neutral (Scandinavian) vessels *Jeanne, Vera, Forsvik* and *Albania* [1916] (*B.C.P.C.*, II, 227).

A special kind of transfer was the sale of a prize to a neutral subject after its condemnation by a prize court. On a case of this kind, the decision of the French *Tribunal de Cassation* of 29 fructidor *an* VII was, according to De Pistoye and Duverdy (I, 320), to the following effect:

> "Les marchandises d'origine ennemie, prises sur l'ennemi par les Français, déclarées de bonne prise et vendues à un neutre, ont le caractère de marchandises neutres".

Section 4. PRODUCE OF THE ENEMY SOIL (*CRÛ ENNEMI*)

As I will set out below *sub* A, Chapter III, section 3 (Contraband), section 3 (Sanctions) under B (Relaxations), pp. 401-413, British prize courts have traditionally assigned a privileged position to goods, even of a contraband character, which were exported as the produce of the soil of a neutral country. I refer to the case of the Dutch ship the *Jonge Pieter* [1781-1783], analysed and followed in that of the Prussian ship the *Apollo (No. 1)* [1802] (4 C.Rob., 158; Roscoe, I, 368), and the cases of the Swedish vessels *Sarah Christina* [1799] (1 C.Rob., 237; Roscoe, I, 125), and *Maria (No. 1)* [1799] (1 C.Rob., 340; Roscoe, I, 152), in which the goods were not condemned, but held liable to pre-emption (comp. *supra*, p. 413).

What I am considering in the present section is, however, in a sense just the opposite, *viz.*, the legal fate of goods in the reverse position of being the produce of the enemy soil, which marks them as goods with an enemy character.

The criterion of the ownership of the seized goods was indeed not the only criterion applied by the prize courts. In addition to that, enemy character could also attach to goods on the ground that they were the produce of the enemy soil, with the legal consequence that such produce also was liable to condemnation in prize as being stamped with enemy character. Evidence of the recognition of this legal principle dates back to an early period. See the case mentioned by Reginald Marsden, pp. 356-357, dating from 1740. Other old precedents are those of the *Phoenix* of 1803 (5 C.Rob., 20; Roscoe, II, 239, footnote (*a*) and the *Vro(u)w Anna Catharina* of 1804 (5 C.Rob., 161).

In the *Phoenix* case concerning a claim on behalf of neutrals for the produce of their property in the Dutch (then enemy) colony of Surinam, Sir William Scott held:

> "Nothing can be more definitively decided and fixed as the principle of this Court and the Supreme Court, than that the possession of the soil does impress upon the owner the character of the country, so far as the produce of that plantation is concerned, in its transportation to any other country, whatever the local residence of the owner may be. This has been so repeatedly decided, both in this and in the Superior Court, that it is no longer open to discussion."

In the case of the *Vro(u)w Anna Catharina* he decided *expressis verbis* that the produce of the land in an enemy country was subject to confiscation, although shipped in time of peace.

The American courts followed the British lead in the case of *Thirty hogsheads of sugar* (or: *Bentzen v. Boyle* [1815] (9 Cranch (Amer.), 191).

This principle of old Anglo-American prize law—to the effect that the produce of land owned or held by the claimants of seized goods in an enemy country, while in the possession or ownership of the person owning or holding such land, even if he was a neutral and resident in a neutral country, was confiscable if captured or seized by a belligerent with which the State where the land was situated was at war— was re-activated during World War I by the British Prize Court in the case of the *Asturian* (*B.C.P.C.*, II, 202).

The same rule was introduced in France in the middle of the 18th century. Art. 3 of a *Règlement* of 21 October 1744 adopted, in effect, the principle that "les marchandises provenant du crû ennemi" would be condemned as good and lawful prize. Comp. on this *Règlement* De Pistoye et Duverdy, vol. II, p. 470.

A special case that arose under that *Règlement* at the end of the 18th century was that of the seizure of cargo on board the Danish merchant ship *Fortuna* by the French corsaire the *Don Quichotte* (De Pistoye and Duverdy, I, 360). This cargo consisted of produce of the soil of the Ionian Island of Zante, which was occupied by Russia at the time of the seizure. The cargo would have come directly within the scope of the *Règlement* if Zante had been enemy territory, but it was in fact only occupied by an enemy. The first question, therefore, was whether enemy-occupied neutral territory was to be placed on the same footing with, and should therefore be assimilated to, enemy territory. But even conceded that this was indeed the solution, the further problem that arose was whether this assimilation was still justified after the island had ceased to be Russian-occupied territory.

In the same case the parties engaged in a discussion of a question of an entirely different nature, *viz.*, whether the *Règlement* was still in force. The *Conseil des prises* by its judgment of 3 ventôse *an* IX (de Pistoye and Duverdy, I, 360) decided that the rule had in the meantime been abrogated by Art. 1 of the *Règlement* of 1778.

The cargo was accordingly released with costs and damages.

CHAPTER III A

THE SUBSTANTIVE LAW OF PRIZE

PREFATORY

I now come to the various specific grounds upon which a belligerent is, or deems itself to be, entitled to seize property at sea. These grounds and a few related subjects were summed up by the *Institut de droit international* in its *Règlement international des prises maritimes* of 1887 (Heidelberg), as amended in 1897 (Copenhagen). §§ 110, 112-118 of the *Règlement* ran as follows:

§ 110. — Aucun navire marchand, ni aucune cargaison appartenant à un particulier, ennemi ou neutre, aucun navire naufragé, échoué ou abandonné, ni aucun bâtiment de pêche, ne peuvent être objets de prise et condamnés qu'en vertu d'un jugement des tribunaux de prises et pour des actes prohibés par le présent règlement.

§ 112. — Les tribunaux de prises ne peuvent condamner des prises ennemies ou neutres que pour les faits suivants:

1°. Transport prohibé en temps de guerre;

2°. Violation de blocus;

3°. Résistance à l'arrêt, à la visite, à la recherche ou à la saisie;

4°. Actes de participation de navires privés à des hostilités des belligérants.

§ 113. — Pour qu'il y ait condamnation du chef de transport prohibé en temps de guerre, il faut:

1°. qu'un transport de contrebande soit à destination d'un belligérant;

2°. qu'un service de transport interdit soit pour son compte;

3°. que l'objet transporté soit lui-même prohibé;

4°. que le navire soit pris en flagrant délit.

§ 114. — Pour qu'il y ait condamnation du chef de violation de blocus, il faut:

1°. Que le blocus soit publié et effectif;

2°. Qu'il ait été porté à la connaissance du navire accusé, et que ce navire ait tenté de violer un tel blocus, selon les dispositions du présent règlement (§§ 43 et 44).

Il n'y a pas lieu à condamnation si un navire a pénétré à travers la ligne d'un blocus, ou dans une mer bloquée, par suite d'un accident, tel qu'une tempête, ou d'une erreur; toutefois ces faits devront être prouvés par le navire qui les allègue.

§ 115. — La résistance d'un navire marchand à l'arrêt, à la visite, à la recherche ou à la saisie, doit être prouvée en fait ou manifestée par des actes; une simple protestation du navire résistant ne pourra motiver la condamnation.

§ 116. — Dans le cas de participation d'un navire privé aux hostilités des belligérants, il faut que la participation soit prouvée et reconnue comme telle.

§ 117. — La contrebande, ainsi que toute chose illégalement transportée sera confisquée, et les personnes et troupes illégalement transportées seront faites prisonnières. Le navire transportant ne sera condamné que:

1°. S'il fait résistance;

2°. S'il transporte illégalement des agents, des militaires ou des dépêches pour un belligérant.

§ 118. — Le navire sera condamné avec sa cargaison:

1°. Dans le cas de violation de blocus (§ 114);

2°. Dans le cas de résistance (§§ 112 et 115);

3°. Dans le cas de participation à des hostilités des belligérants.

Far less traditional than this list drawn up by a scientific body was the enumeration made by one of the belligerents in the last major war preceding the codification of 1908-1909. Art. 37 of Japan's Regulations of 7 March 1904 relating to Capture at Sea (Hurst & Bray, vol. II, Appendix B, pp. 422 *et seq.*) listed as ships liable to capture without regard to their nationality those

" 1. carrying persons who are contraband of war, documents which are contraband of war or articles which are contraband of war;

2. which are not provided with ship's papers, or which have purposely either torn up, thrown away, or secreted their papers, or which produce false papers;

3. which have committed a breach of blockade;

4. which are considered to have been equipped for the use of the hostile State for military purposes;

5. in regard to which there is good reason to believe that they are scouting or carrying information for the benefit of the hostile State, or that their conduct is such as to assist the enemy in some other way;

6. which resist visit or search;

7. which sail under convoy of a ship of war of the hostile State."

This enumeration was parallelled by a series of Articles (40-49), summing up with regard to each of those seven items the consequences which the condemnation of the vessel had for the whole or part of the cargo on board.

I will deal with the subject-matters of this Part A (Substantive Prize Law) in seven sections, devoted respectively to (1) enemy property at sea; (2) enemy goods on neutral vessels, and reversely; (3) contraband of war; (4) blockade running; (5) unneutral service; (6) reserved trade, and a few other, controversial offences against the law of maritime prize, annexed thereto as (6 a) and (6 b); (7) offences consisting in the violation of various belligerents' policing rights, described in the following Part B (pp. 488-570).

The most obvious ground of confiscation is, of course, that the property concerned has enemy character. This ground will accordingly be dealt with first, in section 1 below.

On the elements which determine the character of a ship or her cargo, I refer to my preceding preliminary section II on the problem of the enemy or non-enemy character of prizes (pp. 203-272). The question of the confiscatability of a ship on account of her enemy character sometimes coincides with that of the susceptibility of a neutral ship to condemnation on the ground of her rendering unneutral service to the enemy. This instance of constructive enemy character will not, however, be examined in the present context. It can better be discussed in section 5, *infra*, pp. 456-470.

Section 1. ENEMY PROPERTY AT SEA. THE PRINCIPLE, ATTEMPTS TO ABOLISH IT, ITS GRADUAL MITIGATIONS

(a) *The principle of confiscatability of enemy property at sea*

The principle has been undisputed for centuries: enemy property at sea, both ships and cargoes, is liable to condemnation as prize. This applies especially to private property: public enemy property, in particular warships, fell to the captor State directly as spoils of war without any interference of a prize court being required. The principle was so obvious that initially no intervention by a court was strictly necessary, even in respect of private enemy property. Enemy ships and goods fell to the captor as a matter of course. It was only at a later stage and because control of the activity of privateers was imperative that a clear difference developed between State vessels and State goods, on the one hand, and private ships and cargoes, on the other. Whereas the seizure of private enemy vessels and cargoes came within the jurisdiction of admiralty courts, the capture of warships and other State vessels and State property on board usually remained outside prize jurisdiction and they automatically fell to the captor as booty of war.

(b) *Attempts to abolish the age-old rule*

Private property at sea has always, as a general rule, continued to be subject to confiscation. An attempt by the United States in its treaty with Prussia of 10 September 1785 (Martens, R[2], IV, 37; Parry, 49, 331), Article 23, to completely abolish the traditional rights of capture of private enemy property at sea, laying down that

> "... And all merchant and trading vessels employed in exchanging the products of different places, and thereby rendering the necessaries, conveniences, and comforts of human life more easy to be obtained, and more general, shall be allowed to pass free and unmolested; and neither of the Contracting Powers shall grant or issue any commission to any private armed vessels, empowering them to take or destroy such trading vessels or interrupt such commerce"

has had no lasting effect.

A corresponding provision can no longer be found in a subsequent treaty between the two States of 11 July 1799 (Martens, R[2], VI, 668; Parry, 55, 15):

the new initiative was obviously held to be too radical. The United States has nevertheless repeated its efforts on subsequent occasions in 1856, 1899 and 1907, again without success.

The idea was, however, also revived or advocated by other Powers, generally without gaining sufficient support.

In France, for instance, a proposal to the same effect, combined with a suggestion to abolish the institution of privateering, was in the same historical period (1792) made in a joint proposal of three committees of the revolutionary *Assemblée Nationale* to that Assembly, but it was also not accepted. See on the discussion and ultimate rejection of these suggestions De Pistoye & Duverdy's *Traité*, vol. I, pp. 5-21.

As far as Italy was concerned, I refer to the complicated history of her gradual transformation from a group of independent political entities into a unified kingdom covering the period 1848-1870, described in vol. II of this publication, pp. 94-96, and to the famous controversy amongst Italian lawyers over which of two juridical constructions of the events was the correct one: the theory of a sequence of fusions between members of the group (Anzilotti) or that of the growing paramountcy of a particular member of the group, Sardinia, over all its fellow members by their successive incorporation (Romano). This latter construction would seem to be in line with what happened in 1865-1877 with regard to the problem discussed here. On the Italian side the authorities laid down their intention in this field in a provision of the national *Codice per la marina mercantile*, enacted by *Reale Decreto* of 25 June 1865, No. 2560, to the effect that a general exemption from capture and confiscation would be granted in favour of the merchant fleet of all other Powers, potential future enemies of Italy, which would be prepared to grant the same treatment to Italian ships. This conditional exemption on the basis of reciprocity was laid down in Art. 211 of the *Codice* which provided as follows:

> "La cattura e la preda di navi mercantili di nazione nemica per parte delle navi da guerra dello Stato saranno abolite in via di reciprocità verso quelle Potenze, che adotteranno eguale trattamento a favore della marina mercantile nazionale.
>
> Il trattamento di reciprocità dovrà risultare da leggi locali, da convenzioni diplomatiche o da dichiarazioni fatte dal nemico prima del cominciamento delle ostilità."

On the outbreak of hostilities between Austria and Prussia, and between Austria and Italy in 1866 both German States demonstrated a corresponding preparedness to accept such exemption.

An Austrian *Verordnung* of 13 May 1866 (Martens, N.R.G.[1], XVIII, 308), referring to the Declaration of Paris of 16 April 1856 and professing the intention further to extenuate "die durch die Unsicherheit des öffentlichen Rechts gesteigerten nachtheiligen Einwirkungen eines Krieges auf den Handel zur See", on the footing of reciprocity, provided as follows (Art. 1):

> "Handelsschiffe und ihre Ladungen können aus dem Grunde, dass dieselben einem Lande angehören, mit welchem Österreich im Kriege ist, von österreichischen Kriegsfahrzeugen zur See nicht aufgebracht noch von österreichischen Prisengerichten als gute Prisen erklärt

> werden, wenn die feindliche Macht den österreichischen Handelsschiffen gegenüber die Gegenseitigkeit beobachtet."

The observance of reciprocity was provisionally presumed.

A Prussian *Erlass* of 19 May 1866 (*ibid.*, 309) provided likewise.

On the basis of these two declarations by the German States the Italian Minister of Marine on 20 June 1866 issued a notification (*ibid.*, 309) declaring that the abolition, on a footing of equality, of the capture of enemy merchant ships, as laid down in Art. 211 of the Italian Code, would take full effect in view of the Austrian attitude. This would seem to have been laid down in a bilateral agreement between Austria and Italy of July 1866, implemented on the Italian side by instructions to cruise commanders (see Godfrey Lushington's *Manual of Naval Prize Law* (1866), p. ix, and Thomas Erskine Holland's *Manual*, based on that of Lushington).

This renunciation by Italy of the exercise of the right of prize against enemy private property at sea on the footing of reciprocity was later re-incorporated into the new version of her *Codice per la marina mercantile* of 1877 as Art. 225, which in fact amounted to the renewal of a unilateral legislative offer to future belligerents on a world-wide scale, which went far beyond the grant of days of grace to enemy merchant ships caught in Italian harbours or at sea on the outbreak of hostilities. This new version of the *Codice* was enacted by a Law of 24 May 1877 (*Leggi e Decreti*, v. 52 (1877), pp. 2708 *et seq.*), later substituted by a "testo unico" approved by a *Reale Decreto* of 24 October 1877, No 4166. The later version of the *Codice* of 1877 was treated as an amended version of the pre-war *Codice* of 1865.

For a while the King of Prussia joined in this somewhat "epidemic" harmony by following the example of 1866 after the outbreak of the Franco-German War of 1870: on 18 July of that year, indeed, he enacted, in the name of the North-German Federation, a *Verordnung* (Martens, N.R.G.[1], XIX, 588), decreeing:

> "Französische Handelsschiffe sollen der Aufbringung und Wegnahme durch die Fahrzeuge der Bundes-Kriegsmarine nicht unterliegen",

except, of course, in case they should be equally subject to seizure and confiscation if they were neutral ships. This *Verordnung* was, however, rendered inoperative by a subsequent ordinance, issued from the German Headquarters at Versailles by the same King in his new capacity of German Emperor, on 19 January 1871 (*ibid.*, 590).

France, on her side, did not go as far as that: the French Minister of Marine, by a circular of 26 July 1870 (modified by a new circular of 13 August) merely sent out orders that assured protection to enemy merchant ships which had entered, or would enter, ports of the French Empire in ignorance of the state of war, and to those which had, prior to 19 July 1870, loaded, in enemy or neutral ports, cargoes which were destined for France and were for French account (*ibid.*, 588).

Suggestions to the same effect were made by China to Japan at the commencement of their war of 1894, but did not result in any agreement (comp. S. Takahashi, *International law as applied to the Chino-Japanese war* (Cambridge, 1899), pp. 9 *et seq.*).

As I have already reported in Chapter II, pp. 33 *et seq.*, one of the first activities of the *Institut de droit international* has consisted in advocating on its part in the same period the abolition of the old rule of condemnation of private enemy property at sea. This was done at its first session at The Hague in 1875 in the form of a *vœu* urging the world-wide adoption of the principle of inviolability of private enemy property in maritime war. This *vœu* was confirmed during its second session at Zürich in 1877 in far more imperative wording. However, these "conclusions" of the *Institut* have not produced the desired effect and sound now, after an experience of decades, like a *vox clamantis in deserto.*

The two sets of "conclusions" ran as follows:

"Traitement de la propriété dans la guerre maritime. Principes généraux. Conclusions adoptées à La Haye en 1875.

II. Il est à désirer que le principe de l'inviolabilité de la propriété privée ennemie, naviguant sous pavillon ennemi, soit universellement accepté dans les termes suivants, empruntés aux déclarations de la Prusse, de l'Autriche et de l'Italie en 1866, et sous la réserve ci-après, *sub* III:

'Les navires marchands et leurs cargaisons ne pourront être capturés que s'ils portent de la contrebande de guerre ou s'ils essaient de violer un blocus effectif et déclaré.'

III. Il est entendu que, conformément aux principes généraux qui doivent règler la guerre sur mer aussi bien que sur terre, la disposition précédente n'est pas applicable aux navires marchands qui, directement ou indirectement, prennent part ou sont destinés à prendre part aux hostilités.

Conclusions adoptées à Zürich en 1877.

I. La propriété privée neutre ou ennemie, naviguant sous pavillon ennemi ou sous pavillon neutre, est inviolable" [save the same exceptions, listed *sub* II, of the transport of contraband, participation or capacity of participating in the hostilities, and breach of blockade].

The *vœu* of the *Institut* in favour of the abolition of the capture and confiscation of private enemy property in naval war has been reconfirmed later in § 4 of its *Règlement des prises maritimes*, adopted at Turin (1882), but in a very weakened working:

"La propriété privée est inviolable sous la condition de réciprocité..."

The inviolability of private enemy property in naval war has remained ever since a *pium votum*. In the preamble of its *Manuel* of 1913 (Oxford) the *Institut* has had to acknowledge this:

"L'Institut de droit international, dans sa session de Christiania (1912), a déclaré firmement ses Résolutions antérieures, en ce qui concerne l'abolition de la capture et de la confiscation de la propriété privée ennemie dans la guerre maritime. Mais, constatant, en même temps, que l'acceptation de ce principe n'est pas encore acquise et considérant qu'aussi longtemps qu'elle ne le sera pas, le règlement du droit de capture est indispensable".

A Commission was charged with the task of elaborating provisions for both eventualities. The final *Manuel* of Oxford (1913) was as a consequence still based on the right of capture of private enemy property at sea.

(c) *Gradual mitigation of the principle of confiscatability*

Under general international law certain categories of enemy vessels or their cargoes had in the course of time gradually become exempted from confiscation, and that on account of either (a) their special character or position (such as small fishing vessels, hospital ships, postal correspondence, vessels and cargoes trapped by the outbreak of war), or (b) the circumstance that the cargo was being transported under a neutral flag. On the latter exemption see *infra*, section 2, *sub* c (at p. 299). The former group of exemptions, introduced by custom at different points of time, some already at an early stage, were ultimately sanctioned by the codification of 1907 in Conventions VI, X and XI of the Second Hague Peace Conference. I will confine myself in this introduction to a few historical data of a general character.

The general recognition of the principle of confiscatability entailed, especially in British prize courts, the consequence that, in accordance with the old maxim of English law which denied to enemy subjects the *jus standi in judicio* in British law courts, enemy claimants in prize cases, owners of captured ships and cargoes, were equally precluded, in principle, from claiming their release in British Admiralty Courts. See Story's *Notes on the Principles and Practice of Prize Courts*, edited by F.Th. Pratt in 1854, p. 21. It was only in circumstances in which they were in a position to invoke a special ground of exemption that their *jus standi* was admitted. Such special circumstances were, for example, their holding a British safe-conduct, pass or cartel licence.

The issue of the *jus standi* of enemy claimants was reconsidered much later by the British Prize Court, when it was adjudicating the cases of prizes made during the Crimean War. On that occasion Dr Lushington closely examined the practice which had been followed during previous wars, comp. his judgments concerning the fishing vessel *Froija* [1854] (Spinks, 37) and, especially, the *Panaja Drapaniotisa* [1856] (Spinks, 336; Roscoe, II, 560). The latter was a somewhat complicated case of a ship that had entered the port of Odessa under Serbian colours, had at first been detained by the Russian Government, thereupon been sold by her owner to a Greek merchant Iraclidi in order to defray certain expenses incurred, and was finally captured by a British warship when she was sailing from that port, then blockaded, under the Greek flag. The Queen's Advocate argued that the buyer was a merchant, resident at Odessa and therefore "totally ex-lex", having no *persona standi* (reference to the case of the *De Hoop* (Cornelis, Master) [1799] (1 C.Rob., 196; Roscoe, I, 104)). The buyer argued that he had a trading house in Greece and was only temporarily living in Odessa, and invoked in favour of the release of his vessel the precedents of the *Herman* [1802] (4 C.Rob., 228; Roscoe, I, footnote *a* at p. 270) and the *Jonge Klassina* [1804] (5 C.Rob., 297; Roscoe, I, 485). Dr Lushington found that according to an old judicial practice

> "a claimant must show first that he is entitled to a *locus standi* and is not tainted with the character of enemy and must therefore describe affirmatively the character on which he claims. He must state the place to which he belongs and negative all interests attaching to any person resident in the territory of the enemy".

As the affidavit was defective in this respect and nothing could be expected from further evidence, the *Panaja Drapaniotisa* was condemned as lawful prize.

The chances for enemy nationals of being received as claimants in a British or, at a later stage, an American or Japanese Admiralty Court improved concurrently with the introduction of new exemptions from capture in favour of enemy property, *e.g.*, because they were under the protection of the grant of days of grace at the commencement of hostilities, or of a developing practice of sparing small fishing vessels, and suchlike. The traditional ban on enemy subjects appearing before British and other prize courts was thus increasingly raised with regard to particular groups of claimants, especially at the very end of the pre-codification period about 1900. See the cases of

the *Pedro* (175 U.S. 354), the *Guido* (175 U.S. 382), the *Lola* (175 U.S. 677; Pitt Cobbett's *Cases* I, 1), the *Buena Ventura* (175 U.S. 384), the *Panamá* (176 U.S. 535) and the *Paquete Habana* (189 U.S. 453; Pitt Cobbett's *Cases* I, 1) during the Spanish-American War of 1898.

The principles of mitigation, thus gradually "received" by the international community by the way of judicial decisions and customary State practice up to the very end of the pre-codification period, were thus lifted over the threshold of the 20th century by the way of public and private codification, the former in 1907 at the Second Peace Conference at the Hague, the latter in 1913 at the Oxford session of the *Institut de droit international.* The classes of enemy vessels which the *Institut* considered to be conditionally exempt from condemnation were listed in Arts. 41-49 of its Oxford *Manuel des lois de la guerre maritime dans les rapports entre belligérants* of 1913. This list included hospital ships, cartel ships, vessels charged with a religious, scientific or philanthropic mission, vessels engaged in coastal fishing or in small local shipping, and vessels provided with a safe-conduct or a licence. Art. 53 prescribed a similar exemption in favour of postal correspondence on board an enemy vessel. See for details the data collected in the separate paragraphs 1-9 of the present section of Chapter III.

In addition to those exemptions, the *Manuel* in Arts. 36-40 stipulated certain attenuations of the principle in favour of public or private enemy vessels which (1) find themselves in a belligerent's port on the outbreak of hostilities; (2) have left their last port of departure before that outbreak and enter an enemy port in ignorance of the hostilities; (3) have been prevented by *force majeure* to leave the port of a belligerent within the term fixed by the latter; (4) have left their last port of departure before the outbreak of war and are met at sea in ignorance of the hostilities. These vessels should not be captured and confiscated, but might be "saisis, moyennant l'obligation de les restituer après la guerre sans indemnité, ou à être réquisitionnés, ou même à être détruits, à charge d'indemnité ...".

The attenuations thus stipulated by the *Institut* in 1913 went beyond the traditional leniency granted under the old customary practice to enemy vessels.

What is said here about exemptions in favour of certain groups of enemy vessels applied *mutatis mutandis* equally to enemy cargoes on board such vessels.

One further remark of a general character relates to a case of 1813 concerning the *Hope and other vessels* (1 Dodson, 226; Roscoe, II, 153). In that case the British prize court held that a consul or the admiral on a station had no power to exempt enemy property from capture *propria auctoritate*, but that such an invalid exemption might be ratified by the government of the captors *a posteriori*.

> "The instrument of protection, in order to be effectual, must come from those who have a competent authority to grant such a protection".

The case, reported by De Pistoye & Duverdy in vol. I of their *Traité* at p. 115, was therefore wholly abnormal. It related to the release of the English warship *Elisabeth* by the Governor of the enemy port of Spanish Habana because the ship had entered the harbour of that colony in a helpless state, battered as she was by storm. The Governor's gesture, however courteous, cannot be adduced as a valid precedent in law. See for further details of this extraordinary case the narrative by G.T. Raynal in book xiv, chapter 52 of his *Histoire philosophique et politique des établissements du commerce des Européens dans les deux Indes* (Paris, 1826).

After this introduction I will now pass on to a separate discussion in the following nine paragraphs of each of the individual grounds of exemption.

§ 1. *Vessels sailing under a belligerent licence*

Anxious to maintain as much as possible a strict, systematic order in exposing the subject matters of this publication, as I have endeavoured to do throughout my work, I must confess that I am in some doubt about the justifiability of inserting the issue of the effects of belligerent licences in the present section and paragraph. The reason is clear: the practice of granting licences for engaging in specific overseas transports favoured not only enemy, but allied, neutral and national ships and cargoes as well and should therefore, from a strictly systematic point of view, be treated under different headings, a method which, however, would unduly destroy the unity of the exposé. The system of the grant of licences in England specially related to navigation and the transportation of goods by national vessels, a subject matter which in that country was considered as coming under the international law of prize whereas in other systems of maritime law it rather belonged to the domain of municipal law. Such licences usually contained strict conditions, disregard of which invalidated them, as will be seen from the precedents surveyed below.

These reasons combined determined my decision to deal with licences in general in the present paragraph in spite of my systematic scruples.

What German lawyers in the period of the London Conference on Naval Warfare of 1908-1909 called *Lizenzfahrten* was something quite different from navigation under a belligerent licence in the sense of this paragraph. Whereas such a licence, in the British sense, to sail under British protection was intended to exempt the ships and cargoes concerned from condemnation in prize to which they would otherwise be liable, *Lizenzfahrten* had just the opposite effect of rendering them susceptible of such condemnation as a penalty for their engagement in a maritime trade which would otherwise be closed to them, especially trade between the motherland and the colonies of a belligerent State, or navigation along its coasts. This latter subject will be set out below in section 6, pp. 477 *et seq.*

The practice by belligerent States of permitting national, neutral or even enemy vessels to sail under their licence was in fairly frequent use according to Dodson's note under his report of the *Actaeon* case [1815] at p. 48 of his second volume and the examples of 1807 and 1809, cited in Judge Story's *Notes on the Principles and Practice of Prize Courts* (ed. F.Th. Pratt, London 1854) at pp. 170 *et seq.*

Decisions of British prize courts have dealt with many such cases and have on such occasions defined the limits within which the licences should be respected as a valid ground of exemption from condemnation.

Licences could, as will appear from the following examples, be granted for widely varying purposes:

to exceptionally permit trading with the enemy: the *Jonge Pieter* (Musterdt, Master) [1801] (4 C.Rob., 79; Roscoe, I, 353):

> "In all the cases that have occurred on the question—and there are many—it has been held indubitably clear that a subject cannot trade with the enemy without the special licence of government";

to permit the entry of, or sailing from, a blockaded port: the *Juno (No. 1)* (Beard, Master) [1799] (2 C.Rob., 116; Roscoe, I, 198); the *Mercurius*

(Harmens, Master) [1808] (Edw., 53; Roscoe, II, 15); the *Dankbaarheit* [1812] (1 Dods., 183; Roscoe, II, 146);

or to sail to or from any enemy or normally interdicted port: the *Courier* [1810] (Edw., 249; Roscoe, II, 50), a case complicated by the fact that permission to proceed had been given by the commander of a British cruiser without nautical necessity (Order in Council of 7 January 1807);

to import or export goods from or to an enemy country: the *Vriendschap* (Goverts, Master) [1801] (4 C.Rob., 96; Roscoe, I, 360); the *Jonge Klassina* [1804] (5 C.Rob., 297; Roscoe, I, 485); the *Johan Pieter* (Schwartz, Master) [1810] (Edw., 355; Roscoe, II, 80);

to purchase a vessel from an enemy country: the *Clio* [1805] (6 C.Rob., 67; Roscoe, I, 529);

to sail under any foreign, except the enemy (French) flag: the *Bourse, alias Gute Erwagtung* [1811] (Edw., 370; Roscoe, II, 94):

> "Where French interests clearly appear, the vessel cannot be protected by the mere absence of the French flag";

the *Jonge Clara* (Stevens, Master) [1811] (Edw., 371; Roscoe, II, 95).

The validity of a British licence, its protective effect and the conditions on which that effect depended were examined in various judgments, several of which hinged on the construction of the terms of the licence.

In the *Cosmopolite (No. 2)* (Mathison, Master) [1801] (4 C.Rob., 8; Roscoe, I, 326) Sir William Scott argued with regard to that construction:

> "A licence must be construed with the object of carrying out the intention of the grantor, and small deviations from the terms may be overlooked. But when a licence covers the export of certain enumerated kinds of goods, its protection will be confined to them only."

To the same effect the *Vriendschap* (Goverts, Master) [1801] (*supra*): barilla was not listed in a licence to export commodities to Rouen.

Neither does a licence to go to a specified harbour protect the ship if she is captured on a voyage to another port: the *Manly* [1813] (1 Dods., 257; Roscoe, II, 169).

The terms of a licence were sometimes interpreted in a liberal, sometimes in a more strict sense.

Lenient constructions or applications of licences are exemplified by the following judgments:

the *Mercurius* (Harmens, Master) [1808] (Edw., 53; Roscoe, II, 15): when a vessel, intending to call at a British port in order to obtain a licence to trade with a blockaded port, was captured before reaching that British port, the voyage to the blockaded port was held (in the terminology already then in use) not to be "continuous", and the vessel had to be restored.

In the leading case of the *Goede Hoop* (Pieters, Master) [1809] (Edw., 327; Roscoe, II, 73) Sir William Scott laid down the principles by which his decisions would be governed in questions arising on the capture of vessels sailing under British licence. The licence granted to this Oldenburg vessel, dated 15 November 1808, had—owing to a French embargo and adverse wind—expired on the day of sailing from La Rochelle to Hull (29 June 1809). It authorized her only for a term of six months to sail from French to British ports. The President explained the practice as follows:

> "These licences owe their origin to the general prohibition which declares it to be unlawful for the subjects of this country to trade with the enemies of the King without his permission, for a state of war is a state of interdiction of communication. In former wars this prohibition was attended with very little inconvenience as the greater part of the countries in the neighbourhood remained neutral, and presented to the belligerents various channels of communication, through which they obtained from each other such commodities as they stood in need of."

In the case under consideration he decided for a liberal construction of the licence because "there was clear *bona fides* in the holder";

the Prussian *Cousine Marianne* [1810] (Edw., 346; Roscoe, II, 85), captured on a voyage from Barcelona to London; when a licence is granted to a vessel that bears every appearance of being foreign (*in casu* from Mecklenburg), no inquiry into the ownership of the cargo or the possibility of British interests in her is necessary;

the *Johan Pieter* (Schwarz, Master) [1810] (Edw., 354; Roscoe, II, footnote at p. 80): a licence to bring cargo from Charente in France to England, dating from 1808, was held still to be valid in 1810 because the delay in using it in time was caused by the detention of the ship in Charente by the French authorities;

the *Vro(u)w Cornelia* (Dykstra, Master) [1810] (Edw., 349; Roscoe, II, 87): a licence to transport cargo in one vessel was held also to protect its transportation in two;

the Prussian *Jonge Frederick* [1810] (Edw., 357; Roscoe, II, 90): a licence to load cargo for a voyage from Great Britain to a foreign port also covers her return voyage with the same cargo, if it proved to be unmarketable there;

the *Frau Magdalena* [1811] (Edw., 367; Roscoe, II, 93), a Danish vessel that had a licence for a direct voyage from St. Petersburg to London, but had touched at an intermediate port for orders, and was subsequently captured, was held liable to condemnation unless she proved to have left that port with an identical cargo;

the American *Hector* [1811] (Edw., 379; Roscoe, II, 102): a licence to go to a port of the Kingdom extended also to Ireland;

the *Anna Maria* (Wolgahayer, Master) [1813] (1 Dods., 209; Roscoe, II, 151): her neglect to fulfil the obligation under the licence to call at London before sailing to Rouen was excused by the fact that the Admiral had ordered her to go to Wingo Sound;

the *Aeolus* [1813] (1 Dods., 300; Roscoe, II, 173): despite the expiration of a licence and a refusal of the authorities to renew it, it nevertheless benefitted the holder because he had used due diligence;

the *Wohlforth* [1813] (1 Dods., 305; Roscoe, II, 176): after the original cargo had been spoiled by unavoidable accident, the master took in a fresh cargo of the same kind after the time which the licence was granted had expired; its protection was not thereby forfeited.

The verdict was, on the other hand, more severe in the following cases:

the *Planter's Wensch* [1803] (5 C.Rob., 22; Roscoe, I, 414): a licence granted before the conclusion of peace had no validity after peace was signed in a subsequent war;

the *Jonge Klassina* [1804] (5 C.Rob., 297; Roscoe, I, 485): a licence to import goods from enemy Holland into England, granted to a person in his capacity of a British merchant, was invalidated by the fact that the licensee was likewise the exporter from Holland and by his bond to restore the goods to their owner after the conclusion of peace;

the Mecklenburgh *Catherina Maria* (Brathering, Master) [1809] (Edw., 337; Roscoe, II, footnote at p. 160): a licence to proceed in ballast to a port in the Baltic and there to load a cargo for England did not protect this vessel because she was captured on an outward voyage with cargo; the allegation by the master of compulsion exercised upon him by French authorities in Rostock, even if reliable, was in any case inadmissible as a defence;

the Lübeck *Speculation* [1810] (Edw., 344; Roscoe, II, 83): the licence which was produced appeared to have no bearing on the ship concerned;

the Danish *Minerva* (Davidson, Master) [1811] (Edw., 375; Roscoe, 98): the stipulation that the ship should touch at London was a fundamental condition, disregard of which invalidated the protection of the licence;

the Russian *St. Ivan* [1811] (Edw., 376; Roscoe, II, 100): and the *Vro(u)w Deborah* [1812] (1 Dods., 163; Roscoe, II, 144): a licence obtained subsequently to the date of capture, did not offer protection;

the *Seyerstadt* [1813] (1 Dods., 241; Roscoe, II, 159): even violence by a hostile government against a licensed ship was no justification for contravening the essential terms of a British licence;

the *Gute Hoffnung* [1813] (1 Dods., 251; Roscoe, II, 168): when a licence granted to British merchants for the import of a cargo from a belligerent country did not protect the property of an enemy unless it contained the words, in reference to the goods, "to whomsoever the property may appear to belong": as her licence contained no such customary clause, an inquiry into the ownership of the cargo was held to be necessary.

Also cases of fraud are reported, *e.g.*:

the *Louise Charlotte de Guldeneroni* [1813] (1 Dods., 308; Roscoe, II, 177) was a case of fraudulent alteration of a licence to trade with an enemy country by a change of dates therein; this brought with it that even a *bona fide* holder for value was not protected:

> "The present case may be one of great hardship upon an innocent individual, but I cannot take upon myself to say that a licence which has been vitiated in so material a point can be deemed valid".

The *Actaeon* [1815] (2 Dods., 48; Roscoe, II, 209, with footnote *a* at p. 210) was an American (enemy) vessel that, after having sailed in January 1813 from Norfolk (Virg.) to Cádiz with a shipload of flour on board shipped under a British licence, subsequently returned to Boston under a new licence granted by the British Minister in Spain. After successive boardings by British warships she was finally captured by the British man-of-war *La Hogue* and set on fire on 12 May 1813. Sir William Scott recognized the owners' claim to compensation so that the further proceedings only concerned the fixation of the measure of restitution, rendered difficult by the fact that, before her destruction, the papers of the *Actaeon* had been put aboard another captured American vessel which was later, before she was carried into Halifax, recaptured by the American naval forces.

This case law was continued during the Crimean War under an Order in Council of 29 March 1854 in favour of Russian ships which should have sailed from any foreign port bound for any British port prior to that date.

The operation of that Order was examined by the Prize Court in the case of the *Fenix, otherwise Phoenix* [1854] (Spinks, 1; Roscoe, II, 238): the text of the Order ran as follows:

> "Her Majesty, being compelled to declare war against his Imperial Majesty the Emperor of all the Russias, and being desirous to lessen as much as possible the evils thereof, is pleased, by and with the advice of her Privy Council, to order, and it is hereby ordered, that Russian merchant vessels, in any ports or places within her Majesty's dominions, shall be allowed until the tenth day of May next, six weeks from the date hereof, for loading their cargoes and departing from such ports or places; and that such Russian merchant vessels, if met at sea by any of her Majesty's ships, shall be permitted to continue their voyage, if on examination of their papers it shall appear that their cargoes were taken on board before the expiration of the above term: Provided, that nothing herein contained shall extend or be taken to extend to Russian vessels having on board any officer in the military or naval service of the enemy, or any article prohibited or contraband of war, or any despatch of or to the Russian Government.
>
> And it is hereby further ordered by her Majesty, by and with the advice of her Privy Council as aforesaid, that any Russian merchant vessel which, prior to the date of this Order, shall have sailed from any foreign port bound for any port or place in her Majesty's dominions, shall be permitted to enter such port or place, and to discharge her cargo, and afterwards forthwith to depart without molestation; and that any such vessel, if met at sea by any of her Majesty's ships, shall be permitted to continue her voyage to any port not blockaded.
>
> And the right honourable the Lords Commissioners of her Majesty's Treasury, the Lords Commissioners of the Admiralty, and the Lord Warden of the Cinque Ports, are to give the necessary directions herein as to them may respectively appertain."

The case concerned a Russian barque, belonging to the Finnish port of Björneborg, which was in England in December 1853. Owing to the unsettled state of affairs between England and Russia, the agent of the owners abandoned a voyage to Lisbon and ordered the master instead to sail to Copenhagen with a cargo of coals to be delivered there, it being at the time impossible for the ship to enter her home port Björneborg on account of the ice. The vessel sailed from Hartlepool on 15 February 1854 and put into the harbour of Copenhagen where she delivered the coals for the English fleet on 10 March. War between England and Russia was declared on 29 March 1854, on which, also, the Order in Council was published "allowing Russian merchant vessels, in any ports or places within Her Majesty's Dominions, until the tenth of May, six weeks from the date thereof, for loading their cargoes, and departing from such ports or places". The ship sailed on 10 April in ballast and was captured during that further voyage to her home port. She was condemned as an enemy ship not being within the exceptions of the Order in Council, which appeared to have been misunderstood, for the opinion prevailed at Copenhagen that Finnish ships might proceed to their own ports unmolested up to 10 May.

A footnote at p. 238 of vol. II of Roscoe's collection of reports lists a series of decrees concerning ten other Russian vessels in similar conditions, published by Spinks, but not republished by Roscoe.

Later instances in which the exemption from capture granted by the Order in Council was invoked by Russian shipowners were those of

the *Argo* (Stenman, Master) [1854] (Spinks, 52; Roscoe, II, 294), captured by an English revenue cruiser off the harbour of Cork when sailing under Russian colours, bound on a voyage from Havana to Cork (Ireland) for orders;

the *Odessa* (Wicklund, Master) [1854] (Spinks, 208; Roscoe, II, 462), which had sailed under neutral colours but was in fact Russian: an enemy vessel entering a British port and claiming the protection of the Order in Council must enter under enemy, not under neutral colours; and the protection did not extend to enemy vessels beyond a reasonable time for the discharge of their cargo and their departure;

the *Neptune* (Keetley, Master) [1855] (Spinks, 281; Roscoe, II, 520): a Russian ship that came into a British port under the protection of the same Order in Council, lost that protection if, instead of departing forthwith after discharging her cargo, she remained in that port and was sold there to a British merchant.

I do not enter into this particular aspect of the issue of belligerent licences any further here because it is partly a duplicate of the subject discussed in § 3 *infra*, to which I may therefore refer.

What in British case law was known as the grant and use of licences was parallelled in France by the grant and use of *sauf-conduits*. De Pistoye and Duverdy mention in vol. I of their *Traité des prises maritimes* two judgments of the *Conseil d'Etat* concerning *Le Gioseppino contre le Brave* and *Le Diablotin contre le San Antonio*, and further in vol. II the older decisions

Le navire la Dame Jestok contre le Neptune [*an* VII] (p. 87), a case of transport of a cargo of wine (contraband) to Hamburg in conformity with a Decree of 1 August 1795, in which the prize was released in appeal;

Le Vrouw Jelks contre le Neptune [*an* IX] (p. 88), a case of capture of a vessel protected by a safe-conduct, followed in appeal by her release, in which the captor was condemned to the payment of damages; and

Le Hasard contre l'Elisabeth [*an* X] (p. 88; appeal, p. 328), a case in which a safe-conduct granted in express terms for entering a French harbour was held to be implicitly equally valid for leaving it, an exemption that also applied to her cargo.

Licences, much later, still played a minor rôle in the prize practice of Japan during her war with Russia at the end of the pre-codification period. See Takahashi's report on the cases of the *Australia* (p. 625) and the *Montara* (p. 633), under the heading of his section III at p. 625 "Vessels employed by the hostile government or navigating with the enemy's license".

The system of the levy of "convooien en licenten" in the United Netherlands was a means of providing the Confederation with the necessary financial resources.

The examples quoted above were licences granted to an individual, and made out to him in his name. But a licence could also be implied in a document of a general character.

An exemption of enemy prizes from condemnation as such was indeed in England sometimes decreed not by an individual licence but by a general Order in Council, which then needed interpretation. One of the older instances in which this exemption was claimed, but unsuccessfully, on the strength of such an Order in Council, was that of the *La Flora* [1805] (6 C.Rob., 1; Roscoe, I, 515). It concerned a cargo of Spanish wool, consigned to a merchant of the United Kingdom, seized on its way to England via the port of Emden. The Order in Council of 4 September 1803 directed the restitution of Spanish wool "consigned to this country". The cargo concerned was decreed not to be free under that Order because the immediate destination of the cargo had alone to be regarded:

> "A circuitous ulterior destination to [England], either in the same ship or in other ships, [cannot] be considered in law as one identical consignment [and as bringing] the case within the provisions of the Order in Council. How far it may be proper to allow further relaxation, or what considerations may interfere with such an extension of the indulgence, is a question of policy which ... it would not become this Court to decide ... One consequence of such an extension may be easily foreseen, that if such a circuitous voyage was to be allowed, Spanish wools might with great security find their way into France and Holland for the supply of the manufactures of those countries".

What was at issue in another case, that of the Swedish vessel *Success* [1812] (1 Dods., 131; Roscoe, II, 140), sailing from Gothenburg to Malmö in the coasting trade of Sweden, was an Order in Council of 7 January 1807 with an additional Royal Instruction of 20 June 1810, allowing neutrals to trade with an enemy country except between ports from which British ships were excluded. As a moiety of the ship appeared to be Swedish property and the other moiety to belong to British subjects, the ship was decreed not to be protected by the Order in Council: a ship so trading must be wholly the property of neutrals.

§ 2. *Cartel ships*

Another category of ships which enjoyed a certain measure of protection in naval warfare were enemy cartel ships. A number of them played a role in the beginning of the 19th century. See the case of the *Daifjie* (*Duifje?*) [1800] (3 C.Rob., 139; Roscoe, I, 273), one of two Dutch (enemy) ships, taken in May 1800 on a voyage from Texel to Vlissingen, while sailing there for the purpose of taking on board some exchanged prisoners of war to convey them to England. The ships were claimed as sailing under the protection of a cartel, although cartel ships were generally only exempt when, sailing under enemy flag, they actually carried prisoners of war or returned from that service. Despite this irregularity the two Dutch vessels were restored to the owners because they were found to have been sailing in perfect good faith:

> "It is a practice of no very ancient introduction among the States of Europe to exchange prisoners of war in this manner [*i.e.*, by cartel ships]; it has succeeded to the older practice of ransoming, which succeeded to the still more ancient practice of killing or carrying them into captivity... It is highly proper that [this practice] should be conducted with very delicate honour on both sides, so as to leave no ground of suspicion that a practice introduced for the common benefit of mankind should be made a stratagem of war or become liable to fraudulent abuse. I presume the terms of cartel are usually settled by agreement between the two States. In the present instance we are not informed what these terms of agreement are... Judging without such information, and on general principles, I must lay it down as clear that ships are to be protected in this office *ad eundum et redeundum* both in carrying prisoners and returning from that service. Whether there is any stipulation usually made as to the species of ships to be employed does not appear... A particular circumstance in this case is, that these vessels were not actually employed as cartel ships nor taken *in trajectu* either way, either going or returning, between the ports of the two belligerents; they were not in the actual discharge of those functions, which would entitle them to protection *eundo et redeundo.*"

Other cases were those of *La Gloire* [1803] (5 C.Rob., 192) and the *Carolina* [1807] (6 C.Rob., 336), cited by Roscoe in a footnote *a* at pp. 278-279 of vol. I. These ships were likewise restored to their owners, the *La Gloire* notwithstanding the fact that the Government of France had acted in bad faith on some earlier occasion in detaining a vessel sent regularly as a cartel ship from England to a port in France, and the *Carolina* despite the fact that the contracts for cartel ships had been entered into prior to the outbreak of war, because

> "the actual existence of a war is not essentially necessary to give effect to them, but that it will be sufficient if they are entered into prospectively and in expectation of approaching war."

On the other hand, the *Venus*, a British ship that had sailed to Marseille under cartel for the exchange of prisoners, was condemned [1803] (4 C.Rob., 355; Roscoe, I, 403) because she had engaged in trade:

"Certain it is that the conduct of ships of this description cannot be too narrowly watched ... Cartel ships are subject to a double obligation to both belligerent countries not to trade. To engage in trade may be disadvantageous to the enemy, or to their own country; both countries are mutually engaged to permit no trade to be carried on under a fraudulent use of this intercourse; all trade must, therefore, be held to be prohibited, and it is not without the consent of both governments that vessels engaged on that service can be permitted to take in any goods whatever."

It is this category of ships that was listed by Japan in Art. 35, *sub* 4, of her Regulations relating to Capture at Sea of 7 March 1904, as "vessels employed in connection with the exchange of prisoners".

§ 3. *Days of grace*

As remarked at the end of § 1, *supra*, p. 287, the subject of "days of grace" covers part of the field already surveyed in that paragraph under the heading "Belligerent licences". This is one reason why I will refrain from entering into it in any detail again here. But there is another and more important reason for that: the issue of days of grace belongs so typically to the laws of war that it has already been dealt with in my volume IX on those laws (pp. 294-295).

It is indeed now sanctioned and detailed in Convention VI of 1907 relating to the regime of enemy merchant ships met at sea, or lying in an enemy port at the beginning of hostilities.

This exemption from condemnation is already very old practice. It was originally laid down in special provisions of many bilateral treaties of commerce or peace, already discussed in Chapter IV of Part IX-A (vol. IX) of this publication on the laws of maritime war, section 2, pp. 294-295. Those provisions allowed foreign merchants and other subjects free departure with their belongings from their country of sojourn in case of war between that country and their own. The treaties concerned used to limit that freedom of departure to certain, varying maximum terms (*délais de faveur* or "days of grace"), *e.g.*, six or nine months. Comp. the following instances:

The Netherlands-Portugal, 6 August 1661 (Dumont, VI[2], 366; Parry, 6, 375), Article 16: two years' term for vessels to leave the enemy country;

The Netherlands-France, 27 April 1662 (Dumont, VI[2], 412; Parry, 7, 139), Article 13: six months' term granted to the respective subjects to depart;

The Netherlands-England, peace treaty of Breda of 21/31 July 1667 (Dumont, VII[1], 44; Parry, 10, 231), Article 32: "spatium semestre";

The Netherlands-France, treaty of peace of Nijmegen of 10 August 1678 (Dumont, VII[1], 350; Parry, 14, 365), Article 15: six months, and treaty of commerce of the same date (Dumont, VII[1], 357; Parry, 14, 399), Article 37: nine months;

The Netherlands-Sweden, treaty of commerce of Nijmegen of 2/12 October 1679 (Dumont, VII[1], 437; Parry, 15, 331), Article 2: nine months;

The Netherlands-France, treaty of commerce of Rijswijk of 20 September 1697 (Dumont, VII[2], 386; Parry, 21, 371), Article 14: nine months;
and from a much later date during the 18th century:

England-Russia, treaty of commerce of 20 June/1 July 1766 (Martens, R^2, I, 390; Parry, 43, 365), Article 12:

"Si ce qu'à Dieu ne plaise, la paix venoit à se rompre entre les deux H.P.C., les personnes, les vaisseaux et les marchandises ne seront pas détenues ni confisquées, mais il leur sera accordé pour le moins le terme d'un an pour vendre, disposer ou emporter leurs effets, et se retirer où bien leur semblera ...";

France-Hamburg, separate Article 1 annexed to their treaty of commerce of 1 April 1769 (Martens, R^2, I, 619; Parry, 44, 255): nine months;

France-United States, treaty of 6 February 1778 (Martens, R^2, II, 587; Parry, 46, 417): six months.

The practice of the grant of days of grace was sometimes also referred to by municipal courts, see, *e.g.*, the case of *Lindo v. Rodney* of 1782 (Douglas, 612, note).

The 19th century saw a revival of the old practice, *inter alia*, during the Crimean War: French *Décret impérial* of 27 March 1854 (De Pistoye and Duverdy, *Traité*, vol. II, pp. 467, 471).

At the beginning of a war the belligerents could, and usually did *de facto* relieve the subjects of their enemy of their enemy character by granting them "days of grace" during which their ships would temporarily be exempted from capture. I have dealt with that subject in the context of the laws of war in vol. IX-A of this publication, pp. 294-295, and will briefly return to it in the present volume in another context, *viz.*, in Part A, section 1, *sub c* (Mitigations of the principle of confiscatability).

Belligerents were not in the habit of granting days of grace when the hostilities were *de facto* opened, not by a declaration of war but by the issue of a general Order of Reprisals.

Days of grace have still played a significant rôle in the case law of the Japanese prize courts during the war with Russia, the last possible occasion on which the old practice could re-emerge at the very end of the pre-codification period. Their grant was laid down in a Proclamation by a Japanese Imperial Ordinance No. 20 of 9 February 1904, inserted in Hurst & Bray, II, as Appendix C at p. 445. Its text was to the following effect:

"Art. 1. Russian merchant, ships which happen to be in any Japanese port or harbour at the time of the issue of these rules shall be at liberty, till the 16th February 1904, to discharge or load cargo, and depart.

Art. 2. Russian merchant ships which have left Japan, in accordance with the provision contained in the foregoing Article, and the papers of which, properly certified by the Imperial Japanese authorities, show clearly that the said ships discharged or loaded their cargo and left the ports or harbours of Japan before the aforesaid date, and that they are on their way to the nearest Russian port, leased port, or port of destination, shall not be liable to capture; provided that this measure shall not apply if they have touched at a Russian port or a leased port on their way.

Art. 3. Russian merchant ships which have left a foreign port or harbour for a Japanese port or harbour before the 16th February may enter a Japanese port or harbour,

> discharge their cargo at once in the port or harbour, and leave the country. Russian ships leaving Japan under the conditions mentioned in the above sentence shall be treated in accordance with Article 2.
>
> Art. 4. The provisions of this Ordinance shall not apply to Russian merchant ships carrying articles the export of which is forbidden. Persons, articles, and documents which are contraband of war shall be excluded from the above rules."

I reproduce it here not only because it was the last of the period, but also the most controversial owing to the restrictive construction which the Japanese prize courts have put upon it and the torrent of judgments to which it has given rise.

The fact that in 1904 Japan made prizes prior to a declaration of war and that the Japanese prize courts felt bound to honour the specious grounds on which their Government glossed over the objectionable character of their premature surprise attack (comp. *supra* under General Issues, section 2, p. 175), placed them in a difficult position vis-à-vis the Imperial Ordinance No. 20. That Ordinance was binding upon them and was obeyed in principle, but its implementation was cut down to the strictest possible construction which its literal text permitted (*ibid.*, II, 8). The "grace" was in fact not bestowed on vessels which (the references are to pages in Hurst & Bray, II)

were bound for enemy ports: the *Manchuria (No. 1)* (52);

were bound for an enemy-occupied port (in Corea): the *Ekaterinoslav* (8-9), *Kunst and Albers' claim to cargo ex-Mukden* (35);

were captured before publication of the Ordinance: the *Rossia* (39);

were the property of a State institution such as the Chinese Eastern Railway Company: the *Mukden* (12), the *Argun* (46);

were employed by the enemy government: the *Kotik* (95-96);

were engaged in deep sea fishing: the *Michael* (80), the *Alexander* (86), the *Lesnik* (92) and the *Kotik* (95);

sailed not carrying cargo: the *Rossia* (39).

Moreover, the prize courts emphatically cautioned more than once against the mistaken idea that there was an analogy with the corresponding favour granted to neutral contraband carriers, such as the *Hermes* (50): an ill-advised parallel between an enemy merchant ship and a neutral contraband carrier induced Russian shipowners to lay down the proposition that the simple fact that their ship had left harbour prior to the outbreak of hostilities created a claim to her exemption from condemnation apart from any days of grace. The prize courts have soon disabused the claimants by holding that no consequences in their favour could be derived from that fact as regards the ship's liability to confiscation. In that respect there existed a marked difference from the corresponding case of a neutral ship that had put to sea with a contraband cargo before the outbreak of hostilities: their fate was affected neither by ignorance of the war nor by shipment prior to its outbreak. This was considered self-evident.

In this respect the Japanese attitude has shown a remarkable resemblance to that which I still have reported already on the attitude of the British Prize Courts during World War I, which likewise showed a clear tendency to confine the exemption within the narrowest possible limits. Comp. on that case law my preceding Part IX-A (vol. IX), section 2, p. 295.

§ 4. *Small fishing vessels, etc.*

By an ancient usage among civilised nations, originating centuries ago and gradually ripening into a rule of international law, coastal fishing vessels, pursuing their vocation of catching and bringing-in fish, were little by little exempted from capture as prize of war. But as the binding force of that usage was often contested at the bar, the courts proceeded to trace the history of the exemption in their judgments, referring to a great variety of sources: early treaties entered into between different European States, edicts and ordinances issued by European governments, an old compilation on the "usage and customs of the sea", certain later treaties entered into by the United States and the practice followed in previous wars, all of which went to show the observance of such a usage in actual State practice. Its interruption as between Great Britain and France during the wars of the French Revolution was only temporary, and the exemption was renewed in England by Orders in Council of 1806 and 1810. Since then no examples were found of a denial of the rule by Great Britain or any other European nation. Japan, the last State to join the European society of nations, on the outbreak of her war with China in 1894, issued an ordinance exempting "all boats engaged in coast fisheries" and the parties in the Russo-Japanese War of 1904-1905 also respected the time-honoured principles.

For the majority of the American Supreme Court in the cases of the *Paquete Habana* and the *Lola* [1899] (175 U.S. 677) it was abundantly clear that

> "at the present day, by the general consent of the civilized nations of the world, and independently of any express treaty or other public act, it is an established rule of international law, founded on considerations of humanity to a poor and industrious order of men, and of the mutual convenience of belligerent States, that coast fishing vessels, with their implements and supplies, cargoes and crews, unarmed, and honestly pursuing their peaceful calling of catching and bringing-in fresh fish, are exempt from capture as prize of war. The exemption, of course, does not apply to coast fishermen or their vessels, if employed for a warlike purpose; or in such a way fishing on the high seas, taking whales or seals, or cod, which are not brought fresh to market; or in which their seizure was required by military necessity. The exemption rule was in its capacity as a rule of international law one which, in the British view, Prize Courts administering the law of nations were bound to take judicial notice of and to give effect to, even in the absence of any treaty or public act of their own Government in relation to the matter,"

a doctrine laid down in various judgments, such as the English precedent of *Regina v. Keyn* (2 Ex.D. 63), *West Rand Central Mining Co. v. R.* [1905] (2 K.B., 391), and the American decisions in *Hilton v. Guyot* (159 U.S. 113) and *Scotia* (14 Wallace, 170).

The general attitude of France towards the problem was no different. There also fishing vessels owned by enemy subjects used to enjoy since early days a limited protection from condemnation in prize. Particularly illuminating historical details on the subject were included in the conclusions of the Commissary of the Government Dufaut on the case of the Portuguese *La Nostra Segnora de la Piedad y Animas,* captured by the French privateer *La Carmagnole* (*Traité des prises maritimes*, I, 331 *et seq.*):

> " Le monument le plus ancient ... que nous ait conservé sur ce point le Code des prises est une ordonnance du 1er octobre 1692, rendue sous le règne de Louis XIV. A cette époque, la neutralité parfaite de la pêche était reconnue. L'ordonnance du 1er octobre élognait, à la vérité, de nos parages les pêcheurs anglais, mais elle accordait à ceux qui y seraient rencontrés un sauf-conduit de huit jours pour retourner chez eux; et cette mesure, que les circonstances justifiaient, n'avait pour but que de se garantir de l'espionnage auquel, sous prétexte de la pêche, se livrait un enemi, qui préparait déjà le bombardement de nos places maritimes, exécuté en 1674".

During the American War of Independence the King of France, in a letter to the Admiral of 5 June 1775, expressing his desire to temper the calamities of the Franco-English War by looking after the interests of the fishermen, continued as follows:

> " J'ai pensé que l'exemple que je donnerais à mes ennemis, et qui ne peut avoir d'autres principes que les sentiments d'humanité qui m'animent, les déterminerait à accorder à la pêche les mêmes facilités auxquelles je consentirais à me prêter. En conséquence, j'ai donné ordre à tous les commandants de mes bâtiments, aux armateurs et capitaines des corsaires, de ne point inquiéter, jusqu'à nouvel ordre, les pêcheurs anglais et de ne point arrêter leurs bâtiments, non plus que ceux qui seraient chargés de poisson frais, quand même ce poisson n'aurait pas été pêché à bord de ces bâtiments; pourvu toutefois qu'ils ne soient armés d'aucune arme offensive, et qu'ils ne soient pas convaincus d'avoir donné quelques signaux qui annonceraient une intelligence suspecte avec les bâtiments de guerre ennemis".

The French Commissary continued his historical survey with an additional review of various precedents, of 1709—an agreement between the municipal authorities of Calais and the commander of the Downs to completely exempt their respective fishing-fleets from interference—, of 1780—the annulment by the *Conseil* of an ordonnance of the lower court which had approved the ransoming of the fishing vessel *Jean et Sara*, a decision of the *Comité du Salut Public* of *an* III to return to England, without reciprocity, a number of English fishers detained in France—, and about 1800—a convention between a Spanish and a French Admiral to the effect that no acts of hostility should be committed against their respective fishing fleets, either in the Strait of Gibraltar or in the North Sea. On the authority of all these precedents the capture of the Portuguese fishing vessel *La Nostra Segnora de la Piedad* was invalidated.

The group of exemptions now sanctioned and detailed in Chapter II of Convention XI of The Hague of 1907—relating to boats exclusively destined for coast fishery, or for services of small local navigation, and to vessels charged with religious, scientific or philanthropic missions (see *infra*, § 6)—

dates as a group from much later in the history of prize law than the three mentioned in §§ 1-3 *supra*.

As to the most important category of the three, the following can be stated. Scottish fishing vessels were still seized in 1543 and brought into French ports. The exemption regarding this category of vessels was seldom incorporated into bilateral treaties, but was agreed upon by France and England in an agreement of June/July 1801 (Martens, R^2, VI, 505, 515). It was to a certain extent also respected by the prize courts. Comp., *inter alia*, the judgments concerning fishing vessels rendered by American prize courts in the cases of the *Pedro* and several others during the Spanish-American War of 1898. The United States Court was, however, still divided on the issue in the cases of the *Paquete Habana* [1898] and the *Lola* [1899] (175 U.S. 677), but the reason of the dissent between the judges lay in another field: was an American court empowered to apply rules of international customary law without any incorporation of such rules into the municipal law of the United States? Pitt Cobbett has devoted a detailed analysis to this constitutional problem in his *Cases on International Law* (6th ed., I, 1); a minority in the Court denied such power (*per* Justice Gray).

Vessels belonging to the two other groups of exempted ships—vessels engaged in small local navigation and in religious, charitable or scientific missions—have only acquired protection at a later period and have, as far as I know, in former times hardly played a rôle in the application of the law of prize.

The States General of the United Netherlands have repeatedly issued *placaten* prohibiting the sale of captured fishing vessels: 28 February 1678, 22 October 1705 and 22 May 1706 (*Groot Placaatboek*, V, 1565). They were renewed on 7 November 1803 after a temporary abolition by *Arrêté* of 28 February 1801.

Contrary to a condemnatory judgment against the Dutch fishing vessel *Jonge Jeroen* [1804] (Roscoe, I, at p. 480), Sir William Scott released another fishing vessel, the *Liesbet van den Toll* [1804] (5 C.Rob., 283; Roscoe, I, 479), formerly a Dutch vessel, purchased by a native Dutchman who had become by domicile a subject of Prussia, and which had since been employed in fishing off the Dutch coast. The vessel was held not to have been infected with an enemy character by the fact that, although her owner usually sold his cargoes of fish at sea to English ships, he had once or twice resorted to Dutch ports, because he had done so not for the purpose of selling them there, but merely to procure bait.

During the Crimean War declarations of the Emperor of France of 27 March and 15 April 1854 and corresponding declarations of the other Allied Governments established certain exemptions, for humanitarian reasons, from condemnation in favour of local Russian fishing vessels engaged in the exchange of foodstuffs and fresh fish between the peasants of the coastal area of Arkhangel and those of Finmarken. One of those vessels, the *Dwina*, was captured in the White Sea by a French brig under suspect circumstances. This case was brought before the *Conseil impérial des prises* and later reported by De Pistoye and Duverdy under the heading *La Dwina contre le Beaumanoir* [1854] (*Traité*, II, 501). The ship had availed herself of the authorization she thought was granted her by those declarations to carry provisions from the coast of Arkhangel to Finmarken across the blockading line. However, the claim to that exemption was denied, *inter alia*, because it did not apply to ships *de haut-bord*.

When the prize courts refused to recognize the exemption it was usually on the ground that the fishing vessels involved did not answer the description of small fishing boats and were actually engaged in deep-sea fishing.

That was also the ground on which, still at the end of the pre-codification period, the Japanese prize courts dismissed the claims of the Russian owners of the fishing vessels the *Michael* (Hurst and Bray, II, 80), the *Alexander* (II, 86), the *Lesnik* (II, 92) and the *Kotik* (II, 95).

§ 5. *Hospital ships*

The exemption, now sanctioned and detailed by Convention X of 1907 relative to the adaptation of the principles of the Convention of Geneva to maritime war in respect of hospital ships (Martens, N.R.G.[3], III, 630; Parry, 205, 359), is also of much later date. The exemption from capture in favour of such ships was not yet recognized, even by the Red Cross Conference of 1868. Comp. on this unhappy negative decision, initiated by France, but subsequently reversed at France's own suggestion, Part IX-A (vol. IX) of this publication, Chapter VI, section 6, pp. 302-303.

It goes without saying that hospital ships could not lay claim to this exemption if they abused their special status by assisting the enemy. This was decided in the case of the *Johanna Emilie* [1854] during the Crimean War (Spinks, 12; Roscoe, II, 252), and again, half a century later (1904), by the Japanese Prize Court in the case of the Russian hospital ship *Aryol* (Russian pronunciation of *Orël*; Takahashi, 620; Hurst & Bray, II, 354):

> "A hospital ship is only exempt from capture if... she is engaged solely in the humane work of aiding the sick and the wounded... Yet, her action in communicating the orders of the Commander-in-Chief of the Russian Second Pacific Squadron to other vessels during her outward voyage with the squadron, and her attempt to carry persons in good health,... members of the crew of a captured British steamship, to Vladivostok, were evidently acts in aid of the military operations of the enemy".

What the authorities in the Japanese Navy themselves deemed permissible to do against a foreign hospital ship became apparent, again forty years later, in respect of the Netherlands hospital ship *Op ten Noort* which they first converted to a troop transport and later, in order to cover up this violation of the Conventions, sank in their country's territorial sea on the eve of the capitulation (1945). This incident was, again fifteen years later

(1960-1961) submitted to an arbitral tribunal, called "Property Commission", in virtue of the multilateral peace agreements with Japan of San Francisco (1951). See on this arbitration the *International Law Reports*, vol. 30, pp. 515 *et seq.* and pp. 525 *et seq.*

§ 6. *Ships sailing for scientific, charitable or religious purposes*

Already before the Second Hague Peace Conference of 1907 in its Convention No. XI (Chapter II, Article 4) established an exemption from confiscation in favour of ships "chargés de missions religieuses, scientifiques ou philanthropiques", Japan inserted such an exemption in Article 35, *sub* 2 of her Regulations of 7 March 1904 relating to Capture at Sea. As far as I know, there had not yet been at that time concrete examples of prize ships, declared by any prize court to be so exempt. Article 35, moreover, added to the three categories mentioned *sub* 2 one more category (*sub* 3), *viz.*, that of vessels "used for lighthouse purposes", and (*sub* 4) adopted the far older customary rule in favour of cartel ships under the name "vessels employed in connection with the exchange of prisoners".

§ 7. *Postal correspondence*

Special attention was paid already at an early date to the desirability of introducing the principle that postal correspondence deserves freedom from seizure, as is sanctioned since 1907 by Chapter I (Articles 1 and 2) of Convention XI of The Hague relative to certain restrictions of the exercise of the right of capture in maritime war. The Swedish and Netherlands Governments, recognizing already in their treaty of commerce of 26 November 1675 (Dumont, VII[1], 316; Parry, 14, 41), Article 15, that freedom of correspondence was essential for freedom of trade, indeed agreed in a related field that postal communications through each other's country should thenceforth be restored unimpeded and that they would persuade their respective allies to follow their example.

The *Institut de droit international* endorsed the principle of the inviolability of postal correspondence in Article 53 of its *Manuel* of Oxford (1913), which did not, however, extend the principle to vessels carrying such correspondence:

> "La correspondance postale, quel que soit son caractère officiel ou privé, trouvée en mer sur un bâtiment ennemi, est inviolable, à moins qu'elle ne soit à destination ou en provenance d'un port bloqué.
>
> L'inviolabilité de la correspondance postale ne soustrait pas les paquebots-poste aux lois et coutumes de la guerre sur mer concernant les navires en général. Toutefois la visite n'en doit être effectuée qu'en cas de nécessité avec tous les ménagements et toute la célérité possibles.
>
> S'il y a saisie du navire sur lequel la poste est embarquée, la correspondance est expédiée avec le moins de retard possible par le capteur."

In § 17 of its *Règlement* of 1882 (Turin) the *Institut* had still limited the right to visit such vessels:

"Lorsque le navire à visiter est un paquebot-poste, il ne sera pas visité, si le commissaire du gouvernement dont il porte le pavillon, se trouvant à son bord, déclare par écrit que le paquebot ne transporte ni des dépêches ni des troupes pour l'ennemi, ni de la contrebande de guerre pour le compte ou à destination de l'ennemi".

Japan adopted that rule in Art. 34 of her Regulations of 7 March 1904 relating to Capture at Sea in the following wording:

"In visiting or searching a neutral mailship if the mail officer of the neutral country on board the ship swears in a written document that there are no contraband papers in certain mail bags, those mail bags shall not be searched. In case of grave suspicion, however, this rule does not apply."

(Takahashi, p. 786; Hurst & Bray, vol. II, Appendix B, p. 430).

In its *Argun* decision (Takahashi, p. 573; Hurst & Bray, vol. II, p. 46) the Sasebo Prize Court, answering the petitioners' plea *sub* 3 that "the steamship carried mail and ought, therefore, to be released, in accordance with the opinion of authorities on international law", decided adversely as follows:

"In regard to the enemy's mail ships, it is recognized in International Law that they are liable to capture, unless there be a special agreement between the belligerents. The argument of the advocate is nothing more than an opinion of scholars and cannot as yet be adopted."

On the risk for the belligerents that a too indulgent attitude towards mailships might further their chance of conveying "contraband documents" or even "contraband persons" to the enemy and on the reasonableness of distinguishing ordinary mailships from mailships engaged in a specially organized voyage see *infra*, section 5 on Unneutral service, p. 456.

§ 8. *Personal property of the master, crew or passengers of an enemy vessel*

Although such personal property was often exempted from condemnation (comp. already chapter 276 of the *Consulado de Mar* quoted below, p. 303), a distinction was still made in 1854 between the personal property of an enemy master and that of a neutral master, see the *Aina (No. 2)* (Spinks, 12; Roscoe, II, 251): unlike the case of neutral masters, the Court could not restore personal property to an enemy master without the consent of the captors, which in that case was actually given.

The French *Conseil des prises* specified the rule concerning the personal property of neutral masters in the case of the Swedish vessel *Economie* [*an* IX] (De Pistoye and Duverdy, I, 359) as follows:

"C'est un principe déjà consacré par plusieurs décisions du Conseil que les pacotilles des gens de l'équipage sont exemptes de connaissements, pour la raison bien naturelle que les propriétaires suivent leur propre pacotille, et qu'aucun tiers n'est dans le cas de les réclamer à leur destination."

French judgments consistently recognized the principle that the personal effects of the master of a prize must be restored to him. I cite from a later period [1854] the cases of the *Orione* (*ibid.*, II, 499) and the *Christiane* (*ibid.*, II, 502).

§ 9. *Enemy goods under neutral flag*
The last category to be mentioned in this context is the exemption from confiscation of enemy goods carried on a neutral ship. This special exemption is, however, of such great historical importance and so closely related to the reverse principle of the freedom from confiscation of neutral goods carried on an enemy ship, that I will discuss both situations together in a separate section 2 of this Chapter, *infra*, pp. 299 *et seq.*

Section 2. ENEMY GOODS ON NEUTRAL SHIPS AND NEUTRAL GOODS ON ENEMY SHIPS

Introductory

In this section 2 I will combine the two converse situations of (*a*) enemy goods on board neutral ships and (*b*) neutral goods on board enemy ships, because they are historically so closely interwoven that a sharp distinction of their treatment in two separate sections would be artificial.

This chapter of old prize law is indeed the most complex of all. The problem has dragged itself along from the very inception of naval warfare onward up to the Crimean War, and even after the Declaration of Paris of 1856 it has re-entered the practice of prize law by the backdoor of belligerent reprisals (comp. on this latter subject this Chapter *sub* C, section 3, below, pp. 595-610).

Even a sharp distinction between the varying prize law systems is difficult to make because they were often adopted in different combinations. I will nevertheless start from a grouping of the systems according to the three main leading principles, which I will provisionally indicate as those of (*a*) *separatorum separata fit ratio*; (*b*) unfree ship, unfree goods, and (*c*) free ship, free goods.

The systems *sub* (*b*) and (*c*) were often combined so that the total result was fairly evenly balanced. This was, however, not the case of a combination of system (*b*) with a denial of system (*c*). This combination will be set out *sub* (*d*). It would be a happy circumstance if it were possible to find a red thread through the labyrinth of the historical development of this chapter of international prize law, but it is impossible to sketch a picture of a constant and consistent development because there is none. Small wonder that the opinions of writers differ or are inconclusive even on the question where and when exactly one or the other of these systems was in force. Legal history has in actual fact always exhibited a tangle of opposing principles and this has remained so throughout the centuries until the middle of the 19th century when the main belligerents were at long last, at the beginning of the Crimean War, forced by the looming conflict between themselves and with the neutral States to acquiesce in a compromise. This was first laid down in separate parallel unilateral declarations of England and France on 28/29 March 1854 and finally sanctioned by the famous multilateral Declaration of Paris of 16 April 1856 (Martens, N.R.G.[1], XV, 791; de Clercq, VI, 91; Parry, 115, 1), which in a few short paragraphs, couched in the simplest of wordings, wiped out at one stroke the centuries-long antagonism between the conflicting historical systems (see *supra*, Chapter II, *sub* B). But before that end was reached, a long and winding road of contrary legal principles had to be covered.

The fact that innocent neutral-owned goods were often carried on ships sailing under the flag of a belligerent State and that, inversely, goods belonging to subjects of a belligerent State were carried on ships sailing under neutral colours, has indeed in the course of history given rise to the emergence of these differing systems of prize law.

The solutions which the belligerents have adopted during the Middle Ages in order to solve the problem of how to treat the cases of the interlacement of enemy and neutral interests in the same vessel have varied considerably. In his *Collectanea Maritima* of 1801 Sir Christopher Robinson has brought together masses of data which prove how uncertain the general situation was.

Thus, quoting an Anglo-Portuguese treaty of 1294 (footnote at p. 36), he had to conclude that it did not distinctly state whether a neutral ship conveying enemy's property was liable to confiscation or not:

> "If so, the Ordinance of 1 Edw., A.D. 1294 is in this respect more agreeable to the French Code than the principles of English Courts of Prize, in which, according to Sir H. Martin (1640), it had never been the practice to condemn neutral ships for having enemy's goods on board; but the freight of the enemy's goods condemned was always paid" (Rymer, II, 632).

A mandate of Edward III of 1327 (footnote at p. 37) testifies to the observance of the milder English rule: during the then existing Anglo-Scottish war a Flemish ship that had been taken and brought to Yarmouth was restored to the owners, with a *proviso* concerning enemy's goods (Rymer, IV, 328). A subsequent Anglo-Flemish treaty of 4 August 1370 (Rymer, VI, 659), however, enjoined the subjects of Flanders to abstain entirely from carrying goods of enemies of England in their ships. This was repeated in subsequent Anglo-Flemish treaties of 1417, 1446, 1467 and 1495/6, just as, for that matter, in an Anglo-Danish treaty of 1490.

In her relations with Spain England showed corresponding leniency towards the converse case of entanglement of interests, *viz.*, the presence of neutral Spanish goods on board an enemy's ship (p. 37 and note at p. 38): pursuant to their treaty of 1351 the goods were to be restored (Rymer, V, 717). Chr. Robinson observed on this point:

> "The general principle of law and common sense, that restores neutral goods in an enemy's ship according to the fact of property, gives a corresponding right to take enemy's goods in a neutral vessel (rule of the Consolat). The Anglo-Spanish treaty is said to have deviated from the common principle, and to have granted further privileges to neutral ships in this respect."

An enlargement in 1357 of the terms of the truce with Spain of 1351 established for the first time, according to Mr Schlegel, the rights of the neutral flag for a period of twenty years, on the condition of reciprocity, "de quelconque pais et gens lesdites marchandises seront", but Chr. Robinson was uncertain whether that stipulation referred to enemy produce or to enemy property. But, however that might be, the author considered it as a temporary and special agreement contrary to the tenor of the whole system of Spanish prize laws before and since. The same clause was, indeed, not re-inserted in the subsequent Anglo-Spanish treaties of 1414, 1430 and 1467.

During her war with Spain in 1373 England issued a mandate of restitution of a neutral Portuguese ship similar to that of 1327: the ship was restored subject to a *proviso* regarding enemy's goods (Rymer, VII, 3).

The French practice of confiscation of neutral vessels because they had on board the goods of an enemy was, pursuant to a footnote at pp. 119 *et seq*., introduced for the first time by an *Ordonnance* of 1453 (Art. 42), which deviated directly from the old practice of the Consolat. Sir Leoline Jenkins doubted, however, if this rigid rule had ever been applied in actual practice. He referred to a decision of the *Parlement de Paris* of 1592 which released a ship from neutral Hamburg with enemy goods on board; the Parliament said that opposition to the rule had been voiced from various sides, and that it had been abrogated by disuse; it had never been applied by the courts in the course of forty-nine years and had, for that matter, repeatedly been moderated with specific restrictions. Nonetheless the infection rule was formally re-incorporated into the *Ordonnance de la Marine* of 1681 and considered as binding, subject to exceptions in favour of specified countries. The infection rule was not eliminated from French prize law until 1778, but even this statement is disputed.

The contradictory systems

With reference to my preceding introductory remarks, I will now enter into a separate description of the contradictory systems.

(*a*) *Treatment of the goods according to their own nature*

The oldest system was that adopted by the 14th century Mediterranean (Spanish) *Consulado de Mar* which for a long time has governed the relations between belligerent States and States not involved in the war and their subjects. It was based on a sharp distinction between enemy and non-enemy property ("property of friends"), a distinction which entailed that vessels belonging to subjects of a State at war with the captor State and cargoes belonging to such subjects (hereafter called "enemy" vessels and goods) were liable to confiscation, even if the latter were carried on board a neutral ship, but that, conversely, neutral vessels and neutral cargoes, even when they were carried on board an enemy ship, were exempt from confiscation: *separatorum separata fit ratio*. This was the system, implied in the rules of the *Consulado de Mar* (see for their text below), to which England has long continued to cling in principle, in so far as she did not enter into agreements with other Powers that embodied divergent principles, as she did, for example, with the Republic of the United Netherlands in 1668 and 1674 (see *infra*, p. 323). British prize courts, also, would seem to have continued to adhere in principle to the *Consulado de Mar*. But there are reasons for doubt.

According to Reginald Marsden, at p. ix of his Introduction to vol. I of his *Documents relating to the Law and Custom of the Sea* (1915) in the *Publications of the Navy Records Society* (vol. XLIX), it is indeed not quite clear whether in the old days goods of friends carried in a ship of the enemy were released or whether they shared in England the fate of the ship. In most cases they probably shared that fate, but there are instances of restoration of the goods to their owner by order of the King. Reference is made (at p. 42) to a case of 1296 in which neutral cargo captured in a Flemish (enemy) ship was restored, but Spanish (enemy) goods in the same ship were awarded to the captors. On the other hand, the presence of enemy goods in a ship of friends entailed the condemnation of the ship in a case of 1337 (at p. 66, also taken from the *Close Rolls*, 11 Ed. III, pt. 2, m. 32).

As far as can be retraced, the oldest custom observed by seafaring nations during the 13th and 14th centuries admitted the double principle that enemy merchandise was subject to confiscation even if laden in a ship of "friends" (*i.e.* non-enemies), and that merchandise belonging to friends was to be respected even if laden in an enemy ship. Pardessus, in footnote 4 at p. 303 of vol. II of his *Collection de lois maritimes* asserts that a treaty of 1221 between the cities of Pisa and Arles enunciated the principle that neutral cargo on an enemy ship was free, but that assertion is due to an error: it is indeed incompatible with the text of the said treaty, as given by Muratori, *Antiquitates italicae medii aevi*, vol. IV, col. 398:

> "Et quod Januensium vel aliorum publicorum inimicorum Pisanae Civitatis, si cum Arelatensibus forte in aliquo navigio inventum fuerit a Pisanis, ipsi Arelatenses non facient suum, nec suo nomine defendant. Et si forte aliquis Arelatensis cum Januensi, donec guerra inter Pisanos et Januenses fuerit, a Pisanis inventus fuerit in eorum navibus vel lignis eundo vel redeundo, licet Pisanis hominibus Arelatensibus et res eorum tanquam Januensium offendere et capere et capta retinere et non reddere nec reddi facere. Et propterea haec pax et concordia non rumpatur."

Geffckens' conclusion on the scope of this provision in vol. IV of Von Holtzendorff's *Handbuch des Völkerrechts*, p. 572, was:

> "Also die befreundete Flagge deckt kein Gut des Feindes, und ein Unterthan des befreundeten Staates mit seiner Habe wird auf einem feindlichen Schiffe als Feind behandelt."

Other treaties, of the 14th century, quoted by Pardessus *loco cit.*, are those concluded by King Edward III of England with the sea towns in Biscaya and

Castile in 1351 and with Portuguese sea towns in 1353 (Rymer, III, Part 1, pp. 71, respectively 88).

According to Travers Twiss (*Black Book of the Admiralty*, vol. I, p. 29, footnote 5), the right of confiscating enemy's goods on board neutral vessels seems to have been recognized, both by Christian and Mohammedan Powers, in the early part of the twelfth century. Pardessus, in vol. II of his work (Introduction at p. 122) cites a case in which the Pisans, being at war with Genoa, seized a cargo of alum on board an Egyptian vessel, as being the property of Genoese merchants, but gave it up to the Sultan of Egypt, when it was proved to be neutral property. This customary system of *separatorum separata fit ratio* was, however, often modified by treaty or encroached upon in actual practice. It was laid down in chapter ccxxxi (276 in another numbering) of the *Consulado de Mar*, which ruled that, on the one had, cargo of friends carried on an enemy ship, should be released to its owners, but that, on the other hand, the captor was entitled to demand from the master of a neutral vessel met at sea the delivery of enemy goods on board. The text of this chapter ran in the French translation by Pardessus (II, pp. 303 *et seq.*) as follows:

> "Lorsqu'un navire armé allant ou revenant, ou étant en course, recontrera un navire marchand, si ce dernier appartient à des ennemis, ainsi que sa cargaison, il est inutile d'en parler, parce que chacun est assez instruit pour savoir ce qu'on doit faire, et, dans ce cas, il n'est pas nécessaire de donner de règle [comp. chapters clxxxv-clxxxvii].
>
> Mais, si le navire qui sera pris appartient à des amis, tandis que les marchandises qu'il porte appartiennent à des ennemis, l'amiral du navire armé peut forcer et contraindre le patron du navire qu'il aura pris à lui apporter ce qui appartiendra aux ennemis, et même il peut l'obliger à le garder jusqu'à ce qu'il soit en lieu de sûreté; mais il faut pour cela que l'amiral ou un autre pour lui ait amarré le navire pris à sa poupe en lieu où il n'ait pas crainte que des ennemis le lui enlèvent; à la charge, néanmoins, par l'amiral de payer au patron de ce navire tout le fret qu'il aurait dû recevoir s'il avait porté la cargaison là où il devait la décharger, ou de la manière qui sera écrite sur le registre. Si, par événement, on ne trouve point de registre, le patron doit être cru à son serment sur le montant du fret...
>
> Si le navire appartient à des ennemis et sa cargaison à des amis, les marchands qui s'y trouvent et à qui la cargaison appartiendra en tout ou en partie, doivent s'accorder avec l'amiral pour racheter à un prix convenable et comme ils pourront, ce navire qui est de bonne prise: et il doit leur offrir une composition ou pacte raisonnable, sans leur faire supporter aucune injustice. Mais, si les marchands ne veulent pas faire un accord avec l'amiral, celui-ci a le droit d'amariner le navire et de l'envoyer au lieu où lui-même aura armé, et les marchands sont obligés de payer le fret de ce navire de même que s'il avait porté leur cargaison au lieu pour lequel elle était destinée, et rien de plus.
>
> Si, par événement, les marchands éprouvent quelque lésion en raison de la violence que l'amiral leur aura faite, celui-ci ne doit leur répondre de rien, puisqu'ils n'ont pas voulu faire d'accord avec lui pour le rachat de ce navire qui était de bonne prise; encore par une autre raison, parce que souvent le navire vaut plus que les marchandises qu'il porte.
>
> Mais cependant, si les marchands ont annoncé le désir de faire un accord, comme il est déjà dit ci-dessus, et que l'amiral s'y soit refusé par orgueil ou par esprit de jactance, et, comme il a été dit, emmène avec les marchands la cargaison sur laquelle il n'avait aucun droit, ceux-ci ne sont pas obligés de payer de fret, en tout ni en partie, à cet amiral; au contraire, il est obligé de leur rendre et restituer tout le dommage qu'ils éprouveront ou qu'ils auront possibilité d'éprouver par l'effet de cette violence.

> Mais, lorsque le navire armé se trouve avec le navire capturé en un lieu où les marchands ne pourraient pas réaliser l'accord qu'ils ont fait, si ces marchands sont des hommes connus, et tels qu'il n'y ait point à craindre l'inexécution de l'accord fait avec eux, l'amiral ne doit point leur faire violence; et s'il leur fait violence, il est obligé de payer le dommage qu'ils souffriront: mais si, par événement, les marchands ne sont pas des gens connus, ou ne peuvent pas payer le rachat, l'amiral peut agir comme il a été dit."

As regards the first of the two situations (enemy goods on board a ship of friends), this long chapter ccxxxi (276) of the *Consulado de Mar* thus lays down the captor's right of requiring the neutral vessel to carry her cargo "infra praesidia", that is, to a place where it was safe *prima facie* from recapture, on condition that an agreement on the subject be reached between him and the managing owner, and it gives further rules for the cases

that no agreement can be reached between the admiral and the ship-owner on the amount of the freight due (comp. on this subject further III *sub* C, section 6, B, *infra* p. 630);

that the ship-owner or mariners claim that they have personal property on board;

that the ship-owner refuses to carry the enemy goods to a place of safety: in such a case

> "the admiral may sink or cause to be sunk that vessel, if he chooses to do so, saving always that he ought to save the lives of those on board of her; and no local authority [*i.e.*, probably, no tribunal of a third power] can constrain him to give an account, if any complaint or demand may be anywhere made against him. It is, however, to be understood in such a case that all the cargo which is on board of that ship or vessel or the greater part of it is enemy's property".

As regards the second of the two situations (goods of friends on board an enemy ship), the chapter regulates the case

that the merchants are unwilling to make an arrangement with the admiral: in such a case

> "the said admiral may and ought to take the said ship or vessel in tow, and to carry her to the place where she was fitted out, and the said merchants are bound to pay as much freight to the said ship or vessel as it had carried the said cargo which belongs to them to the place where it ought to have carried it, and otherwise not. And if by chance the said merchants shall be damnified or aggrieved on account of the constraint which the said admiral has applied to them the said admiral is not responsible to them for anything, because the said merchants were not willing to make the said arrangement...; and further for another reason because sometimes the ship or the vessel is worth more than the merchandise which it carries";

and the inverse case that the merchants are desirous to make the arrangement, but the admiral is not willing to make it "from arrogance or pride which is in him" and carries the cargo, in which he has no right, away with him forcibly, together with the merchants; in such a case the merchants were not bound to pay any freight either in whole or in part to the said ship, nor further to the admiral, but on the contrary the admiral was bound to make good and restore all the loss which the merchants should sustain from the use of force, or expect to sustain for any reason.

The question of whether a neutral flag should protect the property of an enemy was consequently decided in chapter 231 of the Consulate of the Sea in the negative. This principle of *separatorum separata fit ratio* seems to have prevailed throughout the cities of the Mediterranean in the 13th century and to have been generally adopted by the traders of the northern and western seas in the 14th century (Travers Twiss, *Black Book*, vol. III, p. 539, footnote).

As far as later British case law on the issue is concerned, I will cite a couple of judgments from the first decades of the 19th century:

the *Catharina Elizabeth* (Le Grange, Master) [1804] (5 C.Rob., 232; Roscoe, I, 458): neutral (American) goods on an enemy (French) ship were in principle to be restored. The solution was more complicated when the master resisted to the captor: then the same rule applied if he was an enemy, so that the neutral cargo was to be released; if, however, the master was a neutral who attempted to rescue the prize, the cargo was liable to confiscation;

the *Fanny* (Lawton, Master) [1814] (1 Dods., 443; Roscoe, II, 202): if a neutral placed goods on an enemy ship which he might presume would be defended by force, he thereby adhered to the belligerent concerned and lost the benefit of his neutrality; the neutral property, if captured, was liable to condemnation, and on recapture was subject to salvage.

These judgements would seem to prove that it had remained an old English jurisprudential tradition to maintain the basic principles of the Consulate of the Sea.

The famous report concerning Great Britain's conflict with Prussia over the Silesian loan (comp. on this conflict Part IX-B (vol. X) of this publication, p. 38), dated 18 January 1753 (*B.F.S.P.*, vol. 20 (1832-1833), at pp. 889 *et seq.*), in which the British Law Officers formulated the Rules on Admiralty jurisdiction, etc. in time of war which in their opinion obtained in the middle of the 18th century, sanctioned in its two introductory rules the two principles surveyed in the present section, still reflecting the main rules of the Consulate of the Sea:

> "Goods of an enemy on board the ship of a friend may be taken.
> Goods of a friend on board the ship of an enemy ought to be restored."

The ensuing rules of this rudimentary codification formulated other familiar principles concerning the seizure of contraband goods going to the enemy, though the property of a friend; the requirement of adjudication of the prize in a regular proceeding by the Court of Admiralty of the State to which the captor belongs, judging by the Law of Nations and treaties; the requirement of good faith in respect of the data contained in the ship's papers; the throwing of papers over board; *etcetera*.

(*b*) *The system of "unfree ship, unfree goods"*
A different system was that introduced by France in the second half of the 16th century. Under that system, contrary to the rule laid down in the Consulate of the Sea, the intertwinement of neutral and enemy interests in the same ship operated to the detriment of neutral owners of goods carried in an enemy ship. This system was first embodied in an Ordinance of King François I of 1543 (Article 42) and subsequently confirmed by an Edict of Henri III of 1584 (Article 69) (see for the text below *sub* (*d*), p. 327). It has since constantly remained the law of France, except during the period 1650-1681, initiated by Art. 6 of a Declaration of 1 February 1650 by which neutral goods on an enemy's ship were declared free (De Pistoye-Duverdy, I, 316). The severe rule of 1584 was, however, reintroduced under the régime of titre IX, livre III, of the *Ordonnance de la Marine* of Louis XIV of 1681, Art. 7 of titre IX of which was especially directed against national and allied property on enemy ships:

"Les marchandises de nos sujets et alliés, qui se trouveront dans un navire ennemi, seront pareillement de bonne prise" (De Pistoye-Duverdy, I, 313).

The exact legal position under the French rules was, however, disputed.

This system of "unfree ship, unfree goods" was one of the manifestations of the doctrine of *infection hostile*: "robe d'ennemi confisque robe d'ami". That doctrine had, for that matter, various possible fields of application—the reason why one has to be on one's guard against misunderstanding when there is talk of the abolition of the old doctrine of hostile infection at a later historical period. It may indeed also be applied to various other cases (on which see below under (*d*)).

Many treaties made an express exception to the rule "unfree ship, unfree goods" for cargoes loaded before the outbreak of war, or within a limited period of time following it. Such treaty provisions were included, *inter alia*, in the Netherlands-French treaty of commerce of Nijmegen of 10 August 1678 (Dumont, VII[1], 357; Parry, 14, 399), Art. 22; the Netherlands-Swedish treaty of commerce of Nijmegen of 2/12 October 1679 (Dumont, VII[1], 437; Parry, 15, 331), Art. 22, and the Netherlands-French treaty of Rijswijk of 20 September 1697 (Dumont, VII[2], 386; Parry, 21, 371), Art. 17. I quote below as an example the full text of the provision obtaining in the treaty of 1678, which also mentions the fate of contraband goods on board:

"Il a été en outre accordé & convenu, que tout ce qui se trouvera chargé par les sujets de S.M. en un Navire des Ennemis desdits Seigneurs Etats, bien que ce ne fût Marchandises de Contrebande, sera confisqué, avec tout ce qui se trouvera audit Navire, sans exception ni réserve; mais d'ailleurs aussi sera libre & affranchy tout ce qui sera & se trouvera dans les Navires appartenans aux Sujets du Roi très Chrétien, encore que la charge ou partie d'icelle fût aux Ennemis desdits Seigneurs Etats, sauf les Marchandises de Contrebande ... Et pour éclaircissement plus particulier de cet Article, il est accordé & convenu de plus, que les cas arrivant que toutes les deux Parties, ou bien l'une d'icelles, fussent engagées en

Guerre, les Biens appartenans aux Sujets de l'autre Partie, & chargez dans les Navires de ceux qui sont devenus Ennemis de toutes les deux, ou de l'une des Parties, ne pourront être confisquées aucunement, à raison ou sous prétexte de cet embarquement dans le Navire Ennemi; & cela s'observera non seulement quand lesdites Denrées y auront été chargées avant la Déclaration, pourvu que ç'ait été dans les tems & les termes qui s'ensuivent; à savoir, si elles ont été chargées dans la Mer Baltique, ou dans celle du Nord, depuis Terneuse en Norvège, jusques au bout de la Manche dans l'espace de quatre semaines, etc."

The solution of this issue by Art. 43 of the London Declaration on Naval Warfare of 1909 amounts to the substitution in this case of the sanction of "confiscation moyennant indemnité" to that of confiscation pure and simple.

Art. 22 of the treaty of commerce and navigation of Nijmegen of 1679 between the Netherlands and Sweden began with the following provision:

"Conventum praeterea est, ut quicquid compertum fuerit oneratum à dictis Subditis & Incolis Suecicis in Navibus hostium Dominorum Ordinum Generalium, quamvis Mercimonia non sint prohibita, Fisco addicatur cum omnibus caeteris, quae in praefata Navi invenientur, sine ulla exceptione vel reservatione, & vice versa liberum & relaxatum sit quicquid vehetur in Navibus Subditorum suae Regiae Majestatis quamvis onus aut pars ejus sit hostium Dominorum Ordinum Generalium, exceptis Mercibus interdictis".

Provisions of this tenor, in almost identical wording, reappear in treaties of a much later period, thus proving their continuity. See the very detailed provision of Art. 23 of the French-Netherlands treaty of commerce, navigation and marine, signed at Versailles on 21 December 1739 (Wenck, I, 414; Rousset, *Recueil*, XIV, 447; Parry, 35, 459).

Although France had upheld the principle "unfree ship, unfree goods" until 1778, save for a short period when it lapsed, this application of the doctrine of hostile infection was often expressly abandoned, at least for a limited period of time, by bilateral treaties, and then only on condition of reciprocity. This relaxation of the rule will be explained below *sub* (*d*).

A corresponding relaxation of the "infection hostile" was stipulated during the peculiar régime of capitulations between Western Powers and the Ottoman Porte. Art. 4 of the Franco-Turkish Capitulation of 28 May 1740 (Noradounghian, I, 277; Strupp, *Urkunden*, I, 48; de Clercq, I, 21) laid down that both French merchants and their sea-borne goods would be free even if carried on enemy vessels:

"Si les marchands français étaient embarqués sur un bâtiment ennemi, pour trafiquer (comme il serait contraire aux lois de vouloir les dépouiller et les faire esclaves, parce qu'ils se seraient trouvés dans un navire ennemi), l'on ne pourra, sous ce prétexte, confisquer leurs biens ni faire esclaves leurs personnes, pourvu que ... etc.".

The rule "unfree ship, unfree goods" was, however, not peculiar to France alone, as it also headed the series of provisions enacted by the British Government in 1665 and 1672 during England's second and third naval wars with the United Netherlands. The text of Article 1 of both Orders in Council concerned ran as follows (Pratt-Lee, p. 249):

> "that where the ship or vessel brought in as prize shall belong to the States of the United Provinces, or any of their subjects or any inhabiting with them, in such case no claim shall be admitted for the goods, but both ship and goods shall receive one and the same judgement, and both be judged and condemned as good and lawful prizes [except for their carrying letters of safe-conduct]."

A special legal problem consisted of the presence of private neutral property on board an enemy public vessel. Was such property to be treated as war booty just as the vessel, or was it governed by the normal rules of prize law? The only judgment of Lord Stowell which seems to have had a bearing on this question was that concerning the *Fanny* [1814] (1 Dods., 443; Roscoe, II, 202), in which such private property was held to share the fate of the carrying vessel. In that case the Prize Court argued that

> "if a neutral places goods on a belligerent ship of force, which he may presume will be defended by force, he thereby adheres to the belligerent and loses the benefit of his neutrality. The neutral property, if captured, is liable to condemnation".

A contrary American precedent *Talbot v. the Ship Amelia* (4 Dallas, 34), which preserved neutral property from condemnation when carried on an enemy vessel, was held to be much too "indistinct" to be followed as a precedent (Roscoe, II, at p. 205, with footnote *a*). In any case this solitary *Fanny* judgment can hardly be considered as a British doctrine and has certainly not been adopted by later legal writers as the true rule of the law of nations. At least, that was the conclusion reached by the German *Prisenhof* in a case arising during World War II concerning a large number of gold ingots rescued by the German army in 1940 from the Dutch *Pilotboat No. 19* (*A.D.* 1919-1942, Case No. 167) in which case it was held that there would be no question of their being automatically qualified as booty of war, but that their legal character had to be determined in the usual way. A corresponding problem arose in the case of the *Visurgis* and the *Siena*, reported in *A.D.* 1938/1940, Case No. 94, arising from a collision between two vessels, one of which had been chartered by a foreign government.

In the case of the Swedish ship *Alte Freundschaff* against the privateer *Le Hardy* [*an* X] (De Pistoye and Duverdy, II, 43) the French *Conseil des prises* was faced with a similar problem, *viz.*, that of the fate of a neutral cargo on board not of an enemy ship, but of a neutral ship that was liable to condemnation on other grounds. This cargo was restored to its owners.

Even the United States could not bend the traditional French doctrine of infection in its Treaty of Amity and Commerce with France of 6 February 1778 (Martens, R^2, II, 587, 603; Parry, 46, 417). Whereas Art. 25 (23) of that treaty upheld the principle of "free ship, free goods", Art. 16 (14) reaffirmed the principle of infection of neutral goods by the enemy character of the carrying vessel. The numbering of the articles of this treaty is somewhat confusing, owing to the fact that on the occasion of the exchange of the instruments of ratification two articles were cancelled by the Contracting Parties (comp. Part VI of this publication, p. 243). The text of the relevant Articles ran as follows:

Art. 16 (14):

"On the contrary it is agreed, that whatever shall be found to be laden by the Subjects and Inhabitants of either Party on any Ship belonging to the Enemys of the other or to their Subjects, the whole although it be not of the Sort of prohibited Goods may be confiscated in the same manner, as if it belonged to the Enemy, except such Goods and Merchandizes as were put on board such Ship before the Declaration of War, or even after such Declaration, if so be it were done without knowledge of such Declaration. So that the Goods of the Subjects and People of either Party, whether they be of the Nature of such as are prohibited or otherwise, which, as is aforesaid, were put on board any Ship belonging to an Enemy before the War, or after the Declaration of the same, without the Knowledge of it, shall no ways be liable to confiscation, but shall well and truely be restored without Delay to the proprietors demanding the same; but so as that, if the said Merchandizes be contraband, it shall not be any Ways lawful to carry them afterwards to any Ports belonging to the Enemy. The two contracting Parties agree, that the Term of two Months being passed after the Declaration of War, their respective Subjects, from whatever Part of the World they come, shall not plead the Ignorance mentioned in this Article".

Art. 25 (23):

"It shall be lawful for all and singular the Subjects of the most Christian King and the Citizens, People and Inhabitants of the said United States to sail with their Ships with all manner of Liberty and Security; no distinction being made, who are the Proprietors of the Merchandizes laden thereon, from any Port to the places of those who now are or hereafter shall be at Emnity with the most Christian King or the United States. It shall likewise be Lawful for the Subjects and Inhabitants aforesaid to sail with the Ships and Merchandizes aforementioned and to trade with the same liberty and security from the Places, Ports and Havens of those who are Enemies of both or either Party without any Opposition or disturbance whatsoever, not only directly from the Places of the Enemy afore mentioned to neutral Places; but also from one Place belonging to an Enemy to another place belonging to an enemy, whether they be under the Jurisdiction of the same Prince or under several; And it is hereby stipulated that free Ships shall also give a freedom to Goods, and that every thing shall be deemed to be free and exempt, which shall be found on board the Ships belonging to the Subjects of either of the Confederates, although the whole lading or any Part thereof should appertain to the Enemies of either, contraband Goods being always excepted. It is also agreed in like manner that the same Liberty be extended to Persons, who are on board a free Ship, with this Effect, that although they be Enemies to both or either Party, they are not to be taken out of that free Ship, unless they are Soldiers and in actual Service of the Enemies."

Specific categories of goods

General

Amongst the goods that have played a prominent part in the history of the law of contraband—whether free goods or (conditional) contraband—I will briefly refer in particular to ship's material or naval stores, sulphur and saltpetre, foodstuffs or "provisions", and coal.

The controversy over such commodities arose partly on the diplomatic level during the negotiation of a treaty of commerce and navigation, and partly on the judicial level in the prize courts. The qualification of specific cargoes as contraband of war or as free goods has indeed much earlier already formed the subject of heated discussion in prize court proceedings, either as a matter of the construction or applicability of treaty provisions or governmental instructions, or, where such provisions or instructions were lacking, as a matter of autonomous evaluation by the judiciary. As has become apparent from Sir George Lee's Ms. Notes, many cases have occurred in which British prize courts were bound by treaty provisions or by Orders in Council or Royal Instructions to King's ships and privateers.

Without entering into too great detail, I will briefly survey below the old British case law concerning, in particular, the four categories of goods referred to above. Pratt has taken the trouble of setting out the subject on a much wider scale, and that in two different ways, *viz.*, first by an elaborate survey of all the goods which had formed the subject of judicial discussion, arranged under a number of leading divisions (pp. xxxi-liv), and further by listing them all alphabetically (pp. lxiii-lxv). The twenty-four pages filled by the first survey give a clear picture of the meticulous care which Pratt has devoted to marshalling the legal and judicial chaos. His survey deals successively with "provisions" (in general; biscuit, brandy, butter, cheese, cod, corn and wheat, oil, rice, salmon, salt, salted provisions and wine), stores (for ship's use), warlike stores (saltpetre, shot), naval stores (anchors, cordage, hemp, cordilla or torse, pass hemp, metals (copper, iron, steel), pitch and tar, resin, sail cloth), tallow, timber (fir timber, balks, boards, planks, masts, pipe staves, oak planks, ruckers, spars, staves), coals, tobacco and wax.

My own survey below will be far more modest. From that survey it will also appear that the judicial classification of a particular commodity as a contraband cargo often depended upon the construction of a treaty provision defining the concept, or upon the problem of its applicability *in concreto*.

The drawing-up of such a survey was hindered by the fact that the *ratio decidendi* of the examined cases was often multiple and not confined to the valuation of the intrinsic nature of certain goods as contraband of war. In so far as the decision of the cases was complicated, *e.g.* by the circumstance that the goods concerned were (or were not) recognized as being the native produce of the neutral shipper's national soil or by the Court's consideration that they were liable to pre-emption irrespective (or in spite) of their essential nature, the judgments could better be discussed elsewhere, *viz.*, in § 3 (Sanctions), under B (Relaxations), *infra*, pp. 401 and 413. This applies, for example, to articles such as pitch and tar, masts and hemp (ship's material or naval stores). See, *inter alia*, as regards hemp: the case of the Swedish vessel *Ringende Jacob* [1798] (1 C.Rob., 89; Roscoe, I, 60): this good was classed as contraband under the Anglo-Danish treaty of 4 July 1780 (Parry, 47, 341); true, the cargo of hemp concerned appeared to be the produce of Russia, but it was claimed for a Danish subject and could not, therefore, invoke the traditional exemption for native produce;

and as regards masts: the case of the Dutch vessel the *Vrijheid (No. 1)* [1778] (Hay and Marriott, 188; Roscoe, I, 13).

0. *Warships as contraband*

In English case law on contraband ships of war have occupied a special place in their capacity as objects of capture and confiscation. They were treated as absolute contraband and condemned when they had been sent for sale to an enemy country. But in order that a ship should suffer that fate, her construction was to be such that there could be no doubt that she had been built for purposes of war. This was found to be undoubtedly so in the cases of the *Richmond* [1804] (5 C.Rob., 325), which the owner had directed to be sold to the enemy with the declared expectation that she would be employed in hostilities against England, knowing her to be particularly adapted for purposes of war, and the *Brutus* [1804] (5 C.Rob., 331, note). But is was denied in those of the *Fanny*, the *Neptune* and the *Raven* (5 C.Rob., Ap. 409). In the latter cases the ships were of ambiguous construction, they had been actually employed in trade and the occasion for selling them had arisen from circumstances. The *Raven* had been formerly a privateer. See on this group of cases of 1804 and the treatment of warships as absolute contraband Pratt-Lee's analysis at pp. xxiii-xxv.

1. *Ships' materials and naval stores*

"Naval stores" as a term was on the whole liberally interpreted against the goods seized in the sense that it was held to include, besides warlike stores, a great many other ship's materials, such as masts, anchors, cordage, planks, etc., to the exclusion, however, of materials for ship's use, provided that the supply on board did not, to an unreasonable extent, exceed what each vessel might be expected to require for its own use. See the dubious case of the *Margaretha Magdalena* [1799] (2 C.Rob., 140), cited by Pratt at p. xxxix of his analysis of the English case law on contraband. Other old cases cited by Pratt-Lee at p. 59. footnote 2, date back to the Nine Years' War (1691): the Swedish vessels *Charles* and *Marie*: set free because planks and tar were not listed as contraband in the Swedish treaty.

Commodities of this kind which were already at an early date and most frequently intercepted were pitch and tar. They formed, for instance, the entire cargo of the Swedish vessel *Med Guds Hielpe*, captured by the English privateer Eagle during the War of the Austrian Succession. They were destined for the use of the French. In that case of 1745, reported for the first time in detail by Sir George Lee in his Ms. Notes of 1750-1758 (Pratt-Lee, at pp. 191 *et seq.*), the then President of the High Court of Admiralty, Sir Henry Penrice (*per Curiam*) argued as follows (*ibid.*, pp. 198-199):

> "Pitch and tar are not enumerated in the 11th Article of the Anglo-Swedish treaty of 21 October 1661 [Dumont, VI^2, 384; Parry, 6, 469], but I think those enumerated were mentioned rather for example than by way of exclusion, and that there are other contraband goods than what are mentioned in that article. Three species of goods:
>
> 1st. For immediate use of war, in the manner they are, and those are contraband.
>
> 2nd. Of a mixed nature, which may be of use for war and for other purposes, and these sometimes are, and sometimes are not contraband.
>
> 3rd. Things for pleasure, and which are of no use in war, and those are not contraband.
>
> Pitch and tar are of a mixed nature; may be used for civil purposes, and also for fitting ships of war.
>
> ...
>
> In the old instructions the 11th and 12th Articles of the Swedish treaty were inserted. Now they are not inserted, and I suppose the reason was, because by the present instructions [of 1744] pitch and tar in Swedish ships are expressly declared to be contraband.
>
> A privateer who pursues his instructions, does right."

As a type of information on which a student of mid-18th century English contraband law has to build his conclusions, I will quote footnote 2 at p. 60 of Pratt-Lee's collection appended, presumably by Pratt, to Sir George Lee's MS. Notes concerning the *St. Nicholas* case of 1745-6 (*ibid.*, pp. 57-60):

> "Pitch and tar, before 1656, doubtful; *Maria*, 1 C.Rob., 372. In the time of Sir L. Jenkins (1674), not generally esteemed contraband, unless prohibited by special notification, *Twee Juffrouwen*, 4 C.Rob., 243, 1750. In the *Med Guds Hielpe* the whole cargo, being pitch and tar, was condemned [See Bourguignon, *Sir William Scott*, pp. 187-188]. *Staadt Embden*, 1 C.Rob., 29; and see case reported *infra*. Held contraband, *Staadt Embden*, 1 C.Rob. 30; *Richmond*, 5 C.Rob., 328; was subject to pre-emption, *Maria*, 1 C.Rob., 373; by Swedish Treaty, *Neptunus*, 6 C.Rob., 405.",

and Sir George Lee's own "report" concerning the case, dated 3 March 1745-6:

> "The Court condemned the pitch and tar, and assigned to have precedents to have laid before him the first day of next Term, as to the condemnation of the ship and the rest of the cargo."

I may be excused for having been unable to keep my attention sufficiently alert while going over more than 200 pages of such "reports".

Pitch and tar continued to haunt the Prize Court rooms in England in later wars. They were, for example, again declared to be contraband of war after their seizure on board the Dutch vessels *Jonge Tobias* [1799] (1 C.Rob., 329; Roscoe, I, 146) and *Maria (No. 1)* [1799] (1 C.Rob., 340; Roscoe, I, 152), the Swedish vessel *Sarah Christina* [1799] (1 C.Rob., 237; Roscoe, I, 125), and the Prussian vessel *Twee Juffrouwen* [1802] (4 C.Rob., 242; Roscoe, I, 384).

Pitch and tar have gained a certain celebrity as a subject of dispute between England and Sweden, as appears from the *Neptunus (No. 5)* [1807] (6 C.Rob., 403; Roscoe, I, 595):

"The right of carrying pitch and tar has long been a subject of such contention; this country, contending that they were to be considered as contraband, Sweden, on the contrary, maintaining that they were not contraband when they were the produce of the exporting country. After long and passionate discussion on this subject, which has irritated the feelings of the two countries for two centuries, a sort of compromise was at length adopted, and the last treaty was formed as a kind of middle term, in which both parties abated something of their original pretensions. It was agreed that these articles should be considered not as absolutely contraband, nor yet as entirely free and innocent, but as liable to the exercise of the right of war, 'that they should be subject to seizure for pre-emption'. This was the substance of the treaty that was formed for the regulation of the trade of Sweden, when that country was at peace and in a state of neutrality towards each of the belligerent powers. That, however, is not the present situation of the two countries, since Sweden has long been engaged with this country in hostility against a common enemy ..."

The general rule was, however, held not to be applicable to this ship because the relevant order of the Government directed all the goods to be restored, and the Court decided that this also applied to the ship.

In some of the cases the argument was not confined to the contraband nature of the goods concerned, but turned on an entirely different issue, *viz.*, certain mitigating practices which the Court had meanwhile introduced, as explained in the *Twee Juffrouwen*:

"In the practice of this Court there is a relaxation, which allows the carrying of those articles, being the produce of the claimant's country, as it has been deemed a harsh exercise of a belligerent right to prohibit the carrying of these articles, which constitute so considerable a part of its native produce and ordinary commerce. But in the same practice this relaxation is understood with a condition that it may be brought in, not for confiscation, but for pre-emption, no unfair compromise. To entitle the party to the benefit of this rule perfect *bona fides* on his part is required."

Since the Court by this reference to a judicial practice which had meanwhile been introduced, digressed from the subject of the contraband nature of certain sea-borne goods, discussed in the present § 1, to issues which belong to a subsequent § 3, I will not enter here into further details of the practice alluded to, but will refer to that § 3, dealing under B (iii), pp. 394 *et seq.*, with certain relaxations of the strict rules.

Another sort of ship's material which often emerged in prize proceedings was hemp, on which a footnote at p. 114 of Pratt-Lee's collection informs us in the following words:

"Hemp ..., under modern law of nations, liable to be seized as contraband in its own nature, formerly of a disputable nature.—*Maria*, 1 C.Rob., 372. Hemp forbidden by Danish treaty, Add. Art. July 4, 1780; *Ringende Jacob*, 1 C.Rob., 90. Hemp contraband.—The *Franklin*, 3 C.Rob., 217."

Besides pitch, tar and hemp, the following naval stores have been the subject of judicial assessment:

— masts: the *Vrijheid (No. 1)* [1778] (Hay and Marriott, 188; Roscoe, I, 13), a Dutch vessel captured while sailing from Riga to the French port of

Rochefort with a cargo of masts on board, destined for the use of the French Government. This case was to be adjudicated under the Anglo-Netherlands treaty of 1/10 December 1674 (Dumont, VII[1], 283; Parry, 13, 255), Art. 4 of which expressly labelled "masts, planks, boards and beams of any kind of wood, and all other materials requisite for building and repairing ships" as free goods. The *Vrijheid* was restored to her Dutch owner together with the value of her cargo, but the naval stores themselves were, in accordance with the precedents, sold for the use of the King (on pre-emption, all freight, expenses and charges, both of the captor and the claimant, to be paid by His Majesty).

This latter practice of pre-emption was also followed in other cases, such as those of a cargo of masts exported from Russia, destined for Holland on the *Staadt Embden* [1798] (1 C.Rob., 26; Roscoe, I, 37), and of a cargo of masts and spars, seized in the *Charlotte* (*No. 2*) [1804] (5 C.Rob., 305; Roscoe, I, 490), a Lübeck ship on a voyage from Russian Riga to French Nantes, although the cargo was the produce of Russia;

— sail cloth (condemned): the *Öster Risöer* [1802] (4 C.Rob., 199; Roscoe, I, 382);

— tallow (restored): the *Neptunus (No. 3)* [1800] (3 C.Rob., 108; Roscoe, I, 264);

— ship's timber: the *Fortune de la Mer* [1745] (Pratt-Lee, 33), seized off Dungeness in 1744 on a voyage from Danzig to Brest, where it was to end. The ship was laden at Danzig, where she had also been built, and had a Prussian master living at Danzig where her two owners also were born and lived. The ship and her cargo were restored, but the capturing privateer had "just cause of seizure" (*ibid.*, pp. 39-40);

the *T'Slots Copenhagen* [1745-1746] (Pratt-Lee, 40), seized eastward of the South Foreland in 1745 on a voyage from Danzig to St. Malo, where the timber was to be delivered. The ship was claimed by her master as being the sole property of a Danish subject residing at Elsenör, the cargo as being the sole property of two merchants, residing in and being the subjects of the City of Danzig. The ship and her cargo were condemned (*ibid.*, pp. 48-49);

the *Endraught* (read *Eendraght* [1798] (1 C.Rob., 22; Roscoe, I, 36) and the *Twende Brödre* [1801] (4 C.Rob., 33; Roscoe, I, 332):

> "with mere respect to such timber as is in its own nature ambiguous, I am disposed to look to the criterion of the destination as an equitable rule of interpretation, taking a fair course between the rights of exportation of native produce on the part of the neutral country, and the defensive rights of the belligerent."

The cargo was finally restored.

French prize courts have, as far as I know, only produced a very few judgments dealing with the contraband nature of specific sea-borne goods.

The jurisprudence concerning "bois de construction" was, moreover, contradictory: whereas such wood was released as not being contraband of war in the case of the (Prussian) *Maria Arendz contre le Contrôleur de la Marine* [*an* VIII] (De Pistoye-Duverdy, I, 116), it was condemned as contraband in that of the (Danish) *Confidentia* [*an* X] (*ibid.*, I, 406).

As in England, tar was qualified as contraband in the relation between France and Sweden, see the case of the (American) *Portland versus Le Diable à Quatre* [*an* VIII] (*ibid.*, II, 66).

As regards, in particular, naval stores a change has gradually come about in the practice of States, as is set out in some detail by Sir William Scott in his judgment of 1799 concerning the *Maria* (No. 1), one of the fleet of Swedish merchantmen, captured in January 1798 by British cruisers while sailing under the convoy of a Swedish ship of war (1 C.Rob., 340; Roscoe, I, 152 *et seq.*, at pp. 161-162). He there remarked as follows:

> "That tar, pitch and hemp ... are liable to be seized as contraband in their own nature cannot, I conceive, be doubted under the modern law of nations, though formerly, when the hostilities of Europe were less naval than they since become, they were of a disputable nature ..." [Referring further to concurrent statements by Valin (p. 68) that naval stores "sont de contrebande aujourd'hui et depuis le commencement de ce siècle, ce qui n'était pas autrefois néanmoins" and Vattel, and to an explanatory article of the Anglo-Danish treaty of 1780, Sir William Scott continued:] "Although it might be shown that the nature of these commodities had been subject to some controversy in the time of Whitlock (1656), when the fundamental treaty [with Sweden] was constructed, ... yet, the exposition which the later judgment and practice of Europe has given upon this subject would in some degree affect and apply what the treaties had been content to leave on that indefinite and disputable footing on which the notions then more generally prevailing in Europe had placed it. Certain is, that in the year 1750 the Lords of Appeal in this country declared pitch and tar, the produce of Sweden, and on board a Swedish ship bound to a French port to be contraband, and subject to confiscation, in the memorable case of the *Med Guds Hielpe*" [1745] (Pratt-Lee, 191; Roscoe, I, 1).

2. *Sulphur and saltpetre*

These articles also constituted the subject of both treaty regulation and judicial decision.

As to the latter see the judgments of:

the *Neptunus* [1807] (6 C.Rob., 403), quoted by Pratt-Lee in a footnote at p. 47, although in this case only pitch and tar are mentioned;

the *Wilhelmina Catharina* [1748] (Pratt-Lee, pp. xl and 180);

the *Jesús (,Maria, Joseph)* [1756] (Burrell, 164; Roscoe, I, 6) concerning a cargo of saltpetre in a Spanish vessel, which was held by the Prize Court, in the absence of treaty provisions, to be liable to condemnation.

For the treaties see the long list in Appendix A of Pratt-Lee where saltpetre is frequently mentioned; sulphur as such can scarcely be found in the contraband surveys.

3. *Foodstuffs or "provisions"* (*commeatus*)

Another category of goods the character of which as contraband of war has often been disputed consisted of various kinds of victuals. The treatment of foodstuffs in the law of contraband has indeed formed the subject of a long controversy and of varying practices. Whereas the belligerents have often prohibited and intercepted the transport of victuals by neutral vessels to their enemy, such transport has in a number of 18th century treaties been expressly declared free. The whole development has been set out in detail by Richard Kleen in his work *Lois et usages de la neutralité d'après le droit international conventionnel et coutumier des Etats civilisés* (Paris, 1898-1900), I, pp. 404-408, and in his study of 1893 *De la contrebande de guerre et des transports interdits aux neutres d'après les principes du droit international contemporain* (Paris), p. 125.

The opinion of continental writers, such as Wolff and Vattel, on the contraband nature of victuals and other "provisions" (*commeatus*) was mild. The English prize court was less lenient. A rule developed according to which foodstuffs were held not in themselves to be contraband, but to be liable to be considered as such under special circumstances, according, *e.g.*, to the state they were in (unmanufactured wheat not so noxious as finished products thereof), to the conditions of the war or of the parties to it, or to their intended use, mainly determined by the character of their port of destination (comp. § 2, *infra*, pp. 352-358): the *Luisa Ulrica* (Muller, Master) [1748] (see Bourguignon, *Sir William Scott*, p. 190), the *Jonge Margaretha* [1799] (1 C.Rob., 189; Roscoe, I, 100) and the *Haabet* [1800] (2 C.Rob., 174; Roscoe, I, 212). See Pratt-Lee, p. xxxiii.

In their analysis of the problem the editors of the *Recueil des arbitrages internationaux*, I, 30 *et seq.*, 161-174, give the arguments advanced by the British Government to justify the striking difference of attitude in their capacity of a neutral Power as compared with that of a belligerent (at p. 32).

In 1549 and 1626 England issued prohibitions to transport articles of food to (enemy) Spanish harbours. On the other hand, the tendency to declare the transportation of victuals in wartime free was reflected in the Treaty of the Pyrenees of 7 November 1659 (Dumont, VI^2, 264; Parry, 5, 325), Art. 12; the French *Ordonnance de la Marine* of August 1681; a protest launched by England in 1710 against a Danish prohibition to transport foodstuffs (Dumont, VIII^1, 345; Parry, 28, 1), Art. 20, and the Conventions which constituted together the Armed Neutrality League of 1780 (*e.g.*, Art. 3 of the Convention between Russia and Denmark, Martens, R^2, III, 189).

An inverse development, however, commenced during the war between Revolutionary France and England in 1793, when first a French Decree of 9 May (Martens, R^2, V, 381) ordered the seizure of neutral merchant ships carrying foodstuffs to England, and England thereupon reciprocated either by entering into treaties against the transport of grain and other victuals by neutrals to France—treaties of alliance with Russia of 25 March 1793 (Martens, R^2, V, 438; Parry, 52, 1), Art. 3; with Spain of 25 May 1793 (Martens, R^2, V, 472; Parry, 52, 41), Art. 4; with Sicily of 12 July 1793

(Martens, R^2, V, 480; Parry, 52, 77), Art. 5; with the Emperor of 30 August 1793 (Martens, R^2, V, 486; Parry, 52, 107), Art. 2; with Prussia of 14 July 1793 (Martens, R^2, V, 483; Parry, 52, 91), Art. 2, and with Portugal of 26 September 1793 (Martens, R^2, V, 518; Parry, 52, 147), Art. 4—or by issuing national instructions against such transport: Instructions for the seizure of corn ships, bound for France, 8 June 1793 (Martens, R^2, V, 586), Art. 1; Order in Council of 6 November 1793 extending the interception of foodstuffs destined for the French colonies, especially in the West Indies (*ibid.*, 600), repealed by subsequent Instructions of 18 August 1794 (*ibid.*, 604), but put in force again by an (unpublished) Order of 1795.

The qualification of victuals as contraband of war gave rise to disputes during the negotiations which led to the conclusion of the Anglo-American Jay Treaty of 19 November 1794 (Martens, R^2, VI, 168; Parry, 52, 243) when the United States negotiator tried in vain to achieve the exclusion of foodstuffs from the concept of contraband.

As appears from the judgment of Sir William Scott in the *Jonge Margaretha* [1799] (1 C.Rob., 189; Roscoe, I, 100), the qualification of human food as contraband of war was already the subject of discussion at an early date. In 1673 the then King's Advocate expressly asserted, upon a formal reference made to him, that by the practice of the English Admiralty corn, wine and oil were liable to be deemed contraband.

In subsequent periods many other provisions have been held liable to confiscation as contraband of war, although they were not so liable generally: the *Frau Margaretha* [1805] (6 C.Rob., 92); the *Richmond* [1804] (5 C.Rob., 325). Their confiscation was justified, in particular, when they were going to a port of naval equipment: the *Jonge Margaretha* (*supra*), the *Zelden Rust* [1805] (6 C.Rob., 93; Roscoe, I, 532); the *Ranger* [1805] (6 C.Rob., 125). When they were not condemned, they were held subject to pre-emption: the *Haabet* [1800] (2 C.Rob., 174).

As Sir Henry Penrice said in his judgment concerning cargo on board the *Nostra Seignora de Pentha de França* [1746] (Pratt-Lee, p. 90), provisions were and always had been esteemed contraband, and the British Government had as far as possible guarded against sending provisions from Ireland to the enemy (Pratt-Lee, pp. 93-94). Doubts sometimes arose about whether a specific good was to be considered as human food or rather as an article of luxury. In other cases it was disputable whether a specific commodity, although contraband of war, came under the rule protecting the native produce of the exporting neutral country. The courts sometimes also differed as to the contraband nature of specific goods. A brief survey of a few articles which were thus passed in review follows.

— Butter: in the *Young Andreas* [1747] (Pratt-Lee, 99).

— Rice: in the *St. Johannes* [1748] (Pratt-Lee, 166).

— Cod, salmon, herrings: in the *Jonge Frederick* [1747] (cited in 1 C.Rob., 193).

— Coffee and pepper: in the *Jesús* [1756] (Burrell, 164; Roscoe, I, 6).
— Oil and lemons: in the *St. Jacob* [1759] (Burrell, 160; Roscoe, I, 6).
— Salt: in the *Jonge Tobias* [1748] (Pratt-Lee, 187, 190-1) and the *Le Mars* [1748] (Pratt-Lee, 141).
— Wheat, flour and meal: in the *Jumfro Sarah* [1747] (Pratt-Lee, 100), the *Vro(u)w Anna Maria* [1747] (Pratt-Lee, 119), and much later the *Goede Vreede* [1780] (see the *Apollo*, 4 C.Rob., 163).
— Cheese was a commodity that in the War of the Austrian Succession was not considered contraband, but rather as an article of luxury and therefore restored: the *Juffro(u)w Magdalena* [1747] (Pratt-Lee, 163, footnote 2, cited in 1 C.Rob., 190), the *Eendraght* [1747] (Pratt-Lee, pp. xxxv-xxxvi), cases of such cargoes destined for Bordeaux.

In later times, however, cheeses were considered to be contraband and were consequently confiscated: the *Jonge Margaretha* [1799] (1 C.Rob., 189; Roscoe, I, 100), a Papenberg ship, carrying Dutch cheeses from Amsterdam to Brest, a port universally known to be one of naval military equipment; the cheeses concerned being used in British ships when foreign cheeses were used at all, and such as were exclusively used in French ships of war (Pratt-Lee, p. xxxvi). Sir William Scott condemned the cheeses, stating as his reasons that they were not the produce and manufacture of the country from which they were exported (Papenberg) (see *infra*, § 3, *sub* B, pp. 401-413), but of Holland, the enemy's ally in the war, and that they were destined for a big port of naval equipment of the enemy where a considerable French fleet was in a state of preparation for sailing on a hostile expedition against England.

To the same effect the *Zelden Rust* [1805] (6 C.Rob., 93; Roscoe, I, 532; Pratt-Lee, p. xxxvi): Dutch cheese taken on an asserted destination from Amsterdam to la Coruña, an ordinary commercial port, but situated in the same bay as Ferroll, an enemy port of naval equipment. The cheese was condemned, having special regard to the proximity of the two ports (see *infra*, § 2, p. 355).

Other cargoes that gave rise to discussion about their nature as articles of luxury rather than of "provisions" were beer, brandy, and wine. Cargoes of this kind were restored as being mere articles of luxury, after their seizure in the *Juffro(u)w Magdalena,* the *E(e)ndraght* and the *Klein(e) David* [1747-1748]. On the contrary, they were condemned as being in their nature a species of provisions in the *Elizabeth Catherina* [1747], the *Margaretha Elizabeth* [1748] and much later the *Edward* [1801], relating to a shipment of wine from one enemy (French) port to another on a Prussian ship (4 C.Rob., 68; Roscoe, I, 350); see Pratt-Lee, pp. xxxiii-xxxv.

An other old case in which, in the absence of relevant treaty provisions and municipal regulations, a British prize court was called upon to decide on the contraband nature of provisions for human consumption was that of the *St. Jacob* [1759] (Burrell, 160; Roscoe, I, 6). It concerned a mixed cargo of foodstuffs and other goods, carried by this Danish vessel towards Le Havre de Grâce. In appeal, the oil on board was held not to be contraband. A quantity of lemons, also on board, was released, but on another ground: it was the property of the ship's master.

There were, of course, many cases of mixed cargoes, some harmless, others harmful to the captor's interests. Thus, in an early case of 1756 relating to various goods, carried by the Spanish vessel *Jesús* from la Coruña to San Sebastián (Burrell, 164; Roscoe, I, 6), the shipload consisted of coffee, saltpetre, dye-wood, pepper and India bail. The saltpetre was held to be liable to condemnation, but the other goods, such as coffee and pepper, were restored to their owners.

4. *Coal*

Coal only became a subject of serious dispute at a later stage, when fuel gained ever-increasing importance in naval warfare.

During the War of the Austrian Succession coals were not yet insisted on by the captors as contraband and, therefore, the Court did not declare its opinion on them further than that they were of great use to the enemy. See the case of the *Young Andreas* [1747] (Pratt-Lee, 99).

An early instance in which a cargo of coal was seized and condemned was the case of the *Fenix* (or *Phoenix*) [1854] (5 C.Rob., 20; Roscoe, II, 239).

Spain and Perú declared coal to be contraband during the War of the Pacific of 1865 (*B.F.S.P.*, vol. 56, pp. 710 and 917).

The coaling of the Russian Baltic fleet with Welsh coal by a large fleet of German vessels in 1904 gave rise to an exchange of views on the diplomatic level between the governments most concerned, also from the aspect of neutrality, see Smith and Sibley in Appendix D to their study *International law as interpreted during the Russo-Japanese War*, at pp. 404 *et seq.*; for besides this prize law aspect of coal—its capacity of being treated as (even absolute) contraband—it has also a marked neutrality aspect, *viz.*, its rôle in the provision of belligerent warships with fuel by neutral Powers in their national waters. I will not enter upon that subject again here because I have dealt with it in Part IX-B (vol. X) of this publication, pp. 175-177. This rôle of coal has been analysed by G.A. Scheltus in his thorough academic thesis of 1907, defended at the University of Utrecht, under the title *Voorziening in de behoefte der belligerenten aan steenkolen* (Meeting the belligerents' need for coal in naval war).

The import which the belligerents in the Russo-Japanese war of 1904 in the very last phase of the consolidation period gave to the concept of contraband appears from the lists inserted by Hurst and Bray in the indexes of their collection of *Russian and Japanese Prize Cases*,

as to the Russian side in vol. I, at pp. 37 and 379, and

as to the Japanese side in vol. II at pp. 469-471.

Other goods discussed in prize court decisions were, *inter alia*,
— resin; the *Santa Boa Ventura* [1747] (Roscoe, I, 433, footnote *a*; Pratt-Lee, 137); the *Nostra Signora de Begona* [1804] (5 C.Rob., 97; Roscoe, I, 433);
— brimstone: the *Carpenter* [1810] (2 Acton 11; Roscoe, I, 433);
— metals, such as iron, copper and steel: the *Ringende Jacob* [1798] (1 C.Rob., 92, note *a*); the *Jonge Margaretha* [1799] (1 C.Rob., 195); the *Charlotte* [1804] (5 C.Rob., 275); the *Hoop* [1801] (Pratt-Lee, p. 59, footnote 2, and xliii-xlv).

Modern technology has contributed greatly to the continual expansion of the range of goods susceptible of seizure and confiscation under the law of contraband, until it reached a pitch of absurdity during World War I. The lists of contraband goods had in the meantime split into two according to their destination, either to the enemy forces (absolute contraband) or to the enemy country (conditional or relative contraband), a distinction upon which comp. § 2, *infra*, p. 347.

(*c*) *The system of "free ship, free goods"*

A third, in a sense opposite, system or the image of that *sub* (*b*), propagated with particular energy by the "freight-carriers of Europe", the United Netherlands and their nationals, protected enemy goods carried on vessels under a neutral flag against confiscation. This system (*c*) was indicated by the simple formula "free ship, free goods".

It was still rejected by Sir William Scott in a judgment of 1799 concerning the *Maria (No. 1)* (Paulsen, Master) (1 C.Rob., 340; Roscoe, I, 152, at p. 156), where the rule "free ship, free goods" was called "an inadmissible rule".

The system under (*a*) was doubtless the most logical but could not hold its own against the two rival systems.

The systems under (*b*) and (*c*) were often combined in treaties of commerce or alliance to the balanced effect of exposing neutral cargoes on enemy vessels to confiscation, but leaving enemy cargoes on neutral ships unaffected.

System (*c*) has in the middle of the 19th century, shortly before the Crimean War (1852), formed the subject of a richly documented Netherlands academic dissertation (in Latin) defended at the University of Utrecht by H. Royaards under the title *De placito "Libera navis libera merx"*.

This maxim was, however, often accompanied by the simultaneous maintenance of the traditional French rule under (*b*) that he "unfree" character of the ship infected the "free" goods on board in all those cases in which France had not expressly abandoned that rule in a bilateral treaty. When that happened and the protection of enemy goods by the neutral flag of the carrier (system *c*) was *not* at the same time conceded, the rules worked as a double-edged sword against neutral interests. See on that fourth system *infra* under (*d*).

The point that occupied the British prize courts to the greatest extent was, as far as I could make out, the question of freight. In the *Emanuel* (Söderström, Master) [1799] (1 C.Rob., 296; Roscoe, I, 141) Sir William Scott enunciated the general principle that when enemy goods were captured on a neutral vessel her owner had the same right against the captors for freight as against the enemy, but he stated expressly that that principle did not apply when the neutral ship was engaged in the coastal trade of the enemy. Comp. also the case of the *Bremen Flugge* [1801] (4 C.Rob., 90; Roscoe, I, 356).

The principle "free ship, free goods" under (*c*) was laid down in a large number of treaties of the 17th and 18th centuries. They are, as far as I see, fairly exhaustively cited and analysed in the above mentioned academic (Latin) thesis of H. Royaards of 1852, arranged in the order of the relevant periods of Europe's political history, *viz.*, at pp. 27 *et seq.* (from about 1600 to the Peace Congress of Utrecht of 1713); pp. 61 *et seq.* (text adopted at that Congress); pp. 71 *et seq.* (up to the Armed Neutrality, divided into the two periods 1713-1756 and 1756-1780); pp. 99 *et seq.* (up to the Final Act of the Congress of Vienna, divided into the three periods 1780-1793, 1793-1801 and 1801-1815); and pp. 150 *et seq.* (subsequent to that Congress).

In view of the extreme importance in the history of the law of maritime prize I will recapitulate below a limited number, selected more or less at random from the available scores of treaties.

Many of them simply embodied a combination of the systems (*b*) and (*c*). Two of them (of 1662 and 1678) were concluded by France just in the period 1650-1681, mentioned above *sub* (*b*).

The principle *sub* (*c*) was already adopted in Henri IV's capitulation with the Sublime Porte of 20 May 1604 (Testa, I, 141), Art. 12;

> "Nous ordonnons et défendons aussi que les vaisseaux français qui seront rencontrés chargés de victuailles, prises ès-pays et seigneuries de nos ennemis, ne puissent être retenus ni confisqués ni les marchandises et mariniers faits esclaves.
> Nous déclarons aussi que les Français qui se trouveront pris sur des vaisseaux de nos sujets qui portent des vivres à nos ennemis, encore que nosdits sujets soient justiciables et leurs vaisseaux confiscables, ne puissent être molestés ni retenus esclaves sous ce prétexte, attendu qu'ils sont passagers ou mariniers gagnant leur vie, et, s'il s'en trouve de retenus et pris de cette façon, qu'ils soient relâchés et mis en liberté."

Further examples were:

18 April 1646, France-the Netherlands (Dumont, VI[1], 342), clause I for a term of four years;

10 May 1655, Marine Treaty, France-Hanse Towns (Parry, 3, 417), Art. 3;

3 November 1655, Louis XIV of France-Cromwell (Parry, 4, 1), Art. 15;

7 November 1659, Treaty of the Pyrenees, France-Spain (Parry, 5, 325), Arts. 19 and 20;

See also the Portuguese-Netherlands treaty of 6 August 1661 (Dumont, VI[2], 366; Parry, 6, 375), Art. 24:

"Bona quaelibet ac Merces, sive ad dictos Regem Ordinesque spectabunt, sive ad utrimvis Populum, si Navibus alterutri Parti inimicis hostibusque creditae ac in iis deprehensae fuerint, non minus quam Naves ipsae in praedam cedant, ac Fisco occupantium addicantur. Naves vero ac res quaecumque, ad Partis utriuslibet Hostem pertinentes, Regis Ordinumque jam dictorum aut utriusque Populi Navibus impositae in eas Fisco nil juris esto, adeoque nec detineantur, nec Possessoribus intervertantur".

27 April 1662, Treaty of Alliance, France-The Netherlands (Dumont, VI[2], 412; Parry, 7, 139), Arts. 35 and 36:

"35. Il a esté en outre accordé & convenu, que tout ce qui se trouvera chargé par les Sujets de Sa Majesté en un Navire des Ennemis desdits Seigneurs Etats, bien que ce ne fût Marchandise de Contrebande, sera confisqué, avec tout ce qui se trouvera audit Navire, sans exception ni réserve; mais d'ailleurs aussi sera libre & affranchi tout se qui sera & se trouvera dans les Navires appertenans aux Sujets du Roi Très-Chrétien, encore que la charge ou partie d'icelle fût aux ennemis desdits Seigneurs Estats; sauf les Marchandises de Contrebande, au regard desquelles on se règlera selon ce qui a esté disposé aux Articles précedens.
36. Tous les Sujets & Habitants desdites Provinces-Unies jouiront réciproquement des mêmes Droits, Libertez & Exemptions en leurs Trafics & Commerces dans les Ports, Rades, Mers & Estats de sadite Majesté; ce qui vient d'estre dit que les Sujets de Sa Majesté jouiront en ceux desdits Seigneurs Estats, & en haute Mer, se devant entendre que l'égalité sera réciproque en toute manière de part & d'autre, & mesme en cas que cy-après lesdits Seigneurs fussent en Paix, Amitié & Neutralité avec aucuns Roys, Princes & Etats, qui devinssent Ennemis de Sa Majesté: chacune des deux Parties devant user réciproquement des mêmes conditions & restrictions exprimées aux Articles du présent Traité, qui régardent le Trafic & le Commerce";

6/16 July 1667, Preliminary Agreement between the Netherlands and Sweden (Dumont, VII[1], 37; Parry, 10, 187), Art. 8:

"Bona sive Merx quaecumque pertinens ad Subditos Foederatorum alterutri, etiam illa, quam ex superiorum Paragraphorum Auctoritate permissam ac neutiquam prohibitam esse constabit, in Navibus *inimicis* fortè deprehensa, in praedam occupanti cedat, ac Fisco addicatur, ulla sine exceptione; Contra tutum omninò & immune à Fisco habeatur quicquid Navigiis ad Foederati alterutrius Subditos pertinentibus concredetur, utcumque sit Parti alterutri Subditos inimicorum, excepta solummodo Merce de Contrabanda ad Portum hostilem destinata ..., sed & *vectores* quoscumque quamvis Subditos inimicos Partis ulterutrius, tutos navigare conveniet ...";

24 February 1677, France-England (Parry, 14, 175), Art. 8;
11 April 1713, Treaty of Commerce and Navigation between England and France (Dumont, VIII[1], 345; Parry, 28, 1), Arts. 17 and 27:

"17. ... les Vaisseaux libres rendront les Marchandises libres.
27. Il a été au contraire convenu et accordé que tout ... ce qui se trouvera chargé par les Sujets et les habitants de part et d'autre en un Navire appartenant aux Ennemis de l'autre, ... sera confisqué comme s'il appartenoit à l'ennemi même ...";

See for the history of the inclusion of Article 17 into the Treaty, the article by G.N. Clark on "Neutral commerce in the War of the Spanish Succession and the Treaty of Utrecht" in vol. 9 of the *British Year Book of International Law* 1928, pp. 69-83, at pp. 78-83.

21 December 1739, France-the Netherlands (Parry, 35, 459), Art. 14;

15 March 1742, France-Denmark (Parry, 36, 267), Art. 14;

7 April 1762, the Separate Convention annexed to the Swedish-Prussian Armistice Convention of Ribnitz (Martens, R^2, I, 38, note; Parry, 42, 166), expressed it in Art. 1 clearly and succinctly as follows:

> "Un vaisseau franc affranchira les effets, et un vaisseau qui ne sera point licite rendra les effets illicites";

26 September 1786, France-Great Britain (Parry, 50, 71), Art. 20;

30 September 1800, France-United States (Parry, 55, 343), Art. 14.

Instances of this combined operation of the systems under (*b*) and (*c*) especially supplied by the United Netherlands in the course of the 17th century are embodied in treaties concluded

with Spain, 17 December 1650 (Dumont, VI^1, 570; Parry, 2, 259), Arts. 13-15;

with England, 17 February 1668 (Dumont, VII^1, 74; Parry, 10, 441), Art. 10, and 1/10 December 1674, the famous Marine Treaty, which held out for more than a century (Dumont, VII^1, 282; Parry, 13, 255), Art. 8;

with Sweden, 26 November 1675 (Dumont, VII^1, 316; Parry, 14, 41), Art. 8, and 2/12 October 1679 (Dumont, VII^1, 437; Parry, 15, 331), Arts. 22 and 23;

with France, 10 August 1678 (Dumont, VII^1, 357; Parry, 14, 399), Arts. 22 and 23, and 20 September 1697 (Dumont, VII^2, 386; Parry, 21, 371), Art. 27.

What the general situation was about 1800 in France appears from pp. 362-364 of vol. I of the De Pistoye and Duverdy's *Traité*. They report there the case of a neutral (Danish) vessel, the *Lisifiord*, laden with a cargo belonging to a subject of the Duke of the (at the time) enemy (French-occupied) territory of Wittenberg and destined for Tuscany, then at war with France, which had been captured by a French privateer (cited in the *Traité* under the heading *Henry Moser contre l'Héraclée)*. A transaction between the master of the *Lisifiord* and the owner of the privateer, later confirmed by the *Conseil des prises*, was in conformity with Art. 1 of the *Règlement* of 1778, according to which

> "Fait défense d'arrêter les navires des puissances neutres, quand même ils sortiraient des ports ennemis ou qu'ils y seraient destinés",

so that only the fate of the cargo remained to be decided. In its judgment of 23 vendémiaire *an* X the *Conseil*, in accordance with the conclusions of the Commissary of the Government, determined that the cargo was good and lawful prize on the ground that the neutral flag did not cover the enemy merchandise on board which was on its way from one enemy port to another: the above-quoted Article 1 did not protect the enemy cargo, nor did it follow from that article that enemy property was protected by a neutral flag. The Commissary, obviously supported by the *Conseil des prises*, based his opinion on Art. 15 of the same *Règlement* of 1778, providing that

> "Veut, au surplus, Sa Majesté, que les dispositions du titre des Prises de l'Ordonnance de la Marine du mois d'août 1681 soient exécutées selon leur forme et teneur, autant et à quoi il n'aura pas été dérogé par le présent règlement",

in conjunction with Art. 7 of titre IX of that *Ordonnance* which laid down in express terms that

> "Tous navires qui se trouveront chargés d'effets appartenant à nos ennemis, et les marchandises de nos sujets ou alliés qui se trouveraient dans un navire ennemi, seront pareillement de bonne prise".

The result of this argument was the complete maintenance of the doctrine of hostile infection in both directions.

These conclusions of the Commissary of the Government and this judgment of the *Conseil* were subject to the strongest censure by the authors of the *Traité* at pp. 362-364; they were rejected as:

> "erronées et contraires au règlement du 26 juillet 1778, tel qu'il a toujours été interprété. Ce règlement, garantissant aux neutres la liberté de faire du commerce avec l'ennemi, a toujours été considéré comme garantissant aussi la liberté des marchandises ennemies chargées sur navires neutres."

How the legal situation and its historical development were looked at in France is also apparent from the interesting conclusion of Portalis, the expert Commissary of the French Government of the *Conseil des prises*, in the case of *Le Corsaire le Hasard contre le navire la Statira* of 6 thermidor *an* VIII [1800], reported in De Pistoye and Duverdy's *Traité des prises maritimes*, II, 121 *et seq.* The *Statira* was a neutral (American) vessel which, after having been captured by an English privateer, was recaptured by the *Hasard*, a French privateer from Port Malo, and brought into a French harbour near Paimpol. The recapture aspect of this case will not be discussed here, but *sub* B, section 7, *infra* pp. 561-563. Neither will I enter here upon another aspect of the case, *viz.*, the fact that the cargo of the *Statira* (60 barrels of turpentine and 40 barrels of tar) was considered and condemned as contraband of war. The only interesting aspect of the case in the present context is Portalis' historical exposé of the development of the legal situation of enemy goods on board a neutral vessel and *vice versa*: how should the *Statira* and her enemy cargo have been treated if the latter had not been qualified as contraband of war? I will reproduce below the whole exposé because it gives the most authoritative and complete survey of the legal chaos which has obtained in this field in the past, also in France, but I will omit from that exposé the passages which concern in particular the presence of contraband goods on board a neutral vessel (whereupon comp. below section 3, § 3, pp. 371-394).

"En droit, la qualité du navire doit-elle être déterminée par celle de la cargaison? [comp. on this strange formulation *supra*, p. 212].

Le consulat de la mer décide 1° qu'on peut enlever les effets hostiles qui se trouvent dans le navire neutre, en payant le nolis et l'hypothèque due au capitaine; 2° que si, dans un navire ennemi, il y a des marchandises qui appartiennent à des neutres, on doit les leur rendre.

Les ordonnances de 1543, art. 42, et de 1584, art. 79, paraissent déclarer de bonne prise le navire neutre qui contient des effets hostiles, et toute marchandise qui se trouve dans un navire ennemi, quoiqu'elle appartienne à un ami. Cette rigueur fut adoucie par la déclaration du 1er février 1650, art. 5: 'Si aucune prise, est-il dit dans cet article, a été faite par aucuns capitaines nos sujets..., les marchandises qui se trouveront appartenir à nos amis, alliés ou sujets, seront rendues et restituées'.

L'ordonnance de la marine (of 1681), titre des Prises, art. 7, rétablit l'ancienne sévérité: 'Tous navires, porte cet article, qui se trouveront chargés d'effets appartenant à nos ennemis, et les marchandises de nos sujets et alliés qui se trouveront dans un navire ennemi seront de bonne prise'.

Le règlement du 23 juillet 1704 porte, en l'art. 5, que, 's'il se trouve sur les vaisseaux neutres des effets appartenant aux ennemis, les vaisseaux et tout le chargement seront de bonne prise'.

Cette rigueur fut de nouveau adoucie par le règlement du 21 octobre 1774, art. 5: 'S'il se trouve, y est-il dit, sur les navires neutres, des marchandises ou effets appartenant aux ennemis, lesdites marchandises ou effets seront de bonne prise, et néanmoins les navires relâchés'.

Le règlement du 26 juillet 1778, art. 1er, s'exprime en ces termes: 'Fait défense Sa Majesté, à tous armateurs, d'arrêter et conduire dans les ports du royaume les navires des puissances neutres, quand même ils sortiraient des ports ennemis ou qu'ils y seraient destinés, à l'exception toutefois...' [the exception relates to the cases of the violation of a blockade and the transportation of contraband goods]; 'se réservant, au surplus, Sa Majesté, de révoquer la liberté portée au présent article, si les puissances ennemies n'accordent pas le réciproque dans le délai de six mois, à compter du jour de la publication du présent règlement'.

La loi du 29 nivôse *an* VI changea toute l'économie de ces dernières dispositions; elle ordonna que l'état des navires, en ce qui concernait leur qualité de neutre ou d'ennemi, serait déterminé par leur cargaison; en conséquence, que tout bâtiment trouvé en mer, chargé, en tout ou en partie, de marchandises provenant d'Angleterre ou de ses possessions, serait déclaré de bonne prise, quel que fût le propriétaire de ces denrées ou marchandises.

Mais la loi du 23 frimaire *an* VIII, en abrogeant celle du 29 nivôse *an* VI, a fait revivre les dispositions du règlement de 1778.

Il résulte du tableau historique des lois, qu'elles ont varié selon les mœurs et les circonstances; que la politique du moment a presque toujours modifié les principes du droit politique; que, dans nos temps modernes, les règlements ont paru constamment incliner vers l'équité générale, et que la nation française peut s'honorer d'avoir eu, dans la dernière guerre, l'initiative des maximes douces et généreuses qui ont prévalu, et d'avoir donné des exemples utiles à tous les peuples.

Cependant, comme tout doit être réciproque entre les diverses nations, on voit que le législateur s'est toujours réservé le droit de devenir plus sévère si les autres nations belligérantes devenaient plus jalouses et moins justes.

Le capteur demande à être jugé d'après la loi du 29 nivôse *an* VI. Il soutient que c'est sous l'empire de cette loi qu'il s'est livré aux entreprises périlleuses de la course, et qu'il a fait la capture du navire *la Statira*. Les lois et les règlements, dit-il, ne peuvent point modifier des droits acquis, et rien ne peut préserver le capteur des effets de la loi du 29 nivôse, sous l'empire de laquelle la capture a été faite. Mon droit, dit le capteur, était acquis avant l'abrogation de cette loi.

Sans examiner le degré de force et d'autorité que l'on doit accorder à la loi du 29 nivôse, je dirai qu'en général les règlements de la course, qui ne portent qu'improprement le nom de loi, et qui par eux-mêmes sont essentiellement variables, *pro temporibus et causis*, sont toujours susceptibles, dans leur application, d'être tempérés par des vues de sagesse et d'équité. J'ajouterai qu'en exécutant des règlements d'une extrême rigueur, il faut plutôt les restreindre que les étendre, et que, dans le choix des divers sens dont ils peuvent être susceptibles, on doit préférer celui qui est le plus favorable à la justice et à la liberté. Le droit ne naît pas des règlements, mais les règlements doivent naître du droit. Conséquemment, les lois ou les règles particulières doivent toujours être exécutées de la manière la plus conforme aux principes de raison universelle, surtout dans les matières appartenant au droit des gens, dans lesquelles les législateurs se sont toujours glorifiés de n'être que les respectueux interprètes de la loi naturelle.

La loi du 29 nivôse veut que la qualité du navire neutre ou ennemi soit déterminée par celle de la cargaison; elle ajoute que tout bâtiment chargé en tout ou en partie de marchandises provenant d'Angleterre ou de ses possessions est de bonne prise. Mais comment doit-on entendre les mots 'en tout ou en partie'? Tout doute est résolu si le chargement est composé en entier de marchandises prohibées ou de contrebande, mais si les marchandises prohibées ou de contrebande ne composent qu'*en partie* le chargement, quelle règle faudra-t-il suivre?"

(*d*) *The double-edged system of hostile infection*

As remarked above under (*b*), the system of hostile infection may be applied in a variety of situations. Apart from the system "unfree ship, unfree goods", set out under (*b*), it can indeed also govern the inverse case of the presence of enemy goods on board neutral vessels, which may entail the condemnation of the latter as well. It further lends itself to application in the case of the transportation of contraband goods on a neutral ship, which may infect other, innocent parts of the cargo as well as the ship herself. It was in particular this last variant of the doctrine of infection which occupied the Judicial Committee of the Privy Council in its decision of 1920 concerning certain cargoes on board the *Kronprinsessan Margareta, Rena, Paranà and Hilding* (*B.C.P.C.*, III, 803), in which that body qualified the origin of the infection doctrine as "rather obscure". Comp. the extract of that judgment in III A, section 3 *infra*, pp. 372-373.

But there are still more applications of the doctrine possible, such as the violation of a blockade, the rendering of unneutral service and other forms of assistance to the enemy by the neutral ship involve innocent cargoes on board the guilty vessel. Innocent goods may also become the victim of illegal resistance by the master of a neutral ship to the regular exercise of the right of visit and search by a belligerent. All such other cases can, however, better be discussed in the chapters where they belong. I will, therefore, confine myself for the moment to the application of the fourth system under which both neutral goods on enemy vessels—*adoption* of the system under (*b*)—and enemy goods on neutral vessels—*denial* of the system under (*c*)—were subject to condemnation, the traditional system under the national legislation of France.

The Edict of King François I of 1543 already laid down this double-edged principle of infection in Art. 42. It was repeated in Art. 69 of the Edict of

King Henri III of 1584 "sur le fait de la marine" (*Collectanea Maritima*, p. 105) in the following prolix wording:

> "Item et pour ce que par cy-devant, soubs couleur des pratiques et intelligences que ont *aucuns* de nos allies et confederez avec nos Ennemis, lorsqu'il y avoit aucune Prise faite sur mer par nos subjets, plusieurs procés se suscitoyent par nosdits alliez, voulant dire que les biens, prins en guerre, leur appartiennent, soubs ombre de *quelque part* et *portion qu'ils avoient avec nosdits Ennemis*, dont se sont ensuyies grosses condemnations à l'encontre de nosdits subjets; au moyen de quoi iceuz nos subiets ont depuis craint esquiper navires en guerre, pour Nos faire fermer et endommager nosdits Ennemis: Nous pour remedier à telles fraudes, et afin que nosdits subiets reprennent leur courage, et ayent meilleur desir et occasion *d'équipper* navires en guerre par mer, avons voulu et ordonné, voulons et ordonnons, que si les navires de nos dicts subjets sont, en temps de guerre, prises par mer d'aucuns Navires appartenans à autres nos subjects ou à nos alliez, confederez ou amis, esquels y ait biens, marchandises, ou gens de nos Ennemis, ou bien aussi Navires de nosdits Ennemis, esquelles y ait personnes, marchandises ou autres biens de nosdits Subiets, Confederez et Alliez, [ou (1543) esquels nosdits subiets, confederez et alliez fussent personniers en quelques portions,] que le tout soit déclaré de bonne prise—et dès à present comme pour lors, avons ainsi déclaré et déclarons par ces presentes, comme si le tout appartenoit à nosdits Ennemis. Mais pourront nosdits Alliez et Confederez faire leur traffic par mer, dedans navires qui soyent de leur obéissance et subjection et par leurs gens et subjets, sans y accueillir nos Ennemis et Adversaires; lesquels biens et marchandises ainsi chargés, ils pourront mener et conduire où bon leur semblera, pourvue que se ne soient munitions de guerre, dont ils voulussent fortifier nosdits ennemis. Auquel cas, nous avons permis et permettons à nos susdits subjets, les prendre, et amener en nos ports et havres, *et lesdites munitions retenir, selon l'estimation raisonable, qui en sera faite par nostredit Admiral* ou son dit Lieutenant."

France has for a very long time remained an advocate of the system "unfree ship, unfree goods", set out under (*b*), but instead of adopting simultaneously as a counterbalance the system "free ship, free goods", set out under (*c*), she repudiated the latter already at an early date and thus created the double-edged system envisaged here under (*d*), which impaired the interests of neutrals along the whole line under the motto "robe d'ennemi confisque robe d'ami" (Edicts of 1543 and 1584, and Louis XIV's *Ordonnance de la Marine* of 1681).

The Spanish king Philip II also adopted this rule in his Ordonnance of 2 August 1590. In several prize court decrees from the (Spanish) Southern Netherlands we find the rule "unfree ship, unfree goods" and "Le batteau non franc, défranchit aussi les biens et marchandises y chargées, sans qu'il soit prins esgard à la quantité ou conditions des propriétaires" (24 September 1605). See on this question F. Pollentier, *De Admiraliteit en de oorlogen ter zee onder de Aartshertogen (1596-1609)*; Brussels 1972, pp. 181 *et seq.*

Although the collision between the various systems of prize law is apparent from the provisions of a vast number of bilateral treaties of the 17th and 18th centuries, when perusing all those provisions, one seldom comes across articles in French treaties which sanctioned *expressis verbis* the double-edged threat to the owners involved in the intermixture of enemy and neutral property in the same ship, designated by the principle of " infection " and the said slogan. This, at first sight slightly amazing, lacuna is, however, easily explainable by the fact that the doctrine was of French origin, as sanctioned by the above-quoted Article 69 of the Edict of March 1584. There is, therefore, no need to look especially into French treaties on prize law for confirmation of the adoption of the infection principle. The treaties concluded by France are, however, significant and interesting in so far as they *deviate* from that principle. The treaties which embody such deviation are curious for their manner of handling the issue. Their drafting technique proves that France always clung to her traditional infection doctrine unless she consented by an express treaty provision, agreed upon with a foreign Power, to derogate from it in favour of the neutral owners of cargo found on board enemy vessels. This particular French drafting technique was applied in many French treaties, exemplified by the Preamble and Art. I of the Franco-Netherlands Treaty of Maritime Commerce and Navigation of 18 April 1646 (Dumont, VI[1], 342), in which the operation of the infection doctrine was maintained in principle, but temporarily suspended in favour of the co-contracting Party. That treaty was the first which granted to the Netherlands exemption (for four years) from the severe infection rule which was otherwise the constant rule of French prize jurisprudence.

The same technique was, for that matter, employed in Art. III of the same treaty for suspending vis-à-vis the Netherlands the operation of another rule of the Edict of 1584, namely, the obligatory naval salute to the French flag (comp. on this subject Part IV of this publication, p. 63).

The relevant provisions (preamble and clause 1) were couched in the following terms:

> " Le Roi voulant, par l'avis de la Reine Régente sa Mère, donner de plus en plus aus Sieurs les Estats Généraux des Provinces-Unies des Pays Bas, des témoignages de sa bienveuillance & de son affection, à l'occasion des plaintes qui ont esté faites plusieurs fois de leur part, sur ce que leurs Sujets estoient troublez dans leur Commerce, à cause que les Vaisseaux de Guerre de Sa Majesté & Capitaines Armateurs prenoient leurs Navires Marchands, lors qu'il s'y rencontroit dedans de la Marchandise appartenant aux Ennemis, & incontinent jugez de bonne prise, suivant l'Ordonnance du feu Roy Henry III de l'an 1584 sur le fait de la Marine. A quoy Sa Majesté voulant pourvoir par un bon Règlement, & en attendant remedier au mieux qu'il luy sera possible, aux inconveniens qui naissent tous les jours de l'execution de ladite Ordonnance, & se relacher de la rigueur d'icelle pour quelque temps en faveur desdits Sieurs les Estats, ...
> (I) Qu'en attendant que l'on ait fait un bon Règlement, on surseoira l'execution des Articles de l'Ordonnance du Roy Henry III de l'an 1584 sur le fait de la Marine, portent que " les Marchandises, appartenantes aux Ennemis, donnent lieu à la confiscation de celles des Amis ", & ne sera plus observée ny pratiquée à l'égard des Sujets des Sieurs les Estats Généraux des Provinces-Unies des Pays-Bas, pendant le temps de quatre années, en telle sorte que les Navires qui trafiqueront avec la Patente de l'Admiral des Provinces-Unies dans la Mer Mediterranée & du Levant, & sur l'Ocean dudit Admiral, ou des Villes & lieux aux Sujets desquels lesdits Navires appartiendront, seront libres, & rendront aussi toute leur charge libre, bien qu'il y eust dedans de la Marchandise; même des grains & legumes appartenans aux Ennemis ... ".

This text was, however, later found by the States General to be ambiguous or at least unclear, and for obvious reasons; did the explanation "en telle sorte, etc." refer to a (temporary) exemption from the principle of "infection hostile", as the main suspension clause seemed to suggest, or did it rather refer to the recognition of the principle "free ship, free goods"?

Insofar as France did not expressly eliminate the provisions of the Edict by treaty, they remained in full effect.

It was this provision which has continued to form the normal legal foundation of French prize practice and jurisprudence in so far as it was not *expressis verbis* set aside by bilateral treaties.

The provision of Art. 42 of 1543 and Art. 69 of 1584 was re-incorporated far more succinctly into Art. 7 of *titre* IX of King Louis XIV's *Ordonnance concernant la Marine* of 1681 as follows:

> "Tous Navires qui se trouveront chargez d'effets appartenans à nos ennemys et les marchandises de nos Sujets ou Alliez qui se trouveront dans un Navire ennemy, seront pareillement de bonne prise."

The severity of this application of the principle of infection was, however, as regards the first of the two suppositions—enemy cargoes on neutral ships—mitigated, on condition of a declaration of reciprocity within six months, in favour of neutral shipowners by Art. 1 of the *Règlement* of King Louis XIV "concernant la navigation des bâtimens neutres en tems de guerre" of 26 July 1778 (Martens, R^2, III, 18), as appears from the following extract:

> "... A l'égard des navires des Etats neutres, qui seroient chargés de marchandises de contrebande destinées à l'ennemi, ils pourront être arrêtés, et lesdites marchandises seront saisies et confisquées; mais les bâtimens et le surplus de leur cargaison [obviously even of enemy property] seront relâchés, à moins que ... etc." (the exception relates to the case when the contraband cargo constitutes three fourths of the entire cargo, a subject on which comp. the following section 3, § 3, pp. 376 *et seq.*).

This mitigation of the traditional French practice was continued by Art. 1 of the *Arrêté* of the *Consuls* of 29 frimaire *an* VIII (20 December 1799) (Martens, R^2, VI, 743) and Art. 53 of the *Arrêté* of 2 prairial *an* XI (22 May 1803) (*ibid.*, VIII, 9).

In her Treaty of Commerce and Marine with the Free Imperial City of Hamburg of 1 April 1769 (Martens, R^2, I, 634; Wenck, III, 752; Parry, 44, 255) France still departed in respect of the City from the traditional principle of infection. Art. 23 expressed this in a similar wording:

> "Les vaisseaux de la ville de Hambourg, sur lesquels il se trouvera des marchandises, appartenantes aux ennemis de Sa Majesté, ne pourront être retenus, amenés ni confisqués, non plus que le reste de leur cargaison, mais seulement les marchandises et denrées de la qualité de celles, spécifiées par l'article 16 [foodstuffs] et par l'article 17 [contraband] appartenantes aux ennemis de la France, seront confisquées, de même que les marchandises de contrebande; Sa Majesté dérogeant, à cet égard, à tous usages et ordonnances à ce contraires, même à celles des années 1536, 1584 et 1681, qui portent, que la robe ennemie confisque la marchandise et le vaisseau ami; bien entendu, que si la partie du chargement, qui se trouvera sujette à confiscation, étoit si considérable, qu'elle ne pût être chargée sur le

navire François, il sera permis, en ce cas, au Capitaine du vaisseau François, de conduire le navire Hambourgeois dans le plus prochain port de France, pour être les denrées et marchandises, sujettes à confiscation, déchargées sans retardement, après quoi le vaisseau de Hambourg, avec le reste de sa cargaison, sera relâché et mis en pleine liberté."

The French Court of Cassation, in office at the time as an appellate tribunal in prize cases, by its decision of 4 pluviôse *an* VII (*Traité*, I, 336), reversed *in parte* the decision of an inferior civil tribunal which had confiscated the whole cargo of a condemned enemy vessel, the *Nordel-Falk*, together with the ship: while upholding the condemnation of the Portuguese (enemy) goods on board, the Court applied Art. 2 of the *Règlement* of 1778 by annulling the condemnation of the other half which belonged to merchants from neutral Switzerland and Geneva. There was, therefore, on that occasion no question of *infection hostile* of the neutral position of the cargo carried on an enemy ship.

Sweden, during her Nordic War of 1700-1721, in her Prize Regulations of 1715, threatened, contrary to system (*c*), the condemnation of enemy goods even under a neutral flag; see Art. 12 (*Collectanea Maritima*, p. 171):

"Tous les effets appartenans à des sujets ennemis, ou envoyez pour leur compte, seront confiscables, dans quelque vaisseau que ce soit qu'ils soient trouvez."

When the first American prize courts during the War of Independence had to decide the fate of enemy goods found on board neutral vessels, they at first adhered to the old rule of the *Consulado de Mar* as the accepted customary law and condemned them. This practice was changed, however, when in November 1780 the *Congressional Instructions* to the captains of Americans ships of war and privateers introduced the contrary principle "free ship, free goods" (comp. Chapter I, section 3, at p. 58). Henceforth the Court of Appeals, which had adopted the old rule, also altered its jurisprudence. In one case, however, that of the Dutch ship *Brunette*, which had been captured prior to the Instructions of 1780, but was adjudicated in appeal in 1781, it still condemned the enemy goods on board on a principle of transitional law (Bourguignon, *The first Federal Appellate Court* (1977), p. 281 with footnote 103).

How unsatisfactory the situation still was at the end of the 18th century also appears from Art. XII of the treaty between the United States and Prussia of 11 July 1799 (Martens, R², VI, 669; Parry, 55, 15) in which the parties, after stating that

"Experience having proved that the principle adopted in the twelfth article of the treaty of 1785 [10 September 1785; Martens, R², IV, 37], according to which free ships make free goods, has not been sufficiently respected during the last two wars, and especially in that which still continues",

proposed

"after the return of a general peace, to agree either separately between themselves, or jointly with other powers alike interested, to concert with the great maritime powers of

> Europe such arrangements and such permanent principles as may serve to consolidate the liberty and the safety of the neutral navigation and commerce in future wars. And if, in the interval, either of the contracting parties should be engaged in a war, in which the other should remain neutral, the ships of war and privateers of the belligerent power shall conduct themselves towards the merchant vessels of the neutral power as favourably as the course of the war then existing may permit, observing the principles and rules of the law of nations, generally acknowledged."

The four systems surveyed above remained in operation side by side in different variations for some centuries until the looming clash between belligerents *inter se* and with neutrals at the beginning of the Crimean War forced the belligerents to adopt a compromise solution, initiated by concurrent instructions issued by the governments of France and England on 29, respectively 28 March 1854 (De Pistoye-Duverdy, II, 468 and 469), on which comp. Chapter II, *supra*, p. 128.

This compromise was finally sanctioned by the Declaration of Paris of 16 April 1856 (de Clercq, VI, 91), paragraphs 2 and 3 of which laid down that

> "2. Le pavillon neutre couvre la marchandise ennemie, à l'exception de la contrebande de guerre.
> 3. La marchandise neutre, à l'exception de la contrebande de guerre, n'est pas saisissable sous pavillon ennemi."

Section 3. CONTRABAND OF WAR

General introduction

One of the most basic issues which arose in this field was the question as to whether the carriage of contraband goods to a belligerent was considered to be an action that involved the international responsibility of the State of the carrier and should therefore be prohibited to its subjects by the latter and prevented, or whether it was an activity which did not entail that responsibility but involved only the carrier himself at whose risk the transport was undertaken, save for the duty of his State to acquiesce in lawful countermeasures taken by the other belligerent party.

This dilemma between State responsibility or only personal risk to the carrier did not play a rôle in the days of the Consulat de Mar (*ca* 1370), because that famous document, based on a strict distinction between enemy and non-enemy property at sea, the first subject to confiscation, the second in principle exempt from it, made no mention of the carriage of contraband.

Many treaties of a later period have, however, introduced an obligation of the Contracting Parties to forbid and prevent their nationals from carrying goods to the enemy of the other, should they themselves remain neutral in a future war. Even at a much later date such prohibitions were still contained in municipal legislation, *e.g.*, in the *Non Intercourse Act* of the United States of 10 May 1810, but the issue of such municipal prohibitions was not mandatory under the customary law of nations. This problem is closely related to the content of the concept of neutrality in earlier centuries. It is indeed of far wider purport since it relates not only to the carriage of contraband, but also to other activities of the citizens, such as the violation of a belligerent blockade and the transport of soldiers or sailors by neutral vessels. As I have already set out this question in Chapter II, *sub* 1 (b) of vol. X of this publication on neutrality law (pp. 33-39), I will not expatiate on it again here, but only recall that many older treaties expressly imposed upon the Contracting Parties the obligation to see to it that their subjects should not carry contraband goods to each other's enemy.

There is nothing surprising in the fact that such prohibitions were included in treaties of alliance, such as that of 5 April 1614 between the United Netherlands and Sweden (Dumont, V^2, 245), but they can also be found in other conventions, such as treaties of peace or of commerce. See, for example, the Special Article annexed to the Netherlands-Spanish peace treaty of Münster of 30 January 1648 (Dumont, VI^1, 429, 439; Parry, 1, 109):

> "... bien entendu que les Seigneurs Estats feront défense expresse, que nuls de leurs subjects ne pourront porter des marchandises de contrebande aux ennemis dudit Seigneur Roy",

a prohibition that was further elaborated in Article 5 of the subsequent Netherlands-Spanish treaty of marine of 17 December 1650 (Parry, 2, 259) laying down that

> "... pour d'autant mieux empescher (ce transport), lesdits Seigneurs Etats en feront deffenses bien expresses par Placats & Edits".

That older practice was, however, gradually abolished, although traces of it can still be found much later.

What at the end of the development remained was the rule that the carriage of contraband to a belligerent country or navy by neutral carriers was an action that exposed them to the risk of repressive counter-action by the adversary and that the neutral Power concerned was under an obligation to acquiesce in such counter-action against its subjects if such action remained within the boundaries of customary international law. See for example, Art. 13 of the Treaty of Commerce and Marine between France and Hamburg of 1 April 1769 (Martens, R^2, I, 634; Wenck, III, 752; Parry, 44, 255) by which the Hamburg Senate undertook, in case of a war between France and third Powers other than the Emperor or the Empire, not to tolerate that its citizens should provide the enemies of the King with arms, munitions of war or other contraband goods (specified in Articles 15 and 16). A secret separate Article (Martens, R^2, I, 653) obliged the Free City to punish those of its citizens who might engage in such prohibited trade, on penalty of losing its advantages under the treaty:

> "En cas de contravention à l'article XIII du traité, touchant tout commerce, illicite en tems de guerre, de la part des bourgeois, habitans ou sujets de Hambourg, le Senat en fera raison et justice, si non ladite ville cessera de jouir de tous les avantages qui lui sont accordés par le présent traité."

The description of the captor's action against the carrier of contraband goods as a "penalty" was often used, for instance in the case of the *Commercen* of 1816 (1 Wheaton, 382; Scott's *Cases on International Law*, p. 765), but the Judicial Committee of the Privy Council rightly objected to that description in its judgment of 1921 concerning the *Prins der Nederlanden (No. 3)* (*B.C.P.C.*, III, 943) in the following passages:

> "The term penalty ..., although often mentioned,... is not in this connection really one which implies that the carriage of contraband is attended with the usual incidents of the commission of an offence. Neutrals who carry contraband do not break the law of nations; they run a risk for adequate gain, and if they are caught, they take the consequences. If they know what they are doing, those consequences may be very serious; if they do not, they may get off merely with some inconvenience or delay. This must suffice them. Having done their best to aid one belligerent by carrying contraband for him, they cannot ask that the other shall pay the penalty for their own success in defeating the attempt by rewarding the neutral carrier as if this venture had succeeded. That would be to encourage the carrying of contraband, whereas it is a thing to be deterred...".

This point of view was in strong contrast with early attitudes of belligerent States, which sometimes threatened even capital punishment against carriers of contraband rather than, or in addition to, confiscating their goods.

From among the many topics of the old law of contraband I will deal below successively with the three principal subjects which can be elucidated by municipal or regional regulations, treaties, prize court decisions and, at a later stage, arbitral awards and the writings of legal authors, *viz.*, (1) the categories of goods that could by their nature be lawfully considered and seized as contraband of war; (2) the question of what destination they must have in order to become subject to condemnation as contraband, and (3) what kinds of sanctions were applied to the carriers of contraband and their goods (and ships).

§ 1. *Categories of goods subject to treatment as contraband of war*

Introduction

Before turning to a brief survey of the various goods which have been legally tested on their nature as contraband of war, I will make a few introductory observations.

Controversies over the classification of particular goods as contraband of war naturally arose in particular with regard to goods *ancipitis usus*, also called of "promiscuous use".

According to Pratt-Lee (p. xxxi) an

> "important consideration in determining the character of the goods which fall under this class [of articles] is that of their destination; for it being impossible to ascertain the final use of an article *ancipitis usus*, it is not an injurious rule which deduces both ways the final use from the immediate destination.—Of this the best criterion will perhaps be the nature of the port to which they are bound.—The question to be determined being whether the articles were intended for the ordinary use of life, or even for mercantile ship's use, or whether they were going with a highly probable destination to military use, the nature and quality of the port to which the articles were going is not an irrational test of the matter of fact on which the distinction is to be applied.—If the port is a general commercial port, it shall be understood that the articles were going for civil use, although occasionally a frigate or other ship of war may be constructed in that port. *Contrà*, if the great predominant character of a port be that of a port of naval military equipment, it shall be intended that the articles were going for military use, although it is possible that the articles may be applied to civil consumption."

I cannot but feel a certain lack of logic in this mixing-up of two entirely differing notions. The same objection, for that matter, applies to a corresponding misconception or at least misformulation in French legislation and jurisprudence (*infra*, p. 351).

As an instance on which this dubious theory was enunciated I quote from the judgment concerning the *Twende Brödre* [1801] (4 C.Rob., 33; Roscoe, I, 332): when a treaty—*in casu* an Anglo-Danish treaty of commerce—stipulates that timber is to be regarded as contraband of war if it is destined for the construction of ships—"bois de construction" (interpreted by the Court as referring to "construction navale")—and when the character of the captured timber is ambiguous, its nature is to be decided by reference to the character of the port of destination (the capture was made on a Danish ship, taken on a voyage from Christiansand to Saint Malo or Brest in France).

Comp. on this subject further § 2 on the destination of contraband, *infra*, p. 344.

In earlier times the concept of contraband of war would seem to have been fairly restricted as it, as a rule, included only goods which were clearly of direct and exclusive use for war purposes.

But there were also more severe concepts; for example, a judgment of 1745 during the War of the Austrian Succession in the case of the Swedish vessel *Med Guds Hielpe* (*infra*), which itself referred back to the older case of the *Arms of Plymouth* of 1692, during the Nine Years' War. In that judgment of 1745, never published until 1856, but known from certain references by Sir William Scott (Lord Stowell), concerning a transport of pitch and tar in a ship bound from Stockholm to Port Louis in France, the President, Sir Henry Penrice (*per Curiam*) said (see Sir George Lee's Ms. Notes as published by F.Th. Pratt in 1856, at p. 198):

> "Pitch and tar are of a mixed nature, they may be used for civil purposes and also for fitting ships of war. Sovereign Princes at war may declare such things to be contraband, and, after notice to their allies, their subjects may certainly seize them. The *Arms of Plymouth*, in 1692, is the strongest case that has been cited for condemning this ship."

The same thought was expressed in other judgments of the same period, the *Tweelinge* [1747-1748] (Pratt-Lee, p. 105):

> "Sovereigns have a right to declare what shall be deemed contraband, and have always done so",

and the *Klein(e) David* [1748] (Pratt-Lee, p. 170):

> "Princes declare sometimes things to be contraband which are not so in their nature, and in those cases notifications thereof are given to other sovereigns."

This sovereign power was exercised in England mainly in the form of Orders in Council or of Royal Instructions to King's ships and privateers, such as those of 15 June 1744.

The texts of these legal enactments are inserted in Appendix B to the same work of Pratt, on the origination of which I have given details in Chapter I, section 3, *supra*, pp. 36-42. Those enactments themselves have been applied, construed or simply referred to by British prize courts in many of the judgments surveyed in Sir George Lee's Notes. See, for example, the case of the *Providentia* [1747] (Pratt-Lee, p. 97) and the abovementioned famous judgment of 1745 (Pratt-Lee, pp. 191-205). The latter, for the rest, besides heeding the national instructions, further also argued on the basis of certain provisions in an international convention, especially Articles 11 and 12 of the Anglo-Swedish treaty of 1661.

Sir George Lee's Ms. Notes recall the existence of many treaties defining the concept of contraband of war, as far as England was concerned—apart from other Anglo-Swedish treaties (of 1654, 1656 and 1664, including some concluded by Cromwell, but later repudiated)—, between England and Portugal of 1654, England and Spain of 1667, England and Holland of 1667 and 1674, England and Denmark of 1670, England and Russia of 1734.

The range of action of treaty provisions on contraband of war was often discussed by British prize courts, *inter alia*, in the *Vierge Marie* [1744], in which the Danzig claimant based this action for restoration of his vessel on the Anglo-Russian treaty of 1734. This foundation of the claim was disputed as insufficient because the vessel was not a Russian ship (Pratt-Lee, pp. 47 and 73). Consequently, the outcome of the prize proceedings often depended on the applicability or the construction of the treaty provisions invoked by the parties. An other instance thereof is the case of a cargo, again of pitch and tar, laden on the account of an Englishman in a Swedish vessel, the *Berg(d)stadt*, bound for France, which was seized by a Spanish privateer (Spain being at the time at war with France), carried to Ostend and condemned there upon a declaration of the Spanish Government that the cargo was contraband. In a letter to the King of England of 29 August 1674, Sir Leoline Jenkins disputed the correctness of that condemnation (see fol. 751 (vol. II) of the description of his *Life* by W. Wynne), arguing that it was not in accordance with § 24 of the Anglo-Spanish treaty of 23 May 1667 (Dumont, VII[1], 31; Parry, 10, 63), which he "explained by subsequent usage", but which was not directly applicable in his opinion because the goods were not laden in an English ship. See on this case Pratt-Lee's work at p. 195.

Sir George Lee's Notes also reveal that the *Arms of Plymouth* case of 1692 was not an isolated case since it was preceded or followed by others, such as the *Arms of Copenhagen* [1691] and the *Unity* [1693] (Pratt-Lee, p. 45).

Article 9 of the King's Instructions to privateers of 1744 enjoined them specifically "not to do anything contrary to any treaties" (Pratt-Lee, p. 97).

As remarked above, the treaties listing the goods to be considered as contraband of war fairly often expressly stated that certain other goods were not to be treated as such. I will cite below a number of treaty provisions enumerating a list of contraband and a list of free goods. From those provisions it seems to appear that a tendency gradually emerged to extend the list of contraband goods according as other goods also showed their usefulness for war purposes. I had already an opportunity of mentioning a number of such additional goods in my survey of treaties concerning raw materials, natural products and other commodities in Part VI of this publication, pp. 570 *et seq.*, *sub* 5.

Although the original contraband lists were still single and almost all contained only those goods that really served war purposes, there were rare early exceptions, such as the Anglo-Netherlands treaty of alliance (against Spain) of Southampton of 17 September 1625 (Dumont, V^2, 478), which in Article 20 declared good and lawful prize even such goods as victuals and metals:

> "Toutes marchandises de contrebande, comme sont munitions de bouche et de guerre, navires, armes, voiles, cordages, or, argent, cuivre, fer, plomb et semblables, de quelque part qu'on les voudra porter en Espagne, ... seront de bonne prise avec les navires et hommes qu'ils porteront."

A great many conventions, however, expressly limited the range of contraband goods to relatively small numbers. The treaty provisions enumerating them were in many cases parallelled by others which contained lists of goods that should in no case be considered as contraband of war, as will appear from my following survey of early provisions, borrowed from treaties dating from the second half of the 17th or the first half of the 18th century.

Another juxtaposition of two different categories of sea-borne goods concerned the more or less harmful nature of the cargoes, listed as contraband of war. This contradistinction (between absolute and conditional or relative contraband) was of later date and will also be exemplified by a number of treaty provisions below.

A further contradistinction in this field is that introduced by Pratt in his retrospective analysis (pp. lxi-lxx) between "contraband as declared by treaty" and "contraband by notification".

Treaty provisions enumerating contraband goods

The author who has set out in the greatest detail the range of contraband goods in English case law up to the middle of the 18th century, Fr.Th. Pratt, in his abovementioned *Law of Contraband of War* (London, 1856), has given an elaborate list of goods, invoked with or without success in English courts by captors or claimants, at pp. xxxi-liv of his work and he has supplemented that survey at pp. lxiii-lxv by an alphabetical list of articles referred to under the head of contraband in the treaties from which he inserted extracts in Appendix A.

This Appendix A (Pratt-Lee, pp. 207-249) gives first a list of provisions obtaining in treaties, dating from 1604 to 1803, between England and a number of alphabetically arranged other States, *viz.*, Algiers, America, Brazil, Denmark, France, Portugal, Russia, Spain, the States General (of the United Netherlands) and Sweden. The list is immediately followed by the full texts of a long series of provisions on contraband matters obtaining in the same, this time chronologically arranged, treaties dating from 1604 to 1827, beginning with Article 20 of a treaty of 18 April 1604 between Spain and the States General and continued in the texts of the relevant articles in the same series of treaties between England and the other States, *viz.*:

Russia (1623, 1734, 1766, 1797, 1801);
Spain (1604, 1630, 1667);
France (1655, 1677, 1713, 1786);
Sweden (1654, 1656, 1661, 1803);
the States General (1667, 1668, 1674);
Denmark (1669, 1670, 1673-4, 1780);
Algiers (1686);
America (1794);
Portugal (1810), and
Brazil (1827).

It has to be borne in mind that these treaty provisions were not confined to the delimitation of the categories of contraband goods, but extended also to other contraband problems. I may be allowed to refer here to the texts thus collected by Sir George Lee (Pratt-Lee, pp. 207-249). Since, however, those collected data extend much further than the simple listing of contraband goods dealt with in this § 1, and are, moreover, too exclusively confined to English treaties with foreign States, I will insert below the texts of a number of geographically more widely selected treaty provisions dealing with that particular subject matter, collected before I could finally lay hands on the work of Pratt-Lee.

The treaty between the Netherlands and Algiers of 1622 (Dumont, V^2, 413) mentioned in general terms "goederen van contrabanda" (Art. 6) and various "verboden waren" (prohibited wares), such as war material (powder, lead, iron, tin, balls and guns) and naval stores or ship's material (oars, boards, masts, sails, cables or ropes, pitch and tar) (Art. 21).

Horses were mentioned in Art. II of the Franco-Netherlands Treaty of Maritime Commerce of 18 April 1646 (Dumont, VI[1], 342) and Art. 6 of the Netherlands-Spanish Treaty of Marine of 17 December 1650 (Dumont, VI[1], 570; Parry, 2, 259), in which saltpetre also appeared as a separate commodity:

Art. 6: (contraband) firearms, such as cannon, bombs, shells, etc., gunpowder, fuses, bullets, *saltpetre*; all other weapons, such as pikes and swords, helmets, cuirasses; *horses*; armour, etc. (even including "*gens de guerre*" as contraband); Art. 7: (free list) corn, vegetables, salt, wine, oil and other foodstuffs.

The Anglo-Netherlands Peace Treaty of Westminster of 5 April 1654 (Dumont, VI[2], 74; Parry, 3, 225) did not mention any specific goods as contraband, but Cromwell and the States General agreed to enter into negotiations on the subject (Art. 7).

The Netherlands-Portuguese treaty of 6 August 1661 (Dumont, VI[2], 366; Parry, 6, 375) formed an exception to the general trend since Art. 12 permitted the Dutch to transport all sorts of contraband from anywhere to anywhere, provided they did not carry *krijgstuig* (implements of war) to the enemies of Portugal from Portuguese ports. The text was worded as follows:

> "Liberum praeterea Belgarum Foederatorum Populo, ac permissum sit praeter Mercis omne genus, Arma etiam, res bellicas, & annonam tam ex Foederatorum Belgii Provinciarum, quam ex aliis quibusvis Portubus ac Terris in quascunque Orbis Regiones, & ad quascunque Gentes transferre tam inimicas Regi Regnoque Lusitanae, quam amicas ac foederatas, nec dicto Regi ejusve subditis aut Ministris huic rei moram aut impedimentum afferre liceat per detentiones, repressalias, pignorationes ullove alio modo sive id directe aperteque sive oblique ac occulte fiat, dummodo dictus Foederatorum Belgarum Populus ex ipsis Portubus Lusitanis Armorum nihil apparatus aut rerum bellicarum ad dicti Regis Regnique Hostes & adversarios transvectet; nec minus iisdem Foederatis Belgis integrum relinquatur ac permittatur, in universam Ditionem dicti Regis quascunque Merces, res etiam ad armaturam, Bellum ac Militarem annonam pertinentes inferre, easque non minus magna quam exigua copia venales exponere, & sive integras simul, sive seorsum & per partes pretio ibidem quocunque vendere, ac pro arbitrio suo permutare, Commerciaque quaevis exercere cum iis Emptoribus Negotiatoribusve, quos ipsi fore sibi potissimum utiles ac commodos arbitrabuntur, nec interpellari aut a proposito eos dimoveri per Regem Regiosque Ministros Propolas, Monopoliorum Exercitores, Fiscum, juridicos Confessus, quemvis alium ullo modo, ullave de causa fas esto; nullo denique Mercimoniorum limite aut regula circumscribantur."

The Netherlands-French Treaty of Alliance of 27 April 1662 (Dumont, VI[2], 412; Parry, 7, 139), Art. 28 (contraband): fire arms, gunpowder, bombs, gun-carriages, swords, horses; Art. 29 (free list): grains, vegetables, oil, wine, salt and foodstuffs in general.

The Anglo-Swedish Treaty of Commerce of 21 October 1661 (Dumont, VI[2], 384; Pratt-Lee, 213; Parry, 6, 469); Art. XI:

"Although in the preceding Articles of this present Treaty, it be forbidden to either Confederate to yield any aid or assistance to the enemies of the other; yet it is not to be so understood, as if either Confederate, having no war with the enemies of the other, might not sail to, or traffic with the said enemies, notwithstanding that the other Confederate be in actual war with them. But it is only provided that no goods called goods of contraband, and particularly, that no money, provisions, weapons, fire-arms, with their appurtenances, fire-balls, gunpowder, match, bullets, spear-heads, swords, lances, pikes, halberts, ordnance, mortar-pieces, petards, grenadoes, rests, bandeliers, saltpetre, pistols, small shot, pots, head-pieces, backs and breasts, or such kind of armour; *soldiers [sic]*; horses, all furniture necessary for horses, holsters, belts, and whatsoever warlike instruments; as also, that no *ships or war*, or convoys, be furnished to the enemy, without peril, in case they be taken, of being adjudged lawful prize, without hope of restitution. And neither of the Confederates shall suffer any of His subjects to give aid, sell or lend ships, or be any way useful to the enemies or rebels of the other, to His prejudice or detriment; but it shall be lawful for either Confederate, His people and subjects, to have commerce with the enemies of the other, and to carry to them all kind of merchandize, not before excepted, without any let or hindrance, unless it be into such ports and places as are besieged by the other, and in such case, it shall be lawful for them to sell their commodities to the besiegers, or other wise to betake themselves to any other port which is not besieged."

The "conventio praevia" of 6/16 July 1667 between the Netherlands and Sweden (Dumont, VII[1], 37; Parry, 10, 187), which contained a special agreement concerning the goods to be mutually considered as contraband of war, listed as such (in Art. 3), *inter alia*, horses and saddles, and excluded from that classification (in Art. 4) money, grains, vegetables, salt, wine, oil, and other victuals; iron, copper and ores; even ship's materials. The text of these provisions was to the following effect:

Art. 3 (contraband):

"Ut verò evitentur penitus atque amoveantur Controversiae & disceptationes, quae ob designandam jam dictam Mercem de Contrabanda oriri aliquando possent, convenit utrimque ac pro re rata habitum est, hoc in numero duci & censeri oportere Arma quaevis ad vim tam propulsandam quam inferendam apta, praesertim quae ignem concipiunt pulvere tormentario, quem dicunt, admoto, aliaque eodem pertinentia, ejus verò generis intelligantur Tormenta Bellica majora & minora omnis generis, quae Canones & Sclopeta vulgo dicuntur, Mortaria, Petardae, Bombae, Granatae, Saucisae, Coronae Picae, Affeutae, Furcae Sclopetatiae, Bandelaria, Pulvis Tormentarius, Fomites sive Lonten, Glades Tormentariae tam ferreae quam plumbeae, Nitrum sive Salpetrae, Enses, Lanceae, Hastae, Hellebardae, Bipennes, Flagella armata, Cuspides, & reliqua id genus Arma ad vim inferendam apta. Tum Cassides, Galeae, Loricae, Thoraces aerei ferreique, Clipei, aliaque arma ad vim arcendam idonea, praeterea ad Bellum instruendum utilia quaecumque, nempe Equi, Ephippia, Sclopetorum Equestrium reconditoria, & quicquid denique utile aut necessarium ad instruendos equos tam Turmarum equestrium, quam rei tormentariae, nisi numero sint admodum exiguo, ut inde conjectura probabilis elici possit, eadem non ad Bellum sed ad alios usus esse destinata."

Art. 4 (free list):

"Merci prohibitae nequaquam accensebuntur Pecunia, Frumenti ac Leguminis genus omne, Sal, Vinum, Oleum, nec quicquid ad victum aut alimentum refertur, sed nec Ferrum, Cuprum, Aes, nec quidquid ad Naves construendas, instruendasve, necessarium est, cujus notae sunt Cannabis, Linteamen velis nauticis aptum, Picis tam liquidae quam arida omne genus, Mali, Trabes, Lignum incurvum, Tabulae navales, Rudentes, Anchorae, vel Anchorarum partes quaelibet, hoc in numero habebuntur, nec aliae Merces, quae pro terrestri vel maritimo Bello formam non acceperunt, multo minus hae, quae ad alium quemvis usum jam apparatae ac conformatae sunt, nec aliud Mercimonii genus quodcumque, quod praecedenti paragrapho designatum non sit. Sed id omne transportari huc illuc licebit, etiam ad illas Nationes quibuscum Foederatorum alter Bello jam nunc involutus est, aut postmodum involvi posset."

Great Britain's Peace Treaty of Breda with the United Netherlands of 21/31 July 1667 (Dumont, VIII[1], 44; Parry, 10, 231) ended with a number of separate articles, No. III of which regulated the carrying of contraband provisionally in conformity with Arts. 26-42 of the treaty with France of 27 April 1662, in preparation of an elaborate Anglo-Netherlands Treaty of Marine. This treaty was entered into on 17 February 1668 (Dumont, VII[1], 74) and included an Art. 18 which provided in general terms for a procedure to complement or revise its provisions should they appear to show lacunae or to have undesirable effects. It was in its turn replaced with a new Treaty of Marine of 1/10 December 1674 (Dumont, VII[1], 283; Parry, 13, 255) which laid down in Articles 3 and 4 that

"3. Under this name of Contraband or prohibited merchandizes shall be comprehended only arms, pieces of ordnance, with all implements belonging to them, fire-balls, powder, match, bullets, pikes, swords, lances, spears, halberds, guns, mortar-pieces, petards, granadoes, musquet-rests, bandeliers, salt-petre, musquets, musquet-shot, helmets, breast-plates, coats of mail, and the like kind of armature, *soldiers*, horses, and all things necessary for the furniture of horses, holsters, belts, and all other warlike instruments whatsoever.

4. These merchandizes following shall not be reckoned among prohibited goods, *viz.*, all kind of cloth; and all other manufactures woven of any kind of wool, flax, silk, cotton, or any other material, all sorts of clothing and vestments, together with the materials whereof they use to be made: gold and silver, as well coined as not coined, tin, iron, lead, copper, and coals; as also wheat, barley, and all other kind of corn or pulse; tobacco, and all kind of spices, salted and smoked flesh, salted and dried fish, butter and cheese, beer, oils, wines, sugars, and all sort of salt; and in general, all provision which serves for the nourishment and sustenance of life; likewise all kind of cotton, hemp, flax, and pitch; and ropes, sails, and anchors, also masts and planks, boards and beams of what sort of wood soever, and all other materials requisite for the building or repairing ships, but they shall be wholly reputed amongst free goods, even as all other wares and commodities which are not comprehended in the next precedent article; so that the same may be freely transported and carried by the subjects of his said Majesty, even unto places in enmity with the said States, as also on the other side, by the subjects of the said States, to places under the obedience of the enemies of his said Majesty; except only towns or places besieged, environed, or invested, in French, blocquées ou investies."

26 November 1675, the Netherlands-Sweden, treaty of commerce (Dumont, VII[1], 316; Parry, 14, 41), Art. 3 (contraband); Art. 4 (free list).

10 August 1678, France-the Netherlands, treaty of commerce (Dumont, VII[1], 357; Parry, 14, 399), Art. 15 (contraband); Art. 16 (free list).

2/12 October 1679, the Netherlands-Sweden, treaty of commerce (Dumont, VII[1], 437; Parry, 15, 331), Art. 15 (contraband); Art. 16 (free list).

19 May 1691, Declaratory Ordinance of King Christian V of Denmark

(Dumont, VII², 292), with an annex specifying contraband goods, repeated in Denmark's treaty with England and the Netherlands of 20/30 June 1691, Art. 2 (Parry, 19, 297), because no specification of contraband goods had ever yet been incorporated in any Danish treaty with the Netherlands.

20 September 1697, France-the Netherlands, treaty of commerce (Dumont, VII², 386; Parry, 21, 371), Art. 20 (contraband); Art. 21 (free list).

Arts. 19 and 20 of the treaty of commerce and navigation concluded between France and Great Britain at the Peace Congress of Utrecht on 11 April 1713—often praised as a paragon of an early 18th century commercial treaty (Dumont, VIII¹, 345; Parry, 28, 1) present an interesting picture of the international conceptions of contraband law prevailing at that period. Art. 19 listed as contraband:

> "les armes, canons, arquebuses, mortiers, pétards, bombes, grenades, saucisses, cercles poissez, affûts, fourchettes, bandoullières, poudre à canon, mèsche, salpêtre, balles, picques, espées, morions, casques, cuirasses, hallebardes, javelines, fourreaux de pistolets, baudriers, chevaux, avec leurs harnois, et tous semblabes genres d'armes et d'instruments de guerre servant à l'usage des troupes."

The free list in Article 20 covered a wide range of goods

> "toutes sortes de drap et tous autre ouvrages de manufactures de laine, de lin, de soye, de cotton, et de toute autre matière, tous genres d'habillemens avec les choses qui servent ordinairement à les faire, or, argent monnoyé et non monnoyé, éstain, fer, plomb, cuivre, laiton, charbons à fourneau, bled, orge, et toute autre sorte de grains et de légumes, la nicotine, vulgairement appellée tabac, toutes sortes de aromates, chairs salées, & fumées, poissons salez, fromage & beurre, bière, huile, vins, sucres, toutes sortes de sels et de provisions servant à la nourriture & à la subsistance des hommes, tous genres de cotton, chanvre lin, poix, tant liquide que sèche, cordages, cables, voiles, toiles propres à faire des voiles, ancres, & parties d'ancre, quelles qu'elles puissent être, mâts de navires, planches, madriers, poûtres de toute sorte d'arbres, & toutes les autres choses nécessaires pour construire ou pour radouber les vaisseaux. On ne regardera pas non plus comme marchandises de contrebande, celles qui n'auront pas pris la forme de quelque instrument ou attirail servant à l'usage de la guerre sur terre ou sur mer, encore moins celles qui sont préparées ou travaillées pour tout autre usage."

The situation remained fairly constant during the further part of the 18th century. See, for instance, Arts. 26 and 27 of the treaty of 23 August 1742 between Denmark-Norway and France (Wenck, I, 591; Parry, 36, 425):

> "26. Sous le genre de marchandises de contrebande sont comprises seulement les armes tant à feu que d'autres sortes avec leurs assortimens, comme canons, mousquets, mortiers, pétards, bombes, grenades, cercles poissés, affûts, fourchettes, bandolières, poudre, mêches, salpétre, balles, piques, épées, morions, casques, cuirasses, halbardes, lances, javelines, chevaux, selles de cheval, fourreaux de pistolets, baudriers, & généralement tous autres assortimens, servant à l'usage de la guerre; de même que le goudron ou poix raisiné, les voiles, chanvres & cordages.
>
> 27. Dans ce genre de marchandises de contrebande l'on ne comprend point les fromens, bleds, & autres grains de quelque nature & espèce qu'ils soient, & beaucoup moins les légumes, huiles, vins, sels, & généralement tout ce qui appartient à la sustentation de la vie. Et ainsi toutes ces choses pourront toujours se vendre & transporter comme les autres

marchandises, même aux lieux tenus par un ennemi de l'une des deux Couronnes, pourvu qu'ils ne soient assiégés ou bloqués",

and Arts. 15 and 16 of the treaty of 1 April 1769 between France and Hamburg (Martens, R[1], I, 290; Wenck, III, 572; Parry, 44, 255): listing among contraband goods, *inter alia*, saltpetre and sulphur, and as free goods: grain, vegetables, wine, oil, salt and other foodstuffs.

On the other hand, the treaty of commerce between Great Britain and Russia of 20 June/1 July 1766 (Martens, R[2], I, 390; Parry, 43, 365) contained no more than a single list of contraband goods (Art. 11):

> "Tous les canons, mortiers, armes à feu, pistolets, bombes, grenades, boulets, balles, fusils, pierres-à-feu, mêches, poudre, salpêtre, souffre, cuirasses, piques, épées, ceinturons, poches à cartouche, selles & brides, au-delà de la quantité qui peut être nécessaire pour l'usage du vaisseau, ou au-delà de celle, que doit avoir chaque homme servant sur le vaisseau & passager, seront réputés munitions ou provisions de guerre, & s'il s'en trouve, ils seront confisqués, selon les lois, comme contrebande ou effets prohibés: mais ni les vaisseaux, ni les passagers, ni les autres marchandises, qui s'y trouveront en même tems, ne seront point détenus, ni empêchés de continuer leur voyage."

Double lists (of "absolute" and of "conditional" contraband) only appeared at a later stage. An early and still rudimentary example of a distinction between two separate lists of contraband was that agreed between the Netherlands and Sweden in the above-quoted Art. 4 of the "conventio praevia" of 6/16 July 1667, a provision which hovered on the borderline between the carriage of contraband and the breach of a blockade. That article also included again soldiers, the main category of "quasi-contraband" (comp. *infra*, p. 457).

The Institut de Droit International

The text of the five paragraphs constituting *sub* A the *Réglementation internationale de la contrebande de guerre*, laid down in its resolution of 1896, which obtained and retained an independent existence beside the general *Règlement* of 1882-1887, ran as follows:

> "§ 1. — Sont articles de contrebande de guerre: 1°. les armes de toute nature; 2°. les munitions de guerre et les explosifs; 3°. le matériel militaire, (objets d'équipement, affûts, uniformes etc. —); 4°. les vaisseaux équipés pour la guerre; 5°. les instruments spécialement faits pour la fabrication immédiate de munitions de guerre; lorsque ces divers objets sont transportés par mer pour le compte et à destination d'un belligérant.
>
> La destination pour l'ennemi est présumée lorsque le transport va à l'un de ses ports, ou bien à un port neutre qui, d'après des preuves évidentes et de fait incontestable, n'est qu'une étape pour l'ennemi, comme but final de la même opération commerciale.
>
> § 2. — Sous la dénomination de munitions de guerre doivent être compris les objets qui, pour servir immédiatement à la guerre n'exigent qu'une simple réunion ou juxtaposition.
>
> § 3. — Un objet ne saurait être qualifié de contrebande à raison de la seule intention de l'employer à aider ou favoriser l'ennemi, ni par cela seul qu'il pourrait être, dans un but militaire, utile à un ennemi ou utilisé par lui, ou qu'il est destiné a son usage.

§ 4. — Sont et demeurent abolies, les prétendues contrebandes désignées sous les noms, soit de contrebande *relative*, concernant des articles (*usus ancipitis*) susceptibles d'être utilisés par un belligérant dans un but militaire, mais dont l'usage est essentiellement pacifique, soit de contrebande *accidentelle*, quand lesdits articles ne servent spécialement aux buts militaires que dans une circonstance particulière.

§ 5. — Néanmoins, le belligérant a, à son choix et à charge d'une équitable indemnité, le droit de séquestre ou de préemption, quant aux objets qui, en chemin vers un port de son adversaire, peuvent également servir à l'usage de la guere et à des usages pacifiques."

These five substantive paragraphs *sub* A were complemented *sub* C with two others of a more general purport:

"§ 9. En cas de saisies ou répressions non justifiées pour cause de contrebande ou de transport, l'Etat du capteur sera tenu aux dommages intérêts et à la restitution des objets.

§ 10. Un transport parti avant la déclaration de la guerre et sans connaissance obligée de son imminence n'est pas punissable."

This *Réglementation* contained, moreover, *sub* B, §§ 6-8, a number of rules under the separate heading "Service de transport", a subject that is as a rule indicated as "unneutral service" and whereupon I therefore refer to section 5, *infra*, p. 456.

In the following pages I will now carry out my plan of exposition outlined *supra*.

Quasi-contraband

A very special category of contraband has for a long time consisted in what was called quasi-contraband or *contrebande par analogie*, *i.e.* the conveyance of passengers, in particular troops or individual soldiers or officers, by neutral vessels to a belligerent country or navy. Such transportation was generally held by the other belligerent to justify their removal from the neutral vessel and often the latter's condemnation in prize on account of that transportation. The term "quasi-contraband" fell gradually into disuse and was replaced by other terms, such as "unneutral service" or "*assistance hostile*", under which they are indicated, *inter alia*, in Articles 45-47 of the London Declaration on Naval Warfare of 26 February 1909. The original version of this type of assistance to the enemy can be found in many 17th and 18th century treaties, the relevant texts of several of which I have quoted in § 1 of the present section 3 (Contraband), *supra* at pp. 337 *et seq*. There is therefore no need to return here to this special type of action, the conveyance of "contraband persons", which I have already discussed from its neutrality aspect in Part IX-B (vol. X) of this publication, pp. 96, 135 and 180, and which I will still examine from its prize law aspect in section 5 (Unneutral service), *infra* at pp. 458 *et seq*. There is the less reason for that because the transport of troops or soldiers is notionally linked not only with the transport of contraband goods, but also with the rule set out in section 2 under A (pp. 301 *et seq*.), concerning the treatment of enemy goods conveyed on neutral vessels. Just as troops and soldiers were sometimes ranked among "goods" in order to subject them to treatment as contraband, so they were sometimes also equalized with "goods" in another context, *viz.*, for the purpose of excepting them from the exemption of enemy goods carried on neutral vessels.

I confine myself, therefore, to quoting here a few legal texts which reflect those two trains of thought, viz.:

Article 32 of the Netherlands-Swedish treaty of commerce and navigation of 2 (12) October 1679 (Parry, 15, 346):

> "De plus pour d'autant mieux prevenir les differents qui pouroient naistre touchant la designation des Marchandises defendue de Contrebande, il a esté declaré, convenu, que soubs ledit nom seront comprises toutes Armes à feu, assortissements d'icelles, etc. ... Est encore prohibé soubs ledit nom le transport de gens de Guerre, de Chevaux, de Harnachements, etc."; and

Article 11 of the French *Ordonnance* of 1681, which enumerated together as subject to confiscation (sic!) "chevaux et équipages qui seront transportez pour le service de nos ennemis...", or Article 22 of the Netherlands-French Treaty of Commerce of Nijmegen of 10 August 1678 (Dumont, VII[1], 357; Parry, 14, 399), expressing the same idea in the following wording:

> "Et comme il a été réglé ci-dessus qu'un navire libre affranchira les denrées y chargées, il a été en outre accordé et convenu que cette liberté s'étendra aussi aux personnes qui se trouveront en un navire libre, à tel effet que, quoiqu'elles fussent ennemis de l'un et de l'autre des Parties, pourtant se trouvans dans le navire libre, n'en pourront estre tirées, si ce n'est qu'ils fussent gens de guerre et effectivement en service desdits ennemis".

How familiar and persistent this idea of quasi-contraband was in former centuries, and still was at the end of the 19th century is also demonstrated by the fact that F.Th. Pratt still discussed the conveyance of despatches and passengers as coming under that denomination within the subject matter of his work of 1856 on the *Law of Contraband of War*, pp. liv-lxi, and that even the *Institut de Droit International* still adhered to the idea in its session of Venice of 1896.

§ 2. *The destination of contraband goods to the enemy. Proof and the system of presumptions. Destination of the ship and destination of the contraband cargo. Growth of the doctrine of continuous voyage*

As I have set out in my General Introduction on contraband of war, p. 331, a few subjects of the law of contraband lend themselves in particular to a spreading of their historical description and analysis over the two successive phases of the pre-codification period, the formative and the consolidation phase. The destination of contraband goods is one of them and accordingly I will apply this temporal division to the discussion of the issue of destination.

1. *The formative period*
Just as in many other fields of prize law, the bodies of case law concerning the destination of merchant ships and their sea-borne cargoes to the enemy, produced by the two principal actors in the field, England and France, show little ressemblance. That is why I will deal separately in the following pages with the jurisprudence, handed down to us in the formative phase by each of the two Powers. In this case I will begin with the case law of France whose prize courts were to a far higher degree subordinate to the national legislation than were their English counterparts which enforced an independent position vis-à-vis their legislative authorities.

As the doctrine on the destination of contraband goods has been developed in particular by English, and at a later stage by American prize courts, the survey of the case law available on the subject will mainly be confined to their jurisprudence.

Introductory observations. When adjudicating upon claims for the condemnation of captured goods as good and lawful prize, early prize tribunals already took great care in assessing the value of the evidence of enemy destination produced by the captor. The captor often felt it impossible to produce direct proof and consequently attempted to substantiate his claim for condemnation of the prize by invoking certain probabilities which justified the presumption that the objects seized were enemy property or destined for the enemy, a presumption which could only be rebutted by adequate counterproof. This amounted to a reversion of the usual division of the burden of proof, which in principle rested on the captor.

Early presumptions of this kind assumed by prize courts were still relatively innocuous, such as, as regards absolute contraband, the transporting vessel being on her way to an enemy or to some place on the territory, or within the occupation boundaries, of the enemy, entailing an unrebuttable presumption of enemy destination—see the *Charlotte* [1804] (5 C.Rob., 305; Roscoe, I, 490)—and as regards conditional contraband, the transporting vessel being on her way to the naval or military forces of the enemy, or to some place of naval or military armament within the occupation of documents, entailing a rebuttable presumption of enemy destination—see, among others, the *Ringende Jacob* [1798] (1 C.Rob., 89; Roscoe, I, 60), the *Jonge Margaretha* [1799] (1 C.Rob., 189; Roscoe, I, 100), the *Edward* [1801] (4 C.Rob., 68; Roscoe, I, 350), and the *Twende Brödre* [1801] (4 C.Rob., 33; Roscoe, I, 332). But presumptions subsequently adduced were not always equally harmless and the system has in later periods, especially during World War I, even led to outright absurdities.

The prize courts were often only too willing to come to the captor's aid by admitting the reasonableness of certain legal presumptions, and thus to condone the reversal of the *onus probandi*. But there arose other controversial points. Was it necessary to show by adequate evidence that the ship and her cargo were on their way to the enemy without calling at an intermediate non-enemy port, or could enemy destination equally be admitted if the enemy destination was only to be reached via a call by the ship at such a non-enemy port? Moreover, what was the relation between the destination of the carrying ship and that of the carried goods? And as far as proof of a specific intention to assist the enemy with the goods was required, whose intention had to be proved, that of the consignor or that of the consignee? Or was no subjective intention necessary at all and could enemy destination be inferred from objective data which justified the conclusion that the cargo would in actual fact reach the enemy? It is this aggregate of problems which is hidden behind the comprehensive heading of this paragraph 2. They are so closely interconnected that they can scarcely be examined in separate sub-paragraphs.

An important element in the conduct of prize proceedings has always been the problem of the destination of the contraband goods in its two variants outlined above and the evidence to be produced as proof of such destination, if need be with the help of circumstantial evidence or legal presumptions. The distinction between those two destinations—to the enemy country in general, respectively to the enemy government or their military or naval forces—has sometimes been expressed as a distinction between "destination de direction" and "destination d'emploi".

Another distinction was that between the ultimate destination of the transporting vessel and that of the transported cargo, a distinction which in its turn led to the introduction of the doctrine of continuous voyage, already well-known from other domains of prize law (*infra*), into the law relating to the transport of contraband.

This basic distinction between the two destinations and the connected application of the doctrine of continuous voyage was developed, in particular, during the American Civil War of 1861-1865, when the Southern States were supplied with necessary goods by neutral traders via the Caribbean islands. It was later expressed in the following wording:

> "The character of contraband of war depends on the final and intentional destination of the cargo and not on the immediate and material destination of the vessel."

The last development preceding and influencing the prize law codification at the London Conference on Naval Warfare of 1908-09 was attributable to a famous incident of 1896 when a Dutch merchant ship, the *Doelwijk*, was captured by the Italian navy, suspected of carrying contraband via the French port of Djibouti on the Red Sea. This incident (*infra*, p. 368) gave rise to a new version of the doctrine:

> "Contraband exists when the vessel is directed towards a neutral port there to discharge the goods destined to proceed by land-route to the enemy country, particularly if the country in question has no outlet on the sea."

It was in the same late period of the 19th century that the *Institut de droit international* tackled the problem of continuous voyage in the law of contraband. Its first attempt to codify the law of contraband of war in general only led to the adoption at its session of Turin (1882) of a few summary and insignificant articles (§§ 30-33, 113 and 117), which were completely silent about such vital issues as the fate of the transporting vessel and the application of the doctrine of continuous voyage to contraband of war.

The latter subject was only examined in the mid-1890's in three consecutive sessions, respectively at Paris (1894), Cambridge (1895) and Venice (1896). An *avant-projet*, discussed and adopted in 1894, included a section 7 (1) establishing a presumption of enemy destination of contraband goods if either they themselves had that destination, directly or indirectly, or the vessel alone had it (*Annuaire de l'I.D.I.*, vol. 13 (1894-1895), p. 102). A subsequent proposal by Perels in 1895 pursuant to which, if contraband goods were *en route* for a neutral port, the presumption should be that their destination was neutral, but that presumption might be overthrown by clear proof from special circumstances or the ship's papers, was not adopted (*Annuaire*, vol. 14 (1895-1896), p. 65). It was only fourteen years after Turin that the *Institut* at its session of 1896 in Venice, resumed its deliberations on contraband and on that occasion finally agreed on the following version of the doctrine of continuous voyage (English translation):

> "Destination for the enemy is presumed when the carriage of the goods is directed towards one of its ports, or towards a neutral port which, by evident proofs arising from incontestable facts, is only a stage in a carriage to the enemy as the final object of the same commercial transaction" (*Annuaire*, vol. 15 (1896), p. 122).

In their case law illustrating the way in which especially the British prize courts have implemented the general principles summarized above they have taken as their natural point of departure that goods in the nature of contraband of war were legally only subject to seizure and confiscation when they were on their way to an enemy destination and when that destination was duly proven, preferably by evidence from the ship herself. Initially the required destination was destination to the enemy without further specification, but concurrently with the expansion of the range of goods potentially useful for war purposes, the courts developed a double differentiation, on the one hand, between absolute and conditional (or relative) contraband and, on the other, between destination to the enemy government, army or navy, and destination to the enemy country at large. The latter destination sufficed for the seizure of absolute contraband, whereas the former was required for the seizure of conditional contraband.

In the present context I must briefly return to the question discussed in § 2 (*supra*, p. 345), whether the destination of a cargo can logically be used as a criterion of its contraband character. I have already expressed my theoretical doubts about the correctness of that theory. But I cannot deny that there are many examples of cases in which British prize courts have held that, if the nature of a cargo as contraband of war was doubtful, the character of its port of destination was decisive of that nature, nor that Pratt, in the analytical part of his work on the *Law of Contraband of War* of 1856, preceding the texts of Sir George Lee's Ms. Notes on the British judgments delivered during the War of the Austrian Succession and the references in those Notes to older judgments, has endorsed that view (at p. xxxi).

What that same author remarked there on the subject was rather superficial. He argued indeed only in the context of his debatable thesis that the character of cargoes as contraband of war depends partly on their nature, partly on their destination. Although it is, of course, perfectly true that goods in the nature of contraband are only liable to condemnation if their destination is hostile, these two aspects should, in my opinion, not be jumbled together in that way, not even terminologically. The full text of his summarizing conclusion is worded as follows:

> "Another important consideration in determining the character of the goods which fall under this class is that of their destination; for it being impossible to ascertain the final use of an article *ancipitis usus*, it is not an injurious rule which deduces both ways the final use from the immediate destination.
>
> Of this the best criterion will perhaps be the nature of the port to which they are bound.
>
> The question to be determined being whether the articles were intended for the ordinary use of life, or even for mercantile ship's use, or whether they were going with a highly probable destination to military use, the nature and quality of the port to which the articles were going is not an irrational test of the matter of fact on which the distinction is to be applied.
>
> If the port is a general commercial port, it shall be understood that the articles were going for civil use, although occasionally a frigate or other ship of war may be constructed in that port. *Contrà*, if the great predominant character of a port be that of a port of naval military equipment, it shall be intended that the articles were going for military use, although it is possible that the articles may be applied to civil consumption."

This is one of the few observations which Pratt devoted to the question of the destination of contraband. Arguments of this kind, in my opinion, demonstrate that this mixing-up of two different elements—the intrinsic nature of certain goods and their actual destination to the enemy—still lacked, in the eighteenth century, satisfactory doctrinal profundity, or at least did not testify to a high degree of legal interest, and this obviously has remained so even in the first half of the nineteenth century.

In the following pages I will therefore attempt to isolate the problem of enemy destination by arranging the available precedents dealing more or less directly with it under a few general headings, and by indicating the situations in which enemy destination could reasonably be presumed, or was invoked by the captor without success.

The issue of the enemy destination of contraband goods as it presented itself to prize courts in the past cannot be dealt with easily because of the extreme variety of the factual, and often very complicated, conditions in which their transportation took place. These differed indeed from case to case and it would take up far too much room to describe the divergent circumstances of each particular transport: the direct or indirect destination of the carrying ship and/or the carried goods, the veracity of the ostensible destination, the character and location of the port of destination, the content of the contract of conveyance, the general disposition, conduct and intention of the consignor, the forwarding address of the consignee, various forms of fraudulent behaviour, such as the use of false papers, deviation of the transporting vessel, etc. The discussion before the prize courts also often revolved around the adequacy or inadequacy of the evidence produced. I will therefore quote below from the ample case law available a freely selected and arranged number of cases from the formative period up to 1815 as examples of the variety of the situations with which the British prize courts were faced in the past and of the specific grounds on which the enemy destination of goods with a contraband nature was claimed by the captor, disputed by the cargo-owner or the master, and admitted or denied by the prize court. There is little reason to arrange the subject of enemy destination strictly according to the successive wars in which England became involved. More suitable is an arrangement according to the various presumptions adduced by the courts or the parties to substantiate the enemy or non-enemy destination of contraband goods in the many cases in which no direct proof thereof could be produced. It is that arrangement which I will apply below.

A few judgments of a more general character may first be dealt with.

According to Sir William Scott in the *Trende Söstre* [1807] (6 C.Rob., footnote at pp. 390 *et seq.*; Roscoe, I, 588) and the *Richmond* [1804] (5 C.Rob., 325), the destination of the cargo was generally presumed to be that of the ship. When the ship was bound to call at more ports than one, the presence on board of merchandise *bona fide* documented to be discharged in a neutral port before the ship would reach the enemy port, should not be considered as a valid reason for seizure. But in the absence of such documentary proof the port least favourable to the neutral was to be regarded as the port of destination of the contraband cargo.

A general observation by Pratt (at p. xxi), apparently, but not very clearly, based on that same *Trende Söstre* case, was to the effect that in the case of "several destinations" of the goods on board

> "it will not be allowed that a vessel, having on board a mixed cargo of contraband and innocent articles, should sail on different destinations, some hostile, others neutral, under the pretence that at such destinations as might be hostile the innocent articles only are intended to be landed and delivered, the contraband articles being destined for an ulterior neutral port."

In the course of prize court proceedings during the War of the Austrian Succession mention was often made of "discretionary destination". Thus, the Swedish vessel *Louissa* [1745-1746] (Pratt-Lee, p. 49) was bound from a

Swedish port near Kalmar to Lisbon, "or any port or place in England or France, as the master should think fit to go to if the voyage was likely to prove long". The lading consisted of various kinds: paving stones, pitch, tar and fir planks; ship and lading belonged for one-eighth to her master. The ship was driven by privateers to the French coast and then proposed to go to Havre de Grâce for a market: during that part of the voyage she was seized. Sir Henry Penrice found no *mala fides* in the master and no intention to aid the enemy, his only intention being to sell the cargo in the best possible market; neither was there any ground for considering the bills of lading as colourable. Under those conditions both ship and cargo were restored to the owners upon giving bail to sell the cargo in Lisbon, as was in fact done.

To the same effect the *Providentia* [1747] (Pratt-Lee, p. 94), a Lübeck-built Russian vessel with naval stores on board, whose voyage was from Riga to Brest, Port Louis, Nantes, Rochefort and Bordeaux "at whichever of those places the master could get the best market".

See also the case of the Danish *Ebenezer* [1747] (Pratt-Lee, p. 136):

> "The papers show she was bound either to England or to France; from the examination it appears that she was then intended for Brest, as the best market, but she does not appear to have been specially destined to Brest... It would be hard to confiscate this ship and cargo, as her destination to France was not certain."

The ship and cargo were restored on security given by the owners to sell the cargo in England.

French jurisprudence during the formative phase. As far as I am aware, old French legislation and jurisprudence have not contributed much to the problem of enemy destination of contraband goods. In their *Traité des prises maritimes*, where one has to look for the subject mainly in section 1 of *chapitre* II of *titre* IV under the heading "Liberté de navigation et de commerce des neutres" (vol. I, pp. 337-364), subsidiarily also in section 3 of that same *chapitre* and *titre* under the heading "Contrebande de guerre" (I, 392-415), and additionally even in *titre* III under the heading "Des temps dans lesquels s'exerce le droit de prise" (I, 214 *et seq.*), the authors De Pistoye and Duverdy as usual begin by citing the text of the laws in force in France, especially those of 1681 (*titre* IX, Article 11) and 1798 (Art. 1), and the treaties on the subject entered into by France (I, 396-401). What, after an exposé of their own view of the matter (I, 401 *et seq.*), they quote as the contribution of old prize courts to the régime of French contraband law is very limited indeed (I, 406-415). The judgments reported there: *Le Statira contre le Hasard* [*an* VIII] (II, 121), the *Confidentia* [*an* X] (I, 406), *Le Portland contre le Diable-à-quatre* [*an* VIII] (I, 408; II, 66), *Le Charles-Antoine contre le Camus* [*an* IX] (I, 408), *L'Etoile de Bonaparte contre le navire il Volante* [1807] (I, 409) and the *Minerve* [*an* IX] (I, 410), hardly touch the subject of enemy destination as they bear on other issues, such as: the contraband character of *bois de construction* and of tar, and the rule that if a neutral State stipulated in a treaty with belligerent A that a certain matter would not be contraband but thereupon in a treaty with belligerent B that it would, belligerent B was also authorized to treat the matter concerned as contraband vis-à-vis the neutral State.

As examples of the view of French prize courts concerning the susceptibility of neutral vessels to seizure in the revolutionary and immediately following post-revolutionary period I will cite a few judgments pronounced by the various authorities which were in charge of prize jurisdiction and are reported by De Pistoye and Duverdy in their *Traité des prises maritimes*. They were passed by

the *Conseil des Prises* in *an* IX in the case of the Ragusan vessel *La Paix contre le Redoutable* (I, 355):

> "les neutres peuvent commercer avec l'ennemi pourvu qu'ils ne portent pas d'articles de contrebande";

the *Tribunal de Cassation*, *an* VII, in the case of the Prussian vessel *Le Ferdinand-Henri contre l'Epervier* (I, 124):

> "On ne peut appliquer la loi du 29 nivôse an VI à un navire chargé de marchandises anglaises, et pris à une époque où cette loi n'était pas promulguée sur les côtes où il a été capturé";

the *Comité de Salut Public*, *an* III, in the case of *Le Corsaire le Passe-Partout contre le navire* [danois] *les Trois Frères* (I, 357):

> "Les marchandises sans destinataires connus, chargées par des neutres à destination d'un port ennemi, saisies sous pavillon neutre, même avec des marchandises reconnues de propriété neutre, sont réputées ennemies et doivent être déclarées de bonne prise";

the *Conseil des Prises*, *an* VIII, in the case of the Danish vessel *La Pandora contre le Requin* (I, 124-129):

> "Un navire neutre destiné pour un pays neutre peut légitimement relâcher dans un port ennemi [Portsmouth] quand il est prouvé qu'il ne renonce pas à sa destination primitive [l'île de Sainte-Croix, possession danoise]. Le rôle d'équipage n'a pas besoin de mentionner les passagers [taken on board at Portsmouth], lorsque les derniers sont porteurs de passe-ports en bonne et due forme. Des passagers d'origine ennemie ne peuvent pas être considerés sujets ennemis lorsque depuis longtemps il sont établis dans un pays neutre, où ils ont acquis le droit de cité, et lorsqu'ils retournent dans ce pays. Lorsqu'une nouvelle loi change les règlements relatifs aux neutres, elle ne doit être appliquée qu'aux navires qui ont eu connaissance avant leur départ";

the *Commissaire du Gouvernement français aux Iles Adriatiques* Dubois, ordering the execution of a judgement of condemnation as good and lawful prize of the Austrian vessel *Gentil-Faucon* and her cargo of cloth, passed by a Commission appointed by him *ad hoc* (I, 356), put aside by the *Conseil des Prises*, *an* VIII, (I, 355-357), recorded under the title *Philandros* [owner of the cloth] *contre La Cybèle* [the capturing French corvette, which brought the prize into Korfú):

> "La prise d'un navire neutre destiné pour un port ennemi [Smyrna] n'est pas valable. Le certificat de neutralité, délivré par un consul de la nation ennemie [Great Britain] n'est pas une cause de prise";

the *Conseil d'Etat* [1816] in the appeal cases of the French privateers *Le Risque-Tout et le Sediman contre Le Gode-Ensight* and *Le Sediman contre l'Etnigkeit* (I, 364):

> "La prise est nulle, lorsqu'il résulte des papiers de bord et de l'instruction que le navire capturé, son chargement, le port d'où il avait été expédié, et celui pour lequel il avait été destiné, étant neutres, quelles que fussent les inductions qu'on dût tirer contre la destination apparente dudit navire, de la conformité de son chargement, de son expédition et de sa navigation, avec d'autres bâtiments prétendus neutres, destinés pour l'Angleterre.
>
> L'ordre que les capteurs prétendent avoir été donné aux corsaires français d'arrêter tous les bâtiments chargés de grain, dans la Baltique, ne peut pas entraîner la confiscation des bâtiments ainsi chargés qui n'avaient pas enfreint les règles de la neutralité, telles qu'elles étaient alors établies".

Old French prize court decrees and their comment by the authors on them on the whole proved difficult to classify under a system of logical exposition, such as the present work endeavours to be.

Another example was the confused case of the *Christiania Colbiornsen* [*an* VII] (I, 123) in which the *Tribunal de Cassation* began, in accordance with Art. 1 of the law of 29 nivôse *an* VI, with the surprising statement that

> "L'état des navires, en ce qui concerne leur qualité de neutre et d'ennemi, sera déterminé par leur cargaison; en conséquence, tout bâtiment trouvé en mer chargé en tout ou en partie de marchandises provenant d'Angleterre ou de ses possessions, sera déclaré de bonne prise, quel que soit le propriétaire de ces denrées ou marchandises",

on which I have already made a critical remark in my preliminary section II on the enemy or neutral character of prizes at p. 212.

What follows in the judgment is an issue of transitional law: the vessel was nevertheless released on the ground that she could not yet have known the law in question at the time the goods were shipped (see my remarks in section 3 of another group of preliminary General Issues, dealing with the temporal limitations of the exercise of the right of prize at p. 192).

The judgment then switches over to the practice of ignoring transfers of enemy ships to neutrals in wartime. This was not, however, as far as I can make out, the *ratio decidendi* in the case under review.

This rule was still inserted in Art. 1 of the *Règlement* of 1778. A change in the law only took place much later, during the Crimean War: see the judgment on the *Orione* [1854], a Russian vessel invalidly transferred to a neutral flag, carrying neutral goods (II, 499). These were released subject to the payment of freight *pro rata itineris*, a decision which was exceptional in the French legal tradition (see my exposé on the freight problem under C, section 6, *sub b*, *infra*, p. 634).

English jurisprudence during the formative phase. Turning now to the more systematic case law of British Admiralty Courts, I will give below a brief survey of the various specific grounds on which the enemy destination of contraband goods was claimed or suspected in England during the formative phase of the pre-codificatory period, beginning with the most general one, *viz.*: — Carriage of contraband under false papers or with a false destination, or other kinds of falsification.

This was one of the main means by which the captor tried to satisfy the prize court. His allegation was that some false statement had been made or some fraud had been committed by the consignor of the cargo in the bill of lading or other ship's papers—untrue declaration of the nature of the goods, false mention by their owner of his own or the consignee's nationality or domicile, false indication of the designation of the goods, etc.

Many such cases were reported by Sir George Lee in his Notes as having occurred during the War of the Austrian Succession. See on (the allegation of) "colourable papers", *e.g.*, the references to the Portuguese *Nostra Seignora de Pentha de França* (Pratt-Lee, p. 90), the Norwegian *Jumfro Sarah* (*ibid.*, p. 100), the Prussian *Fredericus Secundus, Koning van Prussien* (*ibid.*, p. 109), the Swedish *Vro(u)w Anna Maria* (*ibid.*, p. 119), the Danish *Providentia* (*ibid.*, p. 144), the *Araminta* (Stew., 47) and the *Success* (Stew., 79), both quoted in Pratt-Lee, footnote 1 at p. 82.

Instances of this ground of suspicion against the cargo, reported from later wars, especially those against Revolutionary France, were:

the Swedish *Concordia* (Wise, Master) [1798] (1 C.Rob., 119), an instance of "alternative destination" of a cargo, a produce of the native soil of Sweden, ostensibly to Genoa, but suspected of the master's concealment of its real destination to France;

the *Juffrouw Anna* (Greeson, Master) [1799] (1 C.Rob., 124 a; Roscoe, I, 76), an English prize purchased in France;

the Prussian *Carolina* (Hartman, Master) [1800] (3 C.Rob., 75): a "colourable" destination" from Bayonne to Altona, but in fact to Ostend; not admitted to further proof;

the American *Nancy* (Joy, Master) [1800] (3 C.Rob., 82; Roscoe, I, 355, footnote *a*): destination ostensibly to Cowes or Altona, but in fact to enemy-occupied Amsterdam;

another *Nancy* (Knudsen, Master) [1800] (3 C.Rob., 122 *et seq.*, at 125): sailing with false papers;

the *Rosalie and Betty* (Gebhadt, Master) [1800] (2 C.Rob., 343; Roscoe, I, 246): "circumstances covered with suspicion; no neutral behaviour";

the *Graaff Bernstorff* (Belmer, Master) [1800-1803] (3 C.Rob., 109; Roscoe, I, 265): concealment of enemy interest in the cargo with fraudulent intent;

the *Franklin (No. 1)* [1801] (Segerbrath, Master) (3 C.Rob., 217; Roscoe, I, 298), a Prussian ship sailing from Lübeck ostensibly to neutral Lisbon, but actually to the Spanish (enemy) port of Bilbao. The case of this ship was, apart from the place of her capture, complicated by the nature of her cargo (hemp and iron), which was held not to be protected by the customary rule concerning the goods of persons exporting the native produce of their country, so that the ship's destination was the principal element in the case. She was found to have been captured out of her proper course and in a direct course towards one of the Spanish ports in the Bay of Biscay on this side of Cape Finisterre, off Santander. The Court was satisfied that the plan of the voyage was to sail the ship fraudulently, under a false destination, into a Spanish (enemy) port;

the Danish *Neutralitet (No. 2)* [1805] (Zeverver, Master) (6 C.Rob., 30; Roscoe, I, 521): the professed destination was Emden, the real one Ostend;

the *Edward* [1801] (Bartlett, Master) (4 C.Rob., 68; Roscoe, I, 350), a Prussian vessel, ostensibly on a voyage from a French port (Bordeaux) to Emden which, however, in actual fact dissembled her real destination for a French port of naval equipment (Brest), being captured near the Ile des Saints on a course incompatible with her asserted course; moreover, her logbook showed apparent contradictions. She was therefore confiscated with her cargo of wines; although wines were not, in general, included in the concept of contraband, they could be so included on the ground of their destination, *in casu* to a naval port;

the American *Ranger* [1805] (Smith, Master) (6 C.Rob., 125). The cargo of biscuit and flour had been put on board at Bordeaux and was ostensibly documented for Ville Real (Portugal); the real destination, however, was Cádiz, "a place of naval equipment" of the French fleet. The ship was condemned.

— Consignment to ports of different nature, either military-naval or commercial.

A presumption of enemy destination of contraband goods was already long ago attached to the destination of the carrying ship to a military port or a port of naval equipment. See, for example, on the rôle of Brest during the War of the Austrian Succession the cases of the Danzig vessel *Juffro(u)w Susanna* [1746] (Pratt-Lee, pp. 67 *et seq.*, at p. 74):

> "the planks are large and thick, fitted for shipping; this ship was going to Brest, where men-of-war only are built and fitted, and timber carried there must be for fitting men-of-war",

and the Prussian ship *Tweelinge* [1747-1748] (*ibid.*, pp. 105-108):

> "the cargo was to be delivered at Brest, where the men-of-war are built".

On the other hand, the port of Nantes was qualified as a merely mercantile port in two cases of conveyance of a cargo of resin on board the Portuguese vessels *Santa Bona Ventura* [1747] (Roscoe, I, 433, footnote *a*; 5 C.Rob., 98, footnote *a*) and *Nostra Signora de Begona* [1804] (5 C.Rob., 97; Roscoe, I, 433).

Less certain was the character of the port of Bordeaux, see the case of the Prussian *Endraght* (read: *Eendraght*) of 1747 (1 C.Rob., 190 and 195;

Roscoe, I, 103, footnote *a*): its character as a port of naval equipment was denied,

> "though smaller vessels of war may occasionally be built and fitted out there",

but that fact did not warrant condemnation of the prize.

— Consignment to an ordinary commercial port situated in the neighbourhood of a port of naval equipment, or other types of adjacency.

Cases of this kind occurred during the War of the Austrian Succession with regard to destination to the harbours of St. Malo and Brest, and likewise to those of Bayonne and San Sebastián. In those cases two questions arose: (*a*) which of the two neighbouring harbours was the real destination, and (*b*) was the port of that real destination in fact a port of naval equipment? See the *Marlborough* [1741] (Pratt-Lee, pp. 24 *et seq.*, at pp. 32):

> "Bayonne and San Sebastián are very near; the stores may very easily be carried from Bayonne thither. There is great reason to suspect them to be Spanish property; and, being warlike stores, they are liable to seizure and confiscation".

In the *Twende Brödre* (Shall, Master) [1801] (4 C.Rob., 33; Roscoe, I, 332; Pratt-Lee, xx-xxi) the nature of the cargo (fir timber, spars, balks and deals) was such that, if going to Brest, a port of military equipment, it would have been contraband; but if to such a port as St. Malo's, not so. The master's instructions referred to both ports as destinations. The Court held that the words used in them "if you resolve" indicated an ultimate discretion to have been reposed in the master, and decreed restitution because the master had had the firm intention to discharge the lading in St. Malo and not to go to Brest. This was a case of what was called "discretionary destination".

See also the complicated case of the *Eagle* [1803], not reported, but described by Sir William Grant in the appeal case of the *William* (Trefry, Master) [1806] (5 C.Rob., 385 *et seq.*, at p. 401).

— Destination to a bay in which both an enemy and a neutral port are situated.

This was the case of two similar consignments in 1805:

a cargo of Dutch cheese on the *Frau Margaretha* (6 C.Rob., 92; Roscoe, I, 532, footnote *a*) was bound for Quimper: that port, though in the vicinity of Brest, is situated on the opposite side of a projecting headland or promontory, so as not to admit of an immediate communication except by land carriage; for this reason the case was held not to be quite identical with an earlier case relating to the *Jonge Margaretha* [1799] (1 C.Rob., 189; Roscoe, I, 100), and further proof was ordered;

the *Zelden Rust* (6 C.Rob., 93; Roscoe, I, 532; Pratt, xix) was bound for La Coruña near Ferrol; these ports are situated in the same bay; if the supply was permitted to be imported into the bay, it would be impossible to prevent it from going on immediately, and in the same conveyance, to Ferrol: this case resulted in condemnation.

See on these cases Pratt's personal survey of the older case law on the destination of contraband goods which precedes the text of Sir George Lee's Ms. Notes, at pp. xix-xxi of his work on the *Law of Contraband of War*, where he refers to Sir William Scott's judgment in the *Imina* (Bauman Vroom, Master) [1800] (3 C.Rob., 167) to the effect that the transportation of contraband was in principle lawful when the ship was destined to a neutral port, but that certain exceptions had been made.

— Consignment to a port which loses its enemy character.

An originally enemy destination of contraband goods loses that character when the port of destination of the carrying ship subsequently changes its territorial status from enemy to neutral or otherwise non-enemy. This happened in the case of the *Trende Söstre* [1807] (6 C.Rob., footnote at pp. 390 *et seq.*; Roscoe, I, 588; Pratt, pp. xxi-xxii), a Danish vessel captured at the Cape of Good Hope after that Dutch settlement had surrendered to the British forces. On the analogy of the treatment of cases of blockade in corresponding circumstances (the *Lisette* [1806]—a case of capture after the discontinuance of the blockade (comp. section 4, *infra*, p. 441)—and the *Conferenzrath* [1806] (6 C.Rob., 387 and 362; Roscoe, I, 587 and 571), the Court decided that the penalty of confiscation could not be inflicted on goods which were no longer *in delicto*:

> "it is a discharge and a complete acquittal, that long before the time of seizure the goods had lost their noxious character of going as contraband to an enemy's port".

The same solution might have been adopted in the converse case of a territorial change of the port of destination from neutral to enemy.

— Change of destination.

Alteration of the ship's destination during her voyage was suspect, just as was the transfer of ownership of ship or cargo *in transitu*, but there were also excusable and even exculpatory reasons for the owner or master taking such a decision. See, *e.g.*, the case of the *Imina* [1800] (3 C.Rob., 167; Roscoe, I, 289; Pratt, xx), a neutral ship laden in Danzig with a cargo of timber for Amsterdam, but whose master abandoned that voyage and diverted her to (neutral) Emden after he had been apprized of the British blockade of the Dutch town. The ship was captured during the course of that altered voyage to Emden, but was restored to her owner by the Prize Court:

> "The cargo was taken on a voyage to a neutral port. To say that it is nevertheless exposed to condemnation, on account of the original destination as it stood in the mind of the owners, would be carrying the penalty of contraband further than it has been ever carried by this or the Superior Court".

On the other hand, the American *Minerva* [1801] (3 C.Rob. 229; Roscoe, I, 301), captured by the French on a voyage from a Spanish settlement overseas to La Coruña and recaptured by a British ship:

> "This case is to be determined by the nature of the original voyage. If the destination was diverted only in consequence of *vis maior* which the party was unable to resist, I cannot consider it as a defeasance of the original illegality any more than if the diversion had been occasioned by the temporary fury of the elements. In both cases the original movement of the vessel must be considered; to which it must be presumed she would again immediately recur as soon as an opportunity presented itself."

Another instance of deviation from the original course of the ship was that of the American *William* (Trefry, Master) [1806] (5 C.Rob., 385 *et seq.*, at p. 403; Roscoe, I, 505), but that was a case in which the captor's claim was also, and perhaps mainly, based on the owner's involvement in a closed colonial trade (comp. under A, section 6, *infra*, pp. 474-475). This ship, during her voyage from La Gu(a)ira, unloaded her cargo in Marblehead, paid income tax there and after slight repairs reloaded most of her cargo. She thereupon continued her voyage to Spain, but before her arrival there she was captured by a British armed vessel and subsequently brought before the Vice-Admiralty Court of Halifax. The doctrine of continuous voyage, already applicable in England in cases of reserved trade, was, however, held not to apply in the case of *bona fide* interruption of a voyage.

— Sailing without a passport in the form prescribed by treaty.

This category of cases concerned in particular the capture of Swedish vessels with contraband goods on board. This was only one of the grounds on which their enemy destination could be presumed.

In the *St Erick* (Pratt-Lee, p. 85, at p. 89), the Court said:

> "It is evident that this [Swedish] ship had not a proper pass according to the treaty, which is our rule to go by. We can take no notice of private regulations unless they were established by a new treaty between the nations."

However, the sanction was not the condemnation of the ship, but a judicial statement that the privateer was justified in bringing the ship in for want of a pass according to the treaty.

— Destination to rebels

In the *Providence* [1746], a New England ship from Boston, captured by the man-of-war *Sheerness* (Pratt-Lee, pp. 75-85), a case of assistance to Scottish rebels was treated as a contraband case: the Court made no distinction between destination to Scottish rebels and destination to enemies:

> "It is evident that master Sinclair joined with and supported the rebels, who were aided and assisted by the French, who are the King's enemies. Captain Sinclair has acted as a rebel; he delivered the ship up to the rebels ... I cannot distinguish between rebels and enemies; the ship had contraband goods on board, and she was in the enemies' or rebels' hands, and rebels are worse than enemies."

— Export prohibitions in the country of destination.

This brings us to another old variant of doubtful operation of the idea of continuous voyage in England, *viz.*, that of the impact of export prohibitions in force in the port of destination on the fate of prizes.

An interesting feature of old British prize jurisprudence was the rule that even a prohibition of the export of the contraband goods concerned from the country of destination was not a sufficient counter-proof against *prima facie* evidence of enemy destination. See the cases of the *Goede Hoop* (Pieters, Master) [1809] (Roscoe, II, 73, 209; Edw., 327) and the *Actaeon* [1814] (2 Dodson, 48; Roscoe, II, 209), decisions which seem to have already been preceded by an earlier pronouncement in the case of the *Rosalia and Betty* (Roper, Master) [1802], often quoted, but only referred to in a footnote added to the table of appeal cases in 6 C.Rob., p. x.

2. *Further developments during the consolidation phase*

Introduction. After this survey of the French and English case law on enemy destination during the formative phase of the pre-codification period from earlier times up to the restoration of Europe, I will now pass on to the further development of the problem of the destination of contraband goods in the consolidation period from then onward up to the codification of 1907-1909.

A short transitional period, including the Anglo-American War of 1812-1814, leads from the Revolutionary Wars of France to the post-Napoleonic era.

One of the first instances of the seizure of a cargo on board a neutral vessel on the suspicion that it was contraband by nature after the Napoleonic period, which might then possibly have presented a case of early application of the doctrine of continuous voyage to contraband, was the American case of the *Commercen* [1816] (Wheaton, I, 382), a Swedish vessel that conveyed grain from Ireland to Bilbao by special permit for the use of the Irish forces that were operating in those years in Spain. The ship was seized by an American armed vessel during the 1812 war. But the cargo would seem to have been condemned as enemy property and not as contraband with enemy destination, and so the vessel was released.

Another case had already preceded two years earlier: the *Rapid* [1814] (8 Cranch (Amer.), p. 155; Scott's *Cases*, p. 474).

The first half of the 19th century was for the rest of no special interest from the point of view of the law of contraband. The reverse was the case of its second half. In that period indeed a considerable sharpening of the rules on the enemy destination of contraband goods prejudicial to the interests of neutrals commenced as a result of the adoption of the doctrine of continuous voyage. And it is curious to state that this development was marked by events which took place successively in four different continents. It began in Europe, culminated in America, it even spread, though hesitantly, as far as Asia, and finally came to an end in Africa. Not all the stages in this development were judicial. Some were, but others rather bore a legislative or a diplomatic character.

The first of these events occurred during the Crimean War.

(1) *The European variant.* Although the naval operations during the Crimean War seem not to have led to important instances of belligerent action against the conveyance of contraband of war to Russia apart from the general blockade of the Baltic coasts by the Allied forces, there arose a French judicial precedent relating to the seizure of a cargo of saltpetre carried on the Hanoverian vessel *Frau Houwina* [1855], suspected of being involved in a stealthy transport of that article to Russia via Hamburg. The saltpetre was confiscated simply on the ground that the importation of saltpetre into Hamburg was stated to have increased during the war and far exceeded ordinary importation, which justified the surmise that the cargo concerned was intended to be conveyed in transit via Hamburg to Russia either further by sea or over land by rail. This was consequently a clear case of the early application of the doctrine of continuous voyage by France in Europe and it has at the time created a considerable stir. It is of course mentioned by H.W. Briggs in his study of 1925 on *The doctrine of continuous voyage* at pp. 57 and 62.

(2) *The American variant.* Far more important was the development during the American Civil War. American prize law was particularly severe during that war, when neutral traders attempted to convey contraband goods to the Confederate forces via Caribbean territory, such as Spanish ports in Cuba or the harbour of Nassau in the English Bahamas.

Most of the American cases bore a mixed character of involving both the carriage of contraband goods and the intent thereby to break the Northern blockade, but some of them represented instances of either the one or the other of the two offences. H.W. Briggs has distinguished the three possible variants in his study of 1925 on *The doctrine of continuous voyage* (in the Johns Hopkins University Studies in Historical and Political Science, series XLIV, no. 2; Baltimore, 1926). He had good reason to do that because the two forms of encroachment upon belligerent rights are subject to different legal handling as the authors of a volume on *International law as interpreted during the Russo-Japanese War,* F.E. Smith and N.W. Sibley, had already stressed in 1905 at p. 325, where they distinguished the operation of the law of blockade from that of contraband on five specific grounds:

> "Firstly. — Questions arising from the law of contraband occur immediately on the mere outbreak of hostilities, the belligerent right to intercept contraband *in transitu* being a general incident of a state of war. But a belligerent cannot enforce the penalties of violation of blockade without notification, and the allotment of a competent blockading force actually present in the blockaded spot.
>
> Secondly. — In the case of contraband, the noxious articles, whose carriage by the neutral involves the penalty, are of a specified class. In the case of blockade the articles

> which are amenable to the operation of the belligerent right comprise ordinary goods which have no relation to war, as well as those that are peculiarly subservient to it.
>
> Thirdly. — In the case of contraband the penalty, though it may extend to the ship, falls primarily on the cargo. In the case of blockade the usual incidence of the penalty is on the ship, though it may extend to the goods, even, in one case, to the exclusion of the ship.
>
> Fourthly. — The object of contraband is to prohibit imports of a specific kind, while that of blockade is to cut off all imports and all exports.
>
> Fifthly. — In the case of contraband the duration of the penalty to which the neutral is amenable is limited to the outward voyage, except where there are false papers, concealment, or fraud.
>
> In the case of violation of blockade, the duration of the penalty lasts as long as the blockade continues, and, therefore, may attach during the return voyage as well as the outward, unless the blockading squadron have given the vessel an implied permission to enter."

The American cases of the 1860's are particularly famous for their rôle in the development of the doctrine of continuous voyage and the asserted rights of "prévention" and "suite".

The first leading case was that of the *Stephen Hart* [1863], an English schooner captured as prize of war by a United States ship of war on 29 January 1862 at 24°12' N., 82°14' W. off the southern coast of Florida, about 25 miles from Key-West and about 82 miles from Point de Yeacos in Cuba. She was sent under the convoy of a prize crew to the port of New York for adjudication. The sole owners of the ship and her cargo of arms, munition and military clothing were English (two Isaac's in London). They argued that they had not intended to enter any United States port, that the sole destination of ship and cargo was the Cuban port of Cardenas, and that the ship would sail back direct from there to West Africa. The American prize court, however, acting under the *Instructions of the Naval Department of the United States to the Naval Commanders* of 18 August 1862 (which upheld the traditional rule that evidence had first of all to come from the captain) found that there was sufficient evidence that the ship intended to run the blockade of the Southern ports by the Northern forces with a cargo of contraband from a port in neutral Cuba, and that the fact that the ship, when seized, was sailing between two neutral ports (in West Africa and Cuba) was no defence.—A short decree of Justice Betts (Blatchford, II, 379) condemned the ship for the carriage of contraband and violation of the blockade; the detailed judgment, confirmed in appeal by the Supreme Court [1865] (3 Wallace, 559) can be found *ibid.*, pp. 387-434. The Court held in effect in its judgment of 1863, which is worth quoting in full as the legal foundation of the momentous doctrine of "continuous voyage", in this case in the fields of contraband and blockade combined, that what was essential was

> "the destination and intended use of the property laden on board the vessel, and not the incidental, ancillary and temporary voyages of the vessel, which may be but one of the many carriers through which the property is to reach its true and original destination. Nor is the unlawfulness of the transportation of contraband goods determined by deciding the

question as to whether their immediate destination was to a port of the enemy. The proper test to be applied is whether the contraband goods are intended for sale or consumption in the neutral market, or whether the direct and intended object of their transportation is to supply the enemy with them. To justify the capture it is enough that the immediate object of the voyage is to supply the enemy and that the contraband property is certainly destined to this immediate use.

If this is the case, no principle of the law of nations, and no consideration of the rights and interests of lawful neutral commerce, can require that the mere touching at such a neutral port, either for the purpose of making it a new point of departure for the vessel to a port of the enemy or for the purpose of transhipping the contraband cargo into another vessel which may carry it to the destination which was intended for it when it left its port of departure, should exempt the vessel or the contraband cargo from capture as prize of war.

The division of a continuous transportation of contraband goods into several intermediate transportations by means of intermediate voyages by different vessels carrying such goods, cannot make a transportation which is, in fact, a unit, to become several transportations; although in effect the entire transportation of the goods requires several voyages by different vessels, each of which may, in a certain sense and for certain purposes, be said to have its own voyage; and although each of such voyages, except the last one in the circuit, may be between neutral ports. Nor can such a transaction make any of the parts of the entire transportation of the contraband cargo a lawful transportation when the transportation would not have been lawful if it had not been thus divided.

The inception of the voyage completes the offence. From the moment that the vessel with the contraband articles on board quits her port on her way to the hostile destination, she may be legally captured. It is not necessary to wait until the ship and goods are actually endeavouring to enter the enemy's port. The voyage being illegal at its commencement the penalty immediately attaches and continues to the end of the voyage, at least so long as the illegality exists."

The argument that the adoption of new legal rules was theoretically justified by a change in the circumstances—allusion was made to the emergence of railways which "exploded the law" because they made it easy to carry goods to their ultimate enemy destination from an intermediary neutral port—had already been rejected much earlier by Lord Stowell. And as T. Baty observed in the preface to his publication of 1915, cited below, the argument was, moreover, two-edged since the circumstances had also conferred on the belligerents a corresponding advantage in the shape of the modern cruiser with long-range guns which, unlike the old frigate or sloop, could catch almost every merchantman sighted.

This *Stephen Hart* case presented therefore a clear intertwinement of contraband and blockade aspects of the doctrine of continuous voyage. In view of that particular feature of the American cases during the Civil War and the preponderance of their blockade aspect—focused on the asserted rights of "prévention et suite" in the law of blockade—I will refer to them in the present section 3 only cursorily and for the rest deal with them in the following section 4 on blockade.

Another authoritative, but at the same time the most controversial, case falling under the same category of asserted attempts to run the Northern blockade of the Southern ports with contraband cargoes was the *Springbok*

[1862] (5 Wallace, 1; Blatchford P.C., II, 300 and 434-463), a British barque, captured on 3 February 1863 at 25°35' lat. N., 73°40' long. W., between 150 and 200 miles east of the port of Nassau, N.P., while "making for the harbour of Nassau" on her voyage from London. The persons who claimed the cargo of varying nature were again the Isaac's of London, who asserted that she was finally destined for Nassau. Justice Betts again dismissed the claim finding that the ship, after her departure from London, had been making for Nassau under the cover of deceptive and simulated bills of lading and manifest of the cargo:

> "the true destination of the ship and cargo was not to Nassau, a neutral port, and for trade and commerce, but to some port lawfully blockaded by the forces of the United States, with intent to violate such blockade."

This judgment, also, was confirmed by the Supreme Court, but only by the casting vote of Chief Justice Salmon Portland Chase, with four of the eight Associate Justices under the leadership of Justice S. Nelson dissenting. Full details of this famous case can be found in H.W. Brigg's above-mentioned study of 1925. *The doctrine of continuous voyage* (pp. 63-79) and in an earlier publication by T. Baty under the title *Prize law and continuous voyage* (London, 1915), including the opinion of other writers. The author of this latter publication, recalling in his preface some less flattering remarks of a contemporary lawyer on the attitude of the said Chief Justice and disapproving of "the recrudescence of belligerent pretensions" (the title of another of his publications in the *I.L.A. Report* 1905) reproduced not only the text of the judgment, but also (at pp. 31 *et seq.*) the brief in the *Springbok* case by W.M. Evarts (once Secretary of State of the United States); the analysis of the *Springbok* judgment by an anonymous author, a D(octor of) C(ommon) L(aw); Sir Travers Twiss's study on *The doctrine of continuous voyage, as applied to contraband of war and blockade, contrasted with the Declaration of Paris of 1856*, written on behalf of a conference at Antwerp (London, 1877), and (at pp. 116 *et seq.*) the famous *Memorial on Prize Proceedings* of 18 January 1753, being the Report of a Committee nominated by His Britannic Majesty to reply to the statement of reasons formulated by the Court of Berlin concerning certain measures taken with respect to the Silesian loan of 1735 (comp. on this controversy, *supra*, pp. 76-77).

A further famous case concerned the *Peterhoff* [1863], captured on 25 February 1863 off the island of St. Thomas about four and a half miles from the mouth of the harbour; ship and cargo were later claimed by British owners and underwriters. In his judgment of condemnation in this case (referred to in the 1866 appeal proceedings before the U.S. Supreme Court; Blatchford, pp. 381 and 463-550; 5 Wallace, 28; Scott's *Cases*, p. 760) Justice Betts found that:

> "(i) the said ss. was knowingly laden, in whole or in part, with articles of contraband of war and had them in the act of transportation at sea;

(ii) the voyage with the said cargo was not truely destined to the port of Matamoros, a neutral port, and for purposes of trade and commerce, within the authority and intendiment of public law, but on the contrary, was destined for some other port or place, and in aid and for the use of the enemy and in violation of the law of nations;

(iii) the ship's papers were simulated and false as to her real destination."

In the *Bermuda* case [1865] (3 Wallace, 514; Briggs, p. 50), in which Chief Justice Chase, in delivering the unanimous judgment of the Supreme Court, said, on the one hand, that:

> "Neutrals may convey in neutral ships, from one neutral port to another, any goods, whether contraband of war or not, if intended for actual delivery at the port of destination, and to become part of the common stock of the country of the port",

and, on the other, that it was not necessary for the captors to establish, either absolutely or by inference, that the shippers had already at the commencement of the voyage the intention to supply the goods to the enemy, but that it was sufficient to establish:

> "an intention, either formed at the time of the original shipment or afterwards."

The *Gertrude* [1863] (3 Wall., 552) was a case in which the doctrine was invoked, but its application was dismissed. It concerned the capture in 1863 of an English steamer made off one of the Bahama islands, while ostensibly on a voyage from Nassau to St. John, N.B. In that case the Supreme Court said that

> "where goods, destined ultimately for a belligerent port, are being conveyed between two neutral ports by a neutral ship, under a charter made in good faith for that voyage, and without any fraudulent connection on the part of her owners with the ulterior destination of the goods, the ship, though liable to seizure in order to the confiscation of the goods, is not liable to condemnation in prize."

It was, moreover, held, not by a prize court but by the Court of Common Pleas, that if it was proven that the contraband cargo had an ulterior enemy destination different from that of the ship and was to be forwarded there as part of a sole and the same commercial operation, the destination of the ship did not protect the cargo. This decision was made in insurance cases during the American Civil War and thus sanctioned the doctrine of continuous voyage also in the sphere of private law: *Hobbs v. Henning (Law Journal Reports, Common Pleas,* XXXIV, 117); *Seymour v. London and Provincial Marine Insurance Company (ibid.,* XLI, 193; XLII, 111).

The publications on the subject were for the greater part opposed to the application of the doctrine to the carriage of contraband. See, *inter alia*:

Sir Travers Twiss's above-mentioned study of 1877 and his subsequent publication *Belligerent rights on the high seas since the Declaration of Paris* (London, 1884);

the following articles in *A.J.I.L.*:

vol. 1 (Part I) (1907), pp. 61 *et seq.*: Judge Ch. B. Elliott, "The doctrine of continuous voyage", an author who "has almost exhausted the discussion on this branch of the subject", a qualification devised by another author on the subject in

vol. 4 (1910), pp. 823 *et seq.*: L. H. Woolsey, "Early cases on the doctrine of continuous voyage"; and

vol. 9 (1915), pp. 583 *et seq.*: H. Arias, "The doctrine of continuous voyage in the 18th century";

and the *Proceedings of the American Society of International Law,* 1909; or a number of individual publications by

L. Gessner, *Opinion on the condemnation of the cargo of the Springbok by the Supreme Court of the United States of America* (London, 1869);

C. N. Gregory, "The doctrine of continuous voyage" in the 26th *I.L.A. Report* (London, 1910), pp. 120 *et seq.*, and

Th. Baty, "The Portland Ministry and the history of continuous voyage", in the *Law Quarterly Review,* vol. 38 (1922). The Duke of Portland was Prime Minister in England in 1783.

Other cases of application of the doctrine were those of the *Cheshire* [1862] (Blatchford, p. 179) and the *Circassian* [1864] (2 Wallace, 135-160). The latter was a British merchant ship with a lawful cargo on board on a voyage from Bordeaux ostensibly to Havana, but captured on 4 May 1862 off the coast of Cuba while her intended destination was the blockaded port of New Orleans. On this ground she was condemned (*loco cit.*, 177). This condemnatory judgment has later given rise to arbitral proceedings in the Claims Commission of Washington of 1871 (comp. vol. VI of this publication, p. 649). John Bassett Moore has collected the prize cases examined by that Commission in vol. IV., chapter LXVI, pp. 3815-3966 of his six volume work on the *History and digest of the international arbitrations to which the United States has been a party* (Washington, 1898), grouping them under eight different headings.

Amongst the prize cases proper which were brought before the Commission there were: two dealing with contraband: the *Neptune* (Jeffries, Master) (pp. 3843-3885), especially the doctrine of continuous voyage, and the *Springbok* (pp. 3928-3935); four with blockade: the *Susan* (pp. 3885-3890), and the *Essex,* the *Hiawatha* and the *Circassian* (pp. 3901-3923); four with probable cause of seizure: the *Nancy* (Florence, Master), the *Sally* (Choate, Master), the *Diana* (Gardner, Master) and the *Peterhoff* (pp. 3815-3843); and four on captures in neutral waters: the *Sir William Peel,* the *Dashing Wave,* the *Volant* and the *Science* (pp. 3935-3957).

Although the combined cases of 1862 regarding the *Memphis* and the *Ella Warley* (Blatchford, 202 and 204) bore also a substantive character, this couple had a special bearing on the question of the admissibility of the requisitioning of prizes during the proceedings (see my *Le droit des prises de la Grande Guerre* of 1924, p. 1271).

A study which deserves special attention in this context of continuous voyage is L. H. Woolsey's abovementioned article in *A.J.I.L.* 4 (1910), pp. 823 *et seq.* In that article the author argued that the earliest case on record in which the doctrine of continuous voyage was applied at all was precisely a case decided by a British Admiralty Court and related to contraband, *viz.*, that of the *Jesús (, Mary* and *Joseph)* [1756, appeal in 1761] (Burrell-Marsden, p. 164). But that case seems to me hardly convincing and insufficient to refute Baty's general statement of 1915 that the doctrine of continuous voyage was not in origin an English doctrine as far as the carriage of contraband was concerned.

The mixed cargo on the *Jesús* (saltpetre and other innocent colonial produce) had begun its voyage on a French (enemy) East Indiaman to neutral Spanish La Coruña. There it had been transferred to the *Jesús*, one of a number of Spanish coasting vessels made use of to protect French cargoes from British cruisers. This vessel sailed to another Spanish port, San Sebastián, but with the intention (confirmed by her master and crew) to continue the transport to France. The cargo was claimed as the property of a Spanish subject but, according to master and crew, most probably belonged to Frenchmen. Nothing had happened during the first part of the transport (to La Coruña), but on the second part (between La Coruña and San Sebastián) the ship was captured by the British. The saltpetre cargo was condemned in both instances by the Prize Courts, being contraband, whereas the vessel and the innocent parts of the cargo were restored. The case gives the impression that the Courts at that juncture were still in two minds about the application of the novel doctrine on "reserved trade" (the rule of the war of 1756) as a new independent doctrine, in addition to the traditional contraband rule. The curious thing is, in any case, that the doctrine of continuous voyage has not since then been invoked again by a British prize court in support of the condemnation of a contraband cargo for more than forty years (1800).

The cases of the application of the doctrine of continuous voyage to contraband and those of its application to blockade must be contradistinguished because in the latter group its application was seen as the implementation of a wider principle according to which violation of a blockade existed from the moment that a ship left her port of departure with the intent to enter a blockaded port up to the moment of her return home after the successful termination of the enterprise, which might easily include an intermediate sailing through a neutral or non-blockaded port. The rules on contraband differed on this aspect.

Even if one takes the *Jesús* case of 1761 as convincing evidence of an early conscious application by British prize courts of the doctrine of continuous voyage to contraband, one must concede that this case has remained an isolated one for a long time. A series of judgments at the beginning of the 19th century has often been referred to as demonstrating England's adherence to the doctrine in respect of contraband, but as Briggs has rightly argued in his study of 1925 (pp. 31 *et seq.*), they do not really substantiate that view. See the cases of the *Imina* (Bauman Vroom, Master) [1800] (a change of course to neutral Emden on a voyage, originally from Danzig to enemy Amsterdam) (3 C.Rob., 167; Roscoe, I, 289); the *Twende Brödre* [1801] (4 C.Rob., 33; Roscoe, I, 332); the *Eagle* [1803] (not reported, but cited by Sir William Grant in the *William* (Trefry, Master) [1806] (5 C.Rob., 385, 401)); the *Frau Margaretha* [1805] (6 C.Rob., 92; Roscoe, I, 532, note) and the *Zelden Rust* [1805] (6 C.Rob., 93; Roscoe, I, 532).

The English cases which, according to Justice Elliott, had admitted the doctrine in respect of the conveyance of contraband already half a century prior to the American Civil War—the *Maria* (Monses, Master) [1805] (6 C.Rob., 201), the *Charlotte Sophia* [1806] (6 C.Rob., 204, footnote), the *Lisette* [1806] (Steg, Master) (6 C.Rob., 387) and the *Mercurius* (Harmens, Master) [1808] (Edw., 53)—or are mentioned in Harcourt (Historicus)'s *Pamphlet on Nassau trade* (1863), were in my opinion either non-committal or dragged in by the head and shoulders.

On the blockade aspect of the doctrine see further section 4, *infra*, pp. 432-434.

The doctrine of continuous voyage was not new. It had already been applied in England in various other fields, such as slave trading, trading with the enemy and reserved colonial trade.

Its application to 'reserved trade' dates back to the Seven Years' War, hence its name 'Rule of the War of 1756' (comp. section 6, *infra*, pp. 470 *et seq.*). See for instances of this application the appeal case of the *William* (Trefry, Master) [1806] (5 C.Rob., 385; Roscoe, I, 505) and the judgments reviewed in that case—the *Polly* (Lasky, Master) [1800] (2 C.Rob., 361; Roscoe, I, 248); the *Mercury* (Roberts, Master) [1802] (5 C.Rob., 400); the *Eagle* (Weeks, Master) [1803] (cited 5 C.Rob., 401); the *Freeport* [1803] (cited 5 C.Rob., 402); the *Essex* (Orne, Master) [1805] (cited 5 C.Rob., 402-403)—and the case of the American *Maria* (Jackson, Master) [1805] (5 C.Rob., 365; Roscoe, I, 495), sailing from Habana to New Providence with a cargo of colonial produce on board, a considerable part of which, however, proved to be destined for enemy Amsterdam.

Its application to 'trading with the enemy' by British and Allied subjects and to shipments to traders with the enemy organized by them was sanctioned in the cases of the *Jonge Pieter* (Musterdt, Master) [1801] (4 C.Rob., 79; Roscoe, I, 353) and the *Mashona* (10 *Cape Times Law Reports*, 163).

But its application to the carriage of contraband dates from the American Civil War and was initiated by the United States, whose prize courts applied it in the same period also in cases of blockade. Colonial possessions of West-European countries, especially English, in the Caribbean served indeed during the Civil War as intermediate stations for trade between Europe and the Southern Confederate States. Whereas most of the traditional rules of contraband law originated in 17th and 18th century treaties of commerce, the doctrine of continuous voyage in that field has its roots rather in the case law of the United States prize courts in the second half of the 19th century. Thomas Baty was therefore completely right, at least as far as the law of contraband was concerned, when he remarked in his report of 1915 to the International Law Association (vol. XXVI, p. 118) that "nothing surprises one more than to hear the doctrine of the continuous voyage called an English doctrine". The only contribution that the British Government in those years actually made to the doctrine's taking root in the law of contraband was their acquiescence in its application to British property by United States courts under the motto "Let us be prudent neutrals, in order to be potent belligerents".

The Far-Eastern phase of the continuous voyage issue originated in the Franco-Chinese armed conflict of 1885, but on that occasion it was, as far as I know, only discussed at the diplomatic, not on a judicial level. According to F.H. Geffcken in the *Revue de droit international et de législation comparée*, vol. XVII (1885), pp. 148-149, the French Government declared that goods of the nature of contraband, such as rice, destined ultimately for China, would be considered to have hostile destination and consequently be liable to seizure, even if they were carried from a neutral port to neutral Hong-Kong.

The issue arose again during the Sino-Japanese war of 1894 when a neutral British ship, the *Gaelic*, on a voyage from San Francisco to Hong-Kong by way of Yokohama, was searched there for articles which the Japanese alleged might go to China either in the same vessel to Amoy or by transshipment at Hong-Kong to a ship going to China. See Takahashi's *Cases on international law during the Chino-Japansese War* (Cambridge, 1899), pp. 52 *et seq*. Prof. Westlake, in his Introduction to Takahashi's work, though disapproving of Japan's action in that particular case, acknowledged the principle that "where a commercial transaction preconceived from the outset involved the carriage of contraband goods to a belligerent, the goods were liable to seizure even when temporarily going to a neutral port" (Introduction, pp. xix, xxvi). Since the *Gaelic* was allowed to proceed, nothing came of the incident.

A third occasion for the doctrine of continuous voyage in the law of contraband to be applied in the Far East would have been during the Russo-Japanese War of 1904-1905, but it was not done in actual fact.

On the one hand, Russia's Supreme Prize Court dismissed the idea of sanctioning the interception of contraband transports to Japan via neutral ports, as it said in its judgment concerning the German *Tetartos*:

> "The Supreme Prize Court cannot attach any importance to a theory which has never been sanctioned by Russia in international relations, and which throws open the door to all manner of arbitrary decisions" (Hurst & Bray, vol. I, pp. 166 *et seq*., at p. 181).

The Russian Prize Regulations of 1895 also still rejected it.

On the other hand, Japan had a more powerful weapon against her enemy at her disposal in her blockade of the Russian possessions in the Far East, such as Vladivostok and Port Arthur, and did not need to make use of

Articles 15 and 17 of her *Regulations concerning captures at sea* of March 1904, pursuant to which

> "(15) The general rule shall be that the destination of a ship is the destination of her cargo.
> (17) In the case of a ship, the destination of which is not the enemy territory, whether she calls at that destination and discharges cargo or not, if there is reason to believe that the cargo in question is being conveyed to the enemy territory, her voyage shall be regarded as a continuous voyage, and her destination shall be held to have been, from the commencement, the enemy territory",

provisions which might have authorized the Japanese prize courts to apply the doctrine.

Comp. as to Russian judgments those relating to the British *Allanton* [1904] (Hurst and Bray, vol. I, p. 1), the British *Oldhamia* [1904] (*ibid.*, p. 145) and the German *Tetartos* [1904] (*ibid.*, p. 181), and as to Japanese judgments those concerning the British *Sishan* [1904] (vol. II, p. 174), the British *Eastry* [1905] (*ibid.*, p. 299), the British *Lincluden*, sometimes also referred to as *Rincluden* [1905] (*ibid.*, p. 341) and the German *Lydia* [1906] (*ibid.*, p. 359). The Japanese judgments laid down that if a captured neutral vessel proved to have abandoned her original intention to sail to an enemy or blockaded port already before her capture she was to be released because there was no *delictum*. This plea was accepted by the Prize Court in the *Lincluden,* but rejected in the *Lydia*. The latter rejection amounted in actual fact to a limited acceptance of the doctrine of continuous voyage, for what the Sasebo Prize Court told the master was this:

> "you admit that your original intention was to sail with a contraband cargo to the enemy port of Nicolaievsk at the mouth of the Amur River; now you pretend that you had already abandoned that intention before your ship was captured; we do not accept that assertion; on the contrary, we assume that you still had the same intention to carry out your plan by sailing via a neutral port, such as Hong Kong, Loochoo or Shanghai."

From the point of view of legal development Africa has made the most important contribution to the final shaping of the doctrine in the law of contraband after its adoption by the United States during the Civil War.

It was an incident during the Italo-Abyssinian War of 1896 that proved pregnant with ominous consequences for the future of naval war. In that year an Italian warship sighted a Dutch vessel, the *Doelwijk*, that according to her papers was bound for the East, but was intercepted and captured on her course to the French (neutral) port of Djibouti in the Red Sea (Erithrea). She was suspected to be laden with war material destined, after unloading there, to be conveyed in transit through that French colonial territory to the enemy country of land-locked Abyssinia, with which Italy was at war at that time. This was the first case in which a continuous voyage from a neutral seaport over land to an enemy country was at issue. After peace between Italy and Abyssinia was restored, ship and cargo were brought before the Italian prize court, but released to the owners who, however, received no costs and damages. The case produced legal after-effects which had a tremendous impact on the law of prize at the London Conference on Naval Warfare of 1908-1909. The incident led, indeed, to the insertion of a special rule in Article 35 of the Declaration which embodied the compromise solution that the doctrine of continuous voyage should in future be accepted also in case of the conveyance in transit from an intermediate neutral port over land, but exclusively for *absolute* contraband. *Conditional* contraband, on the contrary, should in principle not be so subject to capture and condemnation, with only one single exception, *viz*., that the transport should have a belligerent State without a sea-coast as its final destination, in which case conditional contraband should in future also be liable to confiscation under the doctrine.

The *Doelwijk* case has been analysed in a number of publications. See E. Brusa, "L'affaire du Doelwijk" in *R.G.D.I.P.* IV (1897), pp. 157 *et seq.*; P. Fedozzi in the *Revue de droit international et de législation comparée*, vol. 29 (1897), pp. 55 *et seq.*; G. Diena in the *Journal de droit international privé* 1897, pp. 268 *et seq.*; *Archives diplomatiques* 1897, I, pp. 81 *et seq.*; A. Rémy, *Théorie de la continuité du voyage en matière de blocus et de contrebande de guerre* (Paris, 1902), pp. 62 *et seq.*

The Boer War of the end of the century raised a dispute similar to that of the *Doelwijk*. During this war (end of December 1899 and beginning of January 1900) English warships seized three German mail steamers, the *Herzog*, the *Bundesrath* and the *General*, while bound for the neutral Portuguese port of Lourenço Marques in Delagoa Bay, suspecting them of carrying contraband goods intended to be smuggled from there by inland transportation into the Transvaal and the Orange Free State, both land-locked States. In the course of the diplomatic discussion of the incidents the German Government, referring to the British opposition to the seizure of the *Springbok* in 1863 and the British Admiralty's *Manual of Naval Prize Law* of 1866, asserted that according to recognized principles of international law there could not be contraband of war in trade between neutral ports. The incidents were ended, without prize proceedings, by a settlement (*B.F.S.P.* 1900-1901, pp. 973 *et seq*., at p. 997). Comp. for further details of these cases Briggs's study of 1925, pp. 83-89.

For the rest, no major contribution to the development of the law of contraband has been made during the 19th century. Indeed that period has produced more frequent isolated cases of blockade than important novel cases of the interception of transports of contraband goods, apart from the successive instances of the new development of the doctrine of continuous voyage which I have just sketched and which I cannot but qualify as an ominous devaluation of values once acclaimed. That is why I will otherwise practically ignore the second half of the 19th century as a priod of potential significance for the law of contraband and will deal with that period of successive European wars only cursorily from the point of view of the law of blockade in the following section 4, *infra*, at pp. 451 *et seq.*

There would only be reason still to dwell on further development of the law of contraband at the very end of the consolidation period, by referring to the events reported from an extra-European war, that between Russia and Japan of 1904-1905. Those events are, however, of lesser importance for my theme than what the size of Hurst & Bray's collection, printed in two approximately equivalent volumes of together more than 850 pages, might suggest. Two elaborate indexes in vol. I (Russian cases) at pp. 377-382, and in vol. II (Japanese cases) at pp. 468-475 offer a welcome guide to the various topics with which the prize courts of these two countries have had to deal in the field of contraband and, for that matter, of a lot of other prize law fields as well. But as concerns especially the destination of contraband cargoes there would be little really new to be noted. To such other fields of prize law as were significant due regard will be paid elsewhere in the relevant parts and sections of this volume.

It is only to show what the prize courts concerned thought about the problem of the enemy destination of contraband cargoes and its proof at the very end of the pre-codification period, apart from the continuous voyage issue, that I will add a few data, selected at random from the copious Russian and Japanese case law 1904-05.

To begin with the Russian judgments, I will refer to a few statements in the *Arabia* (vol. I, pp. 42 *et seq.*, at p. 52), where the Supreme Prize Court said that conditional contraband goods could only be condemned when they were being carried for the enemy government, contractors, army, navy, fortresses or bases; the *St. Kilda* (vol. I, pp. 188 *et seq.*): in this case one of the consignees was a Japanese firm at Kobe which in advertisements in English journals styled itself a contractor for the Japanese army and navy; the Libau Prize Court declared that it was not convinced that the Japanese Government or their agents or contractors were not to be the actual recipients of the cargo through the firms and merchants to whom it was consigned, and the Supreme Prize Court repeated that it had always recognized Kobe and Yokohama as commercial ports, and interpreted the expression "naval ports or fortresses" as implying a concentration of armed military forces, *i.e.*, places where military installations are concentrated exclusively, or where they predominate; and the *Prinsesse Marie* (vol. I, p. 276) in which the term consignment "to order" was construed in appeal as referring only to the receivers without any suggestion of an alternative destination to Japanese ports.

As regards the Japanese judgments I choose from a series of eighteen plus eleven contraband cases, digested in vol. II at pp. vi to xiv, their constant references to consignments to an enemy naval or military base, to a base of the enemy forces, to a port in neutral territory but occupied by the enemy, or simply to an enemy port; to false papers or other fraud on the part of the owners of ship or cargo; to adoption by the ship of an unusual, circuitous or otherwise suspicious route; to alteration of the ship's destination during the voyage; to evidence of complicity of some kind; or to consignment "to order".

§ 3. *Sanctions against the transportation of contraband*

Introduction

The obvious sanction against the carriage of contraband goods with enemy destination was early on in all belligerent countries their condemnation as good and lawful prize. This natural sanction was usually attended with certain secondary sanctions, such as the forfeiture of the carrier's freight and his condemnation in the captor's expenses for bringing the prize in, together with the costs of suit. See, for instance, the *Sarah Christina* [1799] (1 C.Rob., 237; Roscoe, I, 125) and the *Öster Risöer* [1802] (4 C.Rob., 199; Roscoe, I, 382):

> "The master of a ship on which contraband goods have been carried is not entitled to freight in respect of such goods, even if he was ignorant of their contraband character."

An additional sanction in earlier periods was the arrest and detention of those on board as prisoners of war, as was provided, for example, by Art. 20 of the Anglo-Netherlands treaty of alliance of Southampton of 17 September 1625 (Dumont, V^2, 478):

> "Toutes marchandises de contrebande, comme sont munitions de bouche et de guerre, navires, armes, etc. ... seront de bonne prise, avec les navires et hommes qu'ils porteront."

The basic central sanction of condemnation of the contraband goods themselves was, however, on the one hand, in several countries extended to other, innocent goods on board and/or to the transporting vessel.

On the other hand, the basic rule was subject to various mitigations or exceptions, such as, *e.g.*, in England, (*a*) the exemption from confiscation of goods which the sender shipped before the war and which were intercepted at sea without he master being aware of the outbreak of hostilities, or other forms of ignorance; (*b*) a prohibition from seizing a vessel on her return or next voyage after delivery of her contraband cargo; (*c*) a special exemption from the sanction in favour of contraband goods sent from the neutral shipper's own country as its native produce; (*d*) an alleviation of the sanction from condemnation to pre-emption, and (*e*) indulgence for small quantities.

These general observations explain the order of treatment of the subject matter of sanctions, as regards the formative period, in two subparagraphs A and B, the extensions in A (pp. 372 *et seq.*), the mitigations and exceptions in B (pp. 394 *et seq.*).

The formative period

A. *Extension of the sanction of confiscation to objects other than the contraband goods themselves.* This extension was one of the variants in which prize regulations or prize court decisions applied the doctrine of "hostile infection", on which I have already made some general remarks in the preceding section 2, pp. 326-331.

In a judgment of 1920 concerning certain cargoes on board the vessels *Kronprinsessan Margaretha, Rena, Paraná* and *Hilding* (*B.C.P.C.*, III, 803) the Judicial Committee of the Privy Council still inquired into the origin of the doctrine of infection, which it held to be "rather obscure". Its argument ran as follows:

> "For about one hundred and fifty years at least the law of prize has contained two settled rules [one enunciating the nullity of transfers in transit, see *supra*, pp. 229-244] and the other condemning, as of contraband, any goods which although not condemnable in themselves, belong or are deemed to belong, when captured, to the same owner as other cargo in the same vessel which itself is liable to condemnation as contraband ..... Their Lordships are fully aware that some Continental jurists have criticized the rule of infection adversely, and that Continental prize courts have not always accepted it, although it has been adopted in the United States and more recently in Japan .... [But British prize courts are bound by earlier judicial decisions; comp. Chapter I, section 5, *supra*, p. 102] .... The history of this rule is obscure. A reference to some of the proclamations in Rymer's *Foedera* suggests that it may have had its origin in the practice followed by the Executive during the seventeenth century in successive wars; and the theories on which writers like Zouch, Bynkershoek and Heineccius appear to proceed seem rather to have been an effort to find in their erudition some *ex post facto* warrant for an accepted rule than an historical statement of the reasons which actually guided those who laid it down ... Sir William Scott found it well settled ....
>
> That the so-called doctrine of infection does not really rest, in spite of many passages which suggest it, on the personal culpability or complicity of the owner of the goods, is shown by the fact that, if it were so, excusable ignorance would be an answer, and for this there is no authority. The term is as old as the Treaty of Utrecht (A.D. 1713), but the doctrine is perhaps unfortunately named. From the figure which describes the goods as contaminated when seized, the mind passes to the analogy of a physical taint, which runs through the entire cargo in consequence of its being in one bottom, and begins on shipment or, at least, on sailing. Hence, "once infected, always infected" is assumed to be the rule, and a buyer would get a tainted parcel, even though he became owner before seizure, and was recognised as such. This is inconsistent with the view that the rule is a penal rule ... [At this point the Judicial Committee would seem to wander from its subject and to stray to an entirely different topic, only to return to the "obscure" doctrine of infection later:] It has been contended that control, and not ownership, is the real test, so that either control, divorced from ownership, when vested in a neutral, will avert condemnation, or bare ownership in an enemy, if devoid of control, will be so innocuous as to neutralise any infection. It may be doubted if this point really arises .... In any case, however, there is a fallacy in the argument .... The rules now applicable adopt the test of ownership, and not that of enemy character. They may be criticized or impugned on other grounds, but if they are recognised, and the question is merely as to their application, they must be accepted as they stand. [There follows a defence of the rule from the point of view of equity, even in cases where its application could only be based on a rule of another order, but equally old, enunciating the nullity of transfers *in transitu* (whereupon comp. *supra*, pp. 229 *et seq.*)]
>
> It has been contended that this is a rule applied for the purpose of determining the

> status of goods, and that it is only so applicable; that it decided whether goods have enemy or neutral character; but not whether they, being neutral and in themselves innocent, can be condemned as having been infected by other cargo which is contraband. No authority has been cited for this proposition. Whether the foundation of the rule be taken to be the tendency of documentary transfers to encourage evasion and fraud so as to defeat a belligerent's right in one way, or the tendency of changes of ownership in transit to make the right of seizure at sea precarious, and so to defeat in another way the correlative belligerent right—namely, the right to obtain a condemnation—the reasoning is equally applicable to such cases of exercise of belligerent rights as those now in question."

In my comprehension the whole argument of the Judicial Committee is rather incoherent as it mixes up different problems. At any rate, it would not seem to contribute much to a clarification of an obscure doctrine.

The doctrine of infection applied to both innocent cargoes and the transporting vessel. As to the latter, there was always a great difference of opinion about the criteria that should be applied for the determination of whether the transporting vessel was liable to condemnation together with the contraband cargo. Apart from an early period during which in England the transportation of contraband seems to have in all cases brought in its train the condemnation of the transporting ship, her confiscatability was at a later stage made dependent on certain conditions, such as the ship's behaviour, the ship owner's or master's knowledge of the enemy destination of the cargo, or common ownership of ship and contraband cargo. French legislation sought the solution rather in a minimum proportion between the contraband cargo and the entire shipload, fixed already at an early stage at three-fourths.

International practice in this field appears, on a closer inquiry, to have been extremely diverse. Rules on the subject were repeatedly included in treaties of commerce and navigation and to widely differing effects.

A number of treaty provisions expressly limited the confiscation to the contraband goods themselves and forbade the attending condemnation of the transporting ship and/or of innocent goods on board, even if they belonged to the contraband-owner. Comp. for the concording texts of such express exemptions from confiscation, guaranteed to the transporting ship and to innocent parts of the cargo, the data given *infra*.

In the following exposé I will attempt to create some order in the available source material by first setting out (*sub* 1°, pp. 373-376) the treaty basis of the sanctions regime and after that (*sub* 2°, pp. 376-394) its basis in municipal legislation and case law. The British and French systems of prize law are, in this field also, so divergent that a further strictly logical arrangement is difficult to achieve.

1. *The treaty basis of the sanctions regime.* A large number of treaties excluded in express terms the special form of infection, of innocent property

by contraband on board the same vessel. See for instances of this rejection of the idea of infection the following treaty provisions:

Algiers-The Netherlands, 15 October 1622 (Dumont, V^2, 413), Art. 5:

> "Que si quelques Corsaires ou Flibustiers de ce Royaume viennent à prendre quelques Vaisseaux Marchands appartenans aux sujets de Leurs Hautes Puissances qui auront des Marchandises de contrebande, elles seront de bonne prise. Mais le Vaisseau, Equipage, Marchandises, & tout ce qui appartiendra aux dits Sujets sera libre & franc, quand même ils auroient combattu, & ce pour le tems d'un an".

Special Article annexed to the Netherlands-Spanish Peace Treaty of 30 January 1648 (Dumont, VI^1, 429; Parry, 1, 1):

> "... en ce que dans lesdits Vaisseaux se trouvent tels Biens, Marchandises, ou Denrées qui son déclarées défenduës & de contrebande, lesdits Biens, Marchandises, ou Denrées défenduës & de contrebande tant seulement seront chargées & confisquées, sans que pour cela le Navire, ny les autres Biens, Marchandises, ou Denrées, estants au Navire, puissent estre molestées, inquiétées, ou confisquées en aucune manière (& réciproquement)".

See also Art. 12 of the subsequent treaty of 17 December 1650 (Dumont, VI^1, 570; Parry, 2, 259):

> "Et au cas que dans lesdits Vaisseaux des Subjets des Provinces Unies se trouvent par le moyen susdit quelques Marchandises de celles declarées cy-dessus de Contrebande, & deffendues, elles seront deschargées, calengées, & confisquées pardevant les Juges de l'Admirauté, ou autres competents, sans que pour cela le Navire, ou autres biens, & Marchandise, & premises, retrouvées au même Navire, puissent être en aucune façon saisies ni confisquées".

Art. 34 of the Franco-Netherlands treaty of 27 April 1662 (Dumont, VI^2, 412; Parry, 7, 139) and Art. 21 of the Franco-Netherlands treaty of commerce of 10 August 1678 (Dumont, VII^1, 357; Parry, 14, 399):

> "Et au cas que dans lesdits Vaisseaux & Barques Françoises destinées vers les Havres des Ennemis desdits Seigneurs Estats, se trouve par les moyens susdits quelques Marchandises & Denrées, de celles qui sont ci-dessus déclarées de Contrebande, & defendues, elles seront déchargées, denoncées & confisquées par devant les Juges de l'Admirauté des Provinces-Unies, ou autres competens, sans que pour cela le Navire & Barque, ou autres Biens, Marchandises & Denrées libres & permises, & trouvées au même Navire, puissent être en aucune façon saisies ni confisquées."

Art. 7 of the Netherlands-Swedish agreement of 6/16 July 1667 (Dumont, VII^1, 37; Parry, 10, 187) and Art. 7 of the Netherlands-Swedish treaty of commerce of 26 November 1675 (Dumont, VII^1, 316; Parry, 14, 41):

> "Quod si constiterit Naves ad Subditos alterutrius pertinentes, quae ex toto vel ex parte Merce interdicta hujusmodi oneratae sint, ad Portum quemcunque hostilem aut ad loca inimicae Ditioni subjecta destinari, Merx omnis ejusmodi prohibita per Judicem competentem Fisco addicetur. Naves ipsae & quod reliquum Mercimonii haud vetiti in iis erit, tutum à Fisco illibatumque permanebit",

and, to cite a few examples from the 18th century for the purpose of illustrating the persistence of the tradition:

Art. 26 of the Franco-British treaty of commerce of Utrecht of 11 April 1713 (Dumont, VIII^1, 345; Parry, 28, 1):

"… Les marchandises deffendues saisies ne pourront aussi être vendues, échangées ou autrement aliénées de quelque manière que ce puisse être, qu'après que le procès aura été fait dans les règles …. et que les Juges de l'Amirauté les auront confisquées par sentence, à la réserve néantmoins tant du vaisseau même que des autres marchandises qui y auront été trouvées, et qui en vertu de ce Traité doivent être censées libres, et sans qu'elles puissent être retenues, sous prétexte qu'elles seroient chargées avec des marchandises deffendues, et encore moins être confisquées comme une prise légitime …";

Art. 11 of the treaty of amity and commerce between England and Russia of 20 June 1766 (Martens, R^2, I, 390; Parry, 43, 365):

"Tous les canons, mortiers, armes à feu, pistolets, bombes, grenades. boulets, balles, fusils, pierres-à-feu, mêches, poudre, salpêtre, souffre, cuirasses, piques, épées, ceinturons, poches à cartouche, selles & brides, au delà de la quantité, qui peut être nécessaire pour l'usage du vaisseau, ou au delà de la quantité, qui peut être nécessaire pour l'usage du vaisseau, ou au delà de celle, que doit avoir chaque homme servant sur le vaisseau & passager, seront réputés munitions ou provisions de guerre, & s'il s'en trouve, ils seront confisqués, selon les loix, comme contrebande ou effets prohibés: mais ni les vaisseaux, ni les passagers, ni les autres marchandises, qui s'y trouveront en même tems, ne seront point détenus, ni empêchés de continuer leur voyage";

Art. 12 of the treaty between France and Spain of 2 January 1768 (Martens, R^2, I, 479; Parry, 44, 55):

"Afin de combiner, autant qu'il est possible, la liberté du commerce avec les précautions nécessaires pour éviter qu'à la faveur des privilèges et exemptions rapportés ci-dessus, on n'en prenne occasion de faire un commerce illégitime et de frauder les droits dûs aux finances des deux Couronnes, il a été établi par l'article XI du Traité d'Utrecht [*supra*, p. 374-375], que toutes les marchandises saisies en contrebande actuelle seront confisquées, sans que pour cela le navire, le Capitaine, et son équipage soient détenus, ni que les autres marchandises de son chargement soient mêlées ni comprises dans la confiscation. En conséquence de quoi il a été convenu entre l'Espagne et la France, que les seuls effets qui seront saisis dans le moment de leur introduction ou exportation en contrebande, seront confisqués; et que de plus, si celui qui les introduit est pris à terre, il sera procédé contre lui, quoi qu'il soit de l'équipage du vaisseau, sans que pour cela on puisse retenir le bâtiment, ni procéder contre le reste de l'équipage";

Art. 17 *in fine* of the treaty of commerce between France and Hamburg of 1 April 1769 (Martens, R^2, I, 634; Parry, 44, 255):

" … mais le navire, ni le reste du chargement ne seront pas sujets à confiscation."

An early exception was Art. 20 of the Anglo-Netherlands treaty of alliance of 17 September 1625 (Dumont, V^2, 478), which sanctioned the simultaneous confiscation of the contraband goods and the transporting ship, without, however, mentioning the other, innocent goods on board.

English treaties sometimes included a general clause that put the co-contracting party on the same footing with a third State. Thus, Art. 40 of England's treaty with Denmark of 1670 stipulated that Danes should have all the privileges which should be granted to the Dutch, to the effect, the claimants asserted, that they might carry naval stores, such as masts, even to an enemy country (Pratt-Lee, pp. 46-47).

Treaty provisions to the opposite effect, sanctioning in express terms the simultaneous condemnation of innocent goods on board the confiscated vessel that belonged to the owner of the contraband goods or the ship owner, were more rare. This points to a general conviction that in default of an express treaty provision which protected the ship and the innocent goods on board, they might be comprised in the condemnation in accordance with the rules developed by the national legislation (France) or the case law (England) of the captor State concerned.

French treaties as a rule contained no stipulation on the issue. This was not necessary because, in this respect also, the French doctrine of infection applied automatically if a treaty did not include an express derogation from it. And in England the case law dominated the scene, although there were treaty provisiones or Royal instructions on the subject in force, which then needed construction with regard to their purport.

When one surveys the situation in earlier centuries, one gets the impression that there has been little evidence of a general line or of consistency in this field of treaty regulation, and that in the course of time the belligerents have become increasingly severe against the carrying of contraband goods by also involving other, innocent cargoes and the ship herself in the confiscation. This development resulted only in part from treaties and for the rest and mainly from national legislation and decisions of belligerent prize courts, which showed a corresponding hardening of the rules (*infra*).

2. *The bases of the sanctions regime in municipal legislation and case law.* As remarked above, the divergence between the national laws and practices in France and England makes it virtually impracticable to reduce the available source material to one common denominator. Because it is much simpler to describe the French system than that observed in England I will, for merely practical reasons, begin my exposé with the former and therefor first deal (*sub* I) with the system that was in force during the formative period up to the 19th century in France, based primarily on national legislation and only secondarily on the constructions and applications of that legislation by French prize courts, and after that (*sub* II) with the vast English case law in the same period, which was less dependent on municipal legislation and pursued its own way through the divergent views with greater freedom.

I. *The situation in France during the formative period.* This situation was dominated by the doctrine of infection, which affected both the innocent goods on board and the transporting vessel. A brief historical survey shows the following picture.

Old French legislation already included a provision which condemned the transporting vessel and innocent goods on board together with her contraband cargo: Royal Edict of March 1584 "concernant les ordonnances et règlements de la juridiction de l'Admirauté", an edict of a hundred articles "qui refondit tous les édits précédents, de 1568, 1572 et 1582" (even amounting to 1373) (Pardessus, vol. IV, pp. 226-285, 295-324). This rule was mitigated in subsequent regulations. As De Pistoye and Duverdy stated in their *Traité* (vol. I, p. 406) on the basis of Art. 1 of the *Règlement* of 26 July 1778, the rule became as follows:

> "Pour que les navires sur lesquels il y a des objets de contrebande puissent être confisqués, ainsi que le surplus de leur cargaison, il faut que les objets de contrebande composent au moins les trois quarts de la cargaison".

Another formulation of the French legal system was that used by M. Portalis, the Commissary of the French Government in his capacity of legal adviser of the *Conseil des Prises* in his exposé relative to the case of *Le corsaire le Hasard contre le navire la Statira* [6 thermidor *an* VIII] (reported by De Pistoye-Duverdy, vol. II, pp. 121 *et seq.*):

> "A l'égard des navires des Etats neutres qui seraient chargés de marchandises de contrebande destinées à l'ennemi, ils pourront être arrêtés, et lesdites marchandises seront saisies et confisquées, mais les bâtiments et le surplus de leur cargaison seront relâchés à moins que lesdites marchandises de contrebande ne composent les trois quarts de la valeur du chargement; auquel cas le navire et la cargaison seront confisqués en entier".

In their summary of that case the authors of the *Traité* described the operation of the principle of infection under the late 18th century legislation of France as follows (vol. II, p. 121):

> "la neutralité d'un navire, aux termes du règlement du 26 juillet 1778, remis en vigueur par la loi du 23 frimaire *an* VIII, ne peut être altérée par sa cargaison, à moins que pour les trois quarts cette cargaison ne soit composée de contrebande de guerre. Aux termes de la loi du 29 nivôse *an* VI, si la neutralité d'un navire peut être détruite par la qualité de la cargaison qui, en tout ou en partie, serait ennemie ou de contrebande, toujours est-il qu'il faudrait que cette partie fût assez considérable pour indiquer la fraude du tout."

From this latter quotation it seems to follow that at that moment the "considerable proportion" was not yet definitively and precisely fixed at three-quarters. Comp., however, the case of *La Thétis contre le Serpent* [*an* X] (*ibid.*, I, 148):

> "La présence d'articles de contrebande de guerre ne peut faire confisquer la cargaison que s'ils en forment plus des trois quarts."

Pardessus (vol. IV, 226) specified this proportion of three-fourths as referring to the value of the contraband goods without mentioning any other possible elements, such as volume or weight.

Other judgments to the same effect were *Le navire Portland contre le corsaire Le Diable-à-quatre* [*an* VIII] (*Traité*, II, 66) and *L'Etoile de Bonaparte contre le navire Il Volante* [1807] (*ibid.*, I, 409). See also the *Minerve* [*an* IX] (*ibid.*, I, 410).

II. *The situation in England during the formative period.* Whereas French practice in respect of the confiscatability of the transporting vessel thus adopted and stuck to the criterion of a specific proportion of the contraband goods on board her in relation to the entire shipload, English prize courts developed a totally different theory. This only took shape, after prolonged vacillation, in the doctrine that the transporting vessel was not subject to confiscation unless on the ground of her own behaviour, especially some form of fraud or falsity, or on the ground that she was owned by the owner of the contraband goods. The latter ground served also as a justification of the condemnation of other, innocent goods on board the vessel.

According to Fr. Th. Pratt, at p. lxix of his analysis of the British case law from early times onward in his *Law of Contraband of War* of 1856, preceding, but based on, Sir George Lee's Ms. Notes, published by him in the same work:

> "By the ancient law of Europe the confiscation was also extended to the vessel, the medium of conveyance and instrument of offense. But in the modern practice of the Court of Admiralty a relaxation has been introduced and a milder rule has been adopted."

The old rule had already been stated and justified by Sir William Scott (Lord Stowell) at the beginning of the 19th century in his judgment concerning the Danish vessel *Neutralitet (No. 1)* [1801] (3 C.Rob., 295; Roscoe, I, 309) as follows:

> "The modern rule of the law of nations is, certainly, that the ship shall not be subject to condemnation for carrying contraband articles. The ancient practice was otherwise and it cannot be denied that it was perfectly defensible on every principle of justice. If to supply the enemy with such articles is a noxious act with respect to the owner of the cargo, the vehicle which is instrumental in effecting that illegal purpose cannot be innocent. The policy of modern times has, however, introduced a relaxation on this point, and the general rule now is that the vessel does not become confiscable for that act. But this rule is liable to exceptions: where a ship belongs to the owner of the cargo or where the ship is going on such service under a false destination or false papers, these circumstances of aggravation have been held to constitute excepted cases out of the modern rule and to continue them under the ancient one. The circumstances of the present case impose a case of exception also, for it is a case of singular misconduct on the part of the asserted ship owners. They are subjects of Denmark, and as such are under the peculiar obligations of a treaty not to carry goods of this nature for the use of the enemies of Great Britain."

See on this point also Bourguignon's *Sir William Scott* (1987), p. 196.

As said above, this practice of condemning the vessel and/or other, innocent goods on board together with the contraband goods was one of the forms in which the idea of "infection" or "taint" of innocuous objects by objects liable to condemnation in prize was materialized. The history of this doctrine in the law of contraband is, however, far from clear, and exhibits a very unstable and confused picture. In order to illustrate how uncertain the legal situation has remained for a long time, I must enter into some detail. I will do this by briefly surveying the development in the successive wars waged by England in the course of the 17th and 18th centuries, but owing to the singular nature of the work of Pratt-Lee-Lloyd, described above (pp. 74), it has cost me great trouble to arrange in a more systematic chronological order the dispersed data, contained in that remarkable doctrinal concoction. I am conscious of the high probability that in engaging in that intellectual exercise, I must almost unavoidably have made mistakes, for which I humbly pray in advance for some indulgence.

The earliest judgments worth recalling are, however, not pronounced by British Admiralty Courts, but date back to the Eighty Years' War between the Netherlands and Spain. Particularly famous is the judgment of the Admiralty College of Amsterdam of 9 September 1604 concerning the capture in 1603 of a Portuguese carrack, the *Catharina*, laden with a valuable cargo from the East Indies, famous because it has given rise to a vigorous theoretical defense of its correctness by the young Dutch lawyer Huigh de Groot (Grotius) in a consultation which has later been published under the title *De jure praedae*. The text of that judgment has been published by W.J.M. van Eysinga in an annex to his paper on "Grotius et la Chine" in *Grotiana*, vol. VII (1936-1939) (comp. vol. IV of this publication, p. 32).

Another judgment of the same period, dating from 1602, this one kept in the Provincial Archives in Zeeland, relates to the capture of another Portuguese vessel, the *San Jago*, on which comp. Roelofsen's study of 1980 on the *Carletti* affair (see *supra*, Chapter I, p. 110).

Passing on now to the execution of my plan to set out in succession what views the Admiralty tribunals took on the extension of the sanction of condemnation to the transporting vessel and/or the innocent cargoes on board during the wars in which England became involved in the course of time, I begin with

—the first three naval wars between England and the States General of the United Netherlands of 1652-1654, 1665-1667 and 1672-1674.

As far as seizures made during these wars are concerned, I have only come across a limited number of texts, either in English or in Dutch.

As Pratt reports at p. xxxvi of his *Law of Contraband of War*, the practice of the English Admiralty Court was already in 1673 to condemn corn as contraband, but no mention was made of the transporting vessel. This was stated by the Advocate General in an opinion, cited many years later in the *Goede Vreede* of 1780 (itself quoted in the *Apollo*, 4 C.Rob., at 163; see Pratt-Lee, p. xxxvi).

Another reference to these wars may be a precedent relating to the *North Star*, a Swedish ship laden with masts, reported by Sir George Lee as having been restored to the claimants in 1684. Although the dating of this judgment (Pratt-Lee, p. 47) arouses doubts—the more so because his Ms. Notes, at pp. 60 and 70-71, quote another judgment of the same name, but this one dated 1694—it is still possible that the late date of 1684 is correct because it was not entirely unusual in the 17th century to insert in treaties of alliance or peace, such as that of 1674, a stipulation concerning the subsequent submission of disputed prize cases to compulsory review by a tribunal, either on the national or on the international level. I refer to the various examples which I have already had occasion to cite in vol. VIII of this publication at pp. 217-220, 277-278, 281 and 319-320, and to which I shall briefly return in the present Chapter III, *sub* C, section 8, *infra*, pp. 664 *et seq.*

—the Nine Years' War

One of the oldest and most famous instances in British case law of the condemnation of a neutral ship by reason of her carrying contraband goods to the enemy occurred during this war. It concerned a Swedish vessel, the *Arms of Plymouth*, laden at Gothenburg with a full cargo of pitch and tar, bound for the enemy France—a case to which reference was made much later by the Court of Admiralty during the War of the Austrian Succession [1745], *infra*. The proceedings in that 1692 case, unearthed by Sir George Lee in his detailed MS. Notes (Pratt-Lee, pp. 193, 198 and 204) took a somewhat unusual course as a consequence of the fact that it implied a few doubtful points: Was the cargo of pitch and tar contraband of war? What was the interrelation between the Royal Instructions then in force and the Anglo-Swedish treaty of 21 October 1661? Would the condemnation of the contraband cargo, if pronounced, bring with it the condemnation of the transporting vessel?

The Admiralty Court began on 4 August 1692 by condemning the cargo as good prize (pp. 193 *in fine* and 204). On 26 October the Lords of Appeal affirmed the sentence and remitted the cause (pp. 194 and 204). But on 17 November the King in Council ordered the proceeds of the sale and all the ship's papers to be restored to the owners (p. 204 *in fine*), obviously on the ground that the condemnation was considered by the Crown not to be warranted under Arts. XI and XII of the Anglo-Swedish treaty of 1661 (text in Pratt-Lee's Appendix A at pp. 213-218 and Dumont, VI^2, 384).

For the rest, it appears from Sir George Lee's MS. Notes that the judgment of 1692 was not the only one on the issue since it was preceded, respectively followed, by other sentences, some condemnatory, others ordering restoration of the vessel. However, on the one hand, the condemnation of the contraband-carrier was often founded on considerations other than her carrying contraband, such as her want of a passport in the exact form prescribed by treaty, or her fraudulent behaviour. On the other hand, the restoration of the vessel had often nothing to do with a rejection of the infection rule because it was rather a consequence of the indulgence rule in favour of the contraband goods themselves, being the produce or manufacture of the exporting neutral country (on this practice comp. *infra*, *sub* B, pp. 401-413). Sometimes also the difference in treatment was attributable to the fact that in one case (the *Med Guds Hielpe*) the whole cargo consisted of contraband, whereas in another (the *North Star* [1694], Pratt-Lee, p. 60) the contraband formed only part of the lading. The legal situation during the Nine Years' War thus exhibits a rather incoherent picture. When a ship was released, her master was often obliged to give security either to sell the cargo in a neutral country, or not to sell it in an enemy's country, or to sell it in England.

Other cases from this war are too summarily reported and show the greatest possible diversity which it is not worthwhile specifying in detail. See the (often defective) reports in Pratt-Lee's collection of cases decided in

1689: the Dutch *Pyed Crow* (p. 140);

1691: the *Charles* (Snock, Master) (p. 55); the Danish *Arms of Copenhagen* (p. 45); the Swedish *Marie* (Nelson, Master) (p. 59); the Danish *Castle Royal of Altona* (p. 118);

1692: the Swedish *Fortune* and the *City of Warsaw* (p. 118);

1693: the *Concordia*, the *Elizabeth* and the *Jacob* (p. 146); the *Unity* (p. 45); the *Vine Grape of Riga* (p. 71);

1694: the *North Star* (pp. 60 and 71-72); and

1696: the *St. Antonio* (pp. 55) and the Swedish *St. Peter* (p. 196).

—the War of the Spanish Succession

During this period from 1701 till 1713 the general rule was that in case of a capture of a vessel laden with, among others, contraband goods, the latter were condemned but the vessel and the 'innocent' rest of the cargo were restored to the owners. A well-known example of this practice was the case of the *Christiana Margaretta* [1702] (Pratt-Lee, p. 202), a ship bound from Denmark to France and laden with various goods, among which there were 14 barrels of tar. Ship and cargo were restored to the Danish owners except the barrels of tar which were condemned as prize. The judgment was based on Article XI of the treaty with Sweden of 21 October 1661 (Parry, vol. 6, p. 469): nothing is contraband but what is enumerated in the treaty.

A series of Swedish ships with their cargoes were restored to the owners upon condition that the contraband goods (pitch, tar, etc.) found on board, should be sold in England: the *Fortune* (Dousoe, Master) [1703] (Pratt-Lee, 203); the *St. Jacob* (Brinch, Master) [1703] (*ibid.*); the *Juffrouw Anna* (Albrecht, Master) [1703] (*ibid.*); the *Warsaw Arms* (Peterson, Master) [1703] (Pratt-Lee, 204) and the *Anna Catharina* (Sparman, Master) [1703] (*ibid.*).

A different treatment was meted out to the *Staden of Stockholm* (1711] (Pratt-Lee, 205) which was restored by the Judge of the Admiralty, but condemned in appeal by the Lords for want of a passport that accorded word for word to the form prescribed by Article XII of the above-mentioned treaty of 1661. This same argument was used in the case of the *Med Guds Hielpe* [1745, 1750], see *infra* p. 382.

—the War of the Austrian Succession.

This had its origin on the Continent in a dispute between the Empress Maria Theresia and King Frederick II of Prussia and was terminated by the Peace Treaty of Breslau of 1742 by which the former was forced to cede her land of Silesia to the latter. It expanded into a much wider armed conflict with a strong naval accent, in which England, Spain, France and the United

Netherlands took part and which was ended by the Peace Treaty of Aachen (Aix-la-Chapelle) of 1748. It was this war which provided the next occasion to decide the issue of infection or "taint" of the contraband carrier and the innocent goods on board by the contraband cargo and their ultimate fate. It is with one of the judgments delivered during that war that Roscoe opened his collection of prize cases in vol. I, p. 1, but his report of this case, the *Med Guds Hielpe* of 1745, is far too summary and one has to look for other documentary sources to get a somewhat clearer picture of how the law of contraband has developed since the famous case of the *Arms of Plymouth* of 1692. One gets the impression that the precedents of the half century between that famous case and the War of the Austrian Succession had fallen into oblivion and that even the Admiralty Courts were not aware of them. This is specifically apparent from the case history of the *Med Guds Hielpe* [1745, confirmed in appeal in 1750], a Swedish vessel condemned for the carriage of a full contraband load of pitch and tar, in accordance with the earlier case of 1692 during the Nine Years' War. This judgment of 1745, reported for the first time *in extenso* in Pratt-Lee's collection (at p. 191) and much later praised by Sir William Scott as "famous" in the *Staadt Embden* (Jacobs, Master [1798] (1 C.Rob., 26; Roscoe, I, 37) and as "memorable" in the *Maria (No. 1)* (Paulsen, Master) [1799] (1 C.Rob., 340; Roscoe, I, 152), had already been preceded by the above-mentioned case of 1702 during the War of the Spanish Succession concerning the Danish *Christiana Margaretta*, but in that case, contrary to what one would be inclined to infer from Roscoe's short reference to it at p. 2 of vol. I of his *Reports,* just the opposite decision had been reached and the ship had been restored. The same had happened in a number of other similar cases during the first years of the War of the Spanish Succession, cited above at p. 381. This liberal practice was continued in several subsequent cases arising during the War of the Austrian Succession in which the ship was likewise restored (*infra*).

The Notes devoted by Sir George Lee to the case history of the *Med Guds Hielpe*, rediscovered by Fr. Th. Pratt and edited in his work of 1856, are revealing. This was a Swedish ship, laden with pitch and tar, bound to the enemy France (Pratt-Lee, pp. 191 *et seq.*). The discussion turned around the applicability of Art. XI of the Anglo-Swedish treaty of 1661 (Dumont, VI^2, 384; Parry, 6, 469; Pratt-Lee, Appendix A, pp. 213 *et seq.*), which prescribed the carrying by merchant ships of a passport directed in the form drawn up by its Art. XII. The text of that judgment of 1745, as reported in Sir George Lee's Notes, again does not make it very clear what was the conclusive *ratio decidendi.* According to the Notes at pp. 196-197 of Pratt-Lee, Sir Henry Penrice, in his first *Per Curiam*, argued as follows:

> "The question is first, whether [the ship] is supplied with a proper pass. The pass she has is very materially different from the form directed by the treaty, for this does not certify the cargo. The Swedish treaty has of late not been so strictly observed as perhaps it was before; possibly some new conventions have been made between England and Sweden, which the Court does not know of."

After these inconclusive passages the report passes on to the second question whether pitch and tar were contraband of war:

> "It is a question of great moment, and deserves to be well considered. Many cases have been quoted, which ought to be looked into. When the prizes belonged to the Crown, the Court might show favour to the claimers, which cannot be shown now the prize is given to the captor, *and that distinction has been well inforced by Dr. Lee.*" (my italics)

Who is speaking here? The way in which the cases are reported in the Notes often makes it difficult to conclude with certainty who is speaking: the President of the Admiralty Court Sir Henry Penrice, the author of the Notes Sir George Lee himself, or their editor Fr. Th. Pratt. Be this as it may, the President is reported to have in a first *Per Curiam* "taken time to consider the case" in the light of Art. XI of the Swedish treaty and Art. 5 of the Royal Instructions in force at the time. The proceedings in the first instance ended with a second *Per Curiam*, dated 9 August 1745 (Pratt-Lee, pp. 198-199) which condemned both ship and cargo. The Lords of Appeal, in their turn, took time to deliberate before giving their sentence. This was finally delivered some five years later, on 29 June 1750 (Pratt-Lee, p. 200). It confirmed the condemnatory judgment of the Court below, contrary to the plea in favour of the vessel by the Attorney General who invoked another, the abovementioned contrary precedent from the War of the Spanish Succession, *Christiana Margaretta* of 1702, in which the Court had restored the ship to her Swedish owners, although the cargo of pitch and tar was condemned. It is interesting to note from this early case history how laboriously the system of *stare decisis* in actual fact worked in prize cases. Not only did it sometimes take years to decide the issue definitively, but the process was, moreover, attended with an open avowal by the Courts of their ignorance of the precedents.

Another example that illustrates the difficulties involved in the process of judicial law-making is Sir Henry Penrice's saying in the case of the Danish *T'Slots Copenhagen* [1745-6] (Pratt-Lee, pp. 40 *et seq.*, at p. 48) that he could not accept the case of the *Vierge Marie* as a binding precedent because this was still before the Lords of Appeal, and they in their turn, were obviously also at a loss about how to decide the contraband cases. On this particular issue comp. further my remarks on the principle of *stare decisis* in Chapter I, section 5, *supra*, pp. 102-106.

Despite the condemnatory judgments in the *Med Guds Hielpe* case, the War of the Austrian Succession would seem to have brought about a more resolute and final break through in favour of the transporting vessel and the innocent goods on board. The harsh rule, which had also already been set aside in the relation between England and the United Netherlands by Art. 7 of their Treaty of Commerce of 1/10 December 1674 (Dumont, VII[1], 282; Parry, 13, 255)—see Sir George Lee's reference to that treaty provision in the case of the Dutch ship *Maria* (Dyrk Tyalfsy, Master) [1747] (Pratt-Lee, p. 133)—, was mitigated, as the editor of Sir George Lee's Ms. Notes stated at pp. lxviii-lxx, as follows:

"The first penalty is, of course, the confiscation of the article itself, of which every case of condemnation affords an example.

By the ancient law of Europe the confiscation was also extended to the vessel, the medium of conveyance, and instrument of offence.

But in the modern practice of the Court of Admiralty a relaxation has been introduced and a milder rule has been adopted. Independent of the forfeiture of the article of contraband, the conveyance of it is, in general, only attended with loss of freight and condemnation in expenses of bringing it in together with the costs of suit.

Where, however, part of the cargo had been restored before the condemnation of the contraband articles, it was considered to have been separated from the ship, and the freight allowed as a charge upon it.

This relaxation, however, is only extended to the property of such parties as may fairly be supposed to be free from all participation in the offence, the known ground on which it was introduced being the supposition that freights of noxious or doubtful articles might be taken without the knowledge of the owner; where, therefore, in the case of the *De Vrow Anna Maria* [Pratt-Lee, p. 119] the contraband goods were put on board the ship by the consent and privity of the owners, it also was included in the same sentence of condemnation.

And if the ship and contraband articles belong to the same owner, they will both fall under the same condemnation.

This will also be the case when the master is part-owner; and, in general, the owners of the ship are bound by his acts, the master being agent for the ship, though not necessarily for the cargo.

The taint of contraband also extends to all property on board belonging to the owners of the contraband articles, but all innocent articles belonging to different owners are entitled to restitution.

It must also be observed that this relaxation of the penalty is a benefit which can only be claimed in fair cases. Thus, when the vessel was sailing with a false destination or involved in an act of ill faith, it was condemned.

Generally speaking, all taint is removed by the discharge of the cargo, or an abandonment of the design: the penalty will, however, attach to the return voyage, if false papers have been used on the outward one; but it will not be allowed to be enforced when the vessel has in the meantime made an intermediate voyage."

A number of cases have indeed occurred during the War of the Austrian Succession in which the ship was not forfeited for carrying contraband and was restored though the cargo was condemned (Pratt-Lee, p. 47).

Exceptions were cases in which, *e.g.*, the ship was chartered by the captain who knew what the cargo was: the *T'Slots Copenhagen* [1745-1746] (pp. 40 *et seq.*, at p. 49). Privity of the owners of the vessel and breach of a treaty provision, just as false destination or false papers, were also admitted as justifying the capture and condemnation of the transporting vessel.

See further on the confused jurisprudence at this stage of the legal development (mid-18th century) the following judgments reported from the War of the Austrian Succession (the references are to the relevant pages in Pratt-Lee):

Cases in which both ship and innocent goods were restored were those of the *Fortune de la Mer* [1745] (pp. 33 *et seq.*, at p. 40); the *Juffro(u)w Susanna* [1746] (pp. 67 *et seq.*, at p. 74); the Lübeck *Providentia* [1747] (pp. 94 *et seq.*, at p. 98).

Cases in which both ship and innocent goods were condemned were the

Hewa [1745-6] (pp. 62 *et seq.*, at p. 67); the *Providence* [1746] (pp. 75 *et seq.*, at p. 85), and the above-mentioned *T'Slots Copenhagen.*

Cases in which the ship was restored but the innocent goods on board were condemned were: the *Fredericus Secundus, Koning van Prussien* [1747] (pp. 109 *et seq.*, at p. 112, resp. 114-115); the Danish *Providentia* [1748] (pp. 144 *et seq.*, at p. 147); the *St. Johannes* [1748] (pp. 166 *et seq.*, at p. 170); the *Nostra Seignora de Pentha de França* [1746] (pp. 90 *et seq.*, at p. 94).

Sometimes the disorderly manner in which the cases are reported hinders any firm conclusion: were, for instance, the innocent goods on board the *Louisa* [1745-6] restored to the claimants together with the ship? Comp. Sir Henry Penrice's first decree at p. 62 (reserving the consideration of the ship and the rest of the cargo to the first day of the Easter Term) with the short note at the bottom of p. 111 (restoration of the ship after hearing further arguments, without any mention of the fate of the innocent goods).

There is much vacillation or variation also in the treatment of additional claims for costs and damages, brought either by the captors or by the owners, or for freight, in cases of restoration of the prize, and of additional Court orders to give security for the sale of released contraband cargoes in England. See, *e.g.*, the case of the Lübeck *Providentia* [1747] at p. 98. Sir Henry Penrice's decree was to the effect that ship and cargo should be restored to the claimers, but that they should give security to sell the goods in England; and that expenses were due to the captors because they had had just cause of seizure. While affirming the lower decree as to the just cause of seizure, the Lords of Appeal reversed it almost three years later (December 1749) on two points: (*a*) as to the costs given to the privateer, both sides having to bear their own expenses; (*b*) as to the security to be given by the claimants for the sale of the contraband cargo in England. And there are many more such decrees to be found in Pratt-Lee, which, however, are so detailed, insignificant or sometimes even incomprehensible that I refrain from venturing further into this jurisprudential mess.

The liability of a neutral merchant vessel to condemnation on the ground of her carrying a contraband cargo was consequently not yet recognized in England in the middle of the 18th century. The Attorney General stated indeed in the appeal case of 1750 concerning the *Med Guds Hielpe* that no instance was mentioned of the condemnation of a ship for having contraband goods on board.

When further trying to infer from Sir George Lee's Ms. Notes and references how often a contraband-carrying ship, claimed by neutrals, was condemned for her action either during this war or during preceding wars, one meets with the difficulty that the Notes do not always make clear whether a condemnation was based on the adoption of the "infection" principle rather than on some other ground, such as fraudulent behaviour, the lack of a passport in the exact prescribed form, or insufficient proof of the ship's neutral character, nor, inversely, to what extent the restoration of the prize was based on the rule in favour of the produce of the soil of the exporting neutral country rather than on a rejection of the "infection" doctrine.

The question of infection of a contraband carrier and innocent cargo on board was for that matter not an isolated problem, confined to the carriage of contraband. It played indeed a much wider part as a corresponding problem arose in other fields, such as trading with the enemy, violation of a blockade, and especially attempts at the rescue of a captured neutral ship by her master and crew. There also, it was questionable whether such rescue attempts by neutral masters and crews, often considered as illegal action on their part, caused the simultaneous condemnation of innocent objects, *in casu*, the cargo of such ships. I refer for this problem to section 7 *sub* B on Recapture, where I distinguished in an introductory § 1, *infra*, p. 542, such rescue from recapture proper. A number of such cases of rescue were surveyed by Sir W. Grant in appeal in the *Franklin* case [1811] (2 Acton, 106; Roscoe, II, 115, at pp. 116 *et seq.*).

A case in which a similar problem arose with respect to trading with the enemy was the *Hoop* (Cornelis, Master) [1799] (1 C.Rob., 196; Roscoe, I, 104).

On the sanctions against violation of a blockade comp. the following passage in Sir William Scott's decree on the *Mercurius* (Gerdes, Master) [1798] (1 C.Rob., 80; Roscoe, I, 54, at p. 57):

> "To maintain that the conduct of the ship will affect the cargo, it will be necessary either to prove that the owners were, or might have been, cognisant of the blockade, before they sent their cargoes; or to show, that the act of the master of the ship personally binds them".

—the Seven Years' War

In different cases during this war which on the one side ended by the Peace Treaty of Paris (10 February 1763) and in which England, France and Spain participated, the question arose whether the ship and/or the innocent part of her cargo were liable to condemnation together with the contraband goods. See the *Il Santo Crucifixo* (Burrell, 160); the *Jesús* (*ibid.*, 164); the *San Juan Baptista (ibid.*, 164); the *Dolphin* (*ibid.*, 181) and the *Ravens* (ibid., 182).

—the War of the American Independence and connected wars of 1775-1784

In the last quarter of the 18th century the political scene in North America changed radically as the result of the revolt of England's colonies there against the mother country, and the entry of the United States of America as a new member with its own ideals into the international community. These events were moreover attended with connected wars between Great Britain, on one side, and three other States, France, Spain and the United Netherlands, on the other.

All the five States involved in those wars might consequently have had occasion to reconsider or, as far as the United States were concerned, to consider their position with regard to the extension of the sanction of condemnation to the contraband carrier and innocent cargoes but, as far as I have been able to verify, none of them seems to have done so in actual fact.

As to England, Hay and Marriott's collection, on which I have reported above in Chapter I, section 5, under England, B, p. 97, does not include any prize court decree which deals with this particular subject. Nor did I come across any special mention of it in the ample survey of the case law of the first American prize court we owe to Bourguignon's meticulous research. And reliable copies of French, Spanish and Dutch judgments are lacking.

—the Coalition Wars against France 1793-1815

English case law on the penalties for the carriage of contraband goods to the enemy did not begin to exhibit a more coherent picture until the period of Sir William Scott (Lord Stowell) since 1798 during these Coalition Wars. Those penalties had a double aspect according to whether the presence of contraband goods in the vessel also "tainted" either the carrying vessel or the innocent goods on board (or possibly both). The question of whether the ship or innocent cargo was on that account liable to condemnation together with the contraband cargo often depended on circumstances of a factual nature which differed from case to case. This fact and the still fairly confused jurisprudence explain why I found it rather difficult to arrange the available source material in a satisfactory manner. The obvious way to distinguish the cases of "infection" of the contraband carrier from those of a "taint" of the innocent cargo would have been if the case law had shown a clearer distinction between the two groups, but they were too closely intermingled. Other forms of grouping—in a strictly chronological order (theoretically recommendable with a view to the principle of *stare decisis*) rather than according to the specific grounds of condemnation together with the contraband, or a detailed survey of the cases rather than an attempt at sketching a comprehensive picture—were, as far as I could see, equally impracticable. That is why I had to choose a free exposé in which each of these aspects might turn up.

From the many instances in which the fate of the vessel had to be determined, I will quote the following cases of a more fundamental nature.

The general rule with regard to innocent goods on board the contraband-carrier that they were not subject to confiscation when they belonged to owners other than the contraband owners unless there were other aggravating circumstances present, can be exemplified by the *Staadt Embden* [1798] (1 C.Rob., 26; Roscoe, I, 37) and the *Ringende Jacob* [1798] (1 C.Rob., 89; Roscoe, I, 60).

The *Staadt Embden* was the complicated case of a ship that was initially captured by the French, was brought by them into the Norwegian port of Christiansund and was there assertedly bought by a neutral, a merchant of Emden. She was later recaptured by the English while sailing with a cargo of masts, deals and planks on a voyage from Riga to Amsterdam. The claims put forward for the ship by the Emden merchant were dismissed. The prize court was of the opinion that there had not been a *bona fide* transfer of the ship in the Norwegian port, and on that ground she was condemned. What remained was a claim for the cargo by Russian merchants at Riga, but this claim was also rejected. At that stage of the proceedings two questions arose:

(a) what was the fate of the non-contraband goods on board?, and

(b) was the relaxation in favour of produce of the shipper's neutral soil applicable?

Ad (a) Sir William Scott decided that non-contraband goods which were part of the same cargo as the contraband goods and were the property of the same owner, must also be condemned and that to escape contagion by the contraband the innocent articles must be the property of different owners.
Ad (b) On this point Sir William Scott refused to recognize the relaxation practice as a universal principle. Comp. on this point, *infra*, under B Relaxations, § iii, pp. 401-413.

The *Ringende Jacob* was a ship sailing under Swedish colours, laden with iron, hemp, tobacco and oak logs, and taken on a voyage from (Russian) Riga to Amsterdam. The Court argued as follows:

> "By the ancient law of Europe [the] consequence [of the ship being affected by the contraband cargo] would have ensued; nor can it be said that such a penalty was unjust, or not supported by the general analogies of law; for the owner of the ship has engaged in an unlawful commerce. But in the modern practice of the Courts of Admiralty of this country, and I believe of other nations also, a milder rule has been adopted; and the carrying of contraband articles is attended only with the loss of freight and expenses, except where the ship belongs to the owner of the contraband cargo, or where the simple misconduct of carrying a contraband cargo has been connected with other malignant and aggravating circumstances".

This latter judgment dealt in addition with several other matters, such as the impact of treaties on the decision, the contraband character of hemp, the traditional exemption of the produce of the neutral shipper's own soil from condemnation, and the alleged breach of blockade by the vessel. These additional issues are discussed at the appropriate place in this systematic survey.

See also the *Sarah Christina* [1799] (1 C.Rob., 237; Roscoe, I, 125):

> "With respect to the [Swedish] ship: if I was satisfied that the ship and cargo belonged to the same person, I must condemn that also, upon the ordinary rule which extends the

penalty of contraband to all the property of the same owner involved in the same unlawful transaction. But I shall restore it under the strong doubt which I entertain, whether the cargo is not, in fact, the property of other persons, I mean French agents, for I suspect it to have been a French speculation throughout. In giving the owner of the ship any benefit from these doubts, I am, perhaps, practising a lenity which would require more apology than, upon strict principle, I might find easy to furnish; but I shall content myself with the restitution of the ship, withholding, as usual on the carriage of contraband, the allowance of freight and expenses."

A footnote *a* at p. 127 of Roscoe refers to another precedent, the *America* (3 C.Rob., 36), a case of fraudulent behaviour;

the *Jonge Tobias* [1799] (1 C.Rob., 329; Roscoe, I, 146):

"Formerly, according to the old practice, the cargo [of tar] would have carried with it the condemnation of the ship, but in later times this practice has been relaxed, and an alteration has been introduced which allows the ship to go free .... This applies only to cases where the owners of the ship and cargo are different persons. Where the owner of the cargo has any interest in the ship, the whole of his property will be involved in the same sentence of condemnation; for where a man is concerned in an illegal transaction the whole of his property embarked in that transaction is liable to confiscation. The proofs are very strong that Mr. S [one of the claimant ship-owners] is the owner of the cargo .... [his share in the ship was condemned on the ground of the same fraudulent discretion which had guided his conduct throughout.] The only question is, whether there is proof that there are more owners of the ship than one. I think that there are other persons concerned in the ship, although they do not appear to be affected with a knowledge of the cargo; the presumption is against them certainly, but that is not sufficient to induce me to go to the length of condemning their shares ...."

Discharge of the contraband goods before the ship was seized relieved her from the penalty of confiscation; this was sometimes called "separation of ship and cargo": the *Immanuel* (Eysenberg, Master) (p. 473) [1799] (2 C.Rob., 186; Roscoe, I, 217) and the *Imina* [1800] (p. 356). This was, according to Pratt's Preface, p. xx, in the latter case expressed as follows:

"Although from the moment of quitting port on a hostile destination the offence is complete, and it is not necessary to wait till the goods are actually endeavouring to enter the enemy's port, yet the variation of the destination having happened, the parties were, after that time, entitled to the benefit of it."

Another case of such "separation" (of ship and goods) was that of the *Öster Risöer* [1802] (4 C.Rob., 199, at p. 200; Roscoe, I, 382).

The act of the master of the ship forfeited the ship because her owner was responsible for acts of the master as his agent: the *Franklin (No. 1)* [1801] (3 C.Rob., 127; Roscoe, I, 298). However, the master was not necessarily also the agent of the cargo owner: the *Imina* (Bauman Vroom, Master) [1800] (3 C.Rob., 167; Roscoe, I, 289), the *Caroline* (Doah, Master) [1808] (6 C.Rob., 461; Roscoe, I, 607).

When the transporting vessel was confiscated together with the contraband cargo, this was in many cases on the ground that she belonged to the owner of the contraband, but there were often also other reasons of an aggravating nature. Thus, in the *Neutralitet (No. 1)* [1801] (3 C.Rob., 295;

Roscoe, I, 309) this Danish ship was found to have sailed under a false destination and the ship owner had shown singular misconduct by contravening directly the prohibitions of the Anglo-Danish treaty. But, said the Court:

> "The confiscation of a ship so engaged will leave the general rule still untouched, that the carriage of contraband works a forfeiture of freight and expenses, but not of the ship."

When the owners of the ship and of the contraband were different people, the ship was indeed held not to be "infected" by the contraband goods and therefore restored, unless there were other, specific aggravating circumstances which led to a contrary conclusion.

The harsh rule also applied when the master or the supercargo on board were only part-owners.

Other grounds of condemnation of the vessel together with the contraband were, *inter alia*,
—her sailing under false or dissembled destination or with false papers: the Prussian *Edward* [1801] (4 C.Rob., 68; Roscoe, I, 350), ostensibly bound from Bordeaux to Emden, but found at sea while on course to Brest; the suspicions were aggravated by apparent contradictions in the logbook;
—fraudulent concealment of dispatches: the *Atalanta* [1808] (6 C.Rob., 440; Roscoe, I, 607);
—other forms of deceit or privity of the ship owner or the master; the *Orozembo* [1807] (6 C.Rob., 435);
—the above mentioned action by the ship owner directly contrary to an express treaty provision which prohibited it: the *Neutralitet (No. 1)* (*supra*).

Confiscation of the innocent goods on board together with the contraband cargo was likewise in most cases motivated by the fact that they belonged to the same person as the contraband owner: they were for that reason considered to be "tainted" by the contraband: "But it is contended that the innocent parts of the cargo also, and the ship herself, will be subject to condemnation, on the known principle, that the infection of contraband extends also to all interests included the same claim, on behalf of the same proprietor" (Sir William Scott in the *Neptunus* [1807] (6 C.Rob., 403).

The situation about 1800 was therefore as follows:

Innocent goods on board were only subject to confiscation if they belonged to the owner of the contraband; all other merchandise was returned to its owner. If the owner of the contraband had any interest in the transporting ship, that interest was also liable to confiscation. The ship was, however, also in other cases subject to confiscation, for instance, if she had offered armed resistance to the captor, if she carried false or simulated papers, or if there were other fraudulent circumstances. If none of these circumstances obtained, the ship was to be restored to her owner, but as a rule no compensation was due to him for the loss of freight or for the seizure. A special reason for the condemnation of the transporting vessel and the whole of her cargo was her resistance to the exercise of the right of visit by a belligerent warship on the ground that she was sailing under the convoy of a warship of her own nationality. See the cases of the *Maria* (Paulsen, Master) [1799] (1 C.Rob., 340-379; Roscoe, I, 152 *et seq.*) and the *Elsabe* (Maas, Master) [1803] (4 C.Rob., 408; Roscoe, I, 167).

Two later cases in which the issue arose were those of

1807 in the *Neptunus (No. 5)* (Bachman, Master) (6 C.Rob., 403; Roscoe, I, 595), carrying another cargo of pitch and tar, and

1808 in the *Mercurius* (Harmens, Master) (Edw., 53).

A difference of opinion arose between the Courts with regard to the *Jungfer Charlotta*, a neutral vessel that was compelled by stress of weather to put into Oporto, where part of her cargo was sold to a Portuguese merchant without being landed there and was later carried on to an enemy's port. In a comparable case, the *Thomyris* [1808] (Edw., 17; Roscoe, II, 6), the Admiralty Court had restored the contraband-carrier to her owner (Roscoe, II, footnote *a* at pp. 9-10) and now followed, 1809, that precedent in the *Jungfer Charlotta*. Although the Lords Commissioners of Appeal did not state any reasons for their contrary decision of 1809 (1 Acton, 171), they must, if I have understood correctly the connection between the two decrees, have reversed the lower decree and condemned the ship on the ground that the continuity of her voyage to an enemy's port had not been broken by her stay in Oporto.

A bird's-eye view of the legal development in this field seems to justify the broad conclusion that roughly three successive historical stages can be distinguished, first that of a very harsh rule—condemnation not only of the contraband goods themselves, but also of the carrying vessel and the innocent goods aboard—, then that of the mitigation of the original practice to varying and uncertain extents—restoration of the ship alone, or of the innocent cargo alone, or of both, and subject to more or less drastic conditions—, and finally that of the gradual retrograde hardening of the position to the detriment of neutrals.

After the original rigorous practice the opinion of subsequent English prize courts seems to have turned to the milder view that the transporting vessel and/or the innocent part of the cargo should be released (albeit without any right to compensation for lost freight). Thus, during the War of the Spanish Succession, in 1702, the *Christiana Margaretta* (Sir Leoline Jenkins, II, 191; cited Roscoe, I, 2) was restored to her owners and, during the Seven Years' War, in 1756, only the saltpetre cargo of the *Jesús (, Maria* and *Joseph*) was condemned, but the ship herself released, together with the other goods on board (Burrell, 164; Roscoe, I, 6).

Subsequent prize court decisions, however, have become again more severe in their treatment of neutral interests, especially in cases where there were aggravating circumstances, such as: resistance to the visit, false or simulated ship's papers or other fraud. Leading cases to this effect are those of a cargo of masts on the already condemned ship *Staadt Embden* [1798] (1 C.Rob., 26; Roscoe, I, 37) and the *Ringende Jacob* [1798] (1 C.Rob., 89; Roscoe, I, 60).

Apart from the question of "infection", the presence of contraband goods on board a neutral ship at any rate affected the ship owner's or master's claim to freight. In the *Öster Risöer* [1802] (4 C.Rob., 199; Roscoe, I, 382) the Court laid down the rule that the master of a ship on which contraband goods had been carried was not entitled to freight in respect of such goods, even if he was ignorant of their contraband character: "if a different rule could be sustained, it might be applied to excuse the carrying of all contraband." Freight to goods condemned was refused. Freight for the goods restored was allowed to be a charge upon that part of the cargo, "the ship and the goods having been separated."

Even the courts which were called upon to adjudicate contraband cases after the codification of 1909 have still shown their interest in the history of the sanctions against the conveyance of contraband.

In the case of the *Håkan* during World War I (*B.C.P.C.* II, 210), confirmed in appeal (*B.C.P.C.* II, 497), Sir Samuel Evans wrote a detailed retrospective monograph on the development of customary law in earlier periods, in connection with the duty imposed upon British courts by the Privy Council in the *Zamora* case (comp. *ibid.*, II, 1) to examine in relevant cases whether an Order in Council constituted an aggravation or an alleviation of the position of neutrals under the existing law of nations. It was, in particular, two judgments of Sir William Scott that were reviewed, namely those concerning the *Jonge Tobias* [1799] (1 C.Rob., 329; Roscoe, I, 146) and the *Neutralitet (No. 1)* [1801] (3 C.Rob., 295; Roscoe, I, 309):

> "The claim of the ship owners for the release of this captured vessel was founded upon a proposition that it is a well established rule of the law of nations that neutral vessels carrying contraband of war are free from capture, subject to certain exceptions in cases where the owners of the vessels were also owners of the contraband, or where they attempt to defraud a belligerent of his belligerent rights to capture the contraband by concealment of destination by departure from the voyage, or by false papers or other similar methods."

In the course of his judgment Sir Samuel Evans gave the following exposé:

> "The ancient practice in this country before the Napoleonic wars—apart from special treaties—was that neutral vessels carrying contraband goods were subject to capture and condemnation, as where the goods themselves .... Sir William Scott said of it that "it cannot be denied, that it was perfectly defensible on every principle of justice. If to supply the enemy with such articles is a noxious act with respect to the owner of the cargo, the vehicle which is instrumental in effecting that legal purpose cannot be innocent"—*vide* the *Neutralitet.*

The confiscation of the ship had been justified by Bynkershoek and other jurists of authority. It is true, however, that by the time of Lord Stowell a relaxation of the practice was introduced whereby the ship was regarded as non-confiscable, except in certain cases of the character already mentioned. But it is to be noted that if the owner of any part of the contraband cargo was also the owner of the ship, or had any share in it, the ship or his share was still held to be subject to confiscation—see the *Jonge Tobias* [1799] [1 C.Rob., 329; Roscoe, I, 146].

It is difficult to ascertain precisely the reasons for the relaxation made in those times. It was probably due partly to the policy of this country in relation to neutral commerce, and to the frequency of treaties dealing with the subject. The legal ground for its introduction, however, was "the supposition that freights or noxious or doubtful articles might be taken, without the personal knowledge of the owner"—see *per* Sir William Scott in the *Neutralitet.*"

The President then passed in review a large number of historical precedents: the French *Règlement* of 26 July 1778 (three-quarters' rule); the Franco-American treaty of 30 September 1800 (Martens, R^2, VII, 96; Parry, 55, 343); the French *Instructions* of 31 March 1854 and 25 July 1870; the practice and prize jurisprudence during the Crimean War and the War of Secession; the wars in Europe of 1864 and 1866 and the Russo-Japanese War; the memoranda prepared for the Naval Conference of London of 1908-09, its results and the attitude of the Maritime Powers since 1909, to conclude from all that data that the Order in Council adopting the half-cargo rule of Art. 40 of the London Declaration was not contrary to the law of nations.

From judgments, dating from the Crimean War, it appears that if no part of the ship's cargo was condemned as contraband, the captor was obliged to pay full compensation unless there had been, at the moment of the capture, certain indications of facts which, if established, would have justified condemnation and reason to believe that they would have been established on closer information. See the cases of the *Ostsee* [1855] (Spinks, 174; Roscoe, II, 432) and the *Leucade* [1855] (Spinks, 217; Roscoe, II, 473).

The very last phase of the pre-codification period has demonstrated the durableness of conceptions which had matured in the past: the contrast between the British and French attitudes towards the problem of extension of the sanction of condemnation of objects other than the contraband goods themselves has indeed lived on in the discrepancy between the Japanese and Russian systems of prize law in 1904-1905, Japan following the British, Russia the French solution.

—the Russo-Japanese War

The Japanese prize courts adhered to the theory developed by the British Admiralty Courts and extended the sanction of confiscation to the transporting vessel and the innocent goods on board when they were the property of the same person as the owner of the contraband cargo. They specified this criterion to the effect that, if this common ownership was established, a possible difference in the destination of the two groups of goods was immaterial. See the case of the *Cargo ex Hsiping, claim of Teng Ming Cheng and others* (Hurst & Bray, vol. II, pp. 140 *et seq.* at p. 153):

> "It is held by the doctrine of International Law and considered by this Court to be in accordance with general principles, that when contraband of war is captured and innocent goods belonging to the owner of the contraband are found on board the same vessel, the innocent goods may be condemned, even though their port of destination be not the same as that of the contraband."

The Russian prize courts, on the other hand, followed the French practice which was also adopted in their Prize Regulations of 14 July 1895 (*loco cit.*, vol. I, Appendix A, pp. 311 *et seq.*), Art. 11(1)(b):

> "Merchant vessels of neutral nationality are liable to condemnation as prizes—
> (1) when such vessels are found carrying to the enemy or to an enemy port—
> (b) other articles of contraband of war [than those *sub (a)*] amounting, in bulk or weight, to more than half of the entire cargo."

This proportion of more or less than half of the whole cargo in bulk or weight was expressly stated in several judgments, for example in the *St. Kilda* case (vol. I, 188), in which only 700 of a total of 4745 tons were contraband goods and the Court accordingly decided that both the ship and the rest of the shipload were to be set free. In other judgments the condemnation and destruction were held justified because the contraband cargo amounted to more than half of the entire shipload: the *Knight Commander* (vol. I, 54), the *Ikhona* (vol. I, 226) and the *Prinsesse Marie* (vol. I, 276).

B. *Relaxations of the sanctions.* Introduction. There are five specific mitigations of the rules governing the sanctions on the carriage of contraband which have been adopted in former centuries.

The strictly limited circumstances in which equitable or practical considerations demanded a relaxation of the harsh rule were in particular the following: (i) the transporting vessel was encountered at sea while her master was still unaware of the outbreak of war, or, possibly, of the classing of her cargo as contraband of war; (ii) the delivery of the contraband goods to the enemy had already taken place and the ship no longer had any such goods on board; (iii) the contraband goods were the produce of the neutral shipper's own soil. In cases like these the harsh sanction was (iv) replaced either with the release of the prize, or with a simple requisition or pre-emption of the contraband goods, a form of relaxation which was also applied exceptionally in other cases. A minor ground of exception was (v) the small quantity of contraband goods on board.

The Courts stressed that these relaxations could only be claimed "in fair cases", in which the claimant could rightly be presumed to have been ignorant of the noxious or dubious nature of the cargo. They would not be granted in favour of vessels or goods sailing with false destination, or involved in other acts of *mala fides*: the *Franklin*, the *Floreat Commercium*, the *Edward*, the *Neutralitet* and the *Vro(u)w Anna Maria*.

Particulars of these instances of exemption granted or refused will be given below.

As far as the practice of exceptional relaxations of the strict principle of confiscatabily of cargoes normally liable to that sanction was concerned, I have not come across decisions of a general character. Occasional pronouncements, however, prove that such relaxations were sometimes also admitted in fields other than the conveyance of contraband goods, such as the rule of the war of 1756 against the engagement of neutrals in the colonial trade of the enemy, normally closed to them. Thus, in the case of the Hamburg *Immanuel* (Eysenberg, master) [1799] (2 C.Rob., 186, at pp. 197 *et seq.*) the question arose whether the claimants could invoke certain relaxations of the said rule in favour of a shipment from Hamburg to Santo Domingo, at that time still a French colony and not yet an independent State, via the French port of Bordeaux, where part of the cargo had been unloaded. In that very complicated case the Court held, *inter alia*, that such relaxation should not be extended by construction.

The same principle was applied in the *Charlotte* case [1804] (5 C.Rob., 305): Russian property and produce carried on a non-Russian vessel was held not to be protected by Art. III, § 2 of the Anglo-Russian treaty of 5 (17) June 1801 (Pratt-Lee, at p. 245), dealing with the relaxation. Comp. *infra*, *sub* B, iii, p. 412.

(i) *Contraband intercepted at sea shortly after the outbreak of hostilities or other cases of ignorance of relevant facts.* Exemption from confiscation of goods, normally liable to seizure under the law of prize, but found at sea at the commencement of hostilities, was sometimes stipulated by treaty. Although this exemption usually had a bearing on the fate of enemy goods laden in a neutral vessel and it is difficult to quote a text to the same effect regarding specifically the case of the transportation of contraband goods, laden or shipped prior to the outbreak of war or to the declaration of their contraband character, the broad idea that goods which under normal circumstances would be subject to the exercise of the right of prize, should not be confiscated if their lading or carriage overseas had been begun before the commencement of the war, was expressed in a number of treaties of commerce. See on this particular variant of exemption my exposé in section 2 of this Chapter, *supra* at p. 309.

In 1745 a shipload of rough timber on board the *Postilion of Bourdeaux* was released on the ground that it was shipped so soon after the outbreak of war that it could not be assumed that the shippers had knowledge thereof when the timber was laden (Pratt-Lee, pp. 38 and 72).

This was only one of the instances in which a neutral owner's ignorance of certain facts was admitted as a ground of exemption of a prize from condemnation. Ignorance was not a general defense, but it was a defense in a number of specified cases. Ignorance could indeed exist as regards a variety of facts, as is apparent from the French prize court decisions reported by

De Pistoye and Duverdy in their *Traité des prises maritimes*, vol. I, pp. 123 *et seq.* and 147 *et seq.* The persons concerned could be ignorant of the enemy character of goods laden in a neutral ship, on that ground liable to seizure under the theory of "hostile infection"; of the enactment of a particular law determining or changing the legal situation; of the neutral character of the maritime area where a capture took place; of the outbreak of hostilities; of a notification by a belligerent that certain articles would be considered as contraband; of the establishment of a blockade, or of the conclusion of peace. Examples of such ignorance reported in the *Traité* were:

the *Christiania Colbiornsen contre le Patriote*, in which the *Tribunal de Cassation* [*an* VIII] (vol. I, p. 123) decided that

> "Est nulle la prise d'un navire appartenant à une nation neutre, quoique chargé de marchandises de provenance ennemie, si, à l'époque du chargement, il n'a pu connaître la loi déclarant de bonne prise tout bâtiment chargé de pareilles marchandises";

La Thétis contre le Serpent, in which the *Conseil des prises* [*an* X] (vol. I, p. 147) held that

> "N'est pas valable une prise faite après la signature d'un traité de paix, même avant sa ratification, alors qu'aucune stipulation spéciale n'est faite à cet égard. Il en est ainsi même quand la paix n'est connue ni du capteur ni du capturé".

The authors even cite in this context a decree of the English Admiralty Court of 1854 (vol. I, p. 132) relating to the *Argo* case, in which Dr Lushington decided that the Order in Council of 29 March 1854 protected a Russian ship that had left the Russian harbours prior to the delay determined by that Order, although she had only taken in cargo subsequent to its date.

Further instances of ignorance, reported in the *Traité*, related to captures made after the expiration of the time-limits during which this would still be permitted, as determined in the peace treaty. See the cases of *La Bellone contre le Porcher* and *La Petite Renommée contre la Nymphe* [*an* XI], in which the *Conseil des prises* decided that

> "Lorsqu'un traité de paix détermine des délais à l'expiration desquels les prises ne seront plus faites valablement, l'ignorance absolue de la paix n'est pas indispensable pour la validité d'une saisie faite dans les délais réservés. Dans les délais où les prises peuvent être encore légitimement faites, la présomption d'ignorance de la paix est de droit, et elle ne doit céder que devant la preuve complète que le capteur a eu une connaissance positive de la paix. Cette connaissance doit être certaine, assurée, indubitable. Elle ne peut résulter de renseignements verbaux, ni même de documents non authentiques fournis par l'ennemi. Elle doit émaner immédiatement ou médiatement de la puissance à laquelle appartient le capteur. Elle peut, néanmoins, résulter de communications faites par la voie de l'ennemi, en vertu d'instructions spéciales et officielles dont il serait porteur".

An English precedent on ignorance was that of the *Öster Risöer* [1802] (4 C.Rob., 199-200), in which the master was totally ignorant of the contents of certain packages. The Court decided—in consent with the King's Advocate that the master was not at liberty to bind himself to a voluntary ignorance, by which, if it could be allowed in one instance, the whole penalty of carrying contraband might be defeated—that the master could not be permitted to aver his ignorance and that he was bound, in time of war, to know the contents of his cargo.

Another English precedent was that of the *John (No. 2)* [1818] (2 Dods., 336; Roscoe, II, 232), an American ship, seized by the British on 5 March 1815 in ignorance by the captor of the conclusion of the Anglo-American Peace Treaty of Ghent, and during his possession lost without negligence of the captor. In this case the Prize Court decreed that under the circumstances the captor was not liable for damages since the fact of the conclusion of peace could not possibly have been known to him.

(ii) *Ships intercepted at sea after the delivery of their contraband cargo on the return voyage*. The rules observed with respect to the confiscatability of neutral vessels which had transported contraband to the enemy on their outward voyage, even during their return voyage have developed in what can only be called a "zig-zag" manner. Chr. Robinson has set out this development in some detail at pp. 63 *et seq.* of his *Collectanea Maritima.* Already in a British Royal Proclamation of 31 December 1626 "to prevent the furnishing the Kinge of Spaine and his subjects with provisions for shippinge, or munition for the warres, and with victuals", there was a passage concerning vessels "returning there in the same way." A confrontation arose in 1644 between England and the Republic of the United Netherlands with regard to three of the latter's ships, the *Bonadventure*, the *Golden Parat* and the *Paul*, which, after having carried contraband cargoes from Dunkirk to the at the time rebellious town of Newcastle, were captured by the British on their return voyage with the proceeds of those cargoes in coal, and condemned as good and lawful prize. The Lords and Commons, assembled in Parliament, refused restitution of the ships on the principle that the proceeds of contraband carried to the enemy on the outward voyage, were liable to condemnation on a return voyage. Subsequently, however, a different practice developed: the sanction of confiscation for the carrying of contraband to the enemy was considered not to attach to ordinary return voyages in Europe (*Adm. Rep.*, I, p. 87). Later again, another change took place: in the *Rosalia* of 14 February 1800 the Court reconsidered the legal situation: the case concerned a successful transportation of contraband to the enemy with false destinations, followed by a return with the proceeds of that contraband (the outward voyage had been to the enemy's colonies and the proceeds consisted of colonial produce). Sir William Scott on that occasion suggested that in future it might perhaps not be unreasonable to distinguish the cases of contraband carried in this manner to the distant settlements of the enemy in the East Indies from ordinary cases between the ports of Europe, and to hold the proceeds of contraband on the return voyage to be liable in the former cases for the offence of the outward voyage, considering the outward and the return destination as one and the same voyage. But Chr. Robinson expressly stated that at the moment of his publication (1801) no case had been decided as yet on the principle of that distinction (*Collectanea Maritima*, p. 67, footnote).

The rules which gradually prevailed were to the following effect.

A ship that had delivered her contraband cargo to the enemy was in general no longer liable to condemnation, when she was captured on her return or on a further voyage: "what a ship did before, will not forfeit her on her cargo upon her return voyage". See the *Imina* [1800] (3 C.Rob., 167; Roscoe, I, 289; Pratt-Lee, footnotes at pp. 82 and 182), a case which was simultaneously one of an original attempt at breaking a blockade with the contraband cargo: "There must be actual *delictum* at the moment of seizure"; the *Lisette* [1807] (6 C.Rob., 387; Roscoe, I, 587) (*infra*).

If, however, the ship had sailed on the outward voyage under false papers, liability to condemnation continued: the *Rosalie and Elizabeth* (or *Rosalia and Betty* (Roper, Master)) [appeal, 1802] (6 C.Rob., footnote at the table of judgments in cases before the Lords Commissioners in Appeal Cases, at p. X):

> "The carriage of contraband outwards with false papers would affect the ship as well as the returned cargo with condemnation".

It is uncertain whether the severe rule also applied in cases in which the ship had in the meantime performed an intermediate voyage to another port: the *Christiansberg* [1807] (6 C.Rob., 376 at pp. 381-382), in which case, in principle, she might no longer be subject to confiscation. The Court discussed this point in connection with its question whether it was not necessary to apply the penalty of confiscation also to "a subsequent voyage":

> "It is objected, that if the penalty is applied to the subsequent voyage, it may travel on with the vessel for ever. In principle, perhaps, it might not unjustly be pursued further than to the immediate voyage".

But then the Court continued:

> "But we all know that in practice it has not been carried further than to the voyage succeeding, which affords the first opportunity of enforcing the law",

and on that ground pronounced the ship and cargo subject to condemnation. The argument again appears to be very unclear. The editor of the report added a footnote at p. 382 referring to an old case recorded in the Reports of the Court of Session in Scotland according to which the penalty could in effect only be applied to the "immediate voyage":

> "when the ships have actually gone in and sold the contraband, it is a *delictum commissum*; and though it might infer a quarrel against the delinquent, whenever he could be found, yet the law of nations hath, for the freedom of trade, abridged it to the immediate return of the same voyage, because quarrels would be multiplied upon pretence of any former voyage",

and he further quoted another British case, the *Randers Bye*, in which the Court refused to extend the penalty farther than to the *next* subsequent voyage.

Another appeal case was that of the *Baltic* [1809] (1 Acton, 25).

On the corresponding right of a belligerent to capture a merchant ship on a return voyage on the ground of her having violated a blockade on her outward voyage (*droit de suite*) see *infra*, section 4 on blockade.

The old rules were, in spite of Art. 38 of the Naval Declaration of London, desinterred by Sir Samuel Evans during World War I in the case of the *Alwina* [1916] (*B.C.P.C.*, II, 186; appeal: III, 54) in which the confused legal situation was retrospectively analysed in detail by Sir Samuel Evans who in his summary of that situation said:

> "The general rule which has been acted upon is that when a neutral vessel carries contraband goods, they are confiscable if captured *in delicto*, and that the vessel also, if it belongs to the same owner, or if the owner has been implicated in a transaction veiled over with false papers or other deceitful devices, is subject to the same penalty. But when the goods have been deposited at the port or place of destination, the ship and cargo upon the return voyage are exempt from the penalty".

Sir Samuel Evans continued as follows:

> "But exceptions were made at the beginning of the 19th century where the outward voyage was made under false papers or with a false destination, or in circumstances where the voyage had been conceived and contrived so as to deceive and practise a fraud upon a belligerent. In these latter cases the vessel and cargo have been held to be affected upon the return voyage also".

Comp. also Sir William Scott's own references to the existing practice in his time in the *Frederick Molke* [1798], which was again a case of breach of a blockade (1 C.Rob., 86; Roscoe, I, 58), *infra*, p. 440.

Further in the same *Alwina* judgment of 1916 Sir Samuel Evans said:

> "According to the principles of prize law, if the goods were never carried or delivered to the enemy at all, and if the intention and voyage have been clearly abandoned before seizure and capture, the offence is dissipated and purged, and neither the goods nor the carrying instrument are subject to the penalty of confiscation, the *delictum* being over. This is the reason, I think, why no authority can be produced to the contrary. A similar principle applies where vessels have intended to run a blockade".

Further references were made in illustration of the application of the doctrine in respect of blockade and contraband respectively, even where the voyage had been abandoned, or its character changed, by force of circumstances outside the voluntary intention of those responsible for the vessel and goods. Both were decided by Sir William Scott in the decisions concerning the *Lisette* [1807] (6 C.Rob., 387; Roscoe, I, 587) and the *Trende Söstre* (Missen, Master) [1807] (6 C.Rob., footnote *a* at pp. 390-393; Roscoe, I, 588). On the former see section 4 *infra* (on blockade), p. 441. The latter was a Danish ship, carrying a contraband cargo of cordage, tar, iron, gin and wine to the Danish settlement of Tranquebar (India) via the Cape of Good Hope, where she was captured on 14 May 1806, that is to say at a moment when that Dutch colony surrendered to the English and the cargo by that fact lost its enemy destination. The Prize Court ordered its release although the intention of the master had not changed.

And after referring to the same policy adopted with regard to this problem by the prize courts of other countries—the cases of the *Sishan* [1904], the *Lincluden* [1905] and the *Lydia* [1906] (Hurst and Bray, *Prize Cases*, II, 174, 341 and 359), the Court concluded:

> "The assumption has always been that the contraband goods have been captured *in delicto* while upon the intended voyage to the enemy destination; or in the case of a capture of a vessel on her return or homeward voyage, the contraband goods had actually been delivered to the enemy or carried to the enemy destination".

When one analyses the trend of the British case law in Sir William Scott's days, one must come to the conclusion that the sanctions on a transportation of contraband goods to the enemy, successfully performed in the past, were not too harsh.

After the unloading of contraband goods the transporting vessel could, in principle, no longer be seized and condemned. This was laid down in the abovementioned case of the *Imina* (Bauman Vroom, Master) [1800] (3 C.Rob., 167; Roscoe, I, 289).

A different practice, however, was initiated with regard to ships that were convicted of having successfully carried contraband to the enemy on her outward voyage with the help of false papers or other fraud; such ships were held liable to confiscation even if they were captured on their return voyage. This applied, for instance, to the *Margaret* [1810], an American ship that was captured on her return voyage from Britanny to Baltimore after having, with the help of false papers which disguised the nature of the cargo and the ship's destination to an enemy colony, delivered on her outward voyage a cargo of gunpowder and other contrabands goods in the (from 1712 to 1810) French colony of Isle de France (Mauritius). The condemnation of this ship by the Prize Court of Barbados was confirmed in appeal by Sir William Grant (1 Acton, 333; Roscoe, II, 113), who decided, moreover, that

> "The principle upon which this and other Prize Courts have generally proceeded to adjudication in cases of this nature appears simply to be this, that if a vessel carried contraband on the outward voyage she is liable to condemnation on the homeward voyage. It is by no means necessary that the cargo should have been purchased by the proceeds of this contraband. Hence we must pronounce against this appeal, the sentence of the Court below being perfectly valid and consistent with the acknowledged principles of general law".

As to the controversial question as to whether a neutral vessel remained liable to condemnation on her return voyage from a previous one on which she had delivered contraband to the enemy, the Yokosuka Prize Court during the Russo-Japanese War of 1904 decided in her favour even though she had succeeded in that delivery with the help of false papers. See the case of the British *Eastry* (Hurst & Bray, II, 299). The ship had carried a cargo of

Cardiff coal to Vladivostok in November 1904. A few months later she was visited and seized by a Japanese warship in the Tsugaru Straits, while avoiding the central channel and keeping close to the shore, declaring that she was on a voyage to Singapore. The Court found after an inquiry that the charterers of the two voyages were different persons and that the vessel's destination on the second voyage was really Singapore, and it released her.

(iii) *Produce of the neutral shipper's native soil. General introductory remarks.* The treatment of articles of a contraband nature being the produce or manufacture of the native soil of the neutral shipper, seized by a belligerent on their way to an enemy destination, is one of those subject matters of early English prize law which cause a student of that branch of the law the most serious difficulties. The documentary sources are either inconclusive or contradictory. They do not permit a firm conclusion on whether a binding rule of law on this matter existed or not, nor, if its existence was recognized, on what its exact scope was. I will begin with an attempt to substantiate this discouraging conclusion by summarizing in the following pages a few selected data from the period 1674-1856.

The practice of exempting contraband goods from confiscation if they were sent by a shipper living in an exporting neutral country whose native produce, growth or manufacture they were, or in a country bordering on such a country, sometimes even in a country farther away but in close trade relations with it (*e.g.* among the Hanse towns), is an old tradition, but it had not become quite clear to me whether and when exactly this exemption was "received" by the international society as a binding rule of law.

The oldest instance of an indulgence in favour of native produce is the one I found mentioned in C. Robinson's *Collectanea Maritima*, at p. 186: Denmark, in a Royal Ordinance of 23 September 1659, permitted neutral merchants to export certain contraband goods from Sweden if carried in ships of their own.

In his letter to the King of England of 29 August 1674 Sir Leoline Jenkins objected to the condemnation of a cargo of pitch and tar on the Swedish vessel *Berg(d)stadt* by the British Admiralty Court (Pratt-Lee, p. 195), but in a wording that creates the impression that the exemption was not yet recognized at that juncture. What the writer said was in effect that he thought it "very improbable" that the Swedes should allow pitch and tar, their native commodities, to be contraband, and that this "could not be imagined".

The same inconclusive formulation was employed seventy years later during the War of the Austrian Succession of the 1740's by Sir Henry Penrice in his judgment of 1745-6 in the *T'Slots Copenhagen* case (Pratt-Lee, pp. 40 *et seq.*, at p. 48):

> "Indeed, it is not probable that any nations should consent to restrain the sale of their own commodities."

Even in 1856 F. Th. Pratt, in his analysis of Sir George Lee's Ms. Notes on the British case law on contraband (pp. xxviii-xxix), was still in doubt what the legal position really was. He began by stating (p. xxvii) that

> "with respect to the condition in which the articles are found, such indulgence is, by the practice of nations, shown, where the articles are in their native and unmanufactured state".

A footnote referred to the *Jonge Margaretha* [1799] (1 C.Rob., 189; Roscoe, I, 100): iron as opposed to anchors and other instruments fabricated out of it. After a further remark that

> "the quantity of an article found on board is a subject considered entitled to much consideration; a moderate quantity of an article, however noxious, such as gunpowder, would be considered as forming part of the ship's stores and intended for its own use, as opposed to a very large quantity of the same article, the supply of which could only be reasonably accounted for as intended for purposes of commerce".

Mr Pratt continued by directly broaching the subject of native produce as follows, at p. xxviii:

> "An exception is also made in favour of articles, which are the growth and produce of the neutral country.
>
> This exception is not, however, founded upon any general principle of international law, as cases are not wanting where such articles have been condemned as contraband; this was done in the celebrated case of the *Med Guds Hielpe*. The cargo here consisted of pitch and tar, the produce of Sweden, and laden on board a Swedish vessel, but which was notwithstanding condemned as contraband; a sentence which was affirmed on appeal.
>
> This exception in favour of articles of the growth and produce of the neutral country is rather a relaxation introduced into the practice of the Court, from the consideration that it would be a harsh exercise of a belligerent right to prohibit the carriage of articles, which might constitute a considerable part of its native produce and ordinary commerce, as would be the case with Sweden with reference to the articles referred to in the case above cited",

and the further observed on the extension of the exemption as follows:

> "This exception is also sometimes extended to the produce of the neighbouring district ...".

Moreover,

> "These exceptions in favour of articles of the growth and produce of the neutral or neighbouring country are also to be understood as subject to the condition that the articles in question may be brought in for pre-emption, which is rather to be considered as a privilege conferred by the belligerent on, than a right to be claimed by, the neutral, and consists in the purchase of the article in question by the government to which the captor belongs after it has been brought in for adjudication, allowance being made for the original price, with a fair, reasonable profit.
>
> This subject was fully discussed in the case of the *Haabet*, the cargo of which consisted of corn going from *Altona to Cádiz*, which had been seized and brought in and bought by the Government.

The Court observed that the right of pre-emption was no peculiar claim of this country, but belonged generally to belligerent nations. The ancient practice was to confiscate such a cargo as the one before the Court entirely; a more mitigated practice prevailed in later times of holding such cargoes subject only to a right of *pre-emption*, that is, to a right of purchase upon a reasonable compensation to the individual. It had never been understood that, on the side of the belligerent, this claim went beyond the case of cargoes avowedly bound to the enemy's ports, or suspected on just grounds to have a concealed destination of that kind; or that, on the side of the neutral, the same exact compensation was to be expected which might have been demanded from the enemy in his own port. The enemy might be distressed by famine, and might be driven by his necessities to pay a famine price for his commodities if it got there; it does not follow that, acting upon the rights of war in intercepting such supplies, the government is under the obligation of paying that price of distress. It is a mitigated exercise of war on which the purchase is made, and no rule has been established that such a purchase should be regulated exactly upon the same terms of profit which would have followed the adventure if no such exercise of war had intervened; it is a reasonable indemnification and a fair profit on the commodity that is due, reference being had to the original price actually paid by the exporter and the expenses which he has incurred.

The usual practice appears to have been for Government to pay the ordinary expenses of captor and claimant; and in determining the remuneration to be paid to the latter for the articles seized, to allow the invoice price and ten per cent. profit, together with the freight."

The native produce issue was raised before the Admiralty Court during the War of the Austrian Succession (1744 *et seq.*) and was given a limited recognition.

But even after its revival during that War it has, as far as I have been able to verify from the available source material, again more or less fallen into oblivion or dozed-off in the period of the Seven Years' War of 1756-1763, and it would seem to have continued for some time in this crepuscular state. Bourguignon, as far as I see, does not mention it in his Part One (Historical development) concerning the case law of the British Vice-Admiralty Courts in the British-American colonies of the time at pp. 37 *et seq.*, nor in Part Two (Legal analysis) *sub* VII (Substantive prize law in America during the Revolution) at pp. 238 *et seq.*, of his standard work of 1977 on *The First Federal Court. The Federal Appellate Prize Court of the American Revolution 1775-1787*. Yet, it might have been a welcome subject of examination in the appeal case from the Vice-Admiralty Court of Rhode Island concerning the *William Galley* (Couwenhoven, Master), which has dragged along from 1745 to 1763 (Bourguignon, footnote 103 at pp. 176-177, referring to Pares' study on *Colonial blockade*, pp. 144-147). And neither have I found in other jurisprudential sources that cover (parts of) the Seven Years' War any clear indication of the application or invocation of the rule by the courts during that war. It has, however, finally re-emerged during the wars of the 1780's and the Coalition Wars against Revolutionary France as from 1793.

British case law on the subject.

After this summary survey of the history of the native produce rule or practice from the 17th to the 19th century, I will now pass on to a more detailed exposé of the cases in which the exemption of contraband goods from condemnation on the ground of their being the native produce of the exporting neutral country was either recognized by the prize court, or alleged by the claimant but dismissed by the court, and I will do that by reviewing them in the historical order of the successive wars of England, commencing with a brief survey of the cases reported from the oldest wars.

Originally the belligerents seized, and the Admiralty tribunals confiscated contraband cargoes shipped by neutrals with enemy destination despite their character of being the native produce of the neutral shipper's country. But

> "in the more modern understanding of this matter, goods of the nature being the produce of Sweden, and the actual property of Swedes, and conveyed by their own navigation, have been deemed in British Courts of Admiralty, upon a principle of indulgence to the native products and ordinary commerce of that country, subject only to the milder rights of pre-occupancy or pre-emption, or to the rights of preventing the goods from being carried to the enemy, and of applying them to your own use, making a just pecuniary compensation for them."

The restoration was indeed already early on made conditional upon an undertaking by the claimant not to sell the contraband goods to the enemy, or to sell them in England. This was the practice during the Nine Years' War in the 1690's, see the cases of the *Charles* [1691], the *Marie* [1691], the *North Star* [1694] and the *St. Antonio* [1696], cited by Sir George Lee in his Notes (Pratt-Lee, pp. 55, 56 and 59-60). The claimant had to give bail or security for that purpose. This practice was continued during the War of the Spanish Succession with regard to a number of Swedish ships and cargoes.

Cases in which pitch and tar, though being the native produce of Sweden and carried on Swedish ships, were not exempted from condemnation during the War of the Spanish Succession were those reported by Pratt-Lee at p. 202: the *Christiana Margaretta* [1702], and at p. 71: the *Charles* [1705], but in all the other cases, dating from 1703, reported at pp. 203 and 204, the cargoes of pitch and tar were still restored on the old condition of their compulsory sale in England: the *Fortune* (Dousoe, Master), the *St. Jacob* (Brinch, Master), the *Juffro(u)w Anna*, the *Warsaw Arms* and the *Anna Catharina*. See also *supra* p. 381.

The condition of security to be given for sale in England was sometimes still imposed by the Judge of the Admiralty during the War of the Austrian Succession, see the case of the *Providentia* [1747] (Pratt-Lee, p. 98), but the reversal of just that part of the decree by the Lords of Appeal seems to confirm another statement by Pratt-Lee (at. p. 196) that the last recorded instances of ordering cargo to be sold in England date from 1706: cases of the *Concordia* and the *Town of Rotterdam*.

—the War of the Austrian Succession

Many cases in which the native produce rule was invoked and either applied or rejected have followed the precedents of the Nine Years' War and the War of the Spanish Succession, but one gets the impression that the

British prize courts of the middle of the 18th century were in complete ignorance of those precedents and thus entirely in the dark as to what their predecessors had resolved on the question.

One of the first cases in which the issue might have been decided by the Lords of Appeal in express terms was that of the famous *Med Guds Hielpe* of 1745-50, only rediscovered by Pratt in the 1850's as reported by Sir George Lee in his Ms. Notes (Pratt's edition, pp. 191-205), but even then the problem of native produce was not discussed in so many words. The case concerned a cargo of pitch and tar, carried on a Swedish vessel, bound from Stockholm to Port Louis in France, where the voyage was to end. It was, therefore, a clear case of native produce of neutral Sweden, exported from thence with enemy destination. After prolonged proceedings in two instances (1745-1750) the cargo was condemned as contraband of war, and the carrying ship with it (on this latter aspect of the case see further this paragraph *sub* A, *supra*, pp. 382-383). The conclusion drawn by Pratt from this fact, *viz.*, that the Admiralty Courts at that time still rejected the exemption rule, seems to me debatable. The discussion in the courts in the *Med Guds Hielpe* case has remained confined to two questions without, it seems, even touching upon the problem of the exemption in favour of native produce, *viz.* (1) was the ship supplied with a proper pass?, and (2) were pitch and tar contraband of war under the law of nations and the Swedish treaty of 1661? The first question was answered in the negative (comp. on this aspect of the case this volume *sub* B, section 1, *infra*, pp. 489-491). The answer to the second question was positive (on this aspect see § *supra*, pp. 311-315). It is, of course, true that the lading of pitch and tar was condemned (together with the ship) despite its character of produce of the native Swedish soil, but that point was, as far as I can see, not specially examined and the case can, therefore, hardly be considered as a conscious basic rejection of the rule on native produce by either Sir Henry Penrice or the Lords. But in any case the validity of the rule was obviously still uncertain in the 1740's.

Other somewhat doubtful cases from the War of the Austrian Succession in which a reference to the native produce rule was made were those of

the Danzig vessel *Fortune de la Mer* [1745] (Pratt-Lee, p. 33), carrying rough timber, claimed by its neutral owner in Danzig; the marginal heading of the case at p. 33 speaks of "produce of neighbouring country", but I fail to see in the notes on the Court's decree of restoration of cargo and vessel anything more explicit than that

> "timber is the product of the country about Dantzick, in which they trade with all nations";

the Danzig vessel *La Vierge Marie* [1744-1745] (cited by Pratt-Lee at pp. 38, 43, 45-48, 70, 73), laden at Riga with masts and other timber, bound for France. The claimants argued that the cargo, which belonged to Russians, was not subject to confiscation by the Russian treaty of 1734, but against that it was contended that the prize could not be privileged by the treaty because the carrying vessel was not a Russian ship. This judgment was in a later case (at p. 48) rejected as a binding precedent as long as the Lords had not adjudged it. However, according to a footnote at p. 38, the Court of Appeal in that case did not go into the question of contraband at all: whereas the ship was restored as Danzig property, the cargo was condemned on the ground of enemy (French) ownership;

the abovementioned Danish *T'Slots Copenhagen* [1745-1746] (Pratt-Lee, p. 40), loaded with timber, taken in at Danzig; cargo and ship were both condemned because the timber was not the growth of Denmark;

the Swedish *Louissa* [1745-1746] (p. 49): again decided, as far as I can see, on grounds different from the native produce issue. The cargo consisted of, *inter alia*, pitch and tar; the ship was bound for Lisbon with a "discretionary destination" (comp. on this concept § 2 *supra*, p. 349); her master only went to Le Havre "by the act of God"; the ship did not have a passport according to the Swedish treaty of 1661. The ship was restored upon giving bail to sell the cargo in Lisbon. An allusion to native produce of neutral Sweden can only be found *in margine* at p. 49. The exemption cases cited in the footnote at that page are not all to the point;

the Danish *Ebenezer* [1747] (p. 136), carrying spars, boards and timber, all of the growth of Norway. This judgment dealt specifically with the issue of native produce:

> "Confiscation of ship and cargo is the highest punishment, and only to be inflicted for a plain attempt to assist the enemy. [The claimants] were only upon a trading voyage with the growth of their own country".

Both ship and cargo were restored. Counsel for the claimants again mixed up two different points by saying:

> "The goods are all of the growth of Norway, and therefore in a Danish ship not contraband".

This formulation was a very familiar, but in my opinion mistaken, way of expressing the rule that, although the goods were of a contraband nature, they came under the exemption granted in favour of native produce.

Small wonder that under the confused terminology and case law the English prize courts often took so much time (five years in the case of the *Med Guds Hielpe*) before making a final decision, in order to have the precedents collected and examined. On different occasions Lord Stowell later, during the Wars with Revolutionary France, also made or ordered such an inquiry.

—The Seven Years' War and subsequent wars

I have not come across cases of the application of the exemption rule in favour of the native produce of the exporting neutral country during the Seven Years' War, but it was later again applied during the American War of Independence and connected wars of the 1780's and during the Coalition

Wars of 1793 *et seq.* against Revolutionary France, and then also in the case of cargoes other than the traditional ones of the earlier period, such as wheat, butter and other victuals, and timber, which the claimant asserted were the produce of the soil of his country. The plea was then sometimes accepted in favour of their owner, even though the goods were not strictly the produce of the shipper's own country, but of a neighbouring friendly country (*infra*).

—The War of the American Independence and connected wars of the 1780's

The first controversial point which arose with respect to the native produce rule concerned the question as to whether the contraband cargo was strictly to be the produce of the exporting country or whether it could also be the produce of a closely related neighbouring country. See on this question the case of the *Juffro(u)w Wobetha* [1781-1782] (Roscoe, I, 370, footnote *a*), carrying a cargo of timber exported from Danzig by Greek merchants. This was condemned in the first instance, because it had been proved to be the produce not of the territory of Danzig, but of the neighbouring Kingdom of Poland, but it was released in appeal to be restored on the ground that Danzig, though a free city, being at that time within the immediate protection of Poland, was entitled to export the commodity concerned as one of its own products.

Another cause of controversy was later the fact that the contraband goods were carried in a neutral vessel that did not fly the flag of the shipper's own State. This controversial point led to far more elaborate argument in the Court than the first one. See on this topic the cases of the *Goede Vreede* [1780], the *Sanctissimo Sacramento* [1781] and the *Jonge Pieter* [1781-1783] (Lords, 24 April 1783), subsequently analysed in the case of the *Apollo (No. 1)* (Bottcher, Master) [1802] (4 C.Rob., 158; Roscoe, I, 368). According to the details given in the latter case by the captors and the King's Advocate, the situation in the *Jonge Pieter* case of the 1780's was as follows:

> "In the *Jonge Pieter*, which was a case of hemp, the property of Prussian subjects, exported from Koningsberg to Bourdeaux, on board a Dutch ship, [the principle that it was required, not only that the cargo should be the produce and the property of the exporting country, but also that it should be exported in the bottoms of that country] was distinctly averred in the printed reasons of appeal. It is true, indeed, that case was restored, but not in opposition to this mode of reasoning. Dutch ships had been particularly privileged by the treaty of 1674, to trade to ports of the enemy, even notwithstanding they had contraband on board. Owing to that circumstance, the cargo being otherwise free, except that it was not on board a Prussian ship, might be considered to derive so much protection from the privilege of the vessel; since Dutch ships might be taken under the treaty, as privileged to carry on such a trade, and might be considered, therefore, to this effect, as the ships of any country from which they were going. In another case in the last war, also, in the *Maria Petronella*, it must be admitted that Russian hemp on board a Prussian ship, was restored. But in that case the cargo was going, as was also the *Jonge Pieter*, on a destination to Bourdeaux, which is a mere mercantile port. The difference of destination is a material circumstance, distinguishing both those cases from the present

case—in which the hemp was going to Amsterdam, the enemy's principal port of naval equipment. On these grounds, the restitution which took place in those cases, will not conclude the present question. On the original principle, under which the relaxation was introduced, this hemp is subject to confiscation."

During the proceedings three precedents were cited, *viz.*, the *Sanctissimo Sacramento*, the *Goede Vreede* and the *Juffro(u)w Wobetha.* In his judgment of 15 January 1802 in the case of the *Apollo (No. 1)* Sir William Scott reasoned as follows:

"On the part of the claimants it was contended, that the relaxation was not so restricted, as was asserted on the other side; that the old rule was departed from, and, by the modern rule, neutral merchants were at liberty to export the produce of their own country, on their own account:—That this being allowed, there was no reason why it might not be in other ships, as well as those of their own country, it being equally in the course of their ordinary commerce to do so. Of the cases cited it was said, that the first was a cargo of Bolognese produce, sold to a merchant of Genoa; it was therefore Bologna hemp, going on Genoa account, and liable on that ground to confiscation. The second was a cargo of wheat, sent by a Swede, who is by treaty disabled from carrying wheat. A vehicle, therefore, was used, which it was unlawful to use; and the total disability of the ship to carry such a cargo, put the cargo into an unlawful state. The third was a cargo of timber from Dantzic, which could hardly be, and was proved not to be, in strictness, the produce of the territory of Dantzic, but of the neighbouring kingdom of Poland. These were cases in which the unfavourable determination proceeded upon grounds that have nothing in common with the present case.

But the case of the *Jonge Pieter* was exactly parallel, being the case of a cargo of hemp on board a foreign ship. On that occasion, the Court thought there ought to have been stronger proof that it was Prussian produce; but decreed the cargo to be restored. That case went up to the Lords, where the sentence of the Court of Admiralty was affirmed. It is therefore a direct precedent binding on this Court; and in conformity to that authority, I shall direct this cargo to be restored."

—The Coalition Wars against Revolutionary France

The traditional exemption of contraband goods, being the native produce of a neutral country, from condemnation was revived again during England's Coalition Wars against France since 1793.

When reading through the judgments of this period one must be on one's guard against misconstruction of their text or their heading. When, for example, they say that this or that commodity is not liable to condemnation in prize, they sometimes mean that the articles concerned do not belong to the category of goods listed as contraband in a Royal Instruction or a treaty, sometimes that, though listed as such, they are exempted from condemnation in virtue of the rule on native produce. And when a certain commodity is declared good and lawful prize, the legal ground for that conclusion may have been either that a doubtful term in an Instruction or treaty must be construed in disfavour of that commodity, or that the claimant's invocation of the rule on native produce in protection of an indubitable contraband good was in casu insufficient to defend it against confiscation. Moreover, the footnotes in Pratt's edition of Sir George Lee's Ms Notes are not always correct: some of the cases listed in the footnotes as instances of the exemption in favour of native growth or produce have, as far as I see, nothing to do with the rule.

The first precedent in the series attracts attention by the fact that Sir William Scott still denied the universal validity of the rule in the *Staadt Embden* case of 1798 (1 C.Rob., 26; Roscoe, I, 37):

> "As to the relaxation in favour of the export of native produce, said to have been sanctioned by a determination upon Russian hemp in the case of the *Jonge Pieter*, I am by no means disposed to consider that case as laying down any such universal principle. There have been many cases in which native articles, going to the enemy's ports on the account of inhabitants of the country which produced them, have been treated as contraband."

Reference was made again to the above-mentioned case of 1747-1750 concerning a cargo of pitch and tar, carried from Stockholm to Port Louis on board the Swedish ship *Med Guds Hielpe*, and claimed by a Russian merchant (Pratt-Lee, 191; Roscoe, I, 1).

Subsequent judgments which dealt with the rule will be surveyed now in their chronological order:

the *Ringende Jacob* [1798] (1 C.Rob., 89; Roscoe, I, 60), relating to a cargo of hemp, classed as contraband under the Anglo-Danish treaty of 4 July 1780 (Parry, 47, 341), carried on a Swedish vessel; in this case as in several others, the issue of native produce arose in addition to the question of contraband nature;

the *Jonge Margaretha* [1799] (1 C.Rob., 189; Roscoe, I, 100), a Papenborg ship, taken on a voyage from Amsterdam to Brest (France), with a cargo of cheeses on board. In this case Sir William Scott formulated the rule as follows:

> "Among the circumstances which tend to preserve provisions from being liable to be treated as contraband, one is that they are of the growth of the country which exports them."

In that case, however, the cheeses were the product of another, and that of a hostile, country (the Republic of the United Netherlands, the involuntary ally of France) and were, therefore, liable to condemnation, the more so because

> "the claimant [had] not only gone out of his way for the supply of the enemy, but [had] assisted the enemy's ally in the war by taking off his surplus commodities."

As far as the carrying ship was concerned, Sir William Scott showed remarkable lenience towards her owner by accepting as extenuating circumstances the fact that

> "he had acted without dissimulation in the case and might have been misled by an inattention to circumstances to which in strictness he ought to have adverted, as well as by something like an irregular indulgence on which he had relied";

In a parallel case—the transport of a cargo of Dutch cheese from Amsterdam to Bordeaux, for the account of a neutral merchant of Altona—, the exemption was applied and the cargo restored: the *Welvaart Kwest* [1799] (Roscoe, I, 103, footnote *a*);

the *Sarah Christina* [1799] (1 C.Rob., 237; Roscoe, I, 125) and the *Maria (No. 1)* (Paulsen, Master) (1 C.Rob., 340; Roscoe, I, 152), two Swedish vessels seized by the British fleet despite their sailing under a Swedish convoy (on this particular feature of the cases see *infra*, pp. 523-526). In these two further cases of 1799 it was decided that a cargo of pitch and tar destined for a hostile port was to be considered as contraband of war unless the goods were the produce of the neutral shipper's own country; in such a case, except where there was want of *bona fides*, they were only subject to pre-emption. The ships were restored, but the freight was forfeited;

the *Franklin (No. 1)* [1801] (3 C.Rob., 217; Roscoe, I, 298; Pratt-Lee, 49, 104), a Prussian ship going with a cargo of hemp and iron from Lübeck ostensibly to Lisbon, but actually to Bilbao. Although Sir William Scott alluded in his judgment to "the favourable considerations which are to a certain degree, and in some known instances, applied to the goods of persons exporting the native commodities of their country", this could not apply to the case of a ship taken out of her proper course, and in a direct course towards one of the Spanish (enemy) ports in the Bay of Biscay;

the *Neutralitet* [1801] (3 C.Rob., 295; Roscoe, I, 309), a Danish vessel taken with a cargo of tar on a voyage from Archangel to Dordrecht. In this case also, Sir William Scott alluded to "cases of proprietors exporting the produce of their own territory or of neighbouring parts", but he rejected an appeal to this exemption in the case on the ground that the carriage of a cargo of tar to Holland was a commerce expressly prohibited by the Danish treaty and that "an article which a Danish ship could not lawfully carry to an enemy's port [could not enjoy the protection of the exemption] even when it was the produce and manufacture of Denmark";

in the *Twende Brödre* [1801] (4 C.Rob., 33; Roscoe, I, 432) Sir William Scott,

> "taking a fair course between the rights of exportation of native produce, on the part of the neutral country, and the defensive rights of the belligerent",

reached a more favourable conclusion with regard to a cargo of fir planks which were restored.

Next comes the abovementioned case of the *Apollo (No. 1)* [1802] (4 C.Rob., 158; Roscoe, I, 368) on which I will report more in detail. It concerned a cargo of hemp, Russian property and the produce of Russia on board a Prussian ship, captured on a voyage from Libau (Courland) to Amsterdam. The cargo was claimed by its owners as, in their opinion, being exempted from condemnation as a produce of Russia, although it actually came from Danzig. This case is very elucidating. The legal situation was amply discussed by the parties and the Admiralty Court.

The captors and the King's Advocate argued that the question was whether hemp, being the produce and property of the exporting country

(Russia), but put on board the vessel of any other than the exporting country (*in casu* Prussia), was liable to confiscation. Their argument ran as follows:

"Hemp is now, by the law of nations, considered as contraband, unless protected by the particular relaxations which have taken place, or by special articles of treaty. The hemp in question is not so protected, but stands on the general footing. The relaxation which has given greater privileges to neutral commerce, was introduced in favor of the exportation of the produce of neutral countries, *being also* the property of the merchant of the exporting country, and exported *in ships* of that country. Where either of these circumstances are wanting, articles of a contraband nature revert to their general liability to confiscation. In the present case, the hemp is not so documented, as to shew it to be even the property of the exporting country: It is described, only at large, "as neutral property!" Under that description, it might be the property of a *Danish* merchant, and as such, would be contraband, by the direct terms of the *Danish* treaty. On this fact, at least, farther proof must be exhibited. But, independent of that fact, it is submitted, this hemp is confiscable—as not being exported in the ship of the exporting country. The relaxation was introduced, principally in favor of the *navigation* of neutral countries: It was accordingly required, not only that the cargo should be the produce and the property of the exporting country, but also that it should be exported in the bottoms of that country."

The claimants of the cargo on their side argued as follows:

"The cases which have been cited, are directly in point; and the distinctions which have been attempted, are not sufficient to defeat the application of those precedents to the present case; under the authority of those decisions, the practice has continued, invariably to this day; no instances can be produced, in which articles of a quality bordering on contraband, but otherwise privileged under the relaxation, have been held to be confiscable, merely because they were not *on board a ship of their own country*.—It was farther contended, that the Russian treaty, which had been signed in June 1801, previous to the sailing of this vessel, was to be taken as removing all doubts on this question, if any could otherwise be entertained; since in that it is expressly declared, "That such articles shall be free in *neutral ships*". This difference, it was said, was observable between the present and the former treaty, that the former only stipulated for the freedom of the navigation of Russia, whereas the terms were studiously extended in the third article of the present treaty to the *commerce*, as well as the navigation."

Against this it was replied that

"the term "neutral ships" must be taken, obviously, to mean only the ships of the contracting country, which *should be then neutral* as not engaged in the war."

Sir William Scott in his turn entered into a thorough review of the precedents and finally took sides with the claimants: see his judgment of 15 January 1802, confirmed by the Lords of Appeal. His argument ran as follows:

"This is the case of hemp, being Russian property and produce, put on board the ship of another neutral country, and destined to Amsterdam. Hemp is certainly liable to be considered as generally contraband; but in relaxation of the strict principle, the general rule now prevailing, is, that being the produce and property of the exporting country, and going in a vessel of that country, it is not liable to confiscation. The question is, Whether, if it is put on board a ship of another country, that circumstance alone will defeat the relaxation, and leave it unprotected to the consequences of its general character? The Treaty lately concluded with Russia must, I think, be laid out in the case. The argument has admitted, that the more ancient treaty included the navigation only: It is said, however, that the late treaty expresses *commerce* also, as well as navigation; but as I understand it, *commerce connected with the navigation:* The extension of the terms is only a more accurate expression of what was before implied. The terms of the other articles of the treaty convince me, that this is the true explanation. The second article stipulates, "That the ships *of a neutral power may*, &c."—then comes the expression on which the distinction is raised, "on board neutral ships"; that is, *ships of either of the contracting nations, being neutral*: as it is expressed in the French version of the same article, "Sur les vaisseaux neutres". If the question rested on this point, I should, without hesitation, express my opinion, that no privilege is conveyed to the mere Russian proprietor of the cargo by this treaty, that cargo being conveyed by a foreign bottom. Although the present question does not depend on this treaty, it may not be improper for me to say, in answer to what has been advanced, as the just interpretation of that treaty, that, in my apprehension, it is perfectly clear that the terms do not point to any thing, but what is confined within the navigation of the two contracting Countries.

The question, then, being abstracted from the treaty, is, Whether hemp, being the produce and property of the country, but put on board the vessel of any other than the exporting country, is liable to confiscation? Reference has been made to the case of the *Jonge Pieter*, in which it was decided, that this circumstance did not render it liable to be considered as contraband. In that case, hemp being Prussian property, was put on board a Dutch ship, and sent to Bourdeaux. It did not appear of what country the hemp was, but it was strongly argued, that, by the old rule, contraband affected the ship as well as the cargo; that the relaxation which had taken place, was introduced in favor of the ship, and as a concession to the navigation of neutral countries, when employed in the exportation of their own produce or manufactures; the cases which did not fall within the reach of this principle, were still subject to condemnation, under the old law; and on this point, three cases were relied on,—the *Sanctissimo Sacramento*, the *Goede Vreede*, and the *Juffrouw Wobetha*" [cargo condemned in the first instance, but restored in appeal].

See also the case of the *Christina Maria* [1802] (4 C.Rob., 166):

"This was a case of a cargo of pitch and tar, being the produce of Sweden, and the property of a Swedish merchant, taken on board a Swedish ship, on a voyage from Stockholm to a Dutch port.
Restored."

The *Twee Juffro(u)wen* [1802] (4 C.Rob., 242; Roscoe, I, 384) was again a case of the export of pitch and tar, the property of a Prussian merchant, from Emden to Dieppe in a Prussian ship. The extended rule was recognized by the Prize Court, but the cargo was condemned because it was not shown to be the produce of the exporting country.

In the *Evert* [1803] (4 C.Rob., 354; Pratt-Lee, p. xxix) the exemption was extended to the Hanse Towns, but in order to avail themselves of the exemption it was incumbent on the claimants to show that the hemp was the growth of the neighbouring district whose produce they were usually employed in exporting in the ordinary course of their trade.

Another case, in which a contraband cargo, the produce of the neutral shipper's native soil, was held not to be in a position to avail itself of the exemption principle was that of the *Charlotte (No. 2)* [1804] (5 C.Rob., 305; Roscoe, I, 490): the cargo of masts and spars (absolute contraband) taken on a Lübeck ship on a voyage from Riga to Nantes, although Russian property and produce, was condemned because, not being on board a Russian ship, it was not within the protection of the Russian treaty.

(iv) *Pre-emption or requisition in lieu of confiscation.* A fourth mitigation of the sanction against the transport of contraband was an intermediary solution where the contraband was neither condemned as good and lawful prize, nor released for further carriage to another, innocent destination, but adjudicated to the captor on condition of payment of its value to the owner.

In cases in which a contraband cargo, for one reason or another, could not lawfully be condemned, *e.g.*, because it had been loaded, or the ship had sailed, before the outbreak of hostilities, the Crown was entitled to acquire the contraband goods by pre-emption or requisition. Instances of this procedure in older prize case law are frequent. See, *e.g.*, the judgments concerning

the *Vrijheid (No. 1)* [1778] (Hay and Marriott, 188; Roscoe, I, 13): a cargo of masts for the French Government, carried by a Dutch ship with destination Rochefort, was to be sold for the use of His British Majesty, all freight, expenses and charges to be paid by him; the ship was free under a treaty of 1 December 1674;

the *Haabet (No. 1)* [1800] (2 C.Rob., 174; Roscoe, I, 212): pre-emption by the British authorities of a cargo of wheat on a Danish ship for a price to be determined in the usual manner by Registrar and Merchants who, however, were instructed by the Court not to include in that price the premium of insurance paid by the non-insured owner;

the *Zacheman* [1804] (5 C.Rob., 152; Roscoe, I, 439): if the cargo on this Swedish ship was to be restored, the British Government had a right of pre-emption; undue delay in the exercise of that right obliged the Government to pay damages in the nature of demurrage.

A special group of instances of pre-emption was constituted by the cases mentioned *sub* (iii) above in which, in accordance with the English practice of older times, contraband goods were exempted from condemnation in prize on the ground that they were the produce of the neutral shipper's own country. See the judgments of 1799 relating to cargoes of pitch and tar on the Swedish vessels

the *Sarah Christina* (1 C.Rob., 237; Roscoe, I, 125): although the contraband cargo of pitch and tar on this Swedish ship was for a hostile (French) port and was therefore in principle liable to condemnation in prize, it might be exempted because it was the produce of the shipper's country, in which case it was subject to pre-emption. However, the exemption from confiscation did not apply in the case of lack of *bona fides* on the part of the shipper, which might be established, *e.g.*, by his ostensibly shipping the goods to a neutral port (*in casu* Cagliari);

the *Maria (No. 1)* (Paulsen, Master) (1 C.Rob., 340; Roscoe, I, 152): a corresponding ruling on exemption in an identical case, complicated by the fact that this Swedish vessel had been searched by the British Navy when sailing under Swedish convoy (see on this aspect of the case *infra*, *sub* B, section 4, pp. 523-526).

This practice of pre-emption was described by Professor C. van Vollenhoven in a discourse of 1915 in the Royal Netherlands Academy of Sciences under a title which sounds peculiar even in Dutch ears: *Naasting, opvordering en beteugeling van koopmansgoederen in den zeeoorlog*, later included in his *Verspreide geschriften*, vol. 2, pp. 290-331 (The Hague, 1934). "Beteugeling" is indeed an expression which only an original thinker and orator as was Van Vollenhoven would invent to indicate this procedure of *de facto* requisition of contraband goods by the capturing belligerent. The word means in effect the "bridling" (of one's passions, of a flood, of price inflation, and so on), in this particular case applied to the appropriation of merchandise. In the said discourse the orator surveyed the cases he had discovered in which the prize courts authorized the captor to appropriate the contraband goods against payment of their value.

(v) *The quantity of contraband goods.* In conformity with what seems to be a universal principle, expressed in Roman law by the formula *de minimis non curat praetor*, small quantities of contraband goods were exempted from confiscation. See, for instance, from the War of the Austrian Succession: the *St. Johannes* [1748] (Pratt-Lee, p. 166, at p. 170):

> "the quantity will make [the herrings] contraband or not",

and the *Daegeraad* [1748] (Pratt-Lee, p. 163): five barrels of herrings were considered rather as ship's provisions than as merchandise;
and from the Revolutionary Wars of France:
the *Wilhelmina Catharina* [1798] (Pratt-Lee, p. 180, at p. 187):

> "a single barrel [of musket shot] would not be contraband, but 4 tons and upwards is".

Pratt himself said at p. xxviii with respect to a load of rough iron:

> "a moderate quantity of an article however noxious ... as, for instance, gunpowder, would be considered as forming part of the ship's stores and intended for its own use, and as such free from condemnation".

Section 4. BLOCKADE AND ITS BREACH

Preface

The available source material on blockade in the past is so copious that it needs some form of systematic arrangement. The result of my reflection on the various possible ways of achieving that end has led me to adopt the following distribution of the material.

This section will be divided into two parts A and B.

Part A will give in sub-section 1 a sketch of the historical origin of blockade as a separate legal institution and its principal elements and resulting controversies (pp. 415-419). Sub-section 2 will contain a summary of the distinction between a war blockade and a pacific blockade (pp. 419-421). Sub-section 3 will follow with a factual survey of the abusive establishment of paper blockades, which was one of the causes of the creation of the Armed Neutrality Leagues of 1780 and 1800 (described in Chapter II, *sub* A, *supra*, pp. 124-128), and its culmination during the first decade of the 19th century in the so-called Continental System (pp. 421-422).

A more elaborate Part B will thereupon present a systematic analysis of the case law on blockade. How I intend to expose that vast subject will appear from my introductory remarks at p. 423 *infra*.

Part A. Legal problems concerning blockades

Sub-section 1. Origin of blockade as a separate legal institution and the main elements of its régime

The blockading of an enemy port or coast by belligerent warships has emerged as a specific practice producing legal effects vis-à-vis neutrals under treaty and international customary law in the beginning of the 17th century. Up till about 1600 belligerents put their claims much higher, *viz.*, by effecting a complete interception of all, even neutral, commerce with their ennemy.

The first occasions on which the establishment of a naval blockade of an enemy port or coast would seem to have been adduced as a specific legal argument to justify the interception of neutral trade in innocent (non-contraband) goods to the enemy, which would otherwise have been unlawful, were two treaties of 1613 and 1614. This has been convincingly demonstrated by the late Leyden professor of international law Dr B. M Telders; in his paper on *De oorsprong der effectieve blokkade*, incorporated in his *Verzamelde Geschriften* (The Hague, 1948), vol. II, p. 165, he indicated as the origin two treaties concluded by Sweden, the first of 1613 with Denmark, the second of 1614 with the Republic of the United Netherlands.

In a publication of much later date (1974), an assistant professor of Utrecht University, Dr Johanna M. Oudendijk, has taken up the matter again in a study under the title 'Blockaded seaports in the history of international law' (*Tijdschrift voor Rechtsgeschiedenis* 1974 (42), pp. 1-22), in which she has retraced the development especially from Netherlands sources.

The abovementioned treaties were the following:

The Swedish-Danish treaty of Knäred of 20 January 1613 (Dumont, V^2, 642; Rymer, Foedera, VII^2, 189), which granted Danish merchants freedom of trade to (Russian) Riga even in time of war, restricted that freedom by a clause by which the King of Denmark ordered that

> "si dehic Urbs Rigensis a Serinitate sua Sueciae obsideri ceperat, durante obsidione, nostri Subditi [*i.e.*, subjects of the King of Denmark] navigatione Rigam prorsus abstineant, et qui contrafecerunt suo id periculo facturi ...".

The Swedish-Netherlands treaty of 5 April 1614 (Dumont, V^2, 245), which in Article 5 prohibited the carriage of contraband to the respective enemies, in Article 6 ruled as follows:

> "Bien entendu toutefois, que par là ne sera point deffendu le Trafic & Commerce libre desdites Provinces Unies, soit pour la Ville de Riga comme pour quelque autre Ville, Pais, & Havres scituez sur la Mer du Nord ou de l'Est qui sont sous l'obéissance des ennemis présens ou futurs de sa Majesté ou de la Couronne de Suède; lequel libre Trafic & Commerce sa Majesté Royale permet auxdits Habitans des Provinces Unies dès maintenant & pour toujours, sans qu'il leur puisse être fait aucun trouble ou empêchement à l'avenir; à moins que sadite Majesté n'eût assiégé [according to a Netherlands text in *Groot Placaat Boek* IV, 275: "tenzij zulke steden te water en te land belegerd en bezet zijn"] la Ville de Riga ou autres Villes scituées sur les Mers du Nord & de l'Est pour les conquérir".

These treaty provisions introduced a new rule of international prize law according to which belligerents would in future only be entitled (apart from the carriage of contraband) to intercept neutral shipping to their enemies if they themselves assumed the burden of closing the enemy ports to foreign shipping by a screen of naval units. This new, mitigated system of cutting neutral trade off from an enemy port or coast has, just as has the interception of contraband of war, a neutrality and a prize law aspect. The former, discussed in Part IX-B (vol. X) of this publication, pp. 33-35, 85-86, concerns the question of whether a neutral Power can be blamed for failing to forbid and prevent ships under its flag from attempting to run a blockade regularly established by a belligerent Power. What is at issue in the present context is, on the other hand, the question of the conditions of validity of a blockade, the essentials of an attempt to violate it, and the sanctions which the blockading Power is entitled to impose upon those attempting it. The history of those aspects of the law of blockade shows a long development of the institution.

The presumably oldest controversy was that relating to the conditions of the siege: was it required, for a blockade to be legally effective vis-à-vis neutrals, that the port was entirely besieged, both by naval units on the seaward side and by armed forces on the landward side? Although there are historical indications that a total siege was initially held necessary, this requirement was later abandoned: penalties against the breach of a blockade were already considered permissible in an early stage when the access to the port was only blockaded by warships. The real purpose of the establishment of a blockade was indeed not so much the conquest of the blockaded town or coastal area, but the interception of all intercourse between it and the outer world by sea. On the other hand, Article I *in fine* of the Treaty of Maritime

Commerce between Louis XIV of France and the States General of the United Netherlands of 18 April 1646 (Dumont, VI[1], 342) would seem to have had especially in view places besieged from the landward side:

> "Ce qui [*i.e.*, confiscation as good and lawful prize] sera aussi sévèrement pratiqué à l'égard de ceux qui auront secouru et jetté des hommes, blez et vivres dans une place attaquée par les armées de Sa Majesté".

It was accepted from the outset that a blockade was violated both by merchant ships attempting to enter and by merchant ships attempting to sail from the port. No difference was made in that respect.

The controversies that arose in later periods concerned the conditions under which the blockade of a port could be deemed to be effective. Prize courts sometimes took that requirement of effectiveness seriously. Thus, in the case of the *De Vier Gebroeders* of 13 November 1759 and 15 July 1760 (Burrell, 159; Roscoe, I, 5) the British Prize Court held that the existence of a blockade must be strictly proved. The Netherlands vessel concerned, with a cargo of brandy and salt sailing to Dunkirk, was therefore released as it did not appear juridically in that case what the state of Dunkirk was, or that His Majesty's fleet lay before it on 2 July 1759, though it was of public knowledge.

Various definitions of effectiveness have in the course of time been put forward.

Another, very thorny controversy arose later as to whether neutral merchant ships were already liable to seizure and confiscation when they had the intention of breaking the blockade, but were still far distant, especially when they were provisionally only sailing on their route to an intermediate non-blockaded port—a special blockade variant of the doctrine of continuous voyage, which had already been applied by England to reserved (colonial) navigation and commerce with the enemy, and which was developed during the American Civil War by the American prize courts concurrently with its application to the carriage of contraband (comp. *supra*, pp. 360 *et seq.*).

These two principal controversies between belligerents and neutrals have played a significant rôle in the history of blockade, which I will set out in greater detail and systematically below in sub-section 1.

At first no specification was given in the treaties of what would constitute the blockade of a port or coast. The simply mentioned a "siege" or "obsidium". A definition of its effectiveness was only introduced when belligerent States showed a growing tendency to attain their purpose by declaring "paper blockades", *i.e.* by proclaiming them simply by decree without a corresponding display of naval force off the port or coast. The definition of effectiveness only became stricter in the course of time.

Article 7 of the Anglo-Netherlands Treaty of Offensive and Defensive

Alliance of Southampton of 17 September 1625 (Dumont, V^2, 478) against Spain still simply entrusted England with the blockade of the rivers of Lisbon and Sanlúcar and the Bay of Cádiz, and the Netherlands with that of the Flemish coast.

Article 7 of the Netherlands-Spanish Treaty of Marine of 17 December 1650 (Dumont, VI^1, 570; Parry, 2, 259) permitted the seizure of ships and cargoes on their way to besieged or blockaded places.

Article 29 of the Franco-Netherlands Treaty of Friendship of 27 April 1662 (Dumont, VI^2, 412; Parry, 7, 139) forbade trade "aux villes et places assiégées, blocquées ou investies".

Article 5 of the Netherlands-Swedish preliminary Agreement concerning contraband of 6/16 July 1667 (Dumont, VII^1, 37; Parry, 10, 187) prohibited the carrying of certain non-contraband goods, such as money, victuals and other provisions,

> "ad munimenta, oppida vel loca praesidio militari instructa, quamdiu ea ipsa per militem foederati alterutrius, respectu locorum in oris maritimis sitorum, tam terra quam mari, obsidione cingi, vel manu armata assideri, continget, animo eadem in postestatem suam redigendi",

a provision repeated in Article 5 of the subsequent Treaty of Commerce of 26 November 1675 (Dumont, VII^1, 316; Parry, 14, 41).

Article 16 of the Franco-Netherlands Treaty of Commerce of Nijmegen of 10 August 1678 (Dumont, VII^1, 357; Parry, 14, 399) again simply prohibited the carriage of "free" goods to blockaded places ("obsidione cincta").

The Anglo-French Treaty of Commerce and Navigation of Utrecht of 11 April 1713 (Dumont, VIII^1, 345; Parry, 28, 1) in Article 20 still described them as "places assiégées, blocquées, et investies".

Detailed definitions of blockaded ports only appeared in later treaties. See in particular Article III, *sub* 3 of the Armed Neutrality Conventions of December 1800 (Russia-Sweden, Martens, R^2, VII, 172; Russia-Denmark, *ibid.*, 181; Russia-Prussia, *ibid.*, 188; Parry, 55, 411, 425 and 427), which defined the requirements of an effective blockade as follows:

> "Que pour déterminer ce qui caractérise un port blocqué, on n'accorde cette dénomination qu'à celui, où il y a, par la disposition de la puissance qui l'attaque avec les vaisseaux arrêtés et suffisamment proches, un danger évident d'entrer",

and added:

> "que tout bâtiment naviguant vers un port blocqué ne pourra être regardé d'avoir contrevenu à la présente convention, que lorsqu'après avoir été averti par le commandant du blocus de l'état du port, il tâchera d'y pénétrer en employant la force ou la ruse".

One has to bear in mind that these strict definitions constituted a reaction to the preceding abuses practised by the belligerent Powers by means of mutual reprisals during the wars of revolutionary France in the 1790's. The political upheaval of Europe caused by these Napoleonic wars and the establishment of the "blocus continental" (Continental System) were, of course, not conducive to a general agreement on the conditions of validity of a naval blockade and on the circumstances in which neutral shipping could be legally penalized for running it.

Belligerents had sometimes expressly warned neutral shipping against attempts to run a blockade. See the Russian Manifesto of 1 May 1772 (Martens, R^2, II, 33-35) relative to the blockade of Turkish ports in the Levant by Russia.

Sub-section 2. War blockade as opposed to pacific blockade

When discussing the law and practice of blockade one has to bear two things in mind: (*a*) that there have been many blockades in peacetime—or even in wartime—which did not constitute direct warlike operations and that it is often difficult to make a sharp distinction between the two; and (*b*) that there have often occurred naval operations, also called "blockades", which were not, however, true blockades in the technical sense. Pacific blockades as meant under (*a*) have been dealt with in some detail in Part VIII of this publication, Chapter III (Measures short of war), section 3, pp. 43 *et seq.* On a perusal of the long lists of blockades which can be found in the *British and Foreign State Papers* one can conclude that a large number of them were no real war blockades. The lists contain blockades instituted (the references to the *B.F.S.P.* which follow are simplified):

by Latin American States (such as Argentina, Bolivia, Brazil and Chile) against ports or coastal stretches of other Latin American States (Bahía in 1823 (10-947); the Banda Oriental of Uruguay in 1825 (13-783, 821, 824, 832, 1029); Pará in 1835 (24-540, 541); Valparaiso in 1838 (26-1054); San Juan de Nicaragua in 1842 (34-1264); Uruguayan and Paraguayan coastal areas in 1864-65 (54-544; 55-295); Cumaná Maturín in 1871 and the mouth of the Orinoco in 1874, 1880; Antofagasta in 1879, Yquique in 1879; Cartagena in 1837, 1885; and mutually by Haiti and the Dominican Republic in 1879, 1883, 1884, 1886, 1888;

by certain Great Powers against Latin American ports and coasts: Mexican ports in 1838; Buenos Aires and Uruguay in 1838, 1845; Tampico and Mazatlán in 1862; Valparaiso and Caldera in 1865 (lifted in the same year) (56-646 *et seq.*); Venezuela in 1871, 1902;

by colonizing European Powers against coastal areas of Africa: Portendick in 1835, 1853, 1887; Mogador in 1844; the west coast in 1849, 1853; Benin in 1852; Porto Novo in 1863; the Gold Coast in 1872; Dahomay in 1876, 1892; the Slave Coast in 1890; Moçambique in 1888; continental Zanzibar in 1888; Madagascar in 1884;

by France in East Asia against Canton in 1839-1840 (29-1069; 34-1260), 1857; Formosa in 1884, and Siam in 1887, 1893;

by Great Powers against Greece: Don Pacifico conflict in 1850; repeated disputes over her definitive territorial extent in Epirus in 1897 and the islands; Crete in 1897 and Montenegro (Dulcigno) in 1880;

and more isolated cases, such as certain action by France and England, more in the nature of an embargo, against the Netherlands during the Belgian insurrection (November 1832, Martens, N.R., XIII, 53, 54); against Norway by Great Britain in 1814 (*B.F.S.P.*, vol. I, Part 2, 1277); against Cádiz, Barcelona, etc. by France in 1823; against Algiers by a British squadron in 1824 (*B.F.S.P.*, vol. 11, p. 185) and by France in 1828 (*ibid.*, vol. 16, p. 1253); against Tangier by a British naval force in 1828-29 (*ibid.*, vol. 15, p. 1091); against Venice and Ancona by Austria in 1848-49 (*ibid.*, vol. 36, p. 935; vol. 37, pp. 282, 283, 286); against the German Baltic ports by Denmark in 1848, 1851, 1874; of the north coast of Spain during the second Carlist War in 1874.

Doubtless war blockades were, apart from the (spurious) "blockades" in the first decade of the 19th century of West-European coasts by Great Britain and of the British Isles by Napoleon in 1806 *et seq.* 1812, 1814 (comp. on this series *infra*, pp. 421-422) and that instituted against Texas by the United States in 1842 (sometimes considered as an illegal or invalid operation), those of

Russian ports in the Baltic and the Black Sea and the mouths of the Danube in 1854, 1856. The declarations of blockade of the Russian ports and coasts can be found in 44 *B.F.S.P.*, pp. 894 *et seq.*: those of the Danube and the Black Sea of 13 June 1854 (894); of the Baltic of 16 June and 11 August 1854 (894 and 896); of the Finnish Gulf of 12 July 1854 (895) and of the White Sea ports of 28 September 1854 (899);

Venice by France in 1859;

Tampico and Mazatlán by the United States in 1864;

the ports of Chile by Spain in 1865 (55 *B.F.S.P.*, p. 296);

Prussian ports by France, and French sea coasts (Rouen, Dieppe) by Prussia in 1870;

the Russian Black Sea ports by Turkey in 1878;

Arica, Callao and Ilo by Chile in 1880;

Cuba and Puerto Rico by the United States in 1898;

East-Asian possessions of Russia by Japan in 1904.

A special type of war blockade was that instituted in 1873 by the Netherlands against the Sultanate of Atjeh (Acheen) on the northern part of the island of Sumatra, because the country concerned had no international personality. Nevertheless, this operation was treated by the Netherlands as an international war blockade. I will return to this case *infra*, p. 451.

The latter groups of war blockades have given rise to prize proceedings.

Blockades which have given rise to captures and prize proceedings reported by Roscoe in vol. I of his *Reports* were established in Europe against the following ports and coasts:

Le Havre (pp. 58, 86, 195, 279, 355);

the Seine (p. 528);

Dunkirk and Ostend (pp. 524, 552);

Amsterdam (pp. 54, 84, 89, 147, 207, 292, 310, 317);

Texel and the Strait of the Vlie (pp. 94, 198);
other Dutch ports, such as Rotterdam (pp. 208, 238, 348);
the Elbe and the Weser (pp. 427, 546, 587);
Spanish ports, such as Cádiz (p. 533) and Alicante (p. 580);
Russian ports and coasts on the Baltic, the Danube and the Black Sea (vol. II, pp. 346, 432, 444 and 560)
and outside Europe against Guadeloupe (p. 63) and Montevideo (vol. I, p. 573).

Examples of coercive measures as meant under (b), which are sometimes also given the appelation of "blockade" but which can perhaps more adequately be called a boycott, are those taken at a much later stage by the United States and other American States against Cuba and the sanctions enacted by the United Nations against South Africa and Rhodesia.

It goes without saying that neither, and indeed still less, can the closure of a national port by the territorial sovereign be qualified as a blockade. Comp. on this operation Part VI of this publication, p. 668 *sub* (V). Lists of historical blockades must therefore always be looked at with a critical eye.

After what I have already said about this whole subject in Part VIII of this publication, I will not elaborate further upon it.

Sub-section 3. Paper blockades as opposed to effective blockades

Neglect of the requirement of effectiveness of a blockade has increasingly led to the establishment of "paper blockades" (*blocus sur le papier*), also called "blocus de cabinet" or "blocus per notificationem". De Pistoye and Duverdy (*Traité des prises maritimes*, vol. I, p. 366) laid the first attempt to establish such a paper blockade on the doorstep of England and the Republic of the United Netherlands which by a Convention of 12 August 1689 (Dumont, VII^2, 238; Parry, 18, 479) declared all the coasts, roadsteads and ports under the sovereignty of the Roi Très-Chrétien to be in a state of blockade, although they had not sent any fleets to establish an effective blockade. A similar proclamation was issued by England at the beginning of the Seven Years' War (1756). This practice reached a climax in the first decade of the 19th century in the so-called "Continental System" by the mutual action of France and England in enacting orders of reprisals against one another. The direct connection between paper blockades and the issuance of mutual reprisals has induced me to deal with this subject in part in the present sub-section, in part in section 3 under C (Law to be applied by the prize courts), *infra*, pp. 602 *et seq*., to which I refer here.

However, even during the lawless period of the Napoleonic Wars and the Continental System, there have been examples of blockades in the traditional sense. Instances thereof are the blockades of the mouths of the Elbe (28 June 1803; *B.F.S.P.* 1815-16, p. 373), the Weser (26 July 1803) and the harbours of France on the English Channel (*Nouvelles politiques de la Haye* 1893, nos. 64 and 67; 1804, no. 69) and the North Sea (9 August 1804) by Great

Britain, and her subsequent blockade of the entrances to the rivers Ems, Weser, Elbe and Trave, declared on 8 April 1806. The notification of the latter measure to neutral Powers is given in a French text in Martens, N.R., I, 436:

> "Il a plu à Sa Majesté de faire savoir aux ministres des puissances neutres résidans à cette cour par le secrétaire d'Etat des affaires Mr. Fox que par ordre de Sa Majesté les mesures nécessaires ont été prises pour blocquer l'embouchure des rivières de l'Ems, du Weser, de l'Elbe et de la Trave, et que dès à présent toutes les mesures autorisées par le droit des gens et par les loix subsistant entre Sa Majesté et les Etats neutres seront prises et exécutées à l'égard des vaisseaux qui tenteraient d'enfreindre le dit blocus."

A similar regular blockade was subsequently, on 26 July 1806, declared by France against Venice (von Halem-Runde, *Sammlung der wichtigsten Aktenstücke zur neuesten Zeitgeschichte*, Oldeburg, 1807, vol. II, 58).

Venice was later, in 1848, again blockaded, together with Trieste, by Austria (Martens, N.R.G.[1], XII, 495-508).

Less regular, or totally irregular were the blockades of all the French-occupied ports in the Adriatic by Russia on 15 March 1806 (Martens, N.R., I, 433) and the closure of the ports of the Adriatic to Russians and Englishmen by Austria on 30 May 1806 (*ibid.*, 434), the closure of the ports and river mouths on the North Sea to the English by Prussia on 26 March 1806 (*ibid.*, 435) and the retaliatory British embargo of 8 April 1806 on Prussian ships which might enter British ports (*ibid.*, 436), and the closure of all harbours between Brest and the Elbe on 16 May 1806 by Great Britain (*ibid.*, 436), lifted on 25 September 1806 (*ibid.*, 439).

The institution of a blockade, however, rapidly degenerated into a mere international abuse when the belligerent Powers, relapsing into practices of earlier centuries, proceeded to declare vast coastal areas blockaded for the purpose of intercepting all overseas trade to their enemy by neutral vessels without to any extent fulfilling the requirement of the effectiveness of their prohibitive measures. These "paper blockades" finally resulted in the establishment of the so-called "Continental System", brought into being by the French Decree of Berlin of 21 November 1806 (*ibid.*, 439), blockading the whole of the British Isles, and the counter-blockade by England of the coasts of France and her Allies on 11/25 November 1807 (*ibid.*, 446, 449), answered by France on 17 December 1807 by the Decree of Milan (*ibid.*, 452).

The whole series of Ordinances and Decrees which led to the establishment of this "Continental System" in 1806-1807, and still elaborated on it in the following years, can be found in Martens, N.R., I, 433-549 under the letters *a-z* and *aa-ww*.

On the disputed validity of these reciprocal measures comp. further section 3, under C, where I will also give the main relevant texts (*infra*, p. 602).

Part B. The case law concerning blockade

Introductory remarks

Naval blockade is one of the methods of warfare which in past centuries has given rise to the largest numbers of prize court decisions, especially regarding cases occurring during the Napoleonic, Crimean and American Civil Wars. They range over a vast field of legal questions, relating to the establishment of a blockade and its notification; the conditions of its validity; the various forms in which a blockade can be violated; the intention of a ship owner or master to break it and their knowledge of its existence as a precondition of sanctions against them; the extent of such sanctions; the suspension or lifting of a blockade; the indebtedness of damages in case of unjustified seizure for an asserted breach of a blockade; the marginal question which of the units forming the blockading squadron are entitled to share in prize money, etc. All those prize court decisions will be surveyed below. A number of them were collected by the British Government in its Memorandum for the Naval Conference of London of 1908/1909 (see J. B. Scott, *The declaration of London, February 26, 1909*; New York 1919, pp. 54-55).

I will group them, in principle, according to the main features of the legal development of the regime of blockade in the successive periods, in four paragraphs: the first comprising the judgments rendered from early days after a short transition period up to the middle of the 19th century (§ 1, p. 424), the second the years of the Crimean War (§ 2, p. 444), the third the period of the American Civil War (§ 3, p. 448), the fourth the last decades of the 19th and the first years of the 20th century preceding the codification of 1907-1909 (§ 4, p. 451).

The first period, during which an incessant stream of judicial pronouncements has shaped the international law of classical blockade, had its centre of gravity in the 1790's and early 1800's (the Revolutionary Wars of France), but it also produced a modest prologue during the Seven Years' War and the American War of Independence and an epilogue in the events of the Anglo-American War of 1812, and an upsurge of blockades mainly as a result of the action of the Holy Alliance against the rebellious colonies of Spain.

In order to create some order in the quotation of relevant instances from the somewhat chaotic spate of early cases, I will further arrange my exposé of the consolidation of the rules of blockade in that long first period regionally—the English cases in § 1, *sub* (*a*), the French in § 1, *sub* (*b*)—and sub-arrange especially the British cases systematically pursuant to the various legal elements which together constitute the régime of classical blockade.

I would very much like to add a number of old Netherlands cases in § 1, *sub* (*c*), but, although the Republic of the United Netherlands has played an important rôle in the history of blockade, I am unable to cite any judgment from the Admiralty Archives, partly owing to the disastrous result of a fire in the Ministry of the Navy in the middle of the 19th century.

The formulation of the rules of customary law which had developed in the course of time, undertaken by the *Institut de droit international* in its *Règlement* of Turin of 1882, will be inserted in § 4, p. 455, *infra*.

§ *1. From early days up to the middle of the 19th century*

As said above I will begin with a bird's-eye view of the old British case law. This will be followed at p. 442 *et seq.* by a corresponding, but much shorter survey of old French legislation and jurisprudence.

These separate surveys are entirely in place in this field because the English system differs in many respects from the continental system and therefore calls for an arrangement of the available material according to its own specific features, especially in respect of the so-called blockades de facto, the essence of a breach of blockade (intention to break it *versus* actual violation *in loco*), the application of the doctrine of continuous voyage to the law of blockade, the extent of the sanction on running a blockade (the so-called *droit de suite*), etc.

The law of blockade has obtained its customary contents in the main during the formative phase of the pre-codification period, but it has suffered a serious drawback during the short period of the paper blockades described under A, *supra*, pp. 421-422 *et seq.*

After Napoleon's fall and the restoration of Europe at the Congress of Vienna of 1814-1815 the legal situation returned to normal, also as regards naval blockades. A few blockades were in fact still declared in the traditional pattern in the course of the following four decades, but those blockades were often of a doubtful legal character, more pacific than war blockades. Thus, the nature of the Franco-Mexican hostilities of 1838-1839, which included a blockade of a number of Mexican ports, was only afterwards characterized as a war blockade by the arbitral award of Queen Victoria of 1 August 1844 (*Pas. Int.*, 21; *R.A.I.*, I, 558).

On the other hand, the so-called Pacific blockade of the 1820's, carried out by the forces of the Holy Alliance, was not at all pacific, but a pure war blockade, intended to suppress the revolt of the Spanish colonies in America against their legitimate ruler Spain according to the then prevailing political principles.

Two other blockades in the Pacific which might give rise to mistaken ideas about their legal character were those carried out by Spain against Chilean ports in 1865 (*B.F.S.P.*, 56, 720), respectively Chile against Arica (Perú) in 1880 (*B.F.S.P.*, 71, 128).

(a) Old British precedents

The vast English case material available compels me to present it in some systematic order, according to the special elements which dominate the cases concerned.

—Extent of the obligatoriness of the European law of blockade

I only came across one decision which dealt with the general problem of the binding character of the customary law of blockade as developed by European nations upon ship and cargo owners resident outside Europe, *viz.*, the case of the *Hurtige Hane (No. 2)* [1801] (3 C.Rob., 324; Roscoe, I, 317), which arose on the blockade of Amsterdam, respecting a cargo shipped in Barbary (Morocco) for that city with false destination to Hamburg:

> "It has been argued that it would be extremely hard on persons residing in the Kingdom of Morocco if they should be held bound by all the rules of the law of nations as it is practised amongst European States. On many accounts undoubtedly they are not to be strictly considered on the same footing as European merchants; they may on some points of the law of nations be entitled to a very relaxed application of the principles established, by long usage, between the States of Europe, holding an intimate and constant intercourse with each other. It is a law made up of a good deal of complex reasoning, though derived from very simple rules, and altogether composing a pretty artificial system, which is not familiar either to their knowledge or their observance. Upon such considerations the Court has, on some occasions, laid it down that the European law of nations is not to be applied in its full rigor to the transactions of persons of the description of the present claimants, and residing in that part of the world. But on a point like this, the breach of a blockade, one of the most universal and simple operations of war in all ages and countries excepting such as were merely savage, no such indulgence can be shown. It must not be understood by them that, if an European army or fleet is blockading a town or port, they are at liberty to trade with that port. If that could be maintained it would render the operation of a blockade perfectly nugatory ... It is not a new operation of war—it is almost as old and as general as war itself ...".

—Establishment of a blockade and its notification

The first mention was by whom a blockade could be established. In the *Rolla* case (Coffin, Master) [1807] (6 C.Rob., 364; Roscoe, I, 573) the Court decided that a blockade must in principle be established by a naval officer acting under the orders of his government; that in the absence of such express instructions, the orders must be presumed to have been given by any naval officer in command of a force stationed at the time in such a way that he could not receive those instructions, and that if a blockade was established by a naval officer without express instructions, his initiative needed approval and adoption by his government, with retroactive effect to the date of the establishment of the blockade.

The *Rolla* judgment refers (at p. 579 of Roscoe, vol. I) to an earlier case concerning the capture of the American merchant ship *Hare* for running the blockade of Cádiz when leaving that port with a return cargo loaded there. The blockade was later declared invalid, as being defective, but Sir W. Grant decreed it susceptible of *post factum* ratification by the government.

Next came the requirement of the notification of its establishment to international shipping, either through the diplomatic channels, or by direct special warning.

In the *Neptunus (No. 2)* (Hempel, Master) [1799] (2 C.Rob., 110; Roscoe, I, 195) the Prize Court laid down that the commander of the blockading force must take all possible measures to inform the authorities of the blockaded ports and the foreign consuls there of the blockade, and that in the case of his acting on governmental instructions, or in the case of approval and adoption of his initiative by his government, the latter must notify that fact to the neutral Powers by the ordinary diplomatic channel and must also inform its own subjects. It was the duty of a foreign government, to which a blockade had been notified, to communicate such notice to its subjects.

In this context the judgments often talk of a blockade *de facto*. Such blockades had to be brought to the knowledge of approaching neutral vessels by a special warning, which needed certification by a notice in the vessel's log-book. See the *Mercurius* [1798] (1 C.Rob., 80; Roscoe, I, 54) and the *Vrouw Judith* [1799] (1 C.Rob., 150; Roscoe, I, 86).

In the *Mercurius* case a warning on the spot was held to be a sufficient notice of a blockade *de facto*. In the *Vrouw Judith* the Court said that the continued existence *de facto* of a blockade was a sufficient notice to all vessels within the blockaded port.

When a blockade was accompanied by a notification thereof to neutrals, it was to be presumed to be in force till the notification was revoked: *Neptunus (No. 1)* (Kuyp, Master) [1799] (1 C.Rob., 170; Roscoe, I, 94).

In other cases a neutral vessel was entitled to a special warning by a blockading warship, and no proof of such warning was to be accepted unless it had been entered in the logbook:

In the *Vro(u)w Johanna (No. 1)* (Okhen, Master) [1799] (2 C.Rob., 109; Roscoe, I, 194) Sir W. Scott decided that until notice of a blockade was revoked, it must be presumed still to be in existence; he held it to be the duty of a country notifying a blockade to notify also the revocation.

On the question whether the establishment of a blockade had to be repeated after the blockading force had temporarily been routed by a superior enemy force but had returned later: see the case of the *Triheten* [1805] (6 C.Rob., 65; Roscoe, I, 534, footnote), *infra*, p. 440.

—No encroachment upon neutral rights

A naval blockade can encroach upon the rights of neutral States in various ways.

It is clear that a belligerent State is prohibited from operating with a naval force against the enemy from neutral waters. Such an action would be a direct infringement of the rights of the neutral State concerned.

Nor would it be permissible for a belligerent State to station a blockading squadron in international waters off a neutral coast for the purpose of cutting off communications between foreign shipping and a neighbouring enemy State.

What is more doubtful is the establishment of a blockading force in an open sea area which gives access to the harbours and coast of both the enemy State and neutral countries, such as happened in the past at the entrance of the Adriatic. An Italian judicial body (*Contenziosa diplomatica*, 1878) gave an opinion against the legality of a blockade of straits which give access to a sea that washes neutral States. See the cases of the *Britannia* and the *Matilde Bellagamba*, cited in the *Proceedings of the International Naval Conference 1908-1909* (Parliamentiary Papers, Miscellaneous No. 5 (1919), Cd. 4555, p. 43). Such a blockade would certainly be unlawful if the intention were to stop traffic also to the neutral countries. But even if such traffic were let through, it would be dubious whether the belligerent's action is legally admissible.

The most famous instances of prize court judgments dealing with this contingency are the two judgments of Sir William Scott of 1800-1801 concerning the capture of two Dutch vessels, both called the *Twee Gebroeders*, made on the Wadden Zee (Shallows) north of the Netherlands province of Groningen by the crews of boats sent from a British warship anchored in the river Easter-Ems. Those Dutch vessels were on their way from East-Frisian waters across the shallows and the Zuiderzee to the city of Amsterdam, which had been declared by the British to be under blockade. Aside from the questions where exactly the captures had taken place and under whose territorial scope the actual places of capture came, the issue was whether the blockade of the port of Amsterdam by a British naval force operating from neutral East-Frisian waters was lawful.

This blockade of Amsterdam from the north-east of about 1800, when the Zuiderzee still existed, caused particular legal difficulties. See Sir William Scott in the *Twee Gebroeders (No. 2)* (Northolt, Master) [1801] (3 C.Rob., 336; Roscoe, I, 323):

> "On the blockade of Amsterdam, this Court has been inclined to hold, generally, that all sea passages to Amsterdam by that great body of water, the Zuyder Zee, were blockaded, supposing these sea passages to be in the possession of the enemy. Such as were in the possession of a neutral, it was of opinion, were not included unless the blockading force could be applied at the interior extremity of their communication. Whether the present capture in question was made in a sea passage to the Zuyder Zee, belonging to the enemy or to a neutral power, will be decided by the considerations which are to be examined in the further pursuit of this question."

Since I have already analysed these two cases from that point of view in General Issues, section 3 on where the right of prize may be exercised (*supra*, pp. 185-188), I confine myself here to briefly dealing with their blockade aspect.

—The requirement of effectiveness

This requirement was already recognized and applied by prize courts in early days. One of the oldest decisions I found and in which the Court drew the practical conclusion from a disregard of that requirement or from the lack of sufficient evidence dates from the Seven Years' War, see the case of the *Vier Gebroeders* [1759-1760] (Burrell, 159; Roscoe, I, 5), quoted in subsection 1, *supra*, p. 417: the Dutch ship was released as it was not strictly proved that Dunkirk was effectively blockaded at the date of her seizure.

Subsequent judgments re-affirmed in various wordings the requirement of effectiveness. Some said that a declaration of a blockade by a commander without an actual investment would not constitute a legal blockade: *Betsey (No. 1)* [1798] (1 C.Rob., 93; Roscoe, I, 63). Others said that

> "a blockade must be maintained by a force sufficient to make entrance into, or egress from, the port hazardous",

or argued as follows:

> "When a port is notified as blockaded, such force should be employed as will prevent vessels from entering or leaving that port. When a neutral vessel left a port which was insufficiently blockaded, and was subsequently captured, she must be restored. Under particular circumstances a single ship may be adequate to maintain the blockade of a port and co-operate with other vessels at the same time in the blockade of another neighbouring port."

See also the case of the *Nancy (Nos. 1 and 2)* [1809] (1 Acton, 57 and 63; Roscoe, II, 106 and 108).

In a later case Dr Lushington held that

> "if a blockade was effective, the Court must not appreciate the number and the disposition of the ships of the blockading force",

and that

> "even a single warship might maintain it."

This case law excluded the legality of "paper blockades".

When Sweden, at war with Russia, had blockaded the Livonian ports of Russia by a proclamation of 28 April 1711 "de claudendis atque obsidendis omnibus illis Portubus Maris Baltici, quos Czarus Moscoviae durante hoc bello occupatos adhuc detinet", G. de Lamberty (*Mémoires pour servir à l'histoire du 18e siècle, etc.*, Amsterdam, nouv. éd. 1735-1740), VI, 467, England and Holland protested, alleging that there was no actual blockade, but presumably without providing sufficient reason. The King of Sweden gave a satisfactory definition of what he considered to be a force strong enough to maintain the blockade.

See on these disputes Chr. Robinson's *Collectanea Maritima* of 1801, footnote at pp. 162-165.

As Deák and Jessup relate in their *Neutrality Laws*, vol. I, p. 190, the blockade of Mexican ports by the then President of Texas, notified on 21 September 1842, was declared by the United States Government null and void, and therefore of no effect, on the ground that no blockading force had appeared.

—Knowledge of the blockade

A number of prize court decisions have applied the rule that no vessel could be held culpable of violating a blockade unless she was aware of its existence. Knowledge of the existence of a blockade could be real or presumed: *Betsey (No. 1)* [1798] (1 C.Rob., 93; Roscoe, I, 63).

In the *Henrick and Maria* [1799] (1 C.Rob., 146; Roscoe, I, 84) the Prize Court stressed the rules that, in order to create a presumption of knowledge of the blockade, the notification was to specify the limits of the blockaded part of the coast and the moment at which the blockade commenced, and that neither the declaration of a blockade, nor its notification to a neutral Power, nor a special warning given to a ship by a blockading warship may mention an extension of the blockade beyond its effective range.

A master was deemed to have had real knowledge if it was proven that he had heard of the blockade in whatever way.

His knowledge was presumed if (i) the blockade had been notified to the competent authorities of the State of the port which the vessel had last left and those authorities had had sufficient time to publish the information in that port prior to the vessel's sailing, see the *Neptunus (No. 2)* [1799] (2 C.Rob., 110; Roscoe, I, 195), the *Adelaide* [1801] (3 C.Rob., 281; Roscoe, I, 306 and 195, footnote) and the *Jonge Petronella* [1799] (2 C.Rob., 131; Roscoe, I, 208); (ii) the blockade, whether notified or not, had been manifestly known in the port last left by the ship—(*ibid.*); (iii) the master refused to obey the summons of a blockading warship.

In the absence of real or presumed knowledge the ship was entitled to special warning by a blockading warship and no proof of that warning was to be accepted unless it had been entered in the logbook—the *Neptunus* (*supra*).

In the *Calypso* [1799] (2 C.Rob., 298; Roscoe, I, 238) the Court held that the notification of the British blockade of the United Provinces must have been known at Rotterdam on 15 April 1799, as the evidence in another case proved that it was known to the Prussian consul at Amsterdam on the 12th.

See also the *Columbia* [1799] (1 C.Rob., 154; Roscoe, I, 89).

—Actions constituting the breach of a blockade

A blockade can be violated by egress as well as by ingress of a blockaded port: the *Vrouw Judith* (Volkerts, Master) [1799] (1 C.Rob., 150; Roscoe, I, 86).

Entering a blockaded port, even in ballast, is illegal: the American *Comet* (Mix, Master) [1808] (Edw., 32; Roscoe, II, 10).

A breach of blockade can only be justified by an absolute and unavoidable necessity compelling a vessel to enter a blockaded port: the *Hurtige Hane (No. 1)* (Dahl, Master) [1799] (2 C.Rob., 124; Roscoe, I, 205).

An overruling compulsion to enter a blockaded port is the only legal excuse. Mere want of provisions is rarely an excuse for so doing: the *Fortuna (No. 2)* (Rhode, Master) [1803] (5 C.Rob., 27; Roscoe, I, 417).

A ship was held guilty of violation of the blockade if—without being compelled thereto by heavy weather or other force majeure—after having been informed of the blockade, (i) she left, or attempted to leave, a blockaded port after the expiry of the term that might have been granted her to sail out; (ii) she entered, or tried to enter, such a port; (iii) she drew near a blockaded port to make inquiries about the continuation of the blockade: the *Spes* (Cornelis, Master) and the *Irene* (Lubben, Master) [1804-1807] (5 C.Rob., 76; Roscoe, I, 427).

In another case, of the *Drie Vrienden* (Cassens, Master) [1813] (1 Dods., 269; Roscoe, II, 91, footnote *a*), the prize was restored, apparently on the ground that the master was justified in leaving the blockaded port to escape confiscation, but the grounds of the judgment are not reported, nor are the facts of the case set out fully in the report.

According to the *Apollo (No. 2)* (Karsdadt, Master) [1804] (5 C.Rob., 286; Roscoe, I, 481) it was the duty of a master to leave the locality of a blockaded port (Dieppe) after he had received notice of the blockade of which he was ignorant and after this warning had been noted in his papers.

In the *Charlotte Christine* (Petersen, Master) [1805] (6 C.Rob., 101) it was held that a ship is guilty of running a blockade if she is hovering in the neighbourhood of a blockaded port in a position fit for availing herself of the first opportunity to enter, to land cargo, or to transship it into lighters or other craft that might succeed in violating the blockade.

In the *Maria (No. 4)* (Monses, Master) case [1805] (6 C.Rob., 201; Roscoe, I, 546) the situation was as follows: during the blockade of the Weser goods were brought in lighters from the Free City of Bremen on that river and transhipped outside the river into a vessel which later went out in ballast. This procedure was held illegal irrespective of whether the exportation took place in lighters or otherwise.

A vessel is not justified in approaching close to a blockaded port to obtain a pilot for a non-blockaded port or channel, and shall in consequence be condemned: the *Arthur* (Rathburn, Master), an American ship captured in the river Ems [1810] (Edw., 202; Roscoe, II, 37).

A neutral (Danish) ship the *Wasser Hundt* (Lorentzen, Master) [1810] (Dods., I, 271, note; Roscoe, II, 91), captured on her way from one enemy port to another with a cargo which she had loaded at one port, but reshipped for the other under alleged apprehension of seizure by the enemy (France), was condemned for breach of blockade, even though there had been immediate and pressing danger of a capture by the enemy, in consequence of which she left the port. The case involved was an instance of trading between ports of the enemy from which British vessels were excluded (comp. on this ground of confiscation (reserved trade) below, pp. 470-477).

A ship was held not to be guilty of violating a blockade in the following circumstances.

Her departure from a blockaded port, laden with a cargo that had been *bona fide* shipped before the commencement of the blockade, was permitted:

the *Vrouw Judith* (Volkerts, Master) [1799] (1 C.Rob., 150; Roscoe, I, 86).

When a ship owner was not in a position, at the moment of his ship's sailing, to know if a blockade previously notified still existed, he was justified in sending her to the proximity of the blockaded port in order to enquire whether the blockade still existed: *Betsey (No. 2)* (Goodhue, Master) [1799] (1 C.Rob., 332; Roscoe, I, 147).

There was no question of running a blockade when (i) the vessel had taken in cargo conveyed to her in lighters which had themselves loaded it in a non-blockaded port after its transport from a blockaded port or coast to such free port over land or on inland waters, or (ii) she transported a cargo finally destined for a blockaded port provided that such cargo was to be discharged in a non-blockaded port—the *Ocean* (Parker, Master) [1804-1807] (3 C.Rob., 297; Roscoe, I, 310) and the *Stert* (Johnson, Master) [1801] (4 C.Rob., 65; Roscoe, I, 348).

The *Mercurius* (Harmens, Master) [1808] (Edw., 53; Roscoe, II, 15) was the case of a vessel instructed at the time of loading to call at a British port in order to enable her to obtain a licence to trade with a blockaded port and captured before reaching that British port. She was restored to her owner because the voyage was not considered to be "continuous".

A vessel which went into a blockaded port under the necessity for repairs and came out again without discharging her cargo, was held not to be liable to condemnation: the American *Charlotta* (Elliot, Master) [1810] (Edw., 252; Roscoe, II, 52).

The *Imina* (Bauman Vroom, Master) [1800] (3 C.Rob., 167; Roscoe, I, 289) was a mixed case of contraband and blockade: a ship with a contraband cargo, sailing from Danzig to Amsterdam, was apprised during her voyage of the blockade of the latter port and therefore altered that voyage to the neutral port of Emden. The capture of ship and cargo on this altered voyage was held unjustified:

> "to say that the cargo is nevertheless exposed to condemnation on account of her original destination as it stood in the mind of the owners, would be carrying the penalty of contraband further than it had been carried by this or the Supreme Court."

Ships were sometimes authorized by a licence to enter a blockaded port. Then, of course, they were not liable to confiscation for the breach of blockade, provided that they kept strictly within the terms and conditions of the licence; neglect or infringement of its terms or conditions divested them of its protective force.

A licence granted to a neutral ship to enter a blockaded port gave an implied permission to take a cargo from such port: the *Juno (No. 1)* (Beard, Master) [1799] (2 C.Rob., 116; Roscoe, I, 198).

A neutral holding a licence to trade with a blockaded port from the Government of Great Britain might substitute one neutral ship for another, but if he substituted an enemy ship for a neutral ship, he was not protected by the licence, and the ship would be liable to condemnation: the Prussian ship *Dankbaarheit* (Forbeck, Master) [1812] (1 Dods., 183; Roscoe, II, 146).

The same destructive effect was attached to the abuse or transgression of the terms or conditions of an indulgence granted by an Order in Council to sail to a blockaded port. Such a case was that of the *Christiansberg* (Vanderweyde, Master) [1807] (6 C.Rob., 376; Roscoe, I, 580): an Order in Council of 7 January 1807 directed by indulgence that ships could leave the blockaded port of Rotterdam in order to carry cargo to some neutral port. Although ostensibly destined to Smyrna, the *Christiansberg* went instead to the enemy port of Alicante, assertedly in distress. There the cargo was disposed of and new cargo taken on board. While sailing on a new destination to Copenhagen the ship was captured. Both she and her new cargo were condemned on the ground that (*a*) the excuse set up for running into Alicante was false and the benefit of the indulgence under the Order in Council could not be invoked, and (*b*) that a ship that had thus infringed the permission to sail out was still on her next voyage liable to condemnation for breach of a blockade (on this subject comp. *infra*, p. 438).

When during the Crimean War the master (Harzaliako) of the *Panaja Drapaniotisa* [1856], sailing in ballast from the port of blockaded Odessa under Greek colours in May 1855, sent a man to the British man-of-war *Niger* to inquire whether he might pass out to the Danube, he got permission to do so, provided that his ship was unladen and that she came alongside the *Niger* first in order to have her papers examined. Their inspection, however, only led to her capture in prize and her dispatch to Malta (Spinks, 336; Roscoe, II, 560).

—Intention to run a blockade. *Droit de prévention.* Doctrine of continuous voyage. Proof of intended destination

A number of British and American judgments posed or confirmed the principle that the mere intention of a merchant vessel to run a blockade was sufficient to render her liable to capture and condemnation as good and lawful prize, when she was met at sea. Those judgments recognized the belligerent's right to prevent in this way the carrying out of that intention. In the *Adula* case [1900] (176 U.S. 361) this principle was recognized as follows:

> "By established British and American usage, a blockade runner is liable to capture at any time after leaving its home port with the intention of running an existing and publicly proclaimed blockade. The same rule applies to the carriage of contraband to a belligerent."

In another judgment the rule was formulated a little more elaborately as follows:

> "When the intention existed to run a blockade should an occasion present itself, the fact of the ship's sailing towards a blockaded port was a manifest act sufficient to put the ship

> *in delicto* until that intention was abandoned. When, however, the ship's papers and the testimony of the master and the crew tallied with an alternative destination, or with the intention of taking inquiries in an open port, not in the vicinity of the blockaded port, about the continuance of the blockade, the ship was to be presumed to have an innocent destination unless she had reached a point irreconcilable with a route towards that open port, or unless, after having been warned, she acted in a manner irreconcilable with such route."

That meant that the intention alone to sail for the purpose of breaking a blockade was sufficient to constitute its violation and that no actual passing of a blockading force was required to justify condemnation of the trespassing vessel. This peculiarity of the English law on blockade was often referred to as the belligerent's "right of prevention" (*droit de prévention*), paralleled by a "droit de suite", exercisable even after the vessel's successful escape from a blockaded port. Comp. *infra*, p. 438.

The intention to enter a blockaded port might be abandoned, but if a vessel was captured in a place which excluded the presumption of such abandonment, she would be condemned: case of the American ship *James Cook* [1810] (Edw., 261; Roscoe, II, 53).

Possible theoretical objections to the doctrine were refuted by Sir William Scott in the following passage in his judgment concerning the *Columbia* [1799] (1 C.Rob., 154; Roscoe, I, 89):

> "It is said that as the vessel has not arrived, the offence was not actually committed, but rested in intention only. On this point I am clearly of opinion that the sailing with an intention of evading the blockade of Texel was beginning to execute that intention, and was an overt act constituting the offence. From that moment the blockade was fraudulently invaded."

The theory that the mere fact that a merchant vessel intended to violate a blockade sufficed to render her liable to capture and condemnation wherever she was on her voyage gave rise to the further theory that she was so liable even if she was still on her way to an intermediate neutral or non-blockaded port. Application of this theory implied the introduction into the law of blockade of the principle of continuous voyage. In a richly documented article in the *A.J.I.L.* IV (1910) on "Early cases on the doctrine of continuous voyages" Professor Lester H. Woolsey has analysed the relevant jurisprudence of the prize courts.

However, the doctrine was not applied in cases where the real destination of the vessel was a neutral (non-blockaded) port from where her cargo would or might reach a blockaded port by land or interior navigation. See, for instance, the following extracts from prize judgments:

the *Stert* [1801] (4 C.Rob., 65; Roscoe, I, 348), concerning a cargo of butter and cheese on its way to the neutral port of Emden for further transportation from there to Holland, during the blockade of Amsterdam, which was claimed by Prussian merchants:

> "The blockade of Amsterdam, which was imposed on the part of this country, was, from the nature of our situation, a mere maritime blockade, effected by force operating only at

> sea. As far as that force could be applied, it was indubitably a good and legal blockade; but as to interior navigation, how is it a blockade at all? Where is the blockading power? Let us suppose the case of the blockade of Havre. Can it be said that, by the maritime blockade of the Seine, the interior access to Havre is blockaded, so that goods belonging to a neutral subject sent from Paris to Havre could be held subject to confiscation by virtue of the blockade? [negative answer] This Court cannot ... take upon itself to say that a legal blockade exists, when no actual blockade can be applied. In the very notion of a complete blockade it is included that the besieging force can apply its power to every point of the blockaded State. If it cannot, it is no blockade of that quarter where its power cannot be brought to bear .... In laying down this rule as applicable to the present case, I proceed upon the supposition that this was a real inland navigation, and not a navigation over the Watt, the character of which might be subject to a different signification. Conceiving this to be a cargo which had gone to Embden on neutral account by an internal canal navigation, where no blockade existed, I shall hold it free of all consequences of blockade."

To the same effect the *Jonge Pieter* [1801] (4 C.Rob., 79; Roscoe, I, 353):

> "The blockade of Amsterdam is, from the nature of the thing, a partial blockade—a blockade by sea; and if the goods were going to Embden, with an ulterior destination by land to Amsterdam, or by an interior canal navigation, it is not, according to my conception, a breach of the blockade."

—Proof of intended destination to a blockaded port

The discussion before the Admiralty Court often turned on the vessel's destination to a blockaded port as a *quaestio facti* which had to be resolved before a decision on her condemnation or release could be made. The requirement of sufficient proof was the more necessary as the intention to run the blockade was sufficient for the condemnation of a ship met at sea even at a considerable distance from the port concerned.

The general principles which governed the valuation of the evidence produced were set out in the judgments concerning the *Haabet (No. 2)* [1805] (6 C.Rob., 54; Roscoe, I, 524) and the *Glierktigheit* [1805] (Roscoe, I, 527, footnote *a*). In those cases the Court held that affidavits of the captors could not be admitted if they contradicted depositions of the crew of the captured vessel on which no doubt arose.

In the *Calypso* [1799] (2 C.Rob., 298; Roscoe, I, 238) the fact that the ship's master had continued to take in cargo after he must have obtained knowledge of the blockade of the United Netherlands and that he had sailed out from Rotterdam notwithstanding, was held to prove his intention to break the blockade.

In the *Shepherdess* [1804] (5 C.Rob., 262; Roscoe, I, 470) allegations by the master of a neutral vessel that he was intoxicated at the crucial time, and by the supercargo that he would not have allowed the master to break the blockade were held insufficient to prevent the condemnation of the ship, together with her cargo, captured while apparently intending the breach of a blockade.

In the *Neutralitet (No. 2)* [1805] (6 C.Rob., 30; Roscoe, I, 521) it was held that if a neutral vessel approached a blockaded port so as to be in a position from which she could enter, there was a legal presumption that such vessel intended to break the blockade.

A neutral cargo destined to Hambourg could be considered as having Altona as her port of destination because the two ports were closely adjacent and commercially connected: see *The Conferenzrath* [1806] (6 C.Rob., 362; Roscoe, I, 571).

—Sanctions on violation of a blockade

Running a blockade, or attempts to run it, exposed the ship to condemnation in prize, but did not necessarily affect the cargo, unless this was the property of the ship owner, or unless the owner of the cargo was cognisant of the intended violation: *Mercurius* (Gerdes, Master) [1798] (1 C.Rob., 80; Roscoe, I, 54). The general, but not universal rule was said to be that when a ship was condemned for breach of blockade, the cargo was subject to the same fate.

This rule was expressed a little differently in the *Panaghia Rhomba* [1858] (Roscoe, II, 635; 12 Moore P.C., 168), in which a number of precedents were cited:

> "the sanction on the violation of a blockade is the condemnation of both the ship and her cargo. When a blockade was, or could have been known by the owners of the cargo or their agents at the moment of loading, there was an irrefutable legal presumption of knowledge of the intention to violate the blockade. When the blockade could not have been known to those owners at the moment of loading, the cargo is to be released."

The ship owner was liable for the acts of his master in attempting to break a blockade: the *Vrouw Judith* [1799] (1 C.Rob., 150; Roscoe, I, 86):

> "The act of the master of the vessel binds the owner in respect to the conduct of the ship as much as if it was committed by the owner himself. There are powers with which the law invests him and if he abuses his trust it is a matter to be settled between him and the person who instituted him master; but his act of violation is, as to the personal consequences, to be considered as the act of the owners."

To the same effect the *Columbia (No. 1)* (Weeks, Master) [1799-1801] (1 C.Rob., 154; Roscoe, I, 89), an American merchant ship sailing from America to Amsterdam via Hamburg. Although the master learned at Cuxhaven that Amsterdam was blockaded, he nevertheless attempted to enter that port, and on that voyage the ship was captured. Condemnation followed: the owners were bound by the act of their master whose knowledge of the blockade was sufficient. Absence of a notice of the blockade was held to be immaterial.

In the *Alexander* [1801] (4 C.Rob., 93; Roscoe, I, 358) condemnation of the ship was decreed on the ground of her attempt to break the blockade of Le Havre during a voyage from Lisbon to Altona, on the pretext of want of provisions; as the inference was that the ship entered the blockaded port in the interests of the cargo, the latter was also liable to condemnation.

In the *Adonis* [1804] (5 C.Rob., 256; Roscoe, I, 467) the Court said:

> "The conduct of a master in endeavouring to run a blockade presumptively binds the owner of the cargo, and when a blockade was known to such owner at the time of shipment, the presumption is conclusive."

In some cases the stringency of the sanction rule was relaxed. Thus in the case of the *Neptunus (No. 4)* (Kuyp, Master) [1800] (3 C.Rob., 173; Roscoe, I, 292) the Court decided that the stringency of the rule on the liability of a principal for the acts of his agent might be mitigated if the principal concerned (*in casu* the owner of the cargo) was *bona fide* ignorant of the existence of the blockade.

To the same effect later the *Jeanne Marie* [1855] (Spinks, 167; Roscoe, II, 457): the rule might be relaxed in case the cargo owner was ignorant of the blockade when he purchased cargo in a blockaded port before the declaration of war, and the cargo was brought out of the blockaded port without knowledge on his part of the blockade.

See also the following cases of 1800 and 1801:

the *Juffro(u)w Maria Schroeder* [1800] (3 C.Rob., 147; Roscoe, I, 279, 356, footnote *a*), a Prussian vessel which had been permitted to enter the blockaded port of Le Hâvre de Grâce and had come out again, passing the blockading force. She was afterwards seized by a cruiser not engaged in the blockade, but was restored on the ground that the blockade had been relaxed. The cargo on board, which had been sent to Le Hâvre in 1797 prior to the establishment of the blockade of that port by England, for the purpose of their forwarding to Paris, had proved to be unmarketable there and had therefore been reshipped. When leaving the French port again afterwards, they were seized, but also released by the Prize Court;

the *Adelaide* [1801] (3 C.Rob., 281; Roscoe, I, 306), in which the Court held that the owner was not bound by the acts of his agent, unless sufficient time had been given him to tranship the goods or to countermand.

No sanction was allowed any longer after the termination of the blockade because a capture made under those conditions was invalid. See *infra*.

The question of the liability of the cargo found on board a ship which had run a blockade to confiscation together with the ship herself was not considered to be an isolated problem. The same question arose in respect of comparable cases, such as the carriage of contraband, the presence on board of despatches to the enemy, attempts of a neutral captain or crew to rescue the prize from the captor, etc. This was argued in the *Franklin* [1811] (*infra*), in which various such comparable cases were quoted. The solution depended on whether the ship and her cargo belonged to the same owner, or whether the owner of the cargo was cognisant of the intended violation. In a case of blockade, the *Mercurius* (Gerdes, Master) [1798] (1 C.Rob. 80; Roscoe, I, 54), the Court argued that "to maintain that the conduct of the ship will affect the cargo, it will be necessary either to prove that the owners (of the cargoes) were, or might have been cognisant of the blockade before they sent (them); or to show that the act of the master of the ship personally binds them. In America there could not have been any knowledge of the blockade; the cargo is innocent in its nature, and set out innocently; the master certainly is the agent of the owner of the vessel and can bind him by his contract or his misconduct; but he is not the agent of the owners of the cargo, unless expressly so constituted by them. In cases of insurance and in revenue cases, where, it is said, the act of the master will affect the cargo, it is to be observed that the ground on which they stand is wholly different. In the former, it is in virtue of an express contract which governs the whole case; and in revenue cases it proceeds from positive laws and the necessary strictness of all fiscal regulations.

It is argued that to exempt the cargo from this responsibility will open the door to fraud, if neutrals are allowed to attempt to trade to blockaded ports with impunity by throwing the blame upon the carrier master, but if such an artifice could be proved, it would establish that *mens rea* in the neutral merchant which would expose his property to confiscation, and it would at the same time be sufficient to cause the master to be considered in the character of agent as well for the cargo as for the chip.

Where a cargo is of a contraband nature it will perhaps justify greater severity, but in cases of contraband it is held that innocent parts of the cargo belonging to other owners shall not be infected. This (*Mercurius* case) is, I think, a parallel case. There is misconduct on the part of the owner of the vessel, but none in the owner of the cargo". [The owners of the cargo were admitted to further proof.]

This particular issue of the responsibility of the cargo in the case of blockade-running is indeed part of a wider problem. This is apparent from the *Franklin* case [1811] (2 Acton, 106; Roscoe, II, 115), relating to an attempt by the neutral master to rescue his ship from the hands of the captor. In that case Sir W. Grant, delivering the judgment in appeal from a sentence of the Vice-Admiralty Court of Gibraltar, held that when ship and cargo were owned by different persons, the cargo was liable to condemnation. During those proceedings various other precedents were invoked. Those quoted for the claimants, in addition to the above-mentioned *Mercurius* case of 1798, dated from 1808 and related to cases of capture of neutral ships for the carriage of dispatches destined to the enemy; the *Atalanta* (6 C.Rob. 440; Roscoe, I, 607), the *Constantia* (Roscoe, I, 613, footnote *a*), the *Susan* (continuation of the same footnote at p. 614) and the *Hope* (further continuation of that footnote at pp. 614 and 615). Sir W. Grant on his part quoted a number of other precedents, dealing with attempts by masters or crews of captured neutral ships to rescue them from the hands of the captor: the *Dispatch* [1801], the *Carmelite* [1802], the *Washington* [1806], the *Mars* [1807] and the *Adonis* [1804], the *ratio decidendi* against the cargo in those cases generally being that the cargo was the property of the ship's owner (comp. on these cases of rescue my observations under B, section 7 (on recapture) *infra*, pp. 542 *et seq.*). Among the precedents quoted by Sir W. Grant, there was one that concerned, in particular, another case of the breach of a blockade, *viz.*, the *Alexander* [1801] (4 C.Rob. 93; Roscoe, I, 358), in which the Court decided that when a ship was captured endeavouring to enter a blockaded port, the inference was that she was entering in the interests of the cargo, which for that reason became liable to confiscation together with the ship. She had, on her voyage from Lisbon, ostensibly to Altona, gone into the port of Le Havre during the blockade under the pretence of requiring provisions.

"I think this case is in effect decided by the decree which has pronounced the ship subject to condemnation for fraudulently attempting to go into a blockaded port; for when the Court decided that, it did in effect decide that the vessel was so going to dispose of this cargo, the inference in all cases being that a ship going into a blockaded port is going with an intention of disposing of the cargo. The Court has already decided that the ship was going in, and that the excuse assigned was a frivolous pretence. The master makes no distinction, nor asserts that he deviated under particular directions, applying to one part of the cargo only, or that when that part was delivered, under instructions unknown to the rest of the shippers, he was to go on to Altona with that part of the cargo which is the subject of the present claims. If that could have been made out, the Court might, perhaps, have given the claimants the benefit of that distinction. The same general cause is assigned for all, and I must suppose the whole cargo was to be there delivered. It is true that the owners of the cargo are not, in general cases, held to be affected by the act of the master, unless he is specially appointed their agent. But it would be impossible to maintain a blockade in cases of this nature, which is directed more against the cargo than against ships, if the Court did not draw the inference that a ship going in fraudulently is going in the service of the cargo, with the knowledge and by the direction of the owner. If any inconvenience arises to the claimants of the cargo from this necessary conclusion, the owners of the vessel or the master are the persons to whom they must look for indemnification."

Cargo condemned.

—Capture on the ship's return voyage

Parallel to the "droit de prévention" prize law practice had developed a "droit de suite", *i.e.*, the right of belligerents to capture ships which had run a blockade on their outward voyage, when they met them on their return voyage, and to have them condemned as good and lawful prize. The enunciation of these two rights combined implied that ships which intended to run an effective blockade were subjected with their cargoes to capture from the beginning until the termination of their voyage. This was already the assumption of the United Netherlands in respect of their Resolution of 26 June 1630 (*Collectanea Maritima*, pp. 158 *et seq.*). A quotation from a declaration reproduced *ibid.*, p. 165, contained in effect the threat that neutral vessels would be confiscated

"quand même on ne les auroit rencontrez que bien loin encore de là [Flanders], de sorte qu'ils pourroient encore changer de route & d'intention, ceci étant fondé sur ce qu'ils ont déjà tenté quelque chose d'illicite, & mis en œuvre, quoi qu'ils ne l'ayent pas achevé, ni porté au dernier point de perfection, à moins que les maîtres & les propriétaires de tels vaisseaux ne fissent voir dûëment qu'ils avoient désisté de leur propre mouvement de leur entreprise & voyage destiné, & celà avant qu'aucun vaisseau de l'Etat les eût vû ou poursuivi, & que ceux-ci trouvassent la chose sans fraude ... et que les vaisseaux revenant des ports de Flandres (sans y avoir été jettez par une extrême nécessité) & quoique rencontrez loin de là dans le Canal ou dans la Mer du Nord par les vaisseaux de l'Etat, quand même ils n'auroient pas été vûs ni poursuivis par ceux-ci en sortant de là, seront aussi confisquez, à cause que tel navires sont censez avoir été pris sur le fait, tant qu'ils

> n'ont point achevé ce voyage, & qu'ils ne se sont point sauvez dans quelque port libre ou apartenant à un Prince neutre. Mais ayant été ... dans un port libre, & étant pris par les vaisseaux de guerre de l'Etat dans un autre voyage, ces vaisseaux & marchandises ne seront point confisquez, à moins qu'ils n'ayent été en sortant des ports de Flandres suivis par les vaisseaux de guerre, & poursuivis jusque dans un autre port que de leur, ou celui de leur destination, & qu'en sortant de nouveau de là, ils ayent été pris en pleine mer".

An exception was only made with regard to cases of a *bona fide* change of destination during the voyage.

The right of a belligerent to capture a merchant ship on her return voyage after the breach of a blockade on her outward voyage was generally recognized by British prize courts. See for some instances in which a ship had succeeded in escaping from a blockaded port and was held to remain subject to capture until the end of her voyage, no matter whether she had, or had not, touched at an intermediary port, the cases of the *Welvaart van Pillaw* [1799] (2 C.Rob., 128; Roscoe, I, 207), a Russian vessel that had broken the blockade of Amsterdam; the *General Hamilton* [1805] (6 C.Rob., 61; Roscoe, I, 528), bought by an American citizen in a blockaded port (comp. *infra*, p. 442); the *Christiansberg* (Vanderweyde, Master) [1807] (6 C.Rob., 376; Roscoe, I, 580), and the *Lisette* [1806] (Steg, Master) (6 C.Rob., 387; Roscoe, I, 587).

In the *General Hamilton* case the Court held that when a ship has broken a blockade, her entry into a port even in distress will not be a termination of her voyage so as to take away her liability to condemnation. In the case of the *Christiansberg* the Court held that the sanction of condemnation only applied when the ship was captured during her first voyage after her offence and not to subsequent ones. The *Christiansberg* had sailed from the blockaded port of Rotterdam under the benefit of an indulgence granted by an Order in Council of 7 January 1807 to vessels going to a neutral port. Bound ostensibly for Smyrna, she had, however, put into Alicante, assertedly, but falsely, in distress; after having sold her cargo of cheese and butter there and taken another cargo on board, she was captured when sailing on a new destination to Copenhagen. Both the ship and her cargo were condemned:

> "Until the vessel had actually entered the interdicted port, nothing appeared, whether she was *in delicto* or not. Cruisers see nothing; she goes in and then the offence is consummated and the intention is for the first time declared. It is not till the vessel comes out again that any opportunity is afforded of vindicating the law, and of enforcing the restriction of this Order. It is objected that if the penalty is applied to the subsequent voyage, it may travel on with the vessel for ever. In principle, perhaps, it might not unjustly be pursued further than to the immediate voyage. But we all know that in practice it has not been carried further than to the voyage succeeding, which affords the first opportunity of enforcing the law."

The question of the confiscatability of the offending vessel on subsequent voyages was once discussed in an old case recorded in the Reports of the Court of Session in Scotland, *Parkman v. Allen* (Stair's Decisions, I, 529), in which the Court held that

> "the law of nations had abridged [the quarrel] to the immediate return on the same voyage, because quarrels would be multiplied upon pretence of any former voyage."

The restriction of the "droit de suite" enunciated in the *Christiansberg* was affirmed in the case of the *Randers Bye* [1808], relating to a ship which had made three consecutive voyages, from Almeira to Marseille, from Marseille to Cette and from Cette to Randers. The first of these voyages had been with ostensible papers to Trieste, which would have made her liable to condemnation for fraud. Her capture on the third voyage on the ground of her offence on the first was declared invalid, although the second voyage had been of very short extent and merely a passage in ballast from one port of that same coast to another for the purpose of taking cargo on board (Roscoe, I, 582, footnote).

—Termination or suspension of a blockade

According to the *Hoffnung (No. 1)* [1805] (6 C.Rob., 112; Roscoe, I, 533) a blockade was terminated when (i) the blockading Government or the naval officer in command of the blockading force so declared, or when (ii) the blockaded port or territory was occupied by the forces of the blockading Power, or when (iii) the blockade was not effectively maintained, or when (iv) it was not applied impartially to the vessels of all nations or when (v) the blockading forces were driven away by a superior force, or when (vi) they were temporarily withdrawn for some other service.

According to other judgments—the *Frederick Molke* [1798] (1 C.Rob., 86; Roscoe, I, 58), the *Columbia* [1799] (1 C.Rob., 154; Roscoe, I, 89)—on the other hand, a blockade was not terminated by the fact that (i) the blockading vessels were temporarily chased away by heavy weather, nor by the fact that (ii) ships occasionally succeeded in entering or leaving a blockaded port.

In the *Neptunus (No. 2)* [1799] (2 C.Rob., 110; Roscoe, I, 195) the Prize Court dealt with the special case that an isolated vessel had been wrongly informed by blockading warships that the blockade had been raised.

In the *Imina* [1799] (Roscoe, I, 290, note) there was the question of the suspension of the blockade of Amsterdam (November 1799).

See the *Columbia* [1799-1801] (1 C.Rob., 154; Roscoe, I, 89):

> "the blockade of Amsterdam was to be considered as legally still existing, although the winds did occasionally blow the blockading squadron off course; it was an accidental change which must take place in every blockade, but the blockade is not therefore suspended."

In the *Triheten* case [1805] (6 C.Rob., 65; Roscoe, I, 534, footnote *a*) it appeared that the British squadron, blockading the Spanish coast, was driven off on 10 April by a superior force. It had to be shown that the actual blockade had again been resumed. Seeing that the *Triheten* was taken on the French coast as long ago as 28 May, the Court was not disposed to hold that the mere act of sailing for Sevilla or Sanlúcar was sufficient to inflict upon the vessel the penalty of breaking the blockade.

After the termination of a blockade a ship could no longer be seized for its violation, neither on her entrance into, nor on her egress from the blockaded port, unless this port was captured and a ship was found in it that had entered in violation of the blockade: the *Lisette* [1806] (6 C.Rob., 387; Roscoe, I, 587). The ship had sailed from the Elbe to Tonningen under a charter-party to take on board a cargo for Malaga, which was to be sent from the Elbe in lighters from Hamburg. The goods were accordingly shipped, the ship sailed on 6 September 1806, was captured on 26 September after the blockade of the Elbe had been notified to be withdrawn on 20 September 1806.

An earlier case was that of the *Charlotte Sophia* [1806] (1 Acton, 46; Roscoe, I, 547-548, footnote b), but that was not considered to be a binding precedent because the judgment turned solely on the construction of Orders in Council.

According to the *Conferenzrath* [1806] (6 C.Rob., 362; Roscoe, I, 571) a Danish vessel intending to break the blockade of Hamburg could not be condemned because that blockade had been raised before she was captured.

—Joint capture of blockade-runners

In order to enable certain ships of a blockading squadron to share in a prize captured by other ships, the former need not have actually pursued the prize; it was sufficient that the whole squadron was acting on a preconcerted plan, and that the ships in question were not prevented from action by any permanent obstacle: the case of the French warship *Guillaume Tell* [1808] (Edw., 6; Roscoe, II, 1).

When a squadron is blockading a port and one ship thereof captures a vessel leaving such a port, all the ships of the blockading squadron, however distant from the place of capture, are entitled to a share of the prize money: case of the *La Henriette* [1815] (2 Dods., 96; Roscoe, II, 215).

—The sale of ships or cargoes in a blockaded port

The *Jeanne Marie* [1855] (Spinks, 167; Roscoe, II, 457) related to the purchase of a cargo in a Russian port which was already blockaded prior to the declaration of war. The cargo-owner was ignorant of the blockade when he brought the cargo out, which was on that ground released.

The validity of the always suspect transfer of a vessel in a blockaded port depended on the question between whom the transfer took place:

the transfer of a ship effected in the blockaded port of Le Havre by a neutral citizen to a another neutral citizen was valid: the *Potsdam* [1801] (4 C.Rob., 89; Roscoe, I, 355); the vessel was permitted to come out in ballast;

a transfer operated by an enemy owner to a neutral buyer was invalid: the *General Hamilton* [1805] (6 C.Rob., 61; Roscoe, I, 528).

(b) Old French legislation and jurisprudence

French case law on blockade ran on the whole parallel to that of British prize courts but was far less extensive.

Art. 1 of the *Règlement* of 26 July 1778 defined blockade-runners as

> "ceux qui porteraient des secours à des places bloquées, investies ou assiègées."

De Pistoye and Duverdy in their *Traité des prises maritimes*, I, 365, formulated the principle that

> "pour qu'il y ait blocus, il faut que la place soit investie par des forces suffisantes pour en rendre l'entrée périlleuse aux navires qui voudraient s'y introduire. Ainsi, tout blocus doit être réel et effectif."

They recognized, however, that that principle had not always been admitted by the Powers of Europe, since in certain wars the belligerents had advanced the claim that neutrals were bound to respect as lawfully blockaded ports, coasts and even entire States before which they had not even posted a single cruiser. The authors called these asserted blockades "blocus fictifs", "blocus de convention", "blocus de cabinet", "blocus sur le papier" or "blocus *per notificationem*". They traced the origin of this practice back to an attempt made in 1689 by England and the United Netherlands, then allied against France (see their Convention of Whitehall of 12/22 August 1689 "pour interdire à tout Etat les relations commerciales avec la France", Dumont, VII^2, 238 or Parry, 18, 479). England repeated this attempt at the beginning of the Seven Years' War of 1756, and by her Order in Council of 16 May 1806, declaring all the coasts of France blockaded from the mouths of the Elbe to Brest, inaugurated the notorious series of measures of retorsion or reprisals, marked by the Decrees of Berlin and Milan, described above *sub* A (pp. 601 *et seq.*). It was against these practices that the Armed Neutrality Leagues of 1780 and 1800 were directed.

Old French case law on blockade, as reported in De Pistoye and Duverdy's *Traité* (my following quotations are from vol. I, pp. 365-391) does not include one single judgment dating from the 18th century. The oldest judgment is that of 13 thermidor *an* IX, just over the threshold of the 19th century (1 August 1801), relating to the Danish vessel *Marthe Magdeleine* (I, 378) which was sailing towards Sevilla with a cargo belonging to the consul of a neutral country in an enemy State (the Batavian Republic), when she was captured by the English naval force blockading the port of Cádiz. The ship was afterwards recaptured by the French privateer *Le Solide*. The fate of the recaptured vessel, for the French *Conseil*, depended on the question of whether she could have been lawfully condemned after her first capture by a British prize court for breach of blockade. The French *Conseil* denied this: the Danish ship was not guilty of running the blockade of Cádiz because she had not yet attempted to cross the blockading line off that town and because the blockade of Cádiz did not entail the blockade of Sevilla—a decision which seems to imply a clear rejection of the *droit de prévention*.

The other French judicial precedents recorded by the authors of the *Traité* all had a bearing on cases from the period 1830-1850 (blockades of the ports of the Regency of Algiers and of the waters of the Argentine-Uruguayan Rio de la Plata—a pacific rather than a war blockade). In those cases the requirement of a notification of the blockade was one of the main issues.

In two decisions of 1845, respectively 1847, recorded in the *Traité* at p. 382 of vol. I, relating to the *Flor del Uruguay* and the *Louisa*, the latter a Sardinian vessel, the *Conseil d'Etat* held that for the seizure of a neutral vessel in a blockaded area to be valid it was not sufficient that the blockade should have been notified to the diplomatic agents of foreign Powers; the vessel herself should have been specially notified of the existence and extent of the blockade and that notification should have been entered in the ship's papers. Such a special notification was mentioned in a number of other prize judgments, dealing with the question in what particular actions the violation of a blockade by a neutral vessel might consist:

the *Carolina* and the *Madonna di Montenero* [1830] (I, 381, 382), persistent attempts to enter the blockaded port of Algiers despite a special warning in the ship's papers;

the *Monte Alègre* and the *Candelaria* [1845] and the *Fortuna* [1847] (I, 385-387), a case of the violation of a convention concluded on 23 April 1839 between the commander of the French blockading force of the Rio de la Plata and the authorities of Montevideo which laid down rules on the navigation of vessels flying the "Oriental" flag during the blockade and exempted the commander from making a special notification to vessels of Montevideo, subject to their obligation to have their papers visaed by French surveillance stations or the French consul;

the *Caïman* [1846] (I, 383), a case of two successive captures of the same vessel, the first when she was caught in the act of running the blockade of Buenos Aires with irregular papers;

the British brig *Fame* [1850] (I, 389), entering the port of Buenos Aires notwithstanding a special warning against it, followed by an attempt to sail out again after the expiration of the term granted to neutral vessels to leave the port;

the *Independencia Americana* [1849] (I, 384), refusal to return to the port of Buenos Aires when attempting to sail out of that blockaded port despite a special warning *in loco*;

the *Aurora* [1849] (I, 384), leaving the same port without ship's papers;

the British *Elisa-Cornish* [1850] (I, 387), departure from the same port with a cargo, despite a notice entered in the ship's papers that she was only allowed to sail out in ballast.

In the case of the Spanish *Comte de Thomar* [1848] (I, 390) the *Conseil d'Etat* called the blockade of the Rio de la Plata a "blocus simple", meaning a blockade without a previous declaration of war, a "pacific blockade" (whereupon comp. vol. VIII of this publication, pp. 43 *et seq.*), and released the vessel because she had not been notified of the establishment of the blockade.

§ 2. *The Crimean War (1853-1856)*

This war was preceded by a Turkish blockade of the coast of Dulcigno in 1852-1853 (42 *B.F.S.P.* 237, 238). After its outbreak Great Britain established a blockade of the Russian ports in the Baltic on 16 June and 11 August 1854 (44 *B.F.S.P.* 894, 896, 899), and France and Great Britain jointly a blockade of the Danube on 13 June 1854, of the Finnish Gulf on 12 July 1854 and of the White Sea on 28 September 1854 (44 *B.F.S.P.* 895, 899).

The blockade of the Baltic ports of Russia during the Crimean War has brought in its train a large number of cases decided by the British Admiralty Court under the then presidency of Dr S. Lushington. It is in particular the first case decided by that judge in the first instance of 27 January 1855 and heard and decided by the Appellate Court in the period from 26 July to 1 August 1855 relating to the Danish schooner *Franciska* [1855] (Roscoe, II, 346) which is illustrative of the state of the law of naval blockade as it was regarded in the middle of the 19th century. I will therefore begin by epitomizing the pronouncements in that case, which are far too lengthy to be quoted in extenso.

The *Franciska (No. 1)* case was chosen by the Court as an instance of ingress into the port of Riga and heard together with that of the *Johanna Maria* (*infra*) as an instance of egress from that port. Spinks has published Dr Lushington's judgment in the *Franciska* case at pp. 111-161 of his collection, Roscoe the appellate decision (*per* Lord Pemberton Leigh) in vol. II of the work at pp. 349-416 (also 10 Moore P.C., 37). I will refer in the following summary to the page numbers in Spinks' collection.

The *Franciska* was one of a group of vessels, all captured in comparable circumstances and further consisting of the *Johanna Maria, Union, Annechina Jantina, Steen Bille, Vrouw Alida, Jeanne Marie* and *Nornen*. She had sailed in March 1854 under Danish colours from Tarragona (Spain) with a cargo of wine and salt to Elsenör for orders and, having arrived there, proceeded on 14 May to Riga, in the vicinity of which port (off Lyser Ort) she was captured on 22 May 1854 by two British warships the *Rosamond* and the *Cruiser*. From Dr Lushington's judgment, which comprises in Spinks' report some fifty pages, I cite the following selection of statements and reasonings.

A high act of sovereignty cannot be imposed by a commander unless he is invested with authority for the purpose. On distant stations he may be presumed to be so invested (p. 113). In Europe this may be different (p. 114), but subsequent adoption by his own government legitimates the acts of a commander (p. 114).

For the maintenance of a blockade it is necessary that ingress and egress cannot take place without imminent risk of capture (pp. 115-124). Testimony of a commander-in-chief is the best, and sometimes conclusive evidence as to the sufficiency of the blockading force (*ibid.*).

The legality of a blockade is not affected by the distance of the blockading force, which may be at any distance convenient for closing the blockaded port (p. 118).

A blockading squadron would invalidate the blockade by capriciously permitting ingress or egress (p. 122) and by an injustifiable absence from the locality (p. 124).

If a blockade has been recently established, neutrals may come out with a cargo laden before the blockade or in ballast (p. 122).

Occasional eluding of a blockading force does not invalidate the blockade, it is violation, but not invalidation (p. 123).

A blockade *de facto* needs no notification (p. 127). The subsequent publication of a *Gazette* cannot affect the legality of a blockade *de facto* previously established (p. 126). Early notification is desirable but not essential to the validity of a blockade *de facto* (pp. 127, 128).

In interpreting documents relaxing a belligerent right the most liberal construction should be adopted (p. 130).

One belligerent cannot concede to another, nor assume to himself, a privilege of commerce prohibited to neutrals (p. 131). A grant of licences which might have such an effect would invalidate a blockade (p. 132). The acts of a subordinate officer cannot affect the character of a blockade, thought an individual claimant might plead such acts as his own special justification (p. 133).

Notice to neutrals of a blockade *de facto* is indispensably necessary, but whatever brings it credibly to their knowledge is sufficient (p. 135).

Unless the blockade is notorious, individual warning is requisite. Knowledge is presumed from notoriety (p. 135). Notoriety precludes neutrals from approaching the port on any pretence whatever (p. 137). Knowledge of the blockade, and not the mode in which such knowledge was communicated, justifies capture (p. 137). The Prize Court receives every kind of evidence, unfettered by the municipal law of evidence (p. 137).

Neutrals are bound to make inquiry and cannot plead ignorance which is wilful (p. 141).

The blockade of Riga and the coast of Courland was sufficiently notorious to throw the *onus* of proving his ignorance on the neutral merchant in each case (p. 147).

Ignorance for which the neutral Government is responsible is no excuse for the individual (p. 158). When the blockade is notorious, and no special ignorance proved, the ship must be condemned (p. 158).

And as regards the special treaty relations between England and the Scandinavian countries:

the treaties with Sweden of 1661 and with Denmark of 1670 confer some specific privilege upon those countries and remain unrevoked. Revocation of one treaty by another can only (p. 151) be inferred when the two cannot reasonably co-exist (p. 149). The interpretation of treaties belongs to the Court of Admiralty, but their variation to the Government (p. 152). A treaty conferring on one neutral a right to trade with blockaded ports would be unjust to other neutrals, and violate the law of neutrality (pp. 153-156). The restrictions of blockade are justified only by necessity, which applies to the neutrals equally (pp. 153-156).

The parallel proceedings in the *Franciska* and *Johanna Maria* cases resulted as to the former in a condemnatory judgment by Dr Lushington which was, however, reversed by the Lords of Appeal, and as to the latter (Spinks, 307; Roscoe, II, 370; 10 Moore P.C., 70) in a condemnation in both instances. The difference of opinion between the courts of first and second instance in the *Franciska* case was not due to any ground of principle but to a different evaluation of factual data, see in particular Roscoe, II, 369. The concordant decisions in the *Johanna Maria* case were based on clear proof of a *de facto* blockade on the day of egress from Riga and of the master's full knowledge of that fact.

The *Franciska* case later gave rise to new proceedings: *Franciska (No. 2)*, finally heard and decided, together with the *Union*, by the Lords of Appeal (*per* Sir John Patteson) (Roscoe, II, 416-432; 10 Moore P.C., 73). As the ship and her cargo, after their condemnation in the first instance, had been sold under a decree of the Court in accordance with the *Prize Court Act* (17 & 18 Vict., c. 18, s. 26), the question arose, after the reversal of Dr Lushington's judgment by the Lords, what reparation was due to the Danish owners. The decision was to the effect that the owners were only entitled to a simple restitution of the net proceeds of the sale after deduction of costs from the gross proceeds.

Other judgments concerning an asserted violation of a blockade hinged on —the requirement of effectiveness:

the *Gerasimo* [1857] (Roscoe, II, 577; 11 Moore P.C., 88): a blockade, *in casu* of the Black Sea, could be established for one single or for several ports, or for an entire coast provided that it remained confined to enemy ports and coasts; it could be intended to prevent either the entry or the egress alone, or both.

The *Gerasimo* was one of three vessels captured for the alleged breach of the blockade of the Black Sea under almost the same circumstances; the two others were the *Aspasia* and the *Achilles*. See on these judgments Roscoe, II, 572 with footnote (*a*), 577 and 599; 11 Moore P.C., 79 and 88;

Naylor v. Taylor (1 Moody and Malkin, 297): as in the *Franciska*, it was held that a blockading force could be stationed at any distance from the enemy's ports or coast which the naval authorities deemed convenient provided that their position did not prevent access to a neutral coast; the true criterion of the legality of a blockade was not the location of the blockading fleet but its capability to maintain the blockade;

—the elements of a breach of blockade:

the *Chrissys* [1856] (Spinks, 343; Roscoe, II, 568): a ship sailing under Greek colours, captured sixty or seventy miles off her course and in the neighbourhood of a blockaded port could not be restored without further proof of its real destination; if this was refused by the claimant, the ship was to be condemned;

—the intention to break a blockade:

the *Aline and Fanny* [1856] (Spinks, 322; Roscoe, II, 537, 554; 10 Moore P.C., 491): a Lübeck vessel that sailed from Lübeck, bound according to the ship's papers to Haparanda in Sweden, at the head of the Gulf of Bothnia, but captured by two British warships for an alleged attempt to break the blockade of the Finnish port of Jacobstadt; the proof of intention was considered insufficient;

—certain relaxations of the strict rules:

the *Jeanne Marie* [1855] (Spinks, 167; Roscoe, II, 457): the cargo of a Dutch ship, which was herself condemned for breach of the blockade of Riga, was held not to be liable to condemnation because its owner, who had purchased the goods in that port before the declaration of war and had brought them out of it after the declaration of the blockade, had had no knowledge of the latter fact;

—the liability of the captor to costs and damages in case of the subsequent release of the prize:

the Danish *Otto and Olaf* [1855] (Spinks, 257; Roscoe, II, 507): every ship leaving a blockaded port with a cargo was held subject to detention without the captor being liable to payment of costs and damages; the prize court could require further proof, but would not enter into an inquiry whether the captured neutral vessel had complied with the requirements of the municipal law of her own country; the preparatory evidence was *in casu* at variance with the documentary evidence;

the Danish *Elize* (or *Elise Wilhelmine*) [1854] (Spinks, 88; Roscoe, II, 327): in this case a customs officer at Leith was condemned in costs and damages for the unjustified seizure of a neutral vessel on her arrival in that port on the ground of an alleged preceding breach of the blockade of Arkhangel;

the Mecklenburg *Ostsee* [1855] (Spinks, 174; Roscoe, II, 432, 436; 9 Moore P.C., 150), captured in the Gulf of Finland for a supposed breach of the blockade of Cronstadt which, however, was not imposed upon that town until after the capture. The ship was released; the captors having acted improperly and without reasonable cause by seizing this neutral vessel that was not by any act of her own, voluntarily or unvoluntarily, open to any fair ground of suspicion, were therefore liable to damages and costs, even if they had acted as a result of an honest mistake. Comp. on this case, in which the Lords of Appeal quoted a number of older precedents, Part C, section 6(*a*) (*infra*, p. 624), where details are also given of the exact assessment of the amount of the reparation due in such cases.

§ *3. The American Civil War*

Whereas the judgments quoted above in §§ 1 and 2, dating from the period of the Napoleonic and Crimean Wars on the whole exhibit a marked continuity in the jurisprudence of, in particular, British prize courts on blockade, a new era was opened during the American Civil War, which established new forms of blockade and a large number of new prize court decisions in its train. The United States instituted such a war blockade by its proclamation of 19 April 1862, on which comp. the case of the *Hiawatha* [1862] (Blatchford, 632). According to the judgment in that case the legal situation, as evaluated by an American court, was as follows:

> "Under the proclamation of blockade of April 19, 1862, it is not necessary to the lawfulness of the capture of a vessel seized for violation of the blockade that a warning should have been previously endorsed on her register, where, at the time of capture, she had entered into or escaped from the blockaded port or possessed knowledge or notice of the blockade.
>
> A blockade of the enemy's ports is as lawful a measure of war in civil warfare as it is in a war between nations foreign to each other.
>
> A notice of a blockade to the officials of a neutral government is a sufficient notice of it to the subjects of such government.
>
> The act of egress is as culpable as the act of ingress, when done in fraud of a blockade.
>
> On notice of a blockade, a neutral vessel has a right to withdraw from the blockaded port with all the cargo honestly laden on board before the commencement of the blockade.
>
> The acts of a master in breach of a blockade affect the cargo equally with the vessel, if the cargo is laden on board after the blockade has become effective as to the vessel.
>
> A warning on the register of a vessel is not necessary to establish notice of a blockade where actual notice of it to the master or owner is satisfactorily made out otherwise."

A great many other judgments, confirmed by the United States Supreme Court, have followed. Comp. on those judgments the long series cited below with indication of the pages where they can be found in Blatchford's collection:

the *Crenshaw*, 23, 631; *Hallie Jackson*, 41; *Forest King*, 45, 596; *Sarah Starz*, 69, 635, 650; *Louisa Agnes*, 107; *Delta*, 133, 654; *Cheshire*, 151, 156, 643; *Major Barbour*, 167, 310; *Empress*, 146, 175, 659; *Mersey*, 187, 658; *William H. Northrop*, 235; *Memphis*, 202, 260, 656; *Albert*, 280, 663; *Maria*,

283; *Ella Warley*, 204, 207, 213, 288; *John Gilpin*, 291, 661; *Belle*, 294 (No. 1); *Sunbeam*, 316, 638, 656; *Napoleon*, 296, 357; *Douro*, 362; *Rising Dawn*, 368; *Isabella Thompson*, 377; *Mary Clinton*, 556; *Stephen Hart*, 379, 387; *Springbok*, 349, 380, 434; and *Peterhoff*, 463-550.

It is in particular the latter three cases that have become famous because of their revolutionary impact upon the traditional law. Their impact on the law of contraband has perhaps been greater than that upon the law of blockade, because in the latter field there existed already an old tradition that the essential element of the offence of blockade-running consisted in the departure of a neutral vessel from a port with the intent to sail to a blockaded harbour, however far distant from the port of departure, and finally to enter it, giving rise to the belligerent's "right of prevention". In so far there was nothing really new in the application to blockade of the idea that two parts of the ship's voyage could constitute one single "continuous voyage". At the same time it meant the introduction into the law of blockade of two elements which are basically foreign to it, *viz.*, the admissibility of the interception of ships which were still on their way to a neutral or other non-blockaded port, often far outside the range of a blockading cordon, if they were presumed to intend to continue their course from such an intermediary port to a blockaded port or coastal area, and the replacement of the only relevant criterion of the destination of the ship with the irrelevant destination of the cargo, even independently of the destination of the ship.

The situation can perhaps be best elucidated by citing two judgments in which the United States Supreme Court applied the doctrine explicitly to cases of vessels sailing for a neutral port but intending to proceed thence to a port in a state of blockade, *viz.*, its decisions in the *Bermuda* [1865] (3 Wall., 514) and the *Adela* [1867] (6 Wall., 266). The *Bermuda* was a British vessel that originally left Liverpool for Bermuda for the purpose of proceeding from there to the port of Nassau in the Bahamas from where her cargo after transshipment was intended to run the blockade of the Confederate ports either by the *Bermuda* herself or by some other vessel (a difference that the Court considered immaterial). The ship was captured *en route* between Bermuda and Nassau and was held to have become subject to seizure and condemnation as soon as she left the territorial waters of Great Britain on the ground that the voyage from Liverpool to the blockaded port was a single voyage. The case of the *Adela* was to the same effect: she was another British ship sailing for Nassau and intended to proceed thence to Charleston, then in the state of blockade. The two cases were discussed in an article in the *A.J.I.L.*, vol. 10 (1916), at pp. 60 and 61 by A. Holtzoff, who argued that the cases did not evolve a new doctrine because the general rule was well-recognized that a ship destined to run a blockade became subject to condemnation as soon as it appeared on the high seas:

> "The fact that the ship was to stop at a non-blockaded port or ports on the way did not affect the situation. The entire voyage from the original point of departure to the ultimate

> destination was a single, continuous voyage. Consequently, to confine the general rule to that part of the voyage which extended from the last intermediate port to the blockaded port, would have been an altogether artificial limitation and not justified in reason."

The *Adela* later came before the American-British Claims Commission of 1871, which disallowed a claim of her owner: see John Basset Moore's *History and digest of the international arbitrations to which the United States has been a party*, vol. 3, pp. 3152 and 3159.

As I have argued in § 2 of section 3 of III A on the destination of contraband goods, *supra*, p. 359, it is difficult to isolate blockade cases occurring during the American Civil War systematically from contraband cases because the judgments often had a bearing upon transports of contraband goods destined for blockaded Southern ports. I therefore refer here to that § 2 which deals with the introduction of the doctrine of continuous voyage by United States courts during that War in respect of cases of the transport of contraband.

In his general study of 1925 on the application of the continuous voyage doctrine H.W. Briggs covered a wider field than blockade-running and the carriage of contraband as he also quoted cases of capture during the first part of the voyage of a ship engaged in a reserved colonial trade under the Rule of the War of 1756 (comp. section 6 *infra*).

Cases reported from different periods relate to seizures effected during the Napoleonic Wars:

the *Columbia* [1799] (1 C.Rob., 154; Roscoe, I, 89);
the *Neptunus (No. 2)* [1799] (2 C.Rob., 110; Roscoe, I, 195);
the *Maria No. 4* [1805] (6 C.Rob., 201; Roscoe, I, 546);
the *Charlotte Sophia* [1806] (6 C.Rob., 204, note; Roscoe, I, 547, note);
the *Lisette* [1806] (6 C.Rob., 387; Roscoe, I, 587);
the *Mercurius* [1808] (Edw., 53; Roscoe, II, 15);
the *Sophia Elizabeth* [1809] (1 Acton, 46; Roscoe, I, 548, note);

during the American Civil War in addition to the cases of the *Hiawatha*, the *Bermuda* and the *Adela*, already cited, those of

the *Memphis* [1862] (Blatchford, 202, 260, 656);
the *Ella Warley* [1862] (Blatchford, 204, 288, 648);
the *Minna* [1863] (Blatchford, 333);
the *Stephen Hart* [1863] (Blatchford, 387);
the *Peterhoff* [1863] (5 Wall., 28; Scott's Cases, 760);
the *Circassian* [1864] (2 Wall., 135);
the *Cheshire* [1862] (Blatchford, 151, 156, 643; 3 Wall., 231; Scott's Cases, 1544);
the *Springbok* [1863] (Blatchford, 434);

and during the Spanish-American War:

the *Adula* [1900] (176 U.S. 361).

§ 4. *The last decades of the pre-codification period*

Referring back to my general observations in Sub-section 2 (*supra*, p. 419), I will finally give a few additional data from the period between the American Civil War and the Codification Conference of 1908-1909. This period of the pre-codification era has been rich in wars. Some of them, as far as I know, have had no significance for the law of prize, others have, but only partly in fields other than the law of blockade. No prize cases seem to have arisen, for example, as a result of the wars of 1864 and 1866 in which Denmark, Prussia, Austria, Sardinia and France were involved, although Denmark has proclaimed a blockade of the Prussian coast in 1864, and Austrian harbours, such as Venice, were blockaded by Sardinian or French naval forces in 1866.

The Netherlands have made some contribution to the modern law of blockade during their colonial war with the Sultanate of Atjeh (Acheen) in the northern part of the island of Sumatra in 1873. In fact, the only judgments ever pronounced by a Netherlands Prize Court in the period between the Crimean War and the Conferences of 1907 and 1908/09 related precisely to three cases of violation of a blockade, *viz.*, that of the coasts of the indigenous State of Atjeh in 1873 by sailing vessels from the Straits Settlements flying the British flag. This blockade was proclaimed by the colonial Governor General on 4 June 1873 and was maintained for a couple of years. The seizures of these three vessels were submitted to the regional prize court, the *Raad van Justitie* in Batavia (comp. this Chapter, *sub* C, section 1, *infra*, p. 587). One of them, the *Kim Ban An*, was released on the ground of neglect by the Dutch cruisers of their (recognized) obligation to warn her by a special notification; the two others, the *Ning Po* and the *Mariners' Hope*, were declared good and lawful prize. The text of the latter judgment can be found in the *Weekblad van het Recht* of 24 September 1874, No. 3760. The judgment stated that the vessel, after having been notified twice of the existence of the blockade on 25 June and 3 July 1873, was nevertheless encountered within three miles of the Netherlands Indies territory and on that ground captured on 4 July. The Court of Justice found that all the obligatory requirements had been fulfilled: the blockade had been notified not only to the vessel individually but also to the Consul General at Singapore and the authorities of the Straits Settlements, and the blockade was effective. The Court rejected in particular the owner's plea that a blockade by cruisers could not be considered effective: it was true that this was asserted by individual writers, but their assertion was not accepted: the validity of the blockade of the Confederate American coast of 2500 miles by cruisers during the Civil War had never been disputed, provided there was obvious danger of capture.

During the Serbo-Turkish and Russo-Turkish Wars of 1877-1878, when there was also a blockade of Durazzo, a high administrative tribunal in Italy (*Contenziosa diplomatica*) pronounced the illegality of the blockade of straits giving access to a sea (the Adriatic) that washes neutral States. This pronouncement on the cases of the *Britannia* and the *Matilde Bellagamba* [1878], which obviously was not a prize court decision, was quoted in the publication *Proceedings of the International Naval Conference 1908-1909* (Parliamentary Papers, Miscellaneous No. 5 (1919), Cd. 4555, p. 43).

On the blockade of Formosa (Tai-Wan) by France in October 1884 and Haiti's proclamation of a blockade of certain of her ports occupied by rebels in 1888, see Smith and Sibley's work on *International law as interpreted during the Russo-Japanese War* (London, 1905), pp. 337 and 338.

During the Spanish-American War of 1898 the United States blockaded the entire northern coast of Cuba and part of its southern coast. No blockade of Guantánamo was ever proclaimed by the President. The proclamation that was issued on 27 June established only a blockade of all ports of the southern coast of Cuba between Cape Frances on the west and Cape Cruz on the east, but as both Santiago and Guantánamo are to the eastward of Cape Cruz, they were not included. It appeared, however, that blockades of Santiago and Guantánamo had already been established in the early part of June by order of Admiral Sampson, commander of the naval forces then investing the ports on the southern coast of Cuba. See the case of the capture of the *Adula*, a British vessel intercepted while sailing from Kingston, Jamaica, with a premeditated intent to violate the blockade of Guantánamo, which her master knew was blockaded. The ship was condemned, see the judgment of the Supreme Court of 26 February 1900 (*per* Mr Justice Brown), 176 U.S. Reports 361 and the *Proceedings of the American Society of International Law* at its meeting of 23 and 24 April 1909, pp. 178-179.

During her war with Russia of 1904-1905 Japan proclaimed a blockade of Russia's leased territory of Port Arthur and Dalny (which according to Smith and Sibley's study of 1905, p. 321, was frequently broken by hundreds of Chinese junks) while Vladivostok was decreed to be in "a state of siege" (*ibid.*, p. 345). Twenty-three neutral vessels were captured by the Japanese during 1904 for attempting to run this blockade (*ibid.*, p. 322 and *infra*).

On their side, the Russians also took many prizes but not on account of a blockade. Their action was aimed at intercepting the carriage of contraband by neutral ships to Japanese ports or against certain forms of unneutral service. See on those Russian captures the appendices F (on the *Allanton* case, *ibid.*, pp. 437 *et seq.*) and K (on Russian acts of interference with neutral shipping, *ibid.*, pp. 464 *et seq.*) of Smith and Sibley's study and the relevant sections 3 and 5 of the present Chapter III under A.

As to Japan's blockade of the Russian possessions Hurst & Bray report in vol. II of their digest at pp. vi and vii only six Japanese judgments, and have printed in full at pp. 171-200 and 217-226 the texts of only nine of the twenty-three blockade cases. The six relate to the French *George* (p. 171), the British *Sishan* (p. 174), the German *Fuping* (pp. 177 and 180), the German *Veteran* (pp. 190 and 199) and the British *King Arthur* (p. 217), whereas three more texts are added concerning the British *Roseley* (pp. 228 and 235), the British *Aphrodite* (p. 241) and the Dutch *Wilhelmina* (p. 248). As appears from p. 227, the texts of all the other cases of carriage of Welsh coal to Vladivostok were omitted because the arguments and the decisions were substantially the same. They related to the neutral vessels *Lethington, Oakley, Burma, Siam, Apollo, Sylviana, Powderham, Severus, Romulus, Easby Atbey, Vegga, Venus* and *Harbarton*. The (traditional) type of cases adjudicated upon in this series is apparent from the following summary of the six.

The *George* was a small French steamship that in August 1904 left Taku with provisions and liquors for Port Arthur, with ostensible destination for Wei-hai-wei, succeeded in anchoring under one of the forts of Port Arthur, in transshipping her cargo there to a Russian vessel and in departing again the same night in ballast back to Taku. On this return voyage she was captured. Both in the first instance and in appeal it was held that the fact that such a capture on an outward voyage after a breach of the blockade inwards was no proof that the blockade was not effective. The ship was condemned because the master knew of the blockade.

The British *Sishan* was a ship, captured on the suspicion of intending to break the blockade. After her condemnation by the prize court of Sasebo she was, despite her failure to produce papers and the presence of a supercargo with full control on board, released in appeal because it was found that that intention, if it had existed, had either been abandoned or not been carried into execution.

The *Fuping* was a German vessel sailing with ostensible destination for Chefoo, having a Russian officer, a large quantity of paper roubles and military stores on board, and was captured out of her course on the way to Port Arthur. Both ship and cargo were condemned.

The *Veteran* was also a German ship, the property of a resident of Chefoo. She was captured on more than one suspicion: the ship's bell had been removed in order to secure secret navigation, she was hovering in the neighbourhood of the blockaded coast, and a change of course. The ship was in both instances condemned with her cargo; this belonged to the charterers of the ship who knew of the intended breach.

The British *King Arthur*, whose owner in Bombay was also her master, was ostensibly bound to Chinese Newchang. She was captured after entering and leaving Port Arthur, and had no success with her defense that the enemy had taken her into that port. The Court decided again that an occasional apparent failure of the vigilance of the blockading fleet was not sufficient to prove that the blockade was not effective. Neither was there ground for release on the plea that the blockade had been raised after the capture but before the hearing of the case by the prize court.

The rules on blockade as formulated by Japan at the outset of her war with Russia can be found in Chapter IV (Arts 21-31) of her Regulations relating to Capture at Sea of 7 March 1904 (Hurst and Bray II, Appendix B, pp. 427 *et seq.*). They deserve reproduction here because they mirror the views of a great maritime Power on the subject at the very end of the pre-codification period and therefore constitute the last authentic formulation of the rules on blockade, as brought about by the long progress of customary development during that period. This blockade, described by S. Takahashi in Part III of his *International Law applied to the Russo-Japanese War* (1908), was moreover, the last actual instance of an effective blockade of the traditional type before this institution fell more or less into disuse in the course of World War I.

Chapter IV.—*Blockade.*

Art. 21. A blockade is valid when the enemy's ports, bays, or coasts are effectively closed, and when it is clearly dangerous for ships to endeavour to leave, enter, or approach them.

Should a fleet, or warship, on account of bad weather, or in order to carry out the purposes of the blockade, leave the blockaded area temporarily, the blockade shall not thereby cease to be valid.

Art. 22. When a blockade is established, the commander of the blockading fleet or warship shall issue a declaration in accordance with Form No. 1, stating the area and the date of enforcement of the blockade.

Art. 23. If a blockade, after having been raised, is enforced anew, or if the area of the blockade is altered, a fresh declaration of blockade must be issued in accordance with the previous Article.

Art. 24. When the commander of a fleet, or warship, issues a declaration of blockade, he must at once follow the procedure mentioned under the following headings:—

1. report the declaration of blockade to the Minister of Marine;

2. transmit the declaration of blockade to the Japanese Ministers resident in the foreign countries adjacent to the blockaded area, and request them to notify the Governments concerned and the various Ministers and Consuls resident in those countries of the fact that a blockade has been established;

3. communicate the declaration of blockade to all foreign Consuls resident in neutral territories adjacent to the blockaded area, and take all necessary steps to make the fact of the blockade generally known;

4. communicate, as far as is possible the declaration of blockade by means of a flag of truce to the proper authorities, and to the Consuls of neutral Powers within the area of blockade.

Art. 25. In cases where the master of a ship has received direct warning from a Japanese warship, or where it is clear that he has become aware, either through public or private information, or by any other means whatsoever, of the existence of the blockade, he shall be held to have received actual notice of the said blockade.

Art. 26. In the following cases the master of a ship shall be held to have received presumptive notice of the blockade:—

1. When the master of a ship must be presumed to have received notice of the blockade owing to notice of its establishment having been given to the proper authorities of the country to which the ship belongs, and a sufficient interval having elapsed for its notification by the said authorities to the inhabitants of that country whether such notification was actually made or not.

2. When the fact of the blockade has been published generally, and the master of a ship must therefore be presumed to have received notice of the blockade.

Art. 27. Ships coming under the following categories shall be held to have committed a breach of blockade outwards:—

1. A ship escaping outwards from the blockaded area or trying to do so.

2. A ship which being outside the blockaded area takes on board, or tries to take on board, cargo from a ship which has committed a breach of blockade outwards.

Art. 28. In cases where a ship comes under any of the following clauses the provisions of the preceding article shall not apply:—

1. When a ship leaves the blockaded area outward bound with the special permission of the Imperial Government, or of the commander of the blockading fleet or warship.

2. When a ship which has entered port during the blockade without having received notice of its establishment leaves port without a cargo.

3. When a ship which was within the blockaded area at the time of the establishment of the blockade leaves port without a cargo.

4. When a ship which had taken cargo on board within the blockaded area before the establishment of the blockade leaves port.

Art. 29. A ship which, having received notice of the blockade, comes under any one of the following clauses shall be held to have committed a breach of blockade inwards:—

1. A ship which, having crossed the line of blockade, enters the blockaded area, or tries to do so.

2. A ship which, whatever the destination given in her papers may be, is in the neighbourhood of the blockaded area, and is for good reason considered to be directing her course towards the interior of that area.

3. A ship which, while outside the blockaded area, tranships her cargo to another, and by causing that other to cross the line of blockade, assists in carrying the said cargo inside the blockaded area, or tries to do so.

4. A ship which sails with the blockaded port as her destination.

Art. 30. In cases where a ship comes under any one of the following clauses, the provisions of the preceding Article shall not apply:—

1. When a ship has received the special permission of the Imperial Government, or of the commander of the blockading fleet or warship.

2. When the master of a ship, hoping to have the good luck to find the blockade raised, and with the intention of changing his destination should this not be the case, makes the blockaded port his destination, and it is considered that there is a reason for leniency on account of the fact that the ship has sailed from an exceedingly remote locality.

3. When it is clear that the master of a ship has already abandoned his intention of making the blockaded port the ship's destination.

4. When, on account of bad weather, lack of provisions or other unavoidable causes, the necessity arises for a ship to put into port, and there being no other port or bay at which she can call, she enters the blockaded area.

Art. 31. When a blockade is raised, the commander of the blockading fleet or warship must at once report the fact to the Minister of Marine, and take all necessary steps to make the fact generally known.

The way in which the *Institut de droit international* regarded the legal situation in the field of blockade in the 1880's appears from §§ 35-44 under II of its *Règlement international des prises maritimes*, adopted at its session of 1882 in Turin:

7.—*Du blocus.*

§ 35.—Le blocus déclaré et notifié est effectif lorsqu'il existe un danger imminent pour l'entrée ou la sortie du port bloqué, à cause d'un nombre suffisant de navires de guerre stationnés ou ne s'écartant que momentanément de leur station.

§ 36.—La déclaration du blocus doit déterminer non seulement les limites du blocus par leurs latitude et longitude, et le moment précis où le blocus commencera, mais encore, éventuellement, le délai qui peut être accordé aux navires de commerce pour décharger, recharger et sortir du port (§ 7).

§ 37.—Le commandant du blocus doit, en outre, notifier la déclaration du blocus aux autorités et aux consuls du lieu bloqué. Les mêmes formalités seront remplies lors du rétablissement d'un blocus qui a cessé d'être effectif, et lorsque le blocus sera étendu à des points nouveaux.

§ 38.—Si les navires bloquants s'éloignent de leur station pour un motif autre que le mauvais temps constaté, le blocus est considéré comme levé; il doit alors être de nouveau déclaré et notifié.

§ 39.—Il est interdit aux navires de commerce d'entrer dans les places et ports qui se trouvent en état de blocus et d'en sortir.

§ 40.—Cependant il est permis aux navires de commerce d'entrer, pour cause de mauvais temps, dans le port bloqué, mais seulement après constatation par le commandant du blocus, de la persistance de la force majeure.

§ 41.—S'il est évident qu'un navire de commerce approchant du port bloqué n'a pas eu connaissance du blocus déclaré et effectif, le commandant du blocus l'en avertira, inscrira l'avertissement dans les papiers de bord du navire averti, tout au moins dans le certificat de nationalité et dans le journal de bord, en marquant la date de l'avertissement, et invitera le navire à s'éloigner du port bloqué, en l'autorisant à continuer son voyage vers un port non bloqué.

§ 42.—On admet l'ignorance du blocus, lorsque le temps écoulé depuis la déclaration du blocus est trop peu considérable pour que le navire en cours de voyage, qui a tenté d'entrer dans le port bloqué, ait pu en être instruit.

§ 43.—Un navire de commerce sera saisi pour violation de blocus lorsqu'il aura essayé par force ou par ruse de pénétrer à travers la ligne de blocus, ou si, après avoir été renvoyé une première fois, il a essayé de nouveau de pénétrer dans le même port bloqué.

§ 44.—Ni le fait qu'un navire de commerce est dirigé sur un port bloqué, ni le simple affrètement, ni la seule destination du navire pour un tel port, ne justifient la saisie pour violation du blocus. En aucun cas, la supposition d'un voyage continue ne peut justifier la condamnation pour violation de blocus.

Section 5. UNNEUTRAL SERVICE

General

What is nowadays called "unneutral service" ("assistance hostile", "neutralitätswidrige" or "feindselige Unterstützung", etc.) is a vaguely circumscribed aggregate of actions, other than the carriage of contraband and the breach of a blockade, by neutral subjects, consisting of multifarious ways of helping a belligerent across the sea. This subject, also, has neutrality and prize law aspects.

One of the neutrality aspects of this kind of activity is the question to what extent a neutral State is legally bound to prohibit and prevent it. Another is the question whether and to what extent, if no such obligation exists, a neutral State is obliged to tolerate that a belligerent State thwarts such activity, *e.g.*, by removing enemy soldiers from a vessel sailing under a neutral flag. Both these questions belong to Part IX-B (vol. X) of this publication, see pp. 85-86 and 96-98.

Although no sharp distinction can be made between the neutrality and the prize law aspects, in this context I will discuss only the typically prize law point of view, *viz.*, the question of the consequences resulting from such activities for their perpetrators as a sanction under the law of prize.

The chief historic example of this type of assistance given to a belligerent Power by neutral or other non-enemy merchant ships is the transport of soldiers or marines to that Power. The concept of unneutral assistance as a separate legal category has indeed begun its career as a, somewhat illogical appendix to the provisions on contraband, inclusive of those providing for their "confiscation" also. This direct connexion has, as a consequence, often in earlier times been called the transport of quasi-contraband or *contrebande par analogie*. It has first been established by bilateral conventions, the provisions of which to all intents and purposes repeat themselves in the history of treaties.

Cases in which the provision concerning the transport of soldiers and other military men was attached to a contraband clause were, *e.g.*, those obtaining in the conventions of

18 April 1646 between France and the United Netherlands (Dumont, VI[1], 342), sub I:

> "excepté toutefois [*i.e.*, from release] les marchandises de contrebande, à savoir poudres, mousquets, etc. ...; même ne pourront porter ny transporter des hommes pour le service des Ennemis; auquel cas le tout sera de bonne prise ...";

17 December 1650 between the Netherlands and Spain (Dumont, VI[1], 570; Parry, 2, 259), Article 6:

> "De plus pour d'autant mieux prevenir les différents qui pourroient naistre touchant la designation des Marchandises deffenduës, et de Contrebande, il a esté déclaré, et convenu, que soubs ledit nom seront comprises toutes Armes à feu, et assortissements d'icelles, comme Canons, mousquets, etc. ... Pareillement sont entendues soubs le mesme nom de Marchandises deffenduës et de Contrebande toutes autres Armes, comme etc. ... Est encore prohibé soubs ledit nom le transport de gens de Guerre, de Chevaux, etc. ...;

2/12 October 1679 between the Netherlands and Sweden (Dumont, VII[1], 437; Parry, 15, 331), Article 22.

Although the treaty clause concerning the transport of troops or individual military men was usually inserted in a provision dealing with contraband cargoes, there were also instances in which it was not appended to such a provision, but to one concerning the freedom of enemy goods on neutral vessels. This analogy between cargoes and soldiers can be found, *inter alia*, in Article 22 of the Franco-Netherlands treaty of commerce of 10 August 1678 (Dumont, VII[1], 350; Parry, 14, 399):

> "Et comme il a été réglé ci-dessus qu'un Navire libre affranchira les Denrées y chargées, il a été en outre accordé & convenu, que cette Liberté s'étendra aussi aux Personnes qui se trouveront en un Navire libre; à tel effet que quoiqu'elles soient Ennemis de l'un & de l'autre des Parties, ou de l'une d'icelles, pourtant se trouvans dans le Navire libre, n'en pourront estre tirées, si ce n'est qu'ils fussent Gens de Guerre, & effectivement en service des dits Ennemis",

and in the corresponding Article 22 of the treaty between the Netherlands and Sweden of 2/12 October 1679 (*supra*):

> "sicut jam circa Navigia & Merces stipulatum est, ut Naves liberae libertatem quoque Mercimoniis vindicent; ita ulterius conventum est, eandem libertatcm ad personas extendi debere, quae Navi libera vehuntur, eo cum effectu, ut quamvis utriusque Partis aut alterius Hostes sint, ex Navi ista libera non extrahantur, nisi milites sint & hostibus effective ministeria sua praestent."

The designation of the persons whose presence on board was held to constitute unneutral service (conveyance of quasi-contraband) was not always the same: "gens de guerre" or soldiers in general in some cases, officers in others. Comp., for example, the difference between the two treaties, concluded between the same Powers (the Netherlands and Sweden) within the space of four years: 26 November 1675 (Dumont, VII[1], 316; Parry, 14, 41), Article 8, in which the expression was "exceptis tantum Ducibus et Officialibus hostilibus", and 2/12 October 1679 (Dumont, VII[1], 437; Parry; 15, 331) Article 22, where the text reads "nisi milites sint & hostibus effective ministeria sua praestent". Not seldom also a difference was made between the transport of troops and that of isolated officers or volunteers.

In the case of the *Julius Caesar* during the French blockade of Mexican ports in 1842, her passengers had to prove that they were not on their way in order to embrace the cause of the Mexican insurgents as *volontaires* (see *R.A.I.*, I, 482 *et seq.*, 492 *et seq.*).

The case law

After this general summary of the elements of unneutral service, I will now turn to a more detailed survey of the case law, in particular that relating to (1) the transportation of troops or military men, (2) the carriage of despatches and (3) the employment of neutral ships by the enemy.

1. Transport of troops or military men

Cases in which the transportation of troops was the ground for condemnation were in Lord Stowell's time those of

the *Carolina* (Nordquist, Master) [1802] (4 C.Rob., 256; Roscoe, I, 385), a Swedish ship, which was chartered in 1798 by a merchant of Livorno to go on a trading voyage to Cività Vecchia and whose master was ordered to hold her there in readiness to be put at the disposal of the French Commissary. After returning from a visit to Rome to solicit the interference of the Swedish consul, he found his ship fitted up as a transport. He then provided for an insurance to be made for the benefit of the owner, took on board 150 dragoons, and sailed with 57 other vessels, not knowing to what destination. At least, such was his alleged report of the events. They sailed in fact to Alexandria where the troops were landed. Subsequently the *Carolina* was captured by the British when they took the town. The ship was later lost in the possession of the captors before she had been brought to adjudication. The court obviously gave no credit to the master's story and rejected the petition of the owners for reparation of the damage:

> "It did not appear that the master made any protest or remonstrance against the service; but rather in proof of his voluntary assent he proceeded to insure the vessel, and to provide the necessary provisions for the voyage. It is now, however, said that this was an act under duress, and that it is a by-gone transaction. On the former part of this representation my opinion is that a man cannot be permitted to aver that he was an involuntary agent in such a transaction. If an act of force, exercised by one belligerent on a neutral ship or person, is to be deemd a sufficient justification for any act done by him contrary to the known duties of the neutral character, there would be no end of any prohibition under the law of nations to carry contraband or to engage in any other hostile act. If any loss is sustained in such a service, the neutral yielding to such demands must seek redress against the government that has imposed the restraint upon him. He has no right to expect that the British Government should pay for the injustice of its public enemy. If this vessel had been taken *in delicto* I should have felt no hesitation in saying that she must have been subject to condemnation. Whether the troops were received on board voluntarily or involuntarily could make no difference." [The argument that it was "a by-gone transaction" was equally dismissed: the ship was liable to condemnation even after the service had ceased, if it was still subservient to purposes of the belligerent];

the *Friendship* (Collard, Master) [1807] (6 C.Rob., 420; Roscoe, I, 599), an American ship, which carried ninety passengers from Baltimore and Annapolis to Bordeaux, among them eighty-four officers and marines, and with hardly any cargo on board. Was this vessel to be considered as a neutral vessel carrying on an innoxious commerce, or as a transport vessel engaged in the immediate military service of the enemy? On the facts of the case the Court decided that the *Friendship* was a transport vessel. I quote from the judgment because it was very elaborate in defining the limits of the right of a belligerent to sanction the conveyance of soldiers by neutrals:

> "The form of the contract of conveyance is of no importance. The substance of the thing is this: whether they are vessels hired by the agents of the Government, for the purpose of conveying soldiers or stores in the service of the State. That is the substance; and it signifies nothing whether the men so conveyed are to be put into action on an immediate action or not. The mere shifting of drafts in detachments ... is an ordinary employment of transport vessels, and it is a distinction totally unimportant, whether this or that case may be connected with the immediate active service of the enemy ... If the contract is not on board, but is industriously concealed from the master, who professes to know nothing about it, or if he wilfully suppresses the fact, though it is in his knowledge, that will not defeat the Courts of the belligerents of their right of putting the proper construction on the act done. This then appears that it was a transaction entered into with the privity and consent of the French Government [a conclusion that was supported by further strong evidence]. It would be a very different case if a vessel appeared to be carrying only a few individual invalided soldiers or discharged sailors taken on board by chance and at their own charge .... If [a military officer in the service of the enemy] was going merely as an ordinary passenger, as other passengers do, and at his own expense, the question would present itself in a different form."

The ship was condemned with all cargo on board;

the *Orozembo* (Brewster, Master) [1807] (6 C.Rob., 430; Roscoe, I, 605), another American vessel that was condemned on a comparable ground. This judgment stressed the inconclusiveness of the number of the transported military persons, who were in fact travelling to French-occupied Dutch Batavia via Portuguese Macao:

> "Number alone is an insignificant circumstance in the considerations on which the principle of law on this subject is built, since fewer persons of high quality and character may be of more importance than a much greater number of persons of lower condition. To send but one veteran general of France to take the command of the forces of Batavia might be a much more noxious act than the conveyance of a whole regiment".

It is worth mentioning that during the Sino-Japanese War of 1894 the transport of "contraband persons", such as soldiers, gave rise to one further application of the doctrine of continuous voyage (on this doctrine comp. section 3 (Contraband), § 2 (Destination), *supra*, pp. 367). This was the case of certain Frenchmen travelling with technical inventions for use in warfare to the Chinese fleet via intermediate ports, first on board the English ss. *Gaelic*, later transhipped to the French ss. *Sydney*. They were removed from this vessel in a Japanese port under protest by the French consul (Takahashi, pp. 52-63; 64-72; Westlake's introduction, pp. xxiii-xxvii; K. Strupp's *Wörterbuch des Völkerrechts und der Diplomatie*, vol. I, 196, *voce* "Chinesisch-Japanischer Krieg"). Comp. vol. X of this publication, pp. 135-136.

A special case was that of the British *Nigretia* [1905] (Hurst & Bray, II, 201, 213), captured on a voyage to Vladivostok with two Russian naval officers on board. They had formerly belonged to a Russian destroyer that had taken refuge in the neutral Chinese harbour of Chefoo and had subsequently been blown up there. They had later been released by the Chinese Government on parole. The passage of the officers, ostensibly as clerks and supercargoes, was arranged by a Russian subject, who chartered the ship for that purpose. She was condemned together with her cargo on the ground of privity of the master and the charterer.

Even the *Institut de droit international* still maintained that close connection between the two groups of 'contraband' in § 34 of its *Règlement international des prises maritimes*, adopted at Turin in 1882:

> "Sont assimilés au transport interdit de contrebande de guerre les transports des troupes pour les opérations militaires sur terre et sur mer de l'ennemi, ainsi que les transports de la correspondance officielle de l'ennemi, par les navires de commerce nationaux, neutres ou ennemis",

and in its *Réglementation internationale de la contrebande de guerre*, adopted at Venice in 1896, in §§ 6-8 of which 'service de transport' was inserted, *sub* B, as a special form of the transport of contraband (see *infra*, pp. 468-469).

It was, however, not only the conveyance of military men to the enemy that caused the other belligerent to arrest a neutral vessel on that account. In the famous *Trent* case of 1861 (*R.A.I.*, I, 492; Wharton, *Digest*, §§ 325 *et seq.*), it was the presence on board of diplomats charged with an important mission,

Mason and Slidell. The British Government strongly protested to the United States Government, but did not succeed in obtaining their release. However, no confiscation of the *Trent* followed. The *Trent* was sailing from a neutral (Spanish Havana) to another neutral (Danish St. Thomas) port.

2. *Carriage of despatches*

A third well-known form of unneutral service was the carrying of important despatches by a neutral vessel to a belligerent. Best known are two cases of 1808, relating to the Bremen vessel *Atalanta* (6 C.Rob., 440-460; Roscoe, I, 607), respectively the American vessel *Caroline* (Doah, Master) (6 C.Rob., 461-470; Roscoe, I, 615). Sir William Scott distinguished the two, confiscating the *Atalanta*, but restoring the *Caroline* (*infra*, pp. 462 *et seq.*). The cause of that distinction was a difference in the degree of noxiousness of the acts of the transporting vessel.

The issue in such cases was what was to be understood by "despatches" and whether particular despatches could reasonably be held to come within the definition. In some of the judgments despatches were described as including "all official communications of official persons on the public affairs of the Government". The seriousness of specific forms of this offence was stressed in the following sentences (6 C.Rob., 455):

> "Nor let it be supposed, that it is an act of light and casual importance. The consequence of such a service is indefinite, infinitely beyond the effect of any contraband that can be conveyed. The carrying of two or three cargoes of stores is necessarily an assistance of a limited nature; but in the transmission of despatches may be conveyed the entire plan of a campaign that may defeat all the projects of the other belligerent in that quarter of the world."

Unlike present-day conditions of telecommunications the transport of despatches by neutral vessels to the captor's enemy was two centuries ago a vital element in warfare. Hence the relative frequency of prize court decisions relating to such transport in the days of Sir William Scott at the end of the 18th and the beginning of the 19th century. A perusal of the cases shows how the introduction of this particular ground of condemnation of neutral vessels has gradually taken root in the customary law of maritime prize. Especially interesting are the exposé given by the President in his very elaborate judgment of 4 March 1808 concerning the Bremen *Atalanta* (Klein, Master) (6 C.Rob., 440 *et seq.*, at pp. 455 *et seq.*; Roscoe, I, 607), and the footnotes appended by Roscoe to his report on the *Caroline* (Doah, Master) (6 C.Rob., 461 *et seq.*). From those reports, supported by a great number of precedents, and the footnotes, it appears that claims for the condemnation of vessels on this ground had already been advanced earlier in several cases:

the *Sally* (Griffiths, Master) [1795] (3 C.Rob., 300, footnote *a*; Roscoe, I, 28 and 610);

the *Constitution* (Tate, Master) [Lords, 1802] (6 C.Rob., at pp. 455-456; Roscoe, I, 610);

the *Hope* (Ferrier, Master) [Lords, 1803] (6 C.Rob., at pp. 456-457; Roscoe, I, 610-611);

the *Lisette* (Petersen, Master) [1807] (6 C.Rob., at pp. 457-458; Roscoe, I, 587 *et seq.*, at p. 611);

the *Trende Söstre* (Missen, Master) [1807] (6 C.Rob., footnote *a* at pp. 390-392; Roscoe, I, 588);

the *Hope* (Jones, Master) [1808] (6 C.Rob., footnote at p. 463; Roscoe, I, 588 *et seq.*, and at p. 611).

Those cases, however, presented specific features which prevented the condemnation of four of the ships. Only the *Constitution* was condemned, because it was also a case of reserved colonial trade between Spanish Havana and Truxillo (comp. *infra*, Section 6, pp. 471). The despatches on the *Sally* from the French Minister in America were of a purely commercial nature and the vessel had sailed before the knowledge of hostilities; what was found on board the *Hope* [1803] was nothing but a receipt, appearing to have been given by the captain, for a packet taken by him from the Governor of Dutch Batavia, to be transmitted to the Dutch Minister in America, and to be forwarded ultimately to Amsterdam, but which had probably been sent by some other American ship lying at Batavia; in the *Lisette*, which was captured on her return voyage, the Court repudiated the testimony of a woman on board that the ship had carried a Dutch packet in the Danish mailbag, because she herself had taken the letters on board by fraud against the master who had conducted himself *optima fide*; and the *Trende Söstre* was released because before her seizure her port of destination (Cape of Good Hope) had ceased to be a colony of the enemy (Holland). But in all those cases the principle of the confiscatability of a vessel which transported enemy despatches was uniformly asserted. That principle itself was exposed by Sir William Scott in the *Atalanta*—a clear case of the fraudulent concealment of despatches, found on a Bremen ship, which was captured in 1807 on a voyage from Batavia to Bremen via the French Isle de France (the old name of Mauritius), where a packet containing despatches from the Government of that island to the Minister of Marine at Paris had been taken on board by the master and one of the supercargoes. The President argued as follows:

> "What might be the consequences of a simple transmission of despatches I am not called upon by the necessities of the present case to decide because I have already pronounced this to be a fraudulent case. That the simple carrying of despatches between the colonies and the mother country of the enemy is a service highly injurious to the other belligerent is most obvious. In the present state of the world, in the hostilities of European powers, it is an object of great importance to preserve the connection between the mother country and her colonies; and to interrupt that connection, on the part of the other belligerent, is one of the most energetic operations of war. The importance of keeping up that connection, for the concentration of troops and for various military purposes, is manifest; and, I may add, for the supply of civil assistance also and support, because the infliction of civil distress, for the purpose of compelling a surrender, forms no inconsiderable part of the operations of war. It is not to be argued, therefore, that the importance of

these despatches might relate only to the civil wants of the colony, and that it is necessary to show a military tendency, because the object of compelling a surrender being a measure of war, whatever is conclusive to that event must also be considered, in the contemplation of law, as an object of hostility, although not produced by operations strictly military .... If a war intervenes, and the other belligerent prevails to interrupt the communication, any person stepping in to lend himself to effect the same purpose under the privilege of an ostensible neutral character, does in fact place himself in the service of the enemy State, and is justly to be considered in that character. Nor let it be supposed that it is an act of light and casual importance. The consequence of such a service is indefinite, infinitely beyond the effect of any contraband that can be conveyed. The carrying of two or three cargoes of stores is necessarily an assistance of a limited nature; but in the transmission of despatches may be conveyed the entire plan of a campaign that may defeat all the projects of the other belligerent in that quarter of the world. ... The case of despatches is very different [from that of contraband]; it is impossible to limit a letter to so small a size as not to be capable of producing the most important consequences in the operations of the enemy. It is a service therefore which, in whatever degree it exists, can only be considered in one character, as an act of the most noxious and hostile nature."

The decision in the *Caroline* (Doah, Master) [1 April 1808] (6 C.Rob., 461; Roscoe, I, 615) re-affirmed the principles set out in the *Atalanta* (6 C.Rob., 440; Roscoe, I, 607), but the circumstances of the new case (an American ship having on board despatches from the Minister and Consul of France in the United States to the Government of France) dit not bring it within the range of the considerations developed in the *Atalanta* judgment of a few weeks previously, because the seized despatches were those sent by an ambassador, situated in a neutral country, to his own government. Sir William Scott began by repeating his earlier finding:

"That the carrying the despatches between the mother country and her colonies is criminal can hardly be doubted; and I have never heard of a claim of privilege of this kind being asserted on the part of any nation or by any individual. On the contrary, the artifices of clandestinity and concealment, with which such acts have always been accompanied, strongly betray the opinion which the individuals themselves entertain of the right,"

and went on by defining the concept of "despatches":

"It has been asked, what are despatches? to which, I think, the answer may safely be returned: that they are all official communications of official persons on the public affairs of the government. The comparative importance of the particular papers is immaterial, since the Court will not construct a scale of relative importance, which in fact it has not the means of doing, with any degree of accuracy or with satisfaction to itself; it is sufficient they relate to the public business of the enemy, be it great or small."

But then he continued his argument by asking whether the legal situation was not different when the despatches did not come from any part of the enemy's territory but "from persons who were, in a peculiar manner, the favourite objects of the protection of the law of nations, ambassadors, resident in a neutral country". He confessed that he had from the outset been "struck very forcibly by the distinction between the two classes of case", made during the proceedings, and he accepted the solidity of the distinction:

"The former cases were cases of neutral ships, carrying the enemy's despatches from his colonies to the mother country. In all such cases you have a right to conclude that the effect of those despatches is hostile to yourself ... But the neutral country has a right to preserve its relations with the enemy, and you are not at liberty to conclude that any communication between them can partake in any degree of the nature of hostility against you ... If there should be private reason to suppose that the confidence in the good faith of the neutral State has a doubtful foundation, that is matter for the caution of the government, to be counteracted by just measures of preventive policy, but is no ground on which this Court can pronounce that the neutral character has violated his duty by bearing despatches ...".

After further development of his reasoning Sir William Scott restored ship and cargo on payment of captor's expenses.

Other precedents, dating from the period of the Napoleonic wars, are those concerning the carrying of despatches on board the Danish *Constantia* (Holbeck, Master) [1808] (6 C.Rob., 461, footnote *a*; Roscoe, I, 613, footnote *a*), and the American vessels the *Susan* and the *Hope* (Jones, Master) [1808] (both in 6 C.Rob., footnote (*a*) at pp. 461-463; Roscoe, I, footnote at p. 614), the *Madison* [1810] (Edw., 224; Roscoe, II, 42), and the *Rapid (No. 1)* [1810] (Edw., 228; Roscoe, II, 45).

The Danish vessel *Constantia* was seized on a voyage from Isle de France to Copenhagen, having on board a packet which was to be delivered to the French Ambassador at Copenhagen, to be forwarded by him to the departments of his Government in France.

The *Susan* and the *Hope* [1808] were among a number of neutral vessels captured on a voyage from Bordeaux to New York.

The *Susan* had a packet on board addressed to the Prefect of the Isle de France, but the master averred his ignorance of its contents; this defence was not accepted as a general rule but might be taken into account if the captain had been made the victim of a deception imposed on him by his private agent or by the government of the enemy; *in casu* the ship was condemned, but the cargo restored, even that part belonging to the owner of the ship, as it did not appear that the master had been appointed agent for the cargo. As to the master's own prayer that he might be allowed his private adventure, the Court refused him its usual indulgence in that respect because the offence had originated chiefly in his misconduct of culpable negligence.

The *Hope* [1808] had on board not only various despatches to the officers of the government in the French West Indian islands and the Isle de France, but also a military officer of high rank who had lately come from Martinique and was returning to that island, but who had come aboard in the disguise of a merchant's clerk; in this case also, the plea of ignorance was rejected and the same decisions were made.

The two cases of 1810 concerning the *Madison* and the *Rapid (No. 1)* related,

the first, to an American vessel which had been captured on a previous voyage by a French privateer and brought under duress into the port of Dieppe, from which she had later sailed in ballast to Baltimore with on board despatches from the enemy government to its consul in the neutral United States: rejecting the charge that she had sailed from a blockaded port and considering that the carrying of despatches of this kind was no ground for condemnation, the ship was restored, subject to the payment of costs;

the second, to another neutral vessel, which carried despatches from a belligerent subject which the master had accepted in a neutral port for conveyance together with a number of private letters; in this case the master's plea of ignorance of the despatches was admitted as an exception to the rigid rule.

In its judgments concerning the *Calchas* [1905] (Hurst & Bray, I, 141) and the *St. Kilda* [1908] (*ibid.*, I, 188), the Russian prize court has much later stressed the difference between enemy despatches and ordinary correspondence:

> "there are no sufficient grounds for condemning a vessel when it is not chartered specially for the purpose of carrying the enemy correspondence, but is merely carrying mails from neutral ports to enemy ports in the course of its voyage, such mails being, moreover, in sealed bags, the contents of which could not be known, and *a fortiori* in cases where the enemy correspondence itself could not affect the military operations of the war",

or (at p. 197):

> "It is only in a limited sense that enemy mails can be admitted to be contraband of war, *i.e.*, despatches and correspondence directed to the enemy commanders and having immediate reference to the operations of war, not diplomatic correspondence, the contents of which up to the present have not been established."

As a further form of assistance to the enemy international practice later added to the main types

the chartering or employment of a neutral ship by a belligerent Government, which was the legal ground of the confiscation of the *Rebecca* in 1811 (2 Acton, 119). In that case it was held that

> "A neutral vessel chartered or employed by a belligerent Government to carry a cargo on its behalf and acting under the orders or direction of that Government or of its officers is liable to condemnation as en enemy ship together with the cargo so carried."

This formula was later changed in Article 46 of the London Declaration of 1909, not to the satisfaction of Sir Samuel Evans (case of the *Thor* of 1904).

The case law has demonstrated that employment of neutral vessels by the enemy can take different forms and show varying degrees of damage to the capturing belligerent. This experience has paved the way to a distinction between graver and lighter instances of assistance and a corresponding distinction between the sanctions permissible in one case and in the other, distinctions which have not been precisely defined until the session of the *Institut de droit international* in Venice of 1896 and the London Conference on Naval Warfare of 1908-1909. The employment can be based on a contract between the belligerent Government and the neutral ship owner, but can also find its origin in an act of mere force by the belligerents. A few instances of such varying forms and degrees of seriousness follow below. The judgments were sometimes very severe against the neutral owners.

The main cases handed down to us through prize proceedings are those relative to another *Carolina* (Nordquist, Master) [1802] (4 C.Rob., 256; Roscoe, I, 385) and to the American *Orozembo* [1807] (6 C.Rob., 420, 430; Roscoe, I, 599, 605) (see *supra*, p. 459).

The *Carolina* was a Swedish ship, captured at the taking of French-occupied Alexandria (Egypt) by the British, and lost in the possession of the captors before she had been brought to adjudication. The ship had had a somewhat adventurous voyage: first from Livorno to Cività Vecchia under a normal charter of 1798, subsequently held up in this port as a consequence of an embargo laid by the French upon all the vessels there, thereupon fitted out as a transport by the French Commissary, and finally sent to Alexandria with a load of French troops on board, who were landed there before the British forces appeared. I will quote a few passages from the *Carolina* judgment:

> "If an act of force, exercised by one belligerent on a neutral ship or person, is to be deemed a sufficient justification for any act done by him, contrary to the known duties of the neutral character, there would be an end of any prohibition under the law of nations to carry contraband, or to engage in any other hostile act. If any loss is sustained in such a service, the neutral yielding to such demands, must seek redress against the government that has imposed the restraint upon him. He has no right to expect that the British government should pay for the injustice of its public enemy. If this vessel had been taken *in delicto*, I should have felt no hesitation in saying that she must have been subject to condemnation. Whether the troops were received on board voluntarily, or involuntarily, could make no difference.
>
> Then as to its being a by-gone transaction,—had she divested herself of the character of a French transport?"

That question was also answered against the ship owners on factual grounds set out in the following judgment.

The American *Orozembo* [1807] (6 C.Rob., 430; Roscoe, I, 605), adjudicated together with the *Friendship*, was confiscated although neither the ship owner nor the master were guilty of any connivance, and even though the master had been employed at the time of the capture in the service of the enemy in transporting military persons first to Macao, and ultimately to Netherlands Batavia. I insert again a few passages from the judgment:

> "That a vessel hired by the enemy for the conveyance of military persons is to be considered as a transport subject to condemnation has been in a recent case (*supra*) held by this Court, and on other occasions. What is the number of military persons that shall constitute such a case it may be difficult to define. In the former case there were many, in the present there are much fewer in number; but I accede to what has been observed in argument, that number alone is an insignificant circumstance in the considerations on which the principle of law on this subject is built, since fewer persons of high quality and character may be of more importance than a much greater number of persons of lower condition. To send out one veteran general of France to take the command of the forces at Batavia might be a much more noxious act than the conveyance of a whole regiment."

The military persons on this ship were only three, and there were, besides, two other persons who were going to be employed in civil capacities in the (French) Government of Batavia.

The Court later continued as follows:

> "It has been argued that the master was ignorant of the character of the service on which he was engaged, and that, in order to support the penalty, it would be necessary that there should be some proof of delinquency in him or his owner. But I conceive that is not necessary; it will be sufficient if there is an injury arising to the belligerent from the employment in which the vessel is found. In the case of the Swedish vessel [the *Carolina* of 1802] there was no *mens rea* in the owner, or in any other person acting under his authority. The master was an involuntary agent, acting under compulsion put upon him by the officers of the French Government, and, so far as intention alone is considered, perfectly innocent. In the same manner, in cases of *bona fide* ignorance, there may be no actual delinquency; but if the service is injurious, that will be sufficient to give the belligerent a right to prevent the thing from being done, or at least repeated, by enforcing the penalty of confiscation."

To the same effect the *Friendship* (Roscoe, I, 599).

The decision sometimes hinged on the interpretation of a treaty provision or an Order in Council. Thus, in 1747, the hiring of a ship upon charter-party by the French was, in the case of the Swedish *Elizabeth Catharina* (Pratt-Lee, 115 *et seq*., at p. 119) construed as "lending the ship to them in the sense of Art. 4 of the Order in Council of 1664".

Another instance of this form of unneutral service was discussed by the Admiralty Court in an earlier case relating to the capture of the Swedish vessel the *Ringende Jacob* [1798] (1 C.Rob., 89; Roscoe, I, 60). Her condemnation was asked for by the captor on the ground that she had been freighted to the enemy, but the Court decided that that act was not "the lending the ship to the enemy" as mentioned in the Swedish treaty of 21 October 1661, forbidding the subjects of either Power to sell or lend their ships for the use and advantage of the enemy of the other; what was meant by that was that it should be forbidden to give up the use and the management of their ships directly to the enemy, or to put them under his absolute power and direction.

English prize courts would seem only seldom to have dismissed a claim of the captor in cases of these kinds. In a much later case, however, that of the *Hanametal* of 1914 (B.C.P.C., I, 347), which carried fugitives from Shanghai to Tsingtao and no cargo, the Supreme Court of Hong-Kong based its release of the ship on the argument that

> "neither the text-books nor the cases on this branch of law, such as that of the *Friendship* of 1807 [(6 C.Rob., 420; Roscoe, I, 559)], give any direct support to the doctrine that the carriage of non-combatants from a belligerent port is an unneutral service".

Far-Eastern wars later produced further examples of the capture of a neutral vessel for asserted unneutral service, namely, in the case of

the *Sydney* during the Sino-Japanese war of 1894-1895 (Takahashi, 64), when two engineers, on their way from the port of Yokohama to Kobé, with the intention of entering the service of China, were removed in the harbour of Kobé from an English vessel by a Japanese warship.

In later times the concept of unneutral service was extended to other forms of action by neutral vessels which no longer had any affinity with the carriage of contraband (comp., *infra*, p. 469).

At the very end of the pre-codification period new cases of employment of neutral vessels by the enemy occurred in the Far East during the Russo-Japanese War of 1904-1905 in their form of chartering on behalf of the Russian Government, sometimes for reconnoitering purposes. The Japanese Regulations of 7 March 1904 relating to Capture at Sea (which still used the obsolete expressions "contraband persons" and "contraband documents") in Arts. 37 and 47 paid special attention to this type of unneutral service indicated as "scouting". See the cases of

the German *Industrie* (Hurst & Bray, II, 323; Takahashi, II, p. 732), chartered by the American owner of a pro-Russian newspaper at Chinese Chefoo, ostensibly employed for collecting news for that paper, but in fact for obtaining intelligence about the Japanese fleet for the Russian Government, by cruising in its neighbourhood;

the French *Quang-Nam* (Hurst & Bray, II, 343; Takahashi, II, 735), plying between Formosa and the Pescadores and captured in the dangerous Hatto Channel in a locality where it was easy to gather information concerning the Japanese defences and the movements of the Japanese fleet;

and the American *Australia* (Hurst & Bray, II, 373), a case of the carrying of various supplies and mails belonging to the Russian Government to ports on the Sea of Okhotsk and the Behring Sea.

—Sanctions against unneutral service

The sanctions imposed upon those guilty of unneutral service were in more serious cases the confiscation of the ship, sometimes also of her cargo. Lord Stowell used to distinguish cases in which either whole troops were involved or where the transport took place on specially chartered ships from others of a more innocent character.

At a much later stage, during the Sino-Japanese War (1894), the sanctions became more severe: in that year the neutral English vessel *Kow-Shing*, which was engaged in the transport of Chinese troops, was even sunk by the Japanese warship *Naniwa*: her activities had resulted in impressing "enemy character" upon her (Takahashi, 24-51).

—Codification by the *Institut de droit international* in 1896

The rules which the *Institut*, in its session of Venice, finally formulated on the subject of unneutral service were inserted in a separate section B (§§ 6-8) of its *Réglementation* on contraband under the heading "service de transport". They ran as follows:

"§ 6.—Il est défendu d'attaquer ou empêcher le transport de diplomates ou de courriers diplomatiques: 1°. neutres; 2°. accrédités auprès de gouvernements neutres; 3°. naviguant sous pavillon neutre entre des ports neutres ou entre un port neutre et le port d'un belligérant.

Au contraire le transport des diplomates d'un ennemi, accrédités auprès de son allié, est, sauf le trafic régulier et ordinaire, interdit: 1°. sur les territoires et eaux des belligérants; 2°. entre leurs possessions; 3°. entre les belligérants alliés.

§ 7.—Sont interdits les transports de troupes, militaires ou agents de guerre d'un ennemi: 1°. dans les eaux des belligérants; 2°. entre leurs autorités, ports, possessions, armées ou flottes; 3°. lorsque le transport se fait pour le compte ou par l'ordre ou le mandat d'un ennemi, ou bien pour lui amener soit des agents avec une commission pour les opérations de la guerre, soit des militaires étant déjà à son service ou des troupes auxiliaires ou enrôlées contrairement à la neutralité,—entre ports neutres, entre ceux d'un neutre et ceux d'un belligérant, d'un point neutre à l'armée ou à la flotte d'un belligérant.

L'interdiction ne s'étend point au transport de particuliers qui ne sont pas encore au service militaire d'un belligérant, lors même qu'ils auraient l'intention d'y entrer, ou qui font le trajet comme simples voyageurs sans connexité manifeste avec le service militaire.

§ 8.—Entre deux autorités d'un ennemi, qui se trouvent sur quelque territoire ou navire lui appartenant ou occupé par lui, est interdit, sauf le trafic régulier et ordinaire, le transport de ses dépêches (communications officielles entre autorités officielles).

L'interdiction ne s'étend pas aux transports soit entre ports neutres, soit en provenance ou à destination de quelque territoire ou autorité neutre."

—The Naval Conference of 1909

In London the following Chapter III on unneutral service was formulated:

ARTICLE 45

A neutral vessel will be condemned and will, in a general way, receive the same treatment as a neutral vessel liable to condemnation for carriage of contraband:

(1) If she is on a voyage specially untertaken with a view to the transport of individual passengers who are embodied in the armed forces of the enemy, or with a view to the transmission of intelligence in the interest of the enemy.

(2) If, to the knowledge of either the owner, the charterer, or the master, she is transporting a military detachment of the enemy, or one or more persons who, in the course of the voyage, directly assist the operations of the enemy.

In the cases specified under the above heads, goods belonging to the owner of the vessel are likewise liable to condemnation.

The provisions of the present article do not apply if the vessel is encountered at sea while unaware of the outbreak of hostilities, or if the master, after becoming aware of the outbreak of hostilities, has had no opportunity of disembarking the passengers. The vessel is deemed to be aware of the existence of a state of war if she left an enemy port subsequently to the outbreak of hostilities, or a neutral port subsequently to the notification of the outbreak of hostilities to the Power to which such port belongs, provided that such notification was made in sufficient time.

ARTICLE 46

A neutral vessel will be condemned and, in a general way, receive the same treatment as would be applicable to her if she were an enemy merchant vessel:

(1) If she takes a direct part in the hostilities;

(2) If she is under the orders or control of an agent placed on board by the enemy Government;

(3) If she is in the exclusive employment of the enemy Government;

(4) If she is exclusively engaged at the time either in the transport of enemy troops or in the transmission of intelligence in the interest of the enemy.

In the cases covered by the present article, goods belonging to the owner of the vessel are likewise liable to condemnation.

ARTICLE 47

Any individual embodied in the armed forces of the enemy who is found on board a neutral merchant vessel, may be made a prisoner of war, even though there be no ground for the capture of the vessel.

Section 6. RULE OF THE WAR OF 1756. CLOSED TRADE. *NAVIGATION RÉSERVÉE*

The rule which became known as the "Rule of the War of 1756" had its origin in the decision of the French Government at the commencement of the Seven Years' War (1756) to remove France's inability to maintain trade-relations with her colonies by granting licences to Dutch vessels to carry French colonial produce, such as sugar, coffee and cocoa, to France, and the reaction thereto by the British Government expressed in a declaration to the Netherlands Government that in the future Great Britain would enforce the rule that a trade in which neutrals were forbidden to engage in time of peace should not be opened to them in time of war (Moore, *Digest*, VII, 383), a rule which was thereupon applied by British prize courts. Although it is true that a similar rule had already been enforced earlier by the United Netherlands in 1604 against Venetian vessels (for taking licences from Spain for a trade that was prohibited to non-Spanish ships and thus making themselves an ally of Spain then at war with the Netherlands) and by England in 1630 against neutral merchantmen carrying on the coasting trade of Spain (R.G. Marsden on "Early prize jurisdiction and prize law in England" in the *English Historical Review*, vol. 25 (1910), p. 244), there would seem to be hardly any direct historical connection between those events and the development during the Seven Years' War.

It is self-evident that the new rule had an independent function only as regards trade in non-contraband cargoes.

The enforcement of the rule hit two classes of neutral transports, those direct between the neutral country and the French colonies, and those which were carried out by the detour of an intermediate neutral port. The latter category of transports complicated the new practice by the introduction of what was to be called the doctrine of continuous voyage: the neutral carriers would be liable to condemnation even if they intended to call at an intermediate non-French port before continuing their voyage to the French port of ultimate destination.

Trade between the belligerent mother country and its colonies was for the rest not the only instance of reserved or closed trade, the belligerent's coasting trade was treated on the same footing. I will deal with these two variants successively.

(*a*) *Colonial trade*

An example of this type of trade was that between Portugal and her Brazilian possessions, expressly prohibited to Dutch traders by Article 21 of the Netherlands-Portuguese treaty of 30 July 1669 (Dumont, VII[1], 114; Parry, 11, 187). On such colonial trade comp. also Articles 21 and 22 of the Anglo-Netherlands treaty of alliance of Southampton of 17 September 1625 (Dumont, V[2], 478), Article 13 of the earlier Netherlands-Portuguese treaty of 6 August 1661 (Dumont, VI[2], 366; Parry, 6, 375) and Article 31 of the Netherlands-Spanish peace treaty of 26 June 1714 (Dumont, VIII[1], 427; Parry, 29, 97). See further Part IV of this publication, p. 20.

This practice of British prize courts, initiated during the Seven Years' War, of condemning neutral, especially Dutch, vessels which availed themselves of a licence granted them by belligerent France in wartime, to entertain traffic and trade with her overseas colonies which was closed to them in time of peace was defended by Sir James Marriott in a publication under the title *The case of the Dutch ships considered.* Published originally during the said war (3rd ed., London, 1759), it was later republished in a 4th edition in 1778 during the American War of Independence.

The unconvincing reasoning developed on that occasion, which included a justification of the continuous voyage doctrine, amounted to the following:

> "In the present war between England and France, the subjects of Holland have no right to cover the property of the enemy of England, going to, or coming from the colonies of that enemy, directly, nor indirectly, to do it, thro 'the medium of the Dutch colonies; nor to carry to the colonies of France directly, nor indirectly, any commodities, altho' neutral property, which have a tendency to support the enemy. They have no such right, by the common principle of neutrality. They have no such right by virtue of subsisting treaties [for example, Articles 1 and 8 of the Anglo-Netherlands treaty of 10 December 1674]. A Dutch ship trading to the colonies of France, without a licence from the French Government, is confiscated as good prize to French captors. Therefore all Dutch ships so licensed are adopted French ships."

Cases and opinions, when consulted on the new practice, Sir George Hay, in an opinion of 31 March 1762 (see Reginald Marsden, *Reports*, 382), approved it as a general principle by answering affirmatively to the question:

> "As this trade is not permitted to be carried on in time of peace by the French, except in French bottoms, will not French property on board neutral vessels be deemed good and lawful prize?",

but he denied the legality in respect of French goods on board Netherlands vessels because such transport was in his opinion free under the Anglo-Netherlands treaty of 1674, a thesis which was contested by Sir James Marriott.

The diplomatic exchanges between the countries most directly concerned and the theoretical support of the proclaimed British measures by such eminent lawyers as Sir James Marriott and Sir George Hay prove that there is little foundation in Justice Ch. B. Elliott's suggestion in *A.J.I.L.* I (1907), p. 62, that the designation of the new practice as the Rule of the War of 1756 "was probably a misnomer since the rule was not appreciably developed until 1793". This may be true, but does not alter the fact that the rule was introduced by England during the Seven Years' War as a counter-measure against certain change of policy by France for her own benefit, but also profitable to neutrals.

Amongst the cases of application of the new rule by British prize courts during the Seven Years' War I cite those of the *Good Christian* [1760] (Burrell, 216-217; Roscoe, I, 11) and the *Yong Vrow* (*sic*; read: *Jonge Vrouw* or *Jonkvrouw*) *Adriana* [1758-1764] (Burrell, 178; Roscoe, I, 8).

What is interesting in the first of these two cases is not only the reasoning in the condemnatory judgment of the Court of first instance, but also the restoration of the ship in appeal on 20 December 1760. The *Good Christian* was a Danish vessel sailing from the then Danish colony of St. Croix to Santo Domingo, then in French hands, but having on board a Dutch pass authorizing trade amongst all the West Indian islands. The bill of lading said the voyage was to be to Santo Domingo, on the account and at the risk of a Danish subject; clearance had been given at St. Croix for Cape François. The condemnation of both the ship and the cargo in the first instance was reversed in appeal on the ground that

> "there [was] not sufficient ground to presume that the voyage in which the ship was taken was allowed by the French King or his officers, or undertaken on any assurance, agreement, or authoritative intimation that the ship would be received at Cape François on the footing of a French ship or treated in such a manner as only French ships have a right to be treated in time of peace".

The ship was accordingly restored with her cargo. In a footnote (*a*) at p. 11 of vol. I of his *Reports*, Roscoe remarked that this case illustrated an attempt to extend the Rule of the War of 1756, by which Dutch ships and cargoes trading to the French West Indian colonies were condemned on the ground that the French Government having given exceptional privileges to the Dutch by allowing them to trade with the French colonies, the Dutch ships were, in fact, incorporated with the French mercantile marine. The author referred to the work by Sir William Burrell who noted in a few lines a number of cases of neutral ships either condemned or restored by the application of this rule. See Sir William Burrell's *Reports* (edited by Reginald G. Marsden) *of cases determined by the High Court of Admiralty, and upon appeal therefrom, temp. Sir Thomas Salusbury and Sir George Hay, Judges, 1758-1774*, pp. 216 and 217.

The second case cited above, the *Jonge Vrouw Adriana*, related to a cargo on board a Dutch ship involved in a complicated operation of the transboarding of colonial products from two French ships lying in the Bay of Cádiz. In their final judgment of 30 June 1764 the Lords held that the transboarding of the West Indian products to the Dutch ship was

> "not done in any fair course of trade or commerce ..., but was a fraudulent contrivance merely on account of the war to continue the original voyage and cover the goods of the enemy to their destined port, entitled to the same privileges and liable to the same duties and consequences as if they had arrived on board the same ship on which they were first laden ..."

It seems to be less certain whether the new Rule of the War of 1756 has already been applied during the Seven Years' War to any appreciable degree in combination with the doctrine of continuous voyage. In an article in *A.J.I.L.* IV (1910), pp. 823 *et seq.*, at p. 834, Professor L.H. Woolsey related that after a study of the original Manuscript Books of "Appeal Cases in Prize Causes" he had only discovered two cases in which the doctrine of continuous voyage appeared to have been applied in instances of reserved colonial trade, *viz.*, the *Africa* [1762] and the *St. Croix* [1763].

Be this as it may, the Rule of the War of 1756 has since been revived, and then sometimes in combination with the doctrine of continuous voyage, around the turn of the 18th century in the period of England's wars of 1793 *et seq.* against revolutionary France, which had in the meantime changed her policy by opening in 1779 trade with her West Indian colonies permanently to all countries. Without entering into too great detail, I will illustrate the further development from the findings of Sir William Scott (later Lord Stowell) which lie at the root of all subsequent English prize court decisions, in which, in the English manner of reasoning, earlier judgments are still constantly invoked as authoritative up to the present day.

Precedents of these days were from

1799-1800: the Danish *Emanuel* (Söderström, Master) (1 C.Rob., 296; Roscoe, I, 141); the Spanish *Princessa* (Zavala, Master) (2 C.Rob., 31, 49); the American *Rebecca* (Moore, Master) (2 C.Rob., 101; Roscoe, I, 303, footnote *a*), in which a motion for a freight claim for a voyage from Surinam to Amsterdam in 1796 with a cargo of colonial produce was refused; and especially the Hamburg ship *Immanuel* (Eysenberg, Master) [1800] (2 C.Rob., 186, 197-198; Roscoe, I, 217, at p. 219). This latter ship, which had taken in cargo in neutral Hamburg, sailed first to Bordeaux, sold part of her cargo there, loaded new goods and was captured on the final part of her voyage to the French West Indian island of Santo Domingo. The cargo loaded in Bordeaux alone was condemned, that loaded in Hamburg not. This case is illustrative of the manner in which the Rule was applied: the transport of cargo from the German town with destination to the French West Indies was perfectly legal in spite of the ship's temporary stay in Bordeaux. Sir William Scott formulated it as follows (at p. 217):

> "Neutral goods captured in direct transit from the mother-country of the enemy to a colony of the enemy are liable to capture and condemnation. The ship in which such goods are carried is restored, but the freight is forfeited",

and (at p. 219):

> "Very different is the case of a trade which the neutral has never possessed, which he holds by no title of use and habit in times of peace, and which, in fact, can obtain in war by no

> other title than by the success of the one belligerent against the other, and at the expense of that very belligerent under whose success he sets up his title; and such I take to be the colonial trade, generally speaking."

Another vessel, captured on the same day as the *Immanuel*, the American *Rose* (Young, Master) [1799], sailing from French-occupied Amsterdam to the French colony of Guadeloupe, showed a slight difference from the *Immanuel* in that she was on a voyage from one enemy country to the colony of another enemy, allied in the war. On that case Sir William Scott was of opinion that this difference did not form a solid distinction on the principle which he had laid down and thought that it would be impossible to maintain the rule of law without applying it also in this context.

1801: the American *Minerva* (Andaulle, Master) (3 C.Rob., 229; Roscoe, I, 301) on a voyage from the Spanish settlement of Languera to La Coruña, captured by the French and recaptured by the English: the original destination was decisive and the cargo was condemned—the ship owner only lost his freight; the Dutch *Jonge Thomas* (3 C. Rob., at p. 233; Roscoe, I, 303, footnote *b*), on a voyage from Amsterdam to Surinam. The Lords of Appeal held that the illegality of this voyage attached as strongly on the ship as on the cargo and pronounced the ship subject to condemnation, on the ground of the illegality of the trade, between the mother country (Holland) and the colony of the enemy.

1802: the Danish *Anna Catharina* (Wupper, Master) (4 C.Rob., 107); the *Rendsborg* (Nyberg, Master) (4 C.Rob., 121), a ship of uncertain nationality;

1804: the British *Abby* (Murchy, Master) (5 C.Rob., 251; Roscoe, I, 464), sailing to the Dutch colony of Demerara prior to the outbreak of hostilities between England and Holland (16 September 1795) and the ensuing change in the territorial sovereignty of the colony.

1805: the American *Maria (No. 3)* (Jackson, Master) (5 C.Rob., 365; Roscoe, I, 495), on a voyage with colonial produce from Havana to Amsterdam via New Providence.

In a number of instances of such colonial trade the cases were complicated by the fact that the transportation was presented as constituting a continuous voyage. In the proceedings against the *Polly* (Lasky, Master) [1800] (2 C.Rob., 361; Roscoe, I, 248) and the *Maria (No. 3)* (*supra*) this was denied by Sir William Scott. The *Polly* case, for example, related to a cargo of sugar and cocoa shipped in Havana, unloaded in the American port of Marblehead, reshipped there later and captured on the vessels's further voyage to Bilbao. He held that under the circumstances there had been a *bona fide* importation into neutral territory and that there was, therefore, no question of a continuous voyage.

On the other hand, in the later case of the American *William (No. 2)* (Trefry, Master) [1806] (5 C.Rob., 385; Roscoe, I, 505) continuous voyage from La Guaira to Spanish Bilbao was held to be proven. In that case he, and the Court of Appeal [Lords, 20 June 1810] (*per* Sir William Grant), applied the doctrine to attempts of neutral shippers to evade the restrictions on colonial trade: the *William* was, indeed, seized by a British cruiser on her voyage from Venezuela to the Spanish mainland via the North American port of Marblehead, where she had unloaded her cargo, but reloaded it after passing the customs.

The application of the Rule of 1756 has, however, gradually become more rare under the new liberal conditions of colonial trade.

The re-introduction of the rule on reserved trade by a British Order in Council of 1793 has met with strong opposition by neutral Powers, in particular the United States, at the end of the 18th century. Comp. on these neutral protests the detailed data in H. W. Briggs's study of 1925 in Johns Hopkins University Studies 1926 (44), pp. 13 *et seq.* and 19 *et seq.* See also H. Arias's article on "The doctrine of continuous voyage in the eighteenth century" in 9 *A.J.I.L.* 1915, pp. 583 *et seq.*

The British Government relaxed its policy a little vis-à-vis European neutrals in 1794 and 1798, but those relaxations, granted as "purely voluntary concessions", never went so far that they permitted direct commerce of neutrals between an enemy mother-country and its colonies. It was especially after the British vice-admiralty courts in the North-American colonies had introduced the practice, despite the decision in the *Polly* case (*supra*), of condemning cargoes involved in reserved colonial trade via intermediate neutral ports, *i.e.* in application of the doctrine of continuous voyage to that trade, that the protests grew in momentum. See G. B. Elliott's article on "The doctrine of continuous voyage" in 2 *A.J.I.L.* 1907, pp. 61 *et seq.*, at p. 65. American shippers demanded the repeal of the Order and freedom to carry goods from French, Spanish and Dutch colonies to American ports and from there, either in the same or in other vessels, to the motherland of those colonies. Their protests against the "palpable abuses" by the British authorities were voiced by the United States Minister Rufus King in a diplomatic note of 17 March 1801 and passed on in another note of 20 August 1806 by James Monroe and William Pinkney to Lords Holland and Auckland in their capacity of commissioners to negotiate a commercial treaty, both reproduced in *B.F.S.P.* 1812-1814 (vol. 1, part 2), pp. 1205 *et seq.*

The continued legal force of the old rule, though applied less and less in the course of time, was not contested even by the London Conference on Naval Warfare, witness Art. 57 (2) of its Declaration of 1909 to the effect that

> "Le cas où le navire neutre se livre à une navigation réservée en temps de paix reste hors de cause et n'est nullement visé par cette règle",

and the rule was again revived during World War I.

The rule was also mentioned by the editors of the *Recueil des arbitrages internationaux* in connection with a dispute of 1863 between Chile and the United States concerning the *Macedonian* (vol. II, p. 196), and discussed in Albéric Rolin's doctrinal note, *ibid.*, pp. 209 *et seq.*

See further F. E. Smith and N. W. Sibley, *International law as interpreted during the Russo-Japanese war* (London, 1905), pp. 140-143.

Engagement of neutral traders in wartime in a trade that was closed to foreign vessels in time of peace was still at issue in two different variants in the days of the Russo-Japanese War of 1904-1905.

The Japanese case of the American *Montara* [1906] (Hurst & Bray, II, 403) related to the involvement of this neutral vessel in the reserved coasting trade of Japan's enemy Russia. What was the legal consequence of that involvement? During the progress of that war the Russian Government permitted two Russian companies to employ foreign ships in their trade in the Kommandorski Islands and along the neighbouring coast. One of those ships, the American *Montara*, left San Francisco in July 1905 and called at various Kamchatkan ports, discharging part of her cargo and taking in furs and other articles. In August she was captured while discharging the remainder of her cargo at Behring Island. The Yokosuka prize court construed this case, in accordance with Article 6 (2) of the Japanese Regulations relating to Capture at Sea, as an instance of the sailing of neutral vessels under the enemy's flag, or "with a special licence from the enemy", thus reviving the old Rule of the War of 1756, and condemned both the ship and her cargo. The Higher Prize Court confirmed that judgment notwithstanding the elaborate argument of the claimants against the lasting validity of the old Rule and despite of the fact that the Acting Chief Justice of the Supreme Court of Hong-Kong in his capacity of arbitrator between the Osaka Shosen Kaisha and the owners of the steamship *Prometheus*, Sir H.S. Berkeley, had expressely refrained from deciding the point of that validity affirmatively (*Hong-Kong Law Reports*, vol. II, Part VI, December 1907, p. 207; Hurst & Bray, II, Appendix I, p. 451):

> "To engage in the coasting trade or interport trade of a belligerent power in time of war is not to engage in a privileged trade or in an illegal trade. For such trade to become so—apart from the consideration whether the principle of what is known as the rule of the war of 1756 is or is not obsolete—the ports traded to must have been totally closed before the war to all subjects of that power and must only have been opened to others after the war and because of the pressure and necessity due to the preponderating naval supremacy of the belligerent enemy".

The Russian case of the German *Thea* [1906] (*ibid.*, I, 96) was of a different type. This vessel was chartered by a Japanese commercial firm and engaged in the Japanese coasting trade. Did that fact render her liable to condemnation after the outbreak of the Russo-Japanese War? The Vladivostok Prize Court gave an affirmative answer, but on appeal the Admiralty Council, sitting as Supreme Prize Court, reversed the decision below on the ground that is was based on a wrong thesis, *viz.*, that the *Thea*, under the charter-party with the Japanese firm, had entered the exclusive service of a Japanese company for a period of nine months and had thus become the property of the enemy in time of war. The Superior Prize Court rejected the argument that, since the *Thea* was employed exclusively in the coasting trade between Japanese ports from the time she was chartered and therefore enjoyed the privileges conceded only to Japanese vessels, she must be deemed to have lost her neutral character. This was insufficient for holding the *Thea* to be a lawful prize: the nationality of a vessel is determined by the laws of the State under the flag of which she sails or to the fleet of which she claims to belong; according to the German law of 1867 the German nationality of the *Thea* was incontestable and could not have been lost by the lease of the vessel to a Japanese company.

(*b*) *Coasting trade*

The doctrine of 'closed trade' in the law of prize was, however, also capable of application to other variants, especially to reserved coasting trade.

See, for example, the case of the *Johanna Tholen* (Osterlo, Master) [1805] (6 C.Rob., 72; Roscoe, I, 531), complicated by the use of false papers, being ostensibly on a voyage from Bordeaux to Emden, but in actual fact to Antwerp for the purpose of delivering her cargo there. Sir William Scott agreed with the King's Advocate "that the carrying on the coasting trade with false papers is ground of condemnation, according to the established doctrine of the Court":

> "If there is any doubt upon the rectitude of that principle, it will be a great satisfaction to my mind to see it corrected by the decision of the Superior Court. Until that is done I shall not be disposed to depart from the rule upon which the Court has hitherto proceeded."

The case was one of carrying on the coasting trade of France to the port of Antwerp. As far as I know, the judgment was not reversed in appeal.

Section 6A. SLAVE TRADE, TRADING WITH THE ENEMY AND OTHER INFRACTIONS OF INTERNATIONAL OR MUNICIPAL LAW

I insert these new subjects in an intercalary section because these grounds of condemnation either have no connection at all with the existence of a state of war, or have such a connection but do not constitute instances of international prize law proper, coming rather under municipal penal law. I will revert to this particular type of prize cases *infra*, *sub* C, section 2, pp. 591-592, in the context of the competence of prize courts to deal with them.

(*a*) *Slave trade*

The prosecution of slavers and the condemnation of their ships and other property has given rise in England to prize court decisions. The oldest precedents seem to be a judgment of the Vice-Admiralty Court of Tortola, one of the Virgin Islands, on the *Amedie* of 1807 and a decree of 1804 by Sir William Scott in the *Abby* case. In another pronouncement by Sir William Scott, in the case of the British slaver *Fortuna* [1811] (1 Dodson, 81], the President made the following statement:

> "It has been establishment that the Court of Prize, though properly purely a Court of the Law of Nations, has a right to notice the municipal law of this country in the case of a British vessel which, in the course of prize proceedings, appears to have been trading in violation of that law, and to reject a claim for her on that account."

From the wording of Sir William's sentences, immediately following that statement, referring to a "late decision" in the *Amedie* case (whereupon comp. Roscoe's footnote *a* at pp. 193-195 of vol. I of his collection), which was said to have meanwhile sanctioned an expansion of the doctrine laid down in the statement, one is inclined to conclude that the President was still in two minds as to the correctness of the expansion alluded to. The manner in which he expressed himself sounded indeed far from convinced:

> "[In the *Amedie* case the court concerned] seems to have gone the length of establishing a principle that any trade contrary to the general law of nations, although not tending to or accompanied with any infraction of the belligerent rights of that country, whose tribunals are called upon to consider it, may subject the vessel employed in that trade to confiscation .... The principle laid down in that case appears to be that the slave trade carried on by a vessel belonging to a subject of the United States is a trade which, being unprotected by the domestic regulations of their legislature and government subjects the vessel engaged in it to condemnation."

Comp. on this further expansion of the doctrine from British to American slave traders p. 592, where the issue is discussed as a problem of the competence of the British prize court to take cognizance of such cases, too.

The *Abby* [1804] (5 C.Rob., 251; Roscoe, I, 464) was a ship that had been fitted out by her owner for a voyage to Africa, there to barter her cargo for slaves and then to carry them to Demerara, at that time still a Dutch colony (see on this somewhat complicated case also p. 479).

See also the *Thomas* [1799] (1 C.Rob., 322). The case concerned a British slave ship, seized by the slaves on board but afterwards retaken by a British frigate. The ship was restored to the former British owner.

In France, the subject was discussed by De Pistoye and Duverdy in their *Traité des prises maritimes*, vol. I, pp. 67-85. They record, however, three cases in which the adjudicating tribunal denied its jurisdiction to deal with the capture of foreign slavers without a special Convention authorizing such action:

the American schooner *Plough-Boy*, a case decised by the Prize Commission of Martinique in 1824 (*loco cit.*, p. 75):

> "il n'y a pas lieu à évoquer cette contravention aux tribunaux de la colonie, les bâtiments américains, comme tous autres bâtiments étrangers, n'étant pas sur ce point justiciables de la France";

the Portuguese brig *Pocha*, a case decided by the Prize Commission of the Ile Bourbon in 1840 (*loco cit.*, pp. 75-76):

> "les opérations de traite faites par le capitaine et les gens du *Pocha*, navire portugais, quelque illicites qu'elles soient, ne sont point, cependant, punissables dans l'espèce par les tribunaux français, parce qu'aucune convention entre la France et le Portugal n'autorise le capture des navires de traité ...",

principles confirmed by the *Conseil d'Etat* in 1847 in the *Notre-Dame-de-Grâce* (*loco cit.*, p. 76).

These judgments constitute the judicial basis of France's opposition to the insistence by other Powers on the creation of a mutual right of interference with slave traders, whereupon com. vol. V of this publication, pp. 246 *et seq.*, at pp. 253 *et seq.*

(*b*) *Trading with the enemy*

It is in particular British prize courts which have developed a detailed case law on trading with the enemy as a major ground of condemnation in prize. This judicial practice, however, has no direct affinity with international law since there is no binding rule of the law of nations in force that obliges belligerent States to forbid and to enforce by a penalty commercial intercourse of their subjects with an enemy State. Comp. on this topic my observations and further details in vol. IX of this publication, pp. 24 *et seq.*

Action in this field by a belligerent State acquires an international aspect only when it is exercised against subjects of an allied State.

A case in which a British prize court condemned a prize on the ground of such trading with the enemy by allied subjects was that of the *Neptunus (No. 5)* (Bachman, Master) [1807] (6 C.Rob., 403; Roscoe, I, 595), a case in which the question turned on the effect of a modified permission of trade with the common enemy in innocent articles on the part of an ally in the war (Swedish vessels on a voyage to Amsterdam).

Another case in which foreign subjects were involved in such trade was that of the *Franklin* (Dana, Master) [1805-1806] (6 C.Rob., 127; Roscoe, I, 539). In that case a British merchant had acted in partnership with a firm in a neutral country which traded with the enemy of Great Britain. The British merchant's share alone was condemned.

The abovementioned *Abby* case (Murchy, Master) [1804] (5 C.Rob., 251; Roscoe, I, 464) was an unusual one in that, apart from its slave trading aspects (*supra sub* a), it concerned a voyage by a British ship via Africa, from where she had sailed in May 1796 to Demerara, which at the moment of her original sailing (11 September 1795) was still a Dutch colony and could not be, at that date, considered as the colony of an enemy, since a state of hostility was not declared until 16 September 1795. The Court observed that, if the vessel had sailed after the latter date, proof by the ship-owner of due diligence to alter the voyage would have been required to exonerate him from the charge of illegal trading with the enemy. The ship was taken off the coast of Demerara after the colony's surrender to the British forces and carried to Martinique, where she was condemned by the Vice-Admiralty Court, apparently for the breach of revenue laws. That condemnation, however, could not be upheld in appeal because the Vice-Admiralty Court in question had in the meantime been abolished. On this question of competence of the Admiralty Court see *sub* C, section 2, *infra*, pp. 593-594.

According to footnote *a* in 4 C.Rob., 262, it had been determined, in several instances, that a British subject cannot come before a Court of Prize to claim property taken in the course of trade which is forbidden by the laws of his country; and in the case of the *Etrusco* [Lords, 1803] it was decided, after long deliberation, that property condemned in consequence of the inadmissibility of such a claim, was to be condemned not to the individual captor, but to the King (comp. on this particular aspect *sub* C, section 2, *infra*, p. 592).

Pursuant to the *Hoop* (Cornelis, Master) [1799] (1 C.Rob., 196; Roscoe, I, 104) it was the established rule of the law of the British Prize Court, confirmed by the judgment of the Supreme Court, that trading with the enemy, except under a royal licence, subjected the property to confiscation in prize; the most eminent exponents of the law sitting in the Supreme Court had uniformly sustained such judgments. This decision listed a number of precedents,

—from the War of the Austrian Succession:
the *Ringende Jacob* [1747, 1750], the *Deergarden* [1747], the *Lady Jane* [1749] and the *Elizabeth* [1749];

—from the American War of Independence:
the *Juffrouw Louisa Margaretha* [1781], the *St. Louis* (*El Allessandro*) [1781], the *Comte de Worontzow* [1781], the *Victoria* [1781], the *Expeditie van Rotterdam* [1782] and the *Bella Giudita* [1785];

—from the Revolutionary Wars of France:
the *Eenigheid*, the *Fortuna*, the *Freeden* and the *William*, all decided in 1795.

Later examples from the period of the Crimean War were:

the *Leucade* (Arronis, Master) [1855] (Spinks, 217; Roscoe, II, 473), a vessel belonging to merchants, subjects of the State of the Ionian Islands, and sailing under Ionian colours from Santa Maura with a cargo of olive oil, bound for Taganrog in the Sea of Azov. Having by reason of stress of weather put in first at Syra and then at Mytilene, she reached Constantinople, where in consequence of the war she was refused clearance for Taganrog. The master therefore changed her destination for Trebizond for which she nominally sailed on 1 May 1854, still having on board the bill of lading to Taganrog. She was subsequently intercepted by a British warship at a distance of 40 miles from the Strait of Kertch in proper course for the Sea of Azov. The proceedings ended with the restoration of the vessel and her cargo to the Ionian merchants: their trade with Russia was found not to be trading with the enemy since the Ionian States were not at war with Russia, their trade was therefore valid and the seizure invalid. But the captor was not liable in costs and damages, as he had not made the capture without reasonable cause: the status of the Ionian States relatively to Great Britain was of a doubtful character and depended upon a difficult construction of public documents (comp. on this case *sub* C, section 6 (A) (Damages), *infra*, p. 625);

the *Neptune* (Keetley, Master) [1855] (Spinks, 281; Roscoe, II, 520), a Russian ship bought by a British merchant in Hull and captured on a voyage from Kertch to Hull where she entered the harbour. But instead of leaving the port forthwith after unloading her cargo, the ship stayed there for some time and was later sold to an Englishman. The buyer disputed the validity of the capture, invoking the Order in Council of 29 March 1854 under the protection of which, he claimed, he had acted. Although that Order in Council exempted certain Russian vessels from condemnation and the Crown used its powers to stay the prize proceedings against the vessel so that she was no longer liable to condemnation, that did not alter the fact that the sale of an enemy vessel by a British subject was illegal trading with the enemy and that, therefore, the buyer must be condemned in costs.

The application of the rule against trading with the enemy was complicated by the adoption at an early stage by British prize courts of the doctrine of continuous voyage in this field long before it was invoked in contraband cases: the Dutch vessel *Jonge Pieter* (Musterdt, Master) [1801] (4 C.Rob., 79; Roscoe, I, 353), for example, committed the offence by sailing to Amsterdam via the neutral port of Emden. In one of the judgments which thus applied the doctrine to trading with the enemy the principle was expressed as follows:

> "All trading with the enemy is unlawful, no matter whether it is carried on directly or through an intermediate port."

On its application to voyages under a belligerent licence, see III A, section 1 under § 1, pp. 281 *et seq.*

(*c*) *Other rare encroachments on municipal law which led to prize court decisions*

An instance of another kind of encroachment upon municipal law that was brought before a British prize court was the case of the *Walsingham Packet*

[1799] (2 C.Rob., 77; Roscoe, I, 189), a vessel which had violated the monopoly of the British East India Company. Comp. on this case III C, section 2 (Competence of prize courts, *infra*, p. 592).

On an asserted breach of British revenue laws see the case of the *Abby* [1804], *supra*, p. 479.

Section 7. IRREGULARITIES COMMITTED BY NON-ENEMY VESSELS ENCROACHING UPON THE POLICING RIGHTS OF THE BELLIGERENTS

Apart from the legal grounds of a substantive nature on which neutral or allied vessels were liable to condemnation in prize, dealt with in the preceding sections, they could also incur that sanction on account of the behaviour of their master during visit or search, or of other irregularities of different kinds. The ship's captain could indeed attempt to thwart the belligerent's right of action in varying ways. This eventuality was already foreseen in the oldest regional codes, such as the Rolls of Oléron and the Black Book of the Admiralty, and in a number of national laws and instructions.

Irregularities committed by the masters of merchant ships which had already earlier on justified their capture by belligerent armed vessels, followed in graver cases by confiscation by the Court of Admiralty, were, *inter alia*, according to old maritime laws:

—refusal to strike their sails on a hailing shot: Article 35 of the *Rôles d'Oléron*, embodying a decree, issued by King John of England at Hastings about 1200; Art. 65 of the French Edict of 1584; Art. 12 of *titre* IX of *livre* III of the *Ordonnance de la Marine* of 1681; Art. 57 of the *Arrêté* of *an* XI;

—resistance of merchant ships to attempts by belligerent armed vessels to capture them was a subject that was already specially dealt with in the oldest sources of maritime law.

What the Black Book of the Admiralty and the *Rôles d'Oléron* laid down on it was embodied in a provision inserted in Part C of the former under Article 35 (vol. I, at pp. 88-131), which reproduced an Ordinance enacted by King John in 1201 at Hastings:

> "Item, it was ordained at Hastynges for lawe and custome of the sea in the tyme of Kyng John, in the second yeare of his raigne by the advice of his temporall lordes, that if the [lieutenant of the King or the admirall of the King or his] lieutenant in any voyage appointed by Common Counsell of the Kingdom did at sea meet with any shyps or vessels laden or empty which would not stryke and lower their sailes, at the command of the Kyng's lieutenant, or the Kyng's admirall, or his lieutenant, but makeing resistance against those of the ffleet, that if they can be taken that they be reputed as enemies, and their shyps, vessells, and goodes taken and forfeited as goodes of enemies, albeit that the maysters or possessors thereof should afterwards come and alleadge the same shyps, vessells, and goodes of friends of our lorde the Kyng, and that the company therein be chastized by imprisonment of their bodies for their rebellion at descretion";

—absence, concealment or jettison of ship's papers: Art. 70 of the French Edict of 1584; Art. 6 of *titre* IX of *livre* III of the *Ordonnance de la Marine* of 1681;
—production of false or contradictory papers, or other fraud. Further details about this subject will be given *sub* B, section 1, *infra*, pp. 497 *et seq.*

Commencing with a few general remarks on English legislation and judicial precedents I will refer to the British Order in Council of 1664 which summed up the main irregularities as follows (Art. 4):

> "That where any ship met withal by any of the King's royal navy or other ships commissioned by his authority shall fight or make resistance, or the master or any of the company shall throw away, burn, tear, or conceal any of the ship's papers or documents, or shall have no papers at all found on board in the said ship, or shall bring or offer to the Court any false or double writing for evidence thereof to clear her or her goods, or any of them, the said ship and goods shall be judged and condemned as good and lawful prize".

To the same effect the Order in Council of 22 May 1672, Article 3.

The old threat by a legislature that severe sanctions would be enforced against those guilty of such irregularities has been renewed ever since and applied by prize courts under the régime of the great many treaties of the 17th and 18th centuries which empowered belligerent warships or privateers to verify the national character, destination and cargo of vessels met at sea, while prescribing the manner in which the operations of visit, search and seizure were to be carried out, and which in their turn threatened the penalty of confiscation against all those who should attempt to thwart the exercise of these belligerent rights.

As will be set out *sub* B, sections 1 and 2, *infra*, pp. 489 and 504, such attempts could take various forms. Thus, the master might show false papers, or throw papers into the sea for the purpose of concealing the nature of the cargo, the character of the owner, or the ship's destination. He might refuse to stop or make an attempt to escape, offer actual resistance to the visiting warship, or even himself undertake aggressive action against it. Although it was not illegal for neutrals to arm their merchantmen, a measure of precaution which might be useful against pirates, the use of their arms against the lawful exercise by belligerent warships of their right of visit and search entailed their capture and perhaps final condemnation as good and lawful prize.

The three main grounds of condemnation

In the following short survey of the subject matter of the present section I will first deal with the Anglo-American legal system.

(*a*) *Special caution against all forms of fraud*
Fraud by persons involved in an overseas transport was in the English tradition always a factor strongly adverse to their claims. Comp., among many others, the case of the *Graaff Bernstorff* [1800] (3 C.Rob., 109; Roscoe, I, 265), in which the neutral (Danish) cargo-owner had suppressed an enemy's interest in the cargo with a fraudulent intent.

The use of false papers or other comparable fraud was a very frequent offence, as appears from many prize court decisions of the past.

Old instances of the War of the Austrian Succession were those of 1747 of the *Elizabeth Catharina* and the *Vro(u)w Anna Maria*, both reported by Pratt-Lee, pp. 115, respectively 119: the master of the first ship, whose pass on board was not according to the Swedish treaty and which was assisting the enemy, had "acted colourably"; as he was a part-owner of the ship, not only his cargo, but also the carrying ship was condemned.

Later cases, dating from the period of England's Wars with revolutionary France, were those of

1799: the Swedish vessels *Sarah Christina* (1 C.Rob., 237; Roscoe, I, 125), *Eenrom* (2 C.Rob., 1; Roscoe, I, 168) and *Calypso* (2 C.Rob., 154), claimed as Danish;

1800: the *Rosalie and Betty* (2 C.Rob., 343);

1800: the Danish *Nancy* (Joy, Master) (3 C.Rob., 82; Roscoe, I, 355, footnote *a*), consignment of a cargo "to Cowes and a market", but with (enemy-occupied) Amsterdam as her actual destination; the *Neptunus* (Moswold, Master) (3 C.Rob., 80), and the *America* (3 C.Rob., 36; Roscoe, I, 127, footnote *a*), in which latter case Sir William Scott said:

> "It is not a new rule that if a ship is going with false papers the owner shall lose his freight. I do not say that if an owner makes out a clear case that he has been duped by the fraud of the master, the Court would in all cases press the rule with the utmost rigour against him",

but held that such a case had not been made out (on this additional aspect comp., *infra*, *sub* C, section 7, pp. 642-663).

In the cases of the Danish *Neutralitet (No. 1)* [1801] (3 C.Rob., 295; Roscoe, I, 309) and the Prussian *Edward* [1801] (4 C.Rob., 68; Roscoe, I, 350), both ships were carrying contraband "with dissembled destination".

Falsity in the ship's papers did not, however, always entail condemnation: thus, in the case of the *Sarah* [1801] (3 C.Rob., 330; Roscoe, I, 318) the false claim of a merchant of Emden as being the owner of the transported goods had been used for the purpose of protecting them from the cruisers of the enemy; this artifice was excused because there was no sinister purpose concealed under that pretence and no enemy's interest was concerned. The cargo was restored, but the captors were allowed the expenses into which the expedient had led them.

The *Johanna Tholen* [1805] (6 C.Rob., 78; Roscoe, I, 531) was a case of reserved coastal trade with false papers.

The *Exchange* [1808] (Edw., 39; Roscoe, II, 13) was an American vessel sailing with a cargo of sugar from French Guadeloupe ostensibly to London, but captured close to Cherbourg; she was condemned for fraud, the cargo sharing her fate.

See further the American case of 1821 relative to the *Amiable Isabelle* (6 Wheaton, 1), and much later again the English case of the *Atlantique* [1854] (Spinks, 104; Roscoe, II, 345) in which Dr Lushington stated that an attempt had been made "to practice a great fraud upon the Court" with the assertion that she was not a Russian ship and that no enemy interest was involved; the claim had, however, meanwhile been withdrawn before the hearing.

In another judgment pronounced during the Crimean War, the *Ocean Bride* [1854] (Spinks, 66; Roscoe, II, 309) Dr Lushington restated the traditional principle of the requirement of good faith as follows:

> "Over and over again Lord Stowell has said, it is not the documents themselves which the Court goes upon,—they must be true, they must be *bona fide*,—it never goes on formalities. This is a broad distinction, which I consider not only indispensable to prize law, but to be one of the most honourable distinctions which exist between a prize court and a municipal court, that a Prize Court looks to what is *bona fide* true, while a Court of law is sometimes bound by formality, which prevents real justice being done in the case".

(b) Resistance to visit and search

Well-known historical instances of resistance opposed by an arrested vessel to a visit by her prospective captor were the English one of the *Fanny* [1814] (1 Dodson, 443; Roscoe, II, 202) and the American one of the *Nereide* [1815] (9 Cranch (Amer.), 388).

A special case was that of the *Elsebé* (Maas, Master) [1804] (5 C.Rob., 173; Roscoe, I, 441), sailing under the protection of the second Swedish convoy and for that reason resisting search.

Deák and Jessup, at p. 209 of Part I of their *Neutrality Law*, give the text of a Notice by the Board of Trade, of as late as March 1904, to mariners regarding visit and search by belligerent warships:

> "Masters of British merchant vessels must immediately stop and heave to when summoned on the high seas to do so by a warship of either belligerent and must not resist being visited and searched for contraband of war by such warship, as any attempt on their part to evade or resist visit or search may be attended with serious consequences to themselves and to their vessels and cargoes."

(c) Jettison or "spoliation" of ship's papers

"Spoliation" of the ship's papers was in the Anglo-American system also frequently ground for suspicion and seizure. See already the Orders in Council of 1664 (Art. 4) and 22 May 1672 (Art. 3) quoted in a footnote by Pratt-Lee at p. 118.

In 1854 the *Johanna Emilie* (Spinks, 12; Roscoe, II, 252), a Russian vessel, assertedly transferred to the flag of Hanover, was condemned by

Dr Lushington on the ground of "spoliation of documents", an expression which he held not to comprise every destruction of ship's papers, but only those of greater importance, effected at a moment when the destruction was particularly suspect, *e.g.*, when the capturing vessel was in sight or when the papers were destroyed after the capture. President Dr Lushington in that case decreed as follows:

> "The legal consequences of destruction or spoliation of papers depend for the most part upon the circumstances of each case, but unless the case is one of grave suspicion, further proof will be allowed",

and remarked that Lord Stowell's judgments gave no direct definition of the term "spoliation". Destruction of papers was not, according to Lord Stowell, under all circumstances to be considered as spoliation.

Dr Lushington further gave an exposé of what in his own view was spoliation and what not, and surveyed the precedents. The act was also called "suppression of papers", see the case of the Austrian *Nina* [1856] (Spinks, 276, 347; Roscoe, II, 514).

The older precedents referred to were the French *Two Brothers* (McClousky, Master) [1799] (1 C. Rob., 131; Roscoe, II, footnote at p. 263), the American *Rising Sun* [1799] (2 C.Rob., 104; Roscoe, II, 263, footnote *u*) and the American *Hunter* [1815] (1 Dodson, 480; Roscoe, II, 208).

In the *Two Brothers* Sir William Scott held that suppression of papers was not a cause of condemnation in England, but that it raised great suspicion: the parties would not be allowed to say that they were only private papers; he discussed the circumstances which might lead to condemnation.

In the *Hunter* Sir William Scott stated that the maritime courts of Europe used to condemn the prize without further proof, but that English prize law had adopted a mitigated version of that practice by deciding that, if all other circumstances were clear, the spoliation alone was not damnatory, in particular not if the act was done by a person for interests of his own that might be benefited by the commission of his injurious act.

Chancellor Kent expatiated on that subject in his *Commentaries on American Law* (12th ed., Boston, 1873), I, p. 158, as follows:

> "The spoliation of papers is [a circumstance of suspicion] still more aggravated and inflamed [than the concealment of material papers]. The fact may exclude further proof and be sufficient to infer guilt; but it does not, in England, as it does by the maritime law of other countries, create an absolute *praesumptio juris et de jure*; and yet a case that escapes with such a brand upon it is saved so as by fire. The Supreme Court of the United States has followed the less rigorous English rule, and held that the spoliation of papers was not, of itself, sufficient ground for condemnation".

After an examination of the case under review the Court concluded:

> "I am of opinion, therefore, that special circumstances do not exist which can take the case out of the rule which is generally applicable to such a state of facts; and I have already stated that rule to be the confiscation of all the property forcibly withheld from inquiry and search".

Cases of the spoliation, mutilation, alteration or destruction of ship's papers which led to the confiscation of the offending ship were in the United States also those reported by Blatchford, *inter alia* relating to the *Zavalla.*

For further details on the subject-matter surveyed above I refer to *sub* B, section 2 (Visit and search), respectively section 1 (Ship's papers), *infra*, pp. 489 and pp. 504.

After the above short survey of the Anglo-American legal system on the subject matter dealt with in the present section 7, the legal situation according to French conceptions remains to be described. That situation relates, in particular, to the grounds of condemnation *sub* (*b*), resistance to visitation, and (*c*), jettison, destruction, suppression, concealment, etc., of ship's papers. A close study of this from Valin's basic work and the two volumes of the study by his successors De Pistoye and Duverdy (*Traité des prises maritimes*) has, however, taught me that an exactly corresponding systematic treatment of the French situation is difficult to achieve. I will therefore abstain from dealing with it here and set out the French system in an independent exposé in section 1 *sub* B (Ship's papers), *infra*, pp. 497 *et seq.*, where I will also explain the cause of this difference in systematic analysis.

CHAPTER III B

MODALITIES OF THE EXERCISE OF THE RIGHT OF CAPTURE

Since it has proved impossible to find a short but comprehensive title covering the differing subjects which deserve treatment as a separate intermediate group of topics leading from those discussed above in III A under the heading "The substantive law of prize" to its procedural aspects to be analysed below in III C under the heading "Procedure" I will abandon further search for such a comprehensive title for the contents of the present III B, and will rather indicate them by a simple enumeration of the various subjects which I intend to discuss here, an enumeration which serves precisely to underline their diversity.

The treaties and other regulations of earlier centuries are full of elaborate provisions as to how commanders of belligerent warships were to behave when exercising their right of visit and search and what measures they were entitled to take, in particular against neutral vessels, if their suspicions were confirmed or not satisfactorily dismissed, or if new grounds for suspicion arose. Provisions of the same tenor had to be observed by privateers (comp. *supra*, General issues, section 1, p. 152).

The object of the visit was to verify the national (enemy or non-enemy) character of the ship, the nature of her cargo, her own or her cargo's destination, etc. That verification was to be made in the first place by an inspection of the ship's papers which were of primary importance in wartime. That is why an equally detailed set of provisions concerning the necessary papers used to be inserted, not only in municipal regulations, but also in old treaties of commerce and navigation.

The following survey will consequently deal successively, in seven sections, with the subjects listed below. Sections 1 and 2 will be devoted to the two basic topics of ship's papers and the belligerents' policing rights of visit and search. Section 3 will follow with an exposé of the different actions which the belligerents can take on the basis of the results of their introductory enquiry. Section 4 will examine in how far the normal course of such actions was affected if it were found that the neutral merchantmen encountered at sea were convoyed by warships sailing under the same flag. Section 5 will deal with the destruction of captured ships or cargoes, an action that at an early stage of the development of the law of prize was still considered to be a very questionable step to take. Section 6 will describe the frequently occurring cases of joint capture. Section 7 concludes III B with a detailed exposé on the subject of the recapture of prize vessels, its legal effect and the award of salvage due on that account to the recaptor.

Section 1. SHIP'S PAPERS

General introduction

The requirement that a merchant vessel must carry specified papers identifying her owner, port of origin, the composition of her crew, her destination and her cargo, is particularly significant in time of war. It is not surprising that so many commercial or other treaties, concluded in earlier centuries, contained provisions on this subject and that such provisions were often very elaborate for the purpose of preventing different kinds of possible fraud as to the ship's nationality, ownership, destination, cargo, etc. on which her ultimate fate might depend. They used to contain requirements relative to the contents of the ship's papers and various guarantees of their veracity, such as an oath by the shipowner or master and the co-signature by a public authority confirming the data set forth in them. Other articles provided for their return to the authorities after a certain lapse of time or after the completion of the voyage (*infra*).

I have already had an opportunity to expatiate on the subject of ship's papers at pp. 70 *et seq.* of Part IV of this publication, and to refer there (at pp. 72-73) to the unusually far-reaching and detailed provisions, imposed on Denmark in 1691 by England and the United Netherlands, during their common Nine Years' War against France, in order to prevent Denmark from assisting their common enemy by means of her commercial fleet. The allied Powers on that occasion foresaw in particular two possible ways in which foreign ship owners might attempt, in collusion with Denmark, to achieve this, *viz.*, either by a transfer of their ships to the Danish flag or by having themselves adopted as Danish citizens. To obviate this latter trick England and the Netherlands demanded an undertaking from Denmark that no naturalization would be granted to foreigners without their previous taking an oath that they would remain domiciled with their family in Denmark for a period of at least ten years. Usually, however, the contents of the treaty clauses relating to the "sea-briefs" or "lettres de mer" (*Literae Commeatus, vulgo Literae Maritimae dictae*), or referred to as "muniments, indentures and cocketts" as in Article 18 of certain Instructions, issued under the reign of King Henry VII of England (Rymer, *Foedera*, XIII, 229), were less detailed.

The exact terms in which the sea-briefs and/or passports that the masters of merchant ships were obliged to carry on board had to be drafted were often prescribed by treaty. An example of such a form, which I have already quoted in full from the Annex to Art. 33 of the Franco-Netherlands treaty of 27 April 1662 (Dumont, VI^2, 412; Parry, 7, 139), issued by the Chief and Super-Intendent of the Navigation and Commerce of France, Caesar, Duke of Vendôme, was reproduced at p. 72 of the said Part IV of this publication.

Another example of such a prescribed form of passport was inserted in the famous Treaty of Marine of 1/10 December 1674 (Dumont, VII^1, 282; Parry, 13, 255), by which, after their third naval war, England's trade relations with the Netherlands were regulated for more than a century (until their fourth and last war of 1780). That treaty dealt, *inter alia*, with

> "the form of the Passport (or Sea-brief) to be asked of, and given by the Lord Admiral, or by those to whom the Exercise of Admiralty Jurisdiction is ordinarily committed, or by the Mayor or other Chief Magistrate, or by the Commissioners or other Principal Officers of the Customs in their respective Ports and Places within His Majesty's Dominions, to the Ships and Vessels sailing out thence, according to the Purport of [its Fifth Article] and by the Burgomasters of the Cities and Ports of the United Netherlands."

The British form of the passport read as follows:

> "To all unto whom these presents shall come, greeting. We ... Lord High Admiral of ..., We ... Lords Commissioners executing the office of the Lord High Admiral of ..., or We ... Judge of the High Court of the Admiralty of ..., or We ... the Mayor, or other Magistrate of ..., or We ... Commissioners, or Principal Officers of the Customs in the city or port of ..., do testify and make known, that ..., master or commander of the ship called the ..., hath appeared before us, and has declared by solemn oath, that the said ship or vessel, containing about ... tons, of which he is at present master or commander, doth belong to the inhabitants of ... within the dominions of the most Serene and Mighty Prince, the King of England, Scotland, France, and Ireland, Defender of the Faith, &c. So help him God. And in this regard it would be most acceptable to us, that the said master or commander be assisted in his just and lawful affairs, we do request you, and every of you, wheresoever the said master or commander shall arrive with his ship, and the goods laden on board and carried in her, that you would please to receive him courteously, and use him kindly, and admit him, upon paying the lawful and usual customs and other duties, to enter into, remain in, and pass from your ports, rivers, and dominions, and there to enjoy all kind of right of navigation, traffic, and commerce, in all places where he shall think fit; which we shall most willingly and readily acknowledge upon all occasions. In testimony and confirmation whereof, we have with our hand signed these presents, and caused them to be sealed with our seal. Dated at ... in ..., the ... day of ... in the year of our Lord ...".

A third example is that which I have taken from the trade relations between England and Sweden. The form of the passport is prescribed by Article 12 of the Anglo-Swedish treaty of 21 October 1661 (Dumont, VI^2, 384; Parry, 6, 469).

The new Instructions which Queen Anne during the War of the Spanish Succession issued on 11 May 1706 again referred to the old Swedish treaty, and that in very stringent wording. Art. 8 thereof prescribed in effect that

> "ships belonging to the subjects of Sweden shall be visited and brought up in case they are not furnished with passports, word for word according to the form prescribed by the

12th Article of the treaty between England and Sweden, or in case there be just cause of suspicion".

In graver cases the English prize courts condemned Swedish vessels which did not conform to that strict requirement, or at least pronounced just cause of seizure, both during the War of the Spanish Succession:

the *Staden of Stockholm* [1711] (Pratt-Lee, at p. 205: restored in the first instance, but condemned in appeal);

and during the War of the Austrian Succession:

the *Med Guds Hielpe* [1745-1750] (*ibid.*, at p. 198);

the *St. Erick* [1746] (*ibid*,, at pp. 85, 89):

> "It is evident this ship had not a proper pass according to the treaty, which is our rule to go by. We can take no notice of private regulations unless they were established by a new treaty between the nations";

the *Elizabeth Catherina* [1747] (*ibid.*, p. 115, at p. 119).

However, the rule was not observed so strictly everywhere, for in the case of the Danish *Anna Catherina* [1745] (Pratt-Lee, at p. 89) the Court held that although this ship did not have a Danish pass in the form prescribed by the treaty with Denmark, she had a pass agreeable to the spirit of that treaty, and that was considered sufficient.

Sometimes the term of validity of the passport was at issue: in the case of the *Nostra Seignora de Pentha de França* [1746] (Pratt-Lee, p. 90, at p. 94), for instance, the Court stated that the treaties had not declared how long passes should be in force.

In the history of old European trade relations with non-European countries the Islamic States of North Africa have played a special rôle. Thus, during negotiations with their old treaty partners in that area, the States General of the United Netherlands had the uncommon experience of having to submit to a special demand of the regional Rulers, the Pasha of Tunis *cum suis*, in November 1622 (Dumont, V^2, 411), *viz.*, that in a treaty dealing with sea-briefs or ship's patents, in addition to their own mention as the chief contracting party in their capacity of supreme representative body of their Confederation, separate mention should be made of Prince Maurice of Orange-Nassau, Captain General and Admiral of the Netherlands as co-contracting Netherlands party. This separate mention of the Prince of Orange was partly due to a lack of confidence of the Tunisian rulers in a collective treaty partner such as "les très illustres et puissans Seigneurs Etats des Pais-Bas", and partly to the special function of the Prince as Admiral of the Netherlands. Arts. 3, 4 and 9 of the treaty recognized the authority of "les Patentes du Sérenissime et Grand Prince Maurice, Prince d'Orange, Comte de Nassau".

Special care was also given to the drawing-up of the so-called Turkish passports in order to avoid disputes and the suspicion of the North African

Barbary States: an Edict of the Netherlands States General of 15 January 1729 restricted their validity to a three years' term, prescribed a new manner of indentation, and threatened severe penalties against those who might sell the passports or give them away, or fail to hand them in again within four weeks after their return to the Admiralty College that had issued them.

Judge Story, in his *Notes on the Principles and Practice of Prize Courts* (ed. Pratt, 1854), pp. 193 *et seq.*, gave a list of seven required ship's papers, *viz.*, (1) a certificate of registry; (2) a passport or sea-letter; (3) a muster roll; (4) a charter party; (5) a bill of lading; (6) invoices; (7) a logbook or ship's journal, and adds as an optional 8th document a policy of insurance, but many additional papers were already in use in those days and their number had increased considerably in the course of time.

This number had already increased to twelve on the eve of the codification, see Article 11 of the Russian Regulations of 20 September 1900, where the Admiralty Council summed them up with the names they carried in the languages of the main seafaring nations (Hurst & Bray, I, Appendix B, 342). See also Article 20 of the Japanese Regulations of 7 March 1904 (*ibid*, II, Appendix B, 425).

The *Institut de droit international* has in its session of Turin (1882) included a few provisions on ship's papers in section 5 of its *Règlement international des prises maritimes*. They were to the following effect:

> § 27.—Les papiers de bord requis en vertu du droit international sont les suivants:
> 1°. Les documents relatifs à la propriété du navire;
> 2°. Le connaissement;
> 3°. Le rôle d'équipage avec l'indication de la nationalité du patron et de l'équipage;
> 4°. Le certificat de nationalité, si les documents mentionnés sous le chiffre 3 n'y suppléent pas;
> 5°. Le journal de bord.
>
> § 28.—Les documents énoncés au précédent article doivent, pour avoir force probante, être rédigés clairement et sans équivoque.
>
> § 29.—Si, dans le constation d'une circonstance déterminante pour la saisie, il y a évidence quant à la nationalité ou la destination du navire, ou quant à la nature de la cargaison, ou quant à la nationalité du patron et de l'équipage, suivant le fait dont il s'agit,—et qu'un papier de bord ordinairement relatif à l'une de ces questions manque—la seule absence de ce papier n'est pas un motif de saisie, pourvu toutefois que les autres papiers de bord soient parfaitement d'accord entre eux sur le point en question.

It was an old principle that the absence of ship's papers exposed a vessel to condemnation. See Chapter XXVI, titre IX, Art. VI of the *Ordonnance de la Marine* of 1681 (Pardessus, IV, 385):

> "Seront encore de bonne prise les vaisseaux avec leur chargement, dans lesquels il ne sera trouvé chartes-parties, connaissemens, ni factures".

The absence of ship's papers on board, their spoliation or the use of false papers by the master have always remained valid grounds of grave suspicion against the vessel. This was the common opinion of prize courts both in

England and in France. Comp. on their judgments my exposé on the old English and French practice *infra*, pp. 497 *et seq*., and section 7 of III A *supra*, pp. 483-487, where I have also given a summary of the situation from another point of view.

Failure to observe scrupulously the rules prescribed by the treaty provisions has sometimes provoked international controversy. I cite as an example, dating from 1713, a dispute which arose between the States General of the United Netherlands and the Swedish Senate (acting for King Charles XII Gustav during his unfortunate war with Russia), when the Swedish Navy captured six Netherlands vessels off the coast of Norway and four of them were confiscated at Göteborg. The decision in those cases was based on the fact that the ship's papers had not been "countersigned" by the Clark of the States General as prescribed by the Netherlands-Swedish treaty of commerce of 12 October 1679 (Dumont, VII^1, 437; Parry, 15, 331). The Swedish Senate admitted that this formality had been neglected during the past thirty years in time of peace, but argued that this did not imply that it could also be dispensed with in wartime (comp. G. de Lamberty, *Mémoires pour servir à l'histoire du 18ème siècle* (Amsterdam, 1735-1740), vol. VIII, pp. 336, 342). The States General retorted by stressing that it was inequitable to bereave the ship owners of any possibility of proving their innocence simply because they had *bona fide* followed a practice that had been in use for thirty years.

Severe penalties were threatened by a Decree of the States General of the United Netherlands of 3 March 1648 against those who should make themselves guilty of fraud by sailing under the cover of double ship's papers.

Special provisions further dealt with merchant ships built in a neutral country that was not the country which issued the *lettre de mer*, and with merchant ships that carried neutral papers after having belonged earlier to enemy owners (*transfert de pavillon*). See for further particulars Art. 31 of the treaty between France and Hamburg of 1769 (Wenck, III, 752; Parry, 44, 255).

A thorough study of the legal provisions relative to ship's papers in the past was presented in 1786 to the Law Faculty of Leiden in a thesis for the doctorate by F.F.L. Pestel, § 13. The sea-briefs customary in the Netherlands differed from those prescribed by Art. 21 of the treaty with France of 1739, but were conformable to those required by Art. 46 of the marine treaty with England of 1674.

I will confine myself further to citing an additional number of obligatory forms of sea-letters prescribed by 17th and 18th century treaties.

From the 17th century:

—France-Spain, treaty of the Pyrenees, 7 November 1659 (Dumont, VI^2, 164), annex to Art. 17 after Art. 124, at p. 280;

—the Netherlands-Sweden, 6/16 July 1667 (Dumont, VII^1, 37; Parry, 10, 187), Art. 6, which, however, was limited to "the usual diploma or a diploma still to be agreed upon"; 26 November 1675 (Dumont, VII[1], 316; Parry, 14, 41), Art. 6; and 2/12 October 1679, Nijmegen (Dumont, VII[1], 437; Parry, 15, 331, at pp. 351, 352), annexes to Art. 20;

—the Netherlands-England, 21/31 July 1667 (Dumont, VII[1], 44; Parry, 10, 231), Art. 36; 17 February 1668 (Dumont, VII[1], 74; Parry, 10, 441), Art. 8;

—the Netherlands-France, 27 April 1662 (Dumont, VI[2], 412; Parry, 7, 139), annex to Art. 33; 10 August 1678, treaty of commerce, Nijmegen (Dumont, VII[1], 357; Parry, 14, 399), annex to Art. 20: form of transport and letter prescribed in the name of Louis, Comte de Vermandois, Admiral of France; 20 September 1697, Rijswijk, treaty of commerce (Dumont, VII[2], 386; Parry, 21, 371): form prescribed in the name of Louis, Comte de Toulouse, Admiral of France;

—England and the Netherlands-Denmark, December 1691, the abovementioned convention which incorporated the Declaratory Ordinance of King Christian V of Denmark-Norway of 19 May 1691 (Dumont, VII[2], 292; Parry, 19, 297); comp. also para. 5 of the "amplifications and elucidations" (Parry, 19, 309) prescribing the drafting of the passports and sea-briefs in the clearest possible terms in order to avoid any ambiguity.

From the 18th century:

—the Netherlands-Denmark, 15 June 1701 (Dumont, VIII[1], 32; Parry, 23, 353), Art. 11;

—France-England, treaty of commerce, Utrecht, 11 April 1713 (Dumont, VIII[1], 345; Parry, 28, 1), Art. 21 with annexes;

—France-the Netherlands, treaty of commerce, Utrecht, 11 April 1713 (Dumont, VIII[1], 377; Parry, 28, 83), Art. 24 and annexes; 21 December 1739 (Wenck, I, 414; Parry 35, 459), Art. 21 and annexes, in the name of the Duke of Penthièvre, Admiral of France;

—France-Denmark/Norway, 23 August 1742 (Wenck, I, 591 *et seq.*, at pp. 637-638; Parry, 36, 425), Art. 21 with annex after Art. 46;

—the Netherlands-the Two Sicilies, 27 August 1753 (Wenck, II, 753; Parry, 40, 111), Art. 26 with annexes after Art. 47;

—France-Hamburg, 1 April 1769 (Wenck, III, 752; Parry, 44, 255), Art. 31; in this case the passports had different contents, one for peace-time, one for wartime;

—France-United States, 6 February 1778 (Parry, 46, 417), annex to Art. 27 (25) (on this double numbering see Part VI of this publication, p. 243).

Many of the treaties quoted above included provisions aimed at giving the belligerents guarantees against fraud, consisting either of the requirement of (*a*) an oath by the ship owner or master, or of (*b*) a certification by the local authority.

Ad (*a*). The texts of such oaths can be found in Pratt-Lee's Appendix B, at pp. 265 and 266, respectively. The oath by the owner concerned the burden and the property of his vessel, the oath by the owners was specially required in the case of joint ownership.

A very elaborate form of oath to be taken by the owners of ship and cargo was annexed to Art. 5 of the "amplifications and elucidations" of the abovementioned convention of 1691 between England and the Netherlands, on the one hand, and Denmark, on the other. Art. 5 itself required the oath, just as the sea-briefs and passports, to be drafted in the clearest possible words in order to rule out any ambiguity, and the annexed oath formula included six detailed assurances concerning the ownership of the vessel, her course to Bordeaux and back, the character of the cargo, etc., all intended to prevent collusion.

Ad (*b*). For a *formula contrasignationis* see the annex of the Netherlands-Swedish treaty of commerce of Nijmegen of 2/12 October 1679 (Dumont, VII[1], 437; Parry, 15, 331 *et seq.*, at pp. 352-353):

> "Nos, &c. ... certificamus hisce, quod hae presentes Literae Maritimae sint veré & certo concessae & extraditae à competentibus Consulibus & Senatu Civitatis ... & quòd, ut genuinae, respectuque Sigillo & subscriptiones suae Authenticae, apud omnes & singulos ad quos quovis modo pertinere poterit, plenum suum vigorem & effectum obtinere meritò debeant.
> Datum loco ..., Die ..., Mense ..., Anno ...".

The latter documents, variously named, had to certify, *inter alia*, that the master had confirmed by oath before the Magistrate of his town or before the Admiralty that the ship under his command appertained to an owner, subject of the Prince under whose auspices she sailed, and to state how many tons she could carry. Such a certification was prescribed, *inter alia*, by the special Article, annexed to the Spanish-Netherlands peace treaty of 30 January 1648 (Dumont, VI[1], 429, 439; Parry, I, 1):

> "étant entendu que les Seigneurs Etats Généraux ... donneront des contremarques pour, au moyen d'icelles, d'autant mieux reconnoistre la validité desdits Passeports de l'Admirauté, afin qu'ils ne puissent estre falsifiés";

Art. 11 *in fine* of the treaty of marine between the same Powers of 17 December 1650 (Dumont, VI[1], 570; Parry, 2, 259) which further laid down that the ship's papers, drawn up according to the prescribed form, should be given "entière foy et créance" provided that the contracting Parties gave "contremarques" against falsification;

Art. 33 *in fine* of the France-Netherlands treaty of 27 April 1662 (Dumont, VI[2], 412; Parry, 7, 139), prescribing a countersign by "Sadite Majesté et lesdits Seigneurs Etats Généraux"; Art. 20 *in fine* of the Netherlands-French treaty of commerce of 10 August 1678 (Dumont, VII[1], 357; Parry, 14, 399); and the annex to Art. 21 of the Franco-Netherlands treaty of 21 December 1739 (Wenck, I, 414 *et seq.*, at p. 436; Parry, 35, 459 *et seq.*, at p. 483), according to which

"... il sera ... permis ... d'envoyer une petite Barque ou Chaloupe à bord des Bâtimens François, & d'y faire entrer deux ou trois hommes seulement, auxquels seront montrez les Passeports & Lettres de Mer, par le Maître ou Patron des Bâtimens François, de la manière ci-dessus spécifiée, suivant le formulaire des Lettres de Mer qui sera inséré à la fin de ce Traité; par lesquels Passeports & Lettres de Mer il puisse apparoir non seulement de la charge, mais aussi du lieu de la demeure & résidence, tant du Maître ou Patron, que du Navire même, afin que par ces deux moyens on puisse connoître s'ils portent des Marchandises de Contrebande, & qu'il apparoisse suffisamment, tant de la qualité du dit Navire, que de son Maître & Patron, auxquels Passeports & Lettres de Mer entière foi & créance devra être donnée; & afin que l'on connoisse mieux la validité des dites Lettres de Mer, & qu'elles ne puissent en aucune manière être falsifiées & contrefaites, il sera donné certaines marques & contreseings de Sa Majesté & des dits Seigneurs Etats Généraux"

and the Admiralty declared as follows:

"Nous ... de l'Admirauté de ... certifions que ..., Maître du Navire nommé au Passeport ci-dessus, a prêté le serment mentionné en icelui.
Fait à ... le ... jour de ... de mille sept-cens ...".

The same purpose (protection of the captor from fraud) was served by provisions which prescribed a periodic renewal of the passports. See, *e.g.*, Art. 32 of France's treaty with the three main Hanse towns of Bremen, Hamburg and Lübeck of 28 September 1716 (Dumont, VIII[1], 478; Parry, 30, 19):

"La preuve de la Patrie ou de la naturalisation, tant des Officiers que de l'équipage, sera établie par les Passeports ou Lettres de Mer, qui contiendront le nom et le port du Navire, le nom & le lieu de naissance & de l'habitation du Propriétaire, ainsi que du Maître ou Commandant du Navire; lesquelles Lettres seront renouvellées chaque année, si le Vaisseau ne fait pas un voyage qui demande un plus long terme, ladite preuve sera pareillement établie par le rôle d'équipage bien & duëment certifié."

Additional authenticated papers were required by Art. 21 of the Franco-English treaty of commerce of 11 April 1713 (Dumont, VIII[1], 345; Parry, 28, 1), mentioning the port from where the ship had sailed, the port towards which she was due to sail, the name of her owner and master and her own name, and the nature of the cargo she was carrying, and by Art. 24 of the treaty of 1 April 1769 between France and Hamburg. Art. 21 of the treaty of 1713 ran as follows:

"Mais pour éviter & prévenir la discorde, & toute sorte d'inimitiez de part & d'autre, il a esté convenu, qu'en cas que l'une des deux Parties se trouvast engagée dans la guerre, les vaisseaux et les bâtiments appartenant aux sujets de l'autre Partie, devront estre munis de Lettres de Mer, qui contiendront le nom, la propriété & la grandeur du vaisseau, de même que le nom et le lieu de l'habitation du maître ou du capitaine de ce vaisseau, en sorte que par là il paroisse que ce vaisseau appartient véritablement aux sujets de l'une ou de l'autre Partie; & ces Lettres de Mer seront accordées & conçues en la manière insérée dans ce Traité. Elles seront aussi renouvellées chaque année, s'il arrive que le vaisseau revienne dans le cours de l'an. Il a été aussi convenu que ces sortes de vaisseaux chargez ne devront pas estre seulement munis de Lettres de Mer ... mais encore de Certificats contenant les espèces de la charge, le lieu d'où le vaisseau est parti & celuy de sa destination, afinque l'on puisse connaître s'il ne porte aucune des marchandises deffendues, ou de contrebande spécifiées dans le 19 Article de ce Traité. Lesquels Certificats seront expédiez par les

Officiers du lieu d'où le vaisseau sortira, selon leur coûtume; il sera libre aussi, si on le désire, & si on le juge à propos, d'exprimer dans lesdites Lettres à qui appartienent les marchandises."

English practice

The English case law on various irregularities in the conduct of ship- or cargo-owners or of ship's masters at sea has been surveyed above in section 7 of III A, pp. 482 *et seq.* They did not relate exclusively to offences committed in respect of ship's papers, but also to various other forms of fraud and to resistance by the master to visit and search. For that reason I will not enter again into this subject here, but refer to that more comprehensive section 7, also for the rôle which ship's papers have played amongst the grounds of condemnation of captured ships and goods.

Ship's papers—passports, manifests, crew-rolls, bills of lading, etc.—have indeed always had an important rôle in the exercise of the right of prize and the adjudication of prizes. It was especially the requirements of their presence on board a visited vessel and of the veracity of their contents, and the question of what sanction should be imposed upon the offenders for their falsification, suppression or "spoliation", which were the issues dealt with in many decisions of British prize courts. These held strictly to the rule that owners could, in principle, only prove the neutral character of the property claimed by the papers that were found on board. See the case of the Russian vessel *Ida* [1854] (Spinks, 26; Roscoe, II, 268, also reproduced by De Pistoye and Duverdy, *Traité*, vol. II, 451) in which the neutral ownership of cargo carried by an enemy ship was to be established.

The use of false papers brought not only the condemnation of the vessel but also the forfeiture of her freight: case of the *America* [1803] (3 C.Rob., 36; Roscoe, I, 127, footnote *a*).

The English precedents are paralleled by French judgments to a corresponding effect. These were chiefly connected with irregularities in the *papiers de bord* and will be discussed below in an independent exposé.

French practice

As to the copious French case law, based on the various legislative enactments in force at the time, De Pistoye and Duverdy's exposé of the subject-matter in their *Traité des prises maritimes* is difficult to follow. Its main content can be found in vol. I under two headings: "Des pièces de bord" (where the title of § 1 "Justification de la neutralité" is missing) (pp. 416-462) and § 2 "De la validité des passeports" (pp. 463-509), and further in vol. II under the surprising heading "De la composition des équipages, Rôle d'équipage" (pp. 30-70). The two groups of data are connected by cross-references from vol. I to vol. II, but that in a manner which makes it very difficult to find in vol. II the cases to which reference is made in vol. I, as a result of the fact that this reference is made not to pages in that vol. II, but to the very complicated system of arrangement of the source material in titles (IV), chapters, sections and paragraphs.

Many judgments dealing with the alleged irregularity of the *papiers de bord* or similar irregular circumstances as grounds of confiscation of prizes are quoted by the authors partly in vol. I, pp. 416-509 under *titre* VI ("Des choses de bonne prise"), chap. II ("Des propriétés neutres"), section IV ("Des pièces de bord"), § 1 ("De la justification de la neutralité"), dealing *sub* (*a*) with "la force probante des papiers de bord et du moment où elles doivent être produites pour faire preuve", *sub* (*b*) with "pièces non signées" and *sub* (*c*) with "connaissements", and § 2 ("De la validité des passeports"), and partly in vol. II, pp. 30-70, in § 4 of the same *titre*, chapter and section. A selection from that mass of information follows below.

As the authors report in vol. I, rules on this particular subject were included in the *Ordonnance de la Marine* of 1681, those of 1694 during the Nine Years' War, 1744 during the War of the Austrian Succession and 1778 during the American War of Independence. The references made to the following pages are to De Pistoye-Duverdy's *Traité*.

French prize law made a distinction between *cabotage* and *voyages de caravane*; see the conclusion of M. Portalis concerning the *Bagatelle* [*an* VIII] (I, 475):

> "Les puissances du Nord ne sont pas dans l'usage de limiter le délai des passeports en matière de caravane ou de grand cabotage. Comme le cabotage se compose d'une multitude de petits voyages intermédiaires, il a été décidé plusieurs fois que le voyage n'était terminé que lorsque le navire était retourné dans les Etats du souverain d'où il était parti".

If a passport for cabotage prescribed a specific order of the ports of call, this order should not be altered: the *Maria* [*an* IX] (I, 470). A passport for cabotage which indicated a specific destination, followed by the words "et autres lieux", authorized putting into every port: *Saint-Jean* [*an* IX] (I, 475).

A *voyage de caravane* was not limited to any prescribed route; the ship could call repeatedly at the same harbour: *Quintus* (I, 473).

A basic requirement according to French law was that every sea-going vessel should carry a sea-brief or passport. There were, however, exceptions to this rule.

The capture of the *Mansoure* and the *Rouge* by the *Nisus* [1828] was declared invalid and the ships were released because it was not customary for coasters to carry ship's papers (I, 423).

On the other hand, an armed coaster without papers, the *Junon* [1829] (I, 424), was condemned even though the arming of coasters was customary in their country (Algiers). The capture, in 1827, in the Levant of a Greek mistick by a French frigate on the ground of her sailing without *papiers de bord* and without a flag, was also declared valid by the *Conseil d'Etat*, even though it was customary in those areas to sail without them (I, 424).

A further basic requirement, laid down in Art. 2 of the *Règlement* of 1778, was that

> "Les navires neutres seront obligés de justifier sur mer de leur nationalité".

However, this strict requirement was held not to apply to French or Allied vessels; these could, therefore, prove their national character by documents that were not on board at the moment of capture: the *Deux-Charlottes* (I, 448) and the *Jonge Cornelis* [1816] (I, 450).

In the *Réussite contre San-Bonaventura* (I, 432), however, proof of their presence on board was held to be more important than their actual submission at the moment of seizure: *L'Antoinette contre le Bordelais* (I, 440), the *Saint Jean* and the *Neptune* (I, 444).

Although the rule that the neutral character of a ship had to be proved by the showing of her *papiers de bord* was on the whole applied very strictly, its rigour was thus mitigated by interpretation: the Danish vessel the *Antoinette*, arrested on a voyage from Copenhagen to the Danish colony of Tranquebar (India), which had not shown her papers in proof of her neutral character at the moment of arrest, was nevertheless recognized as neutral when she produced them as yet later, because it was established that they were actually on board at the moment of seizure.

De Pistoye and Duverdy cite in their volume I, p. 420, another old precedent dating from the Nine Years' War (1693), the *Rédempteur du Monde*, which turned on the continued applicability of an old legal rule, later alleged to have been cancelled by Art. 2 of the *Règlement* of 1778. In the case of 1693 the *Conseil des prises* refused to accept certain papers (*livres de sous-bord*) as supplementary evidence.

Older French prize court judgments have produced a copious case law concerning the validity or nullity of passports and other ship's papers. Without going into too great detail, I will briefly mention the various circumstances under which their validity was questionable.

The nullity of a passport could not be accepted on simple presumptions: the *Furet contre l'Elisabeth* (I, 439). Even if a passport was null and void, the neutral character of the ship could be validly inferred from other documents: the *Constance* (I, 479);

the *Eleonora* (I, 465); as to Sweden a "lettre de franchise" was a valid substitute for a passport;

the *Carolina-Wilhelmina* (I, 466): inside the area of the Baltic—characterized at the time (*an* VIII) as a "mer close"—a certificate of ownership could validly replace a passport, but this was no longer the case when a vessel (*in casu* one under Prussian colours) left that area. To the same effect: *La Paix* (I, 486).

The *Conseil d'Etat* held a passport for the Mediterranean also valid for Constantinople, as being part of the Mediterranean: the *Libérateur contre le Napoléon* [1807] (II, 42).

A passport dit not need to be signed by the Souvereign in person; he could delegate his power (*ibid.*).

A passport delivered for one voyage lacked validity for another voyage if the ship had in the meantime returned to her harbour: *La Paix* (I, 476).

As a rule, for a passport to be recognized as valid, it was required that:

(*a*) it had been made out or delivered by a neutral Prince in a port under his own sovereignty: the *Haabet contre l'Heureux* (I, 239), the *Munster Doris contre le Brave* (I, 477); the *Constance* (I, 479), the *La Famille* (I, 483), the *Charitas* and the *Louise* (both at p. 484), a special ground of nullity being the fact that the ship had not put into a port belonging to her Sovereign for a period of a year.

However, a passport delivered to a vessel while she was not staying in one of the ports of the State that delivered it to her was not always null and void, see the case of the Ragusan ship the *Notre Dame de Bon Conseil* (I, 490), which had left Ragusa with a passport delivered there; owing to the death of her master at Porto Ferraio, a port then under British blockade, which prevented her from sailing, she needed a new passport; this was made out to her by the Senate of Ragusa. The Commissary of the Government Portalis argued:

> "le navire, ne pouvant aller chercher le passe-port, il fallait nécessairement que le passe-port vînt chercher le navire",

and he, consequently, saw no valid ground for her condemnation after her capture by a French privateer.

Comp. also the cases of

the Danish vessel *L'Amitié* (I, 460), sold in Amsterdam by a Dane to another Dane: the buyer could send for a passport from his Sovereign and the passport so delivered to him was valid;

the *Attention* (I, 489), a ship of neutral origin bought by a Dane in an allied country and never since her sale having put into a Danish port;

(*b*) the owner had not failed to apply for a new passport after returning to a port of his Sovereign and had not engaged in navigation in other seas than those mentioned in the passport: the *Christiern-Swerin* (I, 469);

(*c*) the crew-roll had not been altered: the *Bagatelle* (I, 475).

The duration of the validity of a passport was considered in the cases of

the *Bucking* (I, 470): it was not limited to one year if the passport was for cabotage and the ship had not returned to a port of her Sovereign;

the *Maria* (Wilkens, Master) (*ibid.*): her passport was held to have lapsed after more than three years.

The fate of a captured vessel suspected of having enemy character often hinged on a question of proof: was the content of the ship's papers sufficient and convincing?

Depositions by the master and/or his crew were generally held to prevail over contradictory contents of the ship's papers. This was already decided during the Nine Years' War in 1692 by the *Conseil du Roi* with regard to the *Notre-Dame du Pilier* (I, 424), of neutral character according to the ship's papers, but in actual fact an enemy vessel according to the testimony of the crew. To the same effect the judgment in the case of *La Nancy contre l'Enrôleur* (I, 425; II, 206).

But in the case of *Reysiger contre le Courageux* (I, 435) it was held that an expert report that the vessel concerned was an enemy vessel could not prevail over her papers which certified her neutral character. In this same case the Court was faced by the fact of the presence on board of two different passports, one for cabotage, the other for a fixed destination. This fact was not considered as fatal for the vessel because it appeared that the second passport was only to take effect after the expiration of the first.

A decree of the *Conseil du Roi* of 1692 (I, 424) laid down that testimony of the crew that their vessel was an enemy vessel should prevail over ship's papers that stated her neutral character, in particular when the testimony ran counter to the crew's interest: the *Munster Doris contre le Brave* (I, 477) and the *Nancy* (II, 206).

On the other hand, experts' reports concerning the enemy character of a cargo should give way to papers stating its neutrality: the *Gebrüder contre l'Oiseau* (I, 433).

Documents should be judged not according to their name, but to their content: *Fredericka* (I, 438).

The conclusive force of ship's papers must be assessed at the moment of their submission to the captor (I, 424).

Although the captor was obliged to take the ship's papers, he was not precluded from producing other proof if he was unable to submit them to the tribunal.

Other judgments concentrated on various forms of irregularity of the ship's papers.

Such irregularity, which was often the ground for the condemnation of the ship, could consist of various deficiencies.

Unsigned or defectively signed papers were held invalid in the cases of the *Thuyskon* (*Traité*, I, 452), the *Aeolus* (I, 453), the *Liberté* (I, 454), the *Louise-Auguste* (I, 456) and the *Anna* (I, 457).

Another irregularity was the lack of information they gave about the nationality, the domicile or the quality of the ship-owner or of the persons on board.

Contradictions in the ship's papers gave rise to serious doubt: *La Molly contre l'Éole* (I, 426); the *Winyau contre l'Ariège* (I, 429), and so did the carriage of simulated or double papers (*e.g.* French and enemy): the *Saint-Antoine et la Vierge-des-Carmes* (I, 425). Simulated papers, however, were not under all circumstances a valid ground for condemnation, especially not when it was proved that the simulation was intended to deceive the enemy: the *Censor contre l'Entreprise* (I, 445), in which the Prize Court held that although the fact that the ship carried simulated papers was by itself enough to justify her capture, she was to be released when it was discovered that she was sailing with the consent of the French Government which staged the simulation for the purpose of deceiving the enemy: "Le navire le *Censor*, sous pavillon suédois, part pour Riga, port de Russie. Il y carge des mâts et autres bois de construction, pour le compte de la République française. Les circonstances ne permettaient pas de laisser à découvert la véritable destination de ce chargement. On prend la robe suédoise pour cacher la propriété française, et les papiers de bord annoncent que la destination du navire et du chargement est pour Lisbonne.

Tout était simulé dans les papiers trouvés à bord du *Censor*. Mais toute simulation n'est point une fraude. ... La simulation n'a donc pas eu pour objet de faire du mal à autrui, mais seulement de prévenir celui qu'on aurait pu nous faire. ... La prétendue simulation qui a été manifestée dans la cause présente ne pouvait donc jamais devenir une prétexte de confiscation."

See also the case of *Les Deux-Charlottes contre le Flibustier* (I, 448): "... le navire *les Deux-Charlottes* et sa cargaison sont la propriété d'un négociant français, ... ses expéditions danoises étaient simulées et le gouvernement l'avait autorisé à emprunter pavillon neutre.

Il était nécesaire de prendre contre la simulation les précautions. De là, la nécessité de la part des neutres de prouver leur neutralité par les pièces mêmes de bord; mais lorsque le gouvernement lui-même est instruit de la simulation, toutes ces précautions ne sont plus nécessaires. Si les pièces qui prouvent la propriété française étaient à bord, il n'y aurait plus de simulation, ou, du moins, elle serait imparfaite.

Le reproche d'immoralité tombe de lui-même; c'est le gouvernement qui permet cette espèce de ruse de guerre. La question de savoir s'il est permis de tromper un ennemi doit être réléguée dans les écoles; elle peut occuper les moralistes; mais la politique n'est pas encore assez épurée pour rejeter une fraude qui doit avoir une influence utile sur notre commerce et notre prospérité.

Le corsaire capteur est trompé lui-même? Sans doute, ses espérances sont frustrées, et il ne fait pas le bénéfice qu'il aurait pu faire, si la prise eût été ennemie; c'est une de ces chances multipliées que l'on court dans ses sortes d'entreprises.

Le Conseil des prises déclare la prise du navire *les Deux-Charlottes* par le corsaire *le Flibustier* nulle et de nul effet."

In the *Anne-Louise* (II, 69) the fact that her name differed in her passport from that in other ship's papers was not considered to be a ground for condemnation because the captor had not proved that this neutral vessel had been of enemy construction or ownership.

The *John William* (II, 57) was a ship that in 1797 obtained at Embden a passport for one year, and for navigation under a neutral or allied flag and to various places. She was forced to engage a new crew in Amsterdam; having been captured later in the Pas-de-Calais she was released by the Prize Court.

It was especially French case law that abounds in judgments relating to the list of the crew. The validity of such a list was to be judged according to the law of the vessel concerned, not according to French law since this did not apply to foreigners: the *Louise* (I, 484; II, 49).

Other judgments dealing with the validity of the list of the crew were those relating to

the *Carolina-Wilhelmina* (I, 466): a list made out in a port other than that of sailing and with erasions in the text was considered null and void;

the *Maria* (I, 470): the roll had to be made out in the ship's harbour even if the crew was formed elsewhere;

the *Constance* (I, 479): the roll was held valid, although the signature did not mention the capacity of the signing officer;

the *L'Amitié* (I, 460): a change in the crew roll stated by the consul of the neutral State to which the ship belonged in a foreign port was accepted as valid;

the *Engel-Elisabeth* (I, 488), a ship of enemy construction, which after her capture from the British by a French privateer had been sold to a Prussian subject in Amsterdam and had obtained a passport of the King of Prussia there; the lack of designation in the crew-roll of the names, nationality and domicile of those composing the crew did not in this case authorize the condemnation of the vessel because the roll had been drawn up according to her national law and an interrogation of the members of the crew proved that they were neither natives nor inhabitants of an enemy country.

See also the long judgment in the case of the *Pégou* (II, 51) in which the crew list appeared not to have been certified by the authorities in the port of departure; the ship was nevertheless released.

A ship was held to be liable to condemnation when the list of the crew

did not mention their place of birth, nationality and/or domicile: the Swedish ship *Alte Freundschaft contre le Hardi* (II, 43); *La Julie contre l'Anna* (II, 47);

had not been made out by a public officer in the port of sailing: the *Geertruida contre le Juste* (II, 47) (*Tribunal de Cassation*);

differed from the sailors actually on board: *Jeune Guillaume* (II, 48); *Le Portland contre le Diable-à-quatre* (II, 66);

was only valid for one, different journey: the *Républicain* (II, 48);
was made out in a port other than that of departure: the *Carolina-Wilhelmina* (I, 466; II, 49);
was renewed in a neutral port by the local authorities instead of by the Consul of the flag State: the *Frederic* (I, 493; II, 59), although that Consul was empowered to authorize such renewal: the *Bucking* (II, 59);
was altered by the master without a subsequent visa from his national Consul or because that visa was obtained by fraud: the *Juliana* (II, 60);
did not mention the substitution of the original master by another: the *Columbia* (II, 62).

On the other hand, the prize was released in the following cases:
the Ragusan *Compagnie Fidèle* (II, 49): ships which navigated exclusively in the Adriatic did not need a list of their crew;
the *Mercure* (II, 46), which had admitted foreigners on board at sea as passengers without mentioning them on the list of the crew; in spite of that the *Tribunal de Cassation* held the papers to be "en bonne et due forme";
the *Retrieve* (II, 68), whose crew-list was not signed by witnesses, but did carry the signatures of a notary and the naval officer;
the *Goede Verwagting* (II, 58), alterations in whose crew-list were duly stated in her port of stay; no statement by officers in her port of departure was required; comp. also the *Bagatelle* (*ibid.*);
the *Félix=Phénix* (II, 64), whose crew had been renewed in a neutral country, even though the necessity for doing so was not proved.

Section 2. VISIT AND SEARCH

Already the oldest sources of prize law contained provisions dealing with the procedure of the visit of merchant vessels met at sea by a King's ship or a privateer. They were in fact among the very first historical prize law rules obtaining in regional or municipal codes or instructions: comp. the data concerning the *Rôles d'Oléron* and the *Black Book of the Admiralty* in Chapter I, pp. 16-22 *supra*.

The procedure of visitation of ships met at sea was prescribed in detail in Arts. 6 and 7 of Part B of the *Black Book of the Admiralty*. The latter Article ran as follows (Travers Twiss, vol. I, p. 29):

> "Item if any shipp or vessell of the said ffleete hath leave and authority from the admirall to goe from the ffleete about any message or other business, if they meete with or find any forreigne vessels upon the sea or in the enemies' ports, then those of our ffleete ought to ask the masters and governors of such forreigne vessels from whence they are and to examine them well about their ladeing and likewise their papers and documents, and if any thing of suspition be found in such vessells that the goods therein doe belong to the enemies, the said vessells with their masters and governors as also the goods in them shall be brought to the admirall, and if it be found there that they are honest merchants and friends without suspition of colour the goods shall be restored againe to them without damage, otherwise they shall be seized with their goods and ransomed as the maritime law doth will and require".

Resistance to visit or search by neutral vessels was already in the earliest periods a valid ground for their capture:

> "if any of our shipps or vessels doe meete upon the sea or in ports any other vessells which doe make any resistance or defence against those our shipps or vessells, then it is lawfull for our men to assaile the others as enemies, and by force to seize and bring them before the admirall entirely as they have taken them ...".

Art. 8 of Part B of the *Black Book* laid down that

> "se aucune de noz nefs ou vesseaulx encontrent sur la mer ou en ports aucunes autres vesseaulx qui facent rebelletees ou defense encontre ceulx de noz nefs ou vesseaulx, a doncques bien lise a noz gentz les autres comme ennemys assaillir et par forte mayn les prendre et amener entierement comme il y les ont gagnez devant l'admiral." (Ordonnance of Philippe de Valois of 23 March 1338).

Under the very general heading "if a ship or vessel meets with a ship of an enemy", Chapter 243 of the *Consolat de Mar* dealt in actual fact with the conditions under which a merchant ship was entitled to offer resistance to an armed enemy vessel:

> "If any ship or vessel of merchandise shall meet with any other ship or vessel of an enemy, if in the ship or vessel of merchandise aforesaid there shall be a merchant or merchants, the managing owner of the ship or vessel is bound to demand of them, whether they should wish or are willing that he should attack and combat and capture that ship or vessel of the enemy. And if the said merchant or merchants assent to it, all or the greater part, the said managing owner of the ship may well do so, for if the said merchants should suffer any loss or detriment thereby, the managing owner of the ship or vessel is not bound to make them any compensation, nor to make good any of the said loss, if the merchants should sustain any, since they assented and it was done with their good will. But, nevertheless, if the said managing owner of the ship or vessel shall do this ... without the knowledge and without the consent of the said merchants, all or the greater part, of the said merchants shall sustain or have to sustain any loss or prejudice, the said managing owner of the ship is bound to make good, without any dispute, all the said loss or prejudice which etc.".

The chapter further regulated the share in the profit that might thus have been made, to which the different interested persons could lay claim.

Early 16th century Instructions to Admiral of the Sea Sir Edward Haward of 1512 "to guide him during the enterprise to be made against the French King in Guyenne", dealt in twenty-eight articles, *inter alia*, with visitation and search, and with resistance of neutral vessels to those belligerent measures as grounds for condemnation. They have been reproduced from Rymer's *Foedera*, XIII, 229, by Chr. Robinson in his *Collectanea Maritima* of 1801, pp. 1 *et seq.*

The purpose of visit and search was always to verify the ship's national (enemy or neutral) character, her port of destination, the nature or destination of her cargo, the nationality of her crew, etc.

The operation began with a simple visit with the object of controlling the ship's papers, but it could be followed by a search of the vessel and her contents in case any suspicion arose or an existing suspicion was not dispelled.

Seafaring nations often concluded treaties on the subject, in which they made the legality of both operations dependent upon the observance of strict formalities and included guarantees against abuses by the captor. Such provisions were very detailed, relating as they did to the introductory summons, the number of mariners sent to institute the visit and search, the minimum distance between the warship and the merchant ship at which the introductory verification (visit) was to be made, the formalities of the search in case of suspicion, etc. The treaty provisions which will be cited below give some impression of what was customary and compulsory.

The first action by a belligerent warship or privateer, when proceeding to arrest a vessel encountered at sea, was to give a flag, sails or light signal, followed, if necessary, by a warning shot, destined to cause her to stop and to submit to a "visit". On behalf of the Commission for Naval History of the Royal Netherlands Academy of Sciences, R. E.J. Weber has recently (1982) published a volume (XI) on the *Seinboeken voor de Nederlandse oorlogsvloten en konvooien tot 1690* (Signalling-books on behalf of the Netherlands navy and convoys up to 1690).

The visit had to be carried out by a limited number of mariners, sent out in a sloop, while the arresting warship or privateer had to await the result at a distance.

When the inspection of the ship's papers gave no ground of suspicion against the arrested vessel, she was to be allowed to continue her voyage unhindered. This was often laid down in express terms in the treaty provisions concerned, such as those quoted below in section 3, *sub* (*a*).

When, on the other hand, suspicion of deceit or bad faith arose, or an existing suspicion was confirmed or not dispelled, the formal visit of the ship's papers could be followed by a search of the vessel and her cargo, with as little violence as possible. The manner in which such a search had to be effected was sometimes defined by a municipal law—see, *e.g.*, Art. 20 of *titre* IX of the French *Ordonnance de la Marine* of 1681 and a Danish law of 5 April 1710—, but usually again by treaty. Many of the 17th and 18th century treaties cited below indeed expressly prohibited the captor from prizing open packing cases: Art. 39 of the Franco-Netherlands treaty of commerce of 27 April 1662, Art. 7 of the Anglo-Netherlands treaty of marine of 1/10 December 1674, Art. 26 of the Franco-Netherlands treaty of commerce of 10 August 1678, Art. 26 of the Netherlands-Swedish treaty of commerce of 2/12 October 1679, and from the 18th century Art. 24 of the Franco-British treaty of commerce of 31 March/11 April 1713 and Art. 21 of the treaty of 1 April 1769 between France and Hamburg.

Imprisonment of the crew or placing them under restraint was not permitted unless it was absolutely necessary for the security of the captors, who were liable in damages for so doing: the *San Juan Baptista* and the *La Purissima Conceptión* [1803] (5 C.Rob., 33; Roscoe, I, 417).

At later periods the requirement of previous visit and, if necessary, search of suspect ships encountered at sea by a belligerent naval unit or a privateer was frequently incorporated into bilateral treaties of commerce and navigation, peace or alliance.

Those treaty provisions used to be copies of each other and were, as a result, on the whole as like as two peas. I will for that reason abstain from quoting too many texts and simply make below a brief selection from the ample source material available, from successive historical periods and from diverse types of treaty relations—of navigation, alliance or peace; between monarchies *inter se* or between kingdoms and republics, such as the Republic of the United Netherlands.

An early and very detailed provision prescribing the manner in which the visit was to be carried out was that embodied in Article III of the Treaty of Maritime Commerce between France and the Netherlands of 18 April 1646 (Dumont, VI[1], 342), which I will quote in extenso:

> "Pour obvier aux inconveniens qui pourroient arriver lors que les Navires Marchands des Sujets desdits Sieurs Estats seront rencontrez par les Vaisseaux de Guerre de Sa Majesté, ou Capitaines Armateurs, & pour oster tout sujet de differend & contention à l'avenir, lesdits Navires, après avoir abbatu leur pavillon par respect, sitost qu'ils auront reconnu celuy de France, & les Vaisseaux François, qui ne se pourront approcher plus près qu'environ la portée d'un Canon desdits Vaisseaux Marchands Hollandois, lesquels se soutiendront & paroitront sur le bord, au premier signal qui leur sera donné d'un coup de Canon tiré sans balle, sans obligation d'abaisser leurs voiles (Sa Majesté voulant bien encor se relâcher en ce point de l'observation de ladite Ordonnance de 1584, en faveur desdits Sieurs les Estats pendant ledit temps de quatre années, en attendant que ledit Règlement general ait esté fait) afin de donner le loisir aux Vaisseaux de Guerre de Sa Majesté, ou autres Armateurs, d'envoyer leur Chaloupe à bord desdits Navires Marchands, dans lesquelles trois Personnes au plus, pour sçavoir d'eux leur route, & faire apparoir de leur Passeport ou Patente, & s'il n'y a point des Munitions & choses cy-dessus exceptees & deffendues, sans faire autre plus exacte perquisition ny visite, ny que pour ce regard il soit pris aucune sorte de Droits, sous prétexte de salaires, vacations ou présens. Ce qui n'aura lieu neanmoins qu'en Mer & ès Costes étrangères, demeurant en son entier la visite & recherche ordinaire ès Ports & Havres de France, selon qu'il est accoutumé, & ainsi qu'il en a esté bien & dûëment usé par le passé".

Subsequent provisions to the same purport in later conventions of the 17th century were gradually simplified, but they remained virtually the same. See, among others, the articles, inserted in the following treaties:

Spain-The Netherlands, 17 December 1650 (Dumont, VI[1], 570; Parry, 2, 259), Art. 11: the warship or privateer may send out a sloop with two or three men, but must itself remain at the distance of a cannon shot;

France-The Netherlands, 27 April 1662 (Dumont, VI[2], 412; Parry, 7, 139), Art. 33;

England-The Netherlands (Treaty of Marine), 1/10 December 1674 (Dumont, VII[1], 283; Parry, 13, 255), in Article 7 of which the Parties prohibited the breaking-open of chests, and in Art. 14 even deemed it necessary expressly to forbid cruelties in the process of visit and search;

France-the Netherlands (Treaty of Commerce), 10 August 1678 (Dumont, VII[1], 357; Parry, 14, 399), Art. 20; by Art. 25 the commanders of warships and ship owners were obliged thenceforth to deposit a cautionary sum of 15,000 *livres tournois* as a guarantee against their possible molestation of to those on board the merchant vessel, prohibited by Art. 24;

The Netherlands-Sweden, Treaty of Commerce, 2/12 October 1679 (Dumont, VII[1], 437; Parry, 15, 331), Article 20—a provision which the Parties to a later Convention of 20/30 June 1691 (Denmark, on the one hand, England and the Netherlands, on the other; Dumont, VII[2], 292) even declared exemplary for the exercise of the right of visit and which I will, therefore, quote in full:

> "Quod si dictae Naves Suecicae ad Oras Maritimas progressae aut in pleno Mari obviam factae fuerint Navibus dictorum Dominorum Ordinum Generalium, aut armatorum privatorum eorum Subditorum, tum dictae Naves Bellicae ad quaevis evitanda incommoda, maneant extra jactum Tormenti Bellici, mittantque scapham ad Navem Subditorum aut Incolarum Suecicorum, & cum duobus aut tribus solummodo hominibus intrent, quibus monstrentur Salvi-Conductus à Magistro vel Patrono dictae Navis Suecicae, modo uti Articulis praecedentibus expressum est, ut & Literae Maritimae, conceptae juxta formam praesenti Tractatui appositam; ex quibus constare possit, ex Salvo-Conducto quidem de onere, ex Literis Maritimis verò de habitationis in Ditionibus Suecicis loco, & de nomine tam Magistri vel Patroni, quam Navis; ut iis suecicis duobus mediis cognoscatur, an Merx interdicta aliqua insit, & appareat sufficienter qualitas Navis & Magistri vel Patroni ejus: quibus Salvo-Conductui & Literis Maritimis fides adhibeatur plena; eoque magis, quia tam à parte suae Regiae Majestatis, quam Dominorum Ordinum Generalium dabantur Certificationes contrasignatae, ut melius agnoscatur valor, ne ullatenus falsae fiant."

Corresponding versions from the 18th century were those obtaining in the following treaties:

France-Great Britain, Utrecht, 31 March/11 April 1713 (Dumont, VIII[1], 345; Parry, 28, 1), often considered as a paragon of an 18th century treaty of commerce and navigation, Art. 24:

> "Que si les Vaisseaux desdits Sujets ou habitans de leurs Sérénissimes Majestez de part et d'autre estoient rencontrez faisant route sur les côtes, ou en pleine Mer par quelque Vaisseau de guerre de leurs Sérénissimes Majestez ou par quelques Vaisseaux armez par des particuliers, lesdits Vaisseaux de guerre ou Armateurs particuliers, pour éviter tout désordre, demeureront hors de la portée du Canon & pourront envoyer leurs Chaloupes au bord du Vaisseau Marchand qu'ils auront rencontré, et y entrer seulement au nombre de deux ou trois hommes, à qui seront montrées par le Maitre ou Capitaine de ce Vaisseau ou Bâtiment, les Lettres de Mer, qui contiennent la preuve de la propriété du Vaisseau, & conçûes dans la forme insérée au présent Traité; et il sera libre au Vaisseau qui les aura montrées de poursuivre sa route sans qu'il soit permis de le molester & le visiter en façon quelconque, ou de luy donner la chasse, ou de l'obliger à se détourner du lieu de sa destination";

France-the Netherlands, 21 December 1739 (Wenck, I, 414; Parry, 35, 459), Art. 21:

"Que s'ils étoient dans les rades, ou étoient rencontrez en pleine Mer par quelques Vaisseaux des dits Seigneurs Etats, ou d'Armateurs particuliers leurs Sujets, les dits Vaisseaux des Provinces Unies, pour éviter tout désordre, n'approcheront pas plus près des François que de la portée du canon, & il sera seulement permis, dans le premier cas, aux Officiers du Port le plus voisin de la Rade, & dans le second, aux Capitaines des Vaisseaux des Provinces Unies, d'envoyer une petite Barque ou Chaloupe à bord des Bâtimens François, & d'y faire entrer deux ou trois hommes seulement, auxquels seront montrez les Passeports et Lettres de Mer, par le Maître ou Patron des Bâtimens François, de la manière ci-dessus spécifiée, suivant le formulaire des Lettres de Mer qui sera inséré à la fin de ce Traité; par lesquels Passeports & Lettres de Mer il puisse apparoir non seulement de la charge, mais aussi du lieu de la demeure & résidence, tant du Maître ou Patron, que du Navire même, afin que par ces deux moyens on puisse connoître s'ils portent des Marchandises de Contrebande, & qu'il apparoisse suffisamment, tant de la qualité du dit Navire, que de son Maître & Patron, auxquels Passeports & Lettres de Mer entière foi & créance devra être donnée; & afin que l'on connoisse mieux la validité des dites Lettres de Mer, qu'elles ne puissent en aucune manière être falsifiées & contrefaites, il sera donné certaines marques & contreseings de Sa Majesté & des dits Seigneurs Etats Généraux."

France-Denmark/Norway, 23 August 1742 (Wenck, I, 59; Parry, 36, 425), Article 22: prohibition for the warship to draw nearer to the arrested vessel than the range of the "red bullets" discharged from her cannons;

The Netherlands-The Two Sicilies, 27 August 1753 (Wenck, II, 753; Parry, 40, 111), Article 26;

France-Hamburg, 1 April 1769 (Wenck, III, 752; Parry, 44, 255), Article 33.

As far as the relations between European Powers and the Barbary States of Northern Africa were concerned, the modalities of visit in war-time were likewise (but summarily) regulated by treaty. See, *e.g.*, Arts. 3-6 of the treaty between the Netherlands and Tunis of 14 November 1622 (Dumont, V^2, 411) (*supra*, p. 491).

On the procedure in the case of convoy of neutral merchant ships by warships see *infra*, section 4, p. 523.

The rules concerning the visit of merchantmen at sea were severely enforced against privateers who infringed them, for example in the case of the privateer *L'Heureux* [*an* XIII] (Pistoye-Duverdy, I, 239). This privateer had proceeded against the neutral Danish vessel *Haabet* in a totally unlawful manner:

"Lorsqu'un corsaire tire à mitraille sur un navire, sans l'avoir préalablement semoncé, lorsqu'il l'attaque en arborant un faux pavillon, et qu'enfin, au mépris des règles du droit, il ne conserve aucun papier du navire capturé, le capitaine du corsaire et les armateurs doivent être déchus de toute participation à la prise, et, sauf la part revenant aux gens de l'équipage, la prise entière doit être attribuée au gouvernement".

As I have related earlier, the British Board of Trade has still thought it necessary in 1904 to caution mariners against their possible ignoring of summons by belligerent warships on the high seas to stop for visit and search, and to order them immediately to heave to, as any attempt on their part to evade or resist visit or search might be attended with serious consequences to themselves and to their vessels and cargoes (text of the warning in Deák and Jessup, *Neutrality Law*, Part I, p. 209).

The rules of customary law, reflected in the treaty provisions surveyed above, have never been codified in an international convention, but a private codification has been incorporated by the *Institut de droit international* into its comprehensive *Règlement international des prises maritimes*, of Turin, 1882.

The subjects dealt with in the present section 2 were distributed in that Règlement over four separate sections under the headings "Arrêt" (§§ 10-13), "Visite" (§§ 14-18), "Recherche" (§§ 19-22) and "Saisie" (§ 23). The first of these sections describes the formalities required for the arrest of a merchant ship; the second, the aim and formalities of the visit, including its restrictions in the case of the merchant ships' sailing under neutral convoy (§ 16) (*infra*, section 4); the third, the admissible cases and formalities of a search of the arrested vessel, including five cases of suspicion (§ 20); and the fourth, the five cases in which a seizure of the vessel is permitted, including four specific cases of suspicion (§ 23).

Under the first heading "De l'arrêt", the following rules were inserted:

"§ 11.—Le navire de guerre du belligérant, pour inviter le navire de commerce à s'arrêter, se servira comme signal d'un coup de canon de semonce à boulet perdu ou à poudre. Avant ou en même temps, le navire de guerre hissera son pavillon au dessus duquel, en temps de nuit, un fanal sera placé. A ce signal, le navire arrêté hissera son pavillon et se mettra en panne pour attendre la visite. Le navire de guerre enverra alors au navire arrêté une chaloupe montée par un officier accompagné d'un nombre d'hommes suffisant, dont deux ou trois seulement monteront avec l'officier à bord du navire arrêté.

§ 12.—Le navire arrêté ne pourra jamais être requis d'envoyer à bord du navire de guerre son patron ou une personne quelconque, pour montrer ses papiers ou pour toute autre cause.

§ 13.—Le navire de commerce est obligé de s'arrêter; il lui est interdit de continuer sa route. S'il le fait néanmoins, le navire de guerre a le droit de le poursuivre et de l'arrêter de force."

The rules under the second heading "De la visite" were to the following effect:

"§ 14.—Le droit de visite s'exerce dans les eaux des belligérants, en tant qu'elles ne sont pas mises, par traité, à l'abri des faits de guerre, et en haute mer; il s'exerce à l'égard des navires de commerce, mais non à l'égard des navires de guerre d'un Etat neutre, ni à l'égard d'autres navires appartenant ostensiblement à un tel Etat, ni à l'égard des navires de commerce neutres qui sont convoyés par un navire de guerre de leur Etat.

§ 15.—Le droit de visite s'exerce, soit en vue de vérifier la nationalité d'un navire arrêté, soit pour constater s'il fait un transport interdit, soit pour constater une violation du blocus.

§ 16.—Lorsque des navires neutres sont convoyés, ils ne seront pas visités, si le commandant du convoi remet au navire du belligérant qui l'arrête une liste des navires convoyés, et une déclaration signée par lui et portant qu'il ne se trouve à leur bord aucune contrebande de guerre, et quelles sont la nationalité et la destination des navires convoyés.

§ 17.—Lorsque le navire à visiter est un paquebot-poste, il ne sera pas visité, si le commissaire du gouvernement dont il porte le pavillon, se trouvant à son bord, déclare par écrit que le paquebot ne transporte ni des dépêches ni des troupes pour l'ennemi, ni de la contrebande de guerre pour le compte ou à destination de l'ennemi.

§ 18.—La visite à laquelle doit se soumettre tout navire qui n'en est pas exempt en vertu des articles 16 et 17, commence par l'examen des papiers de bord du navire arrêté. Si ces papiers sont trouvés en règle ou s'il ne se présente rien de suspect, le navire arrêté peut continuer sa route. Pourront de même continuer leur route les navires neutres destinés à des expéditions scientifiques, à condition qu'ils observent les lois de la neutralité."

Under the third heading "De la recherche" the *Règlement* laid down the following rules:

"§ 19.—Si les papiers de bord ne sont pas en ordre, ou si la visite opérée a fait naître un soupçon fondé, comme il est dit en l'article qui suit, l'officier qui a opéré la visite est autorisé à procéder à la recherche. Le navire ne peut s'y opposer; s'il s'y oppose néanmoins, la recherche peut être opérée de force.

§ 20.—Il y a coupçon fondé dans les cas suivants:

1°. Lorsque le navire arrêté n'a pas mis en panne sur l'invitation du navire de guerre;

2°. Lorsque le navire arrêté s'est opposé à la visite des cachettes supposées recéler des papiers de bord ou de la contrebande de guerre;

3°. Lorsqu'il a des papiers doubles, ou faux, ou falsifiés, ou secrets, ou que ses papiers sont insuffisants, ou qu'il n'a point de papiers;

4°. Lorsque les papiers ont été jetés à la mer ou détruits de quelque autre façon, surtout si ces faits se sont passés après que le navire a pu s'apercevoir de l'approche du navire de guerre;

5°. Lorsque le navire arrêté navigue sous un pavillon faux.

§ 21.—Il n'est pas permis aux personnes qui sont chargées d'opérer la recherche d'ouvrir ni de rompre des armoires, réduits, caisses, cassettes, tonnes, futailles ou autres cachettes pouvant renfermer une partie de la cargaison, ni d'examiner arbitrairement les objects faisant partie de la cargaison qui se trouvent répandus à découvert dans le navire.

§ 22.—Dans les cas de coupçon mentionnés au § 20, s'il n'y a pas de résistance à la recherche, l'officier qui y procède doit faire ouvrir les réduits par le patron, et faire la recherche dans la cargaison à découvert sur le navire avec le concours du patron."

Section 3. POSSIBLE MEASURES FOLLOWING VISIT AND SEARCH

In this section I will deal successively with the various measures to which the organs of the captor State can theoretically proceed, whether recognized as legally permissible or of disputed legality.

(a) Permission to continue the voyage

When visit and search did not give rise to suspicion, nor corroborated any suspicion which was harboured, the merchant ship was to be permitted to continue her voyage. In many treaties the contracting Parties stipulated indeed that the master of a merchant vessel was only obliged to show his sea-letters and passports in order to enable the visiting warship to make the necessary investigations regarding, *inter alia*, the nature, quantity and destination of the cargo, and that, if no suspicion arose or if existing suspicions were dispelled during the visit, the vessel was to be permitted to continue her course. This was expressly stipulated *e.g.*, in the liberal provisions embodied in Art. 6 of the Swedish-Netherlands treaty of 26 November 1675 (Dumont, VII[1], 316; Parry, 14, 41):

> "Porro ut impediatur, ne Merces in illicitis jam designatae ad Portus hostiles aut ad loca inimicae Ditione subjecta subvehantur, vel etiam ne sub hoc ipso subjectionis impediundae praetextu libertas securitasque Navigationis & Commerciorum detrimenti quid capiat, ab Incolis Subditisque Ditionis alterutrius, ubivis locorum, tam in Portu atque statione Navali alterutrius, quam in aperto Mari nihil omnino requiri aut exigi jus esto, praeter exhibitionem talis Diplomatis, quale utriusque usus hactenus confirmavit, aut quale deinceps per Pacta rei Maritimae utrinque ineunda ratum habebitur, exhiberi ad haec necessum erit Literas Passeportus, in quibus quantitas, qualitasque Mercis, qua Navis onerata est, designetur, & eas quidem indultas ab Officialibus publica authoritate constitutis illic locorum, unde Merx ipsa transportatur, & juxta quas jura, quae pro Mercimoniis transportandis debebantur, persolutae sunt, quod si Navis haec non nihil Mercium vetitarum, quas Contrabanda vocant, vehit, oportebit in Literis Passeportus exprimi atque designari, ea loca ad quae id genus Merces devehendae sunt, post quam exhibitionem scrutationi aut visitationi Naves Mercesque non subjicientur, nec quicquam damni, morae aut molestiae iisdem quocunque sub praetextu objicietur,"

and at a later stage in Art. 21 of the Franco-Danish treaty of commerce of 23 August 1742 (Wenck, I, 59; Parry, 36, 425) which laid down that after an examination of

> "les passeports, contenant un état particulier de leur charge, arrestés & marqués du seing & du scel ordinaire des officiers de l'Amirauté du lieu, dont ils seront premièrement partis avec la déclaration de celui pour lequel ils seront destinés; le tout suivant les modèles qui en seront joints au présent Traîté",

the merchant vessels should be questioned no further:

> "Et leurs Passeports montrés on ne pourra les retarder davantage ni les visiter, ni leur faire obstacle & déplaisir quelconque, sous quelque prétexte que ce soit".

Only reasonable suspicions could motivate further action against the vessel by formally seizing her and/or her cargo as prize and bringing the ship into a port.

In § 18 of its *Règlement international des prises maritimes*, adopted at Turin (1882) and Münich (1883), the *Institut* laid down the following principle:

> "La visite à laquelle doit se soumettre tout navire qui n'en est pas exempt en vertu des articles 16 et 17, commence par l'examen des papiers de bord du navire arrêté. Si ces papiers sont trouvés en règle ou s'il ne se présente rien de suspect, le navire arrêté peut continuer sa route. Pourront de même continuer leur route les navires neutres destinés à des expéditions scientifiques, à condition qu'ils observent les lois de la neutralité."

(b) Formal seizure (capture), followed by bringing the ship into a convenient port for adjudication

This was the normal procedure. But it was not always certain what acts exactly constituted a capture in prize. The general answer was that the conduct necessary to establish the fact of capture could take many forms and that no particular formality was necessary. See the *Esperanza* [1822] (1 Haggard, 85). A ship might be truly captured, although she was neither fired on nor boarded, see the *Rebeckah* (Thompson, Master) [1799] (1 C.Rob., 227; Roscoe, I, 118) and the *Edward and Mary* [1801] (3 C.Rob., 305; Roscoe, I, 312). Old formalities of seizure were retrospectively surveyed in a judgment pronounced in the *Pellworm* case after World War I (B.C.P.C., III, 705, 1053).

A rare and unusual instance of doubt about whether a capture had taken place was that of the neutral merchant vessel *Jonge Jacobus Baumann* (Muller, Master) [1799] (1 C.Rob., 243). The British King's frigate *Apollo* had run ashore and had as a consequence got into serious difficulties. In view of her dangerous position with approximately 175 men on board, an officer and several men boarded the neutral vessel, herself in a perfectly seaworthy condition, and told her master that he must go down to the assistance of the frigate. According to the master's affidavit he did that unsuspectingly and thereupon took the frigate's entire crew on board. The occupants threw overboard some 250 of the 815 hogsheads of wine which the master had loaded in France to be delivered in neutral Hamburg, and later also parts of the cabin stores. On the master's protest about this later action the frigate officer replied that satisfaction would be made to him by the British Government. However, when the *Jonge Jacobus Baumann* had been brought into Yarmouth, partly by her master, partly by an English pilot, she was proceeded against as prize by the persons taken on board from the stranded frigate. In his judgment Sir William Scott did not go into a number of questions which might theoretically arise—were the men of the *Apollo* competent to capture the vessel, if capture it was; what legal value should be attached to the frigate-officer's promise; what blame should attach to the alleged captors for their actions or to the master for his remonstrance—but concentrated on the question of capture itself. Accepting the master's affidavit as veracious, the President decreed that the frigate's crew had never boarded the ship as captors. Lauding the master's co-operation in "preserving so many lives of H.M.'s ship and crew" as "an action of great merit", he restored the ship and awarded the master and the ship owner the fullest possible financial satisfaction.

As the operation of seizure often consisted of a sequence of acts performed by the capturing public or private warship against the merchant ship met at sea, a further question arose as to the exact moment at which the capture was begun or completed. See the case of the *Anna* (La Porte, Master) [1805] (5 C.Rob., 373; Roscoe, I, 499), relating to a seizure in the mouth of the Mississippi river. This question could indeed have special importance for the solution of the controversy over the exact place (neutral or enemy waters, territorial or open sea), where the capture had taken place. Comp. on this type of dispute the observations made in section 3 (General issues), *supra*, pp. 180-197.

The *Institut de droit international* included in its *Règlement international des prises maritimes*, adopted at Turin in 1882, a general provision on the 'Permissibility of seizures' to the following effect:

> "§ 23.—La saisie d'un navire ou d'une cargaison, ennemi ou neutre, n'a lieu que dans les cas suivants:
>
> 1°. Lorsqu'il résulte de la visite que les papiers de bord ne sont pas en ordre;
>
> 2°. Dans tous les cas de soupçon mentionnés au § 20;
>
> 3°. Lorsqu'il résulte de la visite, ou de la recherche, que le navire arrêté fait des transports pour le compte et à destination de l'ennemi;
>
> 4°. Lorsque le navire a été pris en violation de blocus;
>
> 5°. Lorsque le navire a pris part aux hostilités ou est destiné à y prendre part."

Section 8 (§§ 45-57) of the *Règlement* further enumerated under the heading "Des formalités qui suivent la saisie" various measures to be taken by the captor, such as the sealing of hatchways and bunkers by the captor; his making an inventory of the ship's cargo; the compiling of a list of the persons on board; the seizure of all papers, documents and letters found there; the drawing-up of a *procès-verbal* stating the place, time, reasons and further particulars of the seizure; the strict conditions under which an enemy prize might be set on fire or sunk (comp. on this subject § 50 and section 5, *infra*, p. 528); the making of a selection amongst the persons aboard according to whether they might be treated as prisoners of war, must be kept on board the capturing vessel as potential witnesses, might be debarked, or must be transferred to the captured vessel to act as a prize crew.

The text of these provisions ran as follows:

> "§ 45.—Après la saisie, le capteur fermera les écoutilles et la soute aux poudres du navire saisi, et y apposera les scellés. Il fera de même à l'égard de la cargaison, après que celle-ci aura été inventoriée.
>
> § 46.—Il ne sera rien vendu, ni déchargé, ni dérangé, ni en général distrait, consommé ou détérioré de la cargaison.
>
> Si cependant la cargaison consiste en choses pouvant se gâter facilement, ou si ces choses sont avariées, le capteur prendra les mesures les plus convenables pour la conservation de la cargaison, du consentement et en présence du patron, ainsi qu'en présence d'un consul de la nationalité du navire saisi, s'il s'en trouve un dans le voisinage du lieu de la capture. Le commandemant du navire capteur procédera, à cet effet, à l'inspection de la cargaison.
>
> § 47.—Le capteur dressera l'inventaire du navire saisi et de la cargaison, ainsi que la liste des personnes trouvées à bord, et fera passer à bord du navire saisi un équipage suffisant pour s'assurer du navire et y maintenir l'ordre.
>
> § 48.—Le capteur saisira tous les papiers de bord, documents et lettres qui se trouvent sur le navire saisi. Ces papiers, documents et lettres seront réunis dans un paquet revêtu du cachet du commandant du navire de guerre et de celui du patron du navire saisi; il sera dressé inventaire de ces papiers, documents et lettres, et le commandant du navire de

guerre déclarera par écrit, dans le procès-verbal, que ce sont là *tous* les papiers trouvés sur le navire; il y ajoutera une mention indiquant quels papiers manquaient au moment de la saisie et dans quel état se trouvaient les papiers saisis, notamment s'ils paraissent avoir été altérés.

§ 49.—Le capteur dressera procès-verbal de la saisie ainsi que de l'état du navire et de la cargaison, en y mentionnant le jour et l'heure de la saisie; à quelle hauteur elle a eu lieu; la circonstance qui l'a motivée; le nom du navire et celui du patron; le nombre d'hommes composant l'équipage; sous quel pavillon naviguait le navire au moment de l'arrêt et s'il y a eu résistance de la part du navire, et de quelle nature a été sa résistance. Seront joints au procès-verbal les inventaires du navire, de la cargaison et des papiers de bord, avec mention au procès-verbal que les inventaires ont été dressés. Copie du procès-verbal sera transmise à l'autorité militaire supérieure de laquelle relève le navire capturé."

§§ 50 and 51 deal with the special subject of the destruction of enemy prizes (*infra*, section 5).

"§ 52.—Des personnes se trouvant à bord nu navire saisi, les seules qui seront considérées comme prisonniers de guerre sont celles qui font partie de la force militaire de l'ennemi, et celles qui ont assisté l'ennemi ou sont soupçonnées de l'avoir assisté.

§ 53.—Le patron, le subrécargue, le pilote et les autres personnes qu'il pourra être nécessaire d'entendre pour la constatation des faits, seront retenus à bord provisoirement. Ces personnes ne seront autorisées à quitter le bord, après leur déposition, qu'en vertu d'une décision du tribunal instructeur.

§ 54.—Les personnes trouvées et retenues à bord seront nourries et, au besoin, vêtues et soignées par le gouvernement de l'État auquel appartient le navire capteur. Le patron fournira caution pour les frais qui en résulteront, lesquels pourront être remboursés en vertu du jugement.

§ 55.—On laissera aux hommes de l'équipage les effets servant à leur usage personnel.

§ 56.—Il n'est pas permis au capteur de débarquer les hommes de l'équipage qui ne sont pas nécessaires pour l'enquête et qu'il y a lieu de renvoyer immédiatement, faute de place sur le navire capteur ou faute de vivres, sur des terres incultes et inhabitées. Mais il sera permis au capteur de faire passer les hommes à bord de navires neutres ou alliés qu'il pourra rencontrer, et de les débarquer sur des territoires cultivés et habités.

§ 57.—Le capitaine du navire capteur répond du bon traitement et du bon entretien des personnes trouvées à bord du navire saisi, par l'équipage du navire capteur et par celui qui conduit le navire saisi; il ne doit pas tolérer que celles même d'entre ces personnes qui sont prisonniers de guerre soient employées à des travaux avilissants."

A prize was, after her normal capture, to be brought into a port for adjudication. This was regulated by the Institut de droit international in section 9 (§§ 58-62) of its *Règlement* under the heading "Du transport du navire saisi en un port de mer", either the nearest harbour of the captor, or a harbour of an allied power with the seat of a "tribunal d'instruction", or in exceptional circumstances a neutral port:

"§ 58.—Le navire saisi sera conduit dans le port le plus voisin de l'État capteur ou dans un port d'une puissance alliée où se trouvera un tribunal pour instruire à l'égard du navire saisi.

§ 59.—Le navire saisi ne pourra être conduit dans un port d'une puissance neutre que pour cause de péril de mer, ou lorsque le navire de guerre sera poursuivi par une force ennemie supérieure.

§ 60.—Lorsque, pour cause de péril de mer, le navire de guerre s'est réfugié avec le navire saisi dans un port neutre, ils devront quitter ce port aussitôt que possible, après que

> la tempête aura cessé. L'État neutre a le droit et le devoir de surveiller le navire de guerre et le navire saisi durant leur séjour dans le port.
>
> § 61.—Lorsque le navire de guerre s'est réfugié avec le navire saisi dans un port neutre, parce qu'il était poursuivi par une force ennemie supérieure, la prise sera relâchée.
>
> § 62.—Le navire saisi et la cargaison seront, autant que possible, conservés intacts durant leur voyage au port; la cargaison sera close et scellée, sauf dans le cas où la levée des scellés et l'ouverture de la cargaison seraient jugées nécessaires dans l'intérêt de la conservation de celle-ci, avec le consentement du patron."

The bringing of the captured vessel into port was to take place either under the conduct of the capturing ship of war, or by the placing on board the captured ship of a prize crew from the warship. In the latter case a further question could arise as to whether the prize crew put on board by the captor was legally sufficient. See the case of the *Pennsylvania* [1809], a neutral (American) vessel that on a voyage from Trieste on the Adriatic to Canton was captured in the Mediterranean by two British privateers, which sent three persons on board her as a prize crew with orders to bring the ship into Malta for adjudication. As, however, these men were unable to navigate the vessel, her master took over and continued to direct her course according to the instructions of her owners in Philadelphia, refusing to carry the vessel into Malta, as required by the prize master. However, immediately after passing that island, the *Pennsylvania* was boarded by a third British privateer and brought into Malta for adjudication. There the claim of the owners for restoration of the prize was rejected by the local prize court which condemned the ship as having been rescued from the original captors. In appeal, however, the Lords (*per* Sir W. Grant) reversed the sentence below and restored the ship to her owners. The tenor of the judgment [1809] (1 Acton, 33; Roscoe, II, 103) was expressed in the heading as follows:

> "If an insufficient prize crew is placed on board a prize, her master is entitled to navigate her to such port as he pleases in the interest of its owners and the prize is not liable to be condemned if she is a neutral ship and is subsequently captured if there was no resistance to the search and capture and no armed rescue".

The Japanese Regulations of 7 March 1904 relating to Capture at Sea included in Arts. 79 *et seq.* and 92 (Hurst & Bray, II, Appendix B, pp. 436-438) detailed provisions concerning the appointment and duties of a prize master in charge of bringing the prize into a national, or as the case might be, an allied or neutral harbour.

According to an old English rule, the prize had to be brought into a "convenient port". If this obligation was not complied with, either because the captor ignored it completely, or because the chosen port was not "convenient" or was an "improper" port, the owners of the prize were entitled to damages.

In the case of the Portuguese ship *Principe* [1809] (Edw., 70; Roscoe, II, 23) the Court defined the duty of the captor as being "to take a prize into a port suitable for her". This vessel had been brought to Portsmouth because the nearest port on the island of Guernsey was too small. The ship was restored with her cargo to her owners with damages and costs.

Comp. further the cases of the *Wilhelmsberg* [1804] (5 C.Rob., 143; Roscoe, I, 437), the *Anna* (La Porte, Master) [1805] and the *Washington* (Williamson, Master) [1806] (6 C.Rob., 275; Roscoe, I, 555).

Where expenses were incurred by captors, who had reasonable ground for seizure, in consequence of taking a vessel into a port not fit for her, such expenses would be disallowed on restitution of the prize.

During the Crimean War another case arose in which the duty of a captor needed some reformulation. That was the case of the Wallachian merchantman *Gerasimo* [1857] (11 Moore, P.C., 88; Roscoe, II, 577), also referred to *infra sub* C, section 4, p. 617. This vessel was captured by the British naval forces, when she left Galatz through the Sulina mouth of the Danube in July 1854, on account of her breaking the blockade of the Black Sea with a cargo of Indian corn, property of a firm of merchants at Galatz, subjects of the Republic of the Ionian Islands, bound to Austrian Trieste. Dr Lushington's definition was worded as follows:

> "It is the duty of the captor, as soon as possible to send a prize to some convenient port in H.M.'s dominions for adjudication, and to procure the examination in preparatory of the principal officers of the captured vessel, and to deposit in the Admiralty Court all papers found on board the prize."

The obligation to compensate the owners of the prize for their losses also applied when the captor had not acted with the required reasonable speed to submit his prize to adjudication, see the case of the Greek merchantman *Madonna del Burso* [1802] (4 C.Rob., 169; Roscoe, I, 370) and that of the *William (No. 1)* (Stodart, Master) [1802] (4 C.Rob., 214; Roscoe, I, 383).

A prize was, in principle, to be brought into one of the captor's own harbours, but might exceptionally be conducted to a neutral port. See the case of the Russian *Polka* [1854] (Spinks, 57; Roscoe, II, 301). When the commanders of the British warships *Amphion* and *Conflict* were informed that a number of Russian merchant ships anchored in the port of Libau within gunshot of the town, its governor was summoned on 17 May 1854 to surrender within three hours. As the governor declared this impossible and the Russian ships were incapable of sailing to England, they were directed to the neutral port of Memel, where they remained in expectation of the decision of the Prize Court. The Court decided that, although the general rule of law was that a prize should be brought into a port belonging to the captor's own country, the Court would under special circumstances condemn a prize which had been taken into and lay in a neutral port, and allow it to be sold there.

Sections 10 and 11 of the *Règlement* of Turin concluded with two long sets of provisions, under the heading (section 10, §§ 63-84) "De l'organisation et de la procédure du tribunal d'instruction des prises dans le port d'arrivée", and under the heading (section 11, §§ 85-99) "De l'organisation et de la procédure du tribunal des prises maritimes". The latter tribunal was meant to be a national tribunal of the captor State (see *sub* C, section 8, at p. 672).

Section 10 regulated in a series of twenty-two detailed provisions the organization and procedure of the "tribunal d'instruction" in the port of arrival. This tribunal was to be composed of "magistrats de l'ordre judiciaire". It was to be entrusted with the investigation of the case; the conservation of the prize; the appointment of a guard in replacement of the conductor of the prize; the release of seized objects found to be exempt from condemnation in any case; the interrogation of witnesses in the presence of the parties; and the transmission of its final report to the prize tribunal of the first instance, whose organization and procedure were regulated in section 11.

Section 12 (§§ 100 *et seq.*) provided for the creation of one or more international prize tribunals, whereupon comp. further *sub* C, section 8, *infra*, pp. 672-673.

(*c*) *Bringing the prize into port for search without formal seizure*

As appears from British prize court decisions of a much later date, another possible procedure, *viz.*, to bring the vessel into port for the purpose of examining her cargo without a previous formal seizure, was not formally allowed. The permissibility of this alternative procedure when a search was not feasible on the high seas would seem not to have been recognized until a later period. Comp. for example the post-World War I appellate judgment concerning the Netherlands steamships *Bernisse* and *Elve*, sent into Kirkwall by a British warship in 1915 [1920] (B.C.P.C., III, 771):

> "To show [a reasonable ground for the action taken] the Crown relies on two points. First they say that the detention was a legitimate exercise of the right of search. In this war [1914] it has been agreed that search at sea has been practically impossible and sending into port for search has been almost universal."

The

> "question of the right of a belligerent to send a vessel into port for examination instead of examining her at sea, as was the practice in former times",

had still been left in suspense by the Court below (B.C.P.C., III, 517).

A passage in the *Zamora* judgment (appeal 1916, B.C.P.C., II, 1) also testifies to this variation in legal opinion; it mentions indeed that change in the following wording:

> "the practice of bringing a vessel into harbour for the purpose of search—a practice which is justifiable because search at sea is impossible under the conditions of modern warfare—...".

However, the permissibility of this novel practice was still controversial in 1915 as appears from the United States protest addressed by Secretary of State Lansing to the British Government on 21 October/5 November 1915 (*A.J.I.L.*, Special Supplement, 1916, pp. 73 *et seq.*).

German legal parlance called this widely practised operation "Einbringung" as distinguished from "Aufbringung" (seizure).

The only allusion to this procedure I found in British Prize Court decisions in earlier wars was that of Sir William Scott in the *Maria (No. 1)* (Paulsen, Master) of 1799 (1 C.Rob., 340; Roscoe, I, 152 *et seq.*, at pp. 162-163), but that was the famous case of a fleet of Swedish merchantmen carrying pitch, tar, hemp, deals, planks and iron to several ports of France, Portugal and the Mediterranean, and taken in January 1798, while sailing under convoy of a Swedish ship of war, and proceeded against for resistance to visitation and search by British cruisers. On that special occasion Sir William Scott stated that

> "another right accrued—namely, under the Anglo-Swedish treaty of 1661—, that of bringing in for a more deliberate inquiry than could possibly be conducted at sea upon such a number of vessels, even those which professed to carry cargoes with a neutral destination."

(*d*) *Delivery of the contraband goods to the captor at sea instead of seizure of the transporting vessel*

The most normal sanction applied against the transport of contraband goods to the captor's enemy was the seizure of the transporting vessel and her bringing into an, in principle national but possibly also a foreign allied or neutral, port for adjudication of its legal validity. As this procedure was likely to cause considerable financial damage to the ship's owner, the usage was introduced of permitting the ship's master, as an alternative procedure, to deliver the contraband goods to the captor at sea instead and thereupon allowing him to continue his voyage. This was, however, a practice which was initially only permissible in virtue of an express bilateral treaty provision and under specified conditions. Comp., for instance, the following conventions:

Franco-Netherlands treaty of 27 April 1662 (Dumont, VI[2], 412; Parry, 7, 139), Art. 39(2):

> "Si ce n'est que les Marchandises de Contrebande ne fissent qu'une partie de la charge, le Maistre ou Patron du Navire trouvait bon & aggréast de livrer lesdites Marchandises de Contrebande audit capitaine (français), & de poursuivre son voyage, auquel cas ledit Maistre ou Patron ne pourra nullement être empêché de poursuivre sa route & le dessin de son voyage";

Franco-Netherlands treaty of commerce of 10 August 1678 (Dumont, VII[1], 357; Parry, 14, 399), Art. 26;

Netherlands-Swedish treaty of commerce of 2/12 October 1679 (Dumont, VII[1], 437; Parry, 15, 331), Art. 26, which I will quote in full because it places this procedure in a wider context:

> "Si praedictorum Praefectorum aliquis, alterutri Parti inserviens, Navem interceperit prohibitis ejusmodi Mercibus ut supra oneratam, foros illius Navis, in qua ea reperiri contigerit, resignare, cistas, capsa, sarcinas, aut vasa in eadem reserare vel disrumpere, vel partem licet minimam Mercimoniorum distrahere, transportare, immutare aut modo aliquo abalienare, nisi toto prius onere praesentibus Tribunalis Maritimi Officialibus in Terram exposito, & in Inventarium redacto, nefas esto: sin autem non totum sed pars oneris duntaxat in Mercibus prohibitis vel Contrabandis constiterit, easque Praefectus Navis Captori, qui eas deprehenderit extradere se promptum & paratum praestet, in eo casu Captor Navem, ud at Portum sibi commodum deflectat haud coget, quin illico dimittet, neque ulla ratione impediet, quo minus cursum quem instituerat prosequatur."

The subject of the delivery of contraband goods to the captor at sea was regulated in § 33 of the *Règlement international des prises maritimes*, adopted by the *Institut de droit international* at Turin in 1882, as follows:

> "Le navire arrêté pour cause de contrebande de guerre peut continuer sa route, si sa cargaison ne se compose pas, exclusivement ou en majeure partie, de contrebande de guerre, et que le patron soit prêt à livrer celle-ci au navire du belligérant et que le déchargement puisse avoir lieu sans obstacle selon l'avis du commandant du croiseur."

In the course of time this practice has become more general, also without a special treaty provision.

(*e*) *Destruction of the prize*

A further possible measure was that of the destruction of the prize by the capturing cruiser. This measure was fairly often practised when the transporting ship was vested with enemy character and could not be brought into harbour. In view of the growing importance of this practice in later periods I will deal with it in a separate section 5 *infra*, pp. 528-533. There I will also mention a parallel measure, authorized by the Japanese Prize Regulations of 1904, consisting of the destruction, not of the prize itself, but of that of the cruising commander's own warship instead, if the latter's value was inferior to that of the prize.

(*f*) *Release of the prize before adjudication*

Even in older times it was generally admitted in England that the Crown had the right to release captured ships or cargoes without previously submitting the question of the legality of the capture to the prize court. Such cases of administrative release of prizes prior to adjudication have occurred both before and after the *Prize Act* of 1708. The Prize Court examined the question in detail in the *Elsebé* (Maas, Master) [1804] (5 C.Rob., 173;

Roscoe, I, 441, at p. 447), a Swedish vessel captured while sailing under the second Swedish convoy of 1800. In that case Sir William Scott defined the question as follows: "how far can the Crown release at any time before adjudication without consent of the captors?" His answer to this "important question connected with most momentous consequences", which "no reflecting man [could] approach without feeling that he [had] to weigh a matter of extreme delicacy, though perhaps not of equal difficulty", was in conclusion of an elaborate argument in the affirmative.

Early instances of such administrative release were those of

certain Hanse ships captured during their voyage to Spain with contraband cargoes, in respect of which an Order in Council of 27 July 1589 directed the Court of Admiralty how to proceed against them (*Collectanea maritima*, p. 163, note);

certain Portuguese, Danish and Swedish vessels, released, respectively, in 1609, 1689 and 1704 on the ground that they had been captured while sailing under the convoy of their national warships (*infra*);

certain Dutch ships released in 1705 after having been seized and brought in on suspicion of trading with the common enemy.

A later instance of release prior to adjudication was that of the American merchantman *Edwin*, captured in 1801 on her way to the French port of Le Havre together with other vessels and released in virtue of a letter from Lord Hawkesbury to the King's Advocate.

The above-cited judgment of 1804 in the *Elsebé* case contains a detailed argument why

> "all principles of law, all forms of law, all considerations of public policy concur to support the right of release prior to adjudication",

and why one single contrary precedent (*in re* the *St. Jago*) by Lord Kenyon should not be followed.

A contrary view was, however, expressed in the famous Memorandum of the Officers of the Crown of 18 January 1753 on the Silesian Loan dispute with Prussia, according to which

> "The property of prizes being given during the last war to the captors, Our Majesty could not arbitrarily release the capture, but must leave the questions to the proper courts, judging by the law of nations."

It was in particular the incident of the capture of neutral vessels, sailing under the convoy of a national warship, that gave rise to the subsequent release of the prize by the Crown without previous proceedings in the prize court. Such was, *e.g.*, the case of the *Salvador*, which became involved in an engagement with the British Admiral Whetstone while sailing under Swedish colours and the convoy of a Swedish warship, and was for that reason captured. She was subsequently restored to her owners together with some other Swedish vessels on the strength of an Order in Council of 1704 (Roscoe, I, 452, footnote *a*). Later cases of the same type were the *St. Johannes*, one of the first Swedish convoy of 1798, released by the captor under an order from the Lords of the Admiralty;

the *Freya*, sailing under Danish convoy, brought in to Gibraltar, but restored by negotiation with the British Government in 1800, both cited by Roscoe, I, 452, footnote *a.*

Comp. also Chapter II, *supra*, pp. 126-127 and section 4, *infra*, pp. 524-526.

The *Aina (No. 2)* (Nyström, Master) [1854] (Spinks, 12; Roscoe, II, 251) was an instance of the release of an enemy vessel with the consent of the captors: she belonged to her master.

(g) *Ransoming of the prize*

The old practice of attempts by ship owners to achieve the restitution of their ship after her capture by a belligerent privateer by means of the payment of a ransom is documented, *inter alia*, by Chapter 185 of the *Consolat de Mar* (*Black Book*, vol. III, pp. 351-352). This Chapter, under the heading "Of ransom or arrangement with an armed vessel", dealt with the conditions under which a ship owner might ward off as far as possible the untoward consequences of meeting with armed vessels of the enemy. The provisions commence with the following passage:

> "The managing owner of a ship or vessel who in the open sea or in a port, or on any coast, or in other place shall meet with armed vessels of the enemy, may parley with and make a convention with the captains and with the admiral for a quantity of money in order that they may do no harm to him nor to his ship ...".

In a footnote at p. 351 of vol. III of his work Travers Twiss remarks that the use of the term "admiral" in this text suggests that Chapter 185 was not drawn up until after the Fourth Crusade (1202-1204), when the term first came into use. He further relates that it has later become the policy of the British Parliament to disallow the ransoming of captured vessels by inflicting a penalty on any British captor who restored his prize upon ransom and by declaring all ransom bills given by British subjects to be null and void.

There was no rule of international law in force which prohibited the practice of ransoming, but belligerent governments were often inclined to forbid such agreements *sua sponte* and indeed actually forbade them. Thus, England prohibited the acceptance and payment of ransom by § 45 of her *Naval Prize Act*, 1864, except when specially provided for by Order in Council. According to W. Senior in the *Law Quarterly Review*, vol. 34, p. 50, the practice had already turned up in the course of the 16th century.

Particulars concerning the practice of ransom and transactions in prize cases can be found in De Pistoye and Duverdy's *Traité des prises maritimes*, vol. II, pp. 345-364. French legislation included no rule on this subject which submitted such transactions to examination and control by the Commissary of the Government together with the *Conseil des prises*, nor to homologation by that *Conseil.* But in a remarkable conclusion Commissary Portalis argued that the public interest demanded that private transactions concluded between captors and those whose properties were captured should be submitted to such control and homologation in all cases in which the transactions were in actual fact a substitute for a judgment of the *Conseil des prises* on the question of the validity of the capture. This doctrine was based on the multiplicity of the interests involved and the public character of those interest. The rule thus propounded by Mr. Portalis that privateers were not permitted to enter freely into transactions, just as the rule that they were prohibited to ransom prizes at sea, was an indispensable means of insuring "la police de la course".

See for the model of a ransom contract the annex to the Decree of 2 prairial *an* XI in De Pistoye and Duverdy's *Traité*, vol. I, p. 292, in the case of the privateer *Egyptienne* (*ibid.*, p. 288).

(*h*) *Abandonment of the prize*

Instead of destroying his prize the captor could also abandon it, *e.g.*, because it was unseaworthy, or because he preferred to make good his escape on the approach of enemy warships or privateers.

See for a case of abandonment the *Diligentia* (Moller, Master) [1814] (1 Dods., 404; Roscoe, II, 197). In that case Sir William Scott concluded:

> "But if the captor does dismiss what he had before seized upon, the interest of himself and all under him is concluded by his act, and the same vessel lies open to seizure by any other captor ...".

Section 4. NEUTRAL CONVOY

Special international complications were often created by the fact that neutral Powers proceeded to protect their mercantile fleet from unjustified seizures by belligerent warships by escorting them by one or more of their own warships, and that the belligerent, in particular English, warships constantly refused to accept such convoy as a legal ground for abstaining from the normal exercise of their right of visit and search.

The neutrality aspect of this type of international conflict has been treated in Part IX-B (vol. X) of this publication, pp. 179 *et seq.* It has played a significant rôle in the period preceeding the Armed Neutrality Alliances of 1780 and 1800, as set out in Chapter II, *sub* A, pp. 126-127, *supra*, and was given detailed regulation on the side of neutral States in rule 5 of the latter group of treaties, pursuant to which (4/15 December 1800, Martens, R^2, VII, 172):

> "la déclaration de l'officier commandant le vaisseau ou les vaisseaux de la marine royale (suédoise) ou impériale (russe), qui accompagneront le convoi d'un ou de plusieurs bâtimens marchands, que son convoi n'a à bord aucune marchandise de contrebande, doit suffire pour qu'il n'y ait lieu à aucune visite sur son bord ni à celui des bâtimens de son convoi".

England has never submitted to the claim of neutral Powers that the convoy of their merchant ships by one of their warships should exempt them from belligerent visit and search if the neutral commander gave the assurance that the ships under his convoy were engaged in an innocent voyage. A compromise solution between the conflicting views was only reached on paper at the London Conference on Naval Warfare in 1909. See Arts. 61 and 62 of the 1909 Declaration.

The circumstance that the conflict involved a direct confrontation between belligerent and neutral warships and that the former were backed by their government so that the controversy was immediately raised to the diplomatic level as an inter-state dispute was not conducive to an unbiassed adjudication by the belligerent prize court. When one or more of the merchant vessels concerned were seized despite protest by the commander of the convoy, on the ground that the visiting belligerent warship suspected them of falling under the law of prize, the prize court, seized of the capture, used to adjudge the case on the basis of its findings concerning the validity or otherwise of the substantive grounds that prompted the belligerent warship to seize the merchant vessel(s) without paying serious attention to the fact that the neutral commander had protested against the visit itself in disregard of the convoy. This was a matter which did not concern the court since it belonged to the sphere of diplomacy. That is why cases of the seizure of neutral merchant ships sailing under the convoy of a warship of their own country have, to my knowledge, very seldom been adjudicated by a prize court from the aspect of their legality under the rules governing the situation of neutral ships sailing under such convoy. Cases of this type show, consequently, a close conceptual resemblance from this particular point of view to those of captures effected in neutral waters (comp. *supra*, pp. 190-193).

Instances of the visit and seizure of neutral ships despite their sailing under the convoy of warships of their own State are reported from earlier days. See the cases which I have mentioned above in section 3, p. 521, relating to vessels of various neutral nationalities—Portuguese, Danish, Swedish—which after their initial capture were later released (1609, 1689, 1704 and about 1800) on the protests of the neutral governments concerned. It is in particular the series of Swedish convoys which have become famous:

the Swedish ships *Salvador and others*, captured in 1704 after a contest between the convoying Swedish man-of-war and the British Admiral Whetstone;

the *St. Johannes* and the *Maria (No. 1)* (Paulsen, Master), sailing under the first Swedish convoy of 1798 (*infra*);

the *Elsebé* (Maas, Master), part of the second Swedish convoy of 1800 (*infra*).

The settlement of the resulting disputes on this account with neutral Powers took different forms. Some of the initial captures were reversed by the vessel's release by government order, after negotiation with the flag State (1609); others by its release in virtue of an Order in Council (15 August 1689), others on the order of the Lords of the Admiralty, others again by a judgment of the prize court. Amongst the instances which came before the Prize Court were the leading case of the Swedish *Maria (No. 1) and others* [1799] (1 C.Rob., 340-379; Roscoe, I, 152-166) and the *Elsebé* case [1804] (5 C.Rob., 173; Roscoe, I, 441). In the *Maria* case—that of the first Swedish convoy, accompanying a large fleet of merchantmen sailing to French, Portuguese and Mediterranean ports—the Court held that a belligerent's right of search existed even if the neutral ships concerned were sailing under neutral convoy, and that a continued refusal to submit to a search by the arresting cruiser made them in principle liable to condemnation on that ground. In a long-winded argument Sir William Scott rejected all the claimants' pleas against their condemnation: (i) Art. 12 of England's treaty of commerce with Sweden of 1661 did not protect the *Maria* because it had never contemplated the extraordinary case of an armed vessel sailing in company with merchantmen for the express purpose of beating off all inquiry and search; (ii) neither could an exemption be based on the fact that the original intention, under official instructions, to use force against such inquiry and search was never carried into effect; (iii) certain irregularities by the captor (the papers were not immediately taken possession of, and proceedings were not instituted till long after the arrival in port) were not such as would destroy the captor's right of proceeding; (iv) nor was it a legal bar to this right that the captors had proceeded only against the merchant vessels, and not against the Swedish frigate, the principal wrongdoer. See Bourguignon, *Sir William Scott* (Cambridge, 1987), pp. 180-183.

The judgment on the *Maria* was, according to a note in C. Robinson's collection, vol. I, heard in appeal and according to Roscoe's note *in margine* at p. 152 of his vol. I affirmed on 2 July 1802.

I will not return here in any detail to what I have already reported on the history of the controversial issue of the protective force of neutral convoy against the exercise of the belligerent right of visit and seizure in Chapter above, p. 520, and in this Chapter III, section 3 *sub e*, apart from illustrating it by one amongst the most famous historical instances of disputes resulting from encounters between belligerent warships and neutral merchantmen sailing under convoy.

When, in December 1799, the Danish vessel *Freya* was sailing near Gibraltar under the convoy of the Danish frigate *Havfruen* she was nevertheless subjected to a visit from the British warships *Emerald* and *Flora* and brought by them into port after an altercation between the respective warship commanders and a short exchange of fire that caused injury to a

British marine. The diplomatic dispute that followed was provisionally terminated by a "convention préalable" between Great Britain and Denmark, concluded on 29 August 1800 in Copenhagen by which the *Havfruen* and the ships under her convoy were forthwith released, while

> "(Art. 1) La question de droit, relativement à la visite des navires neutres allant sous convois sera renvoyée à une discussion ultérieure."

But

> "(Art. 3) Pour empêcher que de pareilles rencontres ne renouvellent des contestations de la même nature, Sa Majesté danoise suspendra ses convois, jusqu'à ce que les explications ultérieures sur ce même objet ayent pu effectuer une convention définitive".

The diplomatic correspondence concerning this incident is reproduced in Martens, R^2, VII, 127-150, where (pp. 150 *et seq.*) the reaction of the Russian Tsar to this kind of incidents is also related.

When a neutral merchant ship, notwithstanding her sailing under the convoy of a warship of her own State, was captured by a belligerent cruiser, but was subsequently recaptured by the convoying warship, the latter was held entitled to salvage. See the *Galen* case of 1814 (1 Dods., 429; Roscoe, II, 199), reported below, p. 551.

It hardly needs explicit mention that neutral ships sailing under enemy convoy were on that account liable to condemnation.

When the *Institut de droit international* at its session in Turin (1882) adopted a first series of articles of its *Règlement international des prises maritimes*, it included therein a provision dealing with the case of neutral merchant ships convoyed by warships under their national flag. Apart from a general § 14 which excluded the exercise of the right of visit, *inter alia*, with regard to neutral vessels sailing under such convoy, § 16 laid down the following specific rule:

> "Lorsque des navires neutres sont convoyés ils ne seront pas visités, si le commandant du convoi remet au navire du belligérant qui l'arrête une liste des navires convoyés, et une déclaration signée par lui et portant qu'il ne se trouve à leur bord aucune contrebande de guerre, et quelles sont la nationalité et la destination des navires convoyés."

The controversy over the legal consequences of the sailing of neutral merchant ships under the convoy of warships of their own country re-emerged during the Sino-Japanese War of 1894. What was remarkable in the dispute that arose in that year was not only that it was precisely Great Britain, the traditional adversary of the respect for neutral convoy, which invoked the right of neutral States to convoy their merchant fleet, but that, moreover, this claim was raised in the exaggerated form of a "paper convoy", a mere pretension that British ships were under the protection of the British squadron commander in all the seas of the Far East.

The issue of neutral convoy arose again during the Russo-Japanese War of 1904-1905. At pp. 12 and 13 of his work on international law issues during that war Takahashi explained Japan's attitude to neutral convoy by the following general introductory observation:

> "The attitude of Japan in regard to convoy calls for mention. It is not necessary to discuss the big contested differences between the English and Continental principles, but it is noteworthy that Japan ordered naval officers to give credence to the declaration of a convoying officer. The idea was simply that as generosity was the chief object of Japan, she did not wish to search and make actual inspection in order to verify the character of escorted merchantmen and goods, trusting to the honour of neutral officers. This was the main idea of the Japanese in adopting the Continental principle regarding convoy, but she was not in actual cases so lax as to admit exorbitant claims of the right of convoy, such as an English admiral made for all British ships in the China Sea" (*supra*).

The author also discussed the question as to whether the convoy of neutral merchant ships by a warship under the same neutral flag was not to be considered part of a hostile expedition and thus liable to be sunk for a grave form of unneutral service.

The legal provisions which governed during the Russo-Japanese War were —on the Japanese side:

her Regulations of 7 March 1904 relating to Capture at Sea (Hurst & Bray, II, Appendix B, pp. 430-432), which included three provisions dealing with the convoy of neutral vessels by belligerent warships, *viz.*, Arts. 33, 37(7) and 49:

Art. 33 (convoy by warships of the neutral State to which the merchant ships belong):

> "A neutral ship convoyed by a warship of her own country may not be visited or searched if the commander of the convoying warship furnishes a written declaration, over his signature, to the effect that there are on board no persons who are contraband of war, no documents which are contraband of war, and no articles which are contraband of war, and that the papers of the ship are in order, and stating clearly the ship's nationality, her port of departure, and her destination. Cases, however, in which the suspicion is very grave do not come under this category."

Arts 37(7) and 49 (convoy by enemy warships, which render them liable to condemnation):

> Art. 37(7) "ships coming under the following categories are liable to capture without regard to their nationality: ... (7) a ship sailing under convoy of a ship of war of the hostile State";
> Art. 49 "A ship sailing under convoy of a ship of war of the hostile State, and her cargo, shall be condemned."

—on the Russian side:

Art. 6 of her Prize Regulations of 14 July 1895, maintained during the 1904-1905 war (Hurst & Bray, I, Appendix A, at p. 313). Russia adhered to her traditional policy of demanding respect for the neutral flag, in accordance with the principles adopted by the Armed Neutrality Alliance in their two versions of 1780 and 1800, by decreeing in the said Art. 6 that:

"Merchant vessels convoyed by ships of war of an allied or neutral Power are not to be subjected to examination, if the commander of the convoy gives an assurance as to the number of vessels convoyed, the nationality and the destination of their cargoes, and also that there is no contraband of war on board. The stoppage and examination of such vessels is permissible only in the following circumstances:
(1) If the commander of the convoy declines to give the assurance indicated above;
(2) If he states that any of the vessels are not sailing under his convoy; and
(3) If it is evident that a vessel under convoy is preparing to do something which constitutes a breach of neutrality."

Section 5. DESTRUCTION OF PRIZES

The destruction of captured merchant ships, even neutral ones, was not unknown in former times, but it was, as far as neutral vessels or ships sailing under a licence were concerned, certainly not a practice authorized by the belligerent government. It remained an action for which, however excusable under special circumstances, the warship commander was personally responsible.

In the case of the *Mentor* [1799] (1 C.Rob., 175; Roscoe, I, 96), an American ship destroyed by two English warships, the *Centurion* and the *Vulture*, cruising off the Delaware in 1783, after the cessation of hostilities, but before that fact had come to the knowledge of either Admiral Digby's squadron or the *Mentor*, Sir William Scott already decided that the owner of a ship alleged to have been wrongfully destroyed was only entitled to proceed against the officer immediately responsible for the destruction. The same was still held in the later case of the *Ostsee* [1855] (Spinks, 174; Roscoe, II, 432).

An old case of the destruction of a prize on the high seas during the first English coalition war against France in the 1790's had led to arbitral proceedings before a Mixed Claims Commission under Art. VII of the Anglo-American Jay Treaty of 19 November 1794, but that case related rather to a neutrality than to a prize law issue. It concerned in effect the seizure and following destruction of a British vessel, the *Jamaica*, by a French privateer which had originally been equipped in an American (neutral) port. The case thus developed into a dispute between Great Britain and the United States (opinion of 1798). See the *Recueil des arbitrages internationaux*, vol. I, pp. 178-184.

J. Dodson reports two cases from the Anglo-American War of 1812.

The first (of 1815) (2 Dodson 48; Roscoe, II, 209) related to an American vessel, the *Actaeon*, which, after having sailed under a British licence from Norfolk (Virg.) to Cádiz with a cargo of flour, was on her return voyage from Cádiz to Boston, again under the protection of a British licence, captured by the British warship *La Hogue* under the command of captain Capel. The prize was burnt on the order of the commander on 12 May 1813.

Sir William Scott did not contest that the commander had reasonable grounds for ordering the destruction of the prize, but argued that:

> "If a belligerent ship destroys a neutral vessel, the owner thereof is entitled to be put in the same position as he was before the destruction of his vessel, that is, to recover damages and costs. The commander of a belligerent ship may have good reason for destroying a neutral vessel, but this fact does not relieve him from responsibility to the neutral owner for damages".

The only thing that was at stake in this case was, consequently, the determination of the amount, which was rendered difficult by the fact that the ship's papers had been put on board another captured American ship.

The second case reported by Dodson (2, 381; Roscoe, II, 233) [1819] was with regard to another American vessel, the *Felicity*, which, when sailing on the same course, was destroyed by H.M.S. *Endymion* on 1 January 1814 because she was so severely battered by a storm that it was doubtful if she would be able to reach the United States. In this case Sir William Scott gave the following statement of reasons:

> "Taking this vessel and cargo to be merely American, the owners could have no right to complain of this act of hostility, for their property was liable to it in the character it bore at that period of enemy's property. There was no doubt that the *Endymion* had a full right to inflict it if any grave call of public service required it. Regularly a captor is bound by the law of his own country, conforming to the general law of nations, to bring in for adjudication, in order that it may be ascertained whether it be enemy's property; and that mistakes may not be committed by captors, in the eager pursuit of gain, by which injustice may be done to neutral subjects, and national quarrels produced with the foreign States to which they belong. Here is a clear American vessel and cargo, alleged by the claimants themselves to be such, and consequently the property of enemies at that time. They share no inconvenience by not being brought in for the condemnation, which must have followed if it were mere American property; and the captors fully justify themselves to the law of their own country, which prescribes the bringing in, by showing that the immediate service in which they were engaged, that of watching the enemy's ship of war, *the President*, with intent to encounter her, though of inferior force, would not permit them to part with any of their own crew to carry her into a British port. Under this collision of duties nothing was left but to destroy her, for they could not, consistently with their general duty to their own country, or indeed its express injunctions, permit enemy's property to sail away unmolested.
>
> If impossible to bring in, their next duty is to destroy enemy's property. Where doubtful whether enemy's property, and impossible to bring in, no such obligation arises, and the safe and proper course is to dismiss. Where it is neutral, the act of destruction cannot be justified to the neutral owner by the gravest importance of such an act to the public service of the captor's own State; to the neutral it can only be justified, under any such circumstances, by a full restitution in value. These are rules so clear in principle and established in practice that they require neither reasoning nor precedent to illustrate or support them".

French laws contained a provision prohibiting the destruction of prizes in express terms:

> "Faisons défense à peine de la vie à tous Chefs, soldats et matelots de couler à fond les vaisseaux pris ..."

The Italian contribution to the preparatory documentation on behalf of the London Conference on Naval Warfare of 1908-1909 mentioned a case of destruction of a neutral merchantman, the *Fama Argentina* [1859]; see the English Command paper no. 4555, Miscellaneous No. 5 (1909), p. 45.

The *Règlement international des prises maritimes*, adopted by the *Institut de droit international* at Turin in 1882, legalized the destruction of prizes, either by setting them on fire or by sinking them, in § 50, but only as regards enemy vessels, and subject to strict conditions and in five specified cases:

> "Il sera permis au capteur de brûler ou de couler bas le navire ennemi saisi, après avoir fait passer sur le navire de guerre les personnes qui se trouvaient à bord et déchargé autant que possible la cargaison, et après que le commandant du navire capteur aura pris à sa charge les papiers de bord et les objets importants pour l'enquête judiciaire et pour les réclamations des propriétaires de la cargaison en dommages-intérêts, dans les cas suivants:
>
> 1. Lorsqu'il n'est pas possible de tenir le navire à flot, à cause de son mauvais état, la mer étant houleuse;
> 2. Lorsque le navire marche si mal qu'il ne peut pas suivre le navire de guerre et pourrait facilement être repris par l'ennemi;
> 3. Lorsque l'approche d'une force ennemie supérieure fait craindre la reprise du navire saisi;
> 4. Lorsque le navire de guerre ne peut mettre sur le navire saisi un équipage suffisant, sans trop diminuer celui qui est nécessaire à sa propre sûreté;
> 5. Lorsque le port où il serait possible de conduire le navire saisi est trop éloigné,"

and § 51 added:

> "Il sera dressé procès-verbal de la destruction du navire saisi et des motifs qui l'ont amenée; ce procès-verbal sera transmis à l'autorité militaire supérieure et au tribunal d'instruction le plus proche, lequel examinera et, au besoin, complétera les actes y relatifs et les transmettra au tribunal des prises."

The destruction of prizes did not acquire great legal interest until it began to seriously affect neutral ships. The Sino-Japanese War of 1894 already gave rise to the destruction of a neutral prize—the *Kow-shing*, a British ship engaged in the transport of eleven hundred Chinese troops from Shanghai to Taku—by the Japanese warship *Naniwa* (Takahashi, 24-51), but the controversy over this act of destruction started in 1904 during the Russo-Japanese War.

One of the most striking actions on the Russian side during that war was the frequency with which the Russian commanders proceeded to the destruction of captured neutral vessels for various reasons: because there was not sufficient coal to take the prize to a Russian port: the British *Knight Commander* (Hurst & Bray, I, 54); because the prize was stranded near the island of Itarup without a chance of being floated off, and recapture was feared: the British *Oldhamia* (*ibid.*, I, 145); because the ship had refused to obey the order to stop and endeavoured to escape, firing shots at the destroyer: the British *Hipsang* (*ibid.*, I, 21); in view of the extraordinary circumstances—the proximity of the enemy's shores, the remoteness of the ports appointed for receiving prizes, the shortage of coal and the impossibility of supplying coal from the cruisers owing to the high sea running—: the German *Thea* (*ibid.*, I, 96); or in simpler wording in other cases: the German *Tetartos* (*ibid.*, I, 166), the British *Ikhona* (*ibid.*, I, 226) and the Danish *Prinsesse Marie* (*ibid.*, I, 276).

The most elaborate discussion of the admissibility of the destruction of neutral prizes in the light of the relevant provisions of the Russian Regulations relating to Naval Prizes (Articles 21 and 22) is embodied in the judgments concerning the British *St. Kilda* (*ibid.*, I, 188). These provisions ran as follows:

> "(21) In exceptional cases, when the preservation of a captured vessel appears impossible on account of her bad condition or entire worthlessness, the danger of her recapture by the enemy, or the great distance or blockade of ports, or else on account of danger threatening the ship which has made the capture or the success of her operations, it is permissible for the Commander, on his own responsibility, to burn or sink the captured vessel, after he has taken off all persons on board and as much of the cargo as possible, and arranged for the safety of the vessel's papers and any other objects which may be necessary for throwing light on the case at the inquiry to be instituted in accordance with the procedure in prize cases. The Commander will draw up a Report ....
> (22) Captured vessels and cargoes are to be taken by the ship making the capture to Russian ports, or, if there are none near, to ports of an allied Power or to the operating Russian fleet. In case of stress of weather, or other extreme necessity, the ship which has made the capture may take refuge with the captured vessel in the port of a neutral Power ...".

As appears from p. 196, a representative of the Fleet argued in respect of the *St. Kilda* that

> "It was impossible to send [the prize] to Libau; the quantity of coal on board was only one tenth of that which would have been required to reach Libau; it was impossible to obtain coal or to take the steamer to a port of an allied nation; ... to leave the steamer with the cruiser would have endangered the latter and exposed the prize to the risk of recapture by the enemy, who, after the battle of Tsu-shima, might have diverted all their forces in pursuit of the Russian cruisers;"

and asked that the sinking of *St. Kilda* should be declared regular.

On their side the claimants qualified it as illegal. According to them sinking, to which reference is made in Article 21, was applicable only to enemy vessels. The sinking of these latter vessels was, moreover, permissible only in exceptional cases, and in the presence of such circumstances as did not exist at the time when the *St. Kilda* was sunk. She might have been sent to the port of Saigon, belonging to an allied nation, instead of being sunk with her valuable cargo.

The Libau prize court disagreed: in view of Article 21 and also of Articles 18 and 19, in which mention was made of merchant vessels irrespective of their flag, it considered that, given the conditions referred to in Article 21, the sinking of a vessel was admissible whether belonging to the enemy or to a neutral.

> "Such circumstances as the distance from ports to which the vessel could be taken, the risk of recapture by the enemy, and the difficulty of keeping the vessel without interfering with the operations of the cruiser, afforded sufficient grounds to justify the orders of the commander of the *Dniepr* for the sinking of the vessel."

The Supreme Prize Court in its turn reversed the lower judgment, being on grounds of a substantive character, of the opinion that neither the *St. Kilda* herself, nor her cargo were liable to condemnation, so that the claims for compensation should not have been dismissed.

One of the instances of destruction reported by Hurst & Bray in their series was a special one: the case of the British *Cilurnum* (I, 186) as a matter of fact did not relate to the destruction of a captured ship but to the jettison of a cargo of cotton, beans and antimony destined for the Japanese port of Kobe, by order of the commander of the capturing cruiser.

The judgments of the Russian prize courts emphasized that the regularity of sinking a captured ship was a matter only for the superior officer or person who gave the order for the sinking and not for the prize court. See, *inter alia*, the case of the British *Knight Commander* (I, pp. 54 *et seq*., at p. 73).

The British rule was that only enemy merchantmen were liable to destruction in open sea but that neutral vessels could not be destroyed before their confiscation by a prize court. Continental States took a different view as to the latter principle, especially because it was far more difficult for them than for maritime States with overseas dependencies to bring their prizes in to national or, as the case might be, allied or neutral ports. The neutrality aspect of this clash of opinions was considered at the Second Hague Peace Conference of 1907 and there led to the adoption of an Article (23)—not subscribed to, however, by the United Kingdom and the United States—which regulated the conditions of access of prizes to neutral harbours and thus tended to contribute to rendering the asserted inevitability of the destruction of neutral prizes on the high seas less urgent. Comp. on that side of the problem Part IX-B (vol. X) of this publication, p. 178.

It was not until 1909 that the specific naval warfare aspect of the controversy was settled, *viz*., by Arts. 48-54 (Chapter IV) of the London Declaration of 26 February 1909. The solution reached there was, however, again rejected by two of the principal maritime Powers, this time Great Britain and Japan.

The rate of destruction of neutral merchant ships on the high seas before adjudication in prize and, for that matter, often even without any intention on the side of the captor State to submit the capture and the destruction to a prize court, has increased enormously since 1904-1909.

Japan, on her side, as a maritime country, had far less reason than Russia for destroying enemy or non-enemy prizes, but she did include in Art. 91 of her Regulations of 7 March 1904 relating to Capture at Sea a provision defining the exceptional cases in which such destruction would be permitted (Hurst & Bray, II, Appendix B, at p. 438; Takahashi, at p. 334):

"(1) When, owing to her being in an unseaworthy condition, or because of dangers at sea, the ship cannot be navigated.

(2) When there is reason to fear that the ship will be retaken by the enemy.

(3) When the ship cannot be navigated without causing a deficiency in the complement of officers and men requisite to the safety of the warship."

As already stated in section 3, *sub* (*e*), of the present III B, at p. 520, the commanding officer of the capturing warship was in that case granted the extraordinary authority to sink his own ship instead of the prize if the latter was in a better seaworthy condition than the former.

Section 6. JOINT CAPTURE

Joint captures were already dealt with in Part A of the Black Book of the Admiralty, Art. 8. They were in later years often effected under treaties of alliance. This contingency was sometimes regulated in express terms in the treaties themselves. If not, the cases had to be adjudicated upon by the Courts of Admiralty.

Treaty provisions dealing with the subject were, among many others:

Articles 12 *et seq.* and 33 of the Anglo-Netherlands Treaty of Alliance of Southampton of 17 September 1625 (Dumont, V^2, 478):

(12) distribution of the prizes among the participants:

"Si ces Flottes ainsi conjointes & armées, font quelque prinse sur les Ennemis communs en Mer ou à Terre, d'Hommes, de Navires, d'Or, d'Argent, de Marchandises, & d'autres meubles, sera incontinent faict un estat & Registre de toutes telles prinses, en présence & par le moyen des Officiers des deux Flottes ensemble, de bonne foy, & sans en rien cacher ou destourner: lesquels seront par après équitablement partagez à proportion du nombre; & du port des Vaisseaux que sadicte Majesté & lesdits Seigneurs Estats auront réellement, & de faict fourny, pour parformer leur Flotte commune, nonobstant qu'il pourroit arriver que lors de la prinse, nul des Navires de sa Majesté ou *vice versa* desdits Seigneurs Estats s'y seroit rencontré, pourvue que telles prinses ayent esté faictes par une partie des Vaisseaux de la Flotte commune."

(13) and (14) differing rules in the case of land operations:

(13) "Mais si sadicte Majesté de la Grande Bretagne, &c. trouvoit bon de faire embarquer à ses despens une bonne armée, & la descendre quelque part à Terre au Pays de l'Ennemy, afin d'y faire invasion & occuper quelque Ville, ou assiette forte à y loger sadite Armée en seureté, & lieu commode, pour advantager ses desseings: il est accordé que les occupations qui de cette sorte se feront en Terre ferme appartiendront & demeureront purement & simplement à sadite Majesté, nonobstant que la Flotte desdits Seigneurs Estats y poirroit avoir assisté & aydé.

(14) Bien entendu toutesfois, que si à telle descente & execution les Sujects desdits Seigneurs Estats entreviennent, qu'ils auront aussi leur part au butin & meubles, proportionnée de leur nombre à celuy des Subjects de sadicte Majesté, à laquelle seule demeureront tous les acquests immeubles des Isles, Villes, & Terres."

(33) conquests to fall to he conqueror:

"Les Conquestes qui de l'une ou de l'autre Armée se feront demeureront entières à celle qui les aura faites."

Cases which originated in joint captures by naval units and which were brought before a prize court related mainly to the question of whether a capture had been a joint capture in the technical sense, giving a claim to prize money to certain units of the Navy that did not actually take part in the operation but

(*a*) were in sight of it. See the case of the *Arthur* of 21 June 1814 (1 Dodson, 423). It related to an American ship, captured in the river Ems by H.M.S. *Blazer* on 26 December 1809 for a breach of the blockade of that river imposed by the Order in Council of 26 April 1809 (see *sub* A, section 4, *supra*, p. 430). Another unit of the blockading force, the *Paz*, claimed a share in the value of the prize as a joint capture because (i) she had been engaged in a common enterprise (the blockade of the Ems) and (ii) she had been in sight at the moment of capture. The claim was dismissed: although a joint interest in a genuine blockade is clear because

> "the connection between ships so employed is of so intimate a nature, that they may be considered as forming links of the same chain", [the same consideration] "was not applicable to this species of blockade, which was sometimes maintained by a single ship",

or (*b*) were administratively under the command of the Admiral who directed the operation. See the old case during the Seven Years' War of the *La Pacifique* [1758], reported by Reginald Marsden, pp. 370-371. This French ship was captured in March 1758 off Cape Finisterre by H.M.S. *Windsor* under captain Falkner. Admiral Sir Edw. Hawke claimed one-eighth of her value as Admiral under whose supreme command the prize was taken. Captain Falkner opposed this claim because the capture had been a lone-hand operation solely under orders from the Admiralty, without any specific orders by Admiral Hawke. The Admiral's claim was awarded in the first instance but dismissed in appeal. See the report by Burrell, p. 158 and Roscoe, I, 3 [1761, 1764].

Joint captures have formed from early on a subject of discussion by legal writers and divergent prize court decisions defining the cases in which a capture by two or more privateers should be held to have been made jointly and those in which this was not so. The first American prize courts have continued that practice in default of any criterion laid down by a law. It was only in 1782 that Congress passed an Ordinance on the matter. That Ordinance, intended to put an end to the existing uncertainty of the law, established the rule that a joint captor had to be within gunshot at the time the prize surrendered, while permitting deviating agreements previously made between vessels cruising in consort.

Bourguignon reviews five cases of an asserted joint capture in his study of 1777 on the first Federal Court (pp. 268-274, with footnotes 78, 79, 80 and 82), *viz.*, those of

the *Anna Maria* [1780]: captured under an agreement of consortship between captains of privateers containing a clause that it was to remain binding even if the privateers had lost sight of each other, unless they had been separated for forty-eight hours. One of the privateers captured the vessel after a separation of only twenty-four hours. Despite that fact the Court awarded the entire prize to the one privateer that was in sight and actually made the capture, presumably on the ground that such agreements between the captains of privateers did not bind the owners;

the *Mermaid* [1780]: wrecked near the shore of New Jersey and captured by two privateers with the help of a boat from shore. The New Jersey Admiralty Court awarded the entire prize to the owner and crew of the boat, possibly because the boat had reached the *Mermaid* first and her owner and crew were local residents, unlike the crews of the privateers. But this judgment was reversed by the Court of Appeals which ordered the prize to be divided into three equal parts;

the *Barbary* [1780]: the records do not reveal the reasons why the Court of Appeals rejected the claim of those who asserted to be joint captors;

the *Countess of Eglinton* [1783]: captured in 1776 by one swift-sailing privateer while another larger privateer was in sight, both privateers being bound by an agreement between their captains to share equally in all captures. The judgment of the Superior Court of Massachusetts to award 6/7 of the prize to the actual captor and 1/7 to the other privateer, presumably on the ground of its estimation of the relative contribution of the two privateers to the capture, was, however, reversed by the Court of Appeals, which decreed that the prize should be shared equally between the privateers. This was its first decision under the Ordinance of 1782.

On a case of asserted joint assistance in the capture of the Cape of Good Hope by several non-commissioned East-India ships see the report on the *Cape of Good Hope and its dependencies* [1799-1802] (2 C.Rob., 274; Roscoe, I, 227) and on their claim to share in the prize *sub* C, section 7, *infra*, p. 658.

Sir William Scott in his judgment of 1799 referred to two older cases, the *Twee Gesusters* [1783] and *Le Franc* [1795] (see footnote *a* at pp. 230-232 of Roscoe's vol. I).

The *Twee Gesusters* [1783-1785] was a Dutch ship, taken on 31 December 1780 by two armed cruisers, the *Providence*, being commissioned, and the *Spitfire*, not commissioned. The *Providence* first reached the prize, the *Spitfire* then being distant about one English mile. The two cruisers together seized the *Twee Gesusters*; the master of the *Spitfire* was put on board the prize and the *Providence* left the prize with the *Spitfire* to convey her to Dartmouth. The High Court of Admiralty pronounced the *Providence* to be the captor, but found that the *Spitfire* was aiding and abetting, and decreed the *Spitfire* to take half the share she could have been entitled to had she had a commission against the Dutch. On appeal by the *Providence*, the Lords of Appeal pronounced for the King, in his office of Admiral, and that such proportion of the prize as would have belonged to the *Spitfire*, if commissioned, was liable to confiscation as a droit and perquisite of Admiralty (see on these terms *sub* C, section 7 introduction, *infra*, p. 643). The prize was condemned "as taken by the private ship of war the *Providence*, and the non-commissioned ship the *Spitfire*" and was directed to be shared in proportion accordingly.

The *Le Franc* [1793-1795] was a French East India ship taken in 1793 by several vessels composing part of a British East India fleet of seven vessels, one of which, the *Glatton*, had not taken out a letter of marque, the others being commissioned as private ships of war. The share of the *Glatton* was condemned as a droit and perquisite of Admiralty. The other six had sailed as an associated and confederated fleet for mutual defence by particular direction of the East India Company.

See also the *Squirrel* [1783]: a schooner captured by two privateers, one of whom alleged to be the sole captor because the other was not within gunshot at the time of capture in accordance with the Ordinance of Congress. The Courts, however, rejected this allegation.

The annals of prize case law contain a fair number of proceedings on joint captures. See the cases of

the *Vrijheid (No. 2)* [1799] (2 C.Rob., 16; Roscoe, I, 179): to entitle a ship of war to share in the proceeds of a prize, it is not sufficient that such a ship be engaged in a common enterprise with other vessels which have actually taken the prize, but there must be some actual contribution of endeavour by such ship. Sight before a chase begins is not sufficient ground to allow a claim for joint capture;

the *Dordrecht* [1799] (2 C.Rob., 55; Roscoe, I, 187): to entitle soldiers to share in the proceeds of a prize directly captured by the navy, there must be evidence of actual material co-operation by them with the navy;

the *Santa Brigada* [1800] (3 C.Rob., 52; Roscoe, I, 255): the fact that a private ship of war is in sight of the capture of an enemy vessel by a King's ship does not entitle such private ship to be considered a joint captor;

the *Forsigheid*[1801] (3 C.Rob., 311; Roscoe, I, 314) and the *Orion* [1803] (4 C.Rob., 362; Roscoe, I, 407): cases of alleged detachment of ships of a squadron on a separate service by order of the Admiralty;

the *Odin (No. 2)* [1803] (4 C.Rob., 318; Roscoe, I, 397): the principle of constructive joint capture by which a ship of war which was in sight at the time of the capture of an enemy ship was entitled to a share of the prize, did not apply to the case of a boat, or to the ship to which such boat belongs, by reason of such boat being in sight;

the *Nancy* [Lords, 1803] (Roscoe, I, 399, footnote a): alleged joint capture by the warships *Royal Admiral* and *Trusty* from the harbour of St. Helena;

the *La Flore* [1804] (5 C.Rob., 268; Roscoe, I, 474): on the contrary, if a King's ship is in sight at the time of the capture, it is a presumption of law that she is present *animo capiendi*, and is therefore, without further proof, entitled to be considered to be a joint captor;

the *L'Amitié* [1806] (6 C.Rob., 261; Roscoe, I, 551): in order to entitle a vessel not a ship of war (*in casu* two privateers, the *Lark* and the *General Coote*) to share in a prize (*in casu* made by a King's ship, the *Gannet*), there must be an *animus capiendi* proved by some overt act, showing constructive assistence

Guillaume Tell [1808] (Edw., 6; Roscoe, II, 1): in order to enable certain ships of a blockading squadron to share in a prize captured by other ships, the former need not have actually pursued the prize, it being sufficient that the whole squadron was acting on a preconcerted plan, and that the ships in question were not prevented from acting by any permanent obstacle;

the *Bellona* [1809] (Edw., 63; Roscoe, II, 21): a revenue cutter is not entitled to share in a prize merely on the ground of being in sight at the time of the capture;

the *Nordstern* [1809] (1 Acton, 128; Roscoe, II, 109): in order to entitle a vessel other than the actual captor to share in the prize it is not sufficient to prove that the captor and the claimant were associated in a joint enterprise but it must also be proved that the capture was the joint produce of actual co-operation;

the *Le Bon Adventure* [1810] (1 Acton, 211; Roscoe, I, 186, footnote *a*): the issue in this case was whether a vessel commencing a second chase in sight of a fleet of which she had constituted a part before she had been detached by signal upon a former chase, and capturing the second chase at any distance from such a fleet, would be compelled to allow the claim of a whole fleet to share in a prize so made, notwithstanding such fleet afforded no assistance or co-operation in the capture, but actually bore away on another track. The answer was negative;

the *Belle Coquette* [1811] (1 Dodson, 18; Roscoe, I, 398, footnote *a*): there was no proof that the prize was seen from on board the *Tenant*; her claim must therefore depend upon whether the capture had been actually made by her boats; constructive assistance by boats was not sufficient;

the *El Rayo* [1811] (1 Dodson, 42; Roscoe, II, 127): "in a general engagement the whole fleet is entitled to head-money though the formal surrender be made to one ship only; but the surrender must be a continuation of the general engagement";

the *Union* [1813] (1 Dodson, 346; Roscoe, II, 180): if at the time of a capture by one vessel another associated in the chase is not visible owing to fog or darkness such other vessel is entitled to share in the prize if it is proved that at the time of the capture she is still engaged in the common purpose. See also *L'Etoile* [1816] (2 Dodson, 106; Roscoe, II, 182, footnote *a*);

the *Sparkler* [1813] (1 Dodson, 359; Roscoe, II, 187): a ship in sight at the time of capture is entitled to share in the prize from that circumstance alone. The claim is still stronger in favour of a ship which has joined in the pursuit of the prize;

the *John (No. 1)* [1813] (1 Dodson, 363; Roscoe, II, 190): the burden of proof lies upon the party setting up a claim of joint capture;

Genoa and Savona [1815] (2 Dodson, 88; Roscoe, II, 214), adjudicated after the capture of these two towns: a ship of war being *in itinere*, and barely seeing or hearing firing on the land, is not entitled to share in the beneficial results of an attack made by a force with which she had no concerted action or communication;

La Henriette [1815] (2 Dodson, 96; Roscoe, II, 215): where a squadron is blockading a port, and one ship thereof captures a vessel leaving such a port, all the ships of the blockading squadron, however distant from the place of capture, are entitled to a share of the prize-money;

Le Mélanie [1816] (2 Dodson, 122; Roscoe, II, 217): "When a vessel of war is in sight both of a prize and of an actual captor at the moment of capture, there is a presumption that such vessel has caused intimidation to the enemy, and encouragement to the friend. But such presumption is rebuttable by evidence to show that a vessel in sight cannot have been of any assistance having regard to her state and position."

During the Crimean War an Anglo-French Convention of 10 May 1854 laid down rules concerning captures to be made in the course of that war (Martens, N.R.G.[1], XV, 580; *B.F.S.P.* vol. 44, p. 11). Another Anglo-French Convention, acceded to by Sardinia and Turkey, of 10 July 1854 regulated the partition of trophies and booty (Martens, N.R.G.[1], XVI[2], 1 and 2).

A similar Convention was entered into by Austria and Prussia at Berlin on 6 June 1864 (Martens, N.R.G.[1], XX, 254; Parry, 129, 155) with regard to maritime prizes made during their common war against Denmark.

Art. 1 dealt with their respective competence:

> "Wenn eine Prise durch die Seemacht der beiden contrahierenden Staaten gemeinschaftlich gemacht wird, soll die diesfällige Entscheidung den für Prisensachen competenten Behörden desjenigen Staates zustehen, dessen Flagge von dem Officier geführt wird, welcher das Obercommando bei der bezüglichen Action hatte".

Art. 2 added that

> "Wenn eine Prise durch einen Kreuzer der einen der beiden contrahirenden Staaten in Gegenwart und in Sicht eines Kreuzers des andern gemacht wird, und hierdurch zur Einschüchterung des Feindes und zur Ermutigung des Captors beigetragen hat, soll die Entscheidung darüber den Prisenbehörden desjenigen Staates zustehen, dessen Flagge der wirkliche Captor führt".

Art. 3 regulated the case that a merchant ship of co-belligerent A should be seized either by the two co-belligerents jointly or by co-belligerent B; in that case the adjudication should be in favour of the State to which the merchant ship belonged.

Art. 4 laid down the principle of distribution of the proceeds of a jointly captured prize amongst the crews of the warships involved: division

> "in eben so viele Theile, als die Personenzahl der Bemannung der bezüglichen Kriegsschiffe beträgt, ohne Rücksicht auf die Rangstufen derselben".

Section 7. RECAPTURE. SALVAGE

General introduction: doctrinal and historical

The history of this chapter of prize law has formed the subject of extensive research by legal authors as well as by prize courts. The source material relating to this marginal subject of prize law is indeed so vast that it cannot be summarized in detail in the present publication. Recaptures and *recousses recouses* have played a prominent rôle in the history of prize law, both as far as municipal and international relations, and as far as prize court decisions are concerned. The almost disproportionate place which this subject and the connected practice of granting salvage to the recaptors has occupied in the legislation and case law of the main maritime Powers is easily understood in view of the desirability of encouraging such action by privateers and official Navy ships by the promise of a substantial reward. Since the Prize Acts defined rather strictly the conditions of the validity of a claim for salvage, disputes often arose over whether a particular recapture fell within their terms (see *infra*).

The subject matter of the recapture of prizes has always presented two aspects: (*a*) what was the legal effect of such a second capture?, and (*b*) to what extent was salvage due to the recaptors in case of the restoration of the recaptured property to its owner?

Ad (*a*). The main issue, of course, was to whom the ownership of a recaptured prize was to be awarded: to the recaptors, to the original captor, or to its original owner? This question was often discussed under the far from clear formula of whether the recapture was "valid". What that formula obviously was meant to express was to ask whether the prize had not already passed so firmly into the hands of the first captor that there could no longer be any question of a real capture of an object of still uncertain status, but only of a new capture of an object that had become enemy property.

The criteria that determined the status of the prize at the moment of its second capture varied: a true recapture might have become legally impossible either because the prize had remained in the captor's possession for a certain lapse of time, such as twenty-four hours, or because it had been brought by the captor to a safe place where it was protected against enemy attempts to retake it, or because it had already been condemned by the captor's prize court. In such circumstances there could no longer be any question of a recapture proper and the consequential restoration of the recaptured prize to its original owner.

Ad (*b*). The second group of issues related to the questions of who, amongst the many potential recaptors, was entitled to receive salvage, in what proportion was the salvage to be apportioned among them, and, in particular, what was the amount of the salvage to which they might lay claim. The latter question often depended again upon the length of time during which the prize had remained in the hands of the first captor.

As far as the first of the two issues distinguished above under (*a*) is concerned, the legal effect of a recapture has already formed the subject of a judicial decision at a very early date, namely in 1349, when a ship recaptured by the English from the enemy was restored to her original owners. Those proceedings still took place before a common law court. See Reginald Marsden's Introduction to his *Select Pleas in the Court of Admiralty* (London, 1894) in vol. 6 of the Publications of the Selden Society, p. xxxix.

What the *Consulat de Mar* contained on the handling of cases of recapture was laid down in Chapter 245 (in Travers Twiss's *Black Book of the Admiralty*, vol. III, pp. 611-631), in a set of provisions which begins with the following passage:

> "If a ship or vessel should be captured by an enemy, and any ship or vessel of a friend encounters the enemy, who has captured the said ship or vessel, if the said ship or vessel, which has encountered the said enemy, shall recapture, or be able to recapture, by whatever means, the said ship or vessel from the enemy, the said ship or vessel, and all which shall be in her, ought to be recaptured for him or for those to whom they belong, or ought to belong, if any of them are alive, on condition, however, of their giving to those who recaptured her from the said enemy, suitable salvage reward, and according to the maltreatment which they may have undergone, and according to the loss which they may have incurred".

The practice by belligerents of appropriating ships and goods even of neutral or allied subjects that had previously been seized by their enemy, but which their own warships or privateers had later recaptured is very old. Its legality was already asserted in letters of King Edward III of England of 1357 to the King of Portugal (Rymer, *Foedera*, VI, 14) and of King Henry IV of 1401 to the Master of the Teutonic Order of Prussia (Rymer, *Foedera*, VIII, 203). This practice was mitigated in later days, when both British and French prize courts restored the recaptured ships to their original owners, even without salvage, provided the property was not affected by circumstances that would have entailed condemnation in the Court of the enemy. See also the data recorded by Reginald Marsden in his works for the Selden Society and the Naval Records Society.

The French *Code des Prises* of 1784 contained on this subject the following statement:

> "Sa Majesté a jugé pendant la dernière guerre que la reprise du navire neutre faite par un corsaire Français (lorsque le navire neutre n'était pas chargé de marchandises prohibées, ni dans le cas d'être confisqué par l'ennemi) était nulle".

Various Prize Court decisions have applied this rule: *Code des Prises*, II, pp. 725, 1024 and 1049. See the judgments reported by De Pistoye et Duverdy, quoted *infra*, pp. 558-563.

Much attention has been paid in the developing law of maritime prize to the recapture of ships that had previously been captured by the enemy. Such recaptures could be made not only by a public warship of the belligerent to which the prize belonged, but also by a privateer, by an allied naval force or by other "friends", by land forces, by the crew of the prize, or even by private vessels or persons. Elaborate provisions covering these contingencies were often included in municipal ordinances or in treaties. Admiralty Courts have even often had to concern themselves with cases of a double recapture (recapture recovered) or, as French legal parlance expressed it, a *recousse recouse*. This complication of a double recapture, well-known from earlier centuries, has reappeared on a wide scale at a much later date, *viz.*, at the end of World War I, when the Belgian authorities, as a result of the Allied counter-offensive in 1918, had the chance of invoking the old rules on recapture with regard to German vessels and other craft which they had originally seized on the river Scheldt or in the port of Antwerp immediately after Germany's invasion in 1914, but which the German occupant had subsequently recaptured from Belgium, without having the opportunity of removing them from Belgium because on the ground of considerations of neutrality the Netherlands Government refused them freedom of passage over the Netherlands section of the river Scheldt (comp. Part IX-B (vol. X) of this publication, p. 219). I mention these special cases here because the Belgian Prize Court has made a remarkably extensive scrutiny of earlier case law, on which comp. *infra*, pp. 566-568.

In the exposé which follows I will deal first with the juridical distinction between recapture proper and other forms of a second capture (§ 1). I will then give some data on the contributions of legal scholars to the problem of recapture (§ 2). This will be followed by a brief survey of the sources of the law of recapture in treaties (§ 3) and municipal legislation (§ 4). And, after a brief reference to the formulation of the rules on recapture by the *Institut de droit international* in 1887 at its session in Heidelberg (at p. 530), I will end this section 7 and therewith the whole III B with a systematic summary of the Admiralty judgments on the subject of recapture available from a selected group of belligerent States (§ 5).

§ 1. *Recapture proper and other forms of a second capture*

Apart from the more normal cases of recapture, there have occurred other forms which gave rise to controversy.

Thus, a case is reported in which a convoyed neutral merchant ship that had been captured by a belligerent was subsequently recaptured by a warship of the convoy. It was decided that in such a case the recaptors had a claim to a share in the salvage due: the *Wight* [1804] (5 C.Rob., 315; Roscoe, I, 492).

Other cases are reported which can better be qualified as pseudorecaptures. For not all cases of a second capture of the same vessel can be classified as true recaptures.

A distinction must be made between a second seizure of the same ship by the same or another captor after her original release and a genuine recapture of the prize from the hands of the original belligerent. Instances of the first type of seizure are those of the *Mercurius* (Gerdes, Master) [1798] (1 C.Rob., 80; Roscoe, I, 54) and the *Odessa* [1855] (Spinks, 208; Roscoe, II, 462). The *Mercurius* case was an instance of the institution of new proceedings by the officers of the Admiralty following the previous restoration of the ship by consent; such second proceedings, either on the same or on different evidence, were not barred by the previous release, but the second seizor—*in casu* the King in his office of Lord High Admiral, a capacity distinguishable from his regal (*i.e.* royal) character—was subject to the risk of costs and damages. The *Odessa* case concerned a Russian vessel, released on the ground of an Order in Council (granting "days of grace" to enemy vessels on strictly defined conditions), but later captured again because she had failed to conform to those conditions.

Another curious case of two successive captures of the same vessels by competent authorities (two admirals) of the same Power was that of the *Diligentia* [1814] (1 Dodson, 404; Roscoe, II, 197): the first admiral captured them in the mouth of the river Tagus but abandoned them on his return to England, whereupon his appointed successor captured them again, an unusual case that gave rise to a legal battle between the two groups of seamen involved in the captures as to which of them could claim the prizes (comp. on this case under Abandonment, section 3, *supra*, p. 523).

A different variant again is that of two consecutive captures of the same ship, the first by belligerent A, the second by its ally, belligerent B. See on a much later case of this type the judgment concerning the *Fortunata* [1951] during World War II (Prises maritimes 1939-1945, p. 193).

A special form of recapture, or attempt to recapture, was that of an endeavour of the master and crew of a captured neutral vessel to rescue her from the belligerent prize master and crew on board. Such an attempt was considered as an unlawful action, which gave rise to the further question what was the sanction against it in respect of the fate of the ship and her cargo. In English prize proceedings the captors argued that in such cases of rescue the same infection rules should be applied as were accepted in the case of the carriage of contraband.

This particular type of recapture was discussed in appeal by Sir William Grant in the case of the American (neutral) *Franklin* [1811] (2 Acton, 106; Roscoe, II, 115). In that case her master and his crew, and the supercargo on board, had attacked the British prize master and his crew, whom they confined below, while the ship's course was altered for her own port of destination, but in the course of carrying out this intention she was captured again. The ship was in the first instance condemned with her cargo (although this was owned by a different person) by the Vice-Admiralty Court of

Gibraltar in a decree that was subsequently confirmed by the Lords of Appeal (*per* Sir William Grant). The latter found that it was clearly a case of rescue, but one in which the question at issue had never yet arisen. In his argument Sir William Grant reviewed a number of earlier cases of rescue, but concluded on an analysis of those precedents that in none of them had an instance of a genuine rescue by the crew of a captured neutral ship in actual fact occurred, so that the Court was not bound by any of the precedents invoked: as there was no direct authority, the issue should be decided on its own merits by analogy. This led the Lords to a confirmation of the judgment below to the effect that when after the capture of a (neutral) vessel her master attempted a rescue, her cargo was also liable to condemnation if ship and cargo were owned by the same person. The precedents reviewed in this appeal case by Sir William Grant and his fellow judges Sir W. Wynne, Sir W. Scott and Sir J. Nicholl related to the retaking of the Danish *Dispatch* [1801] (3 C.Rob., 278; 1 Acton, 163; Roscoe, I, 305), the *Alexander* [1801] (4 C.Rob., 93; Roscoe, I, 358), the *Carmelite* [1802], the *Adonis* [1804], the *Washington* [1806] and the *Mars* [Lords, June 1807]. For the claimants reference had, in addition, been made to the French (enemy) *Catharina Elizabeth* [1804] (5 C.Rob., 232; Roscoe, I, 458).

The *Dispatch* had been captured by an English cruiser, but her crew had seized an opportunity of retaking her from the British prize master put on board. After her fresh seizure by a French privateer and her following recapture by the original English captor, the British Prize Court was called upon to determine her status. This was deemed to be dependent upon the validity of her first rescue:

> "If neutral crews may be allowed to resort to violence to withdraw themselves out of the possession taken by a lawful cruiser for the purpose of a legal inquiry, and may ... hustle them out of the command of the vessel, the whole business of the detention of neutral ships will become a scene of mutual hostility and contention."

Ship and cargo were pronounced liable to condemnation on the ground that the parties had "declared themselves enemies by this act of hostile opposition to lawful inquiry".

In the *Carmelite*, the *Washington* and the *Mars* it was stressed that ship and cargo were liable to condemnation together if they belonged to the same person(s) (*i.e.*, on the analogy of the sanction against contraband carriers).

The *Alexander* was a case of breach of a blockade in which the owners of the cargo objected that they were not bound by the act of the master. In the *Adonis* the claim of the cargo-owners failed because the purity of their intention was not shown.

The *Catharina Elizabeth* of 1804 was an exceptional case in that it related to an enemy (French) vessel whose master had attempted a rescue. Counsel for the claimants in the subsequent *Franklin* case [1811] cited Sir William Scott as having said in that earlier case that "had [the rescue attempt] been by a neutral master, it would undoubtedly reach the property of his owner", and as having expressed his view that this should "extend also to the confiscation of the whole cargo entrusted to his care". In his report on this case (5 C.Rob., 232; Roscoe, I, 458) Counsel added that "this was merely a *dictum*, the case before the Court not at all comprising such a question." What Sir William Scott really said in the text of his judgment of 1804 included indeed the following passages:

> "That there is any ground for condemnation of the cargo in the conduct of the master cannot be maintained. It could only be the hostile act of a hostile person, who was prisoner of war, and who, unless under parole, had a perfect right to attempt to emancipate himself by seizing his own vessel. If a *neutral* master attempts a rescue, he violates a duty, which is imposed upon him by the law of nations, to submit to come in for inquiry ..., and it would, I think, extend also to the confiscation of the whole cargo entrusted to his care .... With an *enemy* master, the case is very different: no duty is violated by such an act on his part .... But a material fact in this case is, that the master did not attempt to withdraw his property: he seized *the ship of the captor*, and not this vessel."

§ 2. *Literature on recapture*

I will confine myself here to two main publications on the subject of recapture.

There is first the scholarly work by G.F. de Martens, entitled *Essai concernant les armateurs, les prises et surtout les reprises*, which is indeed one of the most detailed studies of the subject. This work was published in Göttingen in 1795. An English translation by Th.H. Horne was published in London in 1801. This work was, in accordance with its title, divided into three chapters, the first two dealing with privateering, the third with recaptures. It sets out in §§ 40-73 the various aspects from which the author had investigated his subject: the state of international legal doctrine; the various contingencies of recapture: of ships belonging to the recaptor's fellow citizens, to allied subjects, to auxiliaries, to persons neutral towards the belligerent recaptor or to persons neutral towards both belligerent powers; the effect of recaptures recovered (*recousses recouses*); the various systems in use: under ancient codes of maritime law, under the clauses of the most-favoured-nation or the treatment of aliens on an equal footing with the proper subjects of the recapturing State, and under the régime of Armed Neutrality; and terminating with a survey of laws enacted, and treaties entered into, by the main maritime powers of the time: France, Spain, Great Britain, the United Provinces of the Low Countries, Denmark, Sweden and the Hanse Towns.

In this work the author related, *inter alia*, in a note at p. 147 the curious old case of the Dutch merchant vessel the *Oude Roos*, dating from the War of the Spanish Succession (1710), captured on 2 December by two Dunkirk privateers, recaptured on 20 December by a Dutch privateer, from which she was recaptured again by another French privateer, which later abandoned her. She finally succeeded in reaching a safe haven. According to a German author particulars about this case could be found in a Dutch publication, A. Verwer's *Nederlants Seerechten*, but de Martens had sought them there in vain.

In another note, at p. 143, G.F. de Martens mentioned another Dutch ship, the *Admirael de Ruyter*, which was freighted during the Seven Years' War to the French to take in sugar at (French) Santo Domingo, was first captured by an English privateer, the *Boyne*, and later recaptured by a French privateer, the *Maréchal de Bellisle*. The English claimed the ship on the assertion that her recapture had been illegal. Although her confiscation could have been foreseen if the English privateer had actually conducted her into a British port, the French *Conseil des Prises* decreed that she should be restored to her owners, a decision of 7 April 1759, confirmed in appeal (Valin, p. 91).

A third note *y* in de Martens's *Essai* at pp. 163 *et seq.* dealt with cases dating from the Austrian War of Succession (1748], respectively the fourth Anglo-Dutch Naval War (1781), and related to the attitudes of England and the Netherlands towards the problem of recapture. The French text of de Martens' note is far from clear. Referring to a certain

> "concession exceptionnelle aux droits des neutres"

he observed that that concession

> "était loin d'être reconnue par les autres pays maritimes; que ni pour la propriété alliée, ni pour la propriété neutre l'Angleterre ne l'a jamais admise que sous la condition de réciprocité et moyennant payement du huitième de la valeur comme droit de recousse, et qu'en ce qui concerne la Hollande, malgré un accord de réciprocité conclu avec l'Angleterre quelques années auparavant [*viz.*, in 1744], elle [la Hollande] a refusé, en 1748, d'admettre cette restriction, pourtant légitime, au droit de recousse de ses capteurs;"

and he continued:

> "qu'un navire anglais le *Lydia* [1781], pris par un armateur français, fut repris par un vaisseau hollandais et conduit à Zierikzee et que l'Angleterre ayant réclamé sa propriété, les Etats-Généraux répondirent que la reprise appartenait *jure belli* aux repreneurs."

As to the relations between other Powers comp. further the preceding treaty of Versailles between France and the Netherlands of 1 May 1781 (Martens, R², III, 340; Parry, 47, 457) and the subsequent treaty between England and Spain of 5 February 1814 (Martens, N.S., II, 240; Parry, 63, 75).

Second comes the joint publication by A. de Pistoye and Ch. Duverdy, *Traité des prises maritimes* (Paris, 1855), a work which sets out the practice in France in vol. 2, titre VII ("Des navires recous sur l'ennemi ou abandonnés par lui"), chapter I (pp. 104-119) as to the recapture of French and allied merchant vessels, and chapter II (pp. 120-139) as to the recapture of neutral merchant vessels. According to the survey by these authors of the French legislation and case law these two contingencies gave rise to different solutions.

§ 3. *Treaties*

The settlement of claims arising from recaptures which might take place in the future has often been regulated in bilateral treaties, such as that between England and The Netherlands of 22 October 1691 (treaty of Whitehall) (Dumont, VII^2, 301; Parry, 19, 361), which regulated the premiums in case of recapture as follows (French version):

"En cas que tel Vaisseau ou Bâtiment soit repris par un Armateur comme ci-dessus, dans l'espace de quarante-huit heures après la première capture, on payera pour la recompense du sauvement la cinquième partie de la valeur du Vaisseau, & de sa charge, Canon & appareil. Et en cas que tel Vaisseau ou Bâtiment ait été quarante-huit heures dans la possession de l'Ennemi, & soit repris dans nonante & six heures, la recompense du sauvement montera à la troisième partie de la valeur susdite. Et si tel Vaisseau ou Bâtiment a été nonante & six heures dans la possession de l'Ennemi, & est ensuite repris par un Armateur de la manière susdite, en ce cas-là il sera payé pour recompense du sauvement, la moitié de la valeur dudit Vaisseau, & de sa charge, Canon & appareil.

En cas que des Vaisseaux ou Bâtimens, comme ci-dessus, soient repris par un Navire de Guerre avant que l'Ennemi les ait menés *intra Praesidia*, c'est-à-dire dans aucun Port de l'Ennemi ou Flotte d'Icelui portant le Pavillon comme ci-dessus, il sera payé comme recompense du sauvement la huitième partie de la valeur dudit Vaisseau & de sa charge, Canon & appareil, qui sera partagée entre ledit Roi & lesdits Etats Généraux selon les proportions dont on est convenu par Traité entre lesdites Parties en cas de prises.

La recompense qui sera faite au Capitaine & Matelots du Navire de Guerre reprenans un Vaisseau ou Bâtiment, comme ci-dessus, sera tirée du prix du sauvement en telle proportion que le Roi de la Grande Bretagne trouvera à propos quand il s'agira d'un Navire de Guerre Anglois, & selon le bon plaisir des Etats Généraux, en cas que le Navire de Guerre leur appartienne, pourvû que telle recompense soit donnée par ledit Roi ou lesdits Etats des portions qui leur sont respectivement affectées de la manière susdite.

Et afin de pouvoir mieux arriver à l'estimation des Vaisseaux susdits & de leurs charges & Canons & appareils, elle sera faite par un nombre égal de Personnes, qui seront choisies pour cela, & en cas qu'elles ne puissent s'accorder là-dessus, le Propriétaire fera lui-même l'estimation du Vaisseau & de sa charge, Canon, & appareil, et sera obligé de les vendre au prix qu'il y aura mis, ou bien l'estimation sera faite par le Repreneur, qui sera obligé de prendre ledit Vaisseau avec son Canon & appareil, & les Marchandises au prix qu'il y mettra.

De plus, il est convenu que si d'autres Princes ou Etats Alliés dudit Roi, ou desdits Etats Généraux, veulent être compris dans cet Accord, les Vaisseaux & Bâtimens leur appartenans seront traitez de la même manière comme il est ci-dessus stipulé."

Detailed rules on the legal effects of a recapture and on the resulting claims of the recaptors for salvage were still embodied in treaties which the United States concluded with foreign Powers in the last decades of the 18th century during their War of Independence. See, *e.g.*:

their treaty of the Hague with the United Netherlands "concernant les reprises", concluded on 8 October 1782 (Martens, R^2, III, 462/463; Parry, 48, 169):

Art. I.

"The Vessells of either of the two Nations, recaptured by the Privateers of the other, shall be restored to the first Proprietor, if such Vessells have not been Four and twenty hours in the Power of the Enemy; provided the Owner of the Vessell recaptured pay therefor one Third of the value of the Vessell, as also of that of the Cargo, the Cannons and Apparel, which Third shall be valued, by agreement, between the Parties interested; or, if they cannot agree thereon among themselves, they shall address themselves to the Officers of the Admiralty of the Place, where the Privateer, who has retaken the Vessell, shall have conducted her.

Art. II.

If the Vessell recaptured has been more than twenty four hours in the Power of the Enemy, she shall belong, entirely, to the Privateer who has retaken her.

Art. III.

In case a Vessell shall have been recaptured by a Vessell of War belonging to the States General of the United Netherlands, or to the United States of America, she shall be restored to the first Owner, he paying a thirtieth Part of the value of the Ship, her Cargo, Cannons and Apparel, if she has been recaptured in the Interval of twenty four hours: and the Tenth part, if she has been captured after the twenty four hours: which sums shall be distributed, in form of gratifications, to the Crews of the Vessells, which shall have retaken her.

The valuation of the said thirtieth parts and tenth parts shall be regulated, according to the Tenour of the first Article of the present Convention.

Art. IV.

The restitution of Prizes, whether they may have been retaken by Vessells of War, or by Privateers, in the meantime and untill requisite sufficient Proofs can be given of the Property of Vessells recaptured, shall be admitted in a reasonable time, under sufficient sureties, for the observation of the afore-said Articles.

Art. V.

The Vessells of War and Privateers, of one and of the other of the two Nations, shall be, reciprocally, both in Europe and in the other Parts of the World, admitted, in the respective Ports of each, with their Prizes, which may be unloaded and sold, according to the formalities used in the State, where the Prize shall have been conducted, as far as may be consistent with the 22nd Article of the Treaty of Commerce: provided always, that the Legality of Prizes, by the Vessells of the Low-Countries, shall be decided conformably to the Laws and Regulations established in the United-Netherlands; as likewise, that of Prizes, made by American Vessells, shall be judged, according to the Laws and Regulations, determined by the United-States of America.

Art. VI

Moreover, it shall be free, for the States-General of the United-Netherlands, as well as for the United-States of America, to make such regulations, as they shall judge necessary, relative to the Conduct, which their respective Vessells and Privateers ought to hold, in relation to the Vessells which they shall have taken and conducted into the Ports of the two Powers;"

Art. 18 of their Treaty of Amity and Commerce with *Sweden* of 3 April 1783 (Martens, R^2, III, 565; Parry, 48, 269):

"If it should happen that the two contracting parties should be engaged in a war at the same time with a common enemy, the following points shall be observed on both sides:

1. If the ships of one of the two nations, retaken by the privateers of the other, have not been in the power of the enemy more than twenty-four hours, they shall be restored to the original owner on payment of one third of the value of the ship and cargo. If, on the

contrary, the vessel retaken has been more than twenty-four hours in the power of the enemy, it shall belong wholly to him who has retaken it.

2. In case, during the interval of twenty-four hours, a vessel be retaken by a man-of-war of either of the two parties, it shall be restored to the original owner on payment of a thirthieth part of the value of the vessel and cargo, and a tenth part if it has been retaken after the twenty-four hours, which sums shall be distributed as a gratification among the crew of the men-of-war that shall have made the recapture.

3. The prizes made in manner above mentioned shall be restored to the owners, after proof made of the property, upon giving security for the part coming to him who has recovered the vessel from the hands of the enemy.

4. The men-of-war and privateers of the two nations shall reciprocally be admitted with their prizes into each other's ports; but the prizes shall not be unloaded or sold there until the legality of a prize made by Swedish ships shall have been determined according to the laws determined according to the laws and regulations established in Sweden, as also that of the prizes made by American vessels shall have been determined according to the laws and regulations established by the United States of America.

5. Moreover, the King of Sweden and the United States of America shall be at liberty to make such regulations as they shall judge necessary respecting the conduct which their men-of-war and privateers respectively shall be bound to observe with regard to vessels which they shall take and carry into the ports of the two powers."

§ 4. *Municipal legislation*

Recapture, its effects and the award of salvage belonged to the relatively rare subject matters of legislation in England, as appears from the judgment of Lord Stowell in the complicated case of the *Ceylon* [1810] (1 Dods. 105, 116; Roscoe, II, 133) discussed below pp. 568. In that case the Court indeed examined in detail the operation of the rules laid down in the *Prize Act* in force at the period.

As far as France was concerned, Art. 5 of Henri III's Edict of 1555 did not adopt the generous rule of the Consulat of the Sea cited *supra* p. 540, but a more rigid rule, that was subsequently reproduced in Art. 61 of Henri III's Edict of March 1584 and in Art. 8 of *titre* IX of *livre* III of Louis XIV's *Ordonnance de la Marine* of August 1681. In the wording of 1584 it ran as follows:

"Si auscun navire de noz subjects pris par noz ennemis a esté entre leurs mains jusques à vingt-quatre heures, et après il soit recoux et repris par aucun de noz navires de guerre, ou aultres de noz subiects, la prise sera déclarée bonne; mais si ladicte reprise est faicte auparavant les vingt-quatre heures, il sera restitué avec tout ce qui estoit dedans; et en aura toutefois le navire de guerre qui l'aura recoussé et repris le tiers".

The *Ordonnance* of 1681 repeated the provision in the following wording:

"Si aucun navire de nos sujets est repris sur nos ennemis, après qu'il aura demeuré entre leurs mains pendant 24 heures, la prise en sera bonne; et si elle est faite avant les 24 heures, il sera restitué au propriétaire avec tout ce qui estoit dedans, à la réserve du tiers qui sera donné au navire qui aura fait la recousse".

It added the following supplementary provision (Art. 9) concerning the case of a prize which had either been abandoned by the enemy or had returned into the possession of its French owners as a result of other causes:

> "Si le navire, sans estre recous, est abandonné par les ennemis, ou si, par tempeste ou autre cas fortuit, il revient en la possession de nos Sujets avant qu'il ait esté conduit dans aucun Port ennemy, il sera rendu au proprétaire qui le réclamera dans l'an et jour, quoy qu'il ait esté plus de vingt-quatre heures entre les mains des ennemis",

a provision still extended analogously by a further Decree of 12 vendémiaire *an* VI (3 October 1797), in its turn reproduced in Art. 55 of the *Arrêté* of 2 prairial *an* XI.

These latter provisions (comp. Grotius, *De jure belli ac pacis*, 1. III, ch. VI, § 3), however, had nothing to do with recapture because they had in view ships captured by the enemy which subsequently either were abandoned by him or escaped him by storm of disaster. This contingency consequently came within the rules governing shipwrecks. They were in conformity with older provisions laid down in ordonnances of the King of Spain (Art. 13 of that of 21 August 1702, resp. Art. 11 of that of 17 November 1718) (referred to by De Pistoye and Duverdy in their *Traité*, vol. II, pp. 217-218).

Neither had the ensuing supplementary provision of Art. 10 of the *Ordonnance* of 1681 anything to do with prize law proper since it lay outside its specific domain: it ordered the restitution to their owners of ships and cargoes recovered from pirates in accordance with the principle *pirata non mutat dominium*, subject to the conditions that their property was reclaimed within a year and a day, and that the reconquerors were rewarded with the allocation to them of one-third of the value of ship and cargo.

Another municipal regulation in France was the *Règlement* on *reprises* of 15 June 1779 (Martens, R^2, III, 128). As appears from the elaborate analysis of the situation in France by De Pistoye and Duverdy in their *Traité*, vol. II, pp. 104 *et seq.*, French legislation has developed a systematic distinction between the treatment of the effects of the recapture of French and allied vessels and of those of the recapture of neutral vessels. It was on these rules that the *Conseil des prises* and the tribunal of appeal of the period based their judicial decisions (*infra*, pp. 558-563).

The States General of the United Netherlands issued a number of *placaten* dealing with recapture in the second half of the 17th century. Bynkershoek, in his *Quaestionum juris publici, libri duo* (Classics of International Law, translation, 1930, pp. 38-43) mentioned the decrees of 4 July 1625, concerning the recompense due to private recaptors; of 22 July 1625 on the reward of warships that recover vessels of private owners; and those of 1 September 1643, 8 February 1645 and 13 April 1677. On 27 November 1666, during the second Anglo-Dutch Naval War, a *placaat* was issued on the recapture of prizes purchased by neutral subjects.

Art. VIII of a *placaat* of 12 January 1781, enacted during the fourth Anglo-Dutch Naval War (Martens, R^2, III, 153), determined the reward owing to recaptors in case of the recapture of a Netherlands ship from the English by *commissievaarders*, merchant ships fitted out at the private expenses of Dutch inhabitants: 1/5 of the value of ship and cargo if the prize was retaken within twenty-four hours; 1/3 if retaken between two and four times that period, and 1/2 if retaken after four times twenty-four hours, whatever the duration of their possession by the enemy.

Bynkershoek considered the differentiation in the reward according to the shorter or longer period of the first capture unreasonable. The *placaten* of the States General of 11 March 1632, 8 February 1645 and 19 April 1659 gave a fixed reward of two-thirds of the value of the ship to the recaptor irrespective of the duration of the first capture (one-ninth in the case of the 1659 *placaat*). Bynkershoek considered this correct and referred to the Consolate of the Sea; both the Consolate and Bynkershoek favoured a reward that depended on "the task being difficult or easy, whether the recaptor fought with courage or not at all, whether he incurred heavy expenses, whether the booty was worth much or little".

The recapture of prizes, which has always occupied a somewhat disproportionate place in national legislations and international treaties, has also been the subject of private codification by the *Institut de droit international* in its *Règlement international des prises maritimes* (Heidelberg, 1887), *viz.*, in its final paragraphs 119-122. They run as follows:

> "119. Tout navire privé, pris en temps de guerre par un navire de guerre d'un belligérant, peut être objet de reprise par un navire de guerre de l'autre belligérant, quelque soit d'ailleurs le temps pendant lequel la prise est restée au pouvoir de l'ennemi avant d'être reprise.
>
> § 120. Toute reprise doit être reconnue comme telle et jugée par le tribunal national des prises maritimes.
>
> § 121. Le repreneur sera tenu de restituer la reprise au propriétaire légitime primitif, sauf le cas où celui-ci l'aurait fait servir à un but interdit par le règlement international.
>
> § 122. Il ne sera accordé de prime pour les recaptures que dans le cas où le navire et la cargaison seront adjugés au propriétaire primitif, lequel même ne restituera que les dépenses occasionnées par la reprise et verifiées par le tribunal national des prises maritimes."

§ 5. *Admiralty judgments*

Introduction

A vast number of cases decided by British Admiralty Courts can be gathered from the various collections of judicial pronouncements. Some of them date back to the middle or the second half of the 18th century. Among them there are a number which have given elaborate historical exposés of the legal régime of recaptured prizes. Such an historical survey can be found, *inter alia*, in the judgment concerning the *Santa Cruz* [1798] (1 C.Rob., 50; Roscoe, I, 39), see *infra*, p. 553.

The situation in France was slightly different from that in England in that the French system was based on municipal legislation whereas the English law was primarily judge-made. Another difference between the two legal systems was that the substantive criteria for the solution of the problem also diverged.

Old British and French judgments, illustrating the practice in these two countries from the middle of the 18th century onward will be digested below, pp. 551 *et seq*., respectively pp. 558 *et seq*.

My original plan to group the available case material in two sections, the first relating to (*a*) the legal effect of a recapture, the second to (*b*) the extent of the award of salvage, has been abandoned. Such a rigid division proved to be scarcely practicable since these two aspects of the problem were more often than not dealt with together in the same judgment. Nevertheless I have contrived to observe a certain order according to where the accent lay, but a strict arrangement of that sort also proved to be difficult. Instead, in view of the mass of the available material, I have applied two other methods of classification, on the one hand, according to the States whose prize tribunals were the authors of the case law, and on the other, according to the successive wars during which the recaptures were made.

On American judgments see *infra*, pp. 563 *et seq*.

I did not have access to sources authentic enough to expatiate upon Spanish and Netherlands case law.

At a much later stage, at the end of World War I, the history of recapture, and especially *recousse recouse*, was re-examined by the Belgian Prize Court in a series of decisions, digested below, pp. 566 *et seq*.

Old British case law

A great many recaptures by both King's ships and privateers have left their traces in British prize court decisions. They dealt with a variety of events and situations. I will begin with the oldest precedents up to the end of the 18th century. Among them are:

during the War of the Austrian Succession:

the *Pretty Betsy* [1743], discussed in Reginald Marsden-Burrell's *Reports of cases* (London, 1885), at pp. 388 *et seq*. This was the case of an English plantation-built brigantine, the property of British subjects, which was first seized by a Spanish-registered ship while bound with a cargo from Portuguese Madeira for Virginia, but was recaptured a few weeks later by the English brig *St.-George*, a merchantship engaged in trade only, not a privateer or letter of marque ship, whose master was subsequently ordered by a British man-of-war to sail back to Madeira. There the brigantine was sold by public auction and bought by the master of the *St.-George* without having been first condemned by a prize court. When the brigantine later entered the port of Liverpool, she was claimed there on behalf of the original owner. The experts, consulted on the issues of ownership and salvage, were of the opinion that the property of the ship and cargo was not altered by the event and that salvage was due to the *St.-George* who retook the *Pretty Betsy*, although she did not have a letter of marque, in the same manner and proportion as if she had been retaken by a privateer, *i.e.* one-third should she have been in possession of the enemy above forty-eight hours and under ninety-six, if above ninety-six hours a moiety;

during the Seven Years' War:

the *Charming Elizabeth* [1757-1760]. This vessel (Marsden-Burrell, p. 197) was a British-owned ship that was captured on her way from Jamaica to London by a French privateer and condemned as prize at Port-au-Prince (Cuba). Some time later she was bought there by the master of an English cartel-ship and sent to Jamaica. On her arrival there she was seized by the English man-of-war *Marlborough* and proceeded against as prize. Both the former owners and the purchaser claimed the ship as their property, but the Vice-Admiralty Judge in Jamaica dismissed both claims and condemned the *Charming Elizabeth* as lawful prize on 24 October 1757. This condemnation was, however, reversed in appeal in 1760: the original British owners got their ship back, subject to the payment to the recaptor of the eighth of her value due for salvage and the usual expenses.—A similar case was that of the *Florence* [1760], recorded *loco cit.*, p. 198.

during the American War of Independence:

the *John* [1778] (Hay and Marriott, 152; Roscoe, I, 12) was an English ship that was retaken from the French by a privateer after having been in possession of the enemy for nearly ninety-six hours without being carried into any port. The question in that case was

> "whether, there being no Act of Parliament to regulate proceedings in cases of French captures and recaptures, the old rules should not be observed in favour of privateers retaking to give a salvage according to the time in the possession of the enemy. That larger salvage has always been allowed to privateers than to the King's ships in all former Acts till the American Act, which now equally confined both to one-eighth salvage. It must have been a slip in the legislature, in the American Act; as the King's ships are doing their duty, fitted out at the public expense, but the privateers at the extraordinary expenses of particulars.
>
> Whether it was a slip or not, in the drawers of the American Acts, yet it would be very awkward to have two different rules; one for American, another for French, recaptures. As in this case the Court is not bound by the Acts in former wars, which expired with them, so it is not bound in this case of French reprisals by the American Act of letters of marque. The divisions of point of time for more or less salvage was always a bad rule, borrowed from the oldest Dutch placarts, and seemed calculated for increasing litigations and disputes. The simplest rule is the best in everything, and the decision in the French cases of recapture should square with the clause in the American Act."

The Court therefore

> "pronounced for an eighth salvage, yet not so as to preclude its discretion to give a greater, and even a very great salvage, in other cases, where there should be very great merit in retaking.
>
> There was no resistance in this case [the *John*] on the part of the enemy; but when the action should be attended with loss of lives and blood, and damage of recaptors, they might expect a proportionable salvage; observing that this country owed much at this time

> to the activity of private armaments; and while privateers observed strictly the law and the King's instructions, in doing no injury to British or neutral innocent subjects, they would meet with every suitable and just encouragement";

the *Renard* [1778] (Hay and Marriott, 222; Roscoe, I, 17), a British ship captured by the French and condemned as prize, thereupon fitted out and employed as a French privateer, but finally retaken by the British privateer *Lark*. An order was made for the restoration of the vessel to her original owners, subject to their paying a moiety of her value to the recaptors as salvage. The Court (*per* Sir James Marriott) was very critical of the prevailing doctrines:

> "There is something ridiculous in the decisive manner each lawyer [respectively Grotius and Bynkershoek] had given his opinion. Grotius might as well have laid down, for a rule, twelve hours, as twenty-four; or forty-eight as twelve. A pedantic man in his closet dictates the law of nations: everybody quotes, and nobody minds him. The usage is plainly as arbitrary as it is uncertain; and who shall decide when dictators disagree? Bynkershoek, as it is natural to every writer or speaker who comes after another, is delighted to contradict Grotius; his rule is, that the prize must not only be brought *infra praesidia*, into the port, and under the guns of the enemy, but so that all hope of recovery is lost. But this rule will not do, it is plain, because the fact is the ship is recovered.
>
> As to Master Brooke's rule [*Abridgement*, Tit. Property, forfeiture 38], there is neither sense nor justice in it. The property, he says, is lost between an Englishman and an Englishman, unless it is retaken in twelve hours; and besides that, it must be reclaimed before sunset. What! when the original owner on land knows nothing of his ship being taken by the enemy at sea? and how, and where, and from whom can he reclaim her? From the enemy? The rule is nonsensical, for it is impossible."

during the Napoleonic wars:

the *Santa Cruz* [1798] (1 C.Rob., 50; Roscoe, I, 39), a ship of the subject of an ally (Portugal), captured by the French, brought by them *infra praesidia* and recaptured by English cruisers.

The rule which prevailed in those days with regard to English ships was held by the Court to apply equally to allied vessels unless the rule applied by the prize court of the ally was less liberal than that of Great Britain, in which case on the principle of reciprocity the law of the ally should be applied. The *onus* lay on the Portuguese claimant to prove the law of his country after adverse *prima facie* evidence by the captors. A somewhat hesitant note added by Roscoe to the heading of the report was to the effect that probably the rule observed at that time was that, in order to divest the owner of his property, the vessel after her capture must have been brought *intra praesidia*. Comp., however, the judgment concerning the *Flad Oyen* [1799] (*infra*). The judgment in the *Santa Cruz* case contains a detailed comparative exposé of the subject in different legal systems.

Another case of 1798, the *Betsey (No. 1)* (1 C.Rob., 93; Roscoe, I, 63) related to an American ship which was captured in April 1794 off French Guadeloupe by an English commander who had instituted a blockade of the island without actual investment, and which was later retaken, together with the island, by the French. The compensation claimed by the neutral ship owner from the original British captors was refused on the ground of *bona fide* possession, and of the defence that irregularities, possibly committed, in order to be taken into account, must be such as to produce irreparable loss, or justly prevent restitution from the recaptors.

Another American ship, the *Two Friends* [1799] (1 C.Rob., 271; Roscoe, I, 130), manned partly by a British crew, was captured by the French, but later recaptured by her crew. The English sailors claimed and were awarded salvage.

The *Good Intent* [1799] (1 C.Rob., 286; Roscoe, I, 137), was an English ship, recaptured from the French captors by an American armed vessel, whose sailors claimed salvage. This was an amicable case, but there was no opposition against the jurisdiction of the Court. As there had been no extraordinary merits in the recapture (the recaptor was strong and the prize offered no resistance), no more than one-sixth of the ship's value was held to be due as salvage.

The *Flad Oyen* [1799] (1 C.Rob., 135; Roscoe, I, 78), was a British vessel recaptured by the English after her seizure by the French and her ensuing condemnation by a French consular prize court in the neutral port of Bergen (Norway): the ship was on recapture restored to her former owner on payment of salvage.

The *Vår Önskan* [1799] (2 C.Rob., 299; Roscoe, I, 239) contained the following passages:

> I know perfectly well that it is not the modern practice of the law of nations to grant salvage on recapture of neutral vessels; and upon this plain principle, that the liberation of a clear neutral from the hand of the enemy is no essential service rendered to him, inasmuch as that same enemy would be compelled by the tribunals of his own country, after he had carried the neutral vessel into port, to release him with costs and damages for the injurious seizure and detention. This proceeds upon the supposition that those tribunals would duly respect the obligations of the law of nations—a presumption which, in the wars of civilized States, each belligerent is bound to entertain in their respective dealings with neutrals. But it being notorious to all Europe, in the present war, that there has been a constant struggle maintained between the governing powers of France, for the time being, and its maritime tribunals, which should most outrage the rights of neutral property, the one by its decrees, or the other by its decisions, the liberation of neutral property out of their possession has been deemed, not only in the judgments of our Courts, but in that of neutrals themselves, a most substantial benefit conferred upon them in a delivery from danger, against which no clearness or innocence of conduct could afford any protection; and a salvage for such service has not only been decreed, but thankfully paid, ever since these wild hostilities have been declared and practiced by France, against all acknowledged principles of the law of nations and of natural justice. When the lawless and irregular practices are shown to have ceased, the rule of paying salvage for the liberation of neutral property must cease likewise."

A footnote by Roscoe refers to old case law, cited in Rymer, *Foedera*, VI, 14 and VIII, 203.

The *Kierlighett* [1800] (3 C.Rob., 96; Roscoe, I, 258), was another case of the recapture of a (British) prize illegally condemned by a French consular prize court in a neutral port, thereupon sold to a neutral purchaser, later recaptured and restored to her original owner. The neutral buyer who was *bona fide* was held entitled to recover such sum as registrar and merchants should consider reasonable for improvements made by him to the vessel (comp. on this case also *supra*, p. 196).

The *Helen* [1801] (3 C.Rob., 224; Roscoe, I, 299), was a case in which the recapture was made by a revenue cutter, acting in virtue of a letter of marque; she was awarded 1/6 of the value as salvage on the footing of a private ship and not only 1/8 on that of a King's ship (*Prize Act* of 1793).

The *Edward and Mary* [1801] (3 C.Rob., 305; Roscoe, I, 312), was a more complicated case. Separated from her convoy, the ship was brought to by a French lugger which came up and told her master to stay by her till the storm moderated. Whilst the lugger, sighted by the British frigate *Arethusa*, was chased and captured, the *Edward and Mary* succeeded in escaping and rejoining the convoy. The Court held that, although in order to constitute a case of capture it is sufficient if a vessel came under the control of an enemy ship and the placing of a prize crew on board is not essential, this particular case presented an instance of rescue without actual "retaking". The case was held, therefore, not to come under the *Act* of 33 Geo. 3, c. 66, but the *Arethusa* was awarded salvage under the general maritime law.

The *Cosmopolite (No. 1)* [1801] (3 C.Rob., 333; Roscoe, I, 321), was an American ship captured by the French, condemned by a French court in Spain, bought there by a Danish merchant and recaptured by an English cruiser. There were two claimants: the Danish buyer and the original American owner. The condemnation of the vessel in a neutral port was decreed to be invalid. But the Court declined to judge of the relation between foreign States and ordered restitution to the Danish purchaser.

The *Franklin (No. 2)* [1801] (4 C.Rob., 147; Roscoe, I, 365), related to a British ship and cargo, bound ostensibly on a voyage from Liverpool to Naples, but captured far out of that course whilst going actually into an (enemy) Spanish port in the Bay of Biscay, compelled thereto, according to the master, by bad weather and a leak in the vessel. In his judgment Sir William Scott distinguished two kinds of salvage, one "military" in rescuing the property from the enemy, the other "civil" in preserving it from distress and peril of the sea, and held that no "military salvage" was due where the property rescued was not in the possession of the enemy, or so nearly as to be certainly and inevitably under his grip. The captors claimed military, or in the alternative civil, salvage:

> "The first question is, whether the captors of this ship and cargo can entitle themselves to be considered as salvors? On their part, two kinds of salvage are claimed. First, a military salvage, as it may be termed, in rescuing the property from the enemy; and secondly, a salvage in preserving it from distress and peril of the sea. The vessel had met with bad weather, and had sprung a leak, and was at the time of capture found very near St. Andero, intending to go into an enemy's port for the preservation of the lives of the crew. Whether the danger appeared so great to the privateer may be doubted, as it has

> turned out that, with the aid of a few more hands, they kept the ship eight days longer at sea, and at last brought her safely into a port of Jersey. The next question that occurs is, whether military salvage is due as for a rescue from the enemy? I think it is not. No case has been cited, and I know of none, in which military salvage has been given, where the property rescued was not in the possession of the enemy, or so nearly as to be certainly and inevitably under his grasp. There has been no case of salvage where the possession, if not absolute, was not almost indefensible, as where the ship had struck, and was so near as to be virtually in the hands and grip of the enemy. In such cases, the same hazard is incurred by the salvor and the same reason exists to hold out a stimulus to recaptors. But as in this case there was no enemy to encounter. The danger to the parties was contingent only, and though probable to occur, had not actually occurred."

[The claim of military salvage could, therefore, not be sustained.]

The *Eleonora Catharina* [1802] (4 C.Rob., 156; Roscoe, I, 367), related to a Russian ship, taken on a voyage from Archangel to London by a French privateer and retaken by a British cruiser in December 1800. The Court kept to the older traditional rule that *neutral* property taken out of the possession of a belligerent was not usually liable to salvage, but admitted that there was an exception when the cruisers and government of the captor State acted irregularly, as they were held to have done in the case under review. The Russian ship was, therefore, decreed to be liable to the payment of salvage. On the contrary, such liability was denied in the case of the *Carlotta* [1803] (5 C.Rob., 55) because the proceedings of the French courts had been conducted with more regularity.

The *Three Friends* [1802] (4 C.Rob., 268; Roscoe, I, 389) was accidentally destroyed by fire after a decree of restitution, the ship having been appraised, but not the cargo. The Court held that salvage on the ship should be decreed on the appraised value, but that the owners of the cargo and the recaptors must bear the loss of the cargo.

In the *Urania* [1804] (5 C.Rob., 148; Roscoe, I, 438) the Court decided that salvage on recapture could be claimed by a non-commissioned vessel. This was a case of asserted joint recapture by a King's ship and a non-commissioned vessel, the *Loyal Briton*. Proceedings were first instituted on the part of the Admiralty as for droits of Admiralty, but they were discontinued, whereupon the *Loyal Briton* demanded salvage in her own right. The Court said:

> "Surely a distinction has always been held in cases of salvage. There must be many cases in which the claims of non-commissioned persons have been allowed for salvage on retaking property out of the hands of the enemy. The words of the *Prize Act* appear to me clearly to recognise such a practice, which direct salvage to be paid on recapture by His Majesty's ships of war, or any privateer, or other ship or vessel or boat under His Majesty's protection and obedience."

The *Wight* [1804] (5 C.Rob., 315; Roscoe, I, 492) was a ship which sailed under convoy of the *Thisbe* on a voyage from Zante to London, was captured by a privateer in passing the narrow channel between Kephalonia and Ithaka, but was recaptured by the *Thisbe*. The Court held that a convoying vessel has a right to salvage for the recapture of a vessel under her charge if such vessel has been in the effectual possession of an enemy. The Court would not entertain a charge of negligence against the convoy as a defence of a salvage claim: such claim must be made to the Lords Commissioners of the Admiralty, but if it was substantiated before them, then the Court would act on their finding.

The *Frederick and Mary Ann* [1805] (6 C.Rob., 213; Roscoe, I, 548) was a case of recapture of a prize ship, the English *Prince*, by a prize crew, put by the privateer *Ceres* on board another prize ship; held, that where a prize crew was put on board a prize from a privateer, and such crew subsequently made another prize, those on the privateer were entitled to share in the second prize.

The *Gage* [1806] (6 C.Rob., 273; Roscoe, I, 554) concerned a British ship found and rescued in a derelict state: the Court held that this was not a case of recapture proper, coming under the *Prize Act*, and awarded a larger amount of salvage (one-fourth).

The *Sansom* [1807] (6 C.Rob., 410) was an American ship that was captured by a Spanish privateer on a voyage from Amsterdam to Falmouth; afterwards she was recaptured and brought to England. In the meantime the *Sansom* had been condemned in Spain for breaking the "blockade of England" and "trading with that country". In very strong language Sir William Scott denied any validity to the Napoleonic decree which instituted the "blockade of England" and held that a service had been rendered to the *Sansom* by rescuing her from the operation of the French decree; he declared salvage to be due.

In the *Pensamiento Feliz* [1809] (Edw., 115; Roscoe, II, 29) the discussion revolved around the question of whether a particular capture was an instance of military salvage. The case concerned the capture of a Portuguese ship, laden with a cargo, the property of British and Portuguese merchants, which put into the harbour of Maros (Spain) because of damage incurred during a voyage from Pernambuco (Brazil) to Liverpool, from where she was subsequently brought out by boats of the English warship *Endymion* which placed four men on board. These men claimed salvage on the restoration of the vessel and her cargo to the respective owners. Were they entitled to any salvage on the grounds that the harbour, though not occupied by France, was in fact under her immediate control, and that considerable benefit had been rendered to the parties interested in the property by this interference of the captors? A question arose as to the nature of the salvage to which they were entitled. The Court recognized the operation as a form of military salvage and awarded the claim. Should this not have been so, then it would have been a case of salvage over which the Instance Court would have had jurisdiction.

The *Henry* [1810] (Edw., 192; Roscoe, II, 32) laid down that personal risk is not a necessary element of recapture; in case a captured ship was purchased by a neutral national from the captor, a belligerent cruiser, for the purpose of restoring her to her British owners, salvage was due.

The *Progress* [1810] (Edw., 210; Roscoe, II, 40), chartered from England to Oporto, was captured by a French cruiser but recaptured at Oporto; salvage was due on the entire freight; the value of the prize was held to be its value at the place of restitution.

The *Friends* [1810] (Edw., 246; Roscoe, II, 48), a British ship chartered to proceed to Lisbon, but on her arrival at the mouth of the river Tagus warned off by a blockading squadron, was subsequently captured by a Spanish ship, but later recaptured by a British cruiser and taken to Portuguese Madeira where the ship and her cargo were sold. The Court held that, as the loss of freight had been caused by a calamity common to ship and cargo, the loss must be divided and a moiety of the freight must be paid by the cargo-owner.

The *Robert Hale* [1810] (Edw., 265; Roscoe, II, 56): no reward is due for recapture when the vessel is released by a belligerent prize court on bail since no effective service had been rendered to the ship owners.

The *Ceylon* [1811] (1 Dods., 105; Roscoe, II, 133) was a case of capture by combined land and sea forces. Comp. for further details *infra* under "Salvage claims", p. 568.

The *Charlotte Caroline* [1812] (1 Dods., 192; Roscoe, II, 149): the right to salvage is not extinguished by subsequent capture and condemnation in the enemy's port when the sentence condemning the prize is overruled by an order of release from the sovereign power of the captor State.

The *Georgiana* [1814] (1 Dods., 397; Roscoe, II, 193): a case analogous to that of the *Ceylon*.

The *Galen* (1814) (Dods., 429; Roscoe, II, 199): a convoy is entitled to a share in a recaptured prize (comp. the *Wight* case of 1804 above).

The *Fanny* [1814] (1 Dods., 443; Roscoe, II, 202) was a case of recapture of neutral property on an armed vessel of a belligerent which the captor might presume would be defended by force; by thus adhering to the enemy the neutral cargo-owner lost the benefit of his neutrality; on recapture of his property he was subject to salvage.

Genoa and *Savona* [1815] (2 Dods., 88; Roscoe, II, 214): a case of joint recapture of these two cities, whereby the actual recapture was made by land forces and restoration was obtained on giving a bill of exchange; yet the facts were construed as a military recapture.

Old French legislation and case law

French legislation and jurisprudence made a sharp distinction between the recapture (*recousse*) of French or allied vessels, on the one hand, and neutral vessels on the other. De Pistoye and Duverdy have analysed the legal situation in France in vol. II of their *Traité* at pp. 104-139. Chapter I of their Titre VII deals with the first group (pp. 104-119), a special sub-paragraph (*a*) at pp. 114-119 being devoted to the case of *recousse-recouse* (double recapture), Chapter II deals with the second group (pp. 120-139). In accordance with their general system of exposition they first outline the development of the legislation on the matter and then follow this up with reports of the available case law.

1. Recapture of French or allied vessels. The subject of the recapture by the French of national or allied ships, captured by the enemy, was regulated successively by Art. 61 of the *Ordonnance* of 1584, Art. 8 of the *Ordonnance* of 1681 and Art. 54 of the *Arrêté* of 2 prairial *an* XI.

The original Art. 61 of 1584 ran as follows:

> "Si aucun navire de nos subjects prins par nos ennemis a esté entre leurs mains jusques à vingt-quatre heurs, et après il soit recoux et repris par aucune de nos nefs de guerre ou aultres de nos subjects, la prinse sera déclarée bonne; mais si la dicte reprise est faicte auparavant les vingt-quatre heures, il sera restitué avec tout ce qui estoit dedans; et en aura toutesfois le navire de guerre, qui l'aura recoussé et repris, le tiers".

Art. 8 of 1681 had the following text:

> "Si un navire de nos sujets est repris sur nos ennemis, après qu'il aura demeuré entre leurs mains pendant vingt-quatre heures, la prise en sera bonne; et, si elle est faite avant les vingt-quatre heures, il sera restitué au propriétaire, avec tout ce qui était dedans, à la réserve du tiers, qui sera donné au navire qui aura fait la recousse".

Art. 54 of the *Arrêté* of *an* XI:

> "Si un navire français ou allié est repris par des corsaires sur les ennemis de l'État, après qu'il aura été vingt-quatre heures entre les mains de ces derniers, il appartiendra en totalité auxdits corsaires; mais, dans le cas où la reprise aura été faite avant les vingt-quatre heures, le droit de recousse ne sera que du tiers de la valeur du navire recous et de sa cargaison.
>
> Lorsque la reprise sera faite par un bâtiment de l'Etat, elle sera restituée aux propriétaires, mais sous la condition qu'ils payeront aux équipages repreneurs le trentième de la valeur de la reprise si elle a été faite avant les vingt-quatre heures, et le dixième. Si la reprise a eu lieu après les vingt-quatre heures, tous les frais relatifs à cette reprise restituée seront à la charge des propriétaires".

This latter Art. 54 of *an* XI differed from the preceding provisions in that it established a distinction between prizes made by privateers and prizes made by King's vessels. Those earlier provisions awarded the whole profit of the recapture to the King's warships on the same footing as with privateers, although, as De Pistoye and Duverdy relate at p. 106, the actual practice of the *Parlements* of Rouen and Bordeaux was diametrically opposed to those provisions. The twenty-four hours' rule of 1584 was, for that matter, conformable to the opinion of authors, such as Loccenius (*De jure maritimo*), and to the usages observed in Holland and in Spain, in which latter country the usage was confirmed by Art. 12 of an Ordinance of 21 August 1702 and Art. 10 of an Ordinance of 17 November 1718 (Abreu, *Tratado sobre presas de mar*). Grotius adopted the same rule, but only as a new rule that was at variance with an older rule according to which the criterion was whether the prize had been brought into safety *intra praesidia hostium* (*De jure belli ac pacis*, 1. III, ch. VI, § 3, no. 3). What the English prize court thought about the twenty four hours' rule appears from my quotation *supra*, p. 553.

Under the regime of these *Ordonnances*, which the French prize courts, of course, were bound to apply, the *Conseil des prises* made the following decisions relating to French, respectively allied (Spanish) vessels in *an* IX:

Le Désiré contre la Tapageuse (II, 110). The French vessel the *Désiré*, sailing under the convoy of the French corvette the *Tapageuse*, but temporarily separated from her and in that condition captured by an enemy warship, was recaptured by the corvette. When the captain and crew of the *Tapageuse* claimed salvage on that account, their claim was dismissed: her action had not been a recapture proper, but rather a dutiful act of protection of the vessel convoyed;

La Notre Dame de Miséricorde contre les Bouches-du-Rhône (II, 112); The allied (Spanish) vessel had, after her capture by the English, remained in their power for thirty-six hours. Although the *Ordonnance* of 1584 did not specifically mention allied ships, they had to be treated in the same manner as French ships:

> "parce que nos alliés, ou nos auxiliaires, faisant cause commune avec nous, notre droit leur devient commun dans une cause commune [reference made to Vattel]".

She was, accordingly, adjudged to her French recaptors;

L'Inesperado et le Sant'Antonio y Animas contre l'Eole (II, 113), two Spanish ships, captured by the English, had remained in their power for more than twenty-four hours: although French *Ordonnances* did not in general apply to foreigners, an exception must be made for allied subjects. The two Spanish vessels were accordingly adjudged to the French recaptors.

Recousse recouse of French or allied ships (vol. II, pp. 114-119). An English ship was captured by a French privateer that held her for three days; the two ships together were subsequently seized by an English vessel which was recaptured by a second French privateer after sixteen hours. These events caused a dispute between the two French privateers. The first privateer argued that the prize belonged to him and that the second privateer could only claim one-third of its value for the recapture. The second privateer, on the other hand, alleged that the first English prize belonged entirely to him and that the first privateer had no right to any salvage. The case was examined in detail by Valin in his *Commentaire* on the basis of Art. 8 of the *Ordonnance de la marine* of 1681 to the effect that the issue was decided in favour of the second privateer, by the *Conseil des prises* in 1695 and in appeal by the *Conseil d'Etat* by three consecutive judgments of 1705, 1706 and 1710. The question was, however, reopened later in 1744 and then decided in favour of the first privateer. This gave rise to a new decision of the *Conseil des prises* of 1748 in favour of the second captor. In order to prevent a repetition of the original dispute, the *Conseil du Roi* issued a new *Arrêt* in the form of a binding regulation, dated 5 November 1748, which laid down that

> "Veut et entend Sa Majesté que les prises des navires ennemis faites par ses vaisseaux ou ceux de ses sujets, armés en course, recouses par les ennemis, et ensuite reprises sur eux, appartiennent en entier au dernier capteur".

See Valin's *Traité*, p. 90, and De Pistoye and Duverdy's *Traité*, II, 116.

2. Recapture of neutral vessels. The principle that neutral vessels, captured by the enemy and recaptured by French privateers or by warships of the State, must be released to their owners if they have behaved as neutrals, was laid down in a judgment of the *Conseil des prises* of 6 thermidor *an* VIII under the heading *Le corsaire Le Hasard contre le navire La Statira* (*an* VIII) (II, 121). The Commissary of the Government appointed to the *Conseil des prises*, in his conclusions on the recapture of the American vessel the *Statira* by the French privateer the *Hasard*, stated that all French laws on the subject

> "ne statuent que sur la recousse d'un navire français par un autre navire français; elles sont absolument étrangères à l'hypothèse d'un navire étranger se prétendant neutre, recous par un navire français. A défaut de lois précises, il faut donc recourir aux maximes générales. D'après ces maximes, un navire neutre doit être respecté par tous les peuples. S'il est opprimé par une des nations belligérantes, ce n'est pas une raison pour que les autres se rendent complices de cette oppression, ou soient autorisées à la détourner à leur profit. De là, un navire étranger se prétendant neutre, et recous par un Français sur l'ennemi, doit être relâché si la neutralité est constatée.
>
> Mais, dira-t-on, pourquoi traiter avec plus de ménagement un navire étranger se prétendant neutre, qu'un navire français?
>
> La raison en est sensible. Dans la supposition sur laquelle les lois ont raisonné et sur laquelle nous raisonnons nous-mêmes, le navire français tombé dans les mains de l'ennemi, aurait été perdu pour toujours s'il n'avait été recous; conséquemment, la reprise de ce navire est une véritable conquête sur l'ennemi même. S'il s'agit, au contraire, d'un navire étranger se prétendant neutre, l'arrestation de ce navire par l'ennemi ne le rend pas subitement propriété ennemie, puisque la confiscation peut n'en être pas prononcée par le magistrat. Jusqu'au jugement qui confisque le navire, qui voyage comme neutre, ne perd ni son caractère ni ses droits. Après l'arrestation, il peut recouvrer sa liberté. Dans un pareil état de choses, la recousse de ce navire ne saurait donc faire passer la propriété dans les mains du Français par lequel cette recousse a été opérée. La question de neutralité demeure toujours entière; elle doit être jugée avant tout.
>
> Tel est la langage de tous les publicistes; telle est la coutume générale de toutes les nations policées."

The American ship was accordingly restored to her master without any cost or damages, despite the fact that her cargo was to be condemned as constituting contraband (*dictum* at p. 127). On this latter aspect of the case, which was discussed at great length by the French Commissary Portalis, see *sub* A, section 2, *supra* pp. 324-326.

In a further case, concerning the recapture of a neutral (Danish) vessel from an English captor by a French privateer in December 1806, both the *Conseil des prises* and the *Conseil d'Etat* established a certain connection between the question of whether the Danish owners were right in refusing to pay to the recaptors an amount as salvage and the question of whether the prize court of the country of the original captor would have been right in condemning the prize. In that case concerning *Le Grand-Napoléon contre le Zufriedenheidt* [1808] (II, 130, 131) the *Conseil* held that the principles it had thus far applied

> "veulent que le navire repris soit jugé comme il aurait dû l'être, si le premier capteur eût pu le traduire devant les autorités de son gouvernement";

that in that case the British prize court should have invalidated the capture, and that, consequently, the Danish owners were justified in refusing to pay any salvage to the recaptors. The Emperor Napoléon confirmed this judgment in the *Conseil d'Etat*:

> "si ce navire avait été conduit en Angleterre, l'Amirauté n'aurait pu sans violer les principes reconnus en matière de prises, prononcer la condemnation du bâtiment ou de sa cargaison".

This basic view on the fate of neutral vessels recaptured by French forces was confirmed three weeks later by the *Conseil des prises* in the case of *Le Kity contre le corsaire le Brave* [*an* VIII] (II, 128), but complemented to the effect that the recaptor could never be condemned in damages and interests toward the owners of the recaptured vessel, since there was always a valid reason for arresting a vessel that had fallen into the hands of the enemy.

A short time later this case law was further supplemented by an express decision in *L'Esther contre le corsaire le Zénodore* [*an* IX] (II, 130) that a neutral (*in casu* Ligurian) vessel recaptured from the enemy should be restored to her owner without any salvage (*droit de recousse*) even after having been in the hands of the enemy for more than twenty-four hours.

Judgments to the same general effect were those of the *Conseil des prises* in the cases of the Danish vessel *Anna-Maria contre le Tigre* [*an* IX] (II, 136) and the Swedish vessel *Charles* [*an* IX] (II, 138). On the argument of the French recaptors that English laws granted a right of salvage to those who recapture a neutral vessel the *Conseil des prises* riposted:

> "Il est indifférent de savoir si les lois anglaises accordent un droit de sauvetage sur la recousse des bâtiments neutres: les lois françaises n'accordent point ce droit".

In the case of the French privateer *Le Coureur contre le Salomon et Betty*, a Hamburg ship that had remained for forty days in the hands of the English, the *Conseil d'Etat* held that she could not have been lawfully condemned by an English prize court [1807] (II, 133).

The case of the Bremen vessel *Les Deux-Sœurs contre le San-Josepho* [1808] (II, 133) was of a somewhat different type in that that vessel, which had sailed from Lisbon in November 1807 bound for Hamburg with an almost entirely neutral cargo of colonial produce and had been captured by a British privateer, the *Union* from Guernsey, before being recaptured by the French privateer *San-Josepho*, would have been condemned by an English Prize Court on the double ground that she was on her way to a German port officially blockaded by the British government, and that the Allies of France were considered in England as enemies.

The issue arose again in 1816 in the case of *L'Asie contre le Diligent* (II, 131-132). The *Asie* was a French vessel that, while sailing from Bordeaux in December 1815 with destination in England, provided with a French and a British licence and laden with Swedish goods, was captured by the British warship *Clarence* and recaptured six days later by the French privateer the *Diligent*. This was not a case of a neutral vessel proper but of a national French vessel put in a postion similar to a neutral ship. When entering the French port of Le Palais with her recaptor and with a pilot on board, the ship was wrecked. Two questions arose: was the recapture valid, and who had to defray the damage incurred? The *Conseil d'Etat* upheld its case law that "la validité de la recousse est subordonnée à la validité de la prise", found that the *Asie* could not have been lawfully condemned by the British prize court should she have been brought before it, and that she should, therefore, be restored to her owners, but only in her wrecked state since there was no proof of any fault on the side of the *Diligent*.

American case law

When during the War of American Independence the questions of the effect of a recapture and the grant of prize salvage arose before the first prize courts of the United States, they were initially confronted by cases involving the recapture of American or, more rarely, French ships which had previously been taken by the British. The latter came under a special protective clause inserted in the Franco-American Treaty of Amity and Commerce of 6 February 1778 (Martens, R^2, II, 587; Parry, 46, 417), Arts. 6 and 7:

> "Le Roi Très Chrétien ... fera tous ses efforts pour recouvrer et faire restituer aux propriétaires légitimes, leurs agens ou mandataires, tous les vaisseaux et effets, qui leur seront pris dans l'étendue de sa jurisdiction" [and inversely].

Two French vessels, the *Le Vern* and the *Maria Theresa*, retaken by American privateers from the British, which were awarded by the lower courts to the recaptors, were restored in 1783 in appeal to the French claimants, subject to their liability to pay to the recaptors the same proportion of salvage as if they had been American ships recaptured (Bourguignon, *The first Federal Court* (1977), pp. 276/277, with footnote 91).

As to the recapture of American ships the legal situation was uncertain in the absence of any treaty or generally accepted rule of customary law. Writers had developed a theory to the effect that the original owner of the recaptured prize could only claim its restoration to him if it had not yet passed into the firm possession of the enemy. What exactly constituted the decisive passing of the property from the owner to the captor was uncertain. It could be the arrival of the prize in some place of security (enemy port or territory, the enemy fleet), its condemnation by an enemy prize court, or even its detention by the enemy during a certain short lapse of time. When, as happened in England during the Seven Years' War, restoration was decreed on a far wider scale or as a general rule, the amount of the salvage due by the owner of the prize to the recaptor increased with the length of time the prize had been in possession of the enemy (1/8, 1/3 or 1/2 of its value). This latter system was adopted by the American Congress, with one exception, *viz.*, that the owner would receive nothing and the recaptor the whole prize if the original capture had been followed by its condemnation by an enemy admiralty court.

This system was revised on 27 March 1781 when Congress adopted the twenty-four hours' rule: if the prize had remained in the possession of the original captors for less than twenty-four hours, it would be restored to its owners subject to payment of one third of its value to the recaptor; if possession by the enemy had lasted for more then twenty-four hours, the recaptors were to receive the full value of the prize. See for details Bourguignon's study, pp. 265-267, and the cases surveyed by him at pp. 267-268 with footnotes 68, 69 and 70 concerning the *Charming Elizabeth*, the *Florence*, the *Bermudas*, the *Charming Sally*, the *Nancy*, the *Pitt*, the *John* and *Hepsabeth*, the *Adventurer* and the *Polly*.

The rules on recapture were laid down in the United States in sections 2 and 3 of the Act of 28 June 1798 "more effectively to protect the Commerce and Coasts of the United States" (Deák-Jessup, II, 1145) and section 6 of the Act of 9 July 1798 (*ibid.*, II, 1146) to the following effect:

> 2. "That whenever any vessel the property of, or employed by any citizen of the United States, or person resident therein, or any goods or effects belonging to any such citizen of resident shall be re-captured by any public armed vessel of the United States, the same shall be restored to the former owner or owners, upon due proof, he or they paying and allowing, as and for salvage to the re-captors, one eighthh part of the value of such vessel, goods and effects, free of all deductions and expenses."
>
> 3. "That whenever any armed vessel, captured and condemned, as aforesaid, shall have been of superior or equal force to the public armed vessel of the United States by which such capture shall have been made, the forfeiture shall be and accrue wholly to the captors: and in other cases, one half thereof shall be to the use of the United States, and the residue to the captors. And all salvage which shall be allowed and recovered upon any vessel, goods or effects re-captured, and to be restored, as aforesaid, shall belong wholly to the officers and crew of the public armed vessel of the United States by which such re-capture shall be made: and the court before whom any condemnation shall be had, as aforesaid, shall and may order the sale of the vessel, goods and effects condemned, to be made at public auction, upon due notice by the marshal of the district in which the same shall be; and all expenses of condemnation and sale, being deducted from the proceeds, the part thereof which shall accrue to the United States, shall be paid into the public treasury, and the residue, and all allowances of salvage, as aforesaid, shall be distributed to, and among the officers and crews therein, in the proportions which the President of the United States shall direct."
>
> 6. "That all vessels, goods and effects, the property of any citizen of the United States, or person resident therein, which shall be recaptured, as aforesaid, shall be restored to the lawful owners, upon payment by them, respectively of a just and reasonable salvage, to be

> determined by the mutual agreement of the parties concerned, or by the decree of any court of the United States having maritime jurisdiction according to the nature of each case: *Provided,* that such allowance shall not be less than one eighth, or exceeding one half of the full value of such recapture, without any deduction. And such salvage shall be distributed to and among the owners, officers and crews of the private armed vessel or vessels entitled thereto, according to any agreement which shall be between them; or in case of no agreement, then by the decree of the court who shall determine upon such salvage."

The Far East

The issue re-emerged again at the end of the pre-codification period when Russia inserted a few provisions on the subject in her Prize Regulations of 14 July 1895 (Hurst & Bray, I, Appendix A, at p. 318), regarding in particular the recapture of prizes by merchant vessels. The admissibility of such recaptures was evidently considered as so normal that those Regulations included three articles (43, 45 and 46), fixing in advance the amount of salvage (called prize-money) that the recaptor could claim, *viz.*, the full value of an enemy prize, respectively the amount from one-eighth to one-fourth of the value of a Russian or foreign prize dependent upon the degree of exceptional difficulty and dangerousness of the recapture.

For the rest, Russia stuck to the differentiating rules laid down in Art. 43 of her Regulations:

> "In regard to Russian and foreign vessels and cargoes [Art. 5 added *sub* 2: and vessels or cargoes of an allied nation] recaptured from the enemy ... the following special Regulations have in addition to be observed:
>
> (1) Property recovered from the enemy, although it may have been condemned already by the enemy as prize, is to be restored, upon a decision of the Prize Court, to the original owner, subject to the obligation of paying the prize-money for the recapture and the expenses incurred in connection with the recapture;
>
> (2) Russian Government ships and cargoes recovered from the enemy are to be restored to the Government without the intervention of a court, upon the order of the competent naval authority; and
>
> (3) Property of a foreigner which is recaptured from the enemy is to be restored to the foreigner, and no claim for prize-money or for the expenses of recapture is to be made against him, if it be proved that the property could not lawfully be considered a prize by the enemy, but ought to have been released; in such a case no prize-money is to be paid for the recapture."

The effect of the recapture of a vessel during Japan's war with Russia was governed by Art. 73 of her Regulations of 7 March 1904 relating to Capture at Sea. Unlike some other national prize laws or practices the Article made no difference as regards the national character of the vessel recaptured, nor did it distinguish between the recapture of merchant vessels and of warships. Art. 73 was indeed worded as follows (Hurst & Bray, II, Appendix B, at p. 435; Takahashi, II, 786):

> "In cases where the commander of a warship retakes a Japanese ship, or a neutral ship which has been captured by the enemy, if the ship in question has not yet been taken into a port of the enemy, or made use of by the hostile State for military purposes, he may release her."

Belgian case law

Although the judgments of the Belgian *Conseil des Prises* after World War I do not belong systematically here in this publication, I will nevertheless mention them here, because of their detailed review of the case law of previous centuries.

As I set out in my preceding exposé, several systems have in past centuries been in force with regard to the legal effect of a recapture. The two best-known systems were that of the twenty-four hours' rule and that of the conduct of a prize into safety *intra praesidia*. The effect further also depended on whether the prize had already, or whether it had not yet, been condemned by the enemy prize court.

The twenty-four hours' rule meant that the original owner could no longer claim restitution of the recaptured prize if it had been in the hands of the captor during that twenty-four hours' term.

The rule concerning conduct *intra praesidia* meant that the original owner was not deprived of his property until the captor had succeeded in bringing the prize into a safe place.

A decree of condemnation by the captor's prize court was held to preclude the restitution of the recaptured prize to its former owner.

Ample information concerning the uncertain state of customary law in earlier periods and the diverging views of writers was after World War I provided by the Belgian *Conseil des prises* in the *Midsland, Zaanstroom* and *Agiena* cases.

In the *Midsland* the *Conseil*, referring to Dalloz's *Répertoire*, *voce* "prises maritimes", no. 198, and De Pistoye-Duverdy, II, p. 120, described the legal situation as follows (*Annuaire Grotius* 1921-22, 183):

> "Suivant la doctrine de certains auteurs et l'ancienne jurisprudence française, en cas de recousse d'un navire neutre, si la prise originaire eût été déclarée valable selon les lois du pays ennemi, le neutre n'ayant plus rien à réclamer, puisque par l'effet de la prise il avait perdu le droit qu'il avait dans le navire, on adjugeait dans ce cas le navire au repreneur; qu'il n'était fait exception à cette règle que si le navire neutre destiné pour un port français avait été arrêté par l'ennemi uniquement à raison des effets de contrebande ou autres qu'il apportait."

The *Conseil* added, however, that

> "—Attendu que la France elle-même abandonna dans la suite toute idée de concession obligatoire et donna, en 1870, des instructions absolues et qui ne comportaient qu'une bien faible restriction au droit de recousse; "la recousse d'un bâtiment national", y est-il dit, "ne donnera lieu à aucun droit sur le bâtiment recous. Si le bâtiment repris est un neutre, il sera considéré comme ennemi, s'il est resté plus de vingt-quatre heures en la possession de l'ennemi. Si le bâtiment n'est pas resté vingt-quatre heures au pouvoir de l'ennemi, il sera relâché purement et simplement";—Que s'il est vrai que ces instructions ajoutaient à l'énoncé de la règle du droit de reprise les mots: "à moins de circonstances exceptionnelles dont Sa Majesté se réserve l'application", il ne s'agit là que de la part laissée à l'initiative gouvernementale, pouvant toujours s'exercer, relativement à l'opportunité de la prise et sous forme de restitution généreusement consentie, et nullement d'une latitude donnée aux tribunaux appelés à statuer sur la validité des prises et qui ont seulement à se demander si la prise est légale d'après les principes du droit international".

In the *Agiena* the *Conseil* returned to the extreme variety of earlier opinions relating to the effect of a recapture in an exposé worth being reproduced *in extenso* (*Annuaire Grotius* 1924, p. 259):

"Attendu que los mots "reprise" ou "recousse" sont synonymes; que dans l'ancienne guerre de course, aujourd'hui abolie, on appelait "aller à la recousse d'un navire" courir après le vaisseau qui s'en était emparé, dans l'intention de l'enlever lui-même avec sa prise ou du moins de l'obliger d'abandonner cette prise pour la lui arracher;

Attendu qu'une pareille opération impliquait naturellement et d'après les principes admis autrefois, que le navire fût repris dans un temps relativement rapproché du moment de sa capture et *notamment dans le délai de vingt-quatre heures, fixé par les usages d'alors*, de telle manière que le navire put être considéré comme se trouvant fermement en la possession du capteur après un tel délai et comme ayant changé de propriétaire; que plus tard on exigea, pour que le propriétaire fût réputé dépouillé de son droit, *que le navire eût été conduit en sûreté par le capteur dans un port intra praesidia* et comme le disaient des décisions de prise anglaises "brought into a place so secure that the owner can have no immediate prospect of recovering it"; que, dans l'affaire du *Santa-Cruz* [1798] (1 C. Rob. 49; Roscoe I, 39), jusqu'en 1798 et relative à des navires portugais, alliés, pris par les Français et repris par les Anglais, le savant jurisconsulte Sir W. Scott n'hésita pas, au point de vue des principes théoriques, à considérer la "deductio intra praesidia" comme la vraie règle qui, à son avis, devait faire décider du dépouillement du propriétaire, encore que d'autres nations, ajoutait-il fussent loin d'être d'accord à ce sujet et se contentassent de suivre la règle des 24 heures *ou telle autre plus rigoureuse*; mais que, quoi qu'il en soit des évolutions subies par le "droit de reprise" dans les différents pays et depuis des temps reculés jusqu'à nos jours, il n'a jamais été mis en doute, au point de vue des principes du droit international, que *tout au moins une sentence de confiscation d'un tribunal des prises* doive avoir pour effet de dépouiller le propriétaire de son droit et mettre obstacle, en cas de recapture sur l'ennemi, à l'obligation de restitution;—Attendu que telle est la règle formelle édictée par les Etats-Unis de l'Amérique dans l'Acte du Congrès de 1800, maintenue en vigueur depuis lors et qui s'applique aussi bien aux navires nationaux ou alliés repris sur l'ennemi, qu'aux navires neutres;—Attendu qu'en ce qui concerne l'Angleterre, l'article 40 du Naval Prize Act de 1864 se borne à stipuler le droit à la restitution au profit des sujets britanniques et que si cette disposition, qui reproduit d'ailleurs des dispositions similaires d'Actes de Parlement antérieurs et remontant à 1649, a pu être interprétée et appliquée dans ce sens que le droit à restitution était acquis, que la reprise eût été effectuée avant ou après une condamnation du navire, c'est à raison de ce que l'Angleterre a entendu favoriser ses sujets nationaux, eu égard au développement sans cesse croissant de la propriété commerciale, mais qu'il ne aurait résulter de cette loi spéciale ainsi édictée par l'Angleterre pour elle-même et de caractère restrictif, que des sujets de puissances alliées ou neutres soient admis à en bénéficier en toute l'étendue où elle a été interprétée et appliquée;—Qu'il est vrai, comme le disait Sir W. Scott dans l'affaire du *Santa-Cruz*, "que la loi maritime de l'Angleterre, ayant adopté une règle plus large de restitution ou de sauvetage par rapport aux propriétés reprises de ses sujets, donne le bénéfice de cette règle à ses alliés jusqu'à ce qu'ils paraissent agir envers la propriété anglaise d'après un principe moins libéral et en pareil cas elle adopte leur règle et les traite selon la mesure de leur justice"; Mais que tout cela n'est vrai que pour autant qu'il n'y ait pas eu condamnation du navire allié par une Cour des prises ennemie, les actes du Parlement ayant remis en vigueur, quant aux sujets anglais seulement, le *jus postliminii* du propriétaire originaire;—Qu'en ce qui concerne les neutres, les cours anglaises ont généralement ordonné la restitution en cas de "reprise" proprement dite, même sans l'indemnité, à moins que le navire n'eût été en danger de condamnation par l'ennemi, auquel cas indemnité était due, mais qu'elles ont toujours considéré que le navire repris n'avait la qualité de neutre qu'en l'absence d'une condamnation par le tribunal des prises de l'ennemi, laquelle opérait juridiquement le dépouillement du propriétaire et le changement de nationalité du navire—[reference to Sir William Scott's decree in the case of the *Charlotte Caroline* [1812] (1 Dodson, 192; Roscoe II, 149)];

Attendu que la législation d'autres pays, tels que la Hollande, le Danemark, l'Espagne, la Suède et le Portugal, a également subi des évolutions mais toujours dans la limite indiquée ci-dessus, c'est-à-dire que le propriétaire était nécessairement dépouillé en vertu d'une sentence de condamnation; Que notamment, alors que l'ordonnance du 28 mars 1810 rendait la propriété danoise ou alliée du Danemark sans avoir égard au temps qu'elle avait pu rester en possession du capteur et moyennant le 1/3 de la valeur comme droit de recousse, la loi du 3 février 1864 est venue disposer au contraire que sont considérés comme bonnes prises les navires danois repris sur l'ennemi;—Attendu que le Code italien de droit maritime promulgué en 1865 établit plusieurs distinctions, suivant qu'il s'agit d'un navire marchand national ou allié repris par un corsaire, ou d'un tel navire repris par un vaisseau de guerre; que ce dernier doit être restitué à son propriétaire sans rémunération, même s'il avait déjà été amené dans un port ennemi; qu'il en est de même d'un navire étranger frété pour compte de l'Etat, mais qu'il n'est pas fait mention d'un navire étranger non frété pour compte de l'Etat, de tout quoi il faut conclure qu'un navire neutre de même qu'un navire national ou allié dont la propriété a passé au belligérant en vertu d'un jugement, ne doit pas être restitué en cas de recapture;—Attendu qu'en France, l'arrêté de prairial an XI s'applique aux navires français ou alliés, à l'exclusion des navires neutres; qu'en ce qui concerne les premiers, rien ne prouve qu'il ait eu pour effet de déroger à ce principe universellement admis, qui veut qu'une sentence de confiscation prononcée par le tribunal des prises compétent, opère mutation du caractère du navire, que le rappel de la règle des 24 heures prouve d'ailleurs que l'on n'a pu envisager una recapture effectuée après un assez long laps de temps, tel que le supposaient généralement les formalités et la procédure de prise d'après les règlements en vigueur; que les navires neutres recous devaient être restitués selon les principes mêmes du droit international, mais que par contre la raison qui obligeait à leur restitution venait à disparaître en cas de recapture, après condamnation par le Tribunal des prises de l'ennemi;—Que dans l'affaire du corsaire *le Hasard contra la Statira* [1800] (Pistoye et Duverdy II, 121) M. Portalis, commissaire du Gouvernement, s'exprimait comme suit, sous l'empire de l'arrêté du prairial: "S'il s'agit au contraire d'un navire étranger se prétendant neutre, l'arrestation de ce navire par l'ennemi ne le rend pas subitement propriété ennemie, puisque la confiscation peut n'en être pas prononcée par le magistrat. Jusqu'au jugement qui confisque, le navire qui voyage comme neutre, ne perd ni son caractère ni ses droits. Après l'arrestation il peut recouvrer sa liberté. Dans un pareil état des choses la recousse de ce navire ne saurait donc faire passer la propriété dans les mains du Français par lequel cette recousse a été opérée. La question de la neutralité demeure toujours entière; elle doit être jugée avant tout. Tel est le langage de tous les publicistes, telle est la coutume de toutes les nations policées. Cela posé, le navire *Statira* n'est pas devenu confiscable par cela seul qu'il a été recous sur l'ennemi"; Attendu que c'est évidemment sous le bénéfice de ces observations si judicieuses et si juridiques qu'a été rendue au cours de la récente guerre de 1914-1918 l'instruction ministérielle de la marine du 30 janvier 1916, en tant qu'elle visait la "recousse".

Salvage claims

A vast case law especially on salvage claims has developed both in England and in France. In both countries this subject was regulated by law, but the contents of those laws diverged.

The situation in England can be exemplified by the famous and complicated old case of the *Ceylon* [1810], decided by Lord Stowell on 26 November 1811 (1 Dodson, 105, 116; Roscoe, II, 133). The *Ceylon* was an English East India ship which was captured by French frigates, sailed to the island of

Johanna in the Indian Ocean, was refitted there and taken to a port in the Isle de France, where she succeeded in repelling an attack by a British squadron and in destroying it with the assistance of other French ships. Having been thereupon dismantled and fitted out as a prison-ship for the purpose of receiving English prisoners of war, she was found in this state at the time of the capture of the island by British army and naval forces.

The solution of the legal questions which arose over the claim of the recaptors to the salvage reward depended on the construction and application of the *Prize Act*, in force at the time, (*a*) Was the *Ceylon* in her new guise as a prison-ship sufficiently "set forth for war" to come within its terms? (*b*) Was the recapture, effected by the conjoint operation of the British army and navy, a recapture under the *Prize Act*, seeing that that *Act* spoke of recapture by boats and ships only? On the basis of a digressive historical review of the development of customary law in the field, including the somewhat unclear terms of Chapter 287 of the Consulat de Mar, Lord Stowell came to the conclusion that the claimed award could be granted:

> "It cannot be forgotten that by the ancient law of Europe the *perductio intra praesidia, intra locum tutum* was a sufficient conversion of the property; that by a later law, a possession of twenty-four hours was sufficient to divest the former owner. This is laid down in the 287th article of the Consulat de Mar, in terms, indeed, not very intelligible in themselves, but which are satisfactorily explained by Grotius (1. III, cap. 6, sec. 3) and his commentator Barbeyrac (I, 5)."

The Court continued by stating that the latter already mentioned the substitution of the twenty-four hours' rule for the *intra praesidia* rule; by quoting the opinions of van Bynkershoek (*Quaestiones juris publici*, I, Ch. V) and Loccenius (*De jure maritimo*, 1. II, ch. 4, sec. 4); by invoking the concurrent views held by a Scottish Court on 15 February 1677 and by the legislator in France—*Ordonnance de la Marine* of 1681, *livre* III, *titre* 9, Art. 8—, and by citing another old England statement by Crompton (*Court de Admiraltie d'Engleterre*, p. 91) to the effect that the ancient law of England was that a possession of 24 hours was a sufficient conversion of the property, and that the owner was divested of his property unless it was reclaimed *ante occasum solis*.

Lord Stowell continued by arguing that according to the ancient law of England, which was in agreement with the ancient law of Europe, there was a total obliteration of the rights of former owners if certain conditions were fulfilled. It was true that England had retracted from the old rules when its commerce increased. During the time of the Usurpation by Oliver Cromwell an alteration was effected by the Ordinance of 1649, which directed a restitution upon salvage to *British* subjects; and the same indulgent rule of law was continued afterwards, when this country became still more commercialized. But the common law still prevailed and controlled the provisions of the Stature, where the enemy had fitted out the prize as a ship of war. In the most recent change of the law it was determined that a vessel belonging to a

British subject lost her national character on capture by the enemy and subsequent conversion into a ship of war.

Lord Stowell's final conclusion on the legal question in the *Ceylon* case was that the fact that the Act of Parliament only mentioned recapture by ships and boats, and not such as were effected by the assistance of land forces was irrelevant, but that, even if the case did not fall within the Act, the Court must still consider it to come under the old rule of the law of nations by which the rights of the owner would be completely divested.

This *Ceylon* case had been preceded by others, such as the *Vår Önskan* (Biedumpel, Master) [1799] (2 C.Rob., 299; Roscoe, I, 239), a Swedish vessel captured by the French on her way to Oporto, recaptured by a British cruiser. Here the issue was whether salvage could also be claimed from a neutral owner. Salvage was *in casu* awarded, contrary to a rule prevailing in former periods, owing to "the rapacious proceedings of French cruisers and French Courts of prize".

Apart from the legal effect of such *recousses recouses* as regards the ultimate adjudication of the property of the vessels concerned, such a series of consecutive captures gave rise to the same question as discussed above with regard to ordinary recaptures, as to how the recaptors were to be recompensed for their action. This reward habitually depended on the period of time during which the prize had remained in possession of the earlier captor.

In the case of the *Actaeon* [1810] (Edw. 254; Roscoe, II, 205, footnote *a*) an American ship not proceeding to a French port, captured by the French, but recaptured by the English, the British Prize Court had to decide whether the usual salvage was due. This ship and some others had no certificates of origin on board as required by the French decrees:

> "On the whole of the circumstances of this case, without looking minutely into the varying policy of France, I think that there is very rational ground to apprehend that the French Prize Court would have considered these ships as legal captures and therefore I shall pronounce for the usual salvage".

CHAPTER III C

PRIZE JURISDICTION

Under this heading I will, after an introductory section on the origin of the function of Admiral and of Admiralty jurisdiction set out the different aspects of the adjudication of prize cases in the following order:
—the organization of prize jurisdiction (section 1);
—the competence of prize courts (section 2);
—the law to be applied by prize courts, national and international (section 3);
—the procedure of prize courts (section 4);
—the possible *dicta* and the effects of a condemnatory judgment (section 5);
—the issues of the indebtedness of (a) reparation ("probable cause"), (b) freight, (c) general average (section 6);
—the allocation of the proceeds of prizes and the award of prize money (section 7); and
—appeal and revision, arbitration (section 8).

Only a few of these subjects have been regulated by the codification of 1907-1909, so that for the greater part they have remained under the regime of either municipal law, or customary or conventional international law.

INTRODUCTORY SECTION. THE ORIGIN OF THE FUNCTION OF THE ADMIRAL AND OF ADMIRALTY JURISDICTION

Admiralty jurisdiction is of very old standing. The Black Book of the Admiralty already provides ample information on the Admiralty of England.

A definition of the status, powers and attributions of the Admiral formed indeed a substantial portion of all the most important old codes of maritime law. See, for example, Arts. 4-18 of Part A of the Black Book (Travers Twiss, vol. I, pp. 1 *et seq.*), Part B thereof on "What the Admiral is to do in time of war at sea or land" (*ibid.*, pp. 24 *et seq.*) and certain Rules and Orders, laid down in Part C (*ibid.*, pp. 40 *et seq.*), which testify, *inter alia*, to limited legislative powers of the Admirals of the North and West on the manner of proceeding to banish "transpassers" (Art. 17), being an Act made at Ipswich under Henry I (1100-1135) and powers of enquiry into the unlawful exaction of customs (Art. 26); the Ordonnance of Philippe de Valois of 23 March 1338 (*ibid.*, pp. 420 *et seq.*) and that of Charles V of France of 7 December 1373 "on the jurisdiction of the Admiralty" (*ibid.*, pp. 430 *et seq.*). These early Ordonnances were followed at a later stage by the French Edict of March 1584 (Pardessus IV, pp. 295 *et seq.*, and Arts. 1-19 of the *Ordonnance de la Marine* of August 1681, livre I, titre 1, Arts. 1 *et seq.* (ibid., 325 *et seq.*).

The oldest mention of an Admiral in English printed law refers back to 1315 in the 8th year of the reign of King Edward II (1307-1327) (Travers Twiss, vol. I, p. xlvi). The first person to whom the designation of High Admiral could fitly apply was Sir John Beauchamp, appointed to be Admiral of all the Fleets on 18 July 1360. Before the time of Sir Thomas Beaufort, who was High Admiral in the first quarter of the 15th century (from 9 Henry IV (1408) to 4 Henry VI (1426)), the office of Admiral was as a rule a temporary office, in most cases for one year, and the command over the Northern and the Western fleets was usually entrusted to different persons. Only exceptionally was the office conferred for life and upon the same person for both fleets. Sir Thomas Beaufort, the youngest natural son of John of Gaunt, who was Admiral of the Northern Fleet since 1403, was by Letters Patent of 21 September 1408 appointed Admiral of both the Northern and the Western Fleets for his life-time (in fact until 1425), an appointment that was confirmed and extended towards Ireland, Aquitaine and Picardy by subsequent Letters Patent of 1409, 1411 and 1413. His successors were John of Lancaster, Duke of Bedford, the third son of King Henry IV, who combined the functions of Lord High Admiral, Lord High Constable and Regent of France (1425-1436), and John Holland, Earl of Huntingdon and since 1443 Duke of Exeter (1436-1446).

Particulars about the origin and development of Admiralty jurisdiction in England have been given by Sir Leoline Jenkins (1623-1685) in his address to the House of Lords in defence in that House of the Bill to ascertain the jurisdiction of the Admiralty, inserted in a publication by William Wynne of the Middle Temple under the title *The life of Sir Leoline Jenkins, Judge of the High Court of Admiralty, and Prerogative Court of Canterbury &c., Ambassador and Plenipotentiary for the General Peace of Cologn and Nimweguen, and Secretary of State to King Charles II, &c.* (2 vols., London, 1724), pp. lxxvi *et seq.*. In that speech Sir Leoline argued that there was already an Admiral in function under Edward III (1327-1377), as was proven by a roll in the Tower, documenting a Patent of Robert de Herle: the Admiral had jurisdiction in maritime causes and over seafaring men. The laws whereby he was to conduct himself were the Laws of Oléron, the Constitutions of the Admiralty, and Imperial Civil Law.

Another roll, 12 Edw. III [1339] (and consequently dating from the same period), provided for the carrying-on of the proceedings and the re-establishment of the judicature that his grandfather Edward I (1272-1307) and his Council had ordained for (1) the preservation of his sovereignty and admiralty in the sea, and (2) the interpreting, declaring and enforcing those laws which his predecessors had made for seafaring men. According to Sir Leoline, Richard I (the Lion-hearted), on his return from the Holy Land and his captivity in Austria (1194), reviewed and reformed the Laws of Oléron and gave them the stamp of the Royal authority. A third record, having the endorsement of 22 Edw. I (1294) and 13 Ric. II (1389), confirmed that already in those days there were maritime laws, statutes and ordinances which conferred *haute justice* upon the Admiral. This continued via an Act of 2 Henry V (1413-1422) till 28 Henry VIII (1509-1547). Although these maritime rules contained certain elements which could take place on land (allusion was made to the sealing of charter-parties for a maritime transport), they were, in virtue of their special nature, reputed by all nations not to belong to the domain of the ordinary municipal law of the land, but to be particularly adapted to adjudication by special Admiralty courts. Sir Leoline stressed that the Bill had in substance the same content as an Act in Council of 1632, subscribed by the twelve judges and the Attorney General, in the presence of the King, and enrolled in the several Courts of Westminster as the Resolution of all the Judges, and as a Standing Rule to be observed for the future. Comp. also Sir Leoline Jenkins' address to the Session of Admiralty within the Cinque Ports of 2 September 1668 at pp. lxxxv *et seq.* of Wynne's publication.

The Black Book of the Admiralty begins with the following words:

> "Puisque [in the sense of "after"] homme est fait Admiral, premièrement lui fault ordonner & substituer desoubz lui, pour etre ses Lieutenants, Députés, & autres Officiers, les plus Loyaulx, Sages, & discrets en la loy marine & anciens coutumes de la mer, qu'il pourra aucun part trouver par ainsi, que par laid de Dieu, & leur bonne & droiture Gouvernail, l'office pourra estre gouverné à l'honneur & proufit du Royalme."

Among the various subjects of maritime law, considered as matters to be regulated by the ancient usage and customs of the sea, were also the questions of prize. They were equally subjected to the jurisdiction of the Lord High Admiral's Lieutenant, Deputy General, or Judge of the High Court of Admiralty, either by virtue of his office, or by special commissions, limited to each particular war, as Chr. Robinson demonstrated at pp. vii and viii of his advertisement preceding his *Collectanea Maritima* of 1801, by quoting historical documents dating back to 1357 (Rymer, *Foedera*, IV, 14) and 1426 (Proclamation of King Henry VI). That of 1357 relates to an early instance of the Admiral's judicial authority to decide the question of "prize or no prize".

A very thorough new investigation into the origin of the office and title of Admiral in England was made in 1894 on behalf of the Selden Society by

Reginald G. Marsden and published in volume 6 of its publications under the title *Select pleas in the Court of Admiralty*. Starting from Stubbs's remark at p. 289 at vol. II of his *Constitutional History* that "the history of the jurisdiction of the Admiral and his court [was] as yet obscure", and from Prynne's assertion (*Animadversions*, p. 106) that there were already Admirals and Admiralty courts with power to try cases, civil and criminal, as early as the time of Henry I (1100-1135), derived from the ancient Saxon kings Alfred, Edgar, Ethelred, and others who had "the dominion of the British ocean", the author made the most scrupulous inquiries into the substantiality of all such claims. His conclusion was to the effect that the title of Admiral did not come into use before the beginning of the 14th century and that the earliest mention of such an officer occurred in connection with the possessions of the English kings in France (Bayonne, 1295) and in a Convention of Bruges of 1297 (claims against France on account of acts of piracy committed against ships of England and Flanders). The presumably oldest evidence of the use of the term in England that Marsden was able to find was a document of 1300 in which Gervase Alard was appointed "Admiral of the Fleet of the Cinque Ports". He assumed that the term had originated in the East—the word "Admiral" is in fact of Arabic origin—, was later adopted by the Genoese and other Mediterranean fleets, and reached England via Gascony in the beginning of the 14th century.

The original term "Admiral" in Arabic had the meaning of "commander" in general (the present word "emir"); the admiral of the sea was called "amîr al-bahr".

According to Marsden's investigations it was not until half a century after the emergence of the term "Admiral" that mention was made of the existence of an Admiral's Court with jurisdiction and then originally in competition with older "port" or "marine" courts, already established in certain seaport towns (as appears from the Domesday mention of the Ipswich Court and the Borough Rolls of Yarmouth), which caused reiterated conflicts of jurisdiction. Those conflicts led to the adoption of certain Statutes in the reign of Richard II (1377-1399) (13 Ric. II, c.5 and 15 Ric. II, c.3). The Charters sometimes exempted specific seaport towns from the jurisdiction of the Admiral, sometimes granted them in express terms an Admiralty jurisdiction of their own.

Marsden's conclusion (at p. xiv) was that the origin of the Admiralty Court could be "traced with tolerable certainty" to the period between 1340 (the naval battle of Sluys, in which the French fleet was destroyed by the English and England gained temporary mastery of the sea) and 1357. See the case of 29 April of the latter year in Rymer's *Foedera*, III, 138, in which King Edward III (1327-1377) rejected a complaint, lodged with him by the King of Portugal about the seizure of certain goods belonging to one of his subjects by an Englishman on a French ship that had earlier taken the spoil from a transporting Portuguese vessel, stating as the ground of his rejection that the Admiral before whom the owner had sued for restitution of the goods had decided that they now belonged to the English captor as good and lawful prize.

Marsden, in his argument (at pp. xiv-xv) paid much attention to the connection between, on the one hand, the defeat of the French navy in the Battle of Sluys and, on the other, the consequent emergence of an Admiralty Court for the purpose of enforcing the claim of Edward III and his progenitors to possession of the "superioritas", "custodia", or "admirallatus maris", as set out in the *Fasciculus de Superioritate Maris* of 1339, p. xxx (Travers Twiss, *Black Book of the Admiralty*, vol. I, pp. 40 *et seq.* and 128 *et seq.*).

Disputes in admiralty cases on the most varying subjects—such as piracy, spoil of wreck, capture of royal fish, and obstruction of rivers—were originally dealt with in various ways, either by common law courts, or by the Chancellor, or by the King's Council, witnessed by frequent writs to sheriffs and commissioners of *oyer et terminer*, acting through trial juries, and adjudicating "secundum legem et consuetudinem regis Angliae" or "secundum legem mercatoriam" or "maritimam". In special cases the trial took place "coram ipso domino rege". Cases of piracy were occasionally also tried before special *ad hoc* tribunals.

The jurisdiction of the Chancellor comprised the grant of letters of reprisal and marque.

Rymer's *Foedera* covering the period of 1325 to 1340 contains a number of treaties dealing with complaints about piracy between English Kings and the Rulers of other seafaring nations such as Flanders, Spain and France in the last two decades of the 13th century.

The origin and subsequent vicissitudes of the office of Admiral in France have also long remained wrapped in historical mist. R.-J. Valin has reported on them in his *Nouveau commentaire sur l'Ordonnance de 1681* (1760; reprint 1981). The term "Admiral" seems to have been in use in early days to designate in France a commander in general, even of land operations. The office of Admiral has not been established in France as a grand office of the Crown until the 14th century: Ordonnance of 7 December 1373. The Admiral was at that juncture vested with a very wide range of attributions. The office continued to exist until 1627, when it was replaced by that of "grand maistre surintendant de la navigation", occupied first by Cardinal de Richelieu, later by Dowager-Queen Anne of Austria. The office of Admiral was re-established in 1667, but with a considerable reduction of the Admiral's competencies. It was again abolished by a law of 15 May 1791, but once more restored in the Napoleonic era by a *Sénatus-consulte* of 18 May 1804, again without the old extensive attributions. The title in 1814 devolved upon Monseigneur le duc d'Angoulême.

Section 1. THE ORGANIZATION OF PRIZE JURISDICTION

The oldest municipal and regional codes already included more or less embryonic provisions concerning the adjudication of prize cases. See, *e.g.*, the extracts from the *Ordonnance* of King Charles V the Wise of France (1364-1380) "sur le faict de l'Admirauté" of 7 December 1373, and from the *Edit* of March 1584 "concernant la juridiction de l'Admirauté de France" and further references to ancient "customs and usages of the sea" in Chr. Robinson's *Collectanea Maritima* of 1801, at pp. 75 *et seq.*, respectively pp. 105 *et seq.*

An old adage, sanctioning one of the most basic principles of prize law, commanded that "toute prise doit être jugée". It was chosen by Luigi Sico as the main title of his study of 1971 concerning *Il giudizio delle prede nel diritto internazionale* in the *Pubblicazioni della Facoltà Giuridica dell'Università di Napoli*, vol. CXIX. The adjudication of prize cases was for that purpose entrusted by maritime powers, from earlier centuries onward, to the Admiral, assisted by Jurors, or to Courts of Admiralty. This was particularly necessary during the period when naval operations against foreign commerce were to a large extent carried out by State-commissioned privateers (comp. Ch. III, section 1 *supra*, pp. 152 *et seq.*).

Also already at an early date the regulation of prize procedure was made the subject of treaty provisions. See, for example, the Franco-English treaty of peace and commerce of Boulogne of 24 May 1497 (*Collectanea Maritima*, p. 83). One of the issues which often caused difficulties was the mode of citation of absent persons. The practice had developed that the citation had to be made "per formam Publici Edicti", but this method had proved in practice to be insufficient and was, therefore, objected to by neutral governments, such as that of the Netherlands in 1644 (see the extract from Sir Leoline Jenkins' work in *Collectanea Maritima*, p. 89, footnote). Originally fourteen, later extended to twenty, days were allowed after the execution of the monition for its return.

National regulations

The organization of prize tribunals has developed differently in different countries. It would lead me too far afield, and it would moreover be a too pretentious undertaking, to attempt to describe the differences in detail. Studies have been devoted to this subject in England, *inter alia*, by E.S. Roscoe, *A history of the English Prize Court* (London, 1924), and in an earlier study by the same author together with T.L. Mears, *A treatise on the Admiralty jurisdiction and practice of the High Court of Justice and on the Vice-Admiralty courts and the Cinque Ports, etc.* (London, 1903). I will therefore confine myself to offering a few selected data which may be useful.

The differences between the national systems of the organization of prize tribunals consisted, *inter alia*, in the varying nature of the body entrusted with the adjudication, either administrative or strictly judicial. The development has increasingly gone in the latter direction.

In its *Règlement international des prises maritimes*, adopted at Munich (1883) and Heidelberg (1887), the *Institut de droit international* distinguished three prize tribunals, *viz.*.

in §§ 63-84 a "tribunal d'instruction des prises dans le port d'arrivée";

in §§ 85-99 a "tribunal (national de première instance) de prises maritimes"; and

in §§ 100-109 a "tribunal international des prises maritimes".

England

There is first the series of Acts of Parliament, Orders in Council and Proclamations that constitute the substratum of British prize adjudication: Prize Acts of

1708 (6 Anne, c. 37);

1793 (33 Geo. III, c. 66);

1803 (43 Geo. III, c. 160);

1805 (45 Geo. III, c. 72), incorporating the Act of 1803;

1834 (3 & 4 Will. IV, c. 41) creating the Privy Council as the Appeal Court in prize cases;

1854 (17 & 18 Vict., c. 18), followed by an Order in Council establishing the High Court of Admiralty and the several Courts of Admiralty within H.M.'s Dominions as Prize Courts;

1864 (27 & 28 Vict., c. 25), a permanent Act for regulating Naval Prize of War of 23 June, which created the High Court of Admiralty and the Vice-Admiralty Prize Courts;

1873 (36 & 37 Vict., c. 66), incorporation of the High Court of Admiralty into the new High Court of Justice;

1891 (54 & 55 Vict., c. 53), *Supreme Court Judicature Act*, section 4: the High Court of Admiralty to be a prize court within the meaning of the Naval Prize Act, 1864, and all prize cases to be assigned to the Probate, Divorce and Admiralty Division;

1894 (57 & 58 Vict., c. 39), an Act to make further provisions for the establishment of Prize Courts, and for other purposes connected therewith of 17 August, which authorized the making of Rules of Court and was followed by an Order in Council of 1898 approving such new Rules.

The following list gives the names of the series of Judges of the British High Court of Admiralty between 1702 and 1873 (Roscoe, p. x of vol. I):

Sir Charles Hedges, 1702-1714

Sir Henry Penrice, 1715-1751

Sir Thomas Salusbury, 1751-1773

Sir George Hay, 1773-1778

Sir James Marriott, 1778-1798
Sir William Scott (Lord Stowell), 1798-1828
Sir Christopher Robinson, 1828-1833 } these two not having
Sir John Nicholl, 1833-1838 } officiated as such
Right Honourable Stephen Lushington, 1838-1867
Sir Robert J. Phillimore, 1867-1873.

In the latter year the High Court of Admiralty was incorporated into the High Court of Justice.

An appeal lay to a superior court under different names, at a later stage to the Judicial Committee of the Privy Council.

France

A Decree of 20 December 1759 instituted a special Council, under the presidency of an Admiral, to hear prize cases; appeals went to the Council of State.

The successive changes which were introduced in the organization of French prize courts are illustrated by the following series of legislative enactments in the period 1793-1798:

14 February 1793 (Martens, R^2, V, 379): the adjudication of prizes provisionally entrusted to the *tribunaux de commerce*;

8 November 1793 (18 brumaire *an* II) (*ibid.*, 384): abolition of that temporary mandate by an arrangement under which prize cases would be settled administratively by the *Conseil exécutif provisoire*;

25 October 1795 (3 brumaire *an* IV) (*ibid.*, 384): return of the adjudication of prizes to the *tribunaux de commerce*, with an appeal regulated by a law of 27 April 1796 (8 floréal *an* IV);

11 January and 11 May 1798 (*ibid.*, 380, note): new proposals to revise the prize laws by transferring jurisdiction to administrative bodies (uncertain whether adopted or not).

More decrees were subsequently issued during the turbulent period of 1800-1813:

Arrêté des Consuls of 27 March 1800 (6 germinal *an* VIII), instituting a *Conseil des prises* in Paris, and

Art. 14 of the Decree of 11 June 1806 "sur l'organisation et les attributions du Conseil d'Etat":

> "Notre Conseil d'Etat connaîtra en outre ...
> 3. des décisions de la comptabilité nationale et du Conseil des prises."

At the beginning of the Crimean War an Imperial Decree of 18 July 1854 instituted a new *Conseil des prises* in Paris (Ortolan, Diplomatie de la Mer, II, 469). For the adjudication of prize cases during the following war between Savoy, backed by France, and Austria a decree of 9 May 1859 laid down in Art. 6 that

> "Les décisions rendues par le Conseil des prises peuvent Nous [*i.e.* to the Emperor] être déférées en notre Conseil d'Etat".

The *Conseil des prises* was made permanent by a Decree of 28 November 1861.

Spain

According to F.J. de Abreu y Bertodano's *Tratado jurídico-político sobre presas de mar* (Cadiz, 1746) and D.A. Azuni's *Droit maritime de l'Europe* (Paris, 1805, 2 vols.), prize proceedings were regulated by the *Ordenanza para navegar en corso* of 1621, later amended by *Cédulas* of 1623/24, 1702 and 1718. The *Intendentes*, or their delegates, judged the prizes brought into Spanish ports; if there was no *Intendente* in the port in question, then the *Intendente* of the province where the port is located, judged the case (Art. 2). On 17 April 1675 a royal decree declared, *inter alia*, that prize proceedings came under the exclusive competence of the War Council.

In the Treaty of Navigation and Commerce, concluded in Vienna on 1 May 1725 (Parry, 32, 105) between the Emperor and Spain, Article XXX entitles subjects of the Emperor to appeal prize judgments to the *Consejo de Comercio* in Madrid.

In 1748 a Royal decree determined that appeals of the judgments of the *Intendentes* lay with the King. In 1772, the functions of the *Intendentes* passed to the *Juntas Económicas de los Departamentos* and in 1779 to the Prize Commissioners. An Ordinance of 14 June 1797 defined in more detail the competence of the prize tribunals. Article VII, for instance, ruled that "if a neutral prize is brought into a Spanish port, and it appears that half or more of the cargo is Spanish property, the Spanish tribunals will be competent to judge the taking of the prize; if less than half the cargo is Spanish property, then the tribunals of the captor will be competent". See Abreu, pp. 169 *et seq.* and 315 *et seq.* (text of the *Ordenanza* of 1718) and Azuni, vol. I, pp. 476 *et seq.* and vol. II, pp. 337-339.

The *Ordenanza de Corso* (of 1801) and the *Ordenanza de Matrículas de Mar* (1802) once again empowered the *Juntas Económicas* to hear prize cases; appeal was possible to the *Capitán General del departamento*, and finally to the Supreme War Council. The Acts of the Royal Council of 1845, and of the Council of State of 1860, ruled that prize cases should come before these bodies; in 1869 this was changed insofar that prize cases should first come before the Tribunal of the Admiralty, and in appeal before the Council of State. Only a few years later the Tribunal of the Admiralty was abolished and prize cases went directly to the Council of State. See on this period I. Pérez y Oliva, *Presas marítimas* (Madrid, 1887).

Italy

According to F. Sassi ("La guerra in corsa e il diritto di preda secondo il diritto veneziano" in the *Rivista di Storia del Diritto Italiano* 1929, pp. 100 *et seq.* and 261 *et seq.*), it was only in the 18th century that prize courts were instituted. During many centuries the Consolato del Mare provided the rules applicable to the making of prizes. In 1350 Venice adopted official rules for the distribution of prize booty (Sassi, p. 265), and in 1338 Sicily had already laid down that prize booty could not be sold without previous Royal consent (p. 283).

In the 18th and early 19th century the organization of prize proceedings in the Italian States differed considerably. Naples entrusted prize proceedings to a tribunal of the Admiralty; this can be found in an Edict of 6 December 1789 which at the same time abolished the Court of the High Admiral. Trieste and Genoa brought prize cases before Commercial Tribunals. In Ancona and Cività Vecchia the local governors decided prize cases; in Livorno the governor was assisted by an Auditeur Civil. Sardinia had a tribunal of the General Captaincy, from which appeals could go to the Supreme Council of the Kingdom (Edict of 30 August 1770). In most States appeals were heard by the Government. See Azuni, vol. II, pp. 341-342.

After unification in the 1860's prize jurisdiction in Italy was rather organized on a administrative footing, see Art. 225 of the *Codice per la Marina Mercantile per il Regno d'Italia* of 25 June 1865, modified by a law of 24 May 1877, and republished on 24 October 1877:

> "Il giudizio per la legittimità delle prede e per la confisca sarà promosso dinanzi ad una speciale Commissione da istituirsi con decreto reale, giusta le norme a prescriversi dal regolamento."

The special Commission was appointed by Royal Decree of 20 June 1866 and was located in Florence. The Commission drew up a set of rules for the conduct of prize cases. Appeal against the decisions of the Commission was possible to the Council of State. See Pérez y Oliva (*Presas marítimas*, Madrid 1887, p. 84).

A very restricted recourse to the *Suprema Corte di Cassazione* was only opened in May 1915.

Germany and Austria

Prize jurisdiction in Germany was, as far as I was able to verify, after her emergence as a national unit, first as a confederation (1815), later in various shapes of a federation (1867, 1870), entrusted to judicial bodies acting in two instances, prior to World War I a *Prisengericht* and an *Oberprisengericht*, both located in Berlin. The organization was based on a Law of 3 May 1884 "betreffend die Prisengerichtsbarkeit" (Martens, N.R.G.[3], X, 504; B.F.S.P. 1900/01, 1009).

This judicial form of organization was also that adopted by the Austrian Empire: see the *Prisengerichtsordnung* enacted, after the outbreak of war with Denmark, by an Imperial Ordinance of 21 March 1864, referring to a preceding Ordinance of 3 March 1864 (B.F.S.P., 1863/64, 552).

Denmark and Sweden

In Denmark prize cases were originally decided in first instance by a tribunal of the Admiralty; appeals were possible with the Council of State. See

Art. 38 of the Treaty between Denmark and France of 23 August 1742 (Parry, 36, 465); the text of this article can be found in most other treaties between Denmark and foreign States. On 1 May 1848 new Prize Rules were enacted, and in 1864 proceedings were changed insofar that appeals should come before the Supreme Court (B.F.S.P., 1863/64, 545).

In Sweden the situation was the same: prize proceedings in first instance were decided by a prize court; appeals went to the Supreme Court.

The organization of prize jurisdiction in The Netherlands

During many years the structure of prize jurisdiction in the Low Countries was very complex. Prizes were adjudicated long before the Netherlands emerged as an independent confederation in the 16th century. A succession of princely houses ruled over Holland and Zeeland, those of Holland (922-1299), Hainault (1299-1349), Bavaria (1349-1433), Burgundy (1433-1482) and Austria (1482-1581). Each of the princes had his own regional judiciary. In 1473 Charles the Bold created the Parliament of Mechlin (the *Grand Conseil de Malines*), a superior tribunal to which an appeal lay from the several provincial courts. Its jurisdiction included the adjudication of prize cases in appeal from their judgments.

Prize proceedings were, for instance, conducted in the courts of Holland when Duke Albrecht of Bavaria was at war with the Frisians and captured their ships. Best known is, however, the Burgundian period, during which appeal proceedings were brought before the *Grand Conseil de Malines* (see Chapter I, section 5, *supra*, pp. 106-109). When the Low Countries had fallen to the house of Austria as a consequence of the marriage between Roman-King Maximilian and Duchess Maria of Burgundy the organizational scene changed: prize jurisdiction was amalgamated into a central judicial body by an Ordonnance of Maximilian, also in the name of his infant son Philippe-le-Beau of 8 January 1488 (comp. Chapter I, section 3, *supra*, pp. 54-55). In the meantime the Roman-King had appointed, 1485, an Admiral of the Fleet (*Amiral de la mer en tous leurs pays et seigneuries*) in the person of Philip of Cleves (1456-1528), on whom a thorough treatise has been written in 1941 by Dr Johanna Oudendijk in vol. VII of the publications of the Commission for Naval History of the Royal Netherlands Academy of Sciences, *Een Bourgondische ridder over den oorlog ter zee* (A Burgundian knight on naval war).

The Ordonnance of 1488 on the new organization of prize jurisdiction in the Low Countries was, in the main unchanged, replaced by a new Ordonnance of 27 December 1540 by Charles V, which in a new Article 18 expressly allowed an appeal to the *Grand Conseil de Malines*:

> "Item, indien yemandt mainteneren wil beswaert te wesene by vonnisse van onsen voorsz. Admirael, of sijnen Generael, of particuliere Stadthouders, deselve sal mogen appelleren voor ons, of voor de geene van onsen voorsz. grooten Raede te Mechelen, op 't pericle van den gewonelijcker boete van quaden appel".

A third law in this series of enactments was the very detailed Instruction of the States General for the Colleges of the Admiralty established in the respective provinces and quarters, of 13 August 1597 (*Groot Placaatboek*, II, pp. 1530-1588) in 99 articles. It was adopted on the advice of Prince Maurice in his capacity of Admiral General and only for the period of a year, but was in fact continued in force since. This Instruction confirmed the existence of five *Admiraliteitscolleges*, one for Southern Holland (at Rotterdam), one for Northern Holland (at Amsterdam), one for Holland's northermost quarter of West-Friesland (at Hoorn or Enkhuizen), one for Zeeland (at Middelburg) and one for Friesland (at Dokkum, later Harlingen). Each of these Colleges was to consist of seven members,

in Holland four of them on the nomination of the States Provincial of Holland and West-Friesland and three from other provinces;

in Zeeland, on a compromise proposal of Prince Maurice, provisionally for a one year's term, in the persons of the seven Councillors Delegate of the States Provincial of Zeeland, who would be bound to take an oath to the States General and to renounce all special commitments towards the States Provincial of Zeeland, and to appoint every month four Councillors from their own circle to adjudicate prize cases together with three Councillors from other provinces. This complicated mode of appointment was connected with the persistent disagreement between the province and the States General about the priority of their respective competences in maritime affairs;

in Friesland, four of them on the nomination of the States Provincial with three qualified and expert persons acquainted with the administration of justice on the nomination by six of the other provinces.

This whole arrangement witnesses to the well-known mutual distrust which is so often manifested in (con)federations.

I will now give some more detail of the history of the Admiralty Colleges.

The Instruction of 1597 consolidated and slightly reformed on a Generalty basis the preceding organization on the provincial level. The new Generalty law determined definitively the number, seat and composition of the five Colleges. The element of reform related in particular to Zeeland province whose Admiralty College (the first, in 1488, established at Veere) had never been recognized by Holland. Although originally intended to have only a short temporary operation, it was in fact accepted as a lasting regulation of the organization of prize jurisdiction in the Republic of the United Netherlands and has remained its legal basis up to the very end in 1795.

As it has proved difficult even for a Dutchman to retrace the vicissitudes of the Admiralty Colleges during the two successive stages of Netherlands prize jurisdiction prior and subsequent to 1795, and as the Republic of the United Netherlands in the course of its confederate existence has played an important rôle in the naval war history of Western Europe, I will begin with a few general data on its early development which I have attempted to describe as accurately as possible with the much appreciated and indeed indispensable help of a number of Dutch archivists and historians.

The archives of the Admiralty Colleges of Holland from the period of the

Republic of the United Netherlands up to 1795 are now in the custody of the General State Archives at The Hague, those relating to the College of the river Maas in their Third Division (State Archives of Southern-Holland), those of the two Northern-Holland Colleges (Amsterdam and the "Noorderkwartier") in their First Division.

On the archives of the five Admiralty Colleges see the inventory by J. de Hullu (The Hague, 1924), and on their jurisdiction S.J. Fockema Andreae, *De Nederlandse Staat onder de Republiek* (Amsterdam, 1961), pp. 26-29.

When the five Admiralty Colleges were abolished in 1795 to be replaced with the *Colleges ter judicature van de convooien en licenten* (Colleges for the adjudication of convoy and licence affairs), their archives were removed to The Hague, where they have remained in the care of the General State Archives.

On the archives of these new bodies see the inventory published in the series Verslagen omtrent 's-Rijks Oude Archieven, 1916, vol. I, pp. 250 *et seq.*

In the period 1795-1811 regional Commissaries and *Substituten-fiscaal* functioned in Hoorn and in Amsterdam, charged with the instruction and preparation of proceedings in prize cases, which were finally to be adjudicated upon at The Hague. The archives of those regional Commissaries are now in the custody of the State Archives for Northern-Holland at Haarlem.

On these provincial archives see the printed inventory published by Th. P. M. van der Fluit (1980-).

The Admiralty of Friesland, created by the States of Friesland as an autonomous provincial body in 1596, but promoted to the rank of a Generalty body in 1597, was first established in Dokkum. It was later (1645) transferred to Harlingen, and it was there that the first ominous fire started in 1771. See on this Admiralty College the data given in the *Encyclopedie van Friesland* (Amsterdam, 1958) *in voce* "Admiraliteit", and on the fire in Harlingen the article in the *Nederlandsche Jaarboeken* 1771, pp. 56-58, referred to in J.J. Kalma's *Repertorium Frieslands Verleden* (Leeuwarden, 1955), *in eadem voce.*

The Admiralty of Zeeland province was not hit by fire, but experienced troubles of a different, political nature, both at its birth and at its death. Its infancy (*a*) was marked by a protracted internal conflict of competence between the provincial and the Generalty authorities, and its old age (*b*) by a series of disturbing international occurrences.

Ad (*a*). The origin. In 1983 F.A. Gooskens of the State Archives in Zeeland published his *De Admiraliteit te Veere, Inventaris van het archief en een kort overzicht van de geschiedenis tot 1559* (The Admiralty at Veere; An inventory of the archives and a brief survey of the developments until 1559).

In this survey Gooskens discusses the competence and the composition of the Admiralty when judging prize cases, and the possibilities of appeal, *inter alia* of cases heard in first instance in Dunkirk and in Flanders (from 1540 Flanders cases in appeal could go directly to the *Grand Conseil de Malines*).

The succeeding years from 1577 to 1587 have been described in H.G. van Grol's *Het beheer van het Zeeuwsche zeewezen* (Flushing, 1936). Veere and Flushing took the side of the Prince of Orange in 1574. In the same year an Instruction was published on the setting up of a provincial government and its competence; in Article 8 of the Instruction the Council of the Admiralty was designated as the forum for "beuytgoederen en prinsen" (booty and prizes); appeal was possible with the "Governors and Councillors". The Zeeland Admiralty then had its seat at Flushing. The Lieutenant-Admiral Willem Bloys van Treslong obtained from the Prince of Orange an agreement that a parallel Admiralty Court should be instituted at Dunkirk which had come over to the Northern Netherlands in 1577; the Dunkirk Admiralty functioned from 1579 until 1583 when the town surrendered to the French.

As appears from a detailed report on the contents of the Zeeland archives, the Admiralty of the province was created in 1584 by a provincial authority, the *College van Gecommitteerde Raden* (Board of Councillors Delegate), which first met in Flushing to draw up an instruction, later issued by them in the name of the Prince of Orange in his capacity as Admiral General of the Confederation: the Admiralty was to have its seat at Flushing and consisted of five members. After the assassination of the Prince in 1584, this set-up was confirmed in a new instruction of 1585, this time enacted by a central authority, Prince Maurice of Orange jointly with the Council of State. The Earl of Leicester, representative of Queen Elizabeth I in the Netherlands, in his turn modified the instruction in 1586: the Admiralty was to consist of seven members and to transfer its seat to Middelburg. Owing to the objection of the States of Zeeland because of the preponderance of Generalty influence in their Admiralty jurisdiction, the scene changed again in 1597, when the organization of prize jurisdiction was determined on a Generalty level by the abovementioned Instruction of the States General. This change was made on a conciliatory proposal of Prince Maurice, himself the *Eerste Edele* (First Nobleman) of the province: the Admiralty was henceforth, and now definitively, to consist of ten instead of seven members. The way they were appointed has been described *supra*.

The situation in the Southern Netherlands has been studied by F. Pollentier who published his *De Admiraliteit en de oorlogen ter zee onder de Aartshertogen (1569-1609)* in 1972 (Brussels). In 1583 Dunkirk continued to be the seat of an Admiralty court, this time for the Southern Netherlands; a similar court could be found in Antwerp. The Archduke Albrecht of Austria drew up a new instruction for the Admiralty in November 1596 but in this

Resolution no mention was made of the competence of the Admiralty in prize matters. An older decree by King Philip II from 2 August 1590 was therefore used as the base for the competence in prize proceedings (p. 181). The beginning of the Twelve Years' Truce between Spain and the Northern Netherlands was also the end of the Admiralty which was dissolved on 1 October 1609; when the Truce ended, in 1621, a new Admiralty for Flanders was set up in Sint-Winoksbergen.

The Zeeland Admiralty played a rather conspicuous rôle during the War of the Spanish Succession (1702-1713). G. N. Clark, in his article in the 1928 *British Year Book of International Law*, mentioned the "uncontrollable ardour of the privateers of Zeeland" and the "callous indifference of the Zeeland Admiralty Court to matters of law" (p. 74). Mrs J. Th. H. Verhees-van Meer, in her dissertation on *De Zeeuwse kaapvaart tijdens de Spaanse successieoorlog 1702-1713* (1986), comes to the conclusion that it was the "uncontrollable ardour of the merchants of Holland and Zeeland" combined with the "callous indifference of the States General to matters of law" in prize proceedings which made prize decisions by the Zeeland Admiralty Court unpredictable (p. 161).

Ad (*b*). The end. The final phase of the existence of a national prize jurisdiction was marked by the impact of international events. All the old Netherlands Admiralty Colleges were officially dissolved under French influence by the States General by a Resolution of 17 February 1795 and replaced with a *Comité tot de zaken van de Marine* (Committee for Marine Affairs), which appointed three Delegate Commissaries to take over the task of the Zeeland Admiralty from Vlissingen as their new seat. This remained so when in 1798 the *Uitvoerend Bewind* (Executive Government) of the newly organised Batavian Republic in its turn replaced the *Comité tot de zaken van de Marine* with a Marine Department. A last move of the Zeeland prize tribunal commenced in 1807 when Vlissingen was ceded to France by a treaty of 11 November 1807 (Martens, R^2, VIII, 718, Art. 6; Parry, 59, 389). The Commissaries changed their seat to Zierikzee, from where they sought temporary refuge in Sommelsdijk in 1809 after the surrender of the island of Schouwen to the English. The Zeeland Admiralty ended definitively when the whole of Zeeland province was ceded to France by a new treaty of 16 March 1810 (Martens, N.R., I, 327; Parry, 61, 135, Art. 6), on the eve of the final incorporation of the whole of Holland into the French Empire on 9 July 1810 (Martens, N.R., I, 338) (comp. on these developments vol. VII of this publication, p. 281).

Prize jurisdiction in Zeeland was organized on two levels, an appeal being open to the Board of Councillors Delegate *in pleno*, called "re-audition". But here again a conflict of competence arose because the Council of State, a confederal body, claimed superintendence over the Admiralty College. The new compromise was to the effect that the appeal should formally lie to the

Council of State; that, however, this Council should delegate its judicial functions to the provisional body of Councillors Delegate, but that the sentences should actually be pronounced by the Admiralty College (instruction of 1586). When, in 1597, by the general Instruction of the States General, the Councillors Delegate themselves obtained a seat in the Admiralty College, their concurrent claim to appellate jurisdiction in prize lapsed *ipso facto*.

The Archivist of the Zeeland section of the State Archives informed me that certain remains of old prize proceedings are still extant in his depository, *inter alia*, a register of the roll of cases examined by the Councillors Delegate during the period 1591-1783 (34 vols), a register of sentences concerning prizes condemned by default during the period 1675-1717 (6 vols), a fragment of a prize court judgment of 1782 in the case of the English prize ship *Endeavour*, and a collection of documents (1600-1605) concerning the seizure of the Portuguese ship *San Jago* and the resulting *Carletti* affair, described by Mr Roelofsen in his study published in a paper of the Netherlands Society for Maritime History (March 1970).

The second period of Netherlands prize jurisdiction began about 1800 when the unsurveyable older French legislation on the subject was rendered operative in Holland and newly enacted French laws and decrees automatically applied in the country after it had become part of the French Empire. Those French legislative intrusions were only very slowly thrown out of the Netherlands Statute Book after Holland's restoration as an independent country in 1813 (comp. on this subject vol. VII of this publication, pp. 281 *et seq*.).

It was only in the third period that a truly national prize jurisdiction reappeared. Jurisdiction over piracy and prize (*zeeroverij en zeebuit*) was at first conferred upon a new Superior Court for Financial and Maritime Affairs, but that has not lasted for long, since this Court was abolished by a law of 24 December 1819 (*Staatsblad*, No. 59) whereby its task was transferred to the ordinary judicature. Jurisdiction in matters of "prize and booty" was, however, in actual fact only belatedly conferred specifically upon the newly created Supreme Court: by Articles 89 and 90 of the Law of 18 April 1827 (*Staatsblad*, No. 20) on the Composition of the Judiciary and the Administration of Justice. Although in principle a Court of Cassation whose competence was confined to the decision of legal questions, it was to act in prize cases as a tribunal judging on both facts and law, and that in two instances, pursuant to Article 368 of another Law, the Code of Civil Procedure of 1828, in the first instance composed of five judges and in the second, called "revision", of seven judges.

The law of 1819 had been preceded by a Royal Decree of 13 December 1818 (*Staatsblad*, No. 40), which contained a new regulation of a more substantive nature in replacement of the French *Arrêté* of 2 prairial *an* XI

(22 May 1803). This Decree dealt exclusively with prize procedure: the bringing-in of prizes, their sale in case of condemnation and, *in extenso*, the apportionment of prize bounty (*prijs- en buitgelden*).

This decree was still in force at the beginning of the fourth period on the outbreak of World War II and Germany's invasion of the Netherlands in May 1940, at least for the Kingdom in Europe, for separate regulations had in the meantime been enacted in the course of the 19th century in the Dutch overseas dominions. One of the (civil) courts, instituted in the Netherlands Indies as prize courts for the adjudication of captures made to the east of the Cape of Good Hope, has actually functioned during the naval blockade in 1873 and following years of the indigenous State of Atjeh (Acheen) (comp. on these cases *supra*, *sub* A, section 4 on blockade, p. 451), and it has even still functioned during World War II in the case of the *Nyugat*.

In the mother country the Supreme Court had never had to adjudicate upon matters of prize during the 19th and the first half of the 20th century. It was not until 1953 that it was seised with a prize case—the only one, ever brought before it. It related to a Hungarian vessel, the *Nyugat*, captured by a Netherlands man-of-war in the Indian ocean in 1941 (on which, for that matter, I have already reported in Part I of this publication, pp. 97 and 151-152). I cannot deal with that case in the present Chapter since it occurred during World War II; for the same reason I cannot enter here into a series of (unimportant) cases, submitted at the commencement of World War II to a civil court, acting as a prize court, on the island of Curaçao.

See on the history of Dutch prize law after 1813 J. H. Zeeman's article on "The Netherlands, the law of neutrality, and prize law" in vol. III of *International law in The Netherlands* (Alphen aan den Rijn/Dobbs Ferry, 1980), pp. 331-379, more especially on pp. 354 *et seq*.

Russia

An Ordinance of 31 December 1787 (Martens, R^1, IV, 507) determined that prize cases should be heard in first instance by a Commission, composed of Ministers, Admirals and Councillors; appeals came before the Imperial Court. Later, prize jurisdiction was, by Art. 50 of the Regulations relating to Naval Prizes of 27 March/8 April 1895 (Appendix A to Hurst & Bray, I, 311-331; B.F.S.P., 1900/01, 861) conferred in the first instance upon prize tribunals established in the ports or with squadron commanders of independent navy divisions, and in appeal upon the Admiralty Council as supreme tribunal. Art. 51 laid down that the tribunals in the ports would be set up by the Minister of Marine in Russian ports or, if necessary, in accord with foreign governments, in the ports of Allied Powers.

Appendix B (Hurst & Bray, I, 331-346; B.F.S.P., 1900/01, 882) gives the text of the Instructions on Procedure in Stopping, Examining, and Detaining, and also in Bringing in and Handing over Captured Vessels and Cargoes, of 20 September 1900 under Article 26 of the 1895 Regulations.

Japan

Japan organized her prize jurisdiction by an Imperial Decree of 20 August 1894, No. 149 (B.F.S.P., 1893/94, 352), concerning the Prize Court, modified by Decrees of 1 March 1904, February and July 1905 and 11 September 1914: Prize Court of the first instance at Sasebo and Supreme Prize Court at Tokyo (Decree of 29 August 1914, No. 174).

The United States

The first American prize court dates from the pre-federal period of the United States as a confederation (comp. vol. II of this publication, p. 177). It owed its existence to a resolution of the Continental Congress of November 1775 and has functioned until May 1787. In that initial period it was still the Congress itself that acted as a court of appeal, at first through special *ad hoc* committees, then from January 1777 through a standing committee, until in January 1780 a court of three judges was established, known as "the Court of Appeals in Cases of Capture", which continued in existence until May 1787. The genesis, history and work of this "pioneer tribunal" have been examined and described by Henry J. Bourguignon in a publication (Philadelphia, 1977) under the title *The First Federal Court. The Federal Appellate Prize Court of the American Revolution 1775-1787.*

Federal district courts were created in 1789 under Art. III of the Constitution.

In 1945 Madeline Russell Robinton published *An introduction to the papers of the New York Prize Court, 1861-1865* (New York, Studies in history, economics and public law edited by the Faculty of Political Science of Columbia University). In Chapter II (pp. 27 *et seq.*) she presents a survey of the district courts existing at the time the Civil War began and especially of those courts which were called upon to deal with Union prize cases. The survey is accompanied by an excellent inventory of the literature on the subject, particularly from the years during and immediately after the Civil War.

As Samuel Blatchford set out in the preface to his collection of *Reports in cases of prize* of 1866 (comp. Chapter I, *supra*, p. 114), the District Court was held by the District Judge. The Circuit was held, as a rule, by a Justice of the Supreme Court specially assigned to the circuit embracing the Court, and the District Judge of the district, sitting either jointly, or either of them sitting alone. In cases which were removed by appeal or writ of error from a District to a Circuit Court, judgment was to be rendered in conformity with the opinion of the Judge of the Supreme Court, presiding in the Circuit Court, *i.e.* in practice by the latter, sitting alone. Whereas up to 3 March 1863 appeals from District Court decrees in prize cases were taken to the Circuit Court in the same manner as appeals from decrees in other cases, this was changed by an Act of Congress of that date which provided that appeals from the District Courts in prize cases should in future go directly to the

Supreme Court. That Act (12 U.S. Statutes at Large, p. 760) was re-enacted on 30 June 1864 (13 U.S. Statutes, p. 310).

Further Acts of Congress on the subject are those of 26 June 1812, 13 February 1813, 17 July 1862, 22 June 1870 and 3 March 1873, which can all be found in the *Federal Statutes Annotated* and the *Statutes at Large*. See in particular the Act of Congress of 30 June 1864, enacted during the Civil War (Robinton, p. 89), and the collections by W. Cranch and Wallace (Chapter I, *supra*, p. 114).

Prize jurisdiction in the United States has followed the old British tradition of truly judicial adjudication. Apart from the fact that the United States Government has begun by promoting, in co-operation with the British Government, the adjudication of controversial prize cases (dating from the War of Independence and the War of 1812) by mixed arbitral commissions (comp. Part VIII of this publication, pp. 275 *et seq.*), it had opted almost from the outset for the judicial variant of prize jurisdiction by courts of law, at first even in three instances.

Section 2. COMPETENCE OF THE PRIZE COURTS

As appears from the oldest codes of maritime law, surveyed in Chapter I above, pp. 34 *et seq.*, the Admirals were from the outset vested with a vast extent of jurisdiction, but that jurisdiction lay originally mainly in the criminal or disciplinary field, such as the trial of mariners who committed felonies or other punishable offences and of pirates. Gradually, however, their competence extended to a wider field. A few references to those old codes may suffice.

A list of criminal offences, to be tried by the Admiral or by a tribunal of 12 jury men in Admiralty and punishable by severe penalties (in graver cases, such as those of theft or mutilation, the cutting of cables, a repeated offence of larceny, etc., by death by hanging, or by cutting off a hand), is contained in Part C of the *Black Book of the Admiralty*—a collection of rules and orders in 39 articles. Another such catalogue of offences is included in the *Inquisition of Queensborough* of 1375.

In the said Part C are also inserted a number of Acts in "matters which belong to the Admiralty", made under the reigns of Henry I (1110-1135) at Gyppswiz (Ipswich), Richard I (1189-1199) at Grimsby, John (1199-1216), Henry III (1216-1272), Edward I (1272-1307) at Hastings, and of later Kings, Edward III (1327-1377), Henry IV (1399-1413) and Edward IV (1461-1483).

Several of them had a very wide scope, directed as they were against the withdrawal of ships and men, arrested for the King's service, from that service—obviously a prototype of the right of angary—; against "forestallers" and "regraters" (buyers-up of corn, fish, etc., at sea for the purpose of selling them by retail at a profit); against the appropriation of salt water by setting up fisheries, weirs, windmills, kiddles, etc.; against the use of false measures, weights and scales, the extortion of new customs by keepers of ports and water bailiffs, the exaction of excessive wages by ship's carpenters, the unlicensed export of grain, etc. This wide mediaeval circumscription of admiralty jurisdiction would seem still to lie at the basis of the vast extent of British admiralty law and jurisdiction in later centuries.

Arts. 18 and 19 of the said Part C, inserting the Act made by Richard I at Grimsby, also mention a "Court of the Admiralty and his Lieutenants" as being at that time a Court of Record ("which privilege appears to have been subsequently wrested from the High Court of Admiralty" and only restored to it by an Act of 24 Vict., c. 10, sec. 14).

Even matters of private law were regulated in those medieval instruments and that on a wide scale. Thus, the same Part C of the *Black Book* dealt, in Art. 21, with the Admiral's jurisdiction over contracts made beyond the seas or within flood-marks; in Art. 33, with wrecks and claims thereto; in Art. 36, with flotsam, jetsam, lagon and with floating vessels or "bona wairiata"; in Art. 37, with gold, silver and jewels found upon a man killed at sea.—The same applies to other old codifications, such as Edward I's Ordinance of Hastings, Art. 32, dealing with jettison and general average in conformity with the rules developed by Roman lawyers and later adopted by the Rhodian Law *de jactu*.

The *Rôles d'Oléron*, inserted in Part C of the *Black Book* (vol. I, pp. 88-131) after Art. 39, in a version of 24 further articles, undoubtedly identical with the oldest version of the Judgments of the Sea (a statement which cannot be upheld as regards ten ensuing articles which are not found in any other version of those Judgments), include no provisions of prize law at all, but deal with the relations between the ship's captain and the ship owner (raising of a mortgage on the ship for the purchase of provisions; an oath of the master and six mariners as a discharge of the suspicion of ill-tackling), between the captain and the crew (wages; diet; medical care of mariners; consultation before sailing; punishment for offences; conditions for leaving the ship; disputes between them), and between the ship owner and the charterer (payment of freight for goods saved in a naufrage; compensation due in case of delay in loading), with the responsability of a pilot, with the jettison of cargo and the felling of masts to save the vessel in case of storm, and with collisions between ships on roadsteads.

The Inquisition of Queensborough (1375), reproduced in Part D of the *Black Book*, is a *mixtum compositum* of old usages relating to wages of mariners, prize bounty, penal provisions, "royal fishes" (whales, sturgeon, porpoise), flotsam and lagon, obstruction of streams by weirs, blindstakes, etc., withdrawal of ships from an arrest by angary, desertion of mariners, the catch of oysters and mussels, etc.

The Wisby *Stads-Lag* also dealt only with subjects other than prize law, such as—in the field of private law—the hiring, loading and unloading, sale and mortgaging of ships, shipwreck, jettison and other devices to save cargoes, etc.

At later periods the competence of prize courts has consisted primarily in the power to adjudicate upon the validity or otherwise of seizures made by the Navy or other qualified organs of their State or by privateers, and to draw the legal conclusions from their findings. However, owing to the organization of the judiciary as a whole, various prize courts, especially those of England, have also been assigned, or have assumed, competence over other cases relating to subject-matters foreign to the law of prize.

Foremost among the matters lying outside the field of prize cases proper was the adjudication of cases of trading with the enemy, carried on by British or even allied subjects. Cases in which the English prize courts have dealt with captures made on this ground are numerous, see, *e.g*, the *De Hoop* (Cornelis, Master) [1799] (1 C.Rob., 196; Roscoe, I, 104), the *Odin (No. 1)* (Hals, Master) [1799] (1 C.Rob., 248; Roscoe, I, 127), the *Jonge Pieter* (Musterdt, Master) [1801] (4 C.Rob., 79; Roscoe, I, 353), and the *Neptunus (No. 5)* (Bachman, Master) [1807] (6 C.Rob., 403; Roscoe, I, 595). American courts have followed the British example: the *Rapid* [1814] (8 Cranch, 155; Scott's *Cases,* 557), and the *Julia* [1814] (8 Cranch, 181). Comp. on this subject Ch. III *sub* A, section 6a, *supra*, p. 479.

Another class of cases in which British prize courts have exercised jurisdiction outside the range of the law of prize proper consisted of captures made of vessels involved in the slave trade. The oldest precedent in this field seems to be the condemnation of the *Amedie* by the Vice-Admiralty Court of Tortola (one of the West-Indian Virgin Islands), confirmed by the Superior Court. This was the case of an American vessel, engaged in the slave trade from Africa's west coast. Comp. on this subject *eod. loco*, p. 478.

But there were still other captures which did not come within the range of prize law proper, such as: illegal traffic in violation of municipal Statutes in general. The historical development of this issue of the competence of prize courts in cases other than prize law proper is somewhat complicated, but it can, I think, be sketched in the following chronological order.

In the case of the *Eliza* (Worsely, Master) [1794; in appeal 1798] (2 C.Rob., at 79) the Prize Court was confronted by the capture of a ship engaged in illegal traffic carried on in violation of the charter of the East India Company. As Sir William Scott set out in the *Walsingham Packet* (Bell, Master) [1799] (2 C.Rob., 77; Roscoe, I, 189), this *Eliza* case was the first in which it had been decided that the Court of Admiralty

> "was bound to take notice of an illegal practice, evidently appearing in the conduct of a British subject, though the illegality arose from a violation of some law merely municipal, and that it was bound to reject the claim of any British subject, whose property had found its way into the hands of a British captor, if the transaction in which that property had been employed was a transaction contrary to British law".

The interest in that *Eliza* case had gone to the private captor, whilst the penalty by the Act of Parliament was given to the Company as a compensation for the damages caused to them as a result of such illegal trade. The course taken by the Court had been the same in the *Enterprise*. However, in a subsequent judgment regarding the *Etrusco*, it was questioned whether these decisions were right, both as to the very wide definition of the extent of prize jurisdiction and to the conveyance of the forfeiture to the private captors instead of to the Crown. That is why, in the *Walsingham Packet* of 1799 (2 C.Rob., 82), Sir William Scott observed that:

> "it was an inquiry worth pursuing: whether a British Court of Admiralty, sitting here, armed with its power from this country, and carrying all its process into effect by the authority of the British Parliament, was not so far a British Court as to be bound to take notice of British Acts of Parliament and the flagrant breach of our municipal laws with respect to the transactions of our own subjects coming incidentally before it."

The *Walsingham Packet* case itself related to a different violation of British law from that committed in the *Eliza* case, *viz*., the carriage of cargo which was illegal under the Statute 13 & 14 Ch. 2, cap. ii, s. 22, prohibiting the carrying of all merchandise on board a packet except under a special allowance (which had not been obtained in the case). Sir William Scott examined whether the goods, admitted to have been put on board for Lisbon for the purpose of trade, came under the allowance of the Act of Parliament; he denied this and consequently rejected the claim of the British and Portuguese cargo-owners. However, in view of the fact that the Lords of Appeal, in the *Etrusco* affair, had left in suspense the question of the final appropriation of the cargo, Sir William Scott also reserved this question for further deliberation. It was ultimately decided by the Lords in a further decision on the *Etrusco* of 1803 (Roscoe, I, 194, footnote *b*; I, 388, footnote *a*) to the effect that the property should be condemned to the Crown.

In a later case, the *Fortuna* (Verissimo, Master) [1811] (1 Dods., 81; Roscoe, I, 193, footnote *a*), Sir William Scott returned to the question with regard to the offence of slave trading. The *Fortuna* was an American vessel which had sailed from New York in July 1810 under American colours and the name *William & Mary*, first to the Portuguese island of Madeira, where she was ostensibly sold to a Portuguese subject, de Souza, and from where she departed under Portuguese colours and the new name *Fortuna*. As I have set out in III A, section 6a, *sub* 1, Sir William Scott in that case made the general statement that:

> "It has been established that the Court of Prize, though properly purely a Court of the Law of Nations, has a right to notice the municipal law of this country in the case of a British vessel which, in the course of prize proceedings, appears to have been trading in violation of that law, and to reject a claim for her on that account", ...

He still expressed his hesitation to adopt the extension of the principle from British to foreign slave traders, but seemed to have ended by acquiescing to the fact that the accepted widened principle appeared to be "that the slave trade carried on by a vessel belonging to a subject of the United States is a trade which, being unprotected by the domestic regulations of their legislature and government, subjects the vessel engaged in it to condemnation."

Uncommon events may sometimes give rise to doubts about the competence of the prize court. This was the case of a cargo from the *Ooster Eems* [1784] (Roscoe, I, 136, footnote *a*). This was a Dutch ship which was stranded on a voyage from Texel to the Netherlands East Indies on the Goodwin Sands. The cargo was sent ashore, but some boxes of silver were deposited with the Prussian consul. The Warden of the Cinque Ports claimed the cargo as enemy property and "perquisite of the Admirall" within his jurisdiction. The master of the *Ooster Eems* obtained a monition from the High Court of Admiralty to arrest the goods and to remove the cause from the Cinque Ports to the Prize Court, where he gave a claim for the cargo as Prussian property. The cargo was condemned by the Prize Court, but released by the Lords of Appeal who held the Court of Admiralty to be without jurisdiction over the goods seized and proceeded against. The review was therefore based on a lack of jurisdiction.

The competence of the Admiralty in France in former periods presents the special feature of having been regulated differently prior and subsequent to 1695. In the period of 1674-1695 the Admiralty lacked jurisdiction to take cognizance of prizes made by a squadron of four or more of the King's warships (*Ordonnances* of 23 February 1674, 4 March 1684 and 15 April 1689, XXII, titre 1, and Instruction of 16 August 1692). This ruling was changed in 1695: the *Règlement* of 9 March of that year abolished that limitation; it has remained in force since then (*Règlements* of 12 May 1702, 12 February 1719, 2 November 1733 and 13 April 1744). During the first period the proceedings had to be carried out by the general "intendants" and commissaries of the Navy.

The competence of prize courts to take cognizance of specific claims also played a minor rôle in old French case law. See, *e.g.*, De Pistoye and Duverdy's *Traité*, vol. II, 445, *in re Avierino contre Thiébault* [1819]. In that case the *Conseil d'Etat* decided that the prize court had no competence to adjudicate on disputes of a private law nature between owners of vessels which had been involved in a joint capture over the partition of their respective *parts de prise*.

Another case is that of the *Christiane* [1854] (*ibid.*, II, 502): the *Conseil des prises* denied its competence to adjudicate on a claim that the captured crew should be set free.

A case in which both the absolute and the relative competence of a prize court were at issue was that of the *Abby* [1804] (5 C.Rob., 251; Roscoe, I, 464). This case related to the disputed competence of the Vice-Admiralty Court of Martinique to deal with a claim based on an offence against the common law of another island (Demerara). The case ended with a verdict of the appellate court that the competence, if it existed, had in any case ceased since the court on Martinique had in the meantime been abolished.

The above survey of the jurisdiction of prize courts in earlier days was confined to their absolute competence. Besides, their relative competence has occasionally given rise to controversy. A few examples of that aspect of their jurisdiction may suffice.

In the *Carel and Magdalena* [1797, 1800] (3 C.Rob., 58; Roscoe, I, 257) a Danish vessel, taken by the British at the capture of Dutch Demerara, remained there, but her papers were sent to the island of Martinique, where proceedings were commenced in the Vice-Admiralty Court of that island, and the ship was condemned. The High Court of Admiralty decided in appeal that:

> "it can never be maintained that the sentence of the Court of Martinique, upon a prize not brought within the sphere of the jurisdiction, is a valid sentence. It is a known distinction between the Courts of Vice-Admiralty and the High Court of Admiralty, that the former have only a local jurisdiction, confined to the adjudication of property brought within their own limits, whilst the authority of the High Court of Admiralty in prize matters extends over the whole of His Majesty's dominions, and operates in every port belonging to them."

The jurisdiction of the Vice-Admiralty Courts has since been put on a new footing, first by 41 Geo. 3, c. 99, and later by the *Naval Prize Act* (27 & 28 Vict., c. 25, sections 3 and 9). Section 4 of the same Act gave the High Court of Admiralty power to enforce a decree or order of a Vice-Admiralty Prize Court. This had already been admitted in the *Picimento* [1803] (4 C.Rob., 360; Roscoe, I, 406), the case of a Portuguese vessel, captured and brought to adjudication in the Vice-Admiralty Court at the Cape of Good Hope. This Court ordered the restitution of the prize, but before this order was executed, the Dutch settlement of the Cape was abandoned by the treaty of Amiens (1802) and the records of the Vice-Admiralty Court were deposited in the Registry of the High Court of Admiralty. This Court sustained its jurisdiction "to aid the process of the Vice-Admiralty Court in order to prevent a total failure of justice."

Technical procedural difficulties arose about 1800 in the case of several ships and cargoes carried into Santo Domingo and proceeded against there in a Court of Admiralty, which condemned them, but this Court was later held not to be vested with competent authority to proceed in prize cases. See the *Huldah* [1801] (3 C.Rob., 235; Roscoe, I, 303). The owners subsequently instituted original proceedings in the High Court of Admiralty, asking for a monition calling on the captors to proceed to adjudication, but they did not do that until a year and nine months after the sentence of condemnation had been passed in the Court of Santo Domingo. On the objection of the captors to this procedure after such a long delay the High Court of Admiralty held the petition admissible:

> "During the existence of the Prize Commission there is no fixed and definite time by which the party can be said to be legally barred from calling on the captor to proceed to adjudication ... I know of no prescribed [temporal] limitation against the admission of a claim ... If [captor] neglects to apply to any tribunal, he would be guilty of a great misdemeanour; if through misapprehension, he applies to an improper tribunal ... he cannot protect himself from the call of the claimant to proceed to adjudication before a competent tribunal. In this case there is no imputation of misconduct [neither by the captor nor by the claimant]. It might be a common error .... There existed something of a difficulty, a sort of cloud of uncertainty in the minds of persons as to the competence of the Court [of Santo Domingo] which might account for some part of the delay. However, the claimant has now applied to [the High Court of Admiralty] and I am of opinion that the Court is under the legal duty of admitting the claim and that it cannot relieve the captor from the obligation of proceeding to adjudication."

The case was accordingly heard on the merits.

Section 3. THE LAW TO BE APPLIED BY THE PRIZE COURTS. REPRISALS ORDERS

The question of the law, in particular the substantive law, to be applied by the prize courts is one of the most basic issues of the law of prizes, not only because its solution may decide the fate of the individual ships and cargoes seized, but also because it has had, as experience proves, an impact, which is hardly reversible, on the whole development of the law of prize.

It is self-evident that already in the oldest sources of prize law provisions must have been inserted concerning the rules which admiralty courts should apply in cases submitted to their jurisdiction. This was in fact the case.

Already in the 14th century, after 12 Edw. III (1339), the legislative authorities of England declared specific legal rules, which had been developed by local tribunals, the so-called "Judgments of the Sea" or Rôles d'Oléron, applicable as the law in maritime causes, and an "Inquisition" at Queensborough in 1375 put on record what exact customs in this field had been observed in the past and should continue to govern such causes in the future (comp. *supra*, pp. 20-21). France and other maritime Powers of the past have produced a spate of legislative enactments on the subject, some of which have even outlived the wear and tear of a few centuries.

Especially in England, the creation of legal rules has taken place in the course of centuries in the form of judge-made law and judicial precedents. Present-day international prize law, as a consequence, shows more than do other chapters of international law, the picture of a legacy of the past.

Since I have dealt with the various sources of the law of prize in Chapter I (*supra*, pp. 10 *et seq.*), I need not again expatiate in any detail in this section on the question of what rules of law the prize courts were bound or accustomed to apply in prize cases submitted to their judgment.

Among the topics relating to the applicable law in prize cases there are naturally also the usual problems of transitional law: the retro-activity of a treaty, the legal situation between the signature and the ratification or coming into force of a treaty, the applicability of an earlier or a later prize law, naval instruction or treaty, but I will not enter upon this general subject of intertemporal law here. Instances can be found in De Pistoye and Duverdy's *Traité des prises maritimes*, vol. I, pp. 129-130, 145-147 and 155, and the English case of the *Argos* [1854], *ibid.*, p. 132.

It was only in the course of time that two specific problems of a general nature emerged from the discussion during the adjudication of prize cases, *viz.*, (*a*) were the courts to apply national or international law and, in case of discrepancy between these two, which of the two prevailed?; (*b*) to what extent was a belligerent justified in deviating from the normal rules on the ground of reprisals?

The answer to the question *sub* (*a*) was far from unanimous owing to the fact that a fundamental difference of opinion determined the solution: whereas Anglo-American judicial doctrine clung, at least theoretically, to the thesis that the task of prize courts consisted of the application of the international law of nations, the continental doctrine inclined to the thesis that they were, as national tribunals, bound in principle by the rules enacted by their national legislative authorities.

The question *sub* (*b*) arose as a major issue in consequence of the reciprocal actions by Napoleon and his opponents, at the beginning of the 19th century. It was revived in the first phase of World War I.

Question (*a*). *Application of municipal law or the law of nations?*

As remarked above, the division of opinion in this respect hovered between the conception that prize courts were entrusted with the mission to adjudge the cases submitted to them by the rules and principles of international prize law, on the one hand, and the feeling that they were, in their capacity of national tribunals, bound to follow their national law, on the other.

This crucial question was discussed and summarily regulated by the *Institut de droit international* at its session of Heidelberg (1887). From section 13, *sub* A (Procès de prise), it appears that the *Institut* has resolutely opted for the duty of prize courts to decide prize cases in accordance with the rules of international law:

> "111.—Les tribunaux de prises sont obligés de juger d'après les règles du droit international".

The fundamental issue had already been discussed for centuries and would also drag on long into the post-codification period. It was especially during World War I that English and German prize courts would state their clear, though diverging, opinions on the subject.

The rôle of prize courts, in particular their attitude towards prize laws and decrees or naval instructions issued by their national authorities has become a matter of controversy both in doctrine and in court rooms during World War I. Whereas in particular the German prize courts as a matter of principle accepted their national *Prisenordnung* as binding upon them even where it might be contrary to international law, British prize courts, in particular, upheld at least the appearance of recognizing, also as a matter of principle, the supremacy of international over municipal prize law. The prize tribunals of other countries generally had nothing to say on this basic problem or were at least far less explicit on it. The attitude of prize courts was often ambivalent. Thus the Prize Court of Yokosuka (Japan) stated, on the one hand, "that the Regulations governing captures at sea of 22 February 1904 have no power to bind a prize court," but, on the other, that it "shall take them as a standard and shall give decisions so as not to conflict with the spirit of the Regulations".

The controversy can best be stated as follows: a prize court either considers itself as an organ of its State, bound to apply the national rules enacted by the legislature or the executive, or it understands its function as that of an impartial instance due to base its decisions exclusively on the law of nations. In practice, however, this fundamental divergence of views is not so absolute as it might appear at first sight. National prize tribunals of the first group are often forced to resort to customary international law in default of explicit municipal rules on a subject, or in order to interpret or complete existing municipal rules by what international custom prescribes. And admiralty courts of the second group are often found to pay no more than lip service to the principle professed, by means of an arbitrary identification of the municipal regulations with the rules prescribed by mandatory international law.

A striking formulation of the doctrine adhered to by the *Prisengericht* of Hamburg at the beginning of World War I regarded two Netherlands vessels, the *Batavier V* and the *Zaanstroom*, seized with their cargoes (*Ents*. I, 118). Without any reference to a specific legal issue, in entirely general terms and categorically, the *Prisengericht* declared that prize courts are national tribunals like all others, whose mandate it is to adjudicate the cases submitted to them in conformity with the rules enacted by their Sovereign without examining whether they accord with existing rules of international law. If they are not in harmony with the law of nations, international responsibility therefore falls, not on the courts, but on their State. An opposite view must be rejected as a matter of principle. This doctrine was couched in the following wording:

"Die Prisengerichte sind nationale Gerichte. Sie sind von ihrem Staate eingesetzt, um festzustellen, ob dessen den Seekrieg führende Organe diejenigen Normen, an die sie sich nach ihren Instruktionen halten sollen, beobachtet haben oder nicht, und um die hiernach gebotenen Folgerungen auszusprechen. Aus dieser ihrer Zweckbestimmung ergibt sich, dass sie nach dem von ihrem Staate gesetzten Rechte zu urteilen haben, gleichviel ob es mit

> bestehenden völkerrechtlichen Sätzen übereinstimmt oder nicht. Ob dies der Fall ist, hierüber zu urteilen, ist nicht Sache des Prisengerichts, sondern des kriegführenden Staates, der allein den anderen Staaten hierfür verantwortlich ist. Die in der älteren Literatur stellenweise vertretene Auffassung, dass die Prisengerichte internationales Recht anzuwenden hätten, auch dann, wenn es nicht Bestandteil ihres nationalen Rechtes geworden sei, ist also grundsätzlich abzulehnen."

That is to say: *iudex servus legis*, also in prize cases.

On the face of it, English judicial doctrine was diametrically opposed to this clear and uncompromising German theory, but one has to be cautious in one's interpretation of what it really means. A close analysis of the *Zamora* case (*B.C.P.C.* I, 309; appeal II, 1) is indispensable for that purpose. The *Zamora* was a Swedish vessel carrying a cargo of neutral-owned copper. This cargo was, at the demand of the Admiralty, requisitioned for the Crown in the first stage of the war against payment of its value. The Court of first instance allowed that requisition, but its decision was quashed in appeal by the Judicial Committee of the Privy Council on the ground that the law of nations did not, in the given circumstances, permit the requisitioning of neutral goods and that basing such a measure on an Order in Council permitting it was vain since the Crown lacks the power of derogating from the prescripts of the law of nations to the detriment of neutrals. This judgment in appeal started from the principle that

> "The Prize Court must ascertain and give effect to a law which is not laid down by any particular State but originates in the practice and usage long observed by civilised nations in their relations towards each other or in express international agreement."

It further proclaimed two important additional principles. The first was

(*a*) that, although a prize court is not bound, and is even forbidden, to obey Orders in Council diverging from international law to the detriment of neutrals, it is doubtless obliged to obey such Orders when the Crown, in virtue of its prerogative of bounty, renounces thereby part of its rights in their favour.

The second was

(*b*) that "it is not disputable that a Prize Court, like any other Court, is bound by the legislative enactments of its own State".

The first of these two practical consequences of the doctrine formulated by the Judicial Committee of the Privy Council in the *Zamora* case was subsequently applied in many other cases, *e.g.* in that of the Netherlands vessel *Alwina* (*B.C.P.C.* II, 186; appeal III, 54), in which Sir Samuel Evans concluded his detailed argument against the vessel by holding that

> "If the law was as I have stated, [the] provisions [of the Orders in Council of 20 August and 29 October 1914] do not operate in extension of it, but, if anything, as a mitigation of the captor's rights. Therefore, according to the Zamora, they are not invalid."

At a later stage, the official judicial doctrine was still complemented with a third principle to the effect

(*c*) that derogation from mandatory rules of international law is permitted even against neutrals when there is just cause for the taking of reprisals against a law-breaking enemy. I basically reject that additional thesis as a clear violation of international law by the British prize courts.

What, in conclusion, remains of the high-sounding principles that a British court of prize is an organ of international and not of municipal law? Disappointingly little. Apart from the first of the three rules stated above (applicability of Orders in Council that mitigate international rules in favour of neutrals), which is perfectly acceptable, and from the third (permissibility of derogations from international law, even to the detriment of neutrals, on the ground of breaches of that law by the enemy), which is wholly rejectable, the evaluation of the veracity of the British doctrine centers on the second of the three rules, *viz.*, that even a British prize court is bound by enactments of its national legislature, Acts of Parliament. The whole theory of respect of British prize courts for international law is then seen to shrivel from a basic axiom relative to the supremacy of the law of nations over municipal law to a simple rule of British constitutional law denying to the Crown the power of acting against the law of nations, a power which is thus reserved to the British Parliament. The fact that, as some British courts have stated in express terms, they would, by applying such Acts of Parliament, divest themselves of their proper function of courts of prize, does not detract from the conclusion that the whole profession of reverence for international law in the accomplishment of their task is of doubtful veracity. This truth is sometimes veiled, but again in vain, by an attempt to identify British prize law with the law of nations.

It thus appears that, whereas the German doctrine—erroneous in its basic attitude—is at least logical in the conclusions drawn therefrom, the English doctrine—correct in its basic attitude—becomes illogical and untrue as a result of the restrictions placed on its application.

Looking at the subject matter discussed above from an historical aspect, one is bound to state that the establishment of courts of admiralty has always had the purpose of guaranteeing that the exercise of the rights of visit and seizure at sea would remain within the bounds of international law as recognized at the time. Treaty provisions can be quoted by which the Contracting Parties agreed on the setting-up of an impartial jurisdiction over prize cases. See, for instance, the provisions quoted in Chapter III C (section 8, p. 665) from treaties of 1662, 1674 and 1679.

When, in January 1763, a Commission appointed by the King of England to formulate a defense against the complaints by the King of Prussia about the illegal capture of Prussian merchant ships by the British Navy, delivered its report, it declared in express terms that

> "any notion of a Prize Court being bound by the Executive Orders of the Crown, or having to administer municipal as opposed to international law, is contrary to the best legal opinion of the day."

As Lord Stowell is known to have said, half a century later in the case of the *Maria No. 1* [1799] (1 C.Rob., 340, at 350), that it was his duty to recognize only those claims of England to the prejudice of neutral Sweden which he would recognize under the same circumstances as appertaining to a belligerent Sweden against a neutral Great Britain, since " the law itself has no locality ". Nevertheless, even Lord Stowell could not bring himself to declaring Orders in Council null and void on account of inconsistency with the law of nations: he indeed evaded such a question by saying that he could not admit a contradiction between Orders in Council and the law of nations, and that it was not fitting for him to suppose such an eventuality. See on this point also, in great detail, Bourguignon in his *Sir William Scott—Lord Stowell*, at pp. 219-222 and 264-273.

In accordance with which law—international or national—,then, must the correctness or incorrectness of the opposing theories outlined above be judged? It seems clear that the national law of the Court concerned cannot be the measuring rod for the solution of this specific question. Nor can theoretical reasoning give an authoritative answer to this problem of positive international law. The only standard by which it might be resolved is international law itself. In that light the question poses the following dilemma: does the positive law of nations leave this basic issue—the essential task of a prize court—to the exclusive competence (domestic jurisdiction) of each belligerent State, or does it give a solution itself, and if so, in what sense? However much I should like to feel able to answer that, according to international law a prize court is a *servus iuris gentium*, I am afraid that I cannot do it because we are faced in this field by a disappointing lacuna, attributable to the regrettable uncertainty of the law. It is juridically imaginable that a neutral State during or after a war seizes the International Court of Justice of a legal action against a belligerent State with the object of obtaining from it a judgment on whether the latter was entitled under international law to have its prize courts adjudicate upon seizures in accordance with its national regulations, irrespective of their conformity with the law of nations, but such an action is highly improbable and would perhaps result in a *non liquet*.

The theory developed by the Judicial Committee of the Privy Council made it necessary for British prize courts, when the occasion arose, to examine whether a specific Order in Council constituted an extension or a mitigation of the traditional rights of belligerents vis-à-vis neutrals. This examination was made in a number of cases, interesting from the standpoint of historico-legal history. When analysing the intrinsic value of the reasoning laid down in these judicial pronouncements, one has, however, always to bear in mind that the " law of nations " by which the admissibility of the Orders in Council concerned was tested was not a generally accepted body of international prize law, but a specific British variant of it, based on British precedents and not seldom contradicted by national conceptions of the law of nations in matters of prize, fostered by other States—a curious identification of a British "law of nations" with a general international law, to the fallacy of which identification British prize courts seem not to be completely blind, and a distinct overestimation of the supposedly unique contribution of British prize courts to the historical development of this branch of international law. A critical comparison of the widely diverging views, expressed in the memoranda submitted by the various governments to the London Conference on Naval Warfare regarding the pre-codification state of the law of prize should have taught them better.

See for more details and prize judgments my "La jurisprudence des prises et le droit des gens" in the *Annuaire Grotius* of 1917.

Question (b). The legal permissibility of reprisals which run counter to the law of nations

British prize jurisprudence has developed a doctrine of its own relative to the admissibility of reprisals which, though in the first place directed against the enemy, were in their side-effects highly detrimental to neutrals. This method of warfare reached its climax during the wars of Revolutionary France at the end of the 18th century and the beginning of the 19th century.

Reprisals were by no means unknown in naval warfare before that period. They date back to earlier wars, the Seven Years' War of 1756 and the American War of Independence of 1776. Roscoe, in his collection of prize cases from 1745 onward, mentions, for example, two British Orders of Reprisals, of 29 July 1778 as against France and of 18 June 1779 as against Spain (comp. his chronological table in vol. I, pp. vii-ix).

One such declaration of reprisals, of 29 July 1778 against France, was referred to by Sir J. Marriott in his judgment of 11 January 1779 in the case of the Swedish ship the *Maria Magdalena* [1779] (Hay & Marriott, 247; Roscoe, I, 20).

This ship was captured when sailing from London to Nantes. Should the cargo have reached it, then it would have become the property of French citizens, but having been seized at sea it had remained the property of the British consignors. There was no British declaration of war as yet against France but only a declaration of general reprisals. This was, however, held by the Court to be equivalent, as to its legal effects, to a declaration of war. The cargo was condemned in accordance with the British Declaration of Reprisals of 29 July 1778.

See also the earlier judgment of 9 December 1778 in the *Renard* (Hay & Marriott, 222; Roscoe, I, 17), a case of recapture of a British ship from the French, in which one reads:

> "In the present case, the state of hostilities [there was no Act in force relative to recaptures from the French] is more favourable to the claimant than a declared war. What is declared, then? Reprisals upon the French King, his subjects, and the inhabitants of his territories.

> But British subjects generally ... are not to make reprisals upon one another; there is no authority for that."

Later Orders of the same purport were issued on 14 February 1793 against France, on 15 September 1795 against Holland, and on 9 November 1796 against Spain. An example of a much later date is that of an Order in Council against Russia of 29 March 1854 (*B.F.S.P.*, vol. 46, p. 37).

On her side, during her Revolutionary Wars at the end of the 18th century, France did the same. The French doctrine in this field was set out in an *Arrêté* of the *Directoire Exécutif* of 2 July 1796 (Martens, R^2, V, 388), by which that body,

> "considérant que s'il est de la loyauté française de respecter les traités ou conventions qui assurent aux puissances neutres ou amies des avantages commerciaux dont le résultat doit être commun aux puissances contractantes, ces mêmes avantages, s'ils tournoient au bénéfice de nos ennemis, soit par la faiblesse de nos alliés ou des neutres, soit par la crainte, par des vues d'intérêt ou par tout autre motif, provoqueroient de fait l'inexécution des articles en vertu desquels ils seroient stipulés",

introduced a system of reciprocity in actual fact by reprisals:

> "Il sera notifié sans délai à toutes les puissances neutres ou alliées, que le pavillon de la République française en usera envers les bâtiments neutres, soit pour la confiscation, soit pour la visite ou préhension, de la même manière qu'elles souffrent que les Anglais en usent à leur égard".

The question of the validity or otherwise of Orders in Council which proclaimed reprisals against illegal actions of the enemy which by their effects violated the rights of neutral States and their subjects was for the first time seriously discussed at length during the period of the Napoleonic wars (1807-1810). It was debated at the time in the British Parliament and assessed by legal writers. Almost all the views expressed by British authorities tended to defend their validity and no judgment of any British Prize Court can, it seems, be cited against it. Several cases were decided in the central British Prize Court and the colonial Prize Courts in the period 1809-1811. In all cases the sentences of condemnation were sustained in appeal, and in none of them was there a pronouncement against the legality of the Orders in Council concerned.

Before summarizing the reasoning laid down in the British case law dating from the first early 19th century wave of reprisals, I will first give a survey of the actual content of the French measures and the English countermeasures, which together established the so-called "Continental System".

The whole series of Ordinances and Decrees which led to the establishment of this "System" in the period 1806-1810 can be found in Martens, N.R., I, 433-549 under the letters *a-z* and *aa-ww*. It still begins with a declaration of the British Government of 21 May 1806 (N.R., I, 438) to the effect that British warships and other commissioned vessels should not arrest and seize any ship navigating on the Baltic Sea. The series then continues with the French Decree of Berlin of 21 November 1806 (*ibid.*, 439), which provoked the first series of reprisals; the English counter-declaration against blockades to the detriment of neutrals of 7 January 1807 (*ibid.*, 444) and certain further English countermeasures of 11 and 25 November 1807 (*ibid.*, 446 and 449); Napoleon's second Decree of 17 December 1807, known as the Decree of Milan (*ibid.*, 452); and Prussia's rupture with England of 1 December 1807 after the Franco-Prussian Peace Treaty of Tilsit (*ibid.*, 454). The United States joined in the struggle between belligerents and neutrals by putting an embargo on all merchant vessels in its harbours (*Embargo Act* of 22 December 1807, complemented on 9 March 1808; *ibid.*, 459).

The French Decree, which started it all, was Napoleon's Decree of Berlin of 21 November 1806 (*B.F.S.P.*, vol. 1820-1821, 466; Edw., App. vii, viii). This Decree ran as follows:

"Napoleon, Emperor of the French, and King of Italy.

Considering,

1. That England does not acknowledge the laws generally observed by all civilised nations.

2. That she regards every individual as an enemy who belongs to an enemy's state, and consequently makes prisoners of war, not only of the crews of ships of war, but also of the crews of merchant vessels, and even supercargoes and merchants who are proceeding in their course of trade.

3. That she extends to merchant ships, and to wares, and to property of private persons, that right of conquest which ought only to be applied to property belonging to the hostile states.

4. That she extends the right of blockade to commercial unfortified towns, and to ports, harbours, and mouths of rivers, which, according to the principles and practice of all civilised nations, is only applicable to fortified places.

That she declares places in a state of blockade, before which she has not a ship of war, though no place can be considered in a state of blockade, unless it is so invested, that approach cannot be attempted without imminent danger.

That she even declares places in a state of blockade, which, with all her forces united, she is incapable of blockading, namely, whole coasts and empires.

5. That this monstrous abuse of the right of blockade has no other object than to obstruct the communication of nations with each other, and to raise the trade and the industry of England, upon the ruin of the trade and industry of the nations of the continent.

6. That, since such is the object of England, whoever is concerned in the commerce of English merchandise on the continent, thereby favours her views, and becomes her accomplice.

7. That this conduct on the part of England, which is only worthy of the earliest ages of barbarism, has redounded to the advantage of that state, and to the injury of all others.

8. That it is a natural right to oppose an enemy with the same weapons he employs, and to combat him by the same means which he employs against others, especially when that enemy disclaims all ideas of justice, and all the liberal sentiments, which have resulted from the civilisation of mankind.

We have resolved to direct against England the same system which she has established by her maritime code. The regulations of the present decree shall therefore be henceforth considered as forming a fundamental law of the empire, until England shall acknowledge that the right of war is the same by land as by sea that it does not extend to private property, of any kind whatever, or to the persons of individuals unconnected with the profession of arms, and that the right of blockade is limited to fortified places, actually invested by a sufficient force. We have therefore decreed, and do hereby decree, as follows:

Article 1. The British Isles are declared in a state of blockade.

2. All trade and all correspondence with the British Isles are prohibited.

Consequently, all letters or packets that are addressed to England, or to Englishmen, or which are written in the English language, shall not henceforth be forwarded by post, but shall be seized.

3. Every individual English subject, of whatever rank or condition, who shall be found in any country occupied by our troops, or the troops of our allies, shall be considered as a prisoner of war.

4. Every magazine, every kind of merchandise, every species of property, be it what it may, which belongs to an English subject, shall be considered as lawful prize.

5. Trade in English merchandise, every species of property, be it what it may, which belongs to an English subject, shall be considered as lawful prize.

5. Trade in English merchandise is prohibited; and all merchandise that belongs to England, or that is the produce of her manufactures or colonies, is declared lawful prize.

6. A moiety of the produce of the confiscated property, which, by the foregoing articles, is declared lawful prize, shall be appropriated to the merchants, to indemnity them for the loss they have sustained from the capture of their merchant vessels by English cruisers.

7. No ship which comes direct from England, or the English colonies, or which shall have been there, after the publication of the present decree, shall be permitted to enter any of our harbours.

8. Every ship trading by means of a false declaration, in contravention of the above-mentioned regulations, shall be detained, and the ship and lading shall be confiscated, as if they were English property.

9. Our Tribunal des Prises at Paris is invested with the power of definitively deciding all questions which may arise within our empire, or in the countries occupied by the French armies, in respect to the execution of our present decree. Our Tribunal des Prises at Milan is invested with the power of definitively deciding such questions as may arise within the limits of our Kingdom of Italy."

It was this Decree of Berlin that was countered by the first British Order in Council of 7 January 1807 (*B.F.S.P.* vol. 1820-1821, p. 468; French translation in Martens, N.R., I, 444), and which, reciprocating the French accusations by listing the violations of the law of nations committed by France and expressing H.M.'s "unwillingness to follow the example of France by proceeding to an extremity so distressing to all Nations not engaged in the war, and carrying on their accustomed trade", yet disposed that

"no Vessel shall be permitted to trade from one Port to another, both of which Ports shall belong to or be in the possession of France or her Allies, or shall be so far under their control as that British Vessels may not freely trade thereat: And the Commanders of His Majesty's Ships of War and Privateers shall be, and are hereby instructed to warn every Neutral Vessel coming from any such Port, and destined to another such Port, to discontinue her voyage, and not to proceed to any such Port; and any Vessel after being so warned, or any Vessel coming from any such Port, after a reasonable time shall have been afforded for receiving information of this His Majesty's Order, which shall be found proceeding to another such Port, shall be captured and brought in, and, together with her cargo, shall be condemned as lawful prize".

A second Order in Council, of 11 November 1807 (*B.F.S.P.*, vol. 1820-1821, p. 469; French translation in Martens, N.R., I, 466)—shortly afterwards modified and supplemented by four very detailed Orders of 25 November 1807 (*B.F.S.P.*, vol. 1820-1821, pp. 475-485, under 7A, 7B, 7C and 7D; French translation in Martens, N.R., I, 449)—elaborated the British countermeasures by declaring the ports of France and of all countries, from which the British flag was excluded, in a state of blockade.

The next step was again taken by Napoleon, who, by his Decree of Milan of 17 December 1807 (Martens, N.R., I, 452; *B.F.S.P.*, vol. 1820-1821, p. 482), ordered measures by way of reciprocity as follows:

"Napoléon, Empereur des Français, Roi d'Italie, et Protecteur de la Confédération du Rhin.

Vu les dispositions arrêtées par le gouvernement Britannique, en date du 11 Novembre dernier, qui assujettissent les bâtiments des puissances neutres, amies et même alliées de l'Angleterre, non seulement à une visite par les croisseurs Anglois, mais encore à une station obligée en Angleterre, et à une imposition arbitraire de tant pour cent sur leur chargement, qui doit être réglée par la législation Angloise; considérant que par ces actes le gouvernement Anglois a dénationalisé les bâtiments de toutes les nations de l'Europe; qu'il n'est au pouvoir d'aucun gouvernement de transiger sur son indépendance et sur ses droits, tous les souverains de l'Europe étant solidaires de la souveraineté et de l'indépendance de leur pavillon; que si, par une foiblesse inexcusable, et qui seroit une tache ineffaçable aux yeux de la postérité, on laissoit passer en principe et consacrer par l'usage une pareille tyrannië, les Anglais en prendroient acte pour l'établir en droit, comme ils ont profité de la tolérance des gouvernements pour établir l'infame principe, que le pavillon ne couvre pas la marchandise, et pour donner à leur droit de blocus une extension arbitraire et attentatoire à la souveraineté de tous les états; Nous avons décrété et décrétons ce qui suit:

Art. I. Tout bâtiment, de quelque nation qu'il soit, qui aura souffert la visite d'un vaisseau Anglois, ou se sera soumis à un voyage en Angleterre ou aura payé une imposition quelconque au gouvernement Anglois, est par cela seul déclaré dénationalisé, a perdu la garantie de son pavillon et est devenu propriété Angloise.

Art. II. Soit que lesdits bâtimens ainsi dénationalisés par les mesures arbitraires du gouvernement Anglois, entrent dans nos ports ou dans ceux de nos alliés, soit qu'ils tombent au pouvoir de nos vaisseaux de guerre ou de nos corsaires, ils sont déclarés de bonne et valable prise.

Art. III. Les isles Britanniques sont déclarées en état de blocus sur mer comme sur terre. Tout bâtiment, de quelque nation qu'il soit, quelque soit son chargement, expédié des ports d'Angleterre ou des colonies Angloises, ou de pays occupés par les troupes Angloises, ou allant en Angleterre, ou dans les colonies Angloises, ou dans des pays occupés par les troupes Angloises, est de bonne prise, comme contrevenant au présent décret; il sera capturé par nos vaisseaux de guerre, ou par nos corsaires, et adjugé au capteur.

Art. IV. Ces mesures, qui ne sont qu'une juste réciprocité pour le système barbare adopté par le gouvernement Anglois, qui assimile sa législation à celle d'Alger, cesseront d'avoir leur effet pour toutes les nations qui sauroient obliger le gouvernement Anglois à respecter leur pavillon. Elles continueront d'être en vigueur pendant tout le tems que ce gouvernement ne reviendra pas aux principes du droit des gens, qui règle les relations des états civilisés dans l'état de guerre; les dispositions du présent décret seront abrogées et nulle par le fait, dès que le gouvernement Anglois sera revenu aux principes du droit des gens qui sont aussi ceux de la justice et de l'honneur.

Art. V. Tous nos ministres sont chargés de l'exécution du présent décret, qui sera inséré au bulletin des lois."

The French measures reached their climax in 1810, when on 19 October, an Imperial Decree (Martens, N.R., I, 322) ordered all English merchandise to be seized and burnt.

I now turn to the case law respecting war reprisals, confining myself for the moment to the first historical wave of such reprisals by illustrating by a number of extracts from the early judgments of the beginning of the 19th century the arguments with which British prize courts of the period considered themselves justified in declaring clearly illegal acts legal. The early case law comprised two elements: (*a*) a prize court was held incompetent to judge whether there was sufficient ground for the enactment of reprisals against the enemy: in that respect the court was bound by the decision of the Government; (*b*) it was, however, competent to assess the inconvenience caused by the reprisals to neutrals, as compared with the seriousness of the injury committed by the enemy. The legal situation was elaborately expressed in Lord Stowell's judgment in the case of the *Fox and others* [1811] (Edw., 311; Roscoe, II, 61), American cornships captured on 15 November 1810 during a voyage from Boston to Cherbourg, in virtue of the Reprisals Order in Council of 26 April 1809, on the ground of their destination being a French port. The situation in that case was as follows.

The claimants, supported by the U.S. Government, did not directly attack the legality or validity of the Reprisals Orders, but argued (i) that these had become extinct, professedly founded as they were upon measures which the enemy himself had already retracted; (ii) that, even if they were to be considered as being still in force, considerations of equity required the exoneration of the owners. Although the Court was, therefore, not strictly called upon to enter into an assessment of the legality and validity of the Orders, yet it did so, and in the course of its argument expatiated on such questions as: its duty towards Orders in Council, on the one hand, and the general law of nations, on the other; the extent of its freedom to deviate from Orders in Council, either accused by the claimants of being at variance with general international law, or invoked by them as mitigation of the more severe rules of that law; its liberty to engage in an independent inquiry of whether there was sufficient cause for the issuance of the reprisals, and whether these had perhaps meanwhile ceased to be operative as the automatic result of the retraction by the enemy of his illegal measures of warfare. The judgment in the *Fox* case is too long to be reproduced *in extenso*, but its significance as a stage in the history of prize law is so great that I will quote below, but not in exactly the same sequence, its most characteristic passages, also in view of the respect, which this judgsment has continued to enjoy in World War I. Those passages indeed demonstrate a juristic rope-dance act, perfectly performed.

> "What would be the duty of the Court under Orders in Council that were repugnant to the law of nations? It has been contended on one side, that the Court would at all events

> be bound to enforce the Orders in Council; on the other, that the Court would be bound to apply the rule of the law of nations adapted to the particular case, in disregard of the Orders in Council. I have not observed, however, that these Orders in Council, in their retaliatory character, have been described in the arguments as at all repugnant to the law of nations, however liable to be so described if merely original and abstract. And therefore it is rather to correct possible misapprehensions on the subject than from the sense of any obligation which the present discussion imposes upon me, that I observe that this Court is bound to administer the law of nations to the subjects of other countries in the different relations in which they may be placed towards this country and its government. This is what other countries have a right to demand for their subjects, and to complain if they receive it not. This is its unwritten law evidenced in the course of its decisions, and collected from the common usage of civilized States. At the same time it is strictly true, that by the constitution of this country, the King in Council possesses legislative rights over this Court, and has power to issue orders and instructions which it is bound to obey and enforce; and these constitute the written law of this Court. These two propositions ... are not at all inconsistent with each other; because these Orders and instructions are presumed to conform themselves, under the given circumstances, to the principles of unwritten law. They are either direct applications of those principles to the cases indicated in them ..., or they are positive regulations, consistent with those principles, applying to matters which require more exact and definite rules than those general principles are capable of furnishing. [The Court further draws a comparison here with the position of Courts of Common Law vis-à-vis Acts of Parliament] ... The Court will not let itself loose into speculations as to what would be its duty under such an emergency, because it cannot, without extreme indecency, presume that any such emergency will happen; .... In the particular case of the orders and instructions which give rise to the present question, the Court has not heard it at all maintained in argument, that as retaliatory orders they are not conformable to such principles, for retaliatory they are. They are so declared in their own language, and in the uniform language of the government which has established them. I have no hesitation in saying that they would cease to be just if they ceased to be retaliatory; and they would cease to be retaliatory from the moment the enemy retracts in a sincere manner those measures of his which they were intended to retaliate."

The judgment dealt in fact for the greater part with the alleged revocation by France of her illegal original Decrees: even if the Court were in a position to ascertain such French action in its own lights, it could find no trace of such a revocation. An inquiry ordered during a suspension of the proceedings for that purpose was without success.

> "And till the State revokes [the original Decrees] this Court is bound to presume that the necessity [of the reprisals] continues to exist. It cannot, without extreme indecency, suppose that they would continue a moment longer than the necessity which produced them .... Their establishment was doubtless a great and signal departure from the ordinary administration of justice in the ordinary state of the exercise of public hostility, but was justified by that extraordinary deviation from the common exercise of hostility in the conduct of the enemy."

Lord Stowell stressed especially the novelty of the Orders in Council: the magnitude, the complexity, the extraordinary nature of the facts to which they owed their origin, the attention which they called for and excited both at home and abroad, and the pledges given by England and accepted by other States.

The Court further observed that "it would not have been within its competence to have applied originally such extraordinary rules because it was hardly possible for it to possess that distinct and certain information of the facts to which alone they were justly applicable."

The justification for retaliatory measures operating also against neutrals was restated in the following wording, which is anything but convincing:

> "Neutrals are prohibited to trade with France because they are prohibited by France from trading with England. England acquires the right, which it would not otherwise possess, to prohibit that intercourse by virtue of the act of France. Having so acquired it, it exercises it to its full extent with entire competence of legal authority."

The whole reasoning of the Court fails to convince any non-British lawyer that an injustice perpetrated by belligerent A against innocent neutrals gives belligerent B the "right" to commit a corresponding injustice against them: a nice and comfortable "right" which a belligerent State arrogates to itself to violate the unquestionable rights of fellow States under the law of nations on the strength of violations of that same law, committed by its enemy!

The *Fox* case is indeed a clear demonstration of the liberty which English prize courts deemed themselves justified in sanctioning at the expense of the innocent, and in no way accessory, neutrals in order to be in a position to cover and excuse unlawful counter-measures by their Government against equally unlawful measures of the French Government. The *Fox* judgment makes the solemn protestation by Sir William Scott in the case of the Swedish *Maria* (Paulsen, Master) [1799] (1 C.Rob., 340 *et seq.*, at pp. 350-351, with footnote at pp. 340-342) sound as mere lip-service to a high principle:

> "It is the duty of the person who sits here to determine the question exactly as he would determine the same question if sitting in Stockholm;—to assert no pretensions on the part of Great Britain which he would not allow to Sweden in the same circumstances, and to impose no duties on Sweden, as a neutral country, which he would not admit to belong to Great Britain in the same character. If, therefore, I mistake the law in this matter, I mistake that which I consider, and which I mean should be considered, as the universal law upon the question: a question regarding one of the most important rights of belligerent nations relatively to neutrals."

After having finally given a negative answer to the question "whether there were any circumstances addressed to equitable consideration that could relieve the claimants from the penal effect of the Orders"—they had been duly warned against trading with France—the Court condemned the *Fox* as good and lawful prize. Even the argument that British vessels themselves were often authorized to trade with France under a licence was ignored as a ground for exonerating the American vessel. Although the President agreed that a blockade, imposed for the purpose of obtaining a commercial monopoly for the private advantage of the State which lays on such blockade, was illegal and void on the very principle upon which it was founded, he was not aware that any such trade between English subjects and France was generally permitted despite the licences which had been granted, not to Britains alone but also to foreigners. Moreover, the Order did not institute an original, independent act of blockade, but was in this instance "a counteracting reflex measure, compelled by the act of the enemy, and as such subject to other considerations arising out of its peculiarly distinctive character."

In the course of its argument the Court laid down a further principle which was echoed in many subsequent prize court decisions, also during World War I:

> "The Court might, from motives of forbearance, or even of policy unmixed with any injustice to other States, have adopted a more indulgent rule than the law of nations would authorize, though it is not at liberty ever to apply a harsher rule than that law warrants."

Here the Court refers to two older cases in which it was free to deviate from stricter rules, *viz*., that of the *Swedish convoy* (= *Maria No. 1* [1799]) and that of the *Lucy* [1809] (Edw., 122), in the latter of which the Order in Council subjected to confiscation all ships transferred by the enemy to neutrals during the war, but the Court—in accordance for the rest, with a similar rule adopted by the enemy—decided that these general terms did not extend to prize ships so transferred by the enemy.

Fr. Th. Pratt summarized the views held at the time on the subject of the permissibility of such reprisals at pp. lxvii-lxviii of his *Law of Contraband of War* as follows:

> "The case of the *Fox and others* was that of several American vessels brought in for condemnation, under the Orders of Council of the 26th April, 1809, imposing a blockade on all parts and places under the Government of France, and which were issued in retaliation of the violent measures adopted by that government against the commerce of this country. The Court expressed its opinion that, as retaliatory measures, they were strictly conformable to the principles of the law of nations, and that it rested with the Government to declare when such orders should be revoked, in consequence of a change in the conduct of the enemy. Till the State revokes these, the Court is bound to presume that the necessity continues to exist, and to enforce their execution [the *Courier*, Edw., 249].
>
> In the similar and subsequent case of the *Snipe and others* [Edw., 381] the same question came before the Court, and the validity of the Orders in Council was upheld on the same grounds.
>
> When, however, the conformity of the proceedings of the Government to the principles of International Law was not so evident, the Court would hardly consider it consistent with the respect due to its own government to imagine that any conduct repugnant to these principles could be adopted by it, and would rather consider it to be a question for negotiation between the neutral government and that of the captors.
>
> Such would appear to have been the case with the American corn ships in the year 1795.
>
> In the month of April of that year an Order in Council had been issued, directing British cruisers to stop and detain all vessels laden, wholly or in part, with corn, flour, meal, and other articles of provision, and bound to any port in France.
>
> Under this order several seizures of American vessels were made, the legality of which became the subject of discussion before a mixed Commission, and ultimately full indemnification was allowed by the commissioners to the claimants [Wheaton, *International Law*, p. 561]."

Bourguignon also gave ample attention to Sir William Scott's handling of the *Fox* case. See his *Sir William Scott—Lord Stowell* on pp. 220-223 and 269-273.

Reprisals Orders have often been applied by British prize courts, without such an application necessarily implying a violation of neutral rights. See, for example, the decisions in the cases of the American *Comet* [1808] (Edw., 32; Roscoe, II, 10), the *Mercurius* (Harmens, Master) under Bremen colours [1808] (Edw., 53; Roscoe, II, 15), the Prussian *Speculation* (Koht, Master) (Edw., 184), the *Nymph* [1810] (*Appeal Cases in Prize Cases*, vol. 42, p. 58), the American *Snipe and others* [1812] (Edw., 381) and the *Arthur* [1814] (1 Dods., 423).

Sometimes the decrees of the prize courts were not concerned with the validity of the Reprisals Orders under international law, but with their interpretation. See, *e.g.*, the case of the *Fenix* (or *Phoenix*) during the Crimean War [1854] (Spinks, 1; Roscoe, II, 238).

Occasionally it happened that a Reprisals Order in Council, invoked by the captors, was brushed aside as basis of the decision because of its mistaken construction by the captors. This caused the release in 1810 of an American ship, the *Luna* (Edw., 190; Roscoe, II, at p. 449), which had been seized during a voyage from New York to San Sebastián. The Order of 26 April 1809, which declared a strict blockade "of all ports and places under the Government of France", was held not to extend to San Sebastián in Spain, even though it was militarily occupied by French forces.

Section 4. PROCEDURE IN PRIZE CASES

Rules on the procedure in prize cases belong to the oldest codified rules of prize law. They were often still in an embryonic form. As I have set out in Chapter I on the sources of the law of maritime prize, such rules already existed early on.

This has remained so in later centuries. Rules on procedure formed even more often than not the main—if not the only—content of municipal prize ordinances even in countries where the substantive law of prize was not so laid down.

See for France the *Ordonnance* of King Charles V the Wise (1364-1380) "sur le faict de l'Admirauté" of 7 December 1373 (often erroneously dated 1400) and the *Edit* of March 1584 "concernant la juridiction de l'Admirauté de France", and further references to ancient customs and usages of the sea in Chr. Robinson's *Collectanea maritima* of 1801, pp. 75 *et seq.*, respectively pp. 105 *et seq.* Other French regulations were inserted in the *Ordonnance de la Marine* of August 1681, *livre* 14; a number of *décrets*, *arrêtés*, *règlements*, etc., dating from the end of the 18th and the beginning of the 19th century, such as the *Arrêté* of 2 prairial *an* XI relative to the procedure in prize cases before the then existing *Conseil des Prises* (set up by an *Arrêté* of 6 germinal *an* VIII); *Règlement* of the *Conseil Impérial des Prises* of 4 June 1859.

Many details concerning the procedure in prize cases before English Admiralty Courts in the last decade of the 18th century and the first half of the 19th century up to the Crimean War can be found in the edition by F. Th. Pratt (London, 1854) of the *Notes* of Judge Joseph Story (1779-1845) *on the principles and practice of Prize Courts ... with a selection of documents and forms, as used in the High Court of Admiralty of England*, with an Appendix to Wheaton's *Admiralty Reports*, vols. I and II, in which the *Notes* were originally published (pp. 13-126; 127-259), especially pp. 175 *et seq.*, 201 *et seq.* They relate to such matters as: a standing commission to examine in preparatory; standing interrogatories; depositions of witnesses; instruments of protest; institution of the suit; evidence; rejection or adjudication of the claim; violation of territory; droits of Admiralty; act of Court; (libel of) appeal (proceedings).

See for the Rules of the Admiralty Court "as determined on 22 February 1664 and 22 May 1672", F. Th. Pratt's *The Law of Contraband* (1856), Appendix B, pp. 249, respectively 251.

The prize courts of Japan and Russia during their Far Eastern War of 1904-1905, have also taken it for granted that they were competent to judge their own competence to take cognizance of the cases brought before them and in particular those of Japan have repeatedly acted accordingly. Their national legislation sometimes emphatically precluded them from dealing with certain classes of claims, whereas in respect of various other classes they could decide according to their own lights.

It is hardly worthwhile quoting the whole series of cases in which the Japanese courts have in fact delivered decrees of inadmissibility or the arguments with which they have contrived to decline or elude the adjudication of claims submitted to them. They can be found in Hurst & Bray's collection, especially at pp. xxii-xxv of their Digest of Cases in vol. II under the heading "Practice". I therefore restrict myself to citing a few of those arguments or subterfuges (the references are to the pages in their collection of texts): use of a language other than Japanese (19); presentation by an attorney other than a Japanese advocate (26) or by one without a formal power of attorney (38, 75); absence of signatures required (19); presentation by someone without personal interest (57), for example, by a consular officer in his capacity of protector of the interests of the subjects of his country (27); presentation by telegram (75, 92); disregard of time limits (21, 92). Their arguments were sometimes brought forward as relating to their own competence rather than to the admissibility of the claim.

A selection from the many British judgments concerning matters of procedure follows below.

There are in particular two principles which dominated the procedural scene of English case law, *viz.*,

(*a*) the very restricted *jus standi in judicio* of enemy subjects;
(*b*) the overriding duty of claimants to act *bona fide*.

ad (*a*) One of the formulations of this principle ran as follows:

> "Our Courts of the Law of Nations are so far British Courts, that no man can sue therein who is a subject of the enemy, unless under particular circumstances that *pro hac vice* discharge him from the character of an enemy; such as his coming under a flag of truce, a cartel, a pass, or some other act of public authority that puts him in the King's peace *pro hac vice*": the *Hoop* [1779] (1 C.Rob. 196, at p. 201; Roscoe, I, 104).

A claimant had therefore to invoke a specific Order in Council or a licence.

ad (*b*) This principle was expressed in the case of the *Maria (No. 2)* [1857] (11 Moore 271; Roscoe, II, 616) as follows:

> "In case of doubt about the national character of a ship, claimed to be the property of a neutral, the rule of the Court was decreed to be that the claimant should produce strict proof of ownership, and that any case of fraud or contrivance or attempt of imposition on the Court in making out his title was fatal to the claimant".

In the *Ocean Bride* [1854] (Spinks, 66; Roscoe, II, 309), Dr. S. Lushington restated and stressed the traditional principle of the requirement of good faith in prize cases as follows:

> "Over and over again Lord Stowell has said, it is not the documents themselves which the Court goes upon—they must be true, they must be *bona fide*—it never goes on formalities. This is a broad distinction, which I consider not only indispensable to prize law, but to be one of the most honourable distinctions which exist between a Prize Court and a municipal court; that a Prize Court looks to that which is *bona fide* true, while a Court of law is sometimes bound by formality, which prevents real justice being done in the case".

Further procedural issues concerned, *inter alia*, the following subject matters:

(c) Duty of the captor to bring his prize before a prize court for adjudication

It was from very early on a basic rule of prize law that a seizure was to be submitted to a prize court within a reasonable time. Doubts could arise about two questions: (i) whether the captor had exercised due speed and (ii) whether the tribunal seised was competent to deal with the capture.

Such doubts arose in actual fact in the case of the *Huldah* [1801] (3 C.Rob., 235; Roscoe, I, 303), in which the claim was not given till a year and nine months after the sentence of condemnation passed in the Court of Santo Domingo and that Court was not vested with competent authority to proceed in prize causes.

(*d*) *Release before adjudication*

Such release was generally held to be permissible: see the *Elsebe* case [1804] (5 C.Rob., 173; Roscoe, I, 441). Comp. *sub* B, section 3 under *f, supra*, p. 520.

(*e*) *Representation of the parties in prize proceedings*

It was in particular the intervention of consular agents on behalf of their nationals that gave rise to discussion in the French prize Court. Such intervention of consuls as legal representations of the parties was held inadmissible.

In a case before the new *Conseil des Prises* of 1854 during the Crimean War concerning the Russian vessel *Orione*, claimed to have been transferred to a neutral (Tuscan) buyer (Pistoye-Duverdy, II, 499, under the heading *L'Orione contre l'Averne*), the *Conseil* decided that intervention by the Tuscan vice-consul at Toulon in the prize proceedings was irreceivable. To the same effect the case of the *Christiane* (*eod. loco*, II, 502) another Russian vessel, sailing under the Danish flag after a simulated sale by the Russian owner to a Dane, allegedly before the Crimean War.

(*f*) *Contents of the affidavits*

An enemy claimant had to show by affidavit the grounds of his claim: the *Fenix* (or *Phoenix*) [1854] (Spinks, 1) and a series of corresponding decisions, cited by Roscoe in a note at p. 238 of vol. II of his *Reports*; the *Panaja Drapaniotisa* [1856] (Spinks, 336; Roscoe, II, 560): the claimant's affidavit had to state his residence and to negative all enemy interest, except where the claim was made under an Order in Council or a licence. A prayer for further proof should, moreover, be founded on a statement of what was intended to be proved. Failure to comply with these requirements rendered the claimant liable for costs and damages.

In the *Apollo (No. 2)* [1804] (5 C.Rob., 286; Roscoe, I, 481) the content of an affidavit was contrary to depositions made in standing interrogations and could, therefore, not be received.

(*g*) *Insurance issues; commissions of appraisal, etc.*

A question, which was raised during the Crimean War, concerned the obligation of captors to insure a prize during the proceedings, in order to avoid their becoming personally liable for its possible loss pending the final adjudication. See the case of the *Franciska (No. 2)* [1856] (10 Moore P.C. 73; Roscoe, II, 416).

Liability for the insurance premium was at issue in
the *Haabet (No. 1)* [1800] (2 C.Rob., 174; Roscoe, I, 212) and
the *Catherine and Anna* [1801] (4 C.Rob., 39; Roscoe, I, 336): as the premium has been paid by the captor for his own security, it is not chargeable against the owner in the case of restitution of the prize.

The case of the *Frau Maria* [1799] (2 C.Rob., 292; Roscoe, I, 235) concerned the costs of appraisal of a prize:

> "A commission of appraisement and sale was an instrument, in the first instance, taken out by captors, and they primarily are answerable for the expenses of the same".

(*h*) *Surety on bail*

In the *Betsey (No. 3)* [1804] (5 C.Rob., 295; Roscoe, I, 484) reduction of the amount of a bail, fixed by agreement, was refused, although the cargo had subsequently proved to be of less value.

Two further judgments of 1811 dealt with the giving of surety.

The first was that of the Dutch *Vreede* (1 Dods. 1; Roscoe, II, 120) relating to a mixed cargo captured in 1799, but not proceeded against until nine years later; the decree was to the effect that a surety given to a bail-bond to answer adjudication on the delivery to the claimant of seized cargo was not released by lapse of time from his liability on such bail-bond.

The second was that of the Danish *Nied Elwin* (1 Dods. 50; Roscoe, II, 130), captured by a British private ship of war in 1806, but returned to the owners by consent in 1807 under bail for the double of her appraised value. In that case the Court held that when bail was only given for the limited purpose of answering adjudication as security pending the decision of all questions before the Court at the time such bail was given, the persons who gave bail for the neutral vessel were not liable in respect of such vessel if war broke out and the vessel thereby became enemy property. The ship was restored by consent, the general cargo too, for four-sevenths, proof remaining required for the remaining three-sevenths:

> "Sureties who gave bail for a neutral vessel are not liable in respect of such vessel if war breaks out and she thereby becomes belligerent property and liable to condemnation on this ground."

(*i*) *Evidence*

A great many judgments dealt with the conclusiveness of proof or with the admission or refusal of further proof. Comp., *e.g.*, the cases of the Danish *Speculation* [1799] (2 C.Rob., 293; Roscoe, I, 237); the *Sarah* [1801]

(3 C.Rob., 330; Roscoe, I, 318); the (Antwerp or Papenburg) *Romeo* [1806] (6 C.Rob., 351; Roscoe, I, 568); the Russian *Fidentia (Nos. 1 and 2)* [1854] (Spinks, 39 and 85; Roscoe, II, 281 and 323); a cargo *ex* the Russian *Abo* [1854] (Spinks, 42; Roscoe, II, 285): no mention in the bill of lading of the person on whose account the goods were shipped; the *Maria (No. 1)* [1855] (Spinks, 321; Roscoe, II, 536): absence of a bill of sale; uncertain ownership; and the Greek *Chrissys* [1856] (Spinks, 343; Roscoe, II, 568): refusal of further proof because the ship was 60 or 70 miles off course.

In the *Otto and Olaf* [1855] (Spinks, 257; Roscoe, II, 507) Dr. Lushington held that

> "where the claim and preparatory evidence is at variance with the documentary, the Court is bound to require further proof".

Detailed rules as to the admission of further proof by the captors were formulated in the *Aline and Fanny* [1856] (Spinks, 322; 10 Moore P.C. 491; Roscoe, II, 537):

> "By the Law of Prize the evidence, whether to acquit or to condemn the ship, must, in the first instance, come from the ship's papers and the primary depositions of the master and crew, and the captors are not, except under circumstances of suspicion, arising from the primary evidence, entitled to adduce any intrinsic opposition".

In the *Nina* [1855] (Spinks, 276/277; appeal 345) the nationality of certain merchants, owners of the ship, was doubtful. The vessel had arrived at Ipswich under Austrian colours in May 1855 and was, after the unloading of her cargo there, seized by the Customs officers as enemy property. It was a case of suppression of papers and prevarication by the master. Further proof was refused because the Court could not restore to a person who claimed as sole owner, when others appeared to have an interest in the property, nor could it allow further proof when it was satisfied that no trustworthy evidence could alter the complexion of the case.

As the sufficiency of proof of ownership is more often than not a *quaestio facti*, I will not expatiate on this aspect of prize court judgments, but only refer to a few decisions dealing with the question.

In the *Magnus* [1798] (1 C.Rob., 31; Roscoe, II, 267, footnote *y*) the parties disagreed on the ownership of a cargo, either enemy (French) or neutral (Swiss): the cargo was condemned subject to search for precedents, but the condemnation became final, no precedents being produced.

In the *Bourse* [1811] (Edw., 370; Roscoe, II, 94), a case of transportation under a belligerent licence, the doubts were caused by the vagueness of the clause "to whomsoever the property may appear to belong."

(*j*) *Requisition of prizes*

One of the most famous procedural disputes in England related to the question of whether prize vessels or goods could legally be requisitioned pending the final adjudication. This controversy arose from the fact that an Order in Council of 26 April 1809 permitted such requisition and that the owners disputed the validity of that Order in the light of customary international law. The Order concerned was issued as an Order of reprisals which, though directed principally against the enemy, in its effects encroached upon the rights and interests of neutrals. Thus the issue was raised in the wider context of the legality of Orders in Council accused of running counter to the law of nations (comp. section 3, *sub* (*b*) *supra*). See the cases of the *Fox* [1811] (Edw. 311; Roscoe, II, 61) before the Prize Court in London, and the *Curlew and Magnet* [1812] (*Stewart's Vice-Admiralty cases* (Nova Scotia), 312). The *Fox* case, in particular, has had an great impact upon the development of British prize law since it averred the principle that Orders in Council were subject to testing by the "law of nations". Comp. on this all-important legal issue my exposé at pp. 606 *et seq*.

See for another instance of requisition the case of a cargo of wheat taken over by the British authorities from the Danish (neutral) merchant ship *Haabet (No. 1)* (2 C.Rob., 174; Roscoe, I, 212). The determination of its value was in the usual manner entrusted to Registrar and Merchants, who were, however, instructed by the Court not to include in the amount of compensation the insurance premium paid by the Danish ship owner.

(*k*) *Sale of the prize during the proceedings*

A case of sale beneath the value of the prize, but without irregularities, or *mala fides*, was that of the *Two Suzannahs* [1799] (2 C.Rob., 132; Roscoe, I, 208).

Provisional sale to the Government of an uninsured prize, referred for appraisal to Registrar and Merchants: *Haabet (No. 1)* [1800] (2 C.Rob., 174; Roscoe, I, 212); *Haabet (No. 2)* [1805] (6 C.Rob., 54; Roscoe, I, 524).

On a case in which the ship's captain had sold parts of the cargo in order to defray the expenses to be made for necessary repairs of his (Swedish) vessel, see the *Hoffnung (No. 3)* [1807] (6 C.Rob., 383; Roscoe, I, 583).

The legal situation during the Crimean War was defined in the *Franciska (No. 2)* [1856] (10 Moore P.C., 73; Roscoe, II, 416), in which the history of the practice of sale was reviewed. The prize had been sold under a decree of the Prize Court pursuant to the *Prize Act* (17 & 18 Victoria, c.18, s.26). When the capture was declared invalid, the Court ordered simple restitution of the proceeds of the sale to the claimants. This decision was, however, reversed in appeal. The Privy Council held that the captors were *bona fide* in possession of the prize during litigation and entitled to the nett proceeds of the sale after deducting from the gross proceeds the marshal's charges, consisting of (i) the expenses of the sale; (ii) reasonable expenses for the care and custody of the property pending adjudication, and (iii) the pilotage, lights and other dues incurred in bringing the ship to England. The practice in former wars in such cases was considered.

American case law has also made its contribution to the legal assessment of the practice of the sale of prizes which had not yet been finally adjudicated. See the cases reported in Blatchford's *Prize Cases* concerning the *Memphis and cargo* [1862] (p. 202); the *Ella Warley and cargo* [1862] (p. 204); the *Peterhoff* [1863] (p. 381) and the *Stephen Hart* [1863] (p. 387). These cases are described in detail in Robinton's *Papers of the New York Prize Court, 1861-1865* (New York, 1945).

(*l*) *Appeal or revision*

An appeal to a superior national court was usually open to the parties. This appeal was regulated differently in different countries and in different periods. During the first period of the existence of the United States as an independent confederation, for instance, prize proceedings there were even organized in three strata.

It would carry me too far afield to enter into the multifarious ways in which the maritime Powers of the past organized their national prize jurisdiction in appeal or revision. I therefore confine myself to a few sparse data on which British case law casts some light.

Several forms of proceedings in prize cases in earlier periods have been collected by F. Th. Pratt in his work of 1856 on the *Law of Contraband of War*, Appendix C, at pp. 269 *et seq.* They include

affidavits, differing in form under differing conditions of seizure;
monitions and returns on the part of captors;
decrees of restitution and of condemnation;
petitions and libels of appeal; desertion of appeal;
decrees reversing, respectively affirming a sentence;
bill of sale by the Marshal ...

By an Act of Parliament of 17 & 18 Vict, c. 18, s. 37, the right of appeal from the High Court of Admiralty in England was limited to three months from the date of the first sentence, liberty being reserved to the Judicial Committee of the Privy Council to allow, upon sufficient cause being shown, the appeal to be presented after the expiration of that period. See the cases of the *Aspasia*, the *Achilles* and the *Gerasimo* [1856-1857] involved in the breach of the blockade of the Black Sea and adjudicated upon in the first instance by three separate sentences, but by a combined judgment in appeal (11 Moore P.C., 79; Roscoe, II, 572).

In the captor's own internal legal order, without any specific treaty obligation, the issue of a possible review of earlier prize court decisions also arose.

Occasionally the attempt to achieve the revision or reversal of a prize court judgment took the form of an application for the rescission of an earlier decree of condemnation, but without success. Thus, in the *Geheimrath* [1798] (Roscoe, II, 115, footnote *a*) the Court of Appeal refused to rescind an earlier decree since

> "this decree being final, it would be contrary to their practice to rescind it, and even when it appeared a fraud had been practised they could not go out of the order of their practice."

The same decision was made in the *Elizabeth* [1811] (2 Acton, 57; Roscoe, II, 115):

> "It is contrary to the practice of the Court of Appeal to rescind a decree of that Court on any ground."

There was one precedent to the contrary: the *Harmony* [1807], but the grounds for the rescission were not stated in the record.

The admissibility of additional proof in new proceedings after a condemnatory judgment—the case of a second capture after rescue—was one of the points discussed in the *Franklin* [1811] (Roscoe, II, 115).

One of the peculiarities of British prize proceedings was for some centuries their organization as a legal battle between the actual captors and the owners of the prize. This was only altered at a very late stage, *viz.*, by the *Prize Court Rules 1914* by which the Crown was substituted for the actual captors as a party to the proceedings. This change played a rôle in the assessment of claims for reparation, put forward by interested parties who had suffered damage as a result of illegal seizures, negligence of the captors, or on other grounds. Comp. on this later development the case of the *Oscar II* [1919] (*B.C.P.C.*, III, 421; appeal, III, 588), and further the details given by the new Naval Prize Tribunal of 1918 in its above-quoted decision of 1918 concerning the *Abonema and several other ships* (*B.C.P.C.*, III, 302).

Section 5. POSSIBLE DICTA. LEGAL EFFECTS OF A CONDEMNATORY JUDGMENT

The examination of a case by the prize court could result in varying decisions.

Thus, the court could deny its jurisdiction to adjudicate upon a cause on the ground that it fell outside its province.

The main types of *dicta* in which prize proceedings might result were, of course, the condemnation of a ship or cargo as good and lawful prize, or their release because there were insufficient grounds for condemnation. On release without adjudication see *sub* B, section 3, p. 520.

Both Sir Nathaniel Lloyd in Appendix C to his Ms. Notes in Pratt-Lee's collection and De Pistoye and Duverdy in their *Traité des prises maritimes* have given the texts of model decrees,

as to England, of restitution, respectively condemnation of prizes, and in appeal, reversing, respectively affirming, sentences of the court below, at pp. 292-293 and 307-309,

and as to France, of condemnation in vol. I, p. 318 (case of *Le Voltigeur contre l'Oack*).

A decree of release might or might not be accompanied by the award of damages. Whether these were due by the captor depended traditionally on the question whether he was justified by a "probable cause" to proceed to the seizure. He might indeed have had sufficient reasons for suspicion, even though a subsequent closer examination of the case by the prize court proved that those reasons were substantively unfounded. The captors were only liable for damages when there had not been such a "probable cause". Many cases in the past were decided on the strength of this principle. See on this subject the following section 6, sub-section *a*.

The question of damages could also arise independently of any preceding formal seizure of a vessel or cargo, simply on the ground that the owners were duped by a diversion or detention of the ship, by the disembarkation and re-embarkation of her cargo, or by the destruction of either after the visit.

British prize courts were further often seized of various other ancillary claims, *e.g.*, for freight or for a contribution to general average, or for salvage in case of the recapture of a prize, or they could become involved in controversies between captors over competing claims to prize bounty.

Decisions on all such diverse types of claim, which were often settled in other countries in administrative procedures outside the court, have already been, or will still be, surveyed in the present volume in the systematic context where they belong.

I will further limit myself to one special subject, *viz.*, the legal effect of a condemnatory prize court decree.

Such a decree always brought about a change of ownership of the prize, or, as the Judicial Committee of the Privy Council expressed it during World War I in its judgment concerning the *Odessa and Woolston* (*B.C.P.C.*, I, 554):

> "The effect of a condemnation is to divest the enemy" [and not only an enemy but also an allied or neutral] "subject of his ownership as from the date of the seizure"—*i.e.* with retroactive effect—, "and to transfer it, as from that date, to the Sovereign or to his grantee. The thing—the "*res*"—is then his for him to deal with as he thinks fit and the proceeding is at an end."

This transfer of ownership of a prize to the capturing State in virtue of a prize court judgment entailed the lapse of all rights previously established with regard to the condemned object on behalf of third parties, such as mortgagees, holders of bottomry bonds and maritime liens, etc. Property shares of neutral owners in a ship that was condemned on the ground of her real or constructive enemy character equally lapsed. See the case of the *Aina (No. 1)* [1854] (Spinks, 8; Roscoe, II, 247): foreigners cannot set up a mortgage deed on the ship against captors, though under certain circumstances lenity should be shown to British merchants. Comp. on this subject section 2 on the Enemy character of ships, *supra*, p. 223.

The *res judicata* regarding the ship extended its effects to the resulting treatment of her cargo.

A judgment of condemnation conferred upon the captor a definite title not only vis-à-vis the former owner, but also vis-à-vis his State, whether enemy, allied or neutral.

The sale of a condemned prize to a neutral accordingly vested him with a good title of ownership: cassation in the case of the *Saint-Vincent* (De Pistoye-Duverdy, I, 320).

The principle that the condemnation of a prize conferred a definite title upon the captor was invoked *ad absurdum* by the Agent of the British Government during the arbitral proceedings, organized by Article VII (2) of the Jay Treaty with the United States of 19 November 1794, when he argued that the Mixed Claims Commission was bound to recognize the final character of judgments rendered by British prize courts and was therefore precluded from examining their validity under the law of nations. Comp. on this controversy my remarks in section 8 below, p. 670, and the analysis by the editors of the *Recueil des arbitrages internationaux*, vol. I, pp. 87-99.

In the *Molly* case [1814] (1 Dods., 394; Roscoe, II, 191) the British prize court was seised by a British subject reclaiming a ship that had been captured by the French, been condemned more than ten years ago by the *Conseil des Prises*, and thereupon sold to a neutral (Spanish) purchaser. Having regard to the lapse of time between the capture and the claim, the Court refused to question the title of the Spanish owner, or inquire into the validity of the condemnation. Spain had been neutral at the moment of capture, but had later become involved in a war with England. At the conclusion of peace Spain had not only been replaced in a position of neutrality vis-à-vis England, but had, moreover, become England's ally against France.

What in the case of the *Schoone Sophie* [1805] (6 C.Rob., 138; Roscoe, I, 545) was at issue was the effect of a peace treaty (of Amiens of 1802) upon a title of acquisition in virtue of the decision of a foreign prize court.

The issue of the international effect of a final condemnatory prize court decree has, as far as I know, seldom given rise to serious controversy: such a final decree transferred the ownership of the prize to the captor, whether a State organ or a privateer. There have, however, occurred cases in which those interested in the prize have attempted to reverse the legal position. Thus, in the neutral Netherlands, the former owner of a prize ship, condemned by the German *Prisengericht*, has resorted to bringing in a civil court in Holland an action against the actual possessor in virtue of a legal title acquired through purchase from the German *Reich*, for the recovery of his former property. The cases I have in view relate to events occurring in the post-World War I period—the *Zeemeeuw* [1918] (as far as I know unreported) and *De Hoop* [1921] (*W.v.h.R.*, 9 August 1922, No, 10907; *Nederlandse Jurisprudentie* 1922, p. 974, digested in *A.D.* 1919-1922, Case No. 347, pp. 487-488).

Section 6. AWARD OF DAMAGES. PROBABLE CAUSE. FREIGHT. GENERAL AVERAGE

(*A*) *Claims for damages*

The obligation of captors to pay compensation to ship or cargo owners who suffered damage or loss as a result of wrongful actions or inaction could be based on a variety of grounds: unjustified search or seizure, bringing of vessels into port for examination, prolonged detention of the prize, undue restriction of those on board, loss of goods by negligence, theft or fire, delay in proceeding against a prize before the prize court, etc.

The most important ground for a claim for reparation was a substantively unfounded capture followed by release of the prize.

According to a long tradition, later sanctioned by Art. 64 of the Declaration on Naval Warfare in London of 1909, the answer to the question of whether the captor was bound to pay compensation to the neutral owner of the ship or her cargo in case of subsequent release of the prize by the prize court depended on whether the warship commander or privateer had "probable (or reasonable) cause" for proceeding to his action. If he had, no compensation was held to be due.

The problem of reparation due for seizures as prize which did not ultimately result in a confiscation of the ship or cargo seized was fairly complicated. The final release of a prize vessel or cargo by a prize court on the ground that there proved to be no substantive legal ground for condemnation indeed by no means implied that reparation was due for the damage caused by any such seizure which *a posteriori* appeared to have been substantively unfounded. For the captor might have had sufficient reasons for his action and in that case of "reasonable (or probable) cause for the seizure" he or his State was not obliged to pay compensation to those interested. That legal principle became especially burdensome for the victims of the seizure in cases in which the prize was lost prior to its adjudication or restoration to the owners.

This side of the law of prize has already long ago been considered in municipal regulations and by admiralty courts. It has become particularly important in cases of destruction of the prize and at a much later stage in particular in consequence of the systematic sinking by German submarines during World War I of prizes that could not be safely brought into a German port.

"Probable cause" was defined by the Supreme Court of the United States in 1813 (*per* Chief Justice Marshall) in *Locke v. U.S.* (7 Cranch, 339) as

> "meaning, according to its usual acceptation, less than evidence which would justify condemnation" and "importing a seizure made under circumstances which warrant suspicion",

and in 1899 (*per* Chief Justice Fuller) in *Olinde Rodrígues* (174 U.S. 510) as follows:

> "Probable cause exists where there are circumstances sufficient to warrant suspicion, though it may turn out that the facts are not sufficient to warrant condemnation. And whether they are or not can not be determined unless the customary proceedings of prize are instituted and enforced".

One of the oldest British precedents in support of the doctrine of "probable cause" is that of the *Elizabeth* of 1809 (1 Acton, 10), in which the reason given by the Lords of Appeal for condemning the captors in costs and damages was that there appeared to have been scarcely any ground for detaining the vessel. The late Judge Story in his *Notes on the Principles and Practice of Prize Courts* (Pratt's edition, p. 35) stated the law as follows:

> "Every capture, whether made by commissioned or non-commissioned ships, is at the peril of the captors. If they capture property without reasonable or justifiable cause, they are liable to a suit for restitution, and may also be mulcted in costs and damages. If the vessel and cargo, or any part thereof, be good prize, they are completely justified. And although the whole property may, upon a hearing, be restored, yet, if there was probable cause of capture, they are not responsible in damages".

This doctrine was applied in all subsequent cases, for example, in the American case of the *George* of 1815 (1 Mason (Amer.), 24) and much later in the British case of the *Ostsee* of 1855 (9 Moore P.C., 150; Spinks, 174; Roscoe, II, 432-457). Even slight grounds of suspicion might suffice. From the last-mentioned judgment in the *Ostsee*, rendered by Dr Lushington during the Crimean War, it becomes clear what the requirement of a "probable cause" meant in actual practice:

> "During the seventeen years that Lord Stowell presided in this Court, and administered the law of nations with regard to war, I believe that out of the many thousand ships and cargoes brought before him, he condemned the captors in costs and damages in only about ten or a dozen cases—not one in a thousand, and Lord Stowell also, as I right well remember, laid it down that he would not condemn the captors in costs and damages upon evidence given before him, without giving them the opportunity of justifying their conduct, and stating, if they thought fit, the grounds on which they made the capture. In my own recollection there are only three cases of restitution with costs and damages. I am well aware that were a seizure has been made without ostensible excuse or reason, justice requires that the persons making the seizure should make good to the party the loss that may have been occasioned by the capture; at the same time, I am of opinion that this is the extremity of the law of nations, which ought not to be adopted except in cases which imperatively require the Court so to do".

One of the rare cases in which the captors were condemned in costs and damages was that of the British ship *Nemesis* [1808] (Edw., 50; Roscoe, II, 441, footnote). They were so condemned for their "vexatious conduct", for which "it was impossible to conceive the least shadow of an excuse" and which "removed all reluctance on the part of the judge to award costs and damages".

Ignorance of the captors, or their mistaken construction of the law, or error of judgment, was held, as a rule, not to defend the captor against a claim of the owners of a released prize for damages. Different prize courts have so decided; see for the application of this additional rule several older cases, such as those relative to the *Betsey (No. 1)* (Murphy, Master) of 1798 (1 C.Rob., 93; Roscoe, I, 63), the *John* (*No. 2*) of 1818 (2 Dodson, 336; Roscoe, II, 232), and the *Cape Nicola Mole* cases of 1801 (Roscoe, II, at p. 444).

In the *John* case the Court ruled as follows:

> "[The captor] cannot plead ignorance of the law in excuse of his act; every man is bound to know his own domestic law, wherever he applies it, and if he mistakes, he is answerable for the effects of his own misapprehension [especially when a naval officer is concerned]".

The *Cape Nicola Mole* cases concerned confiscations pronounced by the Admiralty Court of Santo Domingo which, however, had never been duly invested with jurisdictional powers in cases of maritime prizes.

The only cases in prize courts where captors were exonerated on the ground of ignorance of the law were cases where the construction of the law was so unsettled and indeterminate that anyone without legal training could not be expected to determine the course of law to be pursued. This, it was claimed, was the situation in the case of the *Luna* of 1810 (Edw., 190; Roscoe, II, 449-450, footnote *b*), relating to a neutral vessel which during a voyage to San Sebastián was seized by British captors for alleged breach of the blockade of that town. As the captors had been in *bona fide* doubt whether or not an Order in Council of 26 April 1809, declaring a blockade of "ports and places under the Government of France", extended to San Sebastián which had been for two years under French military occupation, Sir William Scott held during his term of office that it did not so extend, and therefore exempted the captors on the release of the ship from the payment of costs and damages.

The same ground of exemption (a wrong construction placed by the captors upon an Order in Council) later, during the Crimean War, induced Dr Lushington in the above-mentioned case of the *Ostsee* [1855] (Spinks, 174; Roscoe, II, 432) on the release of the ship to her owners, to relieve the captors of costs and damages: looking at the confusion that had arisen respecting the blockade of the Baltic port of Cronstadt and the difficulty that even commanders of Her Majesty's warships experienced in forming their own opinion, Dr Lushington felt that it would in this case go too far to accompany the decree for the restoration of the ship with an additional allocation of costs and damages to her owners at the charge of those commanders.

The *Ostsee* had taken wheat on board in May 1854 in the harbour of Cronstadt and had sailed on 28 May bound to Elsenör for orders. During that voyage she was captured by the British warship *Alban* in the Gulf of Finland on 1 June 1854, approximately twenty-four miles from Dagerort, suspected of an intended breach of the blockade of Cronstadt, and was sent to England for adjudication as prize. The claimants in the proceedings submitted that the capture had taken place without probable cause and that it was not in dispute that their ship was captured for the breach of a blockade which had no existence until nearly a month after the seizure (comp. on this case *sub* A, section 4, *supra*, p. 447). They therefore demanded restitution of the prize with costs and damages. The captors consented to the restitution of the ship and her cargo, but submitted that it ought to be without costs and damages. In that case Dr Lushington stated the principle as follows:

> "If captors improperly and without reasonable cause, but through an honest mistake, seize a vessel, such vessel not being, by any act of her own, voluntary or involuntary, open to any fair ground of suspicion, the captors are liable in damages and costs".

The (Mecklenburg) *Ostsee* was accordingly restored to her owners with costs and damages, but the captors brought the question of damages in appeal before the Judicial Committee of the Privy Council (Roscoe, II, 434). During this appeal the owners of the prize and the captors fought each other with a wealth of precedents, which were later also surveyed by the Judicial Committee of the Privy Council (*per* Lord Pemberton Leigh).

The owners of the *Ostsee* argued that the captors had acted without probable cause and that there had not been a valid blockade when the capture took place. The British precedents they invoked in their favour in order to recover the costs and damages already awarded by Dr Lushington were those of the *Hendrick and Jacob* [1798], cited in the *Betsey (No. 1)* (Murphy, Master) [1798] (1 C.Rob., 93; Roscoe, I, at p. 67); the *Corier Maritimo* [1799] (1 C.Rob., 287; Roscoe, I, 137); the *San Juan Baptista* and the *Purissima Conception* [1803] (5 C.Rob., 33; Roscoe, I, 417); the *Wilhemsberg* [1804] (5 C.Rob., 143; Roscoe, I, 437); the *Zacheman* [1804] (5 C.Rob., 152; Roscoe, I, 439); the *Anna* [1806] (5 C.Rob., 373; Roscoe, I, 499); the *Washington* [1808] (6 C.Rob., 275; Roscoe, I, 555); the *Nuestra Señora de los Dolores* [1809] (Edw., 60; Roscoe, II, 20); the *Actaeon* [1815] (2 Dods., 48; Roscoe, II, 209); and the *Elize*, otherwise *Elise Wilhelmine* [1854] (Spinks, 88; Roscoe, II, 327).

They further referred to Story-Pratt's work on *Prize Courts* (pp. 35, 39, 112) and the American case of the *Eleanor* [1817] (2 Wheaton Americ. Rep., 345). From the *Mentor* [1799] (1 C.Rob., 179; Roscoe, I, 96) they quoted that the fact of the captain of the warship *Alban* having acted under orders of this superior in command, did not exonerate him from responsibility, and from the *Zacheman* that even if the captors had acted *bona fide* and been guilty of no misconduct and a neutral subject had been wronged, the latter would still have to be compensated by the captors, the payment of the compensation being a question resting between the Government and the captors.

The captors on their side distinguished the authorities quoted because these were either cases of capture by privateers or of improper conduct on the part of King's ships, and they adduced on their side other precedents, such as the British *Two Susannahs* [1799] (2 C.Rob., 132; Roscoe, I, 208) and *Felicity* [1819] (2 Dods., 231; Roscoe, II, 233), and the American *Lively* (Gallison, Amer. Rep., 315) and *Marianna Flora* [1826] (11 Wheaton Amer. Rep., 1), as well as the absence on board of the *Ostsee* of the necessary ship's papers.

Surveying the precedents at great length in their turn, quoting the British cases of the *Juffro(u)w Maria Schroeder* [1800] (3 C.Rob., 147; Roscoe, I, 279), the *Triton* [1801] (4 C.Rob., 78; Roscoe, I, 352) and the *William* [1806], certain American precedents, which adopted Story's view (p. 35), and referring even (which happened only very rarely in British prize court decisions) to foreign views (expressed by M. Portalis, Commissary of the French Government appointed to the *Conseil des Prises*, in the cases of the American *Pégou* (De Pistoye-Duverdy, II, 51; Roscoe, II, 437-438) and the *Charming Betsy* [1804] (2 Cranch, 98), the Lords of Appeal reached the conclusion that on the restoration of the *Ostsee* to her owners, they should also receive costs and damages, but only those given in the Court below, not those in appeal.

A decision to the same effect was made in another case adjudicated during the Crimean War, *viz.*, that of the *Leucade* [1855] (Spinks, 217; Roscoe, II, 473), an Ionian vessel sailing from Santa Maura with a cargo of olive oil, bound for Taganrog in the Sea of Azov, which was captured by a British steam-frigate about forty-eight miles from the Straits of Kertch, on the ground of illegal trade with Russia. The capture was held to have been illegal because the vessel was neutral and therefore could not be condemned for trading with the enemy. The question of damages remained. The Court held that the status of the Ionian Islands relatively to Great Britain was of such a doubtful character, and depended to such an extent upon the construction of public documents, that, although the capture was illegal, the captor was not liable to condemnation in costs and damages for capturing her without probable cause.

According to American prize jurisprudence the officer making the capture was personally liable in damages. This was earlier also the position in England—see the case of the *Der Mohr (No. 1)* of 1800 (3 C.Rob., 129;

Roscoe, I, 271), but there the situation changed in 1864, when the Crown was substituted for the individual captors by the *Naval Prize Act* of that year.

When there was no valid ground for confiscation of the prize, and when, moreover, there had been no probable cause for its seizure, reparation was due to the owners of the prize for the damage caused, even if it was lost after the seizure by accident, for example by collision, fire or theft. A case of destruction by fire was that of *Lilley v. Doubleday* of 1881, decided by a court of civil law (L.R. 7 Q.B.D., 510).

A case of theft was that of the *Maria (No. 2)* (Jortz, Master) [1803] (4 C.Rob., 348; Roscoe, I, 401). The *William* (Hastie, Master) [1806] (6 C.Rob., 316; Roscoe, II, 439, footnote *y*) was a case in which the prize had been lost at sea through want of proper nautical care on the part of the captors. In those latter cases Lord Stowell argued that the captors were not insurers, bound to restore the goods of the neutral owners in any event. They were held not to be liable to pay compensation for goods stolen from them if they had fulfilled their duty to take reasonable care of the property; that duty, however, was not limited merely to take as much care as they would use about their own affairs; the law required that there should be no lack of due diligence:

> "When a capture is not justifiable, the captor is answerable for every damage. But in this case the original seizure has been justified by the condemnation of part of the cargo. It is therefore to be considered as a justifiable seizure in which all that the law requires of the captor is that he should be held responsible for due diligence. But on questions of this kind there is one position sometimes advanced, which does not meet with my entire assent, namely that captors are answerable only for such care as they would take of their own property. This, I think, is not a just criterion in such case, for a man may with respect to his own property encounter risks from views of particular advantage or from a natural disposition of rashness which would be entirely unjustified in respect to the custody of the goods of another person which have come to his hands by an act of force ...".

I will conclude this exposé by a systematic summary of the grounds on which damages were awarded or claimed in prize case:

—lack of "reasonable cause", among many others:

Triton [1801] (4 C.Rob., 78; Roscoe, I, 352);

Nuestra Señora de los Dolores [1809] (Edw., 60; Roscoe, II, 20).

—neglect by the captor of his duty to institute proceedings promptly:

Corier Maritimo [1799] (1 C.Rob., 287; Roscoe, I, 137): award of demurrage;

Madonna del Burso [1802] (4 C.Rob., 169; Roscoe, I, 370): other non-licensed articles;

Peacock [1802] (4 C.Rob., 185; Roscoe, I, 381): failure to bring the prize to England immediately after seizure;

Zacheman [1804] (5 C.Rob., 152; Roscoe, I, 439): delay in the exercise by the captor of his right of pre-emption.

—neglect of the captor's obligation to bring the prize into a convenient port for adjudication:

Wilhemsberg [1804] (5 C.Rob., 143; Roscoe, I, 437);

Washington [1806] (6 C.Rob., 275; Roscoe, I, 555).

—negligence of the captor or his agent, causing the loss of the prize:

Der Mohr (No. 1) [1800] (3 C.Rob., 129; Roscoe, I, 271): the prize was lost in coming through the Needles owing to the ignorance and wilfulness of the prize master put on board. The parties were free of any blame, but the principal was held to be civilly answerable for the conduct of his agent. See also the

Der Mohr (No. 2) [1802] (4 C.Rob., 314; Roscoe, I, 395): responsibility of the captor also for freight.

—theft of seized cargo:

in the combined cases of certain cargoes from the *Maria (No. 2)* (Jortz, Master) and the *Vro(u)w Johanna (No. 2)* [1803] (4 C.Rob., 348; Roscoe, I, 401) it was held that if a captor had used due diligence, he was not liable for the loss of captured property. *In casu* the cargoes, ordered by the Court to be restored to their owners, were—after their restoration—stolen from a genuine warehouse where they were kept under the joint locks of the officers of the Customs and agents of the captors.

—putting the crew of the prize vessel under restraint for other than security reasons:

San Juan Baptista and *Purissima Conception* [1803] (5 C.Rob., 33; Roscoe, I, 417).

—sale of the prize beneath its value:

Two Susannahs [1799] (2 C.Rob., 132; Roscoe, I, 208).

—destruction of the prize:

Actaeon [1815] (2 Dods., 48; Roscoe, II, 209): recognition of the duty to compensate; *in casu* merely a question of the measure of damages.

—complaints connected with blockade:

the Danish *Elize* (or *Elise Wilhelmine*) [1854] (Spinks, 88; Roscoe, II, 327): in this case a Customs officer at Leith was condemned in costs and damages for the unjustified seizure of a neutral vessel on her arrival in that port on the ground of an alleged preceding breach of the blockade of Archangel;

the Danish *Otto and Olaf* [1855] (Spinks, 257; Roscoe, II, 507): every ship leaving the blockaded Gulf of Riga with a cargo was held subject to detention without the captor being liable to payment of costs and damages; the Prize Court could require further proof, but would not enter into an inquiry whether the captured neutral vessel had complied with the requirements of the municipal law of her own country; the preparatory evidence was *in casu* at variance with the documentary evidence;

the *Aline and Fanny* from Lübeck [1856] (Spinks, 322; 10 Moore P.C., 491; Roscoe, II, 537), bound from that city to Haparanda (Sweden), but captured by two British warships for an alleged attempt to break the blockade of Jacobstad.

Another issue raised in the prize courts was that of the *quantum* of the damages due. The calculation of the exact amount of the compensation was difficult as it always is in cases of indemnification for an international delinquency (comp. Part VI of this publication, pp. 745 *et seq.*).

I have not come across old prize court decisions on this particular subject, as far as Great Britain was concerned, presumably owing to the fact that the calculation used to be made outside the Court by Registrar and Merchants, (as of 1 May 1781). The problem was, however, considered in the case of the *Actaeon* [1815] (2 Dodson, 48; Roscoe, II, 209), an American vessel sailing under a general British licence between the United States and European ports. After having been repeatedly harassed by British warships, she was finally captured by the *La Hogue* whose captain set her on fire and so destroyed her. The Prize Court awarded the owners damages for unjust deprivation of property, and held as to their measure as follows:

> "The natural rule is, that if a party be unjustly deprived of his property, he ought to be put as nearly as possible in the same state as he was before the deprivation". [After denying that the ship had given ground for suspicion which might have justified the capture as an exception to the general rule, and stating that the claimants were consequently entitled to full compensation, the Court continued:] "The measure of restitution to the claimant is the same, whether the captor has acted from improper motives, or otherwise. Where the terms of the licence are general, it is of no consequence who are the individuals acting under it, [and damages must be awarded] even when the captor was actuated by a sense of public duty".

The case of the *Franciska (No. 2)* [1856] (10 Moore P.C., 73; Roscoe, II, 416) was an instance of the sale of the prize during the proceedings, followed by release of the proceeds because the captor had acted without reasonable cause. In that case the owners were awarded the gross proceeds of the sale subject to proper deductions: expenses of the sale, costs of custody of the prize, pilotage dues, *etcetera.*

In another case, the *Catharine and Anna* [1801] (4 C.Rob., 39; Roscoe, I, 336) it appeared that the captor had insured his prize on its voyage to Europe for adjudication. The captor claimed reimbursement of the premium for that insurance from the owners when they obtained release of the prize to them. The Court refused this: the premiums of insurance were not chargeable against the owners because the captor had paid them for his own security and the owners had nothing to do with the benefit of that insurance.

The fact that so many neutral vessels were destroyed by the Russian cruisers during the Russo-Japanese War of 1904-1905 increased the necessity for the Russian prize courts of developing a system of principles for the assessment of the amount of compensation owing to their owners and those of their cargoes in the case of disapproval of the act of destruction. Such principles were laid down, for example, in the Russian judgments concerning the destruction of the *Thea* [1904] (Hurst & Bray, I, 96 *et seq*., at p. 110), the *Tetartos* [1909] (*ibid*., I, 166 *et seq*., at pp. 184-185) and the *Ikhona* [1908] (*ibid*. I, 226 *et seq*., at pp. 241, 249 *et seq*. and 257 *et seq*.). Apart from discussing the "actual value" of the destroyed ships at the moment of destruction, the arguments turned on the questions of consequential damages and the indebtedness of interest.

See for such an assessment, *e.g*., the decision of the Libau Prize Court [1907] relating to the compensation for the destruction of the German s.s. *Thea*, after her capture and destruction by a Russian squadron in the Pacific Ocean on 12 July 1904; it had, in appeal, been declared unlawful by the Supreme Prize Court (*ibid*., I, 103). According to that decision (*ibid*., I, 109) payment had to be made for the value of the ship and stores, loss of profits, wages and expenses of maintaining the crew, but not for charges incurred for lawyer's fees and valuation, nor for damages claimed as compensation for personal losses and privations by the master and crew and paid by the owners of the ship.

On the measure of damages see the study by E.S. Roscoe (London, 1924) *A history of the English prize court*, pp. 49 and 61.

Marginal issues of adjudication in prize proceedings related to (B) the indebtedness of freight and (C) the apportionment of general average.

(*B*) *Freight claims*

General historical introduction

Freight claims were of various kinds.

Sometimes the ship owner brought a claim against the captor for having lost his freight as a consequence of the capture.

On other occasions the captor brought a claim against the ship owner for having fulfilled by or after the capture the cargo owner's contract with the ship owner. On this matter there existed a marked difference between English and French practice, since France awarded in all cases freight *pro rata itineris* (see *infra*, p. 633).

The various claims could clash or concur, in which case an order of priority had to be established (see *infra*, p. 638).

In other cases the freight was forfeited, together with the cargo, for example because the ship carried contraband to the enemy or intended to enter a blockaded port.

There also occurred cases of pre-emption, instead of confiscation of cargoes. This was done in one of the oldest reported cases on freight claims: the *Vrijheid (No. 1)* [1778] (Hay and Marriott, 188; Roscoe, I, 13).

It concerned a cargo of masts carried from Riga on a Dutch ship. This cargo was found not to be liable to condemnation, but to be subject to pre-emption by the Crown. The Court decreed that the ship owner was entitled to receive freight: the ship was restored to the claimant, together with the value of the cargo; the naval stores on board were sold, according to former precedents, for the use of his Majesty; all freight, expenses and charges, both of the captor and the claimant, were to be paid by his Majesty. The judgment was confirmed by the Lords of Appeal in 1784 (see Roscoe, I, 394, footnote *d*).

Other cases in which the freight problem already arose early on were those of the capture of ships or cargoes, followed by their recapture.

In yet other cases ship owners attempted to enforce their freight claims against the owners of carried cargo in a Prize Court, but such attempts usually failed because the Prize Court considered itself incompetent to deal with such private claims (*infra*, p. 638).

In the following pages I will attempt to illustrate the rather confused rules applied by the Courts by surveying their case law.

The obligation of a captor, either a King's ship or a privateer, to pay freight to the owner of a neutral ship from which he had enemy goods delivered to him is almost as old as prize law itself. The obligation of neutral cargo owners on board an enemy ship towards the captor to arrange the freight issue was already laid down in chapter 276(2) of the *Consulat de Mar*:

> "Si le navire appartient à des ennemis et sa cargaison à des amis, les marchands qui s'y trouvent et à qui la cargaison appartiendra en tout ou en partie, doivent s'accorder avec l'amiral ... Mais, si les marchands ne veulent pas faire un accord avec l'amiral, celui-ci a le droit d'envoyer (le navire) au lieu où lui-même aura armé, et les marchands sont obligés de payer le fret de ce navire de même que s'il avait porté leur cargaison au lieu pour lequel elle était destinée, et rien de plus".

See for the full text of this provision *supra* Ch. III *sub* A, section 2, pp. 303-304.

I will now turn to a more detailed survey of

The different types of freight claims

The main types of freight claims were the following two:

(*a*) claims of captors for freight against neutral owners of cargo carried in a neutral ship;

(*b*) claims of neutral ship owners against captors for earned freight in case of the release of the cargo.

Disputes on the indebtedness of freight, however, did not remain confined to these two basic types, but extended to cases of a different kind, such as:

(*c*) claims of captors, in addition to their claim for condemnation of an enemy chip, for the freight earned by her owner;

(*d*) claims of captors for freight against neutral owners of cargo, carried on an enemy ship, but released;

(*e*) claims of ship-owners for freight against cargo owners.

As far as the main types of claims *sub* (*a*) and (*b*) were concerned, the judgments seem to have all related to neutral, and none to British or allied ships involved in the transport. There seems to be only one old reported British case regarding a British vessel in which somewhat similar questions arose, but that was of a different character as it was a case between the owners of a ship that had been captured but afterwards recaptured, on the one hand, and the owners of her cargo, on the other, and not between the ship-owners and the captors; this was a case of 1810 relating to *The Friends* (Edw. 246; Roscoe, II, 48). See on this unusual case *infra*, p. 640.

The many problems relating to claims for the payment of freight or for the restitution of freight already paid or consigned, have again arisen during World War I and in still greater variety which I have attempted to systematize in my *Le droit des prises de la Grande Guerre* (1924).

(*a*) Freight claims of a captor against the owners of cargoes carried on a neutral ship.

As remarked above (p. 629), there existed a marked difference between the British and the French prize law practice.

The rule developed by British prize courts was to the effect that whenever a captor brought goods to the port of actual destination according to the intent of the contracting parties, he was entitled to the freight on the ground that the contract had been fulfilled, but that in all other cases he was not so entitled, even if the ship had carried out the greater part of her intended voyage. This principle has been acted upon constantly by the British prize courts.

France, however, took a different view in that she clung to the practice of awarding the captor freight in all cases *pro rata itineris* (*infra*, p. 633).

(i) The old rule of English prize law that freight was due to a captor on goods which he brought to their original port of destination, but that a captor did not have such a claim in other cases was a rule from which the courts only very seldom departed in special circumstances by allowing minor deviations from it. It was still regarded by the British Government as the authentic rule of international prize law on the eve of the codification of 1908-1909 (see the preparatory documents of the Conference of London and Scott's *Cases on International Law*, pp. 631-632).

In the *Hoop* [1803] (5 C.Rob., 75n; Roscoe, I, 427n), for example, the Court held that on cargoes restored to foreign merchants without having been carried by the captor to their port of destination no freight was due. But in a comparable case of the same year, the *Vrouw Henrietta* [1803] (Roscoe, I, 427n; 5 C.Rob., 75n), the Court overruled the defense by a London merchant that certain goods had not been brought to London but had been delivered at Plymouth and that, therefore, they had not been carried to the claimant's own port. The parcel of goods concerned was held in this case to be subject to freight.

This was one of the cases in which the strict rule was exceptionally mitigated. This had already been done in a case of 1799 concerning cargo on the Danish vessel *Copenhagen* [1799] (1 C.Rob., 289; Roscoe, I, 138), in which the question arose whether freight was due for the whole voyage or only *pro rata itineris*. This was *in casu* a question between the owners of the ship and the owners of the cargo. The ship had been seized in Milford Haven into which she had been driven by stress of weather and in need of repairs; the cargo was released and sent to its destination by other means of conveyance. On this issue the Court argued:

> "With respect to the freight, some is admitted to be due; as the ship has brought her cargo from Smyrna through much the most considerable part of the voyage. But it is said that in matters of prize the whole freight is always given, and for this reason, because capture is considered as delivery and a captured vessel earns her whole freight. I have already said that this is not merely or originally a matter of prize; the ship was not brought in as such; ...—it is a case of a mixed nature; and the maxim that capture is delivery is not to be taken in the general way in which it has been laid down. It is by no means true, except where the captor succeeds fully to the rights of the enemy, and represents him as to those rights. If a neutral vessel, having enemy's goods, is taken, the captor pays the whole freight because he represents the enemy by possessing himself of the enemy's goods *jure belli*; and although the whole freight has been earned by the completion of the voyage, yet, as the captor by his act of seizure has prevented its completion, his seizure shall operate the same effect as an actual delivery of the goods to the consignee, and shall subject him to the payment of the full freight. But if ship and cargo, being both neutral, are restored, the consequence is only that the ship must proceed on and complete her voyage before she can demand her freight. If the cargo is restored whilst the ship continues under detention, still less reason is there to contend that she has earned her whole freight. Such is the present case .... Under these circumstances it is impossible to say that she has earned more than a freight *pro rata itineris*, which therefore the Registrar and merchants must ascertain in the usual manner".

In his judgment of 1802 concerning the capture of the *Fortuna (No. 1)* (Tadsen, Master) (4 C.Rob., 278; Roscoe, I, 392), Sir William Scott, recalling the earlier judgment in the case of the *Vrijheid* [1784] and further referring to Chapter 273 of the *Consulat de Mar* and the opinion of Van Bynkershoek (*Quaestiones juris publici*, I, ch. 13), stated that the Court of Appeal had recognized as the true rule that

> "the captor who has performed the contract of the vessel is, as a matter of right and *de cursu*, entitled to freight, although, if he has done anything to the injury of the property, or has been guilty of any misconduct, he may remain answerable for the effect of such misconduct or injury, in the way of a set-off against him".

The *Fortuna* case, in which a number of authors and precedents were quoted, related to a cargo, carried by a Danish ship to Lisbon, the original port of destination, where it had been discharged:

> "In such a case I apprehend the rule to be that the captor is entitled to freight, and on the same principle on which he would be held not to be entitled where he did not proceed and

perform the original voyage. The specific contract is performed in the one case, and not performed in the other".

In another *Fortuna* case, of 1809 (Koedt, Master) (Edw., 56; Roscoe, II, 17), the question was whether freight was due to the captor (the Crown) on certain Portuguese goods on board this and other Danish ships, which had been detained under the Danish embargo of 2 September 1807 and afterwards condemned to the Crown. The Court decreed that it was not so due because the captor had not brought the goods to the original port of destination, and added that this principle applied although they had afterwards been sold in England.

In the *Diana* [1803] (Runke, Master] (5 C.Rob., 67; Roscoe, I, 424) the Court upheld the rule that if goods were not carried to their original destination within the intention of the contracting parties, freight should not be due, but it made an exception for cases in which the port to which the goods were brought proved more beneficial than their port of destination, or in which they had almost reached that port: the intention of the parties had been substantially fulfilled, and the goods on the *Diana* had been delivered to their possession in the very country to which they would have wished them to have come.

The case of the *Twilling Riget* [1804] (Metz, Master) [1804] (5 C.Rob., 82; Roscoe, I, 430) was concerned with the calculation of the freight on the restoration of a ship with freight. Objections were made to the mode of calculating the burden applied by Registrar and merchants. The Court acceded to the rule on which they had proceeded, *viz.*, that the charter-party was not the measure by which the captor was in all cases bound, even where no fraud was imputed to the contract itself. Where navigation was rendered so hazardous by the events of war as to raise the price of freight to an extraordinary height, captors were not necessarily bound to that inflated rule of freight. The report of Registrar and merchants was referred back for their consideration.

Exceptions such as these only emphasized the general observance of the rule.

In the *Vro(u)w Anna Catherina (No. 2)* (Mahts, Master) [1806] (6 C.Rob., 269; Roscoe, I, 552) the Court reconfirmed the principle that a captor was only entitled to freight if he brought the cargo to its port of actual destination.

Sir William Scott's decision in the uncommon and complicated case of *The Friends* (Creighton, Master) [1810] (Edw., 246; Roscoe, II, 48) was in the nature of a Solomon's judgment. See on that case *infra*, p. 640.

(ii) French prize courts held a view contrary to the English doctrine and awarded the captor in such cases a "proportional freight", proportional, that is, to the distance covered from the port of departure to the port where the prize was brought in, as compared with the total length of the voyage to the final destination.

This traditional French doctrine concerning the indebtedness of freight *pro rata itineris* was, much later, re-affirmed during the Crimean and Franco-German Wars.

During the Crimean War the question was raised in a case of fraudulent *transfert de pavillon*: *L'Orione contre l'Averne* [1854] (Pistoye-Duverdy, II, 499-501). The cargo of the Russian ship *Orione (ex-Orio)* which had illegally been transferred to a neutral (the Tuscan) flag, was the property of neutral (Dutch) merchants who claimed the release of the cargo under the terms of § 5 of the French declaration of 29 March 1854 (comp. *supra*, p. 231). Recognizing the validity of that claim, the *Conseil des prises* decreed on the question of freight:

> "Considérant que par analogie avec le principe de l'Art. 303 du Code de commerce, relatif au fret des marchandises prises et rachetées, il est équitable de faire payer le fret des marchandises restituées, à raison de l'avancement du voyage, mais en tenant compte aux consignataires des sommes payées à titre d'avance dans la mesure des usages de la place d'Odessa ...".

The neutral goods on board the vessel, which was herself condemned, were released subject to the payment of freight by their owners. In that case the Court decreed a payment in proportion to the distance covered of the voyage.

(*b*) Freight claims of a neutral ship owner against the captor in case of release of a prize

(1) *The rule*. It was generally acknowledged that in cases of the release of a neutral ship the captors were under an obligation to pay to the ship owners or his agent, the master, the freight which the ship had earned before the seizure. This freight was called in the *Juno (No. 2)* [1799] (Roscoe, I, 202) "a charge (or a lien) upon the cargo". Lord Stowell stated the principle as follows:

> "The general principle has been stated very correctly that where a neutral vessel is brought in on account of the cargo, the ship is discharged with full freight because no blame attaches to her; she is ready and able to proceed to the completion of the voyage, and is only stopped by the incapacity of the cargo."

Other cases in which freight was ordered to be paid by the captor were the *Bremen Flugge* (Meyer, Master) [1801] (4 C.Rob., 90; Roscoe, I, 356) and *Der Mohr (No. 2)* (Helmer, Master) [1802] (4 C.Rob., 314; Roscoe, I, 395). On the first case, in which there was some controversy over the order of priority between concurrent claims to the proceeds of the cargo, see *infra*, p. 638. In the second case, in which the ship had been lost through the negligence of the captor's agent and a decree of restitution of the ship's value was made against the captor, the latter was held to be also liable for the freight:

> "On the principle of law I am of opinion that the freight must be taken, as having become as much the property of the neutral claimant, as the ship herself. The captor took *cum*

> *onere*: If the loss had happened by accident only in bringing in, the captor, having made a justifiable seizure, would not have been liable to any restitution, either for the freight, or for the ship; but the Court has already pronounced this loss not to have arisen from any casual misfortune. The freight is as much a part of the loss, as the ship: for he was bound to answer equally for both."

(2) *The exceptions*. However, the rule that freight was due by the captor to the ship owner or his agent, the master, was not absolute and general. It did not apply when the ship had been guilty of unlawful behaviour. This might consist of 1. slave trade; 2. the carrying of false papers; 3. engagement in a colonial or coastal trade which was normally closed to foreign shipping and reserved to national ships; 4. the carriage of contraband goods, at least when such carriage took place with the knowledge of the ship-owner or the master; 5. blockade-running. In such cases "the freight was forfeited". The allowance of freight was so disputed by the captor and withheld by the prize court, *inter alia*, in the following cases and on the following grounds:

1. Forfeiture on the ground of slave trade:

See the case of the *Fortuna* (Verissimo, Master) [1811] (1 Dods., 81; Roscoe, I, 193, footnote *a*), reported above *sub* C, section 2, p. 592, in the context of the competence of prize courts.

2. Forfeiture on the ground of the carrying of false papers:

the *America* [Sherborne, Master) [1800] (3 C.Rob., 36; Roscoe, I, 127, footnote *a*). Sir William Scott said:

> "It is not a new rule that if a ship is going with false papers the owner shall lose his freight. I do not say that if an owner makes out a clear case that he has been duped by the fraud of the master, the Court would in all cases press the rule to the utmost rigour against him".

but held that such a case had not been made out.

3. Forfeiture on the ground of engagement in a reserved trade:

the *Minerva* (Andaulle, Master) [1801] (3 C.Rob., 229; Roscoe, I, 301) and the *Rebecca* (Moore, Master) (1799), cited therein and referred to by Roscoe in a footnote *a* at I, p. 303 (2 C.Rob., 101), in which the motion for the allowance of freight to a neutral (American) ship, taken on a voyage from Dutch Surinam to enemy-occupied Amsterdam, with a cargo of colonial produce, was refused without a formal judgment.

4. Forfeiture on the ground of the carriage of contraband goods.

This was the main ground of the rejection of claims brought by neutral ship owners:

the Swedish *Sarah Christina* (Gorgensen, Master) [1799] (1 C.Rob., 237; Roscoe, I, 125); the Hamburg *Immanuel* (Eysenberg, Master) [1799] (2 C.Rob., 186; Roscoe, I, 217); the Prussian *Minerva* (Andaulle, Master) [1801] (3 C.Rob., 129; Roscoe, I, 301); the Danish *Neutralitet (No. 1)* (Burning, Master) [1801] (3 C.Rob., 295; Roscoe, I, 309) and the (also Scandinavian) *Öster Risöer* (Jurgenson, Master) [1802] (4 C.Rob., 199; Roscoe, I, 382); the American *Franklin (No. 1)* (Segerbrath, Master) [1801]

(3 C.Rob., 217; Roscoe, I, 298); and in later years the famous cases from the American Civil War, such as the *Peterhoff* [1866].

This latter reference leads us to

5. Forfeiture on the ground of breach of a blockade or an intent thereto.

An example of an earlier date is that of the *Fortuna (No. 2)* (Rhode, Master) [1803] (5 C.Rob., 27; Roscoe, I, 417), but reference must in particular be made to the famous later group of mixed cases of contraband and blockade from the American Civil War, especially the abovementioned *Peterhoff* case to which Wheaton referred in a note at p. 394 of vol. II of his collection of United States decisions in his report on the *Commercen* [1816] (*ibid.*, p. 382):

> "Freight and expenses were almost always refused by the British prize courts to a carrier of contraband. There is but one case in the books of an exception to this rule which was of sail cloth carried to Amsterdam, the contraband being in a small quantity amongst a variety of other articles."

In the United States the point was definitively and specifically decided in the case of the *Peterhoff* [1866] (5 Wall. (Amer.), 28; Scott, *Prize cases*, III, 1629), in which freight was refused even though the ship owner was ignorant of the contraband character of the cargo.

(*c*) Claims of the captor of an enemy ship to the freight earned by her owner prior to the capture.

The captor of an enemy ship was generally considered to have a claim, additional to his claim for her confiscation, to the freight earned by her owner before the capture over goods carried by his ship (and, for that matter, to comparable claims against third persons).

The captor was held to be the successor to the enemy ship owner and the freight was looked at as part of the condemned vessel.

In the somewhat unusual case of the Danish ships the *Prosper* and the *Holstein* [1809] (Edw., 72; Roscoe, II, 25), captured on a voyage from Tonningen to Lisbon with cargoes documented as Portuguese property, and ultimately restored as such by consent in the first instance, the adjudication of the question of freight and expenses was reserved. In those subsequent proceedings, which took place after hostilities had broken out between England and Denmark, it was submitted to the Court that in consequence of that development, the freight should be condemned to the Crown. The Court (*per* Lord Stowell) decided that the Crown was indeed entitled to freight as succeeding to the rights of the enemy ship owners, and applied this rule even if the condemnation of the vessels had not yet been finally decreed by a judgment. Such was the situation in the case of the two Danish vessels: they had been detained under the Danish embargo of 1807 prior to the outbreak of hostilities and had not yet been condemned by a decree of the Court prior to that outbreak.

In another (French) case in which the same question arose, the *Christiane*, ex-*Welyet* [1854] (De Pistoye-Duverdy, II, 502), the same decision was made; the condemnation of the ship was decreed to extend to the freight she had earned:

> "Le fret acquis, étant la propriété de l'armement, doit suivre le sort du navire."

During the Franco-German War the *Conseil des prises* decided in the same sense: see the *Joan*, reported by H. Barboux in his *Jurisprudence du Conseil des Prises pendant la guerre de 1870-1871* (Paris, 1872), and the *Vorsetzen* and the *Alma* (see Kiss, *Répertoire*, VI, No. 765).

(*d*) Claims of the captor of neutral goods on board an enemy ship to the freight which their neutral owner on their release still owed to the enemy ship owner.

When a captured enemy ship appeared to have neutral goods on board, English prize courts were already used in early periods to release them to their owners. This practice was in accordance with the principles of the *Consulat de Mar* and contrary to the practice in France where the system of infection of neutral property by enemy property was in force (whereon comp. III *sub* A, section 2, *supra*, pp. 300-301). This English case law, therefore, dates back to long before it was definitively sanctioned during the Crimean War and by the Declaration of Paris of 1856.

The release of neutral goods found in such conditions was, however, subject to the payment by their owner to the captor of the freight which he still owed to the enemy ship owner at the moment of release and which the captor considered as an integral part of the enemy ship.

Sir William Scott explained the legal position in the case of the *Bremen Flugge* [1801] (4 C.Rob., 90; Roscoe, I, 399), whereupon comp. further my paragraph on the question of priority between different freight and other claims, *infra*, p. 638.

> "This is a question concerning a remnant of a cargo, left in the registry, which has been condemned for want of further proof, after the neutral owner of the ship had obtained a sentence of restitution of the vessel, with freight and expenses, decreed to be a charge on the cargo. It is true such a decree passed; but this decree of freight and expenses is not to be taken as exclusive of all further orders of the Court respecting the cargo, nor as giving a decided preference of payment, to the exclusion of other just claims upon it if the fund should prove insufficient to satisfy all demands. On general principles, when condemnation has been obtained, the captor's claims appear to have rather the advantage. It has heretofore been a question of doubt whether the neutral vessel can lawfully carry the property of a belligerent at all. The modern rule, and indeed an ancient rule of this country, has been established on more liberal principles; and it is now held almost universally that the neutral has a right to carry the property of the enemy, but subject to the right of the belligerent to bring in the ship so employed, for the purpose of bringing the cargo to adjudication. It is now, I say, generally held that a neutral vessel so engaged is not exposed to any penalty at all, but that she is entitled to her freight as a lien attaching on the cargo. The captor takes *cum onere*. The freight attaches as a lien, which he must discharge by payment, provided, as it must always be understood, that there are no

unneutral circumstances in the conduct of the ship to induce a forfeiture of this demand. But the expenses of the neutral master appear to me to stand on a somewhat different footing. As to them, this distinction seems to present itself, supposing the law to be that the neutral ship is liable to be brought in. If she can carry the property of the enemy lawfully, on that condition only, I do not know that she is entitled to the expenses incurred in consequence of being so brought in. Putting practice out of the question, which has established an indulgent rule, it does not appear that the neutral master would, on principle merely, be entitled to an indemnification for expenses so incurred. He is bound to know the condition annexed to his right, and to abide the consequences. A more favourable practice has obtained, under which his expenses are usually allowed; and this practice the Court will be disposed to sustain as far as it does not interfere with other rights equally protected by practice and more strongly protected by principle. But it is not a claim which the neutral master is entitled to urge against the captor as a right equally original and equally vested in him, and in the same manner as freight is vested, by the receipt of the cargo on board and the performance of the contract of conveyance. It is said that the cargo was condemned, not as enemy's property, but for want of further proof and the attestation of the asserted owner. Can that make any difference? The legal conclusion will be the same, that condemnation passed because it was not proved to be the property of the neutral claimant; the want of proof of neutral property induces the legal conclusion that it is the property of enemies. The captor is as much entitled as if the cargo had been condemned on affirmative grounds, and in the first instance on positive evidence, that it was the property of the enemy. On these considerations I think the captor is entitled to the priority."

(*e*) Freight claims of the ship owner against the cargo owner.

These are rare reported cases in which the Prize Court dealt with claims of a ship owner against the owner of the cargo. See the abovementioned case under (*a*) of the *Copenhagen* [1799] (p. 632), qualified by the Court as "a case of a mixed nature". But in principle a Prize Court was not competent to adjudicate on such freight claims between private persons, as such competence belonged to the jurisdiction of other, private law tribunals.

(*f*) Order of priority between different freight and other claims.

The order of priority between the master's claim for freight and the captor's claim for restitution of their expenses was first determined in the *Bremen Flugge* (Meyer, Master) [1801] (4 C.Rob., 90; Roscoe, I, 356). This was a question respecting the remaining proceeds of a cargo which had been condemned for want of further proof, the ship having been restored as a neutral ship, with freight and expenses, decreed to be a charge on the cargo.

In the judgment Sir William Scott said, *inter alia*:

"This decree of freight and expenses is not to be taken as exclusive of all further orders of the Court respecting the cargo, nor as giving a decided preference of payment, to the exclusion of other just claims upon it if the fund should prove insufficient to satisfy all demands. On general principles, when condemnation has been obtained, the captor's claims appear to have rather the advantage".

The further argument dealt with other considerations, connecting the case with the situation examined under (*b*), (p. 634), Roscoe in his heading of the case summarized the conclusion as follows:

"When a neutral vessel is restored but the cargo is condemned, and freight is ordered to be paid by the captors, such decree does not give the master of the vessel the right to be paid his expenses in priority over the captors of the remaining proceeds of the cargo".

The issue was considered by Sir William Scott again in the case of the *Vro(u)w Henrica* (Hilck, Master) [1803] (4 C.Rob. 343; Roscoe, I, 399), a Danish ship, captured when sailing from Valencia to London. In that case he ordered his staff to collect the unreported precedents in order to state their trend and, on the basis of that research, concluded as follows:

"I have considered the cases which I directed to be looked up, and I see no reason to alter the opinion which I before expressed, that freight is, in all ordinary cases, a lien which is to take place of all others. The captor takes *cum onere*: It is the allowed privilege of neutral trade to carry the property of the enemy, subject to its capture, and to the temporary detention of his vessel; and if the party does not prevaricate, or conduct himself in any respect with ill-faith, he is entitled to his freight. This is the rule which I am disposed to apply in all cases of neutral ships carrying on their ordinary commerce. It is the general rule, which may nevertheless be liable to be altered by circumstances. There is one class of cases to which I think it *ought not* to be applied—I mean the case of ships carrying on a trade between ports of allied enemies—a trade which may be said to arise in a great measure out of the circumstances of the war, though not altogether; I say not altogether, because such a trade exists in a limited degree in times of peace".

In his further argument Sir William Scott qualified the *Vro(u)w Henrica* case as a "case of mixed nature" to which he would apply a sort of middle judgment, allowing the captor his law expenses, and directing the other expenses to be postponed to the payment of freight.

Roscoe resumed the decision in the following heading:

"When a neutral ship trading between the ports of two belligerents was captured and ordered to be restored, but the cargo condemned, and the proceeds of the cargo are insufficient to pay the freight and the captor's expenses in full, the captor is entitled to his legal expenses as a first charge on the proceeds. The freight should rank next, and before other expenses".

The claimant, the neutral ship-owner, had asked the Court to rule that priority of payment might be given to freight on the authority of the *Bremen Flugge*.

(*g*) The *quantum* of the amount of freight after recapture.

The judgments of 1800 in the *Racehorse* (White, Master) (3 C.Rob., 101; Roscoe, I, 261) and the *Hiram* (Still, Master) (3 C.Rob., 180; Roscoe, I, 295) related to cases concerning the indebtedness of the quantum of freight after a recapture.

In the first case (recapture of a British ship, chartered for a voyage from Lisbon to Dublin and captured on that voyage by a French privateer, afterwards recaptured off Falmouth and brought to that port, where the cargo was delivered) the Court restored the ship to the owner. The cargo owner was to pay the whole freight, less one-eighth deducted for salvage.

In the second case (of another British ship, captured by the French on her outward voyage from Liverpool to Halifax, afterwards recaptured and brought back, not to Liverpool but to Plymouth) the ship owner's application under the charter for a freight *pro rata itineris peracti* was rejected, although the Court conceded that the distance from Plymouth to Liverpool is so short in comparison with the whole projected voyage, that the Court might be justified in considering it in effect the same as if the ship had actually been brought back to Liverpool. The rejection in that case was mainly based on the particular terms of the charter: in his view of the matter Sir William Scott was of opinion that the doctrine of freight *pro rata itineris* could not be maintained.

In the case of the recapture of the *Progress* [Barker, Master) [1810] (Edw., 210; Roscoe, II, 40) salvage was held to be due on the entire freight.

A very special case was that of *The Friends* [Creighton, Master) [1810] (Edw., 246; Roscoe, II, 48). This British vessel had been chartered to deliver a cargo at Lisbon. The ship had prosecuted her voyage to the entrance of the Tagus, when she was warned off by the blockading squadron. After a gale of wind had blown her out to sea, she was captured by a Spanish privateer, but soon afterwards recaptured by a British cruiser and taken to Madeira, where the ship and cargo were sold by the recaptors for the purpose of paying salvage. Both the ship and the cargo were afterwards decreed to be restored. What freight was due under these circumstances? Whereas the ship owner contended that the whole of the freight was due to him, as the ship had actually gone up to the mouth of the port to which she was destined, the owner of the cargo contended that no freight was due, as the cargo was not delivered according to the terms of the charter-party. Placed before that dilemma, Lord Stowell decided by a Solomon's judgment:

> "In this case therefore, loss is unavoidable, and the only question is upon whom the weight of it shall fall. Now, if the incapacity of completing the voyage could be exclusively attributed to one of the parties, it would be proper that the loss should fall there; but the fact is that the calamity is common to both, for both ship and cargo were equally affected by the blockade .... I think therefore that what equity would suggest is that the loss should be divided, and under these circumstances, I shall direct a moiety of the freight to be paid".

*(C) Apportionment of general average (*avarie commune *or* avarie grosse)

Captors were from early times under the obligation to make their contribution to making good the damage of "general average", suffered by the owners of cargo jettisoned by the master, before the capture or during the bringing-in of the prize into port, for the purpose of saving the ship and the remaining cargo from shipwreck. The rules on jettison in general, already laid down in Rhodian and Roman law, were constant elements of the oldest regional codifications of maritime law, but they were far from uniform and differed characteristically from regulation to regulation. Their diversity even gives a clue to the problem of the regional origin of the codification concerned, as I have already observed in Chapter I on the sources of prize law, *supra*, p. 3. Travers Twiss has set out those differences at p. lxxviii of the Introduction to Part III of his *Black Book of the Admiralty*. Those differences amounted to the following. Whereas the original rules of Roman law and the Basilica prescribed a valuation of the goods cast overboard at cost price and that of the goods preserved at the market price prevailing in the port of debarkation, the Assises of Jerusalem ordered the valuation of both groups of cargo at cost price. The Judgments of the Sea of Oléron fixed the value of the jettisoned goods at the price they would have yielded in the port of unloading. The Customs of the Sea of the Consulat (Chapter 52) contained a shifting scale according to whether half the voyage had been completed at the time of the jettison (valuation of the cargo cast overboard at its market price in the port of unloading) or had not been so completed (valuation of such cargo at the cost price in the port of loading). Finally the Ordinance of King Pedro IV of Aragón of 1340 (printed as an annex to the Book of 1494) in its Chapters 28 and 29 again ordered a valuation at the market price in the port of unloading, a detail which might justify the uncertain conclusion that the origin of the Valencian Regulations is of a date prior to 1340.

Judicial precedents concerning claims of the owners of jettisoned cargoes against the owners of the ship or of other parts of the cargo which had safely reached their destination for a proportionate contribution to the general average loss incurred before the capture, were rare in prize cases. Lord Stowell touched upon the subject once in a comparable case, that of the *Hoffnung (No. 3)* (Hardrath, Master) of 1807 (6 C.Rob., 383; Roscoe, I, 583). That case concerned a demand of average on the part of the Admiralty against a neutral (Swedish) vessel which lay in the port of Ilfracombe on the outbreak of hostilities between England and Prussia. Part of the cargo was thereupon seized and condemned as enemy (Prussian) property and sold. The proceeds of the sale were applied to the repair of the ship. The Admiralty's demand was to recover against the ship after her restoration to the Swedish owners the value of that part of the cargo.

The nature of a claim for a proportionate contribution to general average was described clearly by the Privy Council in the case of *Cleary v. McAndrew (Cargo ex Galam)* of 1863 (11 Moore P.C. (N.S. 216)) (comp. also R. Lowndes and G.P. Rudolf's *Law of General Average* etc.). But the specific question of whether captors of cargo in wartime had to take it with the burden of such proportionate contribution seems not to have arisen until during World War I in the *Sørfareren* [1915] and *Chateaubriand* [1916] cases.

In the above survey of reparation and freight claims I have confined myself mainly to citing British and American prize court decisions because their impact on the development of customary prize law is the only really important one and because, moreover, comparable data from the case law of other countries, such as France and the United Netherlands, were not readily available.

Section 7. PROCEEDS OF PRIZES. DROITS OF THE CROWN AND DROITS OF ADMIRALTY. PRIZE BOUNTY

Introduction

The subject of the allocation of condemned prizes or their proceeds to the potential beneficiaries and their apportionment amongst them has been regulated differently in the legislation of the main maritime Powers in the course of history.

The condemnation of a captured vessel or cargo as good and lawful prize always had the effect of divesting the owners of their property and transferring the ownership to the captor. This was hardly debatable in theory. More controversial was the question who exactly was the actual beneficiary of the proceeds.

The answer to this query continually changed in the course of time. Was it the capturing State, conceived as a body corporate or a legal person under civil or administrative law? Or was it one particular organ or branch of government of the capturing State? Or was it a special fund created for the purpose of receiving the proceeds? And, of course, to what particular portion of the proceeds could the real captors lay claim, perhaps differing according to who they were: one or more privateers, a State warship, other State agents, such as port or customs officers, or even private persons?

Privateers have always played a prominent rôle in the distribution of the proceeds of prizes, if only because they assisted their State in its warfare at their own, usually heavy, expense for which they expected and deserved adequate compensation. Hence the antiquity of regulations on this subject, which often also laid down rules concerning the distribution of the proceeds of prizes amongst the various groups of captors. I will, therefore, begin with a few more detailed historical data.

Art. 19 of Part A of the Black Book of the Admiralty, dating presumably from before the naval battle on the Zwin in 1340, ordained as follows:

"Item sil avent que desoubz les gages du Roy sur la mer ou en ports biens des enemys estre gaignez par toute la flotte ou par parcelle dicelles, donques aura et prendra le Roy de toutes maneres diceulx biens la quarte partie, et les seigneurs des nefs une autre quarte partie, et l'autre moitié diceulx biens auront les gaigneurs diceulx, la	"Item if it happens that under the King's pay upon the sea or in ports enemies goods be taken by the whole ffleete, or by part thereof, then the King shall have and take the ffourth part of all manner of the said goods, and the owners of the shipps another fourth part, and the other halfe of the said goods shall belong to those who

quelle moitié doit estre entre eulx également partie ..."	took them, which halfe ought to be shared equally between them ...".

The *Rôles d'Oléron* contained nothing on the subject.

The Inquisition of Queensborough of 1375, instituted "to ascertain the points hereafter written in manner as they have been used in ancient times, by the oath of a number of people, for to keepe and continue firmely for the future the same points, according to the verdict hereafter written" in a series of 81 articles, confirmed "the ancient customs of admiralty" in this field in Arts. 1, 18 and 22. The Admiral always received his share, even when enemy property was captured in his absence (Black Book, Part A, Art. 7); the rest was divided into equal parts between (the owners of) the ship and her master and mariners. But a remark in the Black Book (on Art. 9 of Part A on the grant of prize money to privateers or others "out of the King's pay") casts some doubt upon the continued observance of that rule, which the author declared to be "now [1871] obsolete", though still remaining the foundation of the actual practice at the time.

As remarked above, there was a vast circle of potential beneficiaries of condemned prizes or their proceeds. Who exactly were these potential beneficiaries in the successive historical periods was dependent, amongst other things, on the contemporary systems of public law or current doctrinal public law constructions: the King, the Crown, the Government, the State as the personification of the nation, vested with legal personality also in the domain of private law, the Treasury, the Navy, the Admiral or the Admiralty, a special Naval Fund, warship commanders and crews of warships, privateers, customs officers, port authorities, in exceptional cases even merchant vessels and private captors.

The development in England has led to a curious distinction between "droits of the Crown" and "droits of Admiralty", a unique feature of British prize law, dating back to early days, see *infra*, p. 653. Condemned prizes or their proceeds or estimated value fell, in principle, in part to the King, in part to the Admiral. Moreover, the actual captors, whether officers and crews of King's ships, or owners and crews of privateers, used to be granted varying shares in the proceeds of sold prizes or in their estimated value.

The allotment of the proceeds of prizes, *i.e.* their distribution among the Crown, the Admiral of the Fleet and the actual captors, is indeed one of the oldest elements in regional or national regulations of the exercise of the belligerent right of seizure. The shares to which any of the persons engaged in the operation could lay claim differed according to whether the captures were made by the Admiral and his subordinates, or by privateers or other persons not in the King's pay. The solution was sometimes also dependent on whether the Admiral was present or absent when the prize was made, or on the place where it was made, at sea or in port. These grants were subject to a claim of the Admiral to two shares, if he was present at the capture, but otherwise only one share. Privateers and others not in the King's pay should have what they took, subject to a claim of the Admiral to two shares.

These old rules lie at the root of the peculiar tradition in later English legislation and case law of assigning the proceeds of prizes to the Crown in one of two different capacities, either to the King as the Sovereign, or to "the Crown in its office of Admiralty", with the resulting distinction between "droits of the Crown" and "droits of Admiralty", and the connected practice of awarding "prize bounty", "prize money" or "head money" to the actual captors.

This somewhat mysterious splitting up of the British Monarch into two different capacities has remained obscure for a long time until it was clarified by the results of an historical inquiry by H. C. Rothery in 1857 (1915), cited below, p. 653.

It had already been formulated by Sir William Scott in an early judgment relating to the *Mercurius* (Gerdes, Master) [1798] (1 C.Rob., 80; Roscoe, I, 54), a ship claimed by a merchant of Hambourg, restored to him by consent, but subsequently seized for a second time, in the following terms:

> "The King in his office of Admiralty is the second seizor in this case; and it is said that, as the fountain of all prize, he is to be considered, also as the original captor; but the King holds the office of Lord High Admiral in a capacity distinguishable from his regal character; besides, although he is undoubtedly the fountain of prize, he has conveyed away his interests in it to various persons: to the commanders and crews of his own ships; to his other subjects by his letters of marque; and to the Lord High Admiral of England. It has been declared by high authority that the interest of prize is vested in the captor, and that captors may, against the wish of the Crown, proceed to adjudication."

The question of whether certain captured goods came within the category of "droits of the Admiralty" also arose in the case of cargoes landed from the Dutch vessel *Ooster Eems*, stranded on the Goodwin Sands. This was a case in which the competence of the Admiralty Court, sustained by that Court, was denied by the Lords of Appeal (comp. on this case section 2 above, p. 593). The Warden of the Cinque Ports had claimed the goods as enemy property, which had become "a perquisite of Admiralty" within his jurisdiction, and "droits of Admiralty" [1784] (Roscoe, I, 136, footnote *a*).

This practice by the King, in his "regal character" of being "the fountain of all prize", of "conveying-away" parts of his interest in prizes to himself in his other capacity of Lord High Admiral of England becomes not less enigmatical when one is told that constitutional tradition in the United Kingdom is so strong that even the present Sovereign, Her Majesty Queen Elizabeth II, is, after almost two centuries, still officially styled "the Lord High Admiral", a function paralleled by the office recently conferred upon Queen Elizabeth, the Queen Mother, as "Lord Warden of the Cinque Ports".

The legal situation in England in his days was once again analysed by Sir William Scott in his elaborate judgment of 19 December 1804 (5 R.Rob., 173; Roscoe, I, 441) concerning the *Elsebe* (Maas, Master) and several other neutral vessels, being part of the second Swedish convoy (comp. on this famous case III *sub* B *supra*, section 3 under *f*, p. 520, and section 4, p. 525). In that judgment the position was described by the peculiar formula "Prize is altogether a creature of the Crown", a formula which was changed by Roscoe to "The King is the fountain of all prize."

In the case of the *Rebeckah* (Thompson, Master) [1799] (1 C.Rob., 227; Roscoe, I, 118) the claim of the Admiralty to prize money was allowed; in that case there was an additional circumstance in favour of the claim: the island of St Marcou from where the capture had been made was certified to be "peculiarly under the direction of the Admiralty". The Admiral's claims were qualified as "rights of great antiquity and splendour, and entitled to great attention and respect".

1. *Legislation on the subject*

Before passing to a survey of the case law of the prize courts of England and France (*infra*, pp. 653-660 and pp. 661-663), I will summarise the state of the legislation of the main maritime Powers of the past concerning the allotment of the proceeds of prizes.

England

Even in England the rules were not merely judge-made, for this particular subject matter was one of the more exceptional instances of legislative interference of the British Parliament or Crown with prize affairs.

An Ordinance of Cromwell's Commonwealth of 1649 awarded half of the prize to the actual captors.

On the Order in Council of March 1666 comp. my exposé on the distinction between "droits of the Crown" and "droits of Admiralty" *supra*, p. 655.

An Act of 1693 during the Nine Years' War (4 & 5 W. and M., c.25) laid down that in the case of capture by one of the King's ships one-third of the value of the prize was allotted to her crew, but in the case of capture by a privateer four-fifths of the cargo and the whole ship went to the privateer.

A footnote at p. vii of Roscoe's introduction to vol. I of his *Reports* and his note at p. 450 of that volume concerning the Swedish vessel *Elsebe* [1804] (pp. 441 *et seq.*) relate that such was the rule that remained in force until the end of the Nine Years' War (1697).

After the outbreak of the War of the Spanish Succession a Royal Proclamation of 1 June 1702 awarded to His Majesty's ships one-half of the prize and to privateers the whole benefit thereof, but no general parliamentary regulation would seem to have been enacted during that war.

Such general regulation was, however, laid down in the first general *Prize Act* (the Statute 6 Anne, c.37 (1708)), which for the first time gave to the captors "the whole or sole benefit of the prize", as it was there termed. This practice has been continued in the several *Prize Acts* passed since that time. This is at least what E. S. Roscoe records in his note concerning the *Elsebe*, just mentioned.

According tot the *Dickenson* case of 1776 (Hay & Marriott, pp. 1 *et seq.*), all prizes taken in port were, prior to the *Cruizers Act* of Queen Anne of 1798, condemned to the Lord High Admiral, even if captured by Royal warships (cases of the *St. Nicholas du Tot* and the *John* of 1702). But after that Act the Lord High Admiral had no droits of vessels seized in port by the Queen's men-of-war: cases of the *Voorsigtigheit* and the *Adventure* [1709], the *Hope* [1710], the *Anne Galley* and the *St. Nicholas* [1712]. Proceedings were to be as usual: the prizes were to be condemned in her name, but an Order in Council benefitted the actual captors.

A *Prize Act* used to be passed at the beginning of each war until 1864, when the first permanent *Prize Act* was enacted: 27 & 28 Vict., c.25.

Particulars of the older British practice can still be found in much later prize court judgments, even in some dating from the period of World War I, such as the decision of the Naval Prize Tribunal concerning the *Abonema et al.* [1918] (*B.C.P.C.*, III, 302). In that decision one reads about the older practice and the later changes (p. 309):

> "From ancient times a certain portion of those rights were assigned to maintain the dignity of the Lord High Admiral; hence arose the distinction between droits of the Crown and droits of Admiralty. At the outbreak of war it was the practice of the Crown to grant its interest in any prize taken to the captors thereof—that is, to the officers and men of the ship which effected the capture. This left a few cases, which will be referred to hereafter, of droits of the Crown which had not been granted away; but, putting these aside, the practical distinction was between captures which enured for the benefit of the officers and men of individual ships of His Majesty's Navy or commissioned privateers, on the one hand, and droits of Admiralty on the other.
>
> When the office of Lord High Admiral ceased to be filled, and the Crown in lieu thereof appointed Lords Commissioners of the Admiralty, droits of Admiralty reverted to the Crown, and upon the surrender of the hereditary revenues of the Crown which it has been the practice for recent Monarchs to make upon their accession, and which surrender by his present Majesty is embodied in the Civil List Act, 1910 (10 Edw. 7 & 1 Geo. 5, c. 28), passed to the Exchequer. Hence arose the somewhat paradoxical position that droits of the Crown went to the Navy, and droits of Admiralty to the Exchequer. Before this war the practice was, as already stated, that each captured prize enured, subject to any rights of the Flag officer, for the benefit of the officers and men of the capturing ship or ships; but at the beginning of this war the Crown did not make the usual grant. The Naval Prize Act and the Proclamation thereunder have constituted the droits of the Crown one fund "for the entire benefit and encouragement of the Officers and Men of Our Naval and Marine Forces".

On the further development in 1918 (creation of a Naval Prize Fund and transfer of the jurisdiction in this field from the Prize Courts to a new Naval Prize Tribunal) comp. the detailed data, given in my above-cited work of 1924, § 126, pp. 224-231.

Data on the somewhat nebulous subject of the two kinds of "droits", of the Crown and of the Admiralty, can also still be found in two other judgments relating to the destruction of enemy vessels, respectively the

German auxiliary cruiser *Cap Trafalgar* by the British warship *Carmania* [1916] (*B.C.P.C.*, II, p. 77) and a Turkish troop transport in the Sea of Marmora by *H.M. Submarine E.14* [1919] (*ibid.*, II, 404 and III, 568). In the latter judgment one reads:

> "In the old wars claims for head money rarely came before the courts; the award being made by certificate granted upon depositions made before the Chief-Magistrate at the port to which the captors repaired. In 1854, by 17 & 18 Vict. c.19, s. 7, all parties were permitted to resort to the Court of Admiralty in all cases concerning awards, and finally the *Naval Prize Act*, 1864, makes a decree of the Court compulsory in all cases of Prize bounty".

This *Naval Prize Act*, 1864, regulated the award of prize money in its Articles 42-44. Article 42 ran as follows:

> "If, in relation to any war, Her Majesty is pleased to declare, by Proclamation or Order in Council, her intention to grant prize bounty to the officers and crews of her ships of war, then such of the officers and crew of any of H.M.'s ships of war, as are actually present at the taking or destroying of any armed ship of any of H.M.'s enemies shall be entitled to have distributed among them as prize bounty a sum calculated at the rate of five pounds for each person on board the enemy ship at the beginning of the engagement."

It follows from this text that the provision only related to the taking or destruction of "armed ships of any of H.M.'s enemies", not to enemy merchant vessels or cargoes condemned as good and lawful prize.

The old practice of distributing the proceeds of such vessels and cargoes among the captors was formally abrogated in 1914.

The French system

In France the rules on the grant of prize bounty ("parts de prises") to the captors were initially laid down in Art. 25 of the *Edit* of 1543 and Art. 39 of the *Edit* of March 1584. From the latter it appears that the reward originally promised of one eighth of the value of the prize was insufficient to cover the expenses which privateers necessarily had to incur. Therefor the new Edict rules as follows:

> "Pour ce aussi que plusieurs Bourgeois propriétaires et advitailleurs des Navires nos subietz, nous ont cy-devant fait remonstrer que jaçoit ce qu'ilz facent faire lesdictes Navires, et icelles equipent et fournissent d'artillerie et aultres munitions de guerre et de vivres, pour grever et offencer noz ennemis et adversaires, le tout à grandz frais et despens, neantmoingtz ne leur est baillé huictiesme pour leurs portions des butins qui sont gaignez sur nosdicts ennemis et adversaires, qui n'est chose suffisante, en esgard aux grands frais, mises et despences qui leur convient faire, à faire faire lesdictes Navires, et icelles esquiper, munir, et advituailler, qui est cause que lesdicts Bourgeois propriétaires et advictailleurs ne peuvent mettre sus, et nous servir de grands et puissans Navires, ainsi qu'ilz pourroient faire si desdicts butins raisonnable et competante portion leur estoit distribuee, Nous à ce que doresnavant ils ayent plus grande occasion et vouloir de faire faire et entretenir bons, grands, fortz et puissans vaisseaulx, dont peussions estre serviz et secouruz en noz guerres contre nosdicts ennemis et adversaires, et iceulx amplement esquipper, munir, et garnir de toutes choses requises pour la guerre, avons ordonné et ordonnons qu'iceulx Bourgeois et

aultres, ausquels appartiendront aucuns Navires, apres le dixiesme de nostredict Admiral pris et deduict sur la totalité de la prise et butin que feront lesdicts Navires, auront et prendront la quarte partye du surplus d'icelle prise et butin, soit de marchandises, prisonniers, rançons, et quelles que soient lesdictes prises et butin sans aucune chose en reserver ny excepter, et des trois quartz restans les advitailleurs en auront quart et demy, et les mariniers et autres compaignons de guerre autre quart et demy, pour le partir entre eulx en la maniere accoustumee."

A perusal of De Pistoye and Duverdy's *Traité des prises maritimes* shows that the subject matter of prize money in France has subsequently been regulated in a number of other *Arrêtés* or *Règlements*, *viz.*:

Art. 33 of the French *Ordonnance de la Marine* of 1681, which authorized every member of the crew to stipulate with the shipowner the part he would be entitled to share in the prizes, fixed the amount of prize money in the case of absence of any *contrat de société* (see on these "société pour la course" De Pistoye and Duverdy, *Traité*, I, pp. 214-229) on two-thirds for the crew. The rule was changed by Art. 8 of the *Règlement* of 25 November 1695 and the *Arrêté* of 2 prairial *an* XI (*Traité*, II, pp. 399-400);

a *Règlement* of 27 January 1706 (II, 416), complemented by a *Décret* of 9 September 1806 (II, 417), on joint captures by several privateers, either all French, or partly French and partly Allied;

an *Arrêté* of 6 germinal *an* VIII (II, 443), Arts. 16 *et seq.*, regulating the settlement of possible disputes over the liquidation of prizes;

an *Arrêté* of 9 ventôse *an* IX (II, 427-442), concerning the liquidation and distribution of prizes among captors of the Imperial Marine;

the *Arrêté* of 2 prairial *an* XI, Arts. 99 *et seq.* (II, 397-415), dealing with the distribution of prizes among the crews of privateers and the setting up of a *Conseil de répartition*;

an *Avis* of the *Conseil d'Etat* of 4 April 1809 (II, 432), a document more of a legislative than a judicial nature; and

a *Décret Impérial* of 23 May 1854 (II, 447), promulgating the Franco-British convention of 10 May 1854 "pour régler le mode de jugement et de partage des prises faites dans le cours de la présente guerre" (de Crimée) (II, 472).

Judgments of the French prize courts, based on these *arrêtés* and *décrets*, can be found, interspersed between introductory notes and commentaries of the authors and detailed legislative data, spread over the pp. 403 *et seq.*, 432 *et seq.* and 499-515 of vol. II of the *Traité*.

The authors' commentary (II, 426-427) states, *inter alia*, that, prior to the *Ordonnance* of 28 March 1778, the crews of State warships were only entitled to a bonus ("gratification") on account of their capture of enemy warships, but that the *Ordonnance* granted them full right to such warships.

Most of the judgments concern disputes over alleged joint captures, either by several privateers, or by State warships and privateers together with forces based on land. A special group of cases relates to recaptures ("recousses"), whereupon comp. III *sub* B, section 7, *supra*, p. 558.

I insert here, in a different arrangement, the main provisions on the subject matter obtaining in the *Arrêté* of 2 prairial *an* XI (section II of chapter II of *Titre* IX of the *Traité*, p. 382):

"§1. Du droit des équipages dans les prises. De la formation de la masse partageable. Encouragements à la course.

Art. 91. Le tiers du produit des prises qui auront été faites appartiendra à l'équipage du bâtiment qui les aura faites; mais le montant des avances qui auront été payées sera déduit sur les parts de ceux qui les auront reçues.
Art. 92. Les équipages des bâtiments armés en guerre et marchandises, n'auront que le cinquième des prises, et il ne leur sera fait aucune déduction pour les avances comptées à l'armement, ou pour les mois payés pendant le cours du voyage.
Art. 62. Si le chef conducteur d'un navire pris fait dans sa route quelques autres prises, elles appartiendront à l'armement dont il fait partie, ou à la division à laquelle il est attaché.
Art. 26. Les gratifications suivantes seront payées pour les prises qui seront faites par des corsaires particuliers, savoir:
Navires de commerce chargés de marchandises: quarante francs pour chaque prisonnier amené dans les ports."

What followed in section III of chapter II of *Titre* IX of the *Traité* (Arts. 99-104 of the *Arrêté* of 2 prairial *an* XI) related to the setting-up of a *Conseil de répartition*, whose decisions would be final; the cases in which that *Conseil* could not be convened; the maximum and the reduction of prize money; its award to wounded or mutilated members of the crews and to the widows and orphans of those killed in action; and the prize money owing to mariners landed during a cruise on account of illness.

The complicated history of the *Caisse des Invalides de la Marine* is described by De Pistoye and Duverdy at pp. 389-393 of vol. II of the *Traité*. It was set up by Louis XIV during the Nine Years' War (1688-1697); the contributions due to this fund by way of "prélèvement" from the proceeds of prizes were determined progressively by a long series of decrees dated 1703, 1709, 1713, 1791, *an* III, germinal *an* VIII, 2 prairial *an* XI (Art. 95), 22 May 1816 (Art. 5) when the *Caisse* seems to have been "reconstituted" (*Traité*, II, 391 and 426) and 31 May 1838.

On the "dixième de l'Admiral" see p. 397 of vol. II of the *Traité*. It was abolished in France by an Edict of 1758 during the Seven Years' War. A comparable share in the prize money was reserved in the Netherlands for the Admiral-General of the United Provinces, see *infra*, p. 650.

The Netherlands

The Netherlands as a seafaring nation depended in their first difficult period after independence in 1572 very much on the activities of their privateers ("commissievaarders"). We find therefore a long series of decrees of the States General ("placaten") which regulate the taking of prizes in the several wars fought by the United Provinces and which prescribe in detail the shares of the owners and the crews of the capturing ships. Also, right from the outset, a decree was adopted which awarded a tenth part of the prize money to the Admiral-General of the United Provinces, the Prince of Orange; several times this decree was repeated as it seems that not all provincial Admiralty Colleges "remembered" to deduct this part from the prize proceeds (comp. the "dixième de l'Admiral" in France).

In the Groot Placaatboek (Statute Book of the United Provinces) every volume has a special chapter on "Decrees concerning privateers". The main decrees were the following:

23 May 1624: there was a fixed bonus for taking an enemy ship; the amount of the bonus depended on the size of the captured ship (Groot Placaatboek, I, 972);

4 July 1625 (I, 974), almost identical to the 1624 Decree;

11 March 1632 (I, 976), a reminder of the part due to the Admiral-General; a special premium was promised for the capturing of the colours of the enemy ship, ranging from 1000 guilders for the ensign of the commanding Admiral to 50 guilders for the colours of the ship's stern;

in those years (I, 978) there were special Decrees for capturing enemy ships on inland rivers, especially on the Upper-Rhine (8 August 1625 and 11 June 1639, respectively);

27 August 1672 (III, 232), once again a reminder of the original Decree of 20 July 1602, on the tenth part for the Admiral-General;

31 May 1697 (IV, 217), changing the distribution of prize money: the amount of the bonus now depended on the number of persons constituting the crew of the captured ship and on the amount of munition used during the battle ("pounds of gunpowder and number of cannon-balls", certain small guns being excepted); in exceptional circumstances the relation between the size of the capturing and the captured crew could play a role;

6 June 1702 (V, 300), *idem*;

20 June 1704 (V, 305), *idem*, although the bonus for captures during a certain period within a well-defined zone of the North Sea was raised;

28 July 1705 (V, 306), *idem*;

29 April 1709 (V, 312), explaining in detail some of the rules of the 1705 Decree;

11 December 1747 (VII, 482), a repetition of the older regulations; it concerns a war against the French and the complete proceeds of the ship—after adjudication by the Admiralty Colleges—are promised to the owner and crew of the privateer; a detailed system of bonusses for retaking a ship during a more or less long period of time after the original taking of the ship (a rule that had already been decreed on 13 April 1677); and on

22 February 1793 (IX, 104), a Decree for the war against Revolutionary France. During the time of the Batavian Republic, when the Netherlands were ruled by the French, one Decree on the taking of prizes and the distribution of prize money was published: 2 prairial *an* XI (22 May 1803).

After the liberation of the country and the institution of a monarchy in the Netherlands, the 1803 Decree was replaced by a Decree of 13 December 1818 (Statute Book 1818, No. 44). This Decree repeated the old, well-known rules and was in force until the commencement of the second World War, although in 1838 the Supreme Court of the Netherlands had been asked to produce a concept for a more modern law on the taking of prizes and the distribution of the prize money. The Supreme Court made a draft-Act, but this draft was never laid before Parliament.

During the nineteenth century several Decrees were published on the regulation of prize-making in the then Netherlands East Indies. On 26 June 1829 the Netherlands Decree of 1818 was also declared in force for the East Indies; this was more or less repeated in a Decree of 4 December 1877 (Netherlands Indies Statutebook 1877, No. 242) at the beginning of the Acheen war. On 17 July 1877 a new set of prize regulations had already been enacted for the taking of prizes and the sale of them (No. 284). The 1877 rules were replaced on 28 October 1903 by a new Decree (Netherlands Indies Statute Book 1903, No. 372).

For Surinam and the Netherlands Antilles no special prize decrees were ever enacted.

Spain

There is a long list of Spanish *Ordenanzas* on the distribution of prize money, starting in 1430 with an *Ordenanza* by the Catholic Kings. One of the main points of these Orders is the part of the proceeds that went to the King. In general it was one fifth, although there were different rules for prizes made by official men-of-war of by privateers. In the first category the King could claim anything up to the full proceeds, in the latter category the King claimed two fifths (*Real Cédula* of 1513), one fifth (*Ordenanzas* of 1633 and following years) and, finally, the King ceded even this last fifth to the captor if the latter had borne the full costs of the ship and the crew. See for a detailed survey of all the *Ordenanzas* the *Tratado jurídico-político sobre presas de mar* by Felix Joseph de Abreu y Bertodano (Cadiz, 1746) and *Presas marítimas* by Isidro Pérez y Oliva (Madrid, 1887).

The United States

The United States, in their first stage of their international existence as a confederation of States, laid down their views on the subject in the Act of 2 March 1799 in which Congress formulated statutory provisions on "The produce of prizes taken by the ships of the United States". After some legislative amendments by the Acts of 17 July 1862 and 3 March 1863 Congress adopted the Act of 30 June 1864 "to regulate prize proceedings and the distribution of prize money" (13 Stat. 306, sec. 10). This Act legalized the participation of non-naval vessels in the distribution of the proceeds of the prize in certain cases. See on the development of American legislation in this field the third chapter of Madeline Robinton's book on the New York Prize Court, 1861-1865 (pp. 75 *et seq.*, et 86 *et seq.*).

Japan
However, as appears from S. Takahashi's statement at p. 12 of his *Cases on international law during the Chinese-Japanese War* (Cambridge, 1899) not all naval Powers have adopted the practice of granting prize money to the actual captors. There we read about Japanese practice:

> "In Western countries, it was and has been the usual custom that the whole or a portion of the captured movables should be given to the captors, according to some scale of reward fixed by public authority: USA 1864 *Act* gave the whole of the value to the captors when the vessels making the capture were of equal or inferior force to the prize, but if their force was superior, they were to receive a half only, the rest going to the Treasury—1864 English *Naval Prize Act*: "The captors shall continue to take only such interest (if any) in the proceeds of prizes as may be from time to time granted to them by the Crown". But it is, and has been, the invariable rule in England, in modern times, to surrender the entire proceeds to the officers and men engaged in the capture. The general practice of prize courts is to order a sale of the vessel or goods on condemnation, and the sum thus realized is divided among the captors. But in Japan no prize was to be given to the captors, who are deemed to seize property at sea on the ground of some breach of law connected with it, for the sake of their country and not for their own sake."

On the other hand, Japan's opponents in her two wars of 1894-1895 with China and of 1904-1905 with Russia stuck to the ancient practice. Thus, Takahashi mentions at the same page a decree on the distribution of war booty among captors who are involved in a faulty seizure (comp. *Wörterbuch des Völkerrechts*, Strupp, I, 196).

Russia
Russia's Regulations as to Naval Prizes of 14 July 1895 (Hurst and Bray, I, Appendix A, pp. 319 *et seq.*) contained an elaborate section II, devoted to prize-money, chapter 1 of which (Arts. 35-41) dealt with the right to prize-money itself, chapter 2 (Arts. 42-49) determining its amount and distribution. This section covered under the name of prize-money also the award of salvage in case of recapture (dealt with in this volume in III B, section 7, *supra*, pp. 565) and it related to a wide range of potential beneficiaries: not only commanders of the squadron and divisions and all other persons serving in the Navy, including volunteers, but also land forces on board of ships of war; persons who had assisted the capture of the prize by giving notice and information; persons who had died after the conclusion of the naval operation concerned, or killed before their conclusion, and their widows and descendants; and merchant vessels.

2. *Case law on the subject*

After having given above a broad survey of the legislative sources I will now pass to the judicial side of the subject by dealing with the available case law.

In view of the difference between the legal systems of England and France,

I must review them separately, beginning with the judicial pronouncements of English prize courts.

English case law

After my survey of the origin and development of the English system I will undertake a more detailed summary of the judgments of Sir William Scott (Lord Stowell).

The application of the system presented two different aspects of the problem, as the accent lay sometimes on (*a*) the distinction between "droits of the Crown" and "droits of the Admiralty", and sometimes on (*b*) the grant and distribution of prize money to the actual captors. These two aspects will be discussed separately, although it is difficult to make a strict distinction between the two groups of decisions. I will attempt to arrange them in such a manner that first will be quoted (under *a*) the judgments in which the emphasis lies on the distinction between the two classes of "droits" and then (under *b*) those which turned around the award of prize money.

(*a*) *Distinction between "droits of the Crown" and "droits of Admiralty"*. The origin of the system of allocation and apportionment of prizes in England has remained for a long time shrouded in historical mist. The author to whom we are indebted for dissipating that mist is H.C. Rothery, a former Registrar of the Prize Court, who has undertaken an inquiry into the distinction between the two classes of "droits", "droits of the Crown" and "droits of Admiralty". The results of that inquiry were laid down by the author in a *Report on Prize Droits* which was drawn up in 1857, but was only published in 1915 in a revised and annotated version by E.S. Roscoe under the title *Prize droits, being a report to H.M. Treasury on droits of the Crown and of Admiralty in time of war*.

When perusing the case law concerning this distinction, one gets the curious impression of finding oneself confronted with a sort of secret language, employed by a sect of initiated lawyers. Let me quote in support of this boutade the relevant passages of Sir William Scott's elaborate judgment of 20 March/22 April 1806 in the case of the *Maria Françoise* (Le Bourch, Master) [1806] (6 C.Rob., 282; Roscoe, I, 559), a French ship which had sailed from Europe to the Isle de France prior to the Franco-British declaration of hostilities in March 1803, had been captured off Pondicherry (India) by the cutter *Fox* and carried to Negapatnam where she was first set free by the English admiral of the station in those seas, only to be seized a second time in September 1803 by His Majesty's ship *Sheerness*, which brought the prize to England for adjudication. In this case Sir William Scott argued as follows:

"We now come to the question of interest whether this prize is to be condemned to the captor, or as a droit of office to the Lord High Admiral, or, as that office is now constituted in practice, to the King in his office of Admiralty. It is well known that formerly there was a Lord High Admiral who now exists only in contemplation of law. All rights of prize belong originally to the Crown, and the beneficial interest derived to others can proceed only from the grant of the Crown. It was thought expedient to assign a certain portion of these rights to maintain the dignity of the Lord High Admiral; but during the civil wars, those ancient grants had grown into obscurity; and it is observed by Sir Leoline Jenkins, that it had been the policy of the usurper (Cromwell) to expunge as much as possible from record the very name and office of Lord High Admiral and all rights belonging to it.

[The Earl of Warwick, who was appointed Lord High Admiral by the Parliament and whose appointment was after his resignation removed by the Commons on 28 April 1645, was finally deprived of that office on 23 February 1648, under an Ordinance to the effect that that office and the wardenship of the Cinque Ports should be executed by the Council of State, appointed by the authority of Parliament.]

At the Restoration it became necessary to institute an inquiry into the nature of those rights, for the purpose of ascertaining their just limits. The discussion that took place respecting them is recorded in the works of Sir Leoline Jenkins; and I think it does appear from the history of that transaction that the nature and distinction of those rights had been all but obliterated in the minds of those who might be expected to be best acquainted with them. For the opinions that are reported to have been held by persons of eminence in this profession at that time are in no trifling degree at variance with each other, and contradictory to the understanding which has now for a long time universally prevailed. A very few passages from Sir Leoline Jenkins will be sufficient to justify this remark ...".

After two pages of further quotations, Lord Stowell continued:

"On all these points, it is impossible not to observe that the opinions of those eminent persons, who are not to be named in this Court without great respect, are so inconsistent, so opposite to the Order made in Council, and the interpretation which that Order has always received, that we are induced to conclude that they were speaking on a subject which had gone into some disuse and consequent oblivion, and on which they had not refreshed their memories by recurring to any traces that then existed of the more ancient practice; that their opinions can afford but little light for our guide in the present times, and therefore that the true rule must now be taken from the Order of Council of 1665 [comp. for its contents the text below, p. 655].

It appears to me, I confess, from the tenor of this Order, that the distinction between rights of the Admiral and rights of the Crown is founded in this—that when vessels come in, not under any motive arising out of the occasion of war, but from distress of weather, or want of provisions, or from ignorance of war, and are seized in port, they belong to the Lord High Admiral; but where the hand of violence has been exercised upon them, where the impression arises from acts connected with war, from revolt of their own crew, or from being forced or driven in by the King's ships, they belong to the Crown. This is the broad distinction which is laid down in the Order of Council, and which has since been invariably observed.

It is an opinion which I have occasionally thrown out, that the rights of the Lord High Admiral, though they are to be duly supported, are not to be extended by construction; and for these reasons, that the grants of the Crown differ in this respect from other grants, that they are to be taken strictly, and are not to be interpreted to the benefit of the grantee; and secondly, that the rights of the Crown, being public rights, deposited there for great public purposes, are not to be alienated beyond the precise tenor of the grant. It is said that the captors are grantees also, and that their claims stand in that respect on the same footing with those of the Lord High Admiral; but that description of them is subject to an essential distinction. In the first place, it is to be recollected that the grant to the

Lord High Admiral was made at a time when that office was on a footing which the present state of society and modern policy would scarcely suffer to exist. It is an establishment of ancient times, but little adapted to reasons of modern convenience. This at least we may presume, that if such an office was to be now instituted, some other mode of providing for its support would be resorted to than that of perquisites, which are so fluctuating in their own nature, which supply no regular fund for a permanent establishment, and are in no manner adapted to the exigencies of the public service. The grant, which is now made to those who by a commission execute that office, is accommodated to the necessities of the present times, and is directed under the view of the legislature attending to these present necessities, and to purposes of national concern. Another distinction of rather a more legal nature is, that the grant to the Lord High Admiral, whatever it conveys, carries with it a total and perpetual alienation of the rights of the Crown. They are gone for ever, and separated from the Crown, and nothing short of an Act of Parliament can restore them; whereas the grant to captors is nothing more than a mere temporary transfer of the beneficial interest. The Crown would not be chargeable with a violation of any public law, if if did not issue the grant; and though the practice of issuing it after the commencement of every war has been so constant in later times as to authorize the expectation of the continuance, it still is to be considered as the occasional act of the Crown's bounty, by which not the right but the mere beneficial interest of prize is conveyed for a time; but to return to the Crown and there to remain till again conveyed by a fresh act of royal liberality. Against such captors standing on an interest of that species the construction is the same as it would be against the Crown itself, because they cannot be pronounced against without pronouncing, in effect, that a perpetual alienation of the Crown's right to prize taken under such circumstances had already been made to the Lord High Admiral."

Sir William Scott's conclusion was as follows:

"I am of opinion that [the *Maria Françoise* case] is a case not only *not* within the words of the grant to the Lord High Admiral, but that it is *that* which is specially reserved to the Crown, and consequently that the condemnation [*sic*] ought to pass to the captor".

The full text of the Order in Council of 6 March 1665-1666 to which Sir William Scott referred in his judgment concerning the *Maria Françoise* and to which the distinction between "droits of the Crown" and "droits of Admiralty" has been traced down (already printed at p. 232 of my *Le droit des prises de la Grande Guerre* of 1924) ran as follows (from Roscoe, I, 123, footnote *a*):

Whereas through the long intermission of any war at sea by his Majesty's authority, several doubts have arisen concerning certain rights of the Lord High Admiral in time of hostility, the determination whereof appearing very necessary for the direction as well of his Majesty's officers as of those of the Lord High Admiral; upon full hearing and debate of the particulars hereafter mentioned, the King's counsel, learned in the common law, and likewise the judge of the High Court of Admiralty, and those of his Majesty's and his Royal Highness the Lord High Admiral's counsel in the said High Court of Admiralty, being present his Majesty, present in council, was pleased to declare:

1st. That all ships and goods belonging to enemies coming into any port, creek, or road, of this his Majesty's kingdom of England or of Ireland, by stress of weather or other accident, or by mistake of port, or by ignorance, not knowing of the war, do belong to the Lord High Admiral; but such as shall voluntarily come in, either men of war or merchantmen, upon revolt from the enemy, and such as shall be driven in, and forced into port by the King's men-of-war, and also such ships as shall be seized in any of the ports,

> creeks, or roads, of this kingdom, or of Ireland, before any declaration of war or reprisals by his Majesty, do belong unto his Majesty.
>
> 2nd. That all enemies' ships and goods casually met at sea, and seized by any vessel not commissionated, do belong to the Lord High Admiral.
>
> 3rd. That salvage belongs to the Lord High Admiral for all ships rescued.
>
> 4th. That all ships forsaken by the company belonging to them are the Lord High Admiral's, unless a ship commissionated have given the occasion to such dereliction, and the ship so left be seized by such ship pursuing, or by some other ship commissionated, then in the same company, and in pursuit of the enemy; and the like is to be understood of any goods thrown out of any ship pursued.

Disputes before British prize courts over the question "droits of the Crown" or "droits of Admiralty" have been fairly frequent and some of them are of old date. They were decided on the basis of Proclamations, Orders in Council or Naval Prize Acts which needed interpretation, and then sometimes arose as a result of unusual circumstances.

Mention of the distinction between the two kinds of "droits" has already been made by the Admiralty Court at an early stage. One of the oldest judicial texts is the judgment concerning the *Nostra Signora del Carmen* [1708] (Roscoe, I, footnote at p. 119), seized during the War of the Spanish Succession in the harbour of Gibraltar; by order of the Lieutenant-Governor she was condemned to the Lord High Admiral "as perquisite of Admiralty", although the relevant Act of Parliament of 1708 made no mention of captures in a harbour.

During the Seven Years' War, in the case of the *La Pacifique* [1761/4] (Burrell, 158; Roscoe, I, 3), the Admiral's right to a share in the prize was equally recognized.

Other cases of condemnation as "droits of Admiralty" were those of

the *Twee Gesusters* [1783-85] (Roscoe, I, 230, with footnote *a*), a case of contest between two private armed cruisers, the *Providence* being commissioned against the Dutch and the *Spitfire*, not so commissioned. The Dutch merchant ship chased by both cruisers was first reached by the *Providence*, the *Spitfire* still being distant about one English mile, but the actual capture of the prize took place by both; the master of the *Spitfire* was put on board the *Twee Gesusters* with a prize crew and left by the *Providence* to the *Spitfire* to convey her to Dartmouth. The Court of Admiralty pronounced the *Providence* to be the actual captor but the *Spitfire* to have been aiding and abetting and therefore entitled to take half the share she would have been entitled to if she had had a commission against the Dutch. The Lords of Appeal pronounced for "the interest of the King, in his office of Admiral", held that such proportion of the prize as would have belonged to the *Spitfire*, if commissioned, was liable to confiscation "as a droit and perquisite of Admiralty" and condemned the prize as taken by the two private ships to be shared in proportion accordingly;

the *Melomane* (Colas, Master) [1803] (5 C.Rob., 41; Roscoe, I, 419), captured by a boat hired by the captain of the King's ship the *Dragon* and sent out, manned with part of the *Dragon*'s crew, for the purpose of impressing mariners that were expected to arrive in the homeward-bound ships. Was a prize made by such a boat to be condemned as a "droit of Admiralty" or as a prize to the *Dragon*? This was held to depend upon whether the boat was acting as the boat of the warship;

the *Charlotte (No. 1)* (Witt, Master) [1804] (5 C.Rob., 280; Roscoe, I, 478), a ship captured by a hired armed revenue cutter, the *Duke of York*, commissioned, in accordance with the then existing practice, with a letter of marque, and alleged to have been placed under the command of the warship *Euridice* as her tender. In order to entitle a ship of war to a share of the prize made by such a vessel, the latter must be, so the Court held, have been recognized as a tender to the warship by order of the Admiralty, or have been constantly employed as such. As she was not considered to be a tender to the warship, the latter was not entitled to take interest in the prize, which enured exclusively to the private captors under their commission. The *Charlotte* was condemned as droits of Admiralty;

the abovementioned *Maria Françoise* [1806] an enemy (French) ship, seized in the roadstead of Negapatnam (India) by the King's ship *Sheerness*; the Court decided that an enemy ship seized in a port where she had sought refuge for reasons other than war must be condemned as "droits of Admiralty";

the *Foltina* [1814] (1 Dods., 450; Roscoe, II, 206), a ship taken, together with other ships, in the roadstead of the Danish island of Heligoland, which was conquered and taken possession of by British forces after the island's surrender on 5 September 1807. The official seizure of the ship, lying at anchor, took place on 15 December 1811. Although the conquest of the island had not been regularized by an Anglo-Danish treaty of peace or cession, the vessel was, despite the place of seizure, considered as hostile territory in British possession, condemned as droits of Admiralty.

Cases in which, on the other hand, the qualification of prizes as "droits of Admiralty" was denied were those of

the *Trautmannsdorff* [1795] (Roscoe, I, 119), decided by the Lords of Appeal against the claim of the Admiralty. In that case, related to a capture made in the open sea off "the bold shore" of St. Helena, it had remained doubtful in what manner possession was first taken of the vessel, either by a boat of the warship *Powerful*, or by the act of firing a shot from the fort. It was not disputed that the surrender was made to the fort long before any boat went off to take possession;

the *Rebeckah* (Thompson, Master) [1799] (1 C.Rob., 227; Roscoe, I, 118, footnote at p. 121), captured by a boat's crew from a British naval station, after having been fired at from that station and having struck her flag; it was held that the neutral vessel did not fall under the terms of the Order in Council of 1665-1666, which granted to the Lord High Admiral

> "the benefit of all captures of ships and goods coming into ports, creeks, or roads of England or Ireland, unless they come involuntarily upon revolt, or are driven in by the King's cruisers."

There was no military establishment at the station, which was used solely by the crews of warships lying in the vicinity; therefore, the prize vessel was "not a droit of Admiralty, but lawful maritime prize".

(*b*) *The award of prize money.* The practice of the award of prize bounty (prize money) has continued unchanged for centuries, only the shares allotted to the various groups of claimants have varied in the course of time.

The award or the distribution of prize money has frequently been discussed before British prize courts, although disputes on that account were often disposed of outside Court.

In order to illustrate the types of issues which were discussed in this field in the middle of the 18th century I will briefly report one of the oldest instances of doubtful claims to a share in a prize. During the War of the Austrian Succession (1740-48) a Spanish vessel, the *Nostra Signora de Cabadonga* (6 C.Rob., 305; Roscoe, I, 568, note *a*) was captured by the British warship the *Centurion.* At that moment, this warship had on board several officers of two other British warships, the *Gloucester* and the *Trial Prize*, which had been associated with the *Centurion* on a voyage of discovery under the command of Lord Anson, but which had been destroyed during that voyage as no longer seaworthy. The Court of Admiralty, seized by those officers with a claim to a share in the prize, adjudged them a share in the proceeds of the Spanish vessel according to their ranks with the officers of the *Centurion.* However, this judgment of 1745 was reversed by the Lords on 17 May 1747 on the following grounds: the claimants were not commissioned or warrant officers of, or belonging to the *Centurion*, nor in pay as such, nor aiding or assisting as officers of, or belonging to the *Centurion*, at the time of capture. They, consequently, had no right to a share in the distribution of the prize money with the officers of the *Centurion.*

The conquest by the British in the 1780's of the last remaining Netherlands colony on the coast of India, Negapatnam (Coromandel or eastern coast), gave rise to a dispute in the British Prize Court over the legal status of certain large vessels in the port which had previously carried pennants, but had taken them down out of respect for the King's ships. Subsequently, however, they had been granted permission to hoist the pennants again and it was on that ground that the status of warships was claimed for them. The Prize Court denied them military status and classed them as transports. The mere fact that they were granted permission to hoist the pennants again could not be accepted as proof of their military character as the grant was rather an act of civility and condescension on the part of the British authorities (Roscoe, I, 233, footnote *a*).

Another dispute over the legal qualification of transports arose in the case of the *Cape of Good Hope and its Dependencies* [1799-1802] (2 C.Rob., 274; Roscoe, I, 227). In this case it was decided, that transports were not primarily entitled to share in a prize taken by a squadron to which they were attached. But they might acquire an interest in a prize if they had been given a military character, and become associated with a fighting squadron with an *animus capiendi*.

Later cases in which the courts were seized with claims by captors, or by persons present at a capture, to a share in a prize were those relating to

Le Franc [1793] (Roscoe, I, 231, footnote *a*), a French East India ship, taken by several vessels composing part of a British East India fleet, six of them commissioned as private ships of war, the seventh, the *Glatton*, not provided with a letter of marque. The *Le Franc* was condemned as taken by six private warships and the *Glatton*, but the latter's share was condemned as a droit and perquisite of Admiralty;

Orion (Cushing, Master) [1803] (4 C.Rob., 362; Roscoe, I, 407): an Admiral had no right to a share in a prize captured by a ship of his squadron if such ship acted on a separate service by direction of the Admiralty;

Elsebe (Maas, Master) [1804] (5 C.Rob., 173; Roscoe, I, 441), a case in which the Crown had released a prize before adjudication and the captors disputed the legality of that measure in a suit for prize money (comp. above, *sub* B, section 3);

Frederick and Mary Ann (Andriesen, Master) [1805] (6 C.Rob., 213; Roscoe, I, 548), captured by a British privateer and sent to port with a prize crew from the captor on board; this prize crew managed to take another vessel as prize; their right to a share in the second prize was recognized;

Nostra Signora del Carmen [1806] (6 C.Rob., 302; Roscoe, I, 567): a naval officer on board a warship as a passenger was not entitled to a share in prize money due to the Lord High Admiral even if he worked on the warship during the capture;

Bellona [1809] (Edw., 63; Roscoe, II, 21), a case in which a revenue cutter, the *Falcon*, set up a claim of joint capture together with a King's ship; he failed because a claimant was not entitled to a share in a prize merely on the ground of having been in sight at the time of capture;

La Gloire and others [1810] (Edw., 280; Roscoe, II, 58): head-money ("the reward of immediate personal exertion"), which should be claimed promptly, is only distributable to the actual captors of a vessel, not to those who were merely in sight or in chase;

Pomona [1811] (1 Dods., 25; Roscoe, II, 124): proceeds of prize may be followed wherever they can be traced. Monition was enforced against persons who were at the time, or had been, in possession of prize goods;

Union (No. 1) [1813] (1 Dods., 346; Roscoe, II, 180): if, at the time of a capture by one vessel, another associated in the chase is not visible owing to fog or darkness, such other vessel is entitled to share in the prize if it is proved that at the time of the capture she is still engaged on the common purpose;

John (No. 1) [1813] (1 Dods., 363; Roscoe, II, 190): the burden of proof lies upon the party setting up a claim as joint captor, who in order to establish it must bring very clear proof in support of his case;

El Rayo [1814] (1 Dods., 42; Roscoe, II, 127): in a general engagement the whole fleet is entitled to head-money even if the factual surrender has been made by one ship only, provided that the surrender is a continuation of the general engagement;

Galen [1814] (1 Dods., 429; Roscoe, II, 199): a convoying warship has the right to share in a prize made during the convoy;

La Clorinde [1814] (1 Dods., 436; Roscoe, II, 200): where a vessel was fought and disabled by one ship, and then surrendered without resistance to another, both ships were entitled to share head-money;

Ville de Varsovie [1818] (2 Dods., 301; Roscoe, II, 220): the rules as to head-money differ in the case of associated and unassociated ships. In the case of associated ships it is only necessary to prove that the claimant was part of a general body associated for a common purpose, and was within sufficient distance to give assistance to ships actively engaged;

La Bellone [1818] (2 Dods., 343; Roscoe, II, 227): the parties are not entitled to head-money because the statute does not apply to conjunct expeditions of both army and navy.

During the Crimean War, on 2 June 1854, new Prize and Salvage Regulations were issued in England by an "Act for facilitating the Payment of Her Majesty's Navy, and the Payment and Distribution of Prize, Bounty, Salvage, and other Moneys to and amongst the Officers and Crews of Her Majesty's Ships and Vessels of War; and for the better Regulation of the Accounts relating thereto" (see *B.F.S.P.*, vol. 44, p. 1116 and Story-Pratt, *Notes on the principles and practice of Prize Courts*, p. 152).

A case that was decided under the régime of those new Regulations was that of the *Carl (No. 2)* [1855] (Spinks, 238; Roscoe, II, 497): a warship was deemed entitled to share in all captures made by a tender attached to her in constant employment, however distant she might have been from the tender at the time of the capture. In this case a claim was made by the warship *Impregnable* on the ground that the *Avon* which had made the capture was her tender and that the distribution of prize money should therefore be made not to the *Avon* alone, but to both of them together.

Reference was made by Dr Lushington to the *Charlotte (No. 1)* [1804] (5 C.Rob., 280; Roscoe, I, 478) in which Sir William Scott had decided that in order to entitle a ship of war to a share of a prize made by a vessel alleged to be her tender, it must be shown that the latter had been recognized as such by order of the Admiralty, or had been constantly employed as such. This latter condition was held to be fulfilled in the case of the *Carl*. In his judgment of 1855 the President stated that all the proclamations concerning the award of prize money were silent on captures made by tenders of a warship: the proclamations quoted were those of 1780, 1793, 1803, 1805, 1816 and 1836.

French case law

I will now survey the old French case law on prize money (*parts de prises*) and its distribution among captors, leaving on one side a few marginal judgments dealing with drawing rights of mariners from the *Caisse des Invalides* (II, 412) for their *parts de prises*, and the admissibility of a civil restraint upon such *parts* (II, 415). A certain rôle is in this context assigned by the prize courts to the *contrats de société*, once in frequent use among privateers.

Bellas contre l'Epervier [*an* IX] (De Pistoye-Duverdy, *Traité* II, 403): the rules which provide prize money for mariners disembarked from their ship because of illness, applied equally to the crews of privateers and those of State warships; they need not prove that their illness was contracted on board.

La Favorite contre Les Bouches-du-Rhône [*an* IX]: (II, 417): when two privateers claim the same prize, a partition between them will only take place if (*a*) both have actually contributed to the capture, or (*b*) they have concluded a *contrat de société*; if no such contract exists, the prize belongs to the privateer who has actually operated the seizure.

L'Adolphe contre l'Espérance [*an* IX] (II, 418): if a privateer, meeting the enemy, signals to another who responds, this amounts to the conclusion of a *contrat de société*; if, however, the latter, invited to take part in the combat remains a spectator, such contract is held to be annulled.

La Brillante [*an* IX] (II, 419): the mere presence of a privateer at a seizure by another without any active collaboration, for instance because his bullets do not reach far enough, does not entitle him to a share in the prize.

Le Génie, la Fortune et la Princesse-de-Bologne [1810] (II, 421): if several privateers chase a vessel (*in casu* the Swedish *Aurore*), she must be adjudged to those privateers only who either (*a*) have actually taken part in the combat or (*b*) have prompted the vessel chased by their manoeuvers to lower her flag.

Le Marsouin et consorts contre Le Théophile et consorts [1816] (II, 422): the *Conseil des prises* was held by the *Conseil d'Etat* to be the sole court competent to decide which of several cruisers have cooperated in an assertedly joint capture. If a ship could offer no resistance, the prize must be adjudged to the cruiser which, while the others were present, was the first to board the prize.

The judgment in *L'Espérance contra La Jeune-Abeille* [*an* IX] (II, 424) concerned a case in which it was doubtful whether prize legislation proper applied. Two privateers, not bound by a *contrat de société*, had separately chased four small merchant vessels, one English and three American. The *Conseil* held that in such a situation ordinary civil law applied: each of the privateers was entitled to the prize he made without any obligation to share it with the other, if the latter had not co-operated in the particular capture.

Three other decisions related to co-operation between naval units and landbased forces.

An *Avis* of the *Conseil d'Etat* of 4 April 1809 (II, 432) ruled in favour of a claim of the latter to a share in the prize. The *Avis* was provoked by doubts about the purport of Arts. 13-15 of the *Arrêté* of 9 ventôse *an* IX (II, 431-432): those articles gave no solution for the contingency that a prize was made by a detachment of the land forces alone without the cooperation of a warship. Now it had happened that batteries established on land forced a merchant ship at sea to strike her flag: the question arose whether the land forces concerned were entitled to the prize or whether the prize fell to the State. The *Avis* of the *Conseil d'Etat* was to the following effect:

> "Considérant que bien qu'une batterie de terre qui tire sur un bâtiment ennemi ne remplisse à la rigueur que son devoir, cette réflexion n'a point été appliquée aux bâtiments de l'Etat, et qu'il y a de suffisants motifs pour assimiler les uns aux autres, et pour accorder aux militaires qui servent les batteries une prise qui n'eût point en lieu sans leur fait;—Qu'en cas de concurrence avec des vaisseaux de l'Etat ou des bâtiments armés en course, le même principe doit conduire à établir le partage entre les uns et les autres, eu égard au nombre respectif des canons et des hommes, et dans les proportions de leurs grades, de la manière qui est observée entre plusieurs vaisseaux capteurs,—Est d'avis que les garnisons des forts et batteries de la côte qui, par l'effet seul de leur artillerie, font échouer un bâtiment ennemi ou l'obligent à amener son pavillon, ont droit à la prise, de la même manière qu'un bâtiment de l'Etat qui eût fait ladite prise, et sous la même déduction envers la caisse des Invalides de la marine;—Que lorsque les batteries auront contribué à la prise de vaisseaux ennemis, concurremment avec un ou plusieurs vaisseaux de la marine impériale ou des bâtiments armés en course, les garnisons au service desdites batteries doivent concourir au partage de la prise avec les vaisseaux ou bâtiments cocapteurs, en raison du nombre respectif des canons et des hommes, et en proportion des grades, de la manière qui est prescrite par les lois et règlements généraux pour les prises qui auraient été faites concurremment par plusieurs bâtiments de l'Etat, ou armés en course, et toujours sous la déduction du droit envers la Caisse des invalides de la marine;—Que lorsque le fait de la coopération est contesté par quelques-unes des parties intéressées, notamment lorsqu'il s'agit de savoir si un détachement, ou partie d'un détachement de troupes de terre a contribué à la prise, c'est au Conseil des prises à y statuer, d'après la nature des armes employées par le détachement, la distance à laquelle il se trouvait de l'ennemi, et d'après toutes les autres circonstances de la capture et à régler quels sont ceux qui ont droit à la prise.
>
> Que les mêmes dispositions, dans les mêmes circonstances, s'appliquent aux préposés des douanes qui ont fait une prise ou y ont concouru."

This *Avis* was a deviation from an earlier practice (I, 166).

Art. 17 of the same *Arrêté* of the *Conseil* of 9 ventôse *an* IX ruled on prizes made by detachments on land from a warship or squadron in open sea, that

> "Le produit des prises faites par quelques détachements de l'armée navale ou escadre, qui sera en pleine mer, appartiendra en commun à l'armée navale ou escadre, sans aucune distraction en faveur des vaisseaux qui auront fait ou amariné lesdites prises."

This provision was applied by the *Conseil d'Etat* extensively in 1835 in the case of *Lebrasse contre le Ministre de la Marine* (II, 434). A gunner of the French frigate *La Gazelle*, stationed in the Antilles, was charged to man with four other members of the crew of the *Gazelle*, a coastal battery. This battery captured a slave trader. Their claim to the whole prize was dismissed by the

Conseil d'Etat: they had to share it on an equal footing with the crew of the *Gazelle*.

In the case of *Dufresne contre le Duc-de-Dantzick* [1808] (II, 436) the *Conseil des prises* decided a controvery of a somewhat different type. When a privateer, the *Duc-de-Dantzick*, at anchor in the port of Le Havre, that had not yet completed all the required formalities, asked for authorization to attack an English vessel, the *William Henri*, sighted by the watch service of the port as battered by the storm, the Commissary of the Marine granted the privateer authorization to sail out on condition that it should operate together with three State cruisers, also at anchor in the port. The privateer succeeded in departing first and capturing the *William Henri* and on that account claimed the whole prize. However, that claim was dismissed, he had to share it with the three cruisers which had also taken part in the operation somewhat later, pursuant to Art. 23 of the same *Arrêté* of the Consuls of 9 ventôse *an* IX.

A subsequent judgment of the *Conseil d'Etat* of 1819, *Avierino contre Thiébault* (II, 445) decided on the strength of another *Arrêté*, of 6 germinal *an* VIII, that the ordinary tribunals had exclusive competence to take cognizance of disputes over private interests arising between shipowners concerning their respective shares in the proceeds of the prizes.

On concurrent claims to salvage on account of recaptures (*recousses*) comp. III *sub* B, section 7, *supra*, p. 539).

A detailed study of the French practice on the subject-matter surveyed above has been made by E. Luce, *Du droit aux parts de prises dans la marine française* (Paris, 1922).

Section 8. REVIEW OF NATIONAL PRIZE COURT DECREES. ARBITRATION AND SIMILAR PROCEDURES

Introductory

As I have remarked in section 4 under *litt.* (*1*) above, p. 617 (Procedure), it was only relatively rarely that prize cases were terminated by a decree pronounced in only one single instance. Usually some form of appeal or revision was provided for in the municipal sphere. The modalities of such an appeal or revision differed from country to country and from one historical period to another. After what I have written on this subject in section 4, I refrain from returning to it and entering into any detail. What I propose to do in the present section is to discuss briefly the various forms in which the provisions on the review of prize court decrees overstepped in one way or another the purely national boundaries and introduced an international element into the proceedings. This international element could in its turn be of various kinds. Thus, a treaty could intervene in order to oblige a party or the parties to submit judgments rendered in prize cases to a specific form of national review. Such obligatory review could also take on a more international tinge by a precisely prescribed composition of the body charged with the review. A treaty could also provide for a review by a mixed commission or an ordinary arbitral tribunal. Such a review on the interstate level could be organized *ad hoc*, or might take the "institutional" form of the setting up of a permanent organ ready to take action or to be available should the occasion arise.

The idea of creating an international instance for the adjudication of prize cases was already suggested in 1877 by a scientific body, the *Institut de droit international*, at its session in Zürich. The text of its resolution on this subject (*Annuaire*, vol. II, p. 153, reproduced by Ernest Lehr in his *Tableau général* of 1893, at p. 193) is equivocal: whereas its heading speaks of "un tribunal international", suggesting the creation of one central body, the idea is worked out quite differently in the resolution itself. This provides indeed for the setting up by each of the belligerent States at the beginning of a war of a prize tribunal of international composition, entrusted with the adjudication of captures to be made by its own naval forces, *i.e.*, in fact the creation of two parallel temporary "tribunaux internationaux". Comp. for further details *infra sub* B., p. 673.

The idea of creating a genuine central international court of appeal in prize cases only emerged in a tangible diplomatic form during the Second Peace Conference of The Hague of 1907.

And apart from all these possible modes of organizing the international adjudication or review of prize cases, there occurred extra-ordinary variants of international review, such as the creation of a permanent body to which, as a superior instance of an international nature, the parties might appeal direct from decrees of a national court. On the variant envisaged here—the *Grand Conseil de Malines* of the Burgundian Empire in the 15th century—see *supra* p. 106.

I will outline below under A the various instances of penetration of an international element into the domain of normal national jurisdiction in prize cases, and survey under B the conferment of prize law disputes upon an international body.

A. *Various degrees of internationalization of national prize court decrees*

Many treaties contained the simplest possible form of international element, *viz.*, a mutual undertaking by the parties to ensure that no seizures of property at sea should become final without previous adjudication by their Admiralty Court or other impartial tribunal, and that the judgments should be duly carried out. A few instances of such an undertaking from the many relevant treaty provisions of the past from the 17th century that reflect this unvarying principle are those included in the following treaties:

France-The Netherlands, 27 April 1662 (Dumont, VI[2], 412; Parry, 7, 139), Art. 40, repeated in Art. 27 of their Treaty of Commerce of Nijmegen of 10 August 1678 (Dumont, VII[1], 357; Parry, 14, 399):

> "Sa Majesté voulant que les Sujets desdits Seigneurs Etats Généraux soient traitéz dans tous les pays de son obéissance aussi favorablement que ses propres Sujets, donnera tous les ordres nécessaires pour faire que les Jugemens & Arrests qui seront rendus sur les prises qui auront esté faites à la Mer, soient donnez avec toute justice & équité, par personnes non suspectes, ny intéressées au fait dont sera question; & donnera S.M. des ordres précis & efficaces, afin que tous les Arrests, Jugemens, & Ordres de Justice déjà donnez & à donner, soient promptement et duement exécutez selon leurs formes".

England-The Netherlands, Treaty of Marine of 1/10 December 1674 (Dumont, VII[1], 283; Parry, 13, 255), Art. 11:

> "His Majesty and the said States, being desirous that the subjects of each other may be mutually treated, in all countries under their obedience respectively, with the like kindness as their own subjects, will give all necessary and effectual orders that the judgments upon prizes taken be given according to the rule of justice and equity, by judges beyond all suspicion, and not in any way concerned in the cause under debate; and His Majesty and the said States will likewise give strict orders that all sentences already given, and which shall be thereafter given, be (according to the tenor thereof) duly put in execution, and obtain their effect."

Sweden-The Netherlands, Treaty of Commerce of Nijmegen of 2/12 October 1679 (Dumont, VII[1], 437; Parry, 15, 331), Art. 27, reproducing the text of 10 August 1678, cited above.

Other treaty provisions tended to "internationalize" the prize proceedings in the municipal sphere, for example, by permitting the co-contracting party to demand the review of an unsatisfactory prize court decree of the first instance by a superior national tribunal in case of complaints about the injustice of a lower decision, and/or by prescribing a specific composition of the national body of review. See, *e.g.*, Art. 12 of the abovementioned Anglo-Netherlands Treaty of Marine of 1/10 December 1674:

> "And whensoever the ambassadors of the said Lords the States, or any other of their public ministers resident at the court of his most Serene Majesty of Great Britain, shall complain of the unjustness of sentences which have been given, his Majesty will cause the same to be reviewed and examined in his council, that it may appear whether the orders and precautions prescribed in this treaty have been observed, and have had their due effect, and will also take care that the same be fully provided for, and that right be done to the party complaining, within the space of three months; and likewise, when the ambassadors or other public ministers of his Majesty, resident with the States General, shall complain of the unjustness of sentences, the said States will cause a review and examination thereof to be made in the assembly of the States General, that it may appear whether the orders and precautions prescribed in this treaty have been observed, and have had their due effect, and they will likewise take care that the same be fully provided for, and that right be done to the party complaining within the space of three months; nevertheless, it shall not any ways be lawful to sell or unlade the goods in controversy,

either before the sentence given, or after it, during the review thereof, on either side, unless it be with the consent of the parties interested."

An old instance of the organisation by treaty of a national revision procedure is that agreed upon by the Netherlands and Sweden in Art. 10 of their *Conventio praevia* of 6/16 July 1667 (Dumont, VII[1], 17; Parry, 10, 187). This treaty prescribed a fresh examination of controversial decisions concerning captured Swedish vessels, pronounced in the first instance by the Netherlands Admiralty College, by the same body, but re-inforced for that purpose *ad hoc* by impartial and disinterested extraordinary expert members:

"Quantum vere attinet ad restitutionem Navium Merciumque quarundam Suecanarum, quas per Sententiam solemnem Collegiorum rei maritimae sive Admiralitatis per Foederatum Belgium pro jure captis habitas, ac proinde Fisco addictas esse constabit, cum nomine Regiae Majestatis Sueciae contendatur, urgeaturque solemnes hasce Sententias sub fundamento minus stabili solidoque ac parum validis de causis, quae per Patronos Fisci Admiralitatis in rem suam sint allegatae, latas fuisse, curae erit D.D. Ordinibus ut ejuscemodi Sententiae secundum Leges & Statuta Foederati Belgii per Revisionis, quam vocant, formam, altiori attentiorique indagini permittantur, Judicibusque Admiralitatis Ordinariis, alii extra ordinem, ut fieri consuevit, Judices periti, quique in partibus non sint, adjungantur. Quod, si rationes nonnullas solidas in causam continget proferri, quae conducant ad revocandos fatalium revisionis, aliorumvé defectuum neglectuumvé decursus; post elapsum jam liti persequendae tempus praescriptum, iis locum haud quaquam defore D.D. Ordines pollicentur".

This Preliminary Agreement between the two countries even included a separate Art. 3, intended to avoid excessive costs of such procedure: the States General promised that they would charge the same extra-ordinary judges with all the revision cases:

"Praeterea ne expensae Judicii Revisorii, quod beneficio Paragraphi decimi modo dictae Conventionis praeviae institui poterit, eorum, quorum interest singulis nimis graves sint, vel quemquam à persequendo Jure suo deterreant, promittunt itidem D.D. Ordines sese Causas eorum omnes, quibus Diplomata Revisionis indulserunt, iisdem Judicibus extra ordinem deligendis Judicibusque Admiralitatis Ordinariis adjungendis, junctim decidendas commissuros."

Another treaty between the same Powers a few days later, of 18 July 1667 (Dumont, VII[1], 39; Parry, 10, 197) further contained in Art. V a compromise solution of a dispute which had arisen over the capture of an individual Swedish vessel, the *Christina*, by the Netherlands West India Company off the coast of African Guinea (Cabo Corso): Sweden abandoned her action to recover the vessel with its cargo from the Company, in return for an indemnification of 14.000 rixdollars to be paid by The Netherlands to Sweden for the cession of Cabo Corso and the relinquishment of the claim of Sweden and her Africa Company to the *Christina* and its cargo.

Corresponding treaty provisions for the revision of prize court judgments by the capturing State itself also obtained in the relations between The Netherlands and France and between The Netherlands and England.

As regards France see Art. 42 of the Treaty of 27 April 1662 (Dumont, VI[2], 412; Parry, 7, 139) and Art. 28 of the Treaty of Commerce of Nijmegen of 10 August 1678 (Dumont, VII[1], 357; Parry, 14, 399).

Stipulations to guarantee the effectiveness of prize jurisdiction can be found in many treaties, *e.g.*, to the effect that judgments favourable to the victims of a seizure were to be carried into execution in anticipation of the judgment expected in appeal. See Art. 13 of the Anglo-Netherlands Treaty of Commerce of Westminster of 1/10 December 1674 (Dumont, VII[1], 282; Parry, 13, 255); Art. 29 of the Franco-Netherlands Treaty of Commerce of Nijmegen of 10 August 1678 (see above), identical with Art. 29 of the Netherlands Treaty with Sweden of 2/12 October 1679 (Dumont, VII[1], 437; Parry, 15, 331).

Art. 13 of 1674 (with England) stated:

> "A suit being commenced between the takers of prizes on the one part, and the claimers thereof on the other, and a sentence or decree being given for the party reclaiming, the said sentence or decree (upon security given) shall be put in execution, notwithstanding the appeal made by him that took the prize, which shall not be observed, in case the sentence shall be given against the claimers."

Art. 29 of 1678 (with France):

> "Quand Procez sera meu en première & seconde instance contre ceux qui auront fait des prises en Mer, & les Interessez en icelles, & que lesdits Interessez viendront à obtenir un Jugement ou Arrest favorable, ledit Jugement ou Arrest aura son execution sous caution, nonobstant l'Appel de celui qui aura fait la prise, mais non au contraire; & ce qui est dit au present Article, & aux precedens, pour faire rendre bonne et brieve Justice aux Sujets des Provinces-Unies, sur les prises faites à la Mer par les Sujets de Sa Majesté, sera entendu & pratiqué par les Seigneurs Etats Généraux à l'égard des prises faites par leurs Sujets sur ceux de Sa Majesté."

Another such guarantee was a prohibition to sell the prize pending the revision proceeding. See Art. 41 of the abovementioned Franco-Netherlands Treaty of 27 April 1662 including the following provision:

> "Et lors que les Ambassadeurs desdits Seigneurs Etats Généraux, ou quelqu'autre de leurs Ministres Publics, qui seront à la Cour de Sa Majesté, feront plaintes desdits Jugemens qui auront esté rendus, Sa Majesté fera revoir lesdits Jugemens en son Conseil, pour examiner si les ordres & précautions, contenues au présent Traité auront esté suivies & observées, & pour y faire pourvoir selon la raison; ce qui sera fait dans le temps de trois mois au plus; & néanmoins avant le premier Jugement ny après iceluy pendant la revision, les Biens & effets qui seront réclamez ne pourront estre vendus ny déchargez, si ce n'est du consentement des Parties intéressées pour eviter le déperissement desdites Marchandises."

B. *Conferment of prize law disputes upon an international body*

The review of national prize court decrees was further "internationalized" when foreign members were included in the body entrusted with such review;

even then the instance of appeal could, however, remain in principle a national judicial organ. The review of national prize court decrees was only entirely internationalized when the decision in appeal or revision was conferred upon an international body. For, besides the treaty provisions of different kinds for the review of prize court decisions by a more or less internationalized national body of appeal, there were cases of a settlement of disputes over captures in prize or over national prize court decrees on an international level.

Referring to several incidental references to arbitration in prize cases in the course of this publication and the more systematic review of groups of such cases in vol. VI, pp. 647 *et seq.* and vol. VIII, pp. 276 *et seq.*, I will make in this section a few remarks additional to what I have already summarily said in section 7 of Chapter I, *supra*, pp. 117.

The final adjudication of captures, validated in the first instance by a national prize court, was in actual fact sometimes referred to arbitration, either by an arbitral tribunal of the usual type, or by mixed claims commissions; the latter became especially familiar since 1794.

There have been two historical periods in which the submission of prize cases to international arbitration was agreed upon, or at least discussed, namely, the first part of the second half of the 17th century and the end of the 18th and the beginning of the 19th century. On the developments in both these periods I have already reported in vols VI and VIII of this publication. I will therefore only briefly recapitulate these cases here.

In the first period England and the Netherlands agreed on the submission of a number of private claims, not further specified, to arbitral settlement by their Treaty of Alliance of Whitehall of 4/14 September 1662 (Dumont, VI^2, 422; Parry, 7, 193), but in Article 15 of that treaty an express exception was made for two old prize cases, relating to the *Bonaventura* and the *Bona Esperanza*, which dated back to 1643 (vol. VIII of this publication, p. 319).

By the second of two Netherlands-Danish treaties of 1/11 February 1666 (Dumont, VI^3, 59; Parry, 8, 423) provision was made for arbitral settlement of a dispute over mutual captures of merchant vessels by the Netherlands West India Company and the Danish Company of Glückstadt (vol. VIII, p. 218).

The Netherlands-Swedish Peace Treaty of Nijmegen of 2/12 October 1679 (Dumont, VII^1, 432; Parry, 15, 317) included a separate Article 2, relating to seven Netherlands vessels captured by privateers, the ultimate fate of three of which was left to decision by a Swedish court of revision, that of the four others (captured by an irregular action of Swedish raiders provided with a French commission) to decision by one or more arbitrators. The four which were referred to arbitration concerned the *St. Jacob*, the *Witte Roos*, the *Maria Boodschap* and the *Nieuwe Heeren Logement*. The three others in whose captures only Swedish privateers had been involved were the *Mouthaan*, the *Buys* and the *Hoop*. Comp. on this arbitration the data given in

Part VIII of this publication, p. 219. It was facilitated by the peculiar character of the preceding Netherlands-Swedish war in which the parties had become involved in their capacity of allies of States belonging to opposite camps, despite their mutual "affection", and during which there had even been complete freedom of commerce between them. Article 3 also provided for the payment for requisitioned goods.

The second period is far more famous because it witnessed a renewal of the old ideal of arbitral settlement of international disputes which had fallen into disuse during the 18th century.

After a progressive decline of the institution of international arbitration during that century, it was indeed revived by Great Britain and the United States in their Jay Treaty of 19 November 1794 (Martens, R^2, V, 642; Parry, 52, 243) and it was Article VII, paragraph 2 of that treaty which provided for the submission of prize cases to mixed claims commissions. Since I have referred the discussion of the subjects envisaged by the said Article VII (2) and of certain subsequent arbitral decisions to the present Part IX-C (see Part VIII, p. 320), I must now enter into a few details concerning these cases.

As I have indicated *loco cit.*, the issues which at the time divided Great Britain and the United States in the field of the exercise of the belligerent right of prize presented the familiar traditional features. They were mentioned in La Fontaine's *Pasicrisie internationale*, pp. 1-16, and analysed in great detail by the editors of the *Recueil des arbitrages internationaux*, A. de Lapradelle and N. Politis, in vol. I, pp. 51-217. These authors grouped the cases submitted to the Mixed Commission into four categories dealing respectively with (i) the qualification of the enemy character of private property at sea: case of the *Betsey* (pp. 51-119); (ii) the presumption of the enemy character of such property: cases of the *Fame* (p. 120), the *Farmer*, *Molly*, *Sally* (Griffiths, master) and *Active* (p. 121), *Diana*, *Sally* (Choate, master), *Nancy* and *Sally* (Hayes, master) (pp. 123, 127, 129 and 131); (iii) contraband of war: case of the *Neptune* (pp. 137-178), and (iv) the responsibility of neutral States for the acts of belligerents in their territorial waters: cases of the *Jamaica* (p. 178), *Fanny* (p. 185) and *Elizabeth* (p. 188). In Part VIII of my publication, p. 320, I divided the issues involved in the cases submitted to the Mixed Commission under Article VII (2) of the Jay Treaty under the following seven headings:

(*a*) What criterion determined the enemy or neutral charactzer of prizes?

(*b*) What presumptions justified their qualification as enemy property?

(*c*) What categories of goods could be legally treated as contraband of war?

(*d*) Could foodstuffs be pre-empted by the belligerents?

(*e*) Under what circumstances were the belligerents obliged to pay compensation for a substantively unjustified capture (probable cause)?

(*f*) What was the legal effect of a condemnatory judgment in prize?
(*g*) What were the effects of seizures made in neutral water territory?

Apart from a number of other legal issues, such as the asserted final conclusiveness of condemnatory sentences pronounced by a municipal prize court as *res judicata* in international arbitral proceedings (denied), the asserted requirement of a unanimous vote of the arbitrators in the matter of their competence (also denied), the purport of the rule of "probable cause" of seizure and the calculation of the damage caused by an unjustified seizure, the *Betsey* case *sub* (*a*), from the point of view of substantive prize law, turned on the question whether the temporary residence of the neutral owner of a cargo on enemy territory was sufficient to constitute its enemy character.

The group of cases *sub* (*b*) concerned the admissible presumption of the enemy character of the property seized, distinguished by the editors as either (*sub* A, pp. 120 *et seq.*) "présomptions de condamnation" or (*sub* B, pp. 123 *et seq.*) "présomptions de juste saisie" (probable cause).

The *Neptune* case *sub* (*c*) had a bearing on the legal admissibility of the compulsory pre-emption by the British authorities of a cargo of rice carried for the account of American citizens on an American vessel sailing from Charleston to Bordeaux, in virtue of an English Order in Council of April 1795, issued in the interval between the signature and the exchange of the ratifications of the Jay Treaty.

The group of cases under (*d*) related to a problem on the borderline between neutrality and prize law, namely, the liability of a neutral government for damages caused by captures made by (partly French) privateers, originally equipped in its harbours, and the validity of such captures (comp. vol. X of this publication, p. 56).

The arbitral settlements under Article VII (2) of the Jay Treaty of 1794 were followed twenty years later by further arbitrations under Arts. IV-VII of the Anglo-American Peace Treaty of Ghent of 24 December 1814 (Martens, N.R., II, 76; Parry, 63, 421), but those no longer dealt with prize cases.

An appeal to an international instance for review of a decree made by a national prize court could be staged in different forms. It might be obligatorily superimposed on a previous adjudication in one or more municipal proceedings. It might be restricted to a testing of the legal aspects of the case or also extend to a re-assessment of the facts. It might, just as in all other forms of arbitral settlement, require an evaluation according to strict law, or admit of a solution ex *aequo et bono*. The parties might, as in the case of the *Alabama* claims, prescribe the rules they wished the arbitrators to apply. They might establish an *ad hoc* tribunal or invoke an existing tribunal in which the appeal case was receivable pursuant to its statute, for example, a permanent arbitration tribunal. In short, all the modalities of arbitral settlement which I have analysed in Part VIII of this publication applied also in the case of applications for the international review of municipal prize court decisions.

I draw special attention to the fact that arbitral proceedings were often a continuation of preceding national prize court decisions from which recourse was had to an international arbitral body on the strength of a special agreement, although there were also instances where the cases were brought direct before an arbitral tribunal, commonly a mixed commission, by "prorogation" without a previous national adjudication.

A number of the arbitrations organized under the Jay Treaty were in fact international extension-phases of proceedings which had commenced in the national domain. The same can be said of a number of proceedings initiated before Mixed Claims Commissions which have followed those decided under the Jay Treaty and which I have described in Part VI of this publication, pp. 647 *et seq.* Prize cases have indeed continued at later periods to be intermittently submitted to arbitral settlement.

Such arbitrations, mentioned in the *Pasicrisie internationale*, are those between

France and Mexico of 1844 (p. 20): French captures of Mexican ships during hostilities (war or not?) following the conflict over the Emperor Maximilian (*R.A.I.*, I, 545);

Spain and France of 1852 (p. 26): different groups of captures by both States prior and subsequent to 1 October 1823 (*Veloz-Mariana, Vigie, Victoria et al.*) (*R.A.I.*, I, 598);

Spain and the United States of 1795 (p. 79): captures made during the war, terminated by the Peace Treaty of San Lorenzo (which has remained without effect);

Spain and England of 1823 (p. 88): mutual captures made since 1 July 1808, in the period of the Holy Alliance, and

Brazil and England of 1829 (p. 91): captures of 25 English ships by Brazil in 1826 and 1827, neither of which, however, seem to have ended in a satisfactory result (at least judging from the fact that they are not reported in the *R.A.I.*);

and Argentina and England of 1830 (p. 92): captures by Argentine privateers during the war between Argentina and Brazil of 1829 (*R.A.I.*, II, 637).

The last arbitration mentioned in the *Pasicrisie internationale* was that between the United States and Russia of 1900 (p. 618), which, however, though also concerning a "prise maritime", was not the settlement of a prize case.

Only a very limited number of the awards which have resulted from these arbitrations have functioned as genuine sources of rules of law on maritime prize.

Occasionally very special variants of international review, other than those already mentioned in this section, have occurred. What I have in view here is the exceptional organization of a two-tier judiciary in the old Burgundian Empire of the 15th century in the Low Countries, consisting of a number of provincial courts in Holland, Zeeland, Flanders, etc., superimposed by a common central tribunal in Mechelen (Malines), established by the Duke-Emperor of Burgundy for the purpose of adjudicating upon cases brought before it in appeal from the decisions of the provincial courts. The gradual disclosure of the long-neglected contents of the archives of the *Grand Conseil de Malines* has already shown that among those archives there are still also extant dockets concerning old prize decrees. Comp. on this subject Chapter I, section 5, under The Netherlands, *supra*, pp. 106.

As related in my Introduction *supra* p. 664, one of the first activities of the *Institut de Droit International* consisted of planning the organization of an international prize tribunal. A Commission to study such a plan was already set up at its first session of 1875 at The Hague on the suggestion of the English member Westlake, who was appointed its Rapporteur (*Annuaire*, I, 121). His project was discussed in his absence at the second session of 1877 at Zürich, where the *Institut*, on the proposal of the members Bluntschli and Rolin-Jacquemyns adopted three resolutions on the subject (*Annuaire*, II, 124) and charged its member Bulmerincq with the task of drafting, after the session, a report on the question and on the resolutions adopted (*Annuaire*, II, 121); the text of this report can be found in *Annuaire*, II, 113 *et seq*. The text of the resolutions ran as follows (*Annuaire,* II, 153; *Tableau général-Lehr*, pp. 193-194):

> "L'Institut déclare que le système actuel des tribunaux et de l'administration de la justice en matière de prises est défectueux, et considère comme urgent de porter remède à cet état de choses par une nouvelle institution internationale. Il est d'avis qu'il y a lieu:
> 1. De formuler par traité les principes généraux en matière de prises;
> 2. De remplacer les tribunaux jusqu'ici exclusivement composés de juges appartenant à l'Etat belligérant par des tribunaux internationaux qui donnent aux particuliers interessés de l'Etat neutre ou ennemi de plus amples garanties d'un jugement impartial;
> 3. De s'entendre sur une procédure commune à adopter en matière de prises."

This text was complemented by the following declaration:

> "Toutefois l'Institut croit devoir déclarer que dès à présent il considérerait comme un progrès l'institution de tribunaux mixtes soit de première instance, soit d'appel, sur les bases du projet élaboré par M. Westlake."

The *Institut* and its Commission have not ceased to study and discuss the matter at their sessions of Paris (*Ann.*, III, 109), Oxford (*Ann.*, V. 131), Wiesbaden (*Ann.*, VI, 12, 105, 129, 139, 164, 174), Turin (*Ann.*, VI, 213-223), Munich (*Ann.*, VII, 185-190), Brussels (*Ann.*, VIII, 167) and finally Heidelberg (*Ann.*, IX, 202-217). The provisions regulating the adjudication of prize cases by an international tribunal were adopted at Heidelberg (1887) as a series of articles inserted in Chapter II (Dispositions spéciales), section 12 (De l'organisation de la procédure du tribunal international des prises maritimes), §§ 100-109 of the *Institut*'s *Règlement international des prises maritimes* (*Tableau général-Rolin*, pp. 191 *et seq*.).

The international prize tribunal proposed at Heidelberg was, contrary to the name conferred upon it, not organized as a universal central court of appeal to be created by the community of States, but as a tribunal to be set up by each of the belligerent States at the commencement of each war. The text of the provisions dealing with the constitution and functioning of this international prize tribunal follows below:

> "Au début de chaque guerre chacune des parties belligérantes constitue un tribunal international d'appel en matière de prises maritimes. Chacun de ces tribunaux est composé de cinq membres désignés comme suit:
>
> L'État belligérant nommera lui-même le président et un des membres. Il désignera en outre trois États neutres, qui choisiront chacun un des trois autres membres.
>
> § 101.—Tout procès de prise peut être déféré, sur demande des parties produite dans un délai de vingt jours, au tribunal international d'appel. L'introduction et la justification de l'appel se font en même temps et les délais courent à partir du jour du prononcé du jugement par le tribunal, ce jour non compris.
>
> § 102.—L'appel s'adresse au tribunal national des prises maritimes, lequel le notifie à la partie adverse, qui exige de l'appelant un dépôt de cautionnement pour le payement des frais de justice.
>
> § 103.—La justification de l'appel indique et motive les différents griefs se rapportant à des points déterminés du jugement du tribunal national des prises maritimes.
>
> § 104.—Le tribunal national des prises maritimes, en communiquant le mémoire d'appel à la partie adverse, l'invite à présenter une réplique dans un délai de quinze jours. A l'expiration de ce délai, ledit tribunal envoie les actes et le mémoire d'appel avec la réplique au tribunal international d'appel. Le tribunal national pourra accorder une prorogation de délai pour cause légitime.
>
> § 105.—La procédure devant le tribunal international d'appel est, en général, celle du tribunal des prises maritimes.
>
> § 106.—Le jugement ou l'arrêt de l'instance d'appel sera motivé et rendu en se basant sur un rapport écrit du président du tribunal, et en tenant compte des preuves et faits nouveaux que l'on aurait produits dans la procédure d'appel.
>
> § 107.—Il n'est admis, au sujet de la procédure et du jugement, ni pourvoi ou demande de restitution en entier, ni requêtes et observations des consuls et agents des États.
>
> § 108.—Le jugement d'appel est prononcé en présence des mandataires des parties assignées à cet effet, auxquels, sur leur demande, copie en est donnée. Il sera, en outre, publié dans un ou plusieurs journaux.
>
> § 109.—Après la publication, le tribunal national des prises maritimes sera requis pour l'exécution du jugement."

Later there have been great expectations about the rôle that the International Prize Court, proposed by the Second Peace Conference at The Hague of 1907 and intended to be a general court of appeal, would play in reforming the whole chaotic picture, but these expectations have been frustrated by the events of the years immediately following that Conference and its successor, the London Conference on Naval Warfare of 1908/09. See on those developments vol. VIII of this work, pp. 345-348 and 595-596, and pp. 130 *et seq.* of this volume.

ABBREVIATIONS

A.A.	Reports of International Arbitral Awards
Acton	Th.H. Acton, Privy Council Reports in The English Reports, vol. 12, see p. 80
A.D. (ad)	Annual Digest (and Reports) of Public International Law Cases
A.J.I.L.	American Journal of International Law
Aitzema	L. van Aitzema, Saken van Staet en oorlogh etc (The Hague, 1669-1672) 7 vols
Annuaire I.D.I.	Annuaire de l'Institut de Droit International (1873-)
B.C.P.C.	British and Colonial Prize Cases (London, 1915-1922) 3 vols
B.F.S.P.	British and Foreign State Papers
Bibliotheca Visseriana	Bibliotheca Visseriana dissertationum ius internationale etc (Leyden, 1923-1963) 20 vols
Black Book	The Black Book of the Admiralty with an appendix. Ed. by Travers Twiss (London,1871-1876) 4 vols
Blatchford	Samuel Blatchford, Reports of Cases in Prize, argued and decided in the Circuit and District Courts of the United States (1861-1865) etc, (New York, 1866)
Bulletin I.I.I.	Bulletin de l'Institut intermédiaire international (Haarlem-The Hague, 1923-)
Burrell	William Burrell, see p. 77
Classics	Classics of International Law, (Washington, 1911-) 25 vols.
de Clercq	A. de Clercq, Recueil des traités de la France (Paris, 1864-1907) 22 vols
coll mar	Chr. Robinson, Collectanea maritima (London, 1801)
C(m)d	Command Paper
Cranch	William Cranch, Reports of Cases adjudged by the Supreme Court of the United States, 1801-1815 (Washington City, 1804-) 9 vols
Deák and Jessup	Neutrality laws, regulations and treaties of various countries (Washington, 1939) 2 vols
Dodson (dods)	J. Dodson, see pp. 81, 82
Dumont	J. Dumont, Corps universel diplomatique du droit des gens, 8 vols (The Hague, 1726-1731)
Edwards (edw)	Th. Edwards, see p. 81
ffc	Bourguignon, The First Federal Court etc
Grotiana	A Journal under the auspices of the Foundation Grotiana (Assen, 1980-)
Grotius	Grotius Annuaire International. International Yearbook (The Hague, 1913-1948)
Hurst and Bray (h+b)	Sir Cecil J.B. Hurst and F.E. Bray, Russian and Japanese Prize Cases (London, 1912-1913)
I.L.R.	International Law Reports
Levantsche Handel	K. Heeringa, Bronnen tot de geschiedenis van den Levantschen handel (The Hague, 1910-1917)
Llo.pc	LLoyds prize cases
L.N.T.S	League of Nations Treaty Series
Martens	G.F. de Martens *et alii* (Göttingen, 1791-1975):
	R^1 Recueil des principaux traités, 1st ed., 7 vols, 1791, 1801
	S Supplément au Recueil, 1st ed., 4 vols,1802-1808

	R^2 Recueil de traités, 2nd ed., 8 vols, 1817-1835
	N.R. Nouveau Recueil de traités, 16 vols, 1817-1842
	N.S. Nouveaux Suppléments au Recueil, 3 vols, 1839-1842
	N.R.G. Nouveau Recueil Général de traités 1st series, 20 vols, 1843-1875 2nd series, 35 vols, 1876-1908 3rd series, 41 vols, 1908-1975
Moore pc	E.F. Moore, Privy Council Reports, see p. 80
N.I.L.R.	Netherlands International Law Review
N.J.	Nederlandse Jurisprudentie
Noradounghian	G. Noradounghian, Recueil d'Actes internationaux de l'Empire Ottoman (Paris, 1847-1903)
Ortolan	Th. Ortolan, Règles internationales etc
Parry	C. Parry, Consolidated Treaty Series (New York, 1969-)
Pistoye-Duverdy (p+d)	A. de Pistoye et Ch.Duverdy, Traité des prises maritimes etc. (Paris, 1859) 2 vols
prises mar fra	P. Fauchille, Jurisprudence française en matière de prises maritimes (Paris, 1916)
C. Rob.	Christopher Robinson, see pp. 81, 82
R.G.D.I.P.	Recueil général du droit international public
Roscoe (ros)	E.S. Roscoe, Reports of Prize Cases (London, 1905) 2 vols
Rousset	J. Rousset, Recueil historique d'actes, négociations, mémoires et traités, 21 vols (The Hague, 1728-1755)
Rymer	Th. Rymer, Foedera, 17 vols (London, 1704-1717)
Sirey rec gen	Sirey Recueil Général des lois et des arrêts en matière civile, criminele, commerciale et de droit public (Paris, 1791-)
Scott cases	James Brown Scott, Cases on international law etc
Spinks	Th. Spinks, Report of cases decided during etc, English Reports vol. 164
Stewart	Stewart, Vice-Admiralty Reports
Takah cases	S. Takahashi, Cases on international law etc
Takah ii	S. Takahashi, International Law applied etc
U.N.T.S.	United Nations Treaty Series
US	United States Supreme Court
Wenck	F.A.L. Wenck, Codex iuris gentium, 3 vols (Leipzig, 1781-1795)
Wheaton	H. Wheaton, see p. 83
W.P.N.R.	Weekblad voor privaatrecht, notaris-ambt en registratie
Z.f.V.R.	Zeitschrift für Völkerrecht

BIBLIOGRAPHY

Felix Joseph de Abreu y Bertodano, Tratado jurídico-político sobre pressas de mar, (Cádiz, 1746).

Walter Ashburner, The Rhodian Sea Law, (Oxford, 1909).

D.A. Azuni, Droit maritime de l'Europe, (Paris, 1805; reprint Torino, 1972) 2 vols.

H. Barboux, Jurisprudence du Conseil des prises pendant la guerre 1870-1871, (Paris, 1872).

T. Baty, Prize law and continuous voyage, (London, 1915).

C. van Bijnkershoek, Quaestionum juris publici, libri duo, (Classics, Washington, 1930).

C. van Bijnkershoek, Observationes tumultuariae, (Haarlem, 1926-1962), 5 vols.

E.O. van Boetzelaer, Netherlands international arbitrations between 1581 and 1794, (Leiden, diss., 1929).

Henry J. Bourguignon, The first Federal Court. The Federal Appellate Prize Court of the American Revolution 1775-1787, (Philadelphia, 1977).

Henry J. Bourguignon, Sir William Scott, Lord Stowell. Judge of the High Court of Admiralty, 1798-1828, (Cambridge etc., 1987).

H.W. Briggs, The doctrine of continuous voyage. Vol. XLIV, no.2 Johns Hopkins University Studies in Historical and Political Science, (Baltimore, 1926).

J.G. Büsch, Über das Bestreben der Völker einander in ihrem Seehandel wehe zu tun, (Hamburg, 1800).

A. de Capmany y de Monpalau, Código de las costumbres marítimas de Barcelona, (Madrid, 1791).

Alice Clare Carter, The Dutch Republic; Europe in the Seven Years' War, (Edinburgh, 1971).

Estienne Cleirac, Les us et coutumes de la mar, (Bordeaux, 1641).

Pitt Cobbett, Cases and opinions on international law, (London, 1909-1913) 3 vols.

Auguste Dumas, Étude sur le jugement des prises maritimes en France jusqu'à la suppression de l'office d'Admiral, (Paris, 1908).

C. Dupuis, Le droit de la guerre maritime d'après les conférences de la Haye et Londres, (Paris, 1911).

Antoine Fontanon, Les Edits et Ordonnances des Roys de France depuis S.Louys jusques à présent, (Paris, 1585) 2 vols.

F.A. Gooskens, De Admiraliteit van Veere. Inventaris van het archief en een kort overzicht van de geschiedenis tot 1559, (Middelburg, 1983).

H.G. van Grol, Het beheer van het Zeeuwsche zeewezen, (Vlissingen, 1936).

H. Grotius, De jure belli ac pacis, libri tres, (Paris, 1625).

H. Grotius, De jure praedae, (The Hague, 1868; edited by H.G. Hamaker).

H. Grotius, Mare liberum sive de jure quod Batavis competit ad Indiana commercia, (Leiden, 1609).

Hansisches Urkundenbuch, (Halle, 1876-1939) 11 vols.

M. Hübner, De la saisie des bâtiments neutres, (The Hague, 1759.

C.J.B. Hurst and F.E. Bray, Russian and Japanese cases, being a collection of translations and summaries of the principal cases decided by the Russian and Japanese Prize Courts arising out of the Russo-Japanese war, 1904-1905, (London, 1912-1913, reprinted Buffalo NY, 1972) 2 vols.

Stanley S. Jados, Consulate of the Sea and related documents, (University of Alabama Press, 1975).

E. Kappelhoff-Wulff, Die Zulässigkeit der Ausübung des Prisenrechts während eines Waffenstillstandes, (Hamburg, diss., 1973).

J. Kent, Commentaries on American law, (Boston, 1873, 12th ed. ad).
J.H. Kernkamp, De handel op den vijand, (Utrecht, 1931).
A.-C. Kiss, Répertoire de la pratique française en matière de droit international public, (Paris, 1962-1972) 7 vols.
Richard Kleen, De la contrebande de guerre et des transports interdits aux neutres d'après les principes du droit international contemporain, (Paris, 1893).
Richard Kleen, Lois et usages de la neutralité d'après le droit international conventionnel et coutumier des Etats civilisés, (Paris, 1898-1900) 2 vols.
A. Korthals Altes, Ons oudste zeerecht, (Zwolle, 1976).
Karl Fr. Kriger, Ursprung und Wurzeln der Rôles d'Oléron, (Cologne, 1970).
Johannes Loccenius, De jure maritimo et navali libri tres, (Holmiae, 1652, 2nd ed.).
E. Luce, Du droit aux parts de prises dans la marine française, (Paris, 1922).
Godfrey Lushington, A manual of naval prize law, (London, 1866).
C. la Mache, La guerre de course dans le passé, dans le présent, et dans l'avenir, (Paris, 1901).
James Marriott, The case of the Dutch ships, (London, 1756 (1759)).
Reginald G. Marsden, Documents relating to the law and custom of the Sea, (London, Naval Records Society, vol. 49, 1915).
Reginald G. Marsden, Select pleas in the Court of Admiralty. Vol.I: 1390-1404 and 1527-1545; Vol.II: 1547-1602 in The Publications of the Selden Society, vol. VI and XI, (London, 1892, 1897).
G.F. de Martens, Essai concernant les armateurs, les prises et surtout les reprises, (Göttingen, 1795; English translation by Th.H. Horne, London, 1801).
Moore, John Bassett, A digest of international law, (Washington, 1906) 8 vols.
Moore, John Bassett, History and digest of the international arbitrations to which the United States have been a party, (Washington, 1898) 6 vols.
Moore, John Bassett, International Adjudications ancient and modern.(New York, 1929-1936) 7 vols.
G. Noradounghian, Recueil d'Actes Internationaux de l'Empire Ottoman, (Paris, 1897-1903).
Th. Ortolan, Règles internationales et diplomatie de la mer, (Paris, 1845 (1853), 1864) 2 vols.
Johanna Oudendijk, Een Bourgondische ridder over den oorlog ter zee, (Amsterdam, 1941).
J.M. Pardessus, Collection de lois maritimes antérieures au xviiie siècle, (Paris, 1828-1845) 6 vols.
R. Pares, Colonial blockade and neutral rights, 1739-1763, (Oxford, 1938).
Isidro Pérez y Oliva, Presas marítimas, (Madrid, 1887).
A. de Pistoye et Ch. Duverdy, Traité des prises maritimes, (Paris, 1855, 1859, 2nd ed.).
F. Pollentier, De Admiraliteit en de oorlogen ter zee onder de Aartshertogen (1596-1609), (Brussels, 1972).
Frederic Thomas Pratt, Law of contraband of war with a selection of cases from the papers of the Right Hon. Sir Geo. Lee, LL.D., (London, 1856).
Frederic Thomas Pratt, Notes on the principles and practice of the prize courts, by the late Judge Story, (London, 1854).
Proceedings of the International Naval Conference, held in London, December 1908-February 1909, (London, 1909; Cd. 4555 and 4554).
A. Rémy, Théorie de la continuité du voyage en matière de blocus et de contrebande de guerre, (Paris, 1902).
Chr. Robinson, Collectanea maritima; being a collection of public instruments etc., etc., tending to illustrate the history and practice of prize law, (London, 1801).
Madeline Russell Robinton, An introduction to the papers of the New York Prize Court, 1861-1865, (New York, 1945).
E.S. Roscoe, A History of the English prize court, (London, 1924).
E.S. Roscoe, Reports of the prize cases determined in the High Court of Admiralty- from 1745 to 1859, (London, 1905) 2 vols.

E.S. Roscoe and T.L. Mears, A treaty on the Admiralty jurisdiction and the practice of the High Court of Justice and on the Vice-Admiralty courts and the Cinque Ports, (London, 1903).

H.C. Rothery; E.S. Roscoe editor, Prize droits, being a report to H.M. Treasury on droits of the Crown and the Admiralty in time of war, (London, 1915).

H. Royaards, De placito "Libera navis, libera merx", (Utrecht, diss., 1852).

G.A. Scheltus, Voorziening in de behoefte der belligerenten aan steenkolen, (Utrecht, diss., 1907).

James Brown Scott, Cases on international law principally selected from English and American courts, (St.Paul, 1922).

James Brown Scott, The declaration of London, February 26, 1909, (New York, 1919).

James Brown Scott, Prize cases decided in the United States Supreme Court 1789-1918, (Oxford, 1923) 3 vols.

J. Selden, Vindiciae maris clausi, (London, 1635).

Luigi Sico, "Toute prise doit être jugée", (Naples, 1971).

Robert Sidney Smith, Historia de los Consulados de Mar (1250-1700), (Barcelona, 1978).

Robert Sidney Smith, The Spanish Guild merchant. A history of the Spanish Consulado 1250-1700, (Durham, NC, 1940).

F.E. Smith and N.W. Sibley, International law as interpreted during the Russo-Japanese War, (London, 1907 2nd ed.).

Thomas Spinks, Reports of cases decided during the present war in the Admiralty Prize Court and the Court of Appeal, (London, w.y. [1856]) 2 parts.

Story's Notes, *See* Pratt, Notes.

Sakuy Takahashi, Cases on international law during the Chino-Japanese War, (Cambridge, 1899).

Sakuy Takahashi, International law applied to the Russo-Japanese War, with the decisions of the Japanese Prize Courts, (London, 1908).

Travers Twiss, Belligerent rights on the high seas since the Declaration of Paris, (London, 1884).

Travers Twiss, The Black Book of the Admiralty, (London, 1871-1876) 4 vols.

Travers Twiss, The doctrine of continuous voyage, as applied to contraband of war and blockade, contrasted with the Declaration of Paris of 1856, (London, 1877).

René-Josué Valin, Nouveau Commentaire sur l'Ordonnance de la Marine du mois d'août 1681, (La Rochelle, 1763-1766-1776-1981).

A. Veillon, Die Auswirkungen des Prisenrechts auf die Neutralen, (Winterthur, 1959).

J.Th.H. Verhees-van Meer, De Zeeuwse kaapvaart tijdens de Spaanse successieoorlog 1702-1713, (Leiden, diss., 1986).

J.H.W. Verzijl, Le droit des prises de la grande guerre, (Leiden, 1924).

C. van Vollenhoven, Naasting, opvordering en beteugeling van koopmansgoederen in den zeeoorlog, (Amsterdam, 1915).

R.E.J. Weber, Seinboeken voor de Nederlandse oorlogsvloten en konvooien tot 1690, (Amsterdam, 1982).

William Wynne, The life of Sir Leoline Jenkins, (London, 1724) 2 vols.

C.E. Zachariae (von Lingenthal), Historiae juris Graeco-romani delineatio, (Heidelberg, 1839).

GEOGRAPHICAL NAME INDEX

NAME INDEX

PRIZE CASE INDEX

SUBJECT INDEX

TREATY INDEX

6 July 1688	Denmark-the Netherlands, Berlin, preliminary treaty on navigation, 184
12 August 1689	England-the Netherlands, Whitehall, prohibition of commerce with France, 421, 442
20 June 1691	Denmark-Great Britain-the Netherlands, Copenhagen, commerce, navigation, 219, 340, 494, 495, 508
22 October 1691	England-the Netherlands, Whitehall, (re)capture of vessels, 546
20 September 1697	France-the Netherlands, Rijswijk, peace, 86
20 September 1697	France-Spain, Rijswijk, peace, 86
20 September 1697	France-England, Rijswijk, peace, 86
20 September 1697	France-the Netherlands, Rijswijk, commerce, navigation, 32, 179, 290, 306, 323, 340, 494
20 September 1697	France-England, Rijswijk, peace, 86
15 June 1701	Denmark-the Netherlands, Copenhagen, amity, commerce, navigation, 494
11 April 1713	France-Great Britain, Utrecht, commerce, navigation, 32, 322, 341, 374, 418, 494, 496, 506, 508
11 April 1713	France-the Netherlands, Utrecht, commerce, 32, 494
26 June 1714	Spain-the Netherlands, Utrecht, peace, commerce, navigation, 166, 179, 471
7 September 1714	Empire-France, Baden, peace, 87
6 February 1715	Spain-Portugal, Utrecht, peace, commerce, navigation, 87
28 September 1716	France-Lübeck, Bremen, Hamburg,, Paris, commerce and navigation, 206, 229, 230, 496
1 May 1725	Emperor-Spain, Vienna, commerce, 579
2 December 1734	Great Britain-Russia, St. Petersburg, commerce, navigation, 335, 405
21 December 1739	France-the Netherlands, Versailles, commerce, marine, 32, 307, 323, 494, 495, 508, 509
28 May 1740	France-Ottoman Empire, Constantinpole, capitulation, 307
25 April 1741	France-Sweden, Versailles, commerce, navigation, preliminary treaty, 123
15 March 1742	France-Denmark, Copenhagen, alliance, subsidies, 123, 323
11 June 1774	Austria-Prussia, Breslau, preliminaries peace, 76, 89, 381
28 July 1742	Austria-Prussia, Berlin, peace, 76, 89, 381
23 August 1742	France-Denmark, Copenhagen, commerce, navigation, 123, 183, 341, 494, 509, 512, 581
30 April 1748	France-Great Britain-the Netherlands, Aachen, preliminaries of peace, 177
18 October 1748	France-Great Britain-the Netherlands, Aachen, peace, 89, 382
27 August 1753	the Netherlands-Two Sicilies, The Hague, commerce, 494, 509
7 April 1762	Prussia-Sweden, Ribnitz, peace, armistice, 323
3 November 1762	England-France-Spain, Fontainebleau, peace, 92
10 February 1763	Great Britain-France-Spain-Portugal, Paris, peace, 386
10 June 1763	Spain-France-Sardinia, Paris, Piacenza, territory, 90
20 June 1766	Great Britain-Russia, St. Petersburg, commerce, navigation, 123, 125, 291, 342, 375
2 January 1768	Spain-France, Madrid, interpretation of the family pact of 5 August 1761, 375
1 April 1769	France-Hamburg, Hamburg, commerce, 33, 291, 329, 332, 342, 375, 493, 494, 496, 506, 509